Philips'

NEW WORLD

ATLAS

GEORGE PHILIP

Edited by:
Bill Willett, B.A., Cartographic Editor, George Philip and Son Ltd
Consultant Cartographer Harold Fullard, M.Sc.
Maps prepared by George Philip Cartographic Services Ltd
under the direction of Alan Poynter, M.A., Director of Cartography

Seventh Edition 1986
Reprinted 1988

British Library Cataloguing in Publication Data

Philips' new world atlas. — 7th ed.
  1. Atlases, British
  912   G1021
  ISBN 0 540 05515 8

© 1987 George Philip & Son Ltd

Printed in Hong Kong

Acknowledgements

The illustrations in *The Universe, Earth and Man* have been provided
by the following: Air India, Australian Information Service, Brazilian
Embassy, London, British Aircraft Corporation, British Airways,
British Leyland, British Petroleum, British Rail, British Steel
Corporation, British Tourist Authority, Central Electricity Generating
Board, D. Chanter, Danish Embassy, London, Egypt Air, Fiat
(England) Ltd., Finnish Tourist Bureau, Freightliners Ltd., H. Fullard,
M. H. Fullard, Gas Council Exploration Ltd., Commander H. R.
Hatfield/Astro Books, H. Hawes, Israeli Govt. Tourist Office, Japan
Air Lines, Lufthansa, M.A.T. Transport Ltd., Meteorological Office,
London, Moroccan Tourist Office, N.A.S.A. (Space Frontiers),
National Coal Board, London, National Maritime Museum, London,
Offshore Co., Pan American World Airways, Royal Astronomical
Society, London, Shell International Petroleum Co. Ltd., Swan
Hunter Group, Ltd., Swiss National Tourist Office, B. M. Willett,
Woodmansterne Ltd.

Preface

The Philips' **New World Atlas** has been designed to provide a compact and convenient reference book which is easy to handle and consult.

The maps in the atlas are arranged in continental sections; each is introduced by a physical and political map of the whole continent and these are followed by regional maps at medium scales and larger scale maps of the more densely-populated areas. The contents list to the atlas as a whole not only gives a complete list of maps but also includes an outline map of each of the continents showing the areas covered by the large scale map pages. This will help the reader to find the page required very quickly. The location of a specific place can, of course, be found via the index, where place names are listed alphabetically and the map page number and geographical coordinates for each entry are given.

The name forms on the maps are those that are used locally, or that have been transcribed according to the accepted systems. In the case of China, the Pinyin system for romanization, which is being increasingly used in the west, has been accepted. Well-known and well-used forms (often English conventions) for foreign place names are cross-referenced to the local form in the index and are often given alongside the local form on the map.

Where there are rival claims to territory, international boundaries are drawn to indicate the *de facto* situation. This does not denote international recognition of these boundaries but shows the limits of administration on either side of the line. Boundaries crossing disputed areas in the eastern Mediterranean have been specifically identified.

The maps are complemented by an illustrated 48-page section on the universe, earth and man which provides a broad introduction to the solar system, the evolution of the continents, world climate and weather, population and religions, vegetation patterns and land use, mineral resources and industry, transport and trade.

Contents

Population of Countries

Population of Cities

The Universe, Earth and Man

1	Chart of the Stars
2-3	The Solar System
4	The Earth
5	The Moon
6-7	Time
8-9	The Atmosphere and Clouds
10-11	Climate and Weather
12-13	The Earth from Space
14-15	The Evolution of the Continents
16-17	The Unstable Earth
18-19	The Making of Landscape
20-21	The Earth: Physical Dimensions
22-23	Distances
24-25	Water Resources and Vegetation

26-27	Population
28	Language
29	Religion
30-31	The Growth of Cities
32-33	Food Resources: Vegetable
34	Food Resources: Animal
35	Nutrition
36-37	Mineral Resources I
38-39	Mineral Resources II
40-41	Fuel and Energy
42	Occupations
43	Industry
44-45	Transport
46-47	Trade
48	Wealth

Maps 1-128

World

1	General Reference	
1	The World–Physical	1:150M
2-3	The World Political	1:80M
4-5	The Polar Regions	1:35M
6-7	The Atlantic Ocean Equatorial Scale	1:50M

Europe

8-9	Europe Physical European Organisations	1:17½M 1:40M
10	Europe Political	1:20M
11	The British Isles Political	1:4M
12-13	England and Wales	1:2M
14	Scotland	1:2M
15	Ireland	1:2M
16	The Netherlands, Belgium and Luxembourg	1:2½M
17	France	1:5M
18-19	Northern France	1:2½M
20-21	Southern France	1:2½M
22-23	Central Europe	1:5M
24-25	Germany and Switzerland	1:2½M
26-27	Austria, Czechoslovakia and Hungary	1:2½M
28	Poland	1:2½M
29	Spain and Portugal	1:5M

30-31	Western Spain and Portugal	1:2½M
32-33	Eastern Spain	1:2½M
34-35	The Mediterranean Lands	1:10M
36-37	Italy and the Balkan States Malta	1:5M 1:1M
38-39	Northern Italy and Western Yugoslavia	1:2½M
40-41	Southern Italy	1:2½M

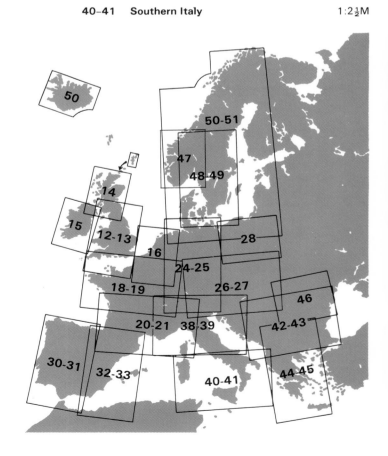

Contents

42–43   Eastern Yugoslavia and Bulgaria   1:2½M

44–45   Greece and Albania   1:2½M

46   Romania   1:2½M

47   Southern Norway   1:2½M

48–49   Denmark and Southern Sweden   1:2½M

50–51   Scandinavia and the Baltic Lands   1:5M
Iceland   1:5M

52–53   The U.S.S.R. in Europe   1:10M

54–55   European Russia Central   1:5M

56–57   European Russia South   1:5M

Asia

58–59   The Union of Soviet Socialist Republics   1:20M

60   Asia
Physical   1:50M

61   Asia
Political   1:50M

62   Israel and West Jordan   1:1M

63   Arabia and The Horn of Africa   1:15M

64–65   The Near and Middle East   1:10M

66–67   South Asia   1:10M

68–69   The Indo-Gangetic Plain   1:6M
S. Asia – Irrigation   1:40M

70   Southern India and Sri Lanka   1:6M

71   Mainland South-East Asia   1:10M
Peninsular Malaysia   1:6M

72–73   The East Indies   1:12½M
Java & Madura   1:7½M

74   Japan   1:10M
Southern Japan   1:5M

75   China   1:20M

76–77   Eastern China and Korea   1:10M

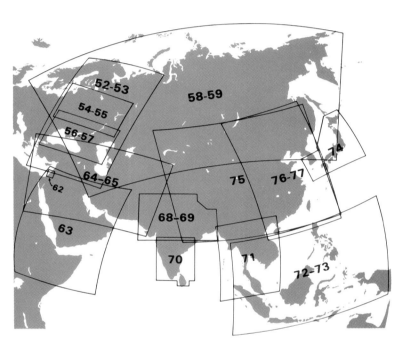

Africa

78   Africa
Physical   1:40M

79   Africa
Political   1:40M

80–81   Northern Africa   1:15M

82–83   North-West Africa   1:8M

84–85   West Africa   1:8M

86–87   The Nile Valley   1:8M
The Nile Delta   1:4M

88–89   Central and Southern Africa   1:15M

90–91   East Africa   1:8M

92–93   Southern Africa   1:8M
Madagascar   1:8M

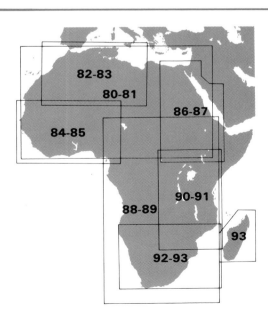

Contents

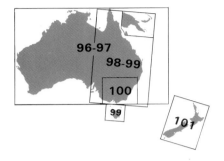

Australasia

94–95	**The Pacific Ocean** Equatorial Scale	1:60M
96–97	**Australia**	1:12M
	Australasia – Political	1:80M
98–99	**Eastern Australia**	1:7½M
	Papua New Guinea	1:12M
100	**South-East Australia**	1:4½M
101	**New Zealand**	1:6M
	Samoa	1:12M
	Fiji and Tonga	1:12M
	New Zealand and Dependencies	1:60M

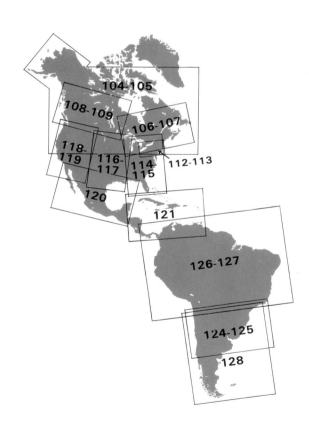

The Americas

102–3	**North America**	
	Physical	1:30M
	Political	1:70M
104–5	**Canada**	1:15M
	Alaska	1:30M
106–7	**Eastern Canada**	1:7M
108–9	**Western Canada**	1:7M
110–11	**The United States**	1:12M
	Hawaii	1:10M
112–13	**North-Eastern United States**	1:2½M
114–15	**The Eastern United States**	1:6M
116–17	**The Middle United States**	1:6M
118–19	**The Western United States**	1:6M
120	**Mexico**	1:12M
	Panama Canal	1:1M
121	**The West Indies**	1:12M
	Bermuda	1:1M
	Leeward Is.	1:8M
	Windward Is.	1:8M
	Trinidad and Tobago	1:8M
	Jamaica	1:8M
122	**South America**	
	Physical	1:30M
123	**South America**	
	Political	1:30M
124–25	**Central South America**	1:8M
126–27	**South America** North	1:16M
128	**South America** South	1:16M

Index

Principal Countries of the World

Country	Area in thousands of square km.	Population in thousands	Density of population per sq. km.	Capital Population in thousands
Afghanistan	647	17 222	27	Kabul (1 036)
Albania	29	2 841	98	Tiranë (202)
Algeria	2 382	20 500	9	Algiers (1 740)
Angola	1 247	8 339	7	Luanda (700)
Argentina	2 767	29 627	11	Buenos Aires (9 927)
Australia	7 687	15 369	2	Canberra (251)
Austria	84	7 549	90	Vienna (1 516)
Bangladesh	144	94 651	657	Dhaka (3 459)
Belgium	31	9 856	318	Brussels (989)
Belize	23	156	5	Belmopan (3)
Benin	113	3 720	33	Porto-Novo (132)
Bhutan	47	1 360	29	Thimphu (60)
Bolivia	1 099	6 082	5	Sucre (63) La Paz (881)
Botswana	600	1 007	2	Gaborone (60)
Brazil	8 512	129 662	15	Brasilia (1 306)
Brunei	6	209	35	Bandar Seri Begawan (58)
Bulgaria	111	8 946	81	Sofia (1 064)
Burkina Faso	274	6 607	24	Ouagadougou (286)
Burma	677	36 750	54	Rangoon (2 276)
Burundi	28	4 540	162	Bujumbura (157)
Cambodia (Kampuchea)	181	6 981	39	Phnom Penh (400)
Cameroon	475	9 165	19	Yaoundé (485)
Canada	9 976	24 907	2	Ottawa (738)
Central African Rep.	623	2 450	4	Bangui (302)
Chad	1 284	4 789	4	Ndjamena (303)
Chile	757	11 682	15	Santiago (4 132)
China	9 597	1 039 677	108	Peking (9 231)
Colombia	1 139	27 190	24	Bogota (4 056)
Congo	342	1 651	5	Brazzaville (422)
Costa Rica	51	2 379	47	San José (272)
Cuba	115	9 884	86	Havana (1 951)
Cyprus	9	655	73	Nicosia (161)
Czechoslovakia	128	15 415	120	Prague (1 186)
Denmark	43	5 118	119	Copenhagen (1 382)
Djibouti	22	332	15	Djibouti (150)
Dominican Republic	49	5 962	121	Santo Domingo (1 313)
Ecuador	284	9 251	32	Quito (881)
Egypt	1 001	45 915	46	Cairo (5 074)
El Salvador	21	5 232	249	San Salvador (429)
Equatorial Guinea	28	381	14	Rey Malabo (37)
Ethiopia	1 222	33680	28	Addis Abeba (1 478)
Fiji	18	670	37	Suva (68)
Finland	337	4 863	14	Helsinki (922)
France	547	54 652	99	Paris (8 510)
French Guiana	91	78	1	Cavenne (39)
Gabon	268	1 127	4	Libréville (252)
Gambia	11	696	63	Banjul (109)
Germany, East	108	16 864	156	East Berlin (1 173)
Germany, West	249	61 638	248	Bonn (294)
Ghana	239	12 700	53	Accra (738)
Greece	132	9 848	75	Athens (3 027)
Greenland	2 176	52	0.02	Godthåb (10)
Guatemala	109	7 699	71	Guatemala (793)
Guinea	246	5 704	23	Conakry (763)
Guinea-Bissau	36	836	23	Bissau (109)
Guyana	215	922	4	Georgetown (188)
Haiti	28	5 201	186	Port-au-Prince (888)
Honduras	112	4 092	37	Tegucigalpa (485)
Hong Kong	1	5 313	5 313	Hong Kong (1 184)
Hungary	93	10 702	115	Budapest (2 067)
Iceland	103	236	2	Reykjavik (84)
India	3 288	732 256	223	Delhi (5 729)
Indonesia	2 027	156 442	77	Jakarta (6 503)
Iran	1 648	42 070	26	Tehran (4 496)
Iraq	435	14 654	34	Baghdad (2 969)
Irish Republic	70	3 508	50	Dublin (525)
Israel	21	4 097	195	Jerusalem (424)
Italy	301	56 836	189	Rome (2 831)
Ivory Coast	322	9 300	29	Abidjan (850)
Jamaica	11	2 260	205	Kingston (671)
Japan	372	119 259	320	Tokyo (8 139)
Jordan	98	3 489	36	Amman (681)
Kenya	583	18 784	32	Nairobi (1 048)
Korea, North	121	19 185	158	Pyöngyang (1 500)
Korea, South	98	39 951	408	Seoul (8 367)
Kuwait	18	1 672	93	Kuwait (775)
Laos	237	4 209	18	Vientiane (90)
Lebanon	10	2 739	274	Beirut (702)
Lesotho	30	1 444	48	Maseru (45)
Liberia	111	2 113	19	Monrovia (306)
Libya	1 760	3 356	2	Tripoli (980)
Luxembourg	3	365	121	Luxembourg (79)
Madagascar	587	9 400	16	Antananarivo (400)
Malawi	118	6 429	54	Lilongwe (103)
Malaysia	330	14 860	45	Kuala Lumpur (938)
Mali	1 240	7 528	6	Bamako (419)
Malta	0.3	377	1 256	Valletta (14)
Mauritania	1 031	1 779	2	Nouakchott (135)
Mauritius	2	993	496	Port Louis (149)
Mexico	1 973	75 103	38	Mexico (14 750)
Mongolia	1 565	1 803	1	Ulan Bator (419)
Morocco	447	22 110	49	Rabat (842)
Mozambique	783	13 311	17	Maputo (384)
Namibia	824	1 040	1	Windhoek (61)
Nepal	141	15 738	112	Katmandu (210)
Netherlands	41	14 362	350	Amsterdam (936)
New Zealand	269	3 203	12	Wellington (343)
Nicaragua	130	3 058	23	Managua (820)
Niger	1 267	6 040	5	Niamey (225)
Nigeria	924	89 022	96	Lagos (1 477)
Norway	324	4 129	13	Oslo (624)
Oman	212	1 131	5	Muscat (25)
Pakistan	804	89 729	112	Islamabad (201)
Panama	76	2 089	27	Panama (655)
Papua New Guinea	462	3 190	7	Port Moresby (123)
Paraguay	407	3 472	8	Asunción (602)
Peru	1 285	18 790	15	Lima (4 601)
Philippines	300	52 055	173	Manila (1 630)
Poland	313	36 571	117	Warsaw (1 641)
Portugal	92	10 056	109	Lisbon (818)
Puerto Rico	9	3 350	372	San Juan (1 086)
Romania	238	22 638	95	Bucharest (1 979)
Rwanda	26	5 700	219	Kigali (116)
Saudi Arabia	2 150	10 421	5	Riyadh (667)
Senegal	196	6 316	32	Dakar (799)
Sierra Leone	72	3 672	51	Freetown (214)
Singapore	0.6	2 502	4 170	Singapore (2 517)
Somali Republic	638	5 269	8	Mogadishu (400)
South Africa	1 221	31 008	25	Pretoria (739) Cape Town (2 517)
Spain	505	38 228	76	Madrid (3 159)
Sri Lanka	66	15 416	234	Colombo (1 412)
Sudan	2 506	20 362	8	Khartoum (561)
Surinam	163	407	2	Paramaribo (151)
Swaziland	17	605	36	Mbabane (23)
Sweden	450	8 331	19	Stockholm (1 409)
Switzerland	41	6 482	158	Bern (289)
Syria	185	9 660	52	Damascus (1 251)
Taiwan	36	18 700	519	Taipei (2 271)
Tanzania	945	20 378	22	Dar-es-Salaam (757)
Thailand	514	49 459	96	Bangkok (5 468)
Togo	56	2 756	49	Lomé (247)
Trinidad and Tobago	5	1 202	240	Port of Spain (66)
Tunisia	164	6 886	42	Tunis (597)
Turkey	781	47 279	61	Ankara (2 239)
Uganda	236	14 625	62	Kampala (332)
United Arab Emirates	84	1 206	14	Abu Dhabi (449)
U.S.S.R.	22 402	272 500	12	Moscow (8 396)
United Kingdom	245	56 377	230	London (6 755)
United States	9 363	234 496	25	Washington (3 061)
Uruguay	178	2 968	17	Montevideo (1 173)
Venezuela	912	16 394	18	Caracas (2 944)
Vietnam	330	57 181	173	Hanoi (2 571)
Western Samoa	3	159	53	Apia (36)
Yemen, North	195	6 232	32	Sana' (448)
Yemen, South	288	2 158	7	Aden (285)
Yugoslavia	256	22 800	89	Belgrade (1 407)
Zaïre	2 345	31 151	13	Kinshasa (2 242)
Zambia	753	6 242	8	Lusaka (641)
Zimbabwe	391	7 740	20	Harare (656)

Principal Cities of the World

The population figures used are from censuses or more recent estimates and are given in thousands for towns and cities over 500,000 (over 750,000 in China, India, the U.S.S.R. and the U.S.A.) Where possible the population of the metropolitan area is given e.g. Greater London, Greater New York, etc.

AFRICA

ALGERIA (1977)
Alger	1 740
Oran	543

ANGOLA (1982)
Luanda	700

CAMEROON (1983)
Douala	708

EGYPT (1976)
El Qâhira	5 074
El Iskandarîya	2 318
El Giza	1 230

ETHIOPIA (1983)
Addis Abeba	1 478

GHANA (1970)
Accra	738

GUINEA (1980)
Conakry	763

IVORY COAST (1976)
Abidjan	850

KENYA (1983)
Nairobi	1 048

MOROCCO (1981)
Casablanca	2 409
Rabat-Salé	842
Fès	562
Marrakech	549

NIGERIA (1975)
Lagos	1 477
Ibadan	847

SENEGAL (1976)
Dakar	779

SOUTH AFRICA (1980)
Johannesburg	1 726
Cape Town	1 491
Durban	961
Pretoria	739
Port Elizabeth	585

SUDAN (1980)
El Khartûm	561

TANZANIA (1978)
Dar-es-Salaam	757

TUNISIA (1984)
Tunis	597

ZAIRE (1975)
Kinshasa	2 242

ZAMBIA (1980)
Lusaka	641

ZIMBABWE (1983)
Harare	681

ASIA

AFGHANISTAN (1979)
Kābul	1 036

BANGLADESH (1982)
Dhaka	3 459
Chittagong	1 388
Khulna	623

BURMA (1977)
Rangoon	2 276

CHINA (1970)
Shanghai	11 860
Beijing	9 231
Tianjin	7 764
Shenyang	2 800
Wuhan	2 560
Guangzhou	2 500
Chongqing	2 400
Nanjing	1 750
Harbin	1 670
Dalian	1 650
Xi'an	1 600
Lanzhou	1 450
Taiyuan	1 350
Qingdao	1 300
Chengdu	1 250
Changchun	1 200
Kunming	1 100
Jinan	1 100
Fushun	1 080
Anshan	1 050
Zhengzhou	1 050
Hangzhou	960
Tangshan	950
Baotou	920
Zibo	850
Changsha	825
Shijiazhuang	800
Qiqihar	760

HONG KONG (1981)
Kowloon	2 450
Hong Kong	1 184
Tsuen Wan	599

INDIA (1981)
Calcutta	9 194
Bombay	8 243
Delhi	5 729
Madras	4 289
Bangalore	2 922
Ahmedabad	2 548
Hyderabad	2 546
Pune	1 686
Kanpur	1 639
Nagpur	1 302
Jaipur	1 015
Lucknow	1 008
Coimbatore	920
Patna	919
Surat	914
Madurai	908
Indore	829
Varanasi	797
Jabalpur	757

INDONESIA (1980)
Jakarta	6 503
Surabaya	2 028
Bandung	1 462
Medan	1 379
Semarang	1 026
Palembang	787
Ujung Pandang	709
Malang	512

IRAN (1976)
Tehrān	4 496
Esfahān	672
Mashhad	670
Tabrīz	599

IRAQ (1970)
Baghdād	2 969

JAPAN (1982)
Tōkyō	11 676
Yokohama	2 848
Ōsaka	2 623
Nagoya	2 093
Kyōto	1 480
Sapporo	1 465
Kobe	1 383
Fukuoka	1 121
Kitakyūshū	1 065
Kawasaki	1 055
Hiroshima	898
Sakai	809
Chiba	756
Sendai	662
Okayama	551
Kumamoto	522
Kagoshima	514
Amagasaki	510
Higashiōsaka	501

JORDAN (1981)
'Ammān	681

KOREA, NORTH (1972)
Pyöngyang	1 500

KOREA, SOUTH (1980)
Sŏul	8 367
Pusan	3 160
Taegu	1 607
Inchŏn	1 085
Kwangju	728
Taejon	652

KUWAIT (1975)
Al-Kuwayt	775

LEBANON (1980)
Bayrūt	702

MALAYSIA (1980)
Kuala Lumpur	938

PAKISTAN (1981)
Karachi	5 103
Lahore	2 922
Faisalabad	1 092
Rawalpindi	806
Hyderabad	795
Multan	730
Gujranwala	597
Peshawar	555

PHILIPPINES (1981)
Manila	1 630
Quezon City	1 166
Davao	610

SAUDI ARABIA (1974)
Ar Riyād	667
Jiddah	561

SINGAPORE (1983)
Singapore	2 517

SRI LANKA (1981)
Colombo	1 412

SYRIA (1982)
Dimashq	1 112
Halab	985

TAIWAN (1981)
Taipei	2 271
Kaohsiung	1 227
Taichung	607
Tainan	595

THAILAND (1982)
Bangkok	5 468

TURKEY (1982)
İstanbul	2 949
Ankara	2 276
İzmir	1 083
Adana	864
Konya	691
Bursa	658
Gaziantep	526

VIETNAM (1973-79)
Phanh Bho Ho Chi Minh	3 420
Hanoi	2 571
Haiphong	1 279

AUSTRALIA AND NEW ZEALAND

AUSTRALIA (1982)
Sydney	3 310
Melbourne	2 837
Brisbane	1 124
Adelaide	960
Perth	948

NEW ZEALAND (1982)
Auckland	839

EUROPE

AUSTRIA (1981)
Wien	1 516

BELGIUM (1983)
Brussel	989

BULGARIA (1982)
Sofiya	1 064

CZECHOSLOVAKIA (1983)
Praha	1 186

DENMARK (1981)
København	1 382

FINLAND (1982)
Helsinki	922

FRANCE (1982)
Paris	8 510
Lyon	1 170
Marseille	1 080
Lille	935
Bordeaux	628
Toulouse	523

GERMANY, EAST (1982)
East Berlin	1 173
Leipzig	557
Dresden	521

GERMANY, WEST (1980)
West Berlin	1 896
Hamburg	1 645
München	1 299
Köln	977
Essen	648
Frankfurt am Main	629
Dortmund	608
Düsseldorf	590
Stuttgart	581
Duisburg	558
Bremen	555
Hannover	535

GREECE (1981)
Athínai	3 027
Thessaloníki	706

HUNGARY (1983)
Budapest	2 067

IRISH REPUBLIC (1981)
Dublin	525

ITALY (1981)
Roma	2 831
Milano	1 635
Napoli	1 211
Torino	1 104
Genova	760
Palermo	700

NETHERLANDS (1983)
Rotterdam	1 025
Amsterdam	936
's-Gravenhage	674

NORWAY (1980)
Oslo	624

POLAND (1983)
Warszawa	1 641
Łodz	848
Kraków	735
Wrocław	631
Poznań	571

PORTUGAL (1981)
Lisboa	818

ROMANIA (1982)
Bucureşti	1 979

SPAIN (1981)
Madrid	3 159
Barcelona	1 753
Valencia	745
Sevilla	646
Zaragoza	572
Málaga	502

SWEDEN (1983)
Stockholm	1 409

SWITZERLAND (1982)
Zürich	705

U.S.S.R. (1983)
Moskva	8 396
Leningrad	4 779
Kiyev	2 355
Tashkent	1 944
Baku	1 638
Kharkov	1 519
Minsk	1 405
Gorkiy	1 382
Novosibirsk	1 370
Sverdlovsk	1 269
Kuybyshev	1 242
Dnepropetrovsk	1 128
Tbilisi	1 125
Odessa	1 097
Yerevan	1 095
Omsk	1 080
Chelyabinsk	1 077
Donetsk	1 055
Perm	1 037
Ufa	1 034
Kazan	1 031
Alma-Ata	1 023
Rostov	977
Volgograd	962
Saratov	887
Riga	867
Krasnoyarsk	845
Zaporozhye	835
Voronezh	831

UNITED KINGDOM (1983)
London	6 754
Birmingham	1 013
Glasgow	751
Leeds	714
Sheffield	543
Liverpool	502

YUGOSLAVIA (1981)
Beograd	1 407
Zagreb	1 175
Skopje	507

SOUTH AMERICA

ARGENTINA (1980)
Buenos Aires	9 927
Córdoba	982
Rosario	955
Mendoza	597
La Plata	560

BOLIVIA (1982)
La Paz	881

BRAZIL (1980)
São Paulo	8 732
Rio de Janeiro	5 539
Belo Horizonte	1 937
Salvador	1 502
Recife	1 433
Fortaleza	1 307
Brasilia	1 306
Pôrto Alegre	1 221
Nova Iguaçu	1 184
Curitiba	943
Belém	934
Goiánia	680
Duque de Caxias	666
São Gonçalo	660
Santo André	634
Campinas	587

CHILE (1983)
Santiago	4 132

COLOMBIA (1978)
Bogotá	4 056
Medellin	1 507
Cali	1 316
Barranquilla	855

ECUADOR (1982)
Guayaquil	1 279
Quito	881

PARAGUAY (1978)
Asunción	602

PERU (1981)
Lima	4 601

URUGUAY (1981)
Montevideo	1 173

VENEZUELA (1980)
Caracas	2 944
Maracaibo	901
Valencia	506

NORTH AMERICA

CANADA (1983)
Toronto	3 067
Montréal	2 862
Vancouver	1 311
Ottawa	738
Edmonton	699
Calgary	634
Winnipeg	601
Québec	580
Hamilton	548

CUBA (1981)
La Habana	1 925

DOMINICAN REP. (1981)
Santo Domingo	1 313

GUATEMALA (1979)
Guatemala	793

HAITI (1982)
Port-au-Prince	888

JAMAICA (1980)
Kingston	671

MEXICO (1979)
Mexico	14 750
Guadalajara	2 468
Netzahualcóyotl	2 331
Monterrey	2 019
Puebla de Zaragoza	711
Ciudad Juárez	625
León de los Aldamas	625
Tijuana	566

NICARAGUA (1981)
Managua	820

PANAMA (1981)
Panama	655

PUERTO RICO (1980)
San Juan	1 086

UNITED STATES (1980)
New York	16 121
Los Angeles	11 498
Chicago	7 870
Philadelphia	5 548
San Francisco	5 180
Detroit	4 618
Boston	3 448
Houston	3 101
Washington	3 061
Dallas	2 975
Cleveland	2 834
Miami	2 644
St. Louis	2 356
Pittsburgh	2 264
Baltimore	2 174
Minneapolis-St. Paul	2 114
Seattle	2 093
Atlanta	2 030
San Diego	1 817
Cincinnati	1 660
Denver	1 621
Milwaukee	1 570
Tampa	1 569
Phoenix	1 509
Kansas City	1 327
Indianapolis	1 306
Portland	1 243
Buffalo	1 243
New Orleans	1 187
Providence	1 096
Columbus	1 093
San Antonio	1 072
Sacramento	1 014
Dayton	1 014
Rochester	971
Salt Lake City	936
Memphis	913
Louisville	906
Nashville	851
Birmingham	847
Oklahoma	834
Greensboro	827
Norfolk	807
Albany	795
Toledo	792
Honolulu	763

Chart of the Stars

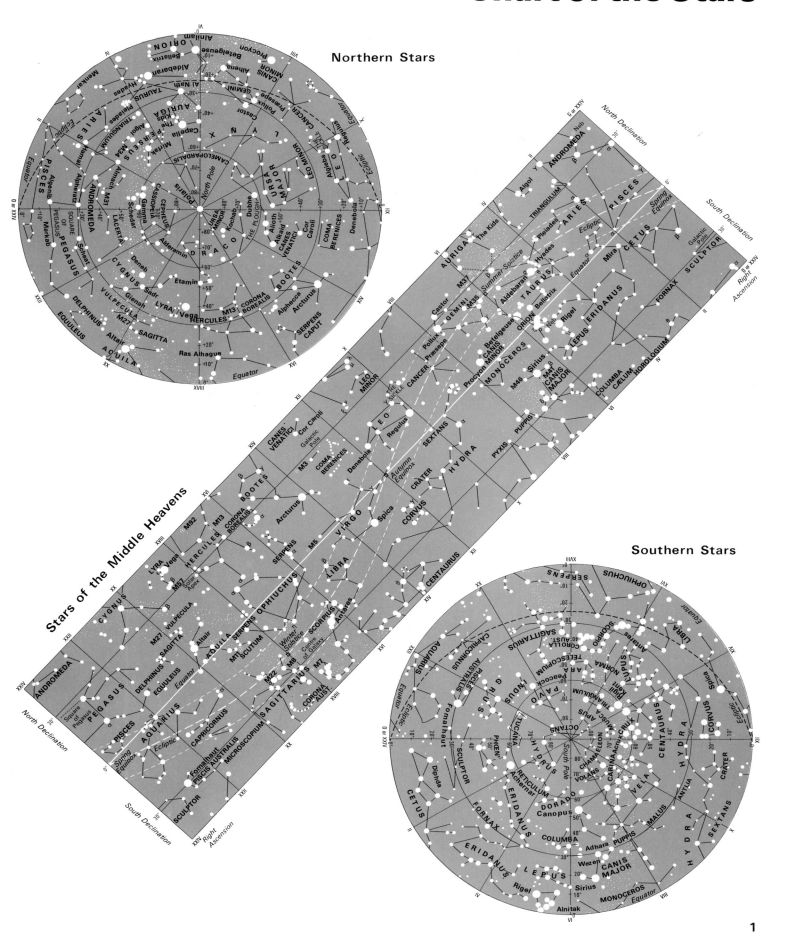

Northern Stars

Stars of the Middle Heavens

Southern Stars

The Solar System

The Solar System is a minute part of one of the innumerable galaxies that make up the universe. Our Galaxy is represented in the drawing to the right and The Solar System (S) lies near the plane of spiral-shaped galaxy, but 27 000 light-years from the centre. The System consists of the Sun at the centre with planets, moons, asteroids, comets, meteors, meteorites, dust and gases revolving around it. It is calculated to be at least 4 700 million years old.

The Solar System can be considered in two parts: the Inner Region planets- Mercury, Venus, Earth and Mars - all small and solid, the Outer Region planets - Jupiter, Saturn, Uranus and Neptune - all gigantic in size, and on the edge of the system the smaller Pluto.

Our galaxy

Inner region planets

Mercury
Venus
Earth
Mars

Outer region planets

Mars
Jupiter
Saturn
Uranus
Neptune
Pluto

The planets

All planets revolve round the Sun in the same direction, and mostly in the same plane. Their orbits are shown (left) - they are not perfectly circular paths.

The table below summarizes the dimensions and movements of the Sun and planets.

The Sun

The Sun has an interior with temperatures believed to be of several million °C brought about by continuous thermo-nuclear fusions of hydrogen into helium. This immense energy is transferred by radiation into surrounding layers of gas the outer surface of which is called the chromosphere. From this "surface" with a temperature of many thousands °C "flames" (solar prominences) leap out into the diffuse corona which can best be seen at times of total eclipse (see photo right). The bright surface of the Sun, the photosphere, is calculated to have a temperature of about 6 000 °C, and when viewed through a telescope has a mottled appearance, the darker patches being called sunspots - the sites of large disturbances of the surface.

Total eclipse of the sun

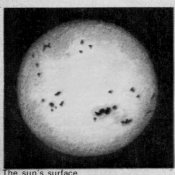
The sun's surface

	Equatorial diameter in km	Mass (earth=1)	Mean distance from sun in millions km	Mean radii of orbit (earth=1)	Orbital inclination	Mean sidereal period (days)	Mean period of rotation on axis (days)	Number of satellites
Sun	1 392 000	332 946	—	—	—	—	25·38	—
Mercury	4 878	0·05	57·9	0·38	7°	87·9	58·6	0
Venus	12 104	0·81	108·2	0·72	3°23'	224·7	243	0
Earth	12 756	1·00	149·6	1·00	—	365·2	0·99	1
Mars	6 794	0·10	227·9	1·52	1°50'	686·9	1·02	2
Jupiter	142 800	317·9	778·3	5·20	1°18'	4332·5	0·41	14 ?
Saturn	120 000	95·1	1 427	9·53	2°29'	10759·2	0·42	11
Uranus	52 000	14·5	2 869	19·17	0°46'	30684·8	0·45	5
Neptune	48 400	17·2	4 496	30·05	1°46'	60190·5	0·67	2
Pluto	3 000 ?	0·001	5 900	39·43	17°1'	91628·6	6·38	1 ?

The Sun's diameter is 109 times greater than that of the Earth.

Distances from sun in millions km

57·9 — Mercury
08·2 — Venus
49·6 — Earth
27·9 — Mars

78·3 — Jupiter

427 — Saturn

2869 — Uranus

4496 — Neptune

5900 — Pluto

Mercury is the nearest planet to the Sun. It is composed mostly of high density metals and probably has an atmosphere of heavy inert gases.

Venus is similar in size to the Earth, and probably in composition. It is, however, much hotter and has a dense atmosphere of carbon dioxide which obscures our view of its surface.

Earth is the largest of the inner planets. It has a dense iron-nickel core surrounded by layers of silicate rock. The surface is approximately $\frac{3}{8}$ land and $\frac{5}{8}$ water, and the lower atmosphere consists of a mixture of nitrogen, oxygen and other gases supplemented by water vapour. With this atmosphere and surface temperatures usually between −50°C and +40°C. life is possible.

Mars, smaller than the Earth, has a noticeably red appearance. Photographs taken by the Mariner probes show clearly the cratered surface and polar ice caps, probably made from frozen carbon dioxide.

The Asteroids orbit the Sun mainly between Mars and Jupiter. They consist of thousands of bodies of varying sizes with diameters ranging from yards to hundreds of miles.

Jupiter is the largest planet of the Solar System. Photographs taken by Voyager I and II have revealed an equatorial ring system and shown the distinctive Great Red Spot and rotating cloud belts in great detail.

Saturn, the second largest planet consists of hydrogen, helium and other gases. The equatorial rings are composed of small ice particles.

Uranus is extremely remote but just visible to the naked eye and has a greenish appearance. A faint equatorial ring system was discovered in 1977. The planet's axis is tilted through 98° from its orbital plane, therefore it revolves in a retrograde manner.

Neptune, yet more remote than Uranus and larger. It is composed of gases and has a bluish green appearance when seen in a telescope. As with Uranus, little detail can be observed on its surface.

Pluto. No details are known of its composition or surface. The existence of this planet was firstly surmised in a computed hypothesis, which was tested by repeated searches by large telescopes until in 1930 the planet was found. Latest evidence seems to suggest that Pluto has one satellite, provisionally named Charon.

The Earth

Seasons, Equinoxes and Solstices

The Earth revolves around the Sun once a year and rotates daily on its axis, which is inclined at $66\frac{1}{2}°$ to the orbital plane and always points into space in the same direction. At midsummer (N.) the North Pole tilts towards the Sun, six months later it points away and half way between the axis is at right angles to the direction of the Sun (right).

Earth data

Maximum distance from the Sun (Aphelion) 152 007 016 km
Minimum distance from the Sun (Perihelion) 147 000 830 km
Obliquity of the ecliptic 23° 27' 08"
Length of year - tropical (equinox to equinox) 365.24 days
Length of year - sidereal (fixed star to fixed star) 365.26 days
Length of day - mean solar day 24h 03m 56s
Length of day - mean sidereal day 23h 56m 04s

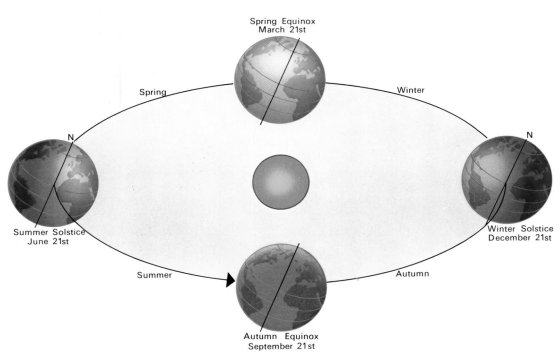

Length of day and night

At the summer solstice in the northern hemisphere, the Arctic has total daylight and the Antarctic total darkness. The opposite occurs at the winter solstice. At the equator, the length of day and night are almost equal all the year, at 30° the length of day varies from about 14 hours to 10 hours and at 50° from about 16 hours to 8 hours.

Apparent path of the Sun

The diagrams (right) illustrate the apparent path of the Sun at A the equator, B in mid latitudes say 45°N, C at the Arctic Circle $66\frac{1}{2}°$ and D at the North Pole where there is six months continuous daylight and six months continuous night

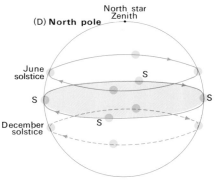

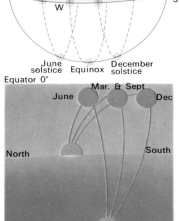

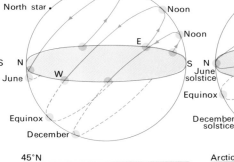

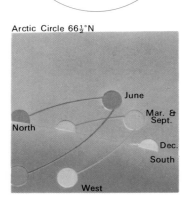

4

The Moon

The Moon rotates slowly making one complete turn on its axis in just over 27 days. This is the same as its period of revolution around the Earth and thus it always presents the same hemisphere ('face') to us. Surveys and photographs from space-craft have now added greatly to our knowledge of the Moon, and, for the first time, views of the hidden hemisphere.

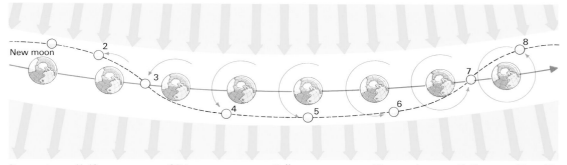

| Crescent moon(2) | Half moon, first quarter(3) | Gibbous moon (4) | Full moon (5) | The waning moon (6) | Half moon, last quarter(7) | The old moon (8) |

Phases of the Moon
The interval between one full Moon and the next is approximately 29½ days - thus there is one new Moon and one full Moon every month. The diagrams and photographs (right) show how the apparent changes in shape of the Moon from new to full arise from its changing position in relation to the Earth and both to the fixed direction of the Sun's rays.

Moon data
Distance from Earth 356 410 km
　　　　　　　　　to 406 685 km
Mean diameter 3 473 km
Mass approx. $\frac{1}{81}$ of that of Earth
Surface gravity $\frac{1}{6}$ of that of Earth
Atmosphere - none, hence no clouds, no weather, no sound.
Diurnal range of temperature at the Equator +200°C

Landings on the Moon
Left are shown the landing sites of the U.S. Apollo programme.
Apollo 11 Sea of Tranquility (1°N 23°E) 1969
Apollo 12 Ocean of Storms (3°S 24°W) 1969
Apollo 14 Fra Mauro (4°S 17°W) 1971
Apollo 15 Hadley Rill (25°N 4°E) 1971
Apollo 16 Descartes (9°S 15°E) 1972
Apollo 17 Sea of Serenity (20°N 31°E) 1972

Eclipses of Sun and Moon
When the Moon passes between Sun and Earth it causes a partial eclipse of the Sun *(right 1)* if the Earth passes through the Moon's outer shadow *(P)*, or a total eclipse *(right 2)*, if the inner cone shadow crosses the Earth's surface.

In a lunar eclipse, the Earth's shadow crosses the Moon and gives either total or partial eclipses.

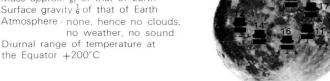

Partial eclipse (1)

Total eclipse (2)

Lunar eclipse

Tides
Ocean water moves around the Earth under the gravitational pull of the Moon, and, less strongly, that of the Sun. When solar and lunar forces pull together - near new and full Moon - high spring tides result. When solar and lunar forces are not combined - near Moon's first and third quarters - low neap tides occur.

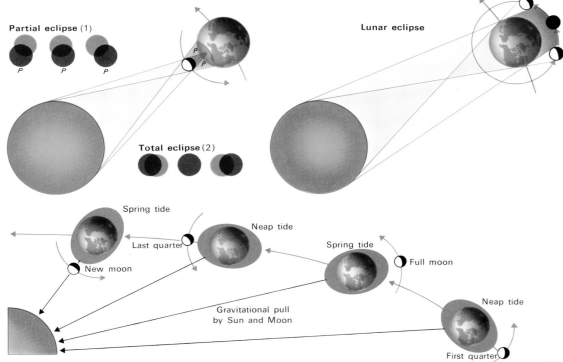

Spring tide
Neap tide
Last quarter
New moon
Spring tide
Full moon
Gravitational pull by Sun and Moon
Neap tide
First quarter

Time

Time measurement
The basic unit of time measurement is the day, one rotation of the earth on its axis. The subdivision of the day into hours and minutes is arbitrary and simply for our convenience. Our present calendar is based on the solar year of $365\frac{1}{4}$ days, the time taken for the earth to orbit the sun. A month was anciently based on the interval from new moon to new moon, approximately $29\frac{1}{2}$ days - and early calendars were entirely lunar.

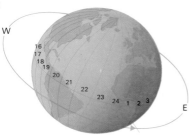
Rotation of the Earth

Greenwich Observatory

Prime Meridian

Rotation

Meridian

Shadow pointing to the north pole

Sun overhead

Shadow pointing to the south pole

The International Date Line
When it is 12 noon at the Greenwich meridian, 180° east it is midnight of the same day while 180° west the day is only just beginning. To overcome this the International Date Line was established, approximately following the 180° meridian. Thus, for example, if one travelled eastwards from Japan (140° East) to Samoa (170° West) one would pass from Sunday night into Sunday morning.

Time zones
The world is divided into 24 time zones, each centred on meridians at 15° intervals which is the longitudinal distance the sun appears to travel every hour. The meridian running through Greenwich passes through the middle of the first zone. Successive zones to the east of Greenwich zone are ahead of Greenwich time by one hour for every 15° of longitude, while zones to the west are behind by one hour.

Night and day
As the earth rotates from west to east the sun appears to rise in the east and set in the west: when the sun is setting in Shanghai on the directly opposite side of the earth New York is just emerging into sunlight. Noon, when the sun is directly overhead, is coincident at all places on the same meridian with shadows pointing directly towards the poles.

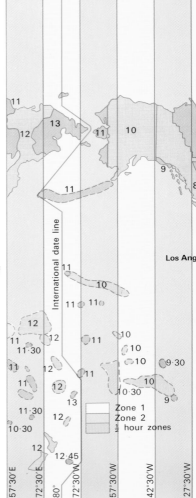

Solar time
The time taken for the earth to complete one rotation about its own axis is constant and defines a day but the speed of the earth along its orbit around the sun is inconstant. The length of day, or 'apparent solar day', as defined by the apparent successive transits of the sun is irregular because the earth must complete more than one rotation before the sun returns to the same meridian.

approx. 1°
approx. 10"

Earth's orbit

Sidereal time
The constant sidereal day is defined as the interval between two successive apparent transits of a star, or the first point of Aries, across the same meridian. If the sun is at the equinox and overhead at a meridian on one day, then the next day the sun will be to the east by approximately 1°; thus the sun will not cross the meridian until about 4 minutes after the sidereal noon.

Towards Aries

Earth's orbit

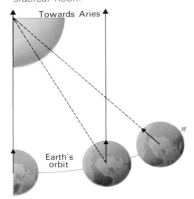
Astronomical clock, Delhi

Kendall's chronometer

Sundials
The earliest record of sundials dates back to 741 BC but they undoubtedly existed as early as 2000 BC although probably only as an upright stick or obelisk. A sundial marks the progress of the sun across the sky by casting the shadow of a central style or gnomon on the base. The base, generally made of stone, is delineated to represent the hours between sunrise and sunset.

Chronometers
With the increase of sea traffic in the 18th century and the need for accurate navigation clockmakers were faced with an intriguing problem. Harrison, an English carpenter, won a British award for designing a clock which was accurate at sea to one tenth of a second per day. He compensated for the effect of temperature changes by incorporating bimetallic strips connected to thin wires and circular balance wheels.

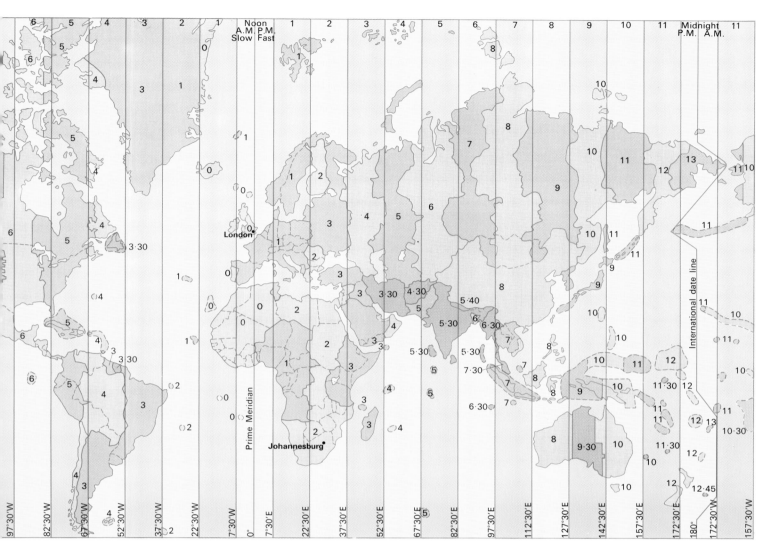

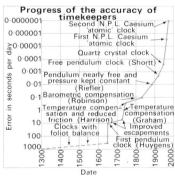

Progress of the accuracy of timekeepers

Error in seconds per day / Date

- Second N.P.L. Caesium 'atomic' clock
- First N.P.L. Caesium 'atomic' clock
- Quartz crystal clock
- Free pendulum clock (Shortt)
- Pendulum nearly free and pressure kept constant (Riefler)
- Barometric compensation (Robinson)
- Temperature compensation and reduced friction (Harrison)
- Temperature compensation (Graham)
- Clocks with foliot balance
- Improved escapements
- First pendulum clock (Huygens)

Vibration of quartz ring

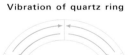

Time difference when travelling by air

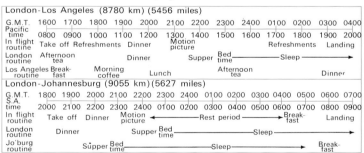

London-Los Angeles (8780 km) (5456 miles)

G.M.T.	1600	1700	1800	1900	2000	2100	2200	2300	2400	0100	0200	0300	0400
Pacific time	0800	0900	1000	1100	1200	1300	1400	1500	1600	1700	1800	1900	2000
In flight routine	Take off	Refreshments	Dinner		Motion picture					Refreshments			Landing
London routine	Afternoon tea			Dinner			Supper	Bed time		Sleep			
Los Angeles routine	Break-fast		Morning coffee		Lunch				Afternoon tea			Dinner	

London-Johannesburg (9055 km) (5627 miles)

G.M.T.	1800	1900	2000	2100	2200	2300	2400	0100	0200	0300	0400	0500	0600	0700
S.A. time	2000	2100	2200	2300	2400	0100	0200	0300	0400	0500	0600	0700	0800	0900
In flight routine	Take off	Dinner	Motion picture		Rest period					Break-fast			Landing	
London routine	Dinner			Supper	Bed time		Sleep							
Jo'burg routine		Supper	Bed time			Sleep						Break-fast		

Chronographs

The invention of the chronograph by Charles Wheatstone in 1842 made it possible to record intervals of time to an accuracy of one sixtieth of a second. The simplest form of chronograph is the stop-watch. This was developed to a revolving drum and stylus and later electrical signals. A recent development is the cathode ray tube capable of recording to less than one ten-thousanth of a second.

Quartz crystal clocks

The quartz crystal clock, designed originally in América in 1929, can measure small units of time and radio frequencies. The connection between quartz clocks and the natural vibrations of atoms and molecules mean that the unchanging frequencies emitted by atoms can be used to control the oscillator which controls the quartz clock. A more recent version of the atomic clock is accurate to one second in 300 years.

International date line

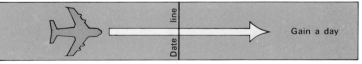

Gain a day

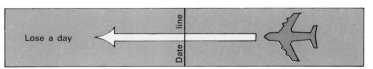

Lose a day

The Atmosphere and Clouds

Earth's thin coating *(right)*
The atmosphere is a blanket of protective gases around the earth providing insulation against otherwise extreme alternations in temperature. The gravitational pull increases the density nearer the earth's surface so that 5/6ths of the atmospheric mass is in the first 15 kms. It is a very thin layer in comparison with the earth's diameter of 12 680 kms., like the cellulose coating on a globe.

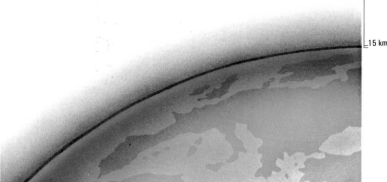

Exosphere(1)
The exosphere merges with the interplanetary medium and although there is no definite boundary with the ionosphere it starts at a height of about 600 kms. The rarified air mainly consists of a small amount of atomic oxygen up to 600 kms. and equal proportions of hydrogen and helium with hydrogen predominating above 2 400 kms.

Ionosphere(2)
Air particles of the ionosphere are electrically charged by the sun's radiation and congregate in four main layers, D, E, F1 and F2, which can reflect radio waves. Aurorae, caused by charged particles deflected by the earth's magnetic field towards the poles, occur between 65 and 965 kms. above the earth. It is mainly in the lower ionosphere that meteors from outer space burn up as they meet increased air resistance.

Stratosphere(3)
A thin layer of ozone contained within the stratosphere absorbs ultra-violet light and in the process gives off heat. The temperature ranges from about -55°C at the tropopause to about -60°C in the upper part, known as the mesosphere, with a rise to about 2°C just above the ozone layer. This portion of the atmosphere is separated from the lower layer by the tropopause.

Troposphere(4)
The earth's weather conditions are limited to this layer which is relatively thin, extending upwards to about 8 kms. at the poles and 15 kms. at the equator. It contains about 85% of the total atmospheric mass and almost all the water vapour. Air temperature falls steadily with increased height at about 1°C for every 100 metres above sea level.

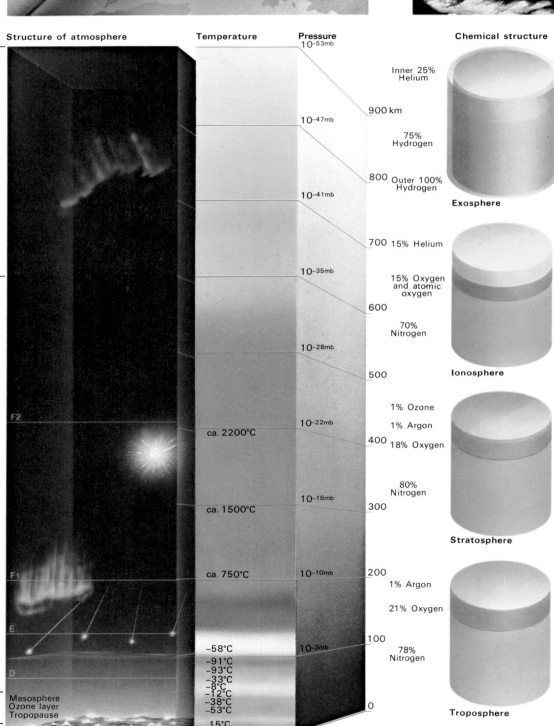

Structure of atmosphere

Temperature

ca. 2200°C
ca. 1500°C
ca. 750°C
-58°C
-91°C
-93°C
-33°C
-8°C
-12°C
-38°C
-53°C
15°C

Mesosphere
Ozone layer
Tropopause

Pressure
10⁻⁵³mb
10⁻⁴⁷mb
10⁻⁴¹mb
10⁻³⁵mb
10⁻²⁸mb
10⁻²²mb
10⁻¹⁶mb
10⁻¹⁰mb
10⁻³mb
10³mb

600 km
15 km

900 km
800 km
700
600
500
400
300
200
100
0

Chemical structure

Inner 25% Helium
75% Hydrogen
Outer 100% Hydrogen

Exosphere

15% Helium
15% Oxygen and atomic oxygen
70% Nitrogen

Ionosphere

1% Ozone
1% Argon
18% Oxygen
80% Nitrogen

Stratosphere

1% Argon
21% Oxygen
78% Nitrogen

Troposphere

Pacific Ocean
Cloud patterns over the Pacific show the paths of prevailing winds.

Circulation of the air

Circulation of the air
Owing to high temperatures in equatorial regions the air near the ground is heated, expands and rises producing a low pressure belt. It cools, causing rain, spreads out then sinks again about latitudes 30° north and south forming high pressure belts.

High and low pressure belts are areas of comparative calm but between them, blowing from high to low pressure, are the prevailing winds. · These are deflected to the right in the northern hemisphere and to the left in the southern hemisphere (Corolis effect). The circulations appear in three distinct belts with a seasonal movement north and south following the overhead sun.

Cloud types

Clouds form when damp air is cooled, usually by rising. This may happen in three ways: when a wind rises to cross hills or mountains; when a mass of air rises over, or is pushed up by another mass of denser air; when local heating of the ground causes convection currents.

Cirrus *(1)* are detached clouds composed of microscopic ice crystals which gleam white in the sun resembling hair or feathers. They are found at heights of 6 000 to 12 000 metres.

Cirrostratus *(2)* are a whitish veil of cloud made up of ice crystals through which the sun can be seen often producing a halo of bright light.

Cirrocumulus *(3)* is another high altitude cloud formed by turbulence between layers moving in different directions.

Altostratus *(4)* is a grey or bluish striated, fibrous or uniform sheet of cloud producing light drizzle.

Altocumulus *(5)* is a thicker and fluffier version of cirro cumulus, it is a white and grey patchy sheet of cloud.

Nimbostratus *(6)* is a dark grey layer of cloud obscuring the sun and causing almost continuous rain or snow.

Cumulus *(7)* are detached heaped up, dense low clouds. The sunlit parts are brilliant white while the base is relatively dark and flat.

Stratus *(8)* forms dull overcast skies associated with depressions and occurs at low altitudes up to 1500 metres.

Cumulonimbus *(9)* are heavy and dense clouds associated with storms and rain. They have flat bases and a fluffy outline extending up to great altitudes.

High clouds

Middle clouds

Low clouds

Thousands of metres

1 Cirrus

2 Cirrostratus

3 Cirrocumulus

4 Altostratus

5 Altocumulus

6 Nimbostratus

7 Cumulus

8 Stratus

9 Cumulonimbus

Climate and Weather

All weather occurs over the earth's surface in the lowest level of the atmosphere, the troposphere. Weather has been defined as the condition of the atmosphere at any place at a specific time with respect to the various elements: temperature, sunshine, pressure, winds, clouds, fog, precipitation. Climate, on the other hand, is the average of weather elements over previous months and years.

Climate graphs *right*
Each graph typifies the kind of climatic conditions one would experience in the region to which it is related by colour to the map. The scale refers to degrees Celsius for temperature and millimetres for rainfall, shown by bars. The graphs show average observations based over long periods of time, the study of which also compares the prime factors for vegetation differences.

Development of a depression *below*
In an equilibrium front between cold and warm air masses (i) a wave disturbance develops as cold air undercuts the warm air (ii). This deflects the air flow and as the disturbance progresses a definite cyclonic circulation with warm and cold fronts is created (iii). The cold front moves more rapidly than the warm front eventually overtaking it, and occlusion occurs as the warm air is pinched out (iv).

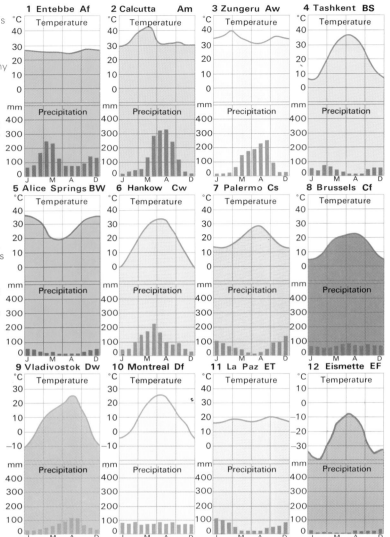

1 Entebbe Af
2 Calcutta Am
3 Zungeru Aw
4 Tashkent BS
5 Alice Springs BW
6 Hankow Cw
7 Palermo Cs
8 Brussels Cf
9 Vladivostok Dw
10 Montreal Df
11 La Paz ET
12 Eismette EF

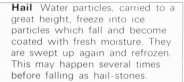

Af Equatorial forest
Am Monsoon forest
Aw Savanna

Tropical climates

| Af | Am | Aw |

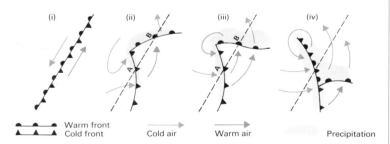

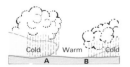
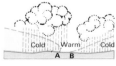
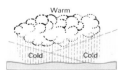

Warm front
Cold front
Cold air
Warm air
Precipitation

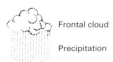

Frontal cloud
Precipitation

The upper diagrams show in plan view stages in the development of a depression.
The cross sections below correspond to stages (ii) to (iv).

Kinds of precipitation

Rain The condensation of water vapour on microscopic particles of dust, sulphur, soot or ice in the atmosphere forms water particles. These combine until they are heavy enough to fall as rain.

Hail Water particles, carried to a great height, freeze into ice particles which fall and become coated with fresh moisture. They are swept up again and refrozen. This may happen several times before falling as hail-stones.

Frost Hoar, the most common type of frost, is precipitated instead of dew when water vapour changes directly into ice crystals on the surface of ground objects which have cooled below freezing point.

Snow is the precipitation of ice in the form of flakes, or clusters, of basically hexagonal ice crystals. They are formed by the condensation of water vapour directly into ice.

10

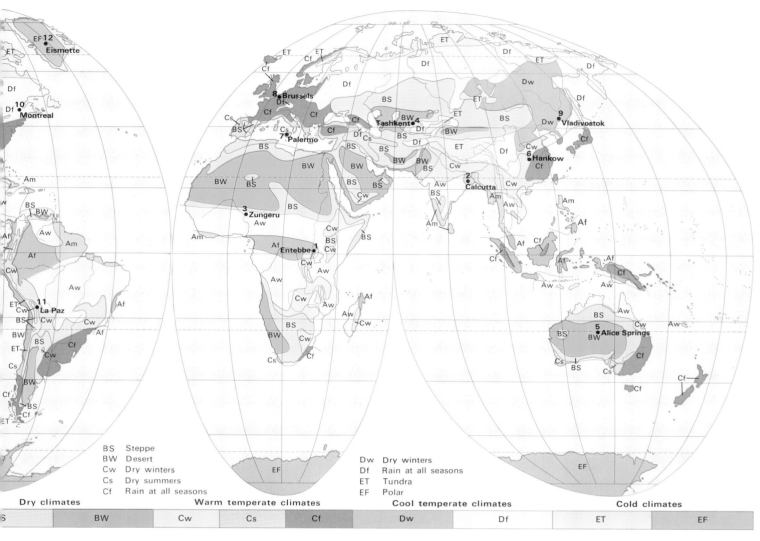

BS Steppe
BW Desert
Cw Dry winters
Cs Dry summers
Cf Rain at all seasons

Dw Dry winters
Df Rain at all seasons
ET Tundra
EF Polar

Dry climates   Warm temperate climates   Cool temperate climates   Cold climates

| S | BW | Cw | Cs | Cf | Dw | Df | ET | EF |

Tropical storm tracks *below*

A tropical cyclone, or storm, is designated as having winds of gale force (60 kph) but less than hurricane force (120 kph). It is a homogenous air mass with upward spiralling air currents around a windless centre, or eye. An average of 65 tropical storms occur each year, over 50% of which reach hurricane force. They originate mainly during the summer over tropical oceans.

Extremes of climate & weather *right*

Tropical high temperatures and polar low temperatures combined with wind systems, altitude and unequal rainfall distribution result in the extremes of tropical rain forests, inland deserts and frozen polar wastes. Fluctuations in the limits of these extreme zones and extremes of weather result in occasional catastrophic heat-waves and drought, floods and storms, frost and snow.

Hurricane devastation

Hot desert

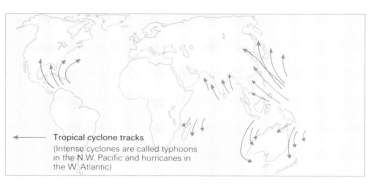

← Tropical cyclone tracks
(Intense cyclones are called typhoons in the N.W. Pacific and hurricanes in the W. Atlantic)

Tornado

Arctic dwellings

11

The Earth from Space

Mount Etna, Sicily *left*
Etna is at the top of the photograph, the Plain of Catania in the centre and the Mediterranean to the right. This is an infra-red photograph; vegetation shows as red, water as blue/black and urban areas as grey. The recent lava flows, as yet with no vegetation, show up as blue/black unlike the cultivated slopes which are red and red/pink.

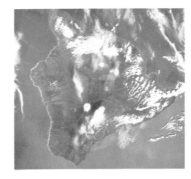

Hawaii, Pacific Ocean *above*
This is a photograph of Hawaii, the largest of the Hawaiian Islands in the Central Pacific. North is at the top of the photograph. The snowcapped craters of the volcanoes Mauna Kea (dormant) in the north centre and Mauna Loa (active) in the south centre of the photograph can be seen. The chief town, Hilo, is on the north east coast.

River Brahmaputra, India *left*
A view looking westwards down the Brahmaputra with the Himalayas on the right and the Khasi Hills of Assam to the left.

Szechwan, China *right*
The River Tachin in the mountainous region of Szechwan, Central China. The lightish blue area in the river valley in the north east of the photograph is a village and its related cultivation.

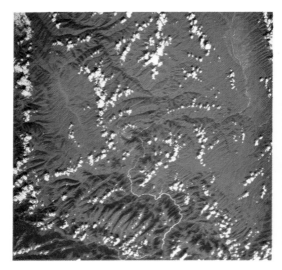

New York, U.S.A. *left*
This infra-red photograph shows the western end of Long Island and the entrance to the Hudson River. Vegetation appears as red, water as blue/black and the metropolitan areas of New York, through the cloud cover, as grey.

The Great Barrier Reef, Australia *right*
The Great Barrier Reef and the Queensland coast from Cape Melville to Cape Flattery. The smoke from a number of forest fires can be seen in the centre of the photograph.

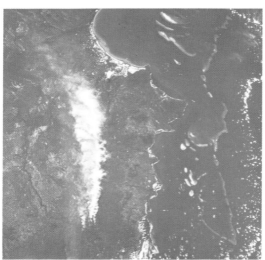

Eastern Himalayas, Asia
above left
A view from Apollo IX looking north-westwards over the snowcapped, sunlit mountain peaks and the head waters of the Mekong, Salween, Irrawaddy and, in the distance, with its distinctive loop, the Brahmaputra.

Atacama Desert, Chile
above right
This view looking eastwards from the Pacific over the Mejillones peninsula with the city of Antofagasta in the southern bay of that peninsula. Inland the desert and salt-pans of Atacama, and beyond, the Andes.

The Alps, Europe *right*
This vertical photograph shows the snow-covered mountains and glaciers of the Alps along the Swiss-Italian-French border. Mont Blanc and the Matterhorn are shown and, in the north, the Valley of the Rhône is seen making its sharp right-hand bend near Martigny. In the south the head waters of the Dora Baltea flow towards the Po and, in the north-west, the Lac d'Annecy can be seen.

The Evolution of the Continents

The origin of the earth is still open to much conjecture although the most widely accepted theory is that it was formed from a solar cloud consisting mainly of hydrogen. Under gravitation the cloud condensed and shrank to form our planets orbiting around the sun. Gravitation forced the lighter elements to the surface of the earth where they cooled to form a crust while the inner material remained hot and molten. Earth's first rocks formed over 3500 million years ago but since then the surface has been constantly altered.

Until comparatively recently the view that the primary units of the earth had remained essentially fixed throughout geological time was regarded as common sense, although the concept of moving continents has been traced back to references in the Bible of a break up of the land after Noah's floods. The continental drift theory was first developed by Antonio Snider in 1858 but probably the most important single advocate was Alfred Wegener who, in 1915, published evidence from geology, climatology and biology. His conclusions are very similar to those reached by current research although he was wrong about the speed of break-up.

The measurement of fossil magnetism found in rocks has probably proved the most influential evidence. While originally these drift theories were openly mocked, now they are considered standard doctrine.

The jigsaw
As knowledge of the shape and structure of the earth's surface grew, several of the early geographers noticed the great similarity in shape of the coasts bordering the Atlantic. It was this remarkable similarity which led to the first detailed geological and structural comparisons. Even more accurate fits can be made by placing the edges of the continental shelves in juxtaposition.

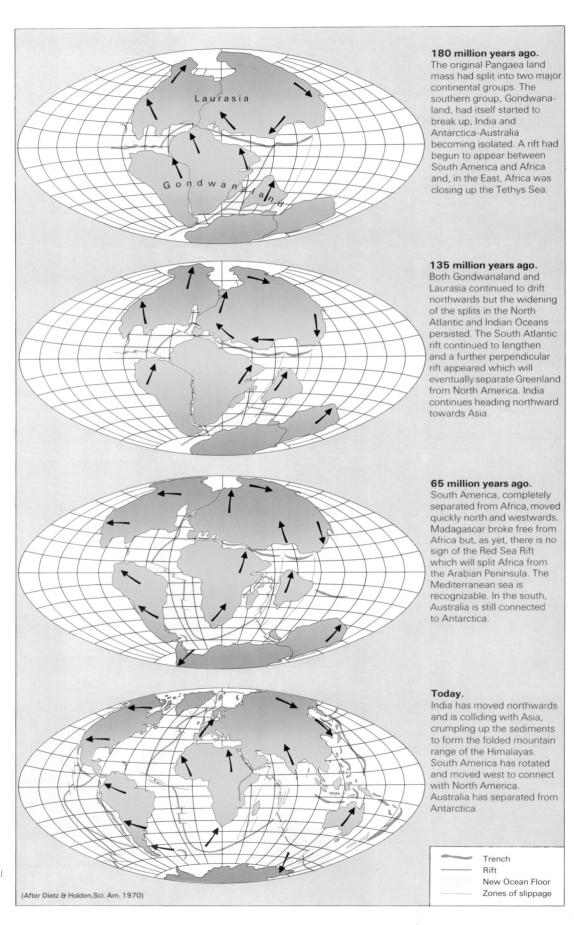

(After Dietz & Holden, Sci. Am. 1970)

180 million years ago.
The original Pangaea land mass had split into two major continental groups. The southern group, Gondwanaland, had itself started to break up, India and Antarctica-Australia becoming isolated. A rift had begun to appear between South America and Africa and, in the East, Africa was closing up the Tethys Sea.

135 million years ago.
Both Gondwanaland and Laurasia continued to drift northwards but the widening of the splits in the North Atlantic and Indian Oceans persisted. The South Atlantic rift continued to lengthen and a further perpendicular rift appeared which will eventually separate Greenland from North America. India continues heading northward towards Asia.

65 million years ago.
South America, completely separated from Africa, moved quickly north and westwards. Madagascar broke free from Africa but, as yet, there is no sign of the Red Sea Rift which will split Africa from the Arabian Peninsula. The Mediterranean sea is recognizable. In the south, Australia is still connected to Antarctica.

Today.
India has moved northwards and is colliding with Asia, crumpling up the sediments to form the folded mountain range of the Himalayas. South America has rotated and moved west to connect with North America. Australia has separated from Antarctica.

～	Trench
—	Rift
	New Ocean Floor
	Zones of slippage

Plate tectonics

The original debate about continental drift was only a prelude to a more radical idea; plate tectonics. The basic theory is that the earth's crust is made up of a series of rigid plates which float on a soft layer of the mantle and are moved about by convection currents in the earth's interior. These plates converge and diverge along margins marked by earthquakes, volcanoes and other seismic activity. Plates diverge from mid-ocean ridges where molten lava pushes upwards and forces the plates apart at a rate of up to 40 mm a year. Converging plates form either a trench, where the oceanic plate sinks below the lighter continental rock, or mountain ranges where two continents collide. This explains the paradox that while there have always been oceans none of the present oceans contain sediments more than 150 million years old.

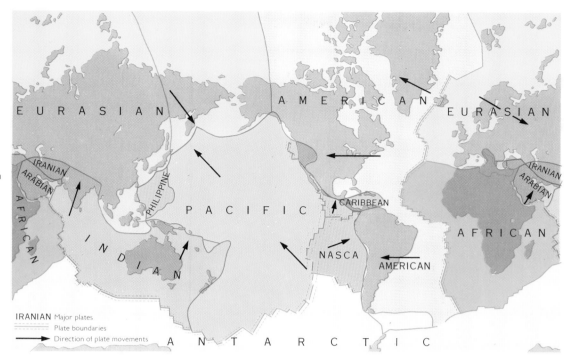

IRANIAN Major plates
- - - - Plate boundaries
→ Direction of plate movements

Trench boundary

The present explanation for the comparative youth of the ocean floors is that where an ocean and a continent meet the ocean plate dips under the less dense continental plate at an angle of approximately 45°. All previous crust is then ingested by downward convection currents. In the Japanese trench this occurs at a rate of about 120 mm a year.

Transform fault

The recent identification of the transform, or transverse, fault proved to be one of the crucial preliminaries to the investigation of plate tectonics. They occur when two plates slip alongside each other without parting or approaching to any great extent. They complete the outline of the plates delineated by the ridges and trenches and demonstrate large scale movements of parts of the earth's surface

Ridge boundary

Ocean rises or crests are basically made up from basaltic lavas for although no gap can exist between plates, one plate can ease itself away from another. In that case hot, molten rock instantly rises from below to fill in the incipient rift and forms a ridge. These ridges trace a line almost exactly through the centre of the major oceans.

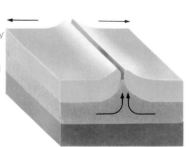

Destruction of ocean plates.

As the ocean plate sinks below the continental plate some of the sediment on its surface is scraped off and piled up on the landward side. This sediment is later incorporated in a folded mountain range which usually appears on the edge of the continent, such as the Andes. Similarly if two continents collide the sediments are squeezed up into new mountains.

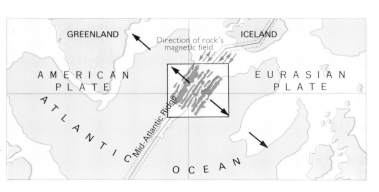

Sea floor spreading

Reversals in direction of the earth's magnetic field have occurred throughout history. As molten rock emerges at the ocean ridges it cools and is magnetised in the direction of the earth's magnetic field. By mapping the ocean floor across the ridge a striped pattern of solidified rock magnetised in alternate directions is produced (see inset area). As the dates of the last few reversals are known the rate of spreading can be calculated (40mm per year in the North Atlantic).

The Unstable Earth

The earth's surface is slowly but continually being rearranged. Some changes such as erosion and deposition are extremely slow but they upset the balance which causes other more abrupt changes often originating deep within the earth's interior. The constant movements vary in intensity, often with stresses building up to a climax such as a particularly violent volcanic eruption or earthquake.

The crust *(below and right)*
The outer layer or crust of the earth consists of a comparatively low density, brittle material varying from 5 km to 50 km deep beneath the continents. This consists predominately of silica and aluminium; hence it is called 'sial'. Extending under the ocean floors and below the sial is a basaltic layer known as 'sima', consisting mainly of silica and magnesium.

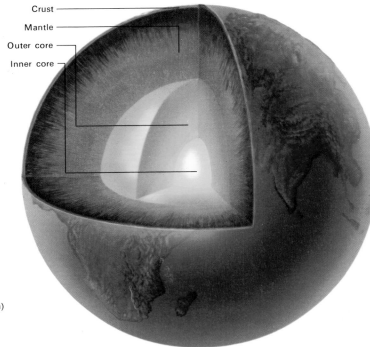

Crust
Mantle
Outer core
Inner core

Continental crust   Ocean crust

Sediment
Granite rock (sial)
Basaltic layer (sima)
Mantle

Volcanoes *(right, below and far right)*
Volcanoes occur when hot liquefied rock beneath the crust reaches the surface as lava. An accumulation of ash and cinders around a vent forms a cone. Successive layers of thin lava flows form an acid lava volcano while thick lava flows form a basic lava volcano. A caldera forms when a particularly violent eruption blows off the top of an already existing cone.

The mantle *(above)*
Immediately below the crust, at the mohorovicic discontinuity line, there is a distinct change in density and chemical properties. This is the mantle - made up of iron and magnesium silicates - with temperatures reaching 1 600 °C. The rigid upper mantle extends down to a depth of about 1 000 km below which is the more viscous lower mantle which is about 1 900 km thick.

The core *(above)*
The outer core, approximately 2 100 km thick, consists of molten iron and nickel at 2 000 °C to 5 000 °C possibly separated from the less dense mantle by an oxidised shell. About 5 000 km below the surface is the liquid transition zone, below which is the solid inner core, a sphere of 2 740 km diameter where rock is three times as dense as in the crust.

Shield volcano   **Cinder cone**   **Hornit cone**   **Caldera**

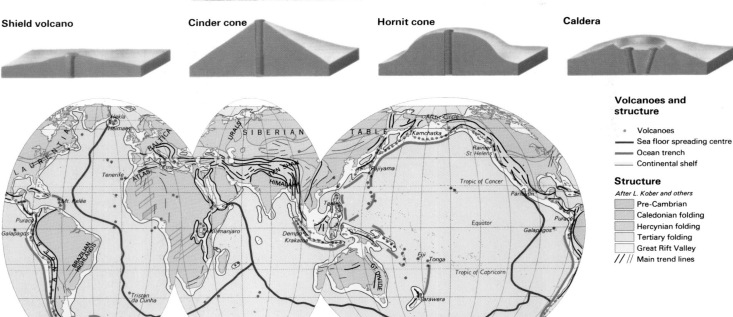

Volcanoes and structure

· Volcanoes
— Sea floor spreading centre
— Ocean trench
— Continental shelf

Structure
After L. Kober and others
Pre-Cambrian
Caledonian folding
Hercynian folding
Tertiary folding
Great Rift Valley
/// // Main trend lines

Major earthquakes in the last 100 years and numbers killed

Year	Location	Killed
1896	Japan (tsunami)	22 000
1906	San Francisco	destroyed
1906	Chile, Valparaiso	22 000
1908	Italy, Messina	77 000
1920	China, Kansu	180 000
1923	Japan, Tokyo	143 000
1930	Italy, Naples	2 100
1931	New Zealand, Napier	destroyed
1931	Nicaragua, Managua	destroyed
1932	China, Kansu	70 000
1935	India, Quetta	60 000
1939	Chile, Chillan	20 000
1939/40	Turkey, Erzincan	30 000
1948	Japan, Fukui	5 100
1956	N. Afghanistan	2 000
1957	W. Iran	10 000
1960	Morocco, Agadir	12 000
1962	N.W. Iran	10 000
1963	Yugoslavia, Skopje	1 000
1966	U.S.S.R., Tashkent	destroyed
1970	N. Peru	66 800
1974	N. Pakistan	10 000
1976	China, Tangshan	650 000
1978	Iran, Tabas	11 000
1980	Algeria, El Asnam	20 000
1985	Mexico City, Mexico	20 000

World distribution of earthquakes

- Major earthquake zones
- Areas experiencing frequent earthquakes

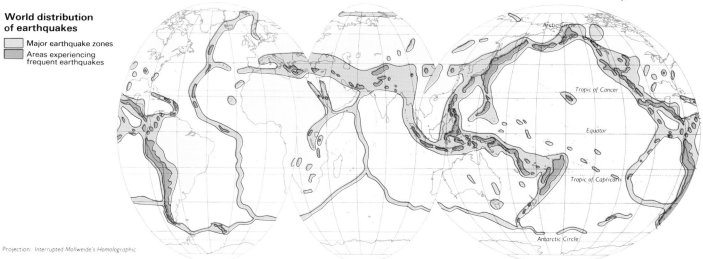

Projection: Interrupted Mollweide's Homolographic

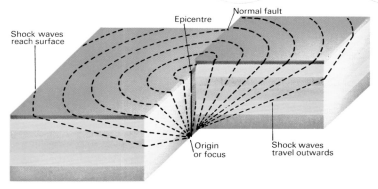

Earthquakes *(right and above)*

Earthquakes are a series of rapid vibrations originating from the slipping or faulting of parts of the earth's crust when stresses within build up to breaking point. They usually happen at depths varying from 8 km to 30 km. Severe earthquakes cause extensive damage when they take place in populated areas destroying structures and severing communications. Most loss of life occurs due to secondary causes i.e. falling masonry, fires or tsunami waves.

Alaskan earthquake, 1964

Tsunami waves *(left)*

A sudden slump in the ocean bed during an earthquake forms a trough in the water surface subsequently followed by a crest and smaller waves. A more marked change of level in the sea bed can form a crest, the start of a Tsunami which travels up to 600 km/h with waves up to 60 m high. Seismographic detectors continuously record earthquake shocks and warn of the Tsunami which may follow it.

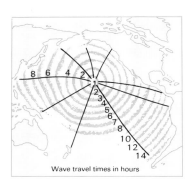

Wave travel times in hours

Seismic Waves *(right)*

The shock waves sent out from the focus of an earthquake are of three main kinds each with distinct properties. Primary (P) waves are compressional waves which can be transmitted through both solids and liquids and therefore pass through the earth's liquid core. Secondary (S) waves are shear waves and can only pass through solids. They cannot pass through the core and are reflected at the core-mantle boundary taking a concave course back to the surface. The core also refracts the P waves causing them to alter course, and the net effect of this reflection and refraction is the production of a shadow zone at a certain distance from the epicentre, free from P and S waves. Due to their different properties P waves travel about 1,7 times faster than S waves. The third main kind of wave is a long (L) wave, a slow wave which travels along the earth's surface, its motion being either horizontal or vertical.

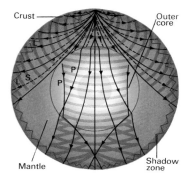

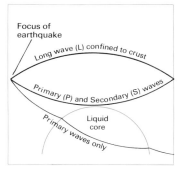

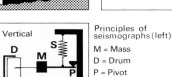

Principles of seismographs (left)

M = Mass
D = Drum
P = Pivot
S = Spring

Seismographs are delicate instruments capable of detecting and recording vibrations due to earthquakes thousands of kilometres away. P waves cause the first tremors. S the second, and L the main shock.

The Making of Landscape

The making of landscape

The major forces which shape our land would seem to act very slowly in comparison with man's average life span but in geological terms the erosion of rock is in fact very fast. Land goes through a cycle of transformation. The diagrams on the right show how a rise in sea level in diagram (2) causes a layer of new rocks formed from the sediments of rivers and the crushed remains of countless animals and plants to be overlain on the original lowlands (1). Millions of years later (3) the waters recede and the new rocks form a plain. Eventually these new rocks are eroded by rain, wind, ice and rivers (4) to once again reveal the original ridges.

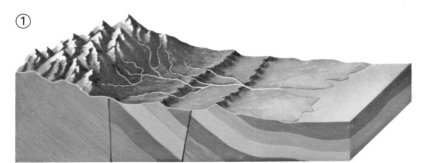
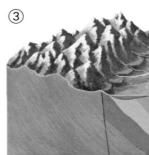

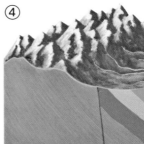

Rivers

Rivers shape the land by three basic processes: erosion, transportation, and deposition. A youthful river flows fast eroding downwards quickly to form a narrow valley (1). As it matures it deposits some debris and erodes laterally to widen the valley (2). In its last stage it meanders across a wide flat flood plain depositing fine particles of alluvium (3).

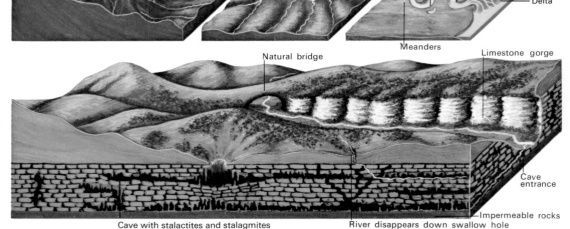

Youthful stage

Mature stage

Ox-bow

Old age stage

Delta

Meanders

Underground water

Water enters porous and permeable rocks from the surface moving downward until it reaches a layer of impermeable rock. Joints in underground rock, such as limestone, are eroded to form underground caves and caverns. When the roof of a cave collapses a gorge is formed. Surface entrances to joints are often widened to form vertical openings called swallow holes.

Natural bridge

Limestone gorge

Cave entrance

Impermeable rocks

Cave with stalactites and stalagmites

River disappears down swallow hole

Wind

Wind action is particularly powerful in arid and semi-arid regions where rock waste produced by weathering is used as an abrasive tool by the wind. The rate of erosion varies with the characteristics of the rock which can cause weird shapes and effects (right). Desert sand can also be accumulated by the wind to form barchan dunes (far right) which slowly travel forward, horns first.

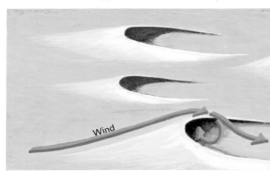

Wind

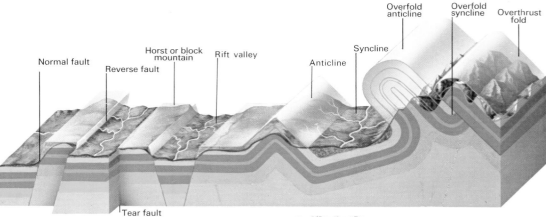

Normal fault · Reverse fault · Horst or block mountain · Rift valley · Anticline · Syncline · Overfold anticline · Overfold syncline · Overthrust fold · Tear fault

Folding and faulting

A vertical displacement in the earth's crust is called a fault or reverse fault; lateral displacement is a tear fault. An uplifted block is called a horst, the reverse of which is a rift valley. Compressed horizontal layers of sedimentary rock fold to form mountains. Those layers which bend up form an anticline, those bending down form a syncline : continued pressure forms an overfold.

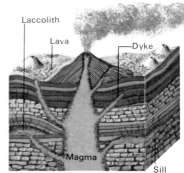

Laccolith · Lava · Dyke · Magma · Sill

Volcanic activity

When pressure on rocks below the earth's crust is released the normally semi-solid hot rock becomes liquid magma. The magma forces its way into cracks of the crust and may either reach the surface where it forms volcanoes or it may collect in the crust as sills dykes or laccoliths. When magma reaches the surface it cools to form lava.

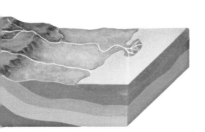

Waves

Coasts are continually changing, some retreat under wave erosion while others advance with wave deposition. These actions combined form steep cliffs and wave cut platforms. Eroded debris is in turn deposited as a terrace. As the water becomes shallower the erosive power of the waves decreases and gradually the cliff disappears. Wave action can also create other features (far right).

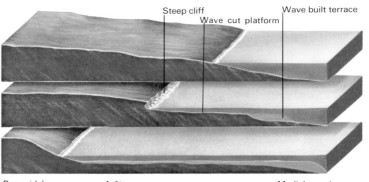

Steep cliff · Wave cut platform · Wave built terrace

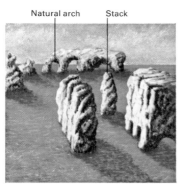

Natural arch · Stack

Ice

These diagrams (right) show how a glaciated valley may have formed. The glacier deepens, straightens and widens the river valley whose interlocking spurs become truncated or cut off. Intervalley divides are frost shattered to form sharp arêtes and pyramidal peaks. Hanging valleys mark the entry of tributary rivers and eroded rocks form medial moraine. Terminal moraine is deposited as the glacier retreats.

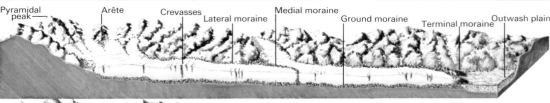

Pyramidal peak · Arête · Crevasses · Lateral moraine · Medial moraine · Ground moraine · Terminal moraine · Outwash plain

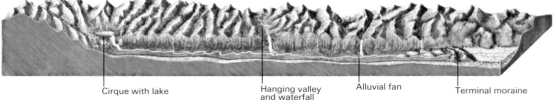

Cirque with lake · Hanging valley and waterfall · Alluvial fan · Terminal moraine

Subsidence and uplift

As the land surface is eroded it may eventually become a level plain - a peneplain, broken only by low hills, remnants of previous mountains. In turn this peneplain may be uplifted to form a plateau with steep edges. At the coast the uplifted wave platform becomes a coastal plain and in the rejuvenated rivers downward erosion once more predominates.

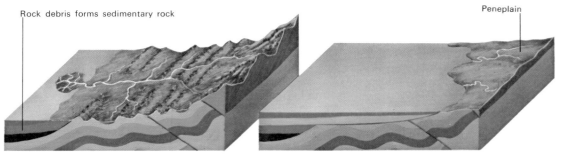

Rock debris forms sedimentary rock · Peneplain

The Earth: Physical Dimensions

Its surface
Highest point on the earth's
surface: Mt. Everest, Tibet -
Nepal boundary   8 848 m
Lowest point on the earth's
surface: The Dead Sea,
Jordan   below sea level 395 m
Greatest ocean depth.:
Challenger Deep, Mariana
Trench   11 022 m
Average height of land   840 m
Average depth of seas
and oceans   3 808 m

Dimensions
Superficial area	510 000 000 km^2
Land surface	149 000 000 km^2
Land surface as % of total area	29·2 %
Water surface	361 000 000 km^2
Water surface as % of total area	70·8 %
Equatorial circumference	40 077 km
Meridional circumference	40 009 km
Equatorial diameter	12 756·8 km
Polar diameter	12 713·8 km
Equatorial radius	6 378·4 km
Polar radius	6 356·9 km
Volume of the Earth	1 083 230 x 10^6 km^3
Mass of the Earth	5·9 x 10^{21} tonnes

The Figure of Earth
An imaginary sea-level surface is
considered and called a geoid. By
measuring at different places the
angles from plumb lines to a fixed
star there have been many
determinations of the shape of parts
of the geoid which is found to be an
oblate spheriod with its axis along
the axis of rotation of the earth.
Observations from satellites have
now given a new method of more
accurate determinations of the
figure of the earth and its local
irregularities.

Land and Sea Hemispheres.
About 85% of the total land area
is contained in the hemisphere
centred on a point between
Paris and Brussels.

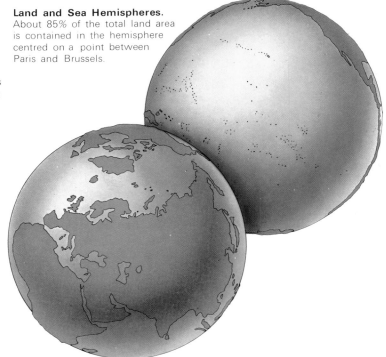

Oceans and Seas
Area in 1000 km²

Pacific Ocean	165 721	North Sea	575
Atlantic Ocean	81 660	Black Sea	448
Indian Ocean	73 442	Red Sea	440
Arctic Ocean	14 351	Baltic Sea	422
Mediterranean Sea	2 966	The Gulf	238
Bering Sea	2 274	St. Lawrence, Gulf of	236
Caribbean Sea	1 942	English Channel & Irish Sea	179
Mexico, Gulf of	1 813	California, Gulf of	161
Okhotsk, Sea of	1 528		
East China Sea	1 248		
Hudson Bay	1 230		
Japan, Sea of	1 049		

Lakes and Inland Seas
Areas in 1000 km²

Caspian Sea, Asia	424·2	Lake Ontario, N.America	19·5
Lake Superior, N.America	82·4	Lake Ladoga, Europe	18·4
Lake Victoria, Africa	69·5	Lake Balkhash, Asia	17·3
Aral Sea (Salt), Asia	63·8	Lake Maracaibo, S.America	16·3
Lake Huron, N.America	59·6	Lake Onega, Europe	9·8
Lake Michigan, N.America	58·0	Lake Eyre (Salt), Australia	9·6
Lake Tanganyika, Africa	32·9	Lake Turkana (Salt), Africa	9·1
Lake Baikal, Asia	31·5	Lake Titicaca, S.America	8·3
Great Bear Lake, N.America	31·1	Lake Nicaragua, C.America	8·0
Great Slave Lake, N.America	28·9	Lake Athabasca, N.America	7·9
Lake Nyasa, Africa	28·5	Reindeer Lake, N.America	6·3
Lake Erie, N.America	25·7	Issyk-Kul, Asia	6·2
Lake Winnipeg, N.America	24·3	Lake Torrens (Salt), Australia	6·1
Lake Chad, Africa	20·7	Koko Nor (Salt), Asia	6·0
		Lake Urmia, Asia	6·0
		Vänern, Europe	5·6

Longest rivers
	km.
Nile, Africa	6 690
Amazon, S.America	6 280
Mississippi-Missouri, N.America	6 270
Yangtze, Asia	4 990
Zaïre, Africa	4 670
Amur, Asia	4 410
Hwang Ho (Yellow), Asia	4 350
Lena, Asia	4 260
Mekong, Asia	4 180
Niger, Africa	4 180
Mackenzie, N.America	4 040
Ob, Asia	4 000
Yenisei, Asia	3 800

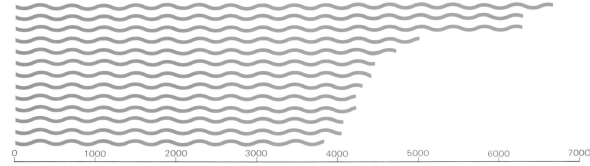

0   1000   2000   3000   4000   5000   6000   7000

The Highest Mountains and the Greatest Depths.

Mount Everest defied the world's greatest mountaineers for 32 years and claimed the lives of many men. Not until 1920 was permission granted by the Dalai Lama to attempt the mountain, and the first successful ascent came in 1953. Since then the summit has been reached several times. The world's highest peaks have now been climbed but there are many as yet unexplored peaks in the Himalayas some of which may be over 7 600 m.

The greatest trenches are the Puerto Rico deep (9 200m). The Tonga (10 822 m) and Mindanao (10 497 m) trenches and the Mariana Trench (11 022 m) in the Pacific. The trenches represent less than 2% of the total area of the sea-bed but are of great interest as lines of structural weakness in the Earth's crust and as areas of frequent earthquakes.

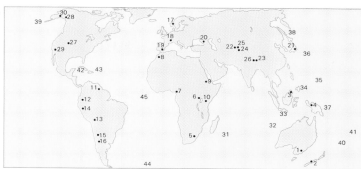

High mountains

Bathyscaphe

Waterfall

Dam

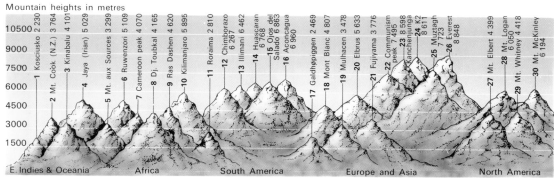

Mountain heights in metres

1 Kosciusko 2 230, 2 Mt. Cook (N.Z.) 3 764, 3 Kinabalu 4 101, 4 Jaya (Irian) 5 029, 5 Mt. aux Sources 3 299, 6 Ruwenzori 5 109, 7 Cameroon peak 4 070, 8 Dj. Toubkal 4 165, 9 Ras Dashen 4 620, 10 Kilimanjaro 5 895, 11 Roraima 2 810, 12 Chimborazo 6 267, 13 Illimani 6 462, 14 Huascaran 6 768, 15 Ojos del Salado 6 863, 16 Aconcagua 6 960, 17 Galdhøpiggen 2 469, 18 Mont Blanc 4 807, 19 Mulhacen 3 478, 20 Elbrus 5 633, 21 Fujiyama 3 776, 22 Communism peak 7 495, 23 Kanchenjunga 8 598, 24 K2 8 611, 25 Muztagh 7 723, 26 Everest 8 848, 27 Mt. Elbert 4 399, 28 Mt. Logan 6 050, 29 Mt. Whitney 4 418, 30 Mt. McKinley 6 194

E. Indies & Oceania — Africa — South America — Europe and Asia — North America

Ocean depths in metres — Sea level

31 Mauritius basin 6 400, 32 W. Australian basin 6 459, 33 Java trench 7 450, 34 Mindanao trench 10 497, 35 Mariana trench 11 022, 36 Japan trench 10 554, 37 Bougainville deep 9 140, 38 Kuril trench 10 542, 39 Aleutian trench 7 822, 40 Kermadec trench 10 047, 41 Tonga trench 10 822, 42 Cayman trough 7 680, 43 Puerto Rico trough 9 200, 44 S. Sandwich trench 8 428, 45 Romanche deep 7 758

Indian Ocean — Pacific Ocean — Atlantic Ocean

Notable Waterfalls
heights in metres

Angel, Venezuela	980
Tugela, S. Africa	853
Mongefossen, Norway	774
Yosemite, California	738
Mardalsfossen, Norway	655
Cuquenan, Venezuela	610
Sutherland, N.Z.	579
Reichenbach, Switzerland	548
Wollomombi, Australia	518
Ribbon, California	491
Gavarnie, France	422
Tyssefallene, Norway	414
Krimml, Austria	370
King George VI, Guyana	366
Silver Strand, California	356
Geissbach, Switzerland	350
Staubbach, Switzerland	299
Trümmelbach, Switzerland	290
Chirombo, Zambia	268
Livingstone, Zaïre	259
King Edward VIII, Guyana	256
Gersoppa, India	253
Vettifossen Norway	250
Kalambo, Zambia	240
Kaieteur, Guyana	226
Maletsunyane, Lesotho	192
Terui, Italy	180
Kabarega, Uganda	122
Victoria, Zimbabwe-Zambia	107
Cauvery, India	97
Boyoma, Zaïre	61
Niagara, N.America	51
Schaffhausen, Switzerland	30

Notable Dams
heights in metres
Africa

Cabora Bassa, Zambezi R.	168
Akosombo Main Dam Volta R.	141
Kariba, Zambezi R.	128
Aswan High Dam, Nile R.	110

Asia

Nurek, Vakhsh R., U.S.S.R.	317
Sayano-Shushensk, U.S.S.R.	245
Bhakra, Sutlej R., India	226
Toktogul, U.S.S.R.	215
Kurobegawa, Kurobe R., Jap.	186
Charvak, Chirchik R., U.S.S.R.	168
Okutadami, Tadami R., Jap.	157
Bratsk, Angara R., U.S.S.R.	125

Oceania

Warragamba, N.S.W., Australia	137
Eucumbene, N.S.W., Australia	116

Europe

Grande Dixence, Switz.	284
Inguri R., U.S.S.R.	272
Vajont, Vajont, R., Italy	261
Mauvoisin, Drance R., Switz.	237
Chirkei, U.S.S.R.	233
Contra, Verzasca R., Switz.	230
Mratinje, Yugoslavia	220
Luzzone, Brenno R., Switz.	208
Tignes, Isère R., France	180
Amir Kabir, Karadj R., U.S.S.R.	180
Vidraru, Arges R., Rom.	165
Kremasta, Acheloos R., Greece	165

North America

Chicoasén, Mexico	261
Alvaro Obregon, Mexico	260
Mica, Columbia R., Can.	242
Oroville, Feather R.,	235
Hoover, Colorado R.,	221
Dworshak, Idaho	219
Glen Canyon, Colorado R.,	216
Daniel Johnson, Can.	214
New Bullards Bar, N. Yuba R.	194
Mossyrock, Cowlitz R.,	184
Shasta, Sacramento R.,	183
W.A.C. Bennett, Canada.	183

Central and South America

Chivor, Colombia	237
Guri, Caroni R., Venezuela.	106

Distances

Kms

Lower-left triangle = distances in kilometres; upper-right triangle = distances in miles. The diagonal labels (Berlin, Bombay, Buenos Aires, Cairo, Calcutta, Caracas, Chicago, Copenhagen, Darwin, Hong Kong, Honolulu, Johannesburg, Lagos, Lisbon …) serve as both the row and column headings.

Kilometres (lower-left triangle)

	Berlin	Bombay	Buenos Aires	Cairo	Calcutta	Caracas	Chicago	Copenhagen	Darwin	Hong Kong	Honolulu	Johannesburg	Lagos	Lisbon	London
Berlin															
Bombay	6288														
Buenos Aires	11909	14925													
Cairo	2890	4355	11814												
Calcutta	7033	1664	16524	5699											
Caracas	8435	14522	5096	10203	15464										
Chicago	7084	12953	9011	3206	12839	4027									
Copenhagen	357	6422	12067	9860	7072	8392	6840								
Darwin	12946	7257	14693	11612	6047	18059	15065	12903							
Hong Kong	8754	4317	18478	8150	2659	16360	12526	8671	4271						
Honolulu	11764	12914	12164	14223	11343	9670	6836	11407	8640	8921					
Johannesburg	8870	6974	8088	6267	8459	11019	13984	9225	10639	10732	19206				
Lagos	5198	7612	7916	3915	9216	7741	9612	5530	14222	11845	16308	4505			
Lisbon	2311	8018	9600	3794	9075	6501	6424	2478	15114	11028	12587	8191	3799		
London	928	7190	11131	3508	7961	7507	6356	952	13848	9623	11632	9071	5017	1588	
Los Angeles	9311	14000	9852	12200	13120	5812	2804	9003	12695	11639	4117	16676	12414	9122	87…
Mexico City	9732	15656	7389	12372	15280	3586	2726	9514	14631	14122	6085	14585	11071	8676	89…
Moscow	1610	5031	13477	2902	5534	9938	8000	1561	11350	7144	11323	9161	6254	3906	24…
Nairobi	6370	4532	10402	3536	6179	11544	12883	6706	10415	8776	17282	2927	3807	6461	68…
New York	6385	12541	8526	9020	12747	3430	1145	6188	16047	12950	7980	12841	8477	5422	55…
Paris	876	7010	11051	3210	7858	7625	6650	1026	13812	9630	11968	8732	4714	1454	3…
Peking	7822	4757	19268	7544	3269	14399	10603	7202	6011	1963	8160	11710	11457	9668	81…
Reykjavik	2385	8335	11437	5266	8687	6915	4757	2103	13892	9681	9787	10938	6718	2948	18…
Rio de Janeiro	10025	13409	1953	9896	15073	4546	8547	10211	16011	17704	13342	7113	6035	7734	92…
Rome	1180	6175	11151	2133	7219	8363	7739	1531	13265	9284	12916	7743	4039	1861	14…
Singapore	9944	3914	15879	8267	2897	18359	15078	9969	3349	2599	10816	8660	11145	11886	108…
Sydney	16096	10160	11800	14418	9138	15343	14875	16042	3150	7374	8168	11040	15519	18178	169…
Tokyo	8924	6742	18362	9571	5141	14164	10137	8696	5431	2874	6202	13547	13480	11149	95…
Toronto	6497	12488	9093	9233	12561	3873	700	6265	15498	12569	7465	13374	8948	5737	57…
Wellington	18140	12370	9981	16524	11354	13122	13451	17961	5325	9427	7513	11761	16050	19575	188…

Miles (upper-right triangle; cut off at right edge)

Row city	Distances to successive columns (Bombay → London → …)
Berlin	3907, 7400, 1795, 4370, 5241, 4402, 222, 8044, 5440, 7310, 5511, 3230, 1436, 5…
Bombay	9275, 2706, 1034, 9024, 8048, 3990, 4510, 2683, 8024, 4334, 4730, 4982, 44…
Buenos Aires	7341, 10268, 3167, 5599, 7498, 9130, 11481, 7558, 5025, 4919, 5964, 69…
Cairo	3541, 6340, 6127, 1992, 7216, 5064, 8838, 3894, 2432, 2358, 2…
Calcutta	9609, 7978, 4395, 3758, 1653, 7048, 5256, 5727, 5639, 4…
Caracas	2502, 5215, 11221, 10166, 6009, 6847, 4810, 4044, 46…
Chicago	4250, 9361, 7783, 4247, 8689, 5973, 3992, 39…
Copenhagen	8017, 5388, 7088, 5732, 3436, 1540, …
Darwin	2654, 5369, 6611, 8837, 9391, 86…
Hong Kong	5543, 6669, 7360, 6853, 59…
Honolulu	11934, 10133, 7821, 72…
Johannesburg	2799, 5089, 56…
Lagos	2360, 3…
Lisbon	9…

5	6047	1000	3958	3967	545	4860	1482	6230	734	6179	10002	5545	4037	11272	**Berlin**
0	9728	3126	2816	7793	4356	2956	5179	8332	3837	2432	6313	4189	7760	7686	**Bombay**
2	4591	8374	6463	5298	6867	11972	7106	1214	6929	9867	7332	11410	5650	6202	**Buenos Aires**
0	7687	1803	2197	5605	1994	4688	3272	6149	1325	5137	8959	5947	5737	10268	**Cairo**
2	9494	3438	3839	7921	4883	2031	5398	9366	4486	1800	5678	3195	7805	7055	**Calcutta**
2	2228	6175	7173	2131	4738	8947	4297	2825	5196	11407	9534	8801	2406	8154	**Caracas**
2	1694	4971	8005	711	4132	6588	2956	5311	4809	9369	9243	6299	435	8358	**Chicago**
4	5912	970	4167	3845	638	4475	1306	6345	951	6195	9968	5403	3892	11160	**Copenhagen**
8	9091	7053	6472	9971	8582	3735	8632	9948	8243	2081	1957	3375	9630	3309	**Darwin**
2	8775	4439	5453	8047	5984	1220	6015	11001	5769	1615	4582	1786	7810	5857	**Hong Kong**
8	3781	7036	10739	4958	7437	5070	6081	8290	8026	6721	5075	3854	4638	4669	**Honolulu**
2	9063	5692	1818	7979	5426	7276	6797	4420	4811	5381	6860	8418	8310	7308	**Johannesburg**
3	6879	3886	2366	5268	2929	7119	4175	3750	2510	6925	9643	8376	5560	9973	**Lagos**
8	5391	2427	4015	3369	903	6007	1832	4805	1157	7385	11295	6928	3565	12163	**Lisbon**
2	5552	1552	4237	3463	212	5057	1172	5778	889	6743	10558	5942	3545	11691	**London**
	1549	6070	9659	2446	5645	6251	4310	6310	6331	8776	7502	5475	2170	6719	**Los Angeles**
		6664	9207	2090	5717	7742	4635	4780	6365	10321	8058	7024	2018	6897	**Mexico City**
			3942	4666	1545	3600	2053	7184	1477	5237	9008	4651	4637	10283	**Moscow**
				7358	4029	5727	5395	5548	3350	4635	7552	6996	7570	8490	**Nairobi**
					3626	6828	2613	4832	4280	9531	9935	6741	356	8951	**New York**
3						5106	1384	5708	687	6671	10539	6038	3738	11798	**Paris**
9	10724						4897	10773	5049	2783	5561	1304	6557	6700	**Peking**
4	14818	6344						6135	2048	7155	10325	5469	2600	10725	**Reykjavik**
6	3364	7510	11842						5725	9763	8389	11551	5180	7367	**Rio de Janeiro**
5	9200	2486	6485	5836						6229	10143	6127	4399	11523	**Rome**
0	12460	5794	9216	10988	8217						3915	3306	9350	5298	**Singapore**
6	7460	3304	8683	4206	2228	7882						4861	9800	1383	**Sydney**
5	7693	11562	8928	7777	9187	17338	9874						6410	5762	**Tokyo**
3	10243	2376	5391	6888	1105	8126	3297	9214						8820	**Toronto**
3	16610	8428	7460	15339	10737	4478	11514	15712	10025						**Wellington**
3	12969	14497	12153	15989	16962	8949	16617	13501	16324	6300					**Miles**
1	11304	7485	11260	10849	9718	2099	8802	18589	9861	5321	7823				
2	3247	7462	12183	574	6015	10552	4184	8336	7080	15047	15772	10316			
4	11100	16549	13664	14405	18987	10782	17260	11855	18545	8526	2226	9273	14194		

Diagonal labels: Mexico City, Moscow, Nairobi, New York, Paris, Peking, Reykjavik, Rio de Janeiro, Rome, Singapore, Sydney, Tokyo, Toronto, Wellington

Water Resources and Vegetation

Water resources and vegetation

Fresh water is essential for life on earth and in some parts of the world it is a most precious commodity. On the other hand it is very easy for industrialised temperate states to take its existence for granted, and man's increasing demand may only be met finally by the desalination of earth's 1250 million cubic kilometres of salt water. 70% of the earth's fresh water exists as ice.

The hydrological cycle

Water is continually being absorbed into the atmosphere as vapour from oceans, lakes, rivers and vegetation transpiration. On cooling the vapour either condenses or freezes and falls as rain, hail or snow. Most precipitation falls over the sea but one quarter falls over the land of which half evaporates again soon after falling while the rest flows back into the oceans.

Distribution of water

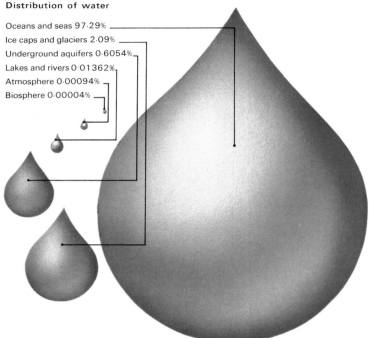

Oceans and seas 97·29%
Ice caps and glaciers 2·09%
Underground aquifers 0·6054%
Lakes and rivers 0·01362%
Atmosphere 0·00094%
Biosphere 0·00004%

Tundra

Mediterranean scrub

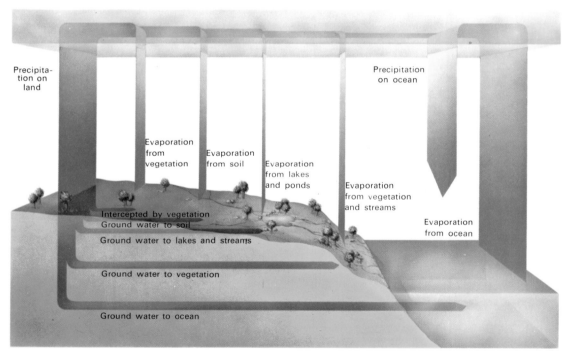

Precipitation on land

Precipitation on ocean

Evaporation from vegetation

Evaporation from soil

Evaporation from lakes and ponds

Evaporation from vegetation and streams

Evaporation from ocean

Intercepted by vegetation
Ground water to soil

Ground water to lakes and streams

Ground water to vegetation

Ground water to ocean

Domestic consumption of water

An area's level of industrialisation, climate and standard of living are all major influences in the consumption of water. On average Europe consumes 636 litres per head each day of which 180 litres is used domestically. In the U.S.A. domestic consumption is slightly higher at 270 litres per day. The graph (right) represents domestic consumption in the U.K.

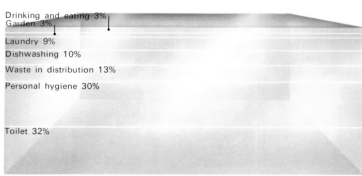

Drinking and eating 3%
Garden 3%
Laundry 9%
Dishwashing 10%
Waste in distribution 13%
Personal hygiene 30%
Toilet 32%

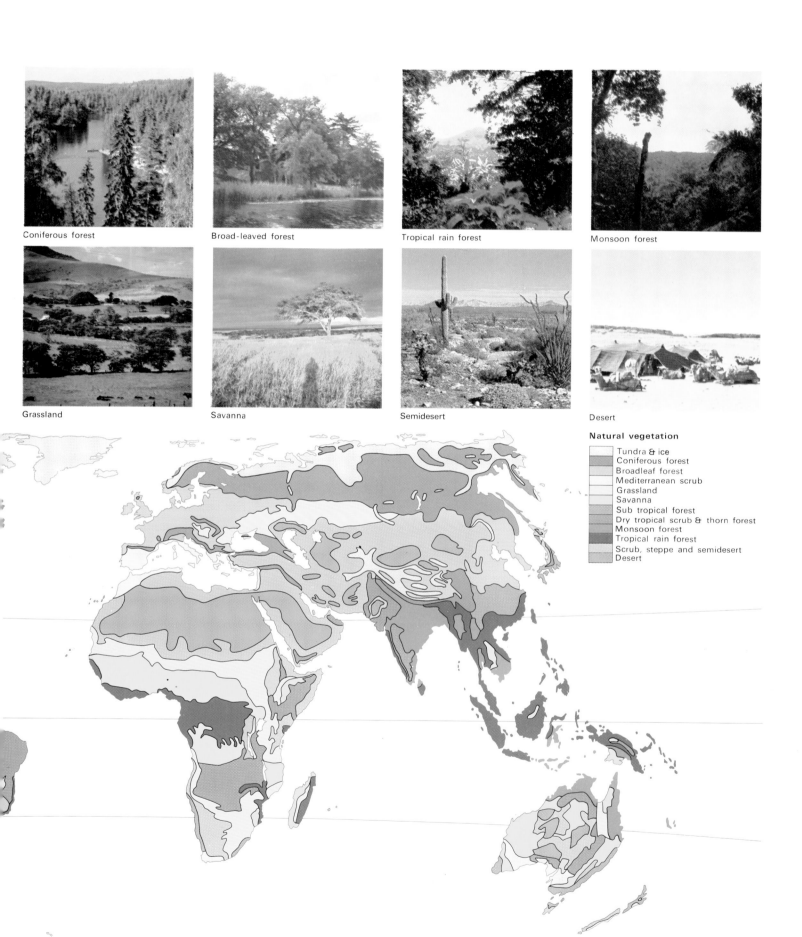

Coniferous forest

Broad-leaved forest

Tropical rain forest

Monsoon forest

Grassland

Savanna

Semidesert

Desert

Natural vegetation

Tundra & ice
Coniferous forest
Broadleaf forest
Mediterranean scrub
Grassland
Savanna
Sub tropical forest
Dry tropical scrub & thorn forest
Monsoon forest
Tropical rain forest
Scrub, steppe and semidesert
Desert

Population

Population distribution
(right and lower right)
People have always been unevenly distributed in the world. Europe has for centuries contained nearly 20 % of the world's population but after the 16-19th century explorations and consequent migrations this proportion has rapidly decreased. In 1750 the Americas had 2 % of the world's total: in 2000 AD they are expected to contain 14%

The most densely populated regions are in India, China and Europe where the average density is between 100 and 200 per km² although there are pockets of extremely high density elsewhere. In contrast French Guiana has less than 1,0 persons per km². The countries in the lower map have been redrawn to make their areas proportional to their populations.

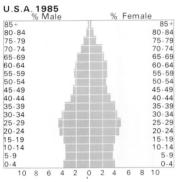

U.S.A. 1985

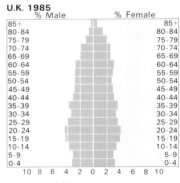

U.K. 1985

Brazil 1985

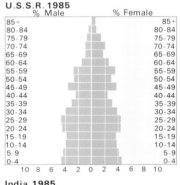

U.S.S.R. 1985

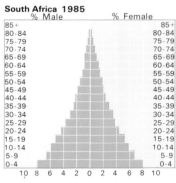

South Africa 1985

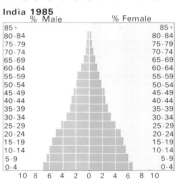

India 1985

Age distribution
The U.K. shows many demographic features characteristic of European countries. Birth and death rates have declined with a moderate population growth - there are nearly as many old as young. In contrast, India and several other countries have few old and many young because of the high death rates and even higher birth rates. It is this excess that is responsible for the world's population explosion.

Increase in urbanisation in developed and developing countries

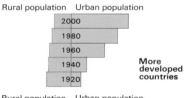

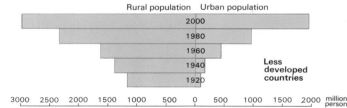

World population distribution

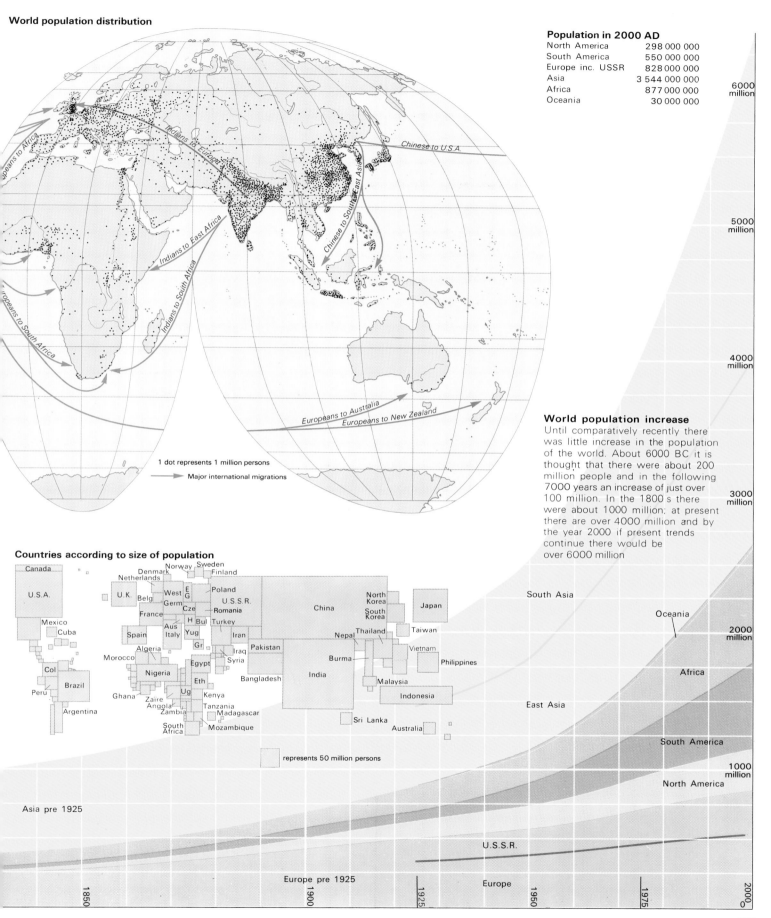

1 dot represents 1 million persons

→ Major international migrations

Europeans to Africa
Indians to Europe
Chinese to U.S.A.
Indians to East Africa
Chinese to South-east Asia
Europeans to South Africa
Indians to South Africa
Europeans to Australia
Europeans to New Zealand

Population in 2000 AD

North America	298 000 000
South America	550 000 000
Europe inc. USSR	828 000 000
Asia	3 544 000 000
Africa	877 000 000
Oceania	30 000 000

World population increase

Until comparatively recently there was little increase in the population of the world. About 6000 BC it is thought that there were about 200 million people and in the following 7000 years an increase of just over 100 million. In the 1800 s there were about 1000 million; at present there are over 4000 million and by the year 2000 if present trends continue there would be over 6000 million

6000 million
5000 million
4000 million
3000 million
2000 million
1000 million

South Asia
Oceania
Africa
East Asia
South America
North America
Asia pre 1925
U.S.S.R.
Europe pre 1925
Europe

1850
1900
1925
1950
1975
2000

Countries according to size of population

Canada
U.S.A.
Mexico
Cuba
Col
Peru
Brazil
Argentina

Norway
Sweden
Denmark
Finland
Netherlands
U.K.
Belg
West Germ
E G
Poland
France
Cze
U.S.S.R.
H Bul Romania
Aus Italy
Yug
Turkey
Spain
Gr
Iran
Algeria
Iraq
Morocco
Egypt
Syria
Pakistan
Nigeria
Eth
Ghana
Ug
Kenya
Zaire
Angola
Tanzania
Zambia
Madagascar
South Africa
Mozambique
Bangladesh
India

China
North Korea
South Korea
Japan
Taiwan
Nepal Thailand
Vietnam
Burma
Philippines
Malaysia
Indonesia
Sri Lanka
Australia

□ represents 50 million persons

27

Language

Languages may be blamed partly for the division and lack of understanding between nations. While a common language binds countries together it in turn isolates them from other countries and groups. Thus beliefs, ideas and inventions remain exclusive to these groups and different cultures develop.

There are thousands of different languages and dialects spoken today. This can cause strife even within the one country, such as India, where different dialects are enough to break down the country into distinct groups.

As a result of colonization and the spread of internationally accepted languages, many countries have superimposed a completely unrelated language in order to combine isolated national groups and to facilitate international understanding, for example Spanish in South America, English in India.

Assyrian (carved)

Ancient Hebrew (painted)

Egyptian hieroglyphic (painted)

Some modern non-latin type faces

Greek
ΑΒΓΔΕΖΗΘΙΚΛΜΝΞΟΠΡΣΤΥΦΧΨΩΣ

Cyrillic
АБВГДЕЖЗИЙІКЛМНОПРСТУФХЦЧШ

Arabic
فى عام ١٨٩٧ وصل إلى إنجلترا أ نموذج

Bengali
১৮৯৭ খ্রীস্টাব্দে আধুনিক মডেলের একটি

Telugu
విను సాయింటికే వచ్చిన యతిధ యేమియు

Japanese
国 土 の 位 置 と 地 形

Chinese
司 父
在 獨
提 子
印 出
芬 有
刷 之
奧 限
業 地
司 位
上 司，
有 能

Related languages

Certain languages showing marked similarities are thought to have developed from common parent languages for example Latin. After the retreat of the Roman Empire wherever Latin had been firmly established it remained as the new nation's language. With no unifying centre divergent development took place and Latin evolved into new languages.

Calligraphy

Writing was originally by a series of pictures, and these gradually developed in styles which were influenced by the tools generally used. Carved alphabets, such as that used by the Sumerians, tended to be angular, while those painted or written tended to be curved, as in Egyptian hieroglyphics development of which can be followed through the West Semitic, Greek and Latin alphabets to our own.

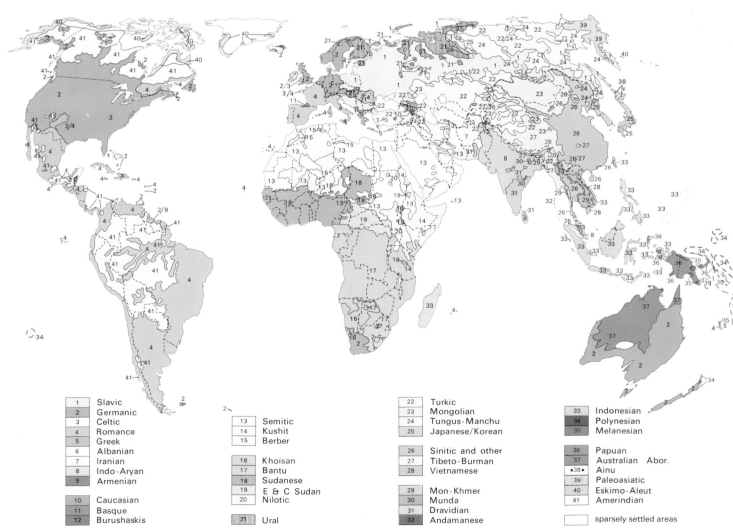

1	Slavic		
2	Germanic		
3	Celtic		
4	Romance		
5	Greek		
6	Albanian		
7	Iranian		
8	Indo-Aryan		
9	Armenian		
10	Caucasian		
11	Basque		
12	Burushaskis		

13	Semitic
14	Kushit
15	Berber
16	Khoisan
17	Bantu
18	Sudanese
19	E & C Sudan
20	Nilotic
21	Ural

22	Turkic
23	Mongolian
24	Tungus-Manchu
25	Japanese/Korean
26	Sinitic and other
27	Tibeto-Burman
28	Vietnamese
29	Mon-Khmer
30	Munda
31	Dravidian
32	Andamanese

33	Indonesian
34	Polynesian
35	Melanesian
36	Papuan
37	Australian Abor.
•38•	Ainu
39	Paleoasiatic
40	Eskimo-Aleut
41	Amerindian
	sparsely settled areas

Religion

Throughout history man has had beliefs in supernatural powers based on the forces of nature which have developed into worship of a god and some cases gods.

Hinduism honours many gods and goddesses which are all manifestations of the one divine spirit, Brahma, and incorporates beliefs such as reincarnation, worship of cattle and the caste system.

Buddhism, an offshoot of Hinduism, was founded in north east India by Gautama Buddha (563-483 BC) who taught that spiritual and moral discipline were essential to achieve supreme peace.

Confucianism is a mixture of Buddhism and Confucius' teachings which were elaborated to provide a moral basis for the political structure of Imperial China and to cover the already existing forms of ancestor worship.

Judaism dates back to c. 13th century B.C. The Jews were expelled from the Holy Land in AD70 and only reinstated in Palestine in 1948.

Islam, founded in Mecca by Muhammad (570-632 AD) spread across Asia and Africa and in its retreat left isolated pockets of adherent communities.

Christianity was founded by Jesus of Nazareth in the 1st century AD The Papal authority, established in the 4th century, was rejected by Eastern churches in the 11th century. Later several other divisions developed eg. Roman Catholicism, Protestantism.

Christian monastery

Jewish holy place

Hindu temple

Mohammedan mosque

Buddhist temple

▲ Roman Catholicism	Shiah Islam
Orthodox and other Eastern Churches	Buddhism
• Protestantism	Hinduism
Sunni Islam	Confucianism
Judaism	
Shintoism	
Primitive religions	
Uninhabited	

The Growth of Cities

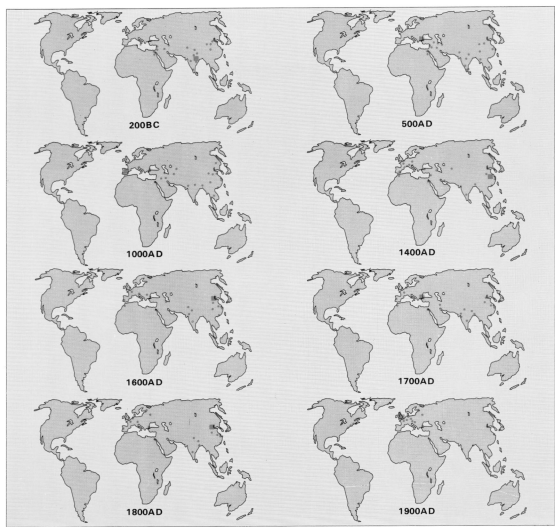

200BC

500AD

1000AD

1400AD

1600AD

1700AD

1800AD

1900AD

Cities through history
The evolution of the semi-perm anent Neolithic settlements into a city took from 5000 until 3500 BC. Efficient communications and exchange systems were developed as population densities increased as high as 30 000 to 50 000 per square kilometre in 2000BC in Egypt and Babylonia, compared with New York City today at 10 000.

■ The largest city in the world
· The twenty five largest cities in the world

Sao Paulo

Increase in urbanisation
The increase in urbanisation is a result primarily of better sanitation and health resulting in the growth of population and secondarily to the movement of man off the land into industry and service occupations in the cities. Generally the most highly developed industrial nations are the most intensely urbanised although exceptions such as Norway and Switzerland show that rural industrialisation can exist.

Increase in urbanisation
The figures on the vertical columns show the urban population as a percentage of the total population for each country in the year shown.

Norway   Japan   Switz.   Sweden   Canada   England and Wales   U.S.A.

1980
1950
1920

Metropolitan areas
A metropolitan area can be defined as a central city linked with surrounding communities by continuous built-up areas controlled by one municipal government. With improved communications the neighbouring communities generally continue to provide the city's work-force. The table (right) compares the total populations of the world's twenty largest cities.

City populations

		1950	1983-5	Projection 2000			1950	1983-5	Projection 2000
1	New York	14 830 192	17 687 400	22 773 000	11	Rio de Janeiro	2 937 000	8 821 845	18 961 000
2	Mexico City	2 967 000	14 750 182	31 025 000	12	Paris	5 525 000	8 706 963	11 330 000
3	Los Angeles	4 046 000	12 190 600	14 154 000	13	Moscow	4 841 000	8 642 000	9 087 000
4	São Paulo	2 227 512	12 183 634	25 796 000	14	Bombay	2 901 000	8 243 405	17 056 000
5	Tokyo	6 275 190	11 746 190	24 172 000	15	Chicago	3 620 962	8 015 900	9 411 000
6	Shanghai	4 300 630	11 185 100	22 677 000	16	Tianjin	2 392 000	7 790 160	9 200 000
7	Buenos Aires	5 251 000	9 967 826	12 104 000	17	Cairo	2 466 000	7 464 000	13 058 000
8	Seoul	1 446 019	9 200 000	14 246 000	18	London	8 348 023	7 379 014	6 860 200
9	Calcutta	4 446 000	9 194 018	16 678 000	19	Chongqing	1 573 000	6 511 130	4 247 000
10	Beijing	2 163 000	9 179 660	19 931 000	20	Jakarta	1 725 000	6 503 449	16 591 000

Major cities
Normally these are not only major centres of population and wealth but also of political power and trade. They are the sites of international airports and characteristically are great ports from which imported goods are distributed using the roads and railways which focus on the city. Their staple trades and industries are varied and flexible and depend on design and fashion rather than raw material production.

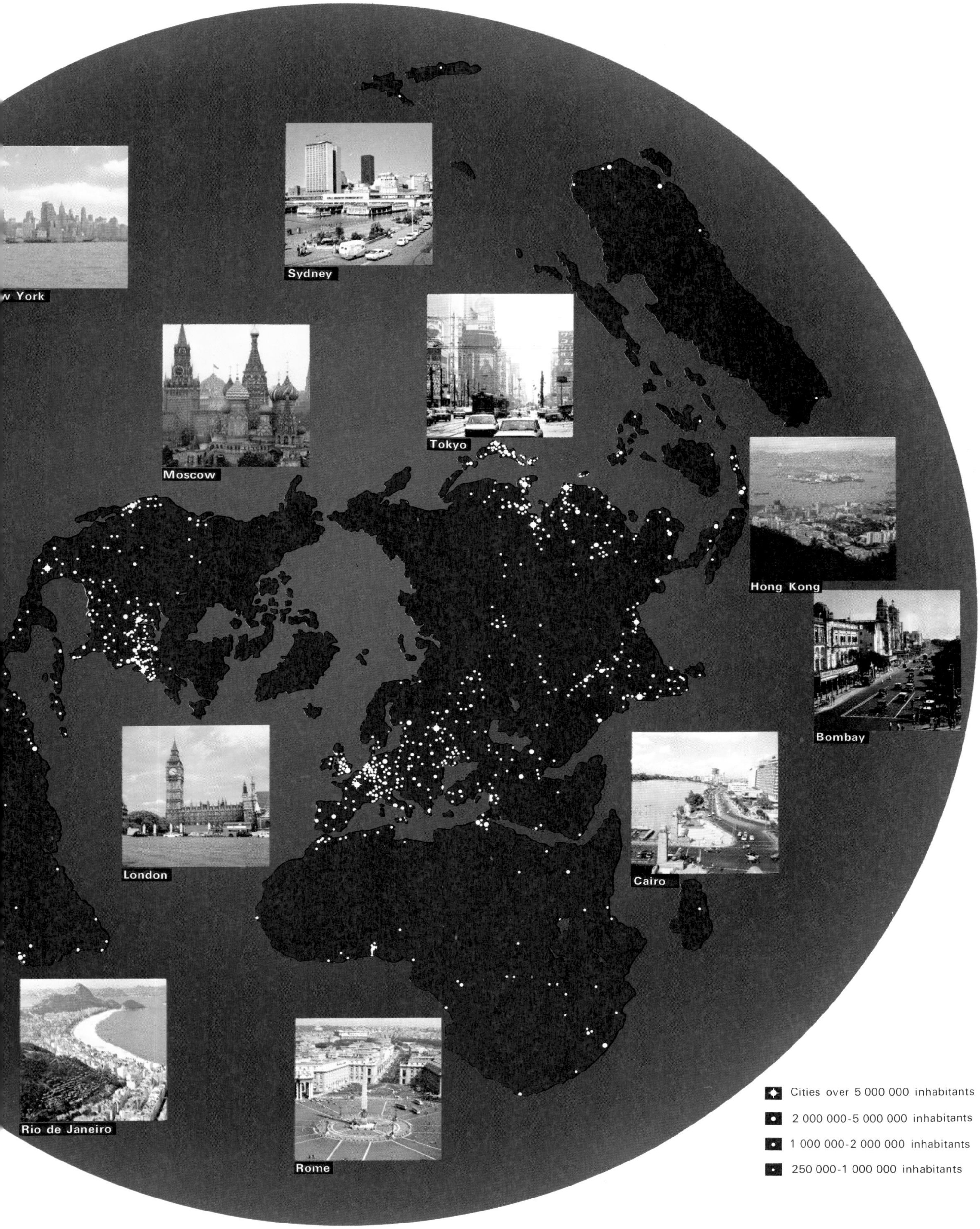
w York
Sydney
Moscow
Tokyo
Hong Kong
Bombay
London
Cairo
Rio de Janeiro
Rome
Cities over 5 000 000 inhabitants
2 000 000-5 000 000 inhabitants
1 000 000-2 000 000 inhabitants
250 000-1 000 000 inhabitants

Food Resources: Vegetable

Cocoa, tea , coffee
These tropical or sub-tropical crops are grown mainly for export to the economically advanced countries. Tea and coffee are the world's principal beverages. Cocoa is used more in the manufacture of chocolate.

Sugar beet, sugar cane
Cane Sugar - a tropical crop - accounts for the bulk of the sugar entering into international trade. Beet Sugar, on the other hand, demands a temperate climate and is produced primarily for domestic consumption.

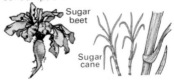

Fruit, wine
With the improvements in canning, drying and freezing, and in transport and marketing, the international trade and consumption of deciduous and soft fruits, citrus fruits and tropical fruits has greatly increased.
Over 80% of grapes are grown for wine and over a half in countries bordering the Mediterranean.

Vegetable oilseeds and oils
Despite the increasing use of synthetic chemical products and animal and marine fats, vegetable oils extracted from these crops grow in quantity, value and importance. Food is the major use- in margarine and cooking fats.

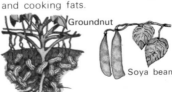

Groundnuts are also a valuable subsistence crop and the meal is used as animal feed. Soya-bean meal is a growing source of protein for humans and animals. The Mediterranean lands are the prime source of olive oil.

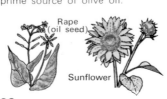

Cocoa	
World Production 1985:	
1 876 thousand tonnes	
Ivory Coast	500
Brazil	419
Ghana	200
Tea	
World Production 1985:	
2 333 thousand tonnes	
India	670
China	465
Sri Lanka	214
Coffee	
World Production 1985:	
6 028 thousand tonnes	
Brazil	1 877
Columbia	660
Indonesia	327

Sugar beet	
World Production 1985:	
283 million tonnes	
U.S.S.R.	82
France	28
W. Germany	21
Sugar cane	
World Production 1985:	
941 million tonnes	
Brazil	246
India	174
Cuba	73

Temperate fruit	
World Production 1985:	
165 million tonnes	
U.S.S.R.	21
Italy	16
China	14
Citrus fruit	
World Production 1985:	
59 million tonnes	
Brazil	15
U.S.A.	9
Spain	3
..... Limits of	
the vine	

Groundnuts	
World Production 1985:	
21 260 thousand tonnes	
China	6 757
India	5 600
U.S.A.	1 800
Soya beans	
World Production 1985:	
101 million tonnes	
U.S.A.	57
Brazil	18
China	11

Rape seed	
World Production 1985:	
18 887 thousand tonnes	
China	5 587
Canada	3 463
India	3 030
Sunflower seed	
World Production 1985:	
19 078 thousand tonnes	
U.S.S.R.	5 230
Argentina	3 430
China	1 901

Cereals
Cereals include those members of the grain family with starchy edible seeds - wheat, maize, barley, oats, rye, rice, millets and sorghums.
  Cereals and potatoes (not a cereal but starch-producing) are the principal source of food for our modern civilisations because of their high yield in bulk and food value per unit of land and labour required. They are also easy to store and transport, and provide food also for animals producing meat, fat, milk and eggs. Wheat is the principal bread grain of the temperate regions in which potatoes are the next most important food source. Rice is the principal cereal in the hotter. humid regions. especially in Asia. Oats, barley and maize are grown mainly for animal feed; millets and sorghums as main subsistence crops in Africa and India.

Maize (or Corn) Needs plenty of sunshine, summer rain or irrigation and frost free for 6 months. Important as animal feed and for human food in Africa, Latin America and as a vegetable and breakfast cereal.

World production 1985 490 million tonnes

Barley Has the widest range of cultivation requiring only 8 weeks between seed time and harvest. Used mainly as animal-feed and by the malting industry.

World production 1985 178 million tonnes

Oats Widely grown in temperate regions with the limit fixed by early autumn frosts. Mainly fed to cattle. The best quality oats are used for oatmeal, porridge and breakfast foods.

World production 1985 45.6 million tonnes

Rice Needs plains or terraces which can be flooded and abundant water in the growing season. The staple food of half the human race. In the husk, it is known as paddy.

World production 1985 466 million tonnes

Wheat The most important grain crop in the temperate regions though it is also grown in a variety of climates e.g. in Monsoon lands as a winter crop.

World production 1985 510 million tonnes

Rye The hardiest of cereals and more resistant to cold, pests and disease than wheat. An important foodstuff in Central and E. Europe and the U.S.S.R.

World production 1985 29.6 million tonnes

Millets The name given to a number of related members of the grass family, of which sorghum is one of the most important. They provide nutritious grain.

World production 1985 109 million tonnes

Potato An important food crop though less nutritious weight for weight than grain crops. Requires a temperate climate with a regular and plentiful supply of rain.

World production 1985 299 million tonnes

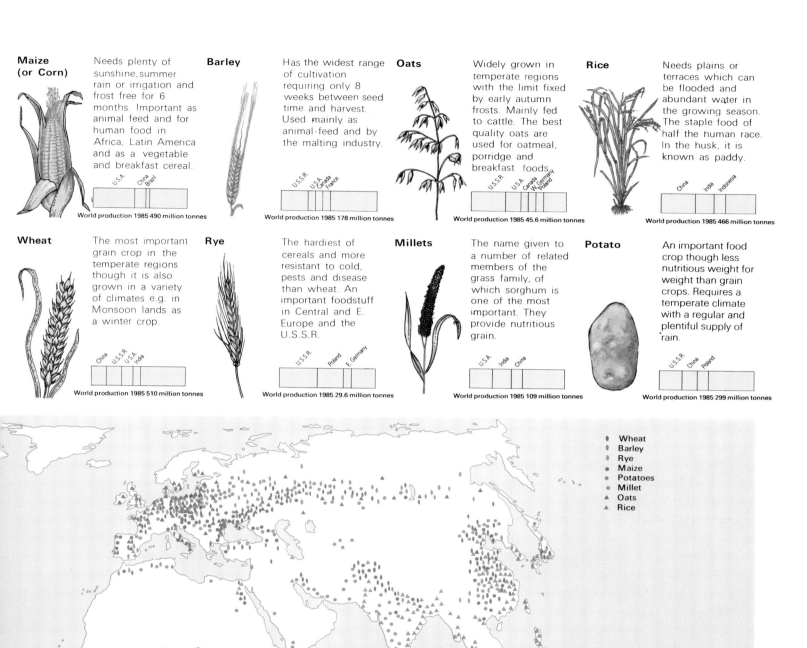

- ♦ Wheat
- ♦ Barley
- ♦ Rye
- ● Maize
- ● Potatoes
- ● Millet
- ▲ Oats
- ▲ Rice

Food Resources: Animal

Food resources: Animal
Meat, milk and allied foods are prime protein-providers and are also sources of essential vitamins. Meat is mainly a product of continental and savannah grasslands and the cool west coasts, particularly in Europe. Milk and cheese, eggs and fish - though found in some quantity throughout the world - are primarily a product of the temperate zones.

Beef cattle
Australia, New Zealand and Argentina provide the major part of international beef exports. Western U.S.A. and Europe have considerable production of beef for their local high demand.

World meat production 1985
97 million head

Dairy Cattle
The need of herds for a rich diet and for nearby markets result in dairying being characteristic of densely-populated areas of the temperate zones - U.S.A., N.W. Europe, N. Zealand and S.E. Australia.

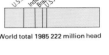

World total 1985 222 million head

Cheese
The principal producers are the U.S.A., W. Europe, U.S.S.R., and New Zealand and principal exporters Netherlands, New Zealand, Denmark and France.

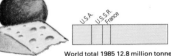

World total 1985 12.8 million tonne

Sheep
Raised mostly for wool and meat, the skins and cheese from their milk are important products in some countries. The merino yields a fine wool and crossbreds are best for meat.

World meat production 1985
6 million tonnes

Pigs
Can be reared in most climates from monsoon to cool temperate. They are abundant in China, the corn belt of the U.S.A. N.W. and C. Europe, Brazil and U.S.S.R.

World meat production 1985
58 million tonnes

Fish
Commercial fishing requires large shoals of fish of one species within reach of markets. Freshwater fishing is also important. A rich source of protein, fish will become an increasingly valuable food source.

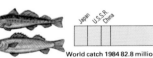

World catch 1984 82.8 million tonnes

Butter
(includes Ghee)
The biggest producers are U.S.S.R., India, U.S.A. and France.

World total 1985 7.6 million tonnes

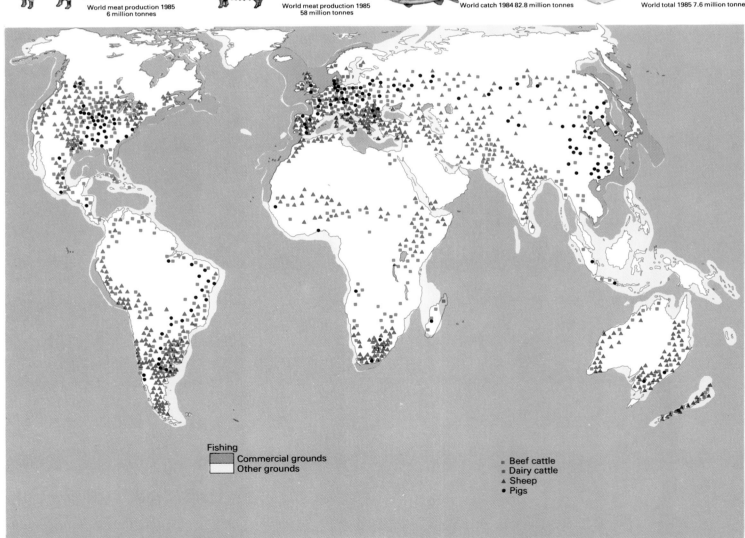

Fishing
Commercial grounds
Other grounds

- Beef cattle
- Dairy cattle
- Sheep
- Pigs

Nutrition

Foodstuffs fall, nutritionally, into three groups - providers of energy, protein and vitamins. Cereals and oil-seeds provide energy and second-class protein'; milk, meat and allied foods provide protein and vitamins, fruit and vegetables provide vitamins, especially Vitamin C, and some energy. To avoid malnutrition, a minimum level of these three groups of foodstuffs is required: the maps and diagrams show how unfortunately widespread are low standards of nutrition and even malnutrition.

Comparison of daily diets

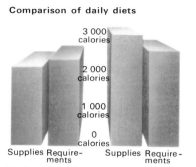

Supplies Requirements — Far East, Near East, Africa & Latin America

Supplies Requirements — Europe, Oceania & North America

Proportions of calories

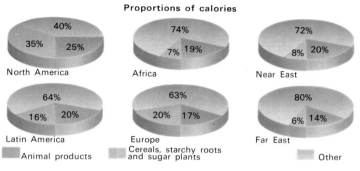

North America 40% 35% 25%

Africa 74% 7% 19%

Near East 72% 8% 20%

Latin America 64% 16% 20%

Europe 63% 20% 17%

Far East 80% 6% 14%

■ Animal products
▨ Cereals, starchy roots and sugar plants
□ Other

Malnutrition

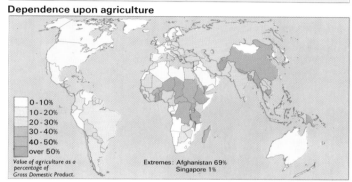

U.S.A. 37% U.K. 38% U.S.S.R. 27% Japan 19%
Egypt 6% India 5% China 10%
Nigeria 4% Ethiopia 8% Indonesia 2%
Brazil 17%
Argentina 21%

under 80%
80-90%
90-100%
100-110%
110-120%
over 120%

Calorie intake as a percentage of needs per person.

Diet: Percentage of calorie intake from meat for selected countries. World average 17%.

Dependence upon agriculture

0-10%
10-20%
20-30%
30-40%
40-50%
over 50%

Value of agriculture as a percentage of Gross Domestic Product.

Extremes: Afghanistan 69% Singapore 1%

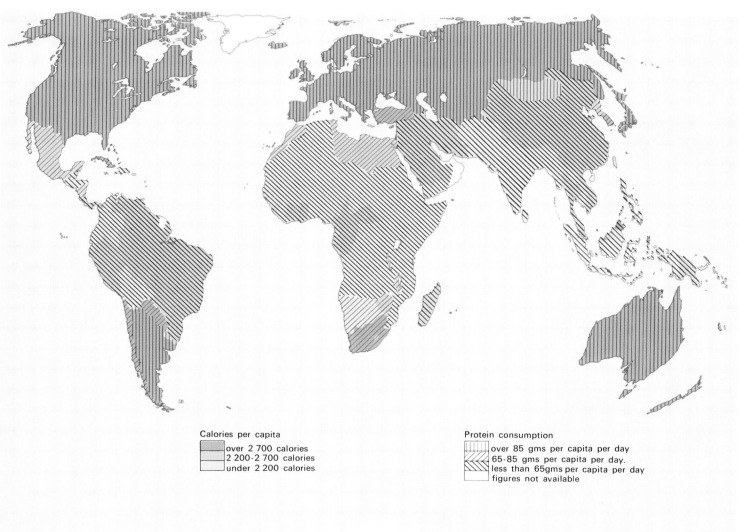

Calories per capita
■ over 2 700 calories
▨ 2 200-2 700 calories
□ under 2 200 calories

Protein consumption
▤ over 85 gms per capita per day
▧ 65-85 gms per capita per day.
▨ less than 65gms per capita per day
□ figures not available

Mineral Resources I

Primitive man used iron for tools and vessels and its use extended gradually until iron, and later steel, became the backbone of the Modern World with the Industrial Revolution in the late 18th Century. At first, local ores were used, whereas today richer iron ores in huge deposits have been discovered and are mined on a large scale, often far away from the areas where they are used; for example, in Western Australia, Northern Sweden, Venezuela and Liberia. Iron smelting plants are today increasingly located at coastal sites, where the large ore carriers can easily discharge their cargo.

Steel is refined iron with the addition of other minerals, giving to the steel their own special properties; for example, resistance to corrosion (chromium, nickel, cobalt), hardness (tungsten, vanadium), elasticity (molybdenum), magnetic properties (cobalt), high tensile strength (manganese) and high ductility (molybdenum).

Production of metal ores used in ferro-alloys

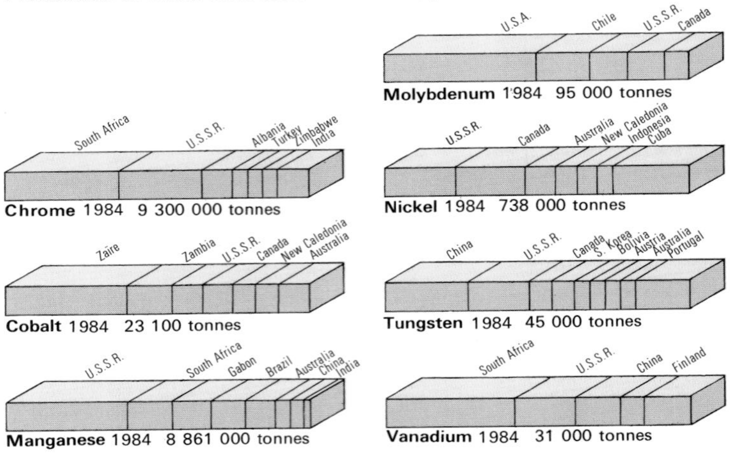

U.S.A.
Chile
U.S.S.R.
Canada
Molybdenum 1984 95 000 tonnes
South Africa
U.S.S.R.
Albania
Turkey
Zimbabwe
India
Chrome 1984 9 300 000 tonnes
U.S.S.R.
Canada
Australia
New Caledonia
Indonesia
Cuba
Nickel 1984 738 000 tonnes
Zaïre
Zambia
U.S.S.R.
Canada
New Caledonia
Australia
Cobalt 1984 23 100 tonnes
China
U.S.S.R.
Canada
S. Korea
Bolivia
Austria
Australia
Portugal
Tungsten 1984 45 000 tonnes
U.S.S.R.
South Africa
Gabon
Brazil
Australia
China
India
Manganese 1984 8 861 000 tonnes
South Africa
U.S.S.R.
China
Finland
Vanadium 1984 31 000 tonnes

Iron and Steel Industry of Western Europe

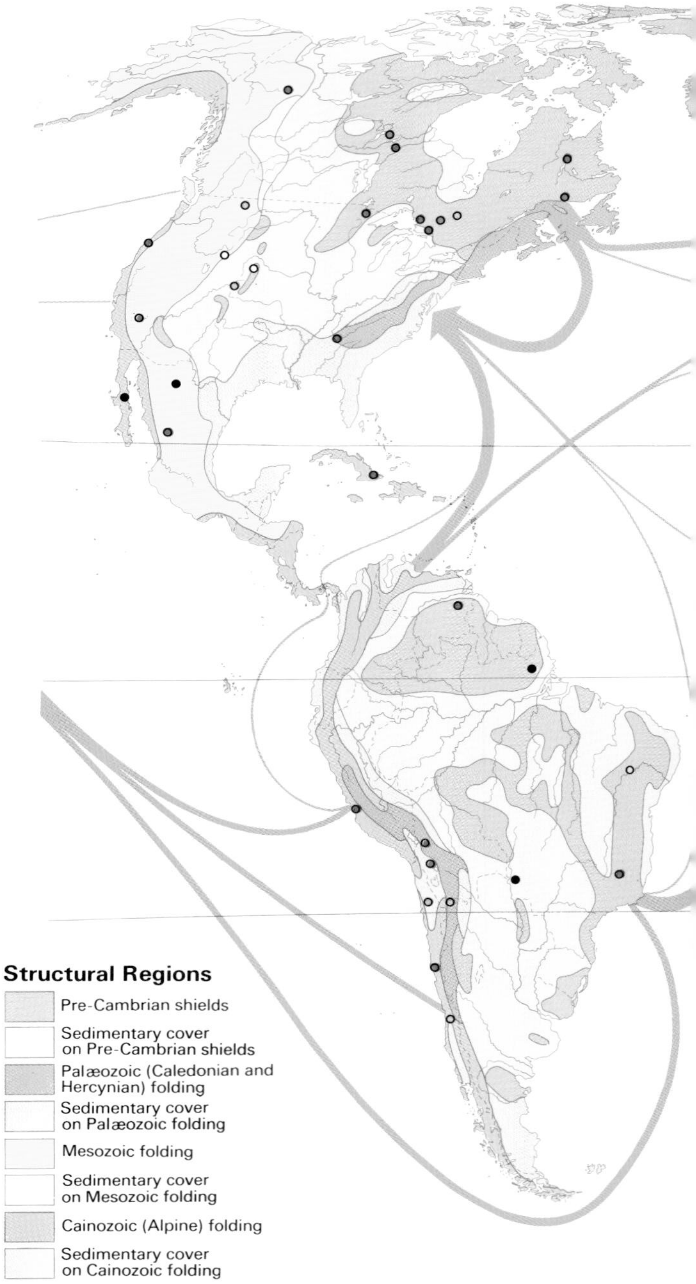

Major Centre
Other Important Centre
Iron ore
Iron and steel plant
Coalfields
Kiruna
Gallivare
Teesside
Sheffield
Scunthorpe
IJmuiden
Dunkerque
South Wales
Salzgitter
The Ruhr
Valenciennes
Esch
Krakow
Ostrava
Genova
Taranto

Sources of Iron ore imported into Western Europe
hundred thousand tonnes

Imports from	Austria	Belgium-Lux	France	Italy	Netherlands	Spain	U.K.	W. Germany
Algeria		7		2				
Australia	1	13	24	17	5	3	31	56
Brazil	7	39	29	67	24	17	23	152
Canada	7	4	13	13	7		35	58
Liberia		12	12	36	5	11		63
Mauritania		18	18	28		4	8	4
U.S.S.R.	13							
Venezuela					4	5	9	5
Others (World)	3	13	12	29	4	2	16	35
France		44					1	
Norway		4			1		11	30
Spain		1	4		7		2	4
Sweden	8	41	27		15		8	20
Total Imports	39	196	139	192	72	42	144	427
Home produced ore	36		150	2		80	4	10

Steep Rock
Vermilion
Mesabi
Gagnon
Marquette
Menominee
Chicago
Gary
Detroit
Hamilton
Buffalo
Cleveland
Pittsburgh
Sparrows Point
Birmingham
Major Centre
Other Important Centre
Iron ore
Iron and steel plant
Coalfields

Iron and Steel Industry of Eastern North America

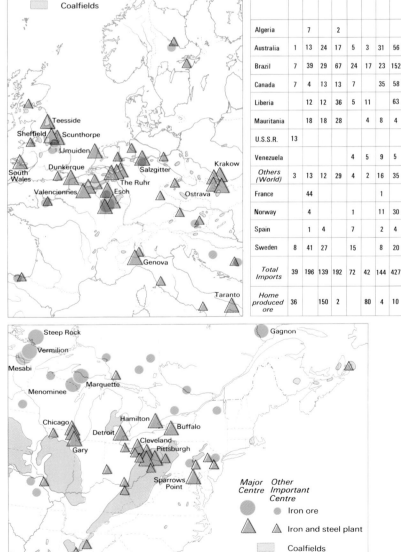

Structural Regions
Pre-Cambrian shields
Sedimentary cover on Pre-Cambrian shields
Palæozoic (Caledonian and Hercynian) folding
Sedimentary cover on Palæozoic folding
Mesozoic folding
Sedimentary cover on Mesozoic folding
Cainozoic (Alpine) folding
Sedimentary cover on Cainozoic folding

World production of pig iron and ferro-alloys

World production 1984 481,0 million tonnes

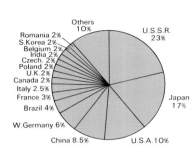

Others 10%
U.S.S.R. 23%
Romania 2%
S.Korea 2%
Belgium 2%
India 2%
Czech. 2%
Poland 2%
U.K. 2%
Canada 2%
Italy 2.5%
France 3%
Brazil 4%
W.Germany 6%
China 8.5%
U.S.A.10%
Japan 17%

Development of world production of pig iron and ferro alloys

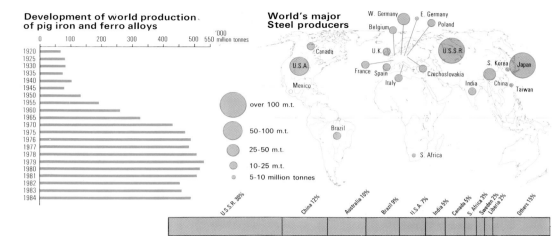

'000 million tonnes

| | 0 | 100 | 200 | 300 | 400 | 500 550 |

1920
1925
1930
1935
1940
1945
1950
1955
1960
1965
1970
1975
1976
1977
1978
1979
1980
1981
1982
1983
1984

World's major Steel producers

W. Germany
E. Germany
Belgium
Poland
Canada
U.K.
U.S.S.R.
U.S.A.
France
Spain
Czechoslovakia
S. Korea
Japan
Mexico
Italy
India
China
Taiwan
Brazil
S. Africa

over 100 m.t.
50-100 m.t.
25-50 m.t.
10-25 m.t.
5-10 million tonnes

U.S.S.R. 30% | China 12% | Australia 10% | Brazil 9% | U.S.A. 7% | India 5% | Canada 5% | S. Africa 3% | Sweden 2% | Liberia 2% | Others 15%

World production of iron ore (Fe content)   World production 1984   495 million tonnes

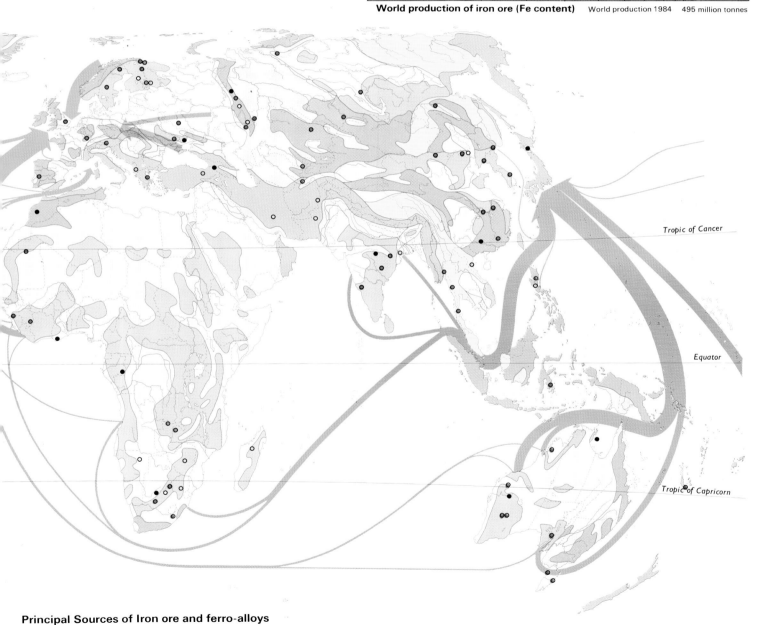

Tropic of Cancer

Equator

Tropic of Capricorn

Principal Sources of Iron ore and ferro-alloys

- Iron
- Chrome
- Cobalt
- Manganese
- Molybdenum
- Nickel
- Tungsten
- Vanadium
- Iron ore trade flow

Mineral Resources II

Antimony – imparts hardness when alloyed to other metals, especially lead.
Uses: type metal, pigments to paints, glass and enamels, fireproofing of textiles

World production 1984 51 600 tonnes

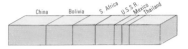

Lead – heavy, soft, malleable, acid resistant.
Uses: storage batteries, sheeting and piping, cable covering, ammunition, type metal, weights, additive to petrol.

World production 1984 3.4 million tonnes

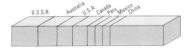

Tin – resistant to attacks by organic acids, malleable.
Uses: canning, foils, as an alloy to other metals (brass and bronze).

World production 1984 194 000 tonnes

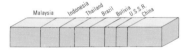

Aluminium – light, resists corrosion, good conductor.
Uses: aircraft, road and rail vehicles, domestic utensils, cables, makes highly tensile and light alloys.

World production 1984 91 million tonnes (of Bauxite)

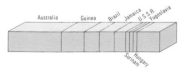

Gold – untarnishable and resistant to corrosion, highly ductile and malleable, good conductor. The pure metal is soft and it is alloyed to give it hardness.
Uses: bullion, coins, jewellery, gold-leaf, electronics.

World production 1984 1 400 tonnes

Copper – excellent conductor of electricity and heat, durable, resistant to corrosion, strong and ductile.
Uses: wire, tubing, brass (with zinc and tin), bronze (with tin), (compounds) – dyeing.

World production 1984 8 300 000 tonnes

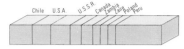

Mercury – the only liquid metal, excellent conductor of electricity
Uses: thermometers, electrical industry, gold and silver ore extraction, (compounds) – drugs, pigments, chemicals, dentistry.

World production 1984 5.5 million kg.

Zinc – hard metal, low corrosion factor.
Uses: brass (with copper and tin), galvanising, diecasting, medicines, paints and dyes.

World production 1984 6.8 million tonnes

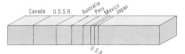

Diamonds – very hard and resistant to chemical attack, high lustre, very rare.
Uses: jewellery, cutting and abrading other materials.

World production 1984 63 million carats

Silver – ductile and malleable, a soft metal and must be alloyed for use in coinage.
Uses: coins, jewellery, photography, electronics, medicines.

World production 1984 12 779 tonnes

World consumption of non-ferrous metals

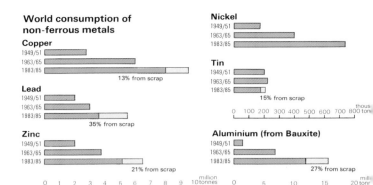

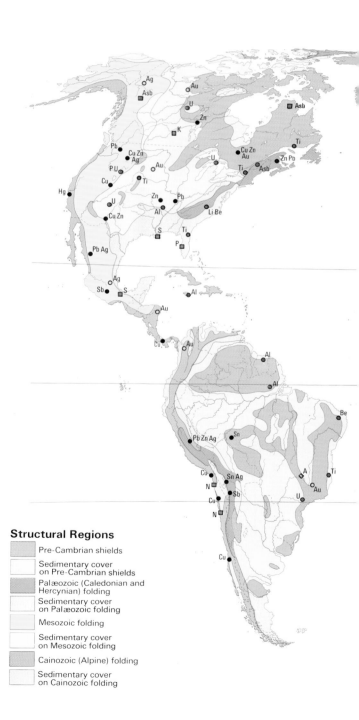

Structural Regions

- Pre-Cambrian shields
- Sedimentary cover on Pre-Cambrian shields
- Palæozoic (Caledonian and Hercynian) folding
- Sedimentary cover on Palæozoic folding
- Mesozoic folding
- Sedimentary cover on Mesozoic folding
- Cainozoic (Alpine) folding
- Sedimentary cover on Cainozoic folding

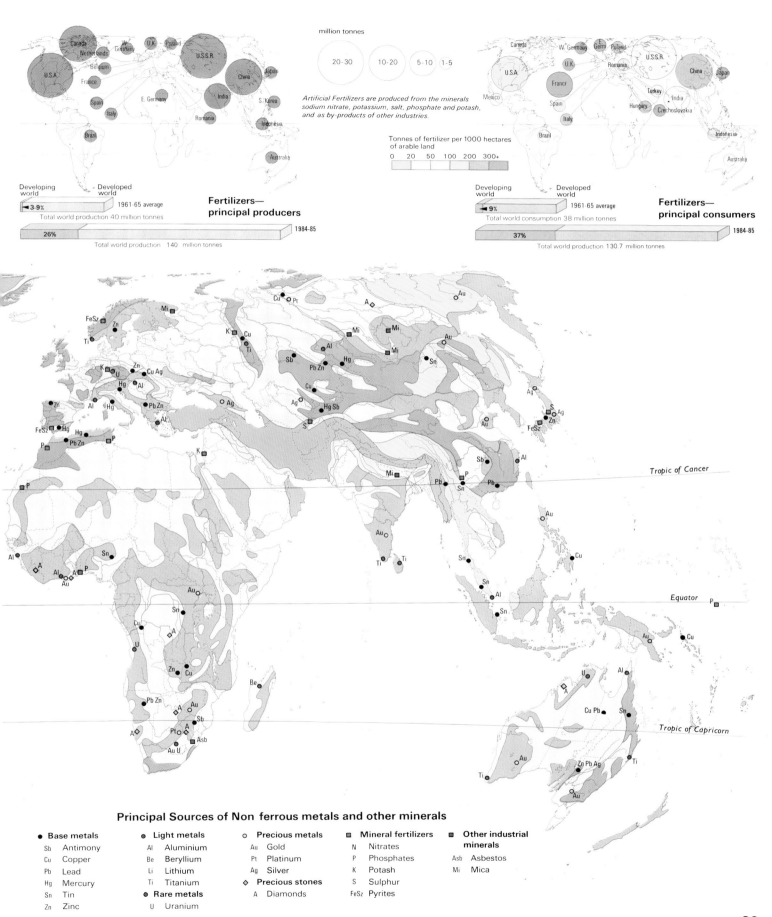

million tonnes

20-30   10-20   5-10   1-5

Artificial Fertilizers are produced from the minerals sodium nitrate, potassium, salt, phosphate and potash, and as by-products of other industries.

Fertilizers— principal producers

Developing world — Developed world

◀ 3.9%   1961-65 average

Total world production 40 million tonnes

26%   1984-85

Total world production 140 million tonnes

Tonnes of fertilizer per 1000 hectares of arable land

0   20   50   100   200   300+

Fertilizers— principal consumers

Developing world — Developed world

◀ 9%   1961-65 average

Total world consumption 38 million tonnes

37%   1984-85

Total world production 130.7 million tonnes

Tropic of Cancer

Equator

Tropic of Capricorn

Principal Sources of Non ferrous metals and other minerals

● Base metals
Sb Antimony
Cu Copper
Pb Lead
Hg Mercury
Sn Tin
Zn Zinc

● Light metals
Al Aluminium
Be Beryllium
Li Lithium
Ti Titanium
● Rare metals
U   Uranium

○ Precious metals
Au Gold
Pt Platinum
Ag Silver
◇ Precious stones
A   Diamonds

▣ Mineral fertilizers
N   Nitrates
P   Phosphates
K   Potash
S   Sulphur
FeSz Pyrites

▪ Other industrial minerals
Asb Asbestos
Mi   Mica

Fuel and Energy

Coal

Coal is the result of the accumulation of vegetation over millions of years. Later under pressure from overlying sediments, it is hardened through four stages: peat, lignite, bituminous coal, and finally anthracite. Once the most important source of power, coal's importance now lies in the production of electricity and as a raw material in the production of plastics, heavy chemicals and disinfectants.

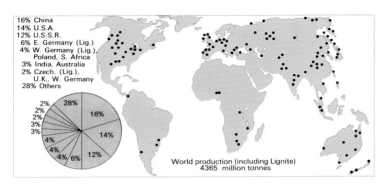

16% China
14% U.S.A.
12% U.S.S.R.
6% E. Germany (Lig.)
4% W. Germany (Lig.), Poland, S. Africa
3% India, Australia
2% Czech. (Lig.), U.K., W. Germany
28% Others

World production (including Lignite) 4365 million tonnes

Coal mine

Oil

Oil is derived from the remains of marine animals and plants, probably as a result of pressure, heat and chemical action. It is a complex mixture of hydrocarbons which are refined to extract the various constituents. These include products such as gasolene, kerosene and heavy fuel oils. Oil is rapidly replacing coal because of easier handling and reduced pollution.

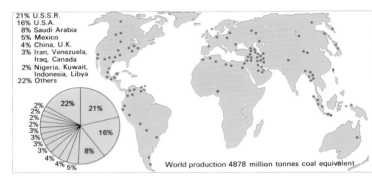

21% U.S.S.R.
16% U.S.A.
8% Saudi Arabia
5% Mexico
4% China, U.K.
3% Iran, Venezuela, Iraq, Canada
2% Nigeria, Kuwait, Indonesia, Libya
22% Others

World production 4878 million tonnes coal equivalent

Oil derrick

Natural gas

Since the early 1960's natural gas (methane) has become one of the largest single sources of energy. By liquefaction its volume can be reduced to 1/600 of that of gas and hence is easily transported. It is often found directly above oil reserves and because it is both cheaper than coal gas and less polluting it has great potential.

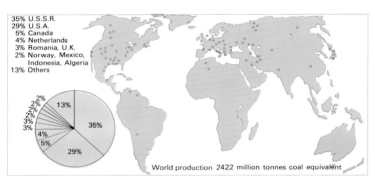

35% U.S.S.R.
29% U.S.A.
5% Canada
4% Netherlands
3% Romania, U.K.
2% Norway, Mexico, Indonesia, Algeria
13% Others

World production 2422 million tonnes coal equivalent

North sea gas rig

Water

Hydro-electric power stations use water to drive turbines which in turn generate electricity. The ideal site is one in which a consistently large volume of water falls a considerable height, hence sources of H.E.P. are found mainly in mountainous areas. Potential sources of hydro-electricity using waves or tides are yet to be exploited widely.

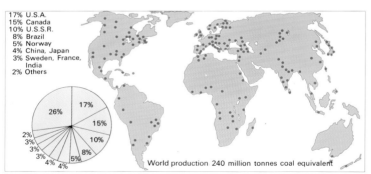

17% U.S.A.
15% Canada
10% U.S.S.R.
8% Brazil
5% Norway
4% China, Japan
3% Sweden, France, India
2% Others

World production 240 million tonnes coal equivalent

Water power

Nuclear energy

The first source of nuclear power was developed in Britain in 1956. Energy is obtained from heat generated by the reaction from splitting atoms of certain elements, of which uranium and plutonium are the most important. Although the initial installation costs are very high the actual running costs are low because of the slow consumption of fuel.

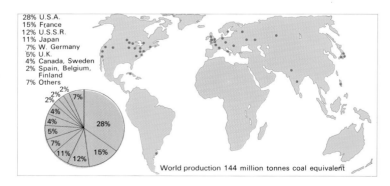

28% U.S.A.
15% France
12% U.S.S.R.
11% Japan
7% W. Germany
5% U.K.
4% Canada, Sweden
2% Spain, Belgium, Finland
7% Others

World production 144 million tonnes coal equivalent

Nuclear power station

40

In a short space of time these two diagrams can change markedly; there can be a cut-back in supply owing to internal political change (Iran), or in consumption by vigorous government action (U.S.A.). The production of North Sea oil has changed the balance of oil trade in the U.K. and Norway but it is very costly to extract, relatively short-lived and is small on a world scale.

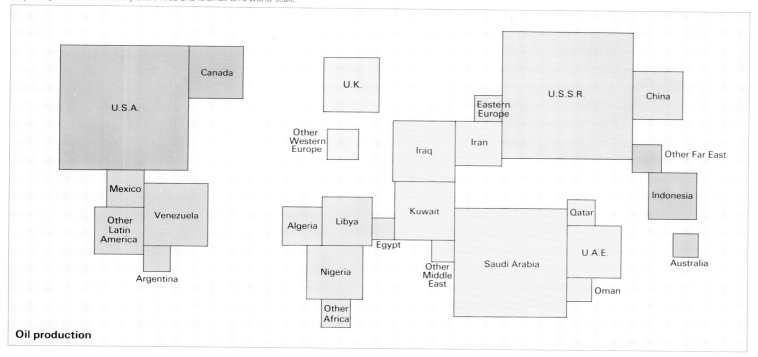

Oil production

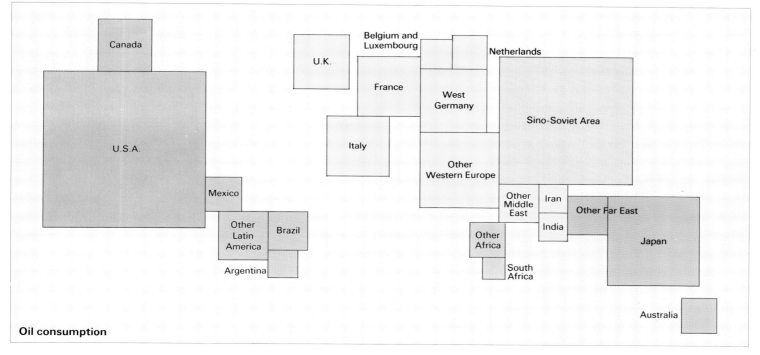

Oil consumption

Oil's new super-powers *above*
When countries are scaled according to their production and consumption of oil they take on new dimensions. At present, large supplies of oil are concentrated in a few countries of the Caribbean, the Middle East and North Africa, except for the vast indigenous supplies of the U.S.A. and U.S.S.R. The Middle East, with 58% of the world's reserves, produces 19% of the world's supply and yet consumes only 3%. The U.S.A.,

despite its great production, has a deficiency of nearly 155 million tons a year, consuming 25% of the world's total. The U.S.S.R., with 9% of world reserves, produces 23% of world output and consumes 15%. Soviet production continues to grow annually although at a decreased rate since the mid-1970's. Japan is the world's third largest oil consumer but 98% of this has to be imported, making it the worlds largest importer.

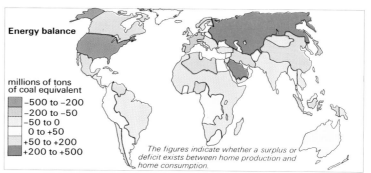

Energy balance

millions of tons
of coal equivalent

- −500 to −200
- −200 to −50
- −50 to 0
- 0 to +50
- +50 to +200
- +200 to +500

The figures indicate whether a surplus or deficit exists between home production and home consumption.

Occupations

Part of the assembly line in a cigarette factory

Manufacturing Employment

The number of people employed in each manufacturing sector is given as a percentage of total manufacturing employment within each country.

Manufacturing Sector	India	Mexico	Japan
Food & tobacco	14.6%	24.1%	10.8%
Precision instruments	0.4%	—	2.3%
Transport equipment	7.0%	9.8%	8.5%
Electrical machinery	5.9%	6.8%	12.8%
General machinery	6.7%	1.1%	11.1%
Non-ferrous metals	0.7%	2.9%	1.4%
Iron & steel	7.0%	11.0%	4.2%
Ceramics & glass	1.3%	4.2%	1.4%
Oil refining & its products	0.5%	0.8%	0.4%
Chemicals & rubber	9.4%	14.1%	5.3%
Paper & paper products	2.0%	5.2%	2.7%
Wood products	0.8%	1.0%	4.1%
Leather goods	0.4%	—	0.4%
Textiles	30.4%	10.0%	7.4%
Others	12.9%	9.0%	27.2%

The table is comparing the manufacturing industries of a low income economy (India), an upper middle income economy (Mexico), and an industrial market economy (Japan).

Percentage of Economically Active Population Engaged in Agriculture, 1965 and 1985

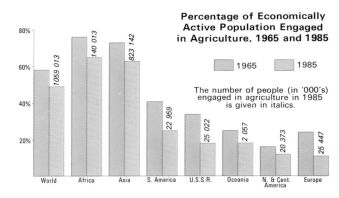

■ 1965 ■ 1985

The number of people (in '000's) engaged in agriculture in 1985 is given in italics.

World 1059 013 · Africa 140 013 · Asia 823 142 · S. America 22 959 · U.S.S.R. 25 022 · Oceania 2 057 · N. & Cent. America 20 373 · Europe 25 447

EMPLOYMENT

Employment by Sector in 1980
Key to Map Colours

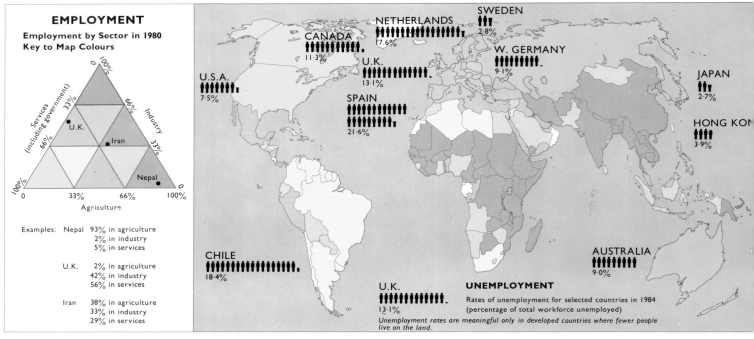

Examples:
- Nepal: 93% in agriculture, 2% in industry, 5% in services
- U.K.: 2% in agriculture, 42% in industry, 56% in services
- Iran: 38% in agriculture, 33% in industry, 29% in services

SWEDEN 2·8%
NETHERLANDS 17·6%
CANADA 11·3%
W. GERMANY 9·1%
U.K. 13·1%
U.S.A. 7·5%
SPAIN 21·6%
JAPAN 2·7%
HONG KONG 3·9%
CHILE 18·4%
AUSTRALIA 9·0%
U.K. 13·1%

UNEMPLOYMENT

Rates of unemployment for selected countries in 1984 (percentage of total workforce unemployed)

Unemployment rates are meaningful only in developed countries where fewer people live on the land.

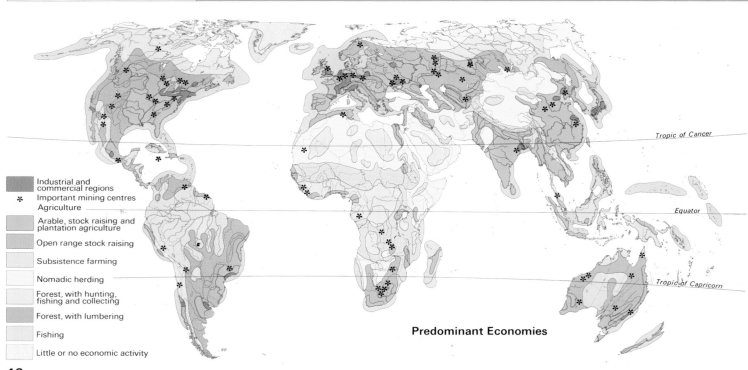

Industrial and commercial regions

* **Important mining centres**

Agriculture
- Arable, stock raising and plantation agriculture
- Open range stock raising
- Subsistence farming
- Nomadic herding
- Forest, with hunting, fishing and collecting
- Forest, with lumbering
- Fishing
- Little or no economic activity

Tropic of Cancer

Equator

Tropic of Capricorn

Predominant Economies

Industry

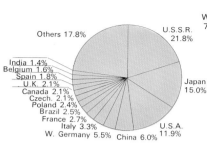

Casting steel ingots

World Steel production

Others 17.8%
U.S.S.R. 21.8%
India 1.4%
Belgium 1.6%
Spain 1.8%
U.K. 2.1%
Canada 2.1%
Czech. 2.1%
Poland 2.4%
Brazil 2.5%
Italy 3.3%
France 2.7%
W. Germany 5.5%
China 6.0%
U.S.A. 11.9%
Japan 15.0%

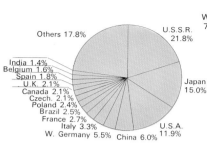

Growth of World Steel production

World production 1984
707 million tonnes

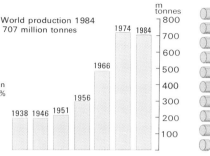

m tonnes
1938 1946 1951 1956 1966 1974 1984

World Steel production per capita

	tonnes/capita
Belgium	1.10
Japan	0.90
W. Germany	0.64
Canada	0.58
U.S.S.R.	0.56
Poland	0.45
Australia	0.37
France	0.35
U.K.	0.27
China	0.04

Principal Areas of Production
- Iron and Steel
- Aluminium

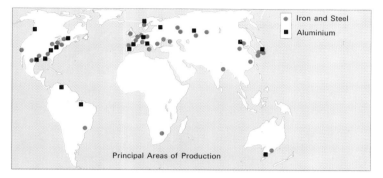

Aluminium

World production 1984 15.9 million tonnes

U.S.A.   U.S.S.R.   Canada   W. Germany   Australia   Norway   Brazil   China   Spain   Venezuela   Others

When compared with bauxite production on p. 38 it is evident that those countries mining bauxite do not necessarily produce proportional quantities of aluminium. For example the U.S.A. mines only 1% of the world's bauxite but is the greatest producer of aluminium. The refining is done where there are abundant sources of cheap electricity, hydro-electricity for example. It takes 15 000 kWh to convert 2 tonnes of alumina to 1 tonne of aluminium.

Principal Areas of Production
- Chemicals
- Cement

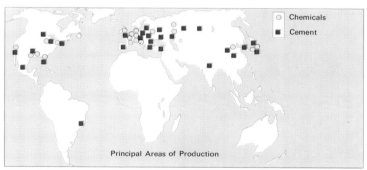

Chemicals

Synthetic Rubber

World production 1983
8257·6 thousand tonnes

U.S.A.	1 985
U.S.S.R.	1 970
Japan	1 003
France	514
W. Germany	432
U.K.	253

Caustic Soda

World production 1983
30.4 million tonnes

U.S.A.	9.3
W. Germany	3.4
U.S.S.R.	2.9
Japan	2.8
China	2.1
Canada	1.5
France	1.4

Cement

World production 1984
890 million tonnes

U.S.S.R.	130.1	Spain	25.5
China	121.1	France	22.7
Japan	78.9	S. Korea	20.4
U.S.A.	70.5	Brazil	19.5
Italy	38.3	Mexico	18.4
India	29.0	Poland	16.6
W. Germany	28.7	U.K.	15.7

Principal Textile Producing Areas
- Cotton Fibre
- Wool
- Cotton yarn
- Wool yarn

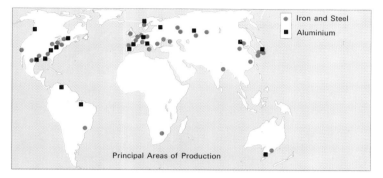

Textiles

Cotton Yarn		Cotton Lint		Wool-greasy		Woollen Yarn	
World production 1983 11 623.8 thousand tonnes		World production 1984 17 794 thousand tonnes		World production 1984 2 888 thousand tonnes		No world total available Thousand tonnes 1983	
China	3 270	China	6 077	Australia	729	U.S.S.R.	447.0
U.S.S.R.	1 659	U.S.A.	2 894	U.S.S.R.	463	Italy	290.8
India	1 180	U.S.S.R.	2 400	New Zealand	363	U.K.	121.2
U.S.A.	1 064	India	1 250	China	187	Japan	110.0
S. Korea	477	Pakistan	990	Argentine	155	France	107.9
Pakistan	448	Brazil	618	S. Africa	109	China	101.0
Japan	438	Turkey	586	Uruguay	91	Belgium	86.7
Egypt	229	Egypt	390	Turkey	63	Poland	81.3
Italy	217	Mexico	257	U.K.	51	Romania	78.8
Poland	177	Sudan	219	U.S.A.	46	W. Germany	76.4

Timber and Paper

Roundwood-coniferous		Roundwood-non-coniferous		Wood Pulp		Paper and Paper Board	
World production 1983 1 187 million m³		World production 1983 1 741 million m³		World production 1983 128 million tonnes		World production 1983 175 million tonnes	
U.S.S.R.	296	India	214	U.S.A.	47.7	U.S.A.	58.8
U.S.A.	277	U.S.A.	158	Canada	19.2	Japan	18.4
Canada	129	Brazil	153	U.S.S.R.	9.2	Canada	13.4
China	111	China	121	Japan	8.8	U.S.S.R.	8.9
Sweden	45	Indonesia	121	Sweden	8.6	W. Germany	8.3
Brazil	37	Nigeria	79	Finland	7.2	Finland	6.4
Finland	31	U.S.S.R.	60	Brazil	3.4	Sweden	6.3
Poland	21	Malaysia	40	W. Germany	2.1	France	5.3
W. Germany	21	Tanzania	39	France	1.9	Italy	4.3
Japan	21	Thailand	37	Norway	1.6	Brazil	3.4

Principal Timber & Paper Producing Areas
- Coniferous softwoods
- Tropical hardwoods
- Temperate hardwoods
- Hardwood and softwoods
- Paper production

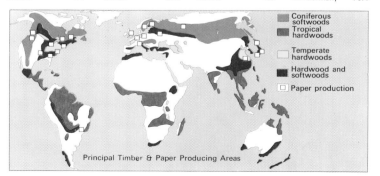

Transport

Japan 9 408	
S. Korea 2 515	
W. Germany 528	
Brazil 460	
Denmark 393	
E. Germany 362	
Poland 320	**World production 1985**
Finland 317	**17.7 million tonnes**
Romania 263	
Italy 241	**Shipbuilding**
France 229	tonnage launched
Yugoslavia 214	in thousand gross registered tons

Shipyards

Aircraft Industry
In 1985 there were approximately 9 400 civil passenger airliners in service. This diagram shows where they were built.

U.S.A. 53%	U.S.S.R. 33%	U.K. 6% Netherlands 3% France 2%

Trade in Aircraft

Exports	*million U.S. $*	Imports	
U.S.A.	11076	W. Germany	3670
W. Germany	3817	U.S.A.	3042
U.K.	2853	U.K.	1699
France	2801	Canada	1192
Italy	1072	Japan	939
Canada	1004	S. Arabia	921
Netherlands	533	Italy	885

Concorde and Boeing 747

Principal shipbuilding centres

Europe

Japan

Principal aircraft manufacturing centres

Motor vehicles World production 1985 43 660 614 vehicles

Production *thousand units*	Exports *million U.S. $*	Imports *million U.S. $*
Japan 11 465	32 798	619
U.S.A. 10 925	14 621	37 587
W. Germany 4045	26 657	7 601
France 3062	9 626	6 987
U.S.S.R. 1900	2 299	2 682
Canada 1829	16 482	14 129
Italy 1601	4 700	4 328
Spain 1309	2 401	1 013
U.K. 1134	4 666	8 721

Locomotive works

Railway vehicles

Exports	*million U.S. $*	Imports	*million U.S. $*
U.S.A.	587.3	U.S.A.	365.7
W. Germany	549.4	Iraq	174.4
Japan	517.4	Indonesia	146.9
France	321.5	Canada	146.9
Canada	173.3	Iran	141.1
U.K.	168.9	Netherlands	94.2
Italy	127.0	Brazil	77.8
Belg.-Lux.	60.0	Egypt	74.1
Switzerland	45.3	W. Germany	70.6
S. Korea	33.8	Yugoslavia	68.8
Sweden	28.9	Tunisia	55.6
Spain	16.2	S. Africa	49.2
Portugal	13.9	Mexico	47.3

Car assembly line

Europe

Principal motor vehicle plants

Principal locomotive building centres

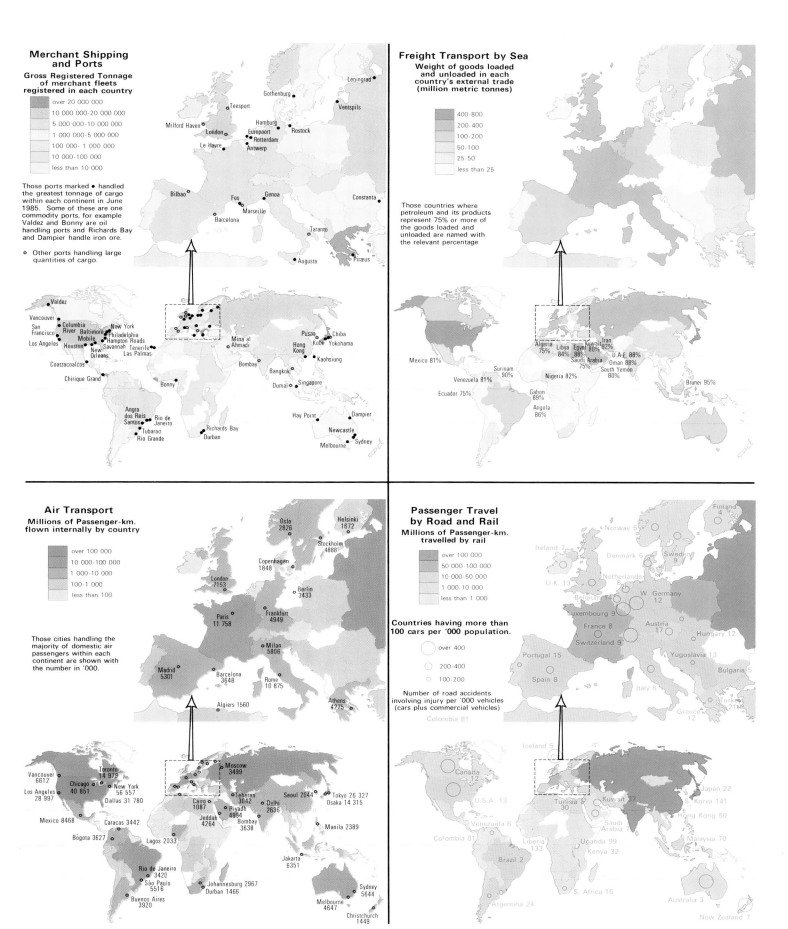

Merchant Shipping and Ports

Gross Registered Tonnage of merchant fleets registered in each country

- over 20 000 000
- 10 000 000-20 000 000
- 5 000 000-10 000 000
- 1 000 000-5 000 000
- 100 000- 1 000 000
- 10 000-100 000
- less than 10 000

Those ports marked ● handled the greatest tonnage of cargo within each continent in June 1985. Some of these are one commodity ports, for example Valdez and Bonny are oil handling ports and Richards Bay and Dampier handle iron ore.

○ Other ports handling large quantities of cargo.

Teesport
Gothenburg
Leningrad
Ventspils
Milford Haven
Hamburg
Rostock
London
Europoort
Rotterdam
Le Havre
Antwerp
Bilbao
Fos
Genoa
Constanta
Marseille
Barcelona
Taranto
Augusta
Piraeus

Valdez
Vancouver
San Francisco
Columbia River
Baltimore
New York
Los Angeles
Houston
Hampton Roads
Mobile
Savannah
Tenerife
New Orleans
Las Palmas
Coatzacoalcos
Chirique Grand
Bonny
Mina al Ahmadi
Pusan
Chiba
Kobe
Yokohama
Hong Kong
Kaohsiung
Bombay
Bangkok
Singapore
Dumai
Angra dos Reis
Santos
Rio de Janeiro
Dampier
Hay Point
Tubarao
Rio Grande
Richards Bay
Durban
Newcastle
Melbourne
Sydney

Freight Transport by Sea

Weight of goods loaded and unloaded in each country's external trade (million metric tonnes)

- 400-800
- 200-400
- 100-200
- 50-100
- 25-50
- less than 25

Those countries where petroleum and its products represent 75% or more of the goods loaded and unloaded are named with the relevant percentage

Mexico 81%
Algeria 75%
Libya 84%
Egypt 80%
Kuwait 92%
Iran
Saudi Arabia 75%
U.A.E. 88%
Oman 88%
Venezuela 81%
Surinam 90%
Nigeria 82%
South Yemen 80%
Brunei 95%
Ecuador 75%
Gabon 89%
Angola 86%

Air Transport

Millions of Passenger-km. flown internally by country

- over 100 000
- 10 000-100 000
- 1 000-10 000
- 100-1 000
- less than 100

Those cities handling the majority of domestic air passengers within each continent are shown with the number in '000.

Oslo 2826
Helsinki 1672
Stockholm 4888
Copenhagen 1848
London 7153
Berlin 3433
Paris 11 758
Frankfurt 4949
Milan 5806
Madrid 5301
Barcelona 3648
Rome 10 875
Algiers 1560
Athens 4275

Vancouver 6612
Toronto 14 978
Moscow 3499
Chicago 40 851
New York 56 557
Los Angeles 28 997
Dallas 31 780
Tokyo 26 327
Osaka 14 315
Seoul 2044
Teheran 3042
Mexico 8468
Cairo 1087
Delhi 2636
Riyadh 4994
Jeddah 4264
Bombay 3638
Caracas 3442
Bogotá 3627
Manila 2389
Lagos 2033
Jakarta 6351
Rio de Janeiro 3420
São Paulo 5516
Johannesburg 2967
Durban 1466
Sydney 5644
Buenos Aires 3920
Melbourne 4647
Christchurch 1449

Passenger Travel by Road and Rail

Millions of Passenger-km. travelled by rail

- over 100 000
- 50 000-100 000
- 10 000-50 000
- 1 000-10 000
- less than 1 000

Countries having more than 100 cars per '000 population.

- ○ over 400
- ○ 200-400
- ○ 100-200

Number of road accidents involving injury per '000 vehicles (cars plus commercial vehicles)

Colombia 81

Finland 4
Norway 5
Ireland 7
Denmark 6
Sweden 9
U.K. 13
Netherlands 8
Belgium 14
W. Germany 12
Luxembourg 9
Austria 17
France 8
Hungary 12
Switzerland 9
Yugoslavia 13
Portugal 15
Bulgaria 5
Spain 8
Italy 6
Turkey 21
Greece 12

Iceland 5
Canada 12
U.S.A. 13
Japan 22
Tunisia 30
Kuwait 37
S. Korea 141
Venezuela 6
Saudi Arabia 7
Hong Kong 50
Colombia 81
Liberia 133
Uganda 99
Kenya 32
Malaysia 70
Brazil 2
S. Africa 16
Australia 3
Argentina 24
New Zealand 7

Trade

Road container lorry.

Oil tanker.

Airfreight.

Road/rail container depot.

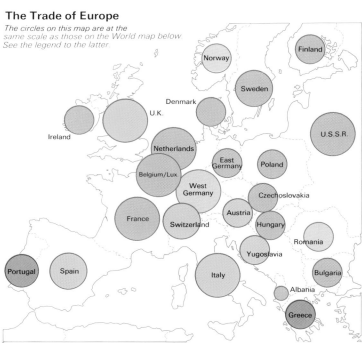
The Trade of Europe
The circles on this map are at the same scale as those on the World map below. See the legend to the latter.

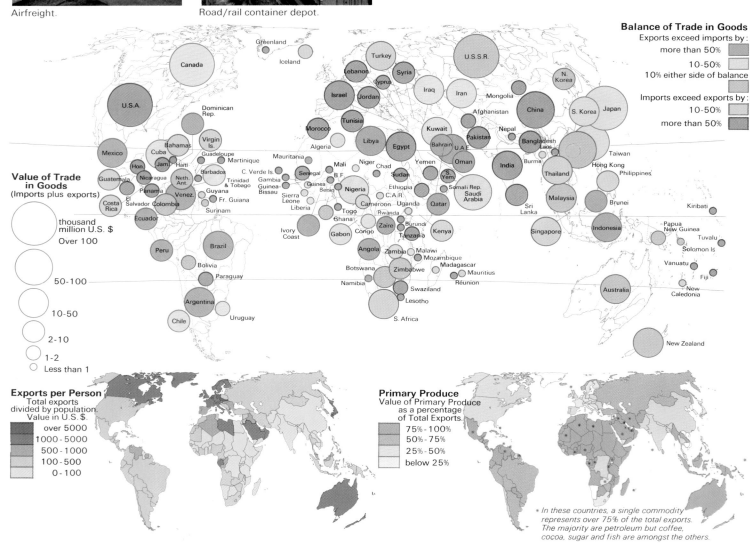

Value of Trade in Goods
(Imports plus exports)

	thousand million U.S. $
	Over 100
	50-100
	10-50
	2-10
	1-2
	Less than 1

Balance of Trade in Goods
Exports exceed imports by :
- more than 50%
- 10-50%
- 10% either side of balance

Imports exceed exports by :
- 10-50%
- more than 50%

Exports per Person
Total exports divided by population. Value in U.S. $.
- over 5000
- 1000 - 5000
- 500 - 1000
- 100 - 500
- 0 - 100

Primary Produce
Value of Primary Produce as a percentage of Total Exports.
- 75% - 100%
- 50% - 75%
- 25% - 50%
- below 25%

* In these countries, a single commodity represents over 75% of the total exports. The majority are petroleum but coffee, cocoa, sugar and fish are amongst the others.

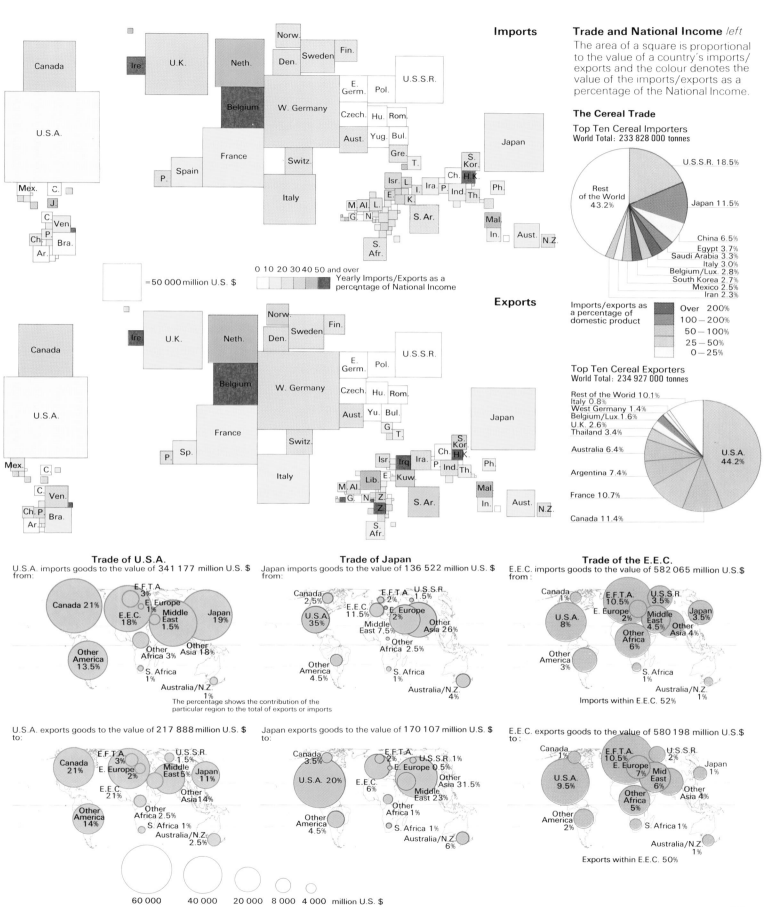

Imports

Exports

Trade and National Income *left*

The area of a square is proportional to the value of a country's imports/exports and the colour denotes the value of the imports/exports as a percentage of the National Income.

The Cereal Trade

Top Ten Cereal Importers
World Total: 233 828 000 tonnes

U.S.S.R. 18.5%
Japan 11.5%
China 6.5%
Egypt 3.7%
Saudi Arabia 3.3%
Italy 3.0%
Belgium/Lux. 2.8%
South Korea 2.7%
Mexico 2.5%
Iran 2.3%
Rest of the World 43.2%

Imports/exports as a percentage of domestic product

Over 200%
100 — 200%
50 — 100%
25 — 50%
0 — 25%

Top Ten Cereal Exporters
World Total: 234 927 000 tonnes

Rest of the World 10.1%
Italy 0.8%
West Germany 1.4%
Belgium/Lux. 1.6%
U.K. 2.6%
Thailand 3.4%
Australia 6.4%
Argentina 7.4%
France 10.7%
Canada 11.4%
U.S.A. 44.2%

0 10 20 30 40 50 and over
Yearly Imports/Exports as a percentage of National Income

=50 000 million U.S. $

Trade of U.S.A.
U.S.A. imports goods to the value of 341 177 million U.S. $ from:

Canada 21%
E.F.T.A. 3%
E. Europe 1%
E.E.C. 18%
Middle East 1.5%
Japan 19%
Other America 13.5%
Other Africa 3%
Other Asia 18%
S. Africa 1%
Australia/N.Z. 1%

The percentage shows the contribution of the particular region to the total of exports or imports

U.S.A. exports goods to the value of 217 888 million U.S. $ to:

Canada 21%
E.F.T.A. 3%
E. Europe 2%
E.E.C. 21%
Middle East 5%
Japan 11%
Other America 14%
Other Africa 2.5%
Other Asia 14%
S. Africa 1%
Australia/N.Z. 2.5%

Trade of Japan
Japan imports goods to the value of 136 522 million U.S. $ from:

Canada 2.5%
E.F.T.A. 2%
U.S.S.R. 1.5%
E.E.C. 11.5%
E. Europe 2%
U.S.A. 35%
Middle East 7.5%
Other Asia 26%
Other Africa 2.5%
Other America 4.5%
S. Africa 1%
Australia/N.Z. 4%

Japan exports goods to the value of 170 107 million U.S. $ to:

Canada 3.5%
E.F.T.A. 2%
U.S.S.R. 1%
E. Europe 0.5%
U.S.A. 20%
E.E.C. 6%
Middle East 23%
Other Asia 31.5%
Other Africa 1%
Other America 4.5%
S. Africa 1%
Australia/N.Z. 6%

Trade of the E.E.C.
E.E.C. imports goods to the value of 582 065 million U.S.$ from:

Canada 1%
E.F.T.A. 10.5%
U.S.S.R. 3.5%
E. Europe 2%
U.S.A. 8%
Middle East 4.5%
Japan 3.5%
Other Africa 6%
Other Asia 4%
Other America 3%
S. Africa 1%
Australia/N.Z. 1%
Imports within E.E.C. 52%

E.E.C. exports goods to the value of 580 198 million U.S.$ to:

Canada 1%
E.F.T.A. 10.5%
U.S.S.R. 2%
E. Europe 7%
U.S.A. 9.5%
Mid East 6%
Japan 1%
Other Africa 5%
Other Asia 4%
Other America 2%
S. Africa 1%
Australia/N.Z. 1%
Exports within E.E.C. 50%

60 000   40 000   20 000   8 000   4 000   million U.S. $

47

Wealth

The living standard of a few highly developed, urbanised, industrialised countries is a complete contrast to the conditions of the vast majority of economically undeveloped, agrarian states. It is this contrast which divides mankind into rich and poor, well fed and hungry. The developing world is still an overwhelmingly agricultural world: over 70% of all its people live off the land and yet the output from that land remains pitifully low. Many Africans, South Americans and Asians struggle with the soil but the bad years occur only too frequently and they seldom have anything left over to save. The need for foreign capital then arises.

National Income
The gap between developing and developed worlds is in fact widening eg. in 1938 the incomes for the United States and India were in the proportions of 1:15; now they are 1:53.

Development aid
The provision of foreign aid, defined as assistance on concessional terms for promoting development, is today an accepted, though controversial aspect of the economic policies of most advanced countries towards less developed countries. Aid for development is based not merely on economic considerations but also on social, political and historical factors. The most important international committee

set up after the war was that of the U.N.; practically all aid however has been given bi-laterally direct from an industrialised country to an under-developed country. Although aid increased during the 1950's the donated proportion of industrialised countries GNP has diminished from 0·5 to 0·4%. Less developed countries share of world trade also decreased and increased population invalidated any progress made:

Incomes per capita in U.S. dollars

Africa $722
Carribean & Latin America $1686
U.S.S.R. $2588
Asia $3933
Oceania $6727
Europe $8652
North America $14 335

INFLATION
Annual average rate of increase 1973-83

0-5%	5-10%	10-15%	15-20%	20-50%	50-100%	over 100%

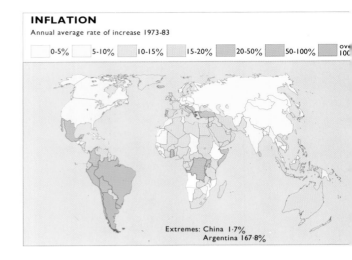

Extremes: China 1·7%
Argentina 167·8%

DEVELOPMENT AID
Development aid received per person in U.S. $, 1979-81 average

0-10$	10-20$	20-50$	50-100$	over 100$

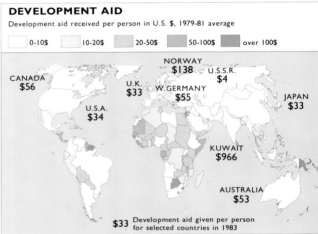

CANADA $56
NORWAY $138
U.S.S.R. $4
U.K. $33
W. GERMANY $55
U.S.A. $34
JAPAN $33
KUWAIT $966
AUSTRALIA $53

$33 Development aid given per person for selected countries in 1983

STANDARDS OF LIVING

THE RICH
- Countries with more than four times the world's average income
- Countries with more than twice the world's average income
- Countries with incomes just above the world's average

THE POOR
- Countries with incomes just below the world's average
- Countries with less than half of the world's average income
- Countries with less than one quarter of the world's average income

- Data not available

The world's average income is just under 2200 US$ per annum. The richest country on a per capita basis is Kuwait with an income over 200 times that of the poorest country, Mali.

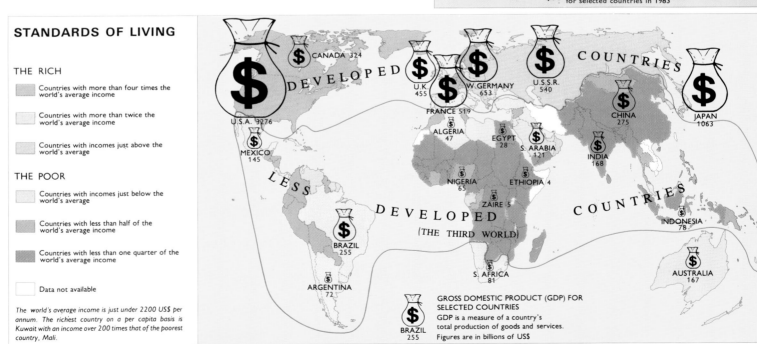

CANADA 324
DEVELOPED COUNTRIES
U.K. 455
W. GERMANY 653
U.S.S.R. 540
FRANCE 519
CHINA 275
JAPAN 1063
U.S.A. 3276
ALGERIA 47
EGYPT 28
S. ARABIA 121
INDIA 168
MEXICO 145
NIGERIA 65
ETHIOPIA 4
ZAIRE 5
LESS DEVELOPED COUNTRIES (THE THIRD WORLD)
INDONESIA 78
BRAZIL 255
S. AFRICA 81
ARGENTINA 72
AUSTRALIA 167

GROSS DOMESTIC PRODUCT (GDP) FOR SELECTED COUNTRIES
GDP is a measure of a country's total production of goods and services.
Figures are in billions of US$

BRAZIL 255

GENERAL REFERENCE

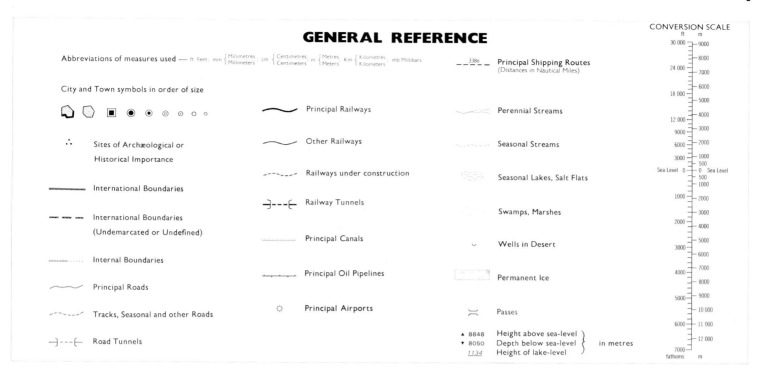

Abbreviations of measures used — ft Feet; mm {Millimetres / Millimeters} cm {Centimetres / Centimeters} m {Metres / Meters} Km {Kilometres / Kilometers} mb Millibars

City and Town symbols in order of size

Sites of Archæological or Historical Importance

International Boundaries

International Boundaries (Undemarcated or Undefined)

Internal Boundaries

Principal Roads

Tracks, Seasonal and other Roads

Road Tunnels

Principal Railways

Other Railways

Railways under construction

Railway Tunnels

Principal Canals

Principal Oil Pipelines

Principal Airports

3386 Principal Shipping Routes (Distances in Nautical Miles)

Perennial Streams

Seasonal Streams

Seasonal Lakes, Salt Flats

Swamps, Marshes

Wells in Desert

Permanent Ice

Passes

▲ 8848 Height above sea-level ⎫
▼ 8050 Depth below sea-level ⎬ in metres
_1134_ Height of lake-level ⎭

CONVERSION SCALE
ft   m
30 000 — 9000
— 8000
24 000 — 7000
— 6000
18 000 — 5000
— 4000
12 000 — 3000
9000 — 2000
6000
3000 — 1000
— 500
Sea Level 0 — 0 Sea Level
— 500
— 1000
1000 — 2000
— 3000
2000 — 4000
— 5000
3000 — 6000
— 7000
4000 — 8000
— 9000
5000 — 10 000
— 11 000
6000 — 12 000
7000
fathoms   m

THE WORLD
Physical
1:150 000 000

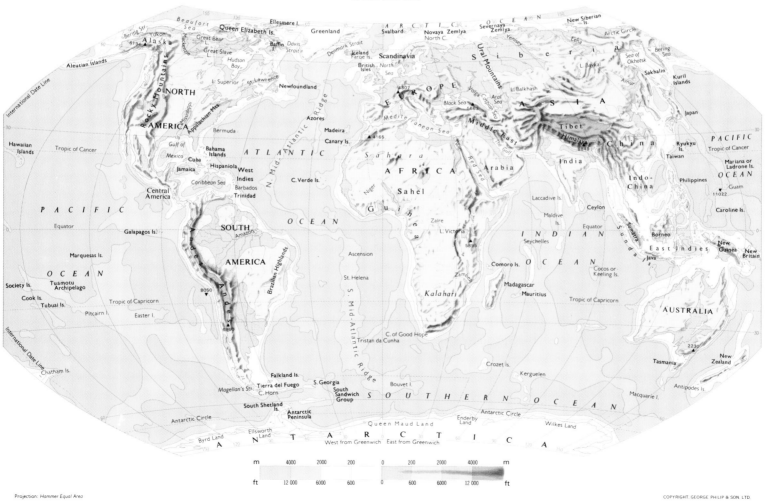

Projection: Hammer Equal Area

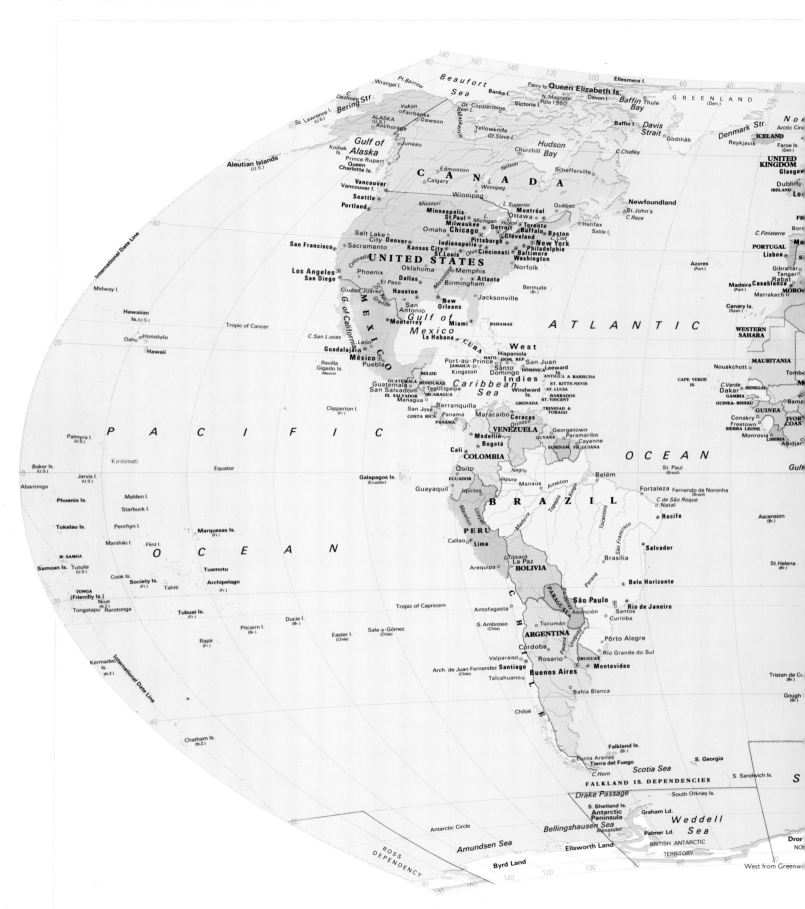

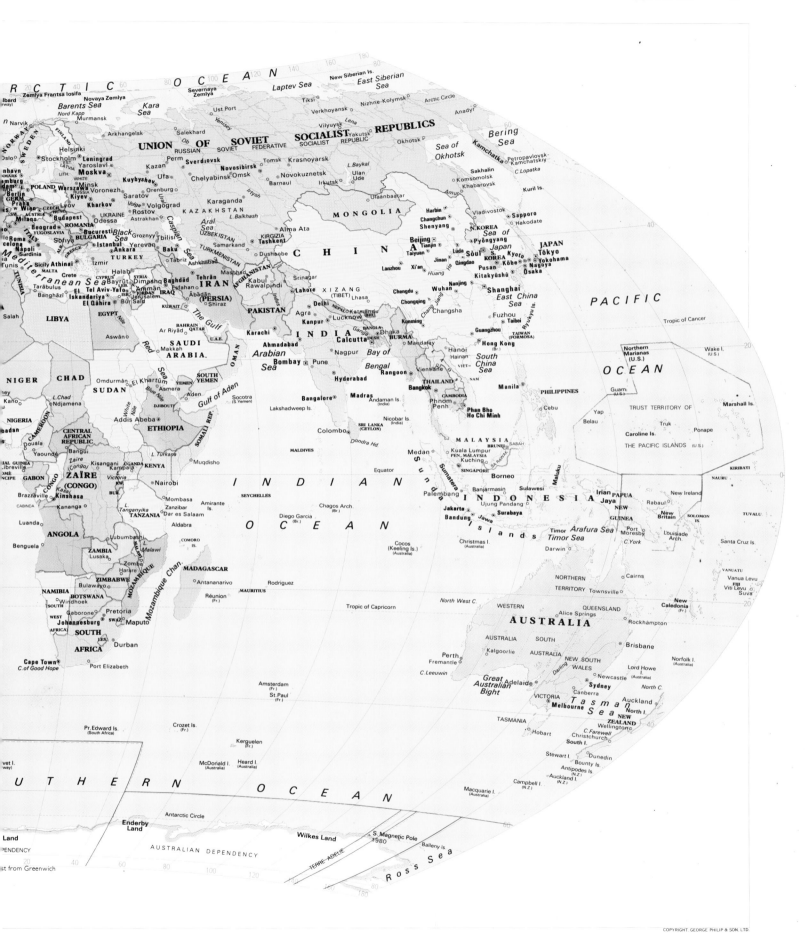

ARCTIC OCEAN

Zemlya Frantsa Iosifa
Ibard
rway) Novaya Zemlya
Nord Kapp   Kara   Severnaya   Laptev Sea   New Siberian Is.   East Siberian
n Narvik Barents Sea   Sea   Zemlya   Sea
   Murmansk   Tiksi   Verkhoyansk   Nizhne-Kolymsk   Arctic Circle
Oslo SWEDEN FINLAND Arkhangelsk Ust Port   Lena   Anadyr
NORWAY   Salekhard   Yenisey Vilyuysk   Yakutsk
   Helsinki   Bering
havn Stockholm Leningrad   Ob   UNION   OF   SOVIET   SOCIALIST   REPUBLIC   REPUBLICS   Sea
DENMARK EST. Yaroslavl   RUSSIAN   SOVIET   FEDERATIVE   Okhotsk   Kamchatka
mburg LATVIA Moskva Kazan   Perm Sverdlovsk   Tomsk Krasnoyarsk   Petropavlovsk-
   LITH. Minsk Kuybyshev Ufa Chelyabinsk Omsk Novosibirsk   L.Baykal   Sea of   Kamchatskiy
Berlin WHITE RUSSIA Voronezh Saratov   Orenburg   Novokuznetsk Irkutsk   Okhotsk   C.Lopatka
GERM. Warszawa Kiyev Volga Volgograd   Barnaul   Ulan Sakhalin   Kuril Is.
ls W Wien POLAND   Ude   Komsomolsk
Praha CZECH. UKRAINE Kharkov KAZAKHSTAN   Karaganda   Ulaanbaatar   Khabarovsk Amur
Milano AUSTRIA Odessa Rostov   Alma Ata   Vladivostok Sapporo
Beograd ROMANIA Astrakhan Aral L.Balkhash   MONGOLIA   Harbin   Hakodate
Roma ITALY Sofiya BULGARIA Black Caspian Sea UZBEKISTAN KIRGIZIA Tashkent   Changchun N.KOREA
celona Sardinia Istanbul Ankara Sea Sea Groznyy Tbilisi Samarkand   Shenyang   Sea of
Napoli GREECE Athinai TURKEY Yerevan Baku TURKMENISTAN Ashkhabad   Beijing Pyongyang Japan
a Sicily MALTA Izmir   Tabriz   Lanzhou CHINA Taiyuan Luda Soul KOREA JAPAN
Tunis Crete CYPRUS Halab   Dimashq Baghdad IRAN Kabul Srinagar   Xi'an Jinan Qingdao Pusan Kyoto Tokyo
Mediterranean Sea Bayrut SYRIA (PERSIA) Tehran Rawalpindi Lahore   Huang Nanjing S. KOREA Kobe Nagoya Yokohama
Tarabulus Tel Aviv-Yafo Amman Baghdad Esfahan AFGHANISTAN Delhi NEPAL Katmandu   Wuhan Kitakyushu Osaka
TUNISIA ISR. JORDAN IRAQ Abadan Shiraz PAKISTAN Agra Lucknow BHU. Chengdu Chang Jiang Shanghai
Salah El Qahira KUWAIT The Gulf BAHRAIN QATAR Kanpur NEPAL   Chongqing East China
LIBYA EGYPT Ar Riyad U.A.E. Karachi INDIA Calcutta Dhaka BANGLA Kunming Changsha Sea
   Aswan SAUDI OMAN   Ahmadabad DESH BURMA Fuzhou
NIGER CHAD Red Makkah ARABIA. Arabian Nagpur Mandalay Guangzhou Taibei
   Omdurman El Khartum Sea Bombay Pune Bengal   Hanoi Hong Kong TAIWAN
Kano L.Chad Blue Nile Asmera YEMEN SOUTH Bangalore Hyderabad Bay of Rangoon VIET- South (FORMOSA)
Ndjamena SUDAN Aden YEMEN Madras Andaman Is. THAILAND NAM China
NIGERIA White Nile DJIBOUTI Lakshadweep Is. (India) Bangkok Sea Manila
badan CAMEROON Addis Abeba Gulf of Aden Colombo SRI LANKA Nicobar Is. CAMBODIA Cebu PHILIPPINES
AL GUINEA GABON CENTRAL ETHIOPIA SOMALI REP. (CEYLON) (India) Phnom PHILIPPINES
NCIPE Yaounde AFRICAN Bangui Muqdisho MALDIVES Dondra Hd. Penh Phan Bho
ZAIRE REPUBLIC Kisangani UGANDA KENYA Ho Chi Minh
Libreville (CONGO) Kasai Victoria Kampala Nairobi I N D I A N MALAYSIA SABAH
Brazzaville Kinshasa Mombasa SEYCHELLES Kuala Lumpur BRUNEI
CABINDA Kananga TANZANIA Zanzibar Dar es Salaam Chagos Arch. Equator PEN. MALAYSIA Kuching
Luanda Tanganyika Amirante Is. (Br.) SINGAPORE Borneo
ANGOLA Kubumbashi Aldabra Diego Garcia O C E A N Medan Palembang Banjarmasin Sulawesi Maluku
   ZAMBIA MALAWI COMORO (Br.) Sumatera INDONESIA Ujung Pandang
Benguela Lusaka Malawi IS.   Jakarta Jawa Surabaya
   Zomba MOZAMBIQUE MADAGASCAR Rodriguez Bandung
NAMIBIA ZIMBABWE Harare Antananarivo MAURITIUS
Windhoek BOTSWANA Bulawayo Mozambique Chan. Reunion (Fr.)
SOUTH Gaborone Pretoria Christmas I. Timor Arafura Sea
WEST Johannesburg SWAZ. Maputo (Australia) Timor Sea
AFRICA SOUTH Durban Tropic of Capricorn NORTHERN Darwin
   AFRICA North West C. WESTERN TERRITORY
Cape Town Port Elizabeth AUSTRALIA Alice Springs QUEENSLAND
C.of Good Hope Amsterdam (Fr.) Great AUSTRALIA SOUTH
   St.Paul (Fr.) Perth Australian Kalgoorlie AUSTRALIA Adelaide NEW SOUTH
Pr.Edward Is. Crozet Is. Fremantle Bight C.Leeuwin WALES Sydney
(South Africa) (Fr.) Kerguelen VICTORIA Canberra
   McDonald I. Heard I. (Fr.) TASMANIA Melbourne Tasman
UTHERN O C E A N (Australia) (Australia) Hobart Sea
Land Antarctic Circle Macquarie I. Campbell I. NEW
ENDENCY Enderby Land AUSTRALIAN DEPENDENCY Wilkes Land S.Magnetic Pole Balleny Is. ZEALAND
t from Greenwich TERRE ADELIE 1980 Ross Sea

PACIFIC

OCEAN

Northern Marianas (U.S.)   Wake I. (U.S.)

Tropic of Cancer

Guam (U.S.)   Marshall Is.

Yap   Truk   Ponape
Belau   TRUST TERRITORY OF
Caroline Is.   THE PACIFIC ISLANDS (U.S.)
                                      KIRIBATI
                                      NAURU

Irian Jaya PAPUA NEW GUINEA New Ireland
   Rabaul New Britain Solomon Is. TUVALU
Port Moresby SOLOMON IS.
C.York Louisiade Arch. Santa Cruz Is.
                                      VANUATU
Cairns   Vanua Levu
                                      FIJI Viti Levu Suva
NORTHERN TERRITORY Townsville New Caledonia (Fr.)
Rockhampton
Brisbane
   Norfolk I. (Australia)
   Lord Howe I. (Australia)
Newcastle North C.
   North I.
   Auckland
Wellington NEW ZEALAND
   C.Farewell
   Christchurch
   South I.
Stewart I. Dunedin
Bounty Is. (N.Z.)
Antipodes Is. (N.Z.)
Auckland Is. (N.Z.)

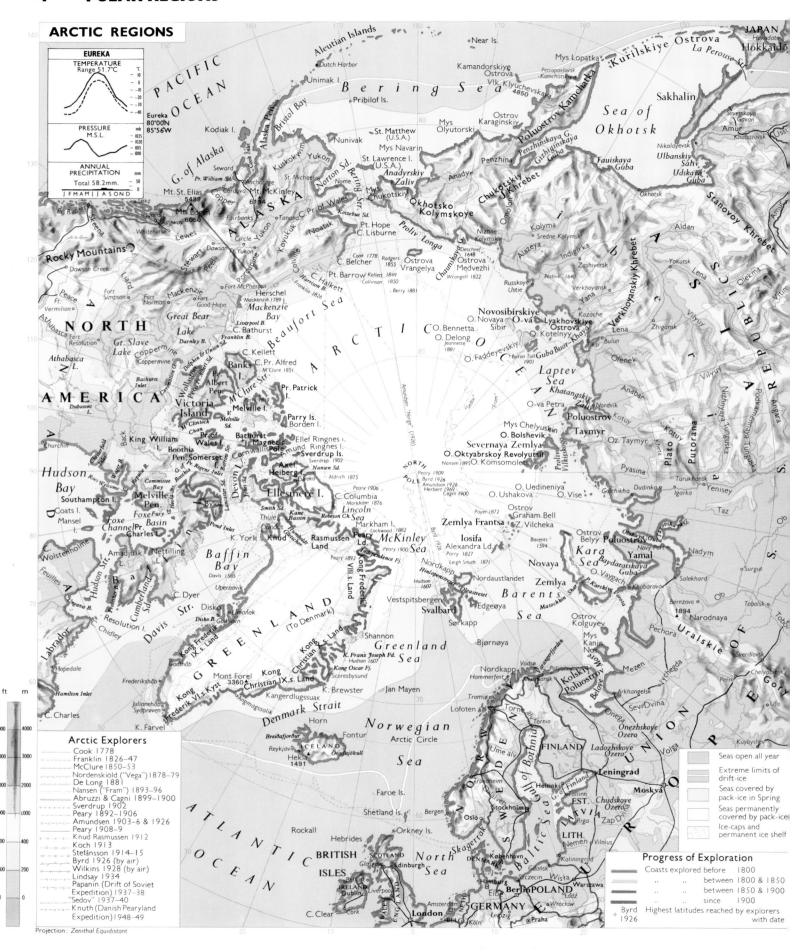

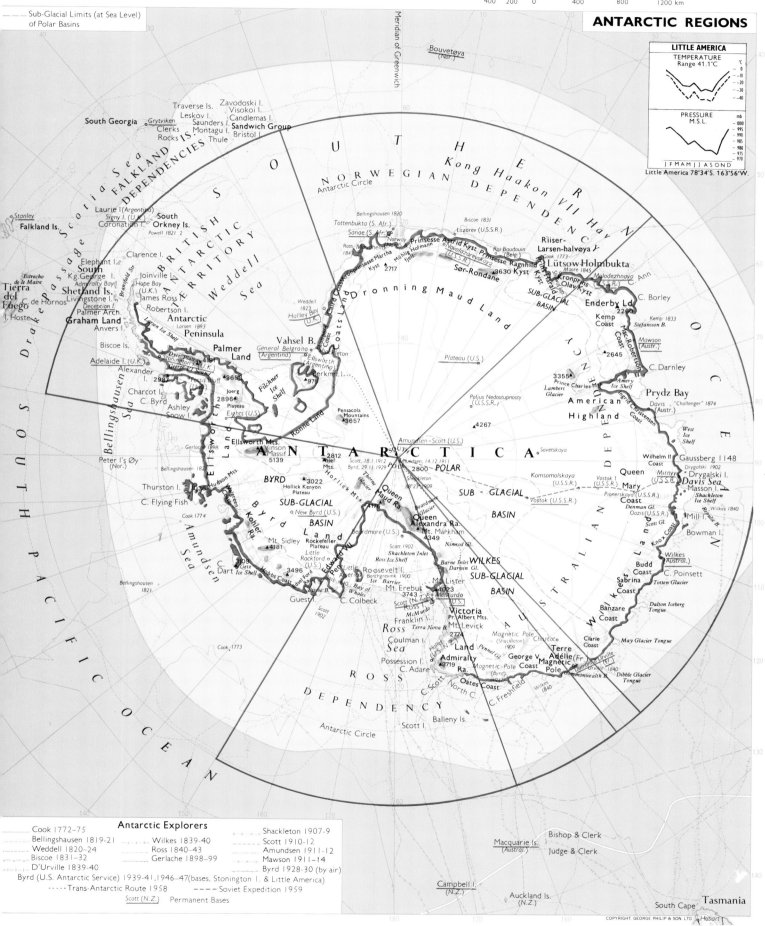

ANTARCTIC REGIONS

1 : 35 000 000

200 100 0 200 400 600 miles
400 200 0 400 800 1200 km

5

LITTLE AMERICA
TEMPERATURE
Range 41.1°C

°C
0
-10
-20
-30
-40

PRESSURE
M.S.L.

mb
1000
995
990
985
980
975
970

J F M A M J J A S O N D

Little America 78°34'S. 163°56'W.

Sub-Glacial Limits (at Sea Level)
of Polar Basins

Bouvetøya
(Nor.)

SOUTHERN

NORWEGIAN DEPENDENCY

Kong Haakon VII Hav

OCEAN

Antarctic Circle

South Georgia
Grytviken
Traverse Is.
Zavodoski I.
Leskov I.
Visokoi I.
Candlemas I.
Clerks
Rocks
Saunders I.
Montagu I.
Bristol I.
Thule
Sandwich Group

Scotia Sea
FALKLAND
DEPENDENCIES

Stanley
Falkland Is.

Laurie I. (Argentina)
Signy I. (U.K.)
Coronation I.
South
Orkney Is.
Powell 1821

BRITISH
ANTARCTIC
TERRITORY

Clarence I.

Bellingshausen 1820
Tottenbukta (S. Afr.)
Sanae (S. Afr.)
Norway
Biscoe 1831
Lazarev (U.S.S.R.)
Prinsesse Astrid Kyst
Prinsesse Ragnhild
Roi Baudouin (Belg.)
Novolazarevskaya
(U.S.S.R.)

Cook 1773
Riiser-
Larsen-halvøya

Lütsow Holmbukta

C. Borley

Tierra
del
Fuego
I. Hoste
C. de Hornos

Elephant I.
South
Kg.George I.
Shetland Is.
Admiralty Bay
Joinville I.
Hope Bay
(U.K.)
James Ross I.
Deception I.
Robertson I.
Livingstone I.

Dronning Maud Land

Sør-Rondane
3630 Kyst
Kronprins
Olav Kyst
SUB-GLACIAL
BASIN

Molodezhnaya
(U.S.S.R.)

Enderby Ld.
2280

Kemp 1833
Stefansson B.

Weddell
Sea

Graham Land
Anvers I.
Antarctic
Peninsula
Larsen 1893

Vahsel B.
General Belgrano
(Argentina)
Ellsworth
(Argentina)
Berkner I.

Weddell
1823
Halley Bay
(U.K.)

Coats Land
Caird Coast

2717
Mühlig Hofmann
fjell

Kemp
Coast

Mawson
(Austr.)
2645

Mac-Robertson

C. Darnley

Adelaide I. (U.K.)
Alexander
I. 2987

Palmer
Land

3653

Filchner
Ice
Shelf

Plateau (U.S.)

3355
Prince Charles Mts.
Lambert Glacier

Amery
Ice
Shelf

Ingrid Christensen
Coast

Prydz Bay

Charcot I.
C. Byrd
Ashley
Snow I.

Joerg
Plateau
2896
Eights (U.S.)

Ronne Land

Pensacola
Mountains
3657

Poljus Nedostupnosty
(U.S.S.R.)

4267

Davis "Challenger" 1874
Davis (Austr.)

American

West
Ice
Shelf

Peter I's Øy
(Nor.)

Bellingshausen

Ellsworth Mts.
Vinson
Massif
5139
Thiel
Mts.

Amundsen-Scott (U.S.)

Highland

Bellingshausen 1821

2812

Scott, 18.1.1912
Byrd, 29.11.1929
POLE

Amundsen, 14.12.1911

2800 POLAR

Soverskaya

Komsomolskaya
(U.S.S.R.)

Wilhelm II
Coast
Queen

Gaussberg 1148

Drygalski 1902

Thurston I.
C. Flying Fish

BYRD
Hollick Kenyon
Plateau
3022

Shackleton
Dec.23 1909

SUB - GLACIAL
BASIN

Vostok I.
(U.S.S.R.)
Vostok (U.S.S.R.)
Pionerskaya (U.S.S.R.)

Mary
Coast

Mirnyy
(U.S.S.R.)

Davis Sea
Masson I.
Shackleton
Ice Shelf
Wilkes 1840

Cook 1774

Kohler
Ra.

SUB-GLACIAL
BASIN

New Byrd (U.S.)

Denman Gl.
Oazis (U.S.S.R.)
Scott Gl.
Mill I. B.

Bowman I.

Bellingshausen
1821

Amundsen
Sea

C. Getz
Dart
Ice Shelf
3496

Hudson Mts.

Byrd
Land

Mt. Sidley
4181
Rockefeller
Plateau
Little
Rockford
(U.S.)

Roosevelt I.

ATKA

Queen
Maud Ra.

Thorne Glacier
Beardmore (U.S.)

Queen
Alexandra Ra.
Mt. Markham
4349

Scott 1902
Nimrod Gl.
Shackleton Inlet

Barne Inlet
Darwin Gl.

WILKES

SUB-GLACIAL
BASIN

Budd
Coast

Sabrina
Coast

Banzare
Coast

Totten Glacier

Wilkes
(Austral.)

C. Poinsett

Dalton Iceberg
Tongue

Clarie
Coast

May Glacier Tongue

Guest I.

Scott
1902

Edward VII
Little
America
(U.S.)

Borchgrevink 1900
Ice Barrier

Bay
of
Whales

Ross Ice Shelf

Mt. Lister
3023
Mt. Erebus
3743
McMurdo
Scott (N.Z.)
McMurdo (U.S.)

C. Colbeck

Victoria
Pr. Albert Mts.
Mt. Levick
2774

Magnetic Pole
(Shackleton)
1909

Terre
Adélie
(Fr.)

Terre Adélie

Magnetic
Pole

Dumont d'Urville (Fr.)
d'Urville 1840

Dibble Glacier
Tongue

Ross
Sea

Franklin I.
Coulman I.

Terra Nova B.

Land

Pennel Gl.

George V
Coast

Commonwealth B.

Possession I.
C. Adare

Admiralty
Ra.

3719

Magnetic Pole
(Byrd)
1947

DEPENDENCY

ROSS

C. Scott
North C.
C. Freshfield

Oates Coast

Wilkes
1840

Scott I.

Balleny Is.

Antarctic Circle

Antarctic Explorers

Cook 1772–75
Bellingshausen 1819-21
Weddell 1820–24
Biscoe 1831–32
D'Urville 1839–40
Byrd (U.S. Antarctic Service) 1939-41,1946-47(bases, Stonington I. & Little America)
Trans-Antarctic Route 1958
Scott (N.Z.) Permanent Bases

Wilkes 1839-40
Ross 1840–43
Gerlache 1898–99

Shackleton 1907-9
Scott 1910-12
Amundsen 1911-12
Mawson 1911–14
Byrd 1928-30 (by air)
Soviet Expedition 1959

Meridian of Greenwich

Macquarie Is.
(Austral.)

Bishop & Clerk
Judge & Clerk

Campbell I.
(N.Z.)

Auckland Is.
(N.Z.)

South Cape

Tasmania
Hobart

COPYRIGHT GEORGE PHILIP & SON LTD.

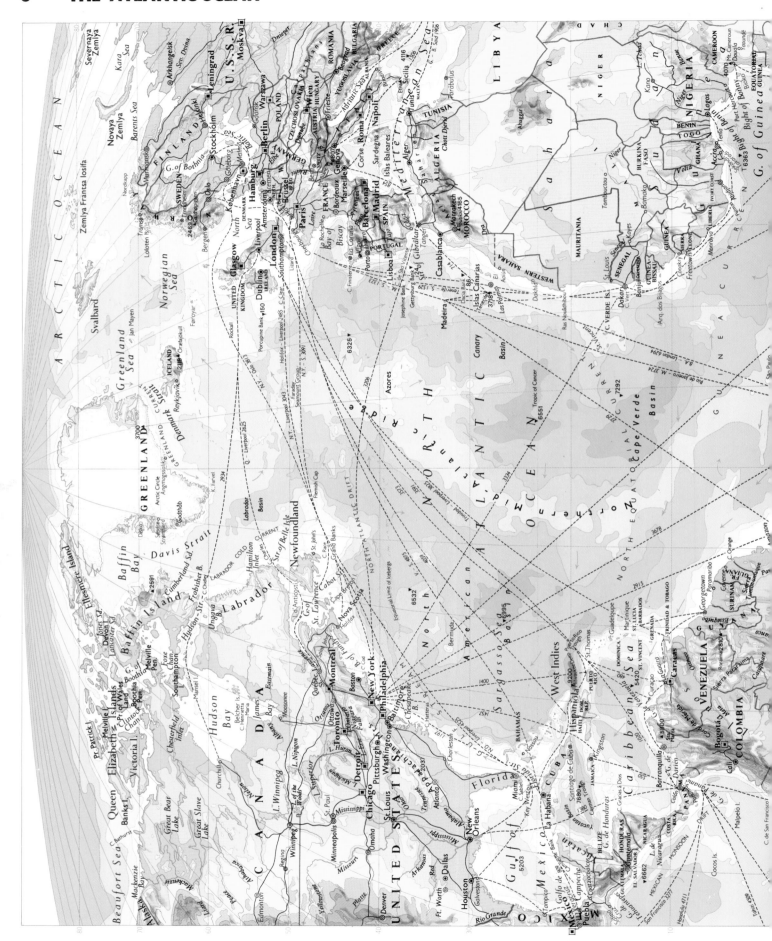

1 : 45 000 000

7

Direction of Currents

COPYRIGHT GEORGE PHILIP & SON LTD.

Principal Shipping Routes
(Distances in Nautical Miles)

3778 - - - - -

Projection : Mollweide

CONGO Brazzaville

(SOUTH
WEST
AFRICA) NAMIBIA

(SOUTH AFRICA)

Cape Town

Agulhas
Basin

Enderby
Land

BENGUELA COLD CURRENT

Angola Basin

Cape
Basin

Dronning Maud Land

S O U T H

A T L A N T I C

O C E A N

Southern

Tropic of Capricorn

Atlantic Indian Ridge

Mid-Atlantic Ridge

Walvis Ridge

St. Helena

Ascension

Brazil Basin

Gough I.

Tristan da Cunha

W E S T   W I N D   D R I F T

S O U T H   E Q U A T O R I A L   C U R R E N T

Equatorial Limit of Icebergs

Coats
Land

Weddell Sea

Antarctic Basin

Fernando de Noronha

Trindade
Martin Vaz

South Sandwich Trench

FALKLAND IS.

DEPENDENCIES

South
Georgia

Scotia Sea

South Orkney Is.

BRITISH

ANTARCTIC

TERRITORY

Recife
Foraleza

Salvador

Belo Horizonte
Rio de Janeiro
São Paulo

B R A Z I L

Brasília

Belém

São Luís

Mato Grosso

Pôrto Alegre

Montevideo
URUGUAY

Río de la Plata

Buenos Aires

Rosário
Córdoba

A R G E N T I N A

Argentine Basin

Pen.
Valdés

Golfo San Matías

Golfo San Jorge

CAPE HORN COLD CURRENT

FALKLAND CURRENT

Falkland Is.

Graham
Land

South Shetland Is.

Antarctic
Peninsula

Palmer
Land

Peter 1st I.

P E R U

Lima

La Paz
BOLIVIA

A n d e s

Santiago
Valparaíso

C H I L E

Concepción

Arch. de los Chonos
Pen. de Taitão

Tierra del Fuego

Drake Passage

S O U T H E R N   O C E A N

Antarctic Circle

Ellsworth Land

PERUVIAN COLD CURRENT

Arch. de
Juan Fernández

S. Ambrosio

ECUADOR
Galapagos

Gulf of Guayaquil

Antarctic
(Southern Pacific)
Basin

Chile Rise

P A C I F I C   O C E A N

South East Pacific Basin

Ross Sea

Byrd Land

m
6000
4000
3000
2000
1500
1000
400
200
0

ft
18 000
12 000
9000
6000
4500
3000
1200
600
0
600

ft
2000 6000
4000 12 000
5000 15 000
6000 18 000
8000 24 000
m

EUROPEAN ORGANIZATIONS
1 : 40 000 000

E.E.C. Members

E.F.T.A. Member

All E.F.T.A. and associated states have
Free Trade Agreements with the E.E.C.

States with Association
Agreement with E.E.C.

Associate Member of E.F.T.A.

States with Trading Agreement
with E.E.C.

Warsaw Pact Countries

The E.E.C. has Trading Agreements with
certain countries in the Mediterranean,
Pacific and Latin American areas.

Arctic Circle

Arctic Circle

NORWEGIAN SE

Iceland

Reykjavik
Hekla
1491
Öræfajökull
2119

3734

Faroe Is.

Rockall

Hebrides

Shetland
Is.

St. Kilda

Orkney
Is.

Lindesnes

British
Isles

Ben Nevis
1343

Edinburgh

NORTH

Ju

Ireland

Belfast

Irish Sea

SEA

Dublin

St. George's
Channel

Snowdon
1085

C.Clear

Frisian Is.

Celtic Sea

Cardiff

Thames

London

Amsterdam

Lands End

Netherlands

Scilly Is.

English Channel

Brussel

English
Channel
Is.

Str. of Dover

Rhine

Western

ATLANTIC

Brittany

Ardennes

Eifel

Taunus

Paris

Seine

Vosges

Black Forest

Loire

OCEAN

Flores

Jura

Zür

Terceira

4861

Bay of
Biscay

Saône

Pico

Azores

Gironde

Massif
Central
Mt. Dore
1886

Mt. Blanc
4807

A

P

São Miguel

C. Finisterre

Cévennes

Rhône

Pa

Cantabrian Mts.

Garonne

Maladetta
3404

Pyrenees

G. of Lion

Ero

Ligurian
Sea

Old Castile

Iberian

Corsica

Douro

Ebro

New
Castile

Madrid

Lisboa

6293

C. da Roca

Peninsula

Tagus

Sardinia

Str. of Bonif

Madeira

Guadiana

Sierra Morena

Balearic
Is.

C. St. Vincent

Guadalquivir

Andalusia

Mulhacén
3478

Sa. Nevada

M E D I T E

C. Trafalgar

Str. of Gibraltar

Gibraltar

Alger

Casablanca

Er Rif

Tunis

Palma

Maritime Atlas

Canary Is.

Plateau of the Shotts

Tenerife

Toubkal
4165

Great Atlas

Saharan Atlas

Gulf
Gabe

Gran
Canaria

Fuerteventura

Sahara

Tropic of Cancer

ft   m

12 000   4000

6000   2000

30

3000   1000

1200   400

600   200

0   0

25

200   600

2000   6000

4000   12 000

m   ft

Projection: Bonne.   20   15   West from Greenwich   0   East from Greenwich   5   10

1:17 500 000

100 0 100 200 300 400 500 miles
100 0 200 400 600 800 km

Nordkapp Nordkinn

Lofoten

L. Inari
Torne älv
Kebnekaise 2123
Lappland
Scandinavia
Umeälv
Indalsälven
Øpiggen 2469
Oslo
Stockholm
Vänern
Mälaren
Vättern
Skaw
Katte gat
København
Gotland

Gulf of Bothnia
Finland
Åland Is.
Helsinki
Gulf of Finland
Lake Ladoga
Svir
L. Onega
Neva Leningrad
L. Chudskoye
Valdai Hills
Dvina
Neman
Vistula
Oder
Berlin
Warszawa
Pripet
Pripet Marshes
Bug
Dniester
Prut

Kanin Peninsula
Kola Peninsula
White Sea
Mezen
N. Dvina
Onega
Pechora
Tundra
Narodnaya 1894
Telpos Iz 1617
Ural Mountains
West Siberian Plain
Ob
Irtysh
Tobol
Kama
Volga
Gorkiy
Oka
Moskva
Rybinsk Res.
Volga
European Plain
Central Russian Uplands
Volga Heights
Obshchi Syrt
Ural
Kirgiz Steppe
Ust Urt Plateau
Karagiye Depression -132
Karu Bogaz

Mts. Praha
Sudetes
Bohemian Forest
Moravia Hts.
Tatra 2655
Carpathians
Danube
Inn
Wien
Bakony Forest
Budapest
Plain of Hungary
Drava
Sava
Tisza
Mures
Transylvanian Alps
Beograd
Morava
Wallachia
Danube
Bucureşti

North European Plain
Ukraine
Kiyevo
Dnieper
Dnieper
Odessa
Dnieper
Crimea
Mouths of the Danube
Sea of Azov
Strait of Kerch
Kuban
Don
Tsimlyansk Res.
Volga
Terek
Caucasus
Elbrus 5633
Transcaucasia
Kura
Baku
Araks
Ararat 5165
Caspian Sea

Dinaric Alps
Adriatic Sea
Dalmatia
Gran Sasso 2914
Apennines
Str. of Otranto
Sofiya
Balkans
Rhodope
Balkan Peninsula
Pindus
Strait of Messina
Etna 3263
Colabria
Sicily
C. Spartivento
Ionian Sea
Ionian Is.
Morea
5121 C. Matapan
Malta
Tripoli
Gulf of Sidra

Black Sea
2211
Istanbul
Bosporus
Sea of Marmara
Dardanelles
Aegean Sea
Athinai
Rhodes
Crete
MEDITERRANEAN SEA

Pontine Mts.
Anatolia
Ankara
Kizil
L. Tuz
Erciyas 3770
Taurus Mts.
Anatolia
Kurdistan
L. Van
L. Urmia
Elburz Mts.
Tehrān
Mesopotamia
Tigris
Euphrates
Baghdad
Halab
Cyprus
Bayrūt
Levant
Syrian Desert
Tel Aviv-Yafo
Dead Sea -395
Nile Delta
Persian Gulf

BALTIC SEA

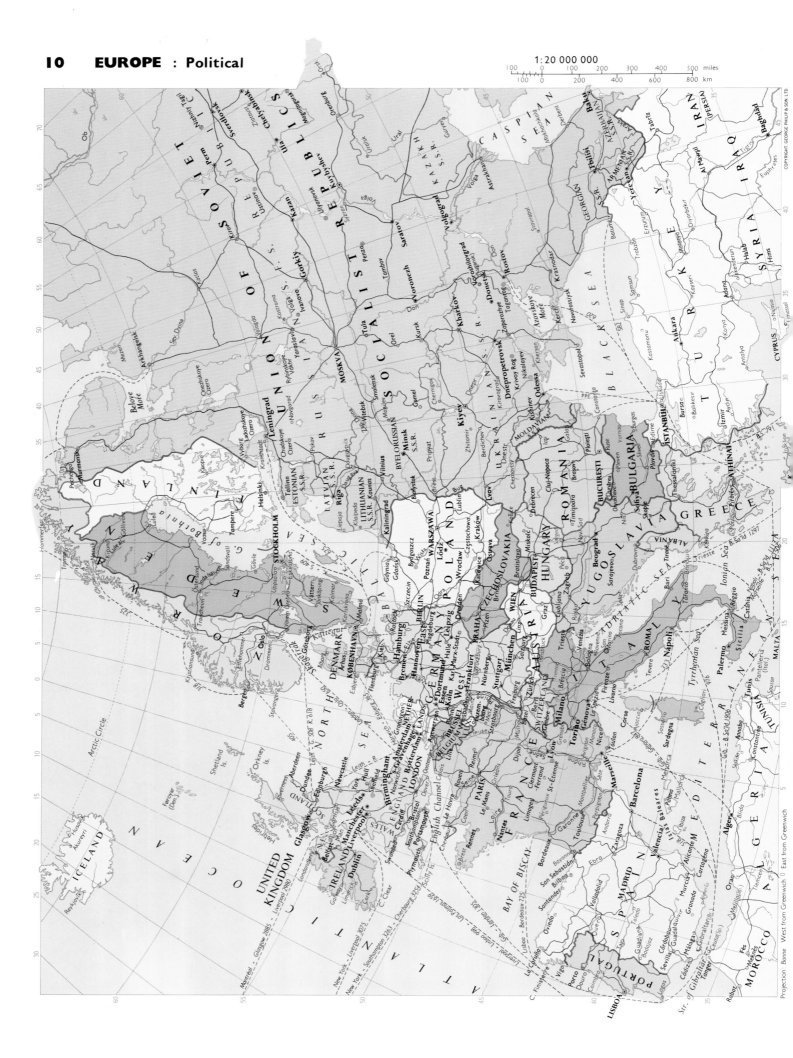

1:20 000 000

The DISTRICTS of Northern Ireland have been numbered and can be identified by reference to this table.

1 Londonderry — 14 Craigavon
2 Limavady — 15 Armagh
3 Coleraine — 16 Newry & Mourne
4 Ballymoney — 17 Banbridge
5 Moyle — 18 Down
6 Larne — 19 Lisburn
7 Ballymena — 20 Antrim
8 Magherafelt — 21 Newtownabbey
9 Cookstown — 22 Carrickfergus
10 Strabane — 23 North Down
11 Omagh — 24 Ards
12 Fermanagh — 25 Castlereagh
13 Dungannon — 26 Belfast

1 Merseyside
2 Greater Manchester
3 West Yorkshire
4 South Yorkshire
5 West Glamorgan
6 Mid Glamorgan
7 South Glamorgan

Projection: Conical with two standard parallels

COPYRIGHT. GEORGE PHILIP & SON. LTD.

1 : 2 000 000

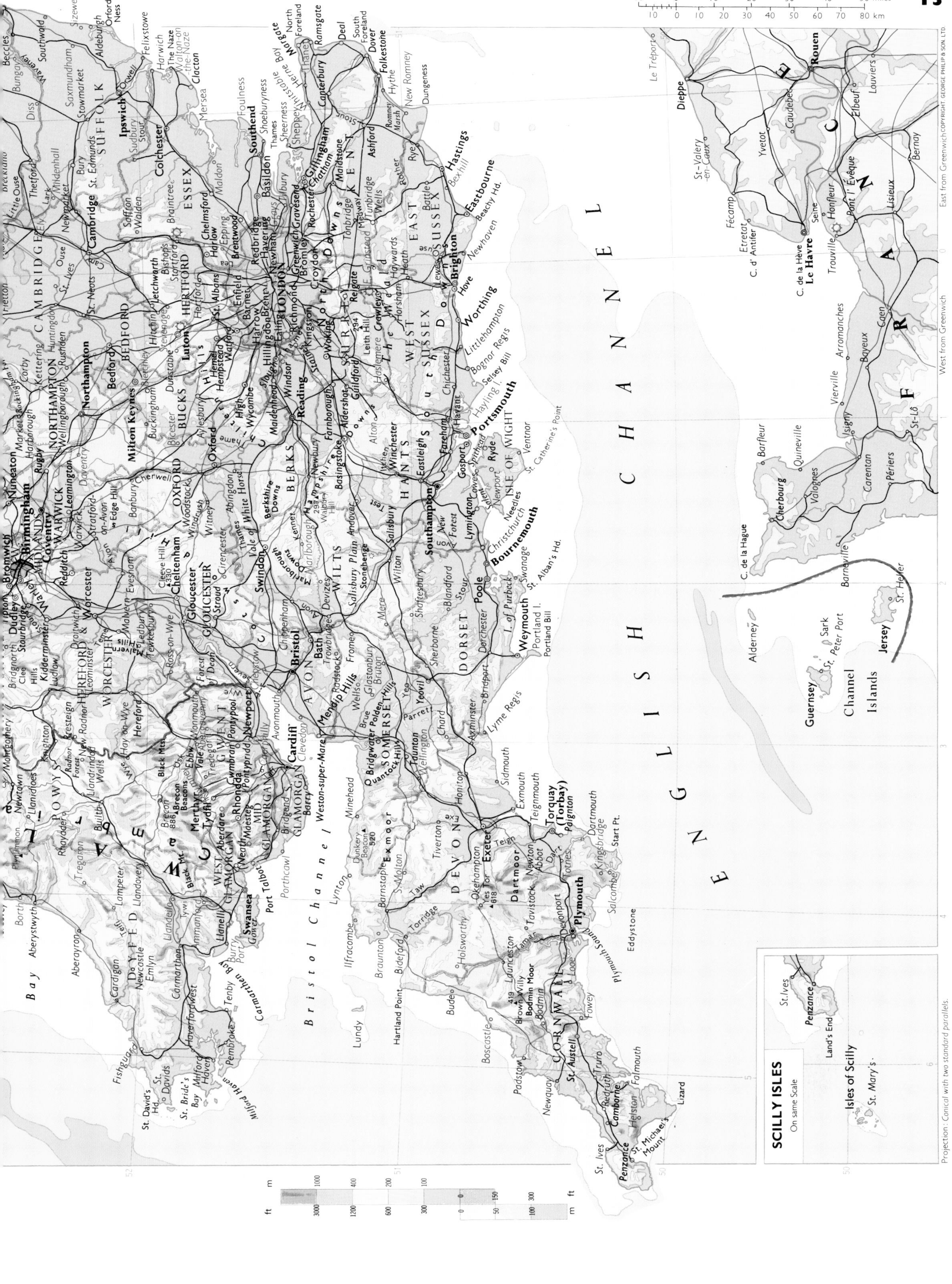

10 0 10 20 30 40 50 miles

10 0 10 20 30 40 50 60 70 80 km

East from Greenwich   COPYRIGHT GEORGE PHILIP & SON LTD.

West from Greenwich

Projection: Conic with two standard parallels

ENGLISH CHANNEL

BRISTOL CHANNEL

Channel Islands

SCILLY ISLES

On same Scale

Isles of Scilly   St. Mary's.

m   ft
3000
1200
600
300
0
0
50
100
300

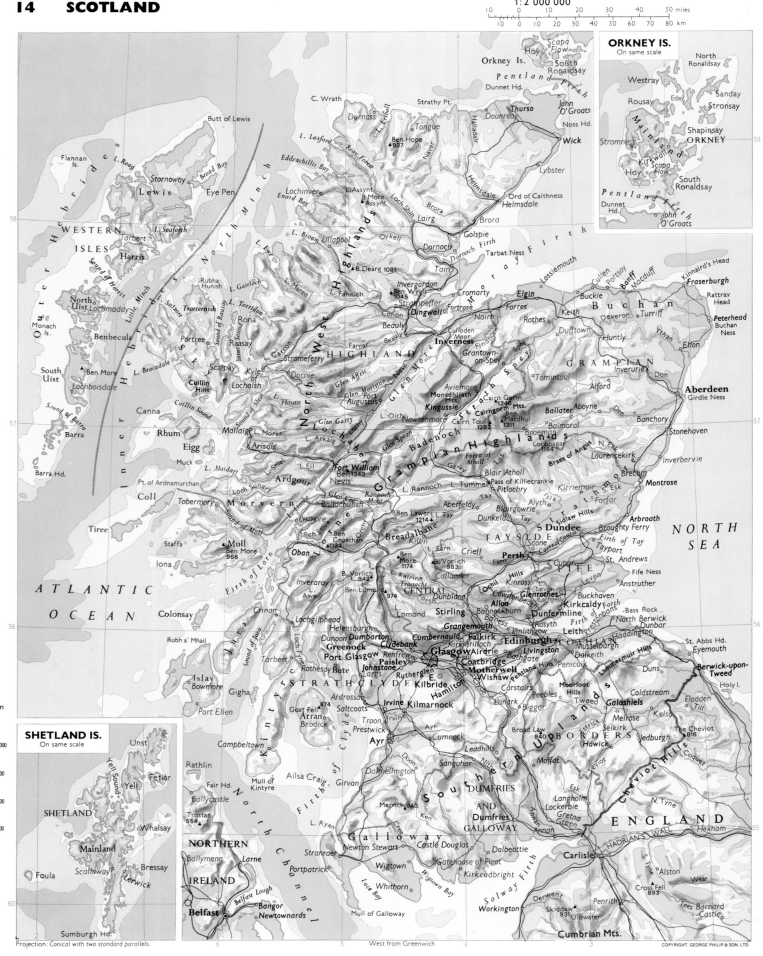

1:2 000 000

ORKNEY IS.
On same scale

SHETLAND IS.
On same scale

Projection: Conical with two standard parallels.

West from Greenwich

COPYRIGHT. GEORGE PHILIP & SON. LTD.

1:2 000 000

10 0 10 20 30 40 50 miles
10 0 10 20 30 40 50 60 70 80 km

ATLANTIC OCEAN

NORTHERN IRELAND

IRELAND

IRISH SEA

St. George's Channel

North Channel

DONEGAL

LONDONDERRY

Belfast

Lisburn

SLIGO

LEITRIM

CAVAN

MONAGHAN

LOUTH

MAYO

ROSCOMMON

LONGFORD

MEATH

CONNACHT

WESTMEATH

DUBLIN

Dublin (Baile Atha Cliath)

Dun Laoghaire

GALWAY

OFFALY

KILDARE

Galway

LAOIS

WICKLOW

CLARE

LEINSTER

CARLOW

Limerick

TIPPERARY

KILKENNY

WEXFORD

MUNSTER

Tralee

Killarney

KERRY

CORK

WATERFORD

Waterford

Cork

Towns underlined in Northern Ireland give their
names to the Districts in which they stand
The remaining Districts are:—

1	Fermanagh	5	Castlereagh
2	Moyle	6	Ards
3	Newtownabbey	7	Down
4	North Down	8	Newry & Mourne

Projection: Conical with two standard parallels.

West from Greenwich

ft   m
3000 — 1000
1200 — 400
600 — 200
300
100 — 300
0 — 0
200 — 600
m   ft

1:2 500 000

10   0   10   20   30   40   50 miles
10 0 10 20 30 40 50 60 70 80 km

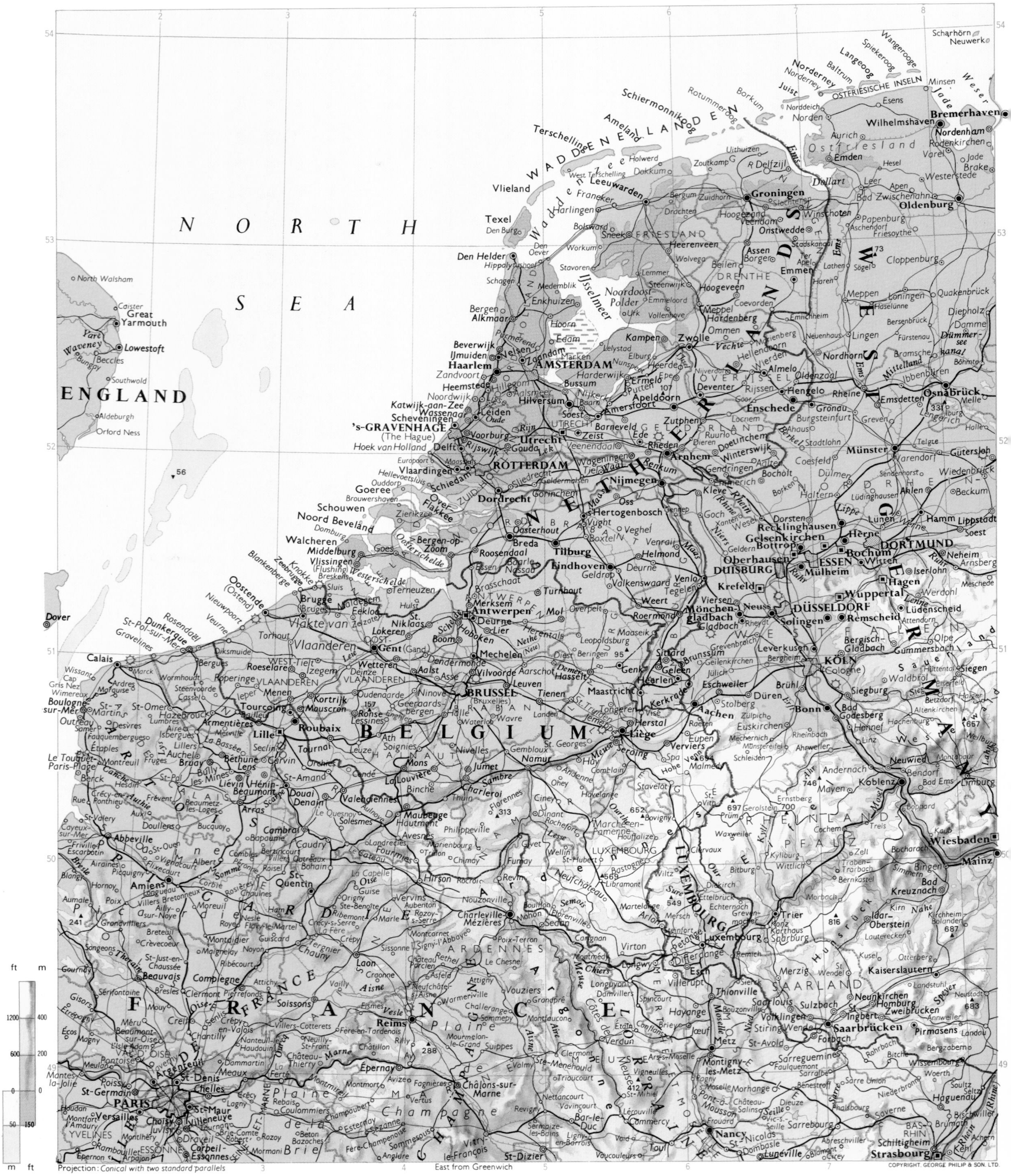

ft   m

NORTH

SEA

ENGLAND

NETHERLANDS

BELGIUM

FRANCE

LUXEMBOURG

GERMANY

AMSTERDAM

's-GRAVENHAGE
(The Hague)

ROTTERDAM

Utrecht

Groningen

Leeuwarden

FRIESLAND

DRENTHE

OVERIJSSEL

GELDERLAND

Arnhem

Nijmegen

Eindhoven

Tilburg

Breda

's-Hertogenbosch

Dordrecht

Middelburg

Vlissingen

Brugge

ANTWERPEN

BRUSSEL

Gent (Gand)

Leuven

Namur

Liège

Charleroi

Mons

VLAANDEREN

BRABANT

HAINAUT

Maastricht

DÜSSELDORF

DORTMUND

KÖLN
(Cologne)

DUISBURG

Essen

Mülheim

Bonn

Koblenz

Wiesbaden

Mainz

Trier

SAARLAND

Saarbrücken

Osnabrück

Münster

Bremerhaven

Wilhelmshaven

Oldenburg

OSTFRIESISCHE INSELN

Emden

PARIS

Versailles

Reims

Amiens

Calais

Boulogne-sur-Mer

Dunkerque

St-Quentin

Laon

Soissons

Compiègne

Beauvais

Lille

Roubaix

Tourcoing

Douai

Valenciennes

Arras

Cambrai

Maubeuge

Charleville-Mézières

Sedan

Luxembourg

Thionville

Metz

Nancy

Strasbourg

ARDENNES

CHAMPAGNE

PICARDIE

ARTOIS

Dover

Great Yarmouth

Lowestoft

Projection: Conical with two standard parallels

East from Greenwich

COPYRIGHT. GEORGE PHILIP & SON. LTD.

1:5 000 000

20 10 0 20 40 60 80 100 miles
40 20 0 40 80 120 160 km

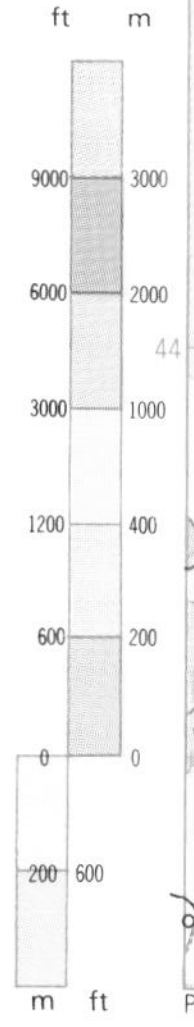

FRENCH DEPARTMENTS

01	Ain
02	Aisne
03	Allier
04	Alpes-de-Haute-Provence
05	Hautes-Alpes
06	Alpes-Maritimes
07	Ardèche
08	Ardennes
09	Ariège
10	Aube
11	Aude
12	Aveyron
13	Bouches-du-Rhône
14	Calvados
15	Cantal
16	Charente
17	Charente-Maritime
18	Cher
19	Corrèze
20	a) Haute-Corse b) Corse-du-Sud
21	Côte-d'Or
22	Côtes-du-Nord
23	Creuse
24	Dordogne
25	Doubs
26	Drôme
27	Eure
28	Eure-et-Loir
29	Finistère
30	Gard
31	Haute-Garonne
32	Gers
33	Gironde
34	Hérault
35	Ille-et-Vilaine
36	Indre
37	Indre-et-Loire
38	Isère
39	Jura
40	Landes
41	Loir-et-Cher
42	Loire
43	Haute-Loire
44	Loire-Atlantique
45	Loiret
46	Lot
47	Lot-et-Garonne
48	Lozère
49	Maine-et-Loire
50	Manche
51	Marne
52	Haute-Marne
53	Mayenne
54	Meurthe-et-Moselle
55	Meuse
56	Morbihan
57	Moselle
58	Nièvre
59	Nord
60	Oise
61	Orne
62	Pas-de-Calais
63	Puy-de-Dôme
64	Pyrénées-Atlantiques
65	Hautes-Pyrénées
66	Pyrénées-Orientales
67	Bas-Rhin
68	Haut-Rhin
69	Rhône
70	Haute-Saône
71	Saône-et-Loire
72	Sarthe
73	Savoie
74	Haute-Savoie
75	Paris
76	Seine-Maritime
77	Seine-et-Marne
78	Yvelines
79	Deux-Sèvres
80	Somme
81	Tarn
82	Tarn-et-Garonne
83	Var
84	Vaucluse
85	Vendée
86	Vienne
87	Haute-Vienne
88	Vosges
89	Yonne
90	Hauts-de-Seine
91	Essonne
92	Seine-St-Denis
93	Seine-St-Denis
94	Val-de-Marne
95	Val-d'Oise

CORSICA On same scale

Corse · Haute-Corse · Corse du Sud

MEDITERRANEAN SEA

ENGLISH CHANNEL

BAY OF BISCAY

GERMANY · SWITZERLAND · BELGIUM

Projection: Conical with two standard parallels

East from Greenwich · West from Greenwich

ft   m

12 000   4000

9000   3000

6000   2000

4500   1500

3000   1000

1200   400

600   200

0   0

200   600

2000   6000

m   ft

DÉPARTEMENTS IN THE PARIS AREA

1 Ville de Paris   3 Val-de-Marne
2 Seine-St-Denis   4 Hauts-de-Seine

Projection: Conical with two standard parallels

West from Greenwich   East from Greenwich

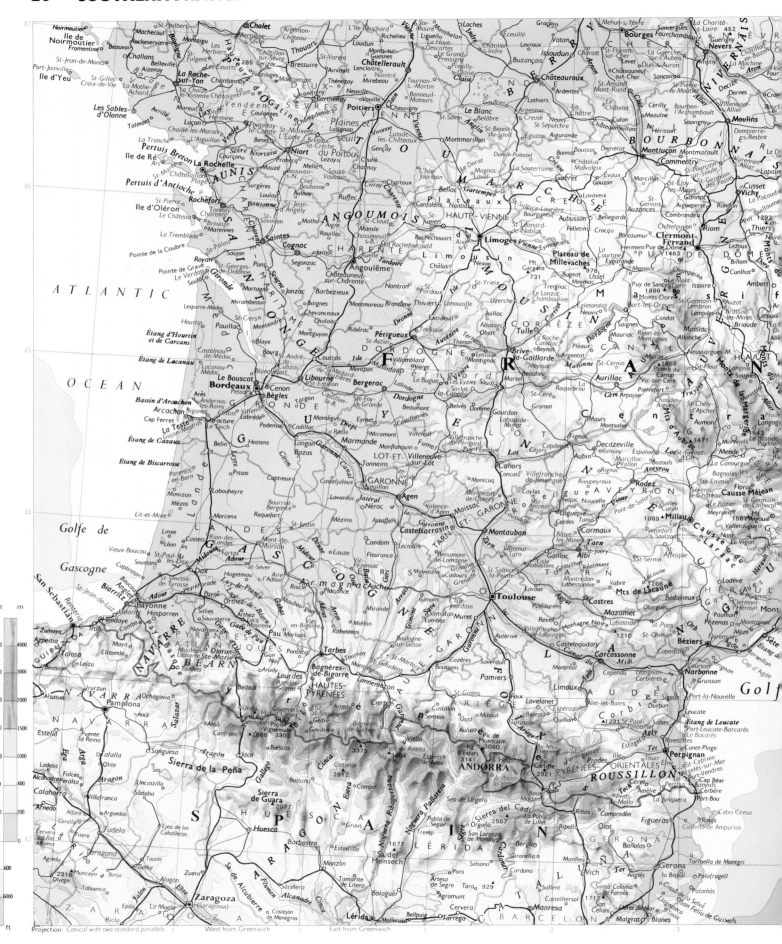

1 : 2 500 000

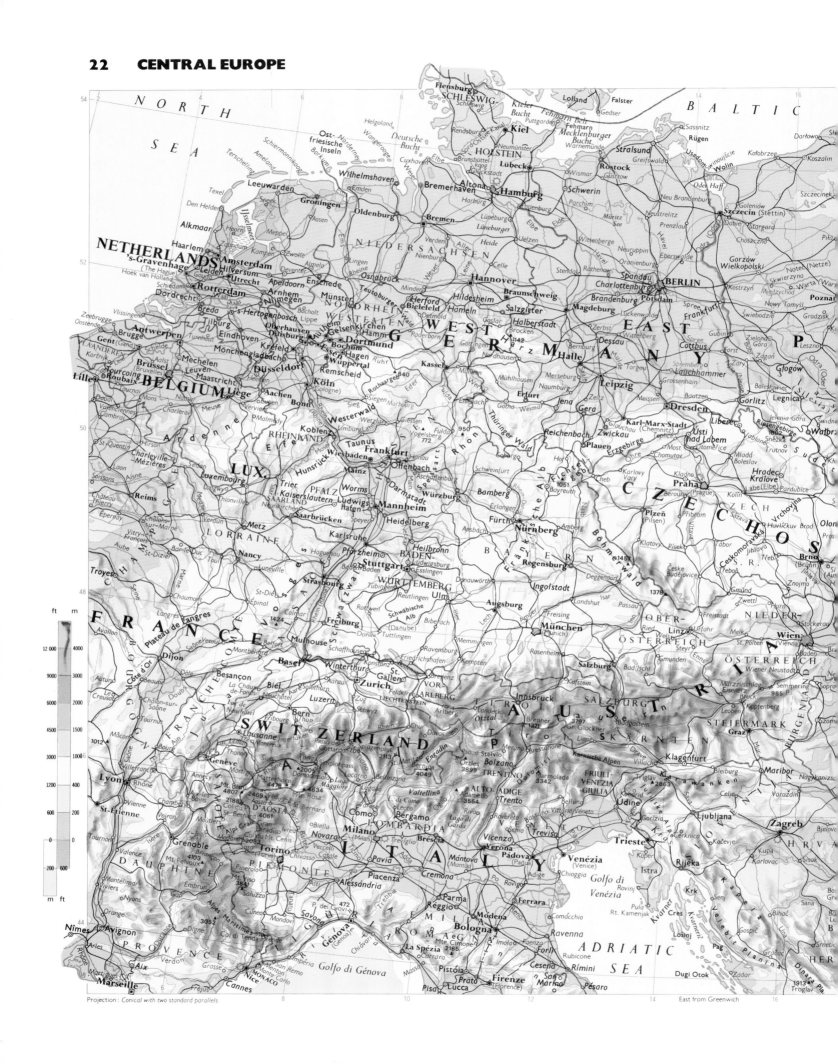

1:5 000 000

50   0   50   100 miles
50   0   50   100   150 km

CENTRAL
EUROPE
POLITICAL
1:25 000 000

Inset map (Central Europe Political):

DENMARK · København · POLAND · Warszawa · U.S.S.R. · NETH · 'S-Gravenhage · Berlin · EAST GERMANY · WEST GERMANY · Brussel · BELGIUM · Bonn · Praha · CZECHOSLOVAKIA · FRANCE · LUX. · Bern · SWITZ. · LIECHT · AUSTRIA · Wien · HUNGARY · Budapest · ROMANIA · ITALY · YUGOSLAVIA · Beograd · București · MONACO · SAN MARINO · Roma · BULGARIA · Sofija

Main map:

Zatoka Gdańska · Wejherowo · Sopot · Gdynia · Gdańsk (Danzig) · Starogard · Elbląg · Malbork · Braniewo · Zelenogradsk · Kaliningrad (Königsberg) · Pregolya · Chernyakhovsk · Gusev · Tyna · LITHUANIAN S.S.R. · Vilnius · Alitus · Varena · Lida · R.S.F.S.R. · Suwałki · ▲309 · Augustów · Gizycko · Ketrzyn · Kwidzyn · Ostróda · Olsztyn · Iława · Mrągowo · Grodno · Sokółka · Mosty · Neman · Novogrudok · BYELORUSSIAN S.S.R. · Grudziądz · Chełmno · Chełmża · Wąbrzeźno · Rypin · Mława · Ciechanów · Ostrołęka · ▲238 · Łomża · Białystok · Volkovysk · Slonim · Bereza · Toruń · Lipno · Płock · Pułtusk · Ostrów Mazowiecka · Brańsk · Hajnówka · Czeremcha · Żabinka · Inowrocław · Noteć · Włocławek · Wisła (Vistula) · Warszawa (Warsaw) · Pruszków · Żyrardów · Mińsk Mazowiecki · Siedlce · Biała Podlaska · Brest · Września · Gniezno · Kutno · Łowicz · Skierniewice · Grójec · Otwock · Łuków · Międzyrzec Podlaski · Pripyat · Turek · Konin · Łęczyca · Zduńska Wola · Łódź · Pilica · Puławy · Włodawa · Kovel · Dubrovitsa · ▲316 · Uzh · Desna · P o l e s y e · Sarny · Korosten · Kalisz · Ostrów Wielkopolski · Tomaszów Mazowiecki · Radom · Kozienice · Chełm · Bug · Kovel · Styr · Goryn · Sluch · Radomyshl · Wieluń · Piotrków Trybunalski · Końskie · Radomsko · Kielce · Ostrowiec Świętokrzyski · Krasnik · Lublin · Zamość · Vladimir Volynskiy · Lutsk · Rovno · Korets · Novograd-Volynskiy · Zhitomir · Kiyev · Borispol · Opole · Częstochowa · Tarnowskie Góry · Zawiercie · Jędrzejów · Pinczów · Sandomierz · Tarnobrzeg · ▲390 · Przeworsk · Kamenka Bugskaya · Radekhov · Brody · Kremenets · Ostrog · Shepetovka · Berdichev · Belaya Tserkov · Zabrze · Bytom · Sosnowiec · Gliwice · Chorzów · Katowice · Kraków · Wisła (Vistula) · Tarnów · Dąbrowa Tarnowska · Rzeszów · Jarosław · Gorodok · Lvov · Zolochev · Ternopol · Starokonstantinov · Kazatin · Vinnitsa · ▲384 · Racibórz · Bielsko-Biała · Wieliczka · Nowy Sącz · Jasło · Krosno · Sanok · Przemyśl · ▲471 · Sambor · Dnestr · Khmelnitsky · U K R A I N I A N S.S.R. · Ostrava · Frýdek-Místek · Český Těšín · ▲1725 · Západné Beskydy · 550 · Vychodné Beskydy · Dukelský Pr. 502 · Drogobych · Borislav · Stryi · Buchach · Chortkov · Zhmerinka · Gottwaldov · Žilina · Tatry · Ružomberok · ▲2655 · SLOVAK S.S.R. · Prešov · ▲1280 · Ivano-Frankovsk · Zaleshchiki · Kamenets-Podolskiy · Dnestr · Mogilev-Podolskiy · Pervomaisk · Nízke Tatry · Košice · Uzhgorod · ▲1881 · Nadvornaya · Kolomyya · Snyatyn · Khotin · Uman · Kremnica · Banská Bystrica · Zvolen · Slovenské Rudohorie · Sátoraljaújhely · Mukachevo · Per-Yablonitse · ▲931 · Chernovtsy · Yedintsy · Soroki · Kotovsk · Bug · Nitra · Banská Štiavnica · Lučenec · Sajó · Bodrog · Beregovo · Khust · ▲2061 · Storozhinets · Dorohoi · Beltsy · MOLDAVIAN S.S.R. · N. Zámky · Miskolc · Hernad · Tokaj · Sighetul · Rădăuți · Botoșani · Dnestr · Hron · Eger · Mezőkövesd · Nyíregyháza · Satu Mare · Baia Mare · Pietrosul ▲2305 · Vatra-Dornei · Suceava · Komárno · Győr · Vác · Esztergom · Hatvan · Jászberény · Hajdúböszörmény · Carei · Someș · Dej · ▲2102 · Pietrosu · Iași · ▲429 · Kishinev · Benderv · Tiraspol · Tatabánya · Újpest · Debrecen · Bistrita · Roman · Vaslui · Odessa · Székesfehérvár · BUDAPEST · Szolnok · Karcag · Mureș · Bistrita · Piatra Neamt · Bârlad · Belgorod-Dnestrovskiy · HUNGARY · Kecskemét · Cegléd · Mezőtúr · Oradea · Cluj-Napoca · Turda · Tirgu Mures · Praid · Odorheiul Secuiesc · Miercurea Ciuc · Bacău · Dunaújváros · Nagykőrös · Salonta · Criș · Aiud · Abrud · Odorheiul · Bretcu · Focșani · Tecuci · Galați · Kalocsa · Kiskunfélegyháza · Békéscsaba · Gyula · Criș Alb · Mții Bihor ▲1848 · Alba-Iulia · Mediaș · Sighișoara · Sfintu Gheorghe · Rimnicu Sărat · Reni · Ismail · Dunăföldvár · Kiskőrös · Hódmezővásárhely · Criș Alb · T r a n s i l v a n i a · Brad · Craiova · Kiskunhalas · Szentes · Brăila · Kagul · Ozero Sasyk · Kiliya · Szekszárd · Baja · Szeged · Makó · Arad · Mureșul · Simeria · Sibiu · Olt · Făgăraș · Brașov · Buzău · Tulcea · 467 · Pécs · Batoszék · Subotica · Timișoara · Lugoj · Hunedoara · Carpații Meridionali · ▲2535 · Vt. Negoiu · Vt. Omul ▲2507 · Cimpina · Prahova · Dunărea (Danube) · Sulina · Mohács · Kikinda · Bečej · Zrenjanin (Petrovgrad) · B a n a t · Caransebeș · Petroșeni 350 · Turnu Roșu · ROMANIA · Târgoviște · Ploiești · Ialomița · Osijek · Novi Sad · Petrovaradin · Vrsač · Reșița · ▲2509 · Peleaga · ▲2518 · Parîngul Mare · Rimnicu Vilcea · Cimpulung · V a l a h i a · Argeș · București (Bucharest) · Constanța · BLACK · Odžak · Brod · Sremska Mitrovica · Porta Orientalis · Mehadia · Tîrgu Jiu · Jiu · Pitești · Dimbovița · Cernavodă · Mamaia · SEA · Bijeljina · Drina · Pančevo · Smederevo · portile de Fier · Orșova · Turnu-Severin · Slatina · Călărași · Tešanj · Tuzla · Zemun · Beograd (Belgrade) · Sava · Morava · Požarevac · Bela Crkva · Vedea · Oltenița · Silistra · Mangalia · Han Pijesak · ▲1346 · Timok · Negotin · Caracal · Olt · Turnu Măgurele · Giurgiu · Ruse (Ruschuk) · Talbukhin · OSLAVIA · Sarajevo · Titovo Užice · Čačak · Kragujevac · Zaječar · Vidin · Lom · Dunărea (Danube) · Corabia · Zimnicea · BULGARIA

COPYRIGHT GEORGE PHILIP & SON LTD.

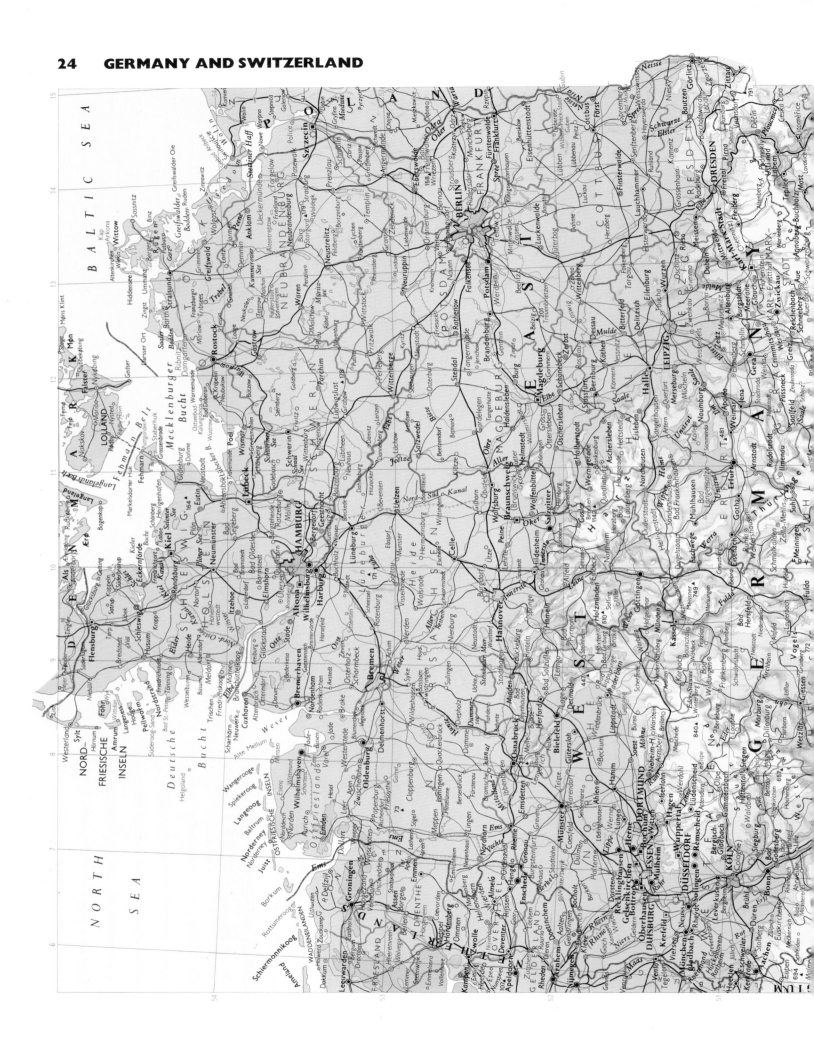

1:2 500 000

East from Greenwich

Conical with two standard parallels

Projection: Conical with two standard parallels

1:2 500 000

10   20   30   40   50 miles
10 0 10 20 30 40 50 60 70 80 km

East from Greenwich

COPYRIGHT GEORGE PHILIP & SON LTD

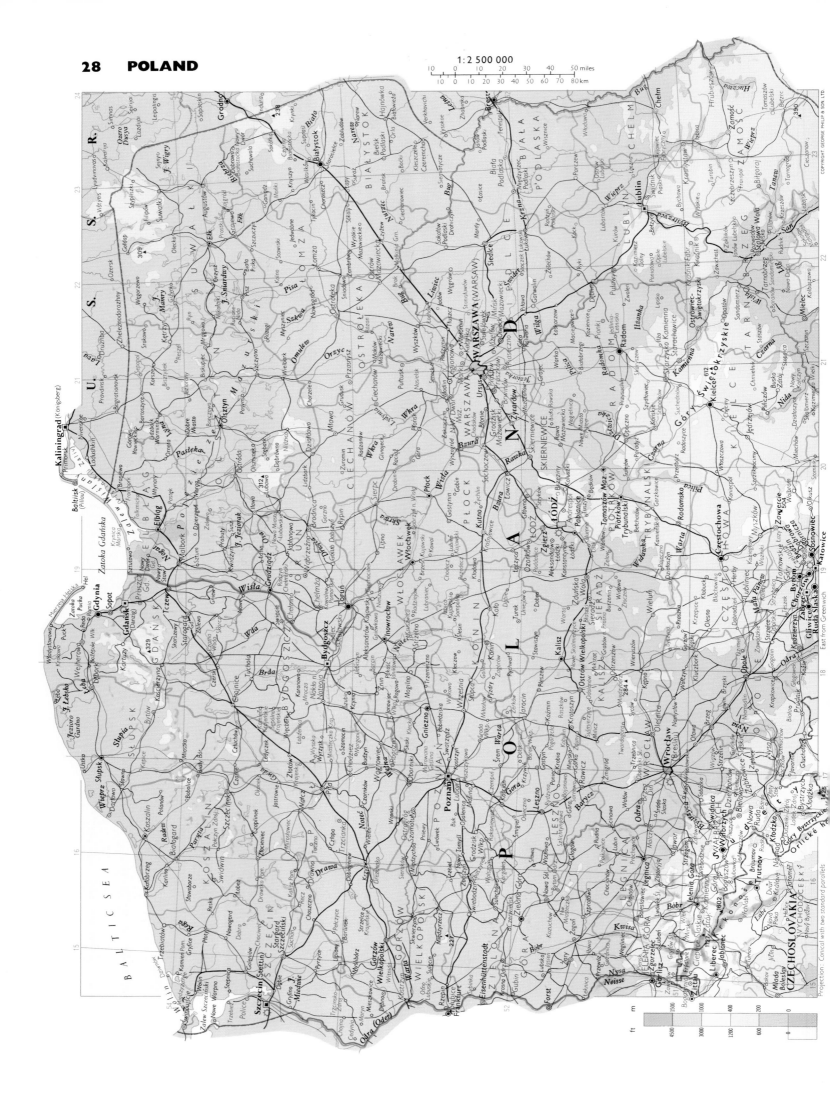

1 : 2 500 000

COPYRIGHT GEORGE PHILIP & SON LTD.

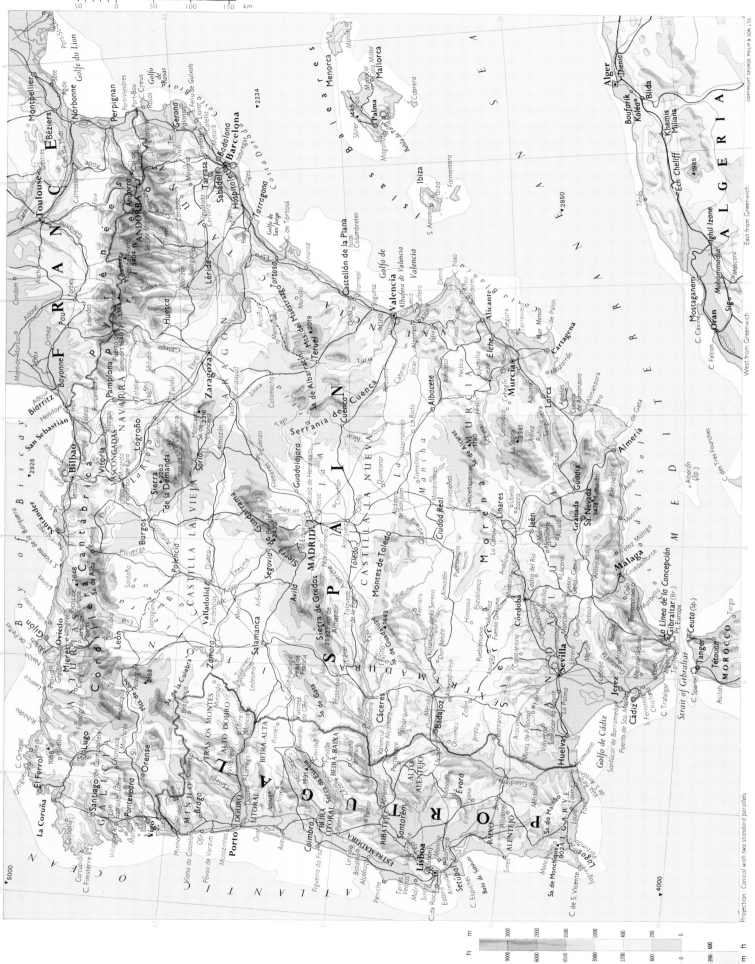

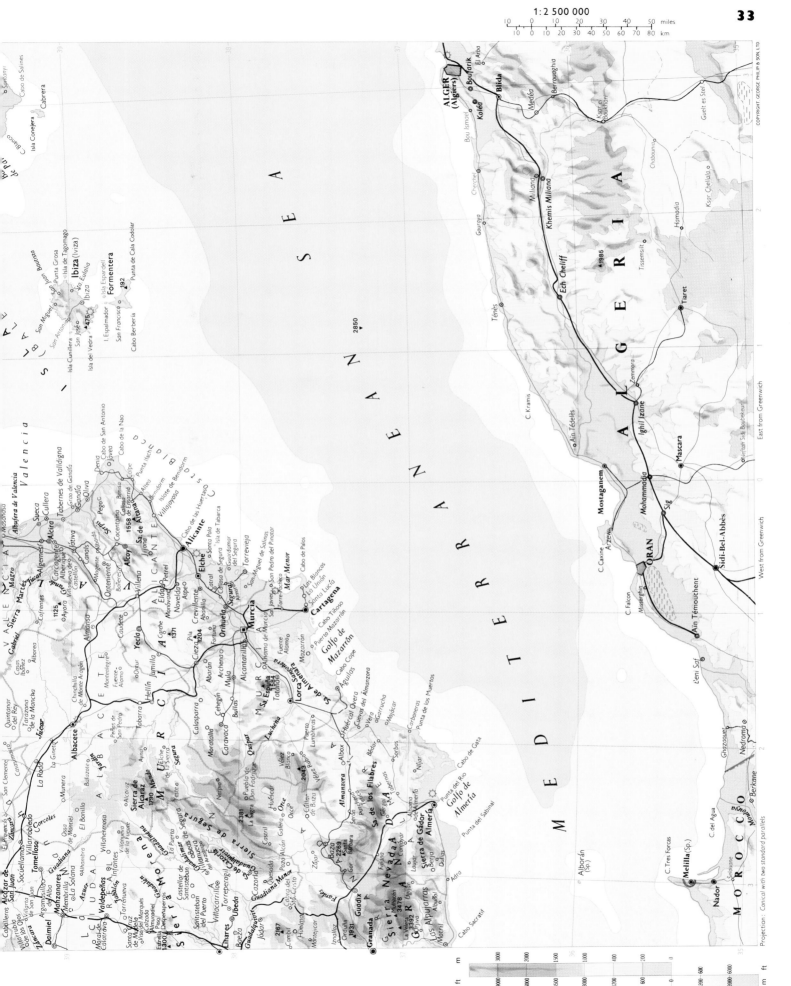

1 : 2 500 000

COPYRIGHT GEORGE PHILIP & SON, LTD

Projection: Conical with two standard parallels

East from Greenwich

West from Greenwich

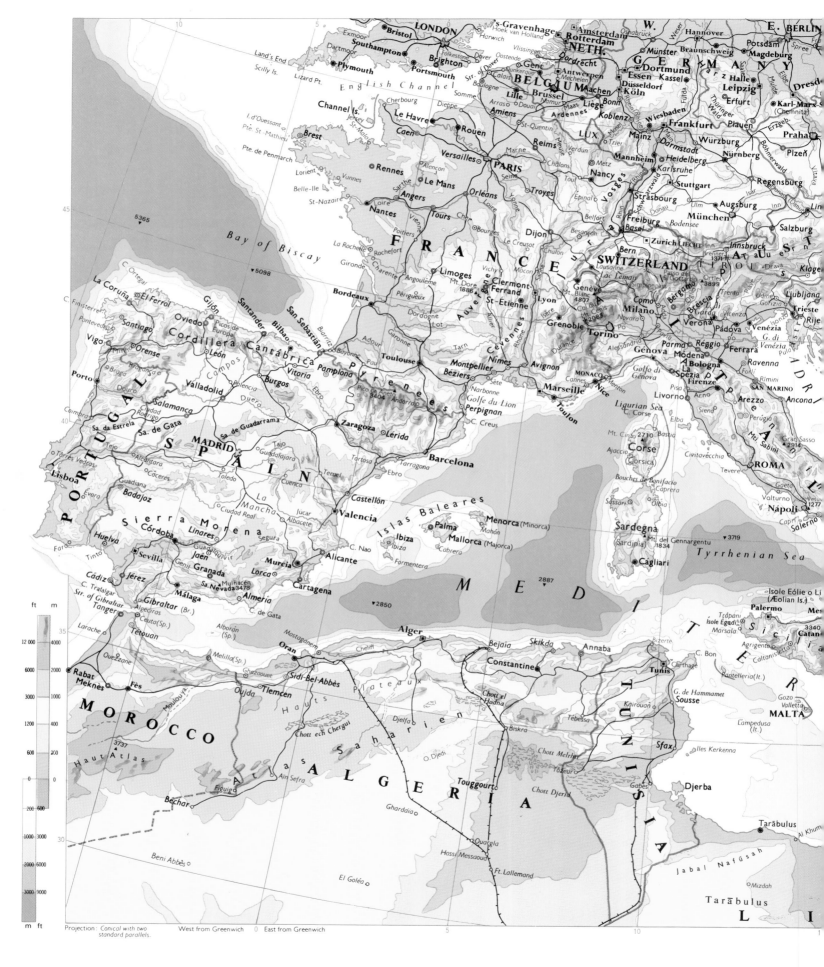

1:10 000 000

50   0   50   100   150   200 miles
50   0   100   200   300 km

35

POLAND
Płock
Poznań
Łódź
Wisła (Vistula)
Warszawa
Brest
Radom
Lublin
Pinsk
Polesye
Chernigov
Konotop
Sumy
Belgorod
Kharkov
Volgograd
Kielce
Lutsk
Rovno
Zhitomir
Kiyev
Pereyaslav-Khmelnitskiy
Poltava
Kremenchug
Belgorod
Kazanskaya
S.F.S.R.
Chorzów
Kraków
Tarnów
Przemyśl
Lvov
Vinnitsa
U.
Berdichev
S.
Belaya Tserkov
S.
Cherkassy
R.
Dnieper
Slavyansk
Artemovsk
Voroshilovgrad
Kamensk-Shakhtinskiy
Tsimlyanskoye Vdkhr.
Ostrava
Jablunkovský Pr.
Cieszyn
Slavkov
Tatry
550
2655
Banská Štiavnica
Miskolc
Košice
Hron
Kolomyya
Chernovtsy
MOLDAVIAN
Kirovograd
Dnepropetrovsk
Krivoy Rog
Zaporozhye
Donetsk
Gorlovka
Makeyevka
Don
Shakhty
Novocherkassk
Rostov
ČHOSLOVAKIA
Bratislava
Vah
Kamenets-Podol'skiy
U.
K
R
A
Pervomaysk
Voznesensk
S.
Zhdanov
(Mariupol)
Taganrog
Azov
Oz. Manych Gudilo
Manych
HUNGARY
Budapest
Kecskemét
Oradea
Cluj-Napoca
Pietrosul
2305
Mogilev-Podol'skiy
Balta
Iași
Bendery
Kishinev
Tiraspol
S.S.R.
Nikolayev
Kherson
Melitopol
Berdyansk
Yeisk
Tikhoretsk
Stavropol
Armavir
Szeged
Hódmezővásárhely
Arad
Pietrosu
2102
Siret
Perekop
Sea of Azov
Kerch
Krasnodar
Maykop
Kuban
Pécs
Subotica
Timișoara
Mureș
ROMANIA
Sibiu
Brașov
(Orașul Stalin)
Galați
Ismail
Odessa
Belgorod
Dnestrovskiy
Karkinitskiy Zaliv
M. Tarkhankut
Yevpatoriya
Krymskaya
(Crimea)
Simferopol
1545
Feodosiya
Novorossiysk
Tuapse
Novi Sad
Petrovaradin
Negoiu
2535
Carpații Meridionali
Brăila
Sulina
Zagreb
Drava
Sombor
Craiova
Ploiești
Bucuresti
Constanța
Sevastopol
Balaklava
Yalta
Sukhumi
Poti
JGOOS
Brod
Banja Luka
Sava
Beograd
Smederevo
Orșova
Porțile de Fier
Turnu-Severin
Pitești
Dunărea
(Danube)
Silistra
Tolbukhin
Dobrich
BLACK SEA
2211
Batumi
BOSNAS
Sarajevo
Drina
Kragujevac
Morava
Vidin
Pleven
Ruse
Tǔrnovo
Varna
İnce Burnu
Sinop
Trabzon
Dalmacija
Mostar
Novi Pazar
Niš
Stara
Planina
Shipchenski Prokhod
Sliven
Burgas
İnebolu
Samsun
Giresun
Tirebolu
Kuzey Anadolu Dağları
Erzincan
Durmitor
2522
CRNA GORA
Sofiya
BULGARIA
Maritsa
Zonguldak
Ereğli
Kastamonu
2565
Çankırı
Çorum
Sivas
Fırat
Laštovo
Dubrovnik
(Ragusa)
Kotor
Cetinje
Shkodra
2764
Skopje
Vardar
Strumica
Musala
2925
Plovdiv
Rhodopi Planina
Edirne
İstanbul
Karadeniz Boğazı
(Bosporus)
İzmit
Bolu
Beypazarı
Kızıl Irmak
Yozgat
Amasya
Tokat
Eleşkirt
SEA
Gargano
Barletta
Bari
Tirana
Elbasan
ALBANIA
Bitola
Sérrai
Kavalla
Tekirdağ
Marmara
Denizi
İznik Gölü
İstanbul
Üsküdar
Bursa
Bilecik
Sakarya
Ankara
Kırşehir
Kızıl
Tuz
Gölü
Kayseri
Erciyas Dağı
3770
Gürün
Malatya
Brindisi
Táranto
Golfo di Táranto
C. Sta. Maria di Leuca
Str. of Otranto
Durrёs
Notia Pindhos
GREECE
Thessaloníki
Olimbos
2917
Alexandroúpolis
Enez
Gelibolu
(Gallipoli)
Çanakkale
Bandırma
Balıkesir
Eskişehir
Kütahya
Sivrihisar
Afyon
Karahisar
Bolvadin
Aksaray
Niğde
Seyhan
Maraş
Gaziantep
La Sila
1929
Kérkira
Kefallinía
Ionian
Sea
Préveza
Aráxthos
Kórinthos
Vólos
Lárissa
Límnos
2033
Gökçeada
Troy
Edremit
Ayvalık
Manisa
Turgutlu
Uşak
Eğridir
Gölü
Konya
Beyşehir
Gölü
Karaman
Ereğli
Tarsus
Mersin
Adana
İskenderun
Osmaniye
Halab
C. Spartivento
C. Messina
Réggio
Zákinthos
Návpaktos
Pátrai
Athínai
Piraiévs
Khíos
Lésvos
Vória
Sporádhes
Évvoia
Sámos
İkaría
İzmir
Aydın
Denizli
Muğla
Burdur
İsparta
Eğridir
Antalya
Toros
Dağları
Silifke
İskenderun Körfezi
Antakya
SYRIA
Hamah
Thívai
Kórinthos
Korinthiakós Kólpos
Síros
Mílos
Kikládhes
Náxos
Íos
Thíra
Dhodhekánisos
Andros
Antalya
Körfezi
Elmalı
3086
Al Lādhiqīyah
Bāniyās
Hims
5121
Pelopónnisos
Kalamata
Spárti
Pílos
Návplion
Olympia
Kíthira
Andikíthira
Khaniá
Íráklion
Ídhi Oros
2456
Kríti
Ródhos
4486
(Kastellórizon)
Megiste
Kárpathos
CYPRUS
Morphou
Nicosia
Famagusta
1951
Larnaca
Limassol
Tarābulus
Bāniyās
3083
Bayrūt
(Beirut)
LEBANON
Dimashq
(Damascus)
ash Shaykh
2814
Jabal ad Durūz
Boṣra
4135
A
N
E
A
N
S
E
A
3174
'Akka
Haifa
(Haifa)
Savdā'
ISRAEL
Tel Aviv-Yafo
Jerusalem
Ammān
JORDAN
Dead Sea
Cyrene
Darnah
Khalīj Bōmba
Tubruq
Rashid
Baḥra el Burullus
Dumyāṭ
Bur Sa'id
El 'Arish
Gaza
Ma'ān
Petra
Al Marj
(Barce)
Banghāzī
Khalīg el Salūm
Matrûh
El 'Alamein
El Iskandarīya
El Mahalla el Kubra
Tanta
El Qantara
Suez
Ismā 'ilīya
Gebel el Tîh
Al 'Aqaba
Elat
Salûm
EL QÂHIRA
El Faiyûm
Suweis
Sinai
2637
Jordan
Khalīj Surt
Barqa
LIBYA
EGYPT
Beni Suef
El Suweis
Canal
Nile
Khalīj es Suweis

COPYRIGHT. GEORGE PHILIP & SON. LTD.

_ _ _ _ _ _   Division between Greeks
and Turks in Cyprus;
Turks to the north.

SWITZERLAND

Lyon
Genève
Annecy
Culoz
Aix-les-Bains
Chambéry
St-Jean
Moutiers
Col du Mt Cenis
2083
Grenoble
Mt Pelvoux
4103
Briançon
Embrun
Gap
Digne
Montélimar
Nyons
Orange
Avignon
Aix
Draguignan
Grasse
Marseille
Toulon
Îles d'Hyères
Martigues
Toulon
Fréjus
St-Tropez
Cannes
Nice
Menton
Monte Carlo
MONACO
Antibes
Côte d'Azur

Passo del S. Gottardo
Domodóssola
Locarno
Lugano
Como
Bergamo
Brescia
Milano (Milan)
LOMBARDIA
Novara
Varese
Busto-Arsizio
PIEMONTE
Torino (Turin)
Chivasso
Casale
Vercelli
Pavia
Piacenza
Pinerolo
Alba
Cuneo
Mondovì
Savona
Savona
Tende
Imperia
San Remo
Riv. di Ponente
GÉNOVA (Genoa)
Chiavári
Riv. di Levante
La Spézia
Massa
Carrara

SWITZERLAND
Matterhorn Mte Ro.
V. D'AOSTA
Gran Paradiso
4061
Bern
Lago
Biella
Ivrea
Mt. Pelat
3052
Alpi Marítime
P. dei Giovi 472
P. Viso
Tánaro
Alessándria

Bolzano
TRENTINO ALTO ADIGE
Trento
Rovereto
Vicenza
Verona
Mántova (Mantua)
Cremona
Parma
Réggio
Módena
EMILIA ROMAGNA
Bologna
Mte. Cimone
2165
Imola
Faenza
Forlì
Cesena
Rímini

Brenner
1371
Merano
Bressanone
Alpi Carniche
Belluno
Vittório Véneto
VENETO
Treviso
Pádova (Padua)
Venézia (Venice)
Golfo di Venézia
Chióggia
Ravenna
Comácchio

FRIULI VENEZIA GIULIA
Údine
Gorízia
Trieste
Koper
Istra
Rijeka (Fiume)
Pula (Pola)

Klagenfurt
Villach
Karawanken
Ljubljana
Cerknica
Kočevje
Kupa
Zagreb
Karlovac
Sisak

Maribor
Drava
Varaždin
Bjelovar
HRV
Krk
Cres
Lošinj
Senj
Kapela
Pag
Gospič
Kremen
1591
Gračac
BOSN
HERC
Dugi Otok
Zadar
Šibenik
Split
Brač
Hvar
Vis
Korčula
Lastovo
Palagruža (Yugoslavia)

DAUPHINÉ
PROVENCE
Verdon

LIGURIAN SEA

C. Corse
Capraia
Piombino
Portoferráio
Elba
Orbetello
Mte. Argentário
Fiora
Civitavécchia

Calvi
Bastia
Mt. Cinto
2710
CORSE (CORSICA) (Fr.)
Ajaccio
Aléria
Sartene
Pto. Vecchio
Bonifacio
Bouches de Bonifacio
Maddalena
Caprera

Asinara
C. Falcone
Golfo dell' Asinara
Porto Torres
Alghero
Sássari
Bosa
Nuoro
Orosei
Tirso
Sorgono
Oristano
Golfo di Oristano
Terralba
Iglésias
Carbónia
2855
Portoscuso
SARDEGNA (SARDINIA)
C. Mte. Santo
Mte. Gennargentu
1834
Arbatax
Jerzu
Cágliari
Golfo di Cágliari
C. Carbonara
C. Spartivento
Golfo di Pálmas

Livorno (Leghorn)
Arno
Pontedera
Pisa
Lucca
Pistóia
Prato
Firenze (Florence)
Prato
Appo. di Porretta
SAN MARINO
Pésaro
Fano
Urbino
Senigállia
Ancona
Loreto
TOSCANA
Siena
Volterra
Cortona
Chiusi
Amiata
1738
Grosseto
L. di Bolsena
Orvieto
Viterbo
L. di Bracciano
Arezzo
Perúgia
Assisi
L. Trasimeno
Fabriano
Macerata
Civitanova
UMBRIA
MARCHE
Foligno
Monti Vettore
Spoleto 2478
Ascoli Piceno
San Benedetto
Téramo
Gran Sasso
2914
L'Aquila
Chieti
Pescara
Ortona
Lánciano
Mte. Amaro
2795
Vasto
Térmoli
ABRUZZI
Rieti
Terni
Tivoli
ROMA (Rome)
Velletri
Ostia
Ánzio
Latina
Frosinone
Sabáudia
Terracina
Fondi
Gaeta
MOLISE
S. Severo
Campobasso
1056
Monte Gargano
Monte S. Ángelo
G. di Manfredónia
Fóggia
Cerignola
Barletta
Trani
Andria
Spinazzola
Corato
Molfetta
Bar
Putignano
Gravina
Matera
Áltamura
CAMPANIA
Caserta
Benevento
Avellino
Nocera
Salerno
Castellammare
Eboli
Potenza
BASILICATA
Agri
Táranto
Golfo di Táranto
Sinni
Nápoli (Naples)
Torre Annunziata
Vesúvio 1277
Ischia
Cápri
Sorrento
Aversa
Volturno
Garigliano
Isole Pónziane
3719

ADRIATIC
SEA

TYRRHENIAN
SEA

Ustica (It.)
Isole Eólie o Lípari
Strómboli
Salina
Lípari
Vulcano
Pisciotta
227

Cosenza
1929
Cariglia
Nicastro
Sambias
CALABRIA
Catanza
Squillace
Pizzo
Palmi
Taurianova
C. Peloro
Réggio
Str. di Messina
C. Spartivento

Trápani
Érice
Castellammare
Palermo
Términi
Cefalù
Mistretta
Monti Nebrodi
Patti
Milazzo
Messina
Isole Egadi
Favignana
Alcamo
Segesta
Marsala
Castelvetrano
Menfi
Selinunte
Sciacca
Platani
Pto. Empédocle
Agrigento
Caltanissetta
Piazza
Enna
Adrano
Etna 3340
Paternò
Giarre
Catánia
Lentini
Augusta
SICILIA
Caltagirone
Favara
Licata
Salso
Gela
Vittória
Ragusa
Módica
Íspica
Noto
Siracusa (Syracuse)
C. Passero
1730

C. Bon
AFRICA

Pantelleria (Ital.)
Lampedusa (Ital.)

Gozo
Comino
Valletta
MALTA
Mdina

MEDIT

MALTA
1:1 000 000

C. S. Dimitri
Gozo (Ghawdex)
Victoria (Rabat)
Comino (Kemmuna)
St. Pauls Bay
239
Mosta
Mdina
Siema
Hamrun
Valletta
Rabat
Luqa
Zurrieq
Marsaxlokk
Birzebbuga

0 5 10miles
0 5 10 15 km

S.E. EUROPE
POLITICAL
1:25 000 000

FRANCE
SWITZ.
LIECHT.
AUSTRIA
Wien
Bern
Venézia
Trieste
SAN MARINO
Corse (Fr.)
ITALY
Roma
Napoli
ADRIATIC SEA
Budapest
HUNGARY
YUGOSLAVIA
Zagreb
Beograd
Tirana
ALBANIA
ROMANIA
Bucureşti
BÚLGARIA
Sofija
Thessaloniki
GREECE
AEGEAN SEA
Athínai
Sicilia
TURKEY
Kriti
U.S.S.R.
MEDITERRANEAN SEA
MALTA

ft   m
12,000 4000
9000   3000
6000   2000
4500   1500
3000   1000
1200   400
600   200
0   0
200   600
m   ft

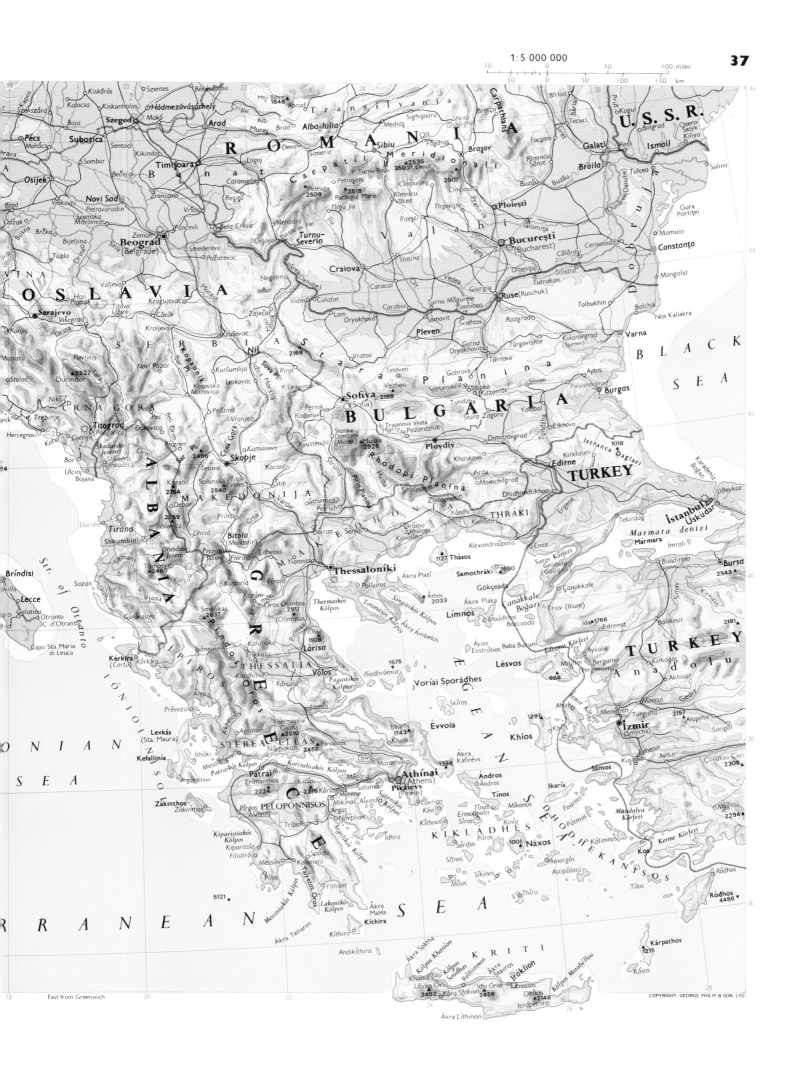

1:5 000 000

50   0   50   100 miles

50   0   50   100   150 km

U.S.S.R.

R O M A N I A

Transilvania

Carpații Meridionali

Carpathians

Mții Bihor
1848

Szentes
Kiskőrös
Kalocsa
Kiskunhalas
Hódmezővásárhely
Békéscsaba
Szekszárd
Baja
Szeged
Makó
Arad
Pécs
Mohács
Subotica
Sombor
Sentao
Kikinda
Timișoara
Bečej
Zrenjanin
Vršac
Osijek
Novi Sad
Petrovaradin
Sremska
Mitrovica
Zemun
Pančevo
Beograd
(Belgrade)
Smederevo
Požarevac

Alba-Iulia
Deva
Simeria
Sibiu
Mediaș
Sighișoara
Brad
Mureș
Crișul
Alb
Abrud
Petroșani
Lugoj
Caransebeș
Reșița
Mehadia
Orșova
Portile de Fier
Turnu-
Severin
Drobeta (Danube)

P. Turnu Roșu
2535
350 Vf. Omul
2507
Negoiu
Brașov
Cîmpulung
Cîmpina
2509
Paringul-Mare
2518
Tîrgu Jiu
Rîmnicu
Vîlcea
Tîrgoviște
Pitești

Focșani
Sîntu
Gheorghiu
Râmnicu
Sărat
Buzău
Buzău
Ploiești

Bîrlad
Tecuci
Galați
Reni
Ismail
Kiliya
Sulina

București
(Bucharest)

V a l a h i a
Arges
Dîmbovița
Ialomița
Olt
Vedea
Craiova
Slatina
Caracal
Oltenița
Giurgiu
Corabia
Turnu Măgurele
Zimnicea
Călărași
Silistra
Cernavodă
Constanța

Mamaia
Gura
Portiței

Tutrakan
Ruse
(Ruschuk)
Tolbukhin
Mangalia
Balchik

B L A C K
S E A

Nos Kaliakra

O S L A V I A
Valjevo
Han
Pijesak
Titovo
Užice
Čačak
Kragujevac
Bor
Negotin
Vidin
Calafat
Lom
Oryakhovo
Korabia
Sômovit
Pleven
Gorna
Oryakhovitsa
Tûrnovo
Türgovishte
Kolarovgrad
(Šumen)
Razgrado
Varna

Sarajevo
Konjic
Stolac
Durmitor
2522
Drina
Plevlja
Kraljevo
Kruševac
Niš
2168
Zaječar
Kosovska
Mitrovica
Leskovac
Pirot
Vratsa
Teteven
Gabrovo
Shipka
Kazanlŭk
Sliven
Polyanovgrad
Burgas

Titograd
(Podgorica)
Cetinje
Đakovica
Peć
Priština
Vranjeo
Sofiya
(Sofia)
2198
Vezhen
Šiptjenski Dag
Stara
Zagora
Yambol
Elkhovo

CRNA GORA
Niкšić
Trebinje
Hercegnovi
Kotor
Bar
Ulcinj
Bojana
Skadarsko
Jezero
(Shkodër)
Beli Drim
Sar Pl.
2496
Kumanovo
Skopje
Kyustendil
Stanke
Dimitrov
(Marek)
Trajanova Vrata
Maritsa
Pazardzhik
Radomir
Pernik
Musala
2925
Plovdiv
Khaskovo
Dimitrovgrad
Kŭrdzhali
Istranca Dağları
1018
Kŭrklareli
Edirne
TURKEY
Karadeniz
Boğazı
Beykoz

A L B A N I A
Tirana
Shkumbini
Elbasan
Debar
2764
Korab
Tetovo
Titov
Veles
Kočani
Štip
Strumica
Petrich
Struma
Pirin Planina
Rhodopi Planina
Smolyan
Zlatograd
Arda
Momchilgrad
Dhidhimótikhon
THRAKI
Komotiní
Ergene
Tekirdağ
İstanbul
Üsküdar
Marmara denizi
Marmara
İmralı

Durrës
Semani
Berati
Jablanica
2259
Ohrid
Ohridsko
Jezero
Prespanko
Jezero
Bitola
(Monastir)
Florína
Édhessa
Dojran
Kilkís
Drama
Philippi
Kaválla
Xánthi
Alexandroúpolis
Enez
Samothráki
1600
Gökçeada
Saros Körfezi
Gelibolu
(Gallipoli)
Bandırma
Bursa
2543

Vlorë
Sazan
Gjirokastër
Smólikas
2637
Korça
Véroia
Yiánnitsa
Thessaloníki
Políyiros
Ákra Platí
Thásos
1127
Singitikós Kólpos
Athos
2033
Ákra Pláka
Límnos
Móudhros
Bozcaada
Troy (Ilium)
Çanakkale
Çanakkale
Boğazı
İda 1766
Edremit
Balıkesir
2181

Brindisi
Lecce
Galatina
Otranto
C. d'Otranto
Capo Sta. Maria
di Leuca
Str. of Otranto
Ioánnina
Píndos
Kalabáka
Tríkkala
Lárisa
Ossa
1978
Kozáni
Oros Olimbos
2917
(Olympus)
Thermaikós
Kólpos
Totonaïos Kólpos
Ákra Ámbelos
Ayios
Evstrátios
Baba Burun
Edremit Körfezi
Ayvalık
Bergama
(Pergamum)
Lésvos
Mitilíni
968
Ídra
Manisa
TURKEY
Anadolu
Akhisar

Kérkira
(Corfu)
Kérkira
THESSALIA
Kardhítsa
Fársala
Vólos
Pagasitikós
Kólpos
1575
Iliodhrómia
Vóriai Sporádhes
Skíros
Skópelos
İzmir
(Smyrna)
2157
Alaşehir

Préveza
Árta
Pínios
Aliákmon
Lamía
Thermopílai
Gióna
2510
Parnassós
2457
Dhírfis
1743
Khalkís
Évvoia
Vóriai Sporádhes
1297
Khíos
Çeşme
Menemen
Turgutlu
Gediz

ÍONIAN
SEA
Kefallinía
Ithákí
Agrínion
Mesolóngion
Patraïkós Kólpos
STEREA
Korinthiakós Kólpos
Návpaktos
Thívai
Marathóno
1398
Ákra
Kafirévs
Ándros
Ándros
Ikaría
Sámos
Kuşadası
Aydın
Ephesus
Çürüksu Çayı
2308

Zákinthos
Zákinthos
Pátrai
Erímanthos
2224
Killíni
2376
Kórinthos
Mykínai
Mégara
Salamís
Mikinai
Athínai
(Athens)
Piraiévs
(Piraeus)
Aíyina
Saronikós
Kólpos
Lávrion
Kéa
Kíthnos
Tínos
Ermoúpolis
Síros
Míkonos
Rinía
Mándalya
Körfezi
2294
Mugla

Kiparissiakós
Kólpos
Kiparissía
Filiatrá
PELOPÓNNISOS
Olympia
Pírgos
Árgos
Trípolis
Návplion
Argolikós
Kólpos
Ídhra
Sérifos
Páros
Sífnos
KIKLÁDHES
Náxos
1001
Amorgós
Astipálaia
Kálimnos
Kos
Kerme Körfezi
Pátmos
DEKÁNISOS

Messíni
Spárti
Kalamáta
Pílos
Taíyetos Óros
5121
Messiniakós Kólpos
Lakonikós
Kólpos
Ákra
Maléa
Kíthira
Kíthira
Andikíthira
Ákra Tainaron
Síkinos
Mílos
Thíra
Folégandros
Tílos
Ródhos
Ródhos
4486

M E D I T E R R A N E A N   S E A

Ákra Spátha
Kólpos Khaníon
Khaniá
Kólpos
Soúdhas
Rethimnon
Lévka Óri
2452
Ákra Sfakíon
Ídhi Óros
2456
Knossós
Iráklion
Kólpos Merabéllou
Dhíkti
2148
Ierápetra
Ákra Líthinon
KRITI
Kárpathos
1215
Kásos

East from Greenwich

COPYRIGHT. GEORGE PHILIP & SON. LTD

18   20   22   24   26

LIGURIAN SEA

Golfo di Génova

CORSE

(CORSICA)

SWITZERLAND

1:2 500 000

10   0   10   20   30   40   50 miles

10   0   10   20   30   40   50   60   70   80 km

39

Innsbruck · Hall · Salzach · Hofgastein · Niedere Tauern · Fohnsdorf · Knittelfeld · Peggau · Weiz · Neudau · Ajka · Devecser

AUSTRIA · STEIERMARK · Graz · Gleisdorf · Fürstenfeld · Güssing · Körmend · Vasvár · Sümeg · Topolca · **HUNGARY**

Bolzano (Bozen) · Marmolada 3342 · Villach · Klagenfurt · Wörther See · Maribor · Sveti · HUNGARY · SOMOGY

VENETO · Belluno · Udine · Gorízia · Ljubljana · **YUGOSLAVIA** · Zagreb · Bjelovar · Virovitica

Pádova (Padua) · Venézia (Venice) · **Golfo di Venézia** · Trieste · Rijeka (Fiume) · Karlovac · Sisak

Ferrara · Ravenna · Rímini · SAN MARINO · **A D R I A T I C   S E A** · Zadar · Split · **BOSNA**

Perúgia · L. Trasimeno · Ancona · Pescara · **HERCEGOVINA**

ROMA (ROME) · Vatican City · L. di Bracciano · Tévere (Tiber) · **ABRUZZI** · Térmoli · Vieste · Monte Sant'Ángelo · **MOLISE**

COPYRIGHT GEORGE PHILIP & SON LTD

1 : 2 500 000

10   20   30   40   50 miles
10 0 10 20 30 40 50 60 70 80 km

ADRIATIC

SEA

G. di Manfredónia

Bari

Brindisi

Strait of Otranto

Lecce

Golfo di
Táranto

BASILICATA

G. di Salerno

G. di
Policastro

CALABRIA

Golfo di
Sant'Eufémia

Golfo di Squillace

Crotone

Catanzaro

IONIAN

Isole Eólie o Lípari (Æolian Is.)

SEA

Messina

Réggio

MEDITERRANEAN SEA

Catánia

Siracusa

ALBANIA

Durrési

Tirana
(Tiranë)

Vlora (Valona)

Kérkira
(Corfu)

COPYRIGHT. GEORGE PHILIP & SON. LTD

ROMANIA

TRANSILVANIA HARGHITA BACĂU VASLUI U.S.S.R.

UKRAINIAN S.S.R.

Turda Cîmpia Turzii Luduş Bond Tîrgu-Mureş MUREŞ Sovata Praid Gheorgheni Comăneşti Moineşti Bacău Crasna Leova Vutcani Valontirovka

Sîlciua Aiud Tîrnăveni Tîrnava Mică Sighişoara Odorheiu Secuiesc Tîrgu Ocna Adjud Zorleni Komrat Chadyr-Lunga Sarata

Trascău Mediaş Agnita Rupea Homorod Gheorghiu-Dej Bîrlad Falciu Bessarabka

ALBA Sebeş Cugir SIBIU Sibiu Făgăraş Braşov (Oraşul Stalin) VRANCEA Focşani Tecuci Kagul Bolgrad Ozero Yalpukh Ozero Kitai Ozero Sasyk

Muntii Făgăraş Muntii Vrancei Rîmnicu Sărat Galaţi Dunay (Dunabe) Ismail Braţul Chilia

PRAHOVA Buzău Brăila BRĂILA Măcin Tulcea Braţul Sulina Sulina

Cîmpulung Rîmnicu Vîlcea VÎLCEA ARGEŞ DÎMBOVIŢA Tîrgovişte Ploieşti IALOMIŢA Braţul Sfîntu Gheorghe

Piteşti BUCUREŞTI (Bucharest) Lacul Razelm

VALAHIA (WALACHIA) GIURGIU CĂLĂRAŞI Constanţa Siutghiol

Craiova DOLJ TELEORMAN Alexandria Giurgiu Dunărea (Danube) Medgidia DOBRUDJA Eforia

Ruse (Ruschuk) Silistra Cernavodă Mangalia Douăzeci Şi Trei August

Turnu Măgurele Zimnicea Svishtov Razgrad Tolbukhin (Dobrich Bazargic) Shabla (Šabla) Kavarna (Cavarna) Nos Kaliakra

Nikopol Pleven Tûrgovishte Kolarovgrad (Shumen) Novi Pazar Balchik Zlatni Pyassatsi

Vratsa BULGARIA Tûrnovo Preslav Varna Drouzhba

Sofiya (Sofia) Gabrovo Sliven Stara Planina (Chatal Balkan) Aytos Nos Emine

Plovdiv (Philippopolis) Kazanlûk Nova Zagora Yambol Burgaski Zaliv Burgas

Pazardzhik Stara Zagora Chirpan Dimitrovgrad Elkhovo Topolovgrad Sozopol

Velingrad Asenovgrad Khaskovo Kharmanli Rezovo

Srednî Rodopi Iztochni Rodopi Kûrdzhali Smolyan Edirne (Adrianople) KIRKLARELI İstranca Dağları Karadeniz Boğazı (Bosporus)

GREECE Drama Xánthi Komotini Kírklareli Vize TEKIRDAĞ TURKEY İSTANBUL Üsküdar Beykoz

B L A C K   S E A

1 : 2 500 000

10 0 10 20 30 40 50 miles
10 0 10 20 30 40 50 60 70 80 km

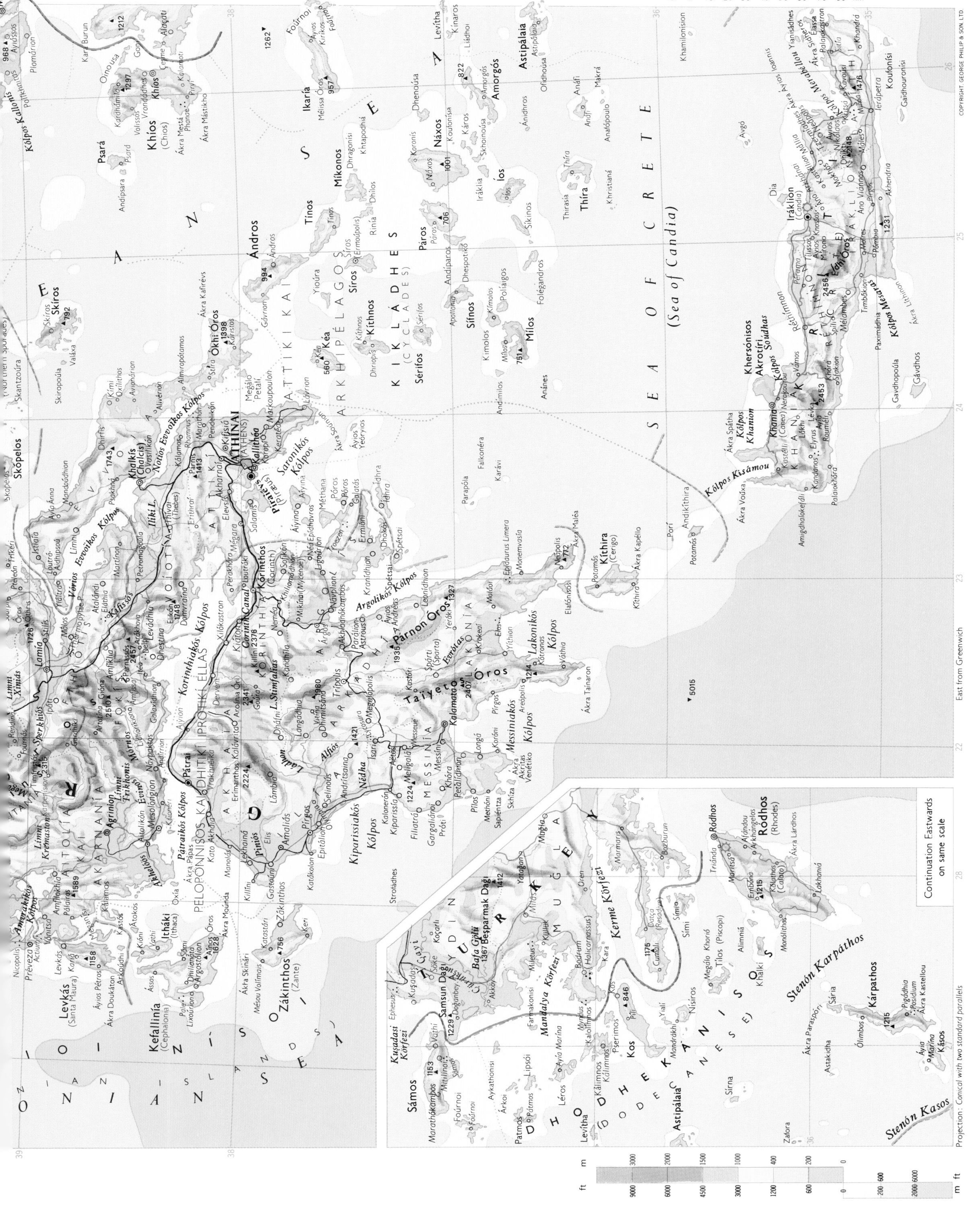

Kárpathos Kallonis
Ayios Efstrátios
968 ▲ Ayiásos
Plomárion
1212 ▲
Kar Burun
Oinoúsa
1297 ▲
Vrondádhos
Khíos (Chios)
Khíos ⊙
Kardhámila
Çeşme ○ Alaçatı
1262 ▲
Foúrnoi
Kiriakós
Levítha
Kínaros
Líadhoi
Astipálaia
Astipálaia
Olfoúsa
Khamilónísion

Psará
Psará
Andípsara
Ákra Mastícho
Ákra Mastí
Vólissos

Ikaría
Ikaría
957 ▲
Mélissa
822 ▲
Amorgós
Amorgós
Dhenoúsa

A E G E A N

S E A

Skópelos
Skiropoúla
Skíros
792 ▲
Skantzoúra

Andros
Andros
Ákra Kafirévs

Tínos
Tínos

Míkonos
Míkonos
Náxos
Náxos
1001 ▲
706 ▲
Páros
Páros
ARKHIPELAGOS
KIKLÁDHES
(CYCLADES)

Síros
Síros
Ermoúpolis
Rínía Dhílos

Kíthnos
Kíthnos
560 ▲ **Kéa**
994 ▲
Yioúra

Sérifos
Sérifos
Sífnos
Sífnos
751 ▲ **Mílos**
Mílos
Kímolos
Andímilos

Thíra
Thíra
Thirasía
Khristianá
Síkinos
Folégandros
Íos

Anáfi Makrá
Andí

S E A   O F   C R E T E
(Sea of Candia)

5015 ▼

Iráklion (Candia)
Iráklion ⊙
2456 ▲
K R I T I
K R E T E
2453 ▲
1231 ▲
Dhía

Khaniá (Canea)
Khaniá ⊙
Kérme Körfezi

Ákra Spátha
Kólpos Soúdhas
Kherrónisos
Akrotíri
Ákra Ródhopoú

Paleókhóra
Gávdhos
Gavdhopoúla

Ákra Lithínon

ATHÍNAI (ATHENS)
ATHÍNAI ⊙
Pireéfs (Piraeus)
1413 ▲
Salamís

Khalkís
Khalkís (Chalcis)
Vasilikón
V 1743 ▲
Iliki L.
Thívai (Thebes)

ATTIKÍ
Saronikós Kólpos
Aíyina
Póros

KORINTHIAKÓS KÓLPOS
Corinth Canal
Kórinthos (Corinth)
2376 ▲
Mikínai (Mycenae)

PELOPÓNNISOS KAÍ DHÍTIKI ELLAS
2457 ▲
ARKADHÍA

Párnon Oros
1935 ▲
Taíyetos Oros
2407 ▲
2404 ▲

LAKONÍA
Lakonikós Kólpos
Argolikós Kólpos
1327 ▲
Spárti (Sparta)

Trípolis
Trípolis

1421 ▲
Kalamáta
Kalamáta
MESSINÍA
Messiniakós Kólpos
1224 ▲

Pírgos
Pírgos
Pátrai
Pátrai ⊙
2224 ▲
Pátraikós Kólpos

AKHAÍA
ÍLIA

Pínios
Pírros
Amalías

Kiparissiakós Kólpos

Kefallinía (Cephalonia)
Kefallinía
Argóstolion
828 ▲
756 ▲

Itháki (Ithaca)

Levkás (Santa Maura)
Levkás

Zákinthos (Zante)
Zákinthos

Amvrakikós Kólpos
Préveza
AKARNANÍA
1589 ▲
AITOLÍA
Mesolóngion
Agrínion
Agrínion

Límni Trikhonís
1158 ▲

Nicópolis
Ágios Pétros

I O N I A N

I S L A N D S

I O N I A N

S E A

Sámos
Sámos
1153 ▲
Kuşadası Körfezi
Ephesus○
Kuşadası

Samsun Dağı
1229 ▲

Baba Gölü
1367 **Beşparmak Dağı**
1412 ▲

T U R K E Y
Y D I N
M U Ğ L A

Menderes

846 ▲

Mandalya Körfezi
Bodrum (Halicarnassus)
Milas
1175 ▲

Kara
Mújla ○

Datça Reşadiye

Kos
Kos
Nísiros
Yalí
Tílos (Piscopi)
Khálki

Rodhos (Rhodes)
Ródhos ⊙
1215 ▲
Líndhos
Ákra Larthós

D H O D E K Á N I S O S
(DODECANESE)

Léros
Léros
Kálimnos
Kálimnos
Pátmos
Pátmos
Lipsói
Astipálaia

Stenón Karpáthos

Kárpathos
Kárpathos
1215 ▲
Ákra Kastéllou

Kásos
Kásos
Stenón Kásos

East from Greenwich

Continuation Eastwards
on same scale

Projection: Conical with two standard parallels

m
3000
2000
1500
1000
400
200
0
ft
9000
6000
4500
3000
1200
600
0

ft
2000 6000
m

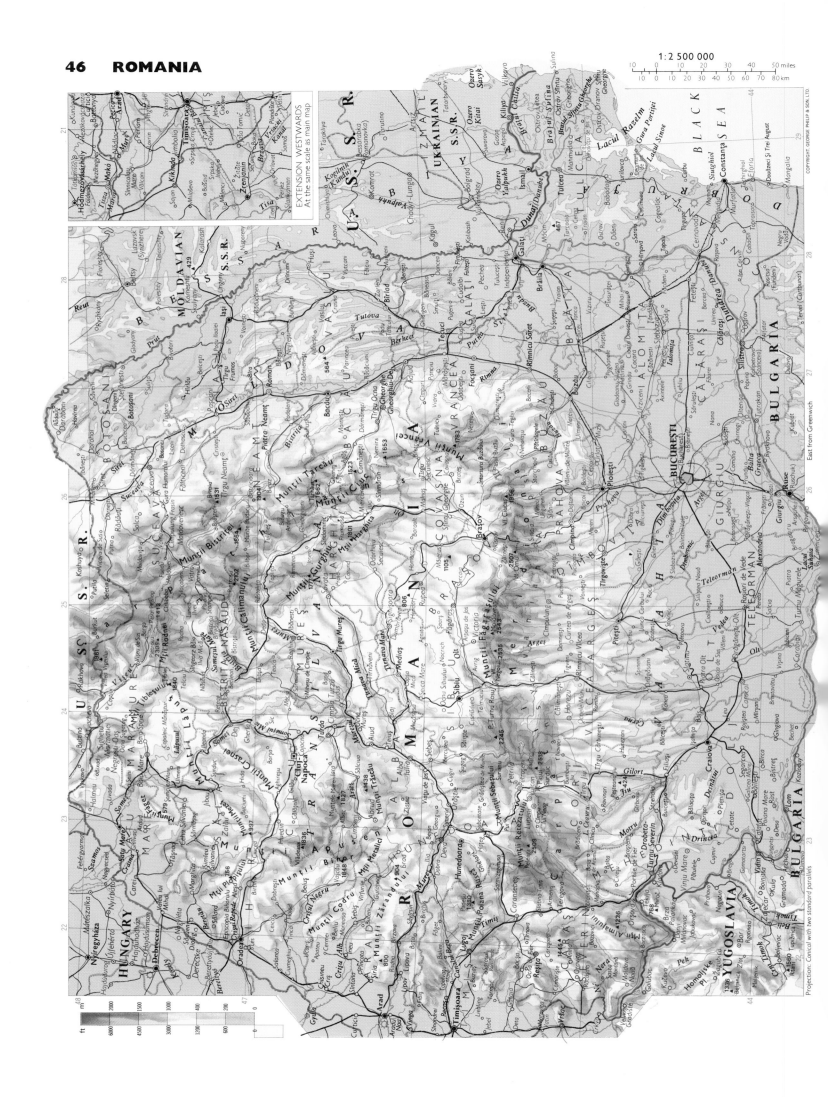

1:2 500 000

EXTENSION WESTWARDS
At the same scale as main map

Projection: Conical with two standard parallels

East from Greenwich

COPYRIGHT GEORGE PHILIP & SON LTD.

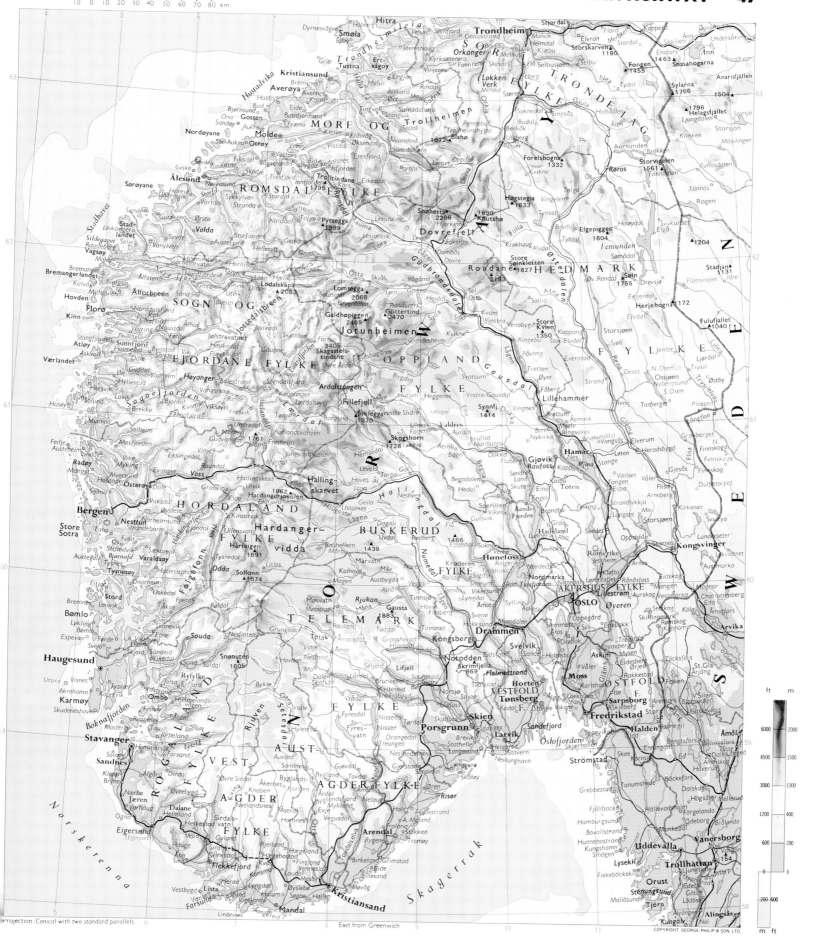

1:2 500 000

Projection: Conical with two standard parallels

East from Greenwich

COPYRIGHT GEORGE PHILIP & SON LTD.

1 : 2 500 000

miles
km

East from Greenwich

Projection: Conical with two standard parallels

BALTIC SEA

GERMANY

POLAND

Gotland · Visby

Öland · Kalmar

KALMAR LÄN

JÖNKÖPINGS LÄN

KRONOBERGS LÄN

BLEKINGE LÄN

ÖSTERGÖTLAND

SKARABORGS LÄN

ÄLVSBORGS LÄN

HALLANDS LÄN

GÖTEBORGS OCH BOHUS

Norrköping · Linköping · Motala · Mjölby · Tranås · Nässjö · Jönköping · Huskvarna · Vetlanda · Västervik · Oskarshamn · Nybro · Växjö · Värnamo · Ljungby · Karlskrona · Ronneby · Karlshamn · Sölvesborg · Kristianstad · Ystad · Simrishamn · Hässleholm · Halmstad · Helsingborg · Landskrona · Lund · Malmö · Trelleborg · Ängelholm · Falkenberg · Varberg · Göteborg · Kungsbacka · Mölndal · Borås · Alingsås · Kinna · Ulricehamn · Falköping · Skara · Lidköping · Mariestad · Skövde · Vänersborg · Trollhättan · Uddevalla · Lysekil

DENMARK

JYLLAND · SJÆLLAND · FYN · LOLLAND · FALSTER · BORNHOLM

Skagen · Frederikshavn · Hjørring · Ålborg · Thisted · Viborg · Randers · Århus · Silkeborg · Herning · Holstebro · Ringkøbing · Esbjerg · Varde · Kolding · Fredericia · Vejle · Horsens · Skanderborg · Haderslev · Åbenrå · Sønderborg · Flensburg · Odense · Svendborg · Middelfart · Nyborg · Korsør · Slagelse · Næstved · Vordingborg · Nykøbing · Maribo · Nakskov · København (Copenhagen) · Roskilde · Helsingør · Frederikssund · Hillerød · Holbæk · Kalundborg · Sorø · Ringsted · Rønne

NORDJYLLANDS AMT · VIBORG AMT · ÅRHUS AMT · RINGKØBING AMT · VEJLE AMT · SØNDERJYLLANDS AMT · FYNS AMT · VESTSJÆLLANDS AMT · STORSTRØMS AMT · FREDERIKSBORG AMT · ROSKILDE AMT

Kattegat · Skagerrak · Jammerbugt · Ålborg Bugt · Store Bælt · Lille Bælt · Femer Bælt · Limfjorden · Læsø · Anholt · Samsø

Kiel · Flensburg · Schleswig · Husum · Rendsburg · Fehmarn · Rügen · Hiddensee · Greifswald · Stralsund · Słupsk · Ustka · Gdynia

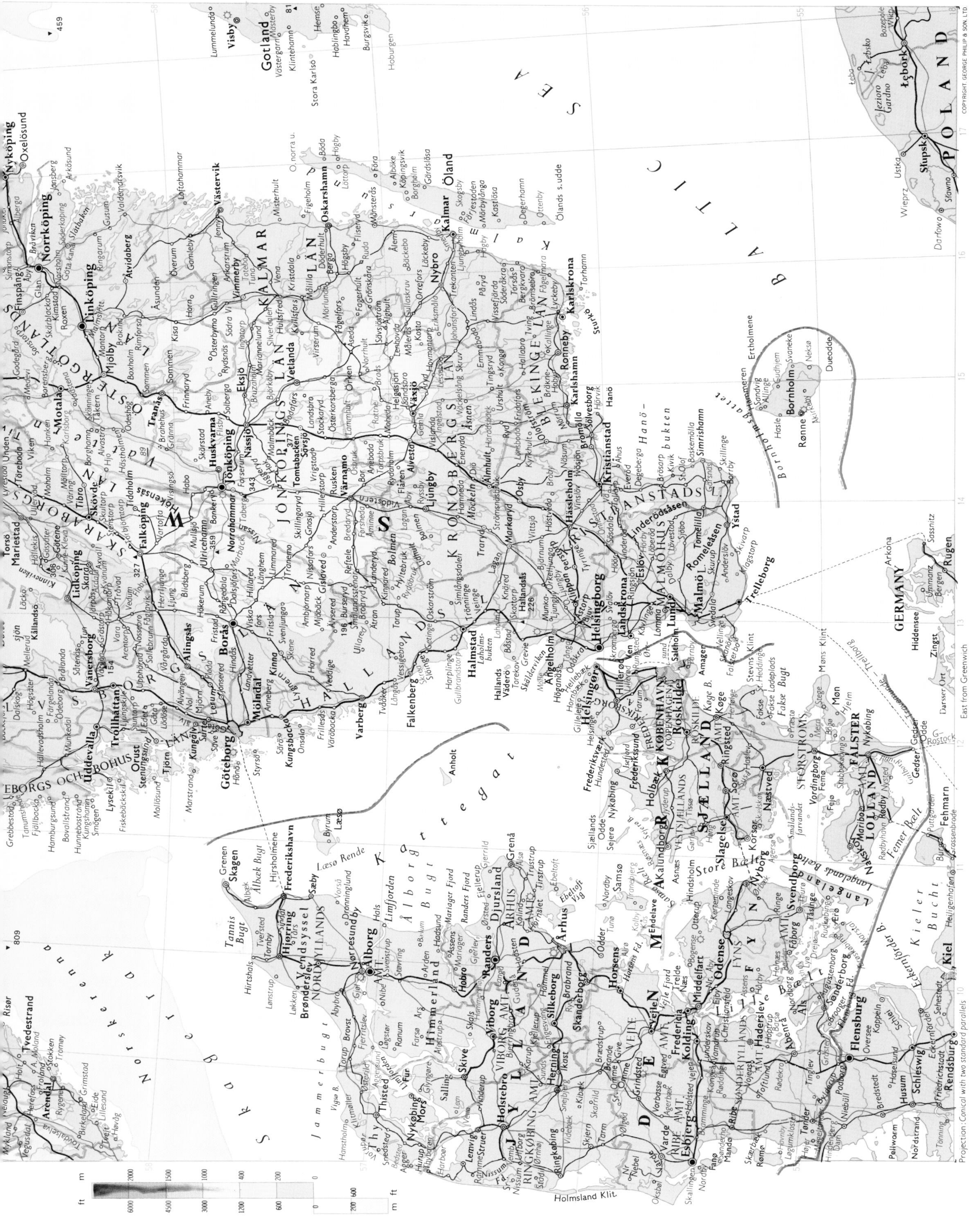

ICELAND
on the same scale
as general map

1:5 000 000

20 10 0 20 40 60 80 100 miles
40 10 0 40 80 120 160 km

BALTIC SEA

GULF OF RIGA — Rīgas Jūras Līcis (Gulf of Riga)

FINLAND · ESTONIAN S.S.R. · LATVIAN S.S.R. · LITHUANIAN S.S.R. · R.S.F.S.R. · POLAND · GERMANY · DENMARK · NORWAY · SWEDEN

HELSINKI (Helsingfors) · Tampere · Turku (Åbo) · Tallinn · Riga · Kaunas · Vilnius · Grodno · Białystok

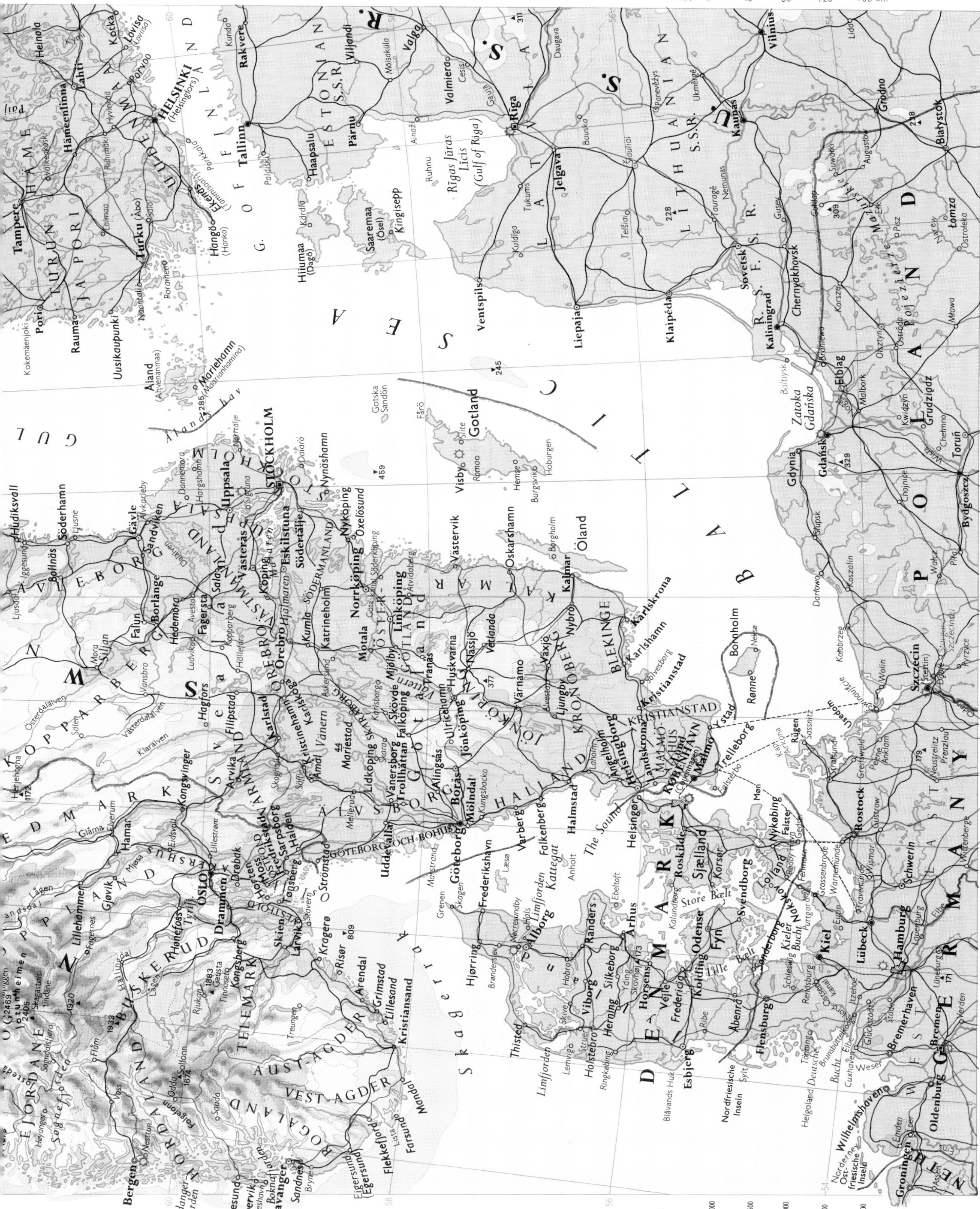

Stockholm · Uppsala · Göteborg · Malmö · København · Oslo · Gotland · Öland · Bornholm

Gdańsk · Gdynia · Szczecin (Stettin) · Bydgoszcz · Toruń · Kaliningrad · Klaipėda · Liepāja · Ventspils

Hamburg · Lübeck · Kiel · Rostock · Bremen · Wilhelmshaven

Projection: Conical with two standard parallels   East from Greenwich

m · ft 6000 4500 3000 1500 1000 400 200 0

1:10 000 000

53

COPYRIGHT GEORGE PHILIP & SON LTD.

1 Kabardino-Balkar A.S.S.R.
2 North Ossetian A.S.S.R.
3 Nakhichevan A.S.S.R. (Azer.)
4 Checheno-Ingush A.S.S.R.
Karagiye Depression

Projection: Conical with two standard parallels
East from Greenwich

Division between Greeks and Turks
in Cyprus: Turks to the North.

K i r g i z   S t e p p e

K A Z A K H   N i z m e n n o s t

KAZAKSKIY

Priyolzhskiy

KALMYK A.S.S.R.

Ergeni Vozvyshennost

C A S P I A N   S E A

Krasnovodsk

Nebit Dag

TEHRÁN

Qom

A l b o r z

E L B U R Z

P E R S I A

I R A N

Baghdād

I R A Q

Astrakhan

Volgograd
(Stalingrad)

Makhachkala

Derbent

BAKU

A Z E R B A I J A N   S.S.R.

Grozny

DAGESTAN

Ordzhonikidze

Tbilisi

GEORGIAN S.S.R.

ARMENIAN S.S.R.

Yerevan

Leninakan

Kirovakan

ADZHAR

ABKHAZIA

Sukhumi

Batumi

Kutaisi

Sochi

Poti

KAVKAZ

Elbrus 5633

Kislovodsk

Pyatigorsk

Stavropol

Armavir

Maykop

Krasnodar

Rostov

Novorossiysk

Kerch

B L A C K   S E A

Sevastopol

Simferopol

Yalta

Feodosiya

Yevpatoriya

Krymskiy P-ov.
(Crimea)

Kherson

Nikolayev

Odessa

Kishinev

MOLDAVIAN S.S.R.

U K R A I N E

KIYEV
(Kiev)

KHARKOV

Donetsk

Zaporozhye

Dnepropetrovsk

Krivoy Rog

Zhdanov

Azovskoye More
(Sea of Azov)

Taganrog

Belgorod

Sumy

Zhitomir

ROMANIA

BUCUREȘTI
(Bucharest)

Brașov

BULGARIA

Varna

Burgas

Constanța

İstanbul

Edirne

Bursa

Ankara

T U R K E Y

A n a d o l u

İzmir
(Smyrna)

Konya

Kayseri

Sivas

Erzurum

Trabzon

Samsun

Zonguldak

Kuzey Anadolu Dağları

Toros Dağları

Adana

Gaziantep

Malatya

Diyarbakır

Dijlah (Tigris)

Nineveh

Al Mawṣil

Kirkūk

SYRIA

Halab

Ḥamāh

Ḥimṣ

Dimashq
(Damascus)

LEBANON

Bayrūt
(Beirut)

Ṭarābulus

M E D I T E R R A N E A N   S E A

CYPRUS

L e v a n t

Dhodhekanisos

Ródhos

Bādiyat ash Shām

MARMARA DENIZI

Çanakkale

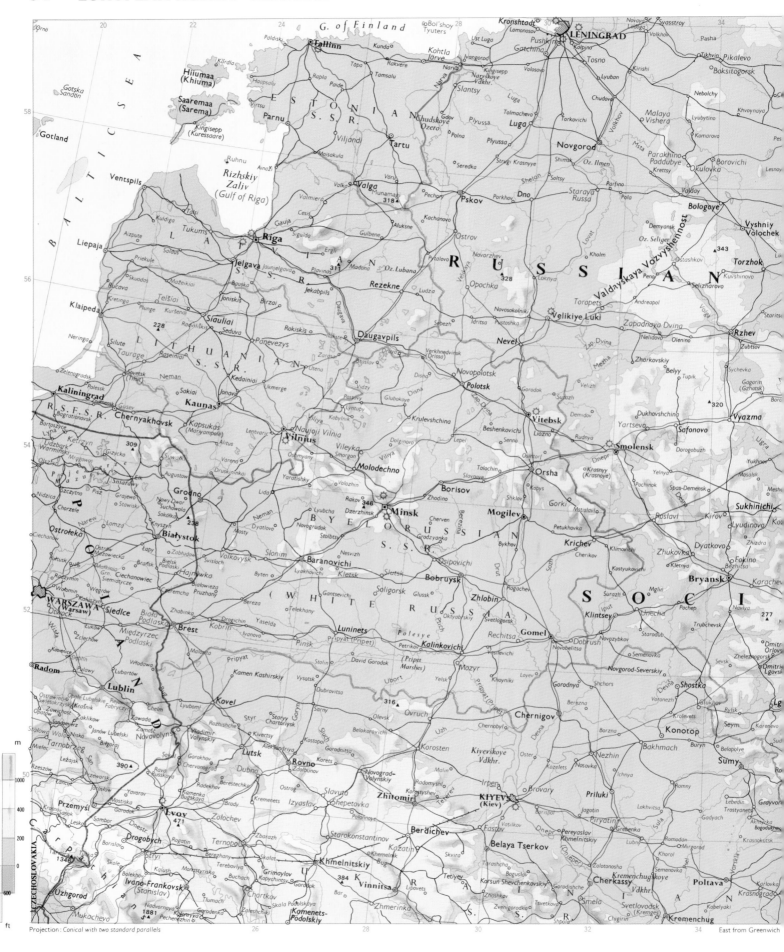

O z. Beloye
Belozersk
Kirillov
Uste
Ozero Kubenskoye
Sheksna
Dyakovskaya
Totma
293
Nikolsk
Murashi
Nagorsk
Vyatka
Peskovka
Krasnoye
Moloma
Belaya Kholunitsa
Chernaya Kholunitsa
Omutninsk
Zolazna
329

Cherepovets
Vologda
Chebsara
Sokol
Sukhona
Suday
Pyshchug
Chernovskoye
Khalturin
Kirov
Kirovo-Chepetsk
Zuyevka
Yar
Glazov
58

Ustyuzhna
Vesyegonsk
Gryazovets
Vokhtoga
Soligalich
Kologriv
Chukhloma
Vokhma
Leninskoye
Kotelnich
Kumeny
Novovyatsk
Vozhgaly
Uni

Breytovo
Rybinskoye Vodokhranilishche
Krasnyy Kholm
Danilov
Buy
Antropovo
Manturovo
Sharya
Unzha
Neya
Vetluga
Shakhunya
Sorvizhi
Nolinsk
Medvedok
Arkul
Urzhum
UDMURT A.S.S.R.
Kilmez
Uva

Volga
Andropov
Tutayev
Kr. Profintern
Makaryev
Uren
Yaransk
Urzhum
Shurma
Kilmez
Mamadysh

Sonkovo
Kashin
Uglich
Kostroma
Nerekhta
Privolzhsk
Zavolzhsk
Volgorechensk
Gorkovskoye Vdkhr.
Yuryevets
Vetluzhskiy
Krasnyye Baki
Tonsha
Yoshkar Ola
MARI
A.S.S.R.
Malmyzh
Mozhga

O **V I E T**   **F E D E R A T I V E**

Kalyazin
293
Rostov
Gavrilov Yam
Ivanovo
Kineshma
Vichuga
Voskresenskoye
Kokhma
Shuya
Chkalovsk
Semenov
Tur_sha
Cheboksary
Krasnogorskiy
Zelenodolsk
Kazan
Vyatskiye Polyany
Kukmor
Sosnovka

O Kimry
Dubna
Pereslavl Zalesskiy
Teykovo
Neri
Yuzha
Zavolzhye
Gorodets
Pravdinsk
Borisoglebskiy
Kozmodemyansk
Volzhsk
Martinskiy Posad
TATAR
Chistopol

Klin
Dmitrov
Krasnozavodsk
Yuryev-Polskiy
Suzdal
Kovrov
Dzerzhinsk
GORKIY (Gorki)
Leninskaya Sloboda
Kstovo
Lyskovo
Yadrin
CHUVASH
A.S.S.R.
Kanash
A. S. S. R.

Solnechnogorsk
Zagorsk
Vladimir
Vyazniki
Volodarsk
Gorbatov
Bogorodsk
Pavlovo
Pyana
Sergach
Shumerlya
Kamskoye Ustye
Kuybyshev
Bilyarsk

Pushkino
Khimki
Mytishchi
Balashikha
Noginsk
Orekhovo-Zuyevo
Pokrov
Sobinka
Krasnaya
Sudogda
Murom
Kulebaki
Arzamas
235
Gagino
Lukoyanov
Ardatov
Alatyr
Kirya
Buinsk
Kuybyshevskoye Vdkhr.
Nurlat

MOSKVA (Moscow)
Lyubertsy
Ramenskoye
Elektrostal
Pavlovskiy-Posad
Yegoryevsk
Kurovskoye
Shatura
Oz. Velikoye
Melenki
Vyksa
Tesha
Mukhtolovo
Pervomaysk
Sarova
Pochinki
Ardatov
Alatyr
Cherdakly

Podolsk
Bronnitsy
Voskresensk
Kolomna
Kolyberevo
Mikhnevo
Spas-Klepiki
Yelatma
Kasimov
Moksha
Temnikov
Krasnoslobodsk
Romodanovo
Sura
Karsun
Novocheremshansk
Dimitrovgrad
54
Sernovodsk

Stupino
Zaraysk
Osery
Solotcha
Tuma
Kadom
MORDOVIAN
A.S.S.R.
Saransk
Inza
Sengiley
Sok

Serpukhov
Kashira
Ryazan
Spassk-Ryazanskiy
Sasovo
Kobylkino
Ruzayevka
Bazarnyy Syzgan
Ulyanovsk
Togliatti
375
Zhigulevsk
Komsomolskiy
Krasnyy Yar

Kaluga
Aleksin
Venev
Mikhaylov
Shilovo
Shatsk
Bednodemyanovsk
Shiringushi
Baryshnikov
Novodevichye
Syzran
Oktyabrsk
Chapayevsk
KUYBYSHEV
Novokuybyshevsk

Tula
Novomoskovsk
Kimovsk
Pavelets
Skopin
Sapozhok
Lukholovo
Nizhniy Lomov
Mokshan
Gorodishche
Syzran
Kashpirovka
Privolzhye

Shchekino
Novotulskiy
Dedilovo
Donskoy
Bogoroditsk
Zametchino
Morshansk
Kamenka
Sura
Sursk
Kuznetsk
351

Uzlovaya
Tovarkovskiy
Kraptvino
Plavsk
Ryazhsk
Chaplygin
Lev Tolstoy
Sosnovka
Zherdevka
Penza
Serdobsk
Khvatovka
Khvalynsk
Pestravka
Bolshaya Glushitsa

293
Mtsensk
Yefremov
Lebedyan
Michurinsk
Kirsanov
Belinskiy (Chembar)
Rtishchevo
Petrovsk
Bazarnyy Karabulak
Volsk
Balakovo
Pugachev

Novosil
Verkhovye
Yelets
Lipetsk
Gryazi
Tambov
Rasskazovo
Kotovsk
Inzhavino
Rtishchevo
Bazarnyy
Gornyy

L **I S T**   **R E P U B L I C**

Livny
Sosna
Zadonsk
Mordovo
Uvarovo
Turki
Arkadak
Atkarsk
Marks
Yershov
Kamenka

Shchigry
Semiluki
Kastornoye
Perlevka
Usman
Ramon
Ertil
Muchkapskiy
Balashov
Balanda
Saratov
Engels
Privolzhskiy
Pushkino
Orlov Gay

Don
Khokhalskiy
VORONEZH
Anna
Gribanovskiy
Arkhangelskoye
Balashov
Samoylovka
Krasnoarmeysk
Volgogradskoye Vdkhr.
Krasnyy Kut
Novouzensk

Staryy Oskol
276
Gubkin
Dobrov
Yelan-Kolenovskiy
Povorino
Novokhopersk
Yelan
Zhirnovsk
Kamenskiy
Krasnyy Yar
358
Rovnoye
Pallasovka
Aleksandrov Gay

Korotoyak
Ostrogozhsk
Georgiu-Dezh
Buturlinovka
239
Uryupinsk
Buzuluk
Kukvidze
Novoannenskiy
Panfilovo
Danilovka
Olovatka
Bol. Uzen

Belgorod
Shebekino
Novyy Oskol
Kamenka
Pavlovsk
Kalach
Ust Buzulukskaya
Medveditsa
Mikhaylovka
Kamyshin
Nikolayevsk
Koztalovka
Mal. Uzen
Furmanovo

Vplokonova
Alekseyevka
Khoper
Kumylzhenskaya
Frolovo
Bykovo
Kaysatskoye
KAZAKH

Volchansk
Pechnezhskoye Vdkhr.
Valuyki
Rossosh
Boguchar
Kazanskaya
Serafimovich
Ilovlya
Ilovlya (Iloulinskaya)
Elton
S.S.R.

Kharkov
Kupyansk
Kupyansk-Uzlovoy
Kantemirovka
Don
Veshenskaya
Kletskiy
Kletskaya
Dubovka
Urda
Dzhanybek

Balakleya
Svatovo
Millerovo
Chertkovo
Chir
Prachalnaya
Volzhskiy
Leninsk
Kapustin Yar

Krasnooskolskoye Vdkhr.
Izyum
Rubezhnoye
Starobelsk
Melovoye
Kamenskiy
Volgograd (Stalingrad)
Krasnoslobodsk

48   COPYRIGHT GEORGE PHILIP & SON. LTD.

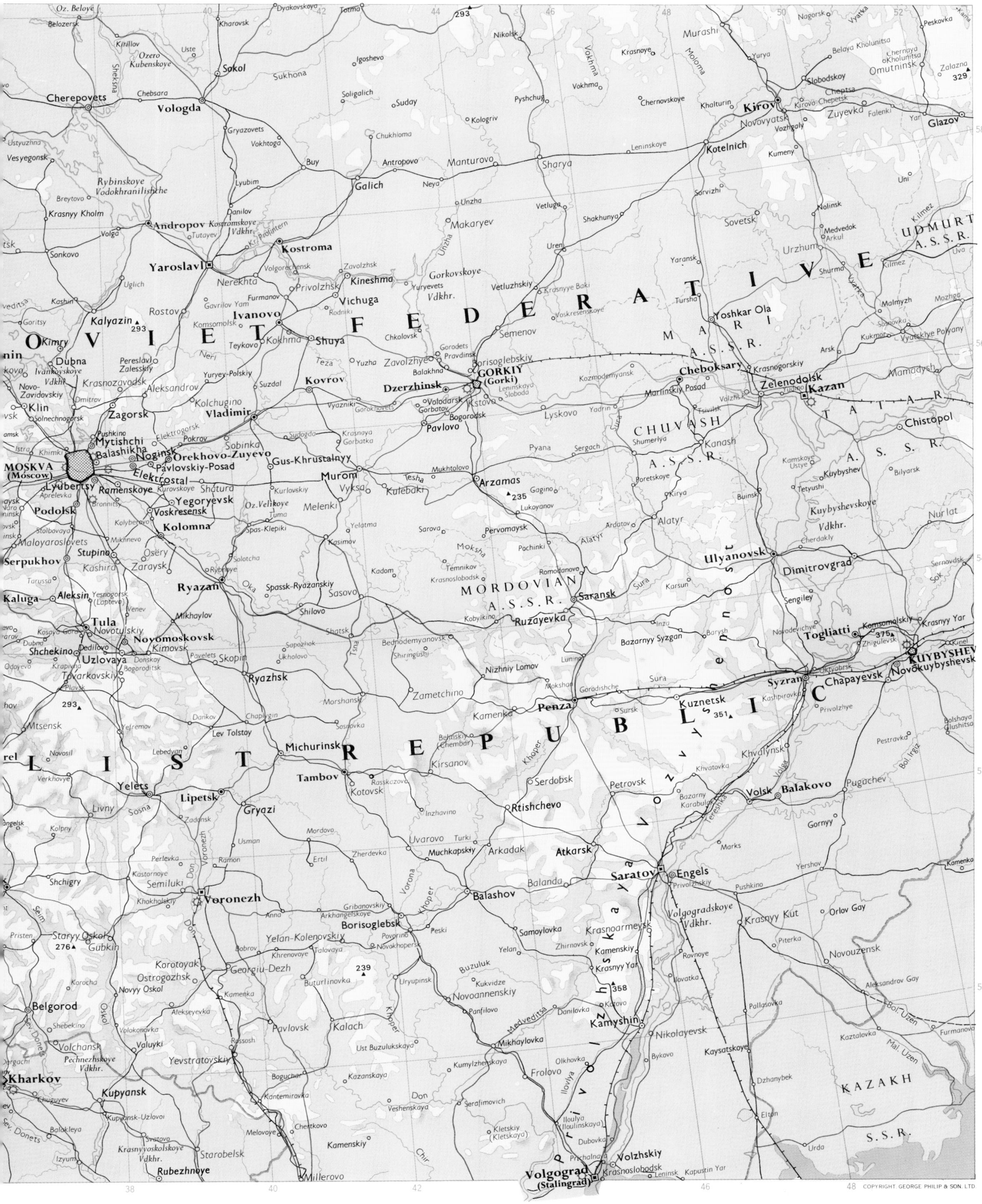

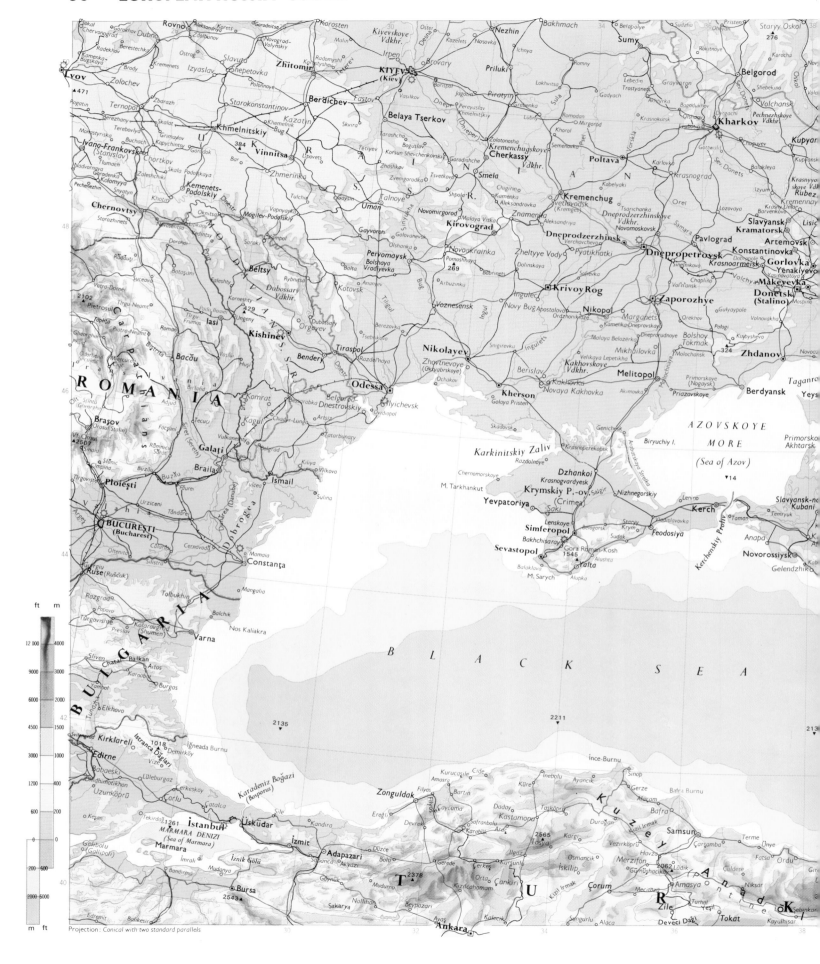

1:5 000 000

50 0 50 100 miles
50 0 50 100 150 km

Yelan-Kolenovskiy
Povorino
Peski
Samoylovka
Krasnoarmeysk
Orlov Gay
Oz. Chalkar
Chalkar
Georgiu-Dezh
Buturlinovka
239
Novokhopersk
Zhirnovsk
Kamenka
Uryupinsk
Buzuluk
Yelan
Krasny Yar
358
Kamennyy
Ravnoye
Piterka
Novouzensk
Dzhambeyty
Ostrogozhsk
Khrenovoye
Talovaya
Novoannenskiy
Ilovatka
Volgogradskoye Vdkhr.
Pallasovka
Aleksandrov Gay
Kushum
Chapayevo
Kalach
Ust Buzulukskaya
Mikhaylovka
Kamyshin
Nikolayevsk
Kaztalovka
Mal. Uzen
Furmanovo
Mergenevskiy
Karsha
Ural
Bol. Uzen
Antonovo
Bazartobe
Kalmykovo
Pavlovsk
Kotovo
Danilovka
Bykovo
Dzhanybek
Kazanskaya
Serafimovich
Kletskiy (Kletskaya)
Volzhskiy
Leninsk
Urda
Elton
Shungay
Makhambet (Yamankhalinka)
Volgograd (Stalingrad)
Krasnoslobodsk
Kapustin Yar
Zelenyy
Topol
Voroshilovgrad (Lugansk)
Krasnoarmeysk
Verkhniy Baskunchak
Akhtubinsk (Petropavlovskiy)
Vladimirovka
Novobogatinskoye
Guryev
Kamensk-Shakhtinskiy
Morozovsk
Chernyshkovskiy
Volga
-28
Belaya Kalitva
Krasnodonetskaya
Tsimlyanskoye Vdkhr.
Kotelnikovo
Kopanovka
Yenotayevka
Kyushyuno
Shakhty
Volgodonsk
Dubovskoye
Obilnoye
Astrakhan
Krasnyy Yar
Novocherkassk
Bolshaya Martynovka
Zavetnoye
KALMYK A.S.S.R.
Kumzyaki
Rostov
Batask
Azov
Proletarskaya
Zimovniki
Remontnoye
Krasnoye
Mumra Liman
Kirovski
-28
Zernograd
Oz. Manych-Gudilo
Elista (Stepnoi)
Kaspiyskiy
Salsk
Leninsk
Pryutnoye
Beloye Ozero
Kultay
Tikhoretsk
Divnoye
Ipatovo
Kalaus
Kuma
Staryy Biryuzyak
CASPIAN SEA
Svetlograd (Petrovskoye)
Arzgir
Budennovsk
O. Kulaly
Mangyshlakskiy Zaliv
Krasnodar
Armavir
Stavropol
831
Blagodarnoye
Vladimirovka
Tyuleniy
M. Tyub Karagan
Fort Shevchenko
P-ov. Mangyshlak
Maykop
Labinsk
Nevinnomyssk
Kursavka
Zelenokumsk (Vorontsovo-Aleksandrovskoye)
Bryanskoye
Shevchenko
Cherkessk
Mineralnyye Vody
Georgievsk
Aleksandriyskaya
Kizlyar
Yessentuki
Pyatigorsk
Prokhladnyy
Mozdok
CHECHENO-INGUSH
Lopatin
Sochi
Kislovodsk
Karachayevsk
Nalchik
Malgobek
Groznyy
Gudermes
Sulak
Makhachkala
Adler
Gagra
KABARDINO-BALKAR A.S.S.R.
Beslan
A.S.S.R.
Kumtorkala
Kaspiysk
ABKHAZ A.S.S.R.
Elbrus 5630
5203
Ordzhonikidze
Buynaksk
Izberbash
Sukhumi
Kazbek 5047
4492
DAGESTAN A.S.S.R.
Derbent
800
Ochamchire
Gali
Dzhvari
GEORGIA
Tebulos
Agvali
Kakhib
Akusha
Dagestanskiye Ogni
Kutaisi
Chiatura
Tskhinvali (Staliniri)
Dusheti
Telavi
S.S.R.
Tbilisi
Mtskheta
Samtredia
Khashuri
Gori
Kvareli
Lagodekhi
Zakataly
Akhty
Khachmas
Poti
Kaspi
Borzhomi
Gurdzhaani
Alazan
Sheki (Nukha)
Kuba
Divichi
Kobuleti
ADZHAR A.S.S.R.
Akhaltsikhe
Signakhi
AZERBAIJAN S.S.R.
Bazar Dyuzi 4466
Baba dag 3629
Batumi
Khulo
Akhalkalaki
Khrami
Rustavi
Iori
Mirzaani
Mingechaurskoye Vdkhr.
Siazan
Hopa
Pazar
Borçka
Kura
Tauz
Mingechaur
Agdash
Geokchay
Sumgait
Görele
Akçaabat
Artvin
Ardahan
Kisir 3192
Çildir
Alaverdi
Shamkhor
Mir-Bashir
Barda
Lyaki
Kazi Magomed
Surakhany
Zyrya
Trabzon
Rize
Kackar 3937
Kirovakan
Kirovabad
BAKU
Tirebolu
Surmene
Oltu
Kars
Dilizhan
Dashkesan
Chanlar
Yevlakh
Kyurdamir
Alyaty
Çakirgat 3063
Narman
Sarikamis
Selim
Aragats 4090
Ozero Sevan
Terter
Agdzhabedi
M. Byandovan
Gümüşane
Bayburt
Ispir
Digor
Echmiadzin
S.S.R.
Yerevan
Kamo
ARMENIAN S.S.R.
Martuni
Agdam
Imishly
Aras
Kağizman
Bayburt

ast from Greenwich

COPYRIGHT GEORGE PHILIP & SON LTD.

R.S.F.S.R.
1. Daghestan A.S.S.R.
2. Kabardino–Balkar A.S.S.R.
3. Mari A.S.S.R.
4. Mordovian A.S.S.R.
5. North Ossetian A.S.S.R.
6. Tatar A.S.S.R.
7. Udmurt A.S.S.R.
8. Chuvash A.S.S.R.
9. Checheno–Ingush A.S.S.R.
AZERBAIJAN
10. Nakhichevan A.S.S.R.
GEORGIA
11. Abkhaz A.S.S.R.
12. Adzhar A.S.S.R.

Projection: Conical Orthomorphic with two standard parallels

East from Greenwich

1:20 000 000

100   0   100   200   300   400   500 miles
100   0   200   400   600   800 km

OCEAN

Ostrov Shmidt
Mys Arkticheskiy
Ostrov Komsomolets
Ostrov Pioner
Ostrov Oktyabrskoy Revolyutsii
965
Severnaya Zemlya
Ostrov Bolshevik
Proliv Vilkitskogo

3800

Ostrova Henrietto
Ostrov Jeanette
Ostrova Delong
Ostrov Zhokhova

La p t e v   Novosibirskiye Ostrova
Ostrov Bennett
Ostrov Faddeyevskiy
Ostrov Novaya Sibir

E a s t   S i b e r i a n   S e a

Ostrov Vrangelya

Chukotskoye More

Mys Dezhneva (East C.)

St. Lawrence I. (U.S.A.)

60

S e a

Ostrov Belkovskiy
Ostrov Malyy Lyakhovskiy
Ostrov Bolshoy Lyakhovskiy
Lyakhovskiye Ostrova
374
Ostrov Kotelnyy
Ostrov Stolbovoy

Proliv Dmitriya Lapteva

Ostrova Medvezhi
Ostrov Aion
Ambarchik
1853
Anadyr

Chukotskiy Khrebet

Providenskoye
Uelon
Anmon
843
Egvekinot
Beringovskiy

Poluostrov Goryustrov Byrranga
1146
Oz. Taymyr
Taymyr

Nordvik
Ust Olenek
Olenek
Tiksi

Mys Buorkhaya
Nizhne Kolymsk
Kolyma
Bolshoy

1742

Koryakskiy Khrebet
2562

Novorybnoye
Uryung-Khaya
Saskylakh

Kyusyur

Chokurdakh
Erdno
Indigirka
Srednekolymsk

Olskon
Parch
Penzhino
Gizhiga

Penzhinskaya Guba

Svedinny

B e r i n g   S e a

Khatanga
Popigay
Anabar
Bulun

Ary
Ust Kuyga
Yana

Ojmyakon
Khond
Uchli
(Otur Kyuyel)

Balygychan
Korkodon

Gizhiginskaya Guba

Poluostrov

Pyasina
Volochanka
Kheta

Kel
(Bysyttakh)
Dzhardzhan

Zashiversk
Ojmyakon
Gora Chen
2682

Seymchan

Zaliv Shelikhova

Kamchatka

Ostrov Bolshoy
Begichev

Zhigansk

Verkhoyansk
2389
Verkhnekolymsk

Khrebet Cherskogo
3147
Ust Nera

Omolon
Nayakhan
Evensk

Mlch-Kyuchevskaya
4750
Kirovskiy

Isk
Gory Putorana
1701

962
Arctic Circle

Y A
Kytyl
Khandyga
2959

Garmanda
Magadan

Ust-Kamchatsk

Noginsk
Yessey
Moyero

Shologontsy

K U
Batamay
(Ust Aldan)

Okhotskaya Perevoz
Okhotsk

1780

Petropavlovsk-Kamchatsky
3456

Tura

Sholoomtsy
Vilyuy
Vilyuysk
Srednevilyuysk

Lena
Aldan
Ytyk-Kyuyel

Nelkan
Ayan

S e a   o f   O k h o t s k

Ostrov Paramushir
Severo-

Nizhnyaya Tunguska
Yukti
Simengo
Chernyshevskiy

Nyurba
Sangar
Namtsy
Maya

Allakh

Chagda

Ostrov Bolshoy Shantar
Sakhalinskiy Zaliv

Ostrov Onekotan

104
Vanavara
Mirnyy
Tuoy-Khaya

Suntar
A. S. S. R.   Yakutsk
Ust Maya
Aim

Chumikan

Nikolayevsk-na-Am.

Okha

Kurilskiye Ostrova

Severo-Yeniseyskiy
Verkhne Kalinina
Lensk
(Mukhtuya)
Olekminsk

Dzhikimde
Ust-Milo
Maya

Tugur
Udskaya Guba

Sakhalin

Ostrova Simushir

Kamennaya
Tunguska
Kuyumba

Buyaga
Olekma
Tommot
2246

Uchur
Khrebet Dzhugdzur

Udskoye
Sredne
Ekimchan

Susuman

Poronaysk
1669
Potonovo

Ostrov Urup

Baykit
Mutaray
Vitim
Kropatkin

Nimnyrskiy
(Vaslevka)
Nagornyy

Torom

Yuzhno-Sakhalinsk
Kholmsk

Ostrov Iturup

Kezhma
Kata
Dubrovskoye
Korshunovo
Mama

Bodaybo
2999
Chara

Chulman

Shimanovsk
Zeya

Nikolskaya
2840
Tambovskoye

Komsomolsk

Sovetskaya Gavan

Kata
Ust-Ilimsk
Makarovo

Karalon
Ust-Nyukzha

Tynda
Zeya

Norskiy
Novochurovka

2078
Khrebet Sikhote Alin

Kirensk
Nizhneangarsk

Ust-Tungir
Skovorodino

Selemdzha
Ekimchan

Melanino

Irkineyeva
Boguchany
Angara
Ust-Kut

Bodarin
Mogocha
Dzhalinda

Novo-Kiyevka
Kukan

2840

Ust-Karenga
Olekma

Ushumun
Yermakovo

Birobidzhan
Khabarovsk
2290

Yeniseysk
Ustye-Chuna
Kondratyevo
Rudnogorsk
Zhelezhnogorsk-Ilimskiy
Nimskiy
Ust-Kut

Vitim
Aksenova
Belogorsk

Chegdomyn
Obluchye

Bikin
Amgu

Kansk
Nevanka
Ilanskiy
Tayshet
Zayarsk

2840
Sosnovka
Vitim
Mogocha

Shimanovsk
Shkotovo

Bira
Lesozavodsk

Olga

Krasnoyarsk
Tulun

Bratsk

Ust-Ilga
Barguzin
Bagdarin

Kocheya
Amazar

Bira
Dalnerechensk

Terney

Vostochnyy Sayan
Artemovsk

Zima
Kazachinskoye

Onguren
Mogocha
Shilka

Sretensk
Shimanovsk

Jiamusi
3669

Nizhneudinsk
Ust-Orda
Buryatskiy

Cheremkhovo
Angarsk
1620
Ulan Ude

Nerchinsk
Nerchinsk Zavod

Olovyannaya

Harbin

Mudanjiang

Ussuriysk

Vladivostok
Nakhodka

J A P A N

Hokkaidō
Sapporo
Hakodate

Tuluri
Munku Sardyk
3491

Irkutsk
Slyudyanka

Petrovsk Zabaykalskiy
Khilok

Borzya
Zabaykalsk

Aleksandrovskiy Zavod

Qiqihar

1054

A. S. S. R.
Samagaltai

Hovsgol Nuur

Torey
Kyakhta

Menzhoull

Harbin

Jilin

Sea   of   JAPAN

Honshū

Kyzyl
Toora-Khem

Zakamensk

Choybalsan

Hulun Nur

Mudanjiang
Changchun

Chongjin
2744

Niigata

Uvs Nuur

Hentiyn Nuruu

Onderhaan

Tamsagbulag

Siping

Jinzhou
Wonsan

Kanazawa
To-yama

Hangayn Nuruu
Ulaanbaatar
(Ulan Bator)
2800

Changchun
1949

Fushun

North

Hyargas Nuur

Ulun

Baruun Urt

Linxi

Shenyang
Anshan

Dandong

P'yongyang

Wonsan
Kaesong

Har Nuur

Ulyasutay
(Javhlant)
Tsetserleg

Saynshand

Chifeng

Yingkou

Sŏul
South
Taejon

Pusan

M O N G O L I A

G O B I

Chengde

Pyongyang
Inch'on

Pusan

3957
Edrengiyn Nuruu

Doulun

Chinhuangdao
Lüda

266
Hami

Tsagaan Olom
Dalandzadgad

Baotou
Zhangjiakou
Beijing

Gaxun Nur

S E R E P U B L I C

COPYRIGHT. GEORGE PHILIP & SON. LTD.

Boundaries of U.S.S.R.
Boundaries of S.S.R.
Boundaries of A.S.S.R.

1:50 000 000

250　0　250　500　750　1000 miles
250　0　500　1000　1500　km

PACIFIC OCEAN

ARCTIC OCEAN

INDIAN OCEAN

C. Dezhneva
Bering Str.
Alaska
Aleutian Is.
7822
Kamchatka Peninsula
Avachnek Vol.
4750
Bering Sea
Sea of Okhotsk
Sredinny Ra.
Kurili Is.
Hokkaido
Sakhalin
Bonin Is.
7056
10 564
Guam
Caroline Is.
New Guinea
Australia

Wrangel I.
Gydan Ra. (Kolyma)
Kolyma
Indigirka
New Siberian Is.
Verkhoyansk Range
Stanovoy Ra.
Lena
Yablonovyi Ra.
Aldan
Amur
Amur
Sikhote Alin Ra.
Shantar
Sea of Japan
La Perouse Str.
Japan
Honshu
Shikoku
Kyushu
Korea Str.
Ryukyu Is.
3776
Tropic of Cancer
3063
Cape Johnson
10 497
Mindanao
Philippine Is.
Luzon
Halmahera
Ceram
Moluccas
Celebes Sea
Banda Sea
Arafura Sea

Central Siberian Plateau
Lower Tunguska
Stony Tunguska
Yenisei
Angara
L. Baikal
Selenga
Sayan Mts.
Plateau of Mongolia
Great Khingan Mts.
Manchurian Plain
Sungari
Korea
Yellow Sea
East China Sea
Formosa
Hainan
G. of Tonkin
Celebes
Sulu Sea
Borneo
Kinabalu
4101
Palawan
Makasar Strait
East Indies
Java Sea
Bali
Flores
Timor
Sumba
Sunda Is.

Taimyr Peninsula
Cheyluskin
Khatanga
Kotuy
Laptev Sea
Severnaya Zemlya
Ob
Yenisei
Irtysh
Tobol
Irtysh
West Siberian Plain
Altai
4506
Belukha
Tien Shan
Turfan Basin
Tarim Basin
Lop Nor
Takla Makan
Koko Nor
Kunlun Shan
Plateau of Tibet
Everest
8848
Tsangpo
Brahmaputra
Irrawaddy
Salween
Mekong
Hwang
Great Plain of China
Po Hai
Yangtze
Si-kiang
Chao Phraya
G. of Thailand
Malay Peninsula
Str. of Malacca
Sumatra
Java
Sunda Str.

Kara Sea
Novaya Zemlya
Barents Sea
Kola Pen.
Kolguyev I.
White Sea
N. Dvina
Ural Mountains
1640
Ob
Narodnaya
1894
Chu
Ili
L. Balkhash
Syr Darya
Aral Sea
Turan Plain
Amu Darya
Pamirs
Stalin Pk.
7495
Communism Pk.
Hindu Kush
Karakoram Ra.
K2
8611
Himalaya
Ganga
Yamuna
Sutlej
Indus
Narmada
Eastern Ghats
Western Ghats
Deccan
Godavari
Krishna
Polk Strait
Ceylon
Equator
C. Comorin
Laccadive Is.
Andaman Is.
Nicobar Is.
Bay of Bengal
India
Gulf of Mannar
Maldive Is.
Chagos Arch.

Greenland
Iceland
Svalbard
North Cape
Scandinavia
Finland
Baltic Sea
North European Plain
Central Russian Uplands
Steppe
Don
Volga
Ural
Caspian Sea
Elburz Mts.
5604
Great Salt Desert
Plateau of Iran
Zagros
The Gulf
G. of Oman
Arabian Sea
Socotra (C. Guardafui)
Ras Asir
G. of Aden
Somali Peninsula
Seychelles
Amirantes

British Isles
North Sea
Rhine
Oder
Elbe
Vistula
Carpathians
Danube
Adriatic Sea
Mediterranean Sea
Cyprus
Anatolia
Taurus Mts.
Black Sea
Bosporus
Caucasus
5633
Pontus
Ararat
5165
Tigris
Euphrates
Mesopotamia
Syrian Desert
Dead Sea
Sinai Pen.
Suez Canal
Red Sea
Nile
Libyan Desert
Arabia
Ar Rub' al Khali
Helmand
Mekran
Arctic Circle

Projection: Bonne

m　6000　4000　2000　1000　400　200　0
ft　18 000　12 000　6000　3000　1200　600　0　600　2000　6000　12 000　18 000　24 000
　　　　　　　　　　　　　　　　　200　2000　4000　6000　8000　m ft

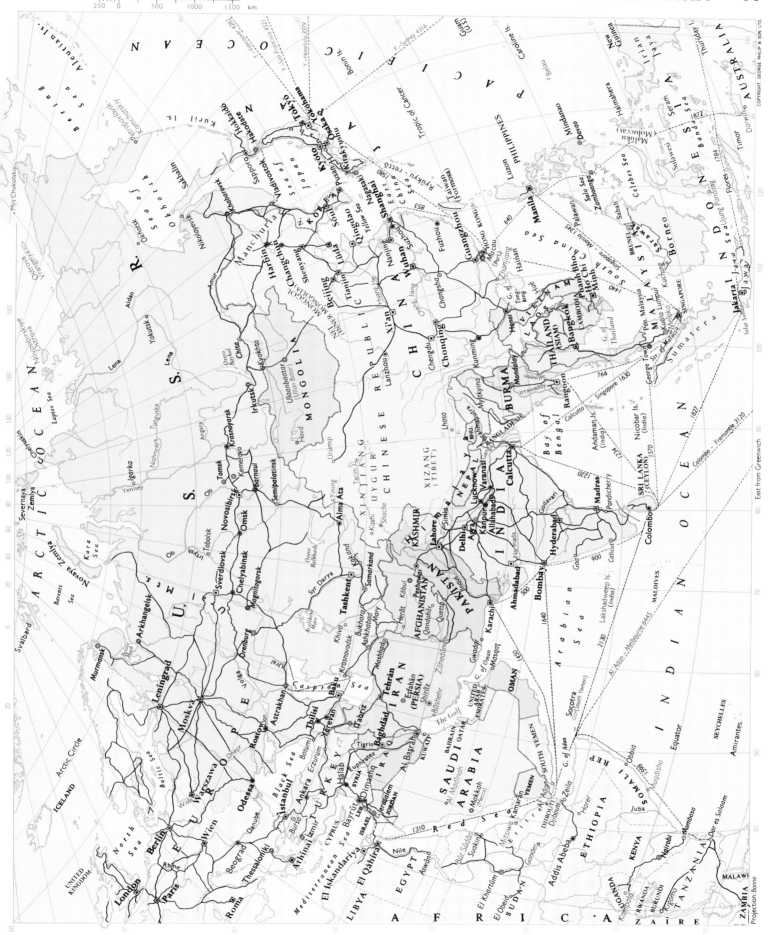

1:50 000 000

Projection: Bonne

1:1 000 000

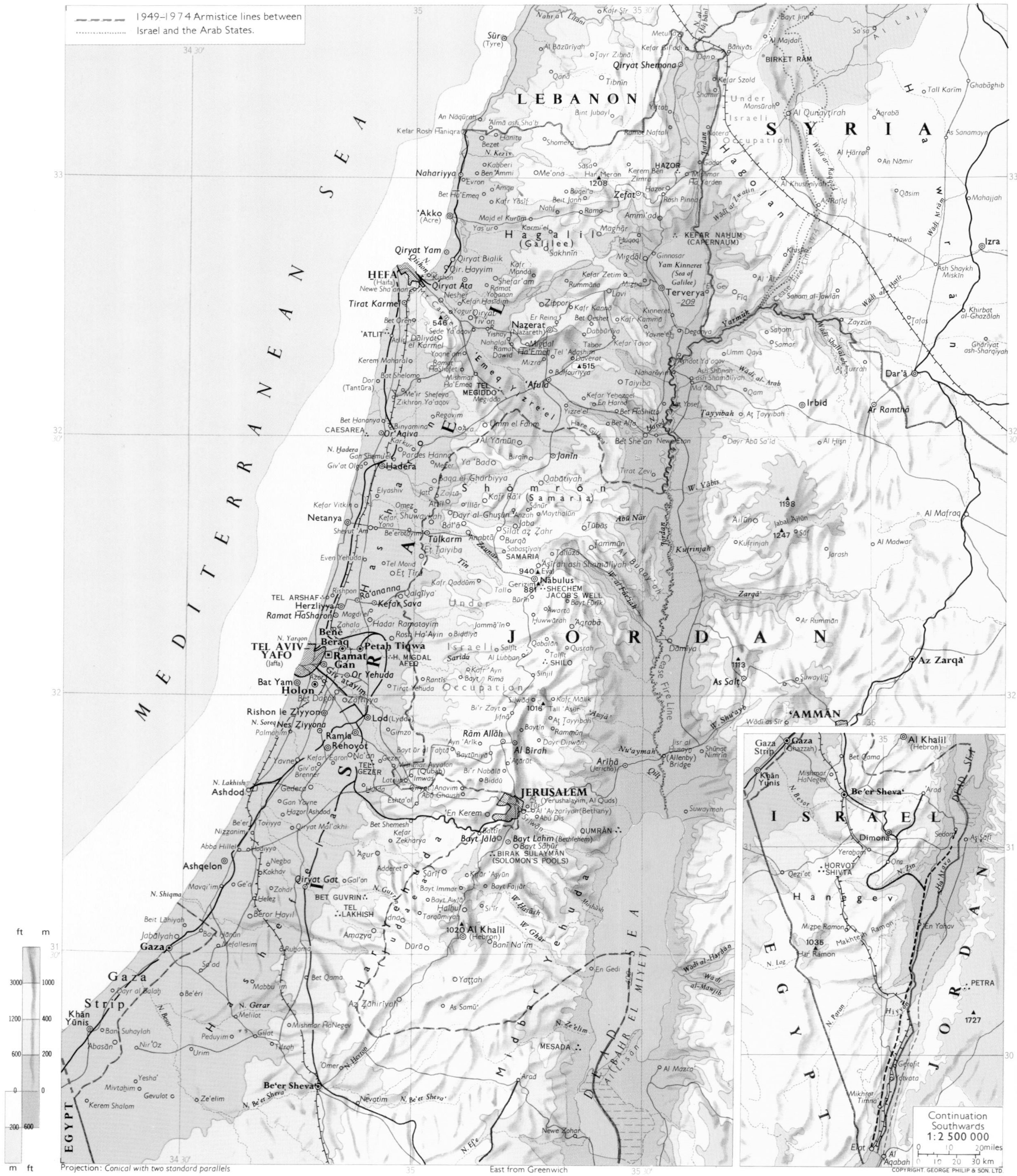

20 miles
km

----- 1949–1974 Armistice lines between
.... Israel and the Arab States.

LEBANON

SYRIA

Sūr
(Tyre)

Qiryat Shemana

BIRKET RAM

Nahariyya

Under
Israeli
Occupation

'Akko
(Acre)

HAZOR

Hagalil
(Galilee)

Zefat

Rosh Pinna

KEFAR NAHUM
(CAPERNAUM)

Qiryat Yam
Qiryat Bialik

HEFA
(Haifa)
Qiryat Ata

Yam Kinneret
(Sea of
Galilee)

Terverya
209

Tirat Karmel

Nazerat
(Nazareth)

Dar'ā

'Afula

Irbid
Ar Ramthā

TEL
MEGIDDO

'Emeq Yizre'el

CAESAREA
Or 'Aqiva

Bet She'an

Janin
Al Mafraq

Hadera

Shomron
(Samaria)

1198
1247

Netanya

Tūlkarm

SAMARIA

Nabulus
SHECHEM
JACOB'S WELL

Zarqā

TEL ARSHAF
Herzliyya
Ramat HaSharon

Under

J O R D A N

TEL AVIV
YAFO
(Jaffa)
Ramat
Gan

Petah Tiqwa

Israeli

Az Zarqā'

Bat Yam
Holon

Occupation

Rishon le Ziyyon
Nes Ziyyona

Ramla
Rehovot

Lod
(Lydda)

Rām Allāh
Al Birah

'AMMĀN

As Salt

Ashdod

TEL
GEZER

JERUSALEM
(Yerushalayim, Al Quds)

Arīhā
(Jericho)

Gaza
Strip
Ghazzah

Al Khalil
(Hebron)

Bayt Lahm
(Bethlehem)

QUMRĀN

BIRAK SULAYMĀN
(SOLOMON'S POOLS)

Khān
Yūnis

Be'er Sheva'

Ashqelon

Qiryat Gat

I S R A E L

Dimona

BET GUVRIN
TEL
LAKHISH

1020 Al Khalil
(Hebron)

Ha negev

Gaza

MESADA

Gaza
Strip
Khān
Yūnis

Be'er Sheva'

HORVOT
SHIVTA

PETRA

Har Ramon
1035

1727

D E A D S E A
(BAHR EL MIYET)

E G Y P T

J O R D A N

EGYPT

MEDITERRANEAN SEA

Continuation
Southwards
1:2 500 000

Elat
Al
'Aqabah

ft m
3000 1000
1200 400
600 200
0 0
200 600
m ft

Projection: Conical with two standard parallels

East from Greenwich

COPYRIGHT GEORGE PHILIP & SON LTD.

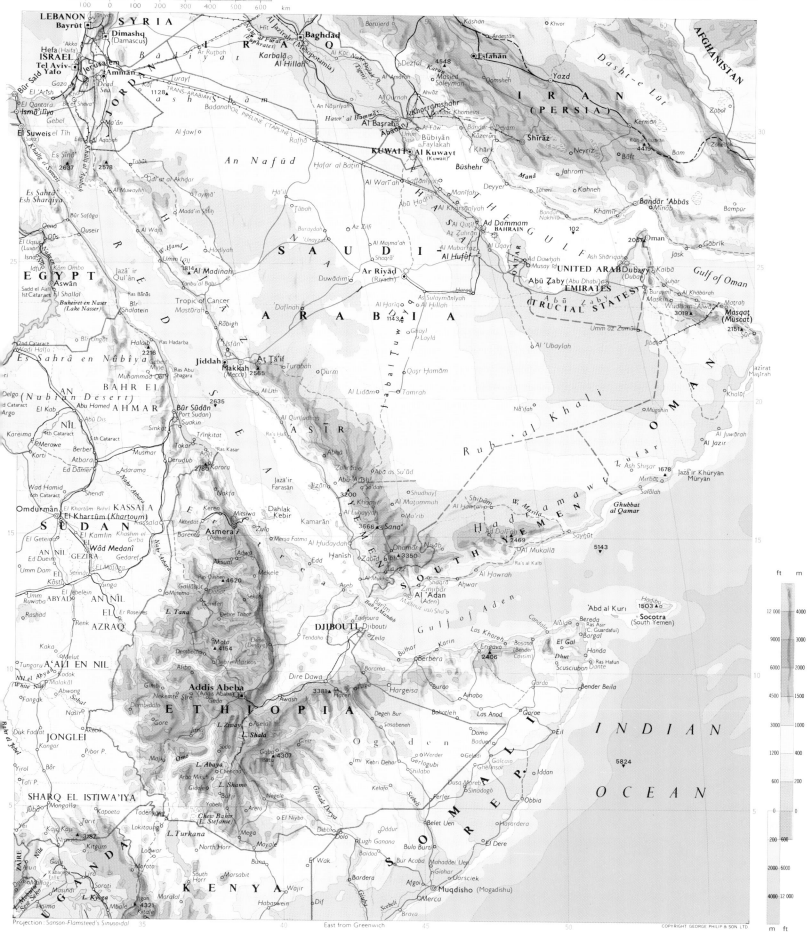

1:15 000 000

100   0   100   200   300   400 miles
100   0   100   200   300   400   500   600   km

LEBANON
Bayrût
SYRIA
'Akko (Haifa)
Hefa (Haifa)
Dimashq (Damascus)
ISRAEL
Tel Aviv-Yafo
Jerusalem
Bûr Sa'îd (Port Said)
Gaza
'Ammân
JORDAN
El Qantara
Be'er Sheva
Ismâ'îlîya
Gebel
El Suweis
Dead Sea
Ma'ân
Es Sînâ'
Khalîg el Suweis
El 'Arîsh
2637   2578
Gebel et Tih
El 'Aqaba

IRAQ
Ar Rutbah
Hît
Jazîrah
Al Furât (Euphrates)
Baghdâd
Karbalâ
Al Hillah
Al Kût
Nahr Dijlah (Tigris)
Mesopotamia
Al 'Amârah
An Nâsirîyah
Al Qurnah
Hawr al Hammâr
Al Basrah
Al Fâw
Abâdân
Būbiyān
Faylakah
Umm Qasr
KUWAIT
Al Kuwayt (Kuwait)
Al Warî'ah
Saffânîyah
Hafar al Bâtin
Rafhâ

Borūjerd
Kâshan
Khvor
Ardestân
Esfahân
4548
Karun
Dezful
Masjed Soleymân
Qomsheh
Ahvâz
Khorramshahr
Bandar-e Khomeinî
Bandar-e Deylam
Būshehr
Deyyer
Tâheri
Mand

IRAN (PERSIA)
Dasht-e Lūt
Yazd
Shîrâz
Neyrîz
Jahrom
Kâhneh
Kermân
Zâbol
Bâft
4419
Bam
Zâhedân
AFGHANISTAN
Bandar 'Abbâs
Khamîr
Mînâb
2057
Gâbrîk
Bampûr
Jâsk

An Nafûd
Qal'at al Akhdar
Tabûk
Al Muwaïlih
Taymâ
Tâbah
Hâ'il
Abû Hadrîyah
Al Kharsânîyah
Al Majma'ah
Az Zilfî
'Unayzah
Buraydah

SAUDI
Al Qatîf
Ad Dammam
BAHRAIN
Az Zulmân
Al Mubarraz
Al Hufûf
Al Uqayt
QATAR
Ad Dawhah
Musay'îd
102
'Omân
Ash Shâriqah
Dubayy (Dubai)
UNITED ARAB
EMIRATES
Abû Zaby (Abu Dhabi)
(TRUCIAL STATES)
Al Khâbûrah
Maskin
Wudhm
'Alwa
3019
Masqat (Muscat)
2151
Matrah

EGYPT
Qenâ
Qûs
Qusêr
El Uqsur (Luxor)
Isnâ
Idfu
Kôm Ombo
Aswân
Sadd el 'Alî
1st Cataract
El Shallâl
Buheiret en Naser (Lake Nasser)
Es Sahrâ Esh Sharqîya
Bûr Safâga
Al Wajh
Jazâ'ir Qul'ân
Ras Bânâs
Bîr Shalatein
Halaib
2216
Ras Hadarba
W. Hamd
Hadîyah
Umm Lajj
1814
Al Madinah
Yanbu' al Bahr
Râbigh
Mastûrah

Dafinah
Duwâdimî
Ar Riyâd (Riyadh)
As Sulaymânîyah
Harad
As Sulaymânîyah
Al Hariq
1143
Al Hillah
ARABIA
Ghayl
Qasr Hamâm
'O Laylâ
Al 'Ubaylah
Umm az Zumûl
Jibal
Jazirat Maşîrah
Khalûf

RED SEA
Tropic of Cancer
Jiddah
Makkah (Mecca)
2565
At Tâ'if
Turabah
Jabal Tuwayq
Durm
OMAN
Al Jûwârah
Al Jâzir

2nd Cataract
Wâdi Halfa
Delgo
3rd Cataract
Abu Hamed
El Kab
AN (Nubian Desert)
Argo
Es Sahrâ en Nûbîya
Kareima
Merowe
4th Cataract
Berber
5th Cataract
Korti
Atbara
Ed Dâmer
NÎL
BAHR EL
AHMAR
Bîr Ungât
Gebel Elba
2216
Muhammad Qol
Ras Abu Shagara
Sinkat
Musmar
Suakin
Trinkitat
Tokar
Derudeb
'Aqîq
'Ras Kasar
2786
Karora
Nafka
Akordat
Keren
Mitsiwa
Adwa
Aksum
Adi Ugri
Barentu
Asmara (Asmera)
Zula
Mersa Fatma
Edd
Al Qunfudhah
Abû 'Arîsh
Jîzân
Sa'dah
3200
Khamîr
Al Matammah
Al Luhayyah
Kamarân
Ma'rib
2635
Bûr Sûdân (Port Sudan)
'ASÎR
Abha
Zahrân
Abâ as Su'ûd
Shudhayf
Na'ifah
Shibâm
Al Hawtah
Rub' al Khali
Mûgshin
Ash Shisar
1678
Jazâ'ir Khûryân Mûryân
Mirbât
Salâlah
Ghubbat al Qamar

SUDAN
KASSALA
Omdurmân
El Khartûm (Khartoum)
Khartûm Bahri
Kassala
Khashm el Girba
Gedaref
El Geteina
Wâd Medanî
GEZIRA
El Managil
Sennâr
El Majâza
Er Roseires
AN NÎL
EL AZRAQ
Ed Dueim
Kôstî
ABYAD
EL
AN NÎL
Umm Ruwaba
El Jebelein
Singa
Rashad
Kaka
Renk
Melut
Tungaru
A'ÂLI EN NIL
Malakâl
Abwong
JONGLEI
Fangak
Nasîr
Kongor
Pibor P.
Bôr
Duk Fadîat
Rahr el Jebel
Yirol
Tali P.
Yei
Kajo Kaji
Torit
SHARQ EL ISTIWA'IYA
Mongalla
Kapoeta
3187
Tadenyang
Lokitaung
L. Turkana
Nimule
3350
Jîzân
Yarîm
YEMEN
Sana
3666
Dhamâr
Zabîd
Ta'izz
Al Mukhâ
Bâb el Mandeb
Perim
Madînat ush Sha'b
Aseb
Barâw
Bulhar
Zeila
Djibouti
DJIBOUTI
Tadjoura
Tendaho
L. Tana
Gonder
Debre Tabor
L. Abaya
Metema
Sekota
Mata
4154
Dembecha
Debre Markos
Alibo
Gimbio
Nekemte
Sire
Addis Abeba (Addis Ababa)
3381
Awash
Harer
Dire Dawa
Jijiga
Hargeisa
Borama
Burao
SOUTH YEMEN
Nişâb
3350
Al Hawrah
Shaqrâ
Zinjibâr
Al 'Adan (Aden)
Ahwar
Gulf of Aden
Al Mukallâ
Ra's al Kalb
5143
Hadramawt
Sayhût
W. Masila
Hadîbû
1503
Socotra (South Yemen)
'Abd al Kuri
Bereda
C. Guardafui
Ras Asir
Aluta
Bargal
Bosaso (Bender Cassim)
Candala
Dhut
Handa
Ras Hafun
Scuschiuan
Dante

2406
Erigavo
El Gal
Las Khoreh
Karin
Berbera
El Gal
Gardo
Ainabo
Bender Beila
SOMALI
REP.
Las Anod
Garoe
Degeh Bur
Bohotleh
Sasabaneh
Werder
Geladi
Galcaio
Gelogubi
Ghelinsor
Shilabo
5824
Eil
Domo
Badweyn
Obbia
INDIAN
OCEAN

ETHIOPIA
Gore
L. Ziway
Asela
L. Shala
Ginir
Goba
4307
Batu
Chencha
Gidole
L. Shamo
Bârî
Ogaden
Ganale Dorya
Imi
Kebri Dehar
Iddan
Dusa Mareb
Sinadogo
Kelafo
Scebeli
Perfer
Belet Uen
Omo
L. Abaya
Arba Minch
Negele
Chew Bahir (L. Stefanie)
Arero
Mega
Moyale
Dolo
Lugh Ganana
Gedo
Bulo Burti
El Dere
Hardardera
Oddur
Bur Acaba
Mahaddei Uen
Giohar
Uarsciek
Muqdisho (Mogadishu)
Merca
Brava

UGANDA
Gulu
ZAIRE
Arua
Moyo
Nimule
Kitgum
Lira
Soroti
4321
Mbale
L. Kyoga
Moroto
Hoima
Masindi
KENYA
Lodwar
South Horr
North Horr
Marsabit
Wajir
Habaswein
Dif
El Wak
Buna
Bardera
Baidoa
Afgoi
Lugh Ganana

East from Greenwich

Projection: Sanson-Flamsteed's Sinusoidal

ft   m
12 000   4000
9000   3000
6000   2000
4500   1500
3000   1000
1200   400
600   200
0   0
200   600
2000   6000
4000   12 000
m   ft

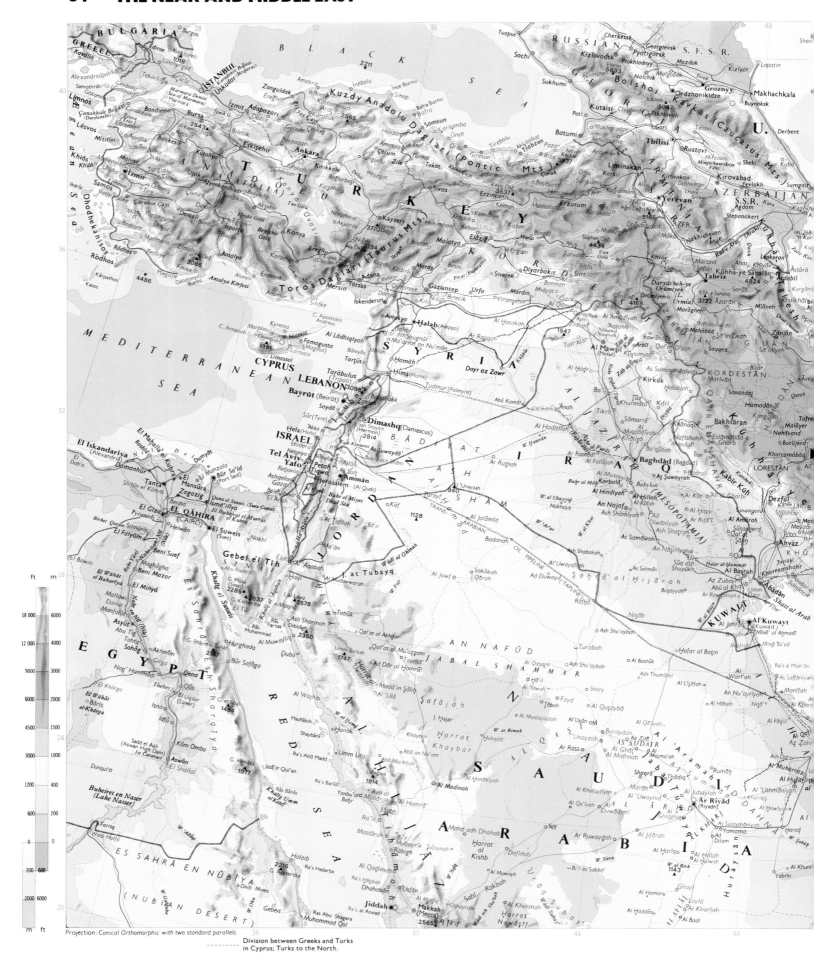

Projection: Conical Orthomorphic with two standard parallels

- - - - - Division between Greeks and Turks
in Cyprus; Turks to the North.

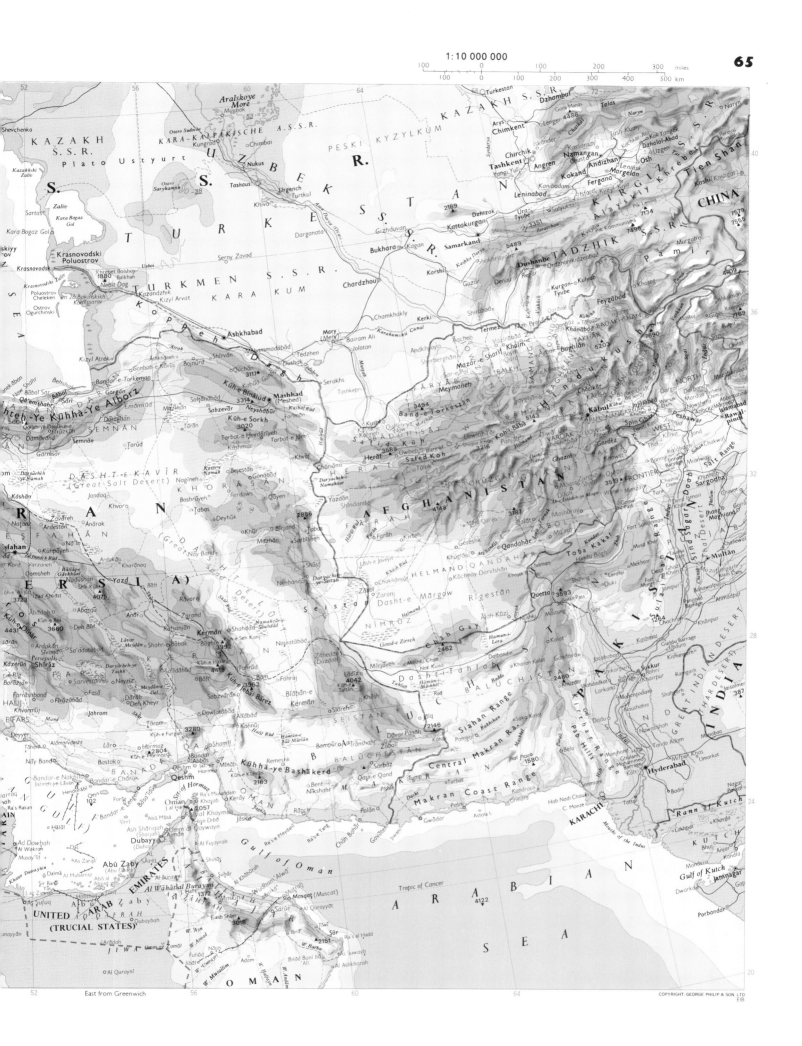

1:10 000 000

100   0   100   200   300 miles
100   0   100   200   300   400   500 km

KAZAKH
S.S.R.

Kazakhskiy
Zaliv

S.
S.
R.

Aralskoye
Moře
Müynak

Ozero Sudoche

KARA-KALPAKISCHE A.S.S.R.
Kungrad
Chimbai

PESKI KYZYLKUM

KAZAKH S.S.R.
Dzhambul
Lenger 4488
Talas

U Z B E K

Nukus

Chimkent
Arys

Turkestan

Naryn

Shevchenko

Chirchik
Tashkent
Yangi Yul'

Kassanson
Iskander

Tash-Kumyr
Gora Manas

Kok Yangak

KARA
Tashaus

Urgench
Turtkul

Khiva

Ozero
Sarykamysh

S.
S.
R.

Gizhduvan
Darganata

Bukhara
Kagan

Samarkand

Dzhizak
Ura-
Tyube

Kokand
Andizhan
Margelan
Fergana

Namangan
Angren

Osh

KIRGIZ
S.S.R.

Ala

yskiy

Khrebet

Naryn

Kanibadam
Leninabad

CHINA

7579

Plato Ustyurt

Kara Bogaz
Gol

Serny Zavod

2169

Kattakurgan

5489

Zeravsan

Pik Lenina
7134

Kommunizma
7495

TADZHIK
S.S.R.

Tien Shan

7555

Kashi (Kashgar)

Kara Bogaz
Gol

Krasnovodski
Poluostrov

T U R K M E N   S.S.R.

Karshi

Guzar

Dushanbe
Ordzhonikidzeabad

Murgab

Sartase

Khrebet Bolshoy
Balkhan

K A R A   K U M

Chardzhou

Denau
Regar

Kurgan-
Tyube
Kulyab

Pamir

4709

Krasnovodsk
Krasnovodski Zaliv

Nebit Dag
1880

Kizyl Arvat

Shirabad

Termez

Khorog

Poluostrov
Cheleken

Kazandzhik

Chamkhakly
Kerki

Mzh Pyandzh

Feyzabad

7189

Ostrov
Ogurchinski

Mary
(Mery)

Bairam Ali
Iolotan

Andkhvoy
Sherberghan

Mazar-e Sharif
Sar-e Pol

BADAKHSHAN

7690

Krasnovodski Zaliv

Kizyl Atrek

Ashkhabad

Mohammadabad

Tedzhen

Serakhs

Tashkepri

Meymaneh

BALKH

Baghlan

5203

TAKHAR

Ashkhaneh

Shirvan

Quchan
3117

Kuh-e Sorkh

Serny Zavod

FARYAB

Kunduz
Khanabad

Kataghan

Bandar-e Torkeman

Bojnurd

Shahrud

Kuh-e Binalud
3314

Mashhad
(Meshed)

Kushk

Qaysar

Band-e Torkestan

Kabul
3494

Charikar
Kapisa

NORTH

Mardan

Abbottabad

SEMNAN

Sabzevar
Neyshabur

Kuh-e Sorkh
3020

Torbat-e Heydariyeh
Torbat-e Jam

Kuh-e Baba 5143

Koh-i-
Baba

Maidan

WARDAK

Kabul

NANGARHAR

Peshawar

Spin Ghar

Islamabad

Rawal-
Pindi

Damavand

Semnan
Torud

Kashmar

Khaf

Safed Kuh

5489

3588

Safed
Koh

Panjao

3216

Ghazni

Gardez

WEST

Kohat

Jand

Bannu

DASHT-E KAVIR
(Great Salt Desert)

Naghineh

KHORASAN

Ferdows

Qayen

Herat

Ghurian

Tulak

ORUZGAN

3787

ZABUL

Moqor

3513

Salt Range

FRONTIER

KAVIR

Nay Band

2886

Tabas

Birjand

Sarbisheh

FARAH

4148

Ghalat

Dehli

FRONTIER

Tank

Sargodha

Kashan

Anarak

Khur

Mazhan

Farah

Kirteh

Gereshk

Qandahar

Toba Kakar

Chaman

Mianwali

Jhang Maghiana

Notanz

Ardestan

Na'in

Deyhuk

Khosf

Nehbandan

Zabol
Zaranj

Dasht-e Margow

QANDAHAR

Muslim Bagh

Duki

Loralai

Chiniot

I R A N

Nay Band

NIMRUZ

Rigestan

Quetta
3593

Fort Sandeman

ESFAHAN

Yazd

Tabas

Lut
Desert

Seistan

Daryacheh-ye
Sistan

HELMAND

Dasht-e Margow

Agha Kuzi

Pishin Lora

1264

Sibi

P E R S I A

3728

Zavareh

Ravar

Shahr-e Babak

Zarand

Namaksar-e
Shahdad

Noshabad

Zahedan
(Duzdab)

BALUCHISTAN

Nushki

Kalat

Kirtha Barrage

Shikarpur

Jacobabad

Sukkur
Rohri

Larkana

FARS

KUH-E DINAR
4431

Kuh-e Hazar
4075

3660

Deh Bid

Lavar

Seh Konj

Rafsanjan

Kerman

Mirjaveh

Dasht-i-Tahlab

Dalbandin
2480

Mohenjodaro

Shahdadkot

Khairpur

Jaisalmer

GREAT INDIAN DESERT

387

Shiraz

Persepolis
Sivand

Sa'adatabad

Kerman

Baghin
3992

Kharan Kalat

Baddo

Ahmadpur
Khanpur

Guddu Barrage

I N D I A

Kazerun

Ardakan

Neyriz

Bam

4419

Kuh-e Jebal Barez
3962

Khash

BALUCHISTAN

Sar Kalat

Nasirabad

Borazjan

Firuzabad

Fasa

Darab
Deh Kheyr

Sabzavaran

SEISTAN

Siahan Range

Saka Kalat

Dadu

Nawabshah

HALIJ
E FARS

Mand

Jahrom

Tarom

Dowlatabad

Afdabad

Kahnuj

Zaboli

2146

Mastung

Pab Hills

Bela

Sehwan

Deyyer

Lar

3280

Kuh-e Furgun

Kahnuj

Hamun-e
Jaz Murian

Bampur
Iranshahr

Davar Panah

Kuhak

Panjgur

Rakhshan

Jhal Jhao
1580

Manjhand

Hyderabad

Nay Band

Bastako
2804

Bandar
Lengeh

Minab
2163

Remeshk

Bent
Nikshahr

Qasr-e Qand
Sarbaz

Tump R

Pishin

Central Makran Ra

Kandrach

Umarkot

BANADAR

Hormoz

Bandar-e Charak

Qeshm

Hormuz

Kuhha-ye Bashakerd

Dashti

Makran Coast Range

Pasni

Hab Nadi Chauki

Tatta

Nagar
Parkar

Bandar-e Nakhilu
Jazireh-ye Lavan

Qeshm

Gulf of
Oman

Polan

Ras-e Meydani

Ormara

C. Monze

KARACHI

Mouths of the Indus

Rann of Kutch

BAIN

Gulf
(Persian Gulf)

Sirri

Abu Musa

Ra's Musandam

Khasab

Jask

Chah Bahar

Ra's-e Tang

Gwadar

Astola I.

KUTCH

Bhuj

Anjar

Kandla

Ad Dawhah
Al Wakrah

Hilal

Halul

Oman

Bandar-e Abbas

Jal Haff
2057

Sul al Khaymah

Umm al Qaywayn

Shinas

Al Khaburah

Wudam
Alwa

Tiwi

Matrah

ARABIAN

Tropic of Cancer

Gulf of Kutch

Jamnagar

Dwarka

Porbandar

Musay'id

As Zarqa

Abu Zaby
(Abu Dhabi)

Dubayy
(Dubai)
Ajman
Al Fujayrah

Al Buraymi

Masqat (Muscat)

4122

Dalma
Abu al Abyad

EMIRATES
Al Wahat al Buraymi

Haffit
1372

Sarur

Ra's al Hadd

Sir Baniyas
Yas I.

Sabkhat Matti

UNITED
ARAB

(TRUCIAL STATES)

As Sufuq

ABU

ZABY

OFRAH

Dubayb

JIWA

Umm az Zamul

2151

Sur

SEA

Al Wakran

Aradah

Al Qurayni

Fuhud

Al 'Ayn

Najih

Al Ushsh

W. Barha

Bilad Bani
Ali

W. Andam

W. Muallim

O M A N

3019

Ibri

Izki

W. Ashkharah

ARABIAN SEA

Continuation Southwards on same scale

Projection: Conical with two standard parallels

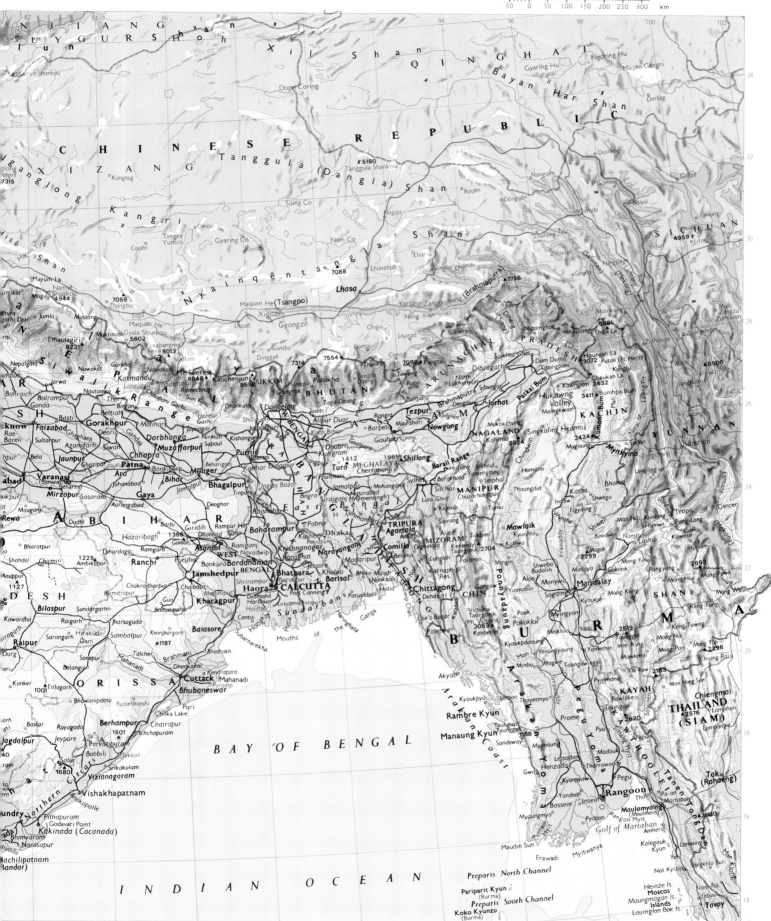

1:10 000 000

50   50   100   150   200 miles
50   0   50   100   150   200   250   300 km

XINJIANG
UYGURS Shan
Xian hah
Xil Shan

CHINESE REPUBLIC

QINGHAI
Ngoring Hu
Gyaring Hu
Maqên Gangri
Darlag

Bayan Har Shan

Doger Coring

XIZANG
Zanglong
7315

Tanggula (Dangla) Shan
5180
Tanggula Shankou

Kangtog

SICHUAN
4959

Yushu
Dainkog
Nanqên

Kangri

Ombu

Tangra Yumco
Coqên
Nam Co
Siling Co

Nagqu

Nyainqêntanglha Shan

Zhxize

7088
Lhari

Lhasa
Lhünzhub

Maquan He (Tsangpo)
Yarlung-Zangbo Jiang (Brahmaputra)

7059
Zhongba
Xigaze
Xaxabangma Feng 8013
Lhazê
Gyangzê

Dhaulagiri 8221
Mt. Everest 8848
Kanchenjunga 8596

SIKKIM

BHUTAN

ARUNACHAL PRADESH

KACHIN
Myitkyina

YUNNAN

Gorakhpur
Darbhanga
Muzaffarpur

Patna
Varanasi (Banaras) (Benares)

BIHAR

BANGLADESH

MEGHALAYA
Shillong
Cherrapunji

NAGALAND

MANIPUR
Imphal

Gaya

WEST BENGAL
Dhaka

TRIPURA
Agartala

MIZORAM

Comilla

CHIN

Asansol
Ranchi
Jamshedpur

Bardhaman
Krishnanagar
Narayanganj

CALCUTTA
Haora
Kharagpur

Barisal
Chittagong

Mandalay

SHAN

BURMA

Balasore

Sundarbans

Mouths of the Ganga

Cuttack
Bhubaneswar

ORISSA

Berhampur

Akyab

KAYAH

THAILAND (SIAM)
Chiengmai

BAY OF BENGAL

Rambre Kyun
Manaung Kyun

Arakan Coast

Prome

Pegu Yoma

Rangoon

Vishakhapatnam
Kakinada (Cocanada)

Bassein
Maulamyaing (Moulmein)

Gulf of Martaban

INDIAN OCEAN

Preparis North Channel
Pariparit Kyun (Burma)
Preparis South Channel
Koko Kyunzu (Burma)

Heinze Is
Moscos
Maungmagan Is.
Islands
Lauingion Bok Is.

Tavoy

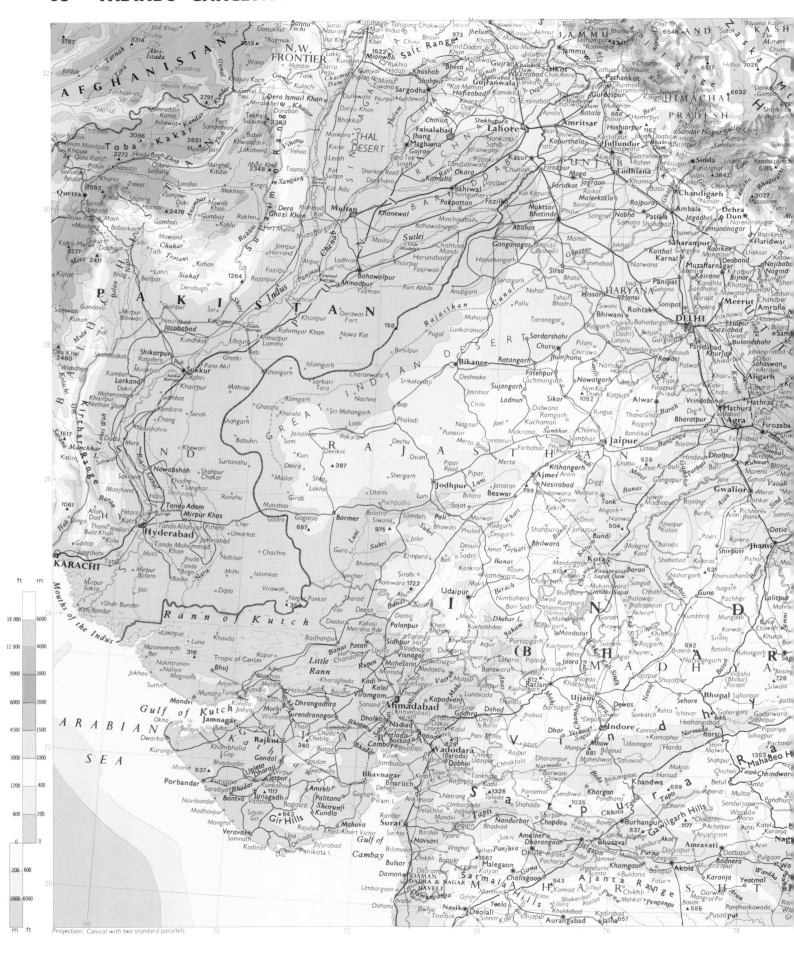

1 : 6 000 000

50   0   50   100   150 miles

50   0   50   100   150   200   250 km

CHINESE REPUBLIC

TIBET

AFGHANISTAN   KASHMIR

PAKISTAN

NEPAL

BANGLA DESH

BURMA

INDIA

Tropic of Cancer

SRI LANKA

S. ASIA: IRRIGATION

1 : 40 000 000

Irrigated Areas

CHINESE REPUBLIC

Xizang Zong   Gangdise Shan   Kangri

La'nga Mapam Yumco Co

Ngangla Rinco

Zhari Namco

Yarlung Zangbo Jiang (Brahmaputra)

Nanda Devi 7066
Nanda Kot 6861

H I M A L A Y A

Mt. Everest 8848   Makalu   Kanchenjunga   SIKKIM   Gangtok   BHUTAN

NEPAL

Katmandu   Lalitpur   Bhaktapur

Annapurna   Dhaulagiri 8172

U T T A R   P R A D E S H

Lucknow   Faizabad   Gorakhpur   Darbhanga   Darjeeling

Sitapur   Basti   Deoria   Motihari   Muzaffarpur   Biratnagar   Shiliguri   Koch Bihar   Gauhati   ASSAM

NPUR   Unnao   Azamgarh   Chhapra   Patna   Munger   Bhagalpur   Purnia   Dinajpur   Rangpur   MEGHALAYA   Garo Hills   Khasi Hills

Allahabad   Varanasi (Banaras, Benares)   Ara   Gaya   B I H A R   Rajmahal Hills   Malda   Bogra   Mymensingh

M A D H Y A   P R A D E S H

Satna   Vindhyachal   Mirzapur-cum-   Rohtas   Hazaribagh   Bokaro   Dhanbad   Asansol   BANGLADESH   DHAKA (Dacca)

Jabalpur   Panna Hills   Kaimur Hills   Dehri   Ranchi   Jamshedpur   Durgapur   Barddhaman   Krishnagar   Jessore   Khulna   Barisal

Raurkela   B E N G A L   Chandannagar   Barakpur   CALCUTTA   Howrah

Bilaspur   Raigarh   Sambalpur   Hirakud Dam   Kharagpur   Midnapur   Sundarbans

Raipur   Bhilai   Mahanadi   O R I S S A   Balasore   Mouths of the Ganga

Durg   Sambalpur   Cuttack   Bhubaneswar

Chilka Lake   Puri   Konarak

B A Y   O F   B E N G A L

The Sandheads

East from Greenwich

COPYRIGHT GEORGE PHILIP & SON LTD

1:6 000 000

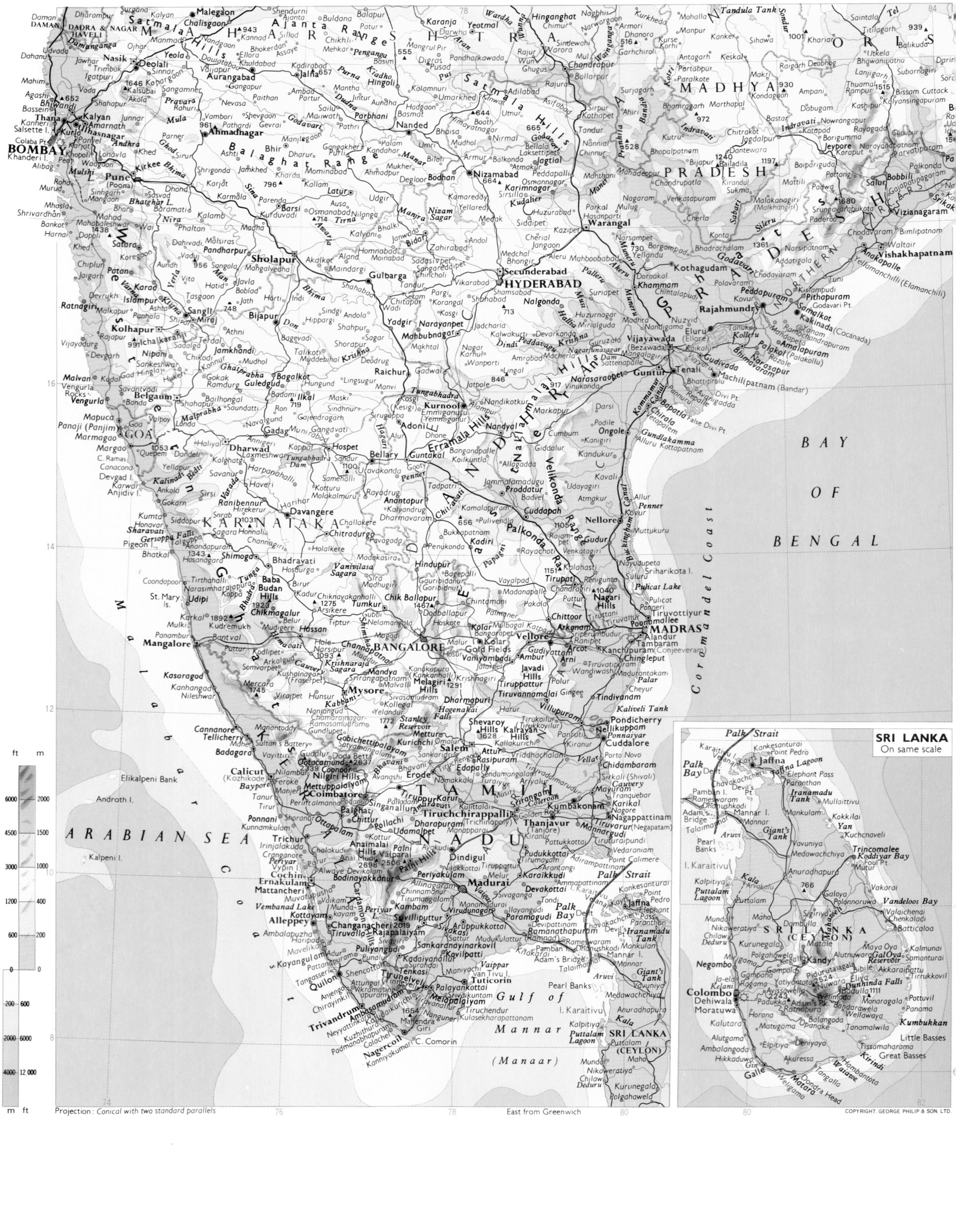

50   0   50   100   150 miles
50   0   50   100   150   200   250 km

ARABIAN SEA

BAY OF BENGAL

MADHYA PRADESH

MAHARASHTRA

KARNATAKA

TAMIL NADU

GOA

BOMBAY

HYDERABAD

BANGALORE

MADRAS

Western Ghats

Eastern Ghats

Nilgiri Hills

Coromandel Coast

Gulf of Mannar

Palk Strait

Palk Bay

SRI LANKA
On same scale

SRI LANKA (CEYLON)

Projection: Conical with two standard parallels

East from Greenwich

COPYRIGHT. GEORGE PHILIP & SON, LTD.

1:10 000 000

PENINSULAR MALAYSIA
AND SINGAPORE
1:6 000 000

Projection: Conical with two standard parallels

East from Greenwich

COPYRIGHT GEORGE PHILIP & SON LTD

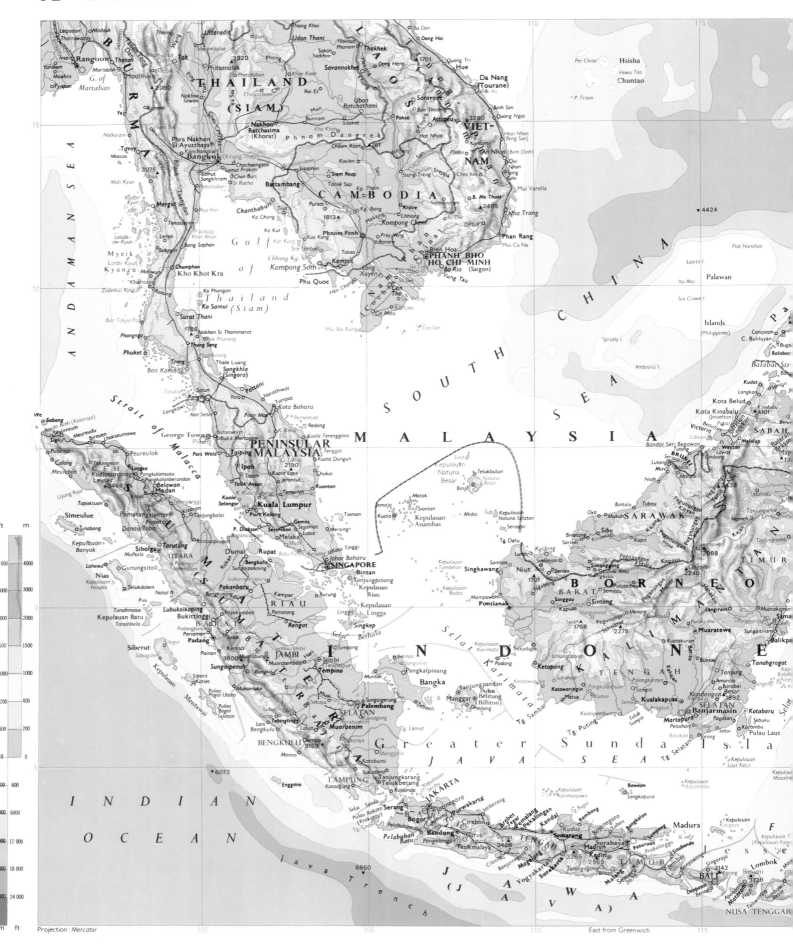

East from Greenwich

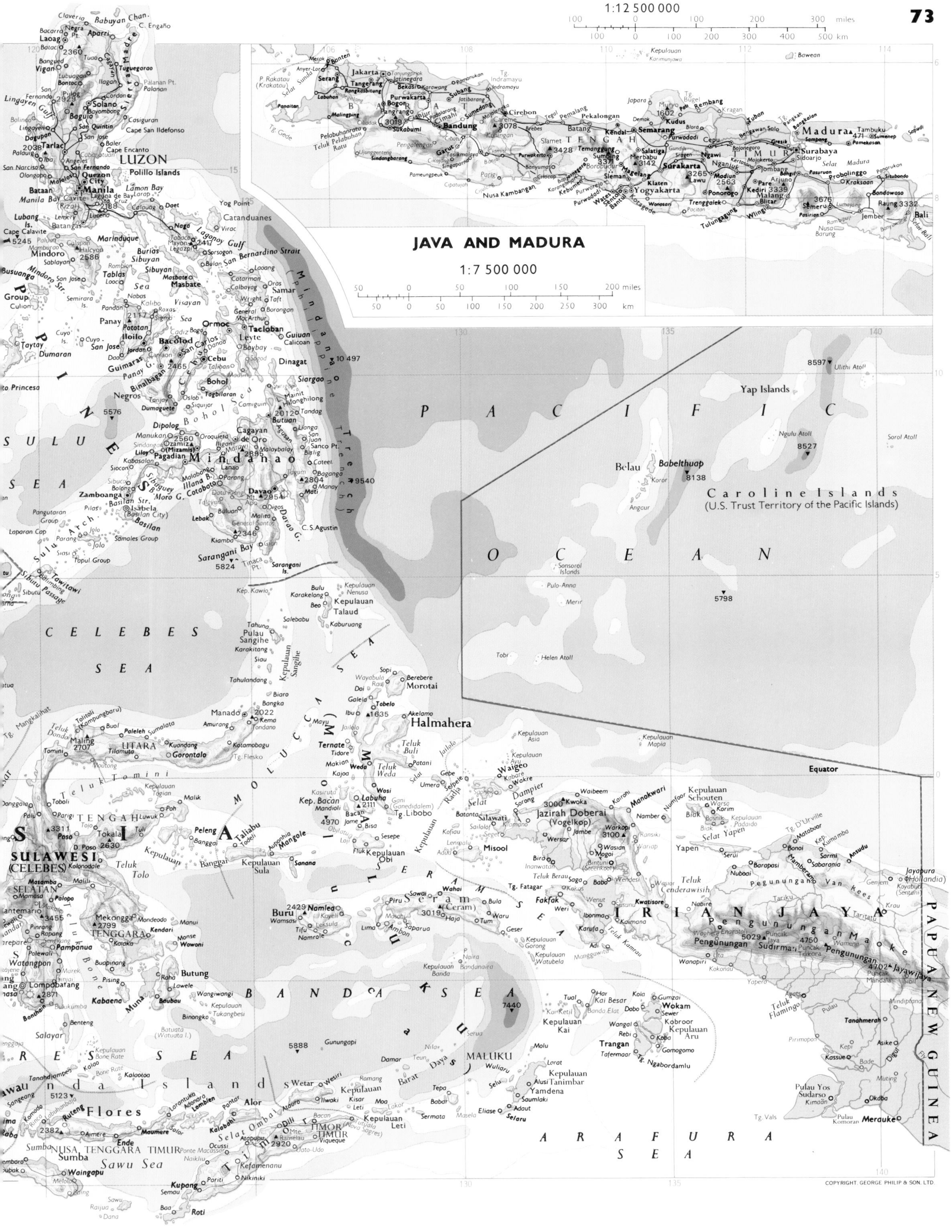

1:12 500 000

100   0   100   200   300 miles
100   0   100   200   300   400   500 km

JAVA AND MADURA

1:7 500 000

50   0   50   100   150   200 miles
50   0   50   100   150   200   250   300 km

LUZON

Manila

PHILIPPINE

Mindoro

Panay

Negros

Cebu

Bohol

Mindanao

Zamboanga

Davao

Jakarta   Bandung   Semarang   Surakarta   Yogyakarta   Surabaya   Madura

T E N G A H   T I M U R

Bali

SULU
SEA

CELEBES
SEA

S U L A W E S I
(CELEBES)

TENGAH

SELATAN

TENGGARA

MOLUCCA SEA

Manado

Gorontalo

Halmahera

Ternate
Tidore

Morotai

PACIFIC   OCEAN

Yap Islands

Belau   Babelthuap

Caroline Islands
(U.S. Trust Territory of the Pacific Islands)

Equator

Waigeo

Jazirah Doberai
(Vogelkop)

Misool

Yapen

Manokwari

Biak

Jayapura
(Hollandia)

I R I A N   J A Y A

Pegunungan Van Rees

Pengunungan Maoke

Pegunungan Sudirman

Jayawijaya

P A P U A   N E W   G U I N E A

Merauke

S E R A M   S E A

Seram
(Ceram)

Buru

Ambon

B A N D A   S E A

Butung

Kabaena

Salayar

Flores

Sumba

NUSA TENGGARA TIMUR

TIMOR
TIMUR

Kupang

Sawu Sea

Kepulauan
Tanimbar

Yamdena

Kepulauan
Kai

Kepulauan
Aru

Trangan

A R A F U R A
S E A

M A L U K U

COPYRIGHT, GEORGE PHILIP & SON, LTD.

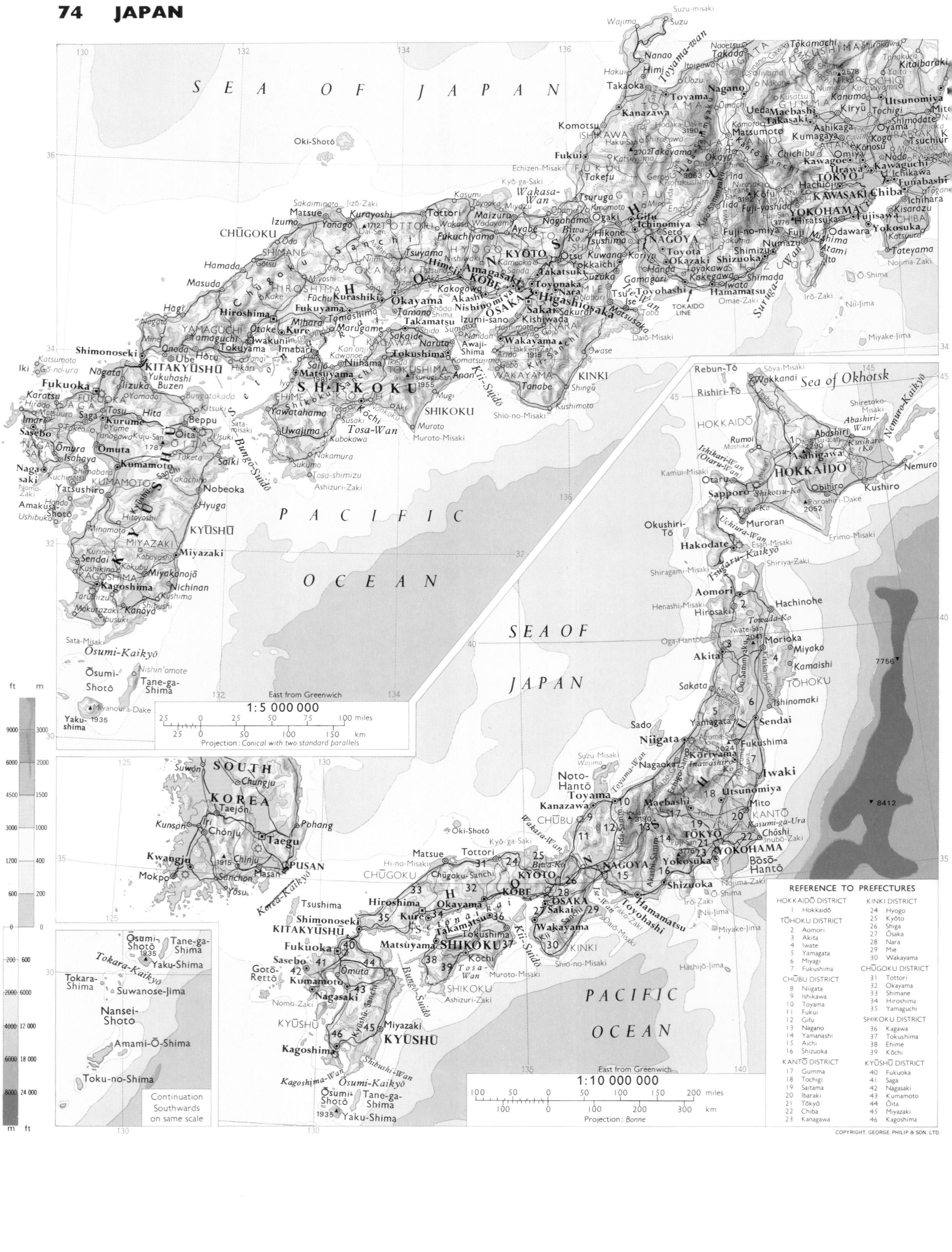

SEA OF JAPAN

PACIFIC OCEAN

CHŪGOKU
SHIKOKU
KYŪSHŪ
HOKKAIDŌ
TŌHOKU
KANTŌ
CHŪBU
KINKI

Sea of Okhotsk

SOUTH KOREA

Major cities and places (main map):

Suzu, Suzu-Misaki, Wajima, Nanao, Himi, Nagano, Takada, Toyama-wan, Takaoka, Toyama, Kanazawa, Komotsu, ISHIKAWA, Fukui, Takefu, Matsumoto, Ueda, Maebashi, Takasaki, Kiryū, Tochigi, Utsunomiya, Kumagaya, Kawagoe, Urawa, TOKYO, KAWASAKI, Chiba, YOKOHAMA, Hiratsuka, Yokosuka, Odawara, Atami, Numazu, Fuji, Mishima, Tateyama, Nojima-Zaki

Izumo, Matsue, Yonago, Kurayoshi, Tottori, Toyooka, Maizuru, Ayabe, Fukuchiyama, KYOTO, Otsu, Kuwana, NAGOYA, Gifu, Ichinomiya, Okazaki, Shizuoka, Hamamatsu, Toyohashi, Tsu, Ise, Iwata, Shimada, Ōmae-Zaki

Hamada, Masuda, HIROSHIMA, Fukuyama, Mihara, Kurashiki, OKAYAMA, HIMEJI, Amagasaki, KOBE, OSAKA, Higashiōsaka, Sakai, Nara, Wakayama, Tanabe, Shingū, Kushimoto

Shimonoseki, KITAKYŪSHŪ, Fukuoka, Karatsu, Saga, Kurume, Hita, Beppu, ŌITA, Saiki, Nobeoka, Hyuga, Kumamoto, Yatsushiro, Minamata, Nobeoka, Miyazaki, Miyakonojō, Nichinan, Kagoshima, Kanoya, Makurazaki, Ibusuki

Ōsumi-Kaikyō, Ōsumi-Shotō, Tane-ga-Shima, Yaku-shima, Miyanoura-Dake, Nishin'omote

SHIMANE, TOTTORI, HYOGO, KYOTO, MIE, OKAYAMA, HIROSHIMA, YAMAGUCHI, EHIME, KAGAWA, TOKUSHIMA, KŌCHI, SHIKOKU, KINKI

Matsuyama, Imabari, Niihama, Takamatsu, Marugame, Tokushima, Kōchi, Uwajima, Nakamura, Sukumo, Muroto, Muroto-Misaki, Ashizuri-Zaki, Tosa-Wan

NAGASAKI, Sasebo, Ōmura, Isahaya, Nagasaki, Shimabara, Amakusa-Shotō, Hondo

HOKKAIDŌ, Rebun-Tō, Rishiri-Tō, Wakkanai, Sōya-Misaki, Rumoi, Abashiri, Abashiri-Wan, Asahigawa, Sapporo, Otaru, Obihiro, Kushiro, Nemuro, Muroran, Hakodate, Okushiri-Tō, Ishikari-Wan, Shikotsu-Ko, Daisetsu-zan 2290, Poroshiri-Dake 2052

Aomori, Hirosaki, Hachinohe, Morioka, Miyako, Kamaishi, Akita, Sakata, Yamagata, Sendai, Ishinomaki, Niigata, Nagaoka, Kōriyama, Fukushima, Iwaki, Mito, Utsunomiya

Sado, Noto-Hantō, Toyama, Kanazawa

TŌHOKU

Tsugaru-Kaikyō, Iwate-San 2041, Towada-Ko, Oga-Hantō

Inset maps:

SOUTH KOREA, Chungju, Taejŏn, Chŏnju, Kunsan, Iri, Kwangju, Mokpo, Yŏsu, Taegu, PUSAN, Masan, Chinju, Pohang, Tsushima, Korea-Kaikyō

Continuation Southwards on same scale

Ōsumi-Shotō, Tane-ga-Shima, Yaku-Shima, Tokara-Kaikyō, Tokara-Shima, Suwanose-Jima, Nansei-Shoto, Amami-Ō-Shima, Toku-no-Shima

Scale bars:

1:5 000 000
25 0 25 50 75 100 miles
25 0 25 50 75 100 125 150 km
Projection: Conical with two standard parallels

1:10 000 000
100 50 0 50 100 150 200 miles
100 0 100 200 300 km
Projection: Bonne

East from Greenwich

Elevation legend (ft / m):

ft	m
9000	3000
6000	2000
4500	1500
3000	1000
1200	400
600	200
0	0
200	600
2000	6000
4000	12 000
6000	18 000
8000	24 000
m	ft

REFERENCE TO PREFECTURES

HOKKAIDŌ DISTRICT	KINKI DISTRICT
1 Hokkaidō	24 Hyogo
TŌHOKU DISTRICT	25 Kyōto
2 Aomori	26 Shiga
3 Akita	27 Ōsaka
4 Iwate	28 Nara
5 Yamagata	29 Mie
6 Miyagi	30 Wakayama
7 Fukushima	**CHŪGOKU DISTRICT**
CHŪBU DISTRICT	31 Tottori
8 Niigata	32 Okayama
9 Ishikawa	33 Shimane
10 Toyama	34 Hiroshima
11 Fukui	35 Yamaguchi
12 Gifu	**SHIKOKU DISTRICT**
13 Nagano	36 Kagawa
14 Yamanashi	37 Tokushima
15 Aichi	38 Ehime
16 Shizuoka	39 Kōchi
KANTŌ DISTRICT	**KYŪSHŪ DISTRICT**
17 Gumma	40 Fukuoka
18 Tochigi	41 Saga
19 Saitama	42 Nagasaki
20 Ibaraki	43 Kumamoto
21 Tōkyō	44 Ōita
22 Chiba	45 Miyazaki
23 Kanagawa	46 Kagoshima

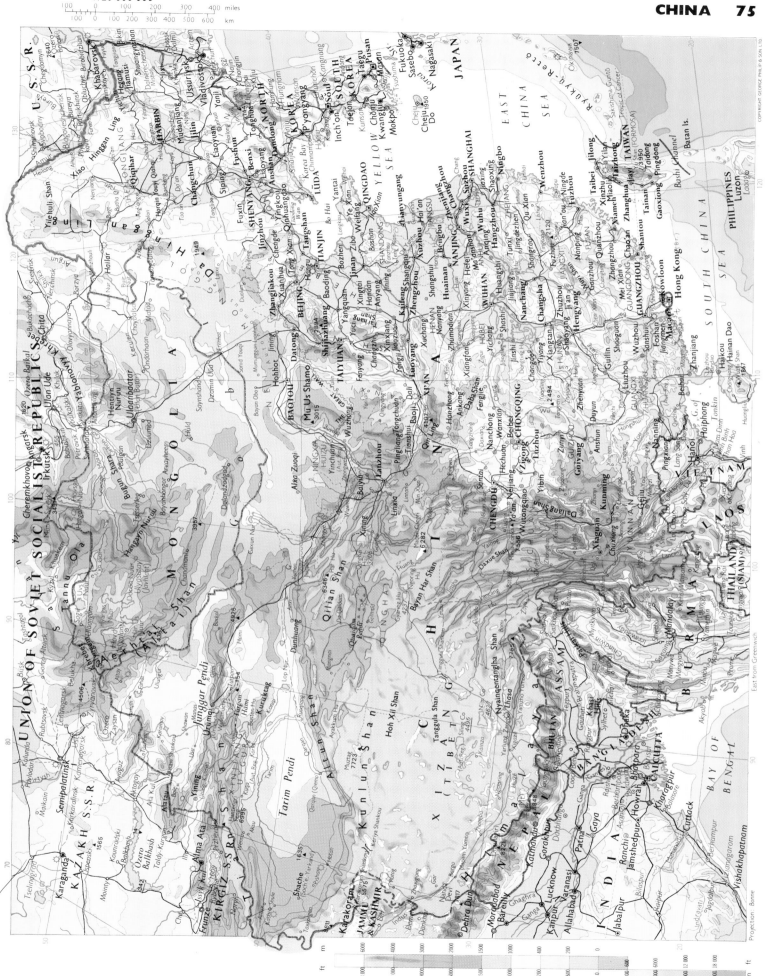

1:20 000 000

Projection: Bonne

East from Greenwich

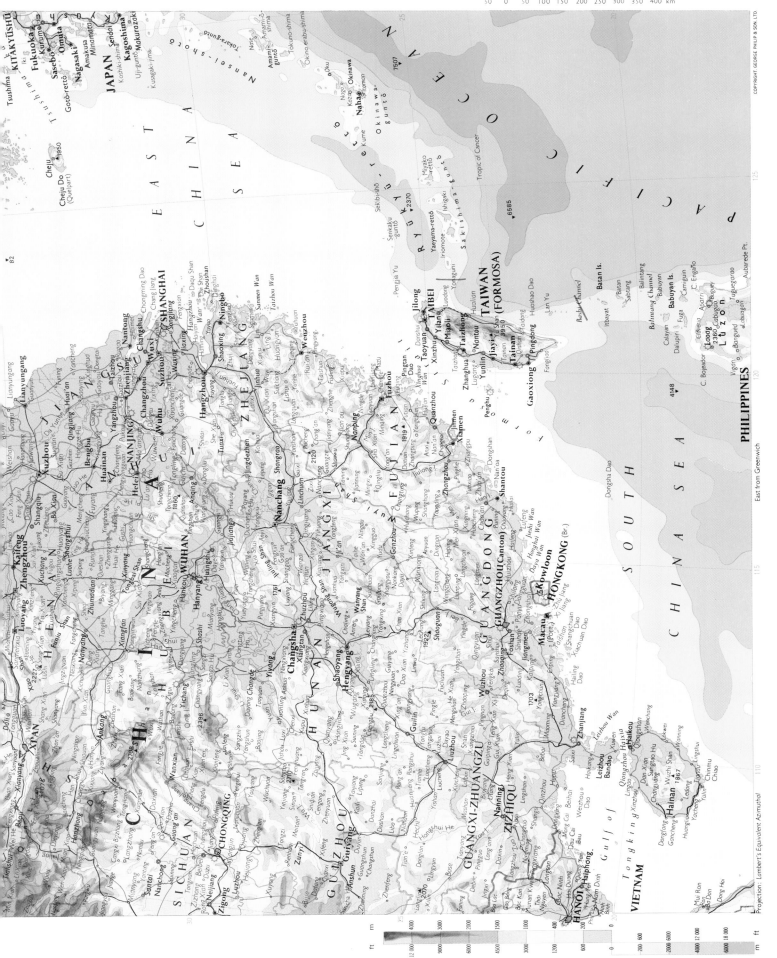

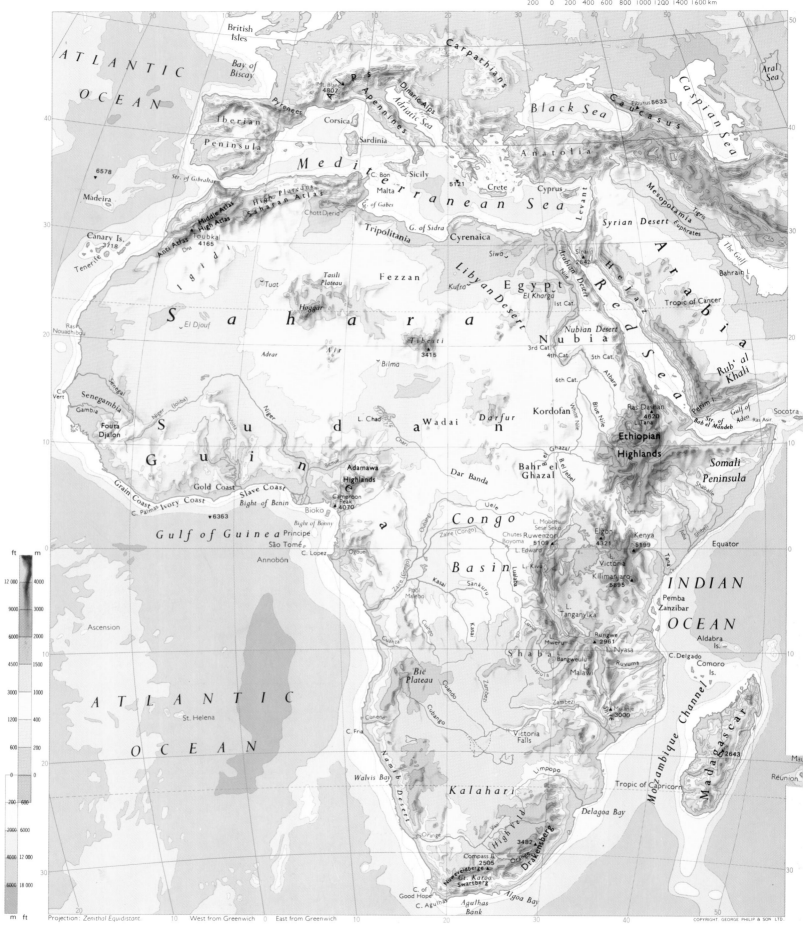

1 : 40 000 000

200   0   200   400   600   800   1000 miles

200   0   200   400   600 800 1000 1200 1400 1600 km

ATLANTIC

OCEAN

British
Isles

Bay of
Biscay

Carpathians

Alps

Mt. Blanc
4807

Pyrenees

Apennines

Dinaric Alps

Adriatic Sea

Corsica

Iberian

Peninsula

Sardinia

Black Sea

Caucasus

Elburus 5633

Caspian Sea

Aral
Sea

Anatolia

6578

Madeira

Str. of Gibraltar

Mediterranean Sea

C. Bon

Sicily

Malta

5121

Crete

Cyprus

Levant

Mesopotamia

Tigris

Euphrates

Middle Atlas

High Atlas

High Plateaux

Saharan Atlas

G. of Gabes

Chott Djerid

Syrian Desert

Arabia

Canary Is.

3718

Tenerife

Anti Atlas

Toubkal
4165

Dra

Igidi

Tuat

Tripolitania

G. of Sidra

Cyrenaica

Siwa

Arabian Desert

Sinai
2642

Hejaz

Red Sea

The Gulf

Bahrain I.

Tasili
Plateau

Fezzan

Egypt

Nile

El Kharga

1st Cat.

Libyan Desert

Kufra

Tropic of Cancer

Ras
Nouadhibou

S   a   h   a   r   a

El Djouf

Hoggar

Adrar

Air

Bilma

Tibesti

3415

Nubian Desert

3rd Cat.

4th Cat.

5th Cat.

Nubia

Rub' al
Khali

Perim I.

C.
Vert

Senegal

Senegambia

Gambia

Foura
Djalon

S   u   d

Niger (Joliba)

Niger

Volta

L. Chad

a   n

Wadai

Chari

Darfur

6th Cat.

Kordofan

White Nile

Blue Nile

Atbara

Ras Dashan
4620

L. Tana

Socotra

Str. of
Bab el Mandeb

Gulf of
Aden

Ras Asir

G   u   i   n   e   a

Grain Coast

Ivory Coast

Gold Coast

Slave Coast

Bight of Benin

Benue

Adamawa
Highlands

Cameroon
Peak
4070

Uele

Bahr el
Ghazal

Dar Banda

Bahr el Ghazal

Ethiopian
Highlands

Somali
Peninsula

Shabelle

C. Palmas

6363

Bight of Bonny

Bioko

Principe

Gulf of Guinea

São Tomé

C. Lopez

Ogoue

Zaire (Congo)

Congo

Ubangi

Zaire (Congo)

L. Mobutu
Sese Seko

Chutes Ruwenzori
Boyoma

L. Edward

Elgon
4321

Kenya
5199

Turkana

Juba

Shibeli

Equator

Annobón

Kasai

Sankuru

Lualaba

L. Kivu

Victoria

Kilimanjaro
5895

Tana

INDIAN

Basin

Ascension

ATLANTIC

St. Helena

OCEAN

Cuanza

Kwango

Cuango

Kasai

L.
Tanganyika

Pemba

Zanzibar

OCEAN

Aldabra
Is.

Mweru

Rungwe
2961

C. Delgado

Comoro
Is.

Shaba

L. Bangweulu

L. Nyasa

Ruvuma

Bié
Plateau

C. Fria

Cunene

Cuando

Cubango

Luapula

Malawi

Zambezi

Mlanje
3000

Mozambique Channel

Madagascar

Mai

Réunion

Walvis Bay

Namib Desert

Orange

Kalahari

Limpopo

Victoria
Falls

Tropic of Capricorn

2643

Vaal

High Veld

3482

Drakensberg

Delagoa Bay

Compass B.
2505

Nuweveldberge

Gt. Karoo

Swartberg

C. of
Good Hope

C. Agulhas

Agulhas
Bank

Algoa Bay

ft   m

12 000   4000

9000   3000

6000   2000

4500   1500

3000   1000

1200   400

600   200

0   0

200   600

2000 6000

4000 12 000

6000 18 000

m ft

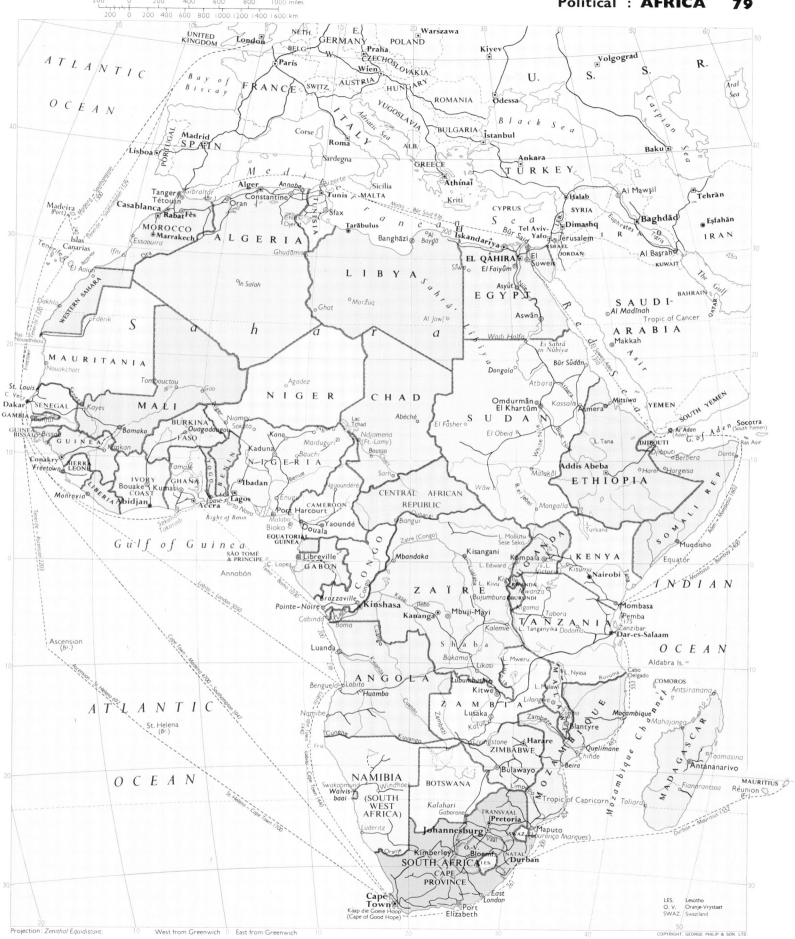

1:40 000 000

200   0   200   400   600   800   1000 miles
200   0   200   400   600   800   1000   1200   1400   1600 km

ATLANTIC

OCEAN

UNITED
KINGDOM   London   NETH.   GERMANY   POLAND   Warszawa
BELG.   Praha   CZECHOSLOVAKIA   Kiyev
Paris   FRANCE   Wien   HUNGARY   Volgograd
Bay of   SWITZ.   AUSTRIA   ROMANIA   Odessa   U. S. S. R.
Biscay   ITALY   YUGOSLAVIA   BULGARIA   İstanbul   Black Sea   Aral
Madrid   Corse   Roma   Adriatic Sea   GREECE   Athínai   TURKEY   Ankara   Baku   Caspian Sea   Sea
SPAIN   Sardegna   Kriti   CYPRUS   Al Mawşil   Tehrān
Lisboa   Madeira   Tanger   Gibraltar   Sicilia   Halab   SYRIA   Dimashq   Esfahān
(Port)   Tétouan   (Br.)   Bizerte   Annaba   MALTA   Tel Aviv-   Baghdād   IRAN
Casablanca   Alger   Constantine   Tunis   Tarābulus   El Iskandarîya   Yafo   Jerusalem   Al Basrah
Rabat Fès   Oran   Sfax   TUNISIA   ISRAEL   JORDAN   KUWAIT   The Gulf
MOROCCO   Chott   El   EL QÂHIRA   El Suweis   BAHRAIN
Marrakech   Djerid   El Faiyûm   SAUDI-   QATAR
Essaouira   ALGERIA   Ghudāmis   Banghâzi   El   Sîwa   Asyût   Madînah   ARABIA   Tropic of Cancer
Ifni   Dra   LIBYA   Bayda   Nile   Aswân   Makkah
WESTERN SAHARA   In Salah   Sahrā'   EGYPT   Wâdi Halfa   Es Sahrâ
El Aaiun   Ghat   Marzûq   Libîya   en Nûbiya   Dongola   Bûr Sûdân
Dakhla   Al Jawf   Atbara   Kassala   Asmera   YEMEN
MAURITANIA   Sahara   Agadez   Omdurmân   SOUTH YEMEN
Nouakchott   Tombouctou   El Khartûm   Al 'Adan   Socotra
St. Louis   Gao   NIGER   CHAD   Abéché   El Fâsher   SUDAN   (Aden)   (South Yemen)   Ras Asir
C. Ver.   SENEGAL   Kayes   MALI   El Obeid   L. Tana   DJIBOUTI   Dante
Dakar   Bamako   BURKINA   Niamey   Ndjamena   Bousso   Djibouti   Berbera
GAMBIA   GUINEA   FASO   Ouagadougou   Kano   (Ft.-Lamy)   Sarh   Addis Abeba   Harer   Hargeisa
BISSAU   Bissau   Kankan   Kaduna   Bauchi   Maiduguri   Nggoundéré   Bangui   Wâw   Bel Jebel   ETHIOPIA
Conakry   SIERRA   Tamale   NIGERIA   Benue   CENTRAL AFRICAN   Mongalla   L. Turkana
Freetown   LEONE   GHANA   BENIN   Ibadan   Enugu   REPUBLIC   Oubangui   L. Mobutu   SOMALI REP.
Monrovia   IVORY   Kumasi   TOGO   Lagos   CAMEROON   Bangui   Sese Seko   Muqdisho
LIBERIA   COAST   Bouake   Accra   Porto Novo   Yaoundé   Zaïre (Congo)   Kisangani   UGANDA   KENYA   INDIAN
Abidjan   Sekondi   Lomé   Port Harcourt   Malabo   Bioko   Douala   Kampala   L. Edward   Nairobi   Equator
Takoradi   Bight of Benin   EQUATORIAL   Libreville   CONGO   Mbandaka   L. Victoria   Kisumu   Mombasa
GUINEA   São Tomé   GABON   L. Kivu   RWANDA   Mwanza   OCEAN
Gulf of Guinea   SÃO TOMÉ & PRÍNCIPE   Brazzaville   ZAÏRE   Bujumbura   BURUNDI   Pemba
Annobón   Lopez   Pointe-Noire   Kinshasa   Ilebo   Kigoma   Tabora   Zanzibar
Ascension   Cabinda   Boma   Mbuji-Mayi   Kananga   TANZANIA   Dodoma   Dar-es-Salaam
(Br.)   Kasai   Shaba   L. Tanganyika
Luanda   Bukama   Kalemie   Cabo
ATLANTIC   ANGOLA   Likasi   L. Mweru   Aldabra Is.
St. Helena   Lubumbashi   L. Malawi   Delgado   COMOROS
(Br.)   Benguela   Lobito   Kitwe   L. Nyasa   Ruvuma   Antsiranana
Namibe   Huambo   ZAMBIA   Lilongwe   MALAWI   Moçambique   Mahajanga
Lusaka   MOZAMBIQUE   Blantyre   MADAGASCAR
Cunene   Livingstone   Harare   Quelimane   Antananarivo
OCEAN   Kuvango   ZIMBABWE   Beira   Toamasina
NAMIBIA   Bulawayo   Chinde   MAURITIUS
(SOUTH   Windhoek   BOTSWANA   Tropic of Capricorn   Réunion (Fr.)
WEST   Swakopmund   Kalahari   Gaborone   Limpopo   Toliara
AFRICA)   Walvis-baai   TRANSVAAL   Pretoria   Maputo (Lourenço Marques)
Lüderitz   Johannesburg   SWAZ.
Oranje   Kimberley   O.V.   Bloem.   NATAL   Durban
SOUTH AFRICA   LES.
CAPE   East
PROVINCE   London
Cape   Kaap die Goeie Hoop   Port
Town   (Cape of Good Hope)   Elizabeth

Projection: Zenithal Equidistant.   West from Greenwich   East from Greenwich

LES.   Lesotho
O. V.   Oranje-Vrystaat
SWAZ.   Swaziland

COPYRIGHT GEORGE PHILIP & SON LTD.

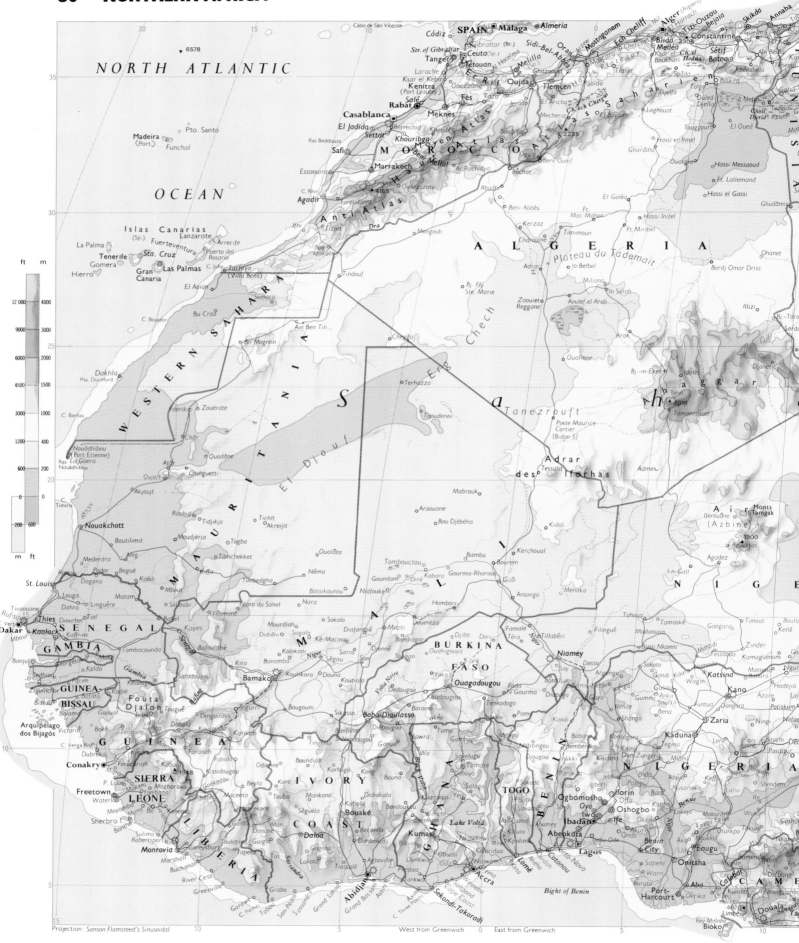

NORTH ATLANTIC

OCEAN

SPAIN

MOROCCO

ALGERIA

WESTERN SAHARA

MAURITANIA

MALI

NIGER

SENEGAL

GAMBIA

GUINEA BISSAU

GUINEA

SIERRA LEONE

LIBERIA

IVORY COAST

GHANA

BURKINA FASO

TOGO

BENIN

NIGERIA

Bight of Benin

Projection: Sanson Flamsteed's Sinusoidal

West from Greenwich   East from Greenwich

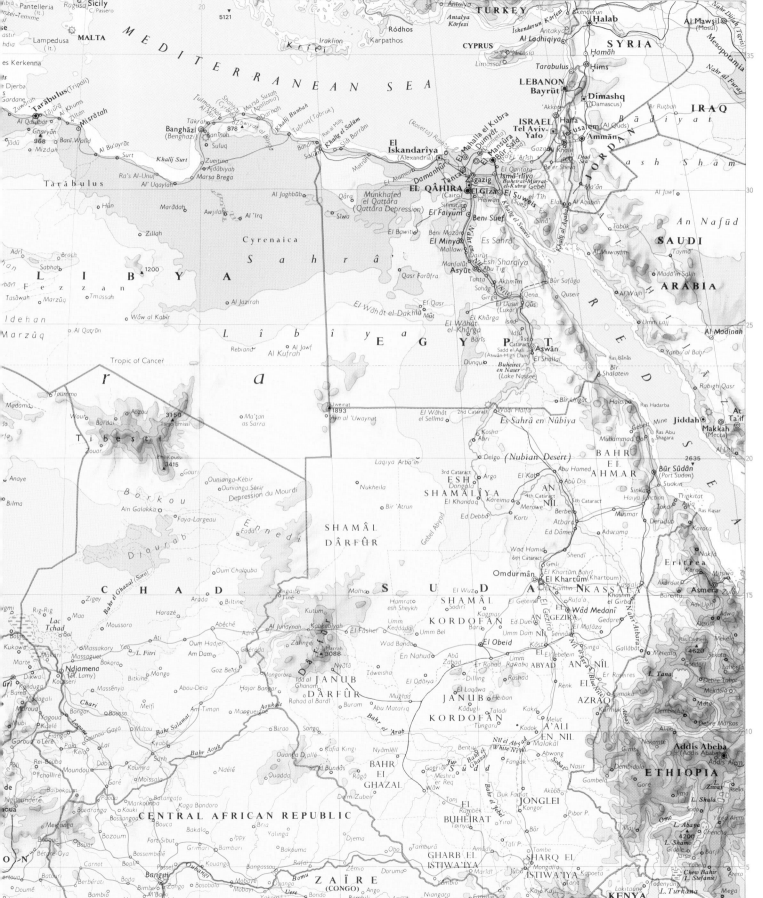

1:15 000 000

100   0   100   200   300   400 miles
100   0   100   200   300   400   500   600 km

MEDITERRANEAN SEA

TURKEY

Antalya
Antalya Körfezi
Ródhos
Karpathos
Iskenderun Körfezi
Antakya
Nahr el Nîl
Al Mawşil
(Mosul)
Halab

CYPRUS
Nicosia
Limassol
Al Ladhiqiya
Hamāh
Ḥimṣ
SYRIA

Tarabulus
LEBANON
Bayrūt
Akkā
Dimashq
(Damascus)
IRAQ

Mesopotamia

Pantelleria
Ragusa   Sicily
C. Passero
MALTA
Lampedusa (It.)

Tarabulus (Tripoli)
Tājūra
Al Khums
Misrātah
Gharyān   968
Mizdah
Al Qubbah   Al Aziziyah

El Iskandariya
(Alexandria)
Damanhûr   El Maḥalla el Kubra
Tantã
Zagazig   El Manṣûra
Dumyât   Pôr Saîd
El 'Arîsh
Gaza
ISRAEL
Tel Aviv-Yafo
Haifa
Jerusalem (Al Quds)
JORDAN
'Ammān
Bādiyat
ash Shām

Banghāzi
(Benghazi)   Bantnah
Suluq   878
Ajdābiyah
Marsa Brega

El Qâhira
(Cairo)
El Gîza
Helwân
Ismā'îliya
El Suweis
(Suez)
Beer Sheva
El Qantara
Dead Sea
Elat
Al 'Aqabah
Ma'ān
Al Jawf

Tarābulus

Al Jaghbūb
Qâra
Munkhafed
el Qattâra
(Qattara Depression)
Siwa
El Faiyûm
Beni Suef

Sinā
Gebel
et Tîh
Tabūk
An Nafūd
SAUDI
ARABIA

Hūn
Marādah

El Bawîti
Beni Mazâr
El Minya
Mallawi
Es Sahrâ
el Gharbîya

Asyûṭ
Abu Tîg
Dairût
Manfalûṭ
Esh Sharqîya

Mada'in Ṣālih
Taymā'

Zillah   1200
Cyrenaica
Sahrâ'

Qasr Farâfra
El Wâhât el-Dakhla   Mûṭ
El Qasr

Tahta
Sohâg
Akhmîm
Girga
El Uqṣur
(Luxor)
Qena
Quseir
Būr Safâga

Al Wajh

LIBYA
Libiya

El Wâhât
el-Khârga
Baris
El Khârga
Isnā
Idfu

Aswân
(Aswân High Dam)
El Shallâl
Ras Bânâs
Bîr
Shalatein

Rabigh Qasr
Al Madînah

Idehan
Marzûq

Tropic of Cancer

Al Kufrah
Rebiana
Al Jawf

Dûnqu
Buheiret
en Naser
(Lake Nasser)

Halaib
Ras Hadarba

Yanbu' al Bahr

Taoummo   3150
Tarso Emissi
3415

Ma'tan
as Sarra
Uweinat
1893
Ayn al 'Uwaynāt

El Wâhât
el Selîma
Wadi Halfa
2nd Cataract

Es Sahrâ en Nûbiya

Bîr Ungât

Gebel Mine
Muhammad Qol
Ras Shagara
Gebel
2635
Jiddah
Makkah
(Mecca)
At Ta'if
Al Lîth

Tibesti
Zouar
Bardai

Nukheila
3rd Cataract

Kosha
Abri
Delgo

(Nubian Desert)

BAHR
EL
AHMAR

Bûr Sûdân
(Port Sudan)
Sinkat
Suakin
Trinkitat
Tokar
Ras Kasar

Ounianga-Kébir
Ounianga Sérir
Depression du Mourdi

Bir 'Atrun

Abu Hamed
Abū Dis
Argo
El Kab
Dongola
El Khandaq
Kareima
Korti
Merowe
Berber
Atbara
Ed Dâmer

4th Cataract
5th Cataract

ESH
SHAMÂLÎYA
AN
NÎL

Haiya Junction
Derudub
Karoka

Anaye

Borkou
Faya-Largeau
Fada
Ennedi

Ed Debba

Wad Hamid
6th Cataract
Shendî
Geili

Adarama
Musmar

Nakfa
Eritrea
Kareb
Mitsiwa

Bilma

Aozou

Diourab

Gebel Abyad

Omdurmân
El Khartûm Bahri
(Khartoum)
El Khartûm

Kassala
Akordat
Barentu
Asmera
Zula
Adi Ugri

Rig-Rig
Mao
Harazé
Biltine
Tiné
Hamrato
esh Sheykh
Sodiri
El Wuz

NKASSALA
SHAMÂL
KORDOFAN

Rufa'a
Khashm
el Girba
Adi Keyih
Adwa
Aksum

CHAD
Lac
Tchad
Bol
Ati
Moussoro

Kutum
Kabkâbiya
Kagmar

Wâd Medanî
EL GEZIRA
Gedaref

Mekele
4620
Metema
Gondar
Sekota

Kukawa
Bosso

Massakory
Yao
L. Fitri

Abéché
Adre
Gereda
Am Dam

DARFUR
3088

El Fasher
Umm
Keddâda
Umm Bel

Wad Banda
En Nahud

El Obeid
Er Rahad
El Mazmûm
Singa
Sennâr

AN
NÎL
EL
AZRAQ

Gallâbât
L. Tana
Debre Tabor
Lalibela

Ndjamena
El Lamy
Chari
Bitkine
Mongo
Bokoro
Massénya

Zalingei
Idd el Ghanam

JANUB
DÂRFÛR

Abû
Zabad
Dilling
Rashad
Heiban
Kadugli
Talodi
Kaka

El Roseires
Kurmuk
Famaka

Dembecha
Debre Markos

Dikwa
Kousséri
Bongor
Melfi

Rahad el Bardî
Buram
Abu Matariq
Mugläd
El Laqâwa

JANUB
KORDOFAN

Tungaru
Kodok
Melut
A'ALI
EN NIL

Gimbi
Nekemte

Addis Abeba
(Addis Ababa)
Addis Alem

Yogoua
Kélo
Lère
Pala
Lai
Kyabé
Sarh

Birao
Songo

Bahr el 'Arab
Bentiu
Nîl el Abyad
(White Nile)
Malakal
Abwong
Sobat
Nasir

ETHIOPIA
Gore

Garoua
Rei-Bouba
Tcholliré
Baïbokoum
Doba
Moundou
Koumra
Moïssala

Ouanda Djallé
Kafia Kingi
Nyamlell
Meshra
er Req
Wâw
Raga

BAHR
EL
GHAZAL
Tur Su d d
Gogrial
Toni
Yirol

L. Abaya
Soddu
Dembidolo
L. Shala

Ngaoundéré

Batangafo
Kaga Bandoro
Bossangoa
Ippy
Bria
Yalinga

Deim Zubeir

EL
BUHEIRAT
Tombe
Amadi
Tali

Bôr

JONGLEI
Pibor P.
Kongor
Duk Faiwil
Akobo

L. Ziway
4200
L. Shamo
Gidole
Burji

Bétaré-Oya
Bouar
Baboua
Bocaranga
Bouca
Bakala
Bambari
Bakouma
Djema
Zémio

Yabelo

CENTRAL AFRICAN REPUBLIC

Tamburâ
Gharb El
Istiwa'iya
Jûba
Sharq El
Istiwa'iya
Kapoeta

Chew Bahir
(L. Stefanie)
Arero

Bétou
Bangui
Bimbo
Zongo
Mobaye
Bosobolo
Mobayi
Bomu
Ouango

ZAÏRE
(CONGO)
Uere
Bondo
Yakoma
Ango

Doruma
Zêmio
Marïdi

Niangara
Dungu
Faradje

Amadi
Kajo Kaji

Lokitaung
Todenyang
L. Turkana

KENYA

COPYRIGHT. GEORGE PHILIP & SON. LTD

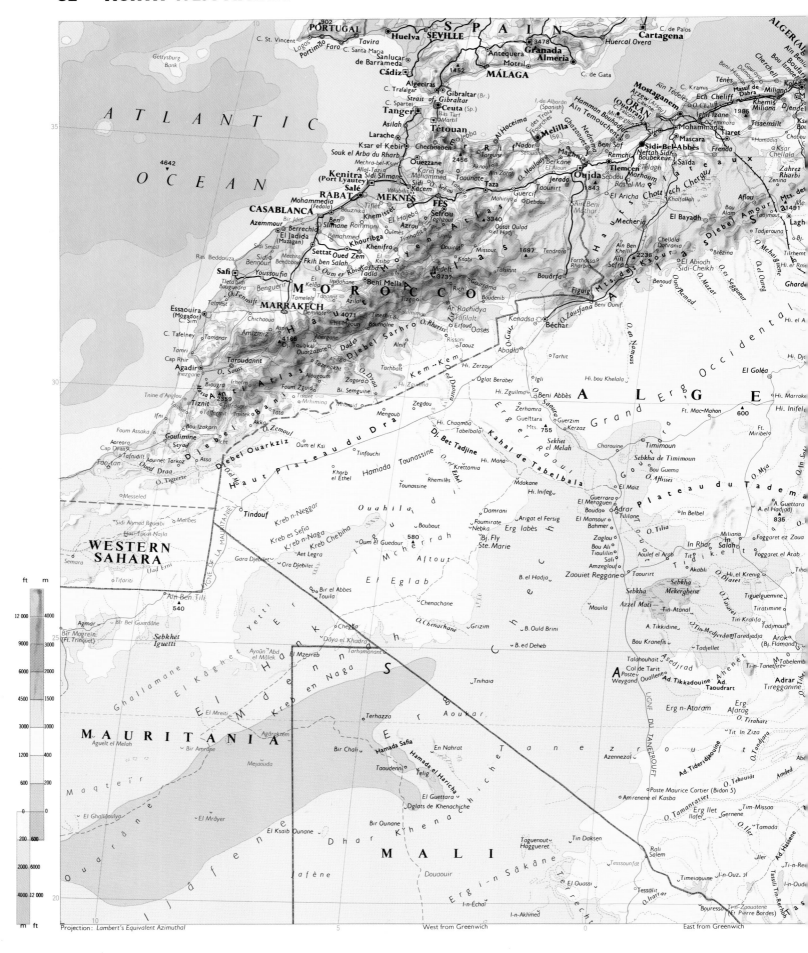

ft m

12 000 — 4000

9000 — 3000

6000 — 2000

4500 — 1500

3000 — 1000

1200 — 400

600 — 200

0 — 0

200 — 600

2000 — 6000

4000 — 12 000

m ft

Projection: Lambert's Equivalent Azimuthal

West from Greenwich   East from Greenwich

1:8 000 000

50   50   100   150   200 miles
50 0 50 100 150 200 250 300 km

SICILY Etna 3340
Marsala   C. Spartivento
Agrigento Caltanissetta **CATANIA**
Ragusa Siracusa C. Passero

M E D I T E R R A N E A N   S E A

Pantelleria (Italian)
Linosa I.
Lampione I. Lampedusa
Valletta **MALTA**

Bizerte (Binzert)
Menzel Bourguiba Mateur Tabarka
Skikda Annaba Béja Halq el Oued
TUNIS Nabeul Menzel-Temime
CONSTANTINE Guelma Hammamet C. Bon
El Eulma Sedrata Zaghouan G. de Hammamet
Sétif Aïn M'lila Souk Ahras El Kef Kalaa-Kebira
Bordj bou Arreridj Oum-el-Bouaghi Maktar **Sousse**
Batna Khenchela Thala Monastir Moknine
Biskra Tébessa Kairouan El Mahdia
Aïn Touta Feriana Sbeitla Djem Rass Kaboudia
Ouled Djellal Négrine Menzel Chaker Djebiniana
Tolga Tamerza **Sfax** Iles Kerkenna
Chott Melrhir **Gafsa** G. de Gabès
El Meghaier Nefta Tozeur **Gabès** Djerba I.
Djamâa Chott Djerid Hamma El Kantara Zarzis
El Oued Douz Médenine
Touggourt Tataouine Bahiret el Bibane

Tarābulus (Tripoli) Al Khums Leptis Magna (Labdah)
Zuwārah Az Zāwiyah Tarhūnah Tāwurghā'
Zliten Misrātah
Jabal Nafūsah Gharyān Bir al Malfa
Nālūt Jādū 968 Wādi Bani Walīd Sabkhat Tāwurghā' Khalij Surt (Gulf of Sidra)
716 Mizdah Surt Es Sider Ra's Al-Unuf
Ghudāmis Daraj AL AL QADDĀHIYAH Marsa Brega
GHARYĀN KHUMS W. Zamzam Ajdābiyah
Al Qaryah ash Sharqīyah Bu Nujaym Al Husayyūt

Banghāzī (Benghazi) Tūkrah Al Abyār
Kurkūrah Suluq

Al Hammādah al Hamrā'
Plateau du Tinrhert Waddān Jabal Waddān Taghrīfat
Jabal as Sawdā' 840 Al Hufrah Hūn Zillah Al Haruj al Aswad
S A B H A Zaltan

Bordj Omar Driss El Bir Adri Barqin Wādi ash Shāti
In Amenas Brach Sumnū 1200
Irhôrharene Umm al'Abīd
Tabelbalet Al Abyaḍ **Sabhah (Sebha)**
Awbārī Ghadir Oāhirah Ar Raml
L I B Y A
Goddua Umm al Aránb
Tasāwuh Trāghān Tarbū
Bir Tin Abunda Marzūq Mu'tan Majjūl
945 W. Barjij Al Hufrah Marqa Wāw al Kabīr

Tassili Ad Edekel Ghāt 1428 Al Barkāt A W B Ā R Ī Al Qatrūn
Adrar 2254 Tin Alkoum Madrusah
Djanet Idehan Marzūq Tajarhī B. Zāmūs 583
Erg Tin Merzouga

Tropic of Cancer

Taiga Madema Sarīr Tibasti
Tamanrasset Tazatat Ghelini
J. Nugayy
Hamada Toummo Tēnērē Tibasti
Mangueni Tummo Dhoba Passe de Kourizo Idd Chiussu
Plateau du Djado Madama Massif d'Afafi Yedri Tuzugu
Djado Latouma Omchi Tarso Emissi 3150 Pic Bette Massif 2286
Chirfa Fezzane Pic Touside 3265 Tarso Ourari Kemet
Sobozo Bardaî Yebbi-Souma Tarso Tieroko 2910
Zouar Sherda **T i b e s t i**
Mabrous Bini Erde
N I G E R **C H A D** Emi Koussi 3415 Gouro

Massif de Terazit

COPYRIGHT. GEORGE PHILIP & SON. LTD.

1:8 000 000

50   50   100   150   200 miles
50   50   100   150   200   250   300 km

NIGER Bosso   Lac
Tchad
CHAD

Arege
Tobo Gashagar
Zari
Kukawa   Baga
Gubio Titiwa   Mongonu
Marte Ngala   Makari
Masbaa Yajua Tokombere Kumshe
Dumboa Dikwa Gwoza Mora
Chibuk Madagali Mokolo
Askira Mkhika
Gombi Malabu Guider
Mubi Mendif
Kaele
Ribaa Song Zummo Binder
Benoué Lere
Garoua
Poli

N. E.
NIGERIA
on same scale
as general map

ALGERIA

Adrar des Iforhas

NIGER

Aïr
(Azbine)

Agadez
(Agadés)

Tahoua

Niamey

SOKOTO

Sokoto   Katsina   Kano

KANO

Maiduguri

BORNO

Zaria

KADUNA

Kaduna

Jos   Plateau

Bauchi

GOMBE

NIGERIA

Abuja

Minna

Bida

Ilorin

Ogbomosho

OYO

IBADAN
Abeokuta

LAGOS

Porto-Novo
Cotonou
Lomé
ACCRA
Tema

Benin
City

BENDEL

Warri

Onitsha

Enugu

ANAMBRA

CROSS
RIVER

Calabar

Port-Harcourt

Aba

Owerri

BENUE

Makurdi

Lafia

Yola

GONGOLA

CAMEROON

DOUALA
Yaoundé

Buea
Limbe

Cameroun 4070

EQUATORIAL GUINEA

BIOKO
(FERNANDO POO)

Bight of Bonny

Slave Coast

Bight of

Benin

Niger

Delta

OF   GUINEA

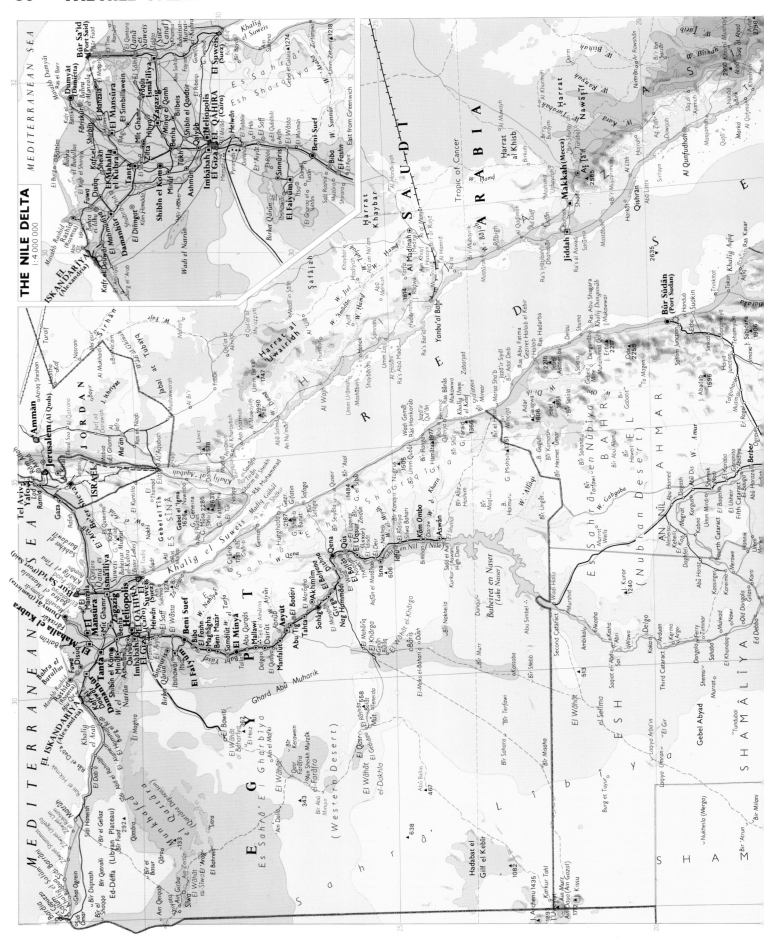

THE NILE DELTA
1:4 000 000

MEDITERRANEAN SEA

1:8 000 000

Projection: Lambert's Equivalent Azimuthal

East from Greenwich

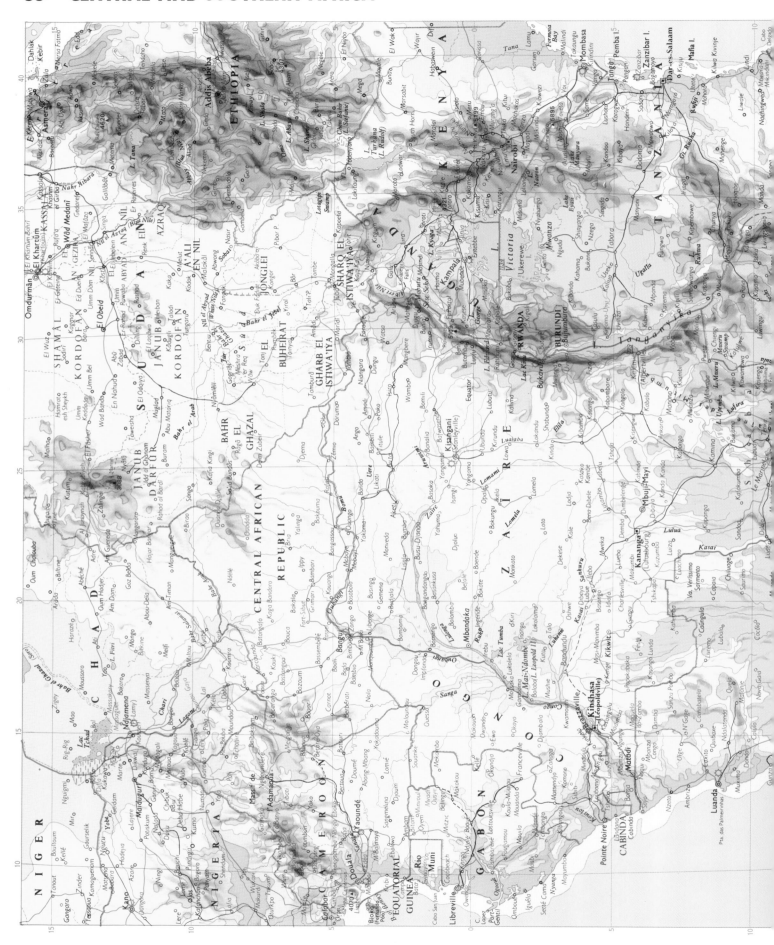

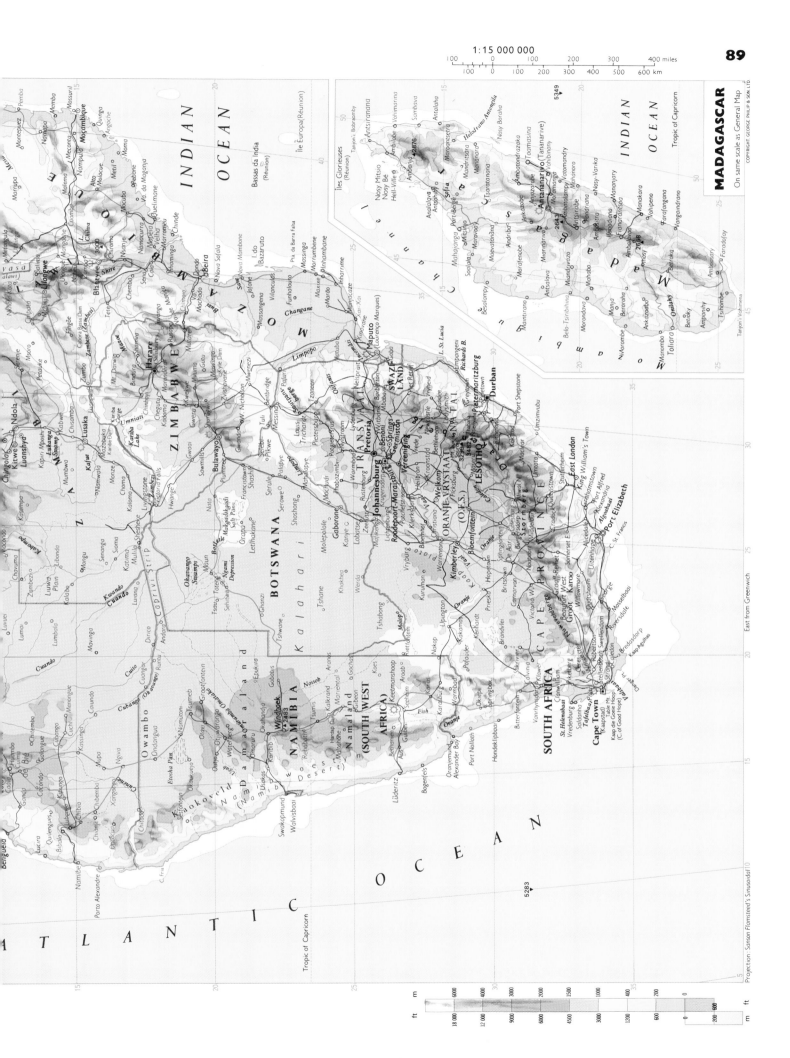

1:15 000 000

100   200   300   400 miles
100   0   100   200   300   400   500   600 km

MADAGASCAR
On same scale as General Map

COPYRIGHT GEORGE PHILIP & SON LTD

INDIAN

OCEAN

Tropic of Capricorn

5349

2643

2876

2638

INDIAN

OCEAN

Tropic of Capricorn

M O Ç A M B I Q U E

INDIAN

OCEAN

Ïle Europa (Reunion)

Bassas da India

Iles Glorieuses
(Reunion)

Nosy Mitsio
Nosy Bé
Hell-Ville

C h a n n e l

M o ç a m b i q u e

Z A M B I A

Harare

ZIMBABWE

Bulawayo

Limpopo

Maputo
(Lourenço Marques)

SWAZI
LAND

NATAL

Pietermaritzburg
Durban

Port Shepstone

Lusaka

Livingstone

Victoria Falls

Kariba Lake

Ndola

Kitwe

B O T S W A N A

K a l a h a r i

Gaborone

Okavango
Swamps

Ngami
Depression

TRANSVAAL

Pretoria
Benoni
Springs
Johannesburg
Vereeniging
Roodepoort-Maraisburg
Klerksdorp
Kimberley
Welkom
Bloemfontein

ORANJE-
VRYSTAAT
(O.F.S.)

LESOTHO

East London

Port Elizabeth

N A M I B I A

(S O U T H   W E S T

A F R I C A)

Windhoek

Walvisbaai
Swakopmund

N a m i b   D e s e r t

Kalahari

C A P E   P R O V I N C E

Groot
Karoo

Great Karoo

SOUTH AFRICA

Cape Town
(Kaapstad)
Kaap die Goeie Hoop
(C. of Good Hope)

Kaap Agulhas

A T L A N T I C   O C E A N

Tropic of Capricorn

East from Greenwich

5283

Projection: Sanson Flamsteed's Sinusoidal 10

m   6000   4000   3000   2000   1500   1000   400   200   0
ft   18 000 12 000 9000   6000   4500   3000   1200   600   0
                                                                m   200–600

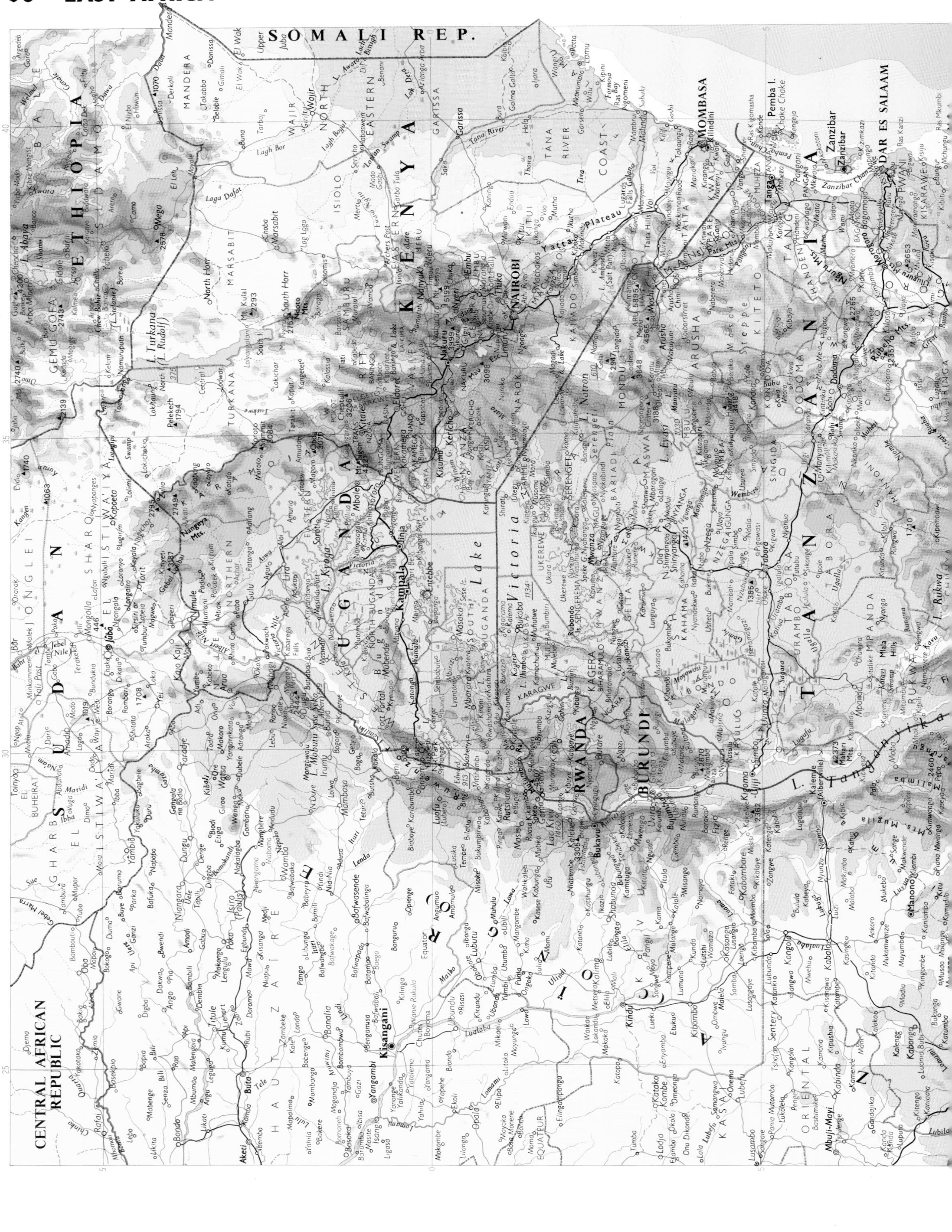

SOMALI REP.

ETHIOPIA

SUDAN

KENYA

UGANDA

TANZANIA

ZAÏRE

RWANDA

BURUNDI

CENTRAL AFRICAN REPUBLIC

NAIROBI

MOMBASA

DAR ES SALAAM

Zanzibar

Pemba I.

L. Victoria

L. Tanganyika

L. Turkana (L. Rudolf)

L. Kyoga

L. Albert

L. Edward

L. Kivu

1:8 000 000

50 0 50 100 150 200 miles

50 0 100 200 300 km

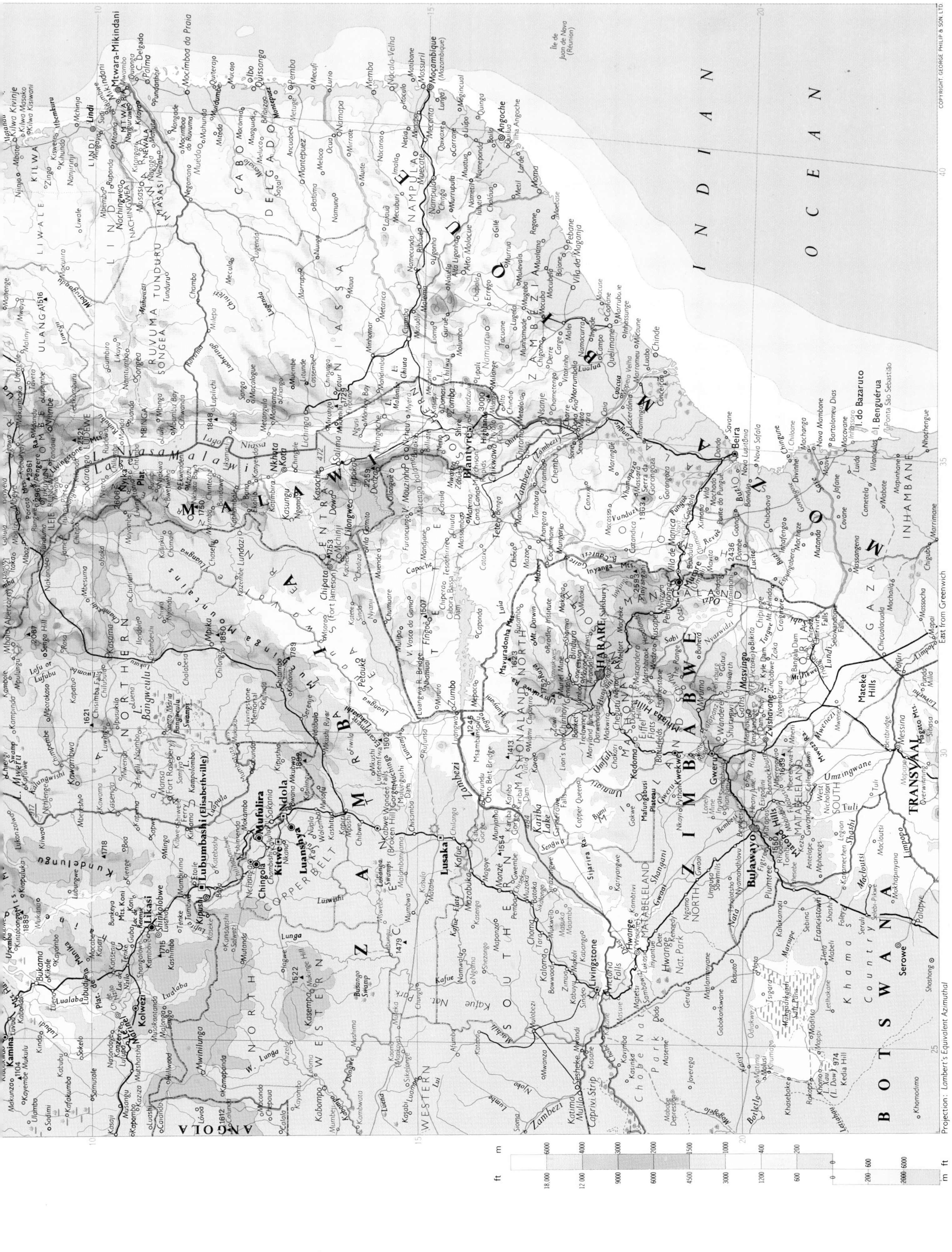

INDIAN OCEAN
ZAMBIA
MALAWI
ZIMBABWE
MOÇAMBIQUE
BOTSWANA
ANGOLA
TRANSVAAL
Lusaka
HARARE (Salisbury)
Bulawayo
Blantyre
Lilongwe
Beira
Lubumbashi (Elisabethville)
Kariba Lake
Victoria Falls
Projection: Lambert's Equivalent Azimuthal
East from Greenwich
COPYRIGHT GEORGE PHILIP & SON LTD.
m 6000 4000 3000 2000 1500 1000 400 200 0
ft 18 000 12 000 9000 6000 4500 3000 1200 600 0
0 200 600 2000 6000 m ft

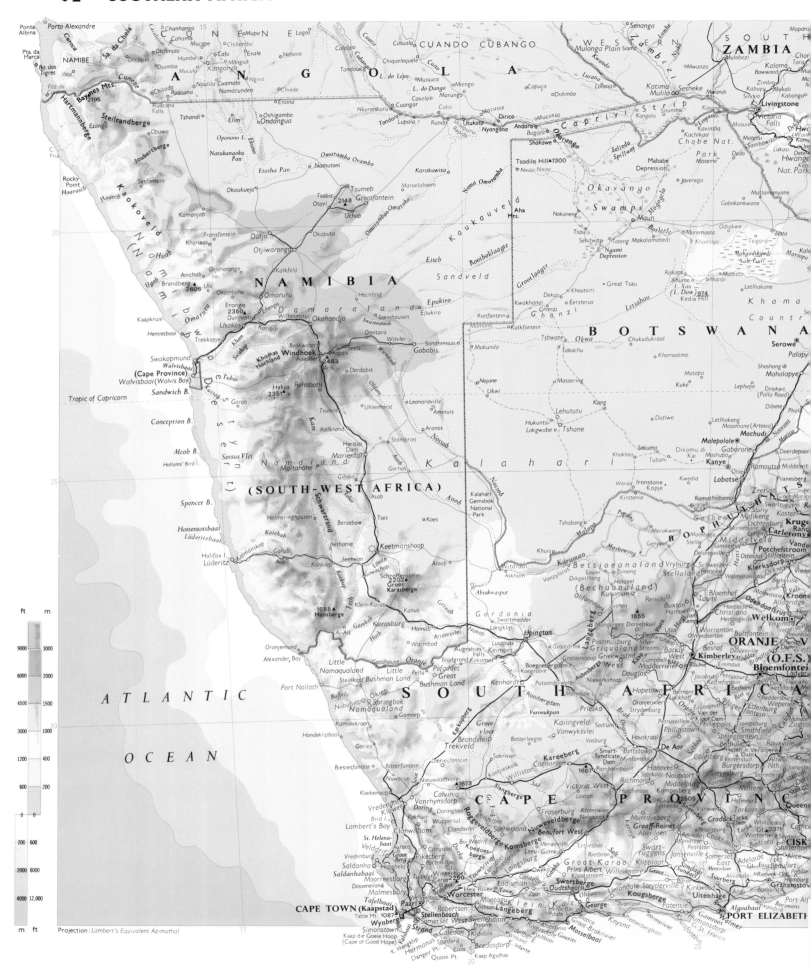

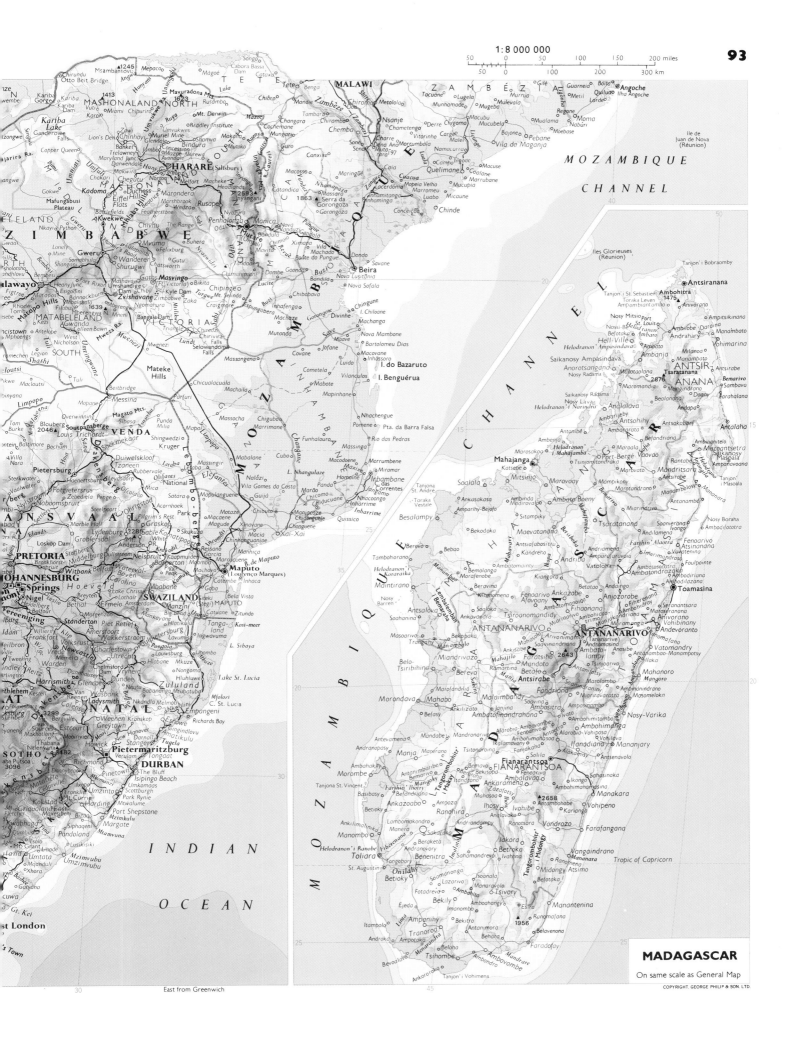

1 : 8 000 000

50   0   100   150   200 miles
50   0   100   200   300 km

MOZAMBIQUE

CHANNEL

TETE

MALAWI   Z A M B É Z I A

MOZAMBIQUE

ZIMBABWE

HARARE (Salisbury)

Beira

Nova Lusitânia

MATABELELAND

SOUTH

VICTORIA

VENDA

SOUTH

PRETORIA

JOHANNESBURG
Springs
Nigel

SWAZILAND

Maputo
(Lourenço Marques)

MAPUTO

NATAL

DURBAN

PIETERMARITZBURG

Lake St. Lucia

INDIAN

OCEAN

East London

Town

East from Greenwich

I. do Bazaruto

I. Benguérua

Pta. da Barra Falsa

Ile de
Juan de Nova
(Réunion)

Angoche

Iles Glorieuses
(Réunion)

Antsiranana

Ambohitra
1475

ANTSIR-
ANANA

Tsaratanana
2876

Mahajanga

Toamasina

ANTANANARIVO

ANTANANARIVO

Antsirabe

2643

FIANARANTSOA

Toliara

Tropic of Capricorn

Faradofay

Tsihombe

MADAGASCAR

On same scale as General Map

EUROPE U. S. S. R.

Leningrad
Moskva
Sverdlovsk
Omsk
Novosibirsk
Tomsk
Irkutsk
Chita
Omsk
Volga
Barnaul
Yenisei
Semipalatinsk
Ozero Baykal
Ulan Ude
Blagoveshchensk Amur
Khabarovsk
Sakhalin
Kamchatka
Komandorskie Is. (U.S.S.R.)
Petropavlovsk
Sea of Okhotsk
Okhotsk

Karaganda
L. Balkhash
Hovd
Ulyasutay
Ulaanbaatar
MONGOLIA
Manchuria
Harbin
Changchun
Vladivostok
Hakodate
La Perouse Strait
10.542
Kuril Trench
Yokohama Vancouver 4280
Kuril Is.
Near
7822
Kiska
Andrean
Aleutian
Aleutian Trench

Aral Sea
Alma Ata
Urumqi
A S I A
Shenyang
N. Antung
KOREA
Sendai
Emperor Seamount Chain
KURO SIWO
7168

Tashkent
Samarkand
Beijing
Tianjin
Luda
Söul's
Pusan
JAPAN
Kyōto
TOKYO
Nagoya
Yokohama
3389

AFGHANISTAN
Kabul
Srinagar
Kunlun Shan
XIZANG (TIBET)
Lhasa
Mt. Everest 8848
CHINA
Xi'an
Lanzhou
Huang He
Jinan
Qingdao
SHANGHAI
Yellow Sea
Kitakyūshū
Nagasaki
Osaka
Shikoku
Fuji San 3776
Honshū Ridge
8412
Japan Trench
10.554

PAKISTAN
Lahore
Delhi
Agra
Kanpur
NEPAL
Chongqing
Wuhan
Chang Jiang
Changsha
Hangzhou
Wenzhou
Fuzhou
Xiamen
East China Sea
Ryūkyū Is.
KURO SIWO
Bonin Is.
Volcano Is.
Midway Is.
6603
Lisiar

Varanasi
Brahmaputra
BANGLA-DESH
Calcutta
INDIA
Chittagong
Mandalay
Kunming
Guangzhou
MACAU (Port.)
HONG KONG
Taibei
Taiwan (Formosa)
Necker Rid

Hyderabad
Cuttack
Ganges
BURMA
Chiengmai
Hanoi
Hainan
C. Engano
Northern Marianas
Wake I. (U.S.)
Marcus I.
P A
Marcus

Madras
Andaman Is.
Mergui Arch.
Rangoon
THAILAND (SIAM)
Bangkok
CAMBODIA
Manila
PHILIPPINES
Samar
Mariana Trench
Guam (U.S.)
11,022
M
U.S. TRUST TERR. OF THE PACIFIC ISLANDS
Bikini Atoll
Marshall Is.

Bay of Bengal
Isthmus of Kra
Phnom Penh
Phanh Bho Ho Chi Minh (Saigon)
C. Camau
South China Sea
Mindoro
Palawan
10,497
Sulu Sea
Yap
Belau
Eniwetok Atoll
i
c
r
o
n
e
s

SRI LANKA
Colombo
Nicobar Is.
1567
Gulf of Thailand
Kinabalu
SABAH
4101
Mindanao
Mindanao Trench
Fed. States of Micronesia
Truk
Ponape
Jaluit
EQUATORIAL
O

PENINSULAR MALAYSIA
George Town
Kuala Lumpur
Melaka
SINGAPORE
SARAWAK
BRUNEI
Natuna
Labuan
Celebes Sea
Caroline Islands
Butaritari
Gilbert Is.
Baker
(U.S)

Nias
Bangka
Palembang
Borneo
Celebes
Buru
Ceram
Halmahera
Dampier Strait
M e l a
n
e
s
NAURU
Banaba
Abariri

INDIAN
Sumatra
Java Sea
Jakarta
Ujung Pandang
Banda Sea
7440
Irian Jaya
5029
PAPUA NEW GUINEA
Bismarck Arch.
New Ireland
9103
Rabaul
New Britain
SOLOMON ISLANDS
9165
Sta. Cruz Is.
TUVALU (Ellice Is.)
Funafuti
Tok
(N

Semarang
Surabaya
Flores Sea
Bali
Lombok
Sumbawa
Sumba
Flores
Timor
Tanimbar Is.
Aru Is.
Madang
Lae
Port Moresby
Honiara
Guadalcanal
Wallis & Futuna (Fr.)
Rotuma

Christmas I. (Austral.)
7450
Java Trench
Torres Strait
Thursday I.
Arafura Sea
C. York
C. Arnhem
Louisiade Arch.
Coral Sea Islands Territory
Vanua Levu
WES
Suvo'
FIJI
244
Tong
Tren

Cocos (Keeling) Is. (Austral.)
Darwin
Ashmore Is.
Larrimah
Wyndham
G. of Carpentaria
Newcastle Waters
Cairns
Brisbane
Coral Sea
VANUATU
Chesterfield Is.
7670
Vanua Levu
10,82

O C E A N
N.W. Cape
Onslow
NORTHERN TERRITORY
Mt. Isa
Townsville
New Caledonia (Fr.)
Noumea
Loyalty Is.
TON
Friend

Shark Bay
Geraldton
Alice Springs
Longreach
AUSTRALIA
QUEENSLAND
Rockhampton
Maryborough
Great Divide
Norfolk I. (Aust.)
10,047
Kermadec Is. (N.Z.)
Kerm
Tren

Perth
Fremantle
Geographe Bay
Albany
WESTERN AUSTRALIA
Kalgoorlie
Oodnadatta
SOUTH AUSTRALIA
L. Eyre
Brisbane
Ipswich
Darling
NEW SOUTH WALES
Sydney
Newcastle
Lord Howe I. (Aust.)
S - A. 1274
Tasman Sea
Auckland
Hamilton
NEW ZEALAND

Cape Town - Fremantle 5615
Great Australian Bight
F - A. 1353
Adelaide
Murray
Canberra
Mt. Kosciusko 2230
Katoomba
Wollongong
1233R
Cook Strait
Palmerston N.
Wellington
Nelson

Amsterdam I. (Fr.)
St. Paul I. (Fr.)
Mid-Indian Ocean
K. George Sd.
Encounter Bay
Ballarat
Geelong
Melbourne
Bass Strait
Launceston
W. 1293
Mt. Cook 3764
Christchurch
Oamaru
Dunedin
Pac

Crozet Is. (Fr.)
Cape Town - Melbourne 5814
Cape Town - Hobart 5838
Indian Rise
TASMANIA
Hobart
AUSTRALIAN CURRENT
Invercargill
Stewart I.
Bounty Is. (N.Z.)
Antipodes Is. (N.Z.)

Kerguelen (Fr.)
Indian-Antarctic Ridge
Auckland Is. (N.Z.)
Macquarie Is. (Austral.)
Campbell I. (N.Z.)

Heard Is. (Aust.)

ft m
18.000 6000
12.000 4000
6000 2000
3000 1000
600 200
0 0
200 600
2000 6000
4000 12.000
6000 18.000
8000 24.000
m ft

Projection: Mollweide's Homolographic

East from Greenwich

____56/5____ Principal Shipping Routes
(Distances in Nautical Miles)

ALASKA   6050   L. Athabaska   GREENLAND
Gulf of Alaska   Churchill   Hudson   C. Farewell
Lol Bay   Sitka   Juneau   Dawson Creek   Lynn Lake   Bay   Belcher Is.   NORTH
Prince of Wales I.   Prince Albert   James   Hamilton Inlet
Prince Rupert   Kitimat   Edmonton   Bay   Labrador   Strait of Belle Isle
Queen Charlotte Is.   C A N A D A   Scheffervelle   Newfoundland
Vancouver   Saskatoon   L. Winnipeg   St. Lawrence   Anticosti   60
Vancouver I.   Victoria   NORTH   AMERICA   Quebec   G. of St. Lawrence   Pr. Edward I.   C. Race
Seattle   Spokane   Regina   Winnipeg   Sault Ste. Marie   Montréal   Fredericton   Saint John   C. Breton I.   Sable I.   Southampton 3091
Tacoma   Helena   Bismarck   Duluth   L. Superior   Ottawa   Toronto   L. Ontario   Boston   C. Sable   New York
Portland   Butte   Missouri   Minneapolis   Michigan   Detroit   Buffalo   Pittsburgh   NEW YORK   ATLANTIC
C. Blanco   Boise   St. Paul   Milwaukee   CHICAGO   Cincinnati   Philadelphia   Baltimore
Mendocino Seascarp   C. Mendocino   Cheyenne   Des Moines   Indianapolis   Washington   40
Sacramento   Salt Lake City   Denver   Kansas   St. Louis   Richmond   Norfolk   OCEAN
Oakland   Colorado   4418   UNITED STATES   Memphis   Atlanta   C. Hatteras
San Francisco   Santa Fé   Oklahoma   Little Rock   Savannah   Bermuda (U.K.)
2419   Los Angeles   El Paso   Dallas   Austin   Jacksonville
San Diego   Ciudad   New   Mobile   Tampa
Murray Seascarp   Juárez   Houston Orleans   Gulf of Mexico   Miami
Guadalupe   6225   San Antonio   Galveston
Hawaiian Is.   Pto. Eugenia   Sierra Madre   Monterrey   Florida   BAHAMAS
(U.S.A.)   Tropic of Cancer   Torreón   Tampico   CUBA   West Indies
Honolulu   Oahu   C.S. Lucas   San Luis Potosí   Mérida   Yucatan   La Habana   Hispaniola 9200
Hawaii   Revilla Gigedo Is.   Guadalajara   Mexico   Veracruz   Channel   HAITI DOM.   St. Thomas (U.S.)
I. (U.S.)   (Mexico)   Puebla   6700   JAMAICA   Kingston   Santo   PUERTO   Virgin Is.   Leeward
PACIFIC   4711   Acapulco   BELIZE   Domingo   RICO   Is.
Clarion Fracture Zone   GUATEMALA   HONDURAS   Caribbean Sea   Guadeloupe   BARBADOS
CURRENT   Guatemala   Tegucigalpa   Curaçao (Ne.)   Martinique   TRINIDAD &
Palmyra Is. (U.S.)   Clipperton Fracture Zone   Clipperton I. (Fr.)   EL SALVADOR   NICARAGUA   Windward   Windward Is.   TOBAGO
Teraina   CENTRAL   Managua   San José   Barranquilla   Maracaibo   Is.
Tabuaeran   AMERICA   PANAMA   Caracas
Kiritimati   COSTA RICA   Colón   Panamá   VENEZUELA   Orinoco
Jarvis I. (U.S.)   Cocos I.   Canal   Medellín   10
Bogotá
KIRIBATI   Malden I.   Cali   COLOMBIA
Starbuck I.   C.S. Francisco
Tongareva   Equator   Galápagos   Quito
Penrhyn Is.   (Ecuador)   Guayaquil   ECUADOR   Manaus
Manihiki   Vostok   Chimborazo 6287   Amazon
Suwarrow Is.   Flint I.   Cuenca   Iquitos   BRAZIL
Marquesas Is.   C. Pariñas   SOUTH
Leeward Is.   Chiclayo   706
Cook   Society Is.   Lobos Is.   Trujillo
Islands   1303   Windward   Tahiti   PERU   AMERICA
(N.Z.)   Manuae   Is.   Tuamotu Archipelago   6369   Lima   Cuzco   L. Titicaca   20
Tahiti – Panamá 4570   Callao   Illampu & Ancohuma
FRENCH POLYNESIA   Arequipa   6866   La Paz   6550
Rarotonga   Southeast   Peru   BOLIVIA
Austral   Pacific Basin   Arica
Seamount Chain   Chile   Iquique   PARAGUAY
Tubuai Is.   Pitcairn I. (U.K.)   Tropic of Capricorn   8050   Antofagasta   Salta   Asunción
(Austral Is.)   Ducie I.   Trench   795   Tucumán
Rapa Iti   Sala-y-Gomez   San Félix (Chile)   Corrientes
Easter Is.   (Chile)   San Ambrosio (Chile)   Paraná   Pto. Alegre
(Chile)   Arch. de Juan Fernández   Córdoba   Santa Fé
East Pacific Ridge   (Chile)   Aconcagua 6960   Rosario   Paysandú
Alejandro Selkirk   Valparaíso   URUGUAY
Pacific-Antarctic Ridge   Robinson Crusoe   Santiago   Buenos Aires   Montevideo
La Plata   Río de la Plata   40
Concepción   ARGENTINA   Mar del Plata
P.A.-Valparaíso   Neuquen   SOUTH
Chile Rise   1414   Buenos Aires – Montevideo   1355   1295
Pacific-   Chonos Arch.   ATLANTIC
WEST WIND DRIFT   Antarctic   P.A.   P. Deseado   Argentine
Basin   G. of Penas   Patagonia   6212   Basin   OCEAN
CAPE HORN CURRENT   Sta. Cruz   Arenas   Falkland Is. (U.K.)   50
Wellington   Punta Arenas   Stanley   South Georgia
I.   Str. of Magellan
Tierra del Fuego
C. Horn
West from Greenwich   COPYRIGHT. GEORGE. PHILIP & SON. LTD.

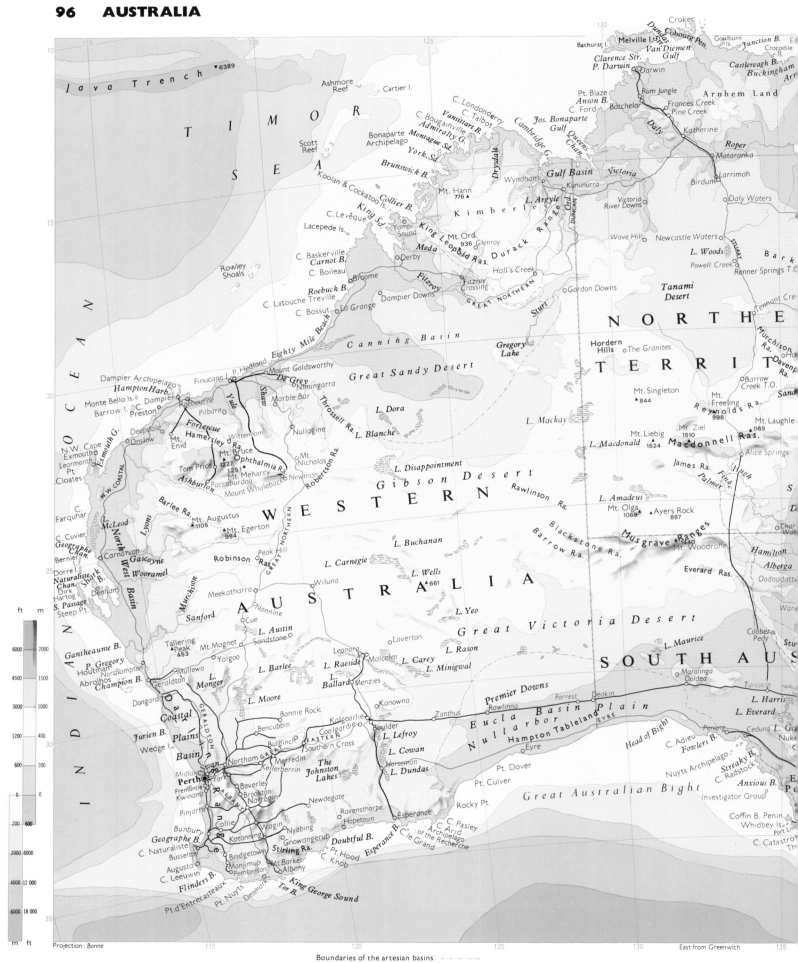

Java Trench ▼6389

TIMOR SEA

INDIAN OCEAN

Ashmore Reef
Cartier I.
Scott Reef
Rowley Shoals

C. Londonderry
C. Talbot
C. Bougainville
Admiralty G.
Vansittart B.
Bonaparte Archipelago
Montague Sd.
York Sd.
Brunswick B.
Koolan & Cockatoo Is.
C. Lévêque
King Sd.
Lacepede Is.
C. Baskerville
Carnot B.
C. Boileau
Roebuck B.
C. Latouche Treville
C. Bossut
La Grange

Croker
Dundas
Cobourg Pen.
Goulburn Is.
Junction B.
Crocodile Is.
Bathurst I.
Melville I.
Van'Diemen Gulf
Clarence Str.
P. Darwin
Darwin
Pt. Blaze
Anson B.
C. Ford
Batchelor
Rum Jungle
Frances Creek
Pine Creek
Castlereagh B.
Buckingham

Arnhem Land
Arn

Jos. Bonaparte Gulf
Cambridge G.
Queens Chan.
Wyndham
Gulf Basin
Kununurra
L. Argyle
Duncan

Daly
Katherine
Roper
Mataranka
Victoria
River Downs
Birdum
Larrimah
Daly Waters

Mt. Hann 776
Kimberley
Mt. Ord 936
Glenroy
Meda
Derby
Hall's Creek
Fitzroy Crossing
Fitzroy
Wave Hill
Newcastle Waters
L. Woods
Powell Creek
Renner Springs T.O.
Bark
Tennant Cre

King Leopold Ras.
Durack Range

Dampier Downs
La Grange

Gordon Downs
GREAT NORTHERN
Sturt

Gregory Lake
Hordern Hills
The Granites

NORTHE
TERRIT

Tanami Desert

Eighty Mile Beach
Canning Basin
Great Sandy Desert

Mt. Singleton
844
Mt. Freeling 998
Reynolds Ra.
Barrow Creek T.O.
Sand

Dampier Archipelago
Hampton Harb.
Finucane I.
P. Hedland
Mount Goldsworthy
De Grey
Nimingarra
Marble Bar
Shaw
Yule
Pilbara
Nullagine
Throssell Ra.
L. Dora
L. Blanche

Mt. Liebig 1169
Mt. Ziel 1510
Macdonnell Ras.
Mt. Laughle
L. Mackay
L. Macdonald 1524
Alice Springs

Monte Bello Is.
Barrow I.
C. Preston
Dampier
Roebourne
Fortescue
Deepdale
Onslow
Hamersley Ra.
Wittenoom
Mt. Enid
Mt. Bruce
Tom Price 1227
Ophthalmia Ra.
Mt. Meharry 1251
Parraburdoo
Ashburton
Mount Whaleback
Newman
Robertson Ra.
Mt. Nicholas

N.W. Cape
Exmouth
Learmonth
Pt. Cloates

Gibson Desert
L. Disappointment

Rawlinson Ra.
James Ra.
Hugh
Finke
Palmer

Mt. Olga 1069
Ayers Rock 867
L. Amadeus
Blackstone Ra.
Musgrave Ranges
Mt. Woodroffe 1440
Hamilton
Alberga
Oodnadat

WESTERN

C. Farquhar
C. McLeod
North West
Barlee Ra.
Mt. Augustus 1105
Mt. Egerton 994
Lyons
GREAT NORTHERN

AUSTRALIA

Everard Ras.

Coober Pedy
Stu

SOUTH AUS

C. Cuvier
Geographe Chan.
Bernier I.
Dorre I.
Naturaliste Chan.
Dirk Hartog I.
S. Passage
Steep Pt.
Shark B.
Denham
Carnarvon
Gascoyne
Wooramel
Murchison
Peak Hill
Robinson
Ras.

L. Buchanan
L. Carnegie
L. Wells 661
L. Yeo
Barrow Ra.

L. Maurice
Maralinga
Oodlea
Tarcoola

Gantheaume B.
P. Gregory
Houtman Abrolhos
Champion B.
Northampton
Geraldton
Dongara
Mullewa
Tallering Peak 453
Mt. Magnet
Yalgoo
L. Barlee
Sandstone
L. Austin
Cue
Nannine
Meekatharra
Sanford
Wiluna
Leonora
Malcolm
Laverton
L. Rason
L. Carey
L. Minigwal

Great Victoria Desert

L. Harris
L. Everard
L. Ga

Coastal
Plains
Basin
Jurien B.
Wedge I.
Dandaragan
L. Monger
L. Moore
Bonnie Rock
Bencubbin
Bullfinch
Southern Cross
EASTERN
Kalgoorlie
Coolgardie
Boulder
L. Lefroy
L. Cowan
Kanowna
L. Raeside
L. Ballard
Menzies

Premier Downs
Rawlinna
Forrest
Deakin
Eucla Basin
Nullarbor Plain
Hampton Tableland
EYRE
Eyre

Zanthus
Zanthus

Penong
Cedun L. Ga
Nuke

Midland
Perth
Fremantle
Kwinana
Swan
York
Northam
GREAT
Merredin
Kellerberrin
Beverley
Brookton
Narrogin
The Johnston Lakes
Norseman
L. Dundas

Pt. Dover
Pt. Culver
Head of Bight
C. Adieu
Fowlers B.
Nuyts Archipelago
C. Radstock
Streaky B.
Anxious B.
Investigator Group

Pinjarra
Newdegate
Ravensthorpe
Hopetoun
Esperance
Rocky Pt.
Great Australian Bight
Coffin B. Penin.
Whidbey Is.
Port L

Bunbury
Collie
Wagin
Nyabing
Gnowangerup
Doubtful B.
C. Pasley
C. Arid
Archipelago of the Recherche
C. le Grand
C. Catastro
Pe

Geographe B.
C. Naturaliste
Busselton
Augusta
C. Leeuwin
Bridgetown
Manjimup
Pemberton
ALBANY
Katanning
Stirling Ra.
Mt. Barker
Albany
Pt. Hood
C. Knob
Esperance B.

Flinders B.
Pt. d'Entrecasteaux
Pt. Nuyts
Denmark
Tor B.
King George Sound

ft   m
6000 2000
4500 1500
3000 1000
1200   400
600   200
0   0
200   600
2000 6000
4000 12 000
6000 18 000
m   ft

Projection: Bonne

Boundaries of the artesian basins ----------

East from Greenwich

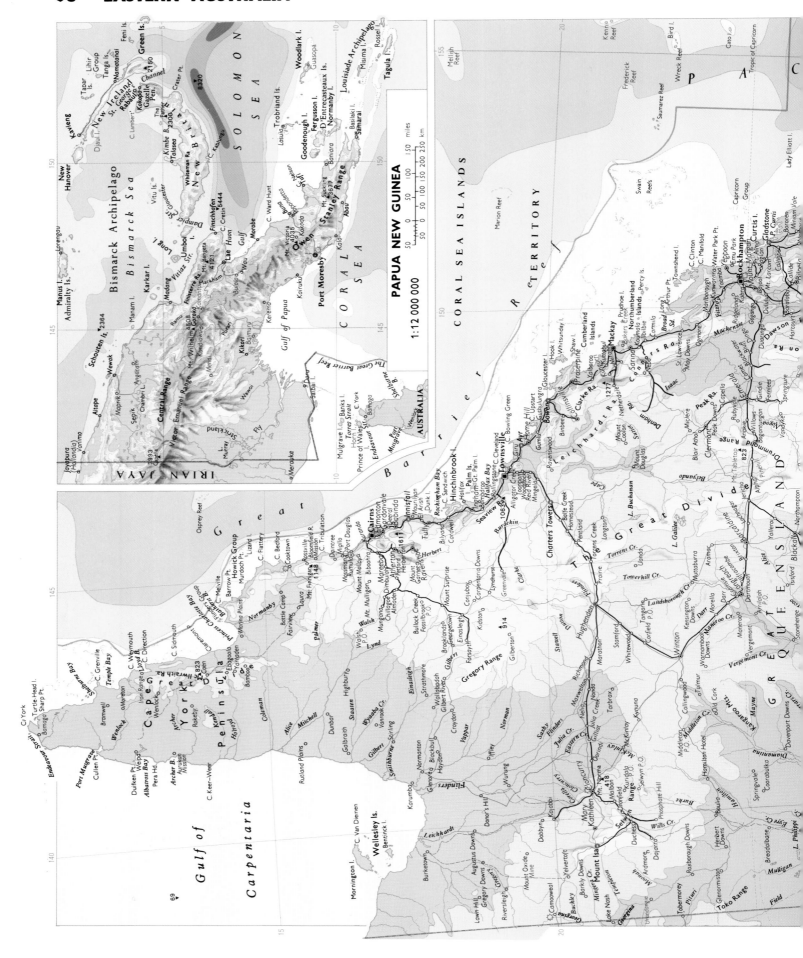

1:7 500 000

PACIFIC OCEAN

Tasman Sea

TASMANIA

Bass Strait

QUEENSLAND

NEW SOUTH WALES

SOUTH AUSTRALIA

VICTORIA

Great Dividing Range

Darling Downs

BRISBANE

SYDNEY

CANBERRA
AUSTRALIAN CAPITAL TERRITORY

MELBOURNE

ADELAIDE

Newcastle

Wollongong

Broken Hill

Maryborough
Gympie

Lake Eyre North

Lake Eyre South

Lake Torrens

Lake Frome

Lake Gairdner

Murray R.

Darling R.

Kangaroo I.

Spencer Gulf

Gulf St Vincent

Flinders Ranges

Grey Range

Barrier Range

Hobart

Launceston

Projection: Bonne

East from Greenwich

COPYRIGHT GEORGE PHILIP & SON LTD

Continuation Southwards

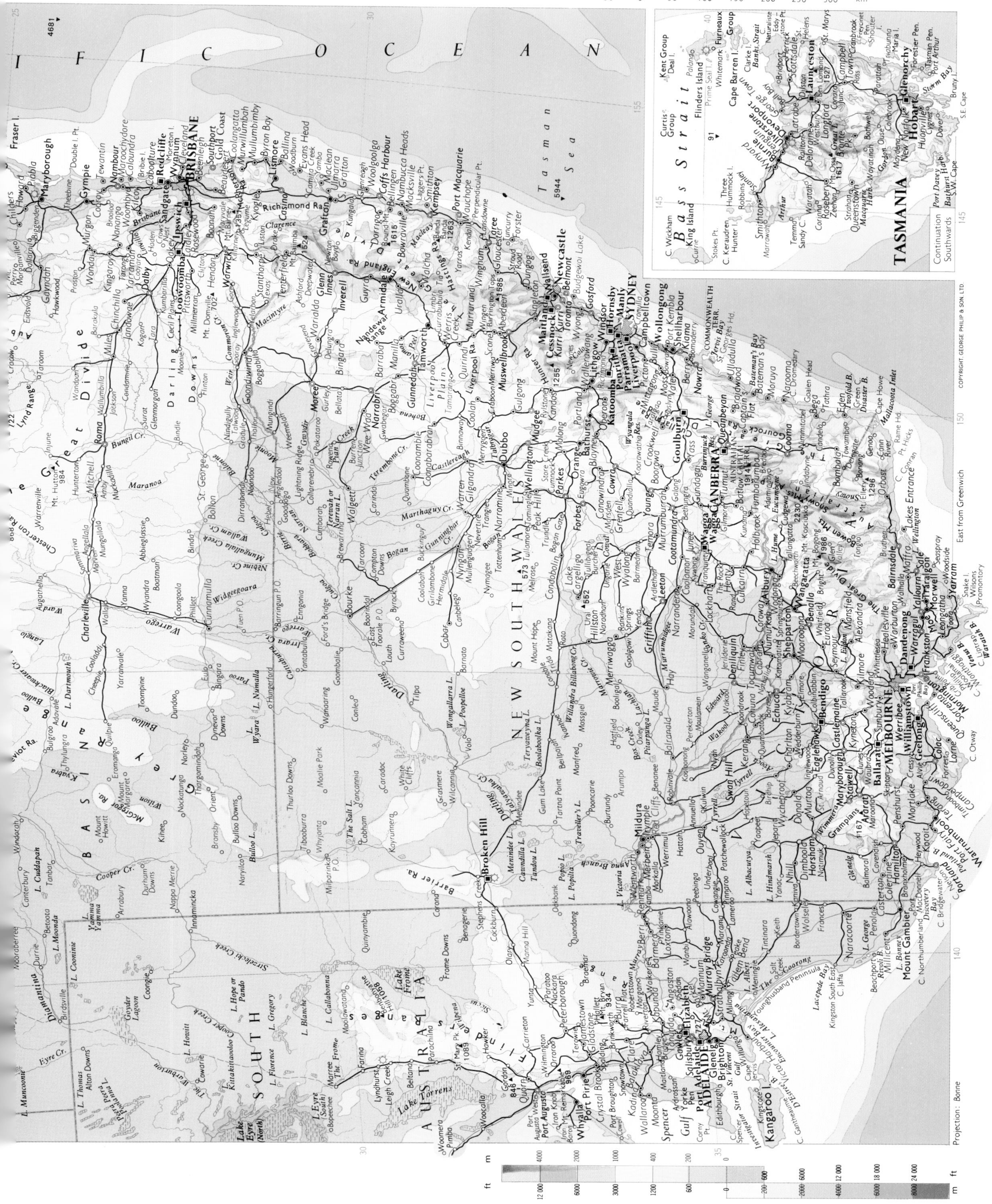

1 : 4 500 000

20 0 20 40 60 80 100 miles
20 0 20 40 60 80 120 160 km

TASMAN SEA

NEW SOUTH WALES

VICTORIA

SOUTH AUSTRALIA

AUSTRALIAN CAPITAL TERRITORY

SYDNEY
Newcastle
Wollongong
Canberra
MELBOURNE
Geelong
Ballarat
Bendigo
Broken Hill
Mildura
Wagga Wagga
Albury
Goulburn
Bathurst
Orange
Dubbo
Parkes
Forbes
Griffith
Maitland
Cessnock
Taree
Lithgow
Katoomba
Penrith
Parramatta
Fairfield
Liverpool
Campbelltown
Cronulla
Manly
Hornsby
Gosford
The Entrance
Nowra
Queanbeyan
Cooma
Eden
Bega
Narrandera
Junee
Temora
Young
Cowra
Cootamundra
Wangaratta
Benalla
Shepparton
Echuca
Castlemaine
Maryborough
Ararat
Hamilton
Horsham
Warrnambool
Portland
Sale
Traralgon
Morwell
Moe
Mudgee
Wellington

Projection: Albers' Equal Area with two standard parallels

East from Greenwich

COPYRIGHT GEORGE PHILIP & SON, LTD.

m ft

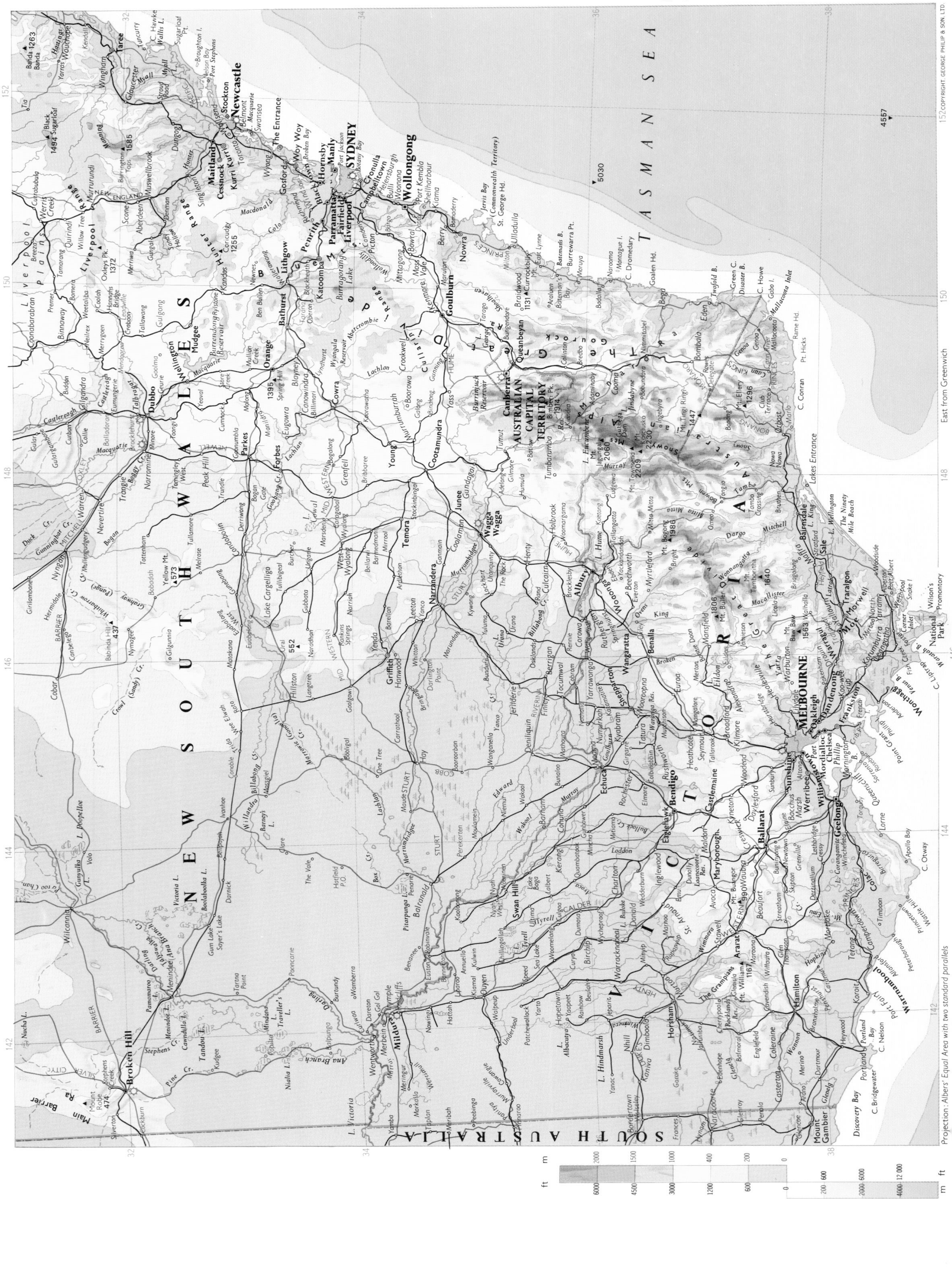

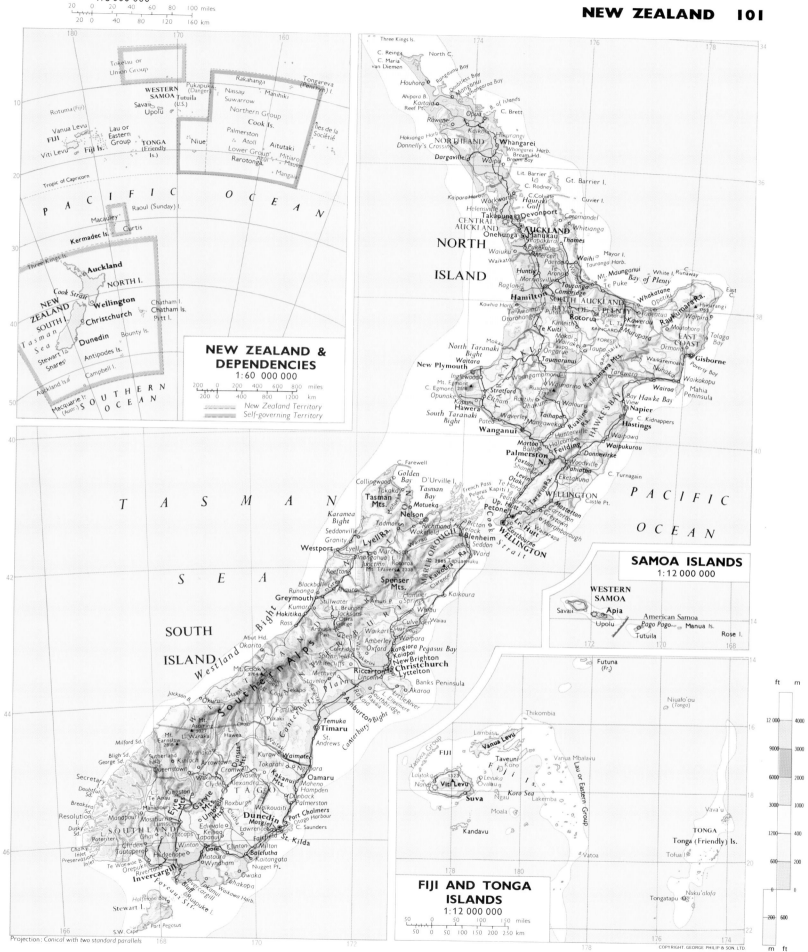

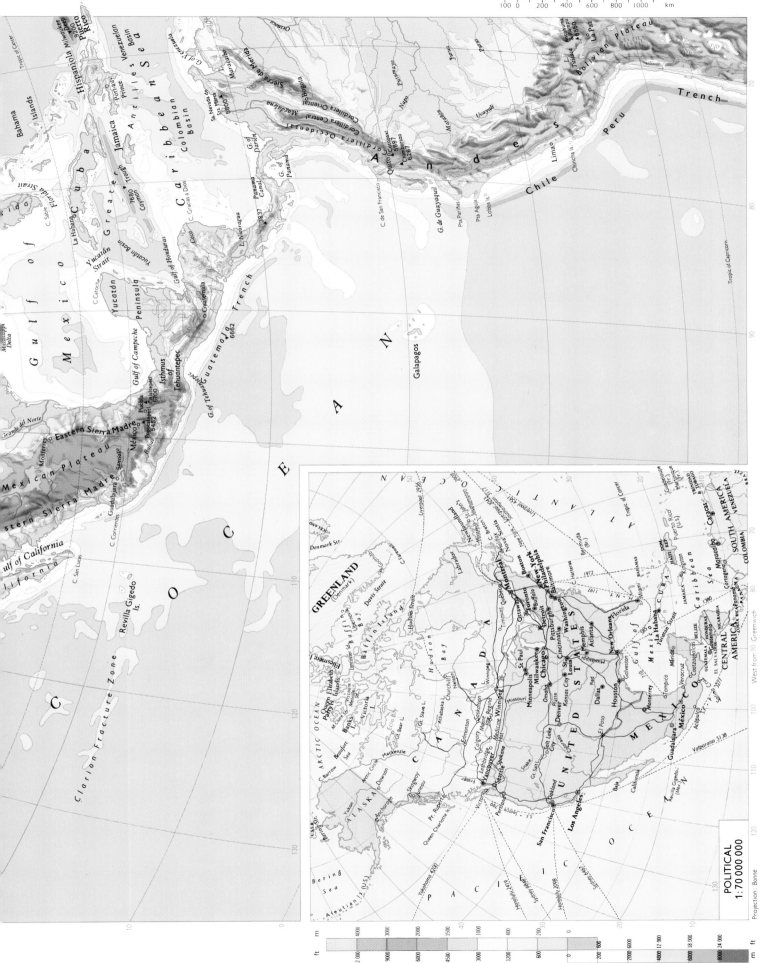

1 : 30 000 000

100   0   100   200   300   400   500   600   700 miles

100   0   200   400   600   800   1000 km

103

Tropic of Cancer

Bahama Islands

Milwaukee Deep 9700
Puerto Rico

Venezuelan Basin

Hispaniola

Cuba

La Habana

Florida Strait

C. Sable

Gulf of Mexico

Mississippi Delta

Yucatán Basin

Yucatán Strait

C. Catoche

Yucatán Peninsula

Gulf of Campeche

Gulf of Honduras

Guatemala

Isthmus of Tehuantepec

Gulf of Tehuantepec

Guatemala Trench 6662

Orizaba 5700

Popocatépetl 5452

México

Eastern Sierra Madre

Western Sierra Madre

Mexican Plateau

Monterrey

Guadalajara

Santiago

Grande del Norte

Gulf of California

California

C. San Lucas

C. Corrientes

Revilla Gigedo Is.

Clarion Fracture Zone

OCEAN

PACIFIC

Jamaica

Greater Antilles

Caribbean Sea

Colombian Basin

Cayo

Trough 7680
Cayman

C. Gracias a Dios

L. Nicaragua

3937

G. of Darién

G. of Panama

Panama Canal

Port-au-Prince

Sta. Marta

Maracaibo

Sierra de Mérida

5800

Cordillera Occidental

Cordillera Central

Cordillera Oriental

Magdalena

Bogotá

Quito

Cotopaxi 5897

Chimborazo 6267

G. de Guayaquil

Pta. Aguja

Lobos Is.

Chincha Is.

Limao

Andes

Chile

Peru Trench

Orinoco

Napo

Putumayo

Marañón

Ucayali

Juruá

Purus

La Paz

Bolivian Plateau

4550

Tropic of Capricorn

Galapagos

N

E

GREENLAND (Denmark)

Denmark Str.

Davis Strait

ICELAND

Liverpool

ARCTIC OCEAN

C. Barrow

Beaufort Sea

Banks I.

Victoria I.

Queen Elizabeth Islands

Baffin Island

Baffin Bay

Hudson Strait

Labrador

Newfoundland

Nova Scotia

ATLANTIC

Tropic of Cancer

Bermuda (Br.)

C. Hatteras

Gt. Bear L.

Gt. Slave L.

Athabaska L.

Reindeer L.

Churchill

Hudson Bay

CANADA

Nelson

Ellesmere I.

Labrador Sea

Montreal

Quebec

Ottawa

Toronto

Buffalo

Detroit

Boston

New York

Philadelphia

Baltimore

Washington

Pittsburgh

Cincinnati

St. Louis

Memphis

Atlanta

New Orleans

Florida

Mackenzie

Yukon

ALASKA (U.S.)

C. Prince of Wales

Bering Sea

Aleutian Is.

PACIFIC OCEAN

Anchorage

Juneau

Skagway

Pr. Rupert

Queen Charlotte Is.

Vancouver

Victoria

Seattle

Spokane

Portland

Fraser

San Francisco

Oakland

Los Angeles

Baja California

Edmonton

Calgary

Lethbridge

Medicine Hat

Regina

Winnipeg

Lake Winnipeg

Saskatoon

Missouri

Minneapolis

St. Paul

Milwaukee

Chicago

Omaha

Kansas City

Denver

Salt Lake City

Platte

Snake

Gt. Salt L.

UNITED STATES

Mississippi

Red

Dallas

Houston

Galveston

El Paso

Monterrey

MEXICO

México

Guadalajara

Acapulco

Tampico

Veracruz

Mérida

Yucatan Strait

Gulf of Mexico

La Habana

CUBA

Miami

BAHAMAS

JAMAICA

Caribbean Sea

HAITI

DOM. REP.

PUERTO RICO (U.S.)

Kingston

GUATEMALA

BELIZE

HONDURAS

EL SALVADOR

NICARAGUA

COSTA RICA

PANAMA

CENTRAL AMERICA

Cartagena

Maracaibo

Caracas

COLOMBIA

VENEZUELA

SOUTH AMERICA

TRINIDAD & TOBAGO

GUADELOUPE (Fr.)

MARTINIQUE (Fr.)

Valparaíso 5138

West from 90 Greenwich

Projection: Bonne

POLITICAL
1 : 70 000 000

m   ft

4000   12 000

3000   9000

1500   6000

1000   4500

400   3000

200   1200

0   600

0

200   600

2000   6000

4000   12 000

6000   18 000

8000   24 000

m   ft

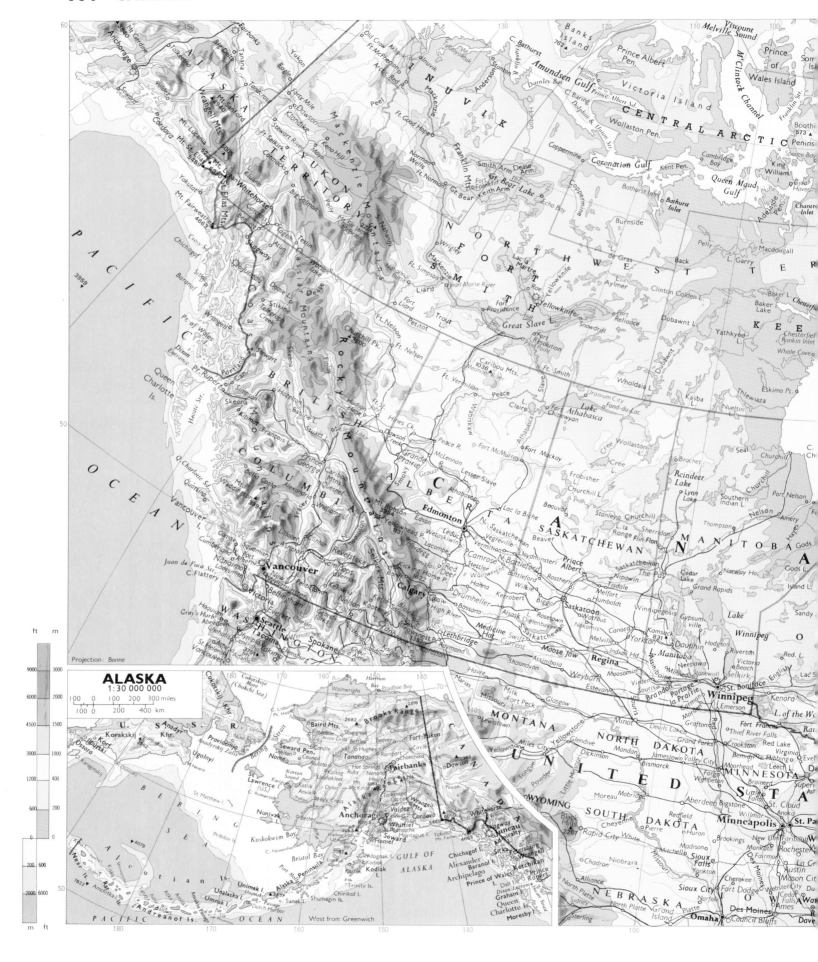

Projection: Bonne

ALASKA
1:30 000 000
100 0 100 200 300 miles
100 0 200   400 km

1:15 000 000

100   50   0   100   200   300   400 miles
100   0   100 200 300 400 500 600   km

Devon Island
Lancaster Sound
Arctic Bay
Bylot I.
Baffin Bay
1890
Brodeur
Peninsula
Milne
Inlet
Pond Inlet
Pond Inlet
2136
Scott I.
C. Hewett
Clyde
Svartenhuk
Halvø
Disko
Disko
B.
Christianshåb
GREENLAND
Angmagssalik
Kong Frederik VI's Kyst
2850
Sukkertoppen
Godthåb
Falkenæsset
Frederikshåb
Ivigtut
Julianehåb
Nanortalik
Kap Farvel

Melville
Peninsula
Hall
Lake
Igloolik
Island
Prince
Charles
I.
Foxe
2591
Cumberland
Peninsula
C. Dyer
Dyer
Broughton
Island
Padloping Island
Pangnirtung
Cumberland Sd.
C. Mercy

Committee B.
Pelly
Bay
Rae Isthmus
Repulse Bay
Wager
B.
Roes Welcome Sd.
Southampton
Coral Harbour
Bell
Pen.
Coats
I.
Mansel
I.
Digges Is.
Salisbury I.
Nottingham I.

VICTORIA
TERRITORIES
FOXE
BASIN
Nettilling
L.
C. Dorchester
Foxe
Channel
BAFFIN
Amadjuak
Amadjuak
L.
Frobisher
Bay
Lake
Harbour
Cape Dorset
Foxe
Penin.
C. Dyer

Hudson Strait
Resolution I.
C. Chidley
Saglouc
(Sugluk)
Invujivak
Koartac
(Notre Dame
de Koartac)
Maricourt
(Wakeham)
Akpatok
I.
Ungava Bay
Arnaud
(Payne Bay)
Payne L.

HUDSON
BAY
257
Ottawa
Is.
Portland
Promontory
Inoucdjouac
(Port Harrison)
PENINSULA
Port Nouveau-Quebec
(George R.)
1676
Hebron
Nutak

Sleeper Is.
King
George Is.
King George Is.
Baker's
Dozen
Is.
Belcher
Is.
C. Henrietta
Maria
Pte.
Louis-XIV
L'Eau Claire
Poste-de-
la-Baleine
(Great Whale River)
Grand Baleine
Kanaaupscow
Feuilles
Loksoak
Ft. Chimo
L. Minto
Mélèzes
Kaniapiskau
George
Whale
NEW
Nain
C. Harrison
Indian Harbour
Hopedale
Rigolet
L. Melville
Cartwright

James Bay
Akimiski
I.
Nouveau Comptoir
(Paint Hills)
Attawapiskat
Eastmain
Ft. George
La Grande
Eastmain
Ft. Rupert
(Rupert
House)
Rupert
Fort Rupert
Charlton I.
Nétapi
L. Albanel
Mistassini
Chibougamau
Scheffervile
Petitsikapau
L.
Lobstick
QUEBEC
COAST OF LABRADOR
Smallwood
Reservoir
Churchill
Falls
North West R.
Goose
Bay
Churchill
Ashuanipi
1128
Gagnon
Romaine
Moisie
Natashquan
Mingan
St-Augustin-
Saguenay
Natashquan
NEWFOUNDLAND
Battle Harb.
Belle Isle
Str. of Belle Isle

Winisk
D
Big
Trout L.
Severn
ONTARIO
Ft. Albany
Moosonee
Albany
Missinaibi
Mattagami
Harricana
Nakina
Oba
Franz
Nottaway
Waswanipi
Senneterre
Matagami
Val d'Or
Bell I.
Chibougamau
Péribonca
L. Albanel
Manicouagan
Sept-Iles
Port-Cartier
I. d'Anticosti
Natashquan
Gulf of
St. Lawrence
Is. de la Madeleine
Pte. de Gaspé
Gaspé
Gulf of St. Lawrence
Cabot Str.
Cape Breton
ST-PIERRE
et MIQUELON
(Fr.)
Grand
Falls
Gander
Bonavista
Grand
Bank
Burgeo
P. aux Basques
Placentia
Trepassey
C. Race
Trinity B.
Carbonear
St. John's
Harbour Grace
Placentia
3809
6309

Thunder Bay
Longlac
Hearst
Cochrane
Kapuskasing
Timmins
Noranda
Rouyn
Kirkland Lake
Haileybury
Cobalt
Témiscamingue
Res. de
Cabonga
La Tuque
Shawinigan
Trois-Rivières
Joliette
Sorel
St. Hyacinthe
MONTRÉAL
Lachine
Hull
North Bay
Pembroke
Ottawa
Arnprior
Cornwall
L. Champlain
Sherbrooke
Thetford Mines
Lévis
Québec
Chicoutimi
Jonquière
Roberval
Dolbeau
L. St-Jean
Saguenay
Rivière-
du-Loup
Rimouski
Matane
Pen. de Gaspé
R. St. Lawrence
Baie-Comeau
Bétsiamites
Campbellton
Dalhousie
Bathurst
Chatham
NEW
BRUNSWICK
Newcastle
Edmundston
St. Léonard
Fredericton
Woodstock
Moncton
Amherst
Springhill
Truro
New Glasgow
Pictou
PR. EDWARD I.
Summerside
Charlottetown
Northumberland Str.
Tignish
Port Hawkesbury
Sydney
Glace Bay
Cape Breton I.
C. North
NOVA SCOTIA
Mulgrave
Windsor
Dartmouth
Halifax
Bridgewater
Liverpool
Shelburne
Yarmouth
C. Sable
Digby
Kentville
B. of Fundy
Saint
John
MAINE
Bangor
Augusta
Portland
Lewiston
VERMONT
NEW
HAMPSHIRE
Concord
Manchester
Lowell
MASS.
Boston
C. Cod
Providence
R. I.
CONN.
New Haven
Bridgeport
Waterbury
Hartford

Sault Ste. Marie
Sudbury
Copper Cliff
North Chan.
Georgian
Bay
Parry
Sound
Orillia
Barrie
Owen Sound
Collingwood
Peterboro
Belleville
Kingston
L. Ontario
TORONTO
Oshawa
Guelph
Kitchener
Stratford
London
Brantford
Hamilton
Niagara
Falls
St. Catharines
Sarnia
Windsor
DETROIT
Toledo
Cleveland
Akron
Youngstown
Erie
Williamsport
PENNSYLVANIA
Scranton
Allentown
Reading
Trenton
NEW JERSEY
NEW YORK
Buffalo
Rochester
Syracuse
Utica
Albany
Schenectady
Glens
Falls
Watertown
Binghamton
Elmira
Jamestown
OHIO
INDIANA
South Bend
Gary
CHICAGO
Evanston
ILLINOIS
Kalamazoo
Grand
Rapids
Muskegon
Saginaw
Flint
Lansing
MICHIGAN
L. Huron
Lake
Michigan
Milwaukee
Racine
Kenosha
Green
Bay
Oshkosh
Appleton
Manitowoc
Sheboygan
WISCONSIN
Wausau
Cheboygan
Petoskey
Traverse
City
Cadillac
Ludington
Manistee
L. Superior
Lake Superior
Marquette
Keweenaw
Bay
Calumet
Houghton
Ironwood
Iron Mt.
Menominee
Escanaba
Sault Ste. Marie
Michipicoten
Heron Bay
Nipigon
Thunder Bay
Worcester
Springfield
Newark
NEW YORK
JERSEY CITY

Worcester
Springfield
Waterbury
Newark
NEW YORK

West from Greenwich

COPYRIGHT. GEORGE PHILIP & SON, LTD.

ATLANTIC OCEAN

N. W. TERRITORIES
MANITOBA
ONTARIO
Q
HUDSON BAY
JAMES BAY
LAKE SUPERIOR
LAKE HURON
LAKE MICHIGAN
LAKE ERIE
LAKE ONTARIO
WISCONSIN
MICHIGAN
ILLINOIS
INDIANA
OHIO
PENNSYLVANIA
NEW YORK
North Belcher Is.
Baker's Dozen Is.
Belcher Islands
Kugong I.
Flaherty I.
Tukarak I.
Innetalling I.
Nastapoka Is.
L. Minto
Akimiski I.
North Twin I.
South Twin I.
Weston I.
Trodely I.
Charlton I.
Long I.
Merry I.
C. Henrietta Maria
C. Lookout
Wabuk Pt.
Winisk
Fort Severn
Severn
Sachigo
Big Trout L.
Winisk
Ekwan
Attawapiskat
Kapiskau
Albany
Fort Albany
Ogoki
Moosonee
Moose Factory
Moose River
Kinoje
Kesagami
Harricana
Missinaibi
Kenogami
Little Current
Lakitusaki
Lake River
Sutton
Shamattawa
Fawn
Pte. Louis-XIV
Poste-de-la-Baleine
Grand Baleine
Lac Bienville
Petite Baleine
L. Guillaume-Delisle
Roggan
Roggan River
Burton
Julian L.
Craven L.
Kanaaupscow
La Grande
Fort George
Duncan L.
Castor
Sakami
Yasinski
Nouveau Comptoir
L. Sakami
Frégate
Boyd L.
Opinaca
Low L.
Eastmain
Lac Rossignol
Rupert B.
Fort Rupert (Rupert House)
Rupert
L. Mesgouez
L. Némiscau
Broadback
L. Dana
L. Evans
L. Troilus
L. Mistassini
Chibougamau
L. Waconichi
L. Opémisca
Matagami
Soscumica
L. Poncheville
L. au Goéland
Waswanipi
L. Olga
Bell
L. Parent
Rés. Gouin
L. Mégiscane
Barraute
Senneterre
Amos
Val-d'Or
Malartic
Cadillac
Rouyn
Noranda
La Sarre
La Reine
Macamic
Taschereau
Kirkland Lake
Abitibi
Iroquois Falls
Cochrane
Timmins
Porcupine
South Porcupine
Smooth Rock Falls
Kapuskasing
Hearst
Mattice
Moonbeam
Smoky Falls
Otter Rapids
Fraserdale
Island Falls
Calstock
Pagwa River
Hornepayne
Hillsport
Longlac
Geraldton
Nakina
Auden
Kowkash
Jellicoe
Beardmore
Armstrong
Collins
L. Nipigon
Nipigon
Cameron Falls
English River
Graham
Ignace
Marmion
Lac des Mille Lacs
Kashabowie
Kakabeka Falls
Thunder Bay
Red Rock
Rossport
Schreiber
Terrace Bay
Marathon
Heron Bay
Slate Is.
St. Ignace
Isle Royale
Grand Portage
Grand Marais
Copper Harbor
Michipicoten I.
Wawa
White River
Hawk Junction
Franz
Esnagi
Dalton
Chapleau
Foleyet
Horwood L.
Missinaibi L.
Elsas
Sultan
Ramsey
Biscotasing
Gogama
Westree
Ramsey L.
Mississagi
Pogamasing
Timagami
Onaping
Elliot Lake
Thessalon
Blind River
Spragge
Copper Cliff
Sudbury
Espanola
Capreol
Sturgeon Falls
Verner
North Bay
Cache Bay
Field
Temiscaming
Latchford
Cobalt
Haileybury
New Liskeard
Englehart
Larder Lake
Swastika
Matachewan
Elk Lake
Ville-Marie
Lorrainville
Lac Simard
Lac Kipawa
Grand Lac Victoria
Outaouais
Lac Dumoine
Dumoine
Rés. Cabonga
PARC PROV. DE LA VÉRENDRYE
Baskatong
Mont-Laurier
Kempt
Rés. Mataouin
Grand-Mère
Shawinigan
Trois-Rivières
Louiseville
Joliette
St-Jérôme
Lachute
Hawkesbury
Buckingham
Hull
Vanier
OTTAWA
MONTRÉAL
Cornwall
Salaberry-de-Valleyfield
Kemptville
Smiths Falls
Perth
Carleton Place
Arnprior
Renfrew
Pembroke
Petawawa
Madawaska
Bancroft
Whitney
Mattawa
Powassan
South River
Burk's Falls
Huntsville
Bracebridge
Gravenhurst
Haliburton
Orillia
Midland
Penetanguishene
Parry Sound
Georgian Bay
Manitoulin I.
Little Current
Killarney
Owen Sound
Wiarton
Tobermory
Lions Head
Southampton
Port Elgin
Kincardine
Walkerton
Wingham
Goderich
Clinton
Stratford
Kitchener
Waterloo
Guelph
Cambridge
Brampton
TORONTO
Oshawa
Bowmanville
Barrie
Lindsay
Peterborough
Cobourg
Port Hope
Trenton
Belleville
Kingston
Brockville
Gananoque
Ogdensburg
Massena
Potsdam
Malone
Plattsburg
Saranac Lake
Tupper Lake
Adirondack Mountains
Lake Placid
Watertown
Carthage
Oswego
Fulton
Syracuse
Auburn
Geneva
Rome
Utica
Amsterdam
Schenectady
Albany
Troy
Saratoga Springs
Glens Falls
Rutland
Gloversville
Oneida
Cortland
Ithaca
Elmira
Corning
Binghamton
Endicott
Oneonta
Catskill Mts.
Kingston
Newark
Rochester
Batavia
Lockport
Niagara Falls
BUFFALO
St. Catharines
HAMILTON
Burlington
Brantford
Dundas
Woodstock
Ingersoll
London
St. Thomas
Simcoe
Tillsonburg
Welland
Port Colborne
Fort Erie
Port Rowan
Port Burwell
Sarnia
Port Huron
Chatham
Wallaceburg
Ridgetown
Leamington
Windsor
Kingsville
Point Pelee
Pelee I.
DETROIT
Dearborn
Pontiac
Mount Clemens
Ann Arbor
Ypsilanti
Monroe
Toledo
Sandusky
Lorain
CLEVELAND
Lakewood
Euclid
Painesville
Ashtabula
Conneaut
Erie
Meadville
Corry
Warren
Jamestown
Dunkirk
Fredonia
Olean
Salamanca
Bradford
Coudersport
Wellsville
Hornell
Dansville
Bath
Sayre
Fremont
Defiance
Napoleon
Bryan
Adrian
Hillsdale
Coldwater
Sturgis
Jackson
Albion
Marshall
Battle Creek
Kalamazoo
Lansing
Owosso
Flint
Saginaw
Bay City
Midland
Lapeer
Alma
Mount Pleasant
Big Rapids
Grand Rapids
Muskegon
Grand Haven
Holland
South Haven
Benton Harbor
Niles
South Bend
Mishawaka
Elkhart
Kendallville
Warsaw
Plymouth
Rochester
Kankakee
Pontiac
Streator
La Salle
Mendota
Joliet
Aurora
Elgin
Harvey
Cicero
CHICAGO
E. Chicago
Gary
Michigan City
Hammond
Waukegan
Highland Park
Evanston
Berwyn
Kenosha
Racine
MILWAUKEE
South Milwaukee
Waukesha
Oconomowoc
Sheboygan
Manitowoc
Two Rivers
Green Bay
Appleton
Menasha
Neenah
Oshkosh
Fond du Lac
Beaver Dam
Watertown
Madison
Baraboo
Portage
Wisconsin Dells
Stevens Point
Wisconsin Rapids
Marshfield
Wausau
Merrill
Antigo
Rhinelander
Tomahawk
Medford
Marinette
Menominee
Escanaba
Gladstone
Iron Mountain
Norway
Iron River
Crandon
Eagle River
Ironwood
Wakefield
Ashland
Washburn
Bayfield
Apostle Is.
Duluth
Superior
Houghton
Hancock
Laurium
Ontonagon
L'Anse
Baraga
Ishpeming
Negaunee
Marquette
Munising
Grand Marais
Au Sable Pt.
Whitefish B.
Newberry
Sault Ste. Marie
St. Joseph I.
Drummond I.
Cheboygan
Petoskey
Charlevoix
Mackinaw City
St. Ignace
Manistique
Traverse City
Alpena
Cadillac
Manistee
Ludington
Grayling
Gaylord
Tawas City
Harrisville
Thunder B.
Saginaw B.
Port Austin
Bad Axe
Sandusky
Lambert's Equivalent Azimuthal
ft
m
4500
1500
3000
1000
1200
400
600
200
0
200
600
2000
6000
4000
12 000
95
90
85
80
75
55
50
45
396
646
604
556
960
1629
1281

1 : 7 000 000

50   0   50   100   150   200 miles
50   0   50 100 150 200 250 300 km

COAST OF
LABRADOR

QUEBEC

NEWFOUNDLAND

NEW
BRUNSWICK

NOVA SCOTIA

PRINCE EDWARD
ISLAND

GULF OF
ST. LAWRENCE

I. d'Anticosti

MAINE

BOSTON

ATLANTIC

OCEAN

Cape Breton Island

SAINT-PIERRE
ET MIQUELON
(Fr.)

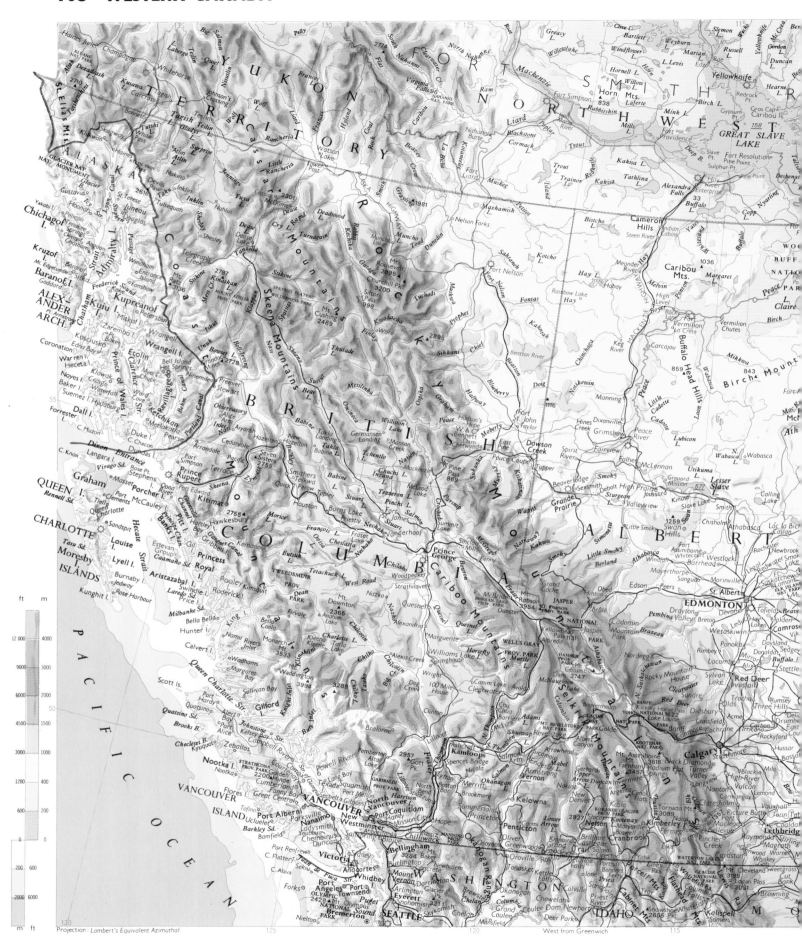

Projection : Lambert's Equivalent Azimuthal   West from Greenwich

1:7 000 000

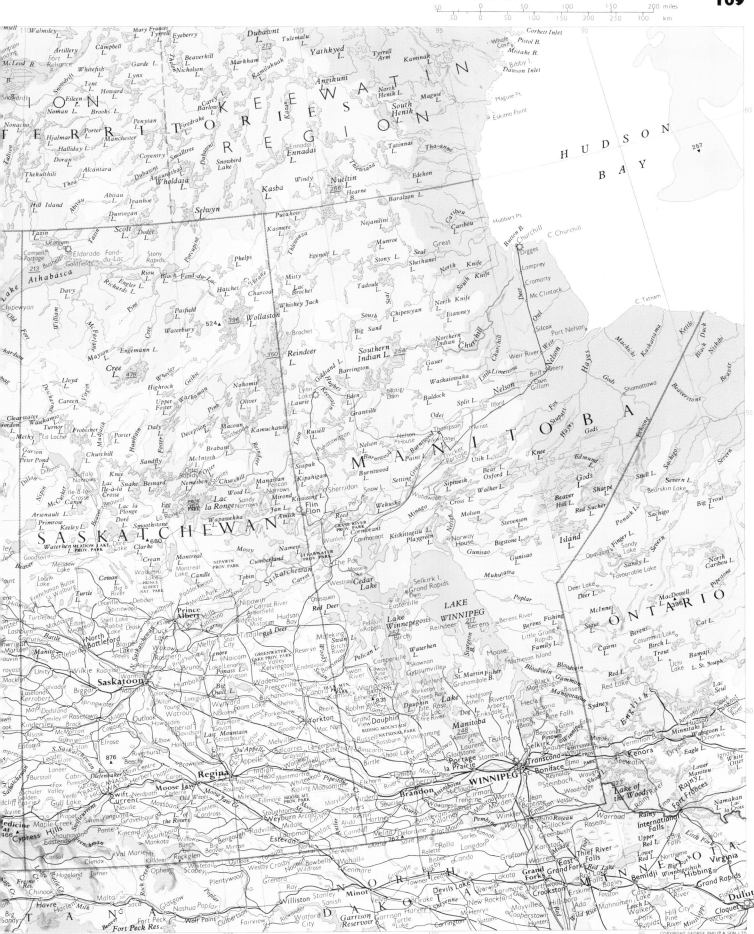

HUDSON BAY

KEEWATIN REGION

TERRITORIES

MANITOBA

SASKATCHEWAN

ONTARIO

Lake Athabasca

Reindeer L.

Lake Winnipeg

Lake Winnipegosis

Saskatoon

Prince Albert

Regina

Moose Jaw

Swift Current

WINNIPEG

Brandon

Portage la Prairie

Selkirk

Yorkton

Kenora

NORTH DAKOTA

MINNESOTA

MONTANA

Minot

Devils Lake

Grand Forks

Bemidji

Duluth

COPYRIGHT GEORGE PHILIP & SON LTD

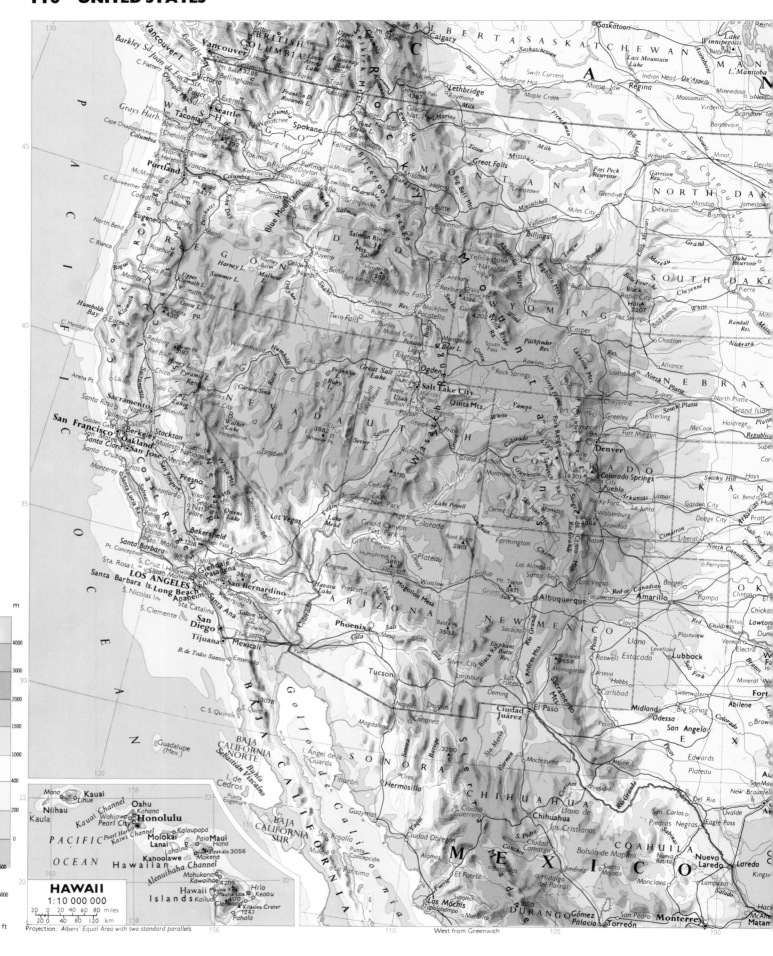

ft m

12 000 4000

9000 3000

6000 2000

4500 1500

3000 1000

1200 400

600 200

0 0

200 600

2000 6000

m ft

HAWAII
1:10 000 000
20 0 20 40 60 80 miles
200 40 80 120 km
Projection: Albers' Equal Area with two standard parallels

West from Greenwich

1:12 000 000

50   0   50   100   150   200   250   300 miles
50   0   50 100 150 200 250 300 350 400 450 km

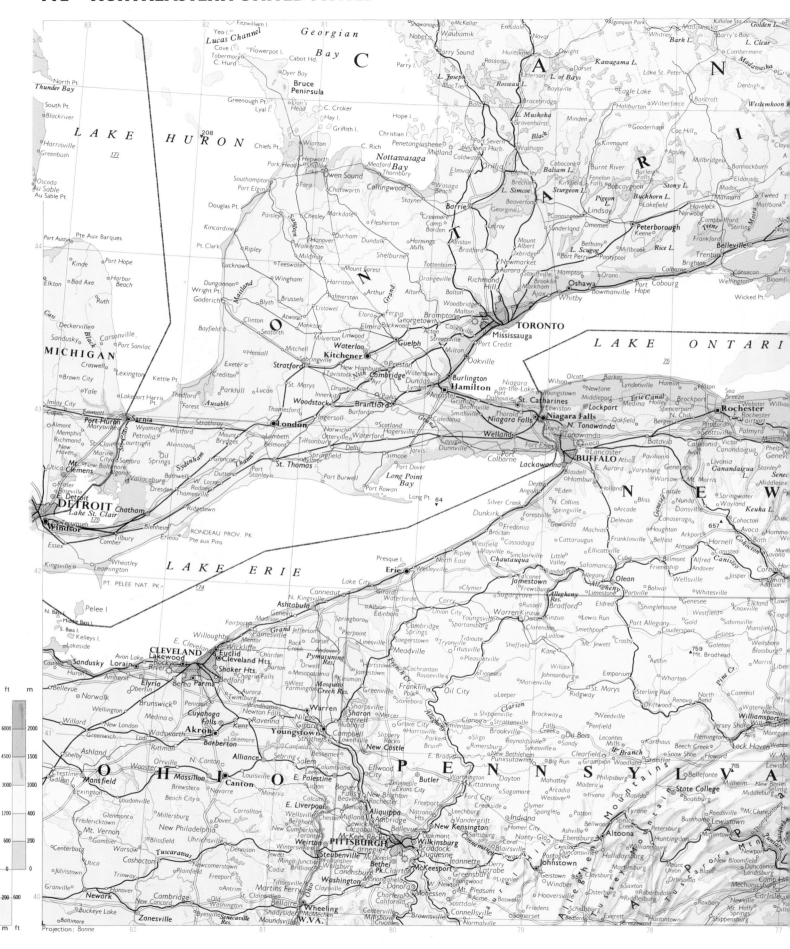

Georgian Bay C

LAKE HURON

208
172

MICHIGAN

O N T A R I O

TORONTO
Mississauga

LAKE ONTARIO
76

Kitchener
Hamilton
St. Catharines
Niagara Falls

Rochester

Port Huron
Sarnia
London

BUFFALO

N E W

Y O R K

657

LAKE ERIE
174

Erie

Long Point Bay
Long Pt. 64

CLEVELAND

759
Mt. Brodhead

O H I O

P E N N S Y L V A N I A

715

PITTSBURGH

ft m
6000 2000
4500 1500
3000 1000
1200 400
600 200
0 0
200 600
m ft

Projection: Bonne

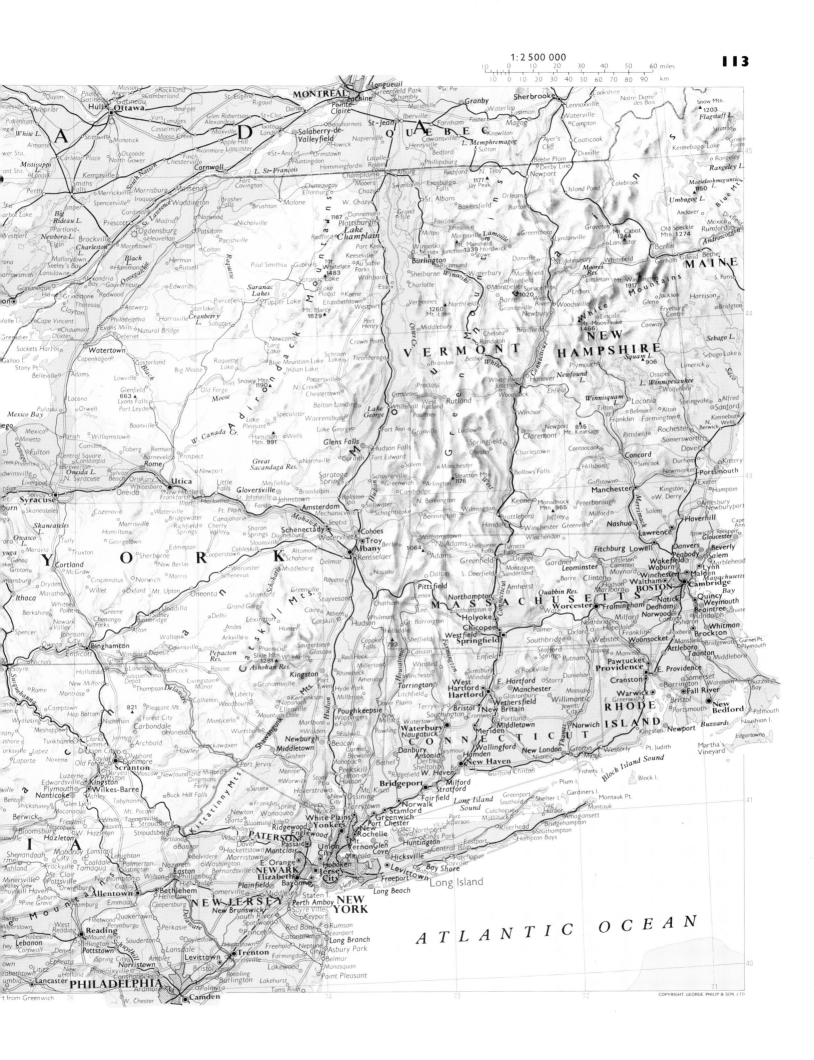

113

1:2 500 000

QUEBEC

Montréal

ONTARIO

Ottawa

NEW HAMPSHIRE

VERMONT

MAINE

BOSTON

MASS.

NEW YORK

TORONTO

LAKE ONTARIO

LAKE ERIE

BUFFALO

Rochester

Hamilton

Niagara Falls

NEW YORK

NEW JERSEY

PHILADELPHIA

DELAWARE

MARYLAND

BALTIMORE

WASHINGTON D.C.

PENNSYLVANIA

PITTSBURGH

Chesapeake Bay

WEST VIRGINIA

VIRGINIA

Richmond

Georgian Bay

LAKE HURON

MICHIGAN

DETROIT

CLEVELAND

OHIO

Columbus

CINCINNATI

LAKE SUPERIOR

Isle Royale

Sault Ste. Marie

LAKE MICHIGAN

Green Bay

MILWAUKEE

CHICAGO

WISCONSIN

INDIANA

INDIANAPOLIS

KENTUCKY

Louisville

1:6 000 000

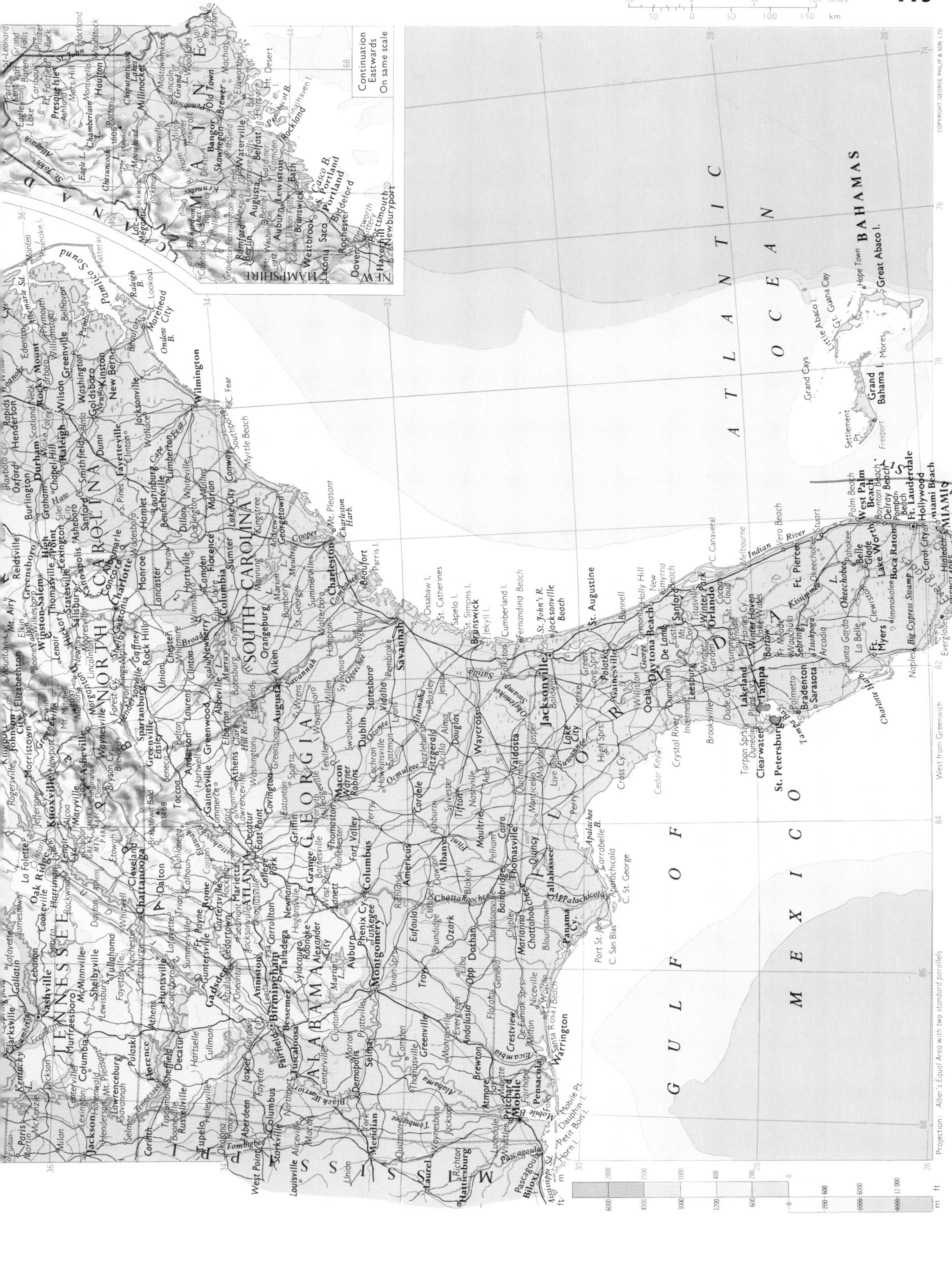

miles
km

Continuation
Eastwards
On same scale

MAINE

NEW HAMPSHIRE

NORTH CAROLINA

SOUTH CAROLINA

GEORGIA

FLORIDA

ALABAMA

MISSISSIPPI

TENNESSEE

KENTUCKY

ATLANTIC OCEAN

GULF OF MEXICO

BAHAMAS

Projection: Alber's Equal Area with two standard parallels

West from Greenwich

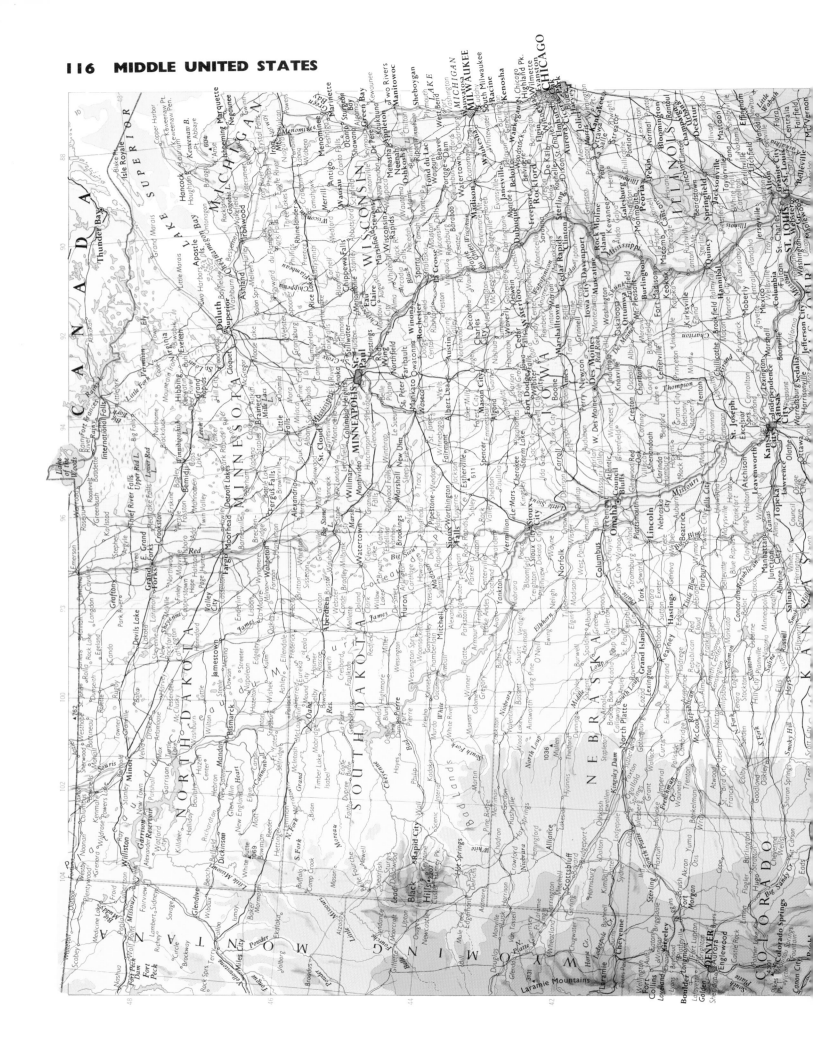

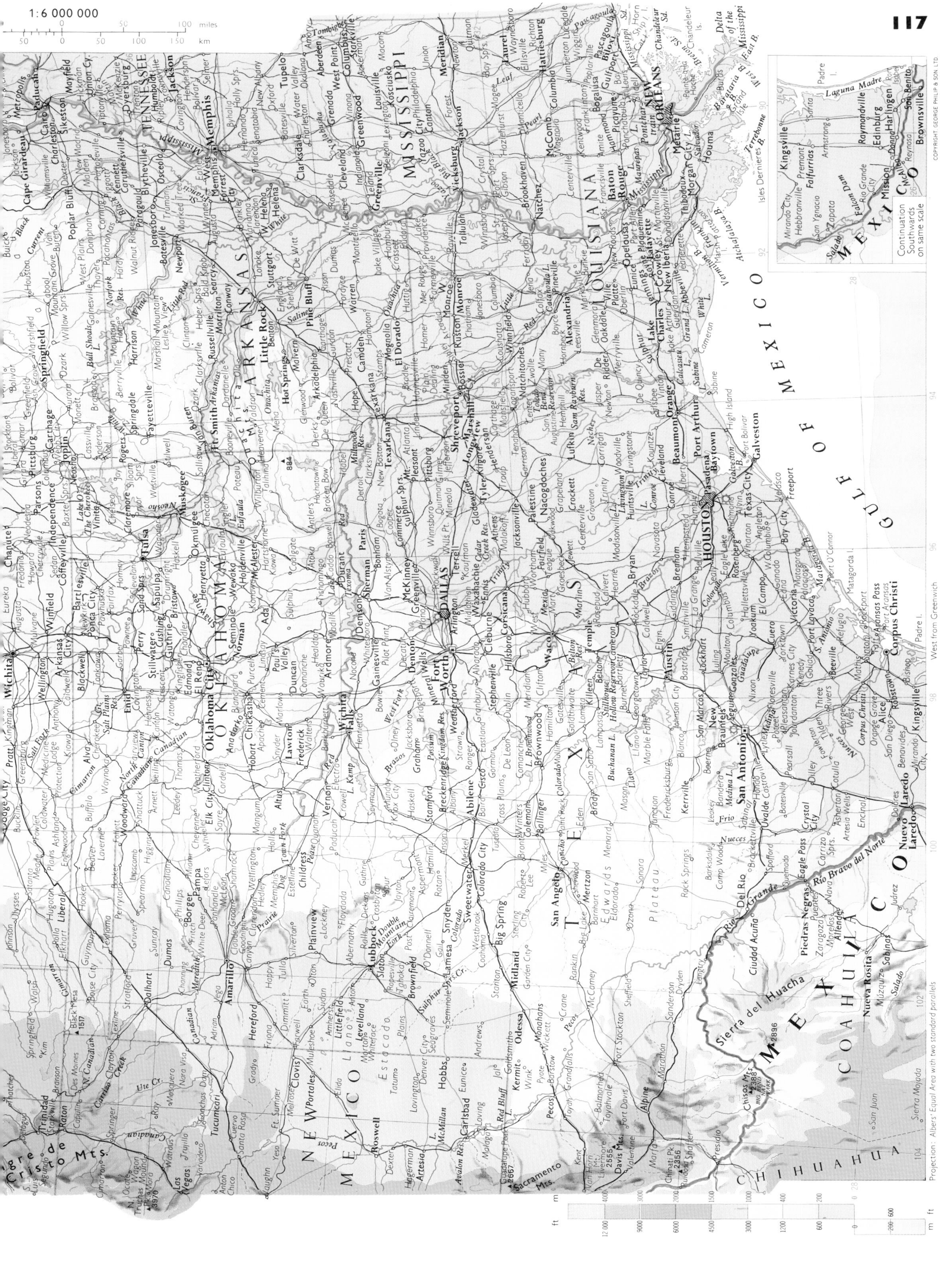

1:6 000 000

50 0 50 100 miles

50 0 50 100 150 km

TENNESSEE

MISSISSIPPI

ARKANSAS

LOUISIANA

OKLAHOMA

TEXAS

NEW MEXICO

COAHUILA

CHIHUAHUA

MEXICO

GULF OF MEXICO

NEW ORLEANS

Baton Rouge

Houston

DALLAS

Fort Worth

San Antonio

Austin

Memphis

Tulsa

Oklahoma City

Wichita

Little Rock

Shreveport

Corpus Christi

Laguna Madre

Continuation Southwards on same scale

West from Greenwich

Projection: Albers' Equal Area with two standard parallels

COPYRIGHT GEORGE PHILIP & SON LTD

Nuevo Laredo · Laredo

Brownsville

m ft

1:6 000 000

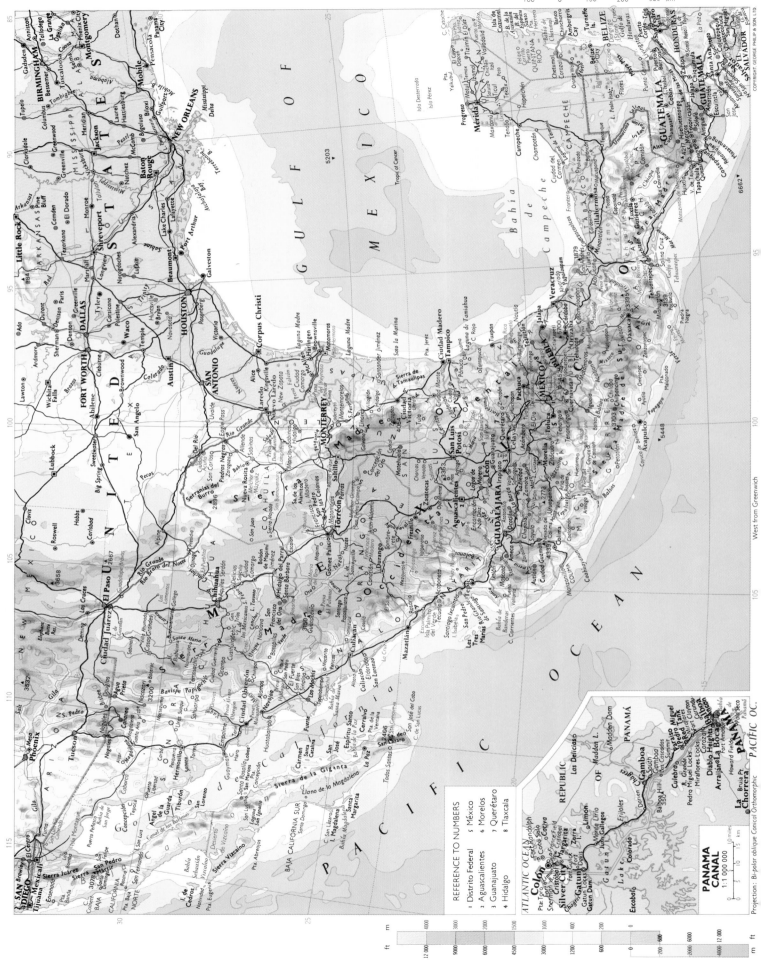

1:12 000 000

PANAMA
CANAL
1:1 000 000

REFERENCE TO NUMBERS
1 Distrito Federal	5 México
2 Aguascalientes	6 Morelos
3 Guanajuato	7 Querétaro
4 Hidalgo	8 Tlaxcala

Projection: Bi-polar oblique Conical Orthomorphic

West from Greenwich

COPYRIGHT GEORGE PHILIP & SON, LTD.

1:12 000 000

100   0   100   200 miles
100   0   100   200   300 km

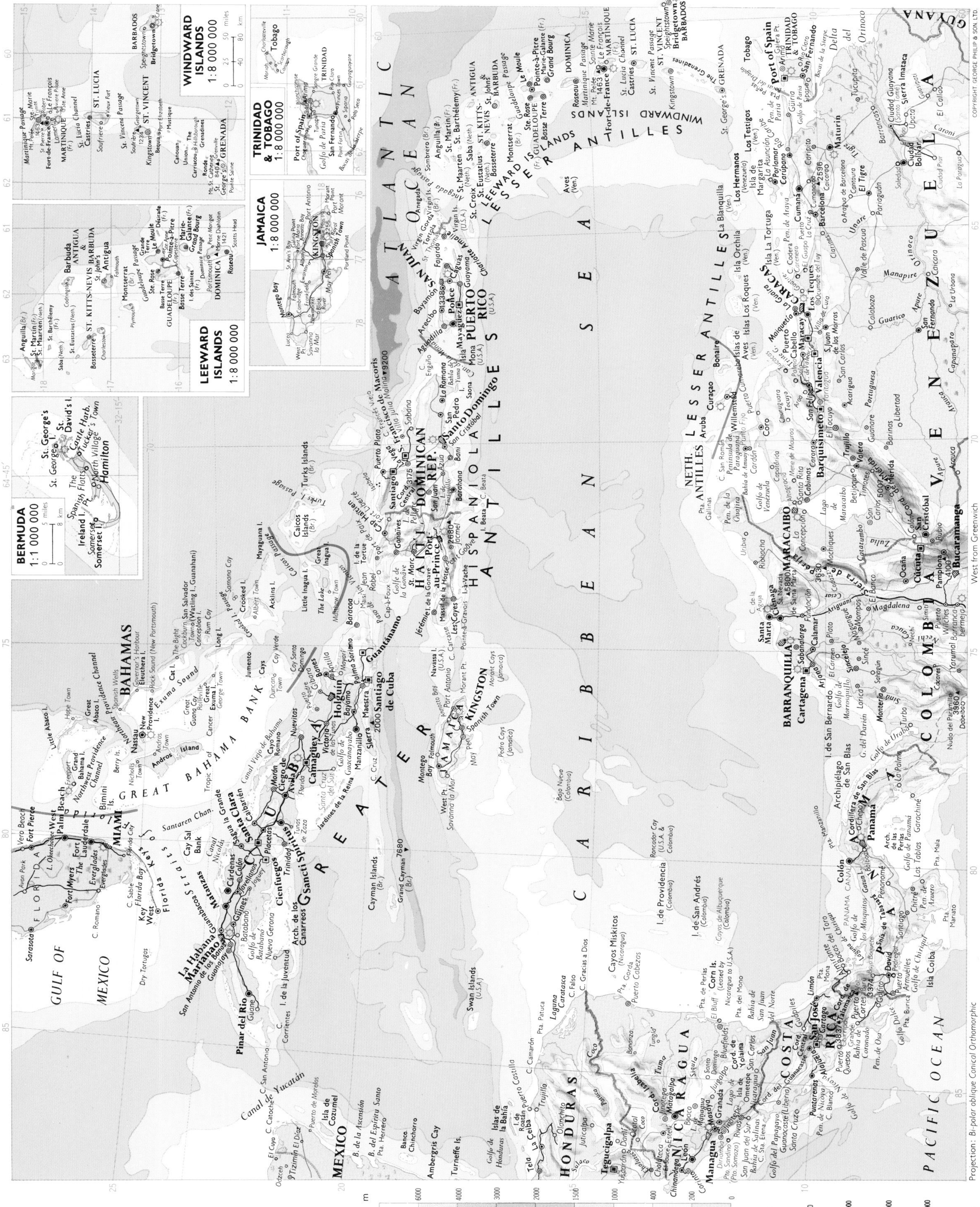

WINDWARD ISLANDS
1:8 000 000

TRINIDAD & TOBAGO
1:8 000 000

JAMAICA
1:8 000 000

LEEWARD ISLANDS
1:8 000 000

BERMUDA
1:1 000 000

ATLANTIC OCEAN

BAHAMAS

GREAT BAHAMA BANK

GULF OF MEXICO

FLORIDA

Miami
Fort Lauderdale
Key West

MEXICO

Yucatán

La Habana
Matanzas
Santa Clara
Cienfuegos
Camagüey
Holguín
Santiago de Cuba

CUBA

GREATER ANTILLES

Cayman Islands

JAMAICA
Kingston

HAITI
Port-au-Prince

DOMINICAN REP.
Santo Domingo

HISPANIOLA

PUERTO RICO (U.S.A.)
San Juan
Ponce

Turks Islands

Caicos Islands

CARIBBEAN SEA

LESSER ANTILLES

LEEWARD ISLANDS

WINDWARD ISLANDS

NETH. ANTILLES

ANTIGUA
GUADELOUPE
DOMINICA
MARTINIQUE
ST. LUCIA
ST. VINCENT
BARBADOS
GRENADA
TRINIDAD & TOBAGO

Aruba
Curaçao
Bonaire

HONDURAS
Tegucigalpa

NICARAGUA
Managua
León

COSTA RICA
San José

PANAMA
Panama
Colón
PANAMA CANAL

COLOMBIA
Barranquilla
Cartagena
Bucaramanga
Cúcuta

VENEZUELA
CARACAS
Maracaibo
Valencia
Barquisimeto
Ciudad Bolívar
Maturín

GUYANA

PACIFIC OCEAN

Projection: Bi-polar oblique Conical Orthomorphic

West from Greenwich

COPYRIGHT GEORGE PHILIP & SON LTD

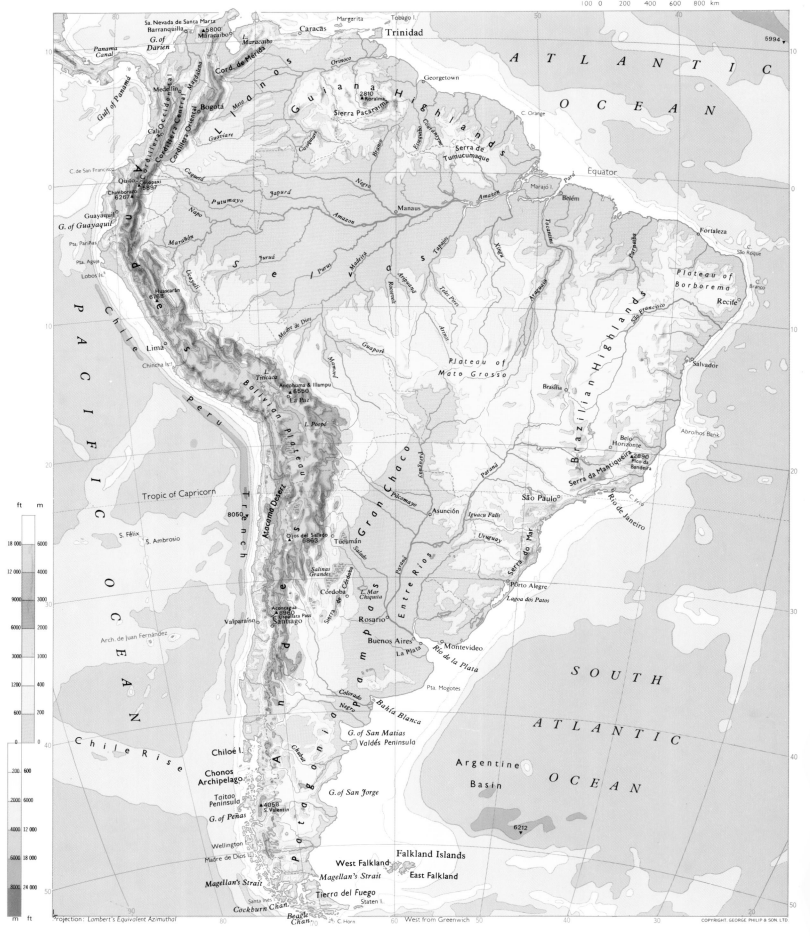

1:30 000 000

100   0   100   200   300   400   500 miles
100   0   200   400   600   800 km

Projection : Lambert's Equivalent Azimuthal   West from Greenwich   COPYRIGHT. GEORGE PHILIP & SON. LTD.

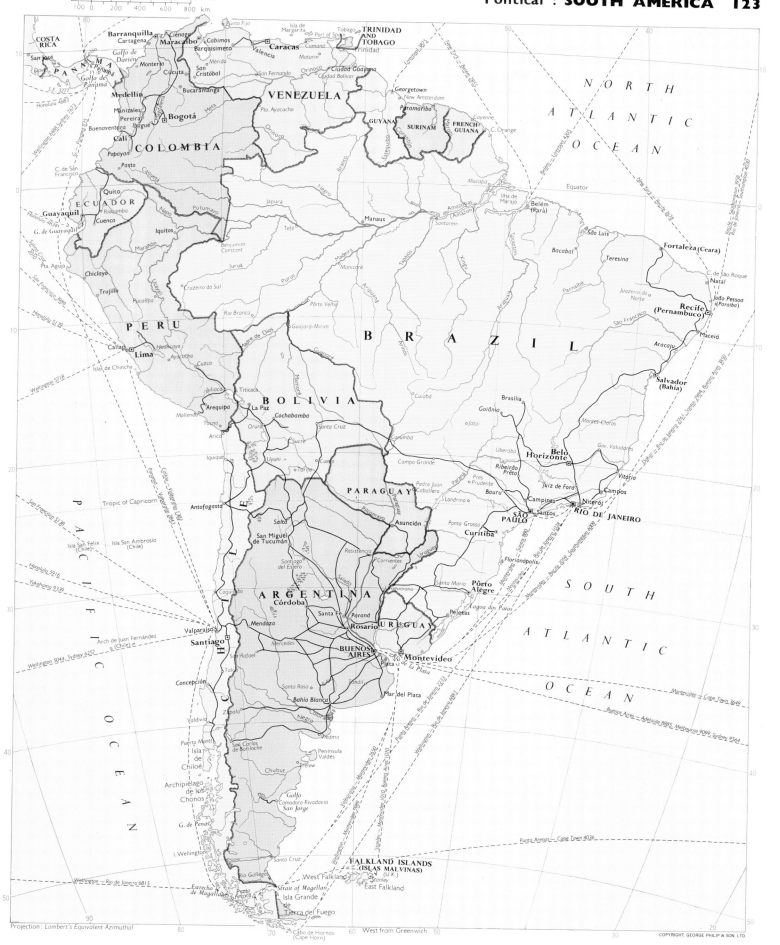

1:30 000 000

100   0   100   200   300   400   500 miles
100   0   200   400   600   800 km

COSTA
RICA
San José

PANAMA
S.F. 3277
Golfo de
Panamá
Honolulu 4683

Barranquilla
Cartagena
Ciénaga
Maracaibo
Barquisimeto
Cabimas
Valencia
Cumaná
Caracas
Golfo de
Darién
Montería
Mérida
San
Cristóbal
Maturín
Medellín
Cúcuta
Bucaramanga
Manizales
Pereira
Ibagué
Bogotá
Buenaventura
Cali
Popayán
C. de San
Francisco

Punta Fijo
Isla de
Margarita
Port of Spain
Trinidad

TRINIDAD
AND
TOBAGO
Tobago

VENEZUELA

Pto. Ayacucho
Orinoco
San Fernando
Ciudad Guayana
Ciudad Bolívar

Georgetown
New Amsterdam
Paramaribo
Cayenne

GUYANA
SURINAM
FRENCH
GUIANA

C. Orange

NORTH

ATLANTIC

OCEAN

COLOMBIA

Equator

Pasto
Caquetá
Putumayo
Japurá
Negro
Amazonas
Ilha de
Marajó
Belém
(Pará)
Macapá

ECUADOR
Quito
Riobamba
Cuenca
Guayaquil
G. de Guayaquil
Napo
Iquitos
Marañón
Tefé
Manaus
Santarem
Amazon
Purus
São Luís
Bacabal
Teresina
Fortaleza (Ceara)

Chiclayo
Trujillo
Pucallpa
Cruzeiro do Sul
Juruá
Madeira
Manicoré
Aripuanã
Tapajós
Xingu
Araguaia
Tocantins
Parnaíba
C. de São Roque
Natal
João Pessoa
(Paraíba)
Recife
(Pernambuco)

PERU
Callao
Lima
Huancayo
Ayacucho
Cuzco
Madre de Dios
Pôrto Velho
Guajará-Mirim
Guaporé
Juazeiro do
Norte

BRAZIL

Maceió
Aracaju

Islas de Chincha
Juliaca
Titicaca
Arequipa
La Paz
Cochabamba
Oruro
Santa Cruz
Corumbá
Cuiabá
Goiânia
Brasília
Montes Claros
São Francisco
Salvador
(Bahia)

BOLIVIA
Sucre
Uyuni
Tarija
Cuevo
Campo Grande
Jataí
Gov. Valadares

Mollendo
Tacna
Arica
Iquique
Antofagasta

Tropic of Capricorn

PARAGUAY
Pedro Juan
Caballero
Pres.
Prudente
Uberaba
Ribeirão
Prêto
Belo
Horizonte
Juiz de Fora
Vitória
Campos

Salta
Asunción
Londrina
Bauru
Campinas
São Paulo
Santos
Niterói
Rio de Janeiro

San Miguel
de Tucumán
Resistencia
Corrientes
Ponta Grossa
Curitiba
Florianópolis

CHILE

Santiago
del Estero
Salado
Uruguayana
Santa María
Pôrto
Alegre
Pelotas
Lagoa dos Patos

Coquimbo
Arch. de Juan Fernández
(Chile)
Valparaíso
Santiago
San Rafael

ARGENTINA
Córdoba
Santa Fe
Paraná
Rosario
URUGUAY
Montevideo
La Plata

Mendoza
Mercedes
BUENOS
AIRES
Rio de la Plata

Talca
Concepción
Santa Rosa
Tandil
Mar del Plata

Zapala
Bahía Blanca
Negro
Colorado

Valdivia
Viedma

Puerto Montt
San Carlos
de Bariloche
Isla
de
Chiloé
Chubut
Trelew

Archipiélago
de los
Chonos
Peninsula
Valdés
Golfo
Comodoro Rivadavia
San Jorge

G. de Penas
Santa Cruz

I. Wellington
FALKLAND ISLANDS
(ISLAS MALVINAS)
(U.K.)
West Falkland
Stanley
East Falkland

Río Gallegos
Estrecho
de Magallanes
Punta
Arenas
Strait of Magellan
Isla Grande
de
Tierra del Fuego

Cabo de Hornos
(Cape Horn)

PACIFIC

OCEAN

SOUTH

ATLANTIC

OCEAN

Montevideo – Cape Town 3649
Buenos Aires – Adelaide 8885, Melbourne 9099, Sydney 9564
Punta Arenas – Cape Town 4036

West from Greenwich

Projection: Lambert's Equivalent Azimuthal

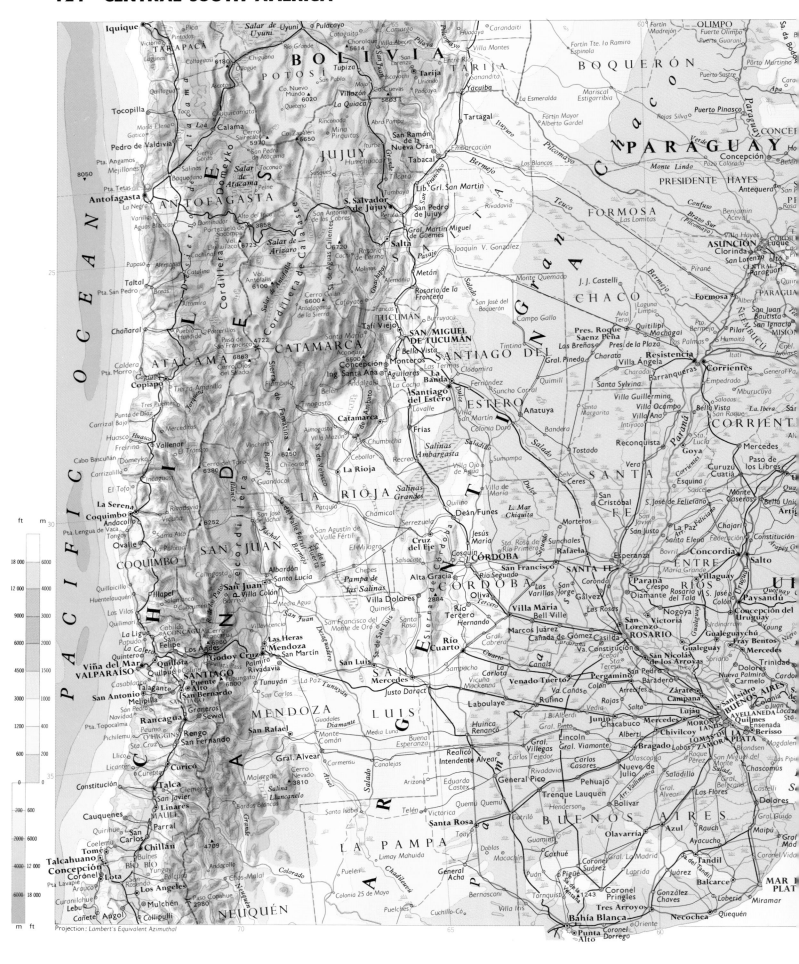

Projection: Lambert's Equivalent Azimuthal

1:8 000 000

50 0 50 100 150 miles

50 0 50 100 150 200 km

BELO HORIZONTE

Vitória

MATO GROSSO DO SUL

Três Lagoas
Andradina
Mirassol
Olímpia
Passos
Congonhas
N. Lima
Itabirito
Itaquari
Vila Velha

Xavantina
Mirandópolis
Aracatuba
S. José do Rio Prêto
Batatais
São Seb. do Paraíso
Oliveira
Cons. Lafaiete
Ouro Prêto
Ponte Nova
Castelo

Panorama
Birigui
Catanduva
Jaboticabal
Ribeirão Prêto
Guaxupé
Represa de Furnas
Campo Belo
Carangola
Muriaé
Cachoeiro de Itapemirim

Adamantina
Penápolis
Tupã
Araraquara
Mococa
Casa Branca
São João del Rei
Ubá
Barbacena
Cataguases
Alegre

Santo Anastácio
SÃO
Lins
São Carlos
Alfenas
Varginha
Três Pontas
Santos Dumont
Leopoldina
Itaperuna
Guarus

Presidente Prudente
Martinópolis
Marilia
Paraguaçu Paulista
Bauru
Jaú
São João da Boa Vista
Araras
Poços de Caldas
Pouso Alegre
Lavras
Juiz de Fora
Além Paraíba
CAMPOS

Paranavaí
Rancharia
Garça
Bariri
PAULO
Pinhal
São Lourenço
Mantiqueira
Três Rios
Paraíba do Sul
Cabo de São Tomé

Nova
Esperança
Assis
Cambará
Rio Claro
Limeira
Mogi-Mirim
Americana
Itajubá
Volta Redonda
RIO DE JANEIRO
Macaé

Londrina
Rolândia
Sertanópolis
Santa Cruz do Rio Pardo
Piracicaba
CAMPINAS
Guaratinguetá
Barra do Piraí
Petrópolis
Nova Friburgo

Maringá
Apucarana
Cornélio Procópio
Jacarèzinho
Ourinhos
Avaré
Botucatu
Jundiaí
Bragança Paulista
Barra Mansa
Nova Iguaçu
DUQUE DE CAXIAS

Cianorte
Mondaguari
Arapongas
Tatuí
Itu
Sorocaba
S. J. dos Campos
Angra dos Reis
NITERÓI
SÃO GONÇALO

Cruzeiro do Oeste
Guaíra
Itapetininga
SÃO PAULO
Mogi das Cruzes
Jacareí
Taubaté
Baía da Ilha Grande
RIO DE JANEIRO
La. de Araruama

BRAZIL
PARANÁ
Itararé
Apiaí
SANTO ANDRÉ
São Vicente
SANTOS
Tropic of Capricorn

Guaíra
Ponta Grossa
Prudentópolis
Palmeira
Castro
Jaguariaíva
Itapeva
Paranapiacaba
Guarujá
Ilha de São Sebastião
Pta. do Boi
Cabo Frio

Guarapuava
Irati
1889
CURITIBA
Antonina
Iguape
Registro
Itanhaém

União da Vitória
Pto. União
Lapa
Paranaguá
Ilha Comprida
Ilha do Cardoso

Rio Negro
Mafra
Guaratuba

Caçador
Rio Negro
São Francisco do Sul

1340
Blumenau
Joinvile

SANTA CATARINA
Brusque
Itajaí

Campos Novos
Rio do Sul

Lajes
Ilha de Santa Catarina
Florianópolis

1808

Vacaria
Tubarão
Laguna
Criciúma
Cabo Santa Marta Grande

Bento Gonçalves
Caxias do Sul
Araranguá

Carazinho
Passo Fundo
Guaporé

Cruz Alta
Guaporé

Vacaria

RIO GRANDE

Santa Maria
Santa Cruz do Sul
Montenegro
Nôvo Hamburgo
Taquara
São Leopoldo
Osorio

Cachoeira do Sul
Rio Pardo
PÔRTO ALEGRE

DO SUL
São Gabriel
Sa. Encantadas

Santana do Livramento
Caçapava do Sul
Camaquã

Dom Pedrito
Camaquã

Bagé
Sa. do Canguçu
Canguçu
Mostardas

Lagoa dos Patos

Pelotas

Melo
Jaguarão
Rio Grande

ATLANTIC

Treinta y Tres
Lagoa Mirim
Santa Vitória do Palmar
Lagoa Mangueira

OCEAN

5304

COPYRIGHT. GEORGE PHILIP & SON. LTD

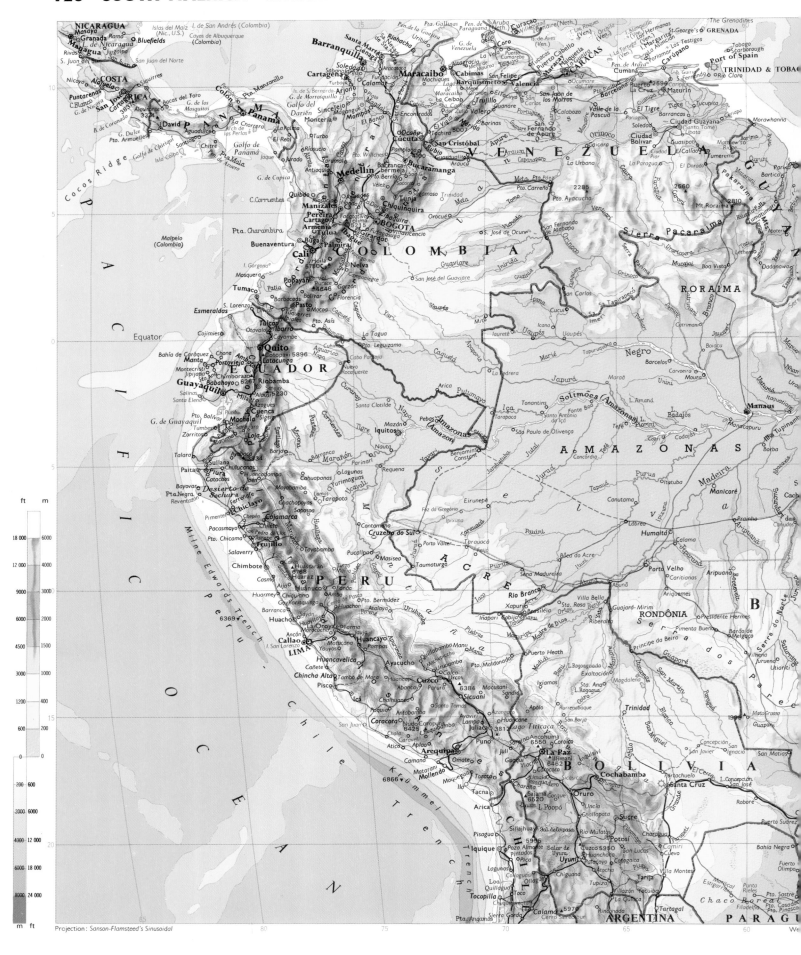

100   0   100   200   300   400   500 miles
100 0 100 200 300 400 500 600 700 800 km

A T L A N T I C

Amsterdam
Paramaribo
Nieuw Amsterdam
Nickerie
Totness
Mana
St. Laurent
Moengo
Albina
Sronnamary
Iracoubo
Kourou
wakoegron
Cayenne
Brokopondo
Kaw
Approuague
C. Orange
Apatou
St. Georges
Oiapoque
SURINAM
FR.
GUIANA
Oiapoque
Camopi
Serra
Tumucumaque
Amapá
Araguari
AMAPÁ

RINAM

Serra
do Navio
Pto. Grande
C. do Norte

Meruma
Macapá

Estuario do
Rio Amazonas
Ilha Caviana

Monte Alegre
Prainha
Almeirim
Gurupá
Afuá
Chaves
C. Curuçá
Salinópolis
Ilha Mexiana

Grande
de Gurupá
Breves
Muaná
Vigia
Bragança

Ilha de
Marajó

Equator

Juruti
Óbidos
Santarém
Pôrto de Móz
Abaetetuba
Belém (Pará)
Igarapé-Açu
Viseu
Turiaçu

A N T I C

Belterra
Aveiro
Altamira
Acará
Cametá
Capim

Guimarães
B. de São Marcos
São Luís (Maranhão)
Barreirinhas

tins
Brasília Legal
Amazonas
Amazonas
Baião
Tucuruí

Rosário
Itupecuru-
Mirim
Tutóia
Luís Correia
Camocim

AMAPÁ
PARÁ
Parnaíba
Granja

Itaituba
Marabá
Bacabal
Coroatá
Miguel Alves
Piripiri
Camocim

Sa. dos Carajás
Icatu
Caxias
União
Campo Maior
Sobral
Maranguape
Fortaleza (Ceará)

Imperatriz
Barra do
Corda
Teresina
Oiticica
Baturité
Aracati
Areia Branca
Macau

MARANHÃO
Grajaú
Senador
Pampeu
Crateús
Quixadá
Russas
Mossoró
Rocas
Fernando de Noronha
(Braz.)

Xingu
Fresco
Sa. do Estrondo
Porto Franco
Colinas
Amarante
Valença
do Piauí
Iguatu
Oros
Caraúbas
RIO GRANDE
Ceará Mirim
Natal

Sa. dos Caiabis
Tocantinópolis
Carolina
Loreto
Floriano
Uruçuí
PIAUÍ
Crato
Juàzeiro
Norte
Sousa
Caicó
Patos
Nova
Cruz
DO NORTE
C. de São Roque

Conceição do
Araguaia
Riachão
Sta. Filomena
São João
do Piauí
Paulistana
Ouricuri
Sertânia
Arcoverde
Caruaru
Pesqueira
Campina Grande
João Pessoa
(Paraíba)
Cabedelo

Araguacema
Pedro Afonso
Caracol
Remanso
Casa Nova
Petrolina
Juàzeiro
Paulo Afonso
PARAÍBA
Penedo
PERNAMBUCO
Garanhuns
Palmares
Maria de Santo Antão
Barreiros
RECIFE
(Pernambuco)

Sa. do Cachimbo
Parnaguá
Campo
Formoso
Queimadas
Senhor do
Bonfim
Pal dos Índios
Rio Largo
Maceió
ALAGOAS
6059

Pôrto Nacional
Natividade
Xique-Xique
Jacobina
Serrinha
Capela
SERGIPE
Aracaju
São Cristóvão
Estância

alegre
Serra formosa
Ilha do Bananal
Sta. Isabel
Manuel Alves
Peixe
Barreiras
Ibotirama
Mundo
Novo
Feira de
Santana
Alagoinhas
Santo Amaro

Serra do Roncador
GOIÁS
BAHIA
Itaberaba
Cachoeira
Salvador (Bahia)

GROSSO
Cuiabá
Montes
São Domingos
Campos Belos
Sta. Maria
da Vitória
Bom Jesus
da Lapa
1850
Itaetê
Sincorá
Valença
São Félix
B. de Todos os Santos

Planalto do
Aruanã
Niquelândia
1678
Posse
Carinhanha
Brumado
Ituaçu
Jequié

Mato Grosso
Mortes
Uruaçu
Januária
Monte Azul
Condeúba
Vitória da
Conquista
Itabuna
Itacaré
Ubaitaba
Ilhéus

Rondonópolis
Baliza
DIST.
FED.
Brasília
Formosa
São Francisco
Salinas
Pedra Azul
Canavieiras

TO GROSSO
Alto
Araguaia
Anápolis
Iuiziânia
Bocaiúva
Jequitinhonha
Belmonte

DO SUL
Jatai
Goiânia
Vianópolis
Pirapora
Teófilo Otoni
Nanuque
Caravelas
Pôrto Seguro

Rio Verde
Morrinhos
Catalão
Patos de
Minas
Curvelo
Diamantina
1340
Prado
Mucuri
Abrolhos

Coxim
Itumbiara
Araguari
Uberlândia
Araxá
MINAS GERAIS
Gov. Valadares
Conceição da Barra

Campo Grande
Agua Clara
Três Lagoas
Nova Granada
Uberaba
Belo Horizonte
2890
Caratinga
Vitória
Trindade
(Braz.)

Dourados
Androlândia
Franca
Ribeirão Prêto
Barbacena
Juiz de Fora
Campos

Ponta Porã
Pres.
Prudente
Marília
Bauru
SÃO PAULO
Piracicaba
Campinas
Petrópolis
Niterói
RIO DE JANEIRO

1:16 000 000

100 50 0 100 200 300 miles
100 0 100 200 300 400 km

PARAGUAY
PARANÁ
MATO GROSSO DO SUL
BRASIL
SANTA CATARINA
RIO GRANDE DO SUL
URUGUAY
BUENOS AIRES
MONTEVIDEO
SANTIAGO
Asunción

RIO DE JANEIRO
SÃO PAULO
Curitiba
Pôrto Alegre
Córdoba
Rosario
Mendoza
Valparaíso
Mar del Plata
Bahía Blanca
Neuquén
Valdivia
Puerto Montt
Comodoro Rivadavia
Río Gallegos
Punta Arenas
Tierra del Fuego

Tropic of Capricorn

Peru—Chile Trench

FALKLAND ISLANDS
(Islas Malvinas)
(Br.)
West Falkland
East Falkland
Stanley

South Georgia (Br.)

SOUTH ATLANTIC OCEAN

Estrecho de Magallanes (Magellan's Str.)
Cabo de Hornos (C. Horn)
Beagle Canal
I. de los Estados (Staten I.)

West from Greenwich

Projection: Sanson-Flamsteed's Sinusoidal

ft   m
18 000 6000
12 000 4000
9000   3000
6000   2000
4500   1500
3000   1000
1200   400
600   200
0   0
200   600
2000   6000
4000   12 000
6000   18 000
8000   24 000
m   ft

INDEX

The number printed in bold type against each entry indicates the map page where the feature can be found. This is followed by its geographical coordinates. The first coordinate indicates latitude, i.e. distance north or south of the Equator. The second coordinate indicates longitude, i.e. distance east or west of the meridian of Greenwich in England (shown as 0° longitude). Both latitude and longitude are measured in degrees and minutes (with 60 minutes in a degree), and appear on the map as horizontal and vertical gridlines respectively. Thus the entry for Paris in France reads.

Paris, France   **19** 48 50 N 2 20 E

This entry indicates that Paris is on page 19, at latitude 48 degrees 50 minutes north (approximately five-sixths of the distance between horizontal gridlines 48 and 49, marked on either side of the page) and at longitude 2 degrees 20 minutes east (approximately one-third of the distance between vertical gridlines 2 and 3, marked at top and bottom of the page). Paris can be found where lines extended from these two points cross on the page. The geographical coordinates are sometimes only approximate but are close enough for the place to be located. Rivers have been indexed to their mouth or confluence.

An open square □ signifies that the name refers to an administrative subdivision of a country while a solid square ■ follows the name of a country. An arrow ⌒ follows the name of a river.

The alphabetical order of names composed of two or more words is governed primarily by the first word and then by the second. This rule applies even if the second word is a description or its abbreviation, R.,L.,I. for example. Names composed of a proper name (Gibraltar) and a description (Strait of) are positioned alphabetically by the proper name. If the same place name occurs twice or more times in the index and all are in the same country, each is followed by the name of the administrative subdivision in which it is located. The names are placed in the alphabetical order of the subdivisions. If the same place name occurs twice or more in the index and the places are in different countries they will be followed by their country names, the latter governing the alphabetical order. In a mixture of these situations the primary order is fixed by the alphabetical sequence of the countries and the secondary order by that of the country subdivisions.

Please refer to the table at the end of the index for the recent place name changes in India, Iran, Mozambique and Zimbabwe.

Abbreviations used in the index:

A. R.–Autonomous Region
A. S. S. R.–Autonomous Soviet Socialist Republic
Afghan.–Afghanistan
Ala.–Alabama
Alas.–Alaska
Alg.–Algeria
Alta.–Alberta
Amer.–America
And. P.–Andhra Pradesh
Arch.–Archipelago
Argent.–Argentina
Ariz.–Arizona
Ark.–Arkansas
Atl. Oc. – Atlantic Ocean
Austral. – Australia
B. – Baie, Bahía, Bay, Bucht, Bugt
B.A. – Buenos Aires
B.C. – British Columbia
Bangla. – Bangladesh
Barr. – Barrage
Bay. – Bayern
Belg. – Belgium
Berks. – Berkshire
Bol. – Bolshoi
Boliv. – Bolivia
Bots. – Botswana
Br. – British
Bri. – Bridge
Bt. – Bight
Bucks. – Buckinghamshire
Bulg. – Bulgaria
C. – Cabo, Cap, Cape, Coast
C. Prov. – Cape Province
Calif. – California
Camb. – Cambodia
Cambs. – Cambridgeshire
Can. – Canada
Cent. – Central
Chan. – Channel
Co. – Country
Colomb. – Colombia
Colo. – Colorado
Conn. – Connecticut
Cord. – Cordillera
Cr. – Creek
Cumb. – Cumbria
Czech. – Czechoslovakia
D.C. – District of Columbia
Del. – Delaware
Dep. – Dependency
Derby. – Derbyshire
Des. – Desert
Dist. – District
Dj. – Djebel
Dumf. & Gall. – Dumfries and Galloway
E. – East
Eng. – England
Fed. – Federal, Federation
Fla. – Florida
For. – Forest
Fr. – France, French
Fs. – Falls
Ft. – Fort

G. – Golfe, Golfo, Gulf, Guba
Ga. – Georgia
Ger. – Germany
Glam. – Glamorgan
Glos. – Gloucestershire
Gr. – Grande, Great, Greater, Group
H.K. – Hong Kong
H.P. – Himachal Pradesh
Hants. – Hampshire
Harb. – Harbor, Harbour
Hd. – Head
Here. & Worcs. – Hereford and Worcester
Herts. – Hertfordshire
Hts. – Heights
Hung. – Hungary
I.o.M. – Isle of Man
I.(s). – Île, Ilha, Insel, Isla, Island, Isle
Id. – Idaho
Ill. – Illinois
Ind. – Indiana
Ind. Oc. – Indian Ocean
Indon. – Indonesia
J. – Jabal, Jabel, Jazira
Junc. – Junction
K. – Kap, Kapp
K. – Kuala
Kal. – Kalmyk A.S.S.R.
Kans. – Kansas
Kep. – Kepulauan
Ky. – Kentucky
L. – Lac, Lacul, Lago, Lagoa, Lake, Limni, Loch, Lough
La. – Lousiana
Lancs. – Lancashire
Leb. – Lebanon
Leics. – Leicestershire
Lim. – Limerick
Lincs. – Lincolnshire
Lit. – Little
Lr. – Lower
Mad. P. – Madhya Pradesh
Madag. – Madagascar
Malay. – Malaysia
Man. – Manitoba
Manch. – Manchester
Maran. – Maranhão
Mass. – Massachusetts
Md. – Maryland
Me. – Maine
Mend. – Mendoza
Mér. – Méridionale
Mich. – Michigan
Mid. – Middle
Minn. – Minnesota
Miss. – Mississippi
Mo. – Missouri
Mong. – Mongolia
Mont. – Montana
Moroc. – Morocco
Mozam. – Mozambique
Mt.(e). – Mont, Monte, Monti, Montaña, Mountain
Mys. – Mysore
N. – Nord, Norte, North, Northern, Nouveau

N.B. – New Brunswick
N.C. – North Carolina
N.D. – North Dakota
N.H. – New Hampshire
N.I. – North Island
N.J. – New Jersey
N. Mex. – New Mexico
N.S. – Nova Scotia
N.S.W. – New South Wales
N.T. – Northern Territory
N.W.T. – North West Territory
N.Y. – New York
N.Z. – New Zealand
Nat. – National
Nat.Park. – National Park
Nebr. – Nebraska
Neth. – Netherlands
Nev. – Nevada
Newf. – Newfoundland
Nic. – Nicaragua
Northants. – Northamptonshire
Northumb. – Northumberland
Notts. – Nottinghamshire
O. – Oued, ouadi
Occ. – Occidentale
O.F.S. – Orange Free State
Okla. – Oklahoma
Ont. – Ontario
Or. – Orientale
Oreg. – Oregon
Os. – Ostrov
Oxon. – Oxfordshire
Oz. – Ozero
P. – Pass, Passo, Pasul, Pulau
P.E.I. – Prince Edward Island
P.N.G. – Papua New Guinea
P.O. – Post Office
P. Rico.–Puerto Rico
Pa. – Pennsylvania
Pac. Oc. – Pacific Ocean
Pak. – Pakistan
Parag. – Paraguay
Pass. – Passage
Pen. – Peninsula, Peninsule
Phil. – Philippines
Pk. – Peak
Plat. – Plateau
P-ov. – Poluostrov
Port. – Portugal, Portuguese
Prom. – Promontory
Prov. – Province, Provincial
Pt. – Point
Pta. – Ponta, Punta
Pte. – Pointe
Qué. – Québec
Queens. – Queensland
R. – Rio, River
R.I. – Rhode Island
R.S.F.S.R. – Russian Soviet Federative Socialist Republic
Ra.(s). – Range(s)
Raj. – Rajasthan
Reg. – Region
Rep. – Republic
Res. – Reserve, Reservoir
Rhld. – Pfz. – Rheinland–Pfalz

S. – San, South
S. Afr. – South Africa
S. Austral. – South Australia
S.C. – South Carolina
S.D. – South Dakota
S.-Holst. – Schleswig-Holstein
S.I. – South Island
S. Leone–Sierra Leone
S.S.R. – Soviet Socialist Republic
Sa. – Serra, Sierra
Sard. – Sardinia
Sask. – Saskatchewan
Scot. – Scotland
Sd. – Sound
Sept. – Septentrionale
Sev. – Severnaja
Sib. – Siberia
Som. – Somerset
Span. – Spanish
Sprs. – Springs
St. – Saint
Sta. – Santa, Station
Staffs. – Staffordshire
Ste. – Sainte
Sto. – Santo
Str. – Strait, Stretto
Switz. – Switzerland
T.O. – Telegraph Office
Tas. – Tasmania
Tenn. – Tennessee
Terr. – Territory
Tex. – Texas
Tg. – Tanjung
Thai. – Thailand
Tipp. – Tipperary
Trans. – Transvaal
U.K. – United Kingdom
U.S.A. – United States of America
U.S.S.R. – Union of Soviet Socialist Republics
Ukr. – Ukraine
Ut.P. – Uttar Pradesh
Utd. – United
V. – Vorota
Va. – Virginia
Vdkhr. – Vodokhranilishche
Venez. – Venezuela
Vic. – Victoria
Viet. – Vietnam
Vol. – Volcano
Vt. – Vermont
W. – Wadi, West
W.A. – Western Australia
W. Isles–Western Isles
W. Va. – West Virginia
Wash. – Washington
Wilts. – Wiltshire
Wis. – Wisconsin
Wlkp. – Wielkopolski
Wyo. – Wyoming
Yorks. – Yorkshire
Yug. – Yugoslavia
Zap. – Zapadnaja
Zimb. – Zimbabwe

A

Name	Map	Lat.	Long.
Aachen	**24**	50 47N	6 4 E
Aâlâ en Nîl □	**87**	8 50N	29 55 E
Aalen	**25**	48 49N	10 6 E
Aalsmeer	**16**	52 17N	4 43 E
Aalst	**16**	50 56N	4 2 E
Aalten	**16**	51 56N	6 35 E
Aarau	**25**	47 23N	8 4 E
Aarberg	**25**	47 2N	7 16 E
Aare →	**25**	47 33N	8 14 E
Aargau □	**25**	47 26N	8 10 E
Aarschot	**16**	50 59N	4 49 E
Aba, Nigeria	**85**	5 10N	7 19 E
Aba, Zaïre	**90**	3 58N	30 17 E
Âbâ, Jazîrat	**87**	13 30N	32 31 E
Ābādān	**64**	30 22N	48 20 E
Abade, Ethiopia	**87**	9 22N	38 3 E
Abade, Iran	**65**	31 8N	52 40 E
Abadin	**30**	43 21N	7 29W
Abadla	**82**	31 2N	2 45W
Abaetetuba	**127**	1 40 S	48 50W
Abagnar Qi	**76**	43 52N	116 2 E
Abai	**125**	25 58 S	55 54W
Abak	**85**	4 58N	7 50 E
Abakaliki	**85**	6 22N	8 2 E
Abakan	**59**	53 40N	91 10 E
Abal Nam	**86**	25 20N	38 37 E
Abalemma	**85**	16 12N	7 50 E
Abanilla	**33**	38 12N	1 3W
Abano Terme	**39**	45 22N	11 46 E
Abarán	**33**	38 12N	1 23W
Abarqū	**65**	31 10N	53 20 E
'Abasān	**62**	31 19N	34 21 E
Abashiri	**74**	44 0N	144 15 E
Abashiri-Wan	**74**	44 0N	144 30 E
Abau	**98**	10 11 S	148 46 E
Abaújszántó	**27**	48 16N	21 12 E
Abay	**58**	49 38N	72 53 E
Abaya L.	**87**	6 30N	37 50 E
Abaza	**58**	52 39N	90 6 E
Abbadia San Salvatore	**39**	42 53N	11 40 E
Abbay (Nîl el Azraq) →	**87**	15 38N	32 31 E
Abbaye, Pt.	**114**	46 58N	88 4W
Abbé, L.	**87**	11 8N	41 47 E
Abbeville, France	**19**	50 6N	1 49 E
Abbeville, La., U.S.A.	**117**	30 0N	92 7W
Abbeville, S.C., U.S.A.	**115**	34 12N	82 21W
Abbiategrasso	**38**	45 23N	8 55 E
Abbieglassie	**99**	27 15 S	147 28 E
Abbotsford, B.C., Can.	**108**	49 5N	122 20W
Abbotsford, Qué., Can.	**113**	45 25N	72 53W
Abbotsford, U.S.A.	**116**	44 55N	90 20W
Abbottabad	**66**	34 10N	73 15 E
Abd al Kūrī	**63**	12 5N	52 20 E
Abéché	**81**	13 50N	20 35 E
Abejar	**32**	41 48N	2 47W
Abekr	**87**	12 45N	28 50 E
Abêlessa	**82**	22 58N	4 47 E
Abengourou	**84**	6 42N	3 27W
Åbenrå	**49**	55 3N	9 25 E
Abensberg	**25**	48 49N	11 51 E
Abeokuta	**85**	7 3N	3 19 E
Aber	**90**	2 12N	32 25 E
Aberaeron	**13**	52 15N	4 16W
Aberayron = Aberaeron	**13**	52 15N	4 16W
Abercorn	**99**	25 12 S	151 5 E
Abercorn = Mbala	**91**	8 46 S	31 17 E
Abercrombie →	**100**	33 54 S	149 8 E
Aberdare	**13**	51 43N	3 27W
Aberdare Ra.	**90**	0 15 S	36 50 E
Aberdeen, Austral.	**99**	32 9 S	150 56 E
Aberdeen, Can.	**109**	52 20N	106 8W
Aberdeen, S. Afr.	**92**	32 28 S	24 2 E
Aberdeen, U.K.	**14**	57 9N	2 6W
Aberdeen, Ala., U.S.A.	**115**	33 49N	88 33W
Aberdeen, Idaho, U.S.A.	**118**	42 57N	112 50W
Aberdeen, S.D., U.S.A.	**116**	45 30N	98 30W
Aberdeen, Wash., U.S.A.	**118**	47 0N	123 50W
Aberdovey	**13**	52 33N	4 3W
Aberfeldy	**14**	56 37N	3 50W
Abergaria-a-Velha	**30**	40 41N	8 32W
Abergavenny	**13**	51 49N	3 1W
Abernathy	**117**	33 49N	101 49W
Abert L.	**118**	42 40N	120 8W
Aberystwyth	**13**	52 25N	4 6W
Abha	**86**	18 0N	42 34 E
Abhayapuri	**69**	26 24N	90 38 E
Abidiya	**86**	18 18N	34 3 E
Abidjan	**84**	5 26N	3 58W
Abilene, Kans., U.S.A.	**116**	39 0N	97 16W
Abilene, Texas, U.S.A.	**117**	32 22N	99 40W
Abingdon, U.K.	**13**	51 40N	1 17W
Abingdon, Ill., U.S.A.	**116**	40 53N	90 23W
Abingdon, Va., U.S.A.	**115**	36 46N	81 56W
Abitau →	**109**	59 53N	109 3W
Abitau L.	**109**	60 27N	107 15W
Abitibi L.	**106**	48 40N	79 40W
Abiy Adi	**87**	13 39N	39 3 E
Abkhaz A.S.S.R. □	**57**	43 0N	41 0 E
Abkit	**59**	64 10N	157 10 E
Abnûb	**86**	27 18N	31 4 E
Åbo	**51**	60 28N	22 15 E
Abo, Massif d'	**83**	21 41N	16 8 E
Abocho	**85**	7 35N	6 56 E
Abohar	**68**	30 10N	74 10 E
Aboisso	**84**	5 30N	3 5W
Aboméy	**85**	7 10N	2 5 E
Abondance	**21**	46 18N	6 42 E
Abong-Mbang	**88**	4 0N	13 8 E
Abonnema	**85**	4 41N	6 49 E
Abony	**27**	47 12N	20 3 E
Aboso	**84**	5 23N	1 57W
Abou-Deïa	**81**	11 20N	19 20 E
Aboyne	**14**	57 4N	2 48W
Abra Pampa	**124**	22 43 S	65 42W
Abrantes	**31**	39 24N	8 7W
Abraveses	**30**	40 41N	7 55W
Abreojos, Pta.	**120**	26 50N	113 40W
Abreschviller	**19**	48 39N	7 6 E
Abrets, Les	**21**	45 32N	5 35 E
Abri, Esh Shimâliya, Sudan	**86**	20 50N	30 27 E
Abri, Janub Kordofân, Sudan	**87**	11 40N	30 21 E
Abrud	**46**	46 19N	23 5 E
Abruzzi □	**39**	42 15N	14 0 E
Absaroka Ra.	**118**	44 40N	110 0W
Abū al Khaşīb	**64**	30 25N	48 0 E
Abū 'Alī	**64**	27 20N	49 27 E
Abu 'Arīsh	**63**	16 53N	42 48 E
Abû Ballas	**86**	24 26N	27 36 E
Abu Deleiq	**87**	15 57N	33 48 E
Abū Dhabī	**65**	24 28N	54 36 E
Abū Dīs	**62**	31 47N	35 16 E
Abû Dis	**86**	19 12N	33 38 E
Abû Dom	**87**	16 18N	32 25 E
Abû Gabra	**87**	11 2N	26 50 E
Abū Ghaush	**62**	31 48N	35 6 E
Abû Gubeiha	**87**	11 30N	31 15 E
Abu Habl, Khawr →	**87**	12 37N	31 0 E
Abu Hamed	**86**	19 32N	33 13 E
Abu Haraz	**87**	14 35N	33 30 E
Abû Haraz	**86**	19 8N	32 18 E
Abû Higar	**87**	12 50N	33 59 E
Abū Kamāl	**64**	34 30N	41 0 E
Abū Madd, Ra's	**64**	24 50N	37 7 E
Abū Markhah	**64**	25 4N	38 22 E
Abu Qir	**86**	31 18N	30 0 E
Abu Qireiya	**86**	24 5N	35 28 E
Abu Qurqâs	**86**	28 1N	30 44 E
Abû Rudies	**86**	29 0N	33 15 E
Abu Salama	**86**	27 10N	35 51 E
Abû Simbel	**86**	22 18N	31 40 E
Abu Tig	**86**	27 4N	31 15 E
Abu Tiga	**87**	12 47N	34 12 E
Abû Zabad	**87**	12 25N	29 10 E
Abū Zābī	**65**	24 28N	54 22 E
Abuja	**85**	9 16N	7 2 E
Abukuma-Gawa →	**74**	38 06N	140 52 E
Abunã	**126**	9 40 S	65 20W
Abunã →	**126**	9 41 S	65 20W
Aburo, Mt.	**90**	2 4N	30 53 E
Abut Hd.	**101**	43 7 S	170 15 E
Abwong	**87**	9 2N	32 14 E
Åby	**49**	58 40N	16 10 E
Aby, Lagune	**84**	5 15N	3 14W
Acámbaro	**120**	20 0N	100 40W
Acanthus	**44**	40 27N	23 47 E
Acaponeta	**120**	22 30N	105 20W
Acapulco	**120**	16 51N	99 56W
Acatlán	**120**	18 10N	98 3W
Acayucan	**120**	17 59N	94 58W
Accéglio	**38**	44 28N	6 59 E
Accomac	**114**	37 43N	75 40W
Accra	**85**	5 35N	0 6W
Accrington	**12**	53 46N	2 22W
Acebal	**124**	33 20 S	60 50W
Aceh □	**72**	4 15N	97 30 E
Acerenza	**41**	40 50N	15 58 E
Acerra	**41**	40 57N	14 22 E
Aceuchal	**31**	38 39N	6 30W
Achalpur	**68**	21 22N	77 32 E
Achenkirch	**26**	47 32N	11 45 E
Achensee	**26**	47 26N	11 45 E
Acher	**68**	23 10N	72 32 E
Achern	**25**	48 37N	8 5 E
Achill	**15**	53 56N	9 55W
Achill Hd.	**15**	53 59N	10 15W
Achill I.	**15**	53 58N	10 5W
Achill Sound	**15**	53 53N	9 55W
Achim	**24**	53 1N	9 2 E
Achinsk	**59**	56 20N	90 20 E
Achol	**87**	6 35N	31 32 E
Acireale	**41**	37 37N	15 9 E
Ackerman	**117**	33 20N	89 8W
Acklins I.	**121**	22 30N	74 0W
Acland, Mt.	**97**	24 50 S	148 20 E
Acme	**108**	51 33N	113 30W
Aconcagua □, Argent.	**124**	32 50 S	70 0W
Aconcagua □, Chile	**124**	32 15 S	70 30W
Aconcagua, Cerro	**124**	32 39 S	70 0W
Aconquija, Mt.	**124**	27 0 S	66 0W
Açores, Is. dos = Azores	**6**	38 44N	29 0W
Acquapendente	**39**	42 45N	11 50 E
Acquasanta	**39**	42 46N	13 24 E
Acquaviva delle Fonti	**41**	40 53N	16 50 E
Acqui	**38**	44 40N	8 28 E
Acre = 'Akko	**62**	32 55N	35 4 E
Acre □	**126**	9 1 S	71 0W
Acre →	**126**	8 45 S	67 22W
Acri	**41**	39 29N	16 23 E
Acs	**27**	47 42N	18 0 E
Actium	**44**	38 57N	20 45 E
Acton	**112**	43 38N	80 3W
Ad Dahnā	**64**	24 30N	48 10 E
Ad Dammām	**64**	26 20N	50 5 E
Ad Dār al Ḩamrā'	**64**	27 20N	37 45 E
Ad Dawhah	**65**	25 15N	51 35 E
Ad Dilam	**64**	23 55N	47 10 E
Ada, Ghana	**85**	5 44N	0 40 E
Ada, Minn., U.S.A.	**116**	47 20N	96 30W
Ada, Okla., U.S.A.	**117**	34 50N	96 45W
Ada, Yugo.	**42**	45 49N	20 9 E
Adaja →	**30**	41 32N	4 52W
Ådalslinden	**48**	63 27N	16 55 E
Adam	**65**	22 15N	57 28 E
Adamaoua, Massif de l'	**85**	7 20N	12 20 E
Adamawa Highlands = Adamaoua, Massif de l'	**85**	7 20N	12 20 E
Adamello, Mt.	**38**	46 10N	10 34 E
Adami Tulu	**87**	7 53N	38 41 E
Adaminaby	**99**	36 0 S	148 45 E
Adams, Mass., U.S.A.	**113**	42 38N	73 8W
Adams, N.Y., U.S.A.	**114**	43 50N	76 3W
Adams, Wis., U.S.A.	**116**	43 59N	89 50W
Adam's Bridge	**70**	9 15N	79 40 E
Adams Center	**113**	43 51N	76 1W
Adams L.	**108**	51 10N	119 40W
Adams, Mt.	**118**	46 10N	121 28W
Adam's Peak	**70**	6 48N	80 30 E
Adamuz	**31**	38 2N	4 32W
Adana	**64**	37 0N	35 16 E
Adanero	**30**	40 56N	4 36W
Adapazarı	**64**	40 48N	30 25 E
Adarama	**87**	17 10N	34 52 E
Adare, C.	**5**	71 0 S	171 0 E
Adaut	**73**	8 8 S	131 7 E
Adavale	**97**	25 52 S	144 32 E
Adda →	**38**	45 8N	9 53 E
Addis Ababa = Addis Abeba	**87**	9 2N	38 42 E
Addis Abeba	**87**	9 2N	38 42 E
Addis Alem	**87**	9 0N	38 17 E
Addison	**112**	42 9N	77 15W
Adebour	**85**	13 17N	11 50 E
Adel	**115**	31 10N	83 28W
Adelaide, Austral.	**97**	34 52 S	138 30 E
Adelaide, Madag.	**93**	32 42 S	26 20 E
Adelaide I.	**5**	67 15 S	68 30W
Adelaide Pen.	**104**	68 15N	97 30W
Adélie, Terre	**5**	68 0 S	140 0 E
Ademuz	**32**	40 5N	1 13W
Aden = Al 'Adan	**63**	12 45N	45 12 E
Aden, G. of	**63**	13 0N	50 0 E
Adendorp	**92**	32 25 S	24 30 E
Adgz	**82**	30 47N	6 30W
Adhoi	**68**	23 26N	70 32 E
Adi	**73**	4 15 S	133 30 E
Adi Daro	**87**	14 20N	38 14 E
Adi Keyih	**87**	14 51N	39 22 E
Adi Kwala	**87**	14 38N	38 48 E
Adi Ugri	**87**	14 58N	38 48 E
Adieu, C.	**96**	32 0 S	132 10 E
Adigala	**87**	10 24N	42 15 E
Adige →	**39**	45 9N	12 20 E
Adigrat	**87**	14 20N	39 26 E
Adilabad	**70**	19 33N	78 20 E
Adin	**118**	41 10N	121 0W
Adin Khel	**65**	32 45N	68 5 E
Adirampattinam	**70**	10 28N	79 20 E
Adirondack Mts.	**114**	44 0N	74 15W
Adjim	**83**	33 47N	10 50 E
Adjohon	**85**	6 41N	2 32 E
Adjud	**46**	46 7N	27 10 E
Adjumani	**90**	3 20N	31 50 E
Adlavik Is.	**107**	55 2N	57 45W
Adler	**57**	43 28N	39 52 E
Admer	**83**	20 21N	5 27 E
Admer, Erg d'	**83**	24 0N	9 5 E
Admiralty B.	**5**	62 0 S	59 0W
Admiralty G.	**96**	14 20 S	125 55 E
Admiralty I.	**104**	57 40N	134 35W
Admiralty Inlet	**118**	48 0N	122 40W
Admiralty Is.	**94**	2 0 S	147 0 E
Admiralty Ra.	**5**	72 0 S	164 0 E
Ado	**85**	6 36N	2 56 E
Ado Ekiti	**85**	7 38N	5 12 E
Adok	**87**	8 10N	30 20 E
Adola	**87**	11 14N	41 44 E
Adonara	**73**	8 15 S	123 5 E
Adoni	**70**	15 33N	77 18W
Adony	**27**	47 6N	18 52 E
Adour →	**20**	43 32N	1 32W
Adra, India	**69**	23 30N	86 42 E
Adra, Spain	**33**	36 43N	3 3W
Adrano	**41**	37 40N	14 49 E
Adrar	**82**	27 51N	0 11W
Adré	**81**	13 40N	22 20 E
Adrī	**83**	27 32N	13 2 E
Ádria	**39**	45 4N	12 3 E
Adrian, Mich., U.S.A.	**114**	41 55N	84 0W
Adrian, Tex., U.S.A.	**117**	35 19N	102 37W
Adriatic Sea	**34**	43 0N	16 0 E
Adua	**73**	1 45 S	129 50 E
Adur	**70**	9 8N	76 40 E
Adwa	**87**	14 15N	38 52 E
Adzhar A.S.S.R. □	**57**	42 0N	42 0 E
Adzopé	**84**	6 7N	3 49W
Ægean Sea	**35**	37 0N	25 0 E
Æolian Is. = Eólie	**41**	38 30N	14 50 E
Aerht'ai Shan	**75**	46 40N	92 45 E
Ærø	**49**	54 52N	10 25 E
Ærøskøbing	**49**	54 53N	10 24 E
Aëtós	**45**	37 15N	21 50 E
Afafi, Massif d'	**83**	22 11N	15 10 E
Afándou	**45**	36 18N	28 12 E
Afarag, Erg	**82**	23 50N	2 47 E
Affreville = Khemis Miliania	**82**	36 11N	2 14 E
Afghanistan ■	**65**	33 0N	65 0 E
Afgoi	**63**	2 7N	44 59 E
'Afīf	**64**	23 53N	42 56 E
Afikpo	**85**	5 53N	7 54 E
Aflisses, O. →	**82**	28 40N	0 50 E
Aflou	**82**	34 7N	2 3 E
Afognak I.	**104**	58 10N	152 50W
Afragola	**41**	40 54N	14 15 E
Afrera	**87**	13 16N	41 5 E
Africa	**78**	10 0N	20 0 E
Afton	**113**	42 14N	75 31W
Aftout	**82**	26 50N	3 45W
Afuá	**127**	0 15 S	50 20W
Afula	**62**	32 37N	35 17 E
Afyonkarahisar	**64**	38 45N	30 33 E
Aga	**86**	30 55N	31 10 E
Agadès = Agadez	**85**	16 58N	7 59 E
Agadez	**85**	16 58N	7 59 E
Agadir	**82**	30 28N	9 35W
Agano →	**74**	37 57N	139 8 E
Agapa	**59**	71 27N	89 15 E
Agar	**68**	23 40N	76 2 E
Agaro	**87**	7 50N	36 38 E
Agartala	**67**	23 50N	91 23 E
Agăş	**46**	46 28N	26 15 E
Agassiz	**108**	49 14N	121 46W
Agats	**73**	5 33 S	138 0 E
Agattu I.	**104**	52 25N	172 30 E
Agbélouvé	**85**	6 35N	1 14 E
Agboville	**84**	5 55N	4 15W
Agdam	**57**	40 0N	46 58 E
Agdash	**57**	40 44N	47 22 E
Agde	**20**	43 19N	3 28 E
Agde, C. d'	**20**	43 16N	3 28 E
Agdzhabedi	**57**	40 5N	47 27 E
Agen	**20**	44 12N	0 38 E
Ager Tay	**83**	20 0N	17 41 E
Agersø	**49**	55 13N	11 12 E
Ageyevo	**55**	54 10N	36 27 E
Agger	**49**	56 47N	8 13 E
Ággius	**40**	40 56N	9 4 E
Aghil Mts.	**69**	36 0N	77 0 E
Aginskoye	**59**	51 6N	114 32 E
Agira	**41**	37 40N	14 30 E
Agly →	**20**	42 46N	3 3 E
Agnibilékrou	**84**	7 10N	3 11W
Agnita	**46**	45 59N	24 40 E
Agnone	**41**	41 49N	14 20 E
Agofie	**85**	8 27N	0 15 E
Agogna →	**38**	45 4N	8 52 E
Agogo	**87**	7 50N	28 45 E
Agon	**18**	49 2N	1 34W
Agön	**48**	61 34N	17 23 E
Ágordo	**39**	46 18N	12 2 E
Agout →	**20**	43 47N	1 41 E
Agra	**68**	27 17N	77 58 E
Agramunt	**32**	41 48N	1 6 E
Agreda	**32**	41 51N	1 55W
Agri →	**41**	40 13N	16 44 E
Ağri Daği	**64**	39 50N	44 15 E
Ağri Karakose	**64**	39 44N	43 3 E
Agrigento	**40**	37 19N	13 33 E
Agrinion	**45**	38 37N	21 27 E
Agrópoli	**41**	40 23N	14 59 E
Água Clara	**127**	20 25 S	52 45W
Agua Prieta	**120**	31 20N	109 32W
Aguadas	**126**	5 40N	75 38W
Aguadilla	**121**	18 27N	67 10W
Aguanish	**107**	50 14N	62 2W
Aguanus →	**107**	50 13N	62 5W
Aguapey →	**124**	29 7 S	56 36W
Aguaray Guazú →	**124**	24 47 S	57 19W
Aguarico →	**126**	0 59 S	75 11W
Aguas →	**32**	41 20N	0 30W
Aguas Blancas	**124**	24 15 S	69 55W
Aguas Calientes, Sierra de	**124**	25 26 S	66 40W
Aguascalientes	**120**	21 53N	102 12W
Aguascalientes □	**120**	22 0N	102 20W
Agudo	**31**	38 59N	4 52
Águeda	**30**	40 34N	8 27
Agueda →	**30**	41 2N	6 56
Aguié	**85**	13 31N	7 46
Aguilafuente	**30**	41 13N	4 7
Aguilar	**31**	37 31N	4 40
Aguilar de Campóo	**30**	42 47N	4 15
Aguilares	**124**	27 26 S	65 35
Aguilas	**33**	37 23N	1 35
Agulaa	**87**	13 40N	39 40
Agulhas, Kaap	**92**	34 52 S	20 0
Agung	**72**	8 20 S	115 28
'Agur	**62**	31 42N	34 55
Agur	**90**	2 28N	32 55
Agusan →	**73**	9 0N	125 30
Agvali	**57**	42 36N	46 8
Aha Mts.	**92**	19 45 S	21 0
Ahaggar	**83**	23 0N	6 30
Ahamansu	**85**	7 38N	0 35
Ahar	**64**	38 35N	47
Ahaus	**24**	52 4N	7
Ahelledjem	**83**	26 37N	6 58
Ahipara B.	**101**	35 5 S	173
Ahiri	**70**	19 30N	80
Ahlen	**24**	51 45N	7 52
Ahmadabad (Ahmedabad)	**68**	23 0N	72 40
Ahmadnagar (Ahmednagar)	**70**	19 7N	74 46
Ahmadpur	**68**	29 12N	71 10
Ahmar Mts.	**87**	9 20N	41 1
Ahoada	**85**	5 8N	6 3
Ahr →	**24**	50 33N	7 1
Ahrensbök	**24**	54 0N	10 3
Ahrweiler	**24**	50 31N	7
Aḩsā', Wāḩat al	**64**	25 50N	49
Ahuachapán	**120**	13 54N	89 5
Åhus	**49**	55 56N	14 1
Ahvāz	**64**	31 20N	48 4
Ahvenanmaa = Åland	**51**	60 15N	20
Ahwar	**63**	13 30N	46 4
Ahzar	**85**	15 30N	3 2
Aichach	**25**	48 28N	11
Aichi □	**74**	35 0N	137 1
Aidone	**41**	37 26N	14 2
Aiello Cálabro	**41**	39 6N	16 1
Aigle	**25**	46 18N	6 5
Aigle, L'	**18**	48 46N	0 3
Aignay-le-Duc	**19**	47 40N	4 4
Aigre	**20**	45 54N	0
Aigua	**125**	34 13 S	54 4
Aigueperse	**20**	46 3N	3
Aigues-Mortes	**21**	43 35N	4
Aigues-Mortes, G. d'	**21**	43 31N	4
Aiguilles	**21**	44 47N	6 5
Aiguillon	**20**	44 18N	0 2
Aiguillon, L'	**20**	46 20N	1
Aigurande	**20**	46 27N	1
Aihui	**75**	50 10N	127
Aija	**126**	9 50 S	77
Aijal	**67**	23 40N	92
Aiken	**115**	33 34N	81
Aillant-sur-Tholon	**19**	47 52N	3
Aillik	**107**	55 11N	59
Ailly-sur-Noye	**19**	49 45N	2
Ailsa Craig	**14**	55 15N	5
'Ailūn	**62**	32 18N	35
Aim	**59**	59 0N	133
Aimere	**73**	8 45 S	121
Aimogasta	**124**	28 33 S	66
Aimorés	**127**	19 30 S	41
Ain □	**21**	46 5N	5
Ain →	**21**	45 45N	5
Ain Banaiyan	**65**	23 0N	51
Aïn Beïda	**83**	35 50N	7
Ain ben Khellil	**82**	33 15N	0
Aïn Ben Tili	**82**	25 59N	9
Aïn Beni Mathar	**82**	34 1N	2
Aïn Benian	**82**	36 48N	2
Ain Dalla	**86**	27 20N	27
Ain Dar	**64**	25 55N	49
Ain el Mafki	**86**	27 30N	28

Aïn Galakka 81 18 10N 18 30 E
Ain Girba 86 29 20N 25 14 E
Aïn M'lila 83 36 2N 6 35 E
Ain Qeiqab 86 29 42N 24 55 E
Aïn-Sefra 82 32 47N 0 37W
Ain Sheikh Murzûk 86 26 47N 27 45 E
Ain Sukhna 86 29 32N 32 20 E
Aïn Tédelès 82 36 0N 0 21 E
Aïn-Témouchent 82 35 16N 1 8W
Aïn Touta 83 35 26N 5 54 E
Ain Zeitûn 86 29 10N 25 48 E
Aïn Zorah 82 34 37N 3 32W
Ainabo 63 9 0N 46 25 E
Ainaži 54 57 50N 24 24 E
Ainos Óros 45 38 10N 20 35 E
Ainsworth 116 42 33N 99 52W
Aïr 85 18 30N 8 0 E
Airaines 19 49 58N 1 55 E
Airdrie 14 55 53N 3 57W
Aire 19 50 37N 2 22 E
Aire →, France 19 49 18N 4 55 E
Aire →, U.K. 12 53 42N 0 55W
Aire, I. del 32 39 48N 4 16 E
Aire-sur-l'Adour 20 43 42N 0 15W
Airvault 18 46 50N 0 8W
Aisch → 25 49 46N 11 1 E
Aisne □ 19 49 42N 3 40 E
Aisne → 19 49 26N 2 50 E
Aitana, Sierra de 33 38 35N 0 24W
Aitape 98 3 11 S 142 22 E
Aitkin 116 46 32N 93 43W
Aitolia Kai Akarnania □ 45 38 45N 21 18 E
Aitolikón 45 38 26N 21 21 E
Aiud 46 46 19N 23 44 E
Aix-en-Provence 21 43 32N 5 27 E
Aix-la-Chapelle = Aachen 24 50 47N 6 4 E
Aix-les-Bains 21 45 41N 5 53 E
Aix-sur-Vienne 20 45 48N 1 8 E
Aiyansh 108 55 17N 129 2W
Áiyina 45 37 45N 23 26 E
Aiyinion 44 40 28N 22 28 E
Aiyion 45 38 15N 22 5 E
Aizenay 18 46 44N 1 38W
Aizpute 54 56 43N 21 40 E
Ajaccio 21 41 55N 8 40 E
Ajaccio, G. d' 21 41 52N 8 40 E
Ajanta Ra. 70 20 28N 75 50 E
Ajax 112 43 50N 79 1W
Ajdâbiyah 83 30 54N 20 4 E
Ajdovščina 39 45 54N 13 54 E
Ajibar 87 10 35N 38 36 E
Ajka 27 47 4N 17 31 E
'Ajmān 65 25 25N 55 30 E
Ajmer 68 26 28N 74 37 E
Ajo 119 32 18N 112 54W
Ajok 87 9 15N 28 28 E
Ak Dağ 64 36 30N 30 0 E
Akaba 85 8 10N 1 2 E
Akabli 82 26 49N 1 31 E
Akaki Beseka 87 8 55N 38 45 E
Akala 87 15 39N 36 13 E
Akaroa 101 43 49 S 172 59 E
Akasha 86 21 10N 30 32 E
Akashi 74 34 45N 135 0 E
Akbou 83 36 31N 4 31 E
Akelamo 73 1 35N 129 40 E
Åkernes 47 58 45N 7 30 E
Akershus fylke □ 47 60 0N 11 10 E
Akeru → 70 17 25N 80 0 E
Aketi 88 2 38N 23 47 E
Akhaïa □ 45 38 5N 21 45 E
Akhalkalaki 57 41 27N 43 25 E
Akhaltsikhe 57 41 40N 43 0 E
Akharnai 45 38 5N 23 44 E
Akhelóös → 45 38 36N 21 14 E
Akhendria 45 34 58N 25 16 E
Akhéron → 44 39 20N 20 29 E
Akhisar 64 38 56N 27 48 E
Akhladhókambos 45 37 31N 22 35 E
Akhmîm 86 26 31N 31 47 E
Akhtopol 43 42 6N 27 56 E
Akhtubinsk (Petropavlovskiy) 57 48 13N 46 7 E
Akhty 57 41 30N 47 45 E
Akhtyrka 54 50 25N 35 0 E
Akimiski I. 106 52 50N 81 30W
Akimovka 56 46 44N 35 0 E
Åkirkeby 49 55 4N 14 55 E
Akita 74 39 45N 140 7 E
Akita □ 74 39 40N 140 30 E
Akjoujt 84 19 45N 14 15W
Akka 82 29 22N 8 9W
'Akko 62 32 55N 35 4 E
Akkol 58 45 0N 75 39 E
Akköy 45 37 30N 27 18 E
Aklampa 85 8 15N 2 10 E
Aklavik 104 68 12N 135 0W
Akmonte 31 37 13N 6 38W
Aknoul 82 34 40N 3 55W
Ako 85 10 19N 10 48 E
Akobo → 87 7 48N 33 3 E
Akola 68 20 42N 77 2 E
Akonolinga 85 3 50N 12 18 E
Akordat 87 15 30N 37 40 E
Akosombo Dam 85 6 20N 0 5 E
Akot, India 68 21 10N 77 10 E
Akot, Sudan 87 6 31N 30 9 E
Akpatok I. 105 60 25N 68 8W
Akranes 50 64 19N 21 58W
Åkrehamn 47 59 15N 5 10 E
Akreijit 84 18 19N 9 11W
Akritas Venétiko, Ákra 45 36 43N 21 54 E
Akron, Colo., U.S.A. 116 40 13N 103 15W
Akron, Ohio, U.S.A. 114 41 7N 81 31W
Akrotiri, Ákra 44 40 26N 25 27 E
Aksai Chih 69 35 15N 79 55 E
Aksaray 64 38 25N 34 2 E
Aksarka 58 66 31N 67 50 E
Aksay 52 51 11N 53 0 E
Akşehir 64 38 18N 31 30 E
Aksenovo Zilovskoye 59 53 20N 117 40 E
Akstafa 57 41 7N 45 27 E
Aksu 75 41 5N 80 10 E
Aksum 87 14 5N 38 40 E
Aktogay 58 46 57N 79 40 E
Aktyubinsk 53 50 17N 57 10 E
Aku 85 6 40N 7 18 E
Akure 85 7 15N 5 5 E
Akureyri 50 65 40N 18 6W
Akusha 57 42 18N 47 30 E
Al Abyār 83 32 9N 20 29 E
Al 'Adan 63 12 45N 45 0 E
Al Amāda03yah 64 37 5N 43 30 E
Al Amārah 64 31 55N 47 15 E
Al 'Aqabah 62 29 31N 35 0 E
Al 'Aramah 64 25 30N 46 0 E
Al Ashkhara 65 21 50N 59 30 E
Al 'Ayzarīyah (Bethany) 62 31 47N 35 15 E
Al 'Azīzīyah 83 32 30N 13 1 E
Al Badī' 64 22 0N 46 35 E
Al Barkāt 83 24 56N 10 14 E
Al Başrah 64 30 30N 47 50 E
Al Bāzūrīyah 62 33 15N 35 16 E
Al Bīrah 62 31 55N 35 12 E
Al Bu'ayrāt 83 31 24N 15 44 E
Al Buqay'ah 62 32 15N 35 30 E
Al Dīwaniyah 64 32 0N 45 0 E
Al Fallūjah 64 33 20N 43 55 E
Al Fāw 64 30 0N 48 30 E
Al Fujayrah 65 25 7N 56 18 E
Al Ghaţghaţ 64 24 40N 46 15 E
Al Hābah 64 27 10N 47 0 E
Al Haddār 64 21 58N 45 57 E
Al Ḩadīthah 64 34 0N 41 13 E
Al Hâmad 64 31 30N 39 30 E
Al Ḩamar 64 22 23N 46 6 E
Al Hamādah al Ḩamrā' 83 29 30N 12 0 E
Al Hamrā 64 24 2N 38 55 E
Al Ḩarīq 64 23 29N 46 27 E
Al Harīr, W. → 62 32 44N 35 59 E
Al Harūj al Aswad 83 27 0N 17 10 E
Al Ḩasakah 64 36 35N 40 45 E
Al Ḩawīyah 64 24 40N 49 15 E
Al Ḩawrah 63 13 50N 47 35 E
Al Ḩawţah 63 16 5N 48 20 E
Al Ḩayy 64 32 5N 46 5 E
Al Ḩillah, Iraq 64 32 30N 44 25 E
Al Ḩillah, Si. Arab. 64 23 35N 46 50 E
Al Hindīyah 64 32 30N 44 10 E
Al Ḩişnn 62 32 29N 35 52 E
Al Hoceïma 82 35 8N 3 58W
Al Ḩudaydah 63 14 50N 43 0 E
Al Ḩufrah, Awbārī, Libya 83 25 32N 14 1 E
Al Ḩufrah, Misrātah, Libya 83 29 5N 18 3 E
Al Hūfuf 64 25 25N 49 45 E
Al Ḩulwah 64 23 24N 46 48 E
Al Husayyāt 83 30 24N 20 37 E
Al 'Idwah 64 27 15N 42 35 E
Al Irq 81 29 5N 21 35 E
Al Ittihad = Madīnat ash Sha'b 63 12 50N 45 0 E
Al Jāfūrah 64 25 0N 50 15 E
Al Jaghbūb 81 29 42N 24 38 E
Al Jahrah 64 29 25N 47 40 E
Al Jalāmīd 64 31 20N 39 45 E
Al Jawf, Libya 81 24 10N 23 24 E
Al Jawf, Si. Arab. 64 29 55N 39 40 E
Al Jazır 63 18 30N 56 31 E
Al Jazirah, Libya 81 26 10N 21 20 E
Al Jazirah, Si. Arab. 64 33 30N 44 0 E
Al Jubayl 64 27 0N 49 50 E
Al Jubaylah 64 24 55N 46 25 E
Al Junaynah 81 13 27N 22 45 E
Al Juwārah 63 19 0N 57 13 E
Al Khābūrah 65 23 57N 57 5 E
Al Khalīl = Hebron 62 31 32N 35 6 E
Al Khalūf 63 20 30N 58 13 E
Al Kharfah 64 22 0N 46 35 E
Al Kharj 64 24 0N 47 0 E
Al Khufayfīyah 64 24 50N 44 35 E
Al Khums 83 32 40N 14 17 E
Al Khums □ 83 31 20N 14 10 E
Al Khurmah 64 21 58N 42 3 E
Al Kufrah 81 24 17N 23 15 E
Al Kūt 64 32 30N 46 0 E
Al Kuwayt 64 29 30N 47 30 E
Al Lādhiqīyah 64 35 30N 35 45 E
Al Lidām 63 20 33N 44 45 E
Al Līth 86 20 9N 40 15 E
Al Lubban 62 32 9N 35 14 E
Al Luḩayyah 63 15 45N 42 40 E
Al Madīnah 64 24 35N 39 52 E
Al-Mafraq 62 32 17N 36 14 E
Al Majma'ah 64 25 57N 45 22 E
Al Manāmāh 65 26 10N 50 30 E
Al Marj 81 32 25N 20 30 E
Al Maşīrah 63 20 25N 58 50 E
Al Matamma 63 16 10N 44 30 E
Al Mawşil 64 36 15N 43 5 E
Al Mazra 62 31 16N 35 31 E
Al Midhnab 64 25 50N 44 18 E
Al Miqdādīyah 64 34 0N 45 0 E
Al Mish'āb 64 28 12N 48 36 E
Al Mubarraz 64 25 30N 49 40 E
Al Muḩarraq 65 26 15N 50 40 E
Al Mukallā 63 14 33N 49 2 E
Al Mukhā 63 13 18N 43 15 E
Al Musayyib 64 32 40N 44 25 E
Al Mustajiddah 64 26 30N 41 50 E
Al Muwayliḩ 64 27 40N 35 30 E
Al Qaddāhīyah 83 31 15N 15 9 E
Al Qadīmah 64 22 20N 39 13 E
Al Qāmishli 64 37 10N 41 10 E
Al Qaryah ash Sharqīyah 83 30 28N 13 40 E
Al Qaşabát 83 32 39N 14 1 E
Al Qaţīf 64 26 35N 50 0 E
Al Qaţrūn 83 24 56N 15 3 E
Al Quaisūmah 64 28 10N 46 20 E
Al Quds 62 31 47N 35 10 E
Al Qunfidha 86 19 3N 41 4 E
Al Quraiyat 65 23 17N 58 53 E
Al Qurnah 64 31 1N 47 25 E
Al 'Ulá 64 26 35N 38 0 E
Al Uqaylah ash Sharqīgah 83 30 12N 19 10 E
Al Uqayr 64 25 40N 50 15 E
Al 'Uthmānīyahyah 64 25 5N 49 22 E
Al 'Uwaynid 64 24 50N 46 0 E
Al' 'Uwayqīlah ash Sharqīgah 64 30 30N 42 10 E
Al 'Uyūn 64 26 30N 43 50 E
Al Wajh 86 26 10N 36 30 E
Al Wakrah 65 25 10N 51 40 E
Al Wari'āh 64 27 51N 47 25 E
Al Wātīyah 83 32 28N 11 57 E
Al Yāmūn 62 32 29N 35 14 E
Ala 38 45 46N 11 0 E
Alabama □ 115 33 0N 87 0W
Alabama → 115 31 8N 87 57W
Alaçati 45 38 16N 26 23 E
Alaejos 30 41 18N 5 13W
Alagna Valsésia 38 45 51N 7 56 E
Alagoa Grande 127 7 3 S 35 35W
Alagoas □ 127 9 0 S 36 0W
Alagoinhas 127 12 7 S 38 20W
Alagón 32 41 46N 1 12W
Alagón → 31 39 44N 6 53W
Alajuela 121 10 2N 84 8W
Alakamisy 93 21 19 S 47 14 E
Alakurtti 52 67 0N 30 30 E
Alameda, Spain 31 37 12N 4 39W
Alameda, Idaho, U.S.A. 118 43 2N 112 30W
Alameda, N. Mex., U.S.A. 119 35 10N 106 43W
Alamitos, Sierra de los 120 37 21N 115 10W
Alamo 119 36 21N 115 10W
Alamogordo 119 32 59N 106 0W
Alamos 120 27 0N 109 0W
Alamosa 119 37 30N 106 0W
Åland 51 60 15N 20 0 E
Aland 70 17 36N 76 35 E
Alandroal 31 38 41N 7 24W
Alandur 70 13 0N 80 15 E
Alange, Presa de 31 38 45N 6 18W
Alanis 31 38 3N 5 43W
Alanya 64 36 38N 32 0 E
Alaotra, Farihin' 93 17 30 S 48 30 E
Alapayevsk 58 57 52N 61 42 E
Alar del Rey 30 42 38N 4 20W
Alaraz 30 40 45N 5 17W
Alaşehir 53 38 23N 28 30 E
Alaska □ 104 65 0N 150 0W
Alaska, G. of 104 58 0N 145 0W
Alaska Highway 108 60 0N 130 0W
Alaska Pen. 104 56 0N 160 0W
Alaska Range 104 62 50N 151 0W
Alássio 38 44 1N 8 10 E
Alataw Shankou 75 45 5N 81 57 E
Alatri 40 41 44N 13 21 E
Alatyr 55 54 45N 46 35 E
Alatyr → 55 54 52N 46 36 E
Alausi 126 2 0 S 78 50W
Álava □ 32 42 48N 2 28W
Alava, C. 118 48 10N 124 40W
Alaverdi 57 41 15N 44 37 E
Alawoona 99 34 45 S 140 30 E
Alayor 32 39 57N 4 8 E
Alazan → 57 41 5N 46 40 E
Alba 38 44 41N 8 1 E
Alba □ 46 46 10N 23 30 E
Alba de Tormes 30 40 50N 5 30W
Alba Iulia 46 46 8N 23 39 E
Albac 46 46 28N 23 1 E
Albacete 33 39 0N 1 50W
Albacete □ 33 38 50N 2 0W
Albacutya, L. 99 35 45 S 141 58 E
Ålbæk 49 57 36N 10 25 E
Ålbæk Bucht 49 57 35N 10 40 E
Albaida 33 38 51N 0 31W
Albalate de las Nogueras 32 40 22N 2 18W
Albalate del Arzobispo 32 41 6N 0 31W
Albania ■ 44 41 0N 20 0 E
Albano Laziale 40 41 44N 12 40 E
Albany, Austral. 96 35 1 S 117 58 E
Albany, Ga., U.S.A. 115 31 40N 84 10W
Albany, Minn., U.S.A. 116 45 37N 94 38W
Albany, N.Y., U.S.A. 114 42 35N 73 47W
Albany, Oreg., U.S.A. 118 44 41N 123 0W
Albany, Tex., U.S.A. 117 32 45N 99 20W
Albany → 106 52 17N 81 31W
Albardón 124 31 20 S 68 30W
Albarracín 32 40 25N 1 26W
Albarracín, Sierra de 32 40 30N 1 30W
Albatross B. 97 12 45 S 141 30 E
Albegna → 39 42 30N 11 11 E
Albemarle 115 35 27N 80 15W
Albemarle Sd. 115 36 0N 76 30W
Albenga 38 44 3N 8 12 E
Alberche → 30 39 58N 4 46W
Alberdi 124 26 14 S 58 20W
Alberes, Mts. 32 42 28N 2 56 E
Alberique 33 39 7N 0 31W
Albersdorf 24 54 8N 9 19 E
Albert 19 50 0N 2 38 E
Albert Canyon 108 51 8N 117 41W
Albert L. 99 35 30 S 139 10 E
Albert, L. = Mobutu Sese Seko, L. 90 1 30N 31 0 E
Albert Lea 116 43 32N 93 20W
Albert Nile → 90 3 36N 32 2 E
Alberta □ 108 54 40N 115 0W
Alberti 124 35 1 S 60 16W
Albertinia 92 34 11 S 21 34 E
Albertirsa 27 47 14N 19 37 E
Alberton 107 46 50N 64 0W
Albertville 21 45 40N 6 22 E
Albertville = Kalemie 90 5 55 S 29 9 E
Alberz, Reshteh-Ye Kūhhā-Ye 65 36 0N 52 0 E
Albi 20 43 56N 2 9 E
Albia 116 41 0N 92 50W
Albina 127 5 37N 54 15W
Albina, Ponta 92 15 52 S 11 44 E
Albino 38 45 47N 9 48 E
Albion, Idaho, U.S.A. 118 42 21N 113 37W
Albion, Mich., U.S.A. 114 42 15N 84 45W
Albion, Nebr., U.S.A. 116 41 47N 98 0W
Albion, Pa., U.S.A. 112 41 53N 80 21W
Albocácer 32 40 21N 0 1 E
Alböke 49 56 57N 16 47 E
Alborán 31 35 57N 3 0W
Alborea 33 39 17N 1 24W
Ålborg 49 57 2N 9 54 E
Ålborg B. 49 56 50N 10 35 E
Albox 33 37 23N 2 8W
Albreda 108 52 35N 119 10W
Albuera, La 31 38 45N 6 49W
Albufeira 31 37 5N 8 15W
Albula → 25 46 38N 9 30 E
Albuñol 33 36 48N 3 11W
Albuquerque 119 35 5N 106 47W
Albuquerque, Cayos de 121 12 10N 81 50W
Alburg 113 44 58N 73 19W
Alburno, Mte. 41 40 32N 15 15 E
Alburquerque 31 39 15N 6 59W
Albury 97 36 3 S 146 56 E
Alby 48 62 30N 15 28 E
Alcácer do Sal 31 38 22N 8 33W
Alcaçovas 31 38 23N 8 9W
Alcalá de Chisvert 32 40 19N 0 13 E
Alcalá de Guadaira 31 37 20N 5 50W
Alcalá de Henares 32 40 28N 3 22W
Alcalá de los Gazules 31 36 29N 5 43W
Alcalá la Real 31 37 27N 3 57W
Alcamo 40 37 59N 12 55 E
Alcanadre 32 42 24N 2 7W
Alcanadre → 32 41 43N 0 12W
Alcanar 32 40 33N 0 28 E
Alcanede 31 39 25N 8 49W
Alcanena 31 39 27N 8 40W
Alcañices 30 41 41N 6 21W
Alcaníz 32 41 2N 0 8W
Alcântara 127 2 20 S 44 30W
Alcántara 31 39 41N 6 57W
Alcantara L. 109 60 57N 108 9W
Alcantarilla 33 37 59N 1 12W
Alcaracejos 31 38 24N 4 58W
Alcaraz 33 38 40N 2 29W
Alcaraz, Sierra de 33 38 40N 2 20W
Alcarria, La 32 40 31N 2 45W
Alcaudete 31 37 35N 4 5W
Alcázar de San Juan 33 39 24N 3 12W
Alcira 33 39 9N 0 30W
Alcoa 115 35 50N 84 0W
Alcobaça 31 39 32N 9 0W
Alcobendas 32 40 32N 3 38W
Alcolea del Pinar 32 41 2N 2 28W
Alcora 32 40 5N 0 14W
Alcoutim 31 37 25N 7 28W
Alcova 118 42 37N 106 52W
Alcoy 33 38 43N 0 30W
Alcubierre, Sierra de 32 41 45N 0 22W
Alcublas 32 39 48N 0 43W
Alcudia 32 39 51N 3 7 E
Alcudia, B. de 32 39 47N 3 15 E
Alcudia, Sierra de la 31 38 34N 4 30W
Aldabra Is. 3 9 22 S 46 28 E
Aldan 59 58 40N 125 30 E
Aldan → 59 63 28N 129 35 E
Aldeburgh 13 52 9N 1 35 E
Aldeia Nova 31 37 55N 7 24W
Alder 118 45 27N 112 3W
Alderney 18 49 42N 2 12W
Aldershot 13 51 15N 0 43W
Aldersyde 108 50 40N 113 53W
Aledo 116 41 10N 90 50W
Alefa 87 11 55N 36 55 E
Aleg 84 17 3N 13 55W
Alegre 125 20 50 S 41 30W
Alegrete 125 29 40 S 56 0W
Aleisk 58 52 40N 83 0 E
Alejandro Selkirk, I. 95 33 50 S 80 15W
Aleksandriya, Ukraine S.S.R., U.S.S.R. 54 50 37N 26 19 E
Aleksandriya, Ukraine S.S.R., U.S.S.R. 56 48 42N 33 3 E
Aleksandriyskaya 57 43 59N 47 0 E
Aleksandrov 55 56 23N 38 44 E
Aleksandrovac, Srbija, Yugo. 42 44 28N 21 13 E
Aleksandrovac, Srbija, Yugo. 42 43 28N 21 3 E
Aleksandrovka 56 48 55N 32 20 E
Aleksandrovo 43 43 14N 24 51 E
Aleksandrovsk-Sakhaliniskiy 59 50 50N 142 20 E
Aleksandrovskiy Zavod 59 50 40N 117 50 E
Aleksandrovskoye 58 60 35N 77 50 E
Aleksandrów Kujawski 28 52 53N 18 43 E
Aleksandrów Łódźki 28 51 49N 19 17 E
Alekseyevka 55 50 43N 38 40 E
Aleksin 55 54 31N 37 9 E
Aleksinac 42 43 31N 21 42 E
Além Paraíba 125 21 52 S 42 41W
Alemania, Argent. 124 25 40 S 65 30W
Alemania, Chile 124 25 10 S 69 55W
Ålen 47 62 51N 11 17 E
Alençon 18 48 27N 0 4 E
Alenuihaha Chan. 110 20 25N 156 0W
Aleppo = Ḩalab 64 36 10N 37 15 E
Aléria 21 42 5N 9 26 E
Alert Bay 108 50 30N 126 55W
Alès 21 44 9N 4 5 E
Aleşd 46 47 3N 22 22 E
Alessándria 38 44 54N 8 37 E
Ålestrup 49 56 42N 9 29 E
Ålesund 47 62 28N 6 12 E
Alet-les-Bains 20 43 0N 2 14 E
Aleutian Is. 104 52 0N 175 0W
Aleutian Trench 94 48 0N 180 0
Alexander 116 47 51N 103 40W
Alexander Arch. 104 57 0N 135 0W
Alexander B. 92 28 36 S 16 33 E
Alexander City 115 32 58N 85 57W
Alexander I. 5 69 0 S 70 0W
Alexandra, Austral. 99 37 8 S 145 40 E
Alexandra, N.Z. 101 45 14 S 169 25 E
Alexandra Falls 108 60 29N 116 18W
Alexandria, B.C., Can. 108 52 35N 122 27W
Alexandria, Ont., Can. 106 45 19N 74 38W
Alexandria, Romania 46 43 57N 25 24 E
Alexandria, S. Afr. 92 33 38 S 26 28 E
Alexandria, Ind., U.S.A. 114 40 18N 85 40W
Alexandria, La., U.S.A. 117 31 20N 92 30W
Alexandria, Minn., U.S.A. 116 45 50N 95 20W
Alexandria, S.D., U.S.A. 116 43 40N 97 45W
Alexandria, Va., U.S.A. 114 38 47N 77 1W

Alexandria = El Iskandarîya	**86**	31 0N	30 0 E
Alexandria Bay	**114**	44 20N	75 52W
Alexandrina, L.	**97**	35 25 S	139 10 E
Alexandroúpolis	**44**	40 50N	25 54 E
Alexis →	**107**	52 33N	56 8W
Alexis Creek	**108**	52 10N	123 20W
Alfambra	**32**	40 33N	1 5W
Alfândega da Fé	**30**	41 20N	6 59W
Alfaro	**32**	42 10N	1 50W
Alfatar	**43**	43 59N	27 13 E
Alfeld	**24**	52 0N	9 49 E
Alfenas	**125**	21 20 S	46 10W
Alfiós →	**45**	37 40N	21 33 E
Alfonsine	**39**	44 30N	12 1 E
Alford	**14**	57 13N	2 42W
Alfred, Me., U.S.A.	**113**	43 28N	70 40W
Alfred, N.Y., U.S.A.	**112**	42 15N	77 45W
Alfreton	**12**	53 6N	1 22W
Alfta	**48**	61 21N	16 4 E
Alga	**58**	49 53N	57 20 E
Algaba, La	**31**	37 27N	6 1W
Algar	**31**	36 40N	5 39W
Ålgård	**47**	58 46N	5 53 E
Algarinejo	**31**	37 19N	4 9W
Algarve	**31**	36 58N	8 20W
Algeciras	**31**	36 9N	5 28W
Algemesí	**33**	39 11N	0 27W
Alger	**82**	36 42N	3 8 E
Algeria ■	**82**	35 10N	3 11 E
Alghero	**40**	40 34N	8 20 E
Algiers = Alger	**82**	36 42N	3 8 E
Algoabaai	**92**	33 50 S	25 45 E
Algodonales	**31**	36 54N	5 24W
Algodor →	**30**	39 55N	3 53W
Algoma, Oreg., U.S.A.	**118**	42 25N	121 54W
Algoma, Wis., U.S.A.	**114**	44 35N	87 27W
Algona	**116**	43 4N	94 14W
Algonac	**112**	42 37N	82 32W
Alhama de Almería	**33**	36 57N	2 34W
Alhama de Aragón	**32**	41 18N	1 54W
Alhama de Granada	**31**	37 0N	3 59W
Alhama de Murcia	**33**	37 51N	1 25W
Alhambra, Spain	**33**	38 54N	3 4W
Alhambra, U.S.A.	**119**	34 2N	118 10W
Alhaurín el Grande	**31**	36 39N	4 41W
Alhucemas = Al-Hoceïma	**82**	35 8N	3 58W
'Alī al Gharbī	**64**	32 30N	46 45 E
Ali Bayramly	**57**	39 59N	48 52 E
Ali Sabieh	**87**	11 10N	42 44 E
Ália	**40**	37 47N	13 42 E
'Alīābād	**65**	28 10N	57 35 E
Aliaga	**32**	40 40N	0 42W
Aliákmon →	**44**	40 30N	22 36 E
Alibag	**70**	18 38N	72 56 E
Alibo	**87**	9 52N	37 5 E
Alibunar	**42**	45 5N	20 57 E
Alicante	**33**	38 23N	0 30W
Alicante □	**33**	38 30N	0 37W
Alice, S. Afr.	**92**	32 48 S	26 55 E
Alice, U.S.A.	**117**	27 47N	98 1W
Alice →, Queens., Austral.	**98**	24 2 S	144 50 E
Alice →, Queens., Austral.	**98**	15 35 S	142 20 E
Alice Arm	**108**	55 29N	129 31W
Alice, Punta dell'	**41**	39 23N	17 10 E
Alice Springs	**96**	23 40 S	133 50 E
Alicedale	**92**	33 15 S	26 4 E
Aliceville	**115**	33 9N	88 10W
Alick Cr. →	**98**	20 55 S	142 20 E
Alicudi, I.	**41**	38 33N	14 20 E
Alida	**109**	49 25N	101 55W
Aligarh, Raj., India	**68**	25 55N	76 15 E
Aligarh, Ut. P., India	**68**	27 55N	78 10 E
Alīgūdarz	**64**	33 25N	49 45 E
Alijó	**30**	41 16N	7 27W
Alimena	**41**	37 42N	14 4 E
Alimnía	**45**	36 16N	27 43 E
Alingsås	**49**	57 56N	12 31 E
Alipur	**68**	29 25N	70 55 E
Alipur Duar	**69**	26 30N	89 35 E
Aliquippa	**114**	40 38N	80 18W
Aliste →	**30**	41 34N	5 58W
Alitus	**54**	54 24N	24 3 E
Alivérion	**45**	38 24N	24 2 E
Aliwal North	**92**	30 45 S	26 45 E
Alix	**108**	52 24N	113 11W
Aljezur	**31**	37 18N	8 49W
Aljustrel	**31**	37 55N	8 10W
Alkamari	**85**	13 27N	11 10 E
Alkmaar	**16**	52 37N	4 45 E
All American Canal	**119**	32 45N	115 0W
Allada	**85**	6 41N	2 9 E
Allah Dad	**68**	25 38N	67 34 E
Allahabad	**69**	25 25N	81 58 E
Allakh-Yun	**59**	60 50N	137 5 E
Allal Tazi	**82**	34 30N	6 20W
Allan	**109**	51 53N	106 4W
Allanche	**20**	45 14N	2 57 E
Allanmyo	**67**	19 30N	95 17 E
Allanridge	**92**	27 45 S	26 40 E
Allanwater	**106**	50 14N	90 10W
Allaqi, Wadi →	**86**	23 7N	32 47 E
Allariz	**30**	42 11N	7 50W
Allassac	**20**	45 15N	1 29 E
Allegan	**114**	42 32N	85 52W
Allegany	**112**	42 6N	78 30W
Allegheny →	**114**	40 27N	80 0W
Allegheny Mts.	**114**	38 0N	80 0W
Allegheny Res.	**112**	42 0N	78 55W
Allègre	**20**	45 12N	3 41 E
Allen, Bog of	**15**	53 15N	7 0W
Allen, L.	**15**	54 12N	8 5W
Allenby (Hussein) Bridge	**62**	31 53N	35 33 E
Allende	**120**	28 20N	100 50W
Allentown	**114**	40 36N	75 30W
Allentsteig	**26**	48 41N	15 20 E
Alleppey	**70**	9 30N	76 28 E
Aller →	**24**	52 57N	9 10 E
Allevard	**21**	45 24N	6 5 E
Alliance, Nebr., U.S.A.	**116**	42 10N	102 50W
Alliance, Ohio, U.S.A.	**114**	40 53N	81 7W
Allier □	**20**	46 25N	3 0 E
Allier →	**19**	46 57N	3 4 E
Allingåbro	**49**	56 28N	10 20 E
Allinge	**49**	55 17N	14 50 E
Alliston	**106**	44 9N	79 52W
Alloa	**14**	56 7N	3 49W
Allos	**21**	44 15N	6 38 E
Alma, Can.	**107**	48 35N	71 40W
Alma, Ga., U.S.A.	**115**	31 33N	82 28W
Alma, Kans., U.S.A.	**116**	39 1N	96 22W
Alma, Mich., U.S.A.	**114**	43 25N	84 40W
Alma, Nebr., U.S.A.	**116**	40 10N	99 25W
Alma, Wis., U.S.A.	**116**	44 19N	91 54W
'Almā ash Sha'b	**62**	33 7N	35 9 E
Alma Ata	**58**	43 15N	76 57 E
Almada	**31**	38 40N	9 9W
Almaden	**98**	17 22 S	144 40 E
Almadén	**31**	38 49N	4 52W
Almagro	**31**	38 50N	3 45W
Almanor, L.	**118**	40 15N	121 11W
Almansa	**33**	38 51N	1 5W
Almanza	**30**	42 39N	5 3W
Almanzor, Pico de	**30**	40 15N	5 18W
Almanzora →	**33**	37 14N	1 46W
Almarcha, La	**32**	39 41N	2 24W
Almaş, Mţii.	**46**	44 49N	22 12 E
Almazán	**32**	41 30N	2 30W
Almazora	**32**	39 57N	0 3W
Almeirim, Brazil	**127**	1 30 S	52 34W
Almeirim, Port.	**31**	39 12N	8 37W
Almelo	**16**	52 22N	6 42 E
Almenar	**32**	41 43N	2 12W
Almenara	**32**	39 46N	0 14W
Almenara, Sierra de	**33**	37 34N	1 32W
Almendralejo	**31**	38 41N	6 26W
Almería	**33**	36 52N	2 27W
Almería □	**33**	37 20N	2 20W
Almería, G. de	**33**	36 41N	2 28W
Almirante	**14**	9 10N	82 30W
Almiropótamos	**45**	38 16N	24 11 E
Almirós	**45**	39 11N	22 45 E
Almodôvar	**31**	37 31N	8 2W
Almodóvar del Campo	**31**	38 43N	4 10W
Almogia	**31**	36 50N	4 32W
Almonaster la Real	**31**	37 52N	6 48W
Almont	**112**	42 53N	83 2W
Almonte	**113**	45 14N	76 12W
Almonte →	**31**	39 41N	6 28W
Almora	**69**	29 38N	79 40 E
Almoradi	**33**	38 7N	0 46W
Almorox	**30**	40 14N	4 24W
Almoustarat	**85**	17 35N	0 8 E
Älmult	**49**	56 33N	14 8 E
Almuñécar	**31**	36 43N	3 41W
Almunia de Doña Godina, La	**32**	41 29N	1 23W
Alnif	**82**	31 10N	5 8W
Alnwick	**12**	55 25N	1 42W
Aloi	**90**	2 16N	33 10 E
Alonsa	**109**	50 50N	99 0W
Alor	**73**	8 15 S	124 30 E
Alor Setar	**71**	6 7N	100 22 E
Alora	**31**	36 49N	4 46W
Alosno	**31**	37 33N	7 7W
Alougoum	**82**	30 17N	6 56W
Alpedrinha	**30**	40 6N	7 27W
Alpena	**114**	45 6N	83 24W
Alpes-de-Haute-Provence □	**21**	44 8N	6 10 E
Alpes-Maritimes □	**21**	43 55N	7 10 E
Alpha	**97**	23 39 S	146 37 E
Alpi Apuane	**38**	44 7N	10 14 E
Alpi Lepontine	**25**	46 22N	8 27 E
Alpi Orobie	**38**	46 7N	10 0 E
Alpi Retiche	**25**	46 30N	10 0 E
Alpiarça	**31**	39 15N	8 35W
Alpine, Ariz., U.S.A.	**119**	33 57N	109 4W
Alpine, Tex., U.S.A.	**117**	30 25N	103 35W
Alps	**22**	47 0N	8 0 E
Alpujarras, Las	**33**	36 55N	3 20W
Alrø	**49**	55 52N	10 5 E
Alsace	**19**	48 15N	7 25 E
Alsask	**109**	51 21N	109 59W
Alsásua	**32**	42 54N	2 10W
Alsen	**48**	63 23N	13 56 E
Alsfeld	**24**	50 44N	9 19 E
Alsónémedi	**27**	47 20N	19 15 E
Alsten	**50**	65 58N	12 40 E
Alta	**50**	69 57N	23 10 E
Alta Gracia	**124**	31 40 S	64 30W
Alta Lake	**108**	50 10N	123 0W
Alta, Sierra	**32**	40 31N	1 30W
Altaelva →	**50**	69 46N	23 45 E
Altafjorden	**50**	70 5N	23 5 E
Altagracia	**126**	10 45N	71 30W
Altai = Aerhatai Shan	**75**	46 40N	92 45 E
Altamaha →	**115**	31 19N	81 17W
Altamira, Brazil	**127**	3 12 S	52 10W
Altamira, Chile	**124**	25 47 S	69 51W
Altamira, Cuevas de	**30**	43 20N	4 5W
Altamont	**113**	42 43N	74 3W
Altamura	**41**	40 50N	16 33 E
Altanbulag	**75**	50 16N	106 30 E
Altar	**120**	30 40N	111 50W
Altata	**120**	24 30N	108 0W
Altavista	**114**	37 9N	79 22W
Altay	**75**	47 48N	88 10 E
Altdorf	**25**	46 52N	8 36 E
Alte Mellum	**24**	53 45N	8 6 E
Altea	**33**	38 38N	0 2W
Altenberg	**24**	50 46N	13 47 E
Altenbruch	**24**	53 48N	8 44 E
Altenburg	**24**	50 59N	12 28 E
Altenkirchen, Germ., E.	**24**	54 38N	13 20 E
Altenkirchen, Germ., W.	**24**	50 41N	7 38 E
Altenmarkt	**26**	47 43N	14 39 E
Altenteptow	**24**	53 42N	13 15 E
Alter do Chão	**31**	39 12N	7 40W
Altkirch	**19**	47 37N	7 15 E
Altmühl →	**25**	48 54N	11 54 E
Alto Adige = Trentino-Alto Adige	**38**	46 30N	11 0 E
Alto Araguaia	**127**	17 15 S	53 20W
Alto Chindio	**91**	16 19 S	35 25 E
Alto Cuchumatanes = Cuchumatanes, Sa. de los	**120**	15 30N	91 10W
Alto del Inca	**124**	24 10 S	68 10W
Alto Ligonha	**91**	15 30 S	38 11 E
Alto Molocue	**91**	15 50 S	37 35 E
Alto Paraná □	**125**	25 0 S	54 50W
Alton, Can.	**112**	43 54N	80 5W
Alton, U.S.A.	**116**	38 55N	90 5W
Alton Downs	**99**	26 7 S	138 57 E
Altona, Austral.	**100**	37 51 S	144 50 E
Altona, Ger.	**24**	53 32N	9 56 E
Altoona	**114**	40 32N	78 24W
Altopáscio	**38**	43 50N	10 40 E
Altötting	**25**	48 14N	12 41 E
Altstätten	**25**	47 22N	9 33 E
Altun Shan	**75**	38 30N	88 0 E
Alturas	**118**	41 36N	120 37W
Altus	**117**	34 30N	99 25W
Alucra	**57**	40 22N	38 47 E
Aluksne	**54**	57 24N	27 3 E
Alùla	**63**	11 50N	50 45 E
Alupka	**56**	44 23N	34 2 E
Alushta	**56**	44 40N	34 25 E
Alusi	**73**	7 35 S	131 40 E
Alustante	**32**	40 36N	1 40W
Alva	**117**	36 50N	98 50W
Alvaiázere	**30**	39 49N	8 23W
Älvängen	**49**	57 58N	12 8 E
Alvarado, Mexico	**120**	18 40N	95 50W
Alvarado, U.S.A.	**117**	32 25N	97 15W
Alvaro Obregón, Presa	**120**	27 55N	109 52W
Alvdal	**47**	62 6N	10 37 E
Alvear	**124**	29 5 S	56 30W
Alverca	**31**	38 56N	9 1W
Alvesta	**49**	56 54N	14 35 E
Alvie	**99**	38 14 S	143 30 E
Alvin	**117**	29 23N	95 12W
Alvinston	**113**	42 49N	81 52W
Alvito	**31**	38 15N	8 0W
Älvros	**48**	62 3N	14 38 E
Älvsborgs län □	**49**	58 30N	12 30 E
Älvsbyn	**50**	65 40N	21 0 E
Älvsered	**49**	57 14N	12 51 E
Alwar	**68**	27 38N	76 34 E
Alwaye	**70**	10 8N	76 24 E
Alxa Zuoqi	**76**	38 50N	105 40 E
Alyangula	**97**	13 55 S	136 30 E
Alyaskitovyy	**59**	64 45N	141 30 E
Alyata	**57**	39 58N	49 25 E
Alyth	**14**	56 38N	3 15W
Alzada	**116**	45 3N	104 22W
Alzano Lombardo	**38**	45 44N	9 43 E
Alzey	**25**	49 48N	8 4 E
Am Dam	**81**	12 40N	20 35 E
Am Géréda	**81**	12 53N	21 14 E
Am-Timan	**81**	11 0N	20 10 E
Amadeus, L.	**96**	24 54 S	131 0 E
Amâdi	**87**	5 29N	30 25 E
Amadi	**90**	3 40N	26 40 E
Amadjuak	**105**	64 0N	72 39W
Amadjuak L.	**105**	65 0N	71 8W
Amadora	**31**	38 45N	9 13W
Amagasaki	**74**	34 42N	135 20 E
Amager	**49**	55 37N	12 35 E
Amakusa-Shotō	**74**	32 15N	130 10 E
Åmål	**48**	59 3N	12 42 E
Amalapuram	**70**	16 35N	81 55 E
Amalfi	**41**	40 39N	14 34 E
Amaliás	**45**	37 47N	21 22 E
Amalner	**68**	21 5N	75 5 E
Amambaí	**125**	23 5 S	55 13W
Amambaí →	**125**	23 22 S	53 56W
Amambay □	**125**	23 0 S	56 0W
Amambay, Cordillera de	**125**	23 0 S	55 45W
Amándola	**39**	42 59N	13 21 E
Amangeldy	**58**	50 10N	65 10 E
Amantea	**41**	39 8N	16 3 E
Amapá	**127**	2 5N	50 50W
Amapá □	**127**	1 40N	52 0W
Amara	**87**	10 25N	34 10 E
Amarante, Brazil	**127**	6 14 S	42 50W
Amarante, Port.	**30**	41 16N	8 5W
Amaranth	**109**	50 36N	98 43W
Amaravati →	**70**	11 0N	78 15 E
Amareleja	**31**	38 12N	7 13W
Amargosa	**127**	13 2 S	39 36W
Amarillo	**117**	35 14N	101 46W
Amaro, Mt.	**39**	42 5N	14 6 E
Amarpur	**69**	25 5N	87 0 E
Amasra	**64**	41 45N	32 30 E
Amassama	**85**	5 1N	6 2 E
Amasya	**64**	40 40N	35 50 E
Amatikulu	**93**	29 3 S	31 33 E
Amatitlán	**120**	14 29N	90 38W
Amatrice	**39**	42 38N	13 16 E
Amazon = Amazonas →	**127**	0 5 S	50 0W
Amazonas □	**126**	4 0 S	62 0W
Amazonas →	**127**	0 5 S	50 0W
Ambad	**70**	19 38N	75 50 E
Ambahakily	**93**	21 36 S	43 41 E
Ambala	**68**	30 23N	76 56 E
Ambalangoda	**70**	6 15N	80 5 E
Ambalapuzha	**70**	9 25N	76 25 E
Ambalavao	**93**	21 50 S	46 56 E
Ambam	**88**	2 20N	11 15 E
Ambanja	**93**	13 40 S	48 27 E
Ambarchik	**59**	69 40N	162 20 E
Ambarijeby	**93**	14 56 S	47 41 E
Ambarnath	**70**	19 12N	73 22 E
Ambaro, Helodranon'	**93**	13 23 S	48 38 E
Ambartsevo	**58**	57 30N	83 52 E
Ambasamudram	**70**	8 43N	77 25 E
Ambato	**126**	1 5 S	78 42W
Ambato Boeny	**93**	16 28 S	46 43 E
Ambato, Sierra de	**124**	28 25 S	66 10W
Ambatofinandrahana	**93**	20 33 S	46 48 E
Ambatolampy	**93**	19 20 S	47 35 E
Ambatondrazaka	**93**	17 55 S	48 28 E
Ambatosoratra	**93**	17 37 S	48 31 E
Ambenja	**93**	15 17 S	46 58 E
Amberg	**25**	49 25N	11 52 E
Ambergris Cay	**120**	18 0N	88 0W
Ambérieu-en-Bugey	**21**	45 57N	5 20 E
Amberley	**101**	43 9 S	172 44 E
Ambert	**20**	45 33N	3 44 E
Ambidédi	**84**	14 35N	11 47W
Ambikapur	**69**	23 15N	83 15 E
Ambikol	**86**	21 20N	30 50 E
Ambinanindrano	**93**	20 5 S	48 23 E
Ambjörnarp	**49**	57 25N	13 17 E
Ambleside	**12**	54 26N	2 58W
Ambo, Ethiopia	**87**	12 20N	37 30 E
Ambo, Peru	**126**	10 5 S	76 10W
Ambodifototra	**93**	16 59 S	49 52 E
Ambodilazana	**93**	18 6 S	49 10 E
Ambohimahasoa	**93**	21 7 S	47 13 E
Ambohimanga	**93**	20 52 S	47 36 E
Ambon	**73**	3 35 S	128 20 E
Amboseli L.	**90**	2 40 S	37 10 E
Ambositra	**93**	20 31 S	47 25 E
Ambovombé	**93**	25 11 S	46 5 E
Amboy	**119**	34 33N	115 51W
Amboyna I.	**72**	7 50N	112 50 E
Ambridge	**112**	40 36N	80 15W
Ambriz	**88**	7 48 S	13 8 E
Ambur	**70**	12 48N	78 43 E
Amby	**99**	26 30 S	148 11 E
Amchitka I.	**104**	51 30N	179 0W
Amderma	**58**	69 45N	61 30 E
Ameca	**120**	20 30N	104 0W
Ameca →	**120**	20 40N	105 15W
Amecameca	**120**	19 7N	98 46W
Ameland	**16**	53 27N	5 45 E
Amélia	**39**	42 34N	12 25 E
Amélie-les-Bains-Palalda	**20**	42 29N	2 41 E
Amen	**59**	68 45N	180 0 E
Amendolaro	**41**	39 58N	16 34 E
American Falls	**118**	42 46N	112 56W
American Falls Res.	**118**	43 0N	112 50W
American Highland	**5**	73 0 S	75 0 E
American Samoa	**101**	14 20 S	170 40W
Americana	**125**	22 45 S	47 20W
Americus	**115**	32 0N	84 10W
Amersfoort, Neth.	**16**	52 9N	5 23 E
Amersfoort, S. Afr.	**93**	26 59 S	29 53 E
Amery	**109**	56 34N	94 3W
Amery Ice Shelf	**5**	69 30 S	72 0 E
Ames	**116**	42 0N	93 40W
Amesbury	**113**	42 50N	70 52W
Amesdale	**109**	50 2N	92 55W
Amfíklia	**45**	38 38N	22 35 E
Amfilokhía	**45**	38 52N	21 9 E
Amfípolis	**44**	40 48N	23 52 E
Ámfissa	**45**	38 32N	22 22 E
Amga	**59**	60 50N	132 0 E
Amga →	**59**	62 38N	134 32 E
Amgu	**59**	45 45N	137 15 E
Amgun →	**59**	52 56N	139 38 E
Amherst, Burma	**67**	16 2N	97 20 E
Amherst, Can.	**107**	45 48N	64 8W
Amherst, Mass., U.S.A.	**113**	42 21N	72 30W
Amherst, Ohio, U.S.A.	**112**	41 23N	82 15W
Amherst, Tex., U.S.A.	**117**	34 0N	102 24W
Amherst I.	**113**	44 8N	76 43W
Amherstburg	**106**	42 6N	83 6W
Amiata, Mte.	**39**	42 54N	11 40 E
Amiens	**19**	49 54N	2 16 E
Amigdhalokefáli	**45**	35 23N	23 30 E
Amindaion	**44**	40 42N	21 42 E
Amirante Is.	**3**	6 0 S	53 0 E
Amisk L.	**109**	54 35N	102 15W
Amite	**117**	30 47N	90 31W
Amizmiz	**82**	31 12N	8 15W
Åmli	**47**	58 45N	8 32 E
Amlwch	**12**	53 24N	4 21W
Amm Adam	**87**	16 20N	36 1 E
'Ammān	**62**	31 57N	35 52 E
Ammanford	**13**	51 48N	4 0W
Ammerån	**48**	63 9N	16 13 E
Ammerån →	**48**	63 9N	16 13 E
Ammersee	**25**	48 0N	11 7 E
Ammi'ad	**62**	32 55N	35 32 E
Amnéville	**19**	49 16N	6 9 E
Amorebieta	**32**	43 13N	2 44W
Amorgós	**45**	36 50N	25 57 E
Amory	**115**	33 59N	88 29W
Amos	**106**	48 35N	78 5W
Åmot, Buskerud, Norway	**47**	59 54N	9 54 E
Åmot, Telemark, Norway	**47**	59 34N	8 0 E
Åmotsdal	**47**	59 37N	8 26 E
Amour, Djebel	**82**	33 42N	1 37 E
Amoy = Xiamen	**76**	24 25N	118 4 E
Ampanihy	**93**	24 40 S	44 45 E
Ampasindava, Helodranon'	**93**	13 40 S	48 15 E
Ampasindava, Saikanosy	**93**	13 42 S	47 55W
Amper	**85**	9 25N	9 40 E
Amper →	**25**	48 30N	11 57 E
Ampère	**83**	35 44N	5 27 E
Ampezzo	**39**	46 25N	12 48 E
Amposta	**32**	40 43N	0 34 E
Ampotaka	**93**	25 3 S	44 41 E
Ampoza	**93**	22 20 S	44 44 E
Amqa	**62**	32 59N	35 10
Amqui	**107**	48 28N	67 27W
Amraoti	**68**	20 55N	77 45
Amreli	**68**	21 35N	71 17
Amrenene el Kasba	**82**	22 10N	0 30
Amritsar	**68**	31 35N	74 57
Amroha	**68**	28 53N	78 30
Amrum	**24**	54 37N	8 21
Amsel	**83**	22 47N	5 29
Amsterdam, Neth.	**16**	52 23N	4 54
Amsterdam, U.S.A.	**114**	42 58N	74 10W
Amsterdam, I.	**3**	37 30 S	77 30
Amstetten	**26**	48 7N	14 51
Amudarya →	**58**	43 40N	59 0
Amund Ringnes I.	**4**	78 20N	96 25W
Amundsen Gulf	**104**	71 0N	124 0W
Amundsen Sea	**5**	72 0 S	115 0W
Amungen	**48**	61 10N	15 40
Amuntai	**72**	2 28 S	115 25
Amur →	**59**	52 56N	141 10
Amurang	**73**	1 5N	124 40
Amuri Pass	**101**	42 31 S	172 11
Amurrio	**32**	43 3N	3 0
Amursk	**59**	50 14N	136 54

Amurzet 59 47 50N 131 5 E
Amusco 30 42 10N 4 28W
Amvrakikós Kólpos 45 39 0N 20 55 E
Amvrosiyevka 57 47 43N 38 30 E
Amzeglouf 82 26 50N 0 1 E
An Nafūd 64 28 15N 41 0 E
An Najaf 64 32 3N 44 15 E
An Nāqūrah 62 33 7N 35 8 E
An Nāşirīyah 64 31 0N 46 15 E
An Nawfalīyah 83 30 54N 17 58 E
An Nhon (Binh Dinh) 71 13 55N 109 7 E
An Nîl □ 86 19 30N 33 0 E
An Nîl el Abyad □ 87 14 0N 32 15 E
An Nîl el Azraq □ 87 12 30N 34 30 E
An Nu'ayrīyah 64 27 30N 48 30 E
An Uaimh 15 53 39N 6 40W
Āna-Sira 47 58 17N 6 25 E
Anabar → 59 73 8N 113 36 E
'Anabtā 62 32 19N 35 7 E
Anaconda 118 46 7N 113 0W
Anacortes 118 48 30N 122 40W
Anadarko 117 35 4N 98 15W
Anadia 30 40 26N 8 27W
Anadolu 64 38 0N 30 0 E
Anadyr 59 64 35N 177 20 E
Anadyr → 59 64 55N 176 5 E
Anadyrskiy Zaliv 59 64 0N 180 0 E
Anáfi 45 36 22N 25 48 E
Anafópoulo 45 36 17N 25 50 E
Anagni 40 41 44N 13 8 E
'Ānah 64 34 25N 42 0 E
Anahim Lake 108 52 28N 125 18W
Anáhuac 120 27 14N 100 9W
Anai Mudi, Mt. 70 10 12N 77 4 E
Anaimalai Hills 70 10 20N 76 40 E
Anakapalle 70 17 42N 83 06 E
Anakie 98 23 32 S 147 45 E
Anaklia 57 42 22N 41 35 E
Analalava 93 14 35 S 48 0 E
Anambar → 68 30 15N 68 50 E
Anambas, Kepulauan 72 3 20N 106 30 E
Anamoose 116 47 55N 100 20W
Anamosa 116 42 7N 91 30W
Anamur 64 36 8N 32 58 E
Anan 74 33 54N 134 40 E
Anand 68 22 32N 72 59 E
Anandpur 69 21 16N 86 13 E
Anánes 45 36 33N 24 9 E
Anantapur 70 14 39N 77 42 E
Anantnag 69 33 45N 75 10 E
Ananyev 56 47 44N 29 47 E
Anapa 56 44 55N 37 25 E
Anápolis 127 16 15 S 48 50W
Anār 65 30 55N 55 13 E
Anārak 65 33 25N 53 40 E
Anatolia = Anadolu 64 38 0N 30 0 E
Anatone 118 46 9N 117 4W
Añatuya 124 28 20 S 62 50W
Anaunethad L. 109 60 55N 104 25W
Anaye 81 19 15N 12 50 E
Ancenis 18 47 21N 1 10W
Anchorage 104 61 10N 149 50W
Ancião 30 39 56N 8 27W
Ancohuma, Nevada 126 16 0 S 68 50W
Ancón 126 11 50 S 77 10W
Ancona 39 43 37N 13 30 E
Ancud 128 42 0 S 73 50W
Ancud, G. de 128 42 0 S 73 0W
Anda 76 46 24N 125 19 E
Andacollo, Argent. 124 37 10 S 70 42W
Andacollo, Chile 124 30 5 S 71 10W
Andalgalá 124 27 40 S 66 30W
Åndalsnes 47 62 35N 7 43 E
Andalucía 31 37 35N 5 0W
Andalusia 115 31 19N 86 30W
Andalusia = Andalucía 31 37 35N 5 0W
Andaman Is. 71 12 30N 92 30 E
Andaman Sea 72 13 0N 96 0 E
Andaman Str. 71 12 15N 92 20 E
Andara 92 18 2 S 21 9 E
Andelot 19 48 15N 5 18 E
Andelys, Les 18 49 15N 1 25 E
Andenne 16 50 30N 5 5 E
Andéranboukane 85 15 26N 3 2 E
Andermatt 25 46 38N 8 35 E
Andernach 24 50 24N 7 25 E
Andernos-les-Bains 20 44 44N 1 6W
Anderslöv 49 55 26N 13 19 E
Anderson, Calif., U.S.A. 118 40 30N 122 19W
Anderson, Ind., U.S.A. 114 40 5N 85 40W
Anderson, Mo., U.S.A. 117 36 43N 94 29W
Anderson, S.C., U.S.A. 115 34 32N 82 40W
Anderson → 104 69 42N 129 0W
Anderson, Mt. 93 25 5 S 30 42 E
Anderstorp 49 57 19N 13 39 E
Andes 126 5 40N 75 53W
Andes, Cord de los 126 20 0 S 68 0W
Andfjorden 50 69 10N 16 20 E
Andhra, L. 70 18 54N 73 32 E
Andhra Pradesh □ 70 16 0N 79 0 E
Andikíthira 45 35 52N 23 15 E
Andímilos 45 36 47N 24 12 E
Andíparos 45 37 0N 25 3 E
Andípaxoi 45 39 9N 20 13 E
Andípsara 45 38 30N 25 29 E
Andirrion 45 38 24N 21 46 E
Andizhan 58 41 10N 72 0 E
Andkhvoy 65 36 52N 65 8 E
Andol 70 17 51N 78 4 E
Andong 76 36 40N 128 43 E
Andorra ■ 32 42 30N 1 30 E
Andorra La Vella 32 42 31N 1 32 E
Andover, U.K. 13 51 13N 1 29W
Andover, N.Y., U.S.A. 112 42 11N 77 48W
Andover, Ohio, U.S.A. 112 41 35N 80 35W
Andrahary, Mt. 93 13 37 S 49 17 E
Andraitx 32 39 39N 2 25 E
Andramasina 93 19 11 S 47 35 E
Andranopasy 93 21 17 S 43 44 E
Andreanof Is. 104 52 0N 178 0W
Andreapol 54 56 40N 32 17 E
Andrespol 28 51 45N 19 34 E
Andrews, S.C., U.S.A. 115 33 29N 79 30W
Andrews, Tex., U.S.A. 117 32 18N 102 33W
Ándria 41 41 13N 16 17 E
Andriba 93 17 30 S 46 58 E
Andrijevica 42 42 45N 19 48 E
Andritsaina 45 37 29N 21 52 E
Androka 93 24 58 S 44 2 E
Ándros 45 37 50N 24 57 E
Andros I. 121 24 30N 78 0W
Andros Town 121 24 43N 77 47W
Andrychów 27 49 51N 19 18 E
Andújar 31 38 3N 4 5W
Aneby 49 57 48N 14 49 E
Anegada I. 121 18 45N 64 20W
Anegada Passage 121 18 15N 63 45W
Anécho 85 6 12N 1 34 E
Anergane 82 31 4N 7 14W
Aneto, Pico de 32 42 37N 0 40 E
Ang Thong 71 14 35N 100 31 E
Angamos, Punta 124 23 1 S 70 32W
Ang'angxi 75 47 10N 123 48 E
Angara → 59 58 30N 97 0 E
Angarab 87 13 11N 37 7 E
Angarsk 59 52 30N 104 0 E
Angaston 99 34 30 S 139 8 E
Ånge 48 62 31N 15 35 E
Angel de la Guarda 120 29 30N 113 30W
Angeles 73 15 9N 120 33 E
Ängelholm 49 56 15N 12 58 E
Angellala 99 26 24 S 146 54 E
Angels Camp 119 38 8N 120 30W
Ängelsberg 48 59 58N 16 0 E
Anger → 87 9 37N 36 6 E
Angereb → 87 13 45N 36 40 E
Ångermanälven → 48 62 40N 18 0 E
Angermünde 24 53 1N 14 0 E
Angers, Can. 113 45 31N 75 29W
Angers, France 18 47 30N 0 35W
Angerville 19 48 19N 2 0 E
Ängesån → 50 66 50N 22 15 E
Anghiari 39 43 32N 12 3 E
Angikuni L. 109 62 0N 100 0W
Angkor 71 13 22N 103 50 E
Anglés 32 41 57N 2 38 E
Anglesey 12 53 17N 4 20W
Anglet 20 43 29N 1 31W
Angleton 117 29 12N 95 23W
Anglin → 20 46 42N 0 52 E
Anglure 19 48 35N 3 50 E
Angmagssalik 4 65 40N 37 20W
Ango 90 4 10N 26 5 E
Angoche 91 16 8 S 40 0 E
Angoche, I. 91 16 20 S 39 50 E
Angol 124 37 56 S 72 45W
Angola, Ind., U.S.A. 114 41 40N 85 0W
Angola, N.Y., U.S.A. 112 42 38N 79 2W
Angola ■ 89 12 0 S 18 0 E
Angoon 108 57 40N 134 40W
Angoram 98 4 4 S 144 4 E
Angoulême 20 45 39N 0 10 E
Angoumois 20 45 50N 0 25 E
Angra dos Reis 125 23 0 S 44 10W
Angren 58 41 1N 70 12 E
Angu 90 3 25N 24 28 E
Anguilla 121 18 14N 63 5W
Angus, Braes of 14 56 51N 3 10W
Anhanduí → 125 21 46 S 52 9W
Anholt 49 56 42N 11 33 E
Anhua 77 28 23N 111 12 E
Anhui □ 75 32 0N 117 0 E
Anhwei □ = Anhui □ 75 32 0N 117 0 E
Ánidhros 45 36 38N 25 43 E
Anie 85 7 42N 1 8 E
Animas 119 31 58N 108 58W
Ånimskog 49 58 53N 12 35 E
Anin 71 15 36N 97 50 E
Anina 42 45 6N 21 51 E
Anivorano 93 18 44 S 48 58 E
Anjangaon 68 21 10N 77 20 E
Anjar 68 23 6N 70 10 E
Anjidiv I. 70 14 40N 74 10 E
Anjou 18 47 20N 0 15W
Anjozorobe 93 18 22 S 47 52 E
Anju 76 39 36N 125 40 E
Anka 85 12 13N 5 58 E
Ankang 75 32 40N 109 1 E
Ankara 64 40 0N 32 54 E
Ankaramena 93 21 57 S 46 39 E
Ankazoabo 93 22 18 S 44 31 E
Ankazobe 93 18 20 S 47 10 E
Ankisabe 93 19 17 S 46 29 E
Anklam 24 53 48N 13 40 E
Anklesvar 68 21 38N 73 3 E
Ankober 87 9 35N 39 40 E
Ankoro 90 6 45 S 26 55 E
Anlu 77 31 15N 113 45 E
Ånn 48 63 19N 12 34 E
Ann Arbor 114 42 17N 83 45W
Ann C., Antarct. 5 66 30 S 50 30 E
Ann C., U.S.A. 114 42 39N 70 37W
Anna, U.S.A. 117 37 28N 89 10W
Anna, U.S.S.R. 55 51 28N 40 23 E
Annaba 83 36 50N 7 46 E
Annaberg-Buchholz 24 50 34N 12 58 E
Annalee → 15 54 3N 7 15W
Annam = Trung-Phan 71 16 30N 107 30 E
Annamitique, Chaîne 71 17 0N 106 0 E
Annan 14 55 0N 3 17W
Annan → 14 54 58N 3 18W
Annapolis 114 38 95N 76 30W
Annapolis Royal 107 44 44N 65 32W
Annapurna 69 28 34N 83 50 E
Anneberg 49 57 32N 12 6 E
Annecy 21 45 55N 6 8 E
Annecy, L. d' 21 45 52N 6 10 E
Annemasse 21 46 12N 6 16 E
Anning 75 24 55N 102 26 E
Anniston 115 33 45N 85 50W
Annobón 79 1 25 S 5 35 E
Annonay 21 45 15N 4 40 E
Annonciation, L' 106 46 25N 74 55W
Annot 21 43 58N 6 38 E
Annotto Bay 121 18 17N 77 3W
Annuello 99 34 53 S 142 55 E
Annville 113 40 18N 76 32W
Annweiler 25 49 12N 7 58 E
Áno Arkhánai 45 35 16N 25 11 E
Áno Porróia 44 41 17N 23 2 E
Áno Viánnos 45 35 2N 25 21 E
Anoka 116 45 10N 93 26W
Anorotsangana 93 13 56 S 47 55 E
Anqing 75 30 30N 117 3 E
Anren 77 26 43N 113 18 E
Ansāb 64 29 11N 44 43 E
Ansai 76 36 50N 109 20 E
Ansbach 25 49 17N 10 34 E
Anse au Loup, L' 107 51 32N 56 50W
Anse, L' 106 46 47N 88 28W
Anseba → 87 16 0N 38 30 E
Anshan 76 41 5N 122 58 E
Anshun 75 26 18N 105 57 E
Ansirabe 93 19 55 S 47 2 E
Ansley 116 41 19N 99 24W
Ansó 32 42 51N 0 48W
Anson 117 32 46N 99 54W
Anson B. 96 13 20 S 130 6 E
Ansongo 85 15 25N 0 35 E
Ansonia 113 41 21N 73 6W
Anstruther 14 56 14N 2 40W
Ansudu 73 2 11 S 139 22 E
Antabamba 126 14 40 S 73 0W
Antakya 64 36 14N 36 10 E
Antalaha 93 14 57 S 50 20 E
Antalya 64 36 52N 30 45 E
Antalya Körfezi 64 36 15N 31 30 E
Antananarivo 93 18 55 S 47 31 E
Antananarivo □ 93 19 0 S 47 0 E
Antanimbaribe 93 21 30 S 44 48 E
Antarctic Pen. 5 67 0 S 60 0W
Antarctica 5 90 0 S 0 0
Antelope 91 21 2 S 28 31 E
Antequera, Parag. 124 24 8 S 57 7W
Antequera, Spain 31 37 5N 4 33W
Antero Mt. 119 38 45N 106 15W
Anthemoús 44 40 31N 23 15 E
Anthony, Kans., U.S.A. 117 37 8N 98 2W
Anthony, N. Mex., U.S.A. 119 32 1N 106 37W
Anti Atlas, Mts. 82 30 0N 8 30W
Antibes 21 43 34N 7 6 E
Antibes, C. d' 21 43 31N 7 7 E
Anticosti, Î. d' 107 49 30N 63 0W
Antifer, C. d' 18 49 41N 0 10 E
Antigo 116 45 8N 89 5W
Antigonish 107 45 38N 61 58W
Antigua 120 14 34N 90 41W
Antigua & Barbuda ■ 121 17 0N 61 50W
Antilla 121 20 40N 75 50W
Antimony 119 38 7N 112 0W
Antioch 118 38 7N 121 45W
Antioche, Pertuis d' 20 46 6N 1 20W
Antioquia 126 6 40N 75 55W
Antipodes Is. 94 49 45 S 178 40 E
Antler 116 48 58N 101 18W
Antler → 109 49 8N 101 0W
Antlers 117 34 15N 95 35W
Antofagasta 124 23 50 S 70 30W
Antofagasta □ 124 24 0 S 69 0W
Antofagasta de la Sierra 124 26 5 S 67 20W
Antofalla 124 25 30 S 68 5W
Antofalla, Salar de 124 25 40 S 67 45W
Anton 117 33 49N 102 5W
Anton Chico 119 35 12N 105 5W
Antongila, Helodrano 93 15 30 S 49 50 E
Antonibé 93 15 7 S 47 24 E
Antonibé, Presqu'île d' 93 14 55 S 47 20 E
Antonina 125 25 26 S 48 42W
Antonito 119 37 4N 106 1W
Antonovo 57 49 25N 51 42 E
Antrain 18 48 28N 1 30W
Antrim 15 54 43N 6 13W
Antrim □ 15 54 55N 6 20W
Antrim, Mts. of 15 54 57N 6 8W
Antrodoco 39 42 25N 13 4 E
Antropovo 55 58 26N 42 51 E
Antsalova 93 18 40 S 44 37 E
Antsiranana 93 12 25 S 49 20 E
Antsohihy 93 14 50 S 47 59 E
Antwerp 113 44 12N 75 36W
Antwerp = Antwerpen 16 51 13N 4 25 E
Antwerpen 16 51 13N 4 25 E
Antwerpen □ 16 51 15N 4 40 E
Anupgarh 68 29 10N 73 10 E
Anuradhapura 70 8 22N 80 28 E
Anvers = Antwerpen 16 51 13N 4 25 E
Anvers I. 5 64 30 S 63 40W
Anvik 104 62 37N 160 20W
Anxi, Fujian, China 77 25 2N 118 12 E
Anxi, Gansu, China 75 40 30N 95 43 E
Anxious B. 96 33 24 S 134 45 E
Anyama 84 5 30N 4 3W
Anyang 76 36 5N 114 21 E
Anyer-Lor 73 6 6 S 105 56 E
Anyi, Jiangxi, China 77 28 49N 115 25 E
Anyi, Shanxi, China 77 35 2N 111 2 E
Anyuan 77 25 9N 115 21 E
'Anzah 62 32 22N 35 12 E
Anzhero-Sudzhensk 58 56 10N 86 0 E
Anzio 40 41 28N 12 37 E
Aoiz 32 42 46N 1 22W
Aomori 74 40 45N 140 45 E
Aomori □ 74 40 45N 140 40 E
Aonla 68 28 16N 79 11 E
Aoreora 82 28 51N 10 53W
Aosta 38 45 43N 7 20 E
Aoudéras 85 17 45N 8 20 E
Aouinet Torkoz 82 28 31N 9 46W
Aoukar 82 23 50N 2 45W
Aouker 84 17 40N 10 0W
Aoulef el Arab 82 26 55N 1 2 E
Apa → 124 22 6 S 58 2W
Apache, Ariz., U.S.A. 119 31 46N 109 6W
Apache, Okla., U.S.A. 117 34 53N 98 22W
Apalachee B. 115 30 0N 84 0W
Apalachicola 115 29 40N 85 0W
Apapa 85 6 25N 3 25 E
Apaporis → 126 1 23 S 69 25W
Aparri 73 18 22N 121 38 E
Apateu 46 46 36N 21 47 E
Apatin 42 45 40N 19 0 E
Apàtity 52 67 34N 33 22 E
Apatzingán 120 19 0N 102 20W
Apeldoorn 16 52 13N 5 57 E
Apen 24 53 12N 7 47 E
Apenam 72 8 35 S 116 13 E
Apennines 9 44 20N 10 20 E
Apia 101 13 50 S 171 50W
Apiacás, Serra dos 126 9 50 S 57 0W
Apizaco 120 19 26N 98 9W
Aplao 126 16 0 S 72 40W
Apo, Mt. 73 6 53N 125 14 E
Apolda 24 51 1N 11 30 E
Apollo Bay 100 38 45 S 143 40 E
Apollonia 45 36 58N 24 43 E
Apollonia = Marsá Susah 81 32 52N 21 59 E
Apolo 126 14 30 S 68 30W
Apostle Is. 116 47 0N 90 30W
Apóstoles 125 28 0 S 56 0W
Apostolovo 56 47 39N 33 39 E
Apoteri 126 4 2N 58 32W
Appalachian Mts. 114 38 0N 80 0W
Appalachicola → 115 29 40N 85 0W
Appennini 41 41 0N 15 0 E
Appennino Ligure 38 44 30N 9 0 E
Appenzell-Ausser Rhoden □ 25 47 23N 9 23 E
Appenzell-Inner Rhoden □ 25 47 20N 9 25 E
Appiano 39 46 27N 11 17 E
Apple Hill 113 45 13N 74 46W
Appleby 12 54 35N 2 29W
Appleton 114 44 17N 88 25W
Approuague 127 4 20N 52 0W
Aprelevka, U.S.S.R. 55 55 33N 37 4 E
Aprelevka, U.S.S.R. 55 55 34N 37 4 E
Apricena 41 41 47N 15 25 E
Aprigliano 41 39 17N 16 19 E
Aprília 40 41 38N 12 38 E
Apsheronsk 57 44 28N 39 42 E
Apt 21 43 53N 5 24 E
Apucarana 125 23 55 S 51 33W
Apulia = Púglia 41 41 0N 16 30 E
Apure → 126 7 37N 66 25W
Apurimac → 126 12 17 S 73 56W
Apuseni, Munţii 46 46 30N 22 45 E
Aqabah = Al 'Aqabah 86 29 13N 35 0 E
'Aqabah, Khalīj al 64 28 15N 33 20 E
Āqcheh 65 37 0N 66 5 E
Āqīq 86 18 14N 38 12 E
Āqīq, Khalīg 86 18 20N 38 10 E
Aqrabā 62 32 9N 35 20 E
Aqrah 64 36 46N 43 45 E
Aquidauana 127 20 30 S 55 50W
Aquila, L' 39 42 21N 13 24 E
Aquiles Serdán 120 28 37N 105 54W
Ar Rachidiya 82 31 58N 4 20W
Ar Rafīd 62 32 57N 35 52 E
Ar Ramādī 64 33 25N 43 20 E
Ar Raml 83 26 45N 19 40 E
Ar Ramthā 62 32 34N 36 0 E
Ar Raqqah 64 36 0N 38 55 E
Ar Rass 64 25 50N 43 40 E
Ar Rifā'ī 64 31 50N 46 10 E
Ar Riyāḍ 64 24 41N 46 42 E
Ar Rummān 62 32 9N 35 48 E
Ar Ruţbah 64 33 0N 40 15 E
Ar Ruwaydah 64 23 40N 44 40 E
Arab, Bahr el → 87 9 50N 29 0 E
Arab, Khalîg el 86 30 55N 29 0 E
Arab, Shatt al 64 30 0N 48 31 E
Arabatskaya Strelka 56 45 40N 35 0 E
Arabba 39 46 30N 11 51 E
Arabia 60 25 0N 45 0 E
Arabian Sea 60 16 0N 65 0 E
Arac 64 41 15N 33 21 E
Aracaju 127 10 55 S 37 4W
Aracataca 126 10 38N 74 9W
Aracati 127 4 30 S 37 44W
Araçatuba 125 21 10 S 50 30W
Aracena 31 37 53N 6 38W
Aracena, Sierra de 31 37 50N 6 50W
Araçuai 127 16 52 S 42 4W
'Arad 62 31 15N 35 12 E
Arad 46 46 10N 21 20 E
Arad □ 42 46 20N 22 0 E
Arada 81 15 0N 20 20 E
Aradu Nou 42 46 8N 21 20 E
Arafura Sea 73 9 0 S 135 0 E
Aragats 57 40 30N 44 15 E
Aragón 32 41 25N 1 0W
Aragón → 32 42 13N 1 44W
Aragona 40 37 24N 13 36 E
Araguacema 127 8 50 S 49 20W
Araguaia → 127 5 21 S 48 41W
Araguari 127 18 38 S 48 11W
Araguari → 127 1 15N 49 55W
Arak 82 25 20N 3 45 E
Arāk 64 34 0N 49 40 E
Arakan Coast 67 19 0N 94 0 E
Arakan Yoma 67 20 0N 94 40 E
Arákhova 45 38 28N 22 35 E
Araks = Aras, Rūd-e → 64 39 10N 47 10 E
Aral Sea = Aralskoye More 58 44 30N 60 0 E
Aralsk 58 46 50N 61 20 E
Aralskoye More 58 44 30N 60 0 E
Aramā, Mţii. de 46 47 10N 22 30 E
Aramac 97 22 58 S 145 14 E
Arambagh 69 22 53N 87 48 E
Aran I. 15 55 0N 8 30W
Aran Is. 15 53 5N 9 42W
Aranda de Duero 32 41 39N 3 42W
Arandelovac 42 44 18N 20 27 E
Aranjuez 30 40 1N 3 40W
Aranos 92 24 9 S 19 7 E
Aransas Pass 117 27 55N 97 9W
Araouane 84 18 55N 3 30W
Arapahoe 116 40 22N 99 53W
Arapey Grande → 124 30 55 S 57 49W
Arapkir 64 39 5N 38 30 E

Arapongas 125 23 29S 51 28W
Araranguá 125 29 0S 49 30W
Araraquara 127 21 50S 48 0W
Ararás, Serra das 125 25 0S 53 10W
Ararat 97 37 16S 143 0E
Ararat, Mt. = Ağri Daği 64 39 50N 44 15E
Araria 69 26 9N 87 33E
Araripe, Chapada do 127 7 20S 40 0W
Araruama, Lagoa de 125 22 53S 42 12W
Aras, Rūd-e → 64 39 10N 47 10E
Arauca 126 7 0N 70 40W
Arauca → 126 7 24N 66 35W
Arauco 124 37 16S 73 25W
Arauco □ 124 37 40S 73 25W
Arawa 87 9 57N 41 58E
Araxá 127 19 35S 46 55W
Araya, Pen. de 126 10 40N 64 0W
Arba Minch 87 6 0N 37 30E
Arbatax 40 39 57N 9 42E
Arbaza 59 52 40N 92 30E
Arbīl 64 36 15N 44 5E
Arboga 48 59 24N 15 52E
Arbois 19 46 55N 5 46E
Arbore 87 5 3N 36 50E
Arborea 40 39 46N 8 34E
Arborfield 109 53 6N 103 39W
Arborg 109 50 54N 97 13W
Arbrå 48 61 28N 16 22E
Arbresie, L' 21 45 50N 4 26E
Arbroath 14 56 34N 2 35W
Arbuckle 118 39 3N 122 2W
Arbus 40 39 30N 8 33E
Arbuzinka 56 47 0N 31 59E
Arc 19 47 28N 5 34E
Arc → 21 45 34N 6 12E
Arcachon 20 44 40N 1 10W
Arcachon, Bassin d' 20 44 42N 1 10W
Arcade 112 42 34N 78 25W
Arcadia, Fla., U.S.A. 115 27 20N 81 50W
Arcadia, La., U.S.A. 117 32 34N 92 53W
Arcadia, Nebr., U.S.A. 116 41 29N 99 4W
Arcadia, Pa., U.S.A. 112 40 46N 78 54W
Arcadia, Wis., U.S.A. 116 44 13N 91 29W
Arcata 118 40 55N 124 4W
Arcévia 39 43 29N 12 58E
Archangel = Arkhangelsk 52 64 40N 41 0E
Archar 42 43 50N 22 54E
Archbald 113 41 30N 75 31W
Archena 33 38 9N 1 16W
Archer → 97 13 28S 141 41E
Archer B. 98 13 20S 141 30E
Archers Post 90 0 35N 37 35E
Archidona 31 37 6N 4 22W
Arci, Monte 40 39 47N 8 44E
Arcidosso 39 42 51N 11 30E
Arcila = Asilah 82 35 29N 6 0W
Arcis-sur-Aube 19 48 32N 4 10E
Arco, Italy 38 45 55N 10 54E
Arco, U.S.A. 118 43 45N 113 16W
Arcola 109 49 40N 102 30W
Arcos 32 41 12N 2 16W
Arcos de los Frontera 31 36 45N 5 49W
Arcos de Valdevez 30 41 55N 8 22W
Arcot 70 12 53N 79 20E
Arcoverde 127 8 25S 37 4W
Arcs, Les 21 43 27N 6 29E
Arctic Bay 105 73 1N 85 7W
Arctic Ocean 4 78 0N 160 0W
Arctic Red River 104 67 15N 134 0W
Arda →, Bulg. 43 41 40N 26 29E
Arda →, Italy 38 44 53N 9 52E
Ardabīl 64 38 15N 48 18E
Ardahan 64 41 7N 42 41E
Ardakān 65 30 20N 52 5E
Årdal, Aust-Agder, Norway 47 58 42N 7 48E
Årdal, Rogaland, Norway 47 59 9N 6 13E
Ardales 31 36 53N 4 51W
Årdalstangen 47 61 14N 7 43E
Ardatov 55 54 51N 46 15E
Ardea 44 40 58N 22 3E
Ardèche □ 21 44 42N 4 16E
Ardèche → 21 44 16N 4 39E
Ardee 15 53 51N 6 32W
Arden 112 44 43N 76 56W
Arden Stby. 49 56 46N 9 52E
Ardennes 16 50 0N 5 10E
Ardennes □ 19 49 35N 4 40E
Ardentes 19 46 45N 1 50E
Ardestān 65 33 20N 52 25E
Ardgour 14 56 45N 5 25W
Ardhas → 44 41 36N 26 25E
Ardila → 31 38 12N 7 28W
Ardino 43 41 34N 25 9E
Ardjuno 73 7 49S 112 34E
Ardlethan 99 34 22S 146 53E
Ardmore, Austral. 98 21 39S 139 11E
Ardmore, Okla., U.S.A. 117 34 10N 97 5W
Ardmore, Pa., U.S.A. 113 39 58N 75 18W
Ardmore, S.D., U.S.A. 116 43 0N 103 40W
Ardnacrusha 15 52 43N 8 38W
Ardnamurchan, Pt. of 14 56 44N 6 14W
Ardore Marina 41 38 11N 16 10E
Ardres 19 50 50N 2 0E
Ardrossan, Austral. 99 34 26S 137 53E
Ardrossan, U.K. 14 55 39N 4 50W
Ards □ 15 54 35N 5 30W
Ards Pen. 15 54 30N 5 25W
Ardud 46 47 37N 22 52E
Ardunac 57 41 8N 42 5E
Åre 48 63 22N 13 15E
Arecibo 121 18 29N 66 42W
Areia Branca 127 5 0S 37 0W
Aremark 47 59 15N 11 42E
Arenas 30 43 17N 4 50W
Arenas de San Pedro 30 40 12N 5 5W
Arendal 47 58 28N 8 46E
Arendsee 24 52 52N 11 27E
Arenys de Mar 32 41 35N 2 33E
Arenzano 38 44 24N 8 40E
Areópolis 45 36 40N 22 22E
Arequipa 126 16 20S 71 30W
Arero 87 4 41N 38 50E
Arès 20 44 47N 1 8W
Arévalo 30 41 3N 4 43W
Arezzo 39 43 28N 11 50E
Arga → 32 42 18N 1 47W
Argalastí 44 39 13N 23 13E
Argamasilla de Alba 33 39 8N 3 5W
Arganda 32 40 19N 3 26W
Arganil 30 40 13N 8 3W
Argelès-Gazost 20 43 0N 0 6W
Argelès-sur-Mer 20 42 34N 3 1E
Argens → 21 43 24N 6 44E
Argent-sur-Sauldre 19 47 33N 2 25E
Argenta, Can. 108 50 20N 116 55W
Argenta, Italy 39 44 37N 11 50E
Argentan 18 48 45N 0 1W
Argentário, Mte. 39 42 23N 11 11E
Argentat 20 45 6N 1 56E
Argentera 38 44 23N 6 58E
Argentera, Monte del 38 44 12N 7 5E
Argenteuil 19 48 57N 2 14E
Argentia 107 47 18N 53 58W
Argentiera, C. dell' 40 40 44N 8 8E
Argentière, L' 21 44 47N 6 33E
Argentina ■ 128 35 0S 66 0W
Argentino, L. 128 50 10S 73 0W
Argenton-Château 18 46 59N 0 27W
Argenton-sur-Creuse 20 46 36N 1 30E
Argeș □ 46 45 0N 24 45E
Argeș → 46 44 30N 25 50E
Arghandab → 66 31 30N 64 15E
Argo 86 19 28N 30 30E
Argolikós Kólpos 45 37 20N 22 52E
Argolís □ 45 37 38N 22 50E
Argonne 19 49 0N 5 20E
Árgos 45 37 40N 22 43E
Árgos Orestikón 44 40 27N 21 26E
Argostólion 45 38 12N 20 33E
Arguedas 32 42 11N 1 36W
Arguello, Pt. 119 34 34N 120 40W
Argun → 59 53 20N 121 28E
Argungu 85 12 40N 4 31E
Argyle 116 48 23N 96 49W
Argyrádhes 44 39 27N 19 58E
Århus 49 56 8N 10 11E
Århus Amtskommune □ 49 56 15N 10 15E
Ariamsvlei 92 28 9S 19 51E
Ariana 83 36 52N 10 12E
Ariano Irpino 41 41 10N 15 4E
Ariano nel Polèsine 39 44 56N 12 5E
Aribinda 85 14 17N 0 52W
Arica, Chile 126 18 32S 70 20W
Arica, Colomb. 126 2 0S 71 50W
Arid, C. 96 34 1S 123 10E
Aridh 64 25 0N 46 0E
Ariège □ 20 42 56N 1 30E
Ariège → 20 43 30N 1 25E
Arieș → 46 46 24N 23 20E
Arilje 42 43 44N 20 7E
Arima 121 10 38N 61 17W
Arinos → 126 10 25S 58 20W
Ario de Rosales 120 19 12N 102 0W
Aripuanã 126 9 25S 60 30W
Aripuanã → 126 5 7S 60 25W
Ariquemes 126 9 55S 63 6W
Arisaig 14 56 55N 5 50W
Arîsh, W. el → 86 31 9N 33 49E
Arissa 87 11 10N 41 35E
Aristazabal I. 108 52 40N 129 10W
Arivaca 119 31 37N 111 25W
Arivonimamo 93 19 1S 47 11E
Ariyalur 70 11 8N 79 8E
Ariza 74 41 19N 2 3W
Arizaro, Salar de 124 24 40S 67 50W
Arizona 124 35 45S 65 25W
Arizona □ 119 34 20N 111 30W
Arizpe 120 30 20N 110 11W
Årjäng 48 59 24N 12 8E
Arjeplog 50 66 3N 18 2E
Arjona, Colomb. 126 10 14N 75 22W
Arjona, Spain 31 37 56N 4 4W
Arka 59 60 15N 142 0E
Arkadak 55 51 58N 43 19E
Arkadelphia 117 34 5N 93 0W
Arkadhía □ 45 37 30N 22 20E
Arkaig, L. 14 56 58N 5 10W
Arkalyk 58 50 13N 66 50E
Arkansas □ 117 35 0N 92 30W
Arkansas → 117 33 48N 91 4W
Arkansas City 117 37 4N 97 3W
Árkathos → 44 39 20N 21 4E
Arkhángelos 45 36 13N 28 7E
Arkhangelsk 52 64 40N 41 0E
Arkhangelskoye 55 51 32N 40 58E
Arkiko 87 15 33N 39 30E
Arklow 15 52 48N 6 10W
Árkoi 45 37 24N 26 44E
Arkona, Kap 24 54 41N 13 26E
Arkonam 70 13 7N 79 43E
Arkösund 49 58 29N 16 56E
Arkoúdhi 45 38 33N 20 43E
Arkticheskiy, Mys 59 81 10N 95 0E
Arkul 55 57 17N 50 3E
Arlanc 20 45 25N 3 42E
Arlanza → 30 42 6N 4 9W
Arlanzón → 30 42 3N 4 17W
Arlberg Pass 25 47 9N 10 12E
Arlee 118 47 10N 114 4W
Arles 21 43 41N 4 40E
Arlington, S. Afr. 93 28 1S 27 53E
Arlington, Oreg., U.S.A. 118 45 48N 120 6W
Arlington, S.D., U.S.A. 116 44 25N 97 4W
Arlington, Va., U.S.A. 114 38 52N 77 5W
Arlington, Wash., U.S.A. 118 48 11N 122 4W
Arlon 16 49 42N 5 49E
Arlöv 49 55 38N 13 5E
Arly 85 11 35N 1 28E
Armagh 15 54 22N 6 40W
Armagh □ 15 54 18N 6 37W
Armagnac 20 43 44N 0 10E
Armançon → 19 47 59N 3 30E
Armavir 57 45 2N 41 7E
Armenia 126 4 35N 75 45W
Armenian S.S.R. □ 57 40 0N 44 0E
Armeniș 46 45 13N 22 17E
Armentières 19 50 40N 2 50E
Armidale 97 30 30S 151 40E
Armour 116 43 20N 98 25W
Armstrong, B.C., Can. 108 50 25N 119 10W
Armstrong, Ont., Can. 106 50 18N 89 4W
Armstrong, U.S.A. 117 26 59N 97 48W
Armur 70 18 48N 78 16E
Arnaia 44 40 30N 23 40E
Arnaouti, C. 64 35 0N 32 20E
Arnarfjörður 50 65 48N 23 40W
Arnaud → 105 60 0N 70 0W
Arnay-le-Duc 19 47 10N 4 27E
Arnedillo 32 42 13N 2 14W
Arnedo 32 42 12N 2 5W
Årnes 50 66 1N 21 31W
Årnes 47 60 7N 11 28E
Arnett 117 36 9N 99 44W
Arnhem 16 51 58N 5 55E
Arnhem B. 96 12 20S 136 10E
Arnhem, C. 97 12 20S 137 30E
Arnhem Land 96 13 10S 134 30E
Arni 70 12 43N 79 19E
Árnissa 44 40 47N 21 49E
Arno → 38 43 41N 10 17E
Arnold, Nebr., U.S.A. 116 41 29N 100 10W
Arnold, Pa., U.S.A. 112 40 36N 79 44W
Arnoldstein 26 46 33N 13 43E
Arnon → 19 47 13N 2 1E
Arnot 109 55 56N 96 41W
Arnøy 50 70 9N 20 40E
Arnprior 106 45 26N 76 21W
Arnsberg 24 51 25N 8 2E
Arnstadt 24 50 50N 10 56E
Aroab 92 26 41S 19 39E
Aroánia Óri 45 37 56N 22 12E
Aroche 31 37 56N 6 57W
Arolsen 24 51 23N 9 1E
Aron → 19 46 50N 3 27E
Arona 38 45 45N 8 32E
Arosa, Ria de → 30 42 28N 8 57W
Arpajon, Cantal, France 20 44 54N 2 28E
Arpajon, Essonne, France 19 48 37N 2 12E
Arpino 40 41 40N 13 35E
Arrabury 99 26 45S 141 0E
Arrah 69 25 35N 84 32E
Arraiján 120 8 56N 79 36W
Arraiolos 31 38 44N 7 59W
Arran 14 55 34N 5 12W
Arrandale 108 54 57N 130 0W
Arras 19 50 17N 2 46E
Arrats → 20 44 6N 0 52E
Arreau 20 42 54N 0 22E
Arrecife 80 28 57N 13 37W
Arrecifes 124 34 06S 60 9W
Arrée, Mts. d' 18 48 26N 3 55W
Arriaga 120 21 55N 101 23W
Arrilalah P.O. 98 23 43S 143 54E
Arromanches-les-Bains 18 49 20N 0 38W
Arronches 31 39 8N 7 16W
Arros, R 20 43 40N 0 2W
Arrou 18 48 6N 1 8E
Arrow, L. 15 54 3N 8 20W
Arrow Rock Res. 118 43 45N 115 50W
Arrowhead 108 50 40N 117 55W
Arrowtown 101 44 57S 168 50E
Arroyo de la Luz 31 39 30N 6 38W
Arroyo Grande 119 35 9N 120 32W
Års 49 56 48N 9 30E
Ars 20 46 13N 1 30W
Ars-sur-Moselle 19 49 5N 6 4E
Arsenault L. 109 55 6N 108 32W
Arsiero 39 45 49N 11 22E
Arsikere 70 13 15N 76 15E
Arsk 55 56 10N 49 50E
Árta 45 39 8N 21 2E
Artá 32 39 41N 3 21E
Árta □ 44 39 15N 21 5E
Arteaga 120 18 50N 102 20W
Arteijo 30 43 19N 8 29W
Artem, Ostrov 57 40 28N 50 20E
Artemovsk, R.S.F.S.R., U.S.S.R. 59 54 45N 93 35E
Artemovsk, Ukraine S.S.R., U.S.S.R. 56 48 35N 38 0E
Artemovski 57 47 45N 40 16E
Artenay 19 48 5N 1 50E
Artern 24 51 22N 11 18E
Artesa de Segre 32 41 54N 1 3E
Artesia 117 32 55N 104 25W
Artesia Wells 117 28 17N 99 18W
Artesian 116 44 2N 97 54W
Arthez-de-Béarn 20 43 29N 0 38W
Arthington 84 6 35N 10 45W
Arthur → 99 41 2S 144 40E
Arthur Pt. 98 22 7S 150 3E
Arthur's Pass 101 42 54S 171 35E
Artigas 124 30 20S 56 30W
Artik 57 40 38N 43 58E
Artillery L. 109 63 9N 107 52W
Artois 19 50 20N 2 30E
Artotina 45 38 42N 22 2E
Artsiz 56 46 4N 29 26E
Artvin 64 41 14N 41 44E
Aru, Kepulauan 73 6 0S 134 30E
Aru Meru □ 90 3 20S 36 50E
Arua 90 3 1N 30 58E
Aruanã 127 14 54S 51 10W
Aruba 121 12 30N 70 0W
Arudy 20 43 7N 0 28W
Arun → 69 26 55N 87 10E
Arunachal Pradesh □ 67 28 0N 95 0E
Aruppukottai 70 9 31N 78 8E
Arusha 90 3 20S 36 40E
Arusha □ 90 4 0S 36 30E
Arusha Chini 90 3 32S 37 20E
Arusi □ 87 7 45N 39 00E
Aruvi → 70 8 48N 79 53E
Aruwimi → 90 1 13N 23 36E
Arvada 118 44 43N 106 6W
Arvakalu 70 8 20N 79 58E
Arvayheer 75 46 15N 102 48E
Arve → 21 46 11N 6 8E
Arvi 68 20 59N 78 16E
Arvida 107 48 25N 71 14W
Arvidsjaur 50 65 35N 19 10E
Arvika 48 59 40N 12 36E
Arxan 75 47 11N 119 57E
Arys 58 42 26N 68 48E
Arzachena 40 41 5N 9 27E
Arzamas 55 55 27N 43 55E
Arzew 82 35 50N 0 23W
Arzgir 57 45 18N 44 23E
Arzignano 39 45 30N 11 20E
Aš 26 50 13N 12 12E
'As Saffānīyah 64 28 5N 48 50E
Aş Şāfī 62 31 2N 35 28E
As Salt 62 32 2N 35 43E
As Samāwah 64 31 15N 45 15E
As Samū' 62 31 24N 35 4E
As Sanamayn 62 33 3N 36 10E
As Sulaymānīyah 64 24 9N 47 18E
As Sulṭan 83 31 4N 17 8E
As Sumaymānīyah 64 35 35N 45 29E
As Summān 64 25 0N 47 0E
As Suwaih 65 22 10N 59 33E
As Suwaydā' 64 32 40N 36 30E
Aş Şuwayrah 64 32 55N 45 0E
Asab 92 25 30S 18 0E
Asaba 85 6 12N 6 38E
Asafo 84 6 20N 2 40W
Asahigawa 74 43 46N 142 22E
Asale, L. 87 14 0N 40 20E
Asamankese 85 5 50N 0 40W
Asansol 69 23 40N 87 1E
Åsarna 48 62 39N 14 22E
Asbe Teferi 87 9 4N 40 49E
Asbesberge 92 29 0S 23 0E
Asbestos 107 45 47N 71 58W
Asbury Park 114 40 15N 74 1W
Ascensión, B. de la 120 19 50N 87 20W
Ascension I. 7 8 0S 14 15W
Aschach 26 48 22N 14 2E
Aschaffenburg 25 49 58N 9 8E
Aschendorf 24 53 2N 7 22E
Aschersleben 24 51 45N 11 28E
Asciano 39 43 14N 11 32E
Ascoli Piceno 39 42 51N 13 34E
Ascoli Satriano 41 41 11N 15 32E
Ascope 126 7 46S 79 8W
Ascotán 124 21 45S 68 17W
Aseb 87 13 0N 42 40E
Åseda 49 57 10N 15 20E
Asedjrad 82 24 51N 1 29E
Asela 87 8 0N 39 0E
Asenovgrad 43 42 1N 24 51E
Aseral 47 58 37N 7 25E
Asfeld 19 49 27N 4 5E
Asfûn el Matâ'na 86 25 26N 32 30E
Åsgårdstrand 47 59 22N 10 27E
Ash Fork 119 35 14N 112 32W
Ash Grove 117 37 21N 93 36W
Ash Shām, Bādiyat 64 32 0N 40 0E
Ash Shāmiyah 64 31 55N 44 35E
Ash Shāriqah 65 25 23N 55 26E
Ash Shaṭrah 64 31 30N 46 10E
Ash Shu'aybah 64 27 53N 42 43E
Ash Shu'bah 64 28 54N 44 44E
Ash Shūnah ash Shamālīyah 62 32 37N 35 34E
Asha 52 55 0N 57 16E
Ashaira 86 21 40N 40 40E
Ashanti □ 85 7 30N 1 30W
Ashburn 115 31 42N 83 40W
Ashburton 101 43 53S 171 48E
Ashburton → 96 21 40S 114 56E
Ashby-de-la-Zouch 12 52 45N 1 29W
Ashcroft 108 50 40N 121 20W
Ashdod 62 31 49N 34 35E
Ashdot Yaaqov 62 32 39N 35 35E
Asheboro 115 35 43N 79 46W
Asherton 117 28 25N 99 43W
Asheville 115 35 39N 82 30W
Asheweig → 106 54 17N 87 12W
Ashford, Austral. 99 29 15S 151 3E
Ashford, U.K. 13 51 8N 0 53E
Ashford, U.S.A. 118 46 45N 122 2W
Ashikaga 74 36 28N 139 29E
Ashizuri-Zaki 74 32 44N 133 0E
Ashkhabad 58 38 0N 57 50E
Ashland, Kans., U.S.A. 117 37 13N 99 43W
Ashland, Ky., U.S.A. 114 38 25N 82 40W
Ashland, Me., U.S.A. 107 46 34N 68 26W
Ashland, Mont., U.S.A. 118 45 41N 106 12W
Ashland, Nebr., U.S.A. 116 41 5N 96 27W
Ashland, Ohio, U.S.A. 114 40 52N 82 20W
Ashland, Oreg., U.S.A. 118 42 10N 122 38W
Ashland, Pa., U.S.A. 113 40 45N 76 22W
Ashland, Va., U.S.A. 114 37 46N 77 30W
Ashland, Wis., U.S.A. 116 46 40N 90 52W
Ashley, N.D., U.S.A. 116 46 3N 99 23W
Ashley, Pa., U.S.A. 113 41 12N 75 55W
Ashley Snow I. 5 73 35S 77 6W
Ashmont 108 54 7N 111 35W
Ashmore Reef 96 12 14S 123 5E
Ashmûn 86 30 18N 30 55E
Ashq'elon 62 31 42N 34 35E
Ashtabula 114 41 52N 80 50W
Ashti 70 18 50N 75 15E
Ashton, S. Afr. 92 33 50S 20 5E
Ashton, U.S.A. 118 44 6N 111 30W
Ashton-under-Lyne 12 53 30N 2 8W
Ashuanipi, L. 107 52 45N 66 15W
Asia 60 45 0N 75 0E
Asia, Kepulauan 73 1 0N 131 13E
Asiago 39 45 52N 11 30E
Asifabad 70 19 20N 79 24E
Asike 73 6 39S 140 24E
Asilah 82 35 29N 6 0W
Asinara, G. dell' 40 41 0N 8 30E
Asinara I. 40 41 5N 8 15E
Asino 58 57 0N 86 0E
'Asīr □ 63 18 40N 42 30E
Asir, Ras 63 11 55N 51 10E
Aska 70 19 2N 84 42E

Asker 47 59 50N 10 26 E
Askersund 49 58 53N 14 55 E
Askim 47 59 35N 11 10 E
Askja 50 65 3N 16 48W
Asl 86 29 33N 32 44 E
Asmār 65 35 10N 71 27 E
Asmera (Asmara) 87 15 19N 38 55 E
Asnæs 49 55 40N 11 0 E
Asni 82 31 17N 7 58W
Aso 74 33 0N 131 5 E
Asola 38 45 12N 10 25 E
Asoteriba, Jebel 86 21 51N 36 30 E
Asotin 118 46 20N 117 3W
Aspe 33 38 20N 0 40W
Aspen 119 39 12N 106 56W
Aspermont 117 33 11N 100 15W
Aspiring, Mt. 101 44 23 S 168 46 E
Aspres 21 44 32N 5 44 E
Aspromonte 41 38 10N 16 0 E
Aspur 68 23 58N 74 7 E
Asquith 109 52 8N 107 13W
Assa 82 28 35N 9 6W
Assâba 84 16 10N 11 45W
Assam □ 67 26 0N 93 0 E
Assamakka 85 19 21N 5 38 E
Asse 16 50 24N 4 10 E
Assekrem 83 23 16N 5 49 E
Assémini 40 39 18N 9 0 E
Assen 16 53 0N 6 35 E
Assens, Fyn, Denmark 49 56 41N 10 3 E
Assens, Fyn, Denmark 49 55 16N 9 55 E
Assini 84 5 9N 3 17W
Assiniboia 109 49 40N 105 59W
Assiniboine → 109 49 53N 97 8W
Assis 125 22 40 S 50 20W
Assisi 39 43 4N 12 36 E
Ássos 45 38 22N 20 33 E
Assus 44 39 32N 26 22 E
Assynt, L. 14 58 25N 5 15W
Astaffort 20 44 4N 0 40 E
Astakidha 45 35 53N 26 50 E
Astara 53 38 30N 48 50 E
Asti 38 44 54N 8 11 E
Astipálaia 45 36 32N 26 22 E
Astorga 30 42 29N 6 8W
Astoria 118 46 16N 123 50W
Åstorp 49 56 6N 12 55 E
Astrakhan 57 46 25N 48 5 E
Astrakhan-Bazàr 53 39 14N 48 30 E
Astudillo 30 42 12N 4 22W
Asturias 30 43 15N 6 0W
Asunción 124 25 10 S 57 30W
Asunción, La 126 11 2N 63 53W
Asutri 87 15 25N 35 45 E
Aswa → 90 3 43N 31 55 E
Aswad, Ras al 86 21 20N 39 0 E
Aswân 86 24 4N 32 57 E
Aswân High Dam = Sadd el Aali 86 24 5N 32 54 E
Asyût 86 27 11N 31 4 E
Asyûti, Wadi → 86 27 11N 31 16 E
Aszód 27 47 39N 19 28 E
At Ţafilah 64 30 45N 35 30 E
At Ta'if 86 21 5N 40 27 E
Aţ Ţur 62 31 47N 35 14 E
Aţ Ţurrah 62 32 39N 35 59 E
Atacama □ 124 27 30 S 70 0W
Atacama, Desierto de 124 24 0 S 69 20W
Atacama, Salar de 124 23 30N 68 20W
Atakor 83 23 27N 5 31 E
Atakpamé 85 7 31N 1 13 E
Atalándi 45 38 39N 22 58 E
Atalaya 126 10 45 S 73 50W
Atami 74 35 5N 139 4 E
Atapupu 73 9 0 S 124 51 E
Atâr 80 20 30N 13 5W
Atara 59 63 10N 129 10 E
Ataram, Erg n- 82 23 57N 2 0 E
Atarfe 31 37 13N 3 40W
Atascadero 119 35 32N 120 44W
Atasu 58 48 30N 71 0 E
Atauro 73 8 10 S 125 30 E
Atbara 86 17 42N 33 59 E
'Atbara → 86 17 40N 33 56 E
Atbasar 58 51 48N 68 20 E
Atchafalaya B. 117 29 30N 91 20W
Atchison 116 39 40N 95 10W
Atebubu 85 7 47N 1 0W
Ateca 32 41 20N 1 49W
Aterno → 39 42 11N 13 51 E
Atesine, Alpi 38 46 55N 11 30 E
Atessa 39 42 5N 14 27 E
Ath 16 50 38N 3 47 E
Ath Thāmāmi 64 27 45N 44 45 E
Athabasca 108 54 45N 113 20W
Athabasca → 109 58 40N 110 50W
Athabasca, L. 109 59 15N 109 15W
Athboy 15 53 37N 6 55W
Athenry 15 53 18N 8 45W
Athens, Can. 113 44 38N 75 57W
Athens, Ala., U.S.A. 115 34 49N 86 58W
Athens, Ga., U.S.A. 115 33 56N 83 24W
Athens, N.Y., U.S.A. 113 42 15N 73 48W
Athens, Ohio, U.S.A. 114 39 25N 82 6W
Athens, Pa., U.S.A. 113 41 57N 76 36W
Athens, Tenn., U.S.A. 115 35 45N 84 38W
Athens, Tex., U.S.A. 117 32 11N 95 48W
Athens = Athinai 45 37 58N 23 46 E
Atherley 112 44 37N 79 20W
Atherton 97 17 17 S 145 30 E
Athiéme 85 6 37N 1 40 E
Athinai 45 37 58N 23 46 E
Athlone 15 53 26N 7 57W
Athni 70 16 44N 75 6 E
Atholl, Forest of 14 56 51N 3 50W
Atholville 107 47 59N 66 43W
Áthos, Mt. 44 40 9N 24 22 E
Athy 15 53 0N 7 0W
Ati, Chad 81 13 13N 18 20 E
Ati, Sudan 87 13 5N 29 2 E
Atiak 90 3 12N 32 2 E
Atico 126 16 14 S 73 40W
Atienza 32 41 12N 2 52W
Atikokan 106 48 45N 91 37W
Atikonak L. 107 52 40N 64 32W
Atka 59 60 50N 151 48 E
Atkarsk 55 51 55N 45 2 E
Atkinson 116 42 35N 98 59W
Atlanta, Ga., U.S.A. 115 33 50N 84 24W
Atlanta, Tex., U.S.A. 117 33 7N 94 8W
Atlantic 116 41 25N 95 0W
Atlantic City 114 39 25N 74 25W
Atlantic Ocean 6 0 0 20 0W
Atlin 104 59 31N 133 41W
Atlin, L. 108 59 26N 133 45W
'Atlit 62 32 42N 34 56 E
Atløy 47 61 21N 4 58 E
Atmakur 70 14 37N 79 40 E
Atmore 115 31 2N 87 30W
Atna → 47 61 44N 10 49 E
Atoka 117 34 22N 96 10W
Átokos 45 38 28N 20 49 E
Atouguia 31 39 20N 9 20W
Atoyac → 120 16 30N 97 31W
Atrak → 65 37 50N 57 0 E
Atran 49 57 7N 12 57 E
Atrauli 68 28 2N 78 20 E
Atri 39 42 35N 14 0 E
Atsbi 87 13 52N 39 50 E
Atsoum, Mts. 85 6 41N 12 57 E
Attalla 115 34 2N 86 5W
Attawapiskat 106 52 56N 82 24W
Attawapiskat → 106 52 57N 82 18W
Attawapiskat, L. 106 52 18N 87 54W
Attendorn 24 51 8N 7 54 E
Attersee 26 47 55N 13 32 E
Attica 114 40 20N 87 15W
Attichy 19 49 25N 3 3 E
Attigny 19 49 28N 4 35 E
Attikamagen L. 107 55 0N 66 30W
Attiki □ 45 38 10N 23 40 E
'Attīl 62 32 23N 35 4 E
Attleboro 114 41 56N 71 18W
Attock 66 33 52N 72 20 E
Attopeu 71 14 48N 106 50 E
Attur 70 11 35N 78 30 E
Atuel → 124 36 17 S 66 50W
Åtvidaberg 49 58 12N 16 0 E
Atwater 119 37 21N 120 37W
Atwood, Can. 112 43 40N 81 1W
Atwood, U.S.A. 116 39 52N 101 3W
Au Sable → 114 44 25N 83 20W
Au Sable Pt. 106 46 40N 86 10W
Aubagne 21 43 17N 5 37 E
Aube □ 19 48 15N 4 0 E
Aube → 19 48 34N 3 43 E
Aubenas 21 44 37N 4 24 E
Aubenton 19 49 50N 4 12 E
Aubigny-sur-Nère 19 47 30N 2 24 E
Aubin 20 44 33N 2 15 E
Aubrac, Mts. d' 20 44 38N 2 58 E
Auburn, Ala., U.S.A. 115 32 37N 85 30W
Auburn, Calif., U.S.A. 118 38 53N 121 4W
Auburn, Ind., U.S.A. 114 41 20N 85 0W
Auburn, N.Y., U.S.A. 114 42 57N 76 39W
Auburn, Nebr., U.S.A. 116 40 25N 95 50W
Auburn Range 99 25 15 S 150 30 E
Auburndale 115 28 5N 81 45W
Aubusson 20 45 57N 2 11 E
Auch 20 43 39N 0 36 E
Auchel 19 50 30N 2 29 E
Auchi 85 7 6N 6 13 E
Auckland 101 36 52 S 174 46 E
Auckland Is. 94 50 40 S 166 5 E
Aude □ 20 43 8N 2 28 E
Aude → 20 43 13N 3 14 E
Auden 106 50 14N 87 53W
Auderville 18 49 43N 1 57W
Audierne 18 48 1N 4 34W
Audincourt 19 47 30N 6 50 E
Audo Ra. 87 6 20N 41 50 E
Audubon 116 41 43N 94 56W
Aue 24 50 34N 12 43 E
Auerbach 24 50 30N 12 25 E
Auffay 18 49 43N 1 07 E
Augathella 97 25 48 S 146 35 E
Augrabies Falls 92 28 35 S 20 20 E
Augsburg 25 48 22N 10 54 E
Augusta, Italy 41 37 14N 15 12 E
Augusta, Ark., U.S.A. 117 35 17N 91 25W
Augusta, Ga., U.S.A. 115 33 29N 81 59W
Augusta, Kans., U.S.A. 117 37 40N 97 0W
Augusta, Me., U.S.A. 107 44 20N 69 46W
Augusta, Mont., U.S.A. 118 47 30N 112 29W
Augusta, Wis., U.S.A. 116 44 41N 91 8W
Augustenborg 49 54 57N 9 53 E
Augusto Cardosa 91 12 40 S 34 50 E
Augustów 28 53 51N 23 00 E
Augustus Downs 98 18 35 S 139 55 E
Augustus, Mt. 96 24 20 S 116 50 E
Aukan 87 15 29N 40 50 E
Aulla 38 44 12N 10 0 E
Aulnay 20 46 2N 0 22W
Aulne → 18 48 17N 4 16W
Aulnoye 19 50 12N 3 50 E
Ault 116 40 40N 104 42W
Ault-Onival 18 50 5N 1 29 E
Aulus-les-Bains 20 42 49N 1 19 E
Aumale 19 49 46N 1 46 E
Aumont-Aubrac 20 44 43N 3 17 E
Auna 85 10 9N 4 42 E
Aundh 70 17 33N 74 23 E
Aunis 20 46 5N 0 50W
Auponhia 73 1 58 S 125 27 E
Aups 21 43 37N 6 15 E
Auraiya 69 26 28N 79 33 E
Aurangabad, Bihar, India 69 24 45N 84 18 E
Aurangabad, Maharashtra, India 70 19 50N 75 23 E
Auray 18 47 40N 3 0W
Aurès 83 35 8N 6 30 E
Aurich 24 53 28N 7 30 E
Aurillac 20 44 55N 2 26 E
Aurlandsvangen 47 60 55N 7 12 E
Auronza 39 46 33N 12 27 E
Aurora, Can. 112 44 0N 79 28W
Aurora, S. Afr. 92 32 40 S 18 29 E
Aurora, Colo., U.S.A. 116 39 44N 104 55W
Aurora, Ill., U.S.A. 114 41 42N 88 12W
Aurora, Mo., U.S.A. 117 36 58N 93 42W
Aurora, Nebr., U.S.A. 116 40 55N 98 0W
Aurora, Ohio, U.S.A. 112 41 21N 81 20W
Aurskog 47 59 55N 11 26 E
Aurukun Mission 98 13 20 S 141 45 E
Aus 92 26 35 S 16 12 E
Aust-Agder fylke □ 47 58 55N 7 40 E
Austad 47 58 58N 7 37 E
Austerlitz = Slavkov 27 49 10N 16 52 E
Austevoll 47 60 5N 5 13 E
Austin, Minn., U.S.A. 116 43 37N 92 59W
Austin, Nev., U.S.A. 118 39 30N 117 1W
Austin, Pa., U.S.A. 112 41 40N 78 7W
Austin, Tex., U.S.A. 117 30 20N 97 45W
Austin, L. 96 27 40 S 118 0 E
Austral Downs 97 20 30 S 137 45 E
Austral Is. = Tubuai Is. 95 23 0 S 150 0W
Austral Seamount Chain 95 24 0 S 150 0W
Australia ■ 94 23 0 S 135 0 E
Australian Alps 97 36 30 S 148 30 E
Australian Cap. Terr. □ 97 35 30 S 149 0 E
Australian Dependency □ 5 73 0 S 90 0 E
Austria ■ 26 47 0N 14 0 E
Austvågøy 50 68 20N 14 40 E
Auterive 20 43 21N 1 29 E
Authie → 19 50 22N 1 38 E
Authon 18 48 12N 0 55 E
Autlán 120 19 40N 104 30W
Autun 19 46 58N 4 17 E
Auvergne 20 45 20N 3 15 E
Auvézère → 20 45 12N 0 50 E
Auxerre 19 47 48N 3 32 E
Auxi-le-Château 19 50 15N 2 8 E
Auxonne 19 47 10N 5 20 E
Auzances 20 46 2N 2 30 E
Auzat 20 45 27N 3 19 E
Avallon 19 47 30N 3 53 E
Avalon Pen. 107 47 30N 53 20W
Avalon Res. 117 32 30N 104 30W
Avanigadda 70 16 0N 80 56 E
Avaré 125 23 4 S 48 58W
Ávas 44 40 57N 25 56 E
Aveiro, Brazil 127 3 10 S 55 5W
Aveiro, Port. 30 40 37N 8 38W
Aveiro □ 30 40 40N 8 35W
Åvej 64 35 40N 49 15 E
Avellaneda 124 34 50 S 58 10W
Avellino 41 40 54N 14 46 E
Averøya 47 63 0N 7 35 E
Aversa 41 40 58N 14 11 E
Avery 118 47 22N 115 56W
Aves, I. de 121 15 45N 63 55W
Aves, Is. de 121 12 0N 67 30W
Avesnes-sur-Helpe 19 50 8N 3 55 E
Avesta 48 60 9N 16 10 E
Aveyron □ 20 44 22N 2 45 E
Aveyron → 20 44 7N 1 5 E
Avezzano 39 42 2N 13 24 E
Avgó 45 35 33N 25 37 E
Aviá Terai 124 26 45 S 60 50W
Aviano 39 46 3N 12 35 E
Avigliana 38 45 7N 7 13 E
Avigliano 41 40 44N 15 41 E
Avignon 21 43 57N 4 50 E
Ávila 30 40 39N 4 43W
Ávila □ 30 40 30N 5 0W
Ávila, Sierra de 30 40 40N 5 0W
Avilés 30 43 35N 5 57W
Avionárion 45 38 31N 24 8 E
Avisio → 39 46 7N 11 5 E
Aviz 31 39 4N 7 53W
Avize 19 48 59N 4 0 E
Avoca, Austral. 100 37 5 S 143 26 E
Avoca, Ireland 15 52 52N 6 13W
Avoca, U.S.A. 112 42 24N 77 25W
Avoca → 100 35 40 S 143 43 E
Avola, Can. 108 51 45N 119 19W
Avola, Italy 41 36 56N 15 7 E
Avon, N.Y., U.S.A. 112 43 0N 77 42W
Avon, S.D., U.S.A. 116 43 0N 98 3W
Avon □ 13 51 30N 2 40W
Avon →, Avon, U.K. 13 51 30N 2 43W
Avon →, Hants., U.K. 13 50 44N 1 45W
Avon →, Warwick, U.K. 13 52 0N 2 9W
Avon Downs 97 19 58 S 137 25 E
Avon, Îles 97 19 37 S 158 17 E
Avon Lake 112 41 28N 82 3W
Avondale 91 17 43 S 30 58 E
Avonlea 109 50 0N 105 0W
Avonmore 113 45 10N 74 58W
Avonmouth 13 51 30N 2 42W
Avramov 43 42 45N 26 38 E
Avranches 18 48 40N 1 20W
Avre → 18 48 47N 1 22 E
Avrig 46 45 43N 24 21 E
Avrillé 20 46 28N 1 28W
Avtovac 42 43 9N 18 35 E
Awag el Baqar 87 10 10N 33 10 E
'Awālī 65 26 0N 50 30 E
Awarja → 70 17 5N 76 15 E
'Awartā 62 32 10N 35 17 E
Awasa, L. 87 7 0N 38 30 E
Awash 87 9 1N 40 10 E
Awash → 87 11 45N 41 5 E
Awaso 84 6 15N 2 22W
Awatere → 101 41 37 S 174 10 E
Awbārī 83 26 46N 12 57 E
Awbārī □ 83 26 35N 12 46 E
Awe, L. 14 56 15N 5 15W
Aweil 87 8 42N 27 20 E
Awgu 85 6 4N 7 24 E
Awjilah 81 29 8N 21 7 E
Ax-les-Thermes 20 42 44N 1 50 E
Axarfjörður 50 66 15N 16 45W
Axel Heiberg I. 4 80 0N 90 0W
Axim 84 4 51N 2 15W
Axintele 46 44 37N 26 47 E
Axiós → 44 40 57N 22 35 E
Axmarsbruk 48 61 3N 17 10 E
Axminster 13 50 47N 3 1W
Axstedt 24 53 26N 8 43 E
Axvall 49 58 23N 13 34 E
Ay 19 49 3N 4 0 E
Ayabaca 126 4 40 S 79 53W
Ayabe 74 35 20N 135 20 E
Ayacucho, Argent. 124 37 5 S 58 20W
Ayacucho, Peru 126 13 0 S 74 0W
Ayaguz 58 48 10N 80 0 E
Ayakudi 70 10 28N 77 56 E
Ayamonte 31 37 12N 7 24W
Ayan 59 56 30N 138 16 E
Ayancık 56 41 57N 34 18 E
Ayas 56 40 10N 32 14 E
Ayaviri 126 14 50 S 70 35W
Āybaq 65 36 15N 68 5 E
Ayenngré 85 8 40N 1 1 E
Ayeritam 71 5 24N 100 15 E
Ayer's Cliff 113 45 10N 72 3W
Ayers Rock 96 25 23 S 131 5 E
Ayguës → 21 44 7N 4 43 E
Ayiá 44 39 43N 22 45 E
Ayia Ánna 45 38 52N 23 24 E
Ayia Marina 45 35 27N 26 53 E
Ayía Marína 45 37 11N 26 48 E
Ayia Paraskeví 44 39 14N 26 16 E
Ayia Rouméli 45 35 14N 23 58 E
Ayiássos 45 39 5N 26 23 E
Áyion Óros 44 40 25N 24 6 E
Áyios Andréas 45 37 21N 22 45 E
Áyios Evstrátios 44 39 34N 24 58 E
Áyios Evstrátios 44 39 30N 25 0 E
Áyios Ioannis, Ákra 45 35 20N 25 40 E
Áyios Kirikos 45 37 34N 26 17 E
Áyios Matthaios 44 39 30N 19 47 E
Áyios Míronos 45 35 15N 25 1 E
Áyios Nikólaos 45 35 11N 25 41 E
Áyios Pétros 45 38 38N 20 33 E
Áyios Yeóryios 45 37 28N 23 57 E
Aykathonisi 45 37 28N 27 0 E
Aykin 52 62 15N 49 56 E
Aylesbury 13 51 48N 0 49W
Aylmer 112 42 46N 80 59W
Aylmer L. 104 64 0N 110 8W
'Ayn al Mubārak 64 24 10N 38 10 E
'Ayn 'Arīk 62 31 54N 35 8 E
'Ayn Zaqqūt 83 29 0N 19 30 E
Ayn Zhālah 64 36 45N 42 35 E
Ayna 33 38 34N 2 3W
Ayolas 124 27 10 S 56 59W
Ayom 87 7 49N 28 23 E
Ayon, Ostrov 59 69 50N 169 0 E
Ayora 33 39 3N 1 3W
Ayr, Austral. 97 19 35 S 147 25 E
Ayr, U.K. 14 55 28N 4 37W
Ayr → 14 55 29N 4 40W
Ayre, Pt. of 12 54 27N 4 21W
Aysha 87 10 50N 42 23 E
Aytos 43 42 42N 27 16 E
Aytoska Planina 43 42 45N 27 30 E
Ayu, Kepulauan 73 0 35N 131 5 E
Ayutla 120 16 58N 99 17W
Ayvalık 64 39 20N 26 46 E
Az Zāhirīyah 62 31 25N 34 58 E
Az Zahrān 64 26 10N 50 7 E
Az Zarqā 62 32 5N 36 4 E
Az Zāwiyah 83 32 52N 12 56 E
Az-Zilfī 64 26 12N 44 52 E
Az Zubayr 64 30 20N 47 50 E
Azambuja 31 39 4N 8 51W
Azamgarh 69 26 5N 83 13 E
Azaouak, Vallée de l' 85 15 50N 3 20 E
Āzārbāijān □ 64 37 0N 44 30 E
Azare 85 11 55N 10 10 E
Azay-le-Rideau 18 47 16N 0 30 E
Azazga 83 36 48N 4 22 E
Azbine = Aïr 85 18 0N 8 0 E
Azeffoun 83 36 51N 4 26 E
Azemmour 82 33 20N 9 20W
Azerbaijan S.S.R. □ 57 40 20N 48 0 E
Azezo 87 12 28N 37 15 E
Azilal, Beni Mallal 82 32 0N 6 30W
Azimganj 69 24 14N 88 16 E
Aznalcóllar 31 37 32N 6 17W
Azogues 126 2 35 S 78 0W
Azor 62 32 2N 34 48 E
Azores 6 38 44N 29 0W
Azov 57 47 3N 39 25 E
Azov Sea = Azovskoye More 56 46 0N 36 30 E
Azovskoye More 56 46 0N 36 30 E
Azovy 58 64 55N 64 35 E
Azpeitia 32 43 12N 2 19W
Azrou 82 33 28N 5 19W
Aztec 119 36 54N 108 0W
Azúa de Compostela 121 18 25N 70 44W
Azuaga 31 38 16N 5 39W
Azuara 32 41 15N 0 53W
Azuer → 31 39 8N 3 36W
Azuero, Pen. de 121 7 30N 80 30W
Azul 124 36 42 S 59 43W
Azzaba 83 36 48N 7 6 E
Azzano Décimo 39 45 53N 12 46 E

B

Ba Don 71 17 45N 106 26 E
Ba Ngoi = Cam Lam 71 11 50N 109 10 E
Ba Xian 76 39 8N 116 22 E
Baa 73 10 50 S 123 0 E
Baamonde 30 43 7N 7 44W
Baarle Nassau 16 51 27N 4 56 E
Baarn 16 52 12N 5 17 E
Bāb el Māndeb 63 12 35N 43 25 E
Baba 43 42 44N 23 59 E
Baba Burnu 44 39 29N 26 2 E
Baba dag 57 41 0N 48 19W
Babadag 46 44 53N 28 44 E
Babaeski 43 41 26N 27 6 E
Babahoyo 126 1 40 S 79 30W
Babana 85 10 31N 3 46 E

Babar, Alg. 83 35 10N 7 6 E
Babar, Indon. 73 8 0 S 129 30 E
Babar, Pak. 68 31 7N 69 32 E
Babarkach 68 29 45N 68 0 E
Babayevo 55 59 24N 35 55 E
Babb 118 48 56N 113 27W
Babenhausen 25 49 57N 8 56 E
Babia Gora 27 49 38N 19 38 E
Babile 87 9 16N 42 11 E
Babinda 98 17 20 S 145 56 E
Babine 108 55 22N 126 37W
Babine → 108 55 45N 127 44W
Babine L. 108 54 48N 126 0W
Babo 73 2 30 S 133 30 E
Babócsa 27 46 2N 17 21 E
Bābol 65 36 40N 52 50 E
Bābol Sar 65 36 45N 52 45 E
Baborów Kietrz 27 50 7N 18 1 E
Baboua 88 5 49N 14 58 E
Babuna 42 41 30N 21 40 E
Babura 85 12 51N 8 59 E
Babušnica 42 43 7N 22 27 E
Babuyan Chan. 73 19 10N 122 0 E
Babylon, Iraq 64 32 40N 44 30 E
Babylon, U.S.A. 113 40 42N 73 20W
Bač 42 45 29N 19 17 E
Bac Kan 71 22 5N 105 50 E
Bac Ninh 71 21 13N 106 4 E
Bac Phan 71 22 0N 105 0 E
Bac Quang 71 22 30N 104 48 E
Bacabal 127 4 15 S 44 45W
Bacan, Kepulauan 73 0 35 S 127 30 E
Bacan, Pulau 73 0 50 S 127 30 E
Bacarès, Le 20 42 47N 3 3 E
Bacarra 73 18 15N 120 37 E
Bacau 73 8 27 S 126 27 E
Bacău 46 46 35N 26 55 E
Bacău □ 46 46 30N 26 45 E
Baccarat 19 48 28N 6 42 E
Bacchus Marsh 100 37 43 S 144 27 E
Bacerac 120 30 18N 108 50W
Băceşti 46 46 50N 27 11 E
Bacharach 25 50 3N 7 46 E
Bachelina 58 57 45N 67 20 E
Bachuma 87 6 48N 35 53 E
Bačina 42 43 42N 21 23 E
Back → 104 65 10N 104 0W
Bačka Palanka 42 45 17N 19 27 E
Bačka Topola 42 45 49N 19 39 E
Bäckefors 49 58 48N 12 9 E
Bački Petrovac 42 45 29N 19 32 E
Backnang 25 48 57N 9 26 E
Backstairs Passage 97 35 40 S 138 5 E
Bacolod 73 10 40N 122 57 E
Bacqueville 18 49 47N 1 0 E
Bacs-Kiskun □ 27 46 43N 19 30 E
Bácsalmás 27 46 8N 19 17 E
Bad → 116 44 22N 100 22W
Bad Aussee 26 47 43N 13 45 E
Bad Axe 106 43 48N 82 59W
Bad Bergzabern 25 49 6N 8 0 E
Bad Bramstedt 24 53 56N 9 53 E
Bad Doberan 24 54 6N 11 55 E
Bad Driburg 24 51 44N 9 0 E
Bad Ems 25 50 22N 7 44 E
Bad Frankenhausen 24 51 21N 11 3 E
Bad Freienwalde 24 52 47N 14 3 E
Bad Godesberg 24 50 41N 7 4 E
Bad Hersfeld 24 50 52N 9 42 E
Bad Hofgastein 26 47 17N 13 6 E
Bad Homburg 25 50 17N 8 33 E
Bad Honnef 24 50 39N 7 13 E
Bad Ischl 26 47 44N 13 38 E
Bad Kissingen 25 50 11N 10 5 E
Bad Kreuznach 25 49 47N 7 47 E
Bad Lands 116 43 40N 102 10W
Bad Langensalza 24 51 6N 10 40 E
Bad Lauterberg 24 51 38N 10 29 E
Bad Leonfelden 26 48 31N 14 18 E
Bad Lippspringe 24 51 47N 8 46 E
Bad Mergentheim 25 49 29N 9 47 E
Bad Münstereifel 24 50 33N 6 46 E
Bad Muskau 24 51 33N 14 43 E
Bad Nauheim 25 50 24N 8 45 E
Bad Oeynhausen 24 52 16N 8 45 E
Bad Oldesloe 24 53 48N 10 22 E
Bad Orb 25 50 16N 9 21 E
Bad Pyrmont 24 51 59N 9 15 E
Bad Reichenhall 25 47 44N 12 53 E
Bad St.-Peter 24 54 23N 8 32 E
Bad Salzuflen 24 52 8N 8 44 E
Bad Segeberg 24 53 58N 10 16 E
Bad Tölz 25 47 43N 11 34 E
Bad Waldsee 25 47 56N 9 46 E
Bad Wildungen 24 51 7N 9 10 E
Bad Wimpfen 25 49 12N 9 10 E
Bad Windsheim 25 49 29N 10 25 E
Badagara 70 11 35N 75 40 E
Badagri 85 6 25N 2 55 E
Badajoz 31 38 50N 6 59W
Badajoz □ 31 38 40N 6 30W
Badakhshan □ 65 36 30N 71 0 E
Badalona 32 41 26N 2 15 E
Badalzai 66 29 50N 65 35 E
Badampahar 69 22 10N 86 10 E
Badanah 64 30 58N 41 30 E
Badas 72 4 33N 114 25 E
Badas, Kepulauan 72 0 45N 107 5 E
Baddo → 66 28 0N 64 20 E
Bade 73 7 10 S 139 35 E
Baden, Austria 27 48 1N 16 13 E
Baden, Can. 112 43 14N 80 40W
Baden, Switz. 25 47 28N 8 18 E
Baden-Baden 25 48 45N 8 15 E
Baden-Württemberg □ 25 48 40N 9 0 E
Badgastein 26 47 7N 13 9 E
Badger 107 49 0N 56 4W
Bādghīsāt □ 65 35 0N 63 0 E
Badia Polèsine 39 45 6N 11 30 E
Badin 68 24 38N 68 54 E
Badnera 68 20 48N 77 44 E
Badogo 84 11 2N 8 13W
Badong 77 31 1N 110 23 E
Badrinath 69 30 45N 79 30 E
Baduen 63 7 15N 47 40 E
Badulla 70 7 1N 81 7 E
Baena 31 37 37N 4 20W
Baeza 33 37 57N 3 25W
Bafa Gölü 45 37 30N 27 29 E
Bafang 85 5 9N 10 11 E
Bafatá 84 12 8N 14 40W
Baffin B. 4 72 0N 64 0W
Baffin I. 105 68 0N 75 0W
Bafia 88 4 40N 11 10 E
Bafilo 85 9 22N 1 22 E
Bafing → 84 13 49N 10 50W
Bafoulabé 84 13 50N 10 55W
Bafoussam 85 5 28N 10 25 E
Bafra 56 41 34N 35 54 E
Bafra, C. 56 41 44N 35 58 E
Bāft, Esfahān, Iran 65 31 40N 55 25 E
Bāft, Kermān, Iran 65 29 15N 56 38 E
Bafut 85 6 6N 10 2 E
Bafwasende 90 1 3N 27 5 E
Bagalkot 70 16 10N 75 40 E
Bagamoyo 90 6 28 S 38 55 E
Bagamoyo □ 90 6 20 S 38 30 E
Baganga 73 7 34N 126 33 E
Bagansiapiapi 72 2 12N 100 50 E
Bagasra 68 21 30N 71 0 E
Bagawi 87 12 20N 34 18 E
Bagdarin 59 54 26N 113 36 E
Bagé 125 31 20 S 54 15W
Bagenalstown = Muine Bheag 15 52 42N 6 57W
Baggs 118 41 8N 107 46W
Baghdād 64 33 20N 44 30 E
Baghelhat 69 22 40N 89 47 E
Bagheria 40 38 5N 13 30 E
Baghīn 65 30 12N 56 45 E
Baghlān 65 36 12N 69 0 E
Baghlān □ 65 36 0N 68 30 E
Bagley 116 47 30N 95 22W
Bagnacavallo 39 44 25N 11 58 E
Bagnara Cálabra 41 38 16N 15 49 E
Bagnères-de-Bigorre 20 43 5N 0 9 E
Bagnères-de-Luchon 20 42 47N 0 38 E
Bagni di Lucca 38 44 1N 10 37 E
Bagno di Romagna 39 43 50N 11 59 E
Bagnoles-de-l'Orne 18 48 32N 0 25W
Bagnoli di Sopra 39 45 13N 11 55 E
Bagnolo Mella 38 45 27N 10 14 E
Bagnols-les-Bains 20 44 30N 3 40 E
Bagnols-sur-Cèze 21 44 10N 4 36 E
Bagnorégio 39 42 38N 12 7 E
Bagolino 38 45 49N 10 28 E
Bagotville 107 48 22N 70 54W
Bagrdan 42 44 5N 21 11 E
Baguio 73 16 26N 120 34 E
Bahabón de Esgueva 32 41 52N 3 43W
Bahadurgarh 68 28 40N 76 57 E
Bahama, Canal Viejo de 121 22 10N 77 30W
Bahamas ■ 121 24 0N 75 0W
Baharîya, El Wâhât al 86 28 0N 28 50 E
Bahau 71 2 48N 102 26 E
Bahawalnagar 68 30 0N 73 15 E
Bahawalpur 68 29 24N 71 40 E
† Bahawalpur □ 68 29 5N 71 3 E
Baheri 69 28 45N 79 34 E
Bahi 90 5 58 S 35 21 E
Bahi Swamp 90 6 10 S 35 0 E
Bahía = Salvador 127 13 0 S 38 30W
Bahía □ 127 12 0 S 42 0W
Bahía Blanca 124 38 35 S 62 13W
Bahía de Caráquez 126 0 40 S 80 27W
Bahía, Islas de la 121 16 45N 86 15W
Bahía Laura 128 48 10 S 66 30W
Bahía Negra 126 20 5 S 58 5W
Bahir Dar 87 11 37N 37 10 E
Bahmer 82 27 32N 0 10W
Bahönye 27 46 25N 17 28 E
Bahr Aouk → 88 8 40N 19 0 E
Bahr el Ahmar □ 86 20 0N 35 0 E
Bahr el Ghazâl □ 87 7 0N 28 0 E
Bahr el Jebel → 87 7 30N 30 30 E
Bahr Salamat → 81 9 20N 18 0 E
Bahr Yûsef → 86 28 25N 30 35 E
Bahra el Burullus 86 31 28N 30 48 E
Bahraich 69 27 38N 81 37 E
Bahrain ■ 65 26 0N 50 35 E
Bai 84 13 35N 3 28W
Baia Mare 46 47 40N 23 35 E
Baia-Sprie 46 47 41N 23 43 E
Baïbokoum 81 7 46N 15 43 E
Baicheng 76 45 38N 122 42 E
Băicoi 46 45 3N 25 52 E
Baidoa 63 3 8N 43 30 E
Baie Comeau 107 49 12N 68 10W
Baie-St-Paul 107 47 28N 70 32W
Baie Trinité 107 49 25N 67 20W
Baie Verte 107 49 55N 56 12W
Baignes 20 45 23N 0 25W
Baigneux-les-Juifs 19 47 31N 4 39 E
Ba'ījī 64 35 0N 43 30 E
Baikal, L. = Baykal, Oz. 59 53 0N 108 0 E
Bailadila, Mt. 70 18 43N 81 15 E
Baile Atha Cliath = Dublin 15 53 20N 6 18W
Bailei 87 6 44N 40 18 E
Bailén 31 38 8N 3 48W
Băileşti 46 44 01N 23 20 E
Bailhongal 70 15 55N 74 53 E
Bailleul 19 50 44N 2 41 E
Bailundo 89 12 10 S 15 50 E
Baimuru 98 7 35 S 144 51 E
Bain-de-Bretagne 18 47 50N 1 40W
Bainbridge, Ga., U.S.A. 115 30 53N 84 34W
Bainbridge, N.Y., U.S.A. 113 42 17N 75 29W
Baing 73 10 14 S 120 34 E
Bainville 116 48 8N 104 10W
Bā'ir 64 30 45N 36 55 E
Baird 117 32 25N 99 25W
Baird Mts. 104 67 10N 160 15W
Bairin Youqi 76 43 30N 118 35 E
Bairin Zuoqi 76 43 58N 119 15 E
Bairnsdale 97 37 48 S 147 36 E
Baise → 20 44 17N 0 18 E
Baissa 85 7 14N 10 38 E
Baitadi 69 29 35N 80 25 E
Baiyin 76 36 45N 104 14 E
Baiyu Shan 76 37 15N 107 30 E
Baiyuda 86 17 35N 32 07 E
Baja 27 46 12N 18 59 E
Baja California 120 31 10N 115 12W
Baja, Pta. 120 29 50N 116 0W
Bajah, Wadi → 86 23 14N 39 20 E
Bajana 68 23 7N 71 49 E
Bajimba, Mt. 99 29 17 S 152 6 E
Bajina Bašta 42 43 58N 19 35 E
Bajmok 42 45 57N 19 24 E
Bajo Nuevo 121 15 40N 78 50W
Bajoga 85 10 57N 11 20 E
Bajool 98 23 40 S 150 35 E
Bak 27 46 43N 16 51 E
Bakala 88 6 15N 20 20 E
Bakar 39 45 18N 14 32 E
Bakchav 58 57 1N 82 5 E
Bakel 84 14 56N 12 20W
Baker, Calif., U.S.A. 119 35 16N 116 8W
Baker, Mont., U.S.A. 116 46 22N 104 12W
Baker, Nev., U.S.A. 118 38 59N 114 7W
Baker, Oreg., U.S.A. 118 44 50N 117 55W
Baker I. 94 0 10N 176 35W
Baker, L. 104 64 0N 96 0W
Baker Lake 104 64 20N 96 3W
Baker Mt. 118 48 50N 121 49W
Baker's Dozen Is. 106 56 45N 78 45W
Bakersfield, Calif., U.S.A. 119 35 25N 119 0W
Bakersfield, Vt., U.S.A. 113 44 46N 72 48W
Bakhchisaray 56 44 40N 33 45 E
Bakhmach 54 51 10N 32 45 E
Bakhtīārī □ 64 32 0N 49 0 E
Bakinskikh Komissarov, im 26 64 39 20N 49 15 E
Bakırköy 43 40 59N 28 53 E
Bakkafjörður 50 66 2N 14 48W
Bakkagerði 50 65 31N 13 49W
Bakony → 27 47 35N 17 54 E
Bakony Forest = Bakony Hegység 27 47 10N 17 30 E
Bakony Hegység 27 47 10N 17 30 E
Bakori 85 11 34N 7 25 E
Bakouma 88 5 40N 22 56 E
Bakov 26 50 27N 14 55 E
Baku 57 40 25N 49 45 E
Bala 112 45 1N 79 37W
Bal'ā 62 32 20N 35 6 E
Bala, L. = Tegid, L. 12 52 53N 3 38W
Balabac I. 72 8 0N 117 0 E
Balabac, Str. 72 7 53N 117 5 E
Balabakk 64 34 0N 36 10 E
Balabalangan, Kepulauan 72 2 20 S 117 30 E
Bălăciţa 46 44 23N 23 8 E
Balaghat 69 21 49N 80 12 E
Balaghat Ra. 70 18 50N 76 30 E
Balaguer 32 41 50N 0 50 E
Balakhna 55 56 25N 43 32 E
Balaklava, Austral. 99 34 7 S 138 22 E
Balaklava, U.S.S.R. 56 44 30N 33 30 E
Balakleya 56 49 28N 36 55 E
Balakovo 55 52 4N 47 55 E
Balanda 55 51 30N 44 40 E
Balangir 69 20 43N 83 35 E
Balapur 68 20 40N 76 45 E
Balashikha 55 55 49N 37 59 E
Balashov 55 51 30N 43 10 E
Balasinor 68 22 57N 73 23 E
Balasore 69 21 35N 87 3 E
Balassagyarmat 27 48 4N 19 15 E
Balât 86 25 36N 29 19 E
Balaton 27 46 50N 17 40 E
Balatonfüred 27 46 58N 17 54 E
Balatonszentgyörgy 27 46 41N 17 19 E
Balazote 33 38 54N 2 09W
Balboa 120 9 0N 79 30W
Balboa Hill 120 9 6N 79 44W
Balbriggan 15 53 35N 6 10W
Balcarce 124 38 0 S 58 10W
Balcarres 109 50 50N 103 35W
Balchik 43 43 28N 28 11 E
Balclutha 101 46 15 S 169 45 E
Bald Knob 117 35 20N 91 35W
Baldock L. 109 56 33N 97 57W
Baldwin, Fla., U.S.A. 115 30 15N 82 10W
Baldwin, Mich., U.S.A. 114 43 54N 85 53W
Baldwinsville 114 43 10N 76 19W
Bale 39 45 4N 13 46 E
Bale □ 87 6 20N 41 30 E
Baleares □ 32 39 30N 3 0 E
Baleares, Islas 32 39 30N 3 0 E
Balearic Is. = Baleares, Islas 32 39 30N 3 0 E
Băleni 46 45 48N 27 51 E
Baler 73 15 46N 121 34 E
Balfe's Creek 98 20 12 S 145 55 E
Balfour 93 26 38 S 28 35 E
Balfouriyya 62 32 38N 35 18 E
Bali, Camer. 85 5 54N 10 0 E
Bali, Indon. 72 8 20 S 115 0 E
Bali □ 72 8 20 S 115 0 E
Bali, Selat 73 8 30 S 114 35 E
Baligród 27 49 20N 22 17 E
Balikesir 64 39 35N 27 58 E
Balikpapan 72 1 10 S 116 55 E
Balimbing 73 5 10N 120 3 E
Baling 71 5 41N 100 55 E
Balipara 67 26 50N 92 45 E
Baliza 127 16 0 S 52 20W
Balkan Mts. = Stara Planina 43 43 15N 23 0 E
Balkan Pen. 9 42 0N 22 0 E
Balkh 65 36 44N 66 47 E
Balkh □ 65 36 30N 67 0 E
Balkhash 58 46 50N 74 50 E
Balkhash, Ozero 58 46 0N 74 50 E
Ballachulish 14 56 40N 5 10W
Balladoran 100 31 52 S 148 39 E
Ballarat 97 37 33 S 143 50 E
Ballard, L. 96 29 20 S 120 10 E
Ballarpur 70 19 50N 79 23 E
Ballater 14 57 2N 3 2W
Ballenas, Canal de las 120 29 10N 113 4
Balleny Is. 5 66 30 S 163
Ballia 69 25 46N 84 1
Ballina, Austral. 97 28 50 S 153 3
Ballina, Mayo, Ireland 15 54 7N 9 1
Ballina, Tipp., Ireland 15 52 49N 8 2
Ballinasloe 15 53 20N 8 1
Ballinger 117 31 45N 99 5
Ballinrobe 15 53 36N 9 1
Ballinskelligs B. 15 51 46N 10
Ballon 18 48 10N 0 1
Ballycastle 15 55 12N 6 1
Ballymena 15 54 53N 6
Ballymena □ 15 54 53N 6
Ballymoney 15 55 5N 6 3
Ballymoney □ 15 55 5N 6 2
Ballyshannon 15 54 30N 8 1
Balmaceda 128 46 0 S 71 5
Balmazújváros 27 47 37N 21 2
Balmoral, Austral. 99 37 15 S 141 4
Balmoral, U.K. 14 57 3N 3 1
Balmorhea 117 31 2N 103 4
Balonne → 97 28 47 S 147 5
Balrampur 69 27 30N 82 2
Balranald 97 34 38 S 143 3
Balş 46 44 22N 24
Balsas → 120 17 55N 102
Bålsta 48 59 35N 17 3
Balston Spa 113 43 0N 73 5
Balta, Romania 46 44 54N 22 3
Balta, U.S.A. 116 48 12N 100
Balta, R.S.F.S.R., U.S.S.R. 57 42 58N 44 3
Balta, Ukraine S.S.R., U.S.S.R. 56 48 2N 29 4
Baltanás 30 41 56N 4
Baltic Sea 51 56 0N 20
Baltīm 86 31 35N 31
Baltimore, Ireland 15 51 29N 9 2
Baltimore, U.S.A. 114 39 18N 76 3
Baltrum 24 53 43N 7 2
Baluchistan □ 65 27 30N 65
Balurghat 69 25 15N 88 4
Balygychan 59 63 56N 154
Bam 65 29 7N 58 1
Bama 85 11 33N 13 4
Bamako 84 12 34N 7 5
Bamba 85 17 5N 1 2
Bambari 88 5 40N 20 3
Bamberg, Ger. 25 49 54N 10 5
Bamberg, U.S.A. 115 33 19N 81
Bambesi 87 9 45N 34 4
Bambey 84 14 42N 16 2
Bambili 90 3 40N 26
Bamboo 98 14 34 S 143 2
Bamenda 85 5 57N 10 1
Bamfield 108 48 45N 125 1
Bāmīān □ 65 35 0N 67
Bamiancheng 76 43 15N 124
Bamkin 85 6 3N 11 2
Bampūr 65 27 15N 60 2
Ban Aranyaprathet 71 13 41N 102 3
Ban Ban 71 19 31N 103 3
Ban Bua Chum 71 15 11N 101
Ban Houei Sai 71 20 22N 100 3
Ban Khe Bo 71 19 10N 104 3
Ban Khun Yuam 71 18 49N 97 5
* Ban Me Thuot 71 12 40N 108
Ban Phai 71 16 4N 102 4
Ban Thateng 71 15 25N 106 2
Baña, Punta de la 32 40 33N 0 4
Banaba 94 0 45 S 169 5
Banadar Daryay Oman □ 65 27 30N 56
Banalia 90 1 32N 25
Banam 71 11 20N 105
Banamba 84 13 29N 7 2
Banana 98 24 28 S 150
Bananal, I. do 127 11 30 S 50 3
Banaras = Varanasi 69 25 22N 83
Banas →, Gujarat, India 68 23 45N 71 2
Banas →, Madhya Pradesh, India 69 24 15N 81 3
Bânâs, Ras. 86 23 57N 35 5
Banbridge 15 54 21N 6
Banbridge □ 15 54 21N 6
Banbury 13 52 4N 1 2
Banchory 14 57 3N 2 3
Bancroft 106 45 3N 77 5
Band 43 46 30N 24 2
Band-e Torkestān 65 35 30N 64
Banda 68 25 30N 80 2
Banda Aceh 72 5 35N 95 2
Banda Banda, Mt. 99 31 10 S 152 2
Banda Elat 73 5 40 S 133
Banda, Kepulauan 73 4 37 S 129 5
Banda, La 124 27 45 S 64
Banda Sea 73 6 0 S 130
Bandama → 84 6 32N 5 3
Bandanaira 73 4 32 S 129 5
Bandanwara 68 26 9N 74 3
Bandar = Machilipatnam 70 16 12N 81 1
Bandār 'Abbās 65 27 15N 56 1
Bandar-e Būshehr 65 28 55N 50 5
Bandar-e Chārak 65 26 45N 54 2
Bandar-e Deylam 64 30 5N 50 1
Bandar-e Lengeh 65 26 35N 54 5
Bandar-e Ma'shur 64 30 35N 49 1
Bandar-e Nakhīlū 65 26 58N 53 3
Bandar-e Rīg 65 29 30N 50 4
Bandar-e Shāh 65 37 0N 54 1
Bandar-e Shāhpūr 64 30 30N 49
Bandar-i-Pahlavī 64 37 30N 49 3
Bandar Seri Begawan 72 4 52N 115
Bandawe 91 11 58 S 34
Bande 30 42 3N 7 5
Bandeira, Pico da 125 20 26 S 41 4
Bandera, Argent. 124 28 55 S 62 2
Bandera, U.S.A. 117 29 45N 99
Banderas, Bahía de 120 20 40N 105 3
Bandia → 70 19 2N 80 2
Bandiagara 84 14 12N 3 2
Bandırma 64 40 20N 28
Bandon 15 51 44N 8 4
Bandon → 15 51 40N 8 4
Bandula 91 19 0 S 33

† *Now part of Punjab* □

* *Renamed Buon Me Thuot*

Bandundu	**88**	3 15 S	17 22 E
Bandung	**73**	6 54 S	107 36 E
Băneasa	**46**	45 56N	27 55 E
Bañeres	**33**	38 44N	0 38W
Banes	**121**	21 0N	75 42W
Bañeza, La	**30**	42 17N	5 54W
Banff, Can.	**108**	51 10N	115 34W
Banff, U.K.	**14**	57 40N	2 32W
Banff Nat. Park	**108**	51 30N	116 15W
Banfora	**84**	10 40N	4 40W
Bang Hieng →	**71**	16 10N	105 10 E
Bang Lamung	**71**	13 3N	100 56 E
Bang Saphan	**71**	11 14N	99 28 E
Bangala Dam	**91**	21 7 S	31 25 E
Bangalore	**70**	12 59N	77 40 E
Bangante	**85**	5 8N	10 32 E
Bangaon	**69**	23 0N	88 47 E
Bangassou	**88**	4 55N	23 7 E
Bangeta, Mt.	**98**	6 21 S	147 3 E
Banggai	**73**	1 40 S	123 30 E
Banggi, P.	**72**	7 17N	117 12 E
Banghāzī	**83**	32 11N	20 3 E
Banghāzi □	**83**	32 7N	20 4 E
Bangil	**73**	7 36 S	112 50 E
Bangjang	**87**	11 23N	32 41 E
Bangka, Pulau, Sulawesi, Indon.	**73**	1 50N	125 5 E
Bangka, Pulau, Sumatera, Indon.	**72**	2 0 S	105 50 E
Bangka, Selat	**72**	2 30 S	105 30 E
Bangkalan	**73**	7 2 S	112 46 E
Bangkinang	**72**	0 18N	101 5 E
Bangko	**72**	2 5 S	102 9 E
Bangkok = Krung Thep	**71**	13 45N	100 35 E
Bangladesh ■	**67**	24 0N	90 0 E
Bangolo	**84**	7 1N	7 29W
Bangor, N. Ireland, U.K.	**15**	54 40N	5 40W
Bangor, Wales, U.K.	**12**	53 13N	4 9W
Bangor, Me., U.S.A.	**107**	44 48N	68 42W
Bangor, Pa., U.S.A.	**113**	40 51N	75 13W
Bangued	**73**	17 40N	120 37 E
Bangui	**88**	4 23N	18 35 E
Banguru	**90**	0 30N	27 10 E
Bangweulu, L.	**91**	11 0 S	30 0 E
Bangweulu Swamp	**91**	11 20 S	30 15 E
Bani	**121**	18 16N	70 22W
Bani →	**84**	14 30N	4 12W
Bani Bangou	**85**	15 3N	2 42 E
Bani, Djebel	**82**	29 16N	8 0W
Banī Na'īm	**62**	31 31N	35 10 E
Banī Suhaylah	**62**	31 21N	34 19 E
Bania	**84**	9 4N	3 6W
Baniara	**98**	9 44 S	149 54 E
Banīnah	**83**	32 0N	20 12 E
Bāniyās	**64**	35 10N	36 0 E
Banja Luka	**42**	44 49N	17 11 E
Banjar	**73**	7 24 S	108 30 E
Banjarmasin	**72**	3 20 S	114 35 E
Banjarnegara	**73**	7 24 S	109 42 E
Banjul	**84**	13 28N	16 40W
Bankeryd	**49**	57 53N	14 6 E
Banket	**91**	17 27 S	30 19 E
Bankilaré	**85**	14 35N	0 44 E
Bankipore	**69**	25 35N	85 10 E
Banks I., B.C., Can.	**108**	53 20N	130 0W
Banks I., N.W.T., Can.	**4**	73 15N	121 30W
Banks I., P.N.G.	**97**	10 10 S	142 15 E
Banks Pen.	**101**	43 45 S	173 15 E
Banks Str.	**99**	40 40 S	148 10 E
Bankura	**69**	23 11N	87 18 E
Bankya	**42**	42 43N	23 8 E
Bann →, Down, U.K.	**15**	54 30N	6 31W
Bann →, Londonderry, U.K.	**15**	55 10N	6 34W
Bannalec	**18**	47 57N	3 42W
Banning	**119**	33 58N	116 52W
Banningville = Bandundu	**88**	3 15 S	17 22 E
Bannockburn, Can.	**112**	44 39N	77 33W
Bannockburn, U.K.	**14**	56 5N	3 55W
Bannockburn, Zimb.	**91**	20 17 S	29 48 E
Bañolas	**32**	42 16N	2 44 E
Banon	**21**	44 2N	5 38 E
Baños de la Encina	**31**	38 10N	3 46W
Baños de Molgas	**30**	42 15N	7 40W
Bánovce	**27**	48 44N	18 16 E
Banská Bystrica	**27**	48 46N	19 14 E
Banská Štiavnica	**27**	48 25N	18 55 E
Bansko	**43**	41 52N	23 28 E
Banswara	**68**	23 32N	74 24 E
Banten	**73**	6 5 S	106 8 E
Bantry	**15**	51 40N	9 28W
Bantry, B.	**15**	51 35N	9 50W
Bantul	**73**	7 55 S	110 19 E
Bantva	**68**	21 29N	70 12 E
Bantval	**70**	12 55N	75 0 E
Banya	**43**	42 33N	24 50 E
Banyak, Kepulauan	**72**	2 10N	97 10 E
Banyo	**85**	6 52N	11 45 E
Banyuls	**20**	42 29N	3 8 E
Banyumas	**73**	7 32 S	109 18 E
Banyuwangi	**73**	8 13 S	114 21 E
Banzare Coast	**5**	68 0 S	125 0 E
Banzyville = Mobayi	**88**	4 15N	21 8 E
Baocheng	**77**	33 12N	106 56 E
Baode	**76**	39 1N	111 5 E
Baoding	**76**	38 50N	115 28 E
Baoji	**77**	34 20N	107 5 E
Baojing	**77**	28 45N	109 41 E
Baokang	**77**	31 54N	111 12 E
Baoshan	**75**	25 10N	99 5 E
Baotou	**76**	40 32N	110 2 E
Baoying	**77**	33 17N	119 20 E
Bap	**68**	27 23N	72 18 E
Bapatla	**70**	15 55N	80 30 E
Bapaume	**19**	50 7N	2 50 E
Bāqa el Gharbīyya	**62**	32 25N	35 2 E
Ba'qūbah	**64**	33 45N	44 50 E
Baquedano	**124**	23 20 S	69 52W
Bar, U.S.S.R.	**56**	49 4N	27 40 E
Bar, Yugo.	**42**	42 8N	19 8 E
Bar Harbor	**107**	44 15N	68 20W
Bar-le-Duc	**19**	48 47N	5 10 E
Bar-sur-Aube	**19**	48 14N	4 40 E
Bar-sur-Seine	**19**	48 7N	4 20 E
Barabai	**72**	2 32 S	115 34 E
Barabinsk	**58**	55 20N	78 20 E
Baraboo	**116**	43 28N	89 46W
Baracoa	**121**	20 20N	74 30W
Baradero	**124**	33 52 S	59 29W
Baraga	**116**	46 49N	88 29W
Barahona, Dom. Rep.	**121**	18 13N	71 7W
Barahona, Spain	**32**	41 17N	2 39W
Barail Range	**67**	25 15N	93 20 E
Baraka →	**86**	18 13N	37 35 E
Barakhola	**67**	25 0N	92 45 E
Barakot	**69**	21 33N	84 59 E
Barakula	**99**	26 30 S	150 33 E
Baralaba	**98**	24 13 S	149 50 E
Baralzon L.	**109**	60 0N	98 3W
Baramati	**70**	18 11N	74 33 E
Baramba	**69**	20 25N	85 23 E
Barameiya	**86**	18 32N	36 38 E
Baramula	**69**	34 15N	74 20 E
Baran	**68**	25 9N	76 40 E
Baranof I.	**104**	57 0N	135 10W
Baranovichi	**54**	53 10N	26 0 E
Baranów Sandomierski	**28**	50 29N	21 30 E
Baranya □	**27**	46 0N	18 15 E
Barão de Melgaço	**126**	11 50 S	60 45W
Baraolt	**46**	46 5N	25 34 E
Barapasi	**73**	2 15 S	137 5 E
Barasat	**69**	22 46N	88 31 E
Barat Daya, Kepulauan	**73**	7 30 S	128 0 E
Barataria B.	**117**	29 15N	89 45W
Baraut	**68**	29 13N	77 7 E
Barbacena	**125**	21 15 S	43 56W
Barbacoas	**126**	1 45N	78 0W
Barbados ■	**121**	13 0N	59 30W
Barban	**39**	45 5N	14 4 E
Barbastro	**32**	42 2N	0 5 E
Barbate	**31**	36 13N	5 56W
Barberino di Mugello	**39**	44 1N	11 15 E
Barberton, S. Afr.	**93**	25 42 S	31 2 E
Barberton, U.S.A.	**114**	41 0N	81 40W
Barbezieux	**20**	45 28N	0 9W
Barbigha	**69**	25 21N	85 47 E
Barbourville	**115**	36 57N	83 52W
Barbuda I.	**121**	17 30N	61 40W
Barca, La	**120**	20 20N	102 40W
Barcaldine	**97**	23 43 S	145 6 E
Barcarrota	**31**	38 31N	6 51W
Barcellona Pozzo di Gotto	**41**	38 8N	15 15 E
Barcelona, Spain	**32**	41 21N	2 10 E
Barcelona, Venez.	**126**	10 10N	64 40W
Barcelona □	**32**	41 30N	2 0 E
Barcelonette	**21**	44 23N	6 40 E
Barcelos	**126**	1 0 S	63 0W
Barcin	**28**	52 52N	17 55 E
Barcoo →	**97**	25 30 S	142 50 E
Barcs	**27**	45 58N	17 28 E
Barczewo	**28**	53 50N	20 42 E
Barda	**57**	40 25N	47 10 E
Bardai	**83**	21 25N	17 0 E
Bardas Blancas	**124**	35 49 S	69 45W
Bardejov	**27**	49 18N	21 15 E
Bardera	**63**	2 20N	42 27 E
Bardi	**38**	44 38N	9 43 E
Bardi, Ra's	**64**	24 17N	37 31 E
Bardia	**81**	31 45N	25 0 E
Bardo	**28**	50 31N	16 42 E
Bardoli	**68**	21 12N	73 5 E
Bardolino	**38**	45 33N	10 43 E
Bardsey I.	**12**	52 46N	4 47W
Bardstown	**114**	37 50N	85 29W
Bareilly	**69**	28 22N	79 27 E
Barentin	**18**	49 33N	0 58 E
Barenton	**18**	48 38N	0 50W
Barents Sea	**4**	73 0N	39 0 E
Barentu	**87**	15 2N	37 35 E
Barfleur	**18**	49 40N	1 17W
Barga, China	**75**	30 40N	81 20 E
Barga, Italy	**38**	44 5N	10 30 E
Bargal	**63**	11 25N	51 0 E
Bargara	**98**	24 50 S	152 25 E
Barge	**38**	44 43N	7 19 E
Barge, La	**118**	42 12N	110 4W
Bargnop	**87**	9 32N	28 25 E
Bargteheide	**24**	53 42N	10 13 E
Barguzin	**59**	53 37N	109 37 E
Barh	**69**	25 29N	85 46 E
Barhaj	**69**	26 18N	83 44 E
Barham	**100**	35 36 S	144 8 E
Barhi	**69**	24 15N	85 25 E
Bari, India	**68**	26 39N	77 39 E
Bari, Italy	**41**	41 6N	16 52 E
Bari Doab	**68**	30 20N	73 0 E
Bariadi □	**90**	2 45 S	34 40 E
Barīm	**63**	12 39N	43 25 E
Barinas	**126**	8 36N	70 15W
Baring C.	**104**	70 0N	117 30W
Baringo	**90**	0 47N	36 16 E
Baringo □	**90**	0 55N	36 0 E
Baringo, L.	**90**	0 47N	36 16 E
Baripada	**69**	21 57N	86 45 E
Bârîs	**86**	24 42N	30 31 E
Barisal	**69**	22 45N	90 20 E
Barisan, Bukit	**72**	3 30 S	102 15 E
Barito →	**72**	4 0 S	114 50 E
Barjac	**21**	44 20N	4 22 E
Barjols	**21**	43 34N	6 2 E
Barjūj, Wadi →	**83**	25 26N	12 12 E
Bark L.	**112**	45 27N	77 51W
Barka = Baraka →	**87**	18 13N	37 35 E
Barkalı	**65**	23 40N	58 0 E
Barker	**112**	43 20N	78 35W
Barkley Sound	**108**	48 50N	125 10W
Barkly Downs	**98**	20 30 S	138 30 E
Barkly East	**92**	30 58 S	27 33 E
Barkly Tableland	**97**	17 50 S	136 40 E
Barkly West	**92**	28 5 S	24 31 E
Barkol, Wadi →	**86**	17 40N	32 0 E
Barksdale	**117**	29 47N	100 2W
Barlee, L.	**96**	29 15 S	119 30 E
Barlee Ra.	**96**	23 30 S	116 0 E
Barletta	**41**	41 20N	16 17 E
Barleur, Pointe de	**18**	49 42N	1 16W
Barlinek	**28**	53 0N	15 15 E
Barlow L.	**109**	62 00N	103 0W
Barmedman	**99**	34 9 S	147 21 E
Barmer	**68**	25 45N	71 20 E
Barmera	**99**	34 15 S	140 28 E
Barmouth	**12**	52 44N	4 3W
Barmstedt	**24**	53 47N	9 46 E
Barnagar	**68**	23 7N	75 19 E
Barnard Castle	**12**	54 33N	1 55W
Barnato	**99**	31 38 S	145 0 E
Barnaul	**58**	53 20N	83 40 E
Barne Inlet	**5**	80 15 S	160 0 E
Barnes	**99**	36 2 S	144 47 E
Barnesville	**115**	33 6N	84 9W
Barnet	**13**	51 37N	0 15W
Barneveld, Neth.	**16**	52 7N	5 36 E
Barneveld, U.S.A.	**113**	43 16N	75 14W
Barneville	**18**	49 23N	1 46W
Barney, Mt.	**97**	28 17 S	152 44 E
Barngo	**99**	25 3 S	147 20 E
Barnhart	**117**	31 10N	101 8W
Barnsley	**12**	53 33N	1 29W
Barnstaple	**13**	51 5N	4 3W
Barnsville	**116**	46 43N	96 28W
Baro	**85**	8 35N	6 18 E
Baro →	**87**	8 26N	33 13 E
Baroda	**68**	25 29N	76 35 E
Baroda = Vadodara	**68**	22 20N	73 10 E
Barpali	**69**	21 11N	83 35 E
Barqin	**83**	27 33N	13 34 E
Barques, Pte. aux	**114**	44 5N	82 55W
Barquinha	**31**	39 28N	8 25W
Barquísimeto	**126**	10 4N	69 19W
Barr	**19**	48 25N	7 28 E
Barra, Brazil	**127**	11 5 S	43 10W
Barra, U.K.	**14**	57 0N	7 30W
Barra do Corda	**127**	5 30 S	45 10W
Barra do Piraí	**125**	22 30 S	43 50W
Barra Falsa, Pta. da	**93**	22 58 S	35 37 E
Barra Hd.	**14**	56 47N	7 40W
Barra Mansa	**125**	22 35 S	44 12W
Barra, Sd. of	**14**	57 4N	7 25W
Barraba	**99**	30 21 S	150 35 E
Barrackpur	**69**	22 44N	88 30 E
Barrafranca	**41**	37 22N	14 10 E
Barranca, Lima, Peru	**126**	10 45 S	77 50W
Barranca, Loreto, Peru	**126**	4 50 S	76 50W
Barrancabermeja	**126**	7 0N	73 50W
Barrancas	**126**	8 55N	62 5W
Barrancos	**31**	38 10N	6 58W
Barranqueras	**124**	27 30 S	59 0W
Barranquilla	**126**	11 0N	74 50W
Barras	**127**	4 15 S	42 18W
Barraute	**106**	48 26N	77 38W
Barre	**114**	44 15N	72 30W
Barreal	**124**	31 33 S	69 28W
Barreiras	**127**	12 8 S	45 0W
Barreirinhas	**127**	2 30 S	42 50W
Barreiro	**31**	38 40N	9 6W
Barreiros	**127**	8 49 S	35 12W
Barrême	**21**	43 57N	6 23 E
Barren I.	**71**	12 17N	93 50 E
Barren, Nosy	**93**	18 25 S	43 40 E
Barretos	**127**	20 30 S	48 35W
Barrhead	**108**	54 10N	114 24W
Barrie	**106**	44 24N	79 40W
Barrier Ra.	**97**	31 0 S	141 30 E
Barrière	**108**	51 12N	120 7W
Barrington, Ill., U.S.A.	**114**	42 8N	88 5W
Barrington, R.I., U.S.A.	**113**	41 43N	71 20W
Barrington L.	**109**	56 55N	100 15W
Barrington Tops	**97**	32 6 S	151 28 E
Barrow	**104**	71 16N	156 50W
Barrow →	**15**	52 10N	6 57W
Barrow Creek T.O.	**96**	21 30 S	133 55 E
Barrow I.	**96**	20 45 S	115 20 E
Barrow-in-Furness	**12**	54 8N	3 15W
Barrow Pt.	**98**	14 20 S	144 40 E
Barrow Ra.	**96**	26 0 S	127 40 E
Barrow Str.	**4**	74 20N	95 0W
Barruecopardo	**30**	41 4N	6 40W
Barruelo	**30**	42 54N	4 17W
Barry	**13**	51 23N	3 19W
Barry's Bay	**106**	45 29N	77 41W
Barsalogho	**85**	13 25N	1 3W
Barsi	**70**	18 10N	75 50 E
Barsø	**49**	55 7N	9 33 E
Barstow, Calif., U.S.A.	**119**	34 58N	117 2W
Barstow, Tex., U.S.A.	**117**	31 28N	103 24W
Barth	**24**	54 20N	12 36 E
Bartica	**126**	6 25N	58 40W
Bartin	**64**	41 38N	32 21 E
Bartle Frere, Mt.	**97**	17 27 S	145 50 E
Bartlesville	**117**	36 50N	95 58W
Bartlett	**117**	30 46N	97 30W
Bartlett, L.	**108**	63 5N	118 20W
Bartolomeu Dias	**91**	21 10 S	35 8 E
Barton-upon-Humber	**12**	53 41N	0 27W
Bartoszyce	**28**	54 15N	20 55 E
Bartow	**115**	27 53N	81 49W
Barumba	**90**	1 3N	23 37 E
Baruth	**24**	52 3N	13 31 E
Barvenkovo	**56**	48 57N	37 0 E
Barwani	**68**	22 2N	74 57 E
Barycz →	**28**	51 42N	16 15 E
Barysh	**55**	53 39N	47 8 E
Bas-Rhin □	**19**	48 40N	7 30 E
Bašaid	**42**	45 38N	20 25 E
Bāsa'idū	**65**	26 35N	55 20 E
Basankusa	**88**	1 5N	19 50 E
Bascuñán, C.	**124**	28 52 S	71 35W
Basel (Basle)	**25**	47 35N	7 35 E
Basel-Stadt □	**25**	47 35N	7 35 E
Baselland □	**25**	47 26N	7 45 E
Basento →	**41**	40 21N	16 50 E
Bashkir A.S.S.R. □	**52**	54 0N	57 0 E
Basilaki I.	**98**	10 35 S	151 0 E
Basilan	**73**	6 35N	122 0 E
Basilan Str.	**73**	6 50N	122 0 E
Basildon	**13**	51 34N	0 29 E
Basilicata □	**41**	40 30N	16 0 E
Basim	**70**	20 3N	77 0 E
Basin	**118**	44 22N	108 2W
Basingstoke	**13**	51 15N	1 5W
Basirhat	**69**	22 40N	88 54 E
Baška	**39**	44 58N	14 45 E
Baskatong, Rés.	**106**	46 46N	75 50W
Baskerville C.	**96**	17 10 S	122 15 E
Basle = Basel	**25**	47 35N	7 35 E
Basmat	**70**	19 15N	77 12 E
Basoda	**68**	23 52N	77 54 E
Basoka	**90**	1 16N	23 40 E
Basongo	**88**	4 15 S	20 20 E
Basque Provinces = Vascongadas	**32**	42 50N	2 45W
Basra = Al Başrah	**64**	30 30N	47 50 E
Bass Rock	**14**	56 5N	2 40W
Bass Str.	**97**	39 15 S	146 30 E
Bassano	**108**	50 48N	112 20W
Bassano del Grappa	**39**	45 45N	11 45 E
Bassar	**85**	9 19N	0 57 E
Basse Santa-Su	**84**	13 13N	14 15W
Basse-Terre	**121**	16 0N	61 40W
Bassée, La	**19**	50 31N	2 49 E
Bassein	**70**	19 26N	72 48 E
Basseterre	**121**	17 17N	62 43W
Bassett, Nebr., U.S.A.	**116**	42 37N	99 30W
Bassett, Va., U.S.A.	**115**	36 48N	79 59W
Bassi	**68**	30 44N	76 21 E
Bassigny	**19**	48 0N	5 10 E
Bassikounou	**84**	15 55N	6 1W
Bassum	**24**	52 50N	8 42 E
Båstad	**49**	56 25N	12 51 E
Bastak	**65**	27 15N	54 25 E
Bastar	**70**	19 15N	81 40 E
Basti	**69**	26 52N	82 55 E
Bastia	**21**	42 40N	9 30 E
Bastia Umbra	**39**	43 4N	12 34 E
Bastide-Puylaurent, La	**20**	44 35N	3 55 E
Bastogne	**16**	50 1N	5 43 E
Bastrop	**117**	30 5N	97 22W
Basuto	**92**	19 50 S	26 25 E
Bat Yam	**62**	32 2N	34 44 E
Bata, Eq. Guin.	**88**	1 57N	9 50 E
Bata, Romania	**46**	46 1N	22 4 E
Bataan	**73**	14 40N	120 25 E
Batabanó	**121**	22 40N	82 20W
Batabanó, G. de	**121**	22 30N	82 30W
Batac	**73**	18 3N	120 34 E
Batagoy	**59**	67 38N	134 38 E
Batak	**43**	41 57N	24 12 E
Batakan	**72**	4 5 S	114 38 E
Batalha	**31**	39 40N	8 50W
Batama	**90**	0 58N	26 33 E
Batamay	**59**	63 30N	129 15 E
Batang, China	**75**	30 1N	99 0 E
Batang, Indon.	**73**	6 55 S	109 40 E
Batangafo	**88**	7 25N	18 20 E
Batangas	**73**	13 35N	121 10 E
Batanta	**73**	0 55 S	130 40 E
Batatais	**125**	20 54 S	47 37W
Batavia	**114**	43 0N	78 10W
Bataysk	**57**	47 3N	39 45 E
Batchelor	**96**	13 4 S	131 1 E
Bateman's B.	**97**	35 40 S	150 12 E
Batemans Bay	**99**	35 44 S	150 11 E
Batesburg	**115**	33 54N	81 32W
Batesville, Ark., U.S.A.	**117**	35 48N	91 40W
Batesville, Miss., U.S.A.	**117**	34 17N	89 58W
Batesville, Tex., U.S.A.	**117**	28 59N	99 38W
Bath, U.K.	**13**	51 22N	2 22W
Bath, Maine, U.S.A.	**107**	43 50N	69 49W
Bath, N.Y., U.S.A.	**114**	42 20N	77 17W
Bathgate	**14**	55 54N	3 38W
Bathurst, Austral.	**97**	33 25 S	149 31 E
Bathurst, Can.	**107**	47 37N	65 43W
Bathurst = Banjul	**84**	13 28N	16 40W
Bathurst B.	**97**	14 16 S	144 25 E
Bathurst, C.	**104**	70 34N	128 0W
Bathurst Harb.	**99**	43 15 S	146 10 E
Bathurst I., Austral.	**96**	11 30 S	130 10 E
Bathurst I., Can.	**4**	76 0N	100 30W
Bathurst In.	**104**	68 10N	108 50W
Bathurst Inlet	**104**	66 50N	108 1W
Batie	**84**	9 53N	2 53W
Batinah	**65**	24 0N	56 0 E
Batlow	**99**	35 31 S	148 9 E
Batman	**64**	37 55N	41 5 E
Batna	**83**	35 34N	6 15 E
Batočina	**42**	44 7N	21 5 E
Batoka	**91**	16 45 S	27 15 E
Baton Rouge	**117**	30 30N	91 5W
Batopilas	**120**	27 0N	107 45W
Batouri	**88**	4 30N	14 25 E
Battambang	**71**	13 7N	103 12 E
Batticaloa	**70**	7 43N	81 45 E
Battipáglia	**41**	40 38N	15 0 E
Battīr	**62**	31 44N	35 8 E
Battle, Can.	**109**	52 58N	110 52W
Battle, U.K.	**13**	50 55N	0 30 E
Battle →	**109**	52 43N	108 15W
Battle Camp	**98**	15 20 S	144 40 E
Battle Creek	**114**	42 20N	85 6W
Battle Harbour	**107**	52 16N	55 35W
Battle Lake	**116**	46 20N	95 43W
Battle Mountain	**118**	40 45N	117 0W
Battlefields	**91**	18 37 S	29 47 E
Battleford	**109**	52 45N	108 15W
Battonya	**27**	46 16N	21 3 E
Batu	**87**	6 55N	39 45 E
Batu Gajah	**71**	4 28N	101 3 E
Batu, Kepulauan	**72**	0 30 S	98 25 E
Batu Pahat	**71**	1 50N	'02 56 E
Batuata	**73**	6 12 S	122 42 E
Batumi	**57**	41 30N	41 30 E
Baturaja	**72**	4 11 S	104 15 E
Baturité	**127**	4 28 S	38 45W
Bau	**72**	1 25N	110 9 E
Baubau	**73**	5 25 S	122 38 E
Bauchi	**85**	10 22N	9 48 E
Bauchi □	**85**	10 30N	10 0 E
Baud	**18**	47 52N	3 1W
Baudette	**116**	48 46N	94 35W
Baugé	**18**	47 31N	0 8W
Baule-Escoublac, La	**18**	47 18N	2 23W
Baume-les-Dames	**19**	47 22N	6 22 E

Baunatal	**24**	51 13N	9 25 E
Baunei	**40**	40 2N	9 41 E
Bauru	**125**	22 10 S	49 0W
Baús	**127**	18 22 S	52 47W
Bauska	**54**	56 24N	25 15 E
Bautzen	**24**	51 11N	14 25 E
Baux, Les	**21**	43 45N	4 51 E
Bavanište	**42**	44 49N	20 53 E
Bavaria = Bayern □	**25**	49 7N	11 30 E
Båven	**48**	59 0N	16 56 E
Bavi Sadri	**68**	24 28N	74 30 E
Bavispe →	**120**	29 30N	109 11W
Baw Baw, Mt.	**100**	37 49 S	146 19 E
Bawdwin	**67**	23 5N	97 20 E
Bawean	**72**	5 46 S	112 35 E
Bawku	**85**	11 3N	0 19W
Bawlake	**67**	19 11N	97 21 E
Baxley	**115**	31 43N	82 23W
Baxter Springs	**117**	37 3N	94 45W
Bay Bulls	**107**	47 19N	52 50W
Bay City, Mich., U.S.A.	**114**	43 35N	83 51W
Bay City, Oreg., U.S.A.	**118**	45 45N	123 58W
Bay City, Tex., U.S.A.	**117**	28 59N	95 55W
Bay de Verde	**107**	48 5N	52 54W
Bay, Laguna de	**73**	14 20N	121 11 E
Bay Minette	**115**	30 54N	87 43W
Bay St. Louis	**117**	30 18N	89 22W
Bay Shore	**114**	40 44N	73 15W
Bay Springs	**117**	31 58N	89 18W
Bay View	**101**	39 25 S	176 50 E
Baya	**91**	11 53 S	27 25 E
Bayamo	**121**	20 20N	76 40W
Bayamón	**121**	18 24N	66 10W
Bayan	**76**	46 5N	127 24 E
Bayan Har Shan	**75**	34 0N	98 0 E
Bayan Hot = Alxa Zuoqi	**76**	38 50N	105 40 E
Bayan Obo	**76**	41 52N	109 59 E
Bayana	**68**	26 55N	77 18 E
Bayanaul	**58**	50 45N	75 45 E
Bayanhongor	**75**	46 8N	102 43 E
Bayard	**116**	41 48N	103 17W
Bayázeh	**65**	33 30N	54 40 E
Baybay	**73**	10 40N	124 55 E
Bayburt	**64**	40 15N	40 20 E
Bayerischer Wald	**25**	49 0N	13 0 E
Bayern □	**25**	49 7N	11 30 E
Bayeux	**18**	49 17N	0 42W
Bayfield, Can.	**112**	43 34N	81 42W
Bayfield, U.S.A.	**116**	46 50N	90 48W
Baykal, Oz.	**59**	53 0N	108 0 E
Baykit	**59**	61 50N	95 50 E
Baykonur	**58**	47 48N	65 50 E
Baymak	**52**	52 36N	58 19 E
Baynes Mts.	**92**	17 15 S	13 0 E
Bayombong	**73**	16 30N	121 10 E
Bayon	**19**	48 30N	6 20 E
Bayona	**30**	42 6N	8 52W
Bayonne, France	**20**	43 30N	1 28W
Bayonne, U.S.A.	**113**	40 41N	74 7W
Bayovar	**126**	5 50 S	81 0W
Baypore →	**70**	11 10N	75 47 E
Bayram-Ali	**58**	37 37N	62 10 E
Bayreuth	**25**	49 56N	11 35 E
Bayrischzell	**25**	47 39N	12 1 E
Bayrūt	**64**	33 53N	35 31 E
Bayt Awlá	**62**	31 37N	35 2 E
Bayt Fajjār	**62**	31 38N	35 9 E
Bayt Fūrīk	**62**	32 11N	35 20 E
Bayt Ḩānūn	**62**	31 32N	34 32 E
Bayt Jālā	**62**	31 43N	35 11 E
Bayt Lahm	**62**	31 43N	35 12 E
Bayt Rīma	**62**	32 2N	35 6 E
Bayt Sāḩūr	**62**	31 42N	35 13 E
Bayt Ummar	**62**	31 38N	35 7 E
Bayt 'ūr al Taḩtā	**62**	31 54N	35 5 E
Baytīn	**62**	31 56N	35 14 E
Baytown	**117**	29 42N	94 57W
Baytūniyā	**62**	31 54N	35 10 E
Bayzo	**85**	13 52N	4 35 E
Baza	**33**	37 30N	2 47W
Bazar Dyuzi	**57**	41 12N	47 50 E
Bazarny Karabulak	**55**	52 15N	46 20 E
Bazarnyy Syzgan	**55**	53 45N	46 40 E
Bazartobe	**57**	49 26N	51 45 E
Bazaruto, I. do	**93**	21 40 S	35 28 E
Bazas	**20**	44 27N	0 13W
Bazhong	**77**	31 52N	106 46 E
Beach	**116**	46 57N	103 58W
Beach City	**112**	40 38N	81 35W
Beachport	**99**	37 29 S	140 0 E
Beachy Head	**13**	50 44N	0 16 E
Beacon	**114**	41 32N	73 58W
Beaconia	**109**	50 25N	96 31W
Beaconsfield	**97**	41 11 S	146 48 E
Beagle, Canal	**128**	55 0 S	68 30W
Bealanana	**93**	14 33N	48 44 E
Beamsville	**112**	43 12N	79 28W
Béar, C.	**20**	42 31N	3 8 E
Bear I.	**15**	51 38N	9 50W
Bear L., B.C., Can.	**108**	56 10N	126 52W
Bear L., Man., Can.	**109**	55 8N	96 0W
Bear L., U.S.A.	**118**	42 0N	111 20W
Bearcreek	**118**	45 11N	109 6W
Beardmore	**106**	49 36N	87 57W
Beardmore Glacier	**5**	84 30 S	170 0 E
Beardstown	**116**	40 0N	90 25W
Béarn	**20**	43 8N	0 36W
Bearpaw Mt.	**118**	48 15N	109 30W
Bearskin Lake	**106**	53 58N	91 2W
Beas de Segura	**33**	38 15N	2 53W
Beasain	**32**	43 3N	2 11W
Beata, C.	**121**	17 40N	71 30W
Beatrice, U.S.A.	**116**	40 20N	96 40W
Beatrice, Zimb.	**91**	18 15 S	30 55 E
Beatrice, C.	**97**	14 20 S	136 55 E
Beatton →	**108**	56 15N	120 45W
Beatton River	**108**	57 26N	121 20W
Beatty	**119**	36 58N	116 46W
Beaucaire	**21**	43 48N	4 39 E
Beauce, Plaine de la	**19**	48 10N	1 45 E
Beauceville	**107**	46 13N	70 46W
Beaudesert	**99**	27 59 S	153 0 E
Beaufort, Austral.	**100**	37 25 S	143 25 E
Beaufort, Malay.	**72**	5 30N	115 40 E
Beaufort, N.C., U.S.A.	**115**	34 45N	76 40W
Beaufort, S.C., U.S.A.	**115**	32 25N	80 40W
Beaufort Sea	**4**	72 0N	140 0W
Beaufort West	**92**	32 18 S	22 36 E
Beaugency	**19**	47 47N	1 38 E
Beauharnois	**106**	45 20N	73 52W
Beaujeu	**21**	46 10N	4 35 E
Beaulieu	**20**	44 59N	1 50 E
Beaulieu →	**108**	62 3N	113 11W
Beauly	**14**	57 29N	4 27W
Beauly →	**14**	57 26N	4 28W
Beaumaris	**12**	53 16N	4 7W
Beaumetz-les-Loges	**19**	50 15N	2 40 E
Beaumont, Dordogne, France	**20**	44 45N	0 46 E
Beaumont, Sarthe, France	**18**	48 13N	0 8 E
Beaumont, U.S.A.	**117**	30 5N	94 8W
Beaumont-de-Lomagne	**20**	43 53N	0 59 E
Beaumont-le-Roger	**18**	49 4N	0 47 E
Beaumont-sur-Oise	**19**	49 9N	2 17 E
Beaune	**19**	47 2N	4 50 E
Beaune-la-Rolande	**19**	48 4N	2 25 E
Beaupréau	**18**	47 12N	1 00W
Beauséjour	**109**	50 5N	96 35W
Beausset, Le	**21**	43 10N	5 46 E
Beauvais	**19**	49 25N	2 8 E
Beauval	**109**	55 9N	107 37W
Beauvoir	**18**	46 55N	2 1W
Beauvoir-sur-Niort	**20**	46 12N	0 30W
Beaver, Alaska, U.S.A.	**104**	66 20N	147 30W
Beaver, Okla., U.S.A.	**117**	36 52N	100 31W
Beaver, Pa., U.S.A.	**112**	40 40N	80 18W
Beaver, Utah, U.S.A.	**119**	38 20N	112 45W
Beaver →, B.C., Can.	**108**	59 52N	124 20W
Beaver →, Sask., Can.	**109**	55 26N	107 45W
Beaver City	**116**	40 13N	99 50W
Beaver Dam	**116**	43 28N	88 50W
Beaver Falls	**114**	40 44N	80 20W
Beaver I.	**106**	45 40N	85 31W
Beaver, R	**106**	55 55N	87 48W
Beaverhill L., Alta., Can.	**108**	53 27N	112 32W
Beaverhill L., Man., Can.	**109**	54 5N	94 50W
Beaverhill L., N.W.T., Can.	**109**	63 2N	104 22W
Beaverlodge	**108**	55 11N	119 29W
Beavermouth	**108**	51 32N	117 23W
Beaverstone →	**106**	54 59N	89 25W
Beaverton	**112**	44 26N	79 9W
Beawar	**68**	26 3N	74 18 E
Bebedouro	**125**	21 0 S	48 25W
Beboa	**93**	17 22 S	44 33 E
Bebra	**24**	50 59N	9 48 E
Beccles	**13**	52 27N	1 33 E
Bečej	**42**	45 36N	20 3 E
Beceni	**46**	45 23N	26 48 E
Becerreá	**30**	42 51N	7 10W
Béchar	**82**	31 38N	2 18W
Bechyně	**26**	49 17N	14 29 E
Beckley	**114**	37 50N	81 8W
Beckum	**24**	51 46N	8 3 E
Bécon	**18**	47 30N	0 50W
Bečva →	**27**	49 31N	17 40 E
Bédar	**33**	37 11N	1 59W
Bédarieux	**20**	43 37N	3 10 E
Bédarrides	**21**	44 2N	4 54 E
Beddouza, Ras	**82**	32 33N	9 9W
Bedele	**87**	8 31N	36 23 E
Bederkesa	**24**	53 37N	8 50 E
Bedeso	**87**	9 58N	40 52 E
Bedford, Can.	**106**	45 7N	72 59W
Bedford, S. Afr.	**92**	32 40 S	26 10 E
Bedford, U.K.	**13**	52 8N	0 29W
Bedford, Ind., U.S.A.	**114**	38 50N	86 30W
Bedford, Iowa, U.S.A.	**116**	40 40N	94 41W
Bedford, Ohio, U.S.A.	**114**	41 23N	81 32W
Bedford, Pa., U.S.A.	**112**	40 1N	78 30W
Bedford, Va., U.S.A.	**114**	37 25N	79 30W
Bedford □	**13**	52 4N	0 28W
Bedford, C.	**97**	15 14 S	145 21 E
Będków	**28**	51 36N	19 44 E
Bednja →	**39**	46 12N	16 25 E
Bednodemyanovsk	**55**	53 55N	43 15 E
Bedónia	**38**	44 28N	9 36 E
Bedourie	**97**	24 30 S	139 30 E
Bedous	**20**	43 0N	0 36W
Będzin	**28**	50 19N	19 7 E
Beech Grove	**114**	39 40N	86 2W
Beechworth	**99**	36 22 S	146 43 E
Beechy	**109**	50 53N	107 24W
Beelitz	**24**	52 14N	12 58 E
Beenleigh	**99**	27 43 S	153 10 E
Be'er Sheva'	**62**	31 15N	34 48 E
Be'er Sheva' →	**62**	31 12N	34 40 E
Be'er Toviyya	**62**	31 44N	34 42 E
Be'eri	**62**	31 25N	34 30 E
Be'erotayim	**62**	32 19N	34 59 E
Beersheba = Be'er Sheva'	**62**	31 15N	34 48 E
Beeskow	**24**	52 9N	14 14 E
Beeston	**12**	52 55N	1 11W
Beetzendorf	**24**	52 42N	11 6 E
Beeville	**117**	28 27N	97 44W
Befale	**88**	0 25N	20 45 E
Befotaka	**93**	23 49 S	47 0 E
Bega	**97**	36 41 S	149 51 E
Bega, Canalul	**42**	45 37N	20 46 E
Bégard	**18**	48 38N	3 18W
* Begemdir & Simen □	**87**	12 55N	37 30 E
Bègles	**20**	44 45N	0 35W
Begna →	**47**	60 41N	10 0 E
Begonte	**30**	43 10N	7 40W
Begu-Sarai	**69**	25 24N	86 9 E
Behbehān	**64**	30 30N	50 15 E
Behror	**68**	27 51N	76 20 E
Behshahr	**65**	36 45N	53 35 E
Bei Jiang →	**75**	23 2N	112 58 E
Bei'an	**75**	48 10N	126 20 E
Beibei	**75**	29 47N	106 22 E
Beihai	**75**	21 28N	109 6 E
Beijing	**76**	39 55N	116 20 E
Beijing □	**76**	39 55N	116 20 E
Beilen	**16**	52 52N	6 27 E
Beilngries	**25**	49 1N	11 27 E
Beilpajah	**99**	32 54 S	143 52 E
Beilul	**87**	13 2N	42 20 E
Beira	**91**	19 50 S	34 52 E
Beirut = Bayrūt	**64**	33 53N	35 31 E
Beit Lāhiyah	**62**	31 32N	34 30 E
Beitaolaizhao	**76**	44 58N	125 58 E
Beitbridge	**91**	22 12 S	30 0 E
Beiuş	**46**	46 40N	22 21 E
Beizhen	**76**	37 20N	118 2 E
Beja	**31**	38 2N	7 53W
Béja	**83**	36 43N	9 12 E
Beja □	**31**	37 55N	7 55W
Bejaia	**83**	36 42N	5 2 E
Béjar	**30**	40 23N	5 46W
Bejestān	**65**	34 30N	58 5 E
Bekasi	**73**	6 20 S	107 0 E
Békés	**27**	46 47N	21 9 E
Békés □	**27**	46 45N	21 0 E
Békéscsaba	**27**	46 40N	21 5 E
Bekily	**93**	24 13 S	45 19 E
Bekoji	**87**	7 40N	39 17 E
Bekok	**71**	2 20N	103 7 E
Bekwai	**85**	6 30N	1 34W
Bela, India	**69**	25 50N	82 0 E
Bela, Pak.	**66**	26 12N	66 20 E
Bela Crkva	**42**	44 55N	21 27 E
Bela Palanka	**42**	43 13N	22 17 E
Bela Vista, Brazil	**124**	22 12 S	56 20W
Bela Vista, Mozam.	**93**	26 10 S	32 44 E
Bélâbre	**20**	46 34N	1 8 E
Belalcázar	**31**	38 35N	5 10W
Belanovica	**42**	44 15N	20 23 E
Belavenona	**93**	24 50 S	47 4 E
Belawan	**72**	3 33N	98 32 E
Belaya →	**52**	56 0N	54 32 E
Belaya Glina	**57**	46 5N	40 48 E
Belaya Kalitva	**57**	48 13N	40 50 E
Belaya Kholunitsa	**55**	58 41N	50 13 E
Belaya, Mt.	**87**	11 25N	36 8 E
Belaya Tserkov	**54**	49 45N	30 10 E
Belceşti	**46**	47 19N	27 7 E
Bełchatów	**28**	51 21N	19 22 E
Belcher, C.	**4**	71 0N	161 0W
Belcher Is.	**106**	56 15N	78 45W
Belchite	**32**	41 18N	0 43W
Belebey	**52**	54 7N	54 7 E
Belém (Pará)	**127**	1 20 S	48 30W
Belén, Argent.	**124**	27 40 S	67 5W
Belén, Parag.	**124**	23 30 S	57 6W
Belen	**119**	34 40N	106 50W
Belene	**43**	43 39N	25 10 E
Bélesta	**20**	42 55N	1 56 E
Belet Uen	**63**	4 30N	45 5 E
Belev	**55**	53 50N	36 5 E
Belfast, S. Afr.	**93**	25 42 S	30 2 E
Belfast, U.K.	**15**	54 35N	5 56W
Belfast, Maine, U.S.A.	**107**	44 30N	69 0W
Belfast, N.Y., U.S.A.	**112**	42 21N	78 9W
Belfast □	**15**	54 35N	5 56W
Belfast, L.	**15**	54 40N	5 50W
Belfield	**116**	46 54N	103 11W
Belfort	**19**	47 38N	6 50 E
Belfort □	**19**	47 38N	6 52 E
Belfry	**118**	45 10N	109 2W
Belgaum	**70**	15 55N	74 35 E
Belgioioso	**38**	45 9N	9 21 E
Belgium ■	**16**	50 30N	5 0 E
Belgorod	**56**	50 35N	36 35 E
Belgorod-Dnestrovskiy	**56**	46 11N	30 23 E
Belgrade	**118**	45 50N	111 10W
Belgrade = Beograd	**42**	44 50N	20 37 E
Belhaven	**115**	35 34N	76 35W
Beli Drim →	**42**	42 6N	20 25 E
Beli Manastir	**42**	45 45N	18 36 E
Beli Timok →	**42**	43 53N	22 14 E
Belice →	**40**	37 35N	12 55 E
Belin	**20**	44 30N	0 47W
Belinga	**88**	1 10N	13 2 E
Belingwe	**91**	20 29 S	29 57 E
Belingwe, N.	**91**	20 37 S	29 55 E
Belinskiy (Chembar)	**55**	53 0N	43 25 E
Belinţ	**42**	45 48N	21 54 E
Belinyu	**72**	1 35 S	105 50 E
Belitung, P.	**72**	3 10 S	107 50 E
Beliu	**46**	46 30N	22 0 E
Belize ■	**120**	17 0N	88 30W
Belize City	**120**	17 25N	88 0W
Beljanica	**42**	44 08N	21 43 E
Belkovskiy, Ostrov	**59**	75 32N	135 44 E
Bell →	**106**	49 48N	77 38W
Bell Bay	**99**	41 6 S	146 53 E
Bell I.	**107**	50 46N	55 35W
Bell-Irving →	**108**	56 12N	129 5W
Bell Peninsula	**105**	63 50N	82 0W
Bell Ville	**124**	32 40 S	62 40W
Bella Bella	**108**	52 10N	128 10W
Bella Coola	**108**	52 25N	126 40W
Bella Unión	**124**	30 15 S	57 40W
Bella Vista, Corrientes, Argent.	**124**	28 33 S	59 0W
Bella Vista, Tucuman, Argent.	**124**	27 10 S	65 25W
Bellac	**20**	46 7N	1 3 E
Bellágio	**38**	45 59N	9 15 E
Bellaire	**114**	40 1N	80 46W
Bellary	**70**	15 10N	76 56 E
Bellata	**99**	29 53 S	149 46 E
Belle Fourche	**116**	44 43N	103 52W
Belle Fourche →	**116**	44 25N	102 19W
Belle Glade	**115**	26 43N	80 38W
Belle-Île	**18**	47 20N	3 10W
Belle Isle	**107**	51 57N	55 25W
Belle-Isle-en-Terre	**18**	48 33N	3 23W
Belle Isle, Str. of	**107**	51 30N	56 30W
Belle, La	**115**	26 45N	81 22W
Belle Plaine, Iowa, U.S.A.	**116**	41 51N	92 18W
Belle Plaine, Minn., U.S.A.	**116**	44 35N	93 48W
Belle Yella	**84**	7 24N	10 0W
Belledonne	**21**	45 30N	6 10 E
Belledune	**107**	47 55N	65 50W
Bellefontaine	**114**	40 20N	83 45W
Bellefonte	**114**	40 56N	77 45W
Bellegarde, Ain, France	**21**	46 4N	5 49 E
Bellegarde, Creuse, France	**20**	45 59N	2 18 E
Bellegarde, Loiret, France	**19**	48 0N	2 26 E
Bellême	**18**	48 22N	0 34 E
Belleoram	**107**	47 31N	55 25W
Belleville, Can.	**106**	44 10N	77 23W
Belleville, Rhône, France	**21**	46 7N	4 45 E
Belleville, Vendée, France	**18**	46 48N	1 28W
Belleville, Ill., U.S.A.	**116**	38 30N	90 0W
Belleville, Kans., U.S.A.	**116**	39 51N	97 38W
Belleville, N.Y., U.S.A.	**113**	43 46N	76 10W
Bellevue, Can.	**108**	49 35N	114 22W
Bellevue, Idaho, U.S.A.	**118**	43 25N	114 23W
Bellevue, Ohio, U.S.A.	**112**	41 20N	82 48W
Bellevue, Pa., U.S.A.	**112**	40 29N	80 3W
Belley	**21**	45 46N	5 41 E
Bellin (Payne Bay)	**105**	60 0N	70 0W
Bellingen	**99**	30 25 S	152 50 E
Bellingham	**118**	48 45N	122 27W
Bellingshausen Sea	**5**	66 0 S	80 0W
Bellinzona	**25**	46 11N	9 1 E
Bellona Reefs	**97**	21 26 S	159 0 E
Bellows Falls	**114**	43 10N	72 30W
Bellpat	**68**	29 0N	68 5 E
Bellpuig	**32**	41 37N	1 1 E
Belluno	**39**	46 8N	12 13 E
Bellville	**117**	29 58N	96 18W
Bellwood	**112**	40 36N	78 21W
Belmar	**113**	40 10N	74 2W
Bélmez	**31**	38 17N	5 17W
Belmont, Austral.	**99**	33 4 S	151 42 E
Belmont, Can.	**112**	42 53N	81 5W
Belmont, U.S.A.	**112**	42 14N	78 3W
Belmonte, Brazil	**127**	16 0 S	39 0W
Belmonte, Port.	**30**	40 21N	7 20W
Belmonte, Spain	**32**	39 34N	2 43W
Belmopan	**120**	17 18N	88 30W
Belmullet	**15**	54 13N	9 58W
Belo Horizonte	**127**	19 55 S	43 56W
Belo-sur-Mer	**93**	20 42 S	44 0 E
Belo-Tsiribihina	**93**	19 40 S	44 30 E
Belogorsk, R.S.F.S.R., U.S.S.R.	**59**	51 0N	128 20 E
Belogorsk, Ukraine S.S.R., U.S.S.R.	**56**	45 3N	34 35 E
Belogradchik	**42**	43 53N	22 15 E
Belogradets	**43**	43 22N	27 18 E
Beloha	**93**	25 10 S	45 3 E
Beloit, Kans., U.S.A.	**116**	39 32N	98 9W
Beloit, Wis., U.S.A.	**116**	42 35N	89 0W
Belokorovichi	**54**	51 7N	28 2 E
Belomorsk	**52**	64 35N	34 30 E
Belonia	**67**	23 15N	91 30 E
Belopolye	**54**	51 14N	34 20 E
Beloretsk	**52**	53 58N	58 24 E
Belovo	**58**	54 30N	86 0 E
Beloye More	**52**	66 30N	38 0 E
Beloye, Oz.	**52**	60 10N	37 35 E
Beloye Ozero	**57**	45 15N	46 50 E
Belozem	**43**	42 12N	25 2 E
Belozersk	**55**	60 0N	37 30 E
Belpasso	**41**	37 37N	15 0 E
Belsito	**40**	37 50N	13 47 E
Beltana	**99**	30 48 S	138 25 E
Belterra	**127**	2 45 S	55 0W
Beltinci	**39**	46 37N	16 20 E
Belton, S.C., U.S.A.	**115**	34 31N	82 39W
Belton, Tex., U.S.A.	**117**	31 4N	97 30W
Belton Res.	**117**	31 8N	97 32W
Beltsy	**56**	47 48N	28 0 E
Belturbet	**15**	54 6N	7 28W
Belukha	**58**	49 50N	86 50 E
Beluran	**72**	5 48N	117 35 E
Beluša	**27**	49 5N	18 27 E
Belušić	**42**	43 50N	21 10 E
Belvedere Maríttimo	**41**	39 37N	15 52 E
Belvès	**20**	44 46N	1 0 E
Belvidere, Ill., U.S.A.	**116**	42 15N	88 55W
Belvidere, N.J., U.S.A.	**113**	40 48N	75 5W
Belvis de la Jara	**31**	39 45N	4 57W
Belyando →	**97**	21 38 S	146 50 E
Belyy	**54**	55 48N	32 51 E
Belyy, Ostrov	**58**	73 30N	71 0 E
Belyy Yar	**58**	58 26N	84 39 E
Belzig	**24**	52 8N	12 36 E
Belzoni	**117**	33 12N	90 30W
Bełżyce	**28**	51 11N	22 17 E
Bemaraha, Lembalemban' i	**93**	18 40 S	44 45 E
Bemarivo	**93**	21 45 S	44 45 E
Bemarivo →	**93**	15 27 S	47 40 E
Bemavo	**93**	21 33 S	45 25 E
Bembéréke	**85**	10 11N	2 43 E
Bembesi	**91**	20 0 S	28 58 E
Bembesi →	**91**	18 57 S	27 47 E
Bembézar →	**31**	37 45N	5 13W
Bemidji	**116**	47 30N	94 50W
Ben 'Ammi	**62**	33 0N	35 7 E
Ben Cruachan	**14**	56 26N	5 8W
Ben Dearg	**14**	57 47N	4 58W
Ben Gardane	**83**	33 11N	11 11 E
Ben Hope	**14**	58 24N	4 36W
Ben Lawers	**14**	56 33N	4 13W
Ben Lomond, Austral.	**97**	41 38 S	147 42 E
Ben Lomond, U.K.	**14**	56 12N	4 39W
Ben Macdhui	**14**	57 4N	3 40W
Ben Mhor	**14**	57 16N	7 21W
Ben More, Central, U.K.	**14**	56 23N	4 31W
Ben More, Strathclyde, U.K.	**14**	56 26N	6 2W
Ben More Assynt	**14**	58 7N	4 51W
Ben Nevis	**14**	56 48N	5 0W
Ben Slimane	**82**	33 38N	7 7W
Ben Vorlich	**14**	56 22N	4 15W
Ben Wyvis	**14**	57 40N	4 35W
Bena	**85**	11 20N	5 50
Bena Dibele	**88**	4 4 S	22 50
Benagalbón	**31**	36 45N	4 15W
Benagerie	**99**	31 25 S	140 22
Benahmed	**82**	33 4N	7 9W
Benalla	**97**	36 30 S	146 0
Benambra, Mt.	**100**	36 31 S	147 34
Benamejí	**31**	37 16N	4 33W
Benanee	**99**	34 31 S	142 52
Benares = Varanasi	**69**	25 22N	83 8
Bénat, C.	**21**	43 5N	6 22
Benavente, Port.	**31**	38 59N	8 49W

* *Renamed Gonder* □

Benavente, Spain **30** 42 2N 5 43W
Benavides, Spain **30** 42 30N 5 54W
Benavides, U.S.A. **117** 27 35N 98 28W
Benbecula **14** 57 26N 7 21W
Bencubbin **96** 30 48S 117 52E
Bend **118** 44 2N 121 15W
Bendel □ **85** 6 0N 6 0E
Bender Beila **63** 9 30N 50 48E
Bendery **56** 46 50N 29 30E
Bendigo **97** 36 40S 144 15E
Bendorf **24** 50 26N 7 34E
Benē Beraq, Israel **62** 32 6N 34 51E
Benē Beraq, Israel **62** 32 6N 34 51E
Bénéna **84** 13 9N 4 17W
Benenitra **93** 23 27S 45 5E
Benešov **26** 49 46N 14 41E
Bénestroff **19** 48 54N 6 45E
Benet **20** 46 22N 0 35W
Benevento **41** 41 7N 14 45E
Benfeld **19** 48 22N 7 34E
Benga **91** 16 11S 33 40E
Bengal, Bay of **60** 15 0N 90 0E
Bengawan Solo → **73** 7 5S 112 35E
Bengbu **75** 32 58N 117 20E
Benghazi = Banghāzī **83** 32 11N 20 3E
Bengkalis **72** 1 30N 102 10E
Bengkulu **72** 3 50S 102 12E
Bengkulu □ **72** 3 48S 102 16E
Bengough **109** 49 25N 105 10W
Benguela **89** 12 37S 13 25E
Benguerir **82** 32 16N 7 56W
Benguérua, I. **93** 21 58S 35 28E
Benha **86** 30 26N 31 8E
Beni **90** 0 30N 29 27E
Beni → **126** 10 23S 65 24W
Beni Abbès **82** 30 5N 2 5W
Beni-Haoua **82** 36 30N 1 30E
Beni Mazâr **86** 28 32N 30 44E
Beni Mellal **82** 32 21N 6 21W
Beni Ounif **82** 32 0N 1 10W
Beni Saf **82** 35 17N 1 15W
Beni Suef **86** 29 5N 31 6E
Beniah L. **108** 63 23N 112 17W
Benicarló **32** 40 23N 0 23E
Benidorm **33** 38 33N 0 9W
Benidorm, Islote de **33** 38 31N 0 9W
Benin ■ **85** 10 0N 2 0E
Benin, Bight of **85** 5 0N 3 0E
Benin City **85** 6 20N 5 31E
Benisa **33** 38 43N 0 03E
Benjamin Aceval **124** 24 58S 57 34W
Benjamin Constant **126** 4 40S 70 15W
Benkelman **116** 40 7N 101 32W
Benkovac **39** 44 2N 15 37E
Benlidi **98** 24 35S 144 50E
Bennett **108** 59 56N 134 53W
Bennett, Ostrov **59** 76 21N 148 56E
Bennettsville **115** 34 38N 79 39W
Bennington **114** 42 52N 73 12W
Benoa **72** 8 50S 115 20E
Bénodet **18** 47 53N 4 7W
Benoni **93** 26 11S 28 18E
Benoud **82** 32 20N 0 16E
Bensheim **25** 49 40N 8 38E
Benson **119** 31 59N 110 19W
Bent **65** 26 20N 59 31E
Benteng **73** 6 10S 120 30E
Bentinck I. **97** 17 3S 139 35E
Bentiu **87** 9 10N 29 55E
Bento Gonçalves **125** 29 10S 51 31W
Benton, Ark., U.S.A. **117** 34 30N 92 35W
Benton, Ill., U.S.A. **116** 38 0N 88 55W
Benton Harbor **114** 42 10N 86 28W
Bentong **71** 3 31N 101 55E
Bentu Liben **87** 8 32N 38 21E
Benue □ **85** 7 30N 7 30E
Benue → **85** 7 48N 6 46E
Benxi **76** 41 20N 123 48E
Beo **73** 4 25N 126 50E
Beograd **42** 44 50N 20 37E
Beowawe **118** 40 35N 116 30W
Beppu **74** 33 15N 131 30E
Berati **44** 40 43N 19 59E
Berau, Teluk **73** 2 30S 132 30E
Berber **86** 18 0N 34 0E
Berbera **63** 10 30N 45 2E
Berbérati **88** 4 15N 15 40E
Berberia, C. del **33** 38 39N 1 24E
Berbice → **126** 6 20N 57 32W
Berceto **38** 44 30N 10 0E
Berchtesgaden **25** 47 37N 12 58E
Berck-sur-Mer **19** 50 25N 1 36E
Berdichev **56** 49 57N 28 30E
Berdsk **58** 54 47N 83 2E
Berdyansk **56** 46 45N 36 50E
Berea, Ky., U.S.A. **114** 37 35N 84 18W
Berea, Ohio, U.S.A. **112** 41 21N 81 50W
Berebere **73** 2 25N 128 45E
Bereda **63** 11 45N 51 0E
Berekum **84** 7 29N 2 34W
Berenice **86** 24 2N 35 25E
Berens → **109** 52 25N 97 2W
Berens I. **109** 52 18N 97 18W
Berens River **109** 52 25N 97 0W
Berestechko **54** 50 22N 25 5E
Bereşti **46** 46 6N 27 50E
Beretău → **46** 46 59N 21 7E
Berettyo → **27** 46 59N 21 7E
Berettyóújfalu **27** 47 13N 21 33E
Berevo, Majunga, Madag. **93** 17 14S 44 17E
Berevo, Tuléar, Madag. **93** 19 44S 44 58E
Bereza **54** 52 31N 24 51E
Berezhany **54** 49 26N 24 58E
Berezina → **54** 52 33N 30 14E
Berezna **55** 51 35N 31 46E
Berezniki **58** 59 24N 56 46E
Berezovka **56** 47 14N 30 55E
Berezovo **58** 64 0N 65 0E
Berg **47** 59 10N 11 18E
Berga, Spain **32** 42 6N 1 48E
Berga, Sweden **49** 57 14N 16 3E
Bergama **64** 39 8N 27 15E
Bérgamo **38** 45 42N 9 40E
Bergantiños **30** 43 20N 8 40W
Bergedorf **24** 53 28N 10 12E
Bergen, Ger. **24** 54 24N 13 26E
Bergen, Neth. **16** 52 40N 4 43E
Bergen, Norway **47** 60 23N 5 20E
Bergen, U.S.A. **112** 43 5N 77 56W
Bergen-op-Zoom **16** 51 30N 4 18E
Bergerac **20** 44 51N 0 30E
Bergheim **24** 50 57N 6 38E
Bergisch-Gladbach **24** 50 59N 7 9E
Bergkvara **49** 56 23N 16 5E
Bergsjö **48** 61 59N 17 3E
Bergues **19** 50 58N 2 24E
Bergum **16** 53 13N 5 59E
Bergvik **48** 61 16N 16 50E
Berhala, Selat **72** 1 0S 104 15E
Berhampore **69** 24 2N 88 27E
Berhampur **70** 19 15N 84 54E
Berheci → **46** 46 7N 27 19E
Bering Sea **94** 58 0N 167 0E
Bering Str. **104** 66 0N 170 0W
Beringen **16** 51 3N 5 14E
Beringovskiy **59** 63 3N 179 19E
Berislav **56** 46 50N 33 30E
Berisso **124** 34 56S 57 50W
Berja **33** 36 50N 2 56W
Berkane **82** 34 52N 2 20W
Berkeley **13** 51 41N 2 28W
Berkeley Springs **114** 39 38N 78 12W
Berkner I. **5** 79 30S 50 0W
Berkovitsa **43** 43 16N 23 8E
Berkshire □ **13** 51 30N 1 20W
Berland → **108** 54 0N 116 50W
Berlanga **31** 38 17N 5 50W
Berleburg **24** 51 3N 8 22E
Berlenga, Ilhas **31** 39 25N 9 30W
Berlin, Ger. **24** 52 32N 13 24E
Berlin, Md., U.S.A. **114** 38 19N 75 12W
Berlin, N.H., U.S.A. **114** 44 29N 71 10W
Berlin, Wis., U.S.A. **114** 43 58N 88 55W
Berlin, E. □ **24** 52 30N 13 30E
Berlin, W. □ **24** 52 30N 13 20E
Bermeja, Sierra **31** 36 30N 5 11W
Bermejo →, Formosa, Argent. **124** 26 51S 58 23W
Bermejo →, San Juan, Argent. **124** 32 30S 67 30W
Bermeo **32** 43 25N 2 47W
Bermillo de Sayago **30** 41 22N 6 8W
Bermuda ■ **121** 32 45N 65 0W
Bern (Berne) **25** 46 57N 7 28E
Bern (Berne) □ **25** 46 45N 7 40E
Bernado **119** 34 30N 106 53W
Bernalda **41** 40 24N 16 44E
Bernalillo **119** 35 17N 106 37W
Bernam → **71** 3 45N 101 5E
Bernardo de Irigoyen **125** 26 15S 53 40W
Bernasconi **124** 37 55S 63 44W
Bernau, Germ., E. **24** 52 40N 13 35E
Bernau, Germ., W. **25** 47 45N 12 20E
Bernay **18** 49 5N 0 35E
Bernburg **24** 51 40N 11 42E
Berndorf **26** 47 59N 16 1E
Berne = Bern **25** 46 57N 7 28E
Berneck **25** 51 3N 11 40E
Berner Alpen **25** 46 27N 7 35E
Bernese Oberland = Oberland **25** 46 27N 7 35E
Bernier I. **96** 24 50S 113 12E
Bernina, Piz **25** 46 20N 9 54E
Bernkastel-Kues **25** 49 55N 7 04E
Beror Hayil **62** 31 34N 34 38E
Béroubouay **85** 10 34N 2 46E
Beroun **26** 49 57N 14 5E
Berounka → **26** 50 0N 13 47E
Berovo **42** 41 38N 22 51E
Berrahal **83** 36 54N 7 33E
Berre, Étang de **21** 43 27N 5 5E
Berrechid **82** 33 18N 7 36W
Berri **99** 34 14S 140 35E
Berriane **82** 32 50N 3 46E
Berrigan **100** 35 38S 145 49E
Berrouaghia **82** 36 10N 2 53E
Berry, Austral. **99** 34 46S 150 43E
Berry, France **19** 47 0N 2 0E
Berry Is. **121** 25 40N 77 50W
Berryville **117** 36 23N 93 35W
Bersenbrück **24** 52 33N 7 56E
Berthold **116** 48 19N 101 45W
Berthoud **116** 40 21N 105 5W
Bertincourt **19** 50 5N 2 58E
Bertoua **88** 4 30N 13 45E
Bertrand **116** 40 35N 99 38W
Berufjörður **50** 64 48N 14 29W
Berwick **114** 41 4N 76 17W
Berwick-upon-Tweed **12** 55 47N 2 0W
Berwyn Mts. **12** 52 54N 3 26W
Berzasca **42** 44 39N 21 58E
Berzence **27** 46 12N 17 11E
Besalampy **93** 16 43S 44 29E
Besançon **19** 47 15N 6 0E
Besar **72** 2 40S 116 0E
Beserah **71** 3 50N 103 21E
Beshenkovichi **54** 55 2N 29 29E
Beška **42** 45 8N 20 6E
Beskydy **27** 49 35N 18 40E
Beslan **57** 43 15N 44 28E
Besna Kobila **42** 42 31N 22 10E
Besnard L. **109** 55 25N 106 0W
Besni **64** 37 41N 37 52E
Besor, N. → **62** 31 28N 34 22E
Beşparmak Dağı **45** 37 32N 27 30E
Bessarabiya **46** 47 0N 28 10E
Bessarabka **56** 46 21N 28 58E
Bessèges **21** 44 18N 4 8E
Bessemer, Ala., U.S.A. **115** 33 25N 86 57W
Bessemer, Mich., U.S.A. **116** 46 27N 90 0W
Bessin **18** 49 21N 1 0W
Bessines-sur-Gartempe **20** 46 6N 1 22E
Bet Alfa **62** 32 31N 35 25E
Bet Dagan **62** 32 1N 34 49E
Bet Guvrin **62** 31 37N 34 54E
Bet Ha'Emeq **62** 32 58N 35 8E
Bet Hashitta **62** 32 31N 35 27E
Bet Qeshet **62** 32 41N 35 21E
Bet She'an **62** 32 30N 35 30E
Bet Shemesh **62** 31 44N 35 0E
Bet Tadjine, Djebel **82** 29 0N 3 30W
Bet Yosef **62** 32 34N 35 33E
Betafo **93** 19 50S 46 51E
Betanzos **30** 43 15N 8 12W
Bétaré Oya **88** 5 40N 14 5E
Bétera **32** 39 35N 0 28W
Bethal **93** 26 27S 29 28E
Bethanien **92** 26 31S 17 8E
Bethany, S. Afr. **92** 29 34S 25 59E
Bethany, U.S.A. **116** 40 18N 94 0W
Bethany = Al Ayzarīyah **62** 31 47N 35 15E
Bethel, Alaska, U.S.A. **104** 60 50N 161 50W
Bethel, Pa., U.S.A. **112** 40 20N 80 2W
Bethel, Vt., U.S.A. **113** 43 50N 72 37W
Bethlehem, S. Afr. **93** 28 14S 28 18E
Bethlehem, U.S.A. **114** 40 39N 75 24W
Bethlehem = Bayt Lahm **62** 31 43N 35 12E
Bethulie **92** 30 30S 25 59E
Béthune **19** 50 30N 2 38E
Béthune → **18** 49 53N 1 9E
Betioky **93** 23 48S 44 20E
Beton Bazoches **19** 48 42N 3 15E
Betong, Malay. **72** 1 24N 111 31E
Betong, Thai. **71** 5 45N 101 5E
Betoota **99** 25 45S 140 42E
Betroka **93** 23 16S 46 0E
Betsiamites **107** 48 56N 68 40W
Betsiamites → **107** 48 56N 68 38W
Betsiboka → **93** 16 3S 46 36E
Betsjoeanaland **92** 26 30S 22 30E
Bettiah **69** 26 48N 84 33E
Bèttola **38** 44 42N 9 32E
Betul **68** 21 58N 77 59E
Betzdorf **24** 50 47N 7 53E
Beuca **46** 44 14N 24 56E
Beuil **21** 44 6N 6 59E
Beulah **116** 47 18N 101 47W
Bevensen **24** 53 5N 10 34E
Beverley, Austral. **96** 32 9S 116 56E
Beverley, U.K. **12** 53 52N 0 26W
Beverly, Mass., U.S.A. **113** 42 32N 70 50W
Beverly, Wash., U.S.A. **118** 46 55N 119 59W
Beverly Hills **119** 34 4N 118 29W
Beverwijk **16** 52 28N 4 38E
Bex **25** 46 15N 7 0E
Beyin **84** 5 1N 2 41W
Beykoz **43** 41 8N 29 7E
Beyla **84** 8 30N 8 38W
Beynat **20** 45 8N 1 44E
Beyneu **58** 45 10N 55 3E
Beypazarı **64** 40 10N 31 56E
Beyşehir Gölü **64** 37 40N 31 45E
Bezdan **42** 45 50N 18 57E
Bezet **62** 33 4N 35 8E
Bezhetsk **55** 57 47N 36 39E
Bezhitsa **54** 53 19N 34 17E
Béziers **20** 43 20N 3 12E
Bezwada = Vijayawada **70** 16 31N 80 39E
Bhadra → **70** 14 0N 75 20E
Bhadrakh **69** 21 10N 86 30E
Bhadravati **70** 13 49N 75 40E
Bhagalpur **69** 25 10N 87 0E
Bhaisa **70** 19 10N 77 58E
Bhakkar **68** 31 40N 71 5E
Bhakra Dam **68** 31 30N 76 45E
Bhamo **67** 24 15N 97 15E
Bhamragarh **70** 19 30N 80 40E
Bhandara **69** 21 5N 79 42E
Bhanrer Ra. **68** 23 40N 79 45E
Bharatpur **68** 27 15N 77 30E
Bharuch **68** 21 47N 73 0E
Bhatghar L. **70** 18 10N 73 48E
Bhatiapara Ghat **69** 23 13N 89 42E
Bhatinda **68** 30 15N 74 57E
Bhatkal **70** 13 58N 74 35E
Bhatpara **69** 22 50N 88 25E
Bhattiprolu **70** 16 7N 80 45E
Bhaun **68** 32 55N 72 40E
Bhaunagar = Bhavnagar **68** 21 45N 72 10E
Bhavani **70** 11 27N 77 43E
Bhavani → **70** 11 0N 78 15E
Bhavnagar **68** 21 45N 72 10E
Bhawanipatna **70** 19 55N 80 10E
Bhera **68** 32 29N 72 57E
Bhilsa = Vidisha **68** 23 28N 77 53E
Bhilwara **68** 25 25N 74 38E
Bhima → **70** 16 25N 77 17E
Bhimavaram **70** 16 30N 81 30E
Bhind **68** 26 30N 78 46E
Bhir **70** 19 4N 75 46E
Bhiwandi **70** 19 20N 73 0E
Bhiwani **68** 28 50N 76 9E
Bhola **69** 22 45N 90 35E
Bhongir **70** 17 30N 78 56E
Bhopal **68** 23 20N 77 30E
Bhor **70** 18 12N 73 53E
Bhubaneswar **69** 20 15N 85 50E
Bhuj **68** 23 15N 69 49E
Bhumibol Dam **72** 17 15N 98 58E
Bhusaval **68** 21 3N 75 46E
Bhutan ■ **69** 27 25N 90 30E
Biafra, B. of = Bonny, Bight of **85** 3 30N 9 20E
Biak **73** 1 10S 136 6E
Biała **28** 50 24N 17 40E
Biała →, Białystok, Poland **28** 53 11N 23 4E
Biała →, Tarnów, Poland **27** 50 3N 20 55E
Biała Piska **28** 53 37N 22 5E
Biała Podlaska **28** 52 4N 23 6E
Biała Podlaska □ **28** 52 0N 23 0E
Biała Rawska **28** 51 48N 20 29E
Białobrzegi **28** 52 27N 21 3E
Białogard **28** 54 2N 15 58E
Białowieża **28** 52 41N 23 49E
Biały Bór **28** 53 53N 16 51E
Białystok **28** 53 10N 23 10E
Białystok □ **28** 53 9N 23 10E
Biancavilla **41** 37 39N 14 50E
Biaro **73** 2 5N 125 26E
Biarritz **20** 43 29N 1 33W
Biasca **25** 46 22N 8 58E
Biba **86** 28 55N 31 0E
Bibala **89** 14 44S 13 24E
Bibane, Bahiret el **83** 33 16N 11 13E
Bibbiena **39** 43 43N 11 50E
Bibby I. **109** 61 55N 93 0W
Biberach **25** 48 5N 9 49E
Bibey → **30** 42 24N 7 13W
Bibiani **84** 6 30N 2 8W
Bibile **70** 7 10N 81 25E
Biboohra **98** 16 56S 145 25E
Bibungwa **90** 2 40S 28 15E
Bic **107** 48 20N 68 41W
Bicaj **44** 42 0N 20 25E
Bicaz **46** 46 53N 26 5E
Biccari **41** 41 23N 15 12E
Biche, La → **108** 59 57N 123 50W
Bichena **87** 10 28N 38 10E
Bicknell, Ind., U.S.A. **114** 38 50N 87 20W
Bicknell, Utah, U.S.A. **119** 38 16N 111 35W
Bida **85** 9 3N 5 58E
Bidar **70** 17 55N 77 35E
Biddeford **107** 43 30N 70 28W
Biddiyā **62** 32 7N 35 4E
Biddū **62** 31 50N 35 8E
Biddwara **87** 5 11N 38 34E
Bideford **13** 51 1N 4 13W
Bidor **71** 4 6N 101 15E
Bié, Planalto de **89** 12 0S 16 0E
Bieber **118** 41 4N 121 6W
Biebrza → **28** 53 13N 22 25E
Biecz **27** 49 44N 21 15E
Biel (Bienne) **25** 47 8N 7 14E
Bielawa **28** 50 43N 16 37E
Bielé Karpaty **27** 49 5N 18 0E
Bielefeld **24** 52 2N 8 31E
Bielersee **25** 47 6N 7 5E
Biella **38** 45 33N 8 3E
Bielsk Podlaski **28** 52 47N 23 12E
Bielsko-Biała **27** 49 50N 19 2E
Bielsko-Biała □ **27** 49 45N 19 15E
Bien Hoa **71** 10 57N 106 49E
Bienfait **109** 49 10N 102 50W
Bienne = Biel **25** 47 8N 7 14E
Bienvenida **31** 38 18N 6 12W
Bienville, L. **106** 55 5N 72 40W
Biescas **32** 42 37N 0 20W
Biese → **24** 52 53N 11 46E
Biesiesfontein **92** 30 57S 17 58E
Bietigheim **25** 48 57N 9 8E
Biferno → **41** 41 59N 15 2E
Big → **107** 54 50N 58 55W
Big B. **107** 55 43N 60 35W
Big Beaver **109** 49 10N 105 10W
Big Belt Mts. **118** 46 50N 111 30W
Big Bend **93** 26 50S 32 2E
Big Bend Nat. Park **117** 29 15N 103 15W
Big Black → **117** 32 0N 91 5W
Big Blue → **116** 39 11N 96 40W
Big Cr. → **108** 51 42N 122 41W
Big Cypress Swamp **115** 26 12N 81 10W
Big Falls **116** 48 11N 93 48W
Big Fork → **116** 48 31N 93 43W
Big Horn **118** 46 11N 107 25W
Big Horn Mts. = Bighorn Mts. **118** 44 30N 107 30W
Big Lake **117** 31 12N 101 25W
Big Moose **113** 43 49N 74 58W
Big Muddy → **116** 48 8N 104 36W
Big Pine **119** 37 12N 118 17W
Big Piney **118** 42 32N 110 3W
Big Quill L. **109** 51 55N 104 50W
Big Rapids **114** 43 42N 85 27W
Big River **109** 53 50N 107 0W
Big Run **112** 40 57N 78 55W
Big Sable Pt. **114** 44 5N 86 30W
Big Sand L. **109** 57 45N 99 45W
Big Sandy **118** 48 12N 110 9W
Big Sandy Cr. → **116** 38 6N 102 29W
Big Sioux → **116** 42 30N 96 25W
Big Spring **117** 32 10N 101 25W
Big Springs **116** 41 4N 102 3W
Big Stone City **116** 45 20N 96 30W
Big Stone Gap **115** 36 52N 82 45W
Big Stone L. **116** 45 30N 96 35W
Big Trout L. **106** 53 40N 90 0W
Biganos **20** 44 39N 0 59W
Bigfork **118** 48 3N 114 2W
Biggar, Can. **109** 52 4N 108 0W
Biggar, U.K. **14** 55 38N 3 31W
Biggenden **99** 25 31S 152 4E
Bighorn → **118** 46 9N 107 28W
Bighorn Mts. **118** 44 30N 107 30W
Bignona **84** 12 52N 16 14W
Bigorre **20** 43 6N 0 5E
Bigstone L. **109** 53 42N 95 44W
Bigtimber **118** 45 53N 110 0W
Bigwa **90** 7 10S 39 10E
Bihać **39** 44 49N 15 57E
Bihar **69** 25 5N 85 40E
Bihar □ **69** 25 0N 86 0E
Biharamulo **90** 2 25S 31 25E
Biharamulo □ **90** 2 30S 31 20E
Biharkeresztes **27** 47 8N 21 44E
Bihor □ **46** 47 0N 22 10E
Bihor, Munţii **46** 46 29N 22 47E
Bijagós, Arquipélago dos **84** 11 15N 16 10W
Bijaipur **68** 26 2N 77 20E
Bijapur, Mad. P., India **70** 18 50N 80 50E
Bijapur, Mysore, India **70** 16 50N 75 55E
Bijār **64** 35 52N 47 35E
Bijeljina **42** 44 46N 19 17E
Bijelo Polje **42** 43 1N 19 45E
Bijie **77** 27 20N 105 16E
Bijnor **68** 29 27N 78 11E
Bikaner **68** 28 2N 73 18E
Bikapur **69** 26 30N 82 7E
Bikin **59** 46 50N 134 20E
Bikini Atoll **94** 12 0N 167 30E
Bikoué **85** 3 55N 11 50E
Bilād Banī Bū 'Ali **65** 22 0N 59 20E
Bilara **68** 26 14N 73 53E
Bilaspur, Mad. P., India **69** 22 2N 82 15E

Bilaspur, Punjab, India 68 31 19N 76 50 E
Bilauk Taung dan 71 13 0N 99 0 E
Bilbao 32 43 16N 2 56W
Bilbeis 86 30 25N 31 34 E
Bilbor 46 47 6N 25 30 E
Bildudalur 50 65 41N 23 36W
Bileća 42 42 53N 18 27 E
Bilecik 64 40 5N 30 5 E
Biłgoraj 28 50 33N 22 42 E
Bilibino 59 68 3N 166 20 E
Bilibiza 91 12 30 S 40 20 E
Bilir 59 65 40N 131 20 E
Bilishti 44 40 37N 21 2 E
Bill 116 43 18N 105 18W
Billabong Creek 100 35 5 S 144 2 E
Billingham 12 54 36N 1 18W
Billings 118 45 43N 108 29W
Billingsfors 48 58 59N 12 15 E
Billiton Is = Belitung 72 3 10 S 107 50 E
Billom 20 45 43N 3 20 E
Bilma 81 18 50N 13 30 E
Bilo Gora 42 45 53N 17 15 E
Biloela 97 24 24 S 150 31 E
Biloxi 117 30 24N 88 53W
Bilpa Morea Claypan 99 25 0 S 140 0 E
Biltine 81 14 40N 20 50 E
Bilyana 98 18 5 S 145 50 E
Bilyarsk 55 54 58N 50 22 E
Bima 73 8 22 S 118 49 E
Bimban 86 24 24N 32 54 E
Bimberi Peak 100 35 44 S 148 51 E
Bimbila 85 8 54N 0 5 E
Bimbo 88 4 15N 18 33 E
Bimini Is. 121 25 42N 79 25W
Bin Xian 77 35 2N 108 4 E
Bina-Etawah 68 24 13N 78 14 E
Binalbagan 73 10 12N 122 50 E
Binalong 100 34 40 S 148 39 E
Binalud, Kuh-e 65 36 30N 58 30 E
Binatang 72 2 10N 111 40 E
Binche 16 50 26N 4 10 E
Binda 99 27 52 S 147 21 E
Bindle 99 27 40 S 148 45 E
Bindura 91 17 18 S 31 18 E
Bingara, N.S.W., Austral. 99 29 52 S 150 36 E
Bingara, Queens., Austral. 99 28 10 S 144 37 E
Bingen 25 49 57N 7 53 E
Bingerville 84 5 18N 3 49W
Bingham 107 45 5N 69 50W
Bingham Canyon 118 40 31N 112 10W
Binghamton 114 42 9N 75 54W
Bingöl 64 38 53N 40 29 E
Binh Dinh = An Nhon 71 13 55N 109 7 E
Binh Son 71 15 20N 108 40 E
Binjai 72 3 20N 98 30 E
Binnaway 99 31 28 S 149 24 E
Binongko 73 5 55 S 123 55 E
Binscarth 109 50 37N 101 17W
Bint Jubayl 62 33 8N 35 25 E
Bintan 72 1 0N 104 0 E
Bintulu 72 3 10N 113 0 E
Bintuni (Steenkool) 73 2 7 S 133 32 E
Binyamina 62 32 32N 34 56 E
Binyang 77 23 12N 108 47 E
Binz 24 54 23N 13 37 E
Binzert = Bizerte 83 37 15N 9 50 E
Bío Bío □ 124 37 35 S 72 0W
Biograd 39 43 56N 15 29 E
Biokovo 42 43 23N 17 0 E
Biougra 82 30 15N 9 14W
Biq'at Bet Netofa 62 32 49N 35 22 E
Bîr Abu Hashim 86 23 42N 34 6 E
Bîr Abu M'nqar 86 26 33N 27 33 E
Bîr Adal Deib 86 22 35N 36 10 E
Bi'r al Malfa 83 31 58N 15 18 E
Bir Aouine 83 32 25N 9 18 E
Bîr 'Asal 86 25 55N 34 20 E
Bir Autrun 81 18 15N 26 40 E
Bi'r Dhu'fân 83 31 59N 14 32 E
Bîr Diqnash 86 31 3N 25 23 E
Bir el Abbes 82 26 7N 6 9W
Bir el Ater 83 34 46N 8 3 E
Bîr el Basur 86 29 51N 25 49 E
Bîr el Gellaz 86 30 50N 26 40 E
Bîr el Shaqqa 86 30 54N 25 1 E
Bîr Fuad 86 30 35N 26 28 E
Bîr Haimur 86 22 45N 33 40 E
Bir Jdid 82 33 26N 8 0W
Bîr Kanayis 86 24 59N 33 15 E
Bîr Kerawein 86 27 10N 28 25 E
Bir Lahrache 83 32 1N 8 12 E
Bîr Maql 86 23 7N 33 40 E
Bîr Misaha 86 22 13N 27 59 E
Bir Mogrein 82 25 10N 11 25W
Bi'r Mubayrīk 64 23 22N 39 8 E
Bîr Murr 86 23 28N 30 10 E
Bi'r Nabālā 62 31 52N 35 12 E
Bîr Nakheila 86 24 1N 30 50 E
Bîr Qatrani 86 30 55N 26 10 E
Bîr Ranga 86 24 25N 35 15 E
Bir, Ras 87 12 0N 43 20 E
Bîr Sahara 86 22 54N 28 40 E
Bîr Seiyâla 86 26 10N 33 50 E
Bir Semguine 82 30 1N 5 39W
Bîr Shalatein 86 23 5N 35 25 E
Bîr Shebb 86 22 25N 29 40 E
Bîr Shût 86 23 50N 35 15 E
Bîr Terfawi 86 22 57N 28 55 E
Bîr Umm Qubûr 86 24 35N 34 2 E
Bîr Ungât 86 22 8N 33 48 E
Bîr Za'farâna 86 29 10N 32 40 E
Bîr Zāmūs 83 24 16N 15 6 E
Bi'r Zayt 62 31 59N 35 11 E
Bîr Zeidûn 86 25 45N 33 40 E
Bira 73 2 3 S 132 2 E
Bîra 46 47 2N 27 3 E
Birak Sulaymān 62 31 42N 35 7 E
Biramféro 84 11 40N 9 10W
Birao 81 10 20N 22 47 E
Birawa 90 2 20 S 28 48 E
Bîrca 46 43 59N 23 36 E
Birch Hills 109 52 59N 105 25W
Birch I. 109 52 26N 99 54W
Birch L., N.W.T., Can. 108 62 4N 116 33W
Birch L., Ont., Can. 106 51 23N 92 18W
Birch L., U.S.A. 106 47 48N 91 43W
Birch Mts. 108 57 30N 113 10W
Birch River 109 52 24N 101 6W
Birchip 99 35 56 S 142 55 E
Birchiş 46 45 58N 22 9 E
Bird 109 56 30N 94 13W
Bird City 116 39 48N 101 33W
Bird I., Austral. 97 22 10 S 155 28 E
Bird I., S. Afr. 92 32 3 S 18 17 E
Bird I. = Aves, I. de 121 12 0N 67 30W
Birdlip 13 51 50N 2 7W
Birdsville 97 25 51 S 139 20 E
Birdum 96 15 39 S 133 13 E
Birecik 64 37 0N 38 0 E
Bireuen 72 5 14N 96 39 E
Birifo 84 13 30N 14 0W
Birigui 125 21 18 S 50 16W
Birk 86 18 8N 41 30 E
Birka 86 22 11N 40 38 E
Birkenfeld 25 49 39N 7 11 E
Birkenhead 12 53 24N 3 1W
Birket Qârûn 86 29 30N 30 40 E
Birkfeld 26 47 21N 15 45 E
Birkhadem 82 36 43N 3 3 E
Bîrlad 46 46 15N 27 38 E
Birmingham, U.K. 13 52 30N 1 55W
Birmingham, U.S.A. 115 33 31N 86 50W
Birmitrapur 69 22 24N 84 46 E
Birni Ngaouré 85 13 5N 2 51 E
Birni Nkonni 85 13 55N 5 15 E
Birnin Gwari 85 11 0N 6 45 E
Birnin Kebbi 85 12 32N 4 12 E
Birnin Kudu 85 11 30N 9 29 E
Birobidzhan 59 48 50N 132 50 E
Birqīn 62 32 27N 35 15 E
Birr 15 53 7N 7 55W
Birrie → 99 29 43 S 146 37 E
Birsilpur 68 28 11N 72 15 E
Birsk 52 55 25N 55 30 E
Birtin 46 46 59N 22 31 E
Birtle 109 50 30N 101 5W
Biryuchiy 56 46 10N 35 0 E
Birzai 54 56 11N 24 45 E
Bîrzava 46 46 7N 21 59 E
Bisa 73 1 15 S 127 28 E
Bisáccia 41 41 0N 15 20 E
Bisacquino 40 37 42N 13 13 E
Bisalpur 69 28 14N 79 48 E
Bisbal, La 32 41 58N 3 2 E
Bisbee 119 31 30N 110 0W
Biscarrosse, Étang de 20 44 21N 1 10W
Biscay, B. of 6 45 0N 2 0W
Biscayne B. 115 25 40N 80 12W
Biscéglie 41 41 14N 16 30 E
Bischofshofen 26 47 26N 13 14 E
Bischofswerda 24 51 8N 14 11 E
Bischwiller 19 48 41N 7 50 E
Biscoe Bay 5 77 0 S 152 0W
Biscoe I. 5 66 0 S 67 0W
Biscostasing 106 47 18N 82 9W
Biševo 39 42 57N 16 3 E
Bisha 87 15 30N 37 31 E
Bisha, Wadi → 86 21 24N 43 26 E
Bishop, Calif., U.S.A. 119 37 20N 118 26W
Bishop, Tex., U.S.A. 117 27 35N 97 49W
Bishop Auckland 12 54 40N 1 40W
Bishop's Falls 107 49 2N 55 30W
Bishop's Stortford 13 51 52N 0 11 E
Bisignano 41 39 30N 16 17 E
Bisina, L. 90 1 38N 33 56 E
Biskra 83 34 50N 5 44 E
Biskupiec 28 53 53N 20 58 E
Bislig 73 8 15N 126 27 E
Bismarck 116 46 49N 100 49W
Bismarck Arch. 94 2 30 S 150 0 E
Bismarck Sea 98 4 10 S 146 50 E
Bismark 24 52 39N 11 31 E
Biso 90 1 44N 31 26 E
Bison 116 45 34N 102 28W
Bispfors 50 63 1N 16 37 E
Bispgården 48 63 2N 16 40 E
Bissagos = Bijagós, Arquipélago dos 84 11 15N 16 10W
Bissau 84 11 45N 15 45W
Bissett 109 51 2N 95 41W
Bissikrima 84 10 50N 10 58W
Bistcho L. 108 59 45N 118 50W
Bistreţu 46 43 54N 23 23 E
Bistrica = Ilirska-Bistrica 39 45 34N 14 14 E
Bistriţa 46 47 9N 24 35 E
Bistriţa → 46 46 30N 26 57 E
Bistriţa Năsăud □ 46 47 15N 24 30 E
Bistriţei, Munţii 46 47 15N 25 40 E
Biswan 69 27 29N 81 2 E
Bisztynek 28 54 8N 20 53 E
Bitam 88 2 5N 11 25 E
Bitburg 25 49 58N 6 32 E
Bitche 19 49 2N 7 25 E
Bitkine 81 11 59N 18 13 E
Bitlis 64 38 20N 42 3 E
Bitola (Bitolj) 42 41 5N 21 10 E
Bitonto 41 41 7N 16 40 E
Bitter Creek 118 41 39N 108 36W
Bitter L. = Buheirat-Murrat-el-Kubra 86 30 15N 32 40 E
Bitterfeld 24 51 36N 12 20 E
Bitterfontein 92 31 0 S 18 32 E
Bitterroot → 118 46 52N 114 6W
Bitterroot Range 118 46 0N 114 20W
Bitti 40 40 29N 9 20 E
Bittou 85 11 17N 0 18W
Biu 85 10 40N 12 3 E
Bivolari 46 47 31N 27 27 E
Bivolu 46 47 16N 25 58 E
Biwa-Ko 74 35 15N 136 10 E
Biwabik 116 47 33N 92 19W
Bixad 46 47 56N 23 28 E
Biyang 77 32 38N 113 21 E
Biysk 58 52 40N 85 0 E
Bizana 93 30 50 S 29 52 E
Bizerte (Binzert) 83 37 15N 9 50 E
Bjargtangar 50 65 30N 24 30W
Bjelasica 42 42 50N 19 40 E
Bjelašnica 42 43 43N 18 9 E
Bjelovar 42 45 56N 16 49 E
Bjerringbro 49 56 23N 9 39 E
Björbo 48 60 27N 14 44 E
Björneborg 48 59 14N 14 16 E
Bjørnøya 4 74 30N 19 0 E
Bjuv 49 56 5N 12 55 E
Blace 42 43 18N 21 17 E
Blachownia 28 50 49N 18 56 E
Black →, Can. 112 44 42N 79 19W
Black →, Ark., U.S.A. 117 35 38N 91 19W
Black →, N.Y., U.S.A. 113 43 59N 76 4W
Black →, Wis., U.S.A. 116 43 52N 91 22W
Black Diamond 108 50 45N 114 14W
Black Forest = Schwarzwald 25 48 0N 8 0 E
Black Hills 116 44 0N 103 50W
Black I. 109 51 12N 96 30W
Black L., Can. 109 59 12N 105 15W
Black L., U.S.A. 114 45 28N 84 15W
Black Mesa, Mt. 117 36 57N 102 55W
Black Mt. = Mynydd Du 13 51 45N 3 45W
Black Mts. 13 51 52N 3 5W
Black Range 119 33 30N 107 55W
Black River 121 18 0N 77 50W
Black River Falls 116 44 23N 90 52W
Black Sea 9 43 30N 35 0 E
Black Sugarloaf, Mt. 100 31 18 S 151 35 E
Black Volta → 84 8 41N 1 33W
Black Warrior → 115 32 32N 87 51W
Blackall 97 24 25 S 145 45 E
Blackball 101 42 22 S 171 26 E
Blackbull 98 17 55 S 141 45 E
Blackburn 12 53 44N 2 30W
Blackduck 116 47 43N 94 32W
Blackfoot 118 43 13N 112 12W
Blackfoot → 118 46 52N 113 53W
Blackfoot River Res. 118 43 0N 111 35W
Blackie 108 50 36N 113 37W
Blackpool 12 53 48N 3 3W
Blackriver 112 44 46N 83 17W
Blacks Harbour 107 45 3N 66 49W
Blacksburg 114 37 17N 80 23W
Blacksod B. 15 54 6N 10 0W
Blackstone 114 37 6N 78 0W
Blackstone → 108 61 5N 122 55W
Blackstone Ra. 96 26 00 S 129 00 E
Blackville 107 46 44N 65 50W
Blackwater 98 23 35 S 148 53 E
Blackwater →, Ireland 15 51 55N 7 50W
Blackwater →, U.K. 15 54 31N 6 35W
Blackwater Cr. → 99 25 56 S 144 30 E
Blackwell 117 36 55N 97 20W
Blaenau Ffestiniog 12 53 0N 3 57W
Blagaj 42 43 16N 17 55 E
Blagodarnoye 57 45 7N 43 37 E
Blagoevgrad (Gorna Dzhumayo) 42 42 2N 23 5 E
Blagoveshchensk 59 50 20N 127 30 E
Blain 18 47 29N 1 45W
Blaine 118 48 59N 122 43W
Blaine Lake 109 52 51N 106 52W
Blainville 19 48 33N 6 23 E
Blair 116 41 38N 96 10W
Blair Athol 97 22 42 S 147 31 E
Blair Atholl 14 56 46N 3 50W
Blairgowrie 14 56 36N 3 20W
Blairmore 108 49 40N 114 25W
Blairsville 112 40 27N 79 15W
Blaj 46 46 10N 23 57 E
Blake Pt. 116 48 12N 88 27W
Blakely 115 31 22N 85 0W
Blâmont 19 48 35N 6 50 E
Blanc, C. 83 37 15N 9 56 E
Blanc, Le 20 46 37N 1 3 E
Blanc, Mont 21 45 48N 6 50 E
Blanca, Bahía 128 39 10 S 61 30W
Blanca Peak 119 37 35N 105 29W
Blanchard 117 35 8N 97 40W
Blanche L., S. Austral., Austral. 97 29 15 S 139 40 E
Blanche L., W. Austral., Austral. 96 22 25 S 123 17 E
Blanco, S. Afr. 92 33 55 S 22 23 E
Blanco, U.S.A. 117 30 7N 98 30W
Blanco → 124 30 20 S 68 42W
Blanco, C., C. Rica 121 9 34N 85 8W
Blanco, C., Spain 33 39 21N 2 51 E
Blanco, C., U.S.A. 118 42 50N 124 40W
Blanda → 50 65 20N 19 40W
Blandford Forum 13 50 52N 2 10W
Blanding 119 37 35N 109 30W
Blanes 32 41 40N 2 48 E
Blanice → 26 49 10N 14 5 E
Blankenberge 16 51 20N 3 9 E
Blankenburg 24 51 46N 10 56 E
Blanquefort 20 44 55N 0 38W
Blanquillo 125 32 53 S 55 37W
Blansko 27 49 22N 16 40 E
Blantyre 91 15 45 S 35 0 E
Blarney 15 51 57N 8 35W
Błaski 28 51 38N 18 30 E
Blatná 26 49 25N 13 52 E
Blatnitsa 43 43 41N 28 32 E
Blato 39 42 56N 16 48 E
Blaubeuren 25 48 24N 9 47 E
Blaydon 12 54 56N 1 47W
Blaye 20 45 8N 0 40W
Blaye-les-Mines 20 44 1N 2 8 E
Blayney 99 33 32 S 149 14 E
Blaze, Pt. 96 12 56 S 130 11 E
Błazowa 27 49 53N 22 7 E
Bleckede 24 53 18N 10 43 E
Bled 39 46 27N 14 7 E
Blednaya, Gora 58 76 20N 65 0 E
Bleiburg 26 46 35N 14 49 E
Blejeşti 46 44 19N 25 27 E
Blekinge län □ 49 56 20N 15 20 E
Blenheim, Can. 112 42 20N 82 0W
Blenheim, N.Z. 101 41 38 S 173 57 E
Bléone → 21 44 5N 6 0 E
Bletchley 13 51 59N 0 44W
Bleymard, Le 20 44 30N 3 42 E
Blida 82 36 30N 2 49 E
Blidet Amor 83 32 59N 5 58 E
Blidö 48 59 37N 18 53 E
Blidsberg 49 57 56N 13 30 E
Bligh Sound 101 44 47 S 167 32 E
Blind River 106 46 10N 82 58W
Blinishti 44 41 52N 19 58 E
Blitar 73 8 5 S 112 11 E
Blitta 85 8 23N 1 6 E
Block I. 114 41 11N 71 35W
Block Island Sd. 113 41 17N 71 35W
Bloemfontein 92 29 6 S 26 14 E
Bloemhof 92 27 38 S 25 32 E
Blois 18 47 35N 1 20 E
Blomskog 48 59 16N 12 2 E
Blönduós 50 65 40N 20 12W
Błonie 28 52 12N 20 37 E
Bloodvein → 109 51 47N 96 43W
Bloody Foreland 15 55 10N 8 18W
Bloomer 116 45 8N 91 30W
Bloomfield, Can. 112 43 59N 77 14W
Bloomfield, Iowa, U.S.A. 116 40 44N 92 26W
Bloomfield, N. Mexico, U.S.A. 119 36 46N 107 59W
Bloomfield, Nebr., U.S.A. 116 42 38N 97 40W
Bloomfield River Mission 98 15 56 S 145 22 E
Bloomington, Ill., U.S.A. 116 40 27N 89 0W
Bloomington, Ind., U.S.A. 114 39 10N 86 30W
Bloomsburg 114 41 0N 76 30W
Blora 73 6 57 S 111 25 E
Blossburg 112 41 40N 77 4W
Blouberg 93 23 8 S 29 0 E
Blountstown 115 30 28N 85 5W
Bludenz 26 47 10N 9 50 E
Blue Island 114 41 40N 87 40W
Blue Lake 118 40 53N 124 0W
Blue Mesa Res. 119 38 30N 107 15W
Blue Mts., Austral. 97 33 40 S 150 0 E
Blue Mts., Ore., U.S.A. 118 45 15N 119 0W
Blue Mts., Pa., U.S.A. 114 40 30N 76 30W
Blue Mud B. 97 13 30 S 136 0 E
Blue Nile = An Nîl el Azraq □ 87 12 30N 34 30
Blue Nile = Nîl el Azraq → 87 15 38N 32 31
Blue Rapids 116 39 41N 96 39W
Blue Ridge Mts. 115 36 30N 80 15W
Blue Stack Mts. 15 54 46N 8 5W
Blueberry → 108 56 45N 120 49W
Bluefield 114 37 18N 81 14W
Bluefields 121 12 20N 83 50W
Bluff, Austral. 98 23 35 S 149 4
Bluff, N.Z. 101 46 37 S 168 20
Bluff, U.S.A. 119 37 17N 109 33
Bluffton 114 40 43N 85 9
Blumenau 125 27 0 S 49 0
Blumenthal 24 53 5N 8 20
Blunt 116 44 32N 100 0
Bly 118 42 23N 121 0
Blyberg 48 61 9N 14 11
Blyth, Can. 112 43 44N 81 26
Blyth, U.K. 12 55 8N 1 32
Blythe 119 33 40N 114 33
Blytheswood 112 42 8N 82 37
Bø 47 59 25N 9 3
Bo 84 7 55N 11 50
Bo Duc 71 11 58N 106 50
Bo Hai 76 39 0N 120 0
Bo Xian 77 33 50N 115 45
Boa Vista 126 2 48N 60 30
Boaco 121 12 29N 85 35
Boal 30 43 25N 6 49
Boatman 99 27 16 S 146 55
Bobai 77 22 17N 109 59
Bobbili 70 18 35N 83 30
Bóbbio 38 44 47N 9 22
Bobcaygeon 106 44 33N 78 33
Böblingen 25 48 41N 9 1
Bobo-Dioulasso 84 11 8N 4 13
Boboc 43 45 13N 26 59
Bobolice 28 53 58N 16 37
Boboshevo 42 42 9N 23 0
Bobov Dol 42 42 20N 23 0
Bóbr → 28 52 4N 15 4
Bobraomby, Tanjon' i 93 12 40 S 49 10
Bobrinets 56 48 4N 32 5
Bobrov 55 51 5N 40 2
Bobruysk 54 53 10N 29 15
Bôca do Acre 126 8 50 S 67 27
Boca, La 120 8 56N 79 30
Boca Raton 115 26 21N 80
Bocaiúva 127 17 7 S 43 49
Bocanda 84 7 5N 4 31
Bocaranga 88 7 0N 15 35
Bocas del Toro 121 9 15N 82 20
Boceguillas 32 41 20N 3 39
Bochnia 27 49 58N 20 27
Bocholt 24 51 50N 6 35
Bochov 26 50 9N 13 3
Bochum 24 51 28N 7 12
Bockenem 24 52 1N 10 8
Boćki 28 52 39N 23 3
Bocşa Montană 42 45 21N 21 47
Boda 88 4 19N 17 26
Böda 49 57 15N 17 3
Bodafors 49 57 48N 14 23
Bodaybo 59 57 50N 114
Boden 50 65 50N 21 42
Bodensee 25 47 35N 9 25
Bodenteich 24 52 49N 10 41
Bodhan 70 18 40N 77 44
Bodinayakkanur 70 10 2N 77 1
Bodinga 85 12 58N 5 1
Bodmin 13 50 28N 4 44
Bodmin Moor 13 50 33N 4 3
Bodrog → 27 48 15N 21 3
Bodrum 64 37 5N 27 3
Bódva → 27 48 19N 20 4
Boegoebergdam 92 29 7 S 22
Boën 21 45 44N 4
Boende 88 0 24 S 21 1
Boerne 117 29 48N 98 4
Boffa 84 10 16N 14
Bogalusa 117 30 50N 89

Bogan → **97** 29 59 S 146 17 E
Bogan Gate **99** 33 7 S 147 49 E
Bogantungan **98** 23 41 S 147 17 E
Bogata **117** 33 26N 95 10W
Bogatić **42** 44 51N 19 30 E
Bogenfels **92** 27 25 S 15 25 E
Bogense **49** 55 34N 10 5 E
Boggabilla **99** 28 36 S 150 24 E
Boggabri **99** 30 45 S 150 0 E
Boggeragh Mts. **15** 52 2N 8 55W
Bognor Regis **13** 50 47N 0 40W
Bogø **49** 54 55N 12 2 E
Bogo **73** 11 3N 124 0 E
Bogodukhov **54** 50 9N 35 33 E
Bogong, Mt. **97** 36 47 S 147 17 E
Bogor **73** 6 36 S 106 48 E
Bogoroditsk **55** 53 47N 38 8 E
Bogorodsk **55** 56 4N 43 30 E
Bogorodskoye **59** 52 22N 140 30 E
Bogoso **84** 5 38N 2 3W
Bogota **126** 4 34N 74 0W
Bogotol **58** 56 15N 89 50 E
Bogra **69** 24 51N 89 22 E
Boguchany **59** 58 40N 97 30 E
Boguchar **57** 49 55N 40 32 E
Bogué **84** 16 45N 14 10W
Boguslav **56** 49 47N 30 53 E
Boguszów **28** 50 45N 16 12 E
Bohain **19** 49 59N 3 28 E
Bohemia **26** 50 0N 14 0 E
Bohemian Forest = Böhmerwald **25** 49 30N 12 40 E
Bohena Cr. → **99** 30 17 S 149 42 E
Bohinjska Bistrica **39** 46 17N 14 1 E
Böhmerwald **25** 49 30N 12 40 E
Bohmte **24** 52 24N 8 20 E
Bohol **73** 9 50N 124 10 E
Bohotleh **63** 8 20N 46 25 E
Boi **85** 9 35N 9 27 E
Boi, Pta. de **125** 23 55 S 45 15W
Boiano **41** 41 28N 14 29 E
Boileau, C. **96** 17 40 S 122 7 E
Boinitsa **42** 43 58N 22 32 E
Boise **118** 43 43N 116 9W
Boise City **117** 36 45N 102 30W
Boissevain **109** 49 15N 100 5W
Boite → **39** 46 5N 12 5 E
Boitzenburg **24** 53 16N 13 36 E
Boizenburg **24** 53 22N 10 42 E
Bojador C. **80** 26 0N 14 30W
Bojana → **42** 41 52N 19 22 E
Bojanowo **28** 51 43N 16 42 E
Bojnūrd **65** 37 30N 57 20 E
Bojonegoro **73** 7 11 S 111 54 E
Boju **85** 7 22N 7 55 E
Boka **42** 45 22N 20 52 E
Boka Kotorska **42** 42 23N 18 32 E
Bokala **84** 8 31N 4 33W
Boké **84** 10 56N 14 17W
Bokhara → **99** 29 55 S 146 42 E
Bokkos **85** 9 17N 9 1 E
Boknafjorden **47** 59 14N 5 40 E
Bokoro **81** 12 25N 17 14 E
Bokote **88** 0 12 S 21 8 E
Bokpyin **71** 11 18N 98 42 E
Boksitogorsk **54** 59 32N 33 56 E
Bokungu **88** 0 35 S 22 50 E
Bol, Chad **81** 13 30N 15 0 E
Bol, Yugo. **39** 43 18N 16 38 E
Bolama **84** 11 30N 15 30W
Bolan Pass **66** 29 50N 67 20 E
Bolaños → **120** 21 14N 104 8W
Bolbec **18** 49 30N 0 30 E
Boldeşti **46** 45 3N 26 2 E
Bole, China **75** 45 11N 81 37 E
Bole, Ethiopia **87** 6 36N 37 20 E
Bolekhov **54** 49 0N 24 0 E
Bolesławiec **28** 51 17N 15 37 E
Bolgatanga **85** 10 44N 0 53W
Bolgrad **56** 45 40N 28 32 E
Boli, China **76** 45 46N 130 31 E
Boli, Sudan **87** 6 2N 28 48 E
Bolinao C. **73** 16 23N 119 55 E
Bolívar, Argent. **124** 36 15 S 60 53W
Bolívar, Colomb. **126** 2 0N 77 0W
Bolivar, Mo., U.S.A. **117** 37 38N 93 22W
Bolivar, Tenn., U.S.A. **117** 35 14N 89 0W
Bolivia ■ **126** 17 6 S 64 0W
Boljevac **42** 43 51N 21 58 E
Bolkhov **55** 53 25N 36 0 E
Bollène **21** 44 18N 4 45 E
Bollnäs **48** 61 21N 16 24 E
Bollon **99** 28 2 S 147 29 E
Bollstabruk **48** 63 1N 17 40 E
Bollullos **31** 37 19N 6 32W
Bolmen **49** 56 55N 13 40 E
Bolobo **88** 2 6 S 16 20 E
Bologna **39** 44 30N 11 20 E
Bologne **19** 48 10N 5 8 E
Bologoye **54** 57 55N 34 0 E
Bolomba **88** 0 35N 19 0 E
Bolong **73** 7 6N 122 16 E
Boloven, Cao Nguyen **71** 15 10N 106 30 E
Bolpur **69** 23 40N 87 45 E
Bolsena **39** 42 40N 11 58 E
Bolsena, L. di **39** 42 35N 11 55 E
Bolshaya Glushitsa **55** 52 24N 50 29 E
Bolshaya Martynovka **57** 47 12N 41 46 E
Bolshaya Vradiyevka **56** 47 50N 30 40 E
Bolshereche **58** 56 4N 74 45 E
Bolshevik, Ostrov **59** 78 30N 102 0 E
Bolshezemelskaya Tundra **52** 67 0N 56 0 E
Bolshoi Kavkas **57** 42 50N 44 0 E
Bolshoy Anyuy → **59** 68 30N 160 49 E
Bolshoy Atlym **58** 62 25N 66 50 E
Bolshoy Begichev, Ostrov **59** 74 20N 112 30 E
Bolshoy Lyakhovskiy, Ostrov **59** 73 35N 142 0 E
Bolshoy Tokmak **56** 47 16N 35 42 E
Bol'shoy Tyuters, Ostrov **54** 59 51N 27 13 E
Bolsward **16** 53 3N 5 32 E
Boltaña **32** 42 28N 0 4 E
Boltigen **25** 46 38N 7 24 E
Bolton, Can. **112** 43 54N 79 45W
Bolton, U.K. **12** 53 35N 2 26W
Bolu **64** 40 45N 31 35 E
Bolvadin **64** 38 45N 31 4 E
Bolzano (Bozen) **39** 46 30N 11 20 E
Bom Despacho **127** 19 43 S 45 15W
Bom Jesus da Lapa **127** 13 15 S 43 25W
Boma **88** 5 50 S 13 4 E
Bomaderry **99** 34 52 S 150 37 E
Bombala **97** 36 56 S 149 15 E
Bombarral **31** 39 15N 9 9W
Bombay **70** 18 55N 72 50 E
Bomboma **88** 2 25N 18 55 E
Bombombwa **90** 1 40N 25 40 E
Bomi Hills **84** 7 1N 10 38W
Bomili **90** 1 45N 27 5 E
Bomokandi → **90** 3 39N 26 8 E
Bomongo **88** 1 27N 18 21 E
Bomu → **88** 4 40N 23 30 E
Bon C. **83** 37 1N 11 2 E
Bonaire **121** 12 10N 68 15W
Bonang **99** 37 11 S 148 41 E
Bonanza **121** 13 54N 84 35W
Bonaparte Archipelago **96** 14 0 S 124 30 E
Boñar **30** 42 52N 5 19W
Bonaventure **107** 48 5N 65 32W
Bonavista **107** 48 40N 53 5W
Bonavista, C. **107** 48 42N 53 5W
Bondeno **39** 44 53N 11 22 E
Bondo **88** 3 55N 23 53 E
Bondoukou **84** 8 2N 2 47W
Bondowoso **73** 7 56 S 113 49 E
Bone Rate **73** 7 25 S 121 5 E
Bone Rate, Kepulauan **73** 6 30 S 121 10 E
Bone, Teluk **73** 4 10 S 120 50 E
Bonefro **41** 41 42N 14 55 E
Bo'ness **14** 56 0N 3 38W
Bong Son = Hoai Nhon **71** 14 28N 109 1 E
Bongandanga **88** 1 24N 21 3 E
Bongor **81** 10 35N 15 20 E
Bongouanou **84** 6 42N 4 15W
Bonham **117** 33 30N 96 10W
Bonifacio **21** 41 24N 9 10 E
Bonifacio, Bouches de **40** 41 12N 9 15 E
Bonin Is. **94** 27 0N 142 0 E
Bonke **87** 6 5N 37 16 E
Bonn **24** 50 43N 7 6 E
Bonnat **20** 46 20N 1 54 E
Bonne Terre **117** 37 57N 90 33W
Bonners Ferry **118** 48 38N 116 21W
Bonnétable **18** 48 11N 0 25 E
Bonneuil-Matours **18** 46 41N 0 34 E
Bonneval **18** 48 11N 1 24 E
Bonneville **21** 46 5N 6 24 E
Bonney, L. **99** 37 50 S 140 20 E
Bonnie Rock **96** 30 29 S 118 22 E
Bonny, France **19** 47 34N 2 50 E
Bonny, Nigeria **85** 4 25N 7 13 E
Bonny → **85** 4 20N 7 10 E
Bonny, Bight of **88** 3 30N 9 20 E
Bonnyville **109** 54 20N 110 45W
Bonoi **73** 1 45 S 137 41 E
Bonorva **40** 40 25N 8 47 E
Bontang **72** 0 10N 117 30 E
Bonthain **73** 5 34 S 119 56 E
Bonthe **84** 7 30N 12 33W
Bontoc **73** 17 7N 120 58 E
Bonyeri **84** 5 1N 2 46W
Bonyhád **27** 46 18N 18 32 E
Booker **117** 36 29N 100 30W
Boolaboolka, L. **99** 32 38 S 143 10 E
Booligal **99** 33 58 S 144 53 E
Boom **16** 51 6N 4 20 E
Boonah **99** 27 58 S 152 41 E
Boone, Iowa, U.S.A. **116** 42 5N 93 53W
Boone, N.C., U.S.A. **115** 36 14N 81 43W
Booneville, Ark., U.S.A. **117** 35 10N 93 54W
Booneville, Miss., U.S.A. **115** 34 39N 88 34W
Boonville, Ind., U.S.A. **114** 38 3N 87 13W
Boonville, Mo., U.S.A. **116** 38 57N 92 45W
Boonville, N.Y., U.S.A. **114** 43 31N 75 20W
Boorindal **99** 30 22 S 146 11 E
Boorowa **99** 34 28 S 148 44 E
Boothia, Gulf of **105** 71 0N 90 0W
Boothia Pen. **104** 71 0N 94 0W
Bootle, Cumb., U.K. **12** 54 17N 3 24W
Bootle, Merseyside, U.K. **12** 53 28N 3 1W
Booué **88** 0 5 S 11 55 E
Bopeechee **99** 29 36 S 137 22 E
Bophuthatswana □ **92** 26 0 S 26 0 E
Boppard **25** 50 13N 7 36 E
Boquete **121** 8 49N 82 27W
Bor **26** 49 41N 12 45 E
Bôr **87** 6 10N 31 40 E
Bor, Sweden **49** 57 9N 14 10 E
Bor, Yugo. **42** 44 8N 22 7 E
Borah, Mt. **118** 44 19N 113 46W
Borama **63** 9 55N 43 7 E
Borang **87** 4 50N 30 59 E
Borås **49** 57 43N 12 56 E
Borāzjān **65** 29 22N 51 10 E
Borba, Brazil **126** 4 12 S 59 34W
Borba, Port. **31** 38 50N 7 26W
Borçka **57** 41 25N 41 41 E
Bordeaux **20** 44 50N 0 36W
Borden **107** 46 18N 63 47W
Borden I. **4** 78 30N 111 30W
Borders □ **14** 55 35N 2 50W
Bordertown **97** 36 19 S 140 45 E
Borðeyri **50** 65 12N 21 6W
Bordighera **38** 43 47N 7 40 E
Bordj bou Arreridj **83** 36 4N 4 45 E
Bordj Bourguiba **83** 32 12N 10 2 E
Bordj el Hobra **83** 32 9N 4 51 E
Bordj Fly Ste. Marie **82** 27 19N 2 32W
Bordj-in-Eker **83** 24 9N 5 3 E
Bordj Menaiel **83** 36 46N 3 43 E
Bordj Messouda **83** 30 12N 9 25 E
Bordj Nili **82** 33 28N 3 2 E
Bordj Omar Driss **83** 28 10N 6 40 E
Bordj Zelfana **83** 32 27N 4 15 E
Borek Wielkopolski **28** 51 54N 17 11 E
Borensberg **49** 58 34N 15 17 E
Borgarnes **50** 64 32N 21 55W
Børgefjellet **50** 65 20N 13 45 E
Borger, Neth. **16** 52 54N 6 44 E
Borger, U.S.A. **117** 35 40N 101 20W
Borghamn **49** 58 23N 14 41 E
Borgholm **49** 56 52N 16 39 E
Bórgia **41** 38 50N 16 30 E
Borgo San Dalmazzo **38** 44 19N 7 29 E
Borgo San Lorenzo **39** 43 57N 11 21 E
Borgo Valsugano **39** 46 3N 11 27 E
Borgomanero **38** 45 41N 8 28 E
Borgonovo Val Tidone **38** 45 1N 9 28 E
Borgorose **39** 42 12N 13 14 E
Borgosésia **38** 45 43N 8 17 E
Borgvattnet **48** 63 26N 15 48 E
Borislav **54** 49 18N 23 28 E
Borisoglebsk **55** 51 27N 42 5 E
Borisoglebskiy **55** 56 28N 43 59 E
Borisov **54** 54 17N 28 28 E
Borispol **54** 50 21N 30 59 E
Borja, Peru **126** 4 20 S 77 40W
Borja, Spain **32** 41 48N 1 34W
Borjas Blancas **32** 41 31N 0 52 E
Borken **24** 51 51N 6 52 E
Borkou **81** 18 15N 18 50 E
Borkum **24** 53 36N 6 42 E
Borlänge **48** 60 29N 15 26 E
Borley, C. **5** 66 15 S 52 30 E
Bormida → **38** 44 23N 8 13 E
Bórmio **38** 46 28N 10 22 E
Borna **24** 51 8N 12 31 E
Borneo **72** 1 0N 115 0 E
Bornholm **49** 55 10N 15 0 E
Bornholmsgattet **49** 55 15N 14 20 E
Borno □ **85** 12 30N 12 30 E
Bornos **31** 36 48N 5 42W
Bornu Yassa **85** 12 14N 12 25 E
Borobudur **73** 7 36 S 110 13 E
Borodino **54** 55 31N 35 40 E
Borogontsy **59** 62 42N 131 8 E
Boromo **84** 11 45N 2 58W
Borongan **73** 11 37N 125 26 E
Bororen **98** 24 13 S 151 33 E
Borotangba Mts. **87** 6 30N 25 0 E
Borovan **43** 43 27N 23 45 E
Borovichi **54** 58 25N 33 55 E
Borovsk **55** 55 12N 36 24 E
Borrby **49** 55 27N 14 10 E
Borriol **32** 40 4N 0 4W
Borroloola **97** 16 4 S 136 17 E
Borşa **46** 47 41N 24 50 E
Borsod-Abaúj-Zemplén □ **27** 48 20N 21 0 E
Bort-les-Orgues **20** 45 24N 2 29 E
Borth **13** 52 29N 4 3W
Borujerd **64** 33 55N 48 50 E
Borzhomi **57** 41 48N 43 28 E
Borzna **54** 51 18N 32 26 E
Borzya **59** 50 24N 116 31 E
Bosa **40** 40 17N 8 32 E
Bosanska Brod **42** 45 10N 18 0 E
Bosanska Dubica **39** 45 10N 16 50 E
Bosanska Gradiška **42** 45 10N 17 15 E
Bosanska Kostajnica **39** 45 11N 16 33 E
Bosanska Krupa **39** 44 53N 16 10 E
Bosanski Novi **39** 45 2N 16 22 E
Bosanski Samac **42** 45 3N 18 29 E
Bosansko Grahovo **39** 44 12N 16 26 E
Bosansko Petrovac **39** 44 35N 16 21 E
Bosaso **63** 11 12N 49 18 E
Boscastle **13** 50 42N 4 42W
Boscotrecase **41** 40 46N 14 28 E
Bose **77** 23 53N 106 35 E
Boshan **76** 36 28N 117 49 E
Boshoek **92** 25 30 S 27 9 E
Boshof **92** 28 31 S 25 13 E
Boshrūyeh **65** 33 50N 57 30 E
Bosilegrad **42** 42 30N 22 27 E
Boskovice **27** 49 29N 16 40 E
Bosna → **42** 45 4N 18 29 E
Bosna i Hercegovina □ **42** 44 0N 18 0 E
Bosnia = Bosna □ **42** 44 0N 18 0 E
Bosnik **73** 1 5 S 136 10 E
Bōsō-Hantō **74** 35 20N 140 20 E
Bosobolo **88** 4 15N 19 50 E
Bosporus = Karadeniz Boğazı **64** 41 10N 29 10 E
Bossangoa **88** 6 35N 17 30 E
Bossekop **50** 69 57N 23 15 E
Bossembélé **81** 5 25N 17 40 E
Bossier City **117** 32 28N 93 48W
Bosso **85** 13 43N 13 19 E
Bossut C. **96** 18 42 S 121 35 E
Bosten Hu **75** 41 55N 87 40 E
Boston, U.K. **12** 52 59N 0 2W
Boston, U.S.A. **114** 42 20N 71 0W
Boston Bar **108** 49 52N 121 30W
Bosut → **42** 45 20N 19 0 E
Boswell, Can. **108** 49 28N 116 45W
Boswell, Okla., U.S.A. **117** 34 1N 95 50W
Boswell, Pa., U.S.A. **112** 40 9N 79 2W
Botad **68** 22 15N 71 40 E
Botevgrad **43** 42 55N 23 47 E
Bothaville **92** 27 23 S 26 34 E
Bothnia, G. of **50** 63 0N 20 0 E
Bothwell, Austral. **99** 42 20 S 147 1 E
Bothwell, Can. **112** 42 38N 81 52W
Boticas **30** 41 41N 7 40W
Botletle → **92** 20 10 S 23 15 E
Botoroaga **46** 44 8N 25 32 E
Botoşani **46** 47 42N 26 41 E
Botoşani □ **46** 47 50N 26 50 E
Botro **84** 7 51N 5 19W
Botswana ■ **92** 22 0 S 24 0 E
Bottineau **116** 48 49N 100 25W
Bottrop **24** 51 34N 6 59 E
Botucatu **125** 22 55 S 48 30W
Botwood **107** 49 6N 55 23W
Bou Alam **82** 33 50N 1 26 E
Bou Ali **82** 27 11N 0 4W
Bou Djébéha **84** 18 25N 2 45W
Bou Guema **82** 28 49N 0 19 E
Bou Ismael **82** 36 38N 2 42 E
Bou Izakarn **82** 29 12N 9 46W
Bou Saâda **83** 35 11N 4 9 E
Bou Salem **83** 36 45N 9 2 E
Bouaké **84** 7 40N 5 2W
Bouar **88** 6 0N 15 40 E
Bouârfa **82** 32 32N 1 58 E
Bouca **88** 6 45N 18 25 E
Boucau **20** 43 32N 1 29W
Bouches-du-Rhône □ **21** 43 37N 5 2 E
Bouda **82** 27 50N 0 27W
Boudenib **82** 31 59N 3 31W
Boufarik **82** 36 34N 2 58 E
Bougainville C. **96** 13 57 S 126 4 E
Bougaroun, C. **83** 37 6N 6 30 E
Bougie = Bejaia **83** 36 42N 5 2 E
Bougouni **84** 11 30N 7 20W
Bouillon **16** 49 44N 5 3 E
Bouïra **83** 36 20N 3 59 E
Boulder, Austral. **96** 30 46 S 121 30 E
Boulder, Colo., U.S.A. **116** 40 3N 105 10W
Boulder, Mont., U.S.A. **118** 46 14N 112 4W
Boulder City **119** 36 0N 114 50W
Boulder Dam = Hoover Dam **119** 36 0N 114 45W
Bouli **84** 15 17N 12 18W
Boulia **97** 22 52 S 139 51 E
Bouligny **19** 49 17N 5 45 E
Boulogne → **18** 47 12N 1 47W
Boulogne-sur-Gesse **20** 43 18N 0 38 E
Boulogne-sur-Mer **19** 50 42N 1 36 E
Bouloire **18** 47 58N 0 33 E
Boulsa **85** 12 39N 0 34W
Boultoum **85** 14 45N 10 25 E
Boumalne **82** 31 25N 6 0W
Bouna **84** 9 10N 3 0W
Boundiali **84** 9 30N 6 20W
Bountiful **118** 40 57N 111 58W
Bounty I. **94** 48 0 S 178 30 E
Bourbon-Lancy **20** 46 37N 3 45 E
Bourbon-l'Archambault **20** 46 36N 3 4 E
Bourbonnais **20** 46 28N 3 0 E
Bourbonne-les-Bains **19** 47 59N 5 45 E
Bourem **85** 17 0N 0 24W
Bourg **20** 45 3N 0 34W
Bourg-Argental **21** 45 18N 4 32 E
Bourg-de-Péage **21** 45 2N 5 3 E
Bourg-en-Bresse **21** 46 13N 5 12 E
Bourg-St.-Andéol **21** 44 23N 4 39 E
Bourg-St.-Maurice **21** 45 35N 6 46 E
Bourganeuf **20** 45 57N 1 45 E
Bourges **19** 47 9N 2 25 E
Bourget **113** 45 26N 75 9W
Bourget, L. du **21** 45 44N 5 52 E
Bourgneuf, B. de **18** 47 3N 2 10W
Bourgneuf-en-Retz **18** 47 2N 1 58W
Bourgneuf-la-Fôret, Le **18** 48 10N 0 59W
Bourgogne **19** 47 0N 4 30 E
Bourgoin-Jallieu **21** 45 36N 5 17 E
Bourgueil **18** 47 17N 0 10 E
Bourke **97** 30 8 S 145 55 E
Bournemouth **13** 50 43N 1 53W
Bourriot-Bergonce **20** 44 7N 0 14W
Bouscat, Le **20** 44 53N 0 32W
Boussac **20** 46 22N 2 13 E
Boussens **20** 43 12N 0 58 E
Bousso **81** 10 34N 16 52 E
Boutilimit **84** 17 45N 14 40W
Boutonne → **20** 45 55N 0 43 E
Bouvet I. = Bouvetøya **7** 54 26 S 3 24 E
Bouvetøya **7** 54 26 S 3 24 E
Bouznika **82** 33 46N 7 6W
Bouzonville **19** 49 17N 6 32 E
Bova Marina **41** 37 59N 15 56 E
Bovalino Marina **41** 38 9N 16 10 E
Bovec **39** 46 20N 13 33 E
Bovigny **16** 50 12N 5 55 E
Bovill **118** 46 58N 116 27W
Bovino **41** 41 15N 15 20 E
Bow Island **108** 49 50N 111 23W
Bowbells **116** 48 47N 102 19W
Bowdle **116** 45 30N 99 40W
Bowen **97** 20 0 S 148 16 E
Bowen → **98** 20 24 S 147 20 E
Bowen Mts. **99** 37 0 S 148 0 E
Bowie, Ariz., U.S.A. **119** 32 15N 109 30W
Bowie, Tex., U.S.A. **117** 33 33N 97 50W
Bowland, Forest of **12** 54 0N 2 30W
Bowling Green, Ky., U.S.A. **114** 37 0N 86 25W
Bowling Green, Ohio, U.S.A. **114** 41 22N 83 40W
Bowling Green, C. **97** 19 19 S 147 25 E
Bowman **116** 46 12N 103 21W
Bowman I. **5** 65 0 S 104 0 E
Bowmans **99** 34 10 S 138 17 E
Bowmanville **106** 43 55N 78 41W
Bowmore **14** 55 45N 6 18W
Bowral **97** 34 26 S 150 27 E
Bowraville **99** 30 37 S 152 52 E
Bowron → **108** 54 3N 121 50W
Bowser L. **108** 56 30N 129 30W
Bowsman **109** 52 14N 101 12W
Bowwood **91** 17 5 S 26 20 E
Boxelder Cr. → **118** 47 20N 108 30W
Boxholm **49** 58 12N 15 3 E
Boxtel **16** 51 36N 5 20 E
Boyabat **56** 41 28N 34 42 E
Boyce **117** 31 25N 92 39W
Boyer → **108** 58 27N 115 57W
Boyle **15** 53 58N 8 19W
Boyne → **15** 53 43N 6 15W
Boyne City **114** 45 13N 85 1W
Boyni Qara **65** 36 20N 67 0 E
Boynton Beach **115** 26 31N 80 3W
Bozburun **45** 36 43N 28 8 E
Bozcaada **44** 39 49N 26 3 E
Bozeman **118** 45 40N 111 0W
Bozen = Bolzano **39** 46 30N 11 20 E
Bożepole Wielkopolski **28** 54 33N 17 56 E
Boževac **42** 44 32N 21 24 E
Bozouls **20** 44 28N 2 43 E
Bozoum **88** 6 25N 16 35 E
Bozovici **46** 44 56N 22 1 E
Bra **38** 44 41N 7 50 E
Brabant □ **16** 50 46N 4 30 E
Brabant L. **109** 55 58N 103 43W

Brabrand 49 56 9N 10 7 E
Brač 39 43 20N 16 40 E
Bracadale, L. 14 57 20N 6 30W
Bracciano 39 42 6N 12 10 E
Bracciano, L. di 39 42 8N 12 11 E
Bracebridge 106 45 2N 79 19W
Brach 83 27 31N 14 20 E
Bracieux 19 47 30N 1 30 E
Bräcke 48 62 45N 15 26 E
Brackettville 117 29 21N 100 20W
Bracki Kanal 39 43 24N 16 40 E
Brad 46 46 10N 22 50 E
Brădano → 41 40 23N 16 51 E
Braddock 112 40 24N 79 51W
Bradenton 115 27 25N 82 35W
Bradford, Can. 112 44 7N 79 34W
Bradford, U.K. 12 53 47N 1 45W
Bradford, Pa., U.S.A. 114 41 58N 78 41W
Bradford, Vt., U.S.A. 113 43 59N 72 9W
Brădiceni 46 45 3N 23 4 E
Bradley, Ark., U.S.A. 117 33 7N 93 39W
Bradley, S.D., U.S.A. 116 45 10N 97 40W
Bradley Institute 91 17 7S 31 25 E
Bradore Bay 107 51 27N 57 18W
Bradshaw 97 15 21 S 130 16 E
Brady 117 31 8N 99 25W
Brædstrup 49 55 58N 9 37 E
Braeside 113 45 28N 76 24W
Braga 30 41 35N 8 25W
Braga □ 30 41 30N 8 30W
Bragado 124 35 2 S 60 27W
Bragança, Brazil 127 1 0 S 47 2W
Bragança, Port. 30 41 48N 6 50W
Bragança □ 30 41 30N 6 45W
Bragança Paulista 125 22 55 S 46 32W
Brahmanbaria 69 23 58N 91 15 E
Brahmani → 69 20 39N 86 46 E
Brahmaputra → 67 24 2N 90 59 E
Braich-y-pwll 12 52 47N 4 46W
Braidwood 99 35 27 S 149 49 E
Brăila 46 45 19N 27 59 E
Brăila □ 46 45 5N 27 30 E
Brainerd 116 46 20N 94 10W
Braintree, U.K. 13 51 53N 0 34 E
Braintree, U.S.A. 113 42 11N 71 0W
Brak → 92 29 35 S 22 55 E
Brake, Niedersachsen, Ger. 24 53 19N 8 30 E
Brake, Nordrhein, Ger. 24 51 43N 9 12 E
Bräkne-Hoby 49 56 14N 15 6 E
Brakwater 92 22 28 S 17 3 E
Brålanda 49 58 34N 12 21 E
Bralorne 108 50 50N 123 45W
Bramberg 25 50 6N 10 40 E
Bramminge 49 55 28N 8 42 E
Brämön 48 62 14N 17 40 E
Brampton 106 43 45N 79 45W
Bramsche 24 52 25N 7 58 E
Bramwell 98 12 8 S 142 37 E
Branco → 126 1 20 S 61 50W
Brande 49 55 57N 9 8 E
Brandenburg 24 52 24N 12 33 E
Brandfort 92 28 40 S 26 30 E
Brandon, Can. 109 49 50N 99 57W
Brandon, U.S.A. 113 43 48N 73 4W
Brandon B. 15 52 17N 10 8W
Brandon, Mt. 15 52 15N 10 15W
Brandsen 124 35 10 S 58 15W
Brandval 47 60 19N 12 1 E
Brandvlei 92 30 25 S 20 30 E
Brandýs 26 50 10N 14 40 E
Branford 113 41 15N 72 48W
Braniewo 28 54 25N 19 50 E
Bransfield Str. 5 63 0 S 59 0W
Brańsk 28 52 44N 22 51 E
Branson, Colo., U.S.A. 117 37 4N 103 53W
Branson, Mo., U.S.A. 117 36 40N 93 18W
Brantford 106 43 10N 80 15W
Brantôme 20 45 22N 0 39 E
Branxholme 99 37 52 S 141 49 E
Branzi 38 46 0N 9 46 E
Bras d'or, L. 107 45 50N 60 50W
Brasiléia 126 11 0 S 68 45W
Brasília 127 15 47 S 47 55 E
Braslav 54 55 38N 27 0 E
Braslovce 39 46 21N 15 3 E
Brașov 46 45 38N 25 35 E
Brașov □ 46 45 45N 25 15 E
Brass 85 4 35N 6 14 E
Brass → 85 4 15N 6 13 E
Brassac-les-Mines 20 45 24N 3 20 E
Brasschaat 16 51 19N 4 27 E
Brassey, Banjaran 72 5 0N 117 15 E
Brasstown Bald, Mt. 115 34 54N 83 45W
Bratislava 27 48 10N 17 7 E
Bratsigovo 43 42 1N 24 22 E
Bratsk 59 56 10N 101 30 E
Brattleboro 114 42 53N 72 37W
Bratul Chilia → 46 45 25N 29 20 E
Bratul Sfintu Gheorghe → 46 45 0N 29 20 E
Bratul Sulina → 46 45 10N 29 20 E
Bratunac 42 44 13N 19 21 E
Braunau 26 48 15N 13 3 E
Braunschweig 24 52 17N 10 28 E
Braunton 13 51 6N 4 9W
Brava 63 1 20N 44 8 E
Bråviken 48 58 38N 16 32 E
Bravo del Norte → 120 25 57N 97 9W
Brawley 119 32 58N 115 30W
Bray 15 53 12N 6 6W
Bray, Pays de 19 49 46N 1 26 E
Bray-sur-Seine 19 48 25N 3 14 E
Brazeau → 108 52 55N 115 14W
Brazil 114 39 32N 87 8W
Brazil ■ 127 10 0 S 50 0W
Brazilian Highlands = Brasil, Planalto 122 18 0 S 46 30W
Brazo Sur → 124 25 21 S 57 42W
Brazos → 117 28 53N 95 23W
Brazzaville 88 4 9 S 15 12 E
Brčko 42 44 54N 18 46 E
Brda → 28 53 8N 18 8 E
Breadalbane, Austral. 98 23 50 S 139 35 E
Breadalbane, U.K. 14 56 30N 4 15W
Breaksea Sd. 101 45 35 S 166 35 E
Bream Bay 101 35 56 S 174 28 E
Bream Head 101 35 51 S 174 36 E
Breas 124 25 29 S 70 24W
Brebes 73 6 52 S 109 3 E
Brechin, Can. 112 44 32N 79 10W
Brechin, U.K. 14 56 44N 2 40W
Breckenridge, Colo., U.S.A. 118 39 30N 106 2W
Breckenridge, Minn., U.S.A. 116 46 20N 96 36W
Breckenridge, Tex., U.S.A. 117 32 48N 98 55W
Břeclav 27 48 46N 16 53 E
Brecon 13 51 57N 3 23W
Brecon Beacons 13 51 53N 3 27W
Breda 16 51 35N 4 45 E
Bredaryd 49 57 10N 13 45 E
Bredasdorp 92 34 33 S 20 2 E
Bredbo 99 35 58 S 149 10 E
Bredstedt 24 54 37N 8 59 E
Bregalnica → 42 41 43N 22 9 E
Bregenz 26 47 30N 9 45 E
Bregovo 42 44 9N 22 39 E
Bréhal 18 48 53N 1 30W
Bréhat, I. de 18 48 51N 3 0W
Breiðafjörður 50 65 15N 23 15W
Breil 21 43 56N 7 31 E
Breisach 25 48 2N 7 37 E
Brejo 127 3 41 S 42 47W
Brekke 47 61 1N 5 26 E
Breloux-la-Crèche 20 46 23N 0 19W
Bremangerlandet 47 61 51N 5 0 E
Bremen 24 53 4N 8 47 E
Bremen □ 24 53 6N 8 46 E
Bremerhaven 24 53 34N 8 35 E
Bremerton 118 47 30N 122 38W
Bremervörde 24 53 28N 9 10 E
Bremnes 47 59 47N 5 8 E
Bremsnes 47 63 6N 7 40 E
Brenes 31 37 32N 5 54W
Brenham 117 30 5N 96 27W
Brenner Pass 26 47 0N 11 30 E
Breno 38 45 57N 10 20 E
Brent, Can. 106 46 2N 78 29W
Brent, U.K. 13 51 33N 0 18W
Brenta → 39 45 11N 12 18 E
Brentwood 13 51 37N 0 19 E
Bréscia 38 45 33N 10 13 E
Breskens 16 51 23N 3 33 E
Breslau = Wrocław 28 51 5N 17 5 E
Bresle → 18 50 4N 1 22 E
Bresles 19 49 25N 2 13 E
Bressanone 39 46 43N 11 40 E
Bressay I. 14 60 10N 1 5W
Bresse, La 19 48 0N 6 53 E
Bresse, Plaine de 19 46 50N 5 10 E
Bressuire 18 46 51N 0 30W
Brest, France 18 48 24N 4 31W
Brest, U.S.S.R. 54 52 10N 23 40 E
Bretagne 18 48 0N 3 0W
Bretçu 46 46 7N 26 18 E
Breteuil, Eur, France 18 48 50N 0 53 E
Breteuil, Oise, France 19 49 38N 2 18 E
Breton 108 53 7N 114 28W
Breton, Pertuis 20 46 17N 1 25W
Breton Sd. 117 29 40N 89 12W
Brett, C. 101 35 10 S 174 20 E
Bretten 25 49 2N 8 43 E
Brevard 115 35 19N 82 42W
Brevik 47 59 4N 9 42 E
Brewarrina 99 30 0 S 146 51 E
Brewer 107 44 43N 68 50W
Brewster, N.Y., U.S.A. 113 41 23N 73 37W
Brewster, Wash., U.S.A. 118 48 10N 119 51W
Brewster, Kap 4 70 7N 22 0W
Brewton 115 31 9N 87 2W
Breyten 93 26 16 S 30 0 E
Breytovo 55 58 18N 37 50 E
Brežice 39 45 54N 15 35 E
Brézina 82 33 4N 1 14 E
Březnice 26 49 32N 13 57 E
Breznik 42 42 44N 22 50 E
Brezno 27 48 50N 19 40 E
Brezovo 43 42 21N 25 5 E
Bria 88 6 30N 21 58 E
Briançon 21 44 54N 6 39 E
Briare 19 47 38N 2 45 E
Bribie I. 97 27 0 S 152 58 E
Bricon 19 48 5N 5 0 E
Bricquebec 18 49 28N 1 38W
Bridgehampton 113 40 56N 72 19W
Bridgend 13 51 30N 3 35W
Bridgeport, Calif., U.S.A. 119 38 14N 119 15W
Bridgeport, Conn., U.S.A. 114 41 12N 73 12W
Bridgeport, Nebr., U.S.A. 116 41 42N 103 10W
Bridgeport, Tex., U.S.A. 117 33 15N 97 45W
Bridger 118 45 20N 108 58W
Bridgeton 114 39 29N 75 10W
Bridgetown, Austral. 96 33 58 S 116 7 E
Bridgetown, Barbados 121 13 0N 59 30W
Bridgetown, Can. 107 44 55N 65 18W
Bridgewater, Can. 107 44 25N 64 31W
Bridgewater, Mass., U.S.A. 113 41 59N 70 56W
Bridgewater, S.D., U.S.A. 116 43 34N 97 29W
Bridgewater, C. 97 38 23 S 141 23 E
Bridgnorth 13 52 33N 2 25W
Bridgton 113 44 5N 70 41W
Bridgwater 13 51 7N 3 0W
Bridlington 12 54 6N 0 11W
Bridport, Austral. 99 40 59 S 147 23 E
Bridport, U.K. 13 50 43N 2 45W
Brie-Comte-Robert 19 48 40N 2 35 E
Brie, Plaine de la 19 48 35N 3 10 E
Briec 18 48 6N 4 0W
Brienne-le-Château 19 48 24N 4 30 E
Brienon 19 48 0N 3 35 E
Brienz 25 46 46N 8 2 E
Brienzersee 25 46 44N 7 53 E
Briey 19 49 14N 5 57 E
Brig 25 46 18N 7 59 E
Brigg 12 53 33N 0 30W
Briggsdale 116 40 40N 104 20W
*Brigham City 118 41 30N 112 1W
Bright 99 36 42 S 146 56 E
Brighton, Austral. 99 35 5 S 138 30 E
Brighton, Can. 106 44 2N 77 44W
Brighton, U.K. 13 50 50N 0 9W
Brighton, U.S.A. 116 39 59N 104 50W
Brignogan-Plage 18 48 40N 4 20W
Brignoles 21 43 25N 6 5 E
Brihuega 32 40 45N 2 52W
Brikama 84 13 15N 16 45W
Brilliant, Can. 108 49 19N 117 38W
Brilliant, U.S.A. 112 40 15N 80 39W
Brilon 24 51 23N 8 32 E
Brindisi 41 40 39N 17 55 E
Brinje 39 45 0N 15 9 E
Brinkley 117 34 55N 91 15W
Brinkworth 99 33 42 S 138 26 E
Brion, Î. 107 47 46N 61 26W
Brionne 18 49 11N 0 43 E
Brionski 39 44 55N 13 45 E
Brioude 20 45 18N 3 24 E
Briouze 18 48 42N 0 23W
Brisbane 97 27 25 S 153 2 E
Brisbane → 99 27 24 S 153 9 E
Brisighella 39 44 14N 11 46 E
Bristol, U.K. 13 51 26N 2 35W
Bristol, Conn., U.S.A. 114 41 44N 72 57W
Bristol, Pa., U.S.A. 113 40 6N 74 52W
Bristol, R.I., U.S.A. 113 41 40N 71 15W
Bristol, S.D., U.S.A. 116 45 25N 97 43W
Bristol, Tenn., U.S.A. 115 36 36N 82 11W
Bristol B. 104 58 0N 160 0W
Bristol Channel 13 51 18N 4 30W
Bristol I. 5 58 45 S 28 0W
Bristol L. 119 34 23N 116 50W
Bristow 117 35 55N 96 28W
British Antarctic Territory □ 5 66 0 S 45 0W
British Columbia □ 108 55 0N 125 15W
British Guiana = Guyana ■ 126 5 0N 59 0W
British Honduras = Belize ■ 120 17 0N 88 30W
British Isles 8 55 0N 4 0W
Brits 93 25 37 S 27 48 E
Britstown 92 30 37 S 23 30 E
Britt 106 45 46N 80 34W
Brittany = Bretagne 18 48 0N 3 0W
Britton 116 45 50N 97 47W
Brive-la-Gaillarde 20 45 10N 1 32 E
Briviesca 32 42 32N 3 19W
Brixton 98 23 32 S 144 57 E
Brlik 58 44 0N 74 5 E
Brno 27 49 10N 16 35 E
Bro 48 59 31N 17 38 E
Broach = Bharuch 68 21 47N 73 0 E
Broad → 115 33 59N 82 39W
Broad B. 14 58 14N 6 16W
Broad Haven 15 54 20N 9 55W
Broad Law 14 55 30N 3 22W
Broad Sd. 97 22 0 S 149 45 E
Broadford 100 37 14 S 145 4 E
Broads, The 12 52 45N 1 30 E
Broadsound Ra. 97 22 50 S 149 30 E
Broadus 116 45 28N 105 27W
Broadview 109 50 22N 102 35W
Broager 49 54 53N 9 40 E
Broaryd 49 57 7N 13 15 E
Brochet 109 57 53N 101 40W
Brochet, L. 109 58 36N 101 35W
Brock 109 51 26N 108 43W
Brocken 24 51 48N 10 40 E
Brockport 114 43 12N 77 56W
Brockton 113 42 8N 71 2W
Brockville 106 44 35N 75 41W
Brockway, Mont., U.S.A. 116 47 18N 105 46W
Brockway, Pa., U.S.A. 112 41 14N 78 48W
Brocton 112 42 25N 79 26W
Brod 42 41 35N 21 17 E
Brodarevo 42 43 14N 19 44 E
Brodeur Pen. 105 72 30N 88 10W
Brodick 14 55 34N 5 9W
Brodnica 28 53 15N 19 25 E
Brody 54 50 5N 25 10 E
Brogan 118 44 14N 117 32W
Broglie 18 49 0N 0 30 E
Brok 28 52 43N 21 52 E
Broken → 100 36 24 S 145 24 E
Broken Bay 100 33 30 S 151 15 E
Broken Bow, Nebr., U.S.A. 116 41 25N 99 35W
Broken Bow, Okla., U.S.A. 117 34 2N 94 43W
Broken Hill 97 31 58 S 141 29 E
Broken Hill = Kabwe 91 14 27 S 28 28 E
Brokind 49 58 13N 15 42 E
Bromfield 13 52 25N 2 45W
Bromley 13 51 20N 0 5 E
Bromölla 49 56 5N 14 28 E
Brønderslev 49 57 16N 9 57 E
Brong-Ahafo 84 7 50N 2 0W
Bronkhorstspruit 93 25 46 S 28 45 E
Bronnitsy 55 55 27N 38 10 E
Bronte, Italy 41 37 48N 14 49 E
Bronte, U.S.A. 117 31 54N 100 18W
Bronte Park 99 42 8 S 146 30 E
Brookfield 116 39 50N 93 4W
Brookhaven 117 31 40N 90 25W
Brookings, Oreg., U.S.A. 118 42 4N 124 10W
Brookings, S.D., U.S.A. 116 44 20N 96 45W
Brooklands 98 18 10 S 144 0 E
Brooklin 112 43 55N 78 55W
Brookmere 108 49 52N 120 53W
Brooks 108 50 35N 111 55W
Brooks B. 108 50 15N 127 55W
Brooks L. 109 61 55N 106 35W
Brooks Ra. 104 68 40N 147 0W
Brooksville 115 28 32N 82 21W
Brookton 96 32 22 S 117 1 E
Brookville 114 39 25N 85 0W
Brooloo 99 26 30 S 152 43 E
Broom, L. 14 57 55N 5 15W
Broome 96 18 0 S 122 15 E
Broons 18 48 20N 2 16W
Brora 14 58 0N 3 50W
Brora → 14 58 4N 3 52W
Brösarp 49 55 43N 14 6 E
Brosna → 15 53 8N 8 0W
Broșteni 46 47 14N 25 43 E
Brothers 118 43 56N 120 39W
Brøttum 47 61 2N 10 34 E
Brou 18 48 13N 1 11 E
Brouage 20 45 52N 1 4W
Broughton Island 105 67 33N 63 0W
Broughty Ferry 14 56 29N 2 50W
Broumov 27 50 35N 16 20 E
Brouwershaven 16 51 45N 3 55 E
Brovary 54 50 34N 30 48 E
Brovst 49 57 6N 9 31 E
Browerville 116 46 3N 94 50W
Brown Willy 13 50 35N 4 34W
Brownfield 117 33 10N 102 15W
Browning 118 48 35N 113 0W
Brownlee 109 50 43N 106 1W
Brownsville, Oreg., U.S.A. 118 44 29N 123 0W
Brownsville, Tenn., U.S.A. 117 35 35N 89 15W
Brownsville, Tex., U.S.A. 117 25 56N 97 25W
Brownwood 117 31 45N 99 0W
Brownwood, L. 117 31 51N 98 35W
Brozas 31 39 37N 6 47W
Bru 47 61 32N 5 11 E
Bruas 71 4 31N 100 46 E
Bruay-en-Artois 19 50 29N 2 33 E
Bruce, Mt. 96 22 37 S 118 8 E
Bruce Pen. 112 45 0N 81 30W
Bruche → 19 48 34N 7 43 E
Bruchsal 25 49 9N 8 39 E
Bruck an der Leitha 27 48 1N 16 47 E
Bruck an der Mur 26 47 24N 15 16 E
Brückenau 25 50 17N 9 48 E
Brue → 13 51 10N 2 59W
Bruges = Brugge 16 51 13N 3 13 E
Brugg 25 47 29N 8 11 E
Brugge 16 51 13N 3 13 E
Brühl 24 50 49N 6 51 E
Brûlé 108 53 15N 117 58W
Brûlon 18 47 58N 0 15W
Brumado 127 14 14 S 41 40W
Brumath 19 48 43N 7 40 E
Brumunddal 47 60 53N 10 56 E
Brundidge 115 31 43N 85 45W
Bruneau 118 42 57N 115 55W
Bruneau → 118 42 57N 115 58W
Brunei = Bandar Seri Begawan 72 4 52N 115 0 E
Brunei ■ 72 4 50N 115 0 E
Brunflo 48 63 5N 14 50 E
Brunico 39 46 50N 11 55 E
Brunkeberg 47 59 26N 8 28 E
Brunna 48 59 52N 17 25 E
Brunnen 25 46 59N 8 37 E
Brunner 101 42 27 S 171 20 E
Brunner, L. 101 42 37 S 171 27 E
Brunnsvik 48 60 12N 15 8 E
Bruno 109 52 20N 105 30W
Brunsbüttelkoog 24 53 52N 9 13 E
Brunswick, Ga., U.S.A. 115 31 10N 81 30W
Brunswick, Md., U.S.A. 114 39 20N 77 38W
Brunswick, Me., U.S.A. 107 43 53N 69 50W
Brunswick, Mo., U.S.A. 116 39 26N 93 10W
Brunswick, Ohio, U.S.A. 112 41 15N 81 50W
Brunswick = Braunschweig 24 52 17N 10 28 E
Brunswick B. 96 15 15 S 124 50 E
Brunswick, Pen. de 128 53 30 S 71 30W
Bruntál 27 50 0N 17 27 E
Bruny I. 97 43 20 S 147 15 E
Brusartsi 42 43 40N 23 5 E
Brush 116 40 17N 103 33W
Brushton 113 44 50N 74 62W
Brusio 25 46 14N 10 8 E
Brusque 125 27 5 S 49 0W
Brussel 16 50 51N 4 21 E
Brussels, Can. 112 43 45N 81 25W
Brussels, Ont., Can. 112 43 44N 81 15W
Brussels = Bruxelles 16 50 51N 4 21 E
Bruthen 99 37 42 S 147 50 E
Bruxelles 16 50 51N 4 21 E
Bruyères 19 48 10N 6 40 E
Brwinów 28 52 9N 20 40 E
Bryagovo 43 41 58N 25 8 E
Bryan, Ohio, U.S.A. 114 41 30N 84 30W
Bryan, Texas, U.S.A. 117 30 40N 96 27W
Bryan, Mt. 99 33 30 S 139 0 E
Bryanka 57 48 32N 38 45 E
Bryansk 54 53 13N 34 25 E
Bryanskoye 57 44 20N 47 10 E
Bryant 116 44 35N 97 28W
Bryne 47 58 44N 5 38 E
Bryson City 115 35 28N 83 25W
Brza Palanka 42 44 28N 22 27 E
Brzava → 42 45 21N 20 45 E
Brzeg 28 50 52N 17 30 E
Brzeg Din 28 51 16N 16 41 E
Brześć Kujawski 28 52 36N 18 55 E
Brzesko 27 49 59N 20 34 E
Brzeszcze 27 49 59N 19 10 E
Brzeziny 28 51 49N 19 42 E
Brzozów 27 49 41N 22 3 E
Bû Athlah 83 30 9N 15 39 E
Bu Craa 80 26 45N 12 50W
Bua Yai 71 15 33N 102 26 E
Buabuq 86 31 29N 25 29 E
Buapinang 73 4 40 S 121 30 E
Buayan 73 6 3N 125 6 E
Buba 84 11 40N 14 59W
Bubanza 90 3 6 S 29 23 E
Bucak 64 37 28N 30 36 E
Bucaramanga 126 7 0N 73 0W
Bucchiánico 39 42 20N 14 10 E
Bucecea 46 47 47N 26 28 E
Buchach 54 49 5N 25 25 E
Buchan 14 57 32N 2 8W
Buchan Ness 14 57 29N 1 48W
Buchanan, Can. 109 51 40N 102 45W
Buchanan, Liberia 84 5 57N 10 2W
Buchanan, L., Queens., Austral. 98 21 35 S 145 52 E
Buchanan, L., W. Australia, Austral. 96 25 33 S 123 2 E
Buchanan, L., U.S.A. 117 30 50N 98 25W
Buchans 107 48 50N 56 52W
Bucharest = București 46 44 27N 26 10 E

Buchholz 24 53 19N 9 51 E
Buchloe 25 48 3N 10 45 E
Bückeburg 24 52 16N 9 2 E
Buckeye 119 33 28N 112 40W
Buckhannon 114 39 2N 80 10W
Buckhaven 14 56 10N 3 2W
Buckie 14 57 40N 2 58W
Buckingham, Can. 106 45 37N 75 24W
Buckingham, U.K. 13 52 0N 0 59W
Buckingham □ 13 51 50N 0 55W
Buckingham B. 97 12 10S 135 40 E
Buckingham Can. 70 14 0N 80 5 E
Buckinguy 99 31 3S 147 30 E
Buckland Newton 13 50 45N 2 25W
Buckley 118 47 10N 122 2W
Bucklin 117 37 37N 99 40W
Bucquoy 19 50 9N 2 43 E
Buctouche 107 46 30N 64 45W
Bucureşti 46 44 27N 26 10 E
Bucyrus 114 40 48N 83 0W
Budafok 27 47 26N 19 2 E
Budalin 67 22 20N 95 10 E
Budapest 27 47 29N 19 5 E
Budaun 68 28 5N 79 10 E
Budd Coast 5 68 0S 112 0 E
Buddusò 40 40 35N 9 18 E
Bude 13 50 49N 4 33W
Budeşti 46 44 13N 26 30 E
Budge Budge 69 22 30N 88 5 E
Búðareyri 50 65 2N 14 13W
Búðir 50 64 49N 23 23W
Budia 32 40 38N 2 46W
Budjala 88 2 50N 19 40 E
Búdrio 39 44 31N 11 31 E
Budva 42 42 17N 18 50 E
Budzyń 28 52 54N 16 59 E
Buea 85 4 10N 9 9 E
Buena Vista, Colo., U.S.A. 119 38 56N 106 6W
Buena Vista, Va., U.S.A. 114 37 47N 79 23W
Buena Vista L. 119 35 15N 119 21W
Buenaventura, Colomb. 126 3 53N 77 4W
Buenaventura, Mexico 120 29 50N 107 30W
Buendia, Pantano de 32 40 25N 2 43W
Buenos Aires 124 34 30S 58 20W
Buenos Aires □ 124 36 30S 60 0W
Buenos Aires, Lago 128 46 35S 72 30W
Buffalo, Mo., U.S.A. 117 37 40N 93 5W
Buffalo, N.Y., U.S.A. 114 42 55N 78 50W
Buffalo, Okla., U.S.A. 117 36 55N 99 42W
Buffalo, S.D., U.S.A. 116 45 39N 103 31W
Buffalo, Wyo., U.S.A. 118 44 25N 106 50W
Buffalo → 108 60 5N 115 5W
Buffalo Head Hills 108 57 25N 115 55W
Buffalo L. 108 52 27N 112 54W
Buffalo Narrows 109 55 51N 108 29W
Buffels → 92 29 36S 17 15 E
Buford 115 34 5N 84 0W
Bug →, Poland 28 52 31N 21 5 E
Bug →, U.S.S.R. 56 46 59N 31 58 E
Buga 126 4 0N 76 15W
Buganda □ 90 0 0N 31 30 E
Buganga 90 0 3S 32 0 E
Bugeat 20 45 36N 1 55 E
Bugel, Tanjung 72 6 26S 111 3 E
Bugojno 42 44 2N 17 25 E
Bugsuk 72 8 15N 117 15 E
Bugt 76 48 47N 121 56 E
Bugue, Le 20 44 55N 0 56 E
Bugulma 52 54 33N 52 48 E
Buguma 85 4 42N 6 55 E
Buguruslan 52 53 39N 52 26 E
Buhăeşti 46 46 47N 27 32 E
Buheirat-Murrat-el-Kubra 86 30 15N 32 40 E
Buhl, Idaho, U.S.A. 118 42 35N 114 54W
Buhl, Minn., U.S.A. 116 47 30N 92 46W
Buhuşi 46 46 41N 26 45 E
Buick 117 37 38N 91 2W
Builth Wells 13 52 10N 3 26W
Buinsk 55 55 0N 48 18 E
Buir Nur 75 47 50N 117 42 E
Buis-les-Baronnies 21 44 17N 5 16 E
Buitrago 30 41 0N 3 38W
Bujalance 31 37 54N 4 23W
Buján 30 42 59N 8 36W
Bujanovac 42 42 28N 21 44 E
Bujaraloz 32 41 29N 0 10W
Buje 39 45 24N 13 39 E
Bujumbura (Usumbura) 90 3 16S 29 18 E
Bük 27 47 22N 16 45 E
Buk 28 52 21N 16 30 E
Bukachacha 59 52 55N 116 50 E
Bukama 91 9 10S 25 50 E
Bukavu 90 2 20S 28 52 E
Bukene 90 4 15S 32 48 E
Bukhara 58 39 48N 64 25 E
Bukima 90 1 50S 33 25 E
Bukittinggi 72 0 20S 100 20 E
Bukkapatnam 70 14 14N 77 46 E
Bukoba 90 1 20S 31 49 E
Bukoba □ 90 1 30S 32 0 E
Bukowno 27 50 17N 19 35 E
Bukuru 85 9 42N 8 48 E
Bukuya 90 0 40N 31 52 E
Bula, Guin.-Biss. 84 12 7N 15 43W
Bula, Indon. 73 3 6S 130 30 E
Bulan 73 12 40N 123 52 E
Bulandshahr 68 28 28N 77 51 E
Bûlâq 86 25 10N 30 38 E
Bulawayo 91 20 7S 28 32 E
Buldana 68 20 30N 76 18 E
Bulgan 75 48 45N 103 34 E
Bulgaria ■ 43 42 35N 25 30 E
Bulgroo 99 25 47S 143 58 E
Bulhar 63 10 25N 44 30 E
Buli, Teluk 73 1 5N 128 25 E
Buliluyan, C. 72 8 20N 117 15 E
Bulki 87 6 11N 36 31 E
Bulkley → 108 55 15N 127 40W
Bull Shoals L. 117 36 40N 93 5W
Bullaque → 31 38 59N 4 17W
Bullas 33 38 2N 1 40W
Bulle 25 46 37N 7 3 E
Buller, Mt. 100 37 10S 146 28 E
Bullfinch 96 30 58S 119 3 E
Bulli 99 34 15S 150 57 E
Bullock Creek 98 17 43S 144 31 E
Bulloo → 97 28 43S 142 30 E
Bulloo Downs 99 28 31S 142 57 E
Bulloo L. 99 28 43S 142 25 E
Bulls 101 40 10S 175 24 E
Bully-les-Mines 19 50 27N 2 44 E
Bulnes 124 36 42S 72 19W
Bulo Burti 63 3 50N 45 33 E
Bulolo 98 7 10S 146 40 E
Bulqiza 44 41 30N 20 21 E
Bulsar 68 20 40N 72 58 E
Bultfontein 92 28 18S 26 10 E
Bulu Karakelong 73 4 35N 126 50 E
Bulukumba 73 5 33S 120 11 E
Bulun 59 70 37N 127 30 E
Bumba 88 2 13N 22 30 E
Bumbiri I. 90 1 40S 31 55 E
Bumble Bee 119 34 8N 112 18W
Bumhpa Bum 67 26 51N 97 14 E
Bumi → 91 17 0S 28 20 E
Buna, Kenya 90 2 58N 39 30 E
Buna, P.N.G. 98 8 42S 148 27 E
Bunazi 90 1 3S 31 23 E
Bunbah, Khalīj 81 32 20N 23 15 E
Bunbury 96 33 20S 115 35 E
Buncrana 15 55 8N 7 28W
Bundaberg 97 24 54S 152 22 E
Bünde 24 52 11N 8 33 E
Bundi 68 25 30N 75 35 E
Bundoran 15 54 24N 8 17W
Bundukia 87 5 14N 30 55 E
Bundure 100 35 10S 146 1 E
Bungendore 100 35 14S 149 30 E
Bungo-Suidō 74 33 0N 132 15 E
Bungoma 90 0 34N 34 34 E
Bungu 90 7 35S 39 0 E
Bungun Shara 75 49 0N 104 0 E
Bunia 90 1 35N 30 20 E
Bunji 69 35 45N 74 40 E
Bunju 72 3 35N 117 50 E
Bunkerville 119 36 47N 114 6W
Bunkie 117 31 1N 92 12W
Bunnell 115 29 28N 81 12W
Buñol 33 39 25N 0 47W
Buntok 72 1 40S 114 58 E
Bununu 85 9 51N 9 32 E
Bununu Dass 85 10 0N 9 31 E
Bunza 85 12 8N 4 0 E
Buol 73 1 15N 121 32 E
Buorkhaya, Mys 59 71 50N 132 40 E
Buqayq 64 26 0N 49 45 E
Buqei'a 62 32 58N 35 20 E
Bur Acaba 63 3 12N 44 20 E
Bûr Fuad 86 31 15N 32 20 E
Bûr Safâga 86 26 43N 33 57 E
Bûr Sa'îd 86 31 16N 32 18 E
Bûr Sûdân 86 19 32N 37 9 E
Bûr Taufiq 86 29 54N 32 32 E
Bura 90 1 4S 39 58 E
Buraimī, Al Wāhāt al 65 24 10N 55 43 E
Burao 63 9 32N 45 32 E
Buras 117 29 20N 89 33W
Buraydah 64 26 20N 44 8 E
Burbank 119 34 9N 118 23W
Burcher 99 33 30S 147 16 E
Burdekin → 98 19 38S 147 25 E
Burdett 108 49 50N 111 32W
Burdur 64 37 45N 30 22 E
Burdwan 69 23 14N 87 39 E
Bure 87 10 40N 37 4 E
Bure → 12 52 38N 1 45 E
Bureba, La 32 42 36N 3 24W
Büren 24 51 33N 8 34 E
Bureya → 59 49 27N 129 30 E
Burford 112 43 7N 80 27W
Burg, Magdeburg, Ger. 24 52 16N 11 50 E
Burg, Schleswig-Holstein, Ger. 24 54 25N 11 10 E
Burg el Arab 86 30 54N 29 32 E
Burg et Tuyur 86 20 55N 27 56 E
Burgas 43 42 33N 27 29 E
Burgaski Zaliv 43 42 30N 27 39 E
Burgdorf, Ger. 24 52 27N 10 0 E
Burgdorf, Switz. 25 47 3N 7 37 E
Burgenland □ 27 47 20N 16 20 E
Burgeo 107 47 37N 57 38W
Burgersdorp 92 31 0S 26 20 E
Burghausen 25 48 10N 12 50 E
Búrgio 40 37 35N 13 18 E
Burglengenfeld 25 49 11N 12 2 E
Burgo de Osma 32 41 35N 3 4W
Burgohondo 30 40 26N 4 47W
Burgos 32 42 21N 3 41W
Burgos □ 32 42 21N 3 42W
Burgstädt 24 50 55N 12 49 E
Burgsteinfurt 24 52 9N 7 23 E
Burgsvik 49 57 3N 18 19 E
Burguillos del Cerro 31 38 23N 6 35W
Burgundy = Bourgogne 19 47 0N 4 30 E
Burhanpur 68 21 18N 76 14 E
Burhou 18 49 45N 2 15W
Buri Pen. 87 15 25N 39 55 E
Burias 73 12 55N 123 5 E
Burica, Pta. 121 8 3N 82 51W
Burigi, L. 90 2 2S 31 22 E
Burin 107 47 1N 55 14W
Bûrîn 62 32 11N 35 15 E
Buriram 71 15 0N 103 0 E
Burji 87 5 29N 37 51 E
Burkburnett 117 34 7N 98 35W
Burke 118 47 31N 115 56W
Burke → 98 23 12S 139 33 E
Burketown 97 17 45S 139 33 E
Burk's Falls 106 45 37N 79 24W
Burley 118 42 37N 113 55W
Burlington, Can. 112 43 18N 79 45W
Burlington, Colo., U.S.A. 116 39 21N 102 18W
Burlington, Iowa, U.S.A. 116 40 50N 91 5W
Burlington, Kans., U.S.A. 116 38 15N 95 47W
Burlington, N.C., U.S.A. 115 36 7N 79 27W
Burlington, N.J., U.S.A. 114 40 5N 74 50W
Burlington, Vt., U.S.A. 114 44 27N 73 14W
Burlington, Wash., U.S.A. 118 48 29N 122 19W
Burlington, Wis., U.S.A. 114 42 41N 88 18W
Burlyu-Tyube 58 46 30N 79 10 E
Burma ■ 67 21 0N 96 30 E
Burnaby I. 108 52 25N 131 19W
Burnet 117 30 45N 98 11W
Burnett → 97 24 45S 152 23 E
Burney 118 40 56N 121 41W
Burnham 112 40 37N 77 34W
Burnie 97 41 4S 145 56 E
Burnley 12 53 47N 2 15W
Burns, Oreg., U.S.A. 118 43 40N 119 4W
Burns, Wyo., U.S.A. 116 41 13N 104 18W
Burns Lake 108 54 20N 125 45W
Burnside → 104 66 51N 108 4W
Burnt River 112 44 41N 78 42W
Burntwood → 109 56 8N 96 34W
Burntwood L. 109 55 22N 100 26W
Burqa 62 32 18N 35 11 E
Burqān 64 29 0N 47 57 E
Burqin 75 47 43N 87 0 E
Burra 97 33 40S 138 55 E
Burragorang, L. 100 33 52S 150 37 E
Burreli 44 41 36N 20 1 E
Burrendong, L. 100 32 45S 149 10 E
Burrewarra Pt. 100 35 50S 150 15 E
Burriana 32 39 50N 0 4W
Burrinjuck Dam 100 35 0S 148 34 E
Burrinjuck Res. 99 35 0S 148 36 E
Burro, Serranías del 120 29 0N 102 0W
Burruyacú 124 26 30S 64 40W
Burry Port 13 51 41N 4 17W
Bursa 64 40 15N 29 5 E
Burseryd 49 57 12N 13 17 E
Burstall 109 50 39N 109 54W
Burton L. 106 54 45N 78 20W
Burton-upon-Trent 12 52 48N 1 39W
Burtundy 99 33 45S 142 15 E
Buru 73 3 30S 126 30 E
Burullus, Bahra el 86 31 25N 31 0 E
Burundi ■ 90 3 15S 30 0 E
Burung 72 0 24N 103 33 E
Bururi 90 3 57S 29 37 E
Burutu 85 5 20N 5 29 E
Burwell 116 41 49N 99 8W
Bury 12 53 36N 2 19W
Bury St. Edmunds 13 52 15N 0 42 E
Buryat A.S.S.R. □ 59 53 0N 110 0 E
Buryn 54 51 13N 33 50 E
Burzenin 28 51 28N 18 47 E
Busalla 38 44 34N 8 58 E
Busango Swamp 91 14 15S 25 45 E
Buşayyah 64 30 0N 46 10 E
Busca 38 44 31N 7 29 E
Bushati 44 41 58N 19 34 E
Bushell 109 59 31N 108 45W
Bushenyi 90 0 35S 30 10 E
Bushnell, Ill., U.S.A. 116 40 32N 90 30W
Bushnell, Nebr., U.S.A. 116 41 18N 103 50W
Busia □ 90 0 25N 34 6 E
Busie 84 10 29N 2 22W
Businga 88 3 16N 20 59 E
Buskerud fylke □ 47 60 13N 9 0 E
Busko Zdrój 28 50 28N 20 42 E
Busoga □ 90 0 5N 33 30 E
Busovača 42 44 6N 17 53 E
Busra ash Shām 64 32 30N 36 25 E
Bussang 19 47 50N 6 50 E
Busselton 96 33 42S 115 15 E
Busseto 38 44 59N 10 2 E
Bussum 16 52 16N 5 10 E
Bustard Hd. 97 24 0S 151 48 E
Busto Arsizio 38 45 40N 8 50 E
Busto, C. 30 43 34N 6 28W
Busu-Djanoa 88 1 43N 21 23 E
Busuanga 73 12 10N 120 0 E
Büsum 24 54 7N 8 50 E
Buta 90 2 50N 24 53 E
Butare 90 2 31S 29 52 E
Bute 14 55 48N 5 2W
Bute Inlet 108 50 40N 124 53W
Butemba 90 1 9N 31 37 E
Butembo 90 0 9N 29 18 E
Butera 41 37 10N 14 10 E
Butha Qi 75 48 0N 122 32 E
Butiaba 90 1 50N 31 20 E
Butler, Mo., U.S.A. 116 38 17N 94 18W
Butler, Pa., U.S.A. 114 40 52N 79 52W
Butom Odrzánski 28 51 44N 15 48 E
Butte, Mont., U.S.A. 118 46 0N 112 31W
Butte, Nebr., U.S.A. 116 42 56N 98 54W
Butterworth 71 5 24N 100 23 E
Button B. 109 58 45N 94 23W
Butuan 73 8 57N 125 33 E
Butuku-Luba 85 3 29N 8 33 E
Butung 73 5 0S 122 45 E
Buturlinovka 55 50 50N 40 35 E
Butzbach 24 50 24N 8 40 E
Bützow 24 53 51N 11 59 E
Buxar 69 25 34N 83 58 E
Buxton, S. Afr. 92 27 38S 24 42 E
Buxton, U.K. 12 53 16N 1 54W
Buxy 19 46 44N 4 40 E
Buy 55 58 28N 41 28 E
Buyaga 59 59 50N 127 0 E
Buynaksk 57 42 48N 47 7 E
Büyük Çekmece 43 41 2N 28 35 E
Büyük Kemikli Burun 44 40 20N 26 15 E
Buzançais 18 46 54N 1 25 E
Buzău 46 45 10N 26 50 E
Buzău □ 46 45 20N 26 30 E
Buzău → 46 45 10N 27 20 E
Buzău, Pasul 46 45 35N 26 12 E
Buzaymah 81 24 50N 22 2 E
Buzen 74 33 35N 131 5 E
Buzet 39 45 24N 13 58 E
Buzi → 91 19 50S 34 43 E
Buziaş 42 45 38N 21 36 E
Buzuluk 52 52 48N 52 12 E
Buzuluk → 55 50 15N 42 7 E
Buzzards Bay 114 41 45N 70 38W
Bwana Mkubwe 91 13 8S 28 38 E
Byala, Ruse, Bulg. 43 43 28N 25 44 E
Byala, Varna, Bulg. 43 42 53N 27 55 E
Byala Slatina 43 43 26N 23 55 E
Byandovan, Mys 57 39 45N 49 28 E
Bychawa 28 51 1N 22 36 E
Byczyna 28 51 7N 18 12 E
Bydgoszcz 28 53 10N 18 0 E
Bydgoszcz □ 28 53 16N 17 33 E
Byelorussian S.S.R. □ 54 53 30N 27 0 E
Byers 116 39 46N 104 13W
Byesville 112 39 56N 81 32W
Bygland 47 58 50N 7 48 E
Byglandsfjord 47 58 40N 7 50 E
Byglandsfjorden 47 58 44N 7 50 E
Byhalia 117 34 53N 89 41W
Bykhov 54 53 31N 30 14 E
Bykle 47 59 20N 7 22 E
Bykovo 57 49 50N 45 25 E
Bylas 119 33 11N 110 9W
Bylderup 49 54 57N 9 6 E
Bylot I. 105 73 13N 78 34W
Byrd, C. 5 69 38S 76 7W
Byrd Land 5 79 30S 125 0W
Byrd Sub-Glacial Basin 5 82 0S 120 0W
Byrock 99 30 40S 146 27 E
Byron, C. 97 28 38S 153 40 E
Byrranga, Gory 59 75 0N 100 0 E
Byrum 49 57 16N 11 0 E
Byske 50 64 57N 21 11 E
Byske älv → 50 64 57N 21 13 E
Bystrzyca →, Lublin, Poland 28 51 21N 22 46 E
Bystrzyca →, Wrocław, Poland 28 51 12N 16 55 E
Bystrzyca Kłodzka 28 50 19N 16 39 E
Byten 54 52 50N 25 27 E
Bytom 28 50 25N 18 54 E
Bytów 28 54 10N 17 30 E
Byumba 90 1 35S 30 4 E
Bzenec 27 48 58N 17 18 E
Bzura → 28 52 25N 20 15 E

C

Ca Mau 71 9 7N 105 8 E
Ca Mau, Mui = Bai Bung 71 8 35N 104 42 E
Caacupé 124 25 23S 57 5W
Caála 89 12 46S 15 30 E
Caamano Sd. 108 52 55N 129 25W
Caazapá 124 26 8S 56 19W
Caazapá □ 125 26 10S 56 0W
Caballeria, C. de 32 40 5N 4 5 E
Cabañaquinta 30 43 10N 5 38W
Cabanatuan 73 15 30N 120 58 E
Cabanes 32 40 9N 0 2 E
Cabano 107 47 40N 68 56W
Čabar 39 45 36N 14 39 E
Cabedelo 127 7 0S 34 50W
Cabeza del Buey 31 38 44N 5 13W
Cabildo 124 32 30S 71 5W
Cabimas 126 10 23N 71 25W
Cabinda 88 5 33S 12 11 E
Cabinda □ 88 5 0S 12 30 E
Cabinet Mts. 118 48 0N 115 30W
Cabo Blanco 128 47 15S 65 47W
Cabo Frio 125 22 51S 42 3W
Cabo Pantoja 126 1 0S 75 10W
Cabonga, Réservoir 106 47 20N 76 40W
Cabool 117 37 10N 92 8W
Caboolture 99 27 5S 152 58 E
Cabora Bassa Dam 91 15 20S 32 50 E
Caborca (Heroica) 120 30 40N 112 10W
Cabot, Mt. 113 44 30N 71 25W
Cabot Strait 107 47 15N 59 40W
Cabra 31 37 30N 4 28W
Cabra del Santo Cristo 33 37 42N 3 16W
Cábras 40 39 57N 8 30 E
Cabrera, I. 33 39 8N 2 57 E
Cabrera, Sierra 30 42 12N 6 40W
Cabri 109 50 35N 108 25W
Cabriel → 33 39 14N 1 3W
Cacabelos 30 42 36N 6 44W
Čačak 42 43 54N 20 20 E
Cáceres, Brazil 126 16 5S 57 40W
Cáceres, Spain 31 39 26N 6 23W
Cáceres □ 31 39 45N 6 0W
Cache Bay 106 46 22N 80 0W
Cachepo 31 37 20N 7 49W
Cachéu 84 12 14N 16 8W
Cachi 124 25 5S 66 10W
Cachimbo, Serra do 127 9 30S 55 0W
Cachoeira 127 12 30S 39 0W
Cachoeira de Itapemirim 125 20 51S 41 7W
Cachoeira do Sul 125 30 3S 52 53W
Cachopo 31 37 20N 7 49W
Cacólo 88 10 9S 19 21 E
Caconda 89 13 48S 15 8 E
Cadarache, Barrage de 21 43 42N 5 47 E
Čadca 27 49 26N 18 45 E
Caddo 117 34 8N 96 18W
Cader Idris 12 52 43N 3 56W
Cadí, Sierra del 32 42 17N 1 42 E
Cadillac, Can. 106 48 14N 78 23W
Cadillac, France 20 44 38N 0 20W
Cadillac, U.S.A. 114 44 16N 85 25W
Cadiz 73 10 57N 123 15 E
Cádiz 31 36 30N 6 20W
Cadiz 112 40 13N 81 0W
Cádiz □ 31 36 36N 5 45W
Cádiz, G. de 31 36 40N 7 0W
Cadomin 108 53 2N 117 20W
Cadotte → 108 56 43N 117 10W
Cadours 20 43 44N 1 2 E
Caen 18 49 10N 0 22W
Caernarfon 12 53 8N 4 17W
Caernarfon B. 12 53 4N 4 40W
Caernarvon = Caernarfon 12 53 8N 4 17W
Caerphilly 13 51 34N 3 13W
Caesarea 62 32 30N 34 53 E
Caeté 127 19 55S 43 40W

Caetité 127 13 50 S 42 32W
Cafayate 124 26 2 S 66 0W
Cafu 92 16 30 S 15 8 E
Cagayan 73 9 39N 121 16 E
Cagayan → 73 18 25N 121 42 E
Cagayan de Oro 73 8 30N 124 40 E
Cagli 39 43 32N 12 38 E
Cágliari 40 39 15N 9 6 E
Cágliari, G. di 40 39 8N 9 10 E
Cagnano Varano 41 41 49N 15 47 E
Cagnes-sur-Mer 21 43 40N 7 9 E
Caguas 121 18 14N 66 4W
Caha Mts. 15 51 45N 9 40W
Cahama 92 16 17 S 14 19 E
Caher 15 52 23N 7 56W
Cahersiveen 15 51 57N 10 13W
Cahore Pt. 15 52 34N 6 11W
Cahors 20 44 27N 1 27 E
Cahuapanas 126 5 15 S 77 0W
Caianda 91 11 2 S 23 31 E
Caibarién 121 22 30N 79 30W
Caicara 126 7 38N 66 10W
Caicó 127 6 20 S 37 0W
Caicos Is. 121 21 40N 71 40W
Caicos Passage 121 22 45N 72 45W
Cainsville 112 43 9N 80 15W
Caird Coast 5 75 0 S 25 0W
Cairn Gorm 14 57 7N 3 40W
Cairn Toul 14 57 3N 3 44W
Cairngorm Mts. 14 57 6N 3 42W
Cairns 97 16 57 S 145 45 E
Cairo, Ga., U.S.A. 115 30 52N 84 12W
Cairo, Illinois, U.S.A. 117 37 0N 89 10W
Cairo = El Qâhira 86 30 1N 31 14 E
Cairo Montenotte 38 44 23N 8 16 E
Caithness, Ord of 14 58 9N 3 37W
Caiundo 89 15 50 S 17 28 E
Caiza 126 20 2 S 65 40W
Cajamarca 126 7 5 S 78 28W
Cajarc 20 44 29N 1 50 E
Cajàzeiras 127 6 52 S 38 30W
Čajetina 42 43 47N 19 42 E
Čajniče 42 43 34N 19 5 E
Çakirgol 57 40 33N 39 40 E
Čakovec 39 46 23N 16 26 E
Cala 31 37 59N 6 21W
Cala → 31 37 38N 6 5W
Cala Cadolar, Punta de 33 38 38N 1 35 E
Calabar 85 4 57N 8 20 E
Calábria □ 41 39 24N 16 30 E
Calaburras, Pta. de 31 36 30N 4 38W
Calaceite 32 41 1N 0 11 E
Calafat 46 43 58N 22 59 E
Calafate 128 50 19 S 72 15W
Calahorra 32 42 18N 1 59W
Calais, France 19 50 57N 1 56 E
Calais, U.S.A. 107 45 11N 67 20W
Calais, Pas de 19 50 57N 1 20 E
Calalaste, Cord. de 124 25 0 S 67 0W
Calama, Brazil 126 8 0 S 62 50W
Calama, Chile 124 22 30 S 68 55W
Calamar, Bolívar, Colomb. 126 10 15N 74 55W
Calamar, Vaupés, Colomb. 126 1 58N 72 32W
Calamian Group 73 11 50N 119 55 E
Calamocha 32 40 50N 1 17W
Calañas 31 37 40N 6 53W
Calanda 32 40 56N 0 15W
Calang 72 4 37N 95 37 E
Calangiánus 40 40 56N 9 12 E
Calapan 73 13 25N 121 7 E
Călăraşi 46 44 12N 27 20 E
Calasparra 33 38 14N 1 41W
Calatafimi 40 37 56N 12 50 E
Calatayud 32 41 20N 1 40W
Calauag 73 13 55N 122 15 E
Calavà, C. 41 38 11N 14 55 E
Calavite, Cape 73 13 26N 120 20 E
Calbayog 73 12 4N 124 38 E
Calbe 24 51 57N 11 47 E
Calca 126 13 22 S 72 0W
Calcasieu L. 117 30 0N 93 17W
Calci 38 43 44N 10 31 E
Calcutta 69 22 36N 88 24 E
Caldaro 39 46 23N 11 15 E
Caldas da Rainha 31 39 24N 9 8W
Caldas de Reyes 30 42 36N 8 39W
Calder → 12 53 44N 1 21W
Caldera 124 27 5 S 70 55W
Caldwell, Idaho, U.S.A. 118 43 45N 116 42W
Caldwell, Kans., U.S.A. 117 37 5N 97 37W
Caldwell, Texas, U.S.A. 117 30 30N 96 42W
Caledon 92 34 14 S 19 26 E
Caledon → 92 30 31 S 26 5 E
Caledon B. 97 12 45 S 137 0 E
Caledonia, Can. 112 43 7N 79 58W
Caledonia, U.S.A. 112 42 57N 77 54W
Calella 32 41 37N 2 40 E
Calemba 92 16 0 S 15 44 E
Calera, La 124 32 50 S 71 10W
Calexico 119 32 40N 115 33W
Calf of Man 12 54 4N 4 48W
Calgary 108 51 0N 114 10W
Calhoun 115 34 30N 84 55W
Cali 126 3 25N 76 35W
Calicoan 73 10 59N 125 50 E
Calicut (Kozhikode) 70 11 15N 75 43 E
Caliente 119 37 36N 114 34W
California, Mo., U.S.A. 116 38 37N 92 30W
California, Pa., U.S.A. 112 40 5N 79 55W
California □ 119 37 25N 120 0W
California, Baja, T.N. □ 120 30 0N 115 0W
California, Baja, T.S. □ 120 25 50N 111 50W
California, Golfo de 120 27 0N 111 0W
California, Lr. = California, Baja 120 25 50N 111 50W
Călimăneşti 46 45 14N 24 20 E
Călimani, Munţii 46 47 12N 25 0 E
Călineşti 46 45 21N 24 18 E
Calingasta 124 31 15 S 69 30W
Calipatria 119 33 8N 115 30W
Calistoga 118 38 36N 122 32W
Calitri 41 40 54N 15 25 E
Callabonna, L. 97 29 40 S 140 5 E
Callac 18 48 25N 3 27W
Callan 15 52 33N 7 25W
Callander 14 56 15N 4 14W
Callao 126 12 0 S 77 0W
Callaway 116 41 20N 99 56W
Callide 98 24 18 S 150 28 E
Calling Lake 108 55 15N 113 12W
Callosa de Ensarriá 33 38 40N 0 8W
Callosa de Segura 33 38 7N 0 53W
Calne 12 51 26N 2 0W
Calola 92 16 25 S 17 48 E
Calore → 41 41 11N 14 28 E
Caloundra 99 26 45 S 153 10 E
Calpe 33 38 39N 0 3 E
Calstock 106 49 47N 84 9W
Caltabellotta 40 37 36N 13 11 E
Caltagirone 41 37 13N 14 30 E
Caltanissetta 41 37 30N 14 3 E
Caluire-et-Cuire 21 45 49N 4 51 E
Calulo 88 10 1 S 14 56 E
Calumet 114 47 14N 88 27W
Calunda 89 12 7 S 23 36 E
Caluso 38 45 18N 7 52 E
Calvados □ 18 49 5N 0 15W
Calvert 117 30 59N 96 40W
Calvert I. 108 51 30N 128 0W
Calvinia 92 31 28 S 19 45 E
Calw 25 48 43N 8 44 E
Calzada Almuradiel 33 38 32N 3 28W
Calzada de Calatrava 31 38 42N 3 46W
Cam → 13 52 21N 0 16 E
Cam Lam 71 11 54N 109 10 E
Cam Ranh 71 11 54N 109 12 E
Camabatela 88 8 20 S 15 26 E
Camacupa 89 11 58 S 17 22 E
Camagüey 121 21 20N 78 0W
Camaiore 38 43 57N 10 18 E
Camaná 126 16 30 S 72 50W
Camaquã → 125 31 17 S 51 47W
Camarat, C. 21 43 12N 6 41 E
Camaret 18 48 16N 4 37W
Camargo 126 20 38 S 65 15 E
Camargue 21 43 34N 4 34 E
Camariñas 30 43 8N 9 12W
Camarón, C. 121 16 0N 85 0W
Camarones 128 44 50 S 65 40W
Camas 118 45 35N 122 24W
Camas Valley 118 43 0N 123 46W
Cambados 30 42 31N 8 49W
Cambará 125 23 2 S 50 5W
Cambay 68 22 23N 72 33 E
Cambay, G. of 68 20 45N 72 30 E
Cambil 33 37 40N 3 33W
Cambo-les-Bains 20 43 22N 1 23W
Cambodia ■ 71 12 15N 105 0 E
Camborne 13 50 13N 5 18W
Cambrai 19 50 11N 3 14 E
Cambria 119 35 39N 121 6W
Cambrian Mts. 13 52 25N 3 52W
Cambridge, Can. 106 43 23N 80 15W
Cambridge, N.Z. 101 37 54 S 175 29 E
Cambridge, U.K. 13 52 13N 0 8 E
Cambridge, Idaho, U.S.A. 118 44 36N 116 40W
Cambridge, Mass., U.S.A. 114 42 20N 71 8W
Cambridge, Md., U.S.A. 114 38 33N 76 2W
Cambridge, Minn., U.S.A. 116 45 34N 93 15W
Cambridge, N.Y., U.S.A. 113 43 2N 73 22W
Cambridge, Nebr., U.S.A. 116 40 20N 100 12W
Cambridge, Ohio, U.S.A. 114 40 1N 81 35W
Cambridge Bay 104 69 10N 105 0W
Cambridge Gulf 96 14 55 S 128 15 E
Cambridge Springs 112 41 47N 80 4W
Cambridgeshire □ 13 52 12N 0 7 E
Cambrils 32 41 8N 1 3 E
Cambuci 125 21 35 S 41 55W
Camden, Ala., U.S.A. 115 31 59N 87 15W
Camden, Ark., U.S.A. 117 33 40N 92 50W
Camden, Me., U.S.A. 107 44 14N 69 6W
Camden, N.J., U.S.A. 114 39 57N 75 7W
Camden, S.C., U.S.A. 115 34 17N 80 34W
Camdenton 117 38 0N 92 45W
Camembert 18 48 53N 0 10 E
Cámeri 38 45 30N 8 40 E
Camerino 39 43 10N 13 4 E
Cameron, Ariz., U.S.A. 119 35 55N 111 31W
Cameron, La., U.S.A. 117 29 50N 93 18W
Cameron, Mo., U.S.A. 116 39 42N 94 14W
Cameron, Tex., U.S.A. 117 30 53N 97 0W
Cameron Falls 106 49 8N 88 19W
Cameron Highlands 71 4 27N 101 22 E
Cameron Hills 108 59 48N 118 0W
Cameroon ■ 88 6 0N 12 30 E
Camerota 41 40 2N 15 21 E
Cameroun → 85 4 0N 9 35 E
Cameroun, Mt. 88 4 13N 9 10 E
Cametá 127 2 12 S 49 30W
Camiguin 73 8 55N 123 55 E
Caminha 30 41 50N 8 50W
Camino 118 38 47N 120 40W
Camira Creek 99 29 15 S 152 58 E
Cammal 112 41 24N 77 28W
Camocim 127 2 55 S 40 50W
Camogli 38 44 21N 9 9 E
Camooweal 97 19 56 S 138 7 E
Camopi → 127 3 10N 52 20W
Camp Crook 116 45 36N 103 59W
Camp Wood 117 29 41N 100 0W
Campagna 41 40 40N 15 5 E
Campana 124 34 10 S 58 55W
Campana, I. 128 48 20 S 75 20W
Campanario 31 38 52N 5 36W
Campania □ 41 40 50N 14 45 E
Campbell 112 41 5N 80 36W
Campbell I. 94 52 30 S 169 0 E
Campbell L. 109 63 14N 106 55W
Campbell River 108 50 5N 125 20W
Campbell Town 99 41 52 S 147 30 E
Campbellford 112 44 18N 77 48W
Campbellsville 114 37 23N 85 21W
Campbellton 107 47 57N 66 43W
Campbelltown 99 34 4 S 150 49 E
Campbeltown 14 55 25N 5 36W
Campeche 120 19 50N 90 32W
Campeche □ 120 19 50N 90 32W
Campeche, Bahía de 120 19 30N 93 0W
Camperdown 99 38 14 S 143 9 E
Camperville 109 51 59N 100 9W
Campi Salentina 41 40 22N 18 2 E
Campidano 40 39 30N 8 40 E
Campillo de Altobuey 32 39 36N 1 49W
Campillo de Llerena 31 38 30N 5 50W
Campillos 31 37 4N 4 51W
Campina Grande 127 7 20 S 35 47W
Campiña, La 31 37 45N 4 45W
Campinas 125 22 50 S 47 0W
Campli 39 42 44N 13 40 E
Campo, Camer. 88 2 22N 9 50 E
Campo, Spain 32 42 25N 0 24 E
Campo Belo 127 20 52 S 45 16W
Campo de Criptana 33 39 24N 3 7W
Campo de Gibraltar 31 36 15N 5 25W
Campo Formoso 127 10 30 S 40 20W
Campo Grande 127 20 25 S 54 40W
Campo Maior 127 4 50 S 42 12W
Campo Maior 31 38 59N 7 7W
Campo Túres 39 46 53N 11 55 E
Campoalegre 126 2 41N 75 20W
Campobasso 41 41 34N 14 40 E
Campobello di Licata 40 37 16N 13 55 E
Campobello di Mazara 40 37 38N 12 45 E
Campofelice 40 37 54N 13 53 E
Camporeale 40 37 53N 13 3 E
Campos 125 21 50 S 41 20W
Campos Belos 127 13 10 S 47 3W
Campos del Puerto 33 39 26N 3 1 E
Campos Novos 125 27 21 S 51 50W
Camprodón 32 42 19N 2 23 E
Campuya → 126 1 40 S 73 30W
Camrose 108 53 0N 112 50W
Camsell Portage 109 59 37N 109 15W
Can Tho 71 10 2N 105 46 E
Canaan 113 42 1N 73 20W
Canada ■ 104 60 0N 100 0W
Cañada de Gómez 124 32 40 S 61 30W
Canadian 117 35 56N 100 25W
Canadian → 117 35 27N 95 3W
Canakkale 44 40 8N 26 30 E
Canakkale Boğazi 44 40 0N 26 0 E
Canal Flats 108 50 10N 115 48W
Canal latéral à la Garonne 20 44 25N 0 15 E
Canalejas 124 35 15 S 66 34W
Canals, Argent. 124 33 35 S 62 53W
Canals, Spain 33 38 58N 0 35W
Canandaigua 114 42 55N 77 18W
Cananea 120 31 0N 110 20W
Canarias, Islas 80 28 30N 16 0W
Canarreos, Arch. de los 121 21 35N 81 40W
Canary Is. = Canarias, Islas 80 29 30N 17 0W
Canaveral, C. 115 28 28N 80 31W
Cañaveras 32 40 27N 2 24W
Canavieiras 127 15 39 S 39 0W
Canbelego 99 31 32 S 146 18 E
Canberra 97 35 15 S 149 8 E
Canby, Calif., U.S.A. 118 41 26N 120 58W
Canby, Minn., U.S.A. 116 44 44N 96 15W
Canby, Ore., U.S.A. 118 45 16N 122 42W
Cancale 18 48 40N 1 50W
Canche → 19 50 31N 1 39 E
Candala 63 11 30N 49 58 E
Candas 30 43 35N 5 45W
Candé 18 47 34N 1 0W
Candela 41 41 8N 15 31 E
Candelaria 125 27 29 S 55 44W
Candelaria, Pta. de la 30 43 45N 8 0W
Candeleda 30 40 10N 5 14W
Candelo 99 36 47 S 149 43 E
Candia = Iráklion 45 35 20N 25 12 E
Candia, Sea of = Crete, Sea of 45 36 0N 25 0 E
Candle L. 109 53 50N 105 18W
Candlemas I. 5 57 3 S 26 40W
Cando 116 48 30N 99 14W
Canea = Khaniá 45 35 30N 24 4 E
Canelli 38 44 44N 8 18 E
Canelones 125 34 32 S 56 17W
Canet-Plage 20 42 41N 3 2 E
Cañete, Chile 124 37 50 S 73 30W
Cañete, Peru 126 13 8 S 76 30W
Cañete, Spain 32 40 3N 1 54W
Cañete de las Torres 31 37 53N 4 19W
Canfranc 32 42 42N 0 31W
Cangas 30 42 16N 8 47W
Cangas de Narcea 30 43 10N 6 32W
Cangas de Onís 30 43 21N 5 8W
Canguaretama 127 6 20 S 35 5W
Canguçu 125 31 22 S 52 43W
Cangxi 77 31 47N 105 59 E
Cangzhou 76 38 19N 116 52 E
Cani, I. 83 36 21N 10 5 E
Canicattì 40 37 21N 13 50 E
Canicattini 41 37 1N 15 3 E
Canim Lake 108 51 47N 120 54W
Canipaan 72 8 33N 117 15 E
Canisteo 112 42 17N 77 37W
Canisteo → 112 42 15N 77 30W
Cañiza, La 30 42 13N 8 16W
Cañizal 30 41 12N 5 22W
Canjáyar 33 37 1N 2 44W
Cankırı 64 40 40N 33 37 E
Cankuzo 90 3 10 S 30 31 E
Canmore 108 51 7N 115 18W
Cann River 99 37 35 S 149 7 E
Canna 14 57 3N 6 33W
Cannanore 70 11 53N 75 27 E
Cannes 21 43 32N 7 0 E
Canning Basin 96 19 50 S 124 0 E
Canning Town 69 22 23N 88 40 E
Cannington 112 44 20N 79 2W
Cannock 12 52 42N 2 2W
Cannon Ball → 116 46 20N 100 38W
Canoe L. 109 55 10N 108 15W
Canon City 116 38 27N 105 14W
Canora 109 51 40N 102 30W
Canosa di Púglia 41 41 13N 16 4 E
Canourgue, Le 20 44 26N 3 13 E
Canowindra 99 33 35 S 148 38 E
Canso 107 45 20N 61 0W
Cantabria, Sierra de 32 42 40N 2 30W
Cantabrian Mts. = Cantábrica, Cordillera 30 43 0N 5 10W
Cantábrica, Cordillera 30 43 0N 5 10W
Cantal □ 20 45 4N 2 45 E
Cantanhede 30 40 20N 8 36W
Cantavieja 32 40 31N 0 25W
Čantavir 42 45 55N 19 46 E
Canterbury, Austral. 99 25 23 S 141 53 E
Canterbury, U.K. 13 51 17N 1 5 E
Canterbury □ 101 43 45 S 171 19 E
Canterbury Bight 101 44 16 S 171 55 E
Canterbury Plains 101 43 55 S 171 22 E
Cantillana 31 37 36N 5 50W
Canton, Ga., U.S.A. 115 34 13N 84 29W
Canton, Ill., U.S.A. 116 40 32N 90 0W
Canton, Mass., U.S.A. 113 42 8N 71 8W
Canton, Miss., U.S.A. 117 32 40N 90 1W
Canton, Mo., U.S.A. 116 40 10N 91 33W
Canton, N.Y., U.S.A. 114 44 32N 75 3W
Canton, Ohio, U.S.A. 114 40 47N 81 22W
Canton, Okla., U.S.A. 117 36 5N 98 36W
Canton, S.D., U.S.A. 116 43 20N 96 35W
Canton = Guangzhou 75 23 5N 113 10 E
• Canton I. 94 2 50 S 171 40W
Canton L. 117 36 12N 98 40W
Cantù 38 45 44N 9 8 E
Canudos 126 7 13 S 58 5W
Canutama 126 6 30 S 64 20W
Canutillo 119 31 58N 106 36W
Canyon, Texas, U.S.A. 117 35 0N 101 57W
Canyon, Wyo., U.S.A. 118 44 43N 110 36W
Canyonlands Nat. Park 119 38 25N 109 30W
Canyonville 118 42 55N 123 14W
Canzo 38 45 54N 9 18 E
Cao Xian 77 34 50N 115 35 E
Cáorle 39 45 36N 12 51 E
Cap-aux-Meules 107 47 23N 61 52W
Cap-Chat 107 49 6N 66 40W
Cap-de-la-Madeleine 106 46 22N 72 31W
Cap-Haïtien 121 19 40N 72 20W
Capa Stilo 41 38 25N 16 35 E
Capáccio 41 40 26N 15 4 E
Capaia 88 8 27 S 20 13 E
Capanaparo → 126 7 1N 67 7W
Capbreton 20 43 39N 1 26W
Capdenac 20 44 34N 2 5 E
Cape → 98 20 49 S 146 51 E
Cape Barren I. 97 40 25 S 148 15 E
Cape Breton Highlands Nat. Park 107 46 50N 60 40W
Cape Breton I. 107 46 0N 60 30W
Cape Charles 114 37 15N 75 59W
Cape Coast 85 5 5N 1 15W
Cape Dorset 105 64 14N 76 32W
Cape Dyer 105 66 30N 61 22W
Cape Fear → 115 34 30N 78 25W
Cape Girardeau 117 37 20N 89 30W
Cape May 114 39 1N 74 53W
Cape Montague 107 46 5N 62 25W
Cape Palmas 84 4 25N 7 49W
Cape Province □ 92 32 0 S 23 0 E
Cape Tormentine 107 46 8N 63 47W
Cape Town (Kaapstad) 92 33 55 S 18 22 E
Cape Verde Is. ■ 6 17 10N 25 20W
Cape Vincent 113 44 9N 76 20W
Cape York Peninsula 97 12 0 S 142 30 E
Capela 127 10 30 S 37 0W
Capella 98 23 2 S 148 1 E
Capella, Mt. 98 5 4 S 141 8 E
Capelle, La 19 49 59N 3 50 E
Capendu 20 43 11N 2 31 E
Capernaum = Kefar Naḥum 62 32 54N 35 32 E
Capestang 20 43 20N 3 2 E
Capim → 127 1 40 S 47 47W
Capitan 119 33 33N 105 41W
Capizzi 41 37 50N 14 26 E
Čapljina 42 43 10N 17 43 E
Capoche → 91 15 35 S 33 0 E
Capraia 38 43 2N 9 50 E
Caprarola 39 42 21N 12 11 E
Capreol 106 46 43N 80 56W
Caprera 40 41 12N 9 28 E
Capri 41 40 34N 14 15 E
Capricorn, C. 97 23 30 S 151 13 E
Capricorn Group 98 23 30 S 151 55 E
Caprino Veronese 38 45 37N 10 47 E
Caprivi Strip 92 18 0 S 23 0 E
Captainganj 69 26 55N 83 45 E
Captain's Flat 99 35 35 S 149 27 E
Captieux 20 44 18N 0 16W
Cápua 41 41 7N 14 15 E
Capulin 117 36 48N 103 59W
Caquetá → 126 1 15 S 69 15W
Caracal 46 44 8N 24 22 E
Caracas 126 10 30N 66 55W
Caracol 127 9 15 S 43 22W
Caradoc 99 30 35 S 143 5 E
Caráglio 38 44 25N 7 25 E
Carajás, Serra dos 127 6 0 S 51 30W
Carangola 125 20 44 S 42 5W
Caransebeş 46 45 28N 22 18 E
Carantec 18 48 40N 3 55W
Carapelle → 41 41 3N 15 55 E
Caraş Severin □ 42 45 10N 22 10 E
Caraşova 42 45 11N 21 51 E
Caratasca, Laguna 121 15 20N 83 40W
Caratinga 127 19 50 S 42 10W
Caraúbas 127 5 43 S 37 33W
Caravaca 33 38 8N 1 52W
Caravággio 38 45 30N 9 39 E
Caravelas 127 17 45 S 39 15W
Caraveli 126 15 45 S 73 25W
Caràzinho 125 28 16 S 52 46W
Carballino 30 42 26N 8 5W
Carballo 30 43 13N 8 41W
Carberry 109 49 50N 99 25W
Carbia 30 42 48N 8 14W
Carbó 120 29 42N 110 58W
Carbon 108 51 30N 113 9W

• *Renamed Abariringa*

Carbonara, C. 40 39 8N 9 30 E
Carbondale, Colo, U.S.A. 118 39 30N 107 10W
Carbondale, Ill., U.S.A. 117 37 45N 89 10W
Carbondale, Pa., U.S.A. 114 41 37N 75 30W
Carbonear 107 47 42N 53 13W
Carboneras 33 37 0N 1 53W
Carboneras de Guadazaón 32 39 54N 1 50W
Carbonia 40 39 10N 8 30 E
Carcabuey 31 37 27N 4 17W
Carcagente 33 39 8N 0 28W
Carcajou 108 57 47N 117 6W
Carcans, Étang d' 20 45 6N 1 7W
Carcasse, C. 121 18 30N 74 28W
Carcassonne 20 43 13N 2 20 E
Carche 33 38 26N 1 9W
Carcross 104 60 13N 134 45W
Cardamom Hills 70 9 30N 77 15 E
Cárdenas, Cuba 121 23 0N 81 30W
Cárdenas, San Luis Potosí, Mexico 120 22 0N 99 41W
Cárdenas, Tabasco, Mexico 120 17 59N 93 21W
Cardenete 32 39 46N 1 41W
Cardiff 13 51 28N 3 11W
Cardigan 13 52 6N 4 41W
Cardigan B. 13 52 30N 4 30W
Cardinal 113 44 47N 75 23W
Cardona, Spain 32 41 56N 1 40 E
Cardona, Uruguay 124 33 53 S 57 18W
Cardoner → 32 41 41N 1 51 E
Cardross 109 49 50N 105 40W
Cardston 108 49 15N 113 20W
Cardwell 98 18 14 S 146 2 E
Careen L. 109 57 0N 108 11W
Carei 46 47 40N 22 29 E
Careme 73 6 55 S 108 27 E
Carentan 18 49 19N 1 15W
Carey, Idaho, U.S.A. 118 43 19N 113 58W
Carey, Ohio, U.S.A. 114 40 58N 83 22W
Carey, L. 96 29 0 S 122 15 E
Carey L. 109 62 12N 102 55W
Careysburg 84 6 34N 10 30W
Cargados Garajos 3 17 0 S 59 0 E
Cargèse 21 42 7N 8 35 E
Carhaix-Plouguer 18 48 18N 3 36W
Carhué 124 37 10 S 62 50W
Caribbean Sea 121 15 0N 75 0W
Cariboo Mts. 108 53 0N 121 0W
Caribou 107 46 55N 68 0W
Caribou →, Man., Can. 109 59 20N 94 44W
Caribou →, N.W.T., Can. 108 61 27N 125 45W
Caribou I. 106 47 22N 85 49W
Caribou Is. 108 61 55N 113 15W
Caribou L., Man., Can. 109 59 21N 96 10W
Caribou L., Ont., Can. 106 50 25N 89 5W
Caribou Mts. 108 59 12N 115 40W
Carignan 19 49 38N 5 10 E
Carignano 38 44 55N 7 40 E
Carinda 99 30 28 S 147 41 E
Cariñena 32 41 20N 1 13W
Carinhanha 127 14 15 S 44 46W
Carini 40 38 9N 13 10 E
Carinola 40 41 11N 13 58 E
Carinthia □ = Kärnten 26 46 52N 13 30 E
Caripito 126 10 8N 63 6W
Caritianas 126 9 20 S 63 6W
Carlbrod = Dimitrovgrad 42 43 0N 22 48 E
Carlentini 41 37 15N 15 2 E
Carleton Place 106 45 8N 76 9W
Carletonville 92 26 23 S 27 22 E
Carlin 118 40 44N 116 5W
Carlingford, L. 15 54 0N 6 5W
Carlinville 116 39 20N 89 55W
Carlisle, U.K. 12 54 54N 2 55W
Carlisle, U.S.A. 114 40 12N 77 10W
Carlitte, Pic 20 42 35N 1 55 E
Carloforte 40 39 10N 8 18 E
Carlos Casares 124 35 32 S 61 20W
Carlos Tejedor 124 35 25 S 62 25W
Carlota, La 124 33 30 S 63 20W
Carlow 15 52 50N 6 58W
Carlow □ 15 52 43N 6 50W
Carlsbad, Calif., U.S.A. 119 33 11N 117 25W
Carlsbad, N. Mex., U.S.A. 117 32 20N 104 14W
Carlyle, Can. 109 49 40N 102 20W
Carlyle, U.S.A. 116 38 38N 89 23W
Carmacks 104 62 5N 136 16W
Carmagnola 38 44 50N 7 42 E
Carman 109 49 30N 98 0W
Carmangay 108 50 10N 113 10W
Carmanville 107 49 23N 54 19W
Carmarthen 13 51 52N 4 20W
Carmarthen B. 13 51 40N 4 30W
Carmaux 20 44 3N 2 10 E
Carmel 113 41 25N 73 38W
Carmel-by-the-Sea 119 36 38N 121 55W
Carmel Mt. 62 32 45N 35 3 E
Carmelo 124 34 0 S 58 20W
Carmen, Colomb. 126 9 43N 75 8W
Carmen, Parag. 125 27 13 S 56 12W
Carmen de Patagones 128 40 50 S 63 0W
Carmen, I. 120 26 0N 111 20W
Cármenes 30 42 58N 5 34W
Carmensa 124 35 15 S 67 40W
Carmi 114 38 6N 88 10W
Carmila 98 21 55 S 149 24 E
* Carmona 31 37 28N 5 42W
Carnarvon, Queens., Austral. 98 24 48 S 147 45 E
Carnarvon, W. Austral., Austral. 96 24 51 S 113 42 E
Carnarvon, S. Afr. 92 30 56 S 22 8 E
Carnarvon Ra. 99 25 15 S 148 30 E
Carnaxide 31 38 43N 9 14W
Carndonagh 15 55 15N 7 16W
Carnduff 109 49 10N 101 50W
Carnegie 112 40 24N 80 4W
Carnegie, L. 96 26 5 S 122 30 E
Carnic Alps = Karnische Alpen 26 46 36N 13 0 E
Carnot 88 4 59N 15 56 E
Carnot B. 96 17 20 S 121 30 E
Carnsore Pt. 15 52 10N 6 20W
Caro 114 43 29N 83 27W
Carol City 115 25 5N 80 16W
Carolina, Brazil 127 7 10 S 47 30W

Carolina, S. Afr. 93 26 5 S 30 6 E
Carolina, La 31 38 17N 3 38W
Caroline I. 95 9 15 S 150 3W
Caroline Is. 94 8 0N 150 0 E
Caron 109 50 30N 105 50W
Caroni → 126 8 21N 62 43W
Carovigno 41 40 42N 17 40 E
Carpathians 46 49 50N 21 0 E
Carpaţii Meridionali 46 45 30N 25 0 E
Carpenédolo 38 45 22N 10 25 E
Carpentaria Downs 98 18 44 S 144 20 E
Carpentaria, G. of 97 14 0 S 139 0 E
Carpentras 21 44 3N 5 2 E
Carpi 38 44 47N 10 52 E
Carpino 41 41 50N 15 51 E
Carpinteria 119 34 25N 119 31W
Carpio 30 41 13N 5 7W
Carrabelle 115 29 52N 84 40W
Carrara 38 44 5N 10 7 E
Carrascosa del Campo 32 40 2N 2 45W
Carrauntohill, Mt. 15 52 0N 9 49W
Carrick-on-Shannon 15 53 57N 8 7W
Carrick-on-Suir 15 52 22N 7 30W
Carrickfergus 15 54 43N 5 50W
Carrickfergus □ 15 54 43N 5 49W
Carrickmacross 15 54 0N 6 43W
Carrieton 99 32 25 S 138 31 E
Carrington 116 47 30N 99 7W
Carrión → 30 41 53N 4 32W
Carrión de los Condes 30 42 20N 4 37W
Carrizal Bajo 124 28 5 S 71 20W
Carrizalillo 124 29 5 S 71 30W
Carrizo Cr. 117 36 30N 103 40W
Carrizo Springs 117 28 28N 99 50W
Carrizozo 119 33 40N 105 57W
Carroll 116 42 2N 94 55W
Carrollton, Ga., U.S.A. 115 33 36N 85 5W
Carrollton, Ill., U.S.A. 116 39 20N 90 25W
Carrollton, Ky., U.S.A. 114 38 40N 85 10W
Carrollton, Mo., U.S.A. 116 39 19N 93 24W
Carrollton, Ohio, U.S.A. 112 40 31N 81 9W
Carron → 14 57 30N 5 30W
Carron, L. 14 57 22N 5 35W
Carrot → 109 53 50N 101 17W
Carrot River 109 53 17N 103 35W
Carrouges 18 48 34N 0 10W
Carruthers 109 52 52N 109 16W
Çarşamba 64 41 15N 36 45 E
Carse of Gowrie 14 56 30N 3 10W
Carsoli 39 42 7N 13 3 E
Carson 116 46 27N 101 29W
Carson City 118 39 12N 119 46W
Carson Sink 118 39 50N 118 40W
Carsonville 114 43 25N 82 39W
Carstairs 14 55 42N 3 41W
Cartagena, Colomb. 126 10 25N 75 33W
Cartagena, Spain 33 37 38N 0 59W
Cartago, Colomb. 126 4 45N 75 55W
Cartago, C. Rica 121 9 50N 85 52W
Cartaxo 31 39 10N 8 47W
Cartaya 31 37 16N 7 9W
Carteret 18 49 23N 1 47W
Cartersville 115 34 11N 84 48W
Carterton 101 41 2 S 175 31 E
Carthage, Ark., U.S.A. 117 34 4N 92 32W
Carthage, Ill., U.S.A. 116 40 25N 91 10W
Carthage, Mo., U.S.A. 117 37 10N 94 20W
Carthage, N.Y., U.S.A. 114 43 59N 75 37W
Carthage, S.D., U.S.A. 116 44 14N 97 38W
Carthage, Texas, U.S.A. 117 32 8N 94 20W
Cartier I. 96 12 31 S 123 29 E
Cartwright 107 53 41N 56 58W
Caruaru 127 8 15 S 35 55W
Carúpano 126 10 39N 63 15W
Caruthersville 117 36 10N 89 40W
Carvin 19 50 30N 2 57 E
Carvoeiro 126 1 30 S 61 59W
Carvoeiro, Cabo 31 39 21N 9 24W
Casa Branca 31 38 29N 8 12W
Casa Grande 119 32 53N 111 51W
Casa Nova 127 9 25 S 41 5W
Casablanca, Chile 124 33 20 S 71 25W
Casablanca, Moroc. 82 33 36N 7 36W
Casacalenda 41 41 45N 14 50 E
Casal di Principe 41 41 0N 14 8 E
Casalbordino 39 42 10N 14 34 E
Casale Monferrato 38 45 8N 8 28 E
Casalmaggiore 38 44 59N 10 25 E
Casalpusterlengo 38 45 10N 9 40 E
Casamance → 84 12 33N 16 46W
Casamássima 41 40 58N 16 55 E
Casarano 41 40 0N 18 10 E
Casares 31 36 27N 5 16W
Casas Grandes 120 30 22N 108 0W
Casas Ibañez 33 39 17N 1 30W
Casasimarro 33 39 22N 2 3W
Casatejada 30 39 54N 5 40W
Casavieja 30 40 17N 4 46W
Cascade, Idaho, U.S.A. 118 44 30N 116 2W
Cascade, Mont., U.S.A. 118 47 16N 111 46W
Cascade Locks 118 45 44N 121 54W
Cascade Ra. 102 47 0N 121 30W
Cascais 31 38 41N 9 25W
Cáscina 38 43 40N 10 32 E
Caselle Torinese 38 45 12N 7 39 E
Caserta 41 41 5N 14 20 E
Cashel 15 52 31N 7 53W
Cashmere 118 47 31N 120 30W
Casiguran 73 16 22N 122 7 E
Casilda 124 33 10 S 61 10W
Casimcea 46 44 45N 28 23 E
Casino 97 28 52 S 153 3 E
Casiquiare → 126 2 1N 67 7W
Caslan 108 54 38N 112 31W
Čáslav 26 49 54N 15 22 E
Casma 126 9 30 S 78 20W
Casola Valsenio 39 44 12N 11 40 E
Cásoli 39 42 7N 14 18 E
Caspe 32 41 14N 0 1W
Casper 118 42 52N 106 20W
Caspian Sea 53 43 0N 50 0 E
Casquets 18 49 46N 2 15W

Cass City 114 43 34N 83 24W
Cass Lake 116 47 23N 94 38W
Cassá de la Selva 32 41 53N 2 52 E
Cassano Iónio 41 39 47N 16 20 E
Cassel 19 50 48N 2 30 E
Casselman 113 45 19N 75 5W
Casselton 116 47 0N 97 15W
Cassiar 108 59 16N 129 40W
Cassiar Mts. 108 59 30N 130 30W
Cassino 40 41 30N 13 50 E
Cassis 21 43 14N 5 32 E
Cassville 117 36 45N 93 52W
Cástagneto Carducci 38 43 9N 10 36 E
Castéggio 38 45 1N 9 8 E
Castejón de Monegros 32 41 37N 0 15W
Castel di Sangro 39 41 47N 14 6 E
Castel San Giovanni 38 45 4N 9 25 E
Castel San Pietro 39 44 23N 11 30 E
Castelbuono 41 37 56N 14 4 E
Casteldelfino 38 44 35N 7 4 E
Castelfiorentino 38 43 36N 10 58 E
Castelfranco Emília 38 44 37N 11 2 E
Castelfranco Véneto 39 45 40N 11 56 E
Casteljaloux 20 44 19N 0 6 E
Castellabate 41 40 18N 14 55 E
Castellammare del Golfo 40 38 2N 12 53 E
Castellammare di Stábia 41 40 47N 14 29 E
Castellammare, G. di 40 38 5N 12 55 E
Castellamonte 38 45 23N 7 42 E
Castellana Grotte 41 40 53N 17 10 E
Castellane 21 43 50N 6 31 E
Castellaneta 41 40 40N 16 57 E
Castellar de Santisteban 33 38 16N 3 8W
Castelleone 38 45 19N 9 47 E
Castelli 124 36 7 S 57 47W
Castelló de Ampurias 32 42 15N 3 4 E
Castellón □ 32 40 15N 0 5W
Castellón de la Plana 32 39 58N 0 3W
Castellote 32 40 48N 0 15W
Castellterssol 32 41 45N 2 8 E
Castelmáuro 41 41 50N 14 40 E
Castelnau-de-Médoc 20 45 2N 0 48W
Castelnaudary 20 43 20N 1 58 E
Castelnovo ne' Monti 38 44 27N 10 26 E
Castelnuovo di Val di Cécina 38 43 12N 10 54 E
Castelo 125 20 33 S 41 14 E
Castelo Branco 30 39 50N 7 31W
Castelo Branco □ 30 39 52N 7 45W
Castelo de Paiva 30 41 2N 8 16W
Castelo de Vide 31 39 25N 7 27W
Castelsarrasin 20 44 2N 1 7 E
Casteltérmini 40 37 32N 13 38 E
Castelvetrano 40 37 40N 12 46 E
Casterton 99 37 30 S 141 30 E
Castets 20 43 52N 1 6W
Castiglione del Lago 39 43 7N 12 3 E
Castiglione della Pescáia 38 42 46N 10 53 E
Castiglione delle Stiviere 38 45 23N 10 30 E
Castiglione Fiorentino 39 43 20N 11 55 E
Castilblanco 31 39 17N 5 5W
Castilla La Nueva 31 39 45N 3 20W
Castilla La Vieja 30 41 55N 4 0W
Castilla, Playa de 31 37 0N 6 33W
Castille = Castilla 30 40 0N 3 30W
Castillon, Barrage de 21 43 53N 6 33 E
Castillon-en-Couserans 20 42 56N 1 1 E
Castillon-la-Bataille 20 44 51N 0 2W
Castillonès 20 44 39N 0 37 E
Castillos 125 34 12 S 53 52W
Castle Dale 118 39 11N 111 1W
Castle Douglas 14 54 57N 3 57W
Castle Harbour 121 32 17N 64 44W
Castle Point 101 40 54 S 176 15 E
Castle Rock, Colo., U.S.A. 116 39 26N 104 50W
Castle Rock, Wash., U.S.A. 118 46 20N 122 58W
Castlebar 15 53 52N 9 17W
Castleblaney 15 54 7N 6 44W
Castlegar 108 49 20N 117 40W
Castlegate 118 39 45N 110 57W
Castlemaine 97 37 2 S 144 12 E
Castlereagh 15 53 47N 8 30W
Castlereagh □ 15 54 33N 5 53W
Castlereagh → 97 30 12 S 147 32 E
Castlereagh B. 96 12 10 S 135 10 E
Castletown 12 54 4N 4 40W
Castletown Bearhaven 15 51 40N 9 54W
Castlevale 98 24 30 S 146 48 E
Castor 108 52 15N 111 50W
Castres 20 43 37N 2 13 E
Castries 121 14 0N 60 50W
Castril 33 37 48N 2 46W
Castro, Brazil 125 24 45 S 50 0W
Castro, Chile 128 42 30 S 73 50W
Castro Alves 127 12 46 S 39 33W
Castro del Río 31 37 41N 4 29W
Castro Marim 31 37 13N 7 26W
Castro Urdiales 32 43 23N 3 11W
Castro Verde 31 37 41N 8 4W
Castrojeriz 30 42 17N 4 9W
Castropol 30 43 32N 7 0W
Castroreale 41 38 5N 15 15 E
Castrovillari 41 39 49N 16 11 E
Castroville 117 29 20N 98 53W
Castuera 31 38 43N 5 37W
Casummit Lake 106 51 29N 92 22W
Cat I., Bahamas 121 24 30N 75 30W
Cat I., U.S.A. 117 30 15N 89 7W
Cat L. 106 51 40N 91 50W
Çata 27 47 58N 18 38 E
Catacáos 126 5 20 S 80 45W
Cataguases 125 21 23 S 42 39W
Catahoula L. 117 31 30N 92 5W
Catalão 127 18 10 S 47 57W
Catalina 107 48 31N 53 4W
Catalonia = Cataluña 32 41 40N 1 15 E
Cataluña 32 41 40N 1 15 E
Catamarca 124 28 30 S 65 50W
Catamarca □ 124 27 0 S 65 50W
Catanduanes 73 13 50N 124 20 E
Catanduva 125 21 5 S 48 58W
Catánia 41 37 31N 15 4 E
Catánia, G. di 41 37 25N 15 8 E

Catanzaro 41 38 54N 16 38 E
Catarman 73 12 28N 124 35 E
Catastrophe C. 96 34 59 S 136 0 E
Cateau, Le 19 50 6N 3 30 E
Cateel 73 7 47N 126 24 E
Cathcart 92 32 18 S 27 10 E
Cathlamet 118 46 12N 123 23W
Catio 84 11 17N 15 15W
Cativa 120 9 21N 79 49W
Catlettsburg 114 38 23N 82 38W
Cato I. 97 23 15 S 155 32 E
Catoche, C. 120 21 40N 87 8W
Catral 33 38 10N 0 47W
Catria, Mt. 39 43 28N 12 42 E
Catrimani 126 0 27N 61 41W
Catskill 114 42 14N 73 52W
Catskill Mts. 114 42 15N 74 15W
Cattaraugus 112 42 22N 78 52W
Cattólica 39 43 58N 12 43 E
Cattólica Eraclea 40 37 27N 13 24 E
Catuala 92 16 25 S 19 2 E
Catur 91 13 45 S 35 30 E
Cauca → 126 8 54N 74 28W
Caucaia 127 3 40 S 38 35W
Caucasus Mts. = Bolshoi Kavkas 57 42 50N 44 0 E
Caudebec-en-Caux 18 49 30N 0 42 E
Caudete 33 38 42N 1 2W
Caudry 19 50 7N 3 22 E
Caulnes 18 48 18N 2 10W
Caulónia 41 38 23N 16 25 E
Caúngula 88 8 26 S 18 38 E
Cauquenes 124 36 0 S 72 22W
Caura → 126 7 38N 64 53W
Cauresi → 91 17 8 S 33 0 E
Causapscal 107 48 19N 67 12W
Caussade 20 44 10N 1 33 E
Cauterets 20 42 52N 0 8W
Caux, Pays de 18 49 38N 0 35 E
Cava dei Tirreni 41 40 42N 14 42 E
Cávado → 30 41 32N 8 48W
Cavaillon 21 43 50N 5 2 E
Cavalaire-sur-Mer 21 43 10N 6 33 E
Cavalerie, La 20 44 0N 3 10 E
Cavalese 39 46 17N 11 29 E
Cavalier 116 48 50N 97 39W
Cavallo, Île de 21 41 22N 9 16 E
Cavally → 84 4 22N 7 32W
Cavan 15 54 0N 7 22W
Cavan □ 15 53 58N 7 10W
Cavárzere 39 45 8N 12 6 E
Cave City 114 37 13N 85 57W
Cavendish 99 37 31 S 142 2 E
Caviana, I. 127 0 10N 50 10W
Cavite 73 14 29N 120 55 E
Cavour 38 44 47N 7 22 E
Cavtat 42 42 35N 18 13 E
Cawndilla, L. 99 32 30 S 142 15 E
Cawnpore = Kanpur 69 26 28N 80 20 E
Caxias 127 4 55 S 43 20W
Caxias do Sul 125 29 10 S 51 10W
Caxine, C. 82 35 56N 0 27W
Caxito 88 8 30 S 13 30 E
Cay Sal Bank 121 23 45N 80 0W
Cayambe 126 0 3N 78 8W
Cayce 115 33 59N 81 10W
Cayenne 127 5 0N 52 18W
Cayes, Les 121 18 15N 73 46W
Cayeux-sur-Mer 19 50 10N 1 30 E
Caylus 20 44 15N 1 47 E
Cayman Is. 121 19 40N 80 30W
* Cayo 120 17 10N 89 0W
Cayo Romano 121 22 0N 78 0W
Cayuga, Can. 112 42 59N 79 50W
Cayuga, U.S.A. 113 42 54N 76 44W
Cayuga L. 114 42 45N 76 45W
Cazalla de la Sierra 31 37 56N 5 45W
Căzăneşti 46 44 36N 27 3 E
Cazaux et de Sanguinet, Étang de 20 44 29N 1 10W
Cazères 20 43 13N 1 5 E
Cazin 39 44 57N 15 57 E
Čazma 39 45 45N 16 39 E
Čazma → 39 45 35N 16 29 E
Cazombo 89 11 54 S 22 56 E
Cazorla 33 37 55N 3 2W
Cazorla, Sierra de 33 38 5N 2 55W
Cea → 30 42 0N 5 36W
Ceamurlia de Jos 43 44 43N 28 47 E
Ceanannus Mor 15 53 42N 6 53W
Ceará = Fortaleza 127 3 43 S 38 35W
Ceará □ 127 5 0 S 40 0W
Ceará Mirim 127 5 38 S 35 25W
Ceauru, L. 46 44 58N 23 11 E
Cebollar 124 29 10 S 66 35W
Cebollera, Sierra de 32 42 0N 2 30W
Cebreros 30 40 27N 4 28W
Cebu 73 10 18N 123 54 E
Ceccano 40 41 34N 13 18 E
Cece 27 46 46N 18 39 E
Cechi 84 6 15N 4 25W
Cecil Plains 99 27 30 S 151 11 E
Cécina 38 43 19N 10 33 E
Cécina → 38 43 19N 10 29 E
Ceclavin 30 39 50N 6 45W
Cedar → 116 41 17N 91 21W
Cedar City 119 37 41N 113 3W
Cedar Creek Res. 117 32 4N 96 5W
Cedar Falls 116 42 39N 92 29W
Cedar Key 115 29 9N 83 5W
Cedar L. 109 53 10N 100 0W
Cedar Rapids 116 42 0N 91 38W
Cedarburg 114 43 18N 87 55W
Cedartown 115 34 1N 85 15W
Cedarvale 108 55 1N 128 22W
Cedarville 118 41 37N 120 13W
Cedeira 30 43 39N 8 2W
Cedral 120 23 50N 100 42W
Cedrino → 40 40 23N 9 44 E
Cedro 127 6 34 S 39 3W
Cedros, I. de 120 28 10N 115 20W
Ceduna 96 32 7 S 133 46 E
Cedynia 28 52 53N 14 12 E
Cefalù 41 38 3N 14 1 E

* Renamed N'gage

* Renamed San Ignacio

HIA

Cega → 30 41 33N 4 46W
Cegléd 27 47 11N 19 47 E
Céglie Messápico 41 40 39N 17 31 E
Cehegín 33 38 6N 1 48W
Cehu-Silvaniei 46 47 24N 23 9 E
Ceiba, La 121 15 40N 86 50W
Ceica 46 46 53N 22 10 E
Ceira → 30 40 13N 8 16W
Cekhira 83 34 20N 10 5 E
Celano 39 42 6N 13 30 E
Celanova 30 42 9N 7 58W
Celaya 120 20 31N 100 37W
Celbridge 15 53 20N 6 33W
Celebes = Sulawesi 73 2 0S 120 0 E
Celebes Sea 73 3 0N 123 0 E
Čelić 42 44 43N 18 47 E
Celina 114 40 32N 84 31W
Celje 39 46 16N 15 18 E
Celldömölk 27 47 16N 17 10 E
Celle 24 52 37N 10 4 E
Celorico da Beira 30 40 38N 7 24W
Cement 117 34 56N 98 8W
Cengong 77 27 13N 108 44 E
Cenis, Col du Mt. 21 45 15N 6 55 E
Ceno → 38 44 4N 10 5 E
Cenon 20 44 50N 0 33W
Centallo 38 44 30N 7 35 E
Center, N.D., U.S.A. 116 47 9N 101 17W
Center, Texas, U.S.A. 117 31 50N 94 10W
Centerfield 119 39 9N 111 56W
Centerville, Ala., U.S.A. 115 32 55N 87 7W
Centerville, Iowa, U.S.A. 116 40 45N 92 57W
Centerville, Miss., U.S.A. 117 31 10N 91 3W
Centerville, Pa., U.S.A. 112 40 3N 79 59W
Centerville, S.D., U.S.A. 116 43 10N 96 58W
Centerville, Tenn., U.S.A. 115 35 46N 87 29W
Centerville, Tex., U.S.A. 117 31 15N 95 56W
Cento 39 44 43N 11 16 E
Central 119 32 46N 108 9W
Central □, Kenya 90 0 30S 37 30 E
Central □, Malawi 91 13 30S 33 30 E
Central □, U.K. 14 56 10N 4 30W
Central □, Zambia 91 14 25S 28 50 E
Central African Republic ■ 88 7 0N 20 0 E
Central City, Ky., U.S.A. 114 37 20N 87 7W
Central City, Nebr., U.S.A. 116 41 8N 98 0W
Central, Cordillera, Colomb. 126 5 0N 75 0W
Central, Cordillera, C. Rica 121 10 10N 84 5W
Central I. 90 3 30N 36 0 E
Central Islip 113 40 49N 73 13W
Central Makran Range 65 26 30N 64 15 E
Central Patricia 106 51 30N 90 9W
Central Ra. 98 5 0S 143 0 E
Central Russian Uplands 9 54 0N 36 0 E
Central Siberian Plateau 59 65 0N 105 0 E
Centralia, Ill., U.S.A. 116 38 32N 89 5W
Centralia, Mo., U.S.A. 116 39 12N 92 6W
Centralia, Wash., U.S.A. 118 46 46N 122 59W
Centúripe 41 37 37N 14 41 E
Cephalonia = Kefallinía 45 38 15N 20 30 E
Cepin 42 45 32N 18 34 E
Ceprano 40 41 33N 13 30 E
Ceptura 46 45 1N 26 21 E
Cepu 73 7 12S 111 31 E
Ceram = Seram 73 3 10S 129 0 E
Ceram Sea = Seram Sea 73 2 30S 128 30 E
Cerbère 20 42 26N 3 10 E
Cerbicales, Îles 21 41 33N 9 22 E
Cerbu 46 44 46N 24 46 E
Cercal 31 37 48N 8 40W
Cercemaggiore 41 41 27N 14 43 E
Cerdaña 32 42 22N 1 35 E
Cerdedo 30 42 33N 8 23W
Cère → 20 44 55N 1 49 E
Cerea 39 45 12N 11 13 E
Ceres, Argent. 124 29 55S 61 55W
Ceres, Italy 38 45 19N 7 22 E
Ceres, S. Afr. 92 33 21S 19 18 E
Céret 20 42 30N 2 42 E
Cerignola 41 41 17N 15 53 E
Cerigo = Kíthira 45 36 15N 23 0 E
Cérilly 20 46 37N 2 50 E
Cerisiers 19 48 8N 3 30 E
Cerizay 18 46 50N 0 40W
Çerkeş 64 40 49N 32 52 E
Cerknica 39 45 48N 14 21 E
Cermerno 42 43 35N 20 25 E
Cerna 46 45 4N 28 17 E
Cerna → 46 44 45N 24 0 E
Cernavodă 46 44 22N 28 3 E
Cernay 19 47 44N 7 10 E
Cernik 42 45 17N 17 22 E
Cerralvo 120 24 20N 109 45 E
Cerreto Sannita 41 41 17N 14 34 E
Cerritos 120 22 27N 100 20W
Cerro 119 36 47N 105 36W
Certaldo 38 43 32N 11 2 E
Cervaro → 41 41 30N 15 52 E
Cervera 32 41 40N 1 16 E
Cervera de Pisuerga 30 42 51N 4 30W
Cervera del Río Alhama 32 42 2N 1 58W
Cérvia 39 44 15N 12 20 E
Cervignano del Friuli 39 45 49N 13 20 E
Cervinara 41 41 2N 14 36 E
Cervione 21 42 20N 9 29 E
Cervo 30 43 40N 7 24W
Cesaro 41 37 50N 14 38 E
Cesena 39 44 9N 12 14 E
Cesenático 39 44 12N 12 22 E
Cēsis 54 57 17N 25 28 E
Česká Lípa 26 50 45N 14 30 E
Česka Socialistická Republika □ 26 49 30N 14 40 E
Česká Třebová 27 49 54N 16 27 E
České Budějovice 26 48 55N 14 25 E
České Velenice 26 48 45N 15 1 E
Ceskomoravská Vrchovina 26 49 30N 15 40 E
Český Brod 26 50 4N 14 52 E
Český Krumlov 26 48 43N 14 21 E
Český Těšin 27 49 45N 18 39 E
Çeşme 45 38 20N 26 23 E
Cessnock 97 32 50S 151 21 E
Cestas 20 44 44N 0 41W
Cestos → 84 5 40N 9 10W
Cetate 46 44 7N 23 2 E
Cétin Grad 39 45 9N 15 45 E
Cetina → 39 43 26N 16 42 E
Cetinje 42 42 23N 18 59 E
Cetraro 41 39 30N 15 56 E
Ceuta 82 35 52N 5 18W
Ceva 38 44 23N 8 3 E
Cévennes 20 44 10N 3 50 E
Ceyhan 64 37 4N 35 47 E
Ceylon = Sri Lanka ■ 70 7 30N 80 50 E
Cèze → 21 44 13N 4 43 E
Cha Pa 71 22 20N 103 47 E
Chabeuil 21 44 54N 5 1 E
Chablais 21 46 20N 6 36 E
Chablis 19 47 47N 3 48 E
Chabounia 82 35 30N 2 38 E
Chacabuco 124 34 40S 60 27W
Chachapoyas 126 6 15S 77 50W
Chachro 68 25 5N 70 15 E
Chaco □ 124 26 30S 61 0W
Chad ■ 81 15 0N 17 15 E
Chad, L. = Tchad, L. 81 13 30N 14 30 E
Chadan 59 51 17N 91 35 E
Chadileuvú → 124 37 46S 66 0W
Chadiza 91 14 45S 32 27 E
Chadron 116 42 50N 103 0W
Chadyr-Lunga 56 46 3N 28 51 E
Chagda 59 58 45N 130 38 E
Chagny 19 46 57N 4 45 E
Chagoda 54 59 10N 35 15 E
Chagos Arch. 60 6 0S 72 0 E
Chágres → 120 9 10N 79 40W
Chāh Bahār 65 25 20N 60 40 E
Chāh Gay Hills 65 29 30N 64 0 E
Chaillé-les-Marais 20 46 25N 1 2W
Chaise-Dieu, La 20 45 20N 3 40 E
Chaize-le-Vicomte, La 18 46 40N 1 18W
Chaj Doab 68 32 15N 73 0 E
Chajari 124 30 42S 58 0W
Chake Chake 90 5 15S 39 45 E
Chakhansur 65 31 10N 62 0 E
Chakhansur □ 65 30 0N 62 0 E
Chakonipau, L. 107 56 18N 68 30W
Chakradharpur 69 22 45N 85 40 E
Chakwal 68 32 56N 72 53 E
Chala 126 15 48S 74 20W
Chalais 20 45 16N 0 3 E
Chalakudi 70 10 18N 76 20 E
Chalcis = Khalkís 45 38 27N 23 42 E
Chaleur B. 107 47 55N 65 30W
Chalhuanca 126 14 15S 73 15W
Chalindrey 19 47 48N 5 26 E
Chaling 77 26 58N 113 30 E
Chalisgaon 70 20 30N 75 10 E
Chalkar 57 50 35N 51 52 E
Chalkar Oz. 57 50 33N 51 45 E
Chalky Inlet 101 46 3S 166 31 E
Challans 18 46 50N 1 52W
Challapata 126 18 53S 66 50W
Challerange 19 49 18N 4 46 E
Challis 118 44 32N 114 25W
Chalna 69 22 36N 89 35 E
Chalon-sur-Saône 19 46 48N 4 50 E
Chalonnes 18 47 20N 0 45W
Châlons-sur-Marne 19 48 58N 4 20 E
Châlus 20 45 39N 0 58 E
Cham 25 49 12N 12 40 E
Chama 119 36 54N 106 35W
Chaman 66 30 58N 66 25 E
Chamarajnagar-Ramasamudram 70 11 52N 76 52 E
Chamartín de la Rosa 32 40 28N 3 40W
Chamba 68 32 35N 76 10 E
Chambal → 69 26 29N 79 15 E
Chamberlain 116 43 50N 99 21W
Chambers 119 35 13N 109 30W
Chambersburg 114 39 53N 77 41W
Chambéry 21 45 34N 5 55 E
Chambly 113 45 27N 73 17W
Chambois 18 48 48N 0 6 E
Chambon-Feugerolles, Le 21 45 24N 4 18 E
Chambord 107 48 25N 72 6W
Chambri L. 98 4 15S 143 10 E
Chamical 124 30 22S 66 27W
Chamonix 21 45 55N 6 51 E
Champa 69 22 2N 82 43 E
Champagne, Can. 108 60 49N 136 30W
Champagne, France 19 49 0N 4 40 E
Champagne, Plaine de 19 49 0N 4 30 E
Champagnole 19 46 45N 5 55 E
Champaign 114 40 8N 88 14W
Champaubert 19 48 50N 3 45 E
Champdeniers 20 46 29N 0 25W
Champeix 20 45 37N 3 8 E
Champion B. 96 28 44S 114 36 E
Champlain, Can. 106 46 27N 72 24W
Champlain, U.S.A. 114 44 59N 73 27W
Champlain, L. 114 44 30N 73 20W
Champotón 120 19 20N 90 50W
Chamusca 31 39 21N 8 29W
Chañaral 124 26 23S 70 40W
Chanasma 68 23 44N 72 5 E
Chandalar 104 67 30N 148 35W
Chandannagar 69 22 52N 88 24 E
Chandausi 68 28 27N 78 49 E
Chandeleur Is. 117 29 48N 88 51W
Chandeleur Sd. 117 29 58N 88 40W
Chandigarh 68 30 43N 76 47 E
Chandler, Can. 107 48 18N 64 46W
Chandler, Ariz., U.S.A. 119 33 20N 111 56W
Chandler, Okla., U.S.A. 117 35 43N 96 53W
Chandmani 75 45 22N 98 2 E
Chandpur, Bangla. 69 23 8N 90 45 E
Chandpur, India 68 29 8N 78 19 E
Chandrapur 70 19 57N 79 25 E
Chang 68 26 59N 68 30 E
Chang Jiang →, Jiangsu, China 75 31 48N 121 10 E
Chang Jiang →, Shanghai, China 75 31 35N 121 15 E
Changanacheri 70 9 25N 76 31 E
Changbai 76 41 25N 128 5 E
Changbai Shan 76 42 20N 129 0 E
Changchiak'ou = Zhangjiakou 76 40 48N 114 55 E
Ch'angchou = Changzhou 75 31 47N 119 58 E
Changchun 76 43 57N 125 17 E
Changde 75 29 4N 111 35 E
Changfeng 77 32 28N 117 10 E
Changhai = Shanghai 75 31 15N 121 26 E
Changjiang 75 19 20N 108 55 E
Changjin-chŏsuji 76 40 30N 127 15 E
Changle 77 25 59N 119 27 E
Changli 76 39 40N 119 13 E
Changning 77 26 28N 112 22 E
Changping 76 40 14N 116 12 E
Changsha 75 28 12N 113 0 E
Changshou 77 29 51N 107 8 E
Changshu 77 31 38N 120 43 E
Changshun 77 26 3N 106 25 E
Changtai 77 24 35N 117 42 E
Changting 75 25 50N 116 22 E
Changyang 77 30 30N 111 10 E
Changzhi 76 36 10N 113 6 E
Changzhou 75 31 47N 119 58 E
Chanhanga 92 16 0S 14 8 E
Chanlar 57 40 25N 46 10 E
Channapatna 70 12 40N 77 15 E
Channel Is., U.K. 18 49 30N 2 40W
Channel Is., U.S.A. 119 33 55N 119 26W
Channel-Port aux Basques 107 47 30N 59 9W
Channing, Mich., U.S.A. 114 46 9N 88 1W
Channing, Tex., U.S.A. 117 35 45N 102 20W
Chantada 30 42 36N 7 46W
Chanthaburi 71 12 38N 102 12 E
Chantilly 19 49 12N 2 29 E
Chantonnay 18 46 40N 1 3W
Chantrey Inlet 104 67 48N 96 20W
Chanute 117 37 45N 95 25W
Chanza → 31 37 32N 7 30W
Chao Hu 77 31 30N 117 30 E
Chao Phraya → 71 13 32N 100 36 E
Chao'an 75 23 42N 116 32 E
Chaoyang, Guangdong, China 75 23 17N 116 30 E
Chaoyang, Liaoning, China 76 41 35N 120 22 E
Chapala 91 15 50S 37 35 E
Chapala, Lago de 120 20 10N 103 20W
Chapayevo 57 50 25N 51 10 E
Chapayevsk 55 53 0N 49 40 E
Chapecó 125 27 14S 52 41W
Chapel Hill 115 35 53N 79 3W
Chapelle-d'Angillon, La 19 47 21N 2 25 E
Chapelle-Glain, La 18 47 38N 1 11W
Chapleau 106 47 50N 83 24W
Chaplin 109 50 28N 106 40W
Chaplino 56 48 8N 36 15 E
Chaplygin 55 53 15N 40 0 E
Chapra 69 25 48N 84 44 E
Châr 80 21 32N 12 45 E
Chara 59 56 54N 118 20 E
Charadai 124 27 35S 60 0W
Charagua 126 19 45S 63 10W
Charaña 126 17 30S 69 25W
Charata 124 27 13S 61 14W
Charcas 120 23 10N 101 20W
Charcoal L. 109 58 49N 102 22W
Charcot I. 5 70 0S 75 0W
Chard 13 50 52N 2 59W
Chardara 58 41 16N 67 59 E
Chardon 112 41 34N 81 17W
Chardzhou 58 39 6N 63 34 E
Charente 20 45 40N 0 5 E
Charente □ 20 45 50N 0 16 E
Charente → 20 45 57N 1 5W
Charente-Maritime □ 20 45 30N 0 35W
Charentsavan 57 40 35N 44 41 E
Chārīkār 65 35 0N 69 10 E
Charité, La 19 47 10N 3 0 E
Chariton → 116 39 19N 92 58W
Charkhari 69 25 24N 79 45 E
Charkhi Dadri 68 28 37N 76 17 E
Charleroi 16 50 24N 4 27 E
Charlerol 112 40 8N 79 54W
Charles, C. 114 37 10N 75 59W
Charles City 116 43 2N 92 41W
Charles L. 109 59 50N 110 33W
Charles Town 114 39 20N 77 50W
Charleston, Ill., U.S.A. 114 39 30N 88 10W
Charleston, Miss., U.S.A. 117 34 2N 90 3W
Charleston, Mo., U.S.A. 117 36 52N 89 20W
Charleston, S.C., U.S.A. 115 32 47N 79 56W
Charleston, W. Va., U.S.A. 114 38 24N 81 36W
Charleston Harb. 115 32 46N 79 55W
Charlestown, S. Afr. 93 27 26S 29 53 E
Charlestown, U.S.A. 114 38 29N 85 40W
Charlesville 88 5 27S 20 59 E
Charleville 97 26 24S 146 15 E
Charleville = Rath Luirc 15 52 21N 8 40W
Charleville-Mézières 19 49 44N 4 40 E
Charlevoix 114 45 19N 85 14W
Charlieu 21 46 10N 4 10 E
Charlotte, Mich., U.S.A. 114 42 36N 84 48W
Charlotte, N.C., U.S.A. 115 35 16N 80 46W
Charlotte Amalie 121 18 22N 64 56W
Charlotte Harbor 115 26 58N 82 4W
Charlotte Waters 96 25 56S 134 54 E
Charlottenberg 48 59 54N 12 17 E
Charlottesville 114 38 1N 78 30W
Charlottetown 107 46 14N 63 8W
Charlton, Austral. 99 36 16S 143 24 E
Charlton, U.S.A. 116 40 59N 93 20W
Charlton I. 106 52 0N 79 20W
Charmes 19 48 22N 6 17 E
Charny 107 46 43N 71 15W
Charolles 21 46 27N 4 16 E
Charost 19 47 0N 2 7 E
Charouine 82 29 0N 0 15W
Charre 91 17 13S 35 10 E
Charroux 20 46 9N 0 25 E
Charters Towers 97 20 5S 146 13 E
Chartre, La 18 47 42N 0 34 E
Chartres 18 48 29N 1 30 E
Chascomús 124 35 30S 58 0W
Chasefu 91 11 55S 33 8 E
Chasovnya-Uchurskaya 59 57 15N 132 50 E
Chasseneuil-sur-Bonnieure 20 45 52N 0 29 E
Chata 68 27 42N 77 30 E
Châtaigneraie, La 18 46 38N 0 45W
Chatal Balkan = Udvoy Balkan 43 42 50N 26 50 E
Château-Chinon 19 47 4N 3 56 E
Château-du-Loir 18 47 40N 0 25 E
Château-Gontier 18 47 50N 0 48W
Château-la-Vallière 18 47 30N 0 20 E
Château-Landon 19 48 8N 2 40 E
Château, Le 20 45 52N 1 12W
Château-Porcien 19 49 31N 4 13 E
Château-Renault 18 47 36N 0 56 E
Château-Salins 19 48 50N 6 30 E
Château-Thierry 19 49 3N 3 20 E
Châteaubourg 18 48 7N 1 25W
Châteaubriant 18 47 43N 1 23W
Châteaudun 18 48 3N 1 20 E
Châteaugiron 18 48 3N 1 30W
Châteauguay 113 45 23N 73 45W
Châteaulin 18 48 11N 4 8W
Châteaumeillant 20 46 35N 2 12 E
Châteauneuf 18 48 35N 1 15 E
Châteauneuf-du-Faou 18 48 11N 3 50W
Châteauneuf-sur-Charente 20 45 36N 0 3W
Châteauneuf-sur-Cher 19 46 52N 2 18 E
Châteauneuf-sur-Loire 19 47 52N 2 13 E
Châteaurenard 21 43 53N 4 51 E
Châteauroux 19 46 50N 1 40 E
Châteaux-Arnoux 21 44 6N 6 0 E
Châtelaillon-Plage 20 46 5N 1 5W
Châtelaudren 18 48 33N 2 59W
Châtelet, Le, Cher, France 20 46 40N 2 20 E
Châtelet, Le, Seine-et-Marne, France 19 48 30N 2 47 E
Châtelguyon 20 45 55N 3 4 E
Châtellerault 18 46 50N 0 30 E
Châtelus-Malvaleix 20 46 18N 2 1 E
Chatfield 116 43 15N 91 58W
Chatham, N.B., Can. 107 47 2N 65 28W
Chatham, Ont., Can. 106 42 24N 82 11W
Chatham, U.K. 13 51 22N 0 32 E
Chatham, La., U.S.A. 117 32 22N 92 26W
Chatham, N.Y., U.S.A. 113 42 21N 73 32W
Chatham Is. 94 44 0S 176 40W
Chatham Str. 108 57 0N 134 40W
Châtillon, Loiret, France 19 47 36N 2 44 E
Châtillon, Marne, France 19 49 5N 3 43 E
Chatillon 38 45 45N 7 40 E
Châtillon-Coligny 19 47 50N 2 51 E
Châtillon-en-Bazois 19 47 3N 3 39 E
Châtillon-en-Diois 21 44 41N 5 29 E
Châtillon-sur-Indre 18 46 59N 1 10 E
Châtillon-sur-Seine 19 47 50N 4 33 E
Châtillon-sur-Sèvre 18 46 56N 0 45W
Chatmohar 69 24 15N 89 15 E
Chatra 69 24 12N 84 56 E
Chatrapur 69 19 22N 85 2 E
Châtre, La 20 46 35N 1 59 E
Chats, L. des 113 45 30N 76 20W
Chatsworth, Can. 112 44 27N 80 54W
Chatsworth, Zimb. 91 19 38S 31 13 E
Chattahoochee 115 30 43N 84 51W
Chattanooga 115 35 2N 85 17W
Chaudanne, Barrage de 21 43 51N 6 32 E
Chaudes-Aigues 20 44 51N 3 1 E
Chauffailles 21 46 13N 4 20 E
Chauk 67 20 53N 94 49 E
Chaukan La 67 27 0N 97 15 E
Chaulnes 19 49 48N 2 47 E
Chaumont, France 19 48 7N 5 8 E
Chaumont, U.S.A. 113 44 4N 76 9W
Chaumont-en-Vexin 19 49 16N 1 53 E
Chaumont-sur-Loire 18 47 29N 1 11 E
Chaunay 20 46 13N 0 9 E
Chauny 19 49 37N 3 12 E
Chausey, Îs. 18 48 52N 1 49W
Chaussin 19 46 59N 5 22 E
Chautauqua 112 42 17N 79 30W
Chauvigny 18 46 34N 0 39 E
Chauvin 109 52 45N 110 10W
Chaux-de-Fonds, La 25 47 7N 6 50 E
Chaves, Brazil 127 0 15S 49 55W
Chaves, Port. 30 41 45N 7 32W
Chavuma 89 13 4S 22 40 E
Chaykovskiy 52 56 47N 54 9 E
Chazelles-sur-Lyon 21 45 39N 4 22 E
Chazy 113 44 52N 73 28W
Cheb (Eger) 26 50 9N 12 28 E
Cheboksary 55 56 8N 47 12 E
Cheboygan 114 45 38N 84 29W
Chebsara 55 59 10N 38 59 E
Chech, Erg 82 25 0N 2 15W
Chechaouen 82 35 9N 5 15W
Chechen, Os. 57 43 59N 47 40 E
Checheno-Ingush A.S.S.R. □ 57 43 30N 45 29 E
Chęciny 28 50 46N 20 28 E
Checleset B. 108 50 5N 127 35W
Checotah 117 35 31N 95 30W
Chedabucto B. 107 45 25N 61 8W
Cheduba I. 67 18 45N 93 40 E
Cheepie 99 26 33S 145 1 E
Chef-Boutonne 20 46 7N 0 4W
Chegdomyn 59 51 7N 133 1 E
Chegga 82 25 27N 5 40W
Chehalis 118 46 44N 122 59W
Cheiron 21 43 49N 6 58 E
Cheju Do 77 33 29N 126 34 E
Chekalin 55 54 10N 36 10 E
Chekiang = Zhejiang □ 75 29 0N 120 0 E
Chela, Sa. da 92 16 20S 13 20 E
Chelan 118 47 49N 120 0W
Chelan, L. 108 48 5N 120 30W
Cheleken 53 39 26N 53 7 E
Chelforó 128 39 0S 66 33W
Chéliff, O. → 82 36 0N 0 8 E
Chelkar 58 47 48N 59 39 E
Chelkar Tengiz, Solonchak 58 48 0N 62 30 E
Chellala Dahrania 82 33 2N 0 1 E
Chelles 19 48 52N 2 33 E
Chełm 28 51 8N 23 30 E
Chełm □ 28 51 15N 23 30 E
Chełmek 27 50 6N 19 16 E
Chełmno 28 53 20N 18 30 E
Chelmsford 13 51 44N 0 29 E

Chelmsford Dam 93 27 55S 29 59 E
Chelmża 28 53 10N 18 39 E
Chelsea, Austral. 100 38 5S 145 8 E
Chelsea, Can. 113 45 30N 75 47W
Chelsea, Okla., U.S.A. 117 36 35N 95 35W
Chelsea, Vt., U.S.A. 113 43 59N 72 27W
Cheltenham 13 51 55N 2 5W
Chelva 32 39 45N 1 0W
Chelyabinsk 58 55 10N 61 24 E
Chemainus 108 48 55N 123 42W
Chemillé 18 47 14N 0 45W
Chemnitz = Karl-Marx-Stadt 24 50 50N 12 55 E
Chemult 118 43 14N 121 47W
Chen, Gora 59 65 16N 141 50 E
Chen Xian 75 25 47N 113 1 E
Chenab → 68 30 23N 71 2 E
Chenachane, O. → 82 25 20N 3 20W
Chenango Forks 113 42 15N 75 51W
Chencha 87 6 15N 37 32 E
Chenchiang = Zhenjiang 75 32 12N 119 24 E
Cheney 118 47 29N 117 34W
Chengbu 77 26 18N 110 16 E
Chengcheng 77 35 8N 109 56 E
Chengde 76 40 59N 117 58 E
Chengdu 75 30 38N 104 2 E
Chenggu 77 33 10N 107 21 E
Chengjiang 75 24 39N 103 0 E
Ch'engtu = Chengdu 75 30 38N 104 2 E
Chengyang 76 36 18N 120 21 E
Chenxi 77 28 2N 110 12 E
Cheo Reo 71 13 25N 108 28 E
Cheom Ksan 71 14 13N 104 56 E
Chepelare 43 41 44N 24 40 E
Chepén 126 7 15S 79 23W
Chepes 124 31 20S 65 35W
Chepo 121 9 10N 79 6W
Cheptsa → 55 58 36N 50 4 E
Cheptulil, Mt. 90 1 25N 35 35 E
Chequamegon B. 116 46 40N 90 30W
Cher □ 19 47 10N 2 30 E
Cher → 18 47 21N 0 29 E
Cheran 69 25 45N 90 44 E
Cherasco 38 44 39N 7 50 E
Cheraw 115 34 42N 79 54W
Cherbourg 18 49 39N 1 40W
Cherchell 82 36 35N 2 12 E
Cherdakly 55 54 25N 48 50 E
Cherdyn 52 60 24N 56 29 E
Cheremkhovo 59 53 8N 103 1 E
Cherepanovo 58 54 15N 83 30 E
Cherepovets 55 59 5N 37 55 E
Chergui, Chott ech 82 34 21N 0 25 E
Cherikov 54 53 32N 31 20 E
Cherkassy 56 49 27N 32 4 E
Cherkessk 57 44 15N 42 5 E
Cherlak 58 54 15N 74 55 E
Chernaya Kholunitsa 55 58 51N 51 52 E
Cherni 43 42 35N 23 18 E
Chernigov 54 51 28N 31 20 E
Chernikovsk 52 54 48N 56 8 E
Chernobyl 54 51 13N 30 15 E
Chernogorsk 59 53 49N 91 18 E
Chernomorskoye 56 45 31N 32 40 E
Chernovskoye 55 58 48N 47 20 E
Chernovtsy 56 48 15N 25 52 E
Chernoye 59 70 30N 89 10 E
Chernyakhovsk 54 54 36N 21 48 E
Chernyshkovskiy 57 48 30N 42 13 E
Chernyshovskiy 59 63 0N 112 30 E
Cherokee, Iowa, U.S.A. 116 42 40N 95 30W
Cherokee, Okla., U.S.A. 117 36 45N 98 25W
Cherokees, L. O'The 117 36 50N 95 12W
Cherquenco 128 38 35S 72 0W
Cherrapunji 67 25 17N 91 47 E
Cherry Creek 118 39 50N 114 58W
Cherryvale 117 37 20N 95 33W
Cherskiy 59 68 45N 161 18 E
Cherskogo Khrebet 59 65 0N 143 0 E
Chertkovo 57 49 25N 40 19 E
Cherven 54 53 45N 28 28 E
Cherven-Bryag 43 43 17N 24 7 E
Chervonograd 54 50 25N 24 10 E
Cherwell → 13 51 46N 1 18W
Chesapeake 114 36 43N 76 15W
Chesapeake Bay 114 38 0N 76 12W
Cheshire □ 12 53 14N 2 30W
Cheshskaya Guba 52 67 20N 47 0 E
Cheslatta L. 108 53 49N 125 20W
Chesley 112 44 17N 81 5W
Chesne, Le 19 49 30N 4 45 E
Cheste 33 39 30N 0 41W
Chester, U.K. 12 53 12N 2 53W
Chester, Calif., U.S.A. 118 40 22N 121 14W
Chester, Ill., U.S.A. 117 37 58N 89 50W
Chester, Mont., U.S.A. 118 48 31N 111 0W
Chester, N.Y., U.S.A. 113 41 22N 74 16W
Chester, Pa., U.S.A. 114 39 54N 75 20W
Chester, S.C., U.S.A. 115 34 44N 81 13W
Chesterfield 12 53 14N 1 26W
Chesterfield, Îles 94 19 52S 158 15 E
Chesterfield In. 104 63 25N 90 45W
Chesterfield Inlet 104 63 30N 90 45W
Chesterton Range 99 25 30S 147 27 E
Chesterville 113 45 6N 75 14W
Chesuncook L. 107 46 0N 69 10W
Chetaibi 83 37 1N 7 20 E
Chéticamp 107 46 37N 60 59W
Chetumal 120 18 30N 88 20W
Chetumal, Bahía de 120 18 40N 88 10W
Chetwynd 108 55 45N 121 36W
Chevanceaux 20 45 18N 0 14W
Cheviot Hills 12 55 20N 2 30W
Cheviot Ra. 99 25 20S 143 45 E
Cheviot, The 12 55 29N 2 8W
Chew Bahir 87 4 40N 36 50 E
Chewelah 118 48 17N 117 43W
Cheyenne, Okla., U.S.A. 117 35 35N 99 40W
Cheyenne, Wyo., U.S.A. 116 41 9N 104 49W
Cheyenne → 116 44 40N 101 15W
Cheyenne Wells 116 38 51N 102 10W
Cheylard, Le 21 44 55N 4 25 E
Chhabra 68 24 40N 76 54 E
Chhatarpur 69 24 55N 79 35 E
Chhindwara 68 22 2N 78 59 E
Chhlong 71 12 15N 105 58 E
Chi → 71 15 11N 104 43 E
Chiamis 73 7 20S 108 21 E
Chiamussu = Jiamusi 75 46 40N 130 26 E
Chiang Mai 71 18 47N 98 59 E
Chiange 89 15 35S 13 40 E
Chiapa → 120 16 42N 93 0W
Chiapas □ 120 17 0N 92 45W
Chiaramonte Gulfi 41 37 1N 14 41 E
Chiaravalle 39 43 38N 13 17 E
Chiaravalle Centrale 41 38 41N 16 25 E
Chiari 38 45 31N 9 55 E
Chiatura 57 42 15N 43 17 E
Chiávari 38 44 20N 9 20 E
Chiavenna 38 46 18N 9 23 E
Chiba 74 35 30N 140 7 E
Chiba □ 74 35 30N 140 20 E
Chibabava 93 20 17S 33 35 E
Chibatu 73 7 6S 107 59 E
Chibemba, Angola 89 15 48S 14 8 E
Chibemba, Angola 92 16 20S 15 20 E
Chibia 89 15 10S 13 42 E
Chibougamau 106 49 56N 74 24W
Chibougamau L. 106 49 50N 74 20W
Chibuk 85 10 52N 12 50 E
Chic-Chocs, Mts. 107 48 55N 66 0W
Chicacole = Srikakulam 70 18 14N 84 4 E
Chicago 114 41 53N 87 40W
Chicago Heights 114 41 29N 87 37W
Chichagof I. 108 58 0N 136 0W
Chichaoua 82 31 32N 8 44W
Chichén Itzá 120 20 40N 88 32W
Chichester 13 50 50N 0 47W
Chichibu 74 36 5N 139 10 E
Ch'ich'ihaerh = Qiqihar 75 47 26N 124 0 E
Chickasha 117 35 0N 98 0W
Chiclana de la Frontera 31 36 26N 6 9W
Chiclayo 126 6 42S 79 50W
Chico 118 39 45N 121 54W
Chico →, Chubut, Argent. 118 44 0S 67 0W
Chico →, Santa Cruz, Argent. 128 50 0S 68 30W
Chicomo 93 24 31S 34 6 E
Chicopee 114 42 6N 72 37W
Chicoutimi 107 48 28N 71 5W
Chidambaram 70 11 20N 79 45 E
Chidenguele 93 24 55S 34 11 E
Chidley C. 105 60 23N 64 26W
Chiede 92 17 15S 16 22 E
Chiefs Pt. 112 44 41N 81 18W
Chiemsee 25 47 53N 12 27 E
Chiengi 91 8 45S 29 10 E
Chienti → 39 43 18N 13 45 E
Chieri 38 45 0N 7 50 E
Chiers → 19 49 39N 5 0 E
Chiese → 38 45 8N 10 25 E
Chieti 39 42 22N 14 10 E
Chifeng 76 42 18N 118 58 E
Chigirin 56 49 4N 32 38 E
Chignecto B. 107 45 30N 64 40W
Chiguana 124 21 0S 67 58W
Chihli, G. of = Bo Hai 76 39 0N 120 0 E
Chihuahua 120 28 40N 106 3W
Chihuahua □ 120 28 40N 106 3W
Chiili 58 44 20N 66 15 E
Chik Bollapur 70 13 25N 77 45 E
Chikhli 68 20 20N 76 18 E
Chikmagalur 70 13 15N 75 45 E
Chikodi 70 16 26N 74 38 E
Chikwawa 91 16 2S 34 50 E
Chilako → 108 53 53N 122 57W
Chilanga 91 15 33S 28 16 E
Chilapa 120 17 40N 99 11W
Chilas 69 35 25N 74 5 E
Chilcotin → 108 51 44N 122 23W
Childers 97 25 15S 152 17 E
Childress 117 34 30N 100 15W
Chile ■ 128 35 0S 72 0W
Chile Rise 95 38 0S 92 0W
Chilecito 124 29 10S 67 30W
Chilete 126 7 10S 78 50W
Chililabombwe 91 12 18S 27 43 E
Chilin = Jilin 76 43 55N 126 30 E
Chilka L. 69 19 40N 85 25 E
Chilko → 108 52 0N 123 40W
Chilko, L. 108 51 20N 124 10W
Chillagoe 97 17 7S 144 33 E
Chillán 124 36 40S 72 10W
Chillicothe, Ill., U.S.A. 116 40 55N 89 32W
Chillicothe, Mo., U.S.A. 116 39 45N 93 30W
Chillicothe, Ohio, U.S.A. 114 39 20N 82 58W
Chilliwack 108 49 10N 121 54W
Chilo 68 27 25N 73 32 E
Chiloane, I. 93 20 40S 34 55 E
Chiloé, I. de 128 42 30S 73 50W
Chilpancingo 120 17 30N 99 30W
Chiltern Hills 13 51 44N 0 42W
Chilton 114 44 1N 88 12W
Chiluage 88 9 30S 21 50 E
Chilubula 91 10 14S 30 51 E
Chilumba 91 10 28S 34 12 E
Chilwa, L. 91 15 15S 35 40 E
Chimacum 118 48 1N 122 46W
Chimay 16 50 3N 4 20 E
Chimbay 58 42 57N 59 47 E
Chimborazo 126 1 29S 78 55W
Chimbote 126 9 0S 78 35W
Chimishliya 46 46 34N 28 44 E
Chimkent 58 42 18N 69 36 E
Chimoio 91 19 4S 33 30 E
Chimpembe 91 9 31S 29 33 E
Chin □ 67 22 0N 93 0 E
Chin Ling Shan = Qinling Shandi 77 33 50N 108 10 E
China 120 25 40N 99 20W
China ■ 75 30 0N 110 0 E
Chinan = Jinan 76 36 38N 117 1 E
Chinandega 121 12 35N 87 12W
Chinati Pk. 117 30 0N 104 25W
Chincha Alta 126 13 25S 76 7W
Chinchilla 99 26 45S 150 38 E
Chinchilla de Monte Aragón 33 38 53N 1 40W
Chinchón 32 40 9N 3 26W
Chinchorro, Banco 120 18 35N 87 20W
Chinchou = Jinzhou 76 41 5N 121 3 E
Chincoteague 114 37 58N 75 21W
Chinde 91 18 35S 36 30 E
Chindwin → 67 21 26N 95 15 E
Chinga 91 15 13S 38 35 E
Chingleput 70 12 42N 79 58 E
Chingola 91 12 31S 27 53 E
Chingole 91 13 4S 34 17 E
Ch'ingtao = Qingdao 76 36 5N 120 20 E
Chinguetti 80 20 25N 12 24W
Chingune 93 20 33S 35 0 E
Chinhae 76 35 9N 128 47 E
Chinhanguanine 93 25 21S 32 30 E
Chiniot 68 31 45N 73 0 E
Chinju 76 35 12N 128 2 E
Chinle 119 36 14N 109 38W
Chinnamanur 70 9 50N 77 24 E
Chinnampo 76 38 52N 125 10 E
Chinnur 70 18 57N 79 49 E
Chino Valley 119 34 54N 112 28W
Chinon 18 47 10N 0 15 E
Chinook, Can. 109 51 28N 110 59W
Chinook, U.S.A. 118 48 35N 109 19W
Chinsali 91 10 30S 32 2 E
Chintamani 70 13 26N 78 3 E
Chióggia 39 45 13N 12 15 E
Chíos = Khíos 45 38 27N 26 9 E
* Chipai L. 106 52 56N 87 53W
Chipata 91 13 38S 32 28 E
Chipatujah 73 7 45S 108 0 E
Chipewyan L. 109 58 0N 98 27W
Chipinga 91 20 13S 32 28 E
Chipiona 31 36 44N 6 26W
Chipley 115 30 45N 85 32W
Chiplun 70 17 31N 73 34 E
Chipman 107 46 6N 65 53W
Chipoka 91 13 57S 34 28 E
Chippawa 112 43 5N 79 2W
Chippenham 13 51 27N 2 7W
Chippewa → 116 44 25N 92 10W
Chippewa Falls 116 44 55N 91 22W
Chiprovtsi 42 43 24N 22 52 E
Chiquián 126 10 10S 77 0W
Chiquimula 120 14 51N 89 37W
Chiquinquira 126 5 37N 73 50W
Chir → 57 48 30N 43 0 E
Chirala 70 15 50N 80 26 E
Chiramba 91 16 55S 34 39 E
Chirawa 68 28 14N 75 42 E
Chirayinkil 70 8 41N 76 49 E
Chirchik 58 41 29N 69 35 E
Chirfa 83 20 55N 12 22 E
Chiricahua Pk. 119 31 53N 109 14W
Chirikof I. 104 55 50N 155 40W
Chiriquí, Golfo de 121 8 0N 82 10W
Chiriquí, Lago de 121 9 10N 82 0W
† Chiriquí, Vol. de 121 8 55N 82 35W
Chirivira Falls 91 21 10S 32 12 E
Chirnogi 46 44 7N 26 32 E
Chirpan 43 42 10N 25 19 E
Chirripó Grande, Cerro 121 9 29N 83 29W
Chisamba 91 14 55S 28 20 E
Chisholm 108 54 55N 114 10W
Chishtian Mandi 68 29 50N 72 55 E
Chisimaio 79 0 22S 42 32 E
Chisimba Falls 91 10 12S 30 56 E
Chisineu Criş 42 46 32N 21 37 E
Chisone → 38 44 49N 7 25 E
Chisos Mts. 117 29 20N 103 15W
Chistopol 55 55 25N 50 38 E
Chita 59 52 0N 113 35 E
Chitapur 70 17 10N 77 5 E
Chitembo 89 13 30S 16 50 E
Chitipa 91 9 41S 33 19 E
Chitokoloki 89 13 50S 23 13 E
Chitorgarh 68 24 52N 74 38 E
Chitrakot 70 19 10N 81 40 E
Chitral 66 35 50N 71 56 E
Chitravati → 70 14 45N 78 15 E
Chitré 121 7 59N 80 27W
Chittagong 67 22 19N 91 48 E
Chittagong □ 67 24 5N 91 0 E
Chittoor 70 13 15N 79 5 E
Chittur 70 10 40N 76 45 E
Chiusa 39 46 38N 11 34 E
Chiusi 39 43 1N 11 58 E
Chiva 33 39 27N 0 41W
Chivasso 38 45 10N 7 52 E
Chivilcoy 124 34 55S 60 0W
Chiwanda 91 11 23S 34 55 E
Chizela 91 13 10S 25 0 E
Chkalov = Orenburg 52 52 0N 55 5 E
Chkolovsk 55 56 50N 43 10 E
Chlumec 26 50 9N 15 29 E
Chmielnik 28 50 37N 20 43 E
Choba 90 2 30N 38 5 E
Chobe National Park 92 18 0S 25 0 E
Chocianów 28 51 27N 15 55 E
Chociwel 28 53 29N 15 21 E
Chodaków 28 52 16N 20 18 E
Chodavaram 70 17 50N 82 57 E
Chodecz 28 52 24N 19 2 E
Chodziez 28 52 58N 16 58 E
Choele Choel 128 39 11S 65 40W
Choisy-le-Roi 19 48 45N 2 24 E
Choix 120 26 40N 108 23W
Chojna 28 52 58N 14 25 E
Chojnice 28 53 42N 17 32 E
Chojnów 28 51 18N 15 58 E
Choke Mts. 87 11 18N 37 15 E
Chokurdakh 59 70 38N 147 55 E
Cholet 18 47 4N 0 52W
Choluteca 121 13 20N 87 14W
Choma 91 16 48S 26 59 E
Chomen Swamp 87 9 20N 37 10 E
Chomu 68 27 15N 75 40 E
Chomutov 26 50 28N 13 23 E
Chon Buri 71 13 21N 101 1 E
Chonan 76 36 48N 127 9 E

* *Renamed Wapikopa, L.*

† *Renamed Barú, Vol.*

Chone 126 0 40S 80 0W
Chong'an 77 27 45N 118 0 E
Chongde 77 30 32N 120 26 E
Chongjin 76 41 47N 129 50 E
Chŏngju 76 39 40N 125 5 E
Chŏngju 76 36 39N 127 27 E
Chongli 76 40 58N 115 15 E
Chongqing 75 29 35N 106 25 E
Chongzuo 77 22 23N 107 20 E
Chŏnju 76 35 50N 127 4 E
Chonming Dao 77 31 40N 121 30 E
Chonos, Arch. de los 128 45 0S 75 0W
Chopda 68 21 20N 75 15 E
Chopim → 125 25 35S 53 5W
Chorley 12 53 39N 2 39W
Chorolque, Cerro 124 20 59S 66 5W
Choroszcz 28 53 10N 22 59 E
Chorrera, La 120 8 50N 79 50W
Chortkov, U.S.S.R. 54 49 2N 25 46 E
Chortkov, U.S.S.R. 56 49 1N 25 42 E
Chŏrwŏn 76 38 15N 127 10 E
Chorzele 28 53 15N 20 55 E
Chorzów 28 50 18N 18 57 E
Chos-Malal 124 37 20S 70 15W
Chosan 76 40 50N 125 47 E
Chōshi 74 35 45N 140 51 E
Choszczno 28 53 7N 15 25 E
Choteau 118 47 50N 112 10W
Chotila 68 22 23N 71 15 E
Chowchilla 119 37 11N 120 12W
Choybalsan 75 48 4N 114 30 E
Christchurch, N.Z. 101 43 33S 172 47 E
Christchurch, U.K. 13 50 44N 1 33W
Christian I. 112 44 50N 80 12W
Christiana 92 27 52S 25 8 E
Christiansfeld 49 55 21N 9 29 E
Christie B. 109 62 32N 111 10W
Christina → 109 56 40N 111 3W
Christmas I., Ind. Oc. 94 10 30S 105 40 E
* Christmas I., Pac. Oc. 95 1 58N 157 27W
Chrudim 26 49 58N 15 43 E
Chrzanów 27 50 10N 19 21 E
Chtimba 91 10 35S 34 13 E
Chu 58 43 36N 73 42 E
Chu → 71 19 53N 105 45 E
Chu Chua 108 51 22N 120 10W
Ch'uanchou = Quanzhou 75 24 55N 118 34 E
Chūbu □ 74 36 45N 137 30 E
Chubut → 128 43 20S 65 5W
Chuchi L. 108 55 12N 124 30W
Chudovo 54 59 10N 31 41 E
Chudskoye, Oz. 54 58 13N 27 30 E
Chūgoku □ 74 35 0N 133 0 E
Chūgoku-Sanchi 74 35 0N 133 0 E
Chuguyev 56 49 55N 36 45 E
Chugwater 116 41 48N 104 47W
Chukai 71 4 13N 103 25 E
Chukhloma 55 58 45N 42 40 E
Chukotskiy Khrebet 59 68 0N 175 0 E
Chukotskoye More 59 68 0N 175 0W
Chula Vista 119 32 39N 117 8W
Chulman 59 56 52N 124 52 E
Chulucanas 126 5 8S 80 10W
Chulym → 58 57 43N 83 51 E
Chumbicha 124 29 0S 66 10W
Chumerna 43 42 45N 25 55 E
Chumikan 59 54 40N 135 10 E
Chumphon 71 10 35N 99 14 E
Chumuare 91 14 31S 31 50 E
Chuna → 59 57 47N 94 37 E
Chun'an 77 29 35N 119 3 E
Chunchŏn 76 37 58N 127 44 E
Chunga 91 15 0S 26 2 E
Chungking = Chongqing 75 29 35N 106 25 E
Chunian 68 30 57N 74 0 E
Chunya 91 8 30S 33 27 E
Chunya □ 90 7 48S 33 0 E
Chuquibamba 126 15 47S 72 44W
Chuquicamata 124 22 15S 69 0W
Chuquisaca □ 126 23 30S 63 30W
Chur 25 46 52N 9 32 E
Churachandpur 67 24 20N 93 40 E
Churchill 109 58 47N 94 11W
Churchill →, Man., Can. 109 58 47N 94 12W
Churchill →, Newf., Can. 107 53 19N 60 10W
Churchill, C. 109 58 46N 93 12W
Churchill Falls 107 53 36N 64 19W
Churchill L. 109 55 55N 108 20W
Churchill Pk. 108 58 10N 125 10W
Churu 68 28 20N 74 50 E
Chushal 69 33 40N 78 40 E
Chusovoy 52 58 15N 57 40 E
Chuvash A.S.S.R. □ 55 55 30N 47 0 E
Ci Xian 76 36 20N 114 25 E
Ciacova 42 45 35N 21 10 E
Cianjur 73 6 51S 107 7 E
Cibadok 73 6 53S 106 47 E
Cibatu 73 7 8S 107 59 E
Cicero 114 41 48N 87 48W
Cidacos → 32 42 21N 1 38W
Cide 56 41 53N 33 1 E
Ciechanów 28 52 52N 20 38 E
Ciechanów □ 28 53 0N 20 30 E
Ciechanowiec 28 52 40N 22 31 E
Ciechocinek 28 52 53N 18 45 E
Ciego de Avila 121 21 50N 78 50W
Ciénaga 126 11 1N 74 15W
Cienfuegos 121 22 10N 80 30W
Cieplice Sląskie Zdrój 28 50 50N 15 40 E
Cierp 20 42 55N 0 40 E
Cíes, Islas 30 42 12N 8 55W
Cieszanów 28 50 14N 23 8 E
Cieszyn 27 49 45N 18 35 E
Cieza 33 38 17N 1 23W
Cifuentes 32 40 47N 2 37W
Cijara, Pantano de 31 39 18N 4 52W
Cijulang 73 7 42S 108 27 E
Cikajang 73 7 25S 107 48 E
Cikampek 73 6 23S 107 28 E
Cilacap 73 7 43S 109 0 E
Çıldır 57 41 10N 43 20 E
Cilician Gates P. 64 37 20N 34 52 E

* *Renamed Kiritimati*

Cîlnicu **46** 44 54N 23 4 E
Cimahi **73** 6 53 S 107 33 E
Cimarron, Kans., U.S.A. **117** 37 50N 100 20W
Cimarron, N. Mex., U.S.A. **117** 36 30N 104 52W
Cimarron → **117** 36 10N 96 17W
Cimone, Mte. **38** 44 10N 10 40 E
Cîmpic Turzii **46** 46 34N 23 53 E
Cîmpina **46** 45 10N 25 45 E
Cîmpulung, Argeş, Romania **46** 45 17N 25 3 E
Cîmpulung, Moldovenesc, Romania **46** 47 32N 25 30 E
Cîmpuri **43** 46 0N 26 50 E
Cinca → **32** 41 26N 0 21 E
Cincer **42** 43 55N 17 5 E
Cincinnati **114** 39 10N 84 26W
Cîndeşti **46** 45 15N 26 42 E
Ciney **16** 50 18N 5 5 E
Cíngoli **39** 43 23N 13 10 E
Cinigiano **39** 42 53N 11 23 E
Cinto, Mt. **21** 42 24N 8 54 E
Ciorani **46** 44 45N 26 25 E
Çiotat, La **21** 43 12N 5 36 E
Čiovo **39** 43 30N 16 17 E
Circeo, Monte **40** 41 14N 13 3 E
Circle, Alaska, U.S.A. **104** 65 50N 144 10W
Circle, Montana, U.S.A. **116** 47 26N 105 35W
Circleville, Ohio, U.S.A. **114** 39 35N 82 57W
Circleville, Utah, U.S.A. **119** 38 12N 112 24W
Cirebon **73** 6 45 S 108 32 E
Cirencester **13** 51 43N 1 59W
Cireşu **46** 44 47N 22 31 E
Cirey-sur-Vezouze **19** 48 35N 6 57 E
Ciriè **38** 45 14N 7 35 E
Cirò **41** 39 23N 17 3 E
Cisco **117** 32 25N 99 0W
Cislău **46** 45 14N 26 20 E
Cisna **27** 49 12N 22 20 E
Cisnădie **46** 45 42N 24 9 E
Cisterna di Latina **40** 41 35N 12 50 E
Cisternino **41** 40 45N 17 26 E
Citeli-Ckaro **57** 41 33N 46 0 E
Citlaltépetl **120** 19 0N 97 20W
Citrusdal **92** 32 35 S 19 0 E
Città della Pieve **39** 42 57N 12 0 E
Città di Castello **39** 43 27N 12 14 E
Città Sant' Angelo **39** 42 32N 14 5 E
Cittadella **39** 45 39N 11 48 E
Cittaducale **39** 42 24N 12 58 E
Cittanova **41** 38 22N 16 5 E
Ciuc, Munţii **46** 46 25N 26 5 E
Ciucaş **46** 45 31N 25 56 E
Ciudad Acuña **120** 29 20N 100 58W
Ciudad Altamirano **120** 18 20N 100 40W
Ciudad Bolívar **126** 8 5N 63 36W
Ciudad Camargo **120** 27 41N 105 10W
Ciudad de Valles **120** 22 0N 99 0W
Ciudad del Carmen **120** 18 38N 91 50W
Ciudad Delicias = Delicias **120** 28 10N 105 30W
Ciudad Guayana **126** 8 0N 62 30W
Ciudad Guerrero **120** 28 33N 107 28W
Ciudad Guzmán **120** 19 40N 103 30W
Ciudad Juárez **120** 31 40N 106 28W
Ciudad Madero **120** 22 19N 97 50W
Ciudad Mante **120** 22 50N 99 0W
Ciudad Obregón **120** 27 28N 109 59W
Ciudad Real **31** 38 59N 3 55W
Ciudad Real □ **31** 38 50N 4 0W
Ciudad Rodrigo **30** 40 35N 6 32W
Ciudad Trujillo = Sto. Domingo **121** 18 30N 70 0W
Ciudad Victoria **120** 23 41N 99 9W
Ciudadela **32** 40 0N 3 50 E
Ciulniţa **46** 44 26N 27 22 E
Cividale del Friuli **39** 46 6N 13 25 E
Cívita Castellana **39** 42 18N 12 24 E
Civitanova Marche **39** 43 18N 13 41 E
Civitavécchia **39** 42 6N 11 46 E
Civitella del Tronto **39** 42 48N 13 40 E
Civray **20** 46 10N 0 17 E
Çivril **64** 38 20N 29 43 E
Cixerri → **40** 39 20N 8 40 E
Cizre **64** 37 19N 42 10 E
Clacton-on-Sea **13** 51 47N 1 10 E
Clain → **18** 46 47N 0 33 E
Claire, L. **108** 58 35N 112 5W
Clairemont **117** 33 9N 100 44W
Clairton **112** 40 18N 79 54W
Clairvaux-les-Lacs **21** 46 35N 5 45 E
Claise → **18** 46 56N 0 42 E
Clamecy **19** 47 28N 3 30 E
Clanton **115** 32 48N 86 36W
Clanwilliam **92** 32 11 S 18 52 E
Clara **15** 53 20N 7 38W
Clare, Austral. **99** 33 50 S 138 37 E
Clare, U.S.A. **114** 43 47N 84 45W
Clare □ **15** 52 20N 9 0W
Clare → **15** 53 22N 9 5W
Clare I. **15** 53 48N 10 0W
Claremont **114** 43 23N 72 20W
Claremont Pt. **98** 14 1 S 143 41 E
Claremore **117** 36 40N 95 37W
Claremorris **15** 53 45N 9 0W
Clarence →, Austral. **97** 29 25 S 153 22 E
Clarence →, N.Z. **101** 42 10 S 173 56 E
Clarence I. **5** 61 10 S 54 0W
Clarence, I. **128** 54 0 S 72 0W
Clarence Str., Austral. **96** 12 0 S 131 0 E
Clarence Str., U.S.A. **108** 55 40N 132 10W
Clarendon, Ark., U.S.A. **117** 34 41N 91 20W
Clarendon, Tex., U.S.A. **117** 34 58N 100 54W
Clarenville **107** 48 10N 54 1W
Claresholm **108** 50 0N 113 33W
Clarie Coast **5** 68 0 S 135 0 E
Clarinda **116** 40 45N 95 0W
Clarion, Iowa, U.S.A. **116** 42 41N 93 46W
Clarion, Pa., U.S.A. **112** 41 12N 79 22W
Clarion → **112** 41 9N 79 41W
Clarion Fracture Zone **95** 20 0N 120 0W
Clark **116** 44 55N 97 45W
Clark Fork **118** 48 9N 116 9W
Clark Fork → **118** 48 9N 116 15W
Clark Hill Res. **115** 33 45N 82 20W
Clark, Pt. **112** 44 4N 81 45W
Clarkdale **119** 34 53N 112 3W
Clarke City **107** 50 12N 66 38W
Clarke, I. **97** 40 32 S 148 10 E
Clarke L. **109** 54 24N 106 54W
Clarke Ra. **98** 20 45 S 148 20 E
Clark's Fork → **118** 45 39N 108 43W
Clark's Harbour **107** 43 25N 65 38W
Clarks Summit **113** 41 31N 75 44W
Clarksburg **114** 39 18N 80 21W
Clarksdale **117** 34 12N 90 33W
Clarkston **118** 46 28N 117 2W
Clarksville, Ark., U.S.A. **117** 35 29N 93 27W
Clarksville, Tenn., U.S.A. **115** 36 32N 87 20W
Clarksville, Tex., U.S.A. **117** 33 37N 94 59W
Clatskanie **118** 46 9N 123 12W
Claude **117** 35 8N 101 22W
Claveria **73** 18 37N 121 4 E
Clay Center **116** 39 27N 97 9W
Clayette, La **21** 46 17N 4 19 E
Claypool **119** 33 27N 110 55W
Claysville **112** 40 5N 80 25W
Clayton, Idaho, U.S.A. **118** 44 12N 114 31W
Clayton, N. Mex., U.S.A. **117** 36 30N 103 10W
Cle Elum **118** 47 15N 120 57W
Clear L. **118** 39 5N 122 47W
Clear, C. **15** 51 26N 9 30W
Clear I. **15** 51 26N 9 30W
Clear Lake, S.D., U.S.A. **116** 44 48N 96 41W
Clear Lake, Wash., U.S.A. **118** 48 27N 122 15W
Clear Lake Res. **118** 41 55N 121 10W
Clearfield, Pa., U.S.A. **114** 41 0N 78 27W
Clearfield, Utah, U.S.A. **118** 41 10N 112 0W
Clearmont **118** 44 43N 106 29W
Clearwater, Can. **108** 51 38N 120 2W
Clearwater, U.S.A. **115** 27 58N 82 45W
Clearwater →, Alta., Can. **108** 52 22N 114 57W
Clearwater →, Alta., Can. **109** 56 44N 111 23W
Clearwater Cr. **108** 61 36N 125 30W
Clearwater, Mts. **118** 46 20N 115 30W
Clearwater Prov. Park **109** 54 0N 101 0W
Cleburne **117** 32 18N 97 25W
Clécy **18** 48 55N 0 29W
Cleethorpes **12** 53 33N 0 2W
Cleeve Cloud **13** 51 56N 2 0W
Clelles **21** 44 50N 5 38 E
Clerks Rocks **5** 56 0 S 34 30W
Clermont, Austral. **97** 22 49 S 147 39 E
Clermont, France **19** 49 23N 2 24 E
Clermont-en-Argonne **19** 49 5N 5 4 E
Clermont-Ferrand **20** 45 46N 3 4 E
Clermont-l'Hérault **20** 43 38N 3 26 E
Clerval **19** 47 25N 6 30 E
Clervaux **16** 50 4N 6 2 E
Cléry-Saint-André **19** 47 50N 1 46 E
Cles **38** 46 21N 11 4 E
Cleveland, Austral. **99** 27 30 S 153 15 E
Cleveland, Miss., U.S.A. **117** 33 43N 90 43W
Cleveland, Ohio, U.S.A. **114** 41 28N 81 43W
Cleveland, Okla., U.S.A. **117** 36 21N 96 33W
Cleveland, Tenn., U.S.A. **115** 35 9N 84 52W
Cleveland, Tex., U.S.A. **117** 30 18N 95 0W
Cleveland □ **12** 54 35N 1 8 E
Cleveland, C. **97** 19 11 S 147 1 E
Cleveland Heights **112** 41 32N 81 30W
Clevelândia **125** 26 24 S 52 23W
Clew B. **15** 53 54N 9 50W
Clewiston **115** 26 44N 80 50W
Clifden, Ireland **15** 53 30N 10 2W
Clifden, N.Z. **101** 46 1 S 167 42 E
Cliff **119** 33 0N 108 36W
Clifton, Austral. **99** 27 59 S 151 53 E
Clifton, Ariz., U.S.A. **119** 33 8N 109 23W
Clifton, Tex., U.S.A. **117** 31 46N 97 35W
Clifton Forge **114** 37 49N 79 51W
Climax **109** 49 10N 108 20W
Clinch → **115** 36 0N 84 29W
Clingmans Dome **115** 35 35N 83 30W
Clint **119** 31 37N 106 11W
Clinton, B.C., Can. **108** 51 6N 121 35W
Clinton, Ont., Can. **106** 43 37N 81 32W
Clinton, N.Z. **101** 46 12 S 169 23 E
Clinton, Ark., U.S.A. **117** 35 37N 92 30W
Clinton, Ill., U.S.A. **116** 40 8N 89 0W
Clinton, Ind., U.S.A. **114** 39 40N 87 22W
Clinton, Iowa, U.S.A. **116** 41 50N 90 12W
Clinton, Mass., U.S.A. **114** 42 26N 71 40W
Clinton, Mo., U.S.A. **116** 38 20N 93 46W
Clinton, N.C., U.S.A. **115** 35 5N 78 15W
Clinton, Okla., U.S.A. **117** 35 30N 99 0W
Clinton, S.C., U.S.A. **115** 34 30N 81 54W
Clinton, Tenn., U.S.A. **115** 36 6N 84 10W
Clinton C. **98** 22 30 S 150 45 E
Clinton Colden L. **104** 63 58N 107 27W
Clintonville **116** 44 35N 88 46W
Clipperton Fracture Zone **95** 19 0N 122 0W
Clipperton, I. **95** 10 18N 109 13W
Clisson **18** 47 5N 1 16W
Clive L. **108** 63 13N 118 54W
Cloates, Pt. **96** 22 43 S 113 40 E
Clocolan **93** 28 55 S 27 34 E
Clodomira **124** 27 35 S 64 14W
Clonakilty **15** 51 37N 8 53W
Clonakilty B. **15** 51 33N 8 50W
Cloncurry **97** 20 40 S 140 28 E
Cloncurry → **98** 18 37 S 140 40 E
Clones **15** 54 10N 7 13W
Clonmel **15** 52 22N 7 42W
Cloppenburg **24** 52 50N 8 3 E
Cloquet **116** 46 40N 92 30W
Clorinda **124** 25 16 S 57 45W
Cloud Peak **118** 44 23N 107 10W
Cloudcroft **119** 33 0N 105 48W
Cloverdale **118** 38 49N 123 0W
Clovis, Calif., U.S.A. **119** 36 47N 119 45W
Clovis, N. Mex., U.S.A. **117** 34 20N 103 10W
Cloyes **18** 48 0N 1 14 E
Cluj-Napoca **46** 46 47N 23 38 E
Cluj □ **46** 46 45N 23 30 E
Clunes **99** 37 20 S 143 45 E
Cluny **21** 46 26N 4 38 E
Cluses **21** 46 5N 6 35 E
Clusone **38** 45 54N 9 58 E
Clutha → **101** 46 20 S 169 49 E
Clwyd □ **12** 53 5N 3 20W
Clwyd → **12** 53 20N 3 30W
Clyde, Can. **105** 70 30N 68 30W
Clyde, N.Z. **101** 45 12 S 169 20 E
Clyde, U.S.A. **112** 43 8N 76 52W
Clyde → **14** 55 56N 4 29W
Clyde, Firth of **14** 55 20N 5 0W
Clydebank **14** 55 54N 4 25W
Clymer **112** 42 3N 79 39W
Côa → **30** 41 5N 7 6W
Coachella **119** 33 44N 116 13W
Coahoma **117** 32 17N 101 20W
Coahuayana → **120** 18 41N 103 45W
Coahuila de Zaragoza □ **120** 27 0N 103 0W
Coal → **108** 59 39N 126 57W
Coalane **91** 17 48 S 37 2 E
Coalcomán **120** 18 40N 103 10W
Coaldale **108** 49 45N 112 35W
Coalgate **117** 34 35N 96 13W
Coalinga **119** 36 10N 120 21W
Coalville, U.K. **12** 52 43N 1 21W
Coalville, U.S.A. **118** 40 58N 111 24W
Coari **126** 4 8 S 63 7W
Coast □ **90** 2 40 S 39 45 E
Coast Mts. **108** 55 0N 129 0W
Coast Ranges **102** 41 0N 123 0W
Coastal Plains Basin **96** 30 10 S 115 30 E
Coatbridge **14** 55 52N 4 2W
Coatepeque **120** 14 46N 91 55W
Coatesville **114** 39 59N 75 55W
Coaticook **107** 45 10N 71 46W
Coats I. **105** 62 30N 83 0W
Coats Land **5** 77 0 S 25 0W
Coatzacoalcos **120** 18 7N 94 25W
Cobadin **46** 44 5N 28 13 E
Cobalt **106** 47 25N 79 42W
Cobán **120** 15 30N 90 21W
Cobar **97** 31 27 S 145 48 E
Cóbh **15** 51 50N 8 18W
Cobija **126** 11 0 S 68 50W
Cobleskill **114** 42 40N 74 30W
Coboconk **112** 44 39N 78 48W
Cobourg **106** 43 58N 78 10W
Cobourg Pen. **96** 11 20 S 132 15 E
Cobram **99** 35 54 S 145 40 E
Cobre **118** 41 6N 114 25W
Coburg **25** 50 15N 10 58 E
Coca **30** 41 13N 4 32W
Cocanada = Kakinada **70** 16 50N 82 11 E
Cocentaina **33** 38 45N 0 27W
Cocha, La **124** 27 50 S 65 40W
Cochabamba **126** 17 26 S 66 10W
Cochem **25** 50 8N 7 7 E
Cochemane **91** 17 0 S 32 54 E
Cochin **70** 9 59N 76 22 E
Cochin China = Nam-Phan **71** 10 30N 106 0 E
Cochise **119** 32 6N 109 58W
Cochran **115** 32 25N 83 23W
Cochrane, Alta., Can. **108** 51 11N 114 30W
Cochrane, Ont., Can. **106** 49 0N 81 0W
Cochrane → **109** 59 0N 103 40W
Cochrane, L. **128** 47 10 S 72 0W
Cockatoo I. **96** 16 6 S 123 37 E
Cockburn **99** 32 5 S 141 0 E
Cockburn, Canal **128** 54 30 S 72 0W
Cockburn I. **106** 45 55N 83 22W
Coco → **121** 15 0N 83 8W
Coco Chan. **71** 13 50N 93 25 E
Coco Solo **120** 9 22N 79 53W
Cocoa **115** 28 22N 80 40W
Cocobeach **88** 0 59N 9 34 E
Cocora **46** 44 45N 27 3 E
Cocos I. **95** 5 25N 87 55W
Cocos Is. **94** 12 10 S 96 55 E
Cod, C. **111** 42 8N 70 10W
Codajás **126** 3 55 S 62 0W
Coderre **109** 50 11N 106 31W
Codigoro **39** 44 50N 12 5 E
Codó **127** 4 30 S 43 55W
Codogno **38** 45 10N 9 42 E
Codróipo **39** 45 57N 13 0 E
Codru, Munţii **46** 46 30N 22 15 E
Cody **118** 44 35N 109 0W
Coe Hill **106** 44 52N 77 50W
Coelemu **124** 36 30 S 72 48W
Coen **97** 13 52 S 143 12 E
Coesfeld **24** 51 56N 7 10 E
Coeur d'Alene **118** 47 45N 116 51W
Cœur d'Alene L. **118** 47 32N 116 48W
Coevorden **16** 52 40N 6 44 E
Coffeyville **117** 37 0N 95 40W
Coffs Harbour **97** 30 16 S 153 5 E
Cofrentes **33** 39 13N 1 5W
Cogealac **46** 44 36N 28 36 E
Coghinas → **40** 40 55N 8 48 E
Coghinas, L. di **40** 40 46N 9 3 E
Cognac **20** 45 41N 0 20W
Cogne **38** 45 37N 7 21 E
Cogolludo **32** 40 59N 3 10W
Cohagen **118** 47 2N 106 36W
Cohoes **114** 42 47N 73 42W
Cohuna **99** 35 45 S 144 15 E
Coiba, I. **121** 7 30N 81 40W
Coig → **128** 51 0 S 69 10W
Coihaique **128** 45 30 S 71 45W
Coimbatore **70** 11 2N 76 59 E
Coimbra, Brazil **126** 19 55 S 57 48W
Coimbra, Port. **30** 40 15N 8 27W
Coimbra □ **30** 40 12N 8 25W
Coín **31** 36 40N 4 48W
Cojimies **126** 0 20N 80 0W
Cojocna **46** 46 45N 23 50 E
Cojutepequé **120** 13 41N 88 54W
Čoka **42** 45 57N 20 12 E
Cokeville **118** 42 4N 111 0W
Col di Tenda **38** 44 7N 7 36 E
Colaba Pt. **70** 18 54N 72 47 E
Colac **97** 38 21 S 143 35 E
Colachel **70** 8 10N 77 15 E
Colares **31** 38 48N 9 30W
Colbeck, C. **5** 77 6 S 157 48W
Colbinabbin **99** 36 38 S 144 48 E
Colborne **112** 44 0N 77 53W
Colby **116** 39 27N 101 2W
Colchagua □ **124** 34 30 S 71 0W
Colchester **13** 51 54N 0 55 E
Coldstream **14** 55 39N 2 14W
Coldwater, Can. **112** 44 42N 79 40W
Coldwater, U.S.A. **117** 37 18N 99 24W
Colebrook, Austral. **99** 42 31 S 147 21 E
Colebrook, U.S.A. **114** 44 54N 71 29W
Coleman, Can. **108** 49 40N 114 30W
Coleman, U.S.A. **117** 31 52N 99 30W
Coleman → **97** 15 6 S 141 38 E
Colenso **93** 28 44 S 29 50 E
Coleraine, Austral. **99** 37 36 S 141 40 E
Coleraine, U.K. **15** 55 8N 6 40 E
Coleraine □ **15** 55 8N 6 40 E
Coleridge, L. **101** 43 17 S 171 30 E
Coleroon → **70** 11 25N 79 50 E
Colesberg **92** 30 45 S 25 5 E
Colfax, La., U.S.A. **117** 31 35N 92 39W
Colfax, Wash., U.S.A. **118** 46 57N 117 28W
Colhué Huapi, L. **128** 45 30 S 69 0W
Cólico **38** 46 8N 9 22 E
Coligny **93** 26 17 S 26 15 E
Colima **120** 19 10N 103 40W
Colima □ **120** 19 10N 103 40W
Colima, Nevado de **120** 19 35N 103 45W
Colina **124** 33 13 S 70 45W
Colina do Norte **84** 12 28N 15 0W
Colinas **127** 6 0 S 44 10W
Colinton **100** 35 50 S 149 10 E
Coll **14** 56 40N 6 35W
Collaguasi **124** 21 5 S 68 45W
Collarada, Peña **32** 42 43N 0 29W
Collarenebri **99** 29 33 S 148 34 E
Collbran **119** 39 16N 107 58W
Colle di Val d'Elsa **39** 43 25N 11 7 E
Colle Salvetti **38** 43 34N 10 27 E
Colle Sannita **41** 41 22N 14 48 E
Collécchio **38** 44 45N 10 10 E
Colleen Bawn **91** 21 0 S 29 12 E
College Park **115** 33 42N 84 27W
Collette **107** 46 40N 65 30W
Collie **96** 33 22 S 116 8 E
Collier B. **96** 16 10 S 124 15 E
Colline Metallifere **38** 43 10N 11 0 E
Collingwood, Austral. **98** 22 20 S 142 31 E
Collingwood, Can. **106** 44 29N 80 13W
Collingwood, N.Z. **101** 40 41 S 172 40 E
Collins **106** 50 17N 89 27W
Collinsville **97** 20 30 S 147 56 E
Collipulli **124** 37 55 S 72 30W
Collo **83** 36 58N 6 37 E
Collonges **21** 46 9N 5 52 E
Collooney **15** 54 11N 8 28W
Colmar **19** 48 5N 7 20 E
Colmars **21** 44 11N 6 39 E
Colmenar **31** 36 54N 4 20W
Colmenar de Oreja **32** 40 6N 3 25W
Colmenar Viejo **30** 40 39N 3 47W
Colne **12** 53 51N 2 11W
Colo → **99** 33 25 S 150 52 E
Cologna Véneta **39** 45 19N 11 21 E
Cologne = Köln **24** 50 56N 9 58 E
Colomb-Béchar = Béchar **82** 31 38N 2 18W
Colombey-les-Belles **19** 48 32N 5 54 E
Colombey-les-Deux-Églises **19** 48 13N 4 50 E
Colômbia **127** 20 10 S 48 40W
Colombia ■ **126** 3 45N 73 0W
Colombo **70** 6 56N 79 58 E
Colombus **119** 31 54N 107 43W
Colome **116** 43 20N 99 44W
Colón, Argent. **124** 32 12 S 58 10W
Colón, Cuba **121** 22 42N 80 54W
Colón, Panama **120** 9 20N 79 54W
Colonella **39** 42 52N 13 50 E
Colonia **124** 34 25 S 57 50W
Colonia Dora **124** 28 34 S 62 59W
Colonial Hts. **114** 37 19N 77 25W
Colonne, C. delle **41** 39 2N 17 11 E
Colonsay, Can. **109** 51 59N 105 52W
Colonsay, U.K. **14** 56 4N 6 12W
Colorado □ **110** 37 40N 106 0W
Colorado →, Argent. **128** 39 50 S 62 8W
Colorado →, Calif., U.S.A. **119** 34 45N 114 40W
Colorado →, Tex., U.S.A. **117** 28 36N 95 58W
Colorado City **117** 32 25N 100 50W
Colorado Desert **110** 34 20N 116 0W
Colorado, I. **120** 9 12N 79 50W
Colorado Plateau **119** 36 40N 110 30W
Colorado R. Aqueduct **119** 34 17N 114 10W
Colorado Springs **116** 38 55N 104 50W
Colorno **38** 44 55N 10 21 E
Colton, N.Y., U.S.A. **113** 44 34N 74 58W
Colton, Wash., U.S.A. **118** 46 41N 117 6W
Columbia, La., U.S.A. **117** 32 7N 92 5W
Columbia, Miss., U.S.A. **117** 31 16N 89 50W
Columbia, Mo., U.S.A. **116** 38 58N 92 20W
Columbia, Pa., U.S.A. **114** 40 2N 76 30W
Columbia, S.C., U.S.A. **115** 34 0N 81 0W
Columbia, Tenn., U.S.A. **115** 35 40N 87 0W
Columbia → **118** 46 15N 124 5W
Columbia Basin **118** 47 30N 118 30W
Columbia, C. **4** 83 0N 70 0W
Columbia City **114** 41 8N 85 30W
Columbia, District of □ **114** 38 55N 77 0W
Columbia Falls **118** 48 25N 114 16W
Columbia Heights **116** 45 5N 93 10W
Columbia, Mt. **108** 52 8N 117 20W
Columbiana **112** 40 53N 80 40W
Columbretes, Is. **32** 39 50N 0 50 E
Columbus, Ga., U.S.A. **115** 32 30N 84 58W
Columbus, Ind., U.S.A. **114** 39 14N 85 55W
Columbus, Kans., U.S.A. **117** 37 15N 94 30W
Columbus, Miss., U.S.A. **115** 33 30N 88 26W
Columbus, Mont., U.S.A. **118** 45 38N 109 14W
Columbus, N.D., U.S.A. **116** 48 52N 102 48W
Columbus, Nebr., U.S.A. **116** 41 30N 97 25W
Columbus, Ohio, U.S.A. **114** 39 57N 83 1W
Columbus, Tex., U.S.A. **117** 29 42N 96 33W
Columbus, Wis., U.S.A. **116** 43 20N 89 2W

Colunga **30** 43 29N 5 16W
Colusa **118** 39 15N 122 1W
Colville **118** 48 33N 117 54W
Colville → **104** 70 25N 151 0W
Colville, C. **101** 36 29S 175 21 E
Colwyn Bay **12** 53 17N 3 44W
Coma **87** 8 29N 36 53 E
Comácchio **39** 44 41N 12 10 E
Comallo **128** 41 0S 70 5W
Comana **46** 44 10N 26 10 E
Comanche, Okla., U.S.A. **117** 34 27N 97 58W
Comanche, Tex., U.S.A. **117** 31 55N 98 35W
Comănești **46** 46 25N 26 26 E
Combahee → **115** 32 30N 80 31W
Combeaufontaine **19** 47 38N 5 54 E
Comber **112** 42 14N 82 33W
Comblain-au-Pont **16** 50 29N 5 35 E
Combles **19** 50 0N 2 50 E
Combourg **18** 48 25N 1 46W
Combronde **20** 45 58N 3 5 E
Comeragh Mts. **15** 52 17N 7 35W
Comet **98** 23 36S 148 38 E
Comilla **69** 23 28N 91 10 E
Comino, C. **40** 40 28N 9 47 E
Comino I. **36** 36 0N 14 20 E
Cómiso **41** 36 57N 14 35 E
Comitán **120** 16 18N 92 9W
Commentry **20** 46 20N 2 46 E
Commerce, Ga., U.S.A. **115** 34 10N 83 25W
Commerce, Tex., U.S.A. **117** 33 15N 95 50W
Commercy **19** 48 46N 5 34 E
Committee B. **105** 68 30N 86 30W
Commonwealth B. **5** 67 0S 144 0 E
Commoron Cr. → **99** 28 22S 150 8 E
Communism Pk. = Kommunisma, Pic **65** 38 40N 72 0 E
Como **38** 45 48N 9 5 E
Como, L. di **38** 46 5N 9 17 E
Comodoro Rivadavia **128** 45 50S 67 40W
Comorin, C. **70** 8 3N 77 40 E
Comoriște **42** 45 10N 21 35 E
Comoro Is. **3** 12 10S 44 15 E
Comox **108** 49 42N 124 55W
Compiègne **19** 49 24N 2 50 E
Compíglia Maríttima **38** 43 4N 10 37 E
Comporta **31** 38 22N 8 46W
Comprida, I. **125** 24 50S 47 42W
Compton Downs **99** 30 28S 146 30 E
Côn Dao **71** 8 45N 106 45 E
Conakry **84** 9 29N 13 49W
Conara Junction **99** 41 50S 147 26 E
Concarneau **18** 47 52N 3 56W
Conceição **91** 18 47S 36 7 E
Conceição da Barra **127** 18 35S 39 45W
Conceição do Araguaia **127** 8 0S 49 2W
Concepción, Argent. **124** 27 20S 65 35W
Concepción, Boliv. **126** 16 15S 62 8W
Concepción, Chile **124** 36 50S 73 0W
Concepción, Parag. **124** 23 22S 57 26W
Concepción □ **124** 37 0S 72 30W
Concepción → **120** 30 32N 113 2W
Concepción del Oro **120** 24 40N 101 30W
Concepción del Uruguay **124** 32 35S 58 20W
Concepción, L. **126** 17 20S 61 20W
Concepción, La = Ri-Aba **85** 3 28N 8 40 E
Concepcion, Pt. **119** 34 27N 120 27W
Concepción, Punta **120** 26 55N 111 59W
Conception B. **92** 23 55S 14 22 E
Conception I. **121** 23 52N 75 9W
Conception, Pt. **119** 34 30N 120 34W
Concession **91** 17 27S 30 56 E
Conchas Dam **117** 35 25N 104 10W
Conche **107** 50 55N 55 58W
Conches **18** 48 51N 2 43 E
Concho **119** 34 32N 109 43W
Concho → **117** 31 30N 99 45W
Conchos → **120** 29 32N 104 25W
Concord, N.C., U.S.A. **115** 35 28N 80 35W
Concord, N.H., U.S.A. **114** 43 12N 71 30W
Concordia **124** 31 20S 58 2W
Concórdia **126** 4 36S 66 36W
Concordia **116** 39 35N 97 40W
Concordia, La **120** 16 8N 92 38W
Concots **20** 44 26N 1 40 E
Concrete **118** 48 35N 121 49W
Condamine → **97** 27 7S 149 48 E
Condat **20** 45 21N 2 46 E
Condé **19** 50 26N 3 34 E
Conde **116** 45 13N 98 5W
Condé-sur-Noireau **18** 48 51N 0 33W
Condeúba **127** 14 52S 42 0W
Condobolin **99** 33 4S 147 6 E
Condom **20** 43 57N 0 22 E
Condon **118** 45 15N 120 8W
Condove **38** 45 8N 7 19 E
Conegliano **39** 45 53N 12 18 E
Conejera, I. **33** 39 11N 2 58 E
Conflans-en-Jarnisy **19** 49 10N 5 52 E
Confolens **20** 46 2N 0 40 E
Confuso → **124** 25 9S 57 34W
Congleton **12** 53 10N 2 12W
Congo = Zaïre → **88** 1 30N 28 0 E
Congo ■ **88** 1 0S 16 0 E
Congo Basin **78** 0 10S 24 30 E
Congonhas **125** 20 30S 43 52W
Congress **119** 34 11N 112 56W
Conil **31** 36 17N 6 10W
Coniston **106** 46 29N 80 51W
Conjeevaram = Kanchipuram **70** 12 52N 79 45 E
Conjuboy **98** 18 35S 144 35 E
Conklin **109** 55 38N 111 5W
Conlea **99** 30 7S 144 35 E
Conn, L. **15** 54 3N 9 15W
Connacht **15** 53 23N 8 40W
Conneaut **114** 41 55N 80 32W
Connecticut □ **114** 41 40N 72 40W
Connecticut → **114** 41 17N 72 21W
Connell **118** 46 36N 118 51W
Connellsville **114** 40 3N 79 32W
Connemara **15** 53 29N 9 45W
Connemaugh → **112** 40 38N 79 42W
Conner, La **118** 48 22N 122 27W
Connerré **18** 48 3N 0 30 E
Connersville **114** 39 40N 85 10W
Connors Ra. **98** 21 40S 149 10 E
Conoble **99** 32 55S 144 33 E
Conon → **14** 57 33N 4 28W
Cononaco → **126** 1 32S 75 35W
Cononbridge **14** 57 32N 4 30W
Conquest **109** 51 32N 107 14W
Conquet, Le **18** 48 21N 4 46W
Conrad **118** 48 11N 112 0W
Conran, C. **99** 37 49S 148 44 E
Conroe **117** 30 15N 95 28W
Conselheiro Lafaiete **125** 20 40S 43 48W
Conshohocken **113** 40 5N 75 18W
Consort **109** 52 1N 110 46W
Constance = Konstanz **25** 47 39N 9 10 E
Constance, L. = Bodensee **25** 47 35N 9 25 E
Constanța **46** 44 14N 28 38 E
Constanța □ **46** 44 15N 28 15 E
Constantina **31** 37 51N 5 40W
Constantine **83** 36 25N 6 42 E
Constitución, Chile **124** 35 20S 72 30W
Constitución, Uruguay **124** 42 0S 57 50W
Consuegra **31** 39 28N 3 36W
Consul **109** 49 20N 109 30W
Contact **118** 41 50N 114 56W
Contai **69** 21 54N 87 46 E
Contamana **126** 7 19S 74 55W
Contarina **39** 45 2N 12 13 E
Contas → **127** 14 17S 39 1W
Contes **21** 43 49N 7 19 E
Contoocook **113** 43 13N 71 45W
Contra Costa **93** 25 9S 33 30 E
Contres **18** 47 24N 1 26 E
Contrexéville **19** 48 6N 5 53 E
Conversano **41** 40 57N 17 8 E
Conway, Ark., U.S.A. **117** 35 5N 92 30W
Conway, N.H., U.S.A. **114** 43 58N 71 8W
Conway, S.C., U.S.A. **115** 33 49N 79 2W
Conway = Conwy **12** 53 17N 3 50W
Conwy **12** 53 17N 3 50W
Conwy → **12** 53 18N 3 50W
Coober Pedy **96** 29 1S 134 43 E
Cooch Behar **69** 26 22N 89 29 E
Cook **116** 47 49N 92 39W
Cook, Bahia **128** 55 10S 70 0W
Cook Inlet **104** 59 0N 151 0W
Cook Is. **95** 17 0S 160 0W
Cook, Mt. **101** 43 36S 170 9 E
Cook Strait **101** 41 15S 174 29 E
Cookeville **115** 36 12N 85 30W
Cookhouse **92** 32 44S 25 47 E
Cookshire **113** 45 25N 71 38W
Cookstown **15** 54 40N 6 43W
Cookstown □ **15** 54 40N 6 43W
Cooksville **112** 43 36N 79 35W
Cooktown **97** 15 30S 145 16 E
Coolabah **99** 31 1S 146 43 E
Cooladdi **99** 26 37S 145 23 E
Coolah **99** 31 48S 149 41 E
Coolamon **99** 34 46S 147 8 E
Coolangatta **99** 28 11S 153 29 E
Coolgardie **96** 30 55S 121 8 E
Coolidge **119** 33 1N 111 35W
Coolidge Dam **119** 33 10N 110 30W
Cooma **97** 36 12S 149 8 E
Coonabarabran **99** 31 14S 149 18 E
Coonamble **97** 30 56S 148 27 E
Coondapoor **70** 13 42N 74 40 E
Coongie **99** 27 9S 140 8 E
Coongoola **99** 27 43S 145 51 E
Cooninie, L. **99** 26 4S 139 59 E
Coonoor **70** 11 21N 76 45 E
Cooper **117** 33 20N 95 40W
Cooper → **115** 33 0N 79 55W
Coopers Cr. → **97** 28 29S 137 46 E
Cooperstown, N.D., U.S.A. **116** 47 30N 98 6W
Cooperstown, N.Y., U.S.A. **114** 42 42N 74 57W
Coorabulka **98** 23 41S 140 20 E
Coorong, The **97** 35 50S 139 20 E
Cooroy **99** 26 22S 152 54 E
Coos Bay **118** 43 26N 124 7W
Cootamundra **97** 34 36S 148 1 E
Cootehill **15** 54 5N 7 5W
Cooyar **99** 26 59S 151 51 E
Cooyeana **98** 24 29S 138 45 E
Copahue Paso **124** 37 49S 71 8W
Copainalá **120** 17 8N 93 11W
Cope **116** 39 44N 102 50W
Cope, Cabo **33** 37 26N 1 28W
Copenhagen = København **49** 55 41N 12 34 E
Copertino **41** 40 17N 18 2 E
Copiapó **124** 27 30S 70 20W
Copiapó → **124** 27 19S 70 56W
Copley **99** 30 36S 138 26 E
Copp L. **108** 60 14N 114 40W
Copparo **39** 44 52N 11 49 E
Copper Center **104** 62 10N 145 25W
Copper Cliff **106** 46 28N 81 4W
Copper Harbor **114** 47 31N 87 55W
Copper Queen **91** 17 29S 29 18 E
Copperbelt □ **91** 13 15S 27 30 E
Coppermine **104** 67 50N 115 5W
Coppermine → **104** 67 49N 116 4W
Coquet → **12** 55 18N 1 45W
Coquilhatville = Mbandaka **88** 0 1N 18 18 E
Coquille **118** 43 15N 124 12W
Coquimbo **124** 30 0S 71 20W
Coquimbo □ **124** 31 0S 71 0W
Corabia **46** 43 48N 24 30 E
Coracora **126** 15 5S 73 45W
Coradi, Is. **41** 40 27N 17 10 E
Coral Gables **115** 25 45N 80 16W
Coral Harbour **105** 64 8N 83 10W
Coral Sea **94** 15 0S 150 0 E
Coral Sea Islands Terr. **97** 20 0S 155 0 E
Corangamite, L. **100** 38 0S 143 30 E
Coraopolis **112** 40 30N 80 10W
Corato **41** 41 12N 16 22 E
Corbeil-Essonnes **19** 48 36N 2 26 E
Corbie **19** 49 54N 2 30 E
Corbières **20** 42 55N 2 35 E
Corbigny **19** 47 16N 3 40 E
Corbin **114** 37 0N 84 3W
Corbones → **31** 37 36N 5 39W
Corby **13** 52 49N 0 31W
Corcoles → **33** 39 40N 3 18W
Corcoran **119** 36 6N 119 35W
Corcubión **30** 42 56N 9 12W
Cordele **115** 31 55N 83 49W
Cordell **117** 35 18N 99 0W
Cordenons **39** 45 59N 12 42 E
Cordes **20** 44 5N 1 57 E
Córdoba, Argent. **124** 31 20S 64 10W
Córdoba, Mexico **120** 18 50N 97 0W
Córdoba, Spain **31** 37 50N 4 50W
Córdoba □, Argent. **124** 31 22S 64 15W
Córdoba □, Spain **31** 38 5N 5 0W
Córdoba, Sierra de **124** 31 10S 64 25W
Cordon **73** 16 42N 121 32 E
Cordova, Ala., U.S.A. **115** 33 45N 87 12W
Cordova, Alaska, U.S.A. **104** 60 36N 145 45W
Corella **32** 42 7N 1 48W
Corella → **98** 19 34S 140 47 E
Corfield **98** 21 40S 143 21 E
Corfu = Kérkira **44** 39 38N 19 50 E
Corgo **30** 42 56N 7 25W
Cori **40** 41 39N 12 53 E
Coria **30** 40 0N 6 33W
Coricudgy, Mt. **100** 32 51S 150 24 E
Corigliano Cálabro **41** 39 36N 16 31 E
Corinna **99** 41 35S 145 10 E
Corinth, Miss., U.S.A. **115** 34 54N 88 30W
Corinth, N.Y., U.S.A. **113** 43 15N 73 50W
Corinth = Kórinthos **45** 38 19N 22 24 E
Corinth Canal **45** 37 58N 23 0 E
Corinth, G. of = Korinthiakós **45** 38 16N 22 30 E
Corinto, Brazil **127** 18 20S 44 30W
Corinto, Nic. **121** 12 30N 87 10W
Corj □ **46** 45 5N 23 25 E
Cork **15** 51 54N 8 30W
Cork □ **15** 51 50N 8 50W
Cork Harbour **15** 51 46N 8 16W
Corlay **18** 48 20N 3 5W
Corleone **40** 37 48N 13 16 E
Corleto Perticara **41** 40 23N 16 2 E
Çorlu **43** 41 11N 27 49 E
Cormack L. **108** 60 56N 121 37W
Cormóns **39** 45 58N 13 29 E
Cormorant **109** 54 14N 100 35W
Cormorant L. **109** 54 15N 100 50W
Corn Is. = Maiz, Is. del **121** 12 0N 83 0W
Cornélio Procópio **125** 23 7S 50 40W
Cornell **116** 45 10N 91 8W
Corner Brook **107** 48 57N 57 58W
Corner Inlet **97** 38 45S 146 20 E
Corníglio **38** 44 29N 10 5 E
Corning, Ark., U.S.A. **117** 36 27N 90 34W
Corning, Calif., U.S.A. **118** 39 56N 122 9W
Corning, Iowa, U.S.A. **116** 40 57N 94 40W
Corning, N.Y., U.S.A. **114** 42 10N 77 3W
Corno, Monte **39** 42 28N 13 34 E
Cornwall, Austral. **99** 41 33S 148 7 E
Cornwall, Can. **106** 45 2N 74 44W
Cornwall □ **13** 50 26N 4 40W
Cornwallis I. **4** 75 8N 95 0W
Corny Pt. **99** 34 55S 137 0 E
Coro **126** 11 25N 69 41W
Coroatá **127** 4 8S 44 0W
Corocoro **126** 17 15S 68 28W
Coroico **126** 16 0S 67 50W
Coromandel **101** 36 45S 175 31 E
Coromandel Coast **70** 12 30N 81 0 E
Corona, Austral. **99** 31 16S 141 24 E
Corona, Calif., U.S.A. **119** 33 49N 117 36W
Corona, N. Mex., U.S.A. **119** 34 15N 105 32W
Coronada **119** 32 45N 117 9W
Coronado, Bahía de **121** 9 0N 83 40W
Coronation **108** 52 5N 111 27W
Coronation Gulf **104** 68 25N 110 0W
Coronation I., Antarct. **5** 60 45S 46 0W
Coronation I., U.S.A. **108** 55 52N 134 20W
Coronda **124** 31 58S 60 56W
Coronel **124** 37 0S 73 10W
Coronel Bogado **124** 27 11S 56 18W
Coronel Dorrego **124** 38 40S 61 10W
Coronel Oviedo **124** 25 24S 56 30W
Coronel Pringles **124** 38 0S 61 30W
Coronel Suárez **124** 37 30S 61 52W
Coronel Vidal **124** 37 28S 57 45W
Çorovoda **44** 40 31N 20 14 E
Corowa **99** 35 58S 146 21 E
Corozal, Belize **120** 18 23N 88 23W
Corozal, Panama **120** 8 59N 79 34W
Corps **21** 44 50N 5 56 E
Corpus **125** 27 10S 55 30W
Corpus Christi **117** 27 50N 97 28W
Corpus Christi L. **117** 28 5N 97 54W
Corque **126** 18 20S 67 41W
Corral de Almaguer **32** 39 45N 3 10W
Corréggio **38** 44 46N 10 47 E
Correntes, C. das **93** 24 6S 35 34 E
Corrèze □ **20** 45 20N 1 45 E
Correze → **20** 45 10N 1 28 E
Corrib, L. **15** 53 5N 9 10W
Corrientes **124** 27 30S 58 45W
Corrientes □ **124** 28 0S 57 0W
Corrientes →, Argent. **124** 30 42S 59 38W
Corrientes →, Peru **126** 3 43S 74 35W
Corrientes, C., Colomb. **126** 5 30N 77 34W
Corrientes, C., Cuba **121** 21 43N 84 30W
Corrientes, C., Mexico **120** 20 25N 105 42W
Corrigan **117** 31 0N 94 48W
Corry **114** 41 55N 79 39W
Corse **21** 42 0N 9 0 E
Corse, C. **21** 43 1N 9 25 E
Corse-du-Sud □ **21** 41 45N 9 0 E
Corsica = Corse **21** 42 0N 9 0 E
Corsicana **117** 32 5N 96 30W
Corté **21** 42 19N 9 11 E
Corte do Pinto **31** 37 42N 7 29W
Cortegana **31** 37 52N 6 49W
Cortez **119** 37 24N 108 35W
Cortina d'Ampezzo **39** 46 32N 12 9 E
Cortland **114** 42 35N 76 11W
Cortona **39** 43 16N 12 0 E
Coruche **31** 38 57N 8 30W
Çorum **64** 40 30N 34 57 E
Corumbá **126** 19 0S 57 30W
Corumbá de Goiás **127** 16 0S 48 50W
Coruña, La **30** 43 20N 8 25W
Coruña, La □ **30** 43 10N 8 30W
Corund **46** 46 30N 25 13 E
Corunna = La Coruña **30** 43 20N 8 25W
Corvallis **118** 44 36N 123 15W
Corvette, L. de la **106** 53 25N 74 3W
Corydon **116** 40 42N 93 22W
Cosalá **120** 24 28N 106 40W
Cosamaloapan **120** 18 23N 95 50W
Cosenza **41** 39 17N 16 14 E
Coșereni **46** 44 38N 26 35 E
Coshocton **114** 40 17N 81 51W
Cosne-sur-Loire **19** 47 24N 2 54 E
Cospeito **30** 43 12N 7 34W
Cosquín **124** 31 15S 64 30W
Cossato **38** 45 34N 8 10 E
Cossé-le-Vivien **18** 47 57N 0 54W
Cosson → **19** 47 30N 1 15 E
Costa Blanca **33** 38 25N 0 10W
Costa Brava **32** 41 30N 3 0 E
Costa del Sol **31** 36 30N 4 30W
Costa Dorada **32** 40 45N 1 15 E
Costa Rica ■ **121** 10 0N 84 0W
Costa Smeralda **40** 41 5N 9 35 E
Costigliole d'Asti **38** 44 48N 8 11 E
Costilla **119** 37 0N 105 30W
Coștiui **46** 47 53N 24 2 E
Coswig **24** 51 52N 12 31 E
Cotabato **73** 7 14N 124 15 E
Cotagaita **124** 20 45S 65 40W
Côte d'Azur **21** 43 25N 6 50 E
Côte d'Or **19** 47 10N 4 50 E
Côte-d'Or □ **19** 47 30N 4 50 E
Côte-St.-André, La **21** 45 24N 5 15 E
Coteau des Prairies **116** 44 30N 97 0W
Coteau du Missouri, Plat. du **116** 47 0N 101 0W
Coteau Landing **113** 45 15N 74 13W
Cotentin **18** 49 30N 1 30W
Côtes de Meuse **19** 49 15N 5 22 E
Côtes-du-Nord □ **18** 48 25N 2 40W
Cotiella **32** 42 31N 0 19 E
Cotina → **42** 43 36N 18 50 E
Cotonou **85** 6 20N 2 25 E
Cotopaxi, Vol. **126** 0 40S 78 30W
Cotronei **41** 39 9N 16 45 E
Cotswold Hills **13** 51 42N 2 10W
Cottage Grove **118** 43 48N 123 2W
Cottbus **24** 51 44N 14 20 E
Cottbus □ **24** 51 43N 13 30 E
Cottonwood **119** 34 48N 112 1W
Cotulla **117** 28 26N 99 14W
Coubre, Pte. de la **20** 45 42N 1 15W
Couches **19** 46 53N 4 30 E
Couço **31** 38 59N 8 17W
Coudersport **114** 41 45N 77 40W
Couëron **18** 47 13N 1 44W
Couesnon → **18** 48 38N 1 32W
Couhe-Vérac **20** 46 18N 0 12 E
Coulanges **19** 47 30N 3 30 E
Coulee City **118** 47 36N 119 18W
Coulman I. **5** 73 35S 170 0 E
Coulommiers **19** 48 50N 3 3 E
Coulon → **21** 43 51N 5 0 E
Coulonge → **106** 45 52N 76 46W
Coulonges **20** 46 28N 0 35W
Council, Alaska, U.S.A. **104** 64 55N 163 45W
Council, Idaho, U.S.A. **118** 44 44N 116 26W
Council Bluffs **116** 41 20N 95 50W
Council Grove **116** 38 41N 96 30W
Courantyne → **126** 5 55N 57 5W
Courçon **20** 46 15N 0 50W
Couronne, C. **21** 43 19N 5 3 E
Cours **21** 46 7N 4 19 E
Coursan **20** 43 14N 3 4 E
Courseulles **18** 49 20N 0 29W
Courtenay **108** 49 45N 125 0W
Courtine, La **20** 45 43N 2 16 E
Courtrai = Kortrijk **16** 50 50N 3 17 E
Courtright **112** 42 49N 82 28W
Courville **18** 48 28N 1 15 E
Coushatta **117** 32 0N 93 21W
Coutances **18** 49 3N 1 28W
Couterne **18** 48 30N 0 25W
Coutras **20** 45 3N 0 8W
Coutts **108** 49 0N 111 57W
Covarrubias **32** 42 4N 3 31W
Covasna **46** 45 50N 26 10 E
Covasna □ **46** 45 50N 26 0 E
Coventry **13** 52 25N 1 31W
Coventry L. **109** 61 15N 106 15W
Covilhã **30** 40 17N 7 31W
Covington, Ga., U.S.A. **115** 33 36N 83 50W
Covington, Ky., U.S.A. **114** 39 5N 84 30W
Covington, Okla., U.S.A. **117** 36 21N 97 36W
Covington, Tenn., U.S.A. **117** 35 34N 89 39W
Cowal, L. **97** 33 40S 147 25 E
Cowan **109** 52 5N 100 45W
Cowan, L. **96** 31 45S 121 45 E
Cowan L. **109** 54 0N 107 15W
Cowangie **99** 35 12S 141 26 E
Cowansville **113** 45 14N 72 46W
Cowarie **99** 27 45S 138 15 E
Cowdenbeath **14** 56 7N 3 20W
Cowes **13** 50 45N 1 18W
Cowra **97** 33 49S 148 42 E
Coxim **127** 18 30S 54 55W
Cox's Bazar **67** 21 26N 91 59 E
Cox's Cove **107** 49 7N 58 5W
Coyuca de Benítez **120** 17 1N 100 8W
Coyuca de Catalan **120** 18 18N 100 41W
Cozad **116** 40 55N 99 57W
Cozumel, Isla de **120** 20 30N 86 40W
Craboon **99** 32 3S 149 30 E
Cracow **99** 25 17S 150 17 E
Cracow = Kraków **27** 50 4N 19 57 E
Cradock **92** 32 8S 25 36 E

Craig, Alaska, U.S.A. **108** 55 30N 133 5W
Craig, Colo., U.S.A. **118** 40 32N 107 33W
Craigavon = Lurgan **15** 54 28N 6 20W
Craigmore **91** 20 28 S 32 50 E
Crailsheim **25** 49 7N 10 5 E
Craiova **46** 44 21N 23 48 E
Cramsie **98** 23 20 S 144 15 E
Cranberry Portage **109** 54 35N 101 23W
Cranbrook, Austral. **99** 42 0 S 148 5 E
Cranbrook, Can. **108** 49 30N 115 46W
Crandon **116** 45 32N 88 52W
Crane, Oregon, U.S.A. **118** 43 21N 118 39W
Crane, Texas, U.S.A. **117** 31 26N 102 27W
Cranston **113** 41 47N 71 27W
Craon **18** 47 50N 0 58W
Craonne **19** 49 27N 3 46 E
Craponne **20** 45 20N 3 51 E
Crasna **46** 46 32N 27 51 E
Crasna → **46** 47 44N 22 35 E
Crasnei, Munţii **46** 47 0N 23 20 E
Crater, L. **118** 42 55N 122 3W
Crater Pt. **98** 5 25 S 152 9 E
Crateús **127** 5 10 S 40 39W
Crati → **41** 39 41N 16 30 E
Crato, Brazil **127** 7 10 S 39 25W
Crato, Port. **31** 39 16N 7 39W
Crau **21** 43 32N 4 40 E
Crawford **116** 42 40N 103 25W
Crawfordsville **114** 40 2N 86 51W
Crawley **13** 51 7N 0 10W
Crazy Mts. **118** 46 14N 110 30W
Crean L. **109** 54 5N 106 9W
Crécy-en-Brie **19** 48 50N 2 53 E
Crécy-en-Ponthieu **19** 50 15N 1 53 E
Crediton **112** 43 17N 81 33W
Cree →, Can. **109** 58 57N 105 47W
Cree →, U.K. **14** 54 51N 4 24W
Cree L. **109** 57 30N 106 30W
Creede **119** 37 56N 106 59W
Creel **120** 27 45N 107 38W
Creighton **116** 42 30N 97 52W
Creil **19** 49 15N 2 34 E
Crema **38** 45 21N 9 40 E
Cremona **38** 45 8N 10 2 E
Crepaja **42** 45 1N 20 38 E
Crépy **19** 49 37N 3 32 E
Crépy-en-Valois **19** 49 14N 2 54 E
Cres **39** 44 58N 14 25 E
Cresbard **116** 45 13N 98 57W
Crescent, Okla., U.S.A. **117** 35 58N 97 36W
Crescent, Oreg., U.S.A. **118** 43 30N 121 37W
Crescent City **118** 41 45N 124 12W
Crescentino **38** 45 11N 8 7 E
Crespino **39** 44 59N 11 51 E
Crespo **124** 32 2 S 60 19W
Cressy **99** 38 2 S 143 40 E
Crest **21** 44 44N 5 2 E
Crested Butte **119** 38 57N 107 0W
Crestline **112** 40 46N 82 45W
Creston, Can. **108** 49 10N 116 31W
Creston, Iowa, U.S.A. **116** 41 0N 94 20W
Creston, Wash., U.S.A. **118** 47 47N 118 36W
Creston, Wyo., U.S.A. **118** 41 46N 107 50W
Crestview **115** 30 45N 86 35W
Creswick **100** 37 25 S 143 58 E
Crete **116** 40 38N 96 58W
Crete = Kríti **45** 35 15N 25 0 E
Crete, La **108** 58 11N 116 24W
Crete, Sea of **45** 36 0N 25 0 E
Cretin, C. **98** 6 40 S 147 53 E
Creus, C. **32** 42 20N 3 19 E
Creuse □ **20** 46 0N 2 0 E
Creuse → **20** 47 0N 0 34 E
Creusot, Le **19** 46 50N 4 24 E
Creuzburg **24** 51 3N 10 15 E
Crevalcore **39** 44 41N 11 10 E
Crèvecœur-le-Grand **19** 49 37N 2 5 E
Crevillente **33** 38 12N 0 48W
Crewe **12** 53 6N 2 28W
Crib Point **99** 38 22 S 145 13 E
Criciúma **125** 28 40 S 49 23W
Crieff **14** 56 22N 3 50W
Crikvenica **39** 45 11N 14 40 E
Crimea = Krymskaya **56** 45 0N 34 0 E
Crimmitschau **24** 50 48N 12 23 E
Crinan **14** 56 6N 5 34W
Cristeşti **46** 47 15N 26 33 E
Cristóbal **120** 9 19N 79 54W
Crişul Alb → **42** 46 42N 21 17 E
Crişul Negru → **46** 46 38N 22 26 E
Crişul Repede → **46** 46 55N 20 59 E
Crivitz **24** 53 35N 11 39 E
Crna Gora **42** 42 10N 21 30 E
Crna Gora □ **42** 42 40N 19 20 E
Crna Reka → **42** 41 33N 21 59 E
Crna Trava **42** 42 49N 22 19 E
Crni Drim → **42** 41 17N 20 40 E
Crni Timok → **42** 43 53N 22 15 E
Črnoljeva Planina **42** 42 20N 21 0 E
Črnomelj **39** 45 33N 15 10 E
Croaghpatrick **15** 53 46N 9 40W
Croatia = Hrvatska □ **39** 45 20N 16 0 E
Crocker, Barisan **72** 5 40N 116 30 E
Crocker I. **96** 11 12 S 132 32 E
Crockett **117** 31 20N 95 30W
Crocodile = Krokodil → **93** 25 26 S 32 0 E
Crocodile Is. **96** 12 3 S 134 58 E
Crocq **20** 45 52N 2 21 E
Croisette, C. **21** 43 13N 5 20 E
Croisic, Le **18** 47 18N 2 30W
Croisic, Pte. du **18** 47 19N 2 31W
Croix, La, L. **106** 48 20N 92 15W
Cromarty, Can. **109** 58 3N 94 9W
Cromarty, U.K. **14** 57 40N 4 2W
Cromer **12** 52 56N 1 18 E
Cromwell **101** 45 3 S 169 14 E
Cronat **19** 46 43N 3 40 E
Cronulla **100** 34 3 S 151 8 E
Crooked →, Can. **108** 54 50N 122 54W
Crooked →, U.S.A. **118** 44 30N 121 16W
Crooked I. **121** 22 50N 74 10W
Crookston, Minn., U.S.A. **116** 47 50N 96 40W
Crookston, Nebr., U.S.A. **116** 42 56N 100 45W
Crooksville **114** 39 45N 82 8W
Crookwell **99** 34 28 S 149 24 E
Crosby, Minn., U.S.A. **116** 46 28N 93 57W
Crosby, N.D., U.S.A. **109** 48 55N 103 18W
Crosby, Pa., U.S.A. **112** 41 45N 78 23W
Crosbyton **117** 33 37N 101 12W
Cross → **85** 4 42N 8 21 E
Cross City **115** 29 35N 83 5W
Cross Fell **12** 54 44N 2 29W
Cross L. **109** 54 45N 97 30W
Cross Plains **117** 32 8N 99 7W
Cross River □ **85** 6 0N 8 0 E
Cross Sound **104** 58 20N 136 30W
Crosse, La, Kans., U.S.A. **116** 38 33N 99 20W
Crosse, La, Wis., U.S.A. **116** 43 48N 91 13W
Crossett **117** 33 10N 91 57W
Crossfield **108** 51 25N 114 0W
Crosshaven **15** 51 48N 8 19W
Croton-on-Hudson **113** 41 12N 73 55W
Crotone **41** 39 5N 17 6 E
Crow → **108** 59 41N 124 20W
Crow Agency **118** 45 40N 107 30W
Crow Hd. **15** 51 34N 10 9W
Crowell **117** 33 59N 99 45W
Crowley **117** 30 15N 92 20W
Crown Point **114** 41 24N 87 23W
Crows Nest **99** 27 16 S 152 4 E
Crowsnest Pass **108** 49 40N 114 40W
Croydon, Austral. **97** 18 13 S 142 14 E
Croydon, U.K. **13** 51 18N 0 5W
Crozet Is. **3** 46 27 S 52 0 E
Crozon **18** 48 15N 4 30W
Cruz Alta **125** 28 45 S 53 40W
Cruz, C. **121** 19 50N 77 50W
Cruz del Eje **124** 30 45 S 64 50W
Cruz, La **120** 23 55N 106 54W
Cruzeiro **125** 22 33 S 45 0W
Cruzeiro do Oeste **125** 23 46 S 53 4W
Cruzeiro do Sul **126** 7 35 S 72 35W
Cry L. **108** 58 45N 129 0W
Crystal Brook **99** 33 21 S 138 12 E
Crystal City, Mo., U.S.A. **116** 38 15N 90 23W
Crystal City, Tex., U.S.A. **117** 28 40N 99 50W
Crystal Falls **114** 46 9N 88 11W
Crystal River **115** 28 54N 82 35W
Crystal Springs **117** 31 59N 90 25W
Csongrád **27** 46 43N 20 12 E
Csongrád □ **27** 46 32N 20 15 E
Csorna **27** 47 38N 17 18 E
Csurgo **27** 46 16N 17 9 E
Cu Lao Hon **71** 10 54N 108 18 E
Cuácua → **91** 17 54 S 37 0 E
Cuamato **92** 17 2 S 15 7 E
Cuamba **91** 14 45 S 36 22 E
Cuando → **89** 14 0 S 19 30 E
Cuando Cubango □ **92** 16 25 S 20 0 E
Cuangar **92** 17 36 S 18 39 E
Cuarto → **124** 33 25 S 63 2W
Cuba, Port. **31** 38 10N 7 54W
Cuba, N. Mex., U.S.A. **119** 36 0N 107 0W
Cuba, N.Y., U.S.A. **112** 42 12N 78 18W
Cuba ■ **121** 22 0N 79 0W
Cubango → **92** 18 50 S 22 25 E
Cuchi **89** 14 37 S 16 58 E
Cúcuta **126** 7 54N 72 31W
Cudahy **114** 42 54N 87 50W
Cudalbi **46** 45 46N 27 41 E
Cuddalore **70** 11 46N 79 45 E
Cuddapah **70** 14 30N 78 47 E
Cuddapan, L. **99** 25 45 S 141 26 E
Cudgewa **99** 36 10 S 147 42 E
Cudillero **30** 43 33N 6 9W
Cue **96** 27 25 S 117 54 E
Cuéllar **30** 41 23N 4 21W
Cuenca, Ecuador **126** 2 50 S 79 9W
Cuenca, Spain **32** 40 5N 2 10W
Cuenca □ **32** 40 0N 2 0W
Cuenca, Serranía de **32** 39 55N 1 50W
Cuerda del Pozo, Pantano de la **32** 41 51N 2 44W
Cuernavaca **120** 18 50N 99 20W
Cuero **117** 29 5N 97 17W
Cuers **21** 43 14N 6 5 E
Cuervo **117** 35 5N 104 25W
Cuevas del Almanzora **33** 37 18N 1 58W
Cuevo **126** 20 15 S 63 30W
Cugir **46** 45 48N 23 25 E
Cuiabá **127** 15 30 S 56 0W
Cuiabá → **127** 17 5 S 56 36W
Cuillin Hills **14** 57 14N 6 15W
Cuillin Sd. **14** 57 4N 6 20W
Cuiluan **76** 47 51N 128 32 E
Cuima **89** 13 25 S 15 45 E
Cuiseaux **21** 46 30N 5 22 E
Cuito → **92** 18 1 S 20 48 E
Cuitzeo, L. de **120** 19 55N 101 5W
Cujmir **46** 44 13N 22 57 E
Culan **20** 46 34N 2 20 E
Culbertson **116** 48 9N 104 30W
Culcairn **99** 35 41 S 147 3 E
Culebra, Sierra de la **30** 41 55N 6 20W
Culgoa → **99** 29 56 S 146 20 E
Culiacán **120** 24 50N 107 23W
Culion **73** 11 54N 120 1 E
Cúllar de Baza **33** 37 35N 2 34W
Cullarin Range **99** 34 30 S 149 30 E
Cullen **14** 57 45N 2 50W
Cullen Pt. **98** 11 57 S 141 54 E
Cullera **33** 39 9N 0 17W
Cullman **115** 34 13N 86 50W
Culloden Moor **14** 57 29N 4 7W
Culoz **21** 45 47N 5 46 E
Culpeper **114** 38 29N 77 59W
Culuene → **127** 12 56 S 52 51W
Culver, Pt. **96** 32 54 S 124 43 E
Culverden **101** 42 47 S 172 49 E
Cumali **45** 36 42N 27 28 E
Cumaná **126** 10 30N 64 5W
Cumberland, B.C., Can. **108** 49 40N 125 0W
Cumberland, Qué., Can. **113** 45 30N 75 24W
Cumberland, Md., U.S.A. **114** 39 40N 78 43W
Cumberland, Wis., U.S.A. **116** 45 32N 92 3W
Cumberland → **115** 36 15N 87 0W
Cumberland I. **115** 30 52N 81 30W
Cumberland Is. **97** 20 35 S 149 10 E
Cumberland L. **109** 54 3N 102 18W
Cumberland Pen. **105** 67 0N 64 0W
Cumberland Plat. **115** 36 0N 84 30W
Cumberland Sd. **105** 65 30N 66 0W
Cumborah **99** 29 40 S 147 45 E
Cumbres Mayores **31** 38 4N 6 39W
Cumbria □ **12** 54 35N 2 55W
Cumbrian Mts. **12** 54 30N 3 0W
Cumbum **70** 15 40N 79 10 E
Cumnock, Austral. **99** 32 59 S 148 46 E
Cumnock, U.K. **14** 55 27N 4 18W
Cuncumén **124** 31 53 S 70 38W
Cunene → **92** 17 20 S 11 50 E
Cúneo **38** 44 23N 7 31 E
Cunillera, I. **33** 38 59N 1 13 E
Cunlhat **20** 45 38N 3 32 E
Cunnamulla **97** 28 2 S 145 38 E
Cuorgnè **38** 45 23N 7 39 E
Cupar, Can. **109** 50 57N 104 10W
Cupar, U.K. **14** 56 20N 3 0W
Cupica, Golfo de **126** 6 25N 77 30W
Čuprija **42** 43 57N 21 26 E
Curaçao **121** 12 10N 69 0W
Curanilahue **124** 37 29 S 73 28W
Curaray → **126** 2 20 S 74 5W
Cure → **19** 47 40N 3 41 E
Curepto **124** 35 8 S 72 1W
Curiapo **126** 8 33N 61 5W
Curicó **124** 34 55 S 71 20W
Curicó □ **124** 34 50 S 71 15W
Curitiba **125** 25 20 S 49 10W
Currabubula **99** 31 16 S 150 44 E
Currais Novos **127** 6 13 S 36 30W
Curralinho **127** 1 45 S 49 46W
Currant **118** 38 51N 115 32W
Curraweena **99** 30 47 S 145 54 E
Currawilla **99** 25 10 S 141 20 E
Current → **117** 37 15N 91 10W
Currie, Austral. **99** 39 56 S 143 53 E
Currie, U.S.A. **118** 40 16N 114 45W
Currie, Mt. **93** 30 29 S 29 21 E
Currituck Sd. **115** 36 20N 75 50W
Currockbilly Mt. **100** 35 25 S 150 0 E
Curtea de Argeş **46** 45 12N 24 42 E
Curtis, Spain **30** 43 7N 8 4W
Curtis, U.S.A. **116** 40 41N 100 32W
Curtis I. **97** 23 35 S 151 10 E
Curuápanema → **127** 2 25 S 55 2W
Curuçá **127** 0 43 S 47 50W
Curuguaty **125** 24 31 S 55 42W
Çürüksu Çayi → **53** 37 27N 27 11 E
Curundu **120** 8 59N 79 38W
Curup **72** 4 26 S 102 13 E
Cururupu **127** 1 50 S 44 50W
Curuzú Cuatiá **124** 29 50 S 58 5W
Curvelo **127** 18 45 S 44 27W
Cushing **117** 35 59N 96 46W
Cushing, Mt. **108** 57 35N 126 57W
Cusihuiriáchic **120** 28 10N 106 50W
Cusna, Monte **38** 44 13N 10 25 E
Cusset **20** 46 8N 3 28 E
Custer **116** 43 45N 103 38W
Cut Bank **118** 48 40N 112 15W
Cuthbert **115** 31 47N 84 47W
Cutro **41** 39 1N 16 58 E
Cuttaburra → **99** 29 43 S 144 22 E
Cuttack **69** 20 25N 85 57 E
Cuvier, C. **96** 23 14 S 113 22 E
Cuvier I. **101** 36 27 S 175 50 E
Cuxhaven **24** 53 51N 8 41 E
Cuyahoga Falls **114** 41 8N 81 30W
Cuyo **73** 10 50N 121 5 E
Cuzco, Boliv. **126** 20 0 S 66 50W
Cuzco, Peru **126** 13 32 S 72 0W
Čvrsnica **42** 43 36N 17 35 E
Cwmbran **13** 51 39N 3 0W
Cyangugu **90** 2 29 S 28 54 E
Cybinka **28** 52 12N 14 46 E
Cyclades = Kikladhes **45** 37 20N 24 30 E
Cygnet **99** 43 8 S 147 1 E
Cynthiana **114** 38 23N 84 10W
Cypress Hills **109** 49 40N 109 30W
Cyprus ■ **64** 35 0N 33 0 E
Cyrenaica **81** 27 0N 23 0 E
Cyrene = Shaḥḥāt **81** 32 40N 21 35 E
Czaplinek **28** 53 34N 16 14 E
Czar **109** 52 27N 110 50W
Czarna →, Piotrkow Trybunalski, Poland **28** 51 18N 19 55 E
Czarna →, Tarnobrzeg, Poland **28** 50 3N 21 21 E
Czarna Woda **28** 53 51N 18 6 E
Czarne **28** 53 42N 16 58 E
Czarnków **28** 52 55N 16 38 E
Czechoslovakia ■ **27** 49 0N 17 0 E
Czechowice-Dziedzice **27** 49 54N 18 59 E
Czeladz **28** 50 16N 19 2 E
Czempiń **28** 52 9N 16 33 E
Czeremcha **28** 52 31N 23 21 E
Czersk **28** 53 46N 17 58 E
Czerwieńsk **28** 52 1N 15 13 E
Czerwionka **27** 50 7N 18 37 E
Częstochowa **28** 50 49N 19 7 E
Częstochowa □ **28** 50 45N 19 0 E
Człopa **28** 53 6N 16 6 E
Człuchów **28** 53 41N 17 22 E
Czyzew **28** 52 48N 22 19 E

D

Da → **71** 21 15N 105 20 E
Da Hinggan Ling **75** 48 0N 121 0 E
Da Lat **71** 11 56N 108 25 E
Da Nang **71** 16 4N 108 13 E
Da Qaidam **75** 37 50N 95 15 E
Da Yunhe, Jiangsu, China **77** 34 25N 120 5 E
Da Yunhe, Zhejiang, China **77** 30 45N 120 35 E
Da'an **76** 45 30N 124 7 E
Dab'a, Râs el **86** 31 3N 28 31 E
Daba Shan **75** 32 0N 109 0 E
Dabai **85** 11 25N 5 15 E
Dabakala **84** 8 15N 4 20W
Dabbūrīya **62** 32 42N 35 22 E
Dabhoi **68** 22 10N 73 20 E
Dąbie, Poland **28** 53 27N 14 45 E
Dąbie, Poland **28** 52 5N 18 50 E
Dabo **72** 0 30 S 104 33 E
Dabola **84** 10 50N 11 5W
Dabou **84** 5 20N 4 23W
Daboya **85** 9 30N 1 20W
Dabrowa Górnicza **28** 50 15N 19 10 E
Dabrowa Tarnówska **27** 50 10N 20 59 E
Dąbrówno **28** 53 27N 20 2 E
Dabus → **87** 10 48N 35 10 E
Dacato → **87** 7 25N 42 40 E
*Dacca **69** 23 43N 90 26 E
*Dacca □ **69** 24 25N 90 25 E
Dachau **25** 48 16N 11 27 E
Dadanawa **126** 2 50N 59 30W
Daday **56** 41 28N 33 27 E
Dade City **115** 28 20N 82 12W
Dades, Oued → **82** 30 58N 6 44W
Dadiya **85** 9 35N 11 24 E
Dadra and Nagar Haveli □ **68** 20 5N 73 0 E
Dadri = Charkhi Dadri **68** 28 37N 76 17 E
Dadu **68** 26 45N 67 45 E
Dāeni **46** 44 51N 28 10 E
Daet **73** 14 2N 122 55 E
Dafang **77** 27 9N 105 39 E
Dagana **84** 16 30N 15 35W
Dagash **86** 19 19N 33 25 E
Dagestan A.S.S.R. □ **57** 42 30N 47 0 E
Dagestanskiye Ogni **57** 42 6N 48 12 E
Daghfeli **86** 19 18N 32 40 E
Dagö = Hiiumaa **54** 58 50N 22 45 E
Dagupan **73** 16 3N 120 20 E
Dahab **86** 28 30N 34 31 E
Dahlak Kebir **87** 15 50N 40 10 E
Dahlenburg **24** 53 11N 10 43 E
Dahlonega **115** 34 35N 83 59W
Dahme, Germ., E. **24** 51 51N 13 25 E
Dahme, Germ., W. **24** 54 13N 11 5 E
Dahomey = Benin ■ **85** 10 0N 2 0 E
Dahra **84** 15 22N 15 30W
Dahra, Massif de **82** 36 7N 1 21 E
Dai Shan **77** 30 25N 122 10 E
Dai Xian **76** 39 4N 112 58 E
Daimiel **33** 39 5N 3 35W
Daingean **15** 53 18N 7 15W
Daintree **98** 16 20 S 145 20 E
Daiō-Misaki **74** 34 15N 136 45 E
Dairût **86** 27 34N 30 43 E
Daitari **69** 21 10N 85 46 E
Dajarra **97** 21 42 S 139 30 E
Dakar **84** 14 34N 17 29W
Dakhla **80** 23 50N 15 53W
Dakhla, El Wâhât el- **86** 25 30N 28 50 E
Dakhovskaya **57** 44 13N 40 13 E
Dakingari **85** 11 37N 4 1 E
Dakor **68** 22 45N 73 11 E
Dakoro **85** 14 31N 6 46 E
Dakota City **116** 42 27N 96 28W
Đakovica **42** 42 22N 20 26 E
Đakovo **42** 45 19N 18 24 E
Dalaba **84** 10 42N 12 15W
Dalachi **76** 36 48N 105 0 E
Dalai Nur **76** 43 20N 116 45 E
Dalandzadgad **75** 43 27N 104 30 E
Dalbandin **65** 29 0N 64 23 E
Dalbeattie **14** 54 55N 3 50W
Dalbosjön **49** 58 40N 12 45 E
Dalby, Austral. **97** 27 10 S 151 17 E
Dalby, Sweden **49** 55 40N 13 22 E
Dale **47** 61 22N 5 23 E
Dalen **47** 59 26N 8 0 E
Dalga **86** 27 39N 30 41 E
Dalhart **117** 36 10N 102 30W
Dalhousie, Can. **107** 48 5N 66 26W
Dalhousie, India **68** 32 38N 76 0 E
Dali, Shaanxi, China **77** 34 48N 109 58 E
Dali, Yunnan, China **75** 25 40N 100 10 E
Daliang Shan **75** 28 0N 102 45 E
Dalias **33** 36 49N 2 52W
Dāliyat el Karmel **62** 32 43N 35 2 E
Dalj **42** 45 29N 18 59 E
Dalkeith **14** 55 54N 3 5W
Dall I. **108** 54 59N 133 25W
Dallarnil **99** 25 19 S 152 2 E
Dallas, Oregon, U.S.A. **118** 45 0N 123 15W
Dallas, Texas, U.S.A. **117** 32 50N 96 50W
Dallol **87** 14 14N 40 17 E
Dalmacija □ **42** 43 20N 17 0 E
Dalmatia = Dalmacija □ **42** 43 20N 17 0 E
Dalmellington **14** 55 20N 4 25W
Dalneretchensk **59** 45 50N 133 40 E
Daloa **84** 7 0N 6 30W
Dalrymple, Mt. **97** 21 1 S 148 39 E
Dalsjöfors **49** 57 46N 13 5 E
Dalskog **49** 58 44N 12 18 E
Dalton, Can. **106** 48 11N 84 1W
Dalton, Ga., U.S.A. **115** 34 47N 84 58W
Dalton, Mass., U.S.A. **113** 42 28N 73 11W
Dalton, Nebr., U.S.A. **116** 41 27N 103 0W
Dalton Iceberg Tongue **5** 66 15 S 121 30 E
Daltonganj **69** 24 0N 84 4 E
Dalvík **50** 65 58N 18 32W
Daly → **96** 13 35 S 130 19 E
Daly L. **109** 56 32N 105 39W
Daly Waters **96** 16 15 S 133 24 E
Dama, Wadi → **86** 27 12N 35 50 E
Daman **68** 20 25N 72 57 E
Daman □ **68** 20 25N 72 58 E
Damanhûr **86** 31 0N 30 30 E
Damar **73** 7 7 S 128 40 E
Damaraland **92** 21 0 S 17 0 E
Damascus = Dimashq **64** 33 30N 36 18 E
Damaturu **85** 11 45N 11 55 E
Damāvand **65** 35 47N 52 0 E
Damāvand, Qolleh-ye **65** 35 56N 52 10 E
Damba **88** 6 44 S 15 20 E

*Renamed Dhaka

Dāmghān 65 36 10N 54 17 E
Dāmienesti 46 46 44N 27 1 E
Damietta = Dumyât 86 31 24N 31 48 E
Daming 76 36 15N 115 6 E
Dāmīya 62 32 6N 35 34 E
Dammarie 19 48 20N 1 30 E
Dammartin 19 49 3N 2 41 E
Damme 24 52 32N 8 12 E
Damodar → 69 23 17N 87 35 E
Damoh 69 23 50N 79 28 E
Damous 82 36 31N 1 42 E
Dampier 96 20 41 S 116 42 E
Dampier Arch. 96 20 38 S 116 32 E
Dampier Downs 96 18 24 S 123 5 E
Dampier, Selat 73 0 40 S 131 0 E
Dampier Str. 98 5 50 S 148 0 E
Damville 18 48 51N 1 5 E
Damvillers 19 49 20N 5 21 E
Dan-Gulbi 85 11 40N 6 15 E
Dan Xian 77 19 31N 109 33 E
Dana 73 11 0 S 122 52 E
Dana, Lac 106 50 53N 77 20W
Danakil Depression 87 12 45N 41 0 E
Danao 73 10 31N 124 1 E
Danbury 114 41 23N 73 29W
Danby L. 119 34 17N 115 0W
Dandeldhura 69 29 20N 80 35 E
Dandenong 99 38 0 S 145 15 E
Dandong 76 40 10N 124 20 E
Danforth 107 45 39N 67 57W
* Danger Is. 95 10 53 S 165 49W
Danger Pt. 92 34 40 S 19 17 E
Dangla 87 11 18N 36 56 E
Dangora 85 11 30N 8 7 E
Dangshan 77 34 27N 116 22 E
Dangtu 77 31 32N 118 25 E
Dangyang 77 30 52N 111 44 E
Daniel 118 42 56N 110 2W
Daniel's Harbour 107 50 13N 57 35W
Danielskull 92 28 11 S 23 33 E
Danielson 113 41 50N 71 52W
Danilov 55 58 16N 40 13 E
Danilovgrad 42 42 38N 19 9 E
Danilovka 55 50 25N 44 12 E
Danissa 90 3 15N 40 58 E
Danja 85 11 21N 7 30 E
Dankalwa 85 11 52N 12 12 E
Dankama 85 13 20N 7 44 E
Dankov 55 53 20N 39 5 E
Danlí 121 14 4N 86 35W
Dannemora, Sweden 48 60 12N 17 51 E
Dannemora, U.S.A. 114 44 41N 73 44W
Dannenberg 24 53 7N 11 4 E
Dannevirke 101 40 12 S 176 8 E
Dannhauser 93 28 0 S 30 3 E
Danshui 77 25 12N 121 25 E
Dansville 114 42 32N 77 41W
Dantan 69 21 57N 87 20 E
Dante 63 10 25N 51 26 E
Danube → 43 45 20N 29 40 E
Danukandi 69 23 32N 90 43 E
Danvers 113 42 34N 70 55W
Danville, Ill., U.S.A. 114 40 10N 87 40W
Danville, Ky., U.S.A. 114 37 40N 84 45W
Danville, Va., U.S.A. 115 36 40N 79 20W
Danzhai 77 26 11N 107 48 E
Danzig = Gdańsk 28 54 22N 18 40 E
Dao 73 10 30N 121 57 E
Dão → 30 40 20N 8 11W
Dao Xian 77 25 36N 111 31 E
Daosa 68 26 52N 76 20 E
Daoud = Aïn Beïda 83 35 44N 7 22 E
Daoulas 18 48 22N 4 17W
Dapong 85 10 55N 0 16 E
Daqing Shan 76 40 40N 111 0 E
Daqu Shan 77 30 25N 122 20 E
Dar al Hamrā, Ad 64 27 22N 37 43 E
Dar es Salaam 90 6 50 S 39 12 E
Dar'ā 62 32 36N 36 7 E
Dārāb 65 28 50N 54 30 E
Darabani 46 48 10N 26 39 E
Daraj 83 30 10N 10 28 E
Daravica 42 42 32N 20 8 E
Daraw 86 24 22N 32 51 E
Darazo 85 11 1N 10 24 E
Darband 66 34 20N 72 50 E
Darbhanga 69 26 15N 85 55 E
Darby 118 46 2N 114 7W
Darda 42 45 40N 18 41 E
Dardanelle 117 35 12N 93 9W
Dardanelles = Canakkale Boğazi 44 40 0N 26 0 E
Darfo 38 45 52N 10 11 E
Dargai 66 34 25N 71 55 E
Dargan Ata 58 40 29N 62 10 E
Dargaville 101 35 57 S 173 52 E
Darhan Muminggan Lianheqi 76 41 40N 110 28 E
Dari 87 5 48N 30 26 E
Darien 120 9 7N 79 46W
Darién, G. del 126 9 0N 77 0W
Darjeeling 69 27 3N 88 18 E
Dark Cove 107 48 47N 54 13W
Darling → 97 34 4 S 141 54 E
Darling Downs 99 27 30 S 150 30 E
Darling Ra. 96 32 30 S 116 0 E
Darlington, U.K. 12 54 33N 1 33W
Darlington, S.C., U.S.A. 115 34 18N 79 50W
Darlington, Wis., U.S.A. 116 42 43N 90 7W
Darlington Point 100 34 37 S 146 1 E
Darłowo 28 54 25N 16 25 E
Dărmăneşti 46 46 21N 26 33 E
Darmstadt 25 49 51N 8 40 E
Darnah 81 32 40N 22 35 E
Darnall 93 29 23 S 31 18 E
Darnétal 18 49 25N 1 10 E
Darney 19 48 5N 6 0 E
Darnick 100 32 48 S 143 38 E
Darnley B. 104 69 30N 123 30W
Darnley, C. 5 68 0 S 69 0 E
Daroca 32 41 9N 1 25W
Darr 98 23 13 S 144 7 E
Darr → 98 23 39 S 143 50 E
Darrington 118 48 14N 121 37W
* Renamed Pakapuka

Darror → 63 10 30N 50 0 E
Darsana 69 23 35N 88 48 E
Darsi 70 15 46N 79 44 E
Darsser Ort 24 54 29N 12 31 E
Dart → 13 50 24N 3 36W
Dart, C. 5 73 6 S 126 20W
Dartmoor 13 50 36N 4 0W
Dartmouth, Austral. 98 23 31 S 144 44 E
Dartmouth, Can. 107 44 40N 63 30W
Dartmouth, U.K. 13 50 21N 3 35W
Dartmouth, L. 99 26 4 S 145 18 E
Dartuch, C. 32 39 55N 3 49 E
Daru 98 9 3 S 143 13 E
Daruvar 42 45 35N 17 14 E
Darvaza 58 40 11N 58 24 E
Darwha 68 20 15N 77 45 E
Darwin 96 12 25 S 130 51 E
Darwin Glacier 5 79 53 S 159 0 E
Daryacheh-ye-Sistan 65 31 0N 61 0 E
Daryapur 68 20 55N 77 20 E
Das 65 25 20N 53 30 E
Dashkesan 57 40 40N 46 0 E
Dasht → 65 25 10N 61 40 E
Dasht-e Kavīr 65 34 30N 55 0 E
Dasht-e Lūt 65 31 30N 58 0 E
Dasht-e Mārgow 65 30 40N 62 30 E
Daska 68 32 20N 74 20 E
Dassa-Zoume 85 7 46N 2 14 E
Dasseneiland 92 33 25 S 18 3 E
Datça 45 36 46N 27 40 E
Datia 68 25 39N 78 27 E
Datian 77 25 40N 117 50 E
Datong, Anhui, China 77 30 48N 117 44 E
Datong, Shanxi, China 76 40 6N 113 18 E
Dattapur 68 20 45N 78 15 E
Datu Piang 73 7 2N 124 30 E
Datu, Tanjung 72 2 5N 109 39 E
Daugava → 54 57 4N 24 3 E
Daugavpils 54 55 53N 26 32 E
Daulatabad 70 19 57N 75 15 E
Daun 25 50 10N 6 53 E
Dauphin 109 51 9N 100 5W
Dauphin I. 115 30 16N 88 10W
Dauphin L. 109 51 20N 99 45W
Dauphiné 21 45 15N 5 25 E
Dauqa 86 19 30N 41 0 E
Daura, Borno, Nigeria 85 11 31N 11 24 E
Daura, Kaduna, Nigeria 85 13 2N 8 21 E
Davangere 70 14 25N 75 55 E
Davao 73 7 0N 125 40 E
Davao, G. of 73 6 30N 125 48 E
Dāvar Panāh 65 27 25N 62 15 E
Davenport, Iowa, U.S.A. 116 41 30N 90 40W
Davenport, Wash., U.S.A. 118 47 40N 118 5W
Davenport Downs 98 24 8 S 141 7 E
Davenport Ra. 96 20 28 S 134 0 E
David 121 8 30N 82 30W
David City 116 41 18N 97 10W
David Gorodok 54 52 4N 27 8 E
Davidson 109 51 16N 105 59W
Davis, Antarct. 5 68 34 S 17 55 E
Davis, U.S.A. 118 38 33N 121 44W
Davis Dam 119 35 11N 114 35W
Davis Inlet 107 55 50N 60 59W
Davis Mts. 117 30 42N 104 15W
Davis Sea 5 66 0 S 92 0 E
Davis Str. 105 65 0N 58 0W
Davos 25 46 48N 9 49 E
Davy L. 109 58 53N 108 18W
Dawa → 87 4 11N 42 6 E
Dawaki, Bauchi, Nigeria 85 9 25N 9 33 E
Dawaki, Kano, Nigeria 85 12 5N 8 23 E
Dawes Ra. 98 24 40 S 150 40 E
Dawson, Can. 104 64 10N 139 30W
Dawson, Ga., U.S.A. 115 31 45N 84 28W
Dawson, N.D., U.S.A. 116 46 56N 99 45W
Dawson → 97 23 25 S 149 45 E
Dawson Creek 108 55 45N 120 15W
Dawson, I. 128 53 50 S 70 50W
Dawson Inlet 109 61 50N 93 25W
Dawson Range 98 24 30 S 149 48 E
Dax 20 43 44N 1 3W
Daxian 75 31 15N 107 23 E
Daxin 77 22 50N 107 11 E
Daxue Shan 75 30 30N 101 30 E
Daye 77 30 6N 114 58 E
Daylesford 100 37 21 S 144 9 E
Dayong 77 29 11N 110 30 E
Dayr Abū Sa'īd 62 32 30N 35 42 E
Dayr al-Ghuṣūn 62 32 21N 35 4 E
Dayr az Zawr 64 35 20N 40 5 E
Dayr Dirwān 62 31 55N 35 15 E
Daysland 108 52 50N 112 20W
Dayton, Ohio, U.S.A. 114 39 45N 84 10W
Dayton, Pa., U.S.A. 112 40 54N 79 18W
Dayton, Tenn., U.S.A. 115 35 30N 85 1W
Dayton, Wash., U.S.A. 118 46 20N 118 10W
Daytona Beach 115 29 14N 81 0W
Dayu 77 25 24N 114 22 E
Dayville 118 44 33N 119 37W
Dazhu 77 30 41N 107 15 E
Dazu 77 29 40N 105 42 E
De Aar 92 30 39 S 24 0 E
De Funiak Springs 115 30 42N 86 10W
De Grey 96 20 12 S 119 12 E
De Land 115 29 1N 81 19W
De Leon 117 32 9N 98 35W
De Pere 114 44 28N 88 1W
De Queen 117 34 3N 94 24W
De Quincy 117 30 30N 93 27W
De Ridder 117 30 48N 93 15W
De Smet 116 44 25N 97 35W
De Soto 116 38 7N 90 33W
De Tour 114 45 59N 83 56W
De Witt 117 34 19N 91 20W
Dead Sea = Miyet, Bahr el 64 31 30N 35 30 E
Deadwood 116 44 23N 103 44W
Deadwood L. 108 59 10N 128 30W
Deakin 96 30 46 S 128 0 E
Deal 13 51 13N 1 25 E
Dealesville 92 28 41 S 25 44 E
Dean, Forest of 13 51 50N 2 35W

Deán Funes 124 30 20 S 64 20W
Dearborn 106 42 18N 83 15W
Dease → 108 59 56N 128 32W
Dease L. 108 58 40N 130 5W
Dease Lake 108 58 25N 130 6W
Death Valley 119 36 19N 116 52W
Death Valley Junc. 119 36 21N 116 30W
Death Valley Nat. Monument 119 36 30N 117 0W
Deauville 18 49 23N 0 2 E
Deba Habe 85 10 14N 11 20 E
Debaltsevo 56 48 22N 38 26 E
Debao 77 23 21N 106 46 E
Debar 42 41 31N 20 30 E
Debden 109 53 30N 106 50W
Debdou 82 33 59N 3 0W
Dębica 27 50 2N 21 25 E
Dęblin 28 51 34N 21 50 E
Debno 28 52 44N 14 41 E
Débo, L. 84 15 14N 4 15W
Debolt 108 55 12N 118 1W
Debrc 42 44 38N 19 53 E
Debre Birhan 87 9 41N 39 31 E
Debre Markos 87 10 20N 37 40 E
Debre May 87 11 20N 37 25 E
Debre Sina 87 9 51N 39 50 E
Debre Tabor 87 11 50N 38 26 E
Debre Zebit 87 11 48N 38 30 E
Debrecen 27 47 33N 21 42 E
Dečani 42 42 30N 20 10 E
Decatur, Ala., U.S.A. 115 34 35N 87 0W
Decatur, Ga., U.S.A. 115 33 47N 84 17W
Decatur, Ill., U.S.A. 116 39 50N 89 0W
Decatur, Ind., U.S.A. 114 40 50N 84 56W
Decatur, Texas, U.S.A. 117 33 15N 97 35W
Decazeville 20 44 34N 2 15 E
Deccan 70 18 0N 79 0 E
Deception I. 5 63 0 S 60 15W
Deception L. 109 56 33N 104 13W
Děčín 26 50 47N 14 12 E
Decize 19 46 50N 3 28 E
Deckerville 112 43 33N 82 46W
Decollatura 41 39 2N 16 21 E
Decorah 116 43 20N 91 50W
Deda 46 46 56N 24 50 E
Dedéagach = Alexandroúpotis 44 40 50N 25 54 E
Dedham 113 42 14N 71 10W
Dedilovo 55 53 59N 37 50 E
Dédougou 84 12 30N 3 25W
Deduru Oya 70 7 32N 79 50 E
Dedza 91 14 20 S 34 20 E
Dee →, Scot., U.K. 14 57 4N 2 7W
Dee →, Wales, U.K. 12 53 15N 3 7W
Deep B. 108 61 15N 116 35W
Deepdale 96 21 42 S 116 10 E
Deepwater 99 29 25 S 151 51 E
Deer → 109 58 23N 94 13W
Deer Lake, Newf., Can. 107 49 11N 57 27W
Deer Lake, Ontario, Can. 109 52 36N 94 20W
Deer Lodge 118 46 25N 112 40W
Deer Park 118 47 55N 117 21W
Deer River 116 47 21N 93 44W
Deeral 98 17 14 S 145 55 E
Deerdepoort 92 24 37 S 26 27 E
Deesa 68 24 18N 72 10 E
Deferiet 113 44 2N 75 41W
Defiance 114 41 20N 84 20W
Deganya 62 32 43N 35 34 E
Degebe → 31 38 13N 7 29W
Degeh Bur 63 8 11N 43 31 E
Degema 85 4 50N 6 48 E
Deggendorf 25 48 49N 12 59 E
Degloor 70 18 34N 77 33 E
Deh Bīd 65 30 39N 53 11 E
Deh Kheyr 65 28 45N 54 40 E
Dehibat 83 32 0N 10 47 E
Dehiwala 70 6 50N 79 51 E
Dehkareqan 64 37 43N 45 55 E
Dehra Dun 68 30 20N 78 4 E
Dehri 69 24 50N 84 15 E
Dehui 76 44 30N 125 40 E
Deinze 16 50 59N 3 32 E
Dej 46 47 10N 23 52 E
Deje 48 59 35N 13 29 E
Dekalb 116 41 55N 88 45W
Dekemhare 87 15 6N 39 0 E
Dekese 88 3 24 S 21 24 E
Del Norte 119 37 40N 106 27W
Del Rio 117 29 23N 100 50W
Delagua 117 37 21N 104 35W
Delai 86 17 21N 36 6 E
Delano 119 35 48N 119 13W
Delareyville 92 26 41 S 25 26 E
Delavan 116 42 40N 88 39W
Delaware 114 40 20N 83 0W
Delaware □ 114 39 0N 75 40W
Delaware → 114 39 20N 75 25W
Delčevo 42 41 58N 22 46 E
Delegate 99 37 4 S 148 56 E
Delémont 25 47 22N 7 20 E
Delft 16 52 1N 4 22 E
Delft I. 70 9 30N 79 40 E
Delfzijl 16 53 20N 6 55 E
Delgado, C. 91 10 45 S 40 40 E
Delgo 86 20 6N 30 40 E
Delhi, Can. 112 42 51N 80 30W
Delhi, India 68 28 38N 77 17 E
Delhi, U.S.A. 113 42 17N 74 56W
Deli Jovan 42 44 13N 22 9 E
Delia 108 51 38N 112 23W
Delice → 64 39 45N 34 15 E
Delicias 120 28 10N 105 30W
Delitzsch 24 51 32N 12 22 E
Dell City 119 31 58N 105 19W
Dell Rapids 116 43 53N 96 44W
Delle 19 47 30N 7 2 E
Dellys 83 36 57N 3 57 E
Delmar 113 42 37N 73 47W
Delmenhorst 24 53 3N 8 37 E
Delmiro Gouveia 127 9 24 S 38 6W
Delnice 39 45 23N 14 50 E
Delong, Ostrova 59 76 40N 149 20 E
Deloraine, Austral. 99 41 30 S 146 40 E

Deloraine, Can. 109 49 15N 100 29W
Delorme, L. 107 54 31N 69 52W
Delphi, Greece 45 38 28N 22 30 E
Delphi, U.S.A. 114 40 37N 86 40W
Delphos 114 40 51N 84 17W
Delportshoop 92 28 22 S 24 20 E
Delray Beach 115 26 27N 80 4W
Delsbo 48 61 48N 16 32 E
Delta, Colo., U.S.A. 119 38 44N 108 5W
Delta, Utah, U.S.A. 118 39 21N 112 29W
Delungra 99 29 39 S 150 51 E
Delvina 44 39 59N 20 4 E
Delvinákion 44 39 57N 20 32 E
Demanda, Sierra de la 32 42 15N 3 0W
Demba 88 5 28 S 22 15 E
Dembecha 87 10 32N 37 30 E
Dembi 87 8 5N 36 25 E
Dembia 90 3 33N 25 48 E
Dembidolo 87 8 34N 34 50 E
Demer → 16 50 57N 4 42 E
Demetrias 44 39 22N 23 1 E
Demidov 54 55 16N 31 30 E
Deming 119 32 10N 107 50W
Demini → 126 0 46 S 62 56W
Demmin 24 53 54N 13 2 E
Demnate 82 31 44N 6 59W
Demonte 38 44 18N 7 18 E
Demopolis 115 32 30N 87 48W
Dempo, Mt. 72 4 2 S 103 15 E
Demyansk 54 57 40N 32 27 E
Den Burg 16 53 3N 4 47 E
Den Haag = 's Gravenhage 16 52 7N 4 17 E
Den Helder 16 52 57N 4 45 E
Den Oever 16 52 56N 5 2 E
Denain 19 50 20N 3 22 E
Denau 58 38 16N 67 54 E
Denbigh 12 53 12N 3 26W
Dendang 72 3 7 S 107 56 E
Dendermonde 16 51 2N 4 5 E
Deneba 87 9 47N 39 10 E
Deng Xian 77 32 34N 112 4 E
Denge 85 12 52N 5 21 E
Dengi 85 9 25N 9 55 E
Denham 96 25 56 S 113 31 E
Denham Ra. 97 21 55 S 147 46 E
Denia 33 38 49N 0 8 E
Deniliquin 97 35 30 S 144 58 E
Denison, Iowa, U.S.A. 116 42 0N 95 18W
Denison, Texas, U.S.A. 117 33 50N 96 40W
Denison Range 97 28 30 S 136 5 E
Denizli 64 37 42N 29 2 E
Denman Glacier 5 66 45 S 99 25 E
Denmark 96 34 59 S 117 25 E
Denmark ■ 49 55 30N 9 0 E
Denmark Str. 6 66 0N 30 0W
Dennison 112 40 21N 81 21W
Denpasar 72 8 45 S 115 14 E
Denton, Mont., U.S.A. 118 47 25N 109 56W
Denton, Texas, U.S.A. 117 33 12N 97 10W
D'Entrecasteaux Is. 98 9 0 S 151 0 E
D'Entrecasteaux Pt. 96 34 50 S 115 57 E
Denu 85 6 4N 1 8 E
Denver 116 39 45N 105 0W
Denver City 117 32 58N 102 48W
Deoband 68 29 42N 77 43 E
Deobhog 70 19 53N 82 44 E
Deogarh 69 21 32N 84 45 E
Deoghar 69 24 30N 86 42 E
Deolali 70 19 58N 73 50 E
Deoli 68 25 50N 75 20 E
Deoria 69 26 31N 83 48 E
Deosai Mts. 69 35 40N 75 0 E
Depew 112 42 55N 78 43W
Deping 76 37 25N 116 58 E
Deposit 113 42 5N 75 23W
Deputatskiy 59 69 18N 139 54 E
Dêqên 75 28 34N 98 51 E
Deqing 77 23 8N 111 42 E
Dera Ghazi Khan 68 30 5N 70 43 E
Dera Ismail Khan 68 31 50N 70 50 E
* Dera Ismail Khan □ 68 32 30N 70 0 E
Derbent 56 42 5N 48 4 E
Derby, Austral. 96 17 18 S 123 38 E
Derby, U.K. 12 52 55N 1 28W
Derby, Conn., U.S.A. 113 41 20N 73 5W
Derby, N.Y., U.S.A. 112 42 40N 78 59W
Derby □ 12 52 55N 1 28W
Derecske 27 47 20N 21 33 E
Derg → 15 54 42N 7 26W
Derg, L. 15 53 0N 8 20W
Dergachi 55 50 9N 36 11 E
Dergaon 67 26 45N 94 0 E
Dermantsi 43 43 8N 24 17 E
Dernieres Isles 117 29 0N 90 45W
Derryveagh Mts. 15 55 0N 8 40W
Derudub 86 17 31N 36 7 E
Derval 18 47 40N 1 41W
Dervéni 45 38 8N 22 25 E
Derventa 42 44 59N 17 55 E
Derwent 109 53 41N 110 58W
Derwent →, Derby, U.K. 12 52 53N 1 17W
Derwent →, N. Yorks., U.K. 12 53 45N 0 57W
Derwentwater, L. 12 54 35N 3 9W
Des Moines, Iowa, U.S.A. 116 41 35N 93 37W
Des Moines, N. Mex., U.S.A. 117 36 50N 103 51W
Des Moines → 116 40 23N 91 25W
Desaguadero →, Argent. 124 34 30 S 66 46W
Desaguadero →, Boliv. 126 18 24 S 67 5W
Deschaillons 107 46 32N 72 7W
Descharme → 109 56 51N 109 13W
Deschutes → 118 45 30N 121 0W
Dese 87 11 5N 39 40 E
Desenzano del Gardo 38 45 28N 10 32 E
Desert Center 119 33 45N 115 27W
Deskenatlata L. 108 60 55N 112 3W
Desna → 54 50 33N 30 32 E
Desnătui → 46 44 15N 23 27 E
Desolación, I. 128 53 0 S 74 0W
Despeñaperros, Paso 33 38 24N 3 30W
Despotovac 42 44 6N 21 30 E
Dessau 24 51 49N 12 15 E
Dessye = Dese 87 11 5N 39 40 E
* Now part of North West Frontier □

D'Estrees B. 99 35 55 S 137 45 E
Desuri 68 25 18N 73 35 E
Desvrès 19 50 40N 1 48 E
Deta 42 45 24N 21 13 E
Detinja → 42 43 51N 19 45 E
Detmold 24 51 55N 8 50 E
Detour Pt. 114 45 37N 86 35W
Detroit, Mich., U.S.A. 106 42 23N 83 5W
Detroit, Tex., U.S.A. 117 33 40N 95 10W
Detroit Lakes 116 46 50N 95 50W
Dett 91 18 38 S 26 50 E
Deurne, Belg. 16 51 12N 4 24 E
Deurne, Neth. 16 51 27N 5 49 E
Deutsche Bucht 24 54 10N 7 51 E
Deutschlandsberg 26 46 49N 15 14 E
Deux-Sèvres □ 18 46 35N 0 20W
Deva 46 45 53N 22 55 E
Devakottai 70 9 55N 78 45 E
Devaprayag 68 30 13N 78 35 E
Dévaványa 27 47 2N 20 59 E
Deveci Daği 56 40 10N 36 0 E
Devecser 27 47 6N 17 26 E
Deventer 16 52 15N 6 10 E
Deveron → 14 57 40N 2 31W
Devesel 46 44 28N 22 41 E
Devgad Baria 68 22 40N 73 55 E
Devgad, I. 70 14 48N 74 5 E
Devils Lake 116 48 5N 98 50W
Devils Paw 108 58 47N 134 0W
Devil's Pt. 70 9 26N 80 6 E
Devin 43 41 44N 24 24 E
Devizes 13 51 21N 2 0W
Devnya 43 43 13N 27 33 E
Devolii → 44 40 57N 20 15 E
Devon 108 53 24N 113 44W
Devon I. 4 75 10N 85 0W
Devonport, Austral. 97 41 10 S 146 22 E
Devonport, N.Z. 101 36 49 S 174 49 E
Devonport, U.K. 13 50 23N 4 11W
Devonshire □ 13 50 50N 3 40W
Dewas 68 22 59N 76 3 E
Dewetsdorp 92 29 33 S 26 39 E
Dewsbury 12 53 42N 1 38W
Dexter, Mo., U.S.A. 117 36 50N 90 0W
Dexter, N. Mex., U.S.A. 117 33 15N 104 25W
Deyhūk 65 33 15N 57 30 E
Deyyer 65 27 55N 51 55 E
Dezadeash L. 108 60 28N 136 58W
Dezfūl 64 32 20N 48 30 E
Dezh Shāhpūr 64 35 30N 46 25 E
Dezhneva, Mys 59 66 5N 169 40W
Dezhou 76 37 26N 116 18 E
Dháfni 45 37 48N 22 1 E
Dhafra 65 23 20N 54 0 E
Dhahaban 86 21 58N 39 3 E
Dhahira 65 23 40N 57 0 E
Dhahiriya = Aẓ Ẓāhirīyah 62 31 25N 34 58 E
Dhahran = Aẓ Ẓahrān 64 26 18N 50 10 E
Dhamar 63 14 30N 44 20 E
Dhamási 44 39 43N 22 11 E
Dhampur 68 29 19N 78 33 E
Dhamtari 69 20 42N 81 35 E
Dhanbad 69 23 50N 86 30 E
Dhankuta 69 26 55N 87 40 E
Dhanora 69 20 20N 80 22 E
Dhar 68 22 35N 75 26 E
Dharampur, Gujarat, India 70 20 32N 73 17 E
Dharampur, Mad. P., India 68 22 13N 75 18 E
Dharapuram 70 10 45N 77 34 E
Dharmapuri 70 12 10N 78 10 E
Dharmavaram 70 14 29N 77 44 E
Dharmsala (Dharamsala) 68 32 16N 76 23 E
Dhaulagiri 69 28 39N 83 28 E
Dhebar, L. 68 24 10N 74 0 E
Dhenkanal 69 20 45N 85 35 E
Dhenoúsa 45 37 8N 25 48 E
Dheskáti 44 39 55N 21 49 E
Dhespotikó 45 36 57N 24 58 E
Dhestina 45 38 25N 22 31 E
Dhidhimótikhon 44 41 22N 26 29 E
Dhíkti 45 35 8N 25 22 E
Dhilianáta 45 38 15N 20 34 E
Dhílos 45 37 23N 25 15 E
Dhimitsána 45 37 36N 22 3 E
Dhírfis 45 38 40N 23 54 E
Dhodhekánisos 45 36 35N 27 0 E
Dhokós 45 37 20N 23 20 E
Dholiana 44 39 54N 20 32 E
Dholka 68 22 44N 72 29 E
Dholpur 68 26 45N 77 59 E
Dhomokós 45 39 10N 22 18 E
Dhond 70 18 26N 74 40 E
Dhoraji 68 21 45N 70 37 E
Dhoxáton 44 41 9N 24 16 E
Dhragonísi 45 37 27N 25 29 E
Dhrangadhra 68 22 59N 71 31 E
Dhriopís 45 37 25N 24 35 E
Dhrol 68 22 33N 70 25 E
Dhubaibah 65 23 25N 54 35 E
Dhubri 69 26 2N 89 59 E
Dhula 63 15 10N 47 30 E
Dhulia 68 20 58N 74 50 E
Dhurm → 86 20 18N 42 53 E
Di Linh, Cao Nguyen 71 11 30N 108 0 E
Dia 45 35 26N 25 13 E
Diablo Heights 120 8 58N 79 34W
Diafarabé 84 14 9N 4 57W
Diala 84 14 10N 10 0W
Dialakoro 84 12 18N 7 54W
Diallassagou 84 13 47N 3 41W
Diamante 124 32 5 S 60 40W
Diamante → 124 34 30 S 66 46W
Diamantina 127 18 17 S 43 40W
Diamantina → 97 26 45 S 139 10 E
Diamantino 127 14 30 S 56 30W
Diamond Harbour 69 22 11N 88 14 E
Diamond Mts. 118 40 0N 115 58W
Diamondville 118 41 51N 110 30W
Diancheng 77 21 30N 111 4 E
Diano Marina 38 43 55N 8 3 E
Dianra 84 8 45N 6 14W
Diapaga 85 12 5N 1 46 E
Diapangou 85 12 5N 0 10 E
Diariguila 84 10 35N 10 2W
Dibaya 88 6 30 S 22 57 E
Dibaya-Lubue 88 4 12 S 19 54 E
Dibbi 87 4 10N 41 52 E
Dibble Glacier Tongue 5 66 8 S 134 32 E
Dibete 92 23 45 S 26 32 E
Dibrugarh 67 27 29N 94 55 E
Dickinson 116 46 50N 102 48W
Dickson 115 36 5N 87 22W
Dickson City 113 41 29N 75 40W
Dickson (Dikson) 58 73 40N 80 5 E
Dicomano 39 43 53N 11 30 E
Didesa, W. → 87 10 2N 35 32 E
Didiéni 84 13 53N 8 6W
Didsbury 108 51 35N 114 10W
Didwana 68 27 23N 17 36 E
Die 21 44 47N 5 22 E
Diébougou 84 11 0N 3 15W
Diefenbaker L. 109 51 0N 106 55W
Diego Garcia 3 7 50 S 72 50 E
Diekirch 16 49 52N 6 10 E
Diélette 18 49 33N 1 52W
Diéma 84 14 32N 9 12W
Diémbéring 84 12 29N 16 47W
Dien Bien 71 21 20N 103 0 E
Diepholz 24 52 37N 8 22 E
Dieppe 18 49 54N 1 4 E
Dieren 16 52 3N 6 6 E
Dierks 117 34 9N 94 0W
Diest 16 50 58N 5 4 E
Dieulefit 21 44 32N 5 4 E
Dieuze 19 48 49N 6 43 E
Differdange 16 49 31N 5 54 E
Dig 68 27 28N 77 20 E
Digba 90 4 25N 25 48 E
Digby 107 44 38N 65 50W
Digges 109 58 40N 94 0W
Digges Is. 105 62 40N 77 50W
Dighinala 67 23 15N 92 5 E
Dighton 116 38 30N 100 26W
Digne 21 44 5N 6 12 E
Digoin 20 46 29N 3 58 E
Digos 73 6 45N 125 20 E
Digranes 50 66 4N 14 44 E
Digras 70 20 6N 77 45 E
Digul → 73 7 7 S 138 42 E
Dihang → 67 27 48N 95 30 E
Dijlah, Nahr → 64 31 0N 47 25 E
Dijon 19 47 20N 5 0 E
Dikala 87 4 45N 31 28 E
Dikkil 87 11 8N 42 20 E
Dikomu di Kai 92 24 58 S 24 36 E
Diksmuide 16 51 2N 2 52 E
Dikwa 85 12 4N 13 30 E
Dila 87 6 21N 38 22 E
Dili 73 8 39 S 125 34 E
Dilizhan 57 40 46N 44 57 E
Dilj 42 45 29N 18 1 E
Dillenburg 24 50 44N 8 17 E
Dilley 117 28 40N 99 12W
Dilling 87 12 3N 29 35 E
Dillingen 25 48 32N 10 29 E
Dillon, Can. 109 55 56N 108 35W
Dillon, Mont., U.S.A. 118 45 9N 112 36W
Dillon, S.C., U.S.A. 115 34 26N 79 20W
Dillon → 109 55 56N 108 56W
Dilston 99 41 22 S 147 10 E
Dimashq 64 33 30N 36 18 E
Dimbokro 84 6 45N 4 46W
Dimboola 99 36 28 S 142 7 E
Dîmboviţa □ 46 45 0N 25 30 E
Dîmboviţa → 46 44 14N 26 13 E
Dîmbovnic → 46 44 28N 25 18 E
Dimbulah 98 17 8 S 145 4 E
Dimitrovgrad, Bulg. 43 42 5N 25 35 E
Dimitrovgrad, U.S.S.R. 55 54 14N 49 39 E
Dimitrovgrad, Yugo. 42 43 0N 22 48 E
Dimitrovo = Pernik 42 42 35N 23 2 E
Dimmitt 117 34 36N 102 16W
Dimo 87 5 19N 29 10 E
Dimona 62 31 2N 35 1 E
Dimovo 42 43 43N 22 50 E
Dinagat 73 10 10N 125 40 E
Dinajpur 69 25 33N 88 43 E
Dinan 18 48 28N 2 2W
Dinant 16 50 16N 4 55 E
Dinapur 69 25 38N 85 5 E
Dinar 64 38 5N 30 15 E
Dinara Planina 39 43 50N 16 35 E
Dinard 18 48 38N 2 6W
Dinaric Alps = Dinara Planina 9 43 50N 16 35 E
Dinder, Nahr ed → 87 14 6N 33 40 E
Dindi → 70 16 24N 78 15 E
Dindigul 70 10 25N 78 0 E
Ding Xian 76 38 30N 114 59 E
Dingbian 76 37 35N 107 32 E
Dingelstädt 24 51 19N 10 19 E
Dinghai 77 30 1N 122 6 E
Dingle 15 52 9N 10 17W
Dingle B. 15 52 3N 10 20W
Dingmans Ferry 113 41 13N 74 55W
Dingnan 77 24 45N 115 0 E
Dingo 98 23 38 S 149 19 E
Dingolfing 25 48 38N 12 30 E
Dingtao 77 35 5N 115 35 E
Dinguiraye 84 11 18N 10 49W
Dingwall 14 57 36N 4 26W
Dingxi 76 35 30N 104 33 E
Dingxiang 76 38 30N 112 58 E
Dinokwe (Palla Road) 92 23 29 S 26 37 E
Dinosaur National Monument 118 40 30N 108 58W
Dinuba 119 36 31N 119 22W
Dio 49 56 37N 14 15 E
Diósgyör 27 48 7N 20 43 E
Diosig 46 47 18N 22 2 E
Diourbel 84 14 39N 16 12W
Diplo 68 24 35N 69 35 E
Dipolog 73 8 36N 123 20 E
Dipşa 46 46 58N 24 27 E
Dir 66 35 08N 71 59 E
Diré 84 16 20N 3 25W
Dire Dawa 87 9 35N 41 45 E
Direction, C. 97 12 51 S 143 32 E
Diriamba 121 11 51N 86 19W
Dirk Hartog I. 96 25 50 S 113 5 E
Dirranbandi 97 28 33 S 148 17 E
Disa 87 12 5N 34 15 E
Disappointment, C. 118 46 20N 124 0W
Disappointment L. 96 23 20 S 122 40 E
Disaster B. 97 37 15 S 150 0 E
Discovery B. 97 38 10 S 140 40 E
Disentis 25 46 42N 8 50 E
Dishna 86 26 9N 32 32 E
Disina 85 11 35N 9 50 E
Disko 4 69 45N 53 30W
Disko Bugt 4 69 10N 52 0W
Disna 54 55 32N 28 11 E
Disna → 54 55 34N 28 12 E
Distrito Federal □ 127 15 45 S 47 45W
Disûq 86 31 8N 30 35 E
Diu 68 20 45N 70 58 E
Dives → 18 49 18N 0 7W
Dives-sur-Mer 18 49 18N 0 8W
Divi Pt. 70 15 59N 81 9 E
Divichi 57 41 15N 48 57 E
Divide 118 45 48N 112 47W
Divinópolis 127 20 10 S 44 54W
Divnoye 57 45 55N 43 21 E
Divo 84 5 48N 5 15W
Diwal Kol 66 34 23N 67 52 E
Dixie 118 45 37N 115 27W
Dixon, Ill., U.S.A. 116 41 50N 89 30W
Dixon, Mont., U.S.A. 118 47 19N 114 25W
Dixon, N. Mex., U.S.A. 119 36 15N 105 57W
Dixon Entrance 108 54 30N 132 0W
Dixonville 108 56 32N 117 40W
Diyarbakir 64 37 55N 40 18 E
Diz Chah 65 35 30N 55 30 E
Djado 83 21 4N 12 14 E
Djado, Plateau du 83 21 29N 12 21 E
Djakarta = Jakarta 73 6 9 S 106 49 E
Djamâa 83 33 32N 5 59 E
Djamba 92 16 45 S 13 58 E
Djambala 88 2 32 S 14 30 E
Djanet 83 24 35N 9 32 E
Djaul I. 98 2 58 S 150 57 E
Djawa = Jawa 73 7 0 S 110 0 E
Djebiniana 83 35 1N 11 0 E
Djelfa 82 34 40N 3 15 E
Djema 90 6 3N 25 15 E
Djendel 82 36 15N 2 25 E
Djeneïene 83 31 45N 10 9 E
Djenné 84 14 0N 4 30W
Djenoun, Garet el 83 25 4N 5 31 E
Djerba 83 33 52N 10 51 E
Djerba, Île de 83 33 56N 11 0 E
Djerid, Chott 83 33 42N 8 30 E
Djibo 85 14 9N 1 35W
Djibouti 87 11 30N 43 5 E
Djibouti ■ 63 12 0N 43 0 E
Djolu 88 0 35N 22 5 E
Djorong 72 3 58 S 114 56 E
Djougou 85 9 40N 1 45 E
Djoum 88 2 41N 12 35 E
Djourab 81 16 40N 18 50 E
Djugu 90 1 55N 30 35 E
Djúpivogur 50 64 39N 14 17W
Djursholm 48 59 25N 18 6 E
Djursland 49 56 27N 10 45 E
Dmitriev-Lgovskiy 54 52 10N 35 0 E
Dmitriya Lapteva, Proliv 59 73 0N 140 0 E
Dmitrov 55 56 25N 37 32 E
Dmitrovsk-Orlovskiy 54 52 29N 35 10 E
Dneiper = Dnepr → 56 46 30N 32 18 E
Dnepr → 56 46 30N 32 18 E
Dneprodzerzhinsk 56 48 32N 34 37 E
Dneprodzerzhinskoye Vdkhr. 56 49 0N 34 0 E
Dnepropetrovsk 56 48 30N 35 0 E
Dneprorudnoye 56 47 21N 34 58 E
Dnestr → 56 46 18N 30 17 E
Dnestrovski = Belgorod 56 50 35N 36 35 E
Dniester = Dnestr → 56 46 18N 30 17 E
Dno 54 57 50N 29 58 E
Doba 81 8 40N 16 50 E
Dobbiaco 39 46 44N 12 13 E
Dobbyn 97 19 44 S 139 59 E
Dobczyce 27 49 52N 20 25 E
Döbeln 24 51 7N 13 10 E
Doberai, Jazirah 73 1 25 S 133 0 E
Dobiegniew 28 52 59N 15 45 E
Doblas 124 37 5 S 64 0W
Dobo 73 5 45 S 134 15 E
Doboj 42 44 46N 18 6 E
Dobra, Konin, Poland 28 51 55N 18 37 E
Dobra, Szczecin, Poland 28 53 34N 15 20 E
Dobra, Dîmboviţa, Romania 43 44 52N 25 40 E
Dobra, Hunedoara, Romania 46 45 54N 22 36 E
Dobre Miasto 28 53 58N 20 26 E
Dobrinishta 43 41 49N 23 34 E
Dobřiš 26 49 46N 14 10 E
Dobrodzień 28 50 45N 18 25 E
Dobropole 56 48 25N 37 2 E
Dobruja 46 44 30N 28 15 E
Dobrush 55 52 28N 30 19 E
Dobrzyń nad Wisłą 28 52 39N 19 22 E
Dobtong 87 6 25N 31 40 E
Dodecanese = Dhodhekánisos 45 36 35N 27 0 E
Dodge Center 116 44 1N 92 50W
Dodge City 117 37 42N 100 0W
Dodge L. 109 59 50N 105 36W
Dodgeville 116 42 55N 90 8W
Dodo 87 5 10N 29 57 E
Dodola 87 6 59N 39 11 E
Dodoma 90 6 8 S 35 45 E
Dodoma □ 90 6 0 S 36 0 E
Dodona 44 39 40N 20 46 E
Dodsland 109 51 50N 108 45W
Dodson 118 48 23N 108 16W
Doetinchem 16 51 59N 6 18 E
Doftana 46 45 11N 25 45 E
Dog Creek 108 51 35N 122 14W
Dog L., Man., Can. 109 51 2N 98 31W
Dog L., Ont., Can. 106 48 18N 89 30W
Doğanbey 45 37 40N 27 10 E
Dogliani 38 44 35N 7 55 E
Dogondoutchi 85 13 38N 4 2 E
Dogran 68 31 48N 73 35 E
Doguéraoua 85 14 0N 5 31 E
Dohad 68 22 50N 74 15 E
Dohazari 67 22 10N 92 5 E
Doi 73 2 14N 127 49 E
Doi Luang 71 18 30N 101 0 E
Doig → 108 56 25N 120 40W
Dois Irmãos, Sa. 127 9 0 S 42 30W
Dojransko Jezero 42 41 13N 22 44 E
Dokka 47 60 49N 10 7 E
Dokka → 47 61 7N 10 0 E
Dokkum 16 53 20N 5 59 E
Dokri 68 27 25N 68 7 E
Dol-de-Bretagne 18 48 34N 1 47W
Doland 116 44 55N 98 5W
Dolbeau 107 48 53N 72 18W
Dole 19 47 7N 5 31 E
Doleib, Wadi → 87 12 10N 33 15 E
Dolgellau 12 52 44N 3 53W
Dolgelley = Dolgellau 12 52 44N 3 53W
Dolginovo 54 54 39N 27 29 E
Dolianova 40 39 23N 9 11 E
Dolinskaya 56 48 6N 32 46 E
Dolj □ 46 44 10N 23 30 E
Dollart 16 53 20N 7 10 E
Dolna Banya 43 42 18N 23 44 E
Dolni Dŭbnik 43 43 24N 24 26 E
Dolo, Ethiopia 87 4 11N 42 3 E
Dolo, Italy 39 45 25N 12 4 E
Dolomites = Dolomiti 39 46 30N 11 40 E
Dolomiti 39 46 30N 11 40 E
Dolores, Argent. 124 36 20 S 57 40W
Dolores, Uruguay 124 33 34 S 58 15W
Dolores, Colo., U.S.A. 119 37 30N 108 30W
Dolores, Tex., U.S.A. 117 27 40N 99 38W
Dolores → 119 38 49N 108 17W
Đolovo 42 44 55N 20 52 E
Dolphin and Union Str. 104 69 5N 114 45W
Dolphin C. 128 51 10 S 59 0W
Dolsk 28 51 59N 17 3 E
Dom Pedrito 125 31 0 S 54 40W
Doma 85 8 25N 8 18 E
Domasi 91 15 15 S 35 22 E
Domazlice 26 49 28N 13 0 E
Dombarovskiy 58 50 46N 59 32 E
Dombasle 19 48 38N 6 21 E
Dombes 21 46 3N 5 0 E
Dombóvár 27 46 21N 18 9 E
Dombrád 27 48 13N 21 54 E
Domburg 16 51 34N 3 30 E
Domel I. = Letsok-aw Kyun 71 11 30N 98 25 E
Domérat 20 46 21N 2 32 E
Domeyko 124 29 0 S 71 0W
Domeyko, Cordillera 124 24 30 S 69 0W
Domfront 18 48 37N 0 40W
Dominador 124 24 21 S 69 20W
Dominica ■ 121 15 20N 61 20W
Dominican Rep. ■ 121 19 0N 70 30W
Dömitz 24 53 9N 11 13 E
Domme 20 44 48N 1 12 E
Domo 63 7 50N 47 10 E
Domodóssola 38 46 6N 8 19 E
Dompaire 19 48 14N 6 14 E
Dompierre-sur-Besbre 20 46 31N 3 41 E
Dompim 84 5 10N 2 5W
Domrémy 19 48 26N 5 40 E
Domsjö 48 63 16N 18 41 E
Domville, Mt. 99 28 1 S 151 15 E
Domvraina 45 38 15N 22 59 E
Domžale 39 46 9N 14 35 E
Don →, India 70 16 20N 76 15 E
Don →, Eng., U.K. 12 53 41N 0 51W
Don →, Scot., U.K. 14 57 14N 2 5W
Don →, U.S.S.R. 57 47 4N 39 18 E
Don Benito 31 38 53N 5 51W
Don Martín, Presa de 120 27 30N 100 50W
Dona Ana 91 17 25 S 35 5 E
Donaghadee 15 54 38N 5 32W
Donald 99 36 23 S 143 0 E
Donalda 108 52 35N 112 34W
Donaldsonville 117 30 2N 91 0W
Donalsonville 115 31 3N 84 52W
Donau → 23 48 10N 17 0 E
Donaueschingen 25 47 57N 8 30 E
Donauwörth 25 48 42N 10 47 E
Donawitz 26 47 22N 15 4 E
Doncaster 12 53 31N 1 9W
Dondo, Angola 88 9 45 S 14 25 E
Dondo, Mozam. 91 19 33 S 34 46 E
Dondo, Teluk 73 0 29N 120 30 E
Dondra Head 70 5 55N 80 40 E
Donegal 15 54 39N 8 8W
Donegal □ 15 54 53N 8 0W
Donegal B. 15 54 30N 8 35W
Donets → 57 47 33N 40 55 E
Donetsk 56 48 0N 37 45 E
Donga 85 7 45N 10 2 E
Dongara 96 29 14 S 114 57 E
Dongargarh 69 21 10N 80 40 E
Donges 18 47 18N 2 4W
Dongfang 77 18 50N 108 33 E
Donggala 73 0 30 S 119 40 E
Donggou 76 39 52N 124 10 E
Dongguan 77 22 58N 113 44 E
Dongguang 76 37 50N 116 30 E
Dongjingcheng 76 44 0N 129 10 E
Donglan 77 24 30N 107 21 E
Dongliu 77 30 13N 116 55 E
Dongola 86 19 9N 30 22 E
Dongou 88 2 0N 18 5 E
Dongping 76 35 55N 116 20 E
Dongshan 77 23 43N 117 30 E
Dongsheng 76 39 50N 110 0 E
Dongtai 77 32 51N 120 21 E
Dongting Hu 75 29 18N 112 45 E
Dongxing 75 21 34N 108 0 E
Dongyang 77 29 13N 120 15 E
Doniphan 117 36 40N 90 50W
Donja Stubica 39 45 59N 16 0 E

Donji Dušnik **42** 43 12N 22 5 E
Donji Miholjac **42** 45 45N 18 10 E
Donji Milanovac **42** 44 28N 22 6 E
Donji Vakuf **42** 44 8N 17 24 E
Donjon, Le **20** 46 22N 3 48 E
Dønna **50** 66 6N 12 30 E
Donna **117** 26 12N 98 2W
Donnaconna **107** 46 41N 71 41W
Donnelly's Crossing **101** 35 42S 173 38 E
Donora **112** 40 11N 79 50W
Donor's Hills **98** 18 42S 140 33 E
Donskoy **55** 53 55N 38 15 E
Donya Lendava **39** 46 35N 16 25 E
Donzère-Mondragon **21** 44 28N 4 43 E
Donzère-Mondragon, Barrage de **21** 44 13N 4 42 E
Donzy **19** 47 20N 3 6 E
Doon → **14** 55 26N 4 41W
Dor (Tantūra) **62** 32 37N 34 55 E
Dora Báltea → **38** 45 11N 8 5 E
Dora, L. **96** 22 0S 123 0 E
Dora Riparia → **38** 45 5N 7 44 E
Dorada, La **126** 5 30N 74 40W
Doran L. **109** 61 13N 108 6W
Dorat, Le **20** 46 14N 1 5 E
Dorchester **13** 50 42N 2 28W
Dorchester, C. **105** 65 27N 77 27W
Dordogne □ **20** 45 5N 0 40 E
Dordogne → **20** 45 2N 0 36W
Dordrecht, Neth. **16** 51 48N 4 39 E
Dordrecht, S. Afr. **92** 31 20S 27 3 E
Dore → **20** 45 50N 3 35 E
Doré L. **109** 54 46N 107 17W
Doré Lake **109** 54 38N 107 36W
Dore, Mt. **20** 45 32N 2 50 E
Dorfen **25** 48 16N 12 10 E
Dorgali **40** 40 18N 9 35 E
Dori **85** 14 3N 0 2W
Doring → **92** 31 54S 18 39 E
Dorion **106** 45 23N 74 3W
Dormaa-Ahenkro **84** 7 15N 2 52W
Dormo, Ras **87** 13 14N 42 35 E
Dornberg **39** 55 45N 13 50 E
Dornbirn **26** 47 25N 9 45 E
Dornes **19** 46 48N 3 18 E
Dornoch **14** 57 52N 4 0W
Dornoch Firth **14** 57 52N 4 0W
Doro **85** 16 9N 0 51W
Dorog **27** 47 42N 18 45 E
Dorogobuzh **54** 54 50N 33 18 E
Dorohoi **46** 47 56N 26 30 E
Döröö Nuur **75** 48 0N 93 0 E
Dorre I. **96** 25 13S 113 12 E
Dorrigo **99** 30 20S 152 44 E
Dorris **118** 41 59N 121 58W
Dorset, Can. **112** 45 14N 78 54W
Dorset, U.S.A. **112** 41 4N 80 40W
Dorset □ **13** 50 48N 2 25W
Dorsten **24** 51 40N 6 55 E
Dortmund **24** 51 32N 7 28 E
Dörtyol **64** 36 52N 36 12 E
Dorum **24** 53 40N 8 33 E
Doruma **90** 4 42N 27 33 E
Dos Bahías, C. **128** 44 58S 65 32W
Dos Cabezas **119** 32 10N 109 37W
Dos Hermanas **31** 37 16N 5 55W
Dosso **85** 13 0N 3 13 E
Dothan **115** 31 10N 85 25W
Douai **19** 50 21N 3 4 E
Douala **88** 4 0N 9 45 E
Douaouir **82** 20 45N 3 0W
Douarnenez **18** 48 6N 4 21W
Douăzeci Şi Trei August **46** 43 55N 28 40 E
Double Island Pt. **99** 25 56S 153 11 E
Doubrava → **26** 49 40N 15 30 E
Doubs □ **19** 47 10N 6 20 E
Doubs → **19** 46 53N 5 1 E
Doubtful B. **96** 34 15S 119 28 E
Doubtful Sd. **101** 45 20S 166 49 E
Doubtless B. **101** 34 55S 173 26 E
Doudeville **18** 49 43N 0 47 E
Doué **18** 47 11N 0 20W
Douentza **84** 14 58N 2 48W
Douglas, S. Afr. **92** 29 4S 23 46 E
Douglas, U.K. **12** 54 9N 4 29W
Douglas, Alaska, U.S.A. **108** 58 23N 134 24W
Douglas, Ariz., U.S.A. **119** 31 21N 109 30W
Douglas, Ga., U.S.A. **115** 31 32N 82 52W
Douglas, Wyo., U.S.A. **116** 42 45N 105 20W
Douglastown **107** 48 46N 64 24W
Douglasville **115** 33 46N 84 43W
Douirat **82** 33 2N 4 11W
Doukáton, Ákra **45** 38 34N 20 30 E
Doulevant **19** 48 22N 4 53 E
Doullens **19** 50 10N 2 20 E
Doumé **88** 4 15N 13 25 E
Douna **84** 13 13N 6 0W
Dounreay **14** 58 34N 3 44W
Dourados **125** 22 9S 54 50W
Dourados → **125** 21 58S 54 18W
Dourdan **19** 48 30N 2 0 E
Douro → **30** 41 8N 8 40W
Douvaine **21** 46 19N 6 16 E
Douz **83** 33 25N 9 0 E
Douze → **20** 43 54N 0 30W
Dove → **12** 52 51N 1 36W
Dove Creek **119** 37 46N 108 59W
Dover, Austral. **99** 43 18S 147 2 E
Dover, U.K. **13** 51 7N 1 19 E
Dover, Del., U.S.A. **114** 39 10N 75 31W
Dover, N.H., U.S.A. **114** 43 12N 70 51W
Dover, N.J., U.S.A. **113** 40 53N 74 34W
Dover, Ohio, U.S.A. **114** 40 32N 81 30W
Dover-Foxcroft **107** 45 14N 69 14W
Dover Plains **113** 41 43N 73 35W
Dover, Pt. **96** 32 32S 125 32 E
Dover, Str. of **18** 51 0N 1 30 E
Dovey → **13** 52 32N 4 0W
Dovrefjell **47** 62 15N 9 33 E
Dowa **91** 13 38S 33 58 E
Dowagiac **114** 42 0N 86 8W
Dowlat Yār **65** 34 30N 65 45 E
Dowlatabad **65** 28 20N 56 40W
Down □ **15** 54 20N 6 0W
Downey **118** 42 29N 112 3W
Downham Market **13** 52 36N 0 22 E
Downieville **118** 39 34N 120 50W
Downpatrick **15** 54 20N 5 43W
Downpatrick Hd. **15** 54 20N 9 21W
Dowshī **65** 35 35N 68 43 E
Doylestown **113** 40 21N 75 10W
Draa, C. **82** 28 47N 11 0W
Draa, Oued → **82** 30 29N 6 1W
Drac → **21** 45 13N 5 41 E
Drachten **16** 53 7N 6 5 E
Drăgăneşti **46** 44 9N 24 32 E
Drăgăneşti-Vlaşca **46** 44 5N 25 33 E
Dragaš **42** 42 5N 20 35 E
Drăgăsani **46** 44 39N 24 17 E
Dragina **42** 44 30N 19 25 E
Dragocvet **42** 44 0N 21 15 E
Dragoman, Prokhod **42** 43 0N 22 53 E
Dragonera, I. **32** 39 35N 2 19 E
Dragovishtitsa (Perivol) **42** 42 22N 22 39 E
Draguignan **21** 43 30N 6 27 E
Drain **118** 43 45N 123 17W
Drake, Austral. **99** 28 55S 152 25 E
Drake, U.S.A. **116** 47 56N 100 21W
Drake Passage **5** 58 0S 68 0W
Drakensberg **93** 31 0S 28 0 E
Dráma **44** 41 9N 24 10 E
Dráma □ **44** 41 20N 24 0 E
Drammen **47** 59 42N 10 12 E
Drangajökull **50** 66 9N 22 15W
Drangedal **47** 59 6N 9 3 E
Dranov, Ostrov **46** 44 55N 29 30 E
Drau = Drava → **26** 46 32N 14 58 E
Drava → **42** 45 33N 18 55 E
Draveil **19** 48 41N 2 25 E
Dravograd **39** 46 36N 15 5 E
Drawa → **28** 52 52N 15 59 E
Drawno **28** 53 13N 15 46 E
Drawsko Pomorskie **28** 53 35N 15 50 E
Drayton Valley **108** 53 12N 114 58W
Dren **42** 43 8N 20 44 E
Drenthe □ **16** 52 52N 6 40 E
Dresden, Can. **112** 42 35N 82 11W
Dresden, Ger. **24** 51 2N 13 45 E
Dresden □ **24** 51 12N 14 0 E
Dreux **18** 48 44N 1 23 E
Drezdenko **28** 52 50N 15 49 E
Driffield **12** 54 0N 0 25W
Driftwood **112** 41 22N 78 9W
Driggs **118** 43 50N 111 8W
Drin i zi → **44** 41 37N 20 28 E
Drina → **42** 44 53N 19 21 E
Drincea → **46** 44 20N 22 55 E
Drînceni **46** 46 49N 28 10 E
Drini → **44** 42 20N 20 0 E
Drinjača → **42** 44 15N 19 8 E
Driva → **47** 62 33N 9 38 E
Drivstua **47** 62 26N 9 47 E
Drniš **39** 43 51N 16 10 E
Drøbak **47** 59 39N 10 39 E
Drobin **28** 52 42N 19 58 E
Drogheda **15** 53 45N 6 20W
Drogichin **54** 52 15N 25 8 E
Drogobych **54** 49 20N 23 30 E
Drohiczyn **28** 52 24N 22 39 E
Droichead Nua **15** 53 11N 6 50W
Droitwich **13** 52 16N 2 10W
Drôme □ **21** 44 38N 5 15 E
Drôme → **21** 44 46N 4 46 E
Dromedary, C. **99** 36 17S 150 10 E
Dronero **38** 44 29N 7 22 E
Dronfield **98** 21 12S 140 3 E
Dronne → **20** 45 2N 0 9W
Dronning Maud Land **5** 72 30S 12 0 E
Dronninglund **49** 57 10N 10 19 E
Dropt → **20** 44 35N 0 6W
Drosendorf **26** 48 52N 15 37 E
Drouzhba **43** 43 15N 28 0 E
Drumbo **112** 43 16N 80 35W
Drumheller **108** 51 25N 112 40W
Drummond **118** 46 40N 113 4W
Drummond I. **106** 46 0N 83 40W
Drummond Ra. **97** 23 45S 147 10 E
Drummondville **106** 45 55N 72 25W
Drumright **117** 35 59N 96 38W
Druskininkai **54** 54 3N 23 58 E
Drut → **54** 53 3N 30 42 E
Druya **54** 55 45N 27 28 E
Druzhina **59** 68 14N 145 18 E
Drvar **39** 44 21N 16 23 E
Drvenik **39** 43 27N 16 3 E
Drwęca → **28** 53 0N 18 42 E
Dry Tortugas **121** 24 38N 82 55W
Dryanovo **43** 42 59N 25 28 E
Dryden, Can. **109** 49 47N 92 50W
Dryden, U.S.A. **117** 30 3N 102 3W
Drygalski I. **5** 66 0S 92 0 E
Drysdale → **96** 13 59S 126 51 E
Drzewiczka → **28** 51 36N 20 36 E
Dschang **85** 5 32N 10 3 E
Du Bois **114** 41 8N 78 46W
Du Quoin **116** 38 0N 89 10W
Duanesburg **113** 42 45N 74 11W
Duaringa **98** 23 42S 149 42 E
Ḍubā **64** 27 10N 35 40 E
Dubai = Dubayy **65** 25 18N 55 20 E
Dubawnt → **109** 64 33N 100 6W
Dubawnt, L. **109** 63 4N 101 42W
Dubayy **65** 25 18N 55 20 E
Dubbo **97** 32 11S 148 35 E
Dubele **90** 2 56N 29 35 E
Dubica **39** 45 11N 16 48 E
Dublin, Ireland **15** 53 20N 6 18W
Dublin, Ga., U.S.A. **115** 32 30N 82 34W
Dublin, Tex., U.S.A. **117** 32 0N 98 20W
Dublin □ **15** 53 24N 6 20W
Dublin B. **15** 53 18N 6 5W
Dubna, U.S.S.R. **55** 54 8N 36 59 E
Dubna, U.S.S.R. **55** 56 44N 37 10 E
Dubno **54** 50 25N 25 45 E
Dubois **118** 44 7N 112 9W
Dubossary **56** 47 15N 29 10 E
Dubossasy Vdkhr. **56** 47 30N 29 0 E
Dubovka **57** 49 5N 44 50 E
Dubovskoye **57** 47 28N 42 46 E
Dubrajpur **69** 23 48N 87 25 E
Dubréka **84** 9 46N 13 31W
Dubrovitsa **54** 51 31N 26 35 E
Dubrovnik **42** 42 39N 18 6 E
Dubrovskoye **59** 58 55N 111 10 E
Dubuque **116** 42 30N 90 41W
Duchang **77** 29 18N 116 12 E
Duchesne **118** 40 14N 110 22W
Duchess **97** 21 20S 139 50 E
Ducie I. **95** 24 40S 124 48W
Duck Lake **109** 52 50N 106 16W
Duck Mt. Prov. Parks **109** 51 45N 101 0W
Duderstadt **24** 51 30N 10 15 E
Dudinka **59** 69 30N 86 13 E
Dudley **13** 52 30N 2 5W
Dudna → **70** 19 17N 76 54 E
Dueñas **30** 41 52N 4 33W
Dueodde **49** 54 59N 15 4 E
Duero → **30** 41 8N 8 40W
Duff Is. **94** 9 53S 167 8 E
Dufftown **14** 57 26N 3 9W
Dugi **39** 44 0N 15 0 E
Dugo Selo **39** 45 51N 16 18 E
Duifken Pt. **97** 12 33S 141 38 E
Duisburg **24** 51 27N 6 42 E
Duiwelskloof **93** 23 42S 30 10 E
Dukati **44** 40 16N 19 32 E
Duke I. **108** 54 50N 131 20W
Dukelsky průsmyk **27** 49 25N 21 42 E
Dukhān **65** 25 25N 50 50 E
Dukhovshchina **54** 55 15N 32 27 E
Dukla **27** 49 30N 21 35 E
Duku, Bauchi, Nigeria **85** 10 43N 10 43 E
Duku, Sokoto, Nigeria **85** 11 11N 4 55 E
Dulce → **124** 30 32S 62 33W
Dulce, Golfo **121** 8 40N 83 20W
Dŭlgopol **43** 43 3N 27 22 E
Dullewala **68** 31 50N 71 25 E
Dülmen **24** 51 49N 7 18 E
Dulovo **43** 43 48N 27 9 E
Dululu **98** 23 48S 150 15 E
Duluth **116** 46 48N 92 10W
Dum Dum **69** 22 39N 88 33 E
Dum Duma **67** 27 40N 95 40 E
Dum Hadjer **81** 13 18N 19 41 E
Dumaguete **73** 9 17N 123 15 E
Dumai **72** 1 35N 101 28 E
Dumaran **73** 10 33N 119 50 E
Dumaring **73** 1 46N 118 10 E
Dumas, Ark., U.S.A. **117** 33 52N 91 30W
Dumas, Tex., U.S.A. **117** 35 50N 101 58W
Dumbarton **14** 55 58N 4 35W
Dumbrăveni **46** 46 14N 24 34 E
Dumfries **14** 55 4N 3 37W
Dumfries & Galloway □ **14** 55 0N 4 0W
Dumka **69** 24 12N 87 15 E
Dümmersee **24** 52 30N 8 21 E
Dumoine → **106** 46 13N 77 51W
Dumoine L. **106** 46 55N 77 55W
Dumraon **69** 25 33N 84 8 E
Dumyât **86** 31 24N 31 48 E
Dumyât, Masabb **86** 31 28N 31 51 E
Dun Laoghaire **15** 53 17N 6 9W
Dun-le-Palestel **20** 46 18N 1 39 E
Dun-sur-Auron **19** 46 53N 2 33 E
Duna → **27** 45 51N 18 48 E
Dunaföldvár **27** 46 50N 18 57 E
Dunaj → **27** 48 5N 17 10 E
Dunajec → **27** 50 15N 20 44 E
Dunajska Streda **27** 48 0N 17 37 E
Dunapatai **27** 46 39N 19 4 E
Dunărea → **46** 45 30N 8 15 E
Dunaszekcsö **27** 46 6N 18 45 E
Dunaújváros **27** 47 0N 18 57 E
Dunav → **42** 44 47N 21 20 E
Dunavtsi **42** 43 57N 22 53 E
Dunback **101** 45 23S 170 36 E
Dunbar, Austral. **98** 16 0S 142 22 E
Dunbar, U.K. **14** 56 0N 2 32W
Dunblane **14** 56 10N 3 58W
Duncan, Can. **108** 48 45N 123 40W
Duncan, Ariz., U.S.A. **119** 32 46N 109 6W
Duncan, Okla., U.S.A. **117** 34 25N 98 0W
Duncan L. **108** 62 51N 113 58W
Duncan, L. **106** 53 29N 77 58W
Duncan Pass. **71** 11 0N 92 30 E
Duncan Town **121** 22 15N 75 45W
Duncannon **112** 40 23N 77 2W
Dundalk, Can. **112** 44 10N 80 24W
Dundalk, Ireland **15** 54 1N 6 25W
Dundalk Bay **15** 53 55N 6 15W
Dundas **106** 43 17N 79 59W
Dundas I. **108** 54 30N 130 50W
Dundas, L. **96** 32 35S 121 50 E
Dundas Str. **96** 11 15S 131 35 E
Dundee, S. Afr. **93** 28 11S 30 15 E
Dundee, U.K. **14** 56 29N 3 0W
Dundoo **99** 27 40S 144 37 E
Dundrum **15** 54 17N 5 50W
Dundrum B. **15** 54 12N 5 40W
Dundwara **68** 27 48N 79 9 E
Dunedin, N.Z. **101** 45 50S 170 33 E
Dunedin, U.S.A. **115** 28 1N 82 45W
Dunedin → **108** 59 30N 124 5W
Dunfermline **14** 56 5N 3 28W
Dungannon, Can. **112** 43 51N 81 36W
Dungannon, U.K. **15** 54 30N 6 47W
Dungannon □ **15** 54 30N 6 55W
Dungarpur **68** 23 52N 73 45 E
Dungarvan **15** 52 6N 7 40W
Dungarvan Bay **15** 52 5N 7 35W
Dungeness **13** 50 54N 0 59 E
Dungo, L. do **92** 17 15S 19 0 E
Dungog **99** 32 22S 151 46 E
Dungu **90** 3 40N 28 32 E
Dungunâb **86** 21 10N 37 9 E
Dungunâb, Khalij **86** 21 5N 37 12 E
Dunhinda Falls **70** 7 5N 81 6 E
Dunhua **76** 43 20N 128 14 E
Dunhuang **75** 40 8N 94 36 E
Dunières **21** 45 13N 4 20 E
Dunk I. **98** 17 59S 146 29 E
Dunkeld **14** 56 34N 3 36W
Dunkerque **19** 51 2N 2 20 E
Dunkery Beacon **13** 51 15N 3 37W
Dunkirk **114** 42 30N 79 18W
Dunkirk = Dunkerque **19** 51 2N 2 20 E
Dunkuj **87** 12 50N 32 49 E
Dunkwa, Central, Ghana **84** 6 0N 1 47W
Dunkwa, Central, Ghana **85** 5 30N 1 0W
Dunlap **116** 41 50N 95 36W
Dunmanus B. **15** 51 31N 9 50W
Dunmore **114** 41 27N 75 38W
Dunmore Hd. **15** 52 10N 10 35W
Dunn **115** 35 18N 78 36W
Dunnellon **115** 29 4N 82 28W
Dunnet Hd. **14** 58 38N 3 22W
Dunning **116** 41 52N 100 4W
Dunnville **112** 42 54N 79 36W
Dunolly **99** 36 51S 143 44 E
Dunoon **14** 55 57N 4 56W
Dunqul **86** 23 26N 31 37 E
Duns **14** 55 47N 2 20W
Dunseith **116** 48 49N 100 2W
Dunsmuir **118** 41 10N 122 18W
Dunstable **13** 51 53N 0 31W
Dunstan Mts. **101** 44 53S 169 35 E
Dunster **108** 53 8N 119 50W
Dunvegan L. **109** 60 8N 107 10W
Duolun **76** 42 12N 116 28 E
Dupree **116** 45 4N 101 35W
Dupuyer **118** 48 11N 112 31W
Duque de Caxias **125** 22 45S 43 19W
Duquesne **112** 40 22N 79 55W
Dūrā **62** 31 31N 35 1 E
Durack Range **96** 16 50S 127 40 E
Durance → **21** 43 55N 4 45 E
Durand **114** 42 54N 83 58W
Durango, Mexico **120** 24 3N 104 39W
Durango, Spain **32** 43 13N 2 40W
Durango, U.S.A. **119** 37 16N 107 50W
Durango □ **120** 25 0N 105 0W
Durant **117** 34 0N 96 25W
Duratón → **30** 41 37N 4 7W
Durazno **124** 33 25S 56 31W
Durazzo = Durrësi **44** 41 19N 19 28 E
Durban, France **20** 43 0N 2 49 E
Durban, S. Afr. **93** 29 49S 31 1 E
Dúrcal **31** 37 0N 3 34W
Đurđevac **42** 46 2N 17 3 E
Düren **24** 50 48N 6 30 E
Durg **69** 21 15N 81 22 E
Durgapur **69** 23 30N 87 20 E
Durham, Can. **106** 44 10N 80 49W
Durham, U.K. **12** 54 47N 1 34W
Durham, U.S.A. **115** 36 0N 78 55W
Durham □ **12** 54 42N 1 45W
Durmitor **34** 43 10N 19 0 E
Durness **14** 58 34N 4 45W
Durrës **44** 41 19N 19 28 E
Durrësi **44** 41 19N 19 28 E
Durrie **99** 25 40S 140 15 E
Durtal **18** 47 40N 0 18W
Duru **90** 4 14N 28 50 E
D'Urville I. **101** 40 50S 173 55 E
D'Urville, Tanjung **73** 1 28S 137 54 E
Duryea **113** 41 20N 75 45W
Dusa Mareb **63** 5 30N 46 15 E
Dûsh **86** 24 35N 30 41 E
Dushak **58** 37 13N 60 1 E
Dushan **77** 25 48N 107 30 E
Dushanbe **58** 38 33N 68 48 E
Dusheti **57** 42 10N 44 42 E
Dusky Sd. **101** 45 47S 166 30 E
Düsseldorf **24** 51 15N 6 46 E
Duszniki-Zdrój **28** 50 24N 16 24 E
Dutch Harbor **104** 53 54N 166 35W
Dutlhe **92** 23 58S 23 46 E
Dutsan Wai **85** 10 50N 8 10 E
Dutton **112** 42 39N 81 30W
Dutton → **98** 20 44S 143 10 E
Duved **48** 63 24N 12 55 E
Duvno **42** 43 42N 17 13 E
Duwādimi **64** 24 35N 44 15 E
Duyun **77** 26 18N 107 29 E
Duzce **64** 40 50N 31 10 E
Duzdab = Zāhedān **65** 29 30N 60 50 E
Dve Mogili **43** 43 35N 25 55 E
Dvina, Sev. **52** 64 32N 40 30 E
Dvinsk = Daugavpils **54** 55 53N 26 32 E
Dvinskaya Guba **52** 65 0N 39 0 E
Dvor **39** 45 4N 16 22 E
Dvorce **27** 49 50N 17 34 E
Dvur Králové **26** 50 27N 15 50 E
Dwarka **68** 22 18N 69 8 E
Dwight, Can. **112** 45 20N 79 1W
Dwight, U.S.A. **114** 41 5N 88 25W
Dyakovskoya **55** 60 5N 41 12 E
Dyatkovo **54** 53 40N 34 27 E
Dyatlovo **54** 53 28N 25 28 E
Dyer, C. **105** 66 40N 61 0W
Dyer Plateau **5** 70 45S 65 30W
Dyersburg **117** 36 2N 89 20W
Dyfed □ **13** 52 0N 4 30W
Dyje → **27** 48 37N 16 56 E
Dynevor Downs **99** 28 10S 144 20 E
Dynów **27** 49 50N 22 11 E
Dysart **109** 50 57N 104 2W
Dzamin Üüd **75** 43 50N 111 58 E
Dzerzhinsk, Byelorussian S.S.R., U.S.S.R. **54** 53 40N 27 1 E
Dzerzhinsk, R.S.F.S.R., U.S.S.R. **55** 56 14N 43 30 E
Dzhalal-Abad **58** 40 56N 73 0 E
Dzhalinda **59** 53 26N 124 0 E
Dzhambeyty **57** 50 15N 52 30 E
Dzhambul **58** 42 54N 71 22 E
Dzhankoi **56** 45 40N 34 20 E
Dzhanybek **57** 49 25N 46 50 E
Dzhardzhan **59** 68 10N 124 10 E
Dzhelinde **59** 70 0N 114 20 E

Dzhetygara **58** 52 11N 61 12 E
Dzhezkazgan **58** 47 44N 67 40 E
Dzhikimde **59** 59 1N 121 47 E
Dzhizak **58** 40 6N 67 50 E
Dzhugdzur, Khrebet **59** 57 30N 138 0 E
Dzhungarskiye Vorota **58** 45 0N 82 0 E
Dzhvari **57** 42 42N 42 4 E
Działdowo **28** 53 15N 20 15 E
Działoszyce **28** 50 22N 20 20 E
Działoszyn **28** 51 6N 18 50 E
Dzierzgoń **28** 53 58N 19 20 E
Dzierzoniów **28** 50 45N 16 39 E
Dzioua **83** 33 14N 5 14 E
Dziwnów **28** 54 2N 14 45 E
Dzungarian Gate = Alataw Shankou **75** 45 5N 81 57 E
Dzuumod **75** 47 45N 106 58 E

E

Eabamet, L. **106** 51 30N 87 46W
Eads **116** 38 30N 102 46W
Eagle, Alaska, U.S.A. **104** 64 44N 141 7W
Eagle, Colo., U.S.A. **118** 39 39N 106 55W
Eagle → **107** 53 36N 57 26W
Eagle Butt **116** 45 1N 101 12W
Eagle Grove **116** 42 37N 93 53W
Eagle L., Calif., U.S.A. **118** 40 35N 120 50W
Eagle L., Me., U.S.A. **107** 46 23N 69 22W
Eagle Lake **117** 29 35N 96 21W
Eagle Nest **119** 36 33N 105 13W
Eagle Pass **117** 28 45N 100 35W
Eagle River **116** 45 55N 89 17W
Eaglehawk **99** 36 39 S 144 16 E
Ealing **13** 51 30N 0 19W
Earl Grey **109** 50 57N 104 43W
Earle **117** 35 18N 90 26W
Earlimart **119** 35 53N 119 16W
Earn → **14** 56 20N 3 19W
Earn, L. **14** 56 23N 4 14W
Earnslaw, Mt. **101** 44 32 S 168 27 E
Earth **117** 34 18N 102 30W
Easley **115** 34 52N 82 35W
East Angus **107** 45 30N 71 40W
East Aurora **112** 42 46N 78 38W
East B. **117** 29 2N 89 16W
East Bengal **67** 24 0N 90 0 E
East Beskids = Vychodné Beskydy **27** 49 30N 22 0 E
East Brady **112** 40 59N 79 36W
East C. **101** 37 42 S 178 35 E
East Chicago **114** 41 40N 87 30W
East China Sea **75** 30 5N 126 0 E
East Coulee **108** 51 23N 112 27W
East Falkland **128** 51 30 S 58 30W
East Grand Forks **116** 47 55N 97 5W
East Greenwich **113** 41 39N 71 27W
East Hartford **113** 41 45N 72 39W
East Helena **118** 46 37N 111 58W
East Indies **72** 0 0 120 0 E
East Jordan **114** 45 10N 85 7W
East Kilbride **14** 55 46N 4 10W
East Lansing **114** 42 44N 84 29W
East Liverpool **114** 40 39N 80 35W
East London **93** 33 0 S 27 55 E
East Orange **114** 40 46N 74 13W
East Pacific Ridge **95** 15 0 S 110 0W
East Pakistan = Bangladesh ■ **67** 24 0N 90 0 E
East Palestine **112** 40 50N 80 32W
East Pine **108** 55 48N 120 12W
East Pt. **107** 46 27N 61 58W
East Point **115** 33 40N 84 28W
East Providence **113** 41 48N 71 22W
East Retford **12** 53 19N 0 55W
East St. Louis **116** 38 37N 90 4W
East Schelde → = Oosterschelde **16** 51 38N 3 40 E
East Siberian Sea **59** 73 0N 160 0 E
East Stroudsburg **113** 41 1N 75 11W
East Sussex □ **13** 51 0N 0 20 E
East Tawas **114** 44 17N 83 31W
Eastbourne, N.Z. **101** 41 19 S 174 55 E
Eastbourne, U.K. **13** 50 46N 0 18 E
Eastend **109** 49 32N 108 50W
Easter I. **95** 27 8 S 109 23W
Easter Islands **95** 27 0 S 109 0W
Eastern □, Kenya **90** 0 0 S 38 30 E
Eastern □, Uganda **90** 1 50N 33 45 E
Eastern Cr. → **98** 20 40 S 141 35 E
Eastern Ghats **70** 14 0N 78 50 E
Eastern Province □ **84** 8 15N 11 0W
Easterville **109** 53 8N 99 49W
Easthampton **113** 42 15N 72 41W
Eastland **117** 32 26N 98 45W
Eastleigh **13** 50 58N 1 21W
Eastmain → **106** 52 27N 78 26W
Eastmain (East Main) **106** 52 10N 78 30W
Eastman, Can. **113** 45 18N 72 19W
Eastman, U.S.A. **115** 32 13N 83 20W
Easton, Md., U.S.A. **114** 38 47N 76 7W
Easton, Pa., U.S.A. **114** 40 41N 75 15W
Easton, Wash., U.S.A. **118** 47 14N 121 8W
Eastport **107** 44 57N 67 0W
Eaton **116** 40 35N 104 42W
Eatonia **109** 51 13N 109 25W
Eatonton **115** 33 22N 83 24W
Eatontown **113** 40 18N 74 7W
Eau Claire, S.C., U.S.A. **115** 34 5N 81 2W
Eau Claire, Wis., U.S.A. **116** 44 46N 91 30W
Eauze **20** 43 53N 0 7 E
Ebagoola **98** 14 15 S 143 12 E
Eban **85** 9 40N 4 50 E
Ebbw Vale **13** 51 47N 3 12W
Ebeggui **83** 26 2N 6 0 E
Ebensburg **112** 40 29N 78 43W
Ebensee **26** 47 48N 13 46 E
Eberbach **25** 49 27N 8 59 E
Eberswalde **24** 52 49N 13 50 E
Ebingen **25** 48 13N 9 1 E
Eboli **41** 40 39N 15 2 E
Ebolowa **88** 2 55N 11 10 E
Ebrach **25** 49 50N 10 30 E
Ébrié, Lagune **84** 5 12N 4 26W
Ebro → **32** 40 43N 0 54 E
Ebro, Pantano del **30** 43 0N 3 58W
Ebstorf **24** 53 2N 10 23 E
Eceabat **44** 40 11N 26 21 E
Éceuillé **18** 47 10N 1 19 E
Echelles, Les **21** 45 27N 5 45 E
Echmiadzin **57** 40 12N 44 19 E
Echo Bay **106** 46 29N 84 4W
Echo Bay (Port Radium) **104** 66 05N 117 55W
Echoing → **109** 55 51N 92 5W
Echternach **16** 49 49N 6 25 E
Echuca **100** 36 10 S 144 20 E
Ecija **31** 37 30N 5 10W
Eckernförde **24** 54 26N 9 50 E
Écommoy **18** 47 50N 0 17 E
Écos **19** 49 9N 1 35 E
Écouché **18** 48 42N 0 10W
Ecuador ■ **126** 2 0 S 78 0W
Ed **49** 58 55N 11 55 E
Ed Dabbura **86** 17 40N 34 15 E
Ed Dâmer **86** 17 27N 34 0 E
Ed Debba **86** 18 0N 30 51 E
Ed-Déffa **86** 30 40N 26 30 E
Ed Deim **87** 10 10N 28 20 E
Ed Dueim **87** 14 0N 32 10 E
Edam, Can. **109** 53 11N 108 46W
Edam, Neth. **16** 52 31N 5 3 E
Edapa!ly **70** 11 19N 78 3 E
Eday **14** 59 11N 2 47W
Edd **87** 14 0N 41 38 E
Eddrachillis B. **14** 58 16N 5 10W
Eddystone **13** 50 11N 4 16W
Eddystone Pt. **99** 40 59 S 148 20 E
Ede, Neth. **16** 52 4N 5 40 E
Ede, Nigeria **85** 7 45N 4 29 E
Édea **88** 3 51N 10 9 E
Edehon L. **109** 60 25N 97 15W
Edekel, Adrar **83** 23 56N 6 47 E
Eden, Austral. **99** 37 3 S 149 55 E
Eden, N.C., U.S.A. **115** 36 29N 79 53W
Eden, N.Y., U.S.A. **112** 42 39N 78 55W
Eden, Tex., U.S.A. **117** 31 16N 99 50W
Eden, Wyo., U.S.A. **118** 42 2N 109 27W
Eden → **12** 54 57N 3 2W
Eden L. **109** 56 38N 100 15W
Edenburg **92** 29 43 S 25 58 E
Edenderry **15** 53 21N 7 3W
Edenton **115** 36 5N 76 36W
Edenville **93** 27 37 S 27 34 E
Eder → **24** 51 15N 9 25 E
Ederstausee **24** 51 11N 9 0 E
Edgar **116** 40 25N 98 0W
Edgartown **113** 41 22N 70 28W
Edge Hill **13** 52 7N 1 28W
Edgefield **115** 33 50N 81 59W
Edgeley **116** 46 27N 98 41W
Edgemont **116** 43 15N 103 53W
Edgeøya **4** 77 45N 22 30 E
Edhessa **44** 40 48N 22 5 E
Edievale **101** 45 49 S 169 22 E
Edina, Liberia **84** 6 0N 10 10W
Edina, U.S.A. **116** 40 6N 92 10W
Edinburg **117** 26 22N 98 10W
Edinburgh **14** 55 57N 3 12W
Edirne **43** 41 40N 26 34 E
Edithburgh **99** 35 5 S 137 43 E
Edjeleh **83** 28 38N 9 50 E
Edmeston **113** 42 42N 75 15W
Edmond **117** 35 37N 97 30W
Edmonds **118** 47 47N 122 22W
Edmonton, Austral. **98** 17 2 S 145 46 E
Edmonton, Can. **108** 53 30N 113 30W
Edmund L. **109** 54 45N 93 17W
Edmundston **107** 47 23N 68 20W
Edna **117** 29 0N 96 40W
Edna Bay **108** 55 55N 133 40W
Edolo **38** 46 10N 10 21 E
Edremit **64** 39 34N 27 0 E
Edsbyn **48** 61 23N 15 49 E
Edsel Ford Ra. **5** 77 0 S 143 0W
Edsele **48** 63 25N 16 32 E
Edson **108** 53 35N 116 28W
Eduardo Castex **124** 35 50 S 64 18W
Edward → **99** 35 0 S 143 30 E
Edward I. **106** 48 22N 88 37W
Edward, L. **90** 0 25 S 29 40 E
Edward VII Pen. **5** 80 0 S 150 0W
Edwards Plat. **117** 30 30N 101 5W
Edwardsville **113** 41 15N 75 56W
Edzo **108** 62 49N 116 4W
Eekloo **16** 51 11N 3 33 E
Ef'e, Nahal **62** 31 9N 35 13 E
Eferding **26** 48 18N 14 1 E
Eferi **83** 24 30N 9 28 E
Effingham **114** 39 8N 88 30W
Eforie Sud **46** 44 1N 28 37 E
Ega → **32** 42 19N 1 55W
Égadi, Ísole **40** 37 55N 12 16 E
Eganville **106** 45 32N 77 5W
Egeland **116** 48 42N 99 6W
Egenolf L. **109** 59 3N 100 0W
Eger **27** 47 53N 20 27 E
Eger → **27** 47 38N 20 50 E
Egersund **47** 58 26N 6 1 E
Egerton, Mt. **96** 24 42 S 117 44 E
Egg L. **109** 55 5N 105 30W
Eggenburg **26** 48 38N 15 50 E
Eggenfelden **25** 48 24N 12 46 E
Égletons **20** 45 24N 2 3 E
Egmont, C. **101** 39 16 S 173 45 E
Egmont, Mt. **101** 39 17 S 174 5 E
Eğridir **64** 37 52N 30 51 E
Eğridir Gölü **64** 37 53N 30 50 E
Egtved **49** 55 38N 9 18 E
Egume **85** 7 30N 7 14 E
Éguzon **20** 46 27N 1 33 E
Egvekinot **59** 66 19N 179 50W
Egyek **27** 47 39N 20 52 E
Egypt ■ **86** 28 0N 31 0 E
Eha Amufu **85** 6 30N 7 46 E
Ehime □ **74** 33 30N 132 40 E
Ehingen **25** 48 16N 9 43 E
Ehrwald **26** 47 24N 10 56 E
Eibar **32** 43 11N 2 28W
Eichstatt **25** 48 53N 11 12 E
Eida **47** 60 32N 6 43 E
Eider → **24** 54 19N 8 58 E
Eidsvold **99** 25 25 S 151 12 E
Eifel **25** 50 10N 6 45 E
Eiffel Flats **91** 18 20 S 30 0 E
Eigg **14** 56 54N 6 10W
Eighty Mile Beach **96** 19 30 S 120 40 E
Eil **63** 8 0N 49 50 E
Eil, L. **14** 56 50N 5 15W
Eildon, L. **99** 37 10 S 146 0 E
Eileen L. **109** 62 16N 107 37W
Eilenburg **24** 51 28N 12 38 E
Ein el Luweiqa **87** 14 5N 33 50 E
Einasleigh **97** 18 32 S 144 5 E
Einasleigh → **98** 17 30 S 142 17 E
Einbeck **24** 51 48N 9 50 E
Eindhoven **16** 51 26N 5 30 E
Einsiedeln **25** 47 7N 8 46 E
Eiríksjökull **50** 64 46N 20 24W
Eirunepé **126** 6 35 S 69 53W
Eisenach **24** 50 58N 10 18 E
Eisenberg **24** 50 59N 11 50 E
Eisenerz **26** 47 32N 14 54 E
Eisenhüttenstadt **24** 52 9N 14 41 E
Eisenkappel **26** 46 29N 14 36 E
Eisenstadt **27** 47 51N 16 31 E
Eiserfeld **24** 50 50N 7 59 E
Eisfeld **24** 50 25N 10 54 E
Eisleben **24** 51 31N 11 31 E
Ejby **49** 55 25N 9 56 E
Eje, Sierra del **30** 42 24N 6 54W
Ejea de los Caballeros **32** 42 7N 1 9W
Ekalaka **116** 45 55N 104 30W
Eket **85** 4 38N 7 56 E
Eketahuna **101** 40 38 S 175 43 E
Ekhínos **44** 41 16N 25 1 E
Ekibastuz **58** 51 50N 75 10 E
Ekimchan **59** 53 0N 133 0W
Ekoli **90** 0 23 S 24 13 E
Eksjö **49** 57 40N 14 58W
Ekwan → **106** 53 12N 82 15W
Ekwan Pt. **106** 53 16N 82 7W
El Aaiún **80** 27 9N 13 12W
El Aat **62** 32 50N 35 45 E
El Abiodh-Sidi-Cheikh **82** 32 53N 0 31 E
El Aïoun **82** 34 33N 2 30W
El 'Aiyat **86** 29 36N 31 15 E
El Alamein **86** 30 48N 28 58 E
El 'Arag **86** 28 40N 26 20 E
El Arahal **31** 37 15N 5 33W
El Arba **82** 36 37N 3 12 E
El Aricha **82** 34 13N 1 10W
El Arīhā **62** 31 52N 35 27 E
El Arish **98** 17 35 S 146 1 E
El 'Arîsh **86** 31 8N 33 50 E
El Arrouch **83** 36 37N 6 53 E
* El Asnam **82** 36 10N 1 20 E
El Astillero **30** 43 24N 3 49W
El Badâri **86** 27 4N 31 25 E
El Bahrein **86** 28 30N 26 25 E
El Ballâs **86** 26 2N 32 43 E
El Balyana **86** 26 10N 32 3 E
El Baqeir **86** 18 40N 33 40 E
El Barco de Ávila **30** 40 21N 5 31W
El Barco de Valdeorras **30** 42 23N 7 0W
El Bauga **86** 18 18N 33 52 E
El Bawiti **86** 28 25N 28 45 E
El Bayadh **82** 33 40N 1 1 E
El Bierzo **30** 42 45N 6 30W
El Bluff **121** 11 59N 83 40W
El Bonillo **33** 38 57N 2 35W
El Cajon **119** 32 49N 117 0W
El Callao **126** 7 18N 61 50W
El Camp **32** 41 5N 1 10 E
El Campo **117** 29 10N 96 20W
El Castillo **31** 37 41N 6 19W
El Centro **119** 32 50N 115 40W
El Cerro, Boliv. **126** 17 30 S 61 40W
El Cerro, Spain **31** 37 45N 6 57W
El Coronil **31** 37 5N 5 38W
El Cuy **128** 39 55 S 68 25W
El Cuyo **120** 21 30N 87 40W
El Dab'a **86** 31 0N 28 27 E
El Deir **86** 25 25N 32 20 E
El Dere **63** 3 50N 47 8 E
El Días **120** 20 40N 87 20W
El Dilingat **86** 30 50N 30 31 E
El Diviso **126** 1 22N 78 14W
El Djem **83** 35 18N 10 42 E
El Djouf **84** 20 0N 11 30 E
El Dorado, Ark., U.S.A. **117** 33 10N 92 40W
El Dorado, Kans., U.S.A. **117** 37 55N 96 56W
El Dorado, Venez. **126** 6 55N 61 37W
El Dorado Springs **117** 37 54N 93 59W
El Eglab **82** 26 20N 4 30W
El Escorial **30** 40 35N 4 7W
El Eulma **83** 36 9N 5 42 E
El Faiyûm **86** 29 19N 30 50 E
El Fâsher **87** 13 33N 25 26 E
El Fashn **86** 28 50N 30 54 E
El Ferrol **30** 43 29N 8 15W
El Fifi **87** 10 4N 25 0 E
El Fuerte **120** 26 30N 108 40W
El Gal **63** 10 58N 50 20 E
El Gebir **87** 13 40N 29 40 E
El Gedida **86** 25 40N 28 30 E
El Geteina **87** 14 50N 32 27 E
El Gezira □ **87** 15 0N 33 0 E
El Gîza **86** 30 0N 31 10 E
El Goléa **82** 30 30N 2 50 E
El Guettar **83** 34 5N 4 38 E
El Hadjira **83** 32 36N 5 30 E
El Hagiz **87** 15 15N 35 50 E
El Hajeb **82** 33 43N 5 13W
El Hammam **86** 30 52N 29 25 E
El Hank **82** 24 30N 7 0W
El Harrache **80** 36 45N 3 5 E

* *Renamed Ech Cheliff*

El Hawata **87** 13 25N 34 42 E
El Heiz **86** 27 50N 28 40 E
El 'Idisât **86** 25 30N 32 35 E
El Iskandarîya **86** 31 0N 30 0 E
El Istwâ'ya □ **87** 5 0N 30 0 E
El Jadida **80** 33 11N 8 17W
El Jebelein **81** 12 40N 32 55 E
El Kab **86** 19 27N 32 46 E
El Kala **83** 36 50N 8 30 E
El Kalâa **82** 32 4N 7 27W
El Kamlin **87** 15 3N 33 11 E
El Kantara, Alg. **83** 35 14N 5 45 E
El Kantara, Tunisia **83** 33 45N 10 58 E
El Karaba **86** 18 32N 33 41 E
El Kef **83** 36 12N 8 47 E
El Khandaq **86** 18 30N 30 30 E
El Khârga **86** 25 30N 30 33 E
El Khartûm **87** 15 31N 32 35 E
El Khartûm □ **87** 16 0N 33 0 E
El Khartûm Bahrî **87** 15 40N 32 31 E
El-Khroubs **83** 36 10N 6 55 E
El Khureiba **86** 28 3N 35 10 E
El Kseur **83** 36 46N 4 49 E
El Ksiba **82** 32 45N 6 1W
El Kuntilla **86** 30 1N 34 45 E
El Laqâwa **81** 11 25N 29 1 E
El Laqeita **86** 25 50N 33 15 E
El Leiya **87** 16 15N 35 28 E
El Mafâza **87** 13 38N 34 30 E
El Mahalla el Kubra **86** 31 0N 31 0 E
El Mahârîq **86** 25 35N 30 35 E
El Mahmûdîya **86** 31 10N 30 32 E
El Maiz **82** 28 19N 0 9W
El-Maks el-Bahari **86** 24 30N 30 40 E
El Manshâh **86** 26 26N 31 50 E
El Mansour **82** 27 47N 0 14W
El Mansûra **86** 31 0N 31 19 E
El Manzala **86** 31 10N 31 50 E
El Marâgha **86** 26 35N 31 10 E
El Masid **87** 15 15N 33 0 E
El Matariya **86** 31 15N 32 0 E
El Meghaier **83** 33 55N 5 58 E
El Meraguen **82** 28 0N 0 7W
El Metemma **87** 16 50N 33 10 E
El Milagro **124** 30 59 S 65 59W
El Milia **83** 36 51N 6 13 E
El Minyâ **86** 28 7N 30 33 E
El Molar **32** 40 42N 3 45W
El Mreyye **84** 18 0N 6 0W
El Obeid **87** 13 8N 30 10 E
El Odaiya **81** 12 8N 28 12 E
El Oro **120** 19 48N 100 8W
El Oro = Sta. María del Oro **120** 25 50N 105 20W
El Oued **83** 33 20N 6 58 E
El Palmito, Presa **120** 25 40N 105 30W
El Panadés **32** 41 10N 1 30 E
El Pardo **30** 40 31N 3 47W
El Paso **119** 31 50N 106 30W
El Pedernoso **33** 39 29N 2 45W
El Pedroso **31** 37 51N 5 45W
El Pobo de Dueñas **32** 40 46N 1 39W
El Portal **119** 37 44N 119 49W
El Prat de Llobregat **32** 41 18N 2 3 E
El Progreso **120** 15 26N 87 51W
El Provencío **33** 39 23N 2 35W
El Pueblito **120** 29 3N 105 4W
El Qâhira **86** 30 1N 31 14 E
El Qantara **86** 30 51N 32 20 E
El Qasr **86** 25 44N 28 42 E
El Quseima **86** 30 40N 34 15 E
El Qusîya **86** 27 29N 30 44 E
El Râshda **86** 25 36N 28 57 E
El Reno **117** 35 30N 98 0W
El Ribero **30** 42 30N 8 30W
El Rîdisiya **86** 24 56N 32 51 E
El Ronquillo **31** 37 44N 6 10W
El Rubio **31** 37 22N 5 0W
El Saff **86** 29 34N 31 16 E
El Salvador ■ **120** 13 50N 89 0W
El Sancejo **31** 37 4N 5 6W
El Sauce **121** 13 0N 86 40W
El Shallal **86** 24 0N 32 53 E
El Simbillawein **86** 30 48N 31 13 E
El Suweis **86** 29 58N 32 31 E
El Thamad **86** 29 40N 34 28 E
El Tigre **126** 8 44N 64 15W
El Tocuyo **126** 9 47N 69 48W
El Tofo **124** 29 22 S 71 18W
El Tránsito **124** 28 52 S 70 17W
El Tûr **86** 28 14N 33 36 E
El Turbio **128** 51 45 S 72 5W
El Uqsur **86** 25 41N 32 38 E
El Vado **32** 41 2N 3 18W
El Vallés **32** 41 35N 2 20 E
El Vigía **126** 8 38N 71 39W
El Wak **90** 2 49N 40 56 E
El Waqf **86** 25 45N 32 15 E
El Wâsta **86** 29 19N 31 12 E
El Weguet **87** 5 28N 42 17 E
El Wuz **81** 15 0N 30 7 E
Elafónisos **45** 36 29N 22 56 E
Elamanchili = Yellamanchilli **70** 17 26N 82 50 E
Elandsvlei **92** 32 19 S 19 31 E
Élassa **45** 35 18N 26 21 E
Elassón **44** 39 53N 22 12 E
Elat **62** 29 30N 34 56 E
Eláthia **45** 38 37N 22 46 E
Elâzığ **64** 38 37N 39 14 E
Elba, Italy **38** 42 48N 10 15 E
Elba, U.S.A. **115** 31 27N 86 4W
Elbasani **44** 41 9N 20 9 E
Elbasani-Berati □ **44** 40 58N 20 0 E
Elbe → **24** 53 50N 9 0 E
Elbert, Mt. **119** 39 5N 106 27W
Elberta **114** 44 35N 86 14W
Elberton **115** 34 7N 82 51W
Elbeuf **18** 49 17N 1 2 E
Elbidtan **64** 38 13N 37 12 E
Elbing = Elbląg **28** 54 10N 19 25 E
Elbląg **28** 54 10N 19 25 E
Elbląg □ **28** 54 15N 19 30 E
Elbow **109** 51 7N 106 35W

Elbrus 57 43 21N 42 30 E
Elburg 16 52 26N 5 50 E
Elburz Mts. = Alborz 65 36 0N 52 0 E
Elche 33 38 15N 0 42W
Elche de la Sierra 33 38 27N 2 3W
Elcho I. 97 11 55S 135 45 E
Elda 33 38 29N 0 47W
Eldon 116 38 20N 92 38W
Eldora 116 42 20N 93 5W
Eldorado, Argent. 125 26 28S 54 43W
Eldorado, Can. 109 59 35N 108 30W
Eldorado, Mexico 120 24 20N 107 22W
Eldorado, Ill., U.S.A. 114 37 50N 88 25W
Eldorado, Tex., U.S.A. 117 30 52N 100 35W
Eldoret 90 0 30N 35 17 E
Eldred 112 41 57N 78 24W
Electra 117 34 0N 99 0W
Elefantes → 93 24 10S 32 40 E
Elektrogorsk 55 55 56N 38 50 E
Elektrostal 55 55 41N 38 32 E
Elele 85 5 5N 6 50 E
Elena 43 42 55N 25 53 E
Elephant Butte Res. 119 33 45N 107 30W
Elephant I. 5 61 0S 55 0W
Elephant Pass 70 9 35N 80 25 E
Eleshnitsa 43 41 52N 23 36 E
Eleuthera 121 25 0N 76 20W
Elevsís 45 38 4N 23 26 E
Elevtheroúpolis 44 40 52N 24 20 E
Elgepiggen 47 62 10N 11 21 E
Elgeyo-Marakwet □ 90 0 45N 35 30 E
Elgin, N.B., Can. 107 45 48N 65 10W
Elgin, Ont., Can. 113 44 36N 76 13W
Elgin, U.K. 14 57 39N 3 20W
Elgin, Ill., U.S.A. 114 42 0N 88 20W
Elgin, N.D., U.S.A. 116 46 24N 101 46W
Elgin, Nebr., U.S.A. 116 41 58N 98 3W
Elgin, Nev., U.S.A. 119 37 21N 114 20W
Elgin, Oreg., U.S.A. 118 45 37N 118 0W
Elgin, Texas, U.S.A. 117 30 21N 97 22W
Elgon, Mt. 90 1 10N 34 30 E
Eliase 73 8 21S 130 48 E
Elida 117 33 56N 103 41W
Elikón, Mt. 45 38 18N 22 45 E
Elin Pelin 43 42 40N 23 36 E
Elisabethville = Lubumbashi 91 11 40S 27 28 E
Elista 57 46 16N 44 14 E
Elizabeth, Austral. 97 34 42S 138 41 E
Elizabeth, U.S.A. 114 40 37N 74 12W
Elizabeth City 115 36 18N 76 16W
Elizabethton 115 36 20N 82 13W
Elizabethtown, Ky., U.S.A. 114 37 40N 85 54W
Elizabethtown, N.Y., U.S.A. 113 44 13N 73 36W
Elizabethtown, Pa., U.S.A. 113 40 8N 76 36W
Elizondo 32 43 12N 1 30W
Ełk 28 53 50N 22 21 E
Ełk → 28 53 41N 22 28 E
Elk City 117 35 25N 99 25W
Elk Island Nat. Park 108 53 35N 112 59W
Elk Lake 106 47 40N 80 25W
Elk Point 109 53 54N 110 55W
Elk River, Idaho, U.S.A. 118 46 50N 116 8W
Elk River, Minn., U.S.A. 116 45 17N 93 34W
Elkhart, Ind., U.S.A. 114 41 42N 85 55W
Elkhart, Kans., U.S.A. 117 37 3N 101 54W
Elkhorn 109 49 59N 101 14W
Elkhorn → 116 41 7N 98 15W
Elkhotovo 57 43 19N 44 15 E
Elkhovo 43 42 10N 26 40 E
Elkin 115 36 17N 80 50W
Elkins 114 38 53N 79 53W
Elko, Can. 108 49 20N 115 10W
Elko, U.S.A. 118 40 50N 115 50W
Ellef Ringnes I. 4 78 30N 102 2W
Ellen, Mt. 119 38 4N 110 56W
Ellendale 116 46 3N 98 30W
Ellensburg 118 47 0N 120 30W
Ellenville 114 41 42N 74 23W
Ellery, Mt. 99 37 28S 148 47 E
Ellesmere I. 4 79 30N 80 0W
Ellesworth Land 5 76 0S 89 0W
Ellice Is. = Tuvalu ■ 94 8 0S 176 0 E
Ellinwood 116 38 27N 98 37W
Elliot 93 31 22S 27 48 E
Elliot Lake 106 46 25N 82 35W
Ellis 116 39 0N 99 39W
Ellisville 117 31 38N 89 12W
Ellon 14 57 21N 2 5W
Ellore = Eluru 70 16 48N 81 8 E
Ells → 108 57 18N 111 40W
Ellsworth 116 38 47N 98 15W
Ellsworth Land 5 76 0S 89 0W
Ellsworth Mts. 5 78 30S 85 0W
Ellwangen 25 48 57N 10 9 E
Ellwood City 114 40 52N 80 19W
Elm 25 46 54N 9 10 E
Elma, Can. 109 49 52N 95 55W
Elma, U.S.A. 118 47 0N 123 30 E
Elmalı 64 36 44N 29 56 E
Elmhurst 114 41 52N 87 58W
Elmina 85 5 5N 1 21W
Elmira, Can. 112 43 36N 80 33W
Elmira, U.S.A. 114 42 8N 76 49W
Elmore 99 36 30S 144 37 E
Elmshorn 24 53 44N 9 40 E
Elmvale 112 44 35N 79 52W
Elne 20 42 36N 2 58 E
Elora 112 43 41N 80 26W
Elos 45 36 46N 22 43 E
Eloy 119 32 46N 111 33W
Éloyes 19 48 6N 6 36 E
Elrose 109 51 12N 108 0W
Elsas 106 48 32N 82 55W
Elsinore, Cal., U.S.A. 119 33 40N 117 15W
Elsinore, Utah, U.S.A. 119 38 40N 112 2W
Elspe 24 51 10N 8 1 E
Elster → 24 51 25N 11 57 E
Elsterwerda 24 51 27N 13 32 E
Eltham 101 39 26S 174 19 E
Elton 57 49 5N 46 52 E
Eluru 70 16 48N 81 8 E
Elvas 31 38 50N 7 10W
Elven 18 47 44N 2 36W
Elverum 47 60 53N 11 34 E
Elvo → 38 45 23N 8 21 E
Elvran 47 63 24N 11 3 E
Elwood, Ind., U.S.A. 114 40 20N 85 50W
Elwood, Nebr., U.S.A. 116 40 38N 99 51W
Ely, U.K. 13 52 24N 0 16 E
Ely, Minn., U.S.A. 116 47 54N 91 52W
Ely, Nev., U.S.A. 118 39 10N 114 50W
Elyashiv 62 32 23N 34 55 E
Elyria 114 41 22N 82 8W
Elyrus 45 35 15N 23 45 E
Elz → 25 48 21N 7 45 E
Emådalen 48 61 20N 14 44 E
Emba 58 48 50N 58 8 E
Emba → 58 45 25N 52 30 E
Embarcación 124 23 10S 64 0W
Embarras Portage 109 58 27N 111 28W
Embóna 45 36 13N 27 51 E
Embrun 21 44 34N 6 30 E
Embu 90 0 32S 37 38 E
Embu □ 90 0 30S 37 35 E
Emden 24 53 22N 7 12 E
'Emeq Yizre'el 62 32 35N 35 12 E
Emerald 97 23 32S 148 10 E
Emerson 109 49 0N 97 10W
Emery 119 38 59N 111 17W
Emery Park 119 32 10N 110 59W
Emi Koussi 83 20 0N 18 55 E
Emilia-Romagna □ 38 44 33N 10 40 E
Emilius, Mte. 38 45 41N 7 23 E
Eminabad 68 32 2N 74 8 E
Emine, Nos 43 42 40N 27 56 E
Emlenton 112 41 11N 79 41W
Emlichheim 24 52 37N 6 51 E
Emmaboda 49 56 37N 15 32 E
Emme → 25 47 0N 7 42 E
Emmeloord 16 52 44N 5 46 E
Emmen 16 52 48N 6 57 E
Emmendingen 25 48 7N 7 51 E
Emmental 25 47 0N 7 35 E
Emmerich 24 51 50N 6 12 E
Emmet 98 24 45S 144 30 E
Emmetsburg 116 43 3N 94 40W
Emmett 118 43 51N 116 33W
Emöd 27 47 57N 20 47 E
Emona 43 42 43N 27 53 E
Empalme 120 28 1N 110 49W
Empangeni 93 28 50S 31 52 E
Empedrado 124 28 0S 58 46W
Emperor Seamount Chain 94 40 0N 170 0 E
Empoli 38 43 43N 10 57 E
Emporia, Kans., U.S.A. 116 38 25N 96 10W
Emporia, Va., U.S.A. 115 36 41N 77 32W
Emporium 114 41 30N 78 17W
Empress 109 50 57N 110 0W
Ems → 24 52 37N 9 26 E
Emsdale 112 45 32N 79 19W
Emsdetten 24 52 11N 7 31 E
Emu 76 43 40N 128 6 E
Emu Park 98 23 13S 150 50 E
En Gedi 62 31 28N 35 25 E
En Gev 62 32 47N 35 38 E
En Harod 62 32 33N 35 22 E
'En Kerem 62 31 47N 35 6 E
En Nahud 87 12 45N 28 25 E
Enafors 48 63 17N 12 20 E
Enana 92 17 30S 16 23 E
Enånger 48 61 30N 17 9 E
Enaratoli 73 3 55S 136 21 E
Enard B. 14 58 5N 5 20W
Encantadas, Serra 125 30 40S 53 0W
Encanto, C. 73 15 45N 121 38 E
Encarnación 125 27 15S 55 50W
Encarnación de Diaz 120 21 30N 102 13W
Enchi 84 5 53N 2 48W
Encinal 117 28 3N 99 25W
Encino 119 34 38N 105 40W
Encounter B. 97 35 45S 138 45 E
Endau 71 2 40N 103 38 E
Endau → 71 2 30N 103 30 E
Ende 73 8 45S 121 40 E
Endeavour 109 52 10N 102 39W
Endeavour Str. 97 10 45S 142 0 E
Endelave 49 55 46N 10 18 E
Enderbury I. 94 3 8S 171 5W
Enderby 108 50 35N 119 10W
Enderby Land 5 66 0S 53 0 E
Enderlin 116 46 37N 97 41W
Endicott, N.Y., U.S.A. 114 42 6N 76 2W
Endicott, Wash., U.S.A. 118 47 0N 117 45W
Endröd 27 46 55N 20 47 E
Enez 44 40 45N 26 5 E
Enfida 83 36 6N 10 28 E
Enfield 13 51 39N 0 4W
Engadin = Engiadina 25 46 51N 10 18 E
Engaño, C., Dom. Rep. 121 18 30N 68 20W
Engaño, C., Phil. 73 18 35N 122 23 E
Engelberg 25 46 48N 8 26 E
Engels 55 51 28N 46 6 E
Engemann L. 109 58 0N 106 55W
Enger 47 60 35N 10 20 E
Enggano 72 5 20S 102 40 E
Enghien 16 50 37N 4 2 E
Engiadina 25 46 51N 10 18 E
Engil 82 33 12N 4 32W
Engkilili 72 1 3N 111 42 E
England 117 34 30N 91 58W
England □ 11 53 0N 2 0W
Englee 107 50 45N 56 5W
Englehart 106 47 49N 79 52W
Engler L. 109 59 8N 106 52W
Englewood, Colo., U.S.A. 116 39 40N 105 0W
Englewood, Kans., U.S.A. 117 37 7N 99 59W
Englewood, N.J., U.S.A. 113 40 54N 73 59W
English → 109 50 35N 93 30W
English Bazar 69 24 58N 88 10 E
English Channel 18 50 0N 2 0W
English River 106 49 14N 91 0W
Enid 117 36 26N 97 52W
Enipévs → 44 39 22N 22 17 E
Eniwetok 94 11 30N 162 15 E
Enkeldoorn 91 19 2S 30 52 E
Enkhuizen 16 52 42N 5 17 E
Enköping 48 59 37N 17 4 E
Enna 41 37 34N 14 15 E
Ennadai 109 61 8N 100 53W
Ennadai L. 109 61 0N 101 0W
Ennedi 81 17 15N 22 0 E
Enngonia 99 29 21S 145 50 E
Ennis, Ireland 15 52 51N 8 59W
Ennis, Mont., U.S.A. 118 45 20N 111 42W
Ennis, Texas, U.S.A. 117 32 15N 96 40W
Enniscorthy 15 52 30N 6 35W
Enniskillen 15 54 20N 7 40W
Ennistimon 15 52 56N 9 18W
Enns 26 48 12N 14 28 E
Enns → 26 48 14N 14 32 E
Enontekiö 50 68 23N 23 37 E
Enping 77 22 16N 112 21 E
Enriquillo, L. 121 18 20N 72 5W
Enschede 16 52 13N 6 53 E
Ensenada, Argent. 124 34 55S 57 55W
Ensenada, Mexico 120 31 50N 116 50W
Enshi 77 30 18N 109 29 E
Ensisheim 19 47 50N 7 20 E
Entebbe 90 0 4N 32 28 E
Enterprise, Can. 108 60 47N 115 45W
Enterprise, Oreg., U.S.A. 118 45 30N 117 18W
Enterprise, Utah, U.S.A. 119 37 37N 113 36W
Entre Ríos, Boliv. 124 21 30S 64 25W
Entre Ríos, Mozam. 91 14 57S 37 20 E
Entre Ríos □ 124 30 30S 58 30W
Entrecasteaux, Pt. d' 96 34 50S 115 56 E
Entrepeñas, Pantano de 32 40 34N 2 42W
Enugu 85 6 20N 7 30 E
Enugu Ezike 85 7 0N 7 29 E
Enumclaw 118 47 12N 122 0W
Envermeières 18 49 54N 1 16 E
Envermeu 18 49 53N 1 15 E
Enz → 25 49 1N 9 6 E
Enza → 38 44 54N 10 31 E
Eólie, I. 41 38 30N 14 50 E
Epanomí 44 40 25N 22 59 E
Epe, Neth. 16 52 21N 5 59 E
Epe, Nigeria 85 6 36N 3 59 E
Épernay 19 49 3N 3 56 E
Épernon 19 48 35N 1 40 E
Ephesus, Turkey 45 37 50N 27 33 E
Ephesus, Turkey 64 38 0N 27 19 E
Ephraim 119 39 21N 111 37W
Ephrata 118 47 20N 119 32W
Epidaurus Limera 45 36 46N 23 0 E
Epila 32 41 36N 1 17W
Épinac-les-Mines 19 46 59N 4 31 E
Épinal 19 48 10N 6 27 E
Episcopia Bihorului 46 47 12N 21 55 E
Epitálion 45 37 37N 21 30 E
Epping 13 51 42N 0 8 E
Epukiro 92 21 40S 19 9 E
Equatorial Guinea ■ 88 2 0S 8 0 E
Er Rahad 87 12 45N 30 32 E
Er Rif 82 35 1N 4 1W
Er Roseires 87 11 55N 34 30 E
Er Yébigué 83 22 30N 17 30 E
Erandol 68 20 56N 75 20 E
Erāwadī Myit = Irrawaddy → 67 15 50N 95 6 E
Erba, Italy 38 45 49N 9 12 E
Erba, Sudan 86 19 5N 36 51 E
Ercha 59 69 45N 147 20 E
Erciyaş Dağı 64 38 30N 35 30 E
Erdao Jiang → 76 43 0N 127 0 E
Erding 25 48 18N 11 55 E
Erdre → 18 47 13N 1 32W
Erebus, Mt. 5 77 35S 167 0 E
Erechim 125 27 35S 52 15W
Ereğli, Turkey 64 41 15N 31 30 E
Ereğli, Turkey 64 37 31N 34 4 E
Erei, Monti 41 37 20N 14 20 E
Erenhot 76 43 48N 111 59 E
Eresma → 30 41 26N 40 45W
Eressós 45 39 11N 25 57 E
Erfenis Dam 92 28 30S 26 50 E
Erfjord 47 59 20N 6 14 E
Erfoud 82 31 30N 4 15W
Erft → 24 51 11N 6 44 E
Erfurt 24 50 58N 11 2 E
Erfurt □ 24 51 10N 10 30 E
Ergani 64 38 17N 39 49 E
Ergene → 43 41 1N 26 22 E
Ergeni Vozyshennost 57 47 0N 44 0 E
Ergli 54 56 54N 25 38 E
Ergun Zuoqi 76 50 47N 121 31 E
Eria → 30 42 3N 5 44W
Eriba 87 16 40N 36 10 E
Eriboll, L. 14 58 28N 4 41W
Érice 40 38 4N 12 34 E
Erie 114 42 10N 80 7W
Erie Canal 112 43 15N 78 0W
Erie, L. 112 42 15N 81 0W
Erieau 112 42 16N 81 57W
Erigavo 63 10 35N 47 20 E
Erikoúsa 44 39 55N 19 14 E
Eriksdale 109 50 52N 98 7W
Erikslund 48 62 31N 15 54 E
Erimanthos 45 37 57N 21 50 E
Erimo-misaki 74 41 50N 143 15 E
Erithraí 45 38 13N 23 20 E
Eritrea □ 87 14 0N 41 0 E
Erjas → 31 39 40N 7 1W
Erlangen 25 49 35N 11 0 E
Ermelo, Neth. 16 52 18N 5 35 E
Ermelo, S. Afr. 93 26 31S 29 59 E
Ermenak 64 36 38N 33 0 E
Ermióni 45 37 23N 23 15 E
Ermoúpolis = Siros 45 37 28N 24 57 E
Ernakulam = Cochin 70 9 59N 76 22 E
Erne → 15 54 30N 8 16W
Erne, Lough 15 54 26N 7 46W
Ernée 18 48 18N 0 56W
Ernstberg 25 50 14N 6 46 E
Erode 70 11 24N 77 45 E
Eromanga 99 26 40S 143 11 E
Erongo 92 21 39S 15 58 E
Erquy 18 48 38N 2 29W
Erquy, Cap d' 18 48 39N 2 29W
Erramala Hills 70 15 30N 78 15 E
Errer → 87 7 32N 42 35 E
Errigal, Mt. 15 55 2N 8 8W
Erris Hd. 15 54 19N 10 0W
Erseka 44 40 22N 20 40 E
Erskine 116 47 37N 96 0W
Erstein 19 48 25N 7 38 E
Ertil 55 51 55N 40 50 E
Ertvågøy 47 63 13N 8 26 E
Eruwa 85 7 33N 3 26 E
Ervy-le-Châtel 19 48 2N 3 55 E
Erwin 115 36 10N 82 28W
Erzgebirge 24 50 25N 13 0 E
Erzin 59 50 15N 95 10 E
Erzincan 64 39 46N 39 30 E
Erzurum 64 39 57N 41 15 E
Es Sahrâ' Esh Sharqîya 86 26 0N 33 30 E
Es Sînâ' 86 29 0N 34 0 E
Es Sûkî 87 13 20N 33 58 E
Esambo 90 3 48S 23 30 E
Esan-Misaki 74 41 40N 141 10 E
Esbjerg 49 55 29N 8 29 E
Escalante 119 37 47N 111 37W
Escalante → 119 37 17N 110 53W
Escalón 120 26 46N 104 20W
Escalona 30 40 9N 4 29W
Escambia → 115 30 32N 87 15W
Escanaba 114 45 44N 87 5W
Esch-sur-Alzette 16 49 32N 6 0 E
Eschallens 25 46 39N 6 38 E
Eschede 24 52 44N 10 13 E
Eschwege 24 51 10N 10 3 E
Eschweiler 24 50 49N 6 14 E
Escobal 120 9 6N 80 1W
Escondido 119 33 9N 117 4W
Escuinapa 120 22 50N 105 50W
Escuintla 120 14 20N 90 48W
Eséka 85 3 41N 10 44 E
Esens 24 53 40N 7 35 E
Esera → 32 42 6N 0 15 E
Eşfahān 65 33 0N 53 0 E
Esgueva → 30 41 40N 4 43W
Esh Sham = Dimashq 64 33 30N 36 18 E
Esh Shamâlîya □ 86 19 0N 29 0 E
Eshowe 93 28 50S 31 30 E
Eshta' ol 62 31 47N 35 0 E
Esiama 84 4 56N 2 25W
Esino → 39 43 39N 13 22 E
Esk →, Dumfries, U.K. 14 54 58N 3 4W
Esk →, N. Yorks., U.K. 12 54 27N 0 36W
Eskifjörður 50 65 3N 13 55W
Eskilstuna 48 59 22N 16 32 E
Eskimo Pt. 109 61 10N 94 15W
Eskişehir 64 39 50N 30 35 E
Esla → 30 41 29N 6 3W
Esla, Pantano del 30 41 29N 6 3W
Eslöv 49 55 50N 13 20 E
Esmeralda, La 124 22 16S 62 33W
Esmeraldas 126 1 0N 79 40W
Espalion 20 44 32N 2 47 E
Espalmador, I. 33 38 47N 1 26 E
Espanola 106 46 15N 81 46W
Espardell, I. del 33 38 48N 1 29 E
Esparraguera 32 41 33N 1 52 E
Espejo 31 37 40N 4 34W
Esperance 96 33 45S 121 55 E
Esperance B. 96 33 48S 121 55 E
Esperanza 124 31 29S 61 3W
Espéraza 20 42 56N 2 14 E
Espevær 47 59 35N 5 7 E
Espichel, C. 31 38 22N 9 16W
Espiel 31 38 11N 5 1W
Espigão, Serra do 125 26 35S 50 30W
Espinal 126 4 9N 74 53W
Espinhaço, Serra do 127 17 30S 43 30W
Espinho 30 41 1N 8 38W
Espinilho, Serra do 125 28 30S 55 0W
Espinosa de los Monteros 30 43 5N 3 34W
Espírito Santo □ 127 20 0S 40 45W
Espíritu Santo, B. del 120 19 15N 87 0W
Espíritu Santo, I. 120 24 30N 110 23W
Espluga de Francolí 32 41 24N 1 7 E
Espuña, Sierra 33 37 51N 1 35W
Espungabera 93 20 29S 32 45 E
Esquel 128 42 55S 71 20W
Esquina 124 30 0S 59 30W
Essaouira (Mogador) 82 31 32N 9 48W
Essarts, Les 18 46 47N 1 12W
Essebie 90 2 58N 30 40 E
Essen, Belg. 16 51 28N 4 28 E
Essen, Ger. 24 51 28N 6 59 E
Essequibo → 126 6 50N 58 30W
Essex, Can. 112 42 10N 82 49W
Essex, U.S.A. 113 44 17N 73 21W
Essex □ 13 51 48N 0 30 E
Esslingen 25 48 43N 9 19 E
Essonne □ 19 48 30N 2 20 E
Essvik 48 62 18N 17 24 E
Estaca, Pta. del 30 43 46N 7 42W
Estadilla 32 42 4N 0 16 E
Estados, I. de Los 128 54 40S 64 30W
Estagel 20 42 47N 2 40 E
Estância 127 11 16S 37 26W
Estancia 119 34 50N 106 1W
Estarreja 30 40 45N 8 35W
Estats, Pic d' 32 42 40N 1 24 E
Estcourt 93 28 58S 29 53 E
Este 39 45 12N 11 40 E
Esteban 30 43 33N 6 5W
Esteli 121 13 9N 86 22W
Estella 32 42 40N 2 0W
Estelline, S.D., U.S.A. 116 44 39N 96 52W
Estelline, Texas, U.S.A. 117 34 35N 100 27W
Estena → 31 39 23N 4 44W
Estepa 31 37 17N 4 52W
Estepona 31 36 24N 5 7W
Esterhazy 109 50 37N 102 5W
Esternay 19 48 44N 3 33 E
Esterri de Aneu 32 42 38N 1 5 E
Estevan 109 49 10N 102 59W

Estevan Group 108 53 3N 129 38W
Estherville 116 43 25N 94 50W
Estissac 19 48 16N 3 48 E
Eston 109 51 8N 108 40W
Estonian S.S.R. □ 54 58 30N 25 30 E
Estoril 31 38 42N 9 23W
Estouk 85 18 14N 1 2 E
Estrada, La 30 42 43N 8 27W
Estrêla, Serra da 30 40 10N 7 45W
Estrella 33 38 25N 3 35W
Estremoz 31 38 51N 7 39W
Estrondo, Serra do 127 7 20 S 48 0W
Esztergom 27 47 47N 18 44 E
Et Tîdra 84 19 45N 16 20W
Eţ Ţîra 62 32 14N 34 56 E
Étables-sur-Mer 18 48 38N 2 51W
Etah 68 27 35N 78 40 E
Étain 19 49 13N 5 38 E
Etamamu 107 50 18N 59 59W
Étampes 19 48 26N 2 10 E
Étang 19 46 52N 4 10 E
Etanga 92 17 55 S 13 00 E
Étaples 19 50 30N 1 39 E
Etawah 68 26 48N 79 6 E
Etawah → 115 34 20N 84 15W
Etawney L. 109 57 50N 96 50W
Eteh 85 7 2N 7 28 E
Ethel, Oued el → 82 28 31N 3 37W
Ethelbert 109 51 32N 100 25W
Ethiopia ■ 63 8 0N 40 0 E
Ethiopian Highlands 78 10 0N 37 0 E
Etive, L. 14 56 30N 5 12W
Etna, Mt. 41 37 45N 15 0 E
Etne 47 59 40N 5 56 E
Etoile 91 11 33 S 27 30 E
Etolin I. 108 56 5N 132 20W
Etosha Pan 92 18 40 S 16 30 E
Etowah 115 35 20N 84 30W
Étrépagny 18 49 18N 1 36 E
Étretat 18 49 42N 0 12 E
Étroits, Les 107 47 24N 68 54W
Etropole 43 42 50N 24 0 E
Ettlingen 25 48 58N 8 25 E
Ettrick Water 14 55 31N 2 55W
Etuku 90 3 42 S 25 45 E
Etzatlán 120 20 48N 104 5W
Eu 18 50 3N 1 26 E
Euabalong West 100 33 3 S 146 23 E
Euboea = Évvoia 45 38 40N 23 40 E
Eucla Basin 96 31 19 S 126 9 E
Euclid 114 41 32N 81 31W
Eucumbene, L. 99 36 2 S 148 40 E
Eudora 117 33 5N 91 17W
Eufaula, Ala., U.S.A. 115 31 55N 85 11W
Eufaula, Okla., U.S.A. 117 35 20N 95 33W
Eufaula, L. 117 35 15N 95 28W
Eugene 118 44 0N 123 8W
Eugenia, Punta 120 27 50N 115 5W
Eugowra 99 33 22 S 148 24 E
Eulo 99 28 10 S 145 3 E
Eunice, La., U.S.A. 117 30 35N 92 28W
Eunice, N. Mex., U.S.A. 117 32 30N 103 10W
Eupen 16 50 37N 6 3 E
Euphrates = Furāt, Nahr al → 64 31 0N 47 25 E
Eure □ 18 49 6N 1 0 E
Eure → 18 49 18N 1 12 E
Eure-et-Loir □ 18 48 22N 1 30 E
Eureka, Can. 4 80 0N 85 56W
Eureka, Calif., U.S.A. 118 40 50N 124 0W
Eureka, Kans., U.S.A. 117 37 50N 96 20W
Eureka, Mont., U.S.A. 118 48 53N 115 6W
Eureka, Nev., U.S.A. 118 39 32N 116 2W
Eureka, S.D., U.S.A. 116 45 49N 99 38W
Eureka, Utah, U.S.A. 118 40 0N 112 9W
Euroa 99 36 44 S 145 35 E
Europa, Picos de 30 43 10N 4 49W
Europa Pt. = Europa, Pta. de 31 36 3N 5 21W
Europa, Pta. de 31 36 3N 5 21W
Europe 8 50 0N 20 0 E
Europoort 16 51 57N 4 10 E
Euskirchen 24 50 40N 6 45 E
Eustis 115 28 54N 81 36W
Eutin 24 54 7N 10 38 E
Eutsuk L. 108 53 20N 126 45W
Eval 62 32 15N 35 15 E
Evale 92 16 33 S 15 44 E
Evanger 47 60 39N 6 7 E
Evans 116 40 25N 104 43W
Evans Head 99 29 7 S 153 27 E
Evans L. 106 50 50N 77 0W
Evans Mills 113 44 6N 75 48W
Evans Pass 116 41 0N 105 35W
Evanston, Ill., U.S.A. 114 42 0N 87 40W
Evanston, Wyo., U.S.A. 118 41 10N 111 0W
Evansville, Ind., U.S.A. 114 38 0N 87 35W
Evansville, Wis., U.S.A. 116 42 47N 89 18W
Évaux-les-Bains 20 46 12N 2 29 E
Eveleth 116 47 29N 92 46W
Even Yahuda 62 32 16N 34 53 E
Evensk 59 62 12N 159 30 E
Evenstad 47 61 25N 11 7 E
Everard, L. 96 31 30 S 135 0 E
Everard Ras. 96 27 5 S 132 28 E
Everest, Mt. 69 28 5N 86 58 E
Everett, Pa., U.S.A. 112 40 2N 78 24W
Everett, Wash., U.S.A. 118 48 0N 122 10W
Everglades, Fla., U.S.A. 115 26 0N 80 30W
Everglades, Fla., U.S.A. 115 25 52N 81 23W
Everglades Nat. Park. 115 25 27N 80 53W
Evergreen 115 31 28N 86 55W
Everson 118 48 57N 122 22W
Evesham 13 52 6N 1 57W
Evian-les-Bains 21 46 24N 6 35 E
Evinayong 88 1 26N 10 35 E
Évinos → 45 38 27N 21 40 E
Evisa 21 42 15N 8 48 E
Evje 47 58 36N 7 51 E
Évora 31 38 33N 7 57W
Évora □ 31 38 33N 7 50W
Évreux 18 49 0N 1 8 E
Evritania □ 45 39 5N 21 30 E
Évron 18 48 10N 0 24W
Évros □ 44 41 10N 26 0 E
Evrótas → 45 36 50N 22 40 E
Évvoia 45 38 30N 24 0 E
Évvoia □ 45 38 40N 23 40 E
Ewe, L. 14 57 49N 5 38W
Ewing 116 42 18N 98 22W
Ewo 88 0 48 S 14 45 E
Exaltación 126 13 10 S 65 20W
Excelsior Springs 116 39 20N 94 10W
Excideuil 20 45 20N 1 4 E
Exe → 13 50 38N 3 27W
Exeter, Can. 112 43 21N 81 29W
Exeter, U.K. 13 50 43N 3 31W
Exeter, Calif., U.S.A. 119 36 17N 119 9W
Exeter, N.H., U.S.A. 113 43 0N 70 58W
Exeter, Nebr., U.S.A. 116 40 43N 97 30W
Exmes 18 48 45N 0 10 E
Exmoor 13 51 10N 3 59W
Exmouth, Austral. 96 21 54 S 114 10 E
Exmouth, U.K. 13 50 37N 3 26W
Exmouth G. 96 22 15 S 114 15 E
Expedition Range 97 24 30 S 149 12 E
Extremadura 31 39 30N 6 5W
Exuma Sound 121 24 30N 76 20W
Eyasi, L. 90 3 30 S 35 0 E
Eyeberry L. 109 63 8N 104 43W
Eyemouth 14 55 53N 2 5W
Eygurande 20 45 40N 2 26 E
Eyjafjörður 50 66 15N 18 30W
Eymet 20 44 40N 0 25 E
Eymoutiers 20 45 40N 1 45 E
Eyrarbakki 50 63 52N 21 9W
Eyre 96 32 15 S 126 18 E
Eyre Cr. → 97 26 40 S 139 0 E
Eyre, L. 97 29 30 S 137 26 E
Eyre Mts. 101 45 25 S 168 25 E
Eyre (North), L. 97 28 30 S 137 20 E
Eyre Pen. 96 33 30 S 137 17 E
Eyre (South), L. 99 29 18 S 137 25 E
Eyzies, Les 20 44 56N 1 1 E
Ez Zeidab 86 17 25N 33 55 E
Ezcaray 32 42 19N 3 0W
Ezine 44 39 48N 26 12 E

F

Fabens 119 31 30N 106 8W
Fåborg 49 55 6N 10 15 E
Fabriano 39 43 20N 12 52 E
Făcăeni 46 44 32N 27 53 E
Facatativá 126 4 49N 74 22W
Fachi 80 18 6N 11 34 E
Facture 20 44 39N 0 58W
Fada 81 17 13N 21 34 E
Fada-n-Gourma 85 12 10N 0 30 E
Fadd 27 46 28N 18 49 E
Faddeyevskiy, Ostrov 59 76 0N 150 0 E
Fāḑilī 64 26 55N 49 10 E
Fadlab 86 17 42N 34 2 E
Faenza 39 44 17N 11 53 E
Fafa 85 15 22N 0 48 E
Fafe 30 41 27N 8 11W
Fagam 85 11 1N 10 1 E
Făgăras 46 45 48N 24 58 E
Făgăras, Munţii 46 45 40N 24 40 E
Fågelsjö 48 61 50N 14 35 E
Fagerhult 49 57 8N 15 40 E
Fagersta 48 60 1N 15 46 E
Făget 46 45 52N 22 10 E
Făget, Munţii 46 47 40N 23 10 E
Fagnano Castello 41 39 31N 16 4 E
Fagnano, L. 128 54 30 S 68 0W
Fagnières 19 48 58N 4 20 E
Fahraj 65 29 0N 59 0 E
Fahūd 65 22 18N 56 28 E
Fair Hd. 15 55 14N 6 10W
Fair Isle 11 59 30N 1 40W
Fairbank 119 31 44N 110 12W
Fairbanks 104 64 50N 147 50W
Fairbury 116 40 5N 97 5W
Fairfax 117 36 37N 96 45W
Fairfield, Austral. 100 33 53 S 150 57 E
Fairfield, Ala., U.S.A. 115 33 30N 87 0W
Fairfield, Calif., U.S.A. 118 38 14N 122 1W
Fairfield, Conn., U.S.A. 113 41 8N 73 16W
Fairfield, Idaho, U.S.A. 118 43 21N 114 46W
Fairfield, Ill., U.S.A. 114 38 20N 88 20W
Fairfield, Iowa, U.S.A. 116 41 0N 91 58W
Fairfield, Mont., U.S.A. 118 47 40N 112 0W
Fairfield, Texas, U.S.A. 117 31 40N 96 0W
Fairford 109 51 37N 98 38W
Fairhope 115 30 35N 87 50W
Fairlie 101 44 5 S 170 49 E
Fairmont, Minn., U.S.A. 116 43 37N 94 30W
Fairmont, W. Va., U.S.A. 114 39 29N 80 10W
Fairmont Hot Springs 108 50 20N 115 56W
Fairplay 119 39 9N 105 40W
Fairport, N.Y., U.S.A. 114 43 8N 77 29W
Fairport, Ohio, U.S.A. 112 41 45N 81 17W
Fairview, Austral. 98 15 31 S 144 17 E
Fairview, Can. 108 56 5N 118 25W
Fairview, N. Dak., U.S.A. 116 47 49N 104 7W
Fairview, Okla., U.S.A. 117 36 19N 98 30W
Fairview, Utah, U.S.A. 118 39 50N 111 0W
Fairweather, Mt. 104 58 55N 137 45W
Faith 116 45 2N 102 4W
Faizabad 69 26 45N 82 10 E
Faizpur 68 21 14N 75 49 E
Fajardo 121 18 20N 65 39W
Fakfak 73 3 0 S 132 15 E
Fakiya 43 42 10N 27 6 E
Fakobli 84 7 23N 7 23W
Fakse 49 55 15N 12 8 E
Fakse B. 49 55 11N 12 15 E
Fakse Ladeplads 49 55 11N 12 9 E
Faku 76 42 32N 123 21 E
Falaise 18 48 54N 0 12W
Falakrón Óros 44 41 15N 23 58 E
Falam 67 23 0N 93 45 E
Falces 32 42 24N 1 48W
Fălciu 46 46 17N 28 7 E
Falcon, C. 82 35 50N 0 50W
Falcon Dam 117 26 50N 99 20W
Falconara Marittima 39 43 37N 13 23 E
Falconer 112 42 7N 79 13W
Faléa 84 12 16N 11 17W
Falenki 55 58 22N 51 35 E
Faleshty 56 47 32N 27 44 E
Falfurrias 117 27 14N 98 8W
Falher 108 55 44N 117 15W
Falkenberg, Ger. 24 51 34N 13 13 E
Falkenberg, Sweden 49 56 54N 12 30 E
Falkensee 24 52 35N 13 6 E
Falkenstein 24 50 27N 12 24 E
Falkirk 14 56 0N 3 47W
Falkland Is. 128 51 30 S 59 0W
Falkland Is. Dependency □ 5 57 0 S 40 0W
Falkland Sd. 128 52 0 S 60 0W
Falkonéra 45 36 50N 23 52 E
Falköping 49 58 12N 13 33 E
Fall Brook 119 33 25N 117 12W
Fall River 114 41 45N 71 5W
Fall River Mills 118 41 1N 121 30W
Fallon, Mont., U.S.A. 116 46 52N 105 8W
Fallon, Nev., U.S.A. 118 39 31N 118 51W
Falls City, Nebr., U.S.A. 116 40 0N 95 40W
Falls City, Oreg., U.S.A. 118 44 54N 123 29W
Falls Creek 112 41 8N 78 49W
Falmouth, Jamaica 121 18 30N 77 40W
Falmouth, U.K. 13 50 9N 5 5W
Falmouth, U.S.A. 114 38 40N 84 20W
False Divi Pt. 70 15 43N 80 50 E
Falset 32 41 7N 0 50 E
Falso, C. 121 15 12N 83 21W
Falster 49 54 45N 11 55 E
Falsterbo 49 55 23N 12 50 E
Fălticeni 46 47 21N 26 20 E
Falun 48 60 37N 15 37 E
Famagusta 64 35 8N 33 55 E
Famatina, Sierra, de 124 27 30 S 68 0W
Family L. 109 51 54N 95 27W
Fan Xian 76 35 55N 115 38 E
Fana, Mali 84 13 0N 6 56W
Fana, Norway 47 60 16N 5 20 E
Fanárion 44 39 24N 21 47 E
Fandriana 93 20 14 S 47 21 E
Fang Xian 77 32 3N 110 40 E
Fangchang 77 31 5N 118 4 E
Fangcheng 77 33 18N 112 59 E
Fangliao 77 22 22N 120 38 E
Fangzheng 76 49 50N 128 48 E
Fani i Madh → 44 41 56N 20 16 E
Fanjiatun 76 43 40N 125 0 E
Fannich, L. 14 57 40N 5 0W
* Fanning I. 95 3 51N 159 22W
Fanny Bay 108 49 27N 124 48W
Fanø 49 55 25N 8 25 E
Fano 39 43 50N 13 0 E
Fanshaw 108 57 11N 133 30W
Fao (Al Fāw) 64 30 0N 48 30 E
Faqirwali 68 29 27N 73 0 E
Fara in Sabina 39 42 13N 12 44 E
Faradje 90 3 50N 29 45 E
Faradofay 93 25 2 S 47 0 E
Farafangana 93 22 49 S 47 50 E
Farâfra, El Wâhât el- 86 27 15N 28 20 E
Farāh 65 32 20N 62 7 E
Farāh □ 65 32 25N 62 10 E
Farahalana 93 14 26 S 50 10 E
Faraid, Gebel 86 23 33N 35 19 E
Faramana 84 11 56N 4 45W
Faranah 84 10 3N 10 45W
Farasān, Jazā'ir 63 16 45N 41 55 E
Faratsiho 93 19 24 S 46 57 E
Fardes → 33 37 35N 3 0W
Fareham 13 50 52N 1 11W
Farewell, C. 101 40 29 S 172 43 E
Farewell C. = Farvel, K. 4 59 48N 43 55W
Fargo 116 46 52N 96 40W
Fari'a → 62 32 12N 35 27 E
Faribault 116 44 15N 93 19W
Faridkot 68 30 44N 74 45 E
Faridpur 69 23 15N 89 55 E
Färila 48 61 48N 15 50 E
Farim 84 12 27N 15 9W
Farīmān 65 35 40N 59 49 E
Farina 99 30 3 S 138 15 E
Faringe 48 59 55N 18 7 E
Fâriskûr 86 31 20N 31 43 E
Farmakonisi 45 37 17N 27 8 E
Farmerville 117 32 48N 92 23W
Farmington, N. Mex., U.S.A. 119 36 45N 108 28W
Farmington, N.H., U.S.A. 113 43 25N 71 7W
Farmington, Utah, U.S.A. 118 41 0N 111 12W
Farmington → 113 41 51N 72 38W
Farmville 114 37 19N 78 22W
Farnborough 13 51 17N 0 46W
Farne Is. 12 55 38N 1 37W
Farnham 113 45 17N 72 59W
Faro, Brazil 127 2 10 S 56 39W
Faro, Port. 31 37 2N 7 55W
Faro □ 31 37 12N 8 10W
Faroe Is. 8 62 0N 7 0W
Farquhar, C. 96 23 50 S 113 36 E
Farrar → 14 57 30N 4 30W
Farrars, Cr. → 98 25 35 S 140 43 E
Farrāshband 65 28 57N 52 5 E
Farrell 114 41 13N 80 29W
Farrell Flat 99 33 48 S 138 48 E
Farrukhabad-cum-Fatehgarh 69 27 30N 79 32 E
Fars □ 65 29 30N 55 0 E
Fársala 44 39 17N 22 23 E
Farsø 49 56 46N 9 19 E
Farsund 47 58 5N 6 55 E
Fartak, Râs 64 28 5N 34 34 E
Fartura, Serra da 125 26 21 S 52 52W
Faru 85 12 48N 6 12 E
Farum 49 55 49N 12 21 E
Farvel, Kap 4 59 48N 43 55W
Farwell 117 34 25N 103 0W
Faryab □ 65 36 0N 65 0 E
Fasā 65 29 0N 53 39 E

* *Renamed Tabuaeran*

Fasano 41 40 50N 17 20 E
Fashoda 87 9 50N 32 2 E
Fastnet Rock 15 51 22N 9 37W
Fastov 54 50 7N 29 57 E
Fatagar, Tanjung 73 2 46 S 131 57 E
Fatehgarh 69 27 25N 79 35 E
Fatehpur, Raj., India 68 28 0N 74 40 E
Fatehpur, Ut. P., India 69 25 56N 81 13 E
Fatesh 55 52 8N 35 57 E
Fatick 84 14 19N 16 27W
Fatima 107 47 24N 61 53W
Fátima 31 39 37N 8 39W
Fatoya 84 11 37N 9 10W
Faucille, Col de la 21 46 22N 6 2 E
Faucilles, Monts 19 48 5N 5 50 E
Faulkton 116 45 4N 99 8W
Faulquemont 19 49 3N 6 36 E
Fauquembergues 19 50 36N 2 5 E
Făurei 46 45 6N 27 19 E
Fauresmith 92 29 44 S 25 17 E
Fauske 50 67 17N 15 25 E
Fåvang 47 61 27N 10 11 E
Favara 40 37 19N 13 39 E
Favignana 40 37 56N 12 18 E
Favignana, I. 40 37 56N 12 18 E
Favone 21 41 47N 9 26 E
Favourable Lake 106 52 50N 93 39W
Fawn → 106 52 22N 88 20W
Faxaflói 50 64 29N 23 0W
Faya-Largeau 81 17 58N 19 6 E
Fayd 64 27 1N 42 52 E
Fayence 21 43 38N 6 42 E
Fayette, Ala., U.S.A. 115 33 40N 87 50W
Fayette, Mo., U.S.A. 116 39 10N 92 40W
Fayette, La 114 40 22N 86 52W
Fayetteville, Ark., U.S.A. 117 36 0N 94 5W
Fayetteville, N.C., U.S.A. 115 35 0N 78 58W
Fayetteville, Tenn., U.S.A. 115 35 8N 86 30W
Fayón 32 41 15N 0 20 E
Fazilka 68 30 27N 74 2 E
Fazilpur 68 29 18N 70 29 E
Fdérik 80 22 40N 12 45W
Feale → 15 52 26N 9 40W
Fear, C. 115 33 51N 78 0W
Feather → 118 38 47N 121 36W
Featherston 101 41 6 S 175 20 E
Featherstone 91 18 42 S 30 55 E
Fécamp 18 49 45N 0 22 E
Fedala = Mohammedia 82 33 44N 7 21W
Federación 124 31 0 S 57 55W
Fedjadj, Chott el 83 33 52N 9 14 E
Fedje 47 60 47N 4 43 E
Fehérgyarmat 27 48 0N 22 30 E
Fehmarn 24 54 26N 11 10 E
Fei Xian 77 35 18N 117 59 E
Feilding 101 40 13 S 175 35 E
Feira de Santana 127 12 15 S 38 57W
Fejér □ 27 47 9N 18 30 E
Fejø 49 54 55N 11 30 E
Fekete → 27 45 47N 18 15 E
Felanitx 33 39 28N 3 9 E
Feldbach 26 46 57N 15 52 E
Feldberg, Germ., E. 24 53 20N 13 26 E
Feldberg, Germ., W. 25 47 51N 7 58 E
Feldkirch 26 47 15N 9 37 E
Feldkirchen 26 46 44N 14 6 E
Felipe Carrillo Puerto 120 19 38N 88 3W
Felixstowe 13 51 58N 1 22 E
Felletin 20 45 53N 2 11 E
Feltre 39 46 1N 11 55 E
Femø 49 54 58N 11 53 E
Femunden 47 62 10N 11 53 E
Fen He → 76 35 36N 110 42 E
Fenelon Falls 112 44 32N 78 45W
Feneroa 87 13 5N 39 3 E
Feng Xian, Jiangsu, China 77 34 43N 116 35 E
Feng Xian, Shaanxi, China 77 33 54N 106 40 E
Fengári 44 40 25N 25 32 E
Fengcheng, Jiangxi, China 77 28 12N 115 48 E
Fengcheng, Liaoning, China 76 40 28N 124 5 E
Fengdu 77 29 55N 107 41 E
Fengfeng 76 36 28N 114 8 E
Fenghua 77 29 40N 121 25 E
Fenghuang 77 27 57N 109 29 E
Fengjie 75 31 5N 109 36 E
Fengkai 77 23 24N 111 30 E
Fengle 77 31 29N 112 29 E
Fengning 76 41 10N 116 33 E
Fengtai 76 39 50N 116 18 E
Fengxian 77 30 55N 121 26 E
Fengxiang 77 34 29N 107 25 E
Fengxin 77 28 41N 115 18 E
Fengyang 77 32 51N 117 29 E
Fengzhen 76 40 25N 113 2 E
Feni Is. 98 4 0 S 153 40 E
Fenit 15 52 17N 9 51W
Fennimore 116 42 58N 90 41W
Fenny 69 22 55N 91 32 E
Feno, C. de 21 41 58N 8 33 E
Fenoarivo Afovoany 93 18 26 S 46 34 E
Fenoarivo Atsinanana 93 17 22 S 49 25 E
Fens, The 12 52 45N 0 2 E
Fenton 114 42 47N 83 44W
Fenyang 76 37 18N 111 48 E
Feodosiya 56 45 2N 35 28 E
Fer, C. de 83 37 3N 7 10 E
Ferdow 65 33 58N 58 2 E
Fère-Champenoise 19 48 45N 4 0 E
Fère-en-Tardenois 19 49 10N 3 30 E
Fère, La 19 49 40N 3 20 E
Ferentino 40 41 42N 13 14 E
Ferfer 63 5 4N 45 9 E
Fergana 58 40 23N 71 19 E
Fergus 106 43 43N 80 24W
Fergus Falls 116 46 18N 96 7W
Fergusson I. 98 9 30 S 150 45 E
Fériana 83 34 59N 8 33 E
Feričanci 42 45 32N 18 0 E
Ferkane 83 34 37N 7 26 E
Ferkéssédougou 84 9 35N 5 6W
Ferlach 26 46 32N 14 18 E
Ferland 106 50 19N 88 27W

Ferlo, Vallée du **84** 15 15N 14 15W
Fermanagh □ **15** 54 21N 7 40W
Fermo **39** 43 10N 13 42 E
Fermoselle **30** 41 19N 6 27W
Fermoy **15** 52 4N 8 18W
Fernán Nuñéz **31** 37 40N 4 44W
Fernández **124** 27 55 S 63 50W
Fernandina Beach **115** 30 40N 81 30W
Fernando de Noronha **127** 4 0 S 33 10W
Fernando Póo = Bioko **85** 3 30N 8 40 E
Ferndale, Calif., U.S.A. **118** 40 37N 124 12W
Ferndale, Wash., U.S.A. **118** 48 51N 122 41W
Fernie **108** 49 30N 115 5W
Fernlees **98** 23 51 S 148 7 E
Fernley **118** 39 36N 119 14W
Feroke **70** 11 9N 75 46 E
Ferozepore **68** 30 55N 74 40 E
Férrai **44** 40 53N 26 10 E
Ferrandina **41** 40 30N 16 28 E
Ferrara **39** 44 50N 11 36 E
Ferrato, C. **40** 39 18N 9 39 E
Ferreira do Alentejo **31** 38 4N 8 6W
Ferreñafe **126** 6 42 S 79 50W
Ferret, C. **20** 44 38N 1 15W
Ferrette **19** 47 30N 7 20 E
Ferriday **117** 31 35N 91 33W
Ferrières **19** 48 5N 2 48 E
Ferriete **38** 44 40N 9 30 E
Ferron **119** 39 3N 111 3W
Ferryland **107** 47 2N 52 53W
Ferté-Bernard, La **18** 48 10N 0 40 E
Ferté, La **19** 48 57N 3 6 E
Ferté-Mace, La **18** 48 35N 0 21W
Ferté-St.-Aubin, La **19** 47 42N 1 57 E
Ferté-Vidame, La **18** 48 37N 0 53 E
Fertile **116** 47 31N 96 18W
Fertilia **40** 40 37N 8 13 E
Fertöszentmiklós **27** 47 35N 16 53 E
Fès **82** 34 0N 5 0W
Feshi **88** 6 8 S 18 10 E
Fessenden **116** 47 42N 99 38W
Feteşti **46** 44 22N 27 51 E
Fethiye **64** 36 36N 29 10 E
Fetlar **14** 60 36N 0 52W
Feuilles → **105** 58 47N 70 4W
Feurs **21** 45 45N 4 13 E
Feyzābād **65** 37 7N 70 33 E
Fezzan **81** 27 0N 15 0 E
Ffestiniog **12** 52 58N 3 56W
Fiambalá **124** 27 45 S 67 37W
Fianarantsoa **93** 21 26 S 47 5 E
Fianarantsoa □ **93** 19 30 S 47 0 E
Fianga **81** 9 55N 15 9 E
Fibiş **42** 45 57N 21 26 E
Fichtelgebirge **25** 50 10N 12 0 E
Ficksburg **93** 28 51 S 27 53 E
Fidenza **38** 44 51N 10 3 E
Field **106** 46 31N 80 1W
Field → **98** 23 48 S 138 0 E
Fieri **44** 40 43N 19 33 E
Fife □ **14** 56 13N 3 2W
Fife Ness **14** 56 17N 2 35W
Fifth Cataract **86** 18 22N 33 50 E
Figeac **20** 44 37N 2 2 E
Figline Valdarno **39** 43 37N 11 28 E
Figtree **91** 20 22 S 28 20 E
Figueira Castelo Rodrigo **30** 40 57N 6 58W
Figueira da Foz **30** 40 7N 8 54W
Figueiró dos Vinhos **30** 39 55N 8 16W
Figueras **32** 42 18N 2 58 E
Figuig **82** 32 5N 1 11W
Fihaonana **93** 18 36 S 47 12 E
Fiherenana **93** 18 29 S 48 24 E
Fiherenana → **93** 23 19 S 43 37 E
Fiji ■ **101** 17 20 S 179 0 E
Fika **85** 11 15N 11 13 E
Filabres, Sierra de los **33** 37 13N 2 20W
Filadélfia **41** 38 47N 16 17 E
Fil'akovo **27** 48 17N 19 50 E
Filchner Ice Shelf **5** 78 0 S 60 0W
Filer **118** 42 30N 114 35W
Filey **12** 54 13N 0 18W
Filiaşi **46** 44 32N 23 31 E
Filiátes **44** 39 38N 20 16 E
Filiatrá **45** 37 9N 21 35 E
Filicudi **41** 38 35N 14 33 E
Filiourí → **44** 41 15N 25 40 E
Filipów **28** 54 11N 22 37 E
Filipstad **48** 59 43N 14 9 E
Filisur **25** 46 41N 9 40 E
Fillmore, Can. **109** 49 50N 103 25W
Fillmore, Calif., U.S.A. **119** 34 23N 118 58W
Fillmore, Utah, U.S.A. **119** 38 58N 112 20W
Filottrano **39** 43 28N 13 20 E
Filyos **56** 41 34N 32 4 E
Filyos → **64** 41 35N 32 10 E
Finale Ligure **38** 44 10N 8 21 E
Finale nell' Emilia **39** 44 50N 11 18 E
Fiñana **33** 37 10N 2 50W
Finch **113** 45 11N 75 7W
Findhorn → **14** 57 38N 3 38W
Findlay **114** 41 0N 83 41W
Finger L. **109** 53 33N 124 18W
Fingõe **91** 15 12 S 31 50 E
Finike **64** 36 21N 30 10 E
Finistère □ **18** 48 20N 4 0W
Finisterre **30** 42 54N 9 16W
Finisterre, C. **30** 42 50N 9 19W
Finisterre Ra. **98** 6 0 S 146 30 E
Finke → **96** 27 0 S 136 10 E
Finland ■ **52** 63 0N 27 0 E
Finland, G. of **52** 60 0N 26 0 E
Finlay → **108** 57 0N 125 10W
Finley, Austral. **99** 35 38 S 145 35 E
Finley, U.S.A. **116** 47 35N 97 50W
Finn → **15** 54 50N 7 55W
Finnigan, Mt. **98** 15 49 S 145 17 E
Finnmark fylke □ **50** 69 30N 25 0 E
Finschhafen **98** 6 33 S 147 50 E
Finse **47** 60 36N 7 30 E
Finsteraarhorn **25** 46 31N 8 10 E
Finsterwalde **24** 51 37N 13 42 E
Finucane I. **96** 20 19 S 118 30 E
Fiora → **39** 42 20N 11 35 E
Fiorenzuola d'Arda **38** 44 56N 9 54 E
Fīq **62** 32 46N 35 41 E
Fire River **106** 48 47N 83 21W
Firebag → **109** 57 45N 111 21W
Firedrake L. **109** 61 25N 104 30W
Firenze **39** 43 47N 11 15 E
Firminy, Aveyron, France **20** 44 32N 2 19 E
Firminy, Loire, France **21** 45 23N 4 18 E
Firozabad **68** 27 10N 78 25 E
Fīrūzābād **65** 28 52N 52 35 E
Fīrūzkūh **65** 35 50N 52 50 E
Firvale **108** 52 27N 126 13W
Fish → **92** 28 7 S 17 45 E
Fisher B. **109** 51 35N 97 13W
Fishguard **13** 51 59N 4 59W
Fishing L. **109** 52 10N 95 24W
Fismes **19** 49 20N 3 40 E
Fitchburg **114** 42 35N 71 47W
Fitero **32** 42 4N 1 52W
Fitjar **47** 59 55N 5 17 E
Fitri, L. **81** 12 50N 17 28 E
Fitz Roy **128** 47 0 S 67 0W
Fitzgerald, Can. **108** 59 51N 111 36W
Fitzgerald, U.S.A. **115** 31 45N 83 16W
Fitzroy →, Queens., Austral. **98** 23 32 S 150 52 E
Fitzroy →, W. Australia, Austral. **96** 17 31 S 123 35 E
Fitzroy Crossing **96** 18 9 S 125 38 E
Fitzwilliam I. **112** 45 30N 81 45W
Fiume = Rijeka **39** 45 20N 14 27 E
Fiumefreddo Brúzio **41** 39 14N 16 4 E
Fivizzano **38** 44 12N 10 11 E
Fizi **90** 4 17 S 28 55 E
Fjæra **47** 59 52N 6 22 E
Fjellerup **49** 56 29N 10 34 E
Fjerritslev **49** 57 5N 9 15 E
Fkih ben Salah **82** 32 32N 6 45W
Flå, Buskerud, Norway **47** 60 25N 9 28 E
Flå, Sør-Trøndelag, Norway **47** 63 13N 10 18 E
Flagler **116** 39 20N 103 4W
Flagstaff **119** 35 10N 111 40W
Flaherty I. **106** 56 15N 79 15W
Flambeau → **116** 45 18N 91 15W
Flamborough Hd. **12** 54 8N 0 4W
Flaming Gorge Dam **118** 40 50N 109 46W
Flaming Gorge L. **118** 41 15N 109 30W
Flamingo, Teluk **73** 5 30 S 138 0 E
Flanders = Flandres **16** 51 10N 3 15 E
Flandre Occidental □ **16** 51 0N 3 0 E
Flandre Orientale □ **16** 51 0N 4 0 E
Flandreau **116** 44 5N 96 38W
Flandres, Plaines des **16** 51 10N 3 15 E
Flannan Is. **11** 58 9N 7 52W
Flåsjön **50** 64 5N 15 40 E
Flat → **108** 61 51N 128 0W
Flat River **117** 37 50N 90 30W
Flatey, Barðastrandarsýsla, Iceland **50** 66 10N 17 52W
Flatey, Suður-Þingeyjarsýsla, Iceland **50** 65 22N 22 56W
Flathead L. **118** 47 50N 114 0W
Flattery, C., Austral. **98** 14 58 S 145 21 E
Flattery, C., U.S.A. **118** 48 21N 124 43W
Flavy-le-Martel **19** 49 43N 3 12 E
Flaxton **116** 48 52N 102 24W
Flèche, La **18** 47 42N 0 5W
Fleetwood **12** 53 55N 3 1W
Flekkefjord **47** 58 18N 6 39 E
Flemington **112** 41 7N 77 28W
Flensborg Fjord **49** 54 50N 9 40 E
Flensburg **24** 54 46N 9 28 E
Flers **18** 48 47N 0 33W
Flesherton **112** 44 16N 80 33W
Flesko, Tanjung **73** 0 29N 124 30 E
Fletton **13** 52 34N 0 13W
Fleurance **20** 43 52N 0 40 E
Fleurier **25** 46 54N 6 35 E
Flin Flon **109** 54 46N 101 53W
Flinders → **97** 17 36 S 140 36 E
Flinders B. **96** 34 19 S 115 19 E
Flinders Group **98** 14 11 S 144 15 E
Flinders I. **97** 40 0 S 148 0 E
Flinders Ranges **97** 31 30 S 138 30 E
Flint, U.K. **12** 53 15N 3 7W
Flint, U.S.A. **114** 43 5N 83 40W
Flint → **115** 30 52N 84 38W
Flint, I. **95** 11 26 S 151 48W
Flinton **99** 27 55 S 149 32 E
Fliseryd **49** 57 6N 16 15 E
Flix **32** 41 14N 0 32 E
Flixecourt **19** 50 0N 2 5 E
Flodden **12** 55 37N 2 8W
Floodwood **116** 46 55N 92 55W
Flora, Norway **47** 63 27N 11 22 E
Flora, U.S.A. **114** 38 40N 88 30W
Florac **20** 44 20N 3 37 E
Florala **115** 31 0N 86 20W
Florence, Ala., U.S.A. **115** 34 50N 87 40W
Florence, Ariz., U.S.A. **119** 33 0N 111 25W
Florence, Colo., U.S.A. **116** 38 26N 105 0W
Florence, Oreg., U.S.A. **118** 44 0N 124 3W
Florence, S.C., U.S.A. **115** 34 12N 79 44W
Florence = Firenze **39** 43 47N 11 15 E
Florence, L. **99** 28 53 S 138 9 E
Florennes **16** 50 15N 4 35 E
Florensac **20** 43 23N 3 28 E
Florenville **16** 49 40N 5 19 E
Flores, Azores **8** 39 13N 31 13W
Flores, Guat. **120** 16 59N 89 50W
Flores, Indon. **73** 8 35 S 121 0 E
Flores I. **108** 49 20N 126 10W
Flores Sea **72** 6 30 S 124 0 E
Floresville **117** 29 10N 98 10W
Floriano **127** 6 50 S 43 0W
Florianópolis **125** 27 30 S 48 30W
Florida, Cuba **121** 21 32N 78 14W
Florida, Uruguay **125** 34 7 S 56 10W
Florida □ **115** 28 30N 82 0W
Florida B. **121** 25 0N 81 20W
Florida Keys **121** 25 0N 80 40W
Florida, Straits of **121** 25 0N 80 0W
Floridia **41** 37 6N 15 9 E
Floridsdorf **27** 48 14N 16 22 E
Flórina **44** 40 48N 21 26 E
Flórina □ **44** 40 45N 21 20 E
Florø **47** 61 35N 5 1 E
Flower Sta. **113** 45 10N 76 41W
Flower's Cove **107** 51 14N 56 46W
Floydada **117** 33 58N 101 18W
Fluk **73** 1 42 S 127 44 E
Flumen → **32** 41 43N 0 9W
Flumendosa → **40** 39 26N 9 38 E
Fluminimaggiore **40** 39 25N 8 30 E
Flushing = Vlissingen **16** 51 26N 3 34 E
Fluviá → **32** 42 12N 3 7 E
Fly → **94** 8 25 S 143 0 E
Flying Fish, C. **5** 72 6 S 102 29W
Foam Lake **109** 51 40N 103 32W
Foča **42** 43 31N 18 47 E
Focşani **46** 45 41N 27 15 E
Fogang **77** 23 52N 113 30 E
Foggaret el Arab **82** 27 13N 2 49 E
Foggaret ez Zoua **82** 27 20N 2 53 E
Fóggia **41** 41 28N 15 31 E
Foggo **85** 11 21N 9 57 E
Foglia → **39** 43 55N 12 54 E
Fogo **107** 49 43N 54 17W
Fogo I. **107** 49 40N 54 5W
Fohnsdorf **26** 47 12N 14 40 E
Föhr **24** 54 40N 8 30 E
Foia **31** 37 19N 8 37W
Foix **20** 42 58N 1 38 E
Foix □ **20** 43 0N 1 30 E
Fojnica **42** 43 59N 17 51 E
Fokino **54** 53 30N 34 22 E
Fokis □ **45** 38 30N 22 15 E
Fokstua **47** 62 7N 9 17 E
Folda, Nord-Trøndelag, Norway **50** 64 41N 10 50 E
Folda, Nordland, Norway **50** 67 38N 14 50 E
Földeák **27** 46 19N 20 30 E
Folégandros **45** 36 40N 24 55 E
Folette, La **115** 36 23N 84 9W
Foleyet **106** 48 15N 82 25W
Folgefonn **47** 60 3N 6 23 E
Foligno **39** 42 58N 12 40 E
Folkestone **13** 51 5N 1 11 E
Folkston **115** 30 55N 82 0W
Follett **117** 36 30N 100 12W
Follónica **38** 42 55N 10 45 E
Follónica, Golfo di **38** 42 50N 10 40 E
Folsom **118** 38 41N 121 7W
Fond-du-Lac **109** 59 19N 107 12W
Fond du Lac **116** 43 46N 88 26W
Fond-du-Lac → **109** 59 17N 106 0W
Fonda **113** 42 57N 74 23W
Fondi **40** 41 21N 13 25 E
Fonfría **30** 41 37N 6 9W
Fongen **47** 63 11N 11 38 E
Fonni **40** 40 5N 9 16 E
Fonsagrada **30** 43 8N 7 4W
Fonseca, G. de **120** 13 10N 87 40W
Fontaine-Française **19** 47 32N 5 21 E
Fontainebleau **19** 48 24N 2 40 E
Fontas → **108** 58 14N 121 48W
Fonte Boa **126** 2 33 S 66 0W
Fontem **85** 5 32N 9 52 E
Fontenay-le-Comte **20** 46 28N 0 48W
Fontur **50** 66 23N 14 32W
Fonyód **27** 46 44N 17 33 E
Foochow = Fuzhou **75** 26 5N 119 16 E
Foping **77** 33 41N 108 0 E
Foppiano **38** 46 21N 8 24 E
Föra **49** 57 1N 16 51 E
Forbach **19** 49 10N 6 52 E
Forbes **97** 33 22 S 148 0 E
Forbesganj **69** 26 17N 87 18 E
Forcados **85** 5 26N 5 26 E
Forcados → **85** 5 25N 5 19 E
Forcall → **32** 40 51N 0 16W
Forcalquier **21** 43 58N 5 47 E
Forchheim **25** 49 42N 11 4 E
Ford City **112** 40 47N 79 31W
Førde **47** 61 27N 5 53 E
Ford's Bridge **99** 29 41 S 145 29 E
Fordyce **117** 33 50N 92 20W
Forécariah **84** 9 28N 13 10W
Forel, Mt. **4** 66 52N 36 55W
Foremost **108** 49 26N 111 34W
Forenza **41** 40 50N 15 50 E
Forest, Can. **112** 43 6N 82 0W
Forest, U.S.A. **117** 32 21N 89 27W
Forest City, Iowa, U.S.A. **116** 43 12N 93 39W
Forest City, N.C., U.S.A. **115** 35 23N 81 50W
Forest City, Pa., U.S.A. **113** 41 39N 75 29W
Forest Grove **118** 45 31N 123 4W
Forestburg **108** 52 35N 112 1W
Forestier Pen. **99** 43 0 S 148 0 E
Forestville, Can. **107** 48 48N 69 2W
Forestville, U.S.A. **114** 44 41N 87 29W
Forez, Mts. du **20** 45 40N 3 50 E
Forfar **14** 56 40N 2 53W
Forges-les-Eaux **19** 49 37N 1 30 E
Forks **118** 47 56N 124 23W
Forlì **39** 44 14N 12 2 E
Forman **116** 46 9N 97 43W
Formazza **38** 46 23N 8 26 E
Formby Pt. **12** 53 33N 3 7W
Formentera **33** 38 43N 1 27 E
Formentor, C. de **32** 39 58N 3 13 E
Fórmia **40** 41 15N 13 34 E
Formigine **38** 44 37N 10 51 E
Formiguères **20** 42 37N 2 5 E
Formosa **124** 26 15 S 58 10W
Formosa = Taiwan ■ **75** 24 0N 121 0 E
Formosa □ **124** 25 0 S 60 0W
Formosa Bay **90** 2 40 S 40 20 E
Formosa, Serra **127** 12 0 S 55 0W
Fornells **32** 40 3N 4 7 E
Fornos de Algodres **30** 40 38N 7 32W
Fornovo di Taro **38** 44 42N 10 7 E
Forres **14** 57 37N 3 38W
Forrest **99** 38 33 S 143 47 E
Forrest City **117** 35 0N 90 50W
Fors **48** 60 14N 16 20 E
Forsa **48** 61 44N 16 55 E
Forsand **47** 58 54N 6 5 E
Forsayth **97** 18 33 S 143 34 E
Forserum **49** 57 42N 14 30 E
Forshaga **48** 59 33N 13 29 E
Forskacka **48** 60 39N 16 54 E
Forsmo **48** 63 16N 17 11 E
Forst **24** 51 43N 14 37 E
Forster **99** 32 12 S 152 31 E
Forsyth, Ga., U.S.A. **115** 33 4N 83 55W
Forsyth, Mont., U.S.A. **118** 46 14N 106 37W
Fort Albany **106** 52 15N 81 35W
Fort Amador **120** 8 56N 79 32W
Fort Apache **119** 33 50N 110 0W
Fort Assiniboine **108** 54 20N 114 45W
Fort Augustus **14** 57 9N 4 40W
Fort Beaufort **92** 32 46 S 26 40 E
Fort Benton **118** 47 50N 110 40W
Fort Bragg **118** 39 28N 123 50W
Fort Bridger **118** 41 22N 110 20W
Fort Chimo **105** 58 6N 68 15W
Fort Chipewyan **109** 58 42N 111 8W
Fort Clayton **120** 9 0N 79 35W
Fort Collins **116** 40 30N 105 4W
Fort-Coulonge **106** 45 50N 76 45W
Fort Davis, Panama **120** 9 17N 79 56W
Fort Davis, U.S.A. **117** 30 38N 103 53W
Fort-de-France **121** 14 36N 61 2W
Fort de Possel = Possel **88** 5 5N 19 10 E
Fort Defiance **119** 35 47N 109 4W
Fort Dodge **116** 42 29N 94 10W
Fort Edward **113** 43 16N 73 35W
Fort Frances **109** 48 36N 93 24W
Fort Franklin **104** 65 10N 123 30W
Fort Garland **119** 37 28N 105 30W
Fort George **106** 53 50N 79 0W
Fort Good-Hope **104** 66 14N 128 40W
Fort Hancock **119** 31 19N 105 56W
Fort Hertz (Putao) **67** 27 28N 97 30 E
Fort Hope **106** 51 30N 88 0W
Fort Huachuca **119** 31 32N 110 30W
Fort Jameson = Chipata **91** 13 38 S 32 28 E
Fort Kent **107** 47 12N 68 30W
Fort Klamath **118** 42 45N 122 0W
Fort Lallemand **83** 31 13N 6 17 E
Fort-Lamy = Ndjamena **81** 12 4N 15 8 E
Fort Laramie **116** 42 15N 104 30W
Fort Lauderdale **115** 26 10N 80 5W
Fort Liard **108** 60 14N 123 30W
Fort Liberté **121** 19 42N 71 51W
Fort Lupton **116** 40 8N 104 48W
Fort Mackay **108** 57 12N 111 41W
Fort McKenzie **107** 57 20N 69 0W
Fort Macleod **108** 49 45N 113 30W
Fort MacMahon **82** 29 43N 1 45 E
Fort McMurray **108** 56 44N 111 7W
Fort McPherson **104** 67 30N 134 55W
Fort Madison **116** 40 39N 91 20W
Fort Meade **115** 27 45N 81 45W
Fort Miribel **82** 29 25N 2 55 E
Fort Morgan **116** 40 10N 103 50W
Fort Myers **115** 26 39N 81 51W
Fort Nelson **108** 58 50N 122 44W
Fort Nelson → **108** 59 32N 124 0W
Fort Norman **104** 64 57N 125 30W
Fort Payne **115** 34 25N 85 44W
Fort Peck **118** 48 1N 106 30W
Fort Peck Dam **118** 48 0N 106 38W
Fort Peck L. **118** 47 40N 107 0W
Fort Pierce **115** 27 29N 80 19W
Fort Pierre **116** 44 25N 100 25W
Fort Pierre Bordes = Ti-n-Zaouatene **82** 20 0N 2 55 E
Fort Plain **113** 42 56N 74 39W
Fort Portal **90** 0 40N 30 20 E
Fort Providence **108** 61 3N 117 40W
Fort Qu'Appelle **109** 50 45N 103 50W
Fort Randolph **120** 9 23N 79 53W
Fort Resolution **108** 61 10N 113 40W
Fort Rixon **91** 20 2 S 29 17 E
Fort Roseberry = Mansa **91** 11 10 S 28 50 E
Fort Rupert (Rupert House) **106** 51 30N 78 40W
Fort Saint **83** 30 19N 9 31 E
Fort St. James **108** 54 30N 124 10W
Fort St. John **108** 56 15N 120 50W
Fort Sandeman **68** 31 20N 69 31 E
Fort Saskatchewan **108** 53 40N 113 15W
Fort Scott **117** 37 50N 94 40W
Fort Severn **106** 56 0N 87 40W
Fort Sherman **120** 9 22N 79 56W
Fort Shevchenko **57** 43 40N 51 20 E
Fort-Sibut **88** 5 46N 19 10 E
Fort Simpson **108** 61 45N 121 15W
Fort Smith, Can. **108** 60 0N 111 51W
Fort Smith, U.S.A. **117** 35 25N 94 25W
Fort Stanton **119** 33 33N 105 36W
Fort Stockton **117** 30 54N 102 54W
Fort Sumner **117** 34 24N 104 16W
Fort Thomas **119** 33 2N 109 59W
Fort Trinquet = Bir Mogrein **80** 25 10N 11 35W
Fort Valley **115** 32 33N 83 52W
Fort Vermilion **108** 58 24N 116 0W
* Fort Victoria **91** 20 8 S 30 49 E
Fort Walton Beach **115** 30 25N 86 40W
Fort Wayne **114** 41 5N 85 10W
Fort William **14** 56 48N 5 8W
Fort Worth **117** 32 45N 97 25W
Fort Yates **116** 46 8N 100 38W
Fort Yukon **104** 66 35N 145 20W
Fortaleza **127** 3 45 S 38 35W
Forteau **107** 51 28N 56 58W
Fortescue → **96** 21 20 S 116 5 E
Forth, Firth of **14** 56 5N 2 55W
Forthassa Rharbia **82** 32 52N 1 18W
Fortore → **39** 41 55N 15 17 E
Fortrose **14** 57 35N 4 10W
Fortuna, Spain **33** 38 11N 1 7W
Fortuna, Cal., U.S.A. **118** 40 38N 124 8W
Fortuna, N.D., U.S.A. **116** 48 55N 103 48W

* *Renamed Masvingo*

Fortune B. 107 47 30N 55 22W
Forûr 65 26 20N 54 30 E
Fos 21 43 26N 4 56 E
Foshan 75 23 4N 113 5 E
Fossacesia 39 42 15N 14 30 E
Fossano 38 44 33N 7 40 E
Fossil 118 45 0N 120 9W
Fossilbrook P.O. 98 17 47 S 144 29 E
Fossombrone 39 43 41N 12 49 E
Fosston 116 47 33N 95 39W
Foster 113 45 17N 72 30W
Foster → 109 55 47N 105 49W
Fostoria 114 41 8N 83 25W
Fougamou 88 1 16 S 10 30 E
Fougères 18 48 21N 1 14W
Foul Pt. 70 8 35N 81 18 E
Foulness I. 13 51 36N 0 55 E
Foulness Pt. 13 51 36N 0 59 E
Foulpointe 93 17 41 S 49 31 E
Foum Assaka 82 29 8N 10 24W
Foum Zguid 82 30 2N 6 59W
Foumban 85 5 45N 10 50 E
Foundiougne 84 14 5N 16 32W
Fountain, Colo., U.S.A. 116 38 42N 104 40W
Fountain, Utah, U.S.A. 118 39 41N 111 37W
Fourchambault 19 47 0N 3 3 E
Fourchu 107 45 43N 60 17W
Fourmies 19 50 1N 4 2 E
Fournás 45 39 3N 21 52 E
Foúrnoi, Greece 45 37 36N 26 32 E
Foúrnoi, Greece 45 37 36N 26 28 E
Fours 19 46 50N 3 42 E
Fouta Djalon 84 11 20N 12 10W
Foux, Cap-à- 121 19 43N 73 27W
Foveaux Str. 101 46 42 S 168 10 E
Fowey 13 50 20N 4 39W
Fowler, Calif., U.S.A. 119 36 41N 119 41W
Fowler, Colo., U.S.A. 116 38 10N 104 0W
Fowler, Kans., U.S.A. 117 37 28N 100 7W
Fowlerton 117 28 26N 98 50W
Fownhope 13 52 0N 2 37W
Fox → 109 56 3N 93 18W
Fox Valley 109 50 30N 109 25W
Foxe Basin 105 68 30N 77 0W
Foxe Channel 105 66 0N 80 0W
Foxe Pen. 105 65 0N 76 0W
Foxen, L. 48 59 25N 11 55 E
Foxpark 118 41 4N 106 6W
Foxton 101 40 29 S 175 18 E
Foyle, Lough 15 55 6N 7 8W
Foynes 15 52 37N 9 5W
Foz 30 43 33N 7 20W
Fóz do Cunene 92 17 15 S 11 48 E
Foz do Gregório 126 6 47 S 70 44W
Foz do Iguaçu 125 25 30 S 54 30W
Frackville 113 40 46N 76 15W
Fraga 32 41 32N 0 21 E
Framingham 113 42 18N 71 26W
Frampol 28 50 41N 22 40 E
Franca 127 20 33 S 47 30W
Francavilla al Mare 39 42 25N 14 16 E
Francavilla Fontana 41 40 32N 17 35 E
France ■ 17 47 0N 3 0 E
Frances 99 36 41 S 140 55 E
Frances → 108 60 16N 129 10W
Frances L. 108 61 23N 129 30W
Franceville 88 1 40 S 13 32 E
Franche-Comté 19 46 30N 5 50 E
Francisco I. Madero, Coahuila, Mexico 120 25 48N 103 18W
Francisco I. Madero, Durango, Mexico 120 24 32N 104 22W
Francofonte 41 37 13N 14 50 E
François, Can. 107 47 35N 56 45W
François, Mart. 121 14 38N 60 57W
François L. 108 54 0N 125 30W
Franeker 16 53 12N 5 33 E
Frankado 87 12 30N 43 12 E
Frankenberg 24 51 3N 8 47 E
Frankenthal 25 49 32N 8 21 E
Frankenwald 25 50 18N 11 36 E
Frankfort, Madag. 93 27 17 S 28 30 E
Frankfort, Ind., U.S.A. 114 40 20N 86 33W
Frankfort, Kans., U.S.A. 116 39 42N 96 26W
Frankfort, Ky., U.S.A. 114 38 12N 84 52W
Frankfort, Mich., U.S.A. 114 44 38N 86 14W
Frankfurt □ 24 52 30N 14 0 E
Frankfurt am Main 25 50 7N 8 40 E
Frankfurt an der Oder 24 52 50N 14 31 E
Fränkische Alb 25 49 20N 11 30 E
Fränkische Rezal → 25 49 11N 11 1 E
Fränkische Saale → 25 50 30N 9 42 E
Fränkische Schweiz 25 49 45N 11 10 E
Franklin, Ky., U.S.A. 115 36 40N 86 30W
Franklin, La., U.S.A. 117 29 45N 91 30W
Franklin, Mass., U.S.A. 113 42 4N 71 23W
Franklin, N.H., U.S.A. 114 43 28N 71 39W
Franklin, N.J., U.S.A. 113 41 9N 74 38W
Franklin, Nebr., U.S.A. 116 40 9N 98 55W
Franklin, Pa., U.S.A. 114 41 22N 79 45W
Franklin, Tenn., U.S.A. 115 35 54N 86 53W
Franklin, Va., U.S.A. 115 36 40N 76 58W
Franklin, W. Va., U.S.A. 114 38 38N 79 21W
* Franklin □ 105 71 0N 99 0W
Franklin B. 104 69 45N 126 0W
Franklin D. Roosevelt L. 118 48 30N 118 16W
Franklin I. 5 76 10 S 168 30 E
Franklin, L. 118 40 20N 115 26W
Franklin Mts. 104 65 0N 125 0W
Franklin Str. 104 72 0N 96 0W
Franklinton 117 30 53N 90 10W
Franklinville 112 42 21N 78 28W
Franks Peak 118 43 50N 109 5W
Frankston 99 38 8 S 145 8 E
Fränsta 48 62 30N 16 11 E
Frantsa Josifa, Zemlya 58 82 0N 55 0 E
Franz 106 48 25N 84 30W
Franz Josef Land = Frantsa Josifa 58 79 0N 62 0 E
Franzburg 24 54 9N 12 52 E
Frascati 40 41 48N 12 41 E
Fraser →, B.C., Can. 108 49 7N 123 11W
Fraser →, Newf., Can. 107 56 39N 62 10W
Fraser I. 97 25 15 S 153 10 E
Fraser Lake 108 54 0N 124 50W
Fraserburg 92 31 55 S 21 30 E
Fraserburgh 14 57 41N 2 0W
Fraserdale 106 49 55N 81 37W
Frashëri 44 40 23N 20 26 E
Frasne 19 46 50N 6 10 E
Frauenfeld 25 47 34N 8 54 E
Fray Bentos 124 33 10 S 58 15W
Frechilla 30 42 8N 4 50W
Fredericia 49 55 34N 9 45 E
Frederick, Md., U.S.A. 114 39 25N 77 23W
Frederick, Okla., U.S.A. 117 34 22N 99 0W
Frederick, S.D., U.S.A. 116 45 55N 98 29W
Frederick Reef 97 20 58 S 154 23 E
Frederick Sd. 108 57 10N 134 0W
Fredericksburg, Tex., U.S.A. 117 30 17N 98 55W
Fredericksburg, Va., U.S.A. 114 38 16N 77 29W
Frederickstown 117 37 35N 90 15W
Fredericton 107 45 57N 66 40W
Fredericton Junc. 107 45 41N 66 40W
Frederikshavn 49 57 28N 10 31 E
Frederikssund 49 55 50N 12 3 E
Fredonia, Ariz., U.S.A. 119 36 59N 112 36W
Fredonia, Kans., U.S.A. 117 37 34N 95 50W
Fredonia, N.Y., U.S.A. 114 42 26N 79 20W
Fredrikstad 47 59 13N 10 57 E
Freehold 113 40 15N 74 18W
Freeland 113 41 3N 75 48W
Freeling, Mt. 96 22 35 S 133 06 E
Freels, C. 107 49 15N 53 30W
Freeman 116 43 25N 97 20W
Freeport, Bahamas 121 26 30N 78 47W
Freeport, Can. 107 44 15N 66 20W
Freeport, Ill., U.S.A. 116 42 18N 89 40W
Freeport, N.Y., U.S.A. 114 40 39N 73 35W
Freeport, Tex., U.S.A. 117 28 55N 95 22W
Freetown 84 8 30N 13 17W
Frégate, L. 106 53 15N 74 45W
Fregenal de la Sierra 31 38 10N 6 39W
Fregene 40 41 50N 12 12 E
Fregeneda, La 30 40 58N 6 54W
Fréhel, C. 18 48 40N 2 20W
Frei 47 63 4N 7 48 E
Freiberg 24 50 55N 13 20 E
Freibourg = Fribourg 25 46 49N 7 9 E
Freiburg, Baden, Ger. 25 48 0N 7 52 E
Freiburg, Niedersachsen, Ger. 24 53 49N 9 17 E
Freire 128 38 54 S 72 38W
Freirina 124 28 30 S 71 10W
Freising 25 48 24N 11 47 E
Freistadt 26 48 30N 14 30 E
Freital 24 51 0N 13 40 E
Fréjus 21 43 25N 6 44 E
Fremantle 96 32 7 S 115 47 E
Fremont, Mich., U.S.A. 114 43 29N 85 59W
Fremont, Nebr., U.S.A. 116 41 30N 96 30W
Fremont, Ohio, U.S.A. 114 41 20N 83 5W
Fremont → 119 38 15N 110 20W
Fremont, L. 118 43 0N 109 50W
French → 114 41 30N 80 2W
French Guiana ■ 127 4 0N 53 0W
French I. 100 38 20 S 145 22 E
French Terr. of Afars & Issas = Djibouti ■ 87 11 30N 42 15 E
Frenchglen 118 42 48N 119 0W
Frenchman → 118 48 24N 107 5W
Frenchman Butte 109 53 35N 109 38W
Frenchman Creek → 116 40 13N 100 50W
Frenda 82 35 2N 1 1 E
Fresco → 127 7 15 S 51 30W
Freshfield, C. 5 68 25 S 151 10 E
Fresnay 18 48 17N 0 1 E
Fresnillo 120 23 10N 103 0W
Fresno 119 36 47N 119 50W
Fresno Alhandiga 30 40 42N 5 37W
Fresno Res. 118 48 40N 110 0W
Freudenstadt 25 48 27N 8 25 E
Frévent 19 50 15N 2 17 E
Freycinet Pen. 97 42 10 S 148 25 E
Freyung 25 48 48N 13 33 E
Fria 84 10 27N 13 38W
Fria, C. 92 18 0 S 12 0 E
Frias 124 28 40 S 65 5W
Fribourg 25 46 49N 7 9 E
Fribourg □ 25 46 40N 7 0 E
Fridafors 49 56 25N 14 39 E
Friedberg, Bayern, Ger. 25 48 21N 10 59 E
Friedberg, Hessen, Ger. 25 50 21N 8 46 E
Friedland 24 53 40N 13 33 E
Friedrichshafen 25 47 39N 9 29 E
Friedrichskoog 24 54 1N 8 52 E
Friedrichsort 24 54 24N 10 11 E
Friedrichstadt 24 54 23N 9 6 E
Friendly (Tonga) Is. 101 22 0 S 173 0W
Friesach 26 46 57N 14 24 E
Friesack 24 52 43N 12 35 E
Friesland □ 16 53 5N 5 50 E
Friesoythe 24 53 1N 7 51 E
Frijoles 120 9 11N 79 48W
Frillesås 49 57 20N 12 12 E
Frinnaryd 49 57 55N 14 50 E
Frio → 117 28 30N 98 10W
Friona 117 34 40N 102 42W
Frisian Is. 24 53 30N 6 0 E
Fristad 49 57 50N 13 0 E
Fritch 117 35 40N 101 35W
Fritsla 49 57 33N 12 47 E
Fritzlar 24 51 8N 9 19 E
Friuli-Venezia Giulia □ 39 46 0N 13 0 E
Friville-Escarbotin 19 50 5N 1 33 E
Frobisher B. 105 62 30N 66 0W
Frobisher Bay 105 63 44N 68 31W
Frobisher L. 109 56 20N 108 15W
Frohavet 50 63 50N 9 35 E
Froid 116 48 20N 104 29W
Frolovo 57 49 45N 43 40 E
Fromberg 118 45 25N 108 58W
Frombork 28 54 21N 19 41 E
Frome 13 51 16N 2 17W
Frome, L. 97 30 45 S 139 45 E
Fromentine 18 46 53N 2 9W
Frómista 30 42 16N 4 25W
Front Range 118 40 0N 105 40W
Front Royal 114 38 55N 78 10W
Fronteira 31 39 3N 7 39W
Frontera 120 18 30N 92 40W
Frontignan 20 43 27N 3 45 E
Frosinone 40 41 38N 13 20 E
Frosolone 41 41 34N 14 27 E
Frostburg 114 39 43N 78 57W
Frostisen 50 68 14N 17 10 E
Frouard 19 48 47N 6 8 E
Frövi 48 59 28N 15 24 E
Frøya 47 63 43N 8 40 E
Fruges 19 50 30N 2 8 E
Frumoasa 46 46 28N 25 48 E
Frunze 58 42 54N 74 46 E
Fruška Gora 42 45 7N 19 30 E
Frutal 127 20 0 S 49 0W
Frutigen 25 46 35N 7 38 E
Frýdek-Místek 27 49 40N 18 20 E
Frýdlant, Severočeský, Czech. 26 50 56N 15 9 E
Frýdlant, Severomoravsky, Czech. 27 49 35N 18 20 E
Fryvaldov = Jeseník 27 50 0N 17 8 E
Fthiótis □ 45 38 50N 22 25 E
Fu Xian, Liaoning, China 76 39 38N 121 58 E
Fu Xian, Shaanxi, China 76 36 0N 109 20 E
Fucécchio 38 43 44N 10 51 E
Fucheng 76 37 50N 116 10 E
Fuchou = Fuzhou 75 26 5N 119 16 E
Fuchuan 77 24 50N 111 5 E
Fuchun Jiang → 77 30 5N 120 5 E
Fúcino, Conca del 39 42 1N 13 31 E
Fuding 77 27 20N 120 12 E
Fuencaliente 31 38 25N 4 18W
Fuengirola 31 36 32N 4 41W
Fuente Álamo 33 38 44N 1 24W
Fuente Álamo 33 37 42N 1 6W
Fuente de Cantos 31 38 15N 6 18W
Fuente de San Esteban, La 30 40 49N 6 15W
Fuente del Maestre 31 38 31N 6 28W
Fuente el Fresno 31 39 14N 3 46W
Fuente Ovejuna 31 38 15N 5 25W
Fuentes de Andalucía 31 37 28N 5 20W
Fuentes de Ebro 32 41 31N 0 38W
Fuentes de León 31 38 5N 6 32W
Fuentes de Oñoro 30 40 33N 6 52W
Fuentesaúco 30 41 15N 5 30W
Fuerte → 120 25 50N 109 25W
Fuerte Olimpo 124 21 0 S 57 51W
Fuerteventura 80 28 30N 14 0W
Fügët, Munţii 46 45 50N 22 9 E
Fugløysund 50 70 15N 20 20 E
Fugou 77 34 3N 114 25 E
Fuhai 75 47 2N 87 25 E
Fuji-no-miya 74 35 10N 138 40 E
Fuji-San 74 35 22N 138 44 E
Fujian □ 75 26 0N 118 0 E
Fujin 76 47 16N 132 1 E
Fujisawa 74 35 22N 139 29 E
Fukien = Fujian □ 75 26 0N 118 0 E
Fukuchiyama 74 35 19N 135 9 E
Fukui 74 36 0N 136 10 E
Fukui □ 74 36 0N 136 12 E
Fukuoka 74 33 39N 130 21 E
Fukuoka □ 74 33 30N 131 0 E
Fukushima 74 37 44N 140 28 E
Fukushima □ 74 37 30N 140 15 E
Fukuyama 74 34 35N 133 20 E
Fulda 24 50 32N 9 41 E
Fulda → 24 51 27N 9 40 E
Fuling 77 29 40N 107 20 E
Fullerton, Calif., U.S.A. 119 33 52N 117 58W
Fullerton, Nebr., U.S.A. 116 41 25N 98 0W
Fulton, Mo., U.S.A. 116 38 50N 91 55W
Fulton, N.Y., U.S.A. 114 43 20N 76 22W
Fulton, Tenn., U.S.A. 115 36 31N 88 53W
Fuluälven 48 61 18N 13 4 E
Fulufjället 48 61 32N 12 41 E
Fumay 19 50 0N 4 40 E
Fumel 20 44 30N 0 58 E
Funabashi 74 35 45N 140 0 E
Funafuti 94 8 30 S 179 0 E
Funchal 80 32 38N 16 54W
Fundación 126 10 31N 74 11W
Fundão 30 40 8N 7 30W
Fundy, B. of 107 45 0N 66 0W
Funing, Jiangsu, China 77 33 45N 119 50 E
Funing, Yunnan, China 77 23 35N 105 45 E
Funiu Shan 77 33 30N 112 20 E
Funsi 84 10 21N 1 54W
Funtua 85 11 30N 7 18 E
Fuping 76 38 48N 114 12 E
Fuqing 77 25 41N 119 21 E
Fur 49 56 50N 9 0 E
Furât, Nahr al → 64 31 0N 47 25 E
Furmanov 55 57 10N 41 9 E
Furmanovo 57 49 42N 49 25 E
Furnas, Represa de 125 20 50 S 45 0W
Furneaux Group 97 40 10 S 147 50 E
Furness, Pen. 12 54 12N 3 10W
Fürstenau 24 52 32N 7 40 E
Fürstenberg 24 53 11N 13 9 E
Fürstenfeld 26 47 3N 16 3 E
Fürstenfeldbruck 25 48 10N 11 15 E
Fürstenwalde 24 52 20N 14 3 E
Fürth 25 49 29N 11 0 E
Furth im Wald 25 49 19N 12 51 E
Furtwangen 25 48 3N 8 14 E
Furudal 48 61 10N 15 11 E
Furusund 48 59 40N 18 55 E
Fury and Hecla Str. 105 69 56N 84 0W
Fusa 47 60 12N 5 37 E
Fusagasuga 126 4 21N 74 22W
Fuscaldo 41 39 25N 16 1 E
Fushan 76 37 30N 121 15 E
Fushë Arrëzi 44 42 4N 20 2 E
Fushun 76 41 50N 123 56 E
Fusong 76 42 20N 127 15 E
Füssen 25 47 35N 10 43 E
Fusui 77 22 40N 107 56 E
Futuna 94 14 25 S 178 20 E
Fuwa 86 31 12N 30 33 E
Fuxin 76 42 5N 121 48 E
Fuyang, Anhui, China 77 33 0N 115 48 E
Fuyang, Zhejiang, China 77 30 5N 119 57 E
Fuyu 76 45 12N 124 43 E
Fuyuan 75 48 20N 134 5 E
Füzesgyarmat 27 47 6N 21 14 E
Fuzhou, Fujian, China 75 26 5N 119 16 E
Fuzhou, Jiangxi, China 75 28 0N 116 25 E
Fylde 12 53 50N 2 58W
Fyn 49 55 20N 10 30 E
Fyne, L. 14 56 0N 5 20W
Fyns Amtskommune □ 49 55 15N 10 30 E
Fyresvatn 47 59 6N 8 10 E

G

Gaanda 85 10 10N 12 27 E
Gabarin 85 11 8N 10 27 E
Gabas → 20 43 46N 0 42W
Gabela 88 11 0 S 14 24 E
Gabès 83 33 53N 10 2 E
Gabès, Golfe de 83 34 0N 10 30 E
Gabgaba, W. 86 22 10N 33 5 E
Gabin 28 52 23N 19 41 E
Gabon ■ 88 0 10 S 10 0 E
Gaborone 92 24 45 S 25 57 E
Gabriels 113 44 26N 74 12W
Gabrovo 43 42 52N 25 19 E
Gacé 18 48 49N 0 20 E
Gach Sārān 65 30 15N 50 45 E
Gacko 42 43 10N 18 33 E
Gadag-Betgeri 70 15 30N 75 45 E
Gadamai 87 17 11N 36 10 E
Gadap 68 25 5N 67 28 E
Gadarwara 68 22 50N 78 50 E
Gadebusch 24 53 41N 11 6 E
Gadein 87 8 10N 28 45 E
Gadhada 68 22 0N 71 35 E
Gádor, Sierra de 33 36 57N 2 45W
Gadsden, Ala., U.S.A. 115 34 1N 86 0W
Gadsden, Ariz., U.S.A. 119 32 35N 114 47W
Gadwal 70 16 10N 77 50 E
Gadyach 54 50 21N 34 0 E
Găeşti 46 44 48N 25 19 E
Gaeta 40 41 12N 13 35 E
Gaeta, G. di 40 41 0N 13 25 E
Gaffney 115 35 3N 81 40W
Gafsa 83 32 24N 8 43 E
Gagarin (Gzhatsk) 54 55 38N 35 0 E
Gagetown 107 45 46N 66 10W
Gagino 55 55 15N 45 1 E
Gagliano del Capo 41 39 50N 18 23 E
Gagnef 48 60 36N 15 5 E
Gagnoa 84 6 56N 5 16W
Gagnon 107 51 50N 68 5W
Gagnon, L. 109 62 3N 110 27W
Gagra 57 43 20N 40 10 E
Gahini 90 1 50 S 30 30 E
Gahmar 69 25 27N 83 49 E
Gai Xian 76 40 22N 122 20 E
Gaibanda 69 25 20N 89 36 E
Gaïdhouronisi 45 34 53N 25 41 E
Gail 117 32 48N 101 25W
Gail → 26 46 36N 13 53 E
Gaillac 20 43 54N 1 54 E
Gaillon 18 49 10N 1 20 E
Gaines 112 41 46N 77 35W
Gainesville, Fla., U.S.A. 115 29 38N 82 20W
Gainesville, Ga., U.S.A. 115 34 17N 83 47W
Gainesville, Mo., U.S.A. 117 36 35N 92 26W
Gainesville, Tex., U.S.A. 117 33 40N 97 10W
Gainsborough 12 53 23N 0 46W
Gairdner L. 96 31 30 S 136 0 E
Gairloch, L. 14 57 43N 5 45W
Gaj 42 45 28N 17 3 E
Gal Oya Res. 70 7 5N 81 30 E
Galachipa 69 22 8N 90 26 E
Galán, Cerro 124 25 55 S 66 52W
Galana → 90 3 9 S 40 8 E
Galangue 89 13 42 S 16 9 E
Galanta 27 48 11N 17 45 E
Galápagos 95 0 0 89 0W
Galas → 71 4 55N 101 57 E
Galashiels 14 55 37N 2 50W
Galatás 45 37 30N 23 26 E
Galaţi 46 45 27N 28 2 E
Galaţi □ 46 45 45N 27 30 E
Galatina 41 40 10N 18 10 E
Galátone 41 40 8N 18 3 E
Galax 115 36 42N 80 57W
Galaxidhion 45 38 22N 22 23 E
Galbraith 98 16 25 S 141 30 E
Galcaio 63 6 30N 47 30 E
Galdhøpiggen 47 61 38N 8 18 E
Galela 73 1 50N 127 49 E
Galera 33 37 45N 2 33W
Galesburg 116 40 57N 90 23W
Galeton 112 41 43N 77 40W
Gali 57 42 37N 41 46 E
Galicea Mare 46 44 4N 23 19 E
Galich 55 58 23N 42 12 E
Galiche 43 43 34N 23 50 E
Galicia 30 42 43N 7 45W
Galilee = Hagalil 62 32 53N 35 18 E
Galilee, L. 98 22 20 S 145 50 E
Galion 112 40 43N 82 48W
Galite, Is. de la 83 37 30N 8 59 E
Galiuro Mts. 119 32 40N 110 30W
Gallabat 81 12 58N 36 11 E
Gallarate 38 45 40N 8 48 E
Gallardon 19 48 32N 1 47 E
Gallatin 115 36 24N 86 27W
Galle 70 6 5N 80 10 E
Gállego → 32 41 39N 0 51W
Gallegos → 128 51 35 S 69 0W
Galley Hd. 15 51 32N 8 56W

* *Now part of Central Arctic and Baffin* □

Galliate 38 45 27N 8 44 E
Gallinas, Pta. 126 12 28N 71 40W
Gallipoli 41 40 8N 18 0 E
Gallipoli = Gelibolu 44 40 28N 26 43 E
Gallipolis 114 38 50N 82 10W
Gällivare 50 67 9N 20 40 E
Gallo, C. 40 38 13N 13 19 E
Gallocanta, Laguna de 32 40 58N 1 30W
Galloway 14 55 0N 4 25W
Galloway, Mull of 14 54 38N 4 50W
Gallup 119 35 30N 108 45W
Gallur 32 41 52N 1 19W
Gal'on 62 31 38N 34 51 E
Galong 99 34 37 S 148 34 E
Galtström 48 62 10N 17 30 E
Galtür 26 46 58N 10 11 E
Galty Mts. 15 52 22N 8 10W
Galtymore 15 52 22N 8 12W
Galva 116 41 10N 90 0W
Galve de Sorbe 32 41 13N 3 10W
Galveston 117 29 15N 94 48W
Galveston B. 117 29 30N 94 50W
Gálvez, Argent. 124 32 0 S 61 14W
Gálvez, Spain 31 39 42N 4 16W
Galway 15 53 16N 9 4W
Galway □ 15 53 16N 9 3W
Galway B. 15 53 10N 9 20W
Gamari, L. 87 11 32N 41 40 E
Gamawa 85 12 10N 10 31 E
Gambaga 85 10 30N 0 28W
Gambat 68 27 17N 68 26 E
Gambela 87 8 14N 34 38 E
Gambia ■ 84 13 25N 16 0W
Gambia → 84 13 28N 16 34W
Gamboa 120 9 8N 79 42W
Gamboli 68 29 53N 68 24 E
» Gambos 89 14 37 S 14 40 E
Gamerco 119 35 33N 108 56W
Gammon → 109 51 24N 95 44W
Gammouda 83 35 3N 9 39 E
Gan 20 43 12N 0 27W
Gan Goriama, Mts. 85 7 44N 12 45 E
Gan Jiang → 75 29 15N 116 0 E
Gan Shemu'el 62 32 28N 34 56 E
Gan Yavne 62 31 48N 34 42 E
Ganado, Ariz., U.S.A. 119 35 46N 109 41W
Ganado, Tex., U.S.A. 117 29 4N 96 31W
Gananoque 106 44 20N 76 10W
Ganaveh 65 29 35N 50 35 E
Gancheng 77 18 51N 108 37 E
Gand = Gent 16 51 2N 3 42 E
Ganda 89 13 3 S 14 35 E
Gandak → 69 25 39N 85 13 E
Gandava 68 28 32N 67 32 E
Gander 107 48 58N 54 35W
Gander L. 107 48 58N 54 35W
Ganderowe Falls 91 17 20 S 29 10 E
Gandesa 32 41 3N 0 26 E
Gandhi Sagar 68 24 40N 75 40 E
Gandi 85 12 55N 5 49 E
Gandia 33 38 58N 0 9W
Gandino 38 45 50N 9 52 E
Gandole 85 8 28N 11 35 E
Ganedidalem = Gani 73 0 48 S 128 14 E
Ganetti 86 18 0N 31 10 E
Ganga → 69 23 20N 90 30 E
Ganga, Mouths of the 69 21 30N 90 0 E
Ganganagar 68 29 56N 73 56 E
Gangapur 68 26 32N 76 49 E
Gangara 85 14 35N 8 29 E
Gangavati 70 15 30N 76 36 E
Gangaw 67 22 5N 94 5 E
Gangdisê Shan 67 31 20N 81 0 E
Ganges 20 43 56N 3 42 E
Ganges = Ganga → 69 23 20N 90 30 E
Gangoh 68 29 46N 77 18 E
Gangtok 69 27 20N 88 37 E
Gani 73 0 48 S 128 14 E
Ganj 68 27 45N 78 57 E
Gannat 20 46 7N 3 11 E
Gannett Pk. 118 43 15N 109 38W
Gannvalley 116 44 3N 98 57W
Ganquan 76 36 20N 109 20 E
Gänserdorf 27 48 20N 16 43 E
Gansu □ 75 36 0N 104 0 E
Ganta (Gompa) 84 7 15N 8 59W
Gantheaume B. 96 27 40 S 114 10 E
Gantheaume, C. 99 36 4 S 137 32 E
Gantsevichi 54 52 49N 26 30 E
Ganyu 77 34 50N 119 8 E
Ganyushkino 57 46 35N 49 20 E
Ganzhou 75 25 51N 114 56 E
Gao □ 85 18 0N 1 0 E
Gao Bang 71 22 37N 106 18 E
Gao'an 77 28 26N 115 17 E
Gaomi 76 36 20N 119 42 E
Gaoping 76 35 45N 112 55 E
Gaoua 84 10 20N 3 8W
Gaoual 84 11 45N 13 25W
Gaoxiong 75 22 38N 120 18 E
Gaoyou 77 32 47N 119 26 E
Gaoyou Hu 77 32 45N 119 20 E
Gaoyuan 76 37 8N 117 58 E
Gap 21 44 33N 6 5 E
Gar 75 32 10N 79 58 E
Garachiné 121 8 0N 78 12W
Garanhuns 127 8 50 S 36 30W
Garawe 84 4 35N 8 0W
Garba Tula 90 0 30N 38 32 E
Garber 117 36 30N 97 36W
Garberville 118 40 11N 123 50W
Gard 63 9 30N 49 6 E
Gard □ 21 44 2N 4 10 E
Gard → 21 43 51N 4 37 E
Garda, L. di 38 45 40N 10 40 E
Gardala 81 5 40N 37 25 E
Gardanne 21 43 27N 5 27 E
Garde L. 109 62 50N 106 13W
Gardelegen 24 52 32N 11 21 E
Garden City, Kans., U.S.A. 117 38 0N 100 45W
Garden City, Tex., U.S.A. 117 31 52N 101 28W
Gardez 66 33 37N 69 9 E
Gardhíki 45 38 50N 21 55 E
Gardiner 118 45 3N 110 42W
Gardiners I. 113 41 4N 72 5W
Gardner 114 42 35N 72 0W
Gardner Canal 108 53 27N 128 8W
Gardnerville 118 38 59N 119 47W
Gardno, Jezioro 28 54 40N 17 7 E
Garešnica 42 45 36N 16 56 E
Garéssio 38 44 12N 8 1 E
Garfield 118 47 3N 117 8W
Gargaliánoi 45 37 4N 21 38 E
Gargano, Mte. 41 41 43N 15 43 E
Gargans, Mt. 20 45 37N 1 39 E
Gargouna 85 15 56N 0 13 E
Garhshankar 68 31 13N 76 11 E
Garibaldi Prov. Park 108 49 50N 122 40W
Garies 92 30 32 S 17 59 E
Garigliano → 40 41 13N 13 44 E
Garissa 90 0 25 S 39 40 E
Garissa □ 90 0 20 S 40 0 E
Garkida 85 10 27N 12 36 E
Garko 85 11 45N 8 53 E
Garland 118 41 47N 112 10W
Garlasco 38 45 11N 8 55 E
Garm 58 39 0N 70 20 E
Garmisch-Partenkirchen 25 47 30N 11 5 E
Garmsār 65 35 20N 52 25 E
Garner 116 43 4N 93 37W
Garnett 116 38 18N 95 12W
Garo Hills 69 25 30N 90 30 E
Garob 92 26 37 S 16 0 E
Garoe 63 8 25N 48 33 E
Garonne → 20 45 2N 0 36W
Garoua (Garwa) 85 9 19N 13 21 E
Garrel 24 52 58N 7 59 E
Garrigues 20 43 40N 3 30 E
Garrison, Mont., U.S.A. 118 46 30N 112 56W
Garrison, N.D., U.S.A. 116 47 39N 101 27W
Garrison, Tex., U.S.A. 117 31 50N 94 28W
Garrison Res. 116 47 30N 102 0W
Garrovillas 31 39 40N 6 33W
Garrucha 33 37 11N 1 49W
Garry → 14 56 47N 3 47W
Garry L. 104 65 58N 100 18W
Garsen 90 2 20 S 40 5 E
Garson → 109 56 20N 110 1W
Garson L. 109 56 19N 110 2W
Gartempe → 20 46 47N 0 49 E
Gartz 24 53 12N 14 23 E
Garu 85 10 55N 0 11W
Garut 73 7 14 S 107 53 E
Garvão 31 37 42N 8 21W
Garvie Mts. 101 45 30 S 168 50 E
Garwa 69 24 11N 83 47 E
Garwolin 28 51 55N 21 38 E
Gary 114 41 35N 87 20W
Garz 24 54 17N 13 21 E
Garzê 75 31 39N 99 58 E
Garzón 126 2 10N 75 40W
Gasan Kuli 58 37 40N 54 20 E
Gascogne 20 43 45N 0 20 E
Gascogne, G. de 32 44 0N 2 0W
Gascony = Gascogne 20 43 45N 0 20 E
Gascoyne → 96 24 52 S 113 37 E
Gascueña 32 40 18N 2 31W
Gash, Wadi → 87 16 48N 35 51 E
Gashaka 85 7 20N 11 29 E
Gashua 85 12 54N 11 0 E
Gaspé 107 48 52N 64 30W
Gaspé, C. 107 48 48N 64 7W
Gaspé, Pén. de 107 48 45N 65 40W
Gaspésie, Parc Prov. de la 107 48 55N 65 50W
Gassaway 114 38 42N 80 43W
Gássino Torinese 38 45 8N 7 50 E
Gassol 85 8 34N 10 25 E
Gastonia 115 35 17N 81 10W
Gastoúni 45 37 51N 21 15 E
Gastoúri 44 39 34N 19 54 E
Gastre 128 42 20 S 69 15W
Gata, C. de 33 36 41N 2 13W
Gata, Sierra de 30 40 20N 6 45W
Gataga → 108 58 35N 126 59W
Gătaia 42 45 26N 21 30 E
Gatchina 54 59 35N 30 9 E
Gateshead 12 54 57N 1 37W
Gatesville 117 31 29N 97 45W
Gaths 91 20 2 S 30 32 E
Gatico 124 22 29 S 70 20W
Gâtinais 19 48 5N 2 40 E
Gâtine, Hauteurs de 20 46 35N 0 45W
Gatineau 113 45 29N 75 39W
Gatineau → 106 45 27N 75 42W
Gatineau, Parc de la 106 45 40N 76 0W
• Gatooma 91 18 20 S 29 52 E
Gattinara 38 45 37N 8 22 E
Gatun 120 9 16N 79 55W
Gatun Dam 120 9 16N 79 55W
Gatun, L. 120 9 7N 79 56W
Gatun Locks 120 9 16N 79 55W
Gaucín 31 36 31N 5 19W
Gauer L. 109 57 0N 97 50W
Gauhati 67 26 10N 91 45 E
Gauja → 54 57 10N 24 16 E
Gaula → 47 63 21N 10 14 E
Gaussberg 5 66 45 S 89 0 E
Gausta 47 59 50N 8 37 E
Gavá 32 41 18N 2 0 E
Gavarnie 20 42 44N 0 3W
Gaväter 65 25 10N 61 31 E
Gavdhopoúla 45 34 56N 24 0 E
Gávdhos 45 34 50N 24 5 E
Gavião 31 39 28N 7 56W
Gävle 48 60 40N 17 9 E
Gävleborgs län □ 48 61 30N 16 15 E
Gavorrano 38 42 55N 10 49 E
Gavray 18 48 55N 1 20W
Gavrilov Yam 55 57 18N 39 49 E
Gávrion 45 37 54N 24 44 E
Gawachab 92 27 4 S 17 55 E
Gawilgarh Hills 68 21 15N 76 45 E
Gawler 97 34 30 S 138 42 E
Gawler Ranges 96 32 30 S 135 45 E
Gaxun Nur 75 42 22N 100 30 E
Gay 52 51 27N 58 27 E
Gaya, India 69 24 47N 85 4 E
Gaya, Niger 85 11 52N 3 28 E
Gaya, Nigeria 85 11 57N 9 0 E
Gaylord 114 45 1N 84 41W
Gayndah 97 25 35 S 151 32 E
Gaysin 56 48 57N 28 25 E
Gayvoron 56 48 22N 29 52 E
Gaza 62 31 30N 34 28 E
Gaza □ 93 23 10 S 32 45 E
Gaza Strip 62 31 29N 34 25 E
Gazaoua 85 13 32N 7 55 E
Gazelle Pen. 98 4 40 S 152 0 E
Gazi 90 1 3N 24 30 E
Gaziantep 64 37 6N 37 23 E
Gazli 58 40 14N 63 24 E
Gbarnga 84 7 19N 9 13W
Gbekebo 85 6 20N 4 56 E
Gboko 85 7 17N 9 4 E
Gbongan 85 7 28N 4 20 E
Gcuwa 93 32 20 S 28 11 E
Gdańsk 28 54 22N 18 40 E
Gdańsk □ 28 54 10N 18 30 E
Gdańska, Zatoka 28 54 30N 19 20 E
Gdov 54 58 48N 27 55 E
Gdynia 28 54 35N 18 33 E
Ge'a 62 31 38N 34 37 E
Gebe 73 0 5N 129 25 E
Gebeit Mine 86 21 3N 36 29 E
Gebel Mûsa 86 28 32N 33 59 E
Gecha 87 7 30N 35 18 E
Gedaref 87 14 2N 35 28 E
Gede, Tanjung 72 6 46 S 105 12 E
Gedera 62 31 49N 34 46 E
Gedo 87 9 2N 37 25 E
Gèdre 20 42 47N 0 2 E
Gedser 49 54 35N 11 55 E
Gedser Odde 49 54 30N 11 58 E
Geelong 97 38 10 S 144 22 E
Geestenseth 24 53 31N 8 51 E
Geesthacht 24 53 25N 10 20 E
Geidam 85 12 57N 11 57 E
Geikie → 109 57 45N 103 52W
Geili 87 16 1N 32 37 E
Geilo 47 60 32N 8 14 E
Geinica 27 48 51N 20 55 E
Geisingen 25 47 55N 8 37 E
Geislingen 25 48 37N 9 51 E
Geita 90 2 48 S 32 12 E
Geita □ 90 2 50 S 32 10 E
Gejiu 75 23 20N 103 10 E
Gel → 87 7 5N 29 10 E
Gel River 87 7 5N 29 10 E
Gela 41 37 6N 14 18 E
Gela, Golfo di 41 37 0N 14 8 E
Geladi 63 6 59N 46 30 E
Gelderland □ 16 52 5N 6 10 E
Geldermalsen 16 51 53N 5 17 E
Geldern 24 51 32N 6 18 E
Geldrop 16 51 25N 5 32 E
Geleen 16 50 57N 5 49 E
Gelehun 84 8 20N 11 40W
Gelendzhik 56 44 33N 38 10 E
Gelibolu 44 40 28N 26 43 E
Gelnhausen 25 50 12N 9 12 E
Gelsenkirchen 24 51 30N 7 5 E
Gelting 24 54 43N 9 53 E
Gemas 71 2 37N 102 36 E
Gembloux 16 50 34N 4 43 E
Gemena 88 3 13N 19 48 E
Gemerek 64 39 15N 36 10 E
Gemona del Friuli 39 46 16N 13 7 E
Gemsa 86 27 39N 33 35 E
Gemu-Gofa □ 87 5 40N 36 40 E
Gemünden 25 50 3N 9 43 E
Gen He → 76 50 16N 119 32 E
Genale 87 6 0N 39 30 E
Gençay 20 46 23N 0 23 E
Gendringen 16 51 52N 6 21 E
Geneina, Gebel 86 29 2N 33 55 E
General Acha 124 37 20 S 64 38W
General Alvear, Buenos Aires, Argent. 124 36 0 S 60 0W
General Alvear, Mendoza, Argent. 124 35 0 S 67 40W
General Artigas 124 26 52 S 56 16W
General Belgrano 124 36 35 S 58 47W
General Cabrera 124 32 53 S 63 52W
General Guido 124 36 40 S 57 50W
General Juan Madariaga 124 37 0 S 57 0W
General La Madrid 124 37 17 S 61 20W
General MacArthur 73 11 18N 125 28 E
General Martin Miguel de Güemes 124 24 35 S 65 0W
General Paz 124 27 45 S 57 36W
General Pico 124 35 45 S 63 50W
General Pinedo 124 27 15 S 61 20W
General Pinto 124 34 45 S 61 50W
General Santos 73 6 5N 125 14 E
General Toshevo 43 43 42N 28 6 E
General Trías 120 28 21N 106 22W
General Viamonte 124 35 1 S 61 3W
General Villegas 124 35 0 S 63 0W
Genesee, Idaho, U.S.A. 118 46 31N 116 59W
Genesee, Pa., U.S.A. 112 42 0N 77 54W
Genesee → 114 42 35N 78 0W
Geneseo, Ill., U.S.A. 116 41 25N 90 10W
Geneseo, Kans., U.S.A. 116 38 32N 98 8W
Geneseo, N.Y., U.S.A. 112 42 49N 77 49W
Geneva, Ala., U.S.A. 115 31 2N 85 52W
Geneva, N.Y., U.S.A. 114 42 53N 77 0W
Geneva, Nebr., U.S.A. 116 40 35N 97 35W
Geneva, Ohio, U.S.A. 114 41 49N 80 58W
Geneva = Genève 25 46 12N 6 9 E
Geneva, L. 114 42 38N 88 30W
Geneva, L. = Léman, Lac 25 46 26N 6 30 E
Genève 25 46 12N 6 9 E
Genève □ 25 46 10N 6 10 E
Gengenbach 25 48 25N 8 0 E
Genichesk 56 46 12N 34 50 E
Genil → 31 37 42N 5 19W
Génissiat, Barrage de 21 46 1N 5 48 E
Genjem 73 2 46 S 140 12 E
Genk 16 50 58N 5 32 E
Genlis 19 47 15N 5 12 E
Gennargentu, Mti. del 40 40 0N 9 10 E
Gennep 16 51 41N 5 59 E
Gennes 18 47 20N 0 17W
Genoa, Austral. 99 37 29 S 149 35 E
Genoa, N.Y., U.S.A. 113 42 40N 76 32W
Genoa, Nebr., U.S.A. 116 41 31N 97 44W
Genoa = Génova 38 44 24N 8 57 E
Génova 38 44 24N 8 56 E
Génova, Golfo di 38 44 0N 9 0 E
Gent 16 51 2N 3 42 E
Genthin 24 52 24N 12 10 E
Geographe B. 96 33 30 S 115 15 E
Geographe Chan. 96 24 30 S 113 0 E
Geokchay 57 40 42N 47 43 E
Georga, Zemlya 58 80 30N 49 0 E
George 92 33 58 S 22 29 E
George → 107 58 49N 66 10W
George, L., N.S.W., Austral. 99 35 10 S 149 25 E
George, L., S. Austral., Austral. 99 37 25 S 140 0 E
George, L., Uganda 90 0 5N 30 10 E
George, L., Fla., U.S.A. 115 29 15N 81 35W
George, L., N.Y., U.S.A. 113 43 30N 73 30W
George River = Port Nouveau 105 58 30N 65 50W
George Sound 101 44 52 S 167 25 E
George Town, Austral. 99 41 5 S 146 49 E
George Town, Bahamas 121 23 33N 75 47W
George Town, Malay. 71 5 25N 100 15 E
George V Coast 5 69 0 S 148 0 E
George VI Sound 5 71 0 S 68 0W
George West 117 28 18N 98 5W
Georgetown, Austral. 97 18 17 S 143 33 E
Georgetown, Ont., Can. 106 43 40N 79 56W
Georgetown, P.E.I., Can. 107 46 13N 62 24W
Georgetown, Gambia 84 13 30N 14 47W
Georgetown, Guyana 126 6 50N 58 12W
Georgetown, Colo., U.S.A. 118 39 46N 105 49W
Georgetown, Ky., U.S.A. 114 38 13N 84 33W
Georgetown, Ohio, U.S.A. 114 38 50N 83 50W
Georgetown, S.C., U.S.A. 115 33 22N 79 15W
Georgetown, Tex., U.S.A. 117 30 40N 97 45W
Georgi Dimitrov 43 42 15N 23 54 E
Georgi Dimitrov, Yazovir 43 42 37N 25 18 E
Georgia □ 115 32 0N 82 0W
Georgia, Str. of 108 49 25N 124 0W
Georgian B. 106 45 15N 81 0W
Georgian S.S.R. □ 57 42 0N 43 0 E
Georgievsk 57 44 12N 43 28 E
Georgina → 97 23 30 S 139 47 E
Georgiu-Dezh 55 51 3N 39 30 E
Gera 24 50 53N 12 11 E
Gera □ 24 50 45N 11 45 E
Geraardsbergen 16 50 45N 3 53 E
Geral de Goiás, Serra 127 12 0 S 46 0W
Geral, Serra 125 26 25 S 50 0W
Geraldine 118 47 36N 110 18W
Geraldton, Austral. 96 28 48 S 114 32 E
Geraldton, Can. 106 49 44N 86 59W
Gérardmer 19 48 3N 6 50 E
Gerede 56 40 45N 32 10 E
Gereshk 65 31 47N 64 35 E
Gérgal 33 37 7N 2 31W
Gerik 71 5 25N 101 0 E
Gering 116 41 51N 103 30W
Gerizim 62 32 13N 35 15 E
Gerlach 118 40 43N 119 27W
Gerlachovka 27 49 11N 20 7 E
Gerlogubi 63 6 53N 45 3 E
German Planina 42 42 20N 22 0 E
Germansen Landing 108 55 43N 124 40W
Germany, East ■ 24 52 0N 12 0 E
Germany, West ■ 24 52 0N 9 0 E
Germersheim 25 49 13N 8 20 E
Germiston 93 26 15 S 28 10 E
Gernsheim 25 49 44N 8 29 E
Gerolstein 25 50 12N 6 40 E
Gerolzhofen 25 49 54N 10 21 E
Gerona 32 41 58N 2 46 E
Gerona □ 32 42 11N 2 30 E
Gerrard 108 50 30N 117 17W
Gers □ 20 43 35N 0 38 E
Gers → 20 44 9N 0 39 E
Gersfeld 24 50 27N 9 57 E
Gersoppa Falls 70 14 12N 74 46 E
Gerufa 92 19 17 S 26 0 E
Geseke 24 51 38N 8 29 E
Geser 73 3 50 S 130 54 E
Gesso → 38 44 24N 7 33 E
Gestro, Wabi → 87 4 12N 42 2 E
Getafe 30 40 18N 3 44W
Gethsémani 107 50 13N 60 40W
Gettysburg, Pa., U.S.A. 114 39 47N 77 18W
Gettysburg, S.D., U.S.A. 116 45 3N 99 56W
Getz Ice Shelf 5 75 0 S 130 0W
Gévaudan 20 44 40N 3 40 E
Gevgelija 42 41 9N 22 30 E
Gévora → 31 38 53N 6 57W
Gex 21 46 21N 6 3 E
Geyikli 44 39 50N 26 12 E
Geyser 118 47 17N 110 30W
Geysir 50 64 19N 20 18W
Ghaghara → 69 25 45N 84 40 E
Ghalla, Wadi el → 87 10 25N 27 32 E
Ghana ■ 85 6 0N 1 0W
Ghansor 69 22 39N 80 1 E
Ghanzi 92 21 50 S 21 34 E
Ghanzi □ 92 21 50 S 21 45 E
Gharbîya, Es Sahrâ el 86 27 40N 26 30 E
Ghard Abû Muharik 86 26 50N 30 0 E
Ghardaïa 82 32 20N 3 37 E
Ghârib, G. 86 28 6N 32 54 E
Ghârib, Râs 86 28 6N 33 18 E
Gharyān 83 32 10N 13 0 E
Gharyān □ 83 30 35N 12 0 E
Ghat 83 24 59N 10 11 E
Ghatal 69 22 40N 87 46 E
Ghatampur 69 26 8N 80 13 E
Ghatprabha → 70 16 15N 75 20 E
Ghayl 64 21 40N 46 20 E

» Renamed Kipungo

• Renamed Kadoma

Ghazal, Bahr el → 81 15 0N 17 0 E
Ghazâl, Bahr el → 87 9 31N 30 25 E
Ghazaouet 82 35 8N 1 50W
Ghaziabad 68 28 42N 77 26 E
Ghazipur 69 25 38N 83 35 E
Ghazni 66 33 30N 68 28 E
Ghaznī □ 65 33 0N 68 0 E
Ghedi 38 45 24N 10 16 E
Ghelari 46 45 38N 22 45 E
Ghèlinsor 63 6 28N 46 39 E
Ghent = Gand 16 51 2N 3 42 E
Gheorghe Gheorghiu-Dej 46 46 17N 26 47 E
Gheorgheni 46 46 43N 25 41 E
Ghergani 46 44 37N 25 37 E
Gherla 46 47 0N 23 57 E
Ghilarza 40 40 8N 8 50 E
Ghisonaccia 21 42 1N 9 26 E
Ghod → 70 18 30N 74 35 E
Ghot Ogrein 86 31 10N 25 20 E
Ghotaru 68 27 20N 70 1 E
Ghotki 68 28 5N 69 21 E
Ghowr □ 65 34 0N 64 20 E
Ghudāmis 83 30 11N 9 29 E
Ghugri 69 22 39N 80 41 E
Ghugus 70 19 58N 79 12 E
Ghulam Mohammad Barrage 68 25 30N 68 20 E
Ghūriān 65 34 17N 61 25 E
Gia Nghia 71 12 0N 107 42 E
Gian 73 5 45N 125 20 E
Giannutri 38 42 16N 11 5 E
Giant Mts. = Krkonoše 26 50 50N 16 10 E
Giant's Causeway 15 55 15N 6 30W
Giarre 41 37 44N 15 10 E
Giaveno 38 45 3N 7 20 E
Gibara 121 21 9N 76 11W
Gibbon 116 40 49N 98 45W
Gibe → 87 7 20N 37 36 E
Gibellina 40 37 48N 13 0 E
Gibeon 92 25 7 S 17 45 E
Gibraléon 31 37 23N 6 58W
Gibraltar 31 36 7N 5 22W
Gibraltar, Str. of 31 35 55N 5 40W
Gibson Des. 96 24 0 S 126 0 E
Gibsons 108 49 24N 123 32W
Giddalur 70 15 20N 78 57 E
Giddings 117 30 11N 96 58W
Gidole 87 5 40N 37 25 E
Gien 19 47 40N 2 36 E
Giessen 24 50 34N 8 40 E
Gifatin, Geziret 86 27 10N 33 50 E
Gifhorn 24 52 29N 10 32 E
Gifu 74 35 30N 136 45 E
Gifu □ 74 35 40N 137 0 E
Gigant 57 46 28N 41 20 E
Giganta, Sa. de la 120 25 30N 111 30W
Gigen 43 43 40N 24 28 E
Gigha 14 55 42N 5 45W
Giglio 38 42 20N 10 52 E
Gignac 20 43 39N 3 32 E
Gigüela → 33 39 8N 3 44W
Gijón 30 43 32N 5 42W
Gil I. 108 53 12N 129 15W
Gila → 119 32 43N 114 33W
Gila Bend 119 33 0N 112 46W
Gila Bend Mts. 119 33 15N 113 0W
Gilan □ 64 37 0N 48 0 E
Gilău 46 46 45N 23 23 E
Gilbert → 97 16 35 S 141 15 E
Gilbert Is. 94 1 0N 176 0 E
Gilbert Plains 109 51 9N 100 28W
Gilbert River 98 18 9 S 142 52 E
Gilberton 98 19 16 S 143 35 E
Gilf el Kebîr, Hadabat el 86 23 50N 25 50 E
Gilford I. 108 50 40N 126 30W
Gilgandra 97 31 43 S 148 39 E
Gilgil 90 0 30 S 36 20 E
Gilgit 69 35 50N 74 15 E
Giljeva Planina 42 43 9N 20 0 E
Gillam 109 56 20N 94 40W
Gilleleje 49 56 8N 12 19 E
Gillette 116 44 20N 105 30W
Gilliat 98 20 40 S 141 28 E
Gillingham 13 51 23N 0 34 E
Gilmer 117 32 44N 94 55W
Gilmore 99 35 20 S 148 12 E
Gilmour 106 44 48N 77 37W
Gilo → 87 8 10N 33 15 E
Gilort → 46 44 38N 23 32 E
Gilroy 119 37 1N 121 37W
Gimbi 87 9 3N 35 42 E
Gimigliano 41 38 58N 16 32 E
Gimli 109 50 40N 97 0W
Gimo 48 60 11N 18 12 E
Gimone → 20 44 0N 1 6 E
Gimont 20 43 38N 0 52 E
Gimzo 62 31 56N 34 56 E
Gin → 70 6 5N 80 7 E
Gin Gin 99 25 0 S 151 58 E
Ginâh 86 25 21N 30 30 E
Gindie 98 23 44 S 148 8 E
Gineta, La 33 39 8N 2 1W
Gîngiova 46 43 54N 23 50 E
Ginir 87 7 6N 40 40 E
Ginosa 41 40 35N 16 45 E
Ginzo de Limia 30 42 3N 7 47W
Giohar 63 2 48N 45 30 E
Gióia del Colle 41 40 49N 16 55 E
Gióia, G. di 41 38 30N 15 50 E
Gióia Táuro 41 38 26N 15 53 E
Gioiosa Iónica 41 38 20N 16 19 E
Gióna, Óros 45 38 38N 22 14 E
Giong, Teluk 73 4 50N 118 20 E
Giovi, Passo dei 38 44 33N 8 57 E
Giovinazzo 41 41 10N 16 40 E
Gippsland 97 37 45 S 147 15 E
Gir Hills 68 21 0N 71 0 E
Girab 68 26 2N 70 38 E
Giraltovce 27 49 7N 21 32 E
Girard, Kans., U.S.A. 117 37 30N 94 50W
Girard, Ohio, U.S.A. 112 41 10N 80 42W
Girard, Pa., U.S.A. 112 42 1N 80 21W
Girardot 126 4 18N 74 48W
Girdle Ness 14 57 9N 2 2W
Giresun 64 40 55N 38 30 E
Girga 86 26 17N 31 55 E
Giridih 69 24 10N 86 21 E
Girifalco 41 38 49N 16 25 E
Girilambone 99 31 16 S 146 57 E
Giro 85 11 7N 4 42 E
Giromagny 19 47 44N 6 50 E
Gironde □ 20 44 45N 0 30W
Gironde → 20 45 32N 1 7W
Gironella 32 42 2N 1 53 E
Giru 98 19 30 S 147 5 E
Girvan 14 55 15N 4 50W
Gisborne 101 38 39 S 178 5 E
Gisenyi 90 1 41 S 29 15 E
Giske 47 62 30N 6 3 E
Gislaved 49 57 19N 13 32 E
Gisors 19 49 15N 1 47 E
Gitega (Kitega) 90 3 26 S 29 56 E
Giuba → 63 1 30N 42 35 E
Giugliano in Campania 41 40 55N 14 12 E
Giulianova 39 42 45N 13 58 E
Giurgeni 46 44 45N 27 48 E
Giurgiu 46 43 52N 25 57 E
Giv'at Brenner 62 31 52N 34 47 E
Giv'atayim 62 32 4N 34 49 E
Give 49 55 51N 9 13 E
Givet 19 50 8N 4 49 E
Givors 21 45 35N 4 45 E
Givry 19 46 41N 4 46 E
Giyon 87 8 33N 38 1 E
Giza = El Gîza 86 30 1N 31 11 E
Gizhiga 59 62 3N 160 30 E
Gizhiginskaya, Guba 59 61 0N 158 0 E
Giżycko 28 54 2N 21 48 E
Gizzeria 41 38 57N 16 10 E
Gjegjan 44 41 58N 20 3 E
Gjerstad 47 58 54N 9 0 E
Gjirokastra 44 40 7N 20 10 E
Gjoa Haven 104 68 20N 96 8W
Gjøl 49 57 4N 9 42 E
Gjøvik 47 60 47N 10 43 E
Glace Bay 107 46 11N 59 58W
Glacier B. 108 58 30N 136 10W
Glacier Nat. Park, Can. 108 51 15N 117 30W
Glacier Nat. Park, U.S.A. 118 48 35N 113 40W
Glacier Park 118 48 30N 113 18W
Glacier Peak Mt. 118 48 7N 121 7W
Gladewater 117 32 30N 94 58W
Gladstone, Austral. 99 33 15 S 138 22 E
Gladstone, Can. 109 50 13N 98 57W
Gladstone, U.S.A. 114 45 52N 87 1W
Gladwin 114 43 59N 84 29W
Gladys L. 108 59 50N 133 0W
Glafsfjorden 48 59 30N 12 37 E
Głagów Małapolski 27 50 10N 21 56 E
Gláma 50 65 48N 23 0W
Glåma → 47 59 12N 10 57 E
Glamoč 39 44 3N 16 51 E
Glan 49 58 37N 16 0 E
Glarus 25 47 3N 9 4 E
Glasco, Kans., U.S.A. 116 39 25N 97 50W
Glasco, N.Y., U.S.A. 113 42 3N 73 57W
Glasgow, U.K. 14 55 52N 4 14W
Glasgow, Ky., U.S.A. 114 37 2N 85 55W
Glasgow, Mont., U.S.A. 118 48 12N 106 35W
Glastonbury, U.K. 13 51 9N 2 42W
Glastonbury, U.S.A. 113 41 42N 72 27W
Glauchau 24 50 50N 12 33 E
Glazov 55 58 9N 52 40 E
Gleisdorf 26 47 6N 15 44 E
Gleiwitz = Gliwice 28 50 22N 18 41 E
Glen 113 44 7N 71 10W
Glen Affric 14 57 15N 5 0W
Glen Canyon Dam 119 37 0N 111 25W
Glen Canyon Nat. Recreation Area 119 37 30N 111 0W
Glen Coe 12 56 40N 5 0W
Glen Cove 113 40 51N 73 37W
Glen Garry 14 57 3N 5 7W
Glen Innes 97 29 44 S 151 44 E
Glen Lyon 113 41 10N 76 7W
Glen Mor 14 57 12N 4 37 E
Glen Moriston 14 57 10N 4 58W
Glen Orchy 14 56 27N 4 52W
Glen Spean 14 56 53N 4 40W
Glen Ullin 116 46 48N 101 46W
Glénans, Îles. de 18 47 42N 4 0W
Glenburnie 100 37 51 S 140 50 E
Glencoe, Can. 112 42 45N 81 43W
Glencoe, S. Afr. 93 28 11 S 30 11 E
Glencoe, U.S.A. 116 44 45N 94 10W
Glendale, Ariz., U.S.A. 119 33 40N 112 8W
Glendale, Calif., U.S.A. 119 34 7N 118 18W
Glendale, Oreg., U.S.A. 118 42 44N 123 29W
Glendale, Zimb. 91 17 22 S 31 5 E
Glendive 116 47 7N 104 40W
Glendo 116 42 30N 105 0W
Glenelg 99 34 58 S 138 31 E
Glenelg → 99 38 4 S 140 59 E
Glengarriff 15 51 45N 9 33W
Glengyle 98 24 48 S 139 37 E
Glenmora 117 31 1N 92 34W
Glenmorgan 99 27 14 S 149 42 E
Glenns Ferry 118 43 0N 115 15W
Glenorchy 99 42 49 S 147 18 E
Glenore 98 17 50 S 141 12 E
Glenormiston 98 22 55 S 138 50 E
Glenreagh 99 30 2 S 153 1 E
Glenrock 118 42 53N 105 55W
Glenrothes 14 56 12N 3 11W
Glens Falls 114 43 20N 73 40W
Glenties 15 54 48N 8 18W
Glenville 114 38 56N 80 50W
Glenwood, Alta., Can. 108 49 21N 113 31W
Glenwood, Newf., Can. 107 49 0N 54 58W
Glenwood, Ark., U.S.A. 117 34 20N 93 30W
Glenwood, Hawaii, U.S.A. 110 19 29N 155 10W
Glenwood, Iowa, U.S.A. 116 41 7N 95 41W
Glenwood, Minn., U.S.A. 116 45 38N 95 21W
Glenwood Sprs. 118 39 39N 107 21W
Glina 39 45 20N 16 6 E
Glinojeck 28 52 49N 20 21 E
Glittertind 47 61 40N 8 32 E
Gliwice 28 50 22N 18 41 E
Globe 119 33 25N 110 53W
Glodeanu Siliştea 46 44 50N 26 48 E
Glödnitz 26 46 53N 14 7 E
Glodyany 46 47 45N 27 31 E
Gloggnitz 26 47 41N 15 56 E
Głogów 28 51 37N 16 5 E
Glogowek 28 50 21N 17 53 E
Glorieuses, Îles 93 11 30 S 47 20 E
Glossop 12 53 27N 1 56W
Gloucester, Austral. 99 32 0 S 151 59 E
Gloucester, U.K. 13 51 52N 2 15W
Gloucester, U.S.A. 113 42 38N 70 39W
Gloucester, C. 98 5 26 S 148 21 E
Gloucester I. 98 20 0 S 148 30 E
Gloucestershire □ 13 51 44N 2 10W
Gloversville 114 43 5N 74 18W
Glovertown 107 48 40N 54 03W
Główno 28 51 59N 19 42 E
Głubczyce 27 50 13N 17 52 E
Glubokiy 57 48 35N 40 25 E
Glubokoye 54 55 10N 27 45 E
Glùbovo 43 42 8N 25 55 E
Głuchołazy 28 50 19N 17 24 E
Glücksburg 24 54 48N 9 34 E
Glückstadt 24 53 46N 9 28 E
Glukhov 54 51 40N 33 58 E
Glussk 54 52 53N 28 41 E
Glyngøre 49 56 46N 8 52 E
Gmünd, Kärnten, Austria 26 46 54N 13 31 E
Gmünd, Niederösterreich, Austria 26 48 45N 15 0 E
Gmunden 26 47 55N 13 48 E
Gnarp 48 62 3N 17 16 E
Gnesta 48 59 3N 17 17 E
Gniew 28 53 50N 18 50 E
Gniewkowo 28 52 54N 18 25 E
Gniezno 28 52 30N 17 35 E
Gnjilane 42 42 28N 21 29 E
Gnoien 24 53 58N 12 41 E
Gnosjö 49 57 22N 13 43 E
Gnowangerup 96 33 58 S 117 59 E
Go Cong 71 10 22N 106 40 E
Goa 70 15 33N 73 59 E
Goa □ 70 15 33N 73 59 E
Goageb 92 26 49 S 17 15 E
Goalen Hd. 99 36 33 S 150 4 E
Goalpara 69 26 10N 90 40 E
Goalundo Ghat 69 23 50N 89 47 E
Goaso 84 6 48N 2 30W
Goat Fell 14 55 37N 5 11W
Goba 87 7 1N 39 59 E
Gobabis 92 22 30 S 19 0 E
Gobi 75 44 0N 111 0 E
Gobichettipalayam 70 11 31N 77 21 E
Gobo 87 5 40N 31 10 E
Goch 24 51 40N 6 9 E
Gochas 92 24 59 S 18 55 E
Godavari → 70 16 25N 82 18 E
Godavari Point 70 17 0N 82 20 E
Godbout 107 49 20N 67 38W
Godda 69 24 50N 87 13 E
Goddua 83 26 26N 14 19 E
Godech 42 43 1N 23 4 E
Godegård 49 58 43N 15 8 E
Goderich 106 43 45N 81 41W
Goderville 18 49 38N 0 22 E
Godhavn 4 69 15N 53 38W
Godhra 68 22 49N 73 40 E
Gödöllö 27 47 38N 19 25 E
Godoy Cruz 124 32 56 S 68 52W
Gods → 109 56 22N 92 51W
Gods L. 109 54 40N 94 15W
Godthåb 4 64 10N 51 35W
Godwin Austen (K2) 69 36 0N 77 0 E
Goeie Hoop, Kaap die 92 34 24 S 18 30 E
Goéland, L. au 106 49 50N 76 48W
Goeree 16 51 50N 4 0 E
Goes 16 51 30N 3 55 E
Gogama 106 47 35N 81 43W
Gogango 98 23 40 S 150 2 E
Gogebic, L. 116 46 20N 89 34W
Gogha 68 21 40N 72 20 E
Gogolin 28 50 30N 18 0 E
Gogra = Ghaghara → 67 26 0N 84 20 E
Gogriâl 87 8 30N 28 8 E
Goiânia 127 16 43 S 49 20W
Goiás 127 15 55 S 50 10W
Goiás □ 127 12 10 S 48 0W
Góis 30 40 10N 8 6W
Goisern 26 47 38N 13 38 E
Gojam □ 87 10 55N 36 30 E
Gojeb, Wabi → 87 7 12N 36 40 E
Gojra 68 31 10N 72 40 E
Gokak 70 16 11N 74 52 E
Gokarannath 69 27 57N 80 39 E
Gokarn 70 14 33N 74 17 E
Gökçeada 44 40 10N 25 50 E
Gokteik 67 22 26N 97 0 E
Gokurt 68 29 40N 67 26 E
Gola 69 28 3N 80 32 E
Golakganj 69 26 8N 89 52 E
Golaya Pristen 56 46 29N 32 32 E
Golchikha 4 71 45N 83 30 E
Golconda 118 40 58N 117 32W
Gold Beach 118 42 25N 124 25W
Gold Coast, Austral. 99 28 0 S 153 25 E
Gold Coast, W. Afr. 85 4 0N 1 40W
Gold Hill 118 42 28N 123 2W
Gold River 108 49 46N 126 3 E
Gołdap 28 54 19N 22 18 E
Goldberg 24 53 34N 12 6 E
Golden, Can. 108 51 20N 117 59W
Golden, U.S.A. 116 39 42N 105 15W
Golden Bay 101 40 40 S 172 50 E
Golden Gate 118 37 54N 122 30W
Golden Hinde 108 49 40N 125 44W
Golden Lake 112 45 34N 77 21W
Golden Prairie 109 50 13N 109 37W
Golden Rock 70 10 45N 78 48 E
Golden Vale 15 52 33N 8 17W
Goldendale 118 45 53N 120 48W
Goldfield 119 37 45N 117 13W
Goldfields 109 59 28N 108 29W
Goldsand L. 109 57 2N 101 8W
Goldsboro 115 35 24N 77 59W
Goldsmith 117 32 0N 102 40W
Goldthwaite 117 31 25N 98 32W
Golegã 31 39 24N 8 29W
Golęniów 28 53 35N 14 50 E
Golfito 121 8 41N 83 5W
Golfo Aranci 40 41 0N 9 35 E
Goliad 117 28 40N 97 22W
Golija, Crna Gora, Yugo. 42 43 5N 18 45 E
Golija, Srbija, Yugo. 42 43 22N 20 15 E
Golina 28 52 15N 18 4 E
Göllersdorf 27 48 29N 16 7 E
Golo → 21 42 31N 9 32 E
Golovanevsk 56 48 25N 30 30 E
Golspie 14 57 58N 3 58W
Golub Dobrzyń 28 53 7N 19 2 E
Golubac 42 44 38N 21 38 E
Golyam Perelik 43 41 36N 24 33 E
Golyama Kamchiya → 43 43 10N 27 55 E
Goma, Rwanda 90 2 11 S 29 18 E
Goma, Zaïre 90 1 37 S 29 10 E
Gomare 92 19 25 S 22 8 E
Gomati → 69 25 32N 83 11 E
Gombari 90 2 45N 29 3 E
Gombe 85 10 19N 11 2 E
Gombe → 90 4 38 S 31 40 E
Gombi 85 10 12N 12 30 E
Gomel 54 52 28N 31 0 E
Gomera 80 28 7N 17 14W
Gómez Palacio 120 25 40N 104 0W
Gommern 24 52 5N 11 47 E
Gomogomo 73 6 39 S 134 43 E
Gomotartsi 42 44 6N 22 57 E
Gomphoi 44 39 31N 21 27 E
Gonābād 65 34 15N 58 45 E
Gonaïves 121 19 20N 72 42W
Gonâve, G. de la 121 19 29N 72 42W
Gonbab-e Kāvūs 65 37 20N 55 25 E
Gönc 27 48 28N 21 14 E
Gonda 69 27 9N 81 58 E
Gondal 68 21 58N 70 52 E
Gonder 87 12 39N 37 30 E
Gondia 69 21 23N 80 10 E
Gondola 91 19 10 S 33 37 E
Gondomar, Port. 30 41 10N 8 35W
Gondomar, Spain 30 42 7N 8 45W
Gondrecourt-le-Château 19 48 26N 5 30 E
Gonghe 75 36 18N 100 32 E
Gongola □ 85 8 0N 12 0 E
Gongola → 85 9 30N 12 4 E
Goniadz 28 53 30N 22 44 E
Goniri 85 11 30N 12 15 E
Gonnesa 40 39 17N 8 27 E
Gónnos 44 39 52N 22 29 E
Gonnosfanadiga 40 39 30N 8 39 E
Gonzales, Calif., U.S.A. 119 36 35N 121 30W
Gonzales, Tex., U.S.A. 117 29 30N 97 30W
González Chaves 124 38 02 S 60 05W
Good Hope, C. of = Goeie Hoop, K. die 92 34 24 S 18 30 E
Goodenough I. 98 9 20 S 150 15 E
Gooderham 106 44 54N 78 21W
Goodeve 109 51 4N 103 10W
Gooding 118 43 0N 114 44W
Goodland 116 39 22N 101 44W
Goodnight 117 35 4N 101 13W
Goodooga 99 29 3 S 147 28 E
Goodsoil 109 54 24N 109 13W
Goodsprings 119 35 51N 115 30W
Goole 12 53 42N 0 52W
Goolgowi 99 33 58 S 145 41 E
Goombalie 99 29 59 S 145 26 E
Goonda 91 19 48 S 33 57 E
Goondiwindi 97 28 30 S 150 21 E
Goor 16 52 13N 6 33 E
Gooray 99 28 25 S 150 2 E
Goose → 107 53 20N 60 35W
Goose Bay 107 53 15N 60 20W
Goose L. 118 42 0N 120 30W
Gooty 70 15 7N 77 41 E
Gopalganj, Bangla. 69 23 1N 89 50 E
Gopalganj, India 69 26 28N 84 30 E
Göppingen 25 48 42N 9 40 E
Gor 33 37 23N 2 58W
Góra, Leszno, Poland 28 51 40N 16 31 E
Góra, Płock, Poland 28 52 39N 20 6 E
Góra Kalwaria 28 51 59N 21 14 E
Gorakhpur 69 26 47N 83 23 E
Goražde 42 43 38N 18 58 E
Gorbatov 55 56 12N 43 2 E
Gorbea, Peña 32 43 1N 2 50W
Gorda, Punta 121 14 20N 83 10W
Gordon, Austral. 99 32 7 S 138 20 E
Gordon, U.S.A. 116 42 49N 102 12W
Gordon → 99 42 27 S 145 30 E
Gordon Downs 96 18 48 S 128 33 E
Gordon L., Alta., Can. 109 56 30N 110 25W
Gordon L., N.W.T., Can. 108 63 5N 113 11W
Gordonia 92 28 13 S 21 10 E
Gordonvale 98 17 5 S 145 50 E
Gore 99 28 17 S 151 30 E
Goré 81 7 59N 16 31 E
Gore, Ethiopia 87 8 12N 35 32 E
Gore, N.Z. 101 46 5 S 168 58 E
Gore Bay 106 45 57N 82 28W
Gorey 15 52 41N 6 18W
Gorgān 65 36 55N 54 30 E
Gorgona 38 43 27N 9 52 E
Gorgona, I. 126 3 0N 78 10W
Gorgora 87 12 15N 37 17 E
Gorham 113 44 23N 71 10W
Gori 57 42 0N 44 7 E
Gorinchem 16 51 50N 4 59 E
Goritsy 55 57 4N 36 43 E
Gorízia 39 45 56N 13 37 E
Górka 28 51 39N 16 58 E
Gorki 54 54 17N 30 59 E

Gorki = Gorkiy 55 56 20N 44 0 E
Gorkiy 55 56 20N 44 0 E
Gorkovskoye Vdkhr. 55 57 2N 43 4 E
Gørlev 49 55 30N 11 15 E
Gorlice 27 49 35N 21 11 E
Görlitz 24 51 10N 14 59 E
Gorlovka 56 48 19N 38 5 E
Gorman 117 32 15N 98 43W
Gorna Oryakhovitsa 43 43 7N 25 40 E
Gornja Radgona 39 46 40N 16 2 E
Gornja Tuzla 42 44 35N 18 46 E
Gornji Grad 39 46 20N 14 52 E
Gornji Milanovac 42 44 00N 20 29 E
Gornji Vakuf 42 43 57N 17 34 E
Gorno Ablanovo 43 43 37N 25 43 E
Gorno-Altaysk 58 51 50N 86 5 E
Gorno Slinkino 58 60 5N 70 0 E
Gornyatski 52 67 32N 64 3 E
Gornyy 55 51 50N 48 30 E
Gorodenka 56 48 41N 25 29 E
Gorodets 55 56 38N 43 28 E
Gorodische 55 53 13N 45 40 E
Gorodishche 56 49 17N 31 27 E
Gorodnitsa 54 50 46N 27 19 E
Gorodnya 54 51 55N 31 33 E
Gorodok, Byelorussia, U.S.S.R. 54 55 30N 30 3 E
Gorodok, Ukraine, U.S.S.R. 54 49 46N 23 32 E
Goroka 98 6 7 S 145 25 E
Gorokhov 54 50 30N 24 45 E
Gorokhovets 55 56 13N 42 39 E
Gorom Gorom 85 14 26N 0 14W
Goromonzi 91 17 52 S 31 22 E
Gorong, Kepulauan 73 4 5 S 131 25 E
Gorongosa, Sa. da 91 18 27 S 34 2 E
Gorongose → 93 20 30 S 34 40 E
Gorontalo 73 0 35N 123 5 E
Goronyo 85 13 29N 5 39 E
Górowo Iławeckie 28 54 17N 20 30 E
Gorron 18 48 25N 0 50W
Gort 15 53 4N 8 50W
Gorumahisani 69 22 20N 86 24 E
Gorzkowice 28 51 13N 19 36 E
Gorzno 28 53 12N 19 38 E
Gorzów Ślaski 28 51 3N 18 22 E
Gorzów Wielkopolski 28 52 43N 15 15 E
Gorzów Wielkopolski □ 28 52 45N 15 30 E
Gosford 99 33 23 S 151 18 E
Goshen, S. Afr. 92 25 50 S 25 0 E
Goshen, Ind., U.S.A. 114 41 36N 85 46W
Goshen, N.Y., U.S.A. 113 41 23N 74 21W
Goslar 24 51 55N 10 23 E
Gospič 39 44 35N 15 23 E
Gosport 13 50 48N 1 8W
Gostivar 42 41 48N 20 57 E
Gostyń 28 51 50N 17 3 E
Gostynin 28 52 26N 19 29 E
Göta älv → 49 57 42N 11 54 E
Göteborg 49 57 43N 11 59 E
Götene 49 58 32N 13 30 E
Gotha 24 50 56N 10 42 E
Gothenburg 116 40 58N 100 8W
Gotland 49 57 30N 18 33 E
Gotō-Rettō 74 32 55N 129 5 E
Gotse Delchev (Nevrokop) 43 41 43N 23 46 E
Göttingen 24 51 31N 9 55 E
Gottwaldov (Zlin) 27 49 14N 17 40 E
Goubangzi 76 41 20N 121 52 E
Gouda 16 52 1N 4 42 E
Goudiry 84 14 15N 12 45W
Gough I. 7 40 10 S 9 45W
Gouin Rés. 106 48 35N 74 40W
Gouitafla 84 7 30N 5 53W
Goula Touila 82 21 50N 1 57W
Goulburn 97 34 44 S 149 44 E
Goulburn → 100 36 6 S 144 55 E
Goulburn Is. 96 11 40 S 133 20 E
Goulia 84 10 1N 7 11W
Goulimine 82 28 56N 10 0W
Goulmina 82 31 41N 4 57W
Gouménissa 44 40 56N 22 37 E
Gounou-Gaya 81 9 38N 15 31 E
Goúra 45 37 56N 22 20 E
Gourara 82 29 0N 0 30 E
Gouraya 82 36 31N 1 56 E
Gourdon 20 44 44N 1 23 E
Gouré 85 14 0N 10 10 E
Gouri 81 19 36N 19 36 E
Gourits → 92 34 21 S 21 52 E
Gourma Rharous 85 16 55N 1 50W
Gournay-en-Bray 19 49 29N 1 44 E
Gourock Ra. 99 36 0 S 149 25 E
Goursi 84 12 42N 2 37W
Gouverneur 113 44 18N 75 30W
Gouzon 20 46 12N 2 14 E
Govan 109 51 20N 105 0W
Gove 97 12 25 S 136 55 E
Governador Valadares 127 18 15 S 41 57W
Gowan Ra. 98 25 0 S 145 0 E
Gowanda 114 42 29N 78 58W
Gowd-e Zirreh 65 29 45N 62 0 E
Gower, The 13 51 35N 4 10W
Gowna, L. 15 53 52N 7 35W
Gowrie, Carse of 14 56 30N 3 10W
Goya 124 29 10 S 59 10W
Goyllarisquisga 126 10 31 S 76 24W
Goz Beîda 81 12 10N 21 20 E
Goz Regeb 87 16 3N 35 33 E
Gozdnica 28 51 28N 15 4 E
Gozo (Ghawdex) 36 36 0N 14 13 E
Graaff-Reinet 92 32 13 S 24 32 E
Grabow 24 53 17N 11 31 E
Grabów 28 51 31N 18 7 E
Gračac 39 44 18N 15 57 E
Gračanica 42 44 43N 18 18 E
Graçay 19 47 10N 1 50 E
Grace 118 42 38N 111 46W
Graceville 116 45 36N 96 23W
Gracias a Dios, C. 121 15 0N 83 10W
Gradačac 42 44 52N 18 26 E
Gradeška Planina 42 41 30N 22 15 E
Gradets 43 42 46N 26 30 E
Grado, Italy 39 45 40N 13 20 E
Grado, Spain 30 43 23N 6 4W
Gradule 99 28 32 S 149 15 E
Grady 117 34 52N 103 15W
Graeca, Lacul 46 44 5N 26 10 E
Graénalon, L. 50 64 10N 17 20W
Grafenau 25 48 51N 13 24 E
Gräfenberg 25 49 39N 11 15 E
Grafton, Austral. 97 29 38 S 152 58 E
Grafton, U.S.A. 116 48 30N 97 25W
Grafton, C. 97 16 51 S 146 0 E
Gragnano 41 40 42N 14 30 E
Graham, Can. 106 49 20N 90 30W
Graham, N.C., U.S.A. 115 36 5N 79 22W
Graham, Tex., U.S.A. 117 33 7N 98 38W
Graham → 108 56 31N 122 17W
Graham Bell, Os. 58 80 5N 70 0 E
Graham I. 108 53 40N 132 30W
Graham Land 5 65 0 S 64 0W
Graham Mt. 119 32 46N 109 58W
Grahamdale 109 51 23N 98 30W
Grahamstown 92 33 19 S 26 31 E
Grahovo 42 42 40N 18 40 E
Graïba 83 34 30N 10 13 E
Graie, Alpi 38 45 30N 7 10 E
Grain Coast 84 4 20N 10 0W
Grajaú 127 5 50 S 46 4W
Grajaú → 127 3 41 S 44 48W
Grajewo 28 53 39N 22 30 E
Gral. Martin Miguel de Gäemes 124 24 50 S 65 0W
Gramada 42 43 49N 22 39 E
Gramat 20 44 48N 1 43 E
Grammichele 41 37 12N 14 37 E
Grámmos, Óros 44 40 18N 20 47 E
Grampian □ 14 57 0N 3 0W
Grampian Mts. 14 56 50N 4 0W
Grampians, Mts. 99 37 0 S 142 20 E
Gran Canaria 80 27 55N 15 35W
Gran Chaco 124 25 0 S 61 0W
Gran Paradiso 38 45 33N 7 17 E
Gran Sasso d'Italia 39 42 25N 13 30 E
Granada, Nic. 121 11 58N 86 0W
Granada, Spain 33 37 10N 3 35W
Granada, U.S.A. 117 38 5N 102 20W
Granada □ 31 37 18N 3 0W
Granard 15 53 47N 7 30W
Granbury 117 32 28N 97 48W
Granby 106 45 25N 72 45W
Grand →, Mo., U.S.A. 116 39 23N 93 6W
Grand →, Mo., U.S.A. 116 39 23N 93 6W
Grand →, S.D., U.S.A. 116 45 40N 100 32W
Grand Bahama 121 26 40N 78 30W
Grand Bank 107 47 6N 55 48W
Grand Bassam 84 5 10N 3 49W
Grand Béréby 84 4 38N 6 55W
Grand-Bourge 121 15 53N 61 19W
Grand Canyon 119 36 3N 112 9W
Grand Canyon National Park 119 36 15N 112 20W
Grand Cayman 121 19 20N 81 20W
Grand Cess 84 4 40N 8 12W
Grand-Combe, La 21 44 13N 4 2 E
Grand Coulee 118 47 48N 119 1W
Grand Coulee Dam 118 48 0N 118 50W
Grand Erg Occidental 82 30 20N 1 0 E
Grand Erg Oriental 83 30 0N 6 30 E
Grand Falls 107 48 56N 55 40W
Grand Forks, Can. 108 49 0N 118 30W
Grand Forks, U.S.A. 116 48 0N 97 3W
Grand-Fougeray 18 47 44N 1 43W
Grand Haven 114 43 3N 86 13W
Grand I. 106 46 30N 86 40W
Grand Island 116 40 59N 98 25W
Grand Isle 117 29 15N 89 58W
Grand Junction 119 39 0N 108 30W
Grand L., N.B., Can. 107 45 57N 66 7W
Grand L., Newf., Can. 107 53 40N 60 30W
Grand L., Newf., Can. 107 49 0N 57 30W
Grand L., U.S.A. 117 29 55N 92 45W
Grand Lac Victoria 106 47 35N 77 35W
Grand Lahou 84 5 10N 5 0W
Grand Lake 118 40 20N 105 54W
Grand-Lieu, Lac de 18 47 6N 1 40W
Grand-Luce, Le 18 47 52N 0 28 E
Grand Manan I. 107 44 45N 66 52W
Grand Marais, Can. 116 47 45N 90 25W
Grand Marais, U.S.A. 114 46 39N 85 59W
Grand Mère 106 46 36N 72 40W
Grand Popo 85 6 15N 1 57 E
Grand Portage 106 47 58N 89 41W
Grand-Pressigny, Le 18 46 55N 0 48 E
Grand Rapids, Can. 109 53 12N 99 19W
Grand Rapids, Mich., U.S.A. 114 42 57N 86 40W
Grand Rapids, Minn., U.S.A. 116 47 15N 93 29W
Grand St.-Bernard, Col. du 25 45 53N 7 11 E
Grand Teton 118 43 54N 111 50W
Grand Valley 118 39 30N 108 2W
Grand View 109 51 10N 100 42W
Grandas de Salime 30 43 13N 6 53W
Grande →, Jujuy, Argent. 124 24 20 S 65 2W
Grande →, Mendoza, Argent. 124 36 52 S 69 45W
Grande →, Boliv. 126 15 51 S 64 39W
Grande →, Bahia, Brazil 127 11 30 S 44 30W
Grande →, Minas Gerais, Brazil 127 20 6 S 51 4W
Grande →, Spain 33 39 6N 0 48W
Grande →, U.S.A. 117 25 57N 97 9W
Grande, B. 128 50 30 S 68 20W
Grande Baie 107 48 19N 70 52W
Grande Baleine → 106 55 20N 77 50W
Grande Cache 108 53 53N 119 8W
Grande, Coxilha 125 28 18 S 51 30W
Grande de Santiago → 120 21 20N 105 50W
Grande-Entrée 107 47 30N 61 40W
Grande, La 118 45 15N 118 0W
Grande-Motte, La 21 43 23N 4 3 E
Grande Prairie 108 55 10N 118 50W
Grande-Rivière 107 48 26N 64 30W
Grande-Saulde → 19 47 22N 1 55 E
Grande-Vallée 107 49 14N 65 8W
Grandes-Bergeronnes 107 48 16N 69 35W
Grandfalls 117 31 21N 102 51W
Grandoe Mines 108 56 29N 129 54W
Grândola 31 38 12N 8 35W
Grandpré 19 49 20N 4 50 E
Grandview 118 46 13N 119 58W
Grandvilliers 19 49 40N 1 57 E
Graneros 124 34 5 S 70 45W
Grange, La, Ga., U.S.A. 115 33 4N 85 0W
Grange, La, Ky., U.S.A. 114 38 20N 85 20W
Grange, La, Tex., U.S.A. 117 29 54N 96 52W
Grangemouth 14 56 1N 3 43W
Granger, U.S.A. 118 46 25N 120 5W
Granger, Wyo., U.S.A. 118 41 35N 109 58W
Grängesberg 48 60 6N 15 1 E
Grangeville 118 45 57N 116 4W
Granite City 116 38 45N 90 3W
Granite Falls 116 44 45N 95 35W
Granite Pk. 118 45 8N 109 52W
Granity 101 41 39 S 171 51 E
Granja 127 3 7 S 40 50W
Granja de Moreruela 30 41 48N 5 44W
Granja de Torrehermosa 31 38 19N 5 35W
Gränna 49 58 1N 14 28 E
Granollers 32 41 39N 2 18 E
Gransee 24 53 0N 13 10 E
Grant 116 40 53N 101 42W
Grant City 116 40 30N 94 25W
Grant, Mt. 118 38 34N 118 48W
Grant, Pt. 100 38 32 S 145 6 E
Grant Range Mts. 119 38 30N 115 30W
Grantham 12 52 55N 0 39W
Grantown-on-Spey 14 57 19N 3 36W
Grants 119 35 14N 107 51W
Grants Pass 118 42 30N 123 22W
Grantsburg 116 45 46N 92 44W
Grantsville 118 40 35N 112 32W
Granville, France 18 48 50N 1 35W
Granville, N.D., U.S.A. 116 48 18N 100 48W
Granville, N.Y., U.S.A. 114 43 24N 73 16W
Granville L. 109 56 18N 100 30W
Grao de Gandía 33 39 0N 0 7W
Grapeland 117 31 30N 95 31W
Gras, L. de 104 64 30N 110 30W
Graskop 93 24 56 S 30 49 E
Gräsö 48 60 28N 18 35 E
Grass → 109 56 3N 96 33W
Grass Range 118 47 0N 109 0W
Grass River Prov. Park 109 54 40N 100 50W
Grass Valley, Calif., U.S.A. 118 39 18N 121 0W
Grass Valley, Oreg., U.S.A. 118 45 22N 120 48W
Grassano 41 40 38N 16 17 E
Grasse 21 43 38N 6 56 E
Graubünden (Grisons) □ 25 46 45N 9 30 E
Graulhet 20 43 45N 1 58 E
Graus 32 42 11N 0 20 E
Grave, Pte. de 20 45 34N 1 4W
Gravelbourg 109 49 50N 106 35W
Gravelines 19 51 0N 2 10 E
's-Gravenhage 16 52 7N 4 17 E
Gravenhurst 112 44 52N 79 20W
Gravesend, Austral. 99 29 35 S 150 20 E
Gravesend, U.K. 13 51 25N 0 22 E
Gravina di Púglia 41 40 48N 16 25 E
Gravois, Pointe-à- 121 16 15N 73 56W
Gravone → 21 41 58N 8 45 E
Gray 19 47 27N 5 35 E
Grayling 114 44 40N 84 42W
Grayling → 108 59 21N 125 0W
Grays Harbor 118 46 55N 124 8W
Grays L. 118 43 8N 111 30W
Grayson 109 50 45N 102 40W
Graz 26 47 4N 15 27 E
Grazalema 31 36 46N 5 23W
Grdelica 42 42 55N 22 3 E
Greasy L. 108 62 55N 122 12W
Great Abaco I. 121 26 25N 77 10W
Great Australia Basin 97 26 0 S 140 0 E
Great Australian Bight 96 33 30 S 130 0 E
Great Bahama Bank 121 23 15N 78 0W
Great Barrier I. 101 36 11 S 175 25 E
Great Barrier Reef 97 18 0 S 146 50 E
Great Barrington 113 42 11N 73 22W
Great Basin 118 40 0N 116 30W
Great Bear → 104 65 0N 124 0W
Great Bear L. 104 65 30N 120 0W
Great Bena 113 41 57N 75 45W
Great Bend 116 38 25N 98 55W
Great Blasket I. 15 52 5N 10 30W
Great Britain 8 54 0N 2 15W
Great Bushman Land 92 29 20 S 19 20 E
Great Central 108 49 20N 125 10W
Great Divide, The 100 35 0 S 149 17 E
Great Dividing Ra. 97 23 0 S 146 0 E
Great Exuma I. 121 23 30N 75 50W
Great Falls, Can. 109 50 27N 96 1W
Great Falls, U.S.A. 118 47 27N 111 12W
Great Fish →, C. Prov., S. Afr. 92 31 30 S 20 16 E
Great Fish →, C. Prov., S. Afr. 92 33 28 S 27 5 E
Great Guana Cay 121 24 0N 76 20W
Great Harbour Deep 107 50 25N 56 32W
Great I. 109 58 53N 96 35W
Great Inagua I. 121 21 0N 73 20W
Great Indian Desert = Thar Desert 68 28 0N 72 0 E
Great Lake 97 41 50 S 146 40 E
Great Orme's Head 12 53 20N 3 52W
Great Ouse → 12 52 47N 0 22 E
Great Palm I. 98 18 45 S 146 40 E
Great Plains 102 47 0N 105 0W
Great Ruaha → 90 7 56 S 37 52 E
Great Salt Lake 102 41 0N 112 30W
Great Salt Lake Desert 118 40 20N 113 50W
Great Salt Plains Res. 117 36 40N 98 15W
Great Sandy Desert 96 21 0 S 124 0 E
Great Scarcies → 84 9 0N 13 0W
Great Slave L. 108 61 23N 115 38W
Great Smoky Mt. Nat. Park 115 35 39N 83 30W
Great Stour → 13 51 15N 1 20 E
Great Victoria Des. 96 29 30 S 126 30 E
Great Wall 76 38 30N 109 30 E
Great Whernside 12 54 9N 1 59W
Great Winterhoek 92 33 07 S 19 10 E
Great Yarmouth 12 52 40N 1 45 E
Greater Antilles 121 17 40N 74 0W
Greater London □ 13 51 30N 0 5W
Greater Manchester □ 12 53 30N 2 15W
Greater Sunda Is. 72 7 0 S 112 0 E
Grebbestad 49 58 42N 11 15 E
Grebenka 54 50 9N 32 22 E
Greco, Mte. 40 41 48N 14 0 E
Gredos, Sierra de 30 40 20N 5 0W
Greece ■ 44 40 0N 23 0 E
Greeley, Colo., U.S.A. 116 40 30N 104 40W
Greeley, Nebr., U.S.A. 116 41 36N 98 32W
Green →, Ky., U.S.A. 114 37 54N 87 30W
Green →, Utah, U.S.A. 119 38 11N 109 53W
Green B. 114 45 0N 87 30W
Green Bay 114 44 30N 88 0W
Green C. 99 37 13 S 150 1 E
Green Cove Springs 115 29 59N 81 40W
Green Is. 98 4 35 S 154 10 E
Green Island 101 45 55 S 170 26 E
Green River 119 38 59N 110 10W
Greenbush, Mich., U.S.A. 112 44 35N 83 19W
Greenbush, Minn., U.S.A. 116 48 46N 96 10W
Greencastle 114 39 40N 86 48W
Greene 113 42 20N 75 45W
Greenfield, Ind., U.S.A. 114 39 47N 85 51W
Greenfield, Iowa, U.S.A. 116 41 18N 94 28W
Greenfield, Mass., U.S.A. 114 42 38N 72 38W
Greenfield, Miss., U.S.A. 117 37 28N 93 50W
Greenfield Park 113 45 29N 73 29W
Greenland □ 4 66 0N 45 0W
Greenland Sea 4 73 0N 10 0W
Greenock 14 55 57N 4 46W
Greenore 15 54 2N 6 8W
Greenore Pt. 15 52 15N 6 20W
Greenport 113 41 5N 72 23W
Greensboro, Ga., U.S.A. 115 33 34N 83 12W
Greensboro, N.C., U.S.A. 115 36 7N 79 46W
Greensburg, Ind., U.S.A. 114 39 20N 85 30W
Greensburg, Kans., U.S.A. 117 37 38N 99 20W
Greensburg, Pa., U.S.A. 114 40 18N 79 31W
Greenville, Liberia 84 5 1N 9 6W
Greenville, Ala., U.S.A. 115 31 50N 86 37W
Greenville, Calif., U.S.A. 118 40 8N 121 0W
Greenville, Ill., U.S.A. 116 38 53N 89 22W
Greenville, Me., U.S.A. 107 45 30N 69 32W
Greenville, Mich., U.S.A. 114 43 12N 85 14W
Greenville, Miss., U.S.A. 117 33 25N 91 0W
Greenville, N.C., U.S.A. 115 35 37N 77 26W
Greenville, Ohio, U.S.A. 114 40 5N 84 38W
Greenville, Pa., U.S.A. 114 41 23N 80 22W
Greenville, S.C., U.S.A. 115 34 54N 82 24W
Greenville, Tenn., U.S.A. 115 36 13N 82 51W
Greenville, Tex., U.S.A. 117 33 5N 96 5W
Greenwater Lake Prov. Park 109 52 32N 103 30W
Greenwich, U.K. 13 51 28N 0 0
Greenwich, Conn., U.S.A. 113 41 1N 73 38W
Greenwich, N.Y., U.S.A. 113 43 2N 73 36W
Greenwich, Ohio, U.S.A. 112 41 1N 82 32W
Greenwood, Can. 108 49 10N 118 40W
Greenwood, Miss., U.S.A. 117 33 30N 90 4W
Greenwood, S.C., U.S.A. 115 34 13N 82 13W
Gregory 116 43 14N 99 20W
Gregory → 98 17 53 S 139 17 E
Gregory Downs 98 18 35 S 138 45 E
Gregory, L. 97 28 55 S 139 0 E
Gregory Lake 96 20 10 S 127 30 E
Gregory Ra. 97 19 30 S 143 40 E
Greiffenberg 24 53 6N 13 57 E
Greifswald 24 54 6N 13 23 E
Greifswalder Bodden 24 54 12N 13 35 E
Greifswalder Oie 24 54 15N 13 55 E
Grein 26 48 14N 14 51 E
Greiner Wald 26 48 30N 15 0 E
Greiz 24 50 39N 12 12 E
Gremikha 52 67 50N 39 40 E
Grenå 49 56 25N 10 53 E
Grenada 117 33 45N 89 50W
Grenada ■ 121 12 10N 61 40W
Grenade 20 43 47N 1 17 E
Grenadines 121 12 40N 61 20W
Grenen 49 57 44N 10 40 E
Grenfell, Austral. 99 33 52 S 148 8 E
Grenfell, Can. 109 50 30N 102 56W
Grenoble 21 45 12N 5 42 E
Grenora 116 48 38N 103 54W
Grenville, C. 97 12 0 S 143 13 E
Grenville Chan. 108 53 40N 129 46W
Gréoux-les-Bains 21 43 45N 5 52 E
Gresham 118 45 30N 122 25W
Gresik 73 7 13 S 112 38 E
Grëssoney St. Jean 38 45 49N 7 47 E
Gretna Green 14 55 0N 3 3W
Greven 24 52 7N 7 36 E
Grevená 44 40 4N 21 25 E
Grevená □ 44 40 2N 21 25 E
Grevenbroich 24 51 6N 6 32 E
Grevenmacher 16 49 41N 6 26 E
Grevesmühlen 24 53 51N 11 10 E
Grevie 49 56 22N 12 46 E
Grey → 101 42 27 S 171 12 E
Grey, C. 97 13 0 S 136 35 E
Grey Range 97 27 0 S 143 30 E
Grey Res. 107 48 20N 56 30W
Greybull 118 44 30N 108 3W
Greytown, N.Z. 101 41 5 S 175 29 E
Greytown, S. Afr. 93 29 1 S 30 36 E
Gribanovskiy 55 51 28N 41 50 E
Gribbell I. 108 53 23N 129 0W
Gridley 118 39 27N 121 47W
Griekwastad 92 28 49 S 23 15 E
Griffin 115 33 17N 84 14W
Griffith 97 34 18 S 146 2 E
Grillby 48 59 38N 17 15 E
Grim, C. 97 40 45 S 144 45 E
Grimari 88 5 43N 20 6 E
Grimaylov 54 49 20N 26 5 E
Grimma 24 51 14N 12 44 E
Grimmen 24 54 6N 13 2 E
Grimsby 112 43 12N 79 34W
Grimsby, Greater 12 53 35N 0 5W
Grimsey 50 66 33N 18 0W
Grimshaw 108 56 10N 117 40W
Grimstad 47 58 22N 8 35 E
Grindelwald 25 46 38N 8 2 E
Grindsted 49 55 46N 8 55 E

Grindu 46 44 44N 26 50 E
Grinnell 116 41 45N 92 43W
Griñón 30 40 13N 3 51W
Grintavec 39 46 22N 14 32 E
Grip 47 63 16N 7 37 E
Griqualand East 93 30 30 S 29 0 E
Griqualand West 92 28 40 S 23 30 E
Grisolles 20 43 49N 1 19 E
Grisslehamn 48 60 5N 18 49 E
Griz Nez, C. 19 50 50N 1 35 E
Grmeč Planina 39 44 43N 16 16 E
Groais I. 107 50 55N 55 35W
Groblersdal 93 25 15 S 29 25 E
Grobming 26 47 27N 13 54 E
Grocka 42 44 40N 20 42 E
Gródek 28 53 6N 23 40 E
Grodkow 28 50 43N 17 21 E
Grodno 54 53 42N 23 52 E
Grodzisk Mázowiecki 28 52 7N 20 37 E
Grodzisk Wielkopolski 28 52 15N 16 22 E
Grodzyanka 54 53 31N 28 42 E
Groesbeck 117 31 32N 96 34W
Groix 18 47 38N 3 29W
Groix, I. de 18 47 38N 3 28W
Grójec 28 51 50N 20 58 E
Gronau, Niedersachsen, Ger. 24 52 5N 9 47 E
Gronau, Nordrhein-Westfalen, Ger. 24 52 13N 7 2 E
Grong 50 64 25N 12 8 E
Groningen 16 53 15N 6 35 E
Groningen □ 16 53 16N 6 40 E
Grönskåra 49 57 5N 15 43 E
Groom 117 35 12N 100 59W
Groot → 92 33 45 S 24 36 E
Groot Berg → 92 32 47 S 18 8 E
Groot-Brakrivier 92 34 2 S 22 18 E
Groot Karoo 92 32 35 S 23 0 E
Groote Eylandt 97 14 0 S 136 40 E
Grootfontein 92 19 31 S 18 6 E
Grootlaagte → 92 20 55 S 21 27 E
Gros C. 108 61 59N 113 32W
Grosa, P. 33 39 6N 1 36 E
Grósio 38 46 18N 10 17 E
Grosne → 21 46 42N 4 56 E
Gross Glockner 26 47 5N 12 40 E
Gross Ottersleben 24 52 5N 11 33 E
Grossenbrode 24 54 21N 11 4 E
Grossenhain 24 51 17N 13 32 E
Grosseto 38 42 45N 11 7 E
Grossgerungs 26 48 34N 14 57 E
Groswater B. 107 54 20N 57 40W
Groton, Conn., U.S.A. 113 41 22N 72 12W
Groton, S.D., U.S.A. 116 45 27N 98 6W
Grottáglie 41 40 32N 17 25 E
Grottaminarda 41 41 5N 15 4 E
Grottammare 39 42 59N 13 52 E
Grouard Mission 108 55 33N 116 9W
Grouin, Pointe du 18 48 43N 1 51W
Groundhog → 106 48 45N 82 58W
Grouse Creek 118 41 44N 113 57W
Grove City 112 41 10N 80 5W
Groveton, N.H., U.S.A. 114 44 34N 71 30W
Groveton, Tex., U.S.A. 117 31 5N 95 4W
Grožnjan 39 45 22N 13 43 E
Groznyy 57 43 20N 45 45 E
Grubišno Polje 42 45 44N 17 12 E
Grudovo 43 42 21N 27 10 E
Grudusk 28 53 3N 20 38 E
Grudziądz 28 53 30N 18 47 E
Gruissan 20 43 8N 3 7 E
Grumo Áppula 41 41 2N 16 43 E
Grums 48 59 22N 13 5 E
Grünberg 24 50 37N 8 55 E
Grundy Center 116 42 22N 92 45W
Grungedal 47 59 44N 7 43 E
Gruver 117 36 19N 101 20W
Gruyères 25 46 35N 7 4 E
Gruža 42 43 54N 20 46 E
Gryazi 55 52 30N 39 58 E
Gryazovets 55 58 50N 40 10 E
Grybów 27 49 36N 20 55 E
Grycksbo 48 60 40N 15 29 E
Gryfice 28 53 55N 15 13 E
Gryfino 28 53 16N 14 29 E
Gryfow Śl. 28 51 2N 15 24 E
Grythyttan 48 59 41N 14 32 E
Grytviken 5 53 50 S 37 10W
Gstaad 25 46 28N 7 18 E
Guacanayabo, G. de 121 20 40N 77 20W
Guachípas → 124 25 40 S 65 30W
Guadajoz → 31 37 50N 4 51W
Guadalajara, Mexico 120 20 40N 103 20W
Guadalajara, Spain 32 40 37N 3 12W
Guadalajara □ 32 40 47N 3 0W
Guadalcanal, Solomon Is. 94 9 32 S 160 12 E
Guadalcanal, Spain 31 38 5N 5 52W
Guadalén → 31 38 5N 3 32W
Guadales 124 34 30 S 67 55W
Guadalete → 31 36 35N 6 13W
Guadalhorce → 31 36 41N 4 27W
Guadalimar → 33 38 5N 3 28W
Guadalmena → 33 38 19N 2 56W
Guadalmez → 31 38 46N 5 4W
Guadalope → 32 41 15N 0 3W
Guadalquivir → 31 36 47N 6 22W
Guadalupe, Spain 31 39 27N 5 17W
Guadalupe, U.S.A. 119 34 59N 120 33W
Guadalupe → 117 28 30N 96 53W
Guadalupe Bravos 120 31 20N 106 10W
Guadalupe I. 95 21 20N 118 50W
Guadalupe Pk. 119 31 50N 105 30W
Guadalupe, Sierra de 31 39 28N 5 30W
Guadarrama, Sierra de 30 41 0N 4 0W
Guadeloupe 121 16 20N 61 40W
Guadeloupe Passage 121 16 50N 62 15W
Guadiamar → 31 36 55N 6 24W
Guadiana → 31 37 14N 7 22W
Guadiana Menor → 33 37 56N 3 15W
Guadiaro → 31 36 17N 5 17W
Guadiato → 31 37 48N 5 5W
Guadiela → 32 40 22N 2 49W
Guadix 33 37 18N 3 11W
Guafo, Boca del 128 43 35 S 74 0W
Guaíra 125 24 5 S 54 10W
Guaira, La 126 10 36N 66 56W
Guaitecas, Islas 128 44 0 S 74 30W
Guajará-Mirim 126 10 50 S 65 20W
Guajira, Pen. de la 126 12 0N 72 0W
Gualdo Tadino 39 43 14N 12 46 E
Gualeguay 124 33 10 S 59 14W
Gualeguaychú 124 33 3 S 59 31W
Guam 94 13 27N 144 45 E
Guaminí 124 37 1 S 62 28W
Guamúchil 120 25 25N 108 3W
Guan Xian 75 31 2N 103 38 E
Guanabacoa 121 23 8N 82 18W
Guanacaste, Cordillera del 121 10 40N 85 4W
Guanaceví 120 25 40N 106 0W
Guanahani = San Salvador, I. 121 24 0N 74 40W
Guanajay 121 22 56N 82 42W
Guanajuato 120 21 0N 101 20W
Guanajuato □ 120 20 40N 101 20W
Guanare 126 8 42N 69 12W
Guandacol 124 29 30 S 68 40W
Guane 121 22 10N 84 7W
Guang'an 77 30 28N 106 35 E
Guangde 77 30 54N 119 25 E
Guangdong □ 75 23 0N 113 0 E
Guanghua 75 32 22N 111 38 E
Guangshun 77 26 8N 106 21 E
Guangxi Zhuangzu Zizhiqu □ 75 24 0N 109 0 E
Guangyuan 77 32 26N 105 51 E
Guangze 77 27 30N 117 12 E
Guangzhou 75 23 5N 113 10 E
Guanipa → 126 9 56N 62 26W
Guantánamo 121 20 10N 75 14W
Guantao 76 36 42N 115 25 E
Guanyun 77 34 20N 119 18 E
Guápiles 121 10 10N 83 46W
Guaporé → 126 11 55 S 65 4W
Guaqui 126 16 41 S 68 54W
Guara, Sierra de 32 42 19N 0 15W
Guarapari 125 20 40 S 40 30W
Guarapuava 125 25 20 S 51 30W
Guaratinguetá 125 22 49 S 45 9W
Guaratuba 125 25 53 S 48 38W
Guarda 30 40 32N 7 20W
Guarda □ 30 40 40N 7 20W
Guardafui, C. = Asir, Ras 63 11 55N 51 16 E
Guardamar del Segura 33 38 5N 0 39W
Guardavalle 41 38 31N 16 30 E
Guardia, La 30 41 56N 8 52W
Guardiagrele 39 42 11N 14 11 E
Guardo 30 42 47N 4 50W
Guareña 31 38 51N 6 6W
Guareña → 30 41 29N 5 23W
Guaria □ 124 25 45 S 56 30W
Guarujá 125 24 2 S 46 25W
Guarus 125 21 44 S 41 20W
Guasdualito 126 7 15N 70 44W
Guasipati 126 7 28N 61 54W
Guastalla 38 44 55N 10 40 E
Guatemala 120 14 40N 90 22W
Guatemala ■ 120 15 40N 90 30W
Guatire 126 10 28N 66 32W
Guaviare → 126 4 3N 67 44W
Guaxupé 125 21 10 S 47 5W
Guayama 121 17 59N 66 7W
Guayaquil 126 2 15 S 79 52W
Guayaquil, G. de 126 3 10 S 81 0W
Guaymas 120 27 59N 110 54W
Guazhou 77 32 17N 119 21 E
Guba 91 10 38 S 26 27 E
Gûbâl 86 27 30N 34 0 E
Gúbbio 39 43 20N 12 34 E
Gubin 28 51 57N 14 43 E
Gubio 85 12 30N 12 42 E
Gubkin 55 51 17N 37 32 E
Guča 42 43 46N 20 15 E
Guchil 71 5 35N 102 10 E
Gudalur 70 11 30N 76 29 E
Gudata 57 43 7N 40 10 E
Gudenå 49 56 27N 9 40 E
Gudermes 57 43 24N 46 5 E
Gudhjem 49 55 12N 14 58 E
Gudiña, La 30 42 4N 7 8W
Gudivada 70 16 30N 81 3 E
Gudiyatam 70 12 57N 78 55 E
Gudur 70 14 12N 79 55 E
Guebwiller 19 47 55N 7 12 E
Guecho 32 43 21N 2 59W
Guékédou 84 8 40N 10 5W
Guelma 83 36 25N 7 29 E
Guelph 106 43 35N 80 20W
Guelt es Stel 82 35 12N 3 1 E
Guelttara 82 29 23N 2 10W
Guemar 83 33 30N 6 49 E
Guéméné-Penfao 18 47 38N 1 50W
Guéméné-sur-Scorff 18 48 4N 3 13W
Guéné 85 11 44N 3 16 E
Guer 18 47 54N 2 8W
Güera, La 80 20 51N 17 0W
Guérande 18 47 20N 2 26W
Guerche, La 18 47 57N 1 16W
Guerche-sur-l'Aubois, La 19 46 58N 2 56 E
Guercif 82 34 14N 3 21W
Guéréda 81 14 31N 22 5 E
Guéret 20 46 11N 1 51 E
Guérigny 19 47 6N 3 10 E
Guernica 32 43 19N 2 40W
Guernsey, Chan. Is. 18 49 30N 2 35W
Guernsey, U.S.A. 116 42 19N 104 45W
Guerrara, Oasis, Alg. 83 32 51N 4 22 E
Guerrara, Saoura, Alg. 82 28 5N 0 8W
Guerrero □ 120 17 30N 100 0W
Guerzim 82 29 39N 1 40W
Guest I. 5 76 18 S 148 0W
Gueugnon 21 46 36N 4 4 E
Gueydan 117 30 3N 92 30W
Guglionesi 41 41 55N 14 54 E
Gui Jiang → 77 23 30N 111 15 E
Gui Xian 77 23 8N 109 35 E
Guia Lopes da Laguna 125 21 26 S 56 7W
Guichi 77 30 39N 117 27 E
Guider 85 9 56N 13 57 E
Guidimouni 85 13 42N 9 31 E
Guidong 77 26 7N 113 57 E
Guiglo 84 6 45N 7 30W
Guijo de Coria 30 40 6N 6 28W
Guildford 13 51 14N 0 34W
Guilford 107 45 12N 69 25W
Guilin 75 25 18N 110 15 E
Guillaumes 21 44 5N 6 52 E
Guillestre 21 44 39N 6 40 E
Guilvinec 18 47 48N 4 17W
Guimarães, Braz. 127 2 9 S 44 42W
Guimarães, Port. 30 41 28N 8 24W
Guimaras 73 10 35N 122 37 E
Guinea ■ 84 10 20N 10 0W
Guinea-Bissau ■ 84 12 0N 15 0W
Guinea, Gulf of 85 3 0N 2 30 E
Güines 121 22 50N 82 0W
Guingamp 18 48 34N 3 10W
Guipavas 18 48 26N 4 29W
Guiping 75 23 21N 110 2 E
Guipúzcoa □ 32 43 12N 2 15W
Guir, O. → 82 31 29N 2 17W
Güiria 126 10 32N 62 18W
Guiscard 19 49 40N 3 0 E
Guise 19 49 52N 3 35 E
Guitiriz 30 43 11N 7 50W
Guiuan 73 11 5N 125 55 E
Guixi 77 28 16N 117 15 E
Guiyang, Guizhou, China 75 26 32N 106 40 E
Guiyang, Hunan, China 77 25 46N 112 42 E
Guizhou □ 75 27 0N 107 0 E
Gujan-Mestras 20 44 38N 1 4W
Gujarat □ 68 23 20N 71 0 E
Gujranwala 68 32 10N 74 12 E
Gujrat 68 32 40N 74 2 E
Gukovo 57 48 1N 39 58 E
Gulargambone 100 31 20 S 148 30 E
Gulbarga 70 17 20N 76 50 E
Gulbene 54 57 8N 26 52 E
Guledgud 70 16 3N 75 48 E
Gulf Basin 96 15 20 S 129 0 E
Gulfport 117 30 21N 89 3W
Gulgong 99 32 20 S 149 49 E
Gulistan 68 30 30N 66 35 E
Gull Lake 109 50 10N 108 29W
Gullringen 49 57 48N 15 44 E
Gulma 85 12 40N 4 23 E
Gülpinar 44 39 32N 26 10 E
Gulshad 58 46 45N 74 25 E
Gulsvik 47 60 24N 9 38 E
Gulu 90 2 48N 32 17 E
Gulwe 90 6 30 S 36 25 E
Gulyaypole 56 47 45N 36 21 E
Gum Lake 99 32 42 S 143 9 E
Gumal → 68 31 40N 71 50 E
Gumbaz 68 30 2N 69 0 E
Gumel 85 12 39N 9 22 E
Gumiel de Hizán 32 41 46N 3 41W
Gumlu 98 19 53 S 147 41 E
Gumma □ 74 36 30N 138 20 E
Gummersbach 24 51 2N 7 32 E
Gummi 85 12 4N 5 9 E
Gümüsane 64 40 30N 39 30 E
Gümüşhaciköy 56 40 50N 35 18 E
Gumzai 73 5 28 S 134 42 E
Guna 68 24 40N 77 19 E
Guna Mt. 87 11 50N 37 40 E
Gundagai 99 35 3 S 148 6 E
Gundelfingen 25 48 33N 10 22 E
Gundih 73 7 10 S 110 56 E
Gundlakamma → 70 15 30N 80 15 E
Gungu 88 5 43 S 19 20 E
Gunisao → 109 53 56N 97 53W
Gunisao L. 109 53 33N 96 15W
Gunnedah 97 30 59 S 150 15 E
Gunning 100 34 47 S 149 14 E
Gunnison, Colo., U.S.A. 119 38 32N 106 56W
Gunnison, Utah, U.S.A. 118 39 11N 111 48W
Gunnison → 119 39 3N 108 30W
Guntakal 70 15 11N 77 27 E
Guntersville 115 34 18N 86 16W
Guntur 70 16 23N 80 30 E
Gunung-Sitoli 72 1 15N 97 30 E
Gunungapi 73 6 45 S 126 30 E
Gunupur 70 19 5N 83 50 E
Günz → 25 48 27N 10 16 E
Gunza 88 10 50 S 13 50 E
Günzburg 25 48 27N 10 16 E
Gunzenhausen 25 49 6N 10 45 E
Guo He → 77 32 59N 117 10 E
Guoyang 77 33 32N 116 12 E
Gupis 69 36 15N 73 20 E
Gura 68 25 12N 71 39 E
Gura Humorului 46 47 35N 25 53 E
Gura-Teghii 46 45 30N 26 25 E
Gurag 87 8 20N 38 20 E
Gürchañ 64 34 55N 49 25 E
Gurdaspur 68 32 5N 75 31 E
Gurdon 117 33 55N 93 10W
Gurdzhaani 57 41 43N 45 52 E
Gurgaon 68 28 27N 77 1 E
Gurghiu, Munţii 46 46 41N 25 15 E
Gurk → 26 46 35N 14 31 E
Gurkha 69 28 5N 84 40 E
Gurley 99 29 45 S 149 48 E
Gurun 71 5 49N 100 27 E
Gurupá 127 1 25 S 51 35W
Gurupá, I. Grande de 127 1 25 S 51 45W
Gurupi → 127 1 13 S 46 6W
Guryev 57 47 5N 52 0 E
Gus-Khrustalnyy 55 55 42N 40 44 E
Gusau 85 12 12N 6 40 E
Gusev 54 54 35N 22 10 E
Gushan 76 39 50N 123 35 E
Gushi 77 32 11N 115 41 E
Gushiago 85 9 55N 0 15W
Gusinje 42 42 35N 19 50 E
Gúspini 40 39 32N 8 38 E
Gusselby 48 59 38N 15 14 E
Güssing 27 47 3N 16 20 E
Gustanj 39 46 36N 14 49 E
Gustine 119 37 14N 121 0 E
Güstrow 24 53 47N 12 12 E
Gusum 49 58 16N 16 30 E
Guta = Kalárovo 27 47 54N 18 0 E
Gütersloh 24 51 54N 8 25 E
Guthalongra 98 19 52 S 147 50 E
Guthega Dam 100 36 20 S 148 27 E
Guthrie 117 35 55N 97 30W
Guttenberg 116 42 46N 91 10W
Guyana ■ 126 5 0N 59 0W
Guyang 76 41 0N 110 5 E
Guyenne 20 44 30N 0 40 E
Guymon 117 36 45N 101 30W
Guyra 99 30 15 S 151 40 E
Guyuan 76 36 0N 106 20 E
Guzhen 77 33 22N 117 18 E
Guzmán, Laguna de 120 31 25N 107 25W
Gwa 67 17 36N 94 34 E
Gwaai 91 19 15 S 27 45 E
Gwabegar 99 30 31 S 149 0 E
Gwadabawa 85 13 28N 5 15 E
Gwādar 66 25 10N 62 18 E
Gwagwada 85 10 15N 7 15 E
Gwalior 68 26 12N 78 10 E
Gwanda 91 20 55 S 29 0 E
Gwandu 85 12 30N 4 41 E
Gwane 90 4 45N 25 48 E
Gwaram 85 10 15N 10 25 E
Gwarzo 85 12 20N 8 55 E
Gwda → 28 53 3N 16 44 E
Gweebarra B. 15 54 52N 8 21W
Gweedore 15 55 4N 8 15W
* Gwelo 91 19 28 S 29 45 E
Gwent □ 13 51 45N 2 55W
Gwi 85 9 0N 7 10 E
Gwinn 114 46 15N 87 29W
Gwio Kura 85 12 40N 11 2 E
Gwol 84 10 58N 1 59W
Gwoza 85 11 5N 13 40 E
Gwydir → 97 29 27 S 149 48 E
Gwynedd □ 12 53 0N 4 0W
Gyaring Hu 75 34 50N 97 40 E
Gydanskiy P-ov. 58 70 0N 78 0 E
Gyland 47 58 24N 6 45 E
Gympie 97 26 11 S 152 38 E
Gyoda 74 36 10N 139 30 E
Gyoma 27 46 56N 20 50 E
Gyöngyös 27 47 48N 20 0 E
Györ 27 47 41N 17 40 E
Györ-Sopron □ 27 47 40N 17 20 E
Gypsum Pt. 108 61 53N 114 35W
Gypsumville 109 51 45N 98 40W
Gyttorp 48 59 31N 14 58 E
Gyula 27 46 38N 21 17 E
Gzhatsk = Gagarin 54 55 30N 35 0 E

H

Ha 'Arava 62 30 50N 35 20 E
Haag 25 48 11N 12 12 E
Haapamäki 50 62 18N 24 28 E
Haapsalu 54 58 56N 23 30 E
Haarlem 16 52 23N 4 39 E
Haast → 101 43 50 S 169 2 E
Hab Nadi Chauki 66 25 0N 66 50 E
Habana, La 121 23 8N 82 22W
Habaswein 90 1 2N 39 30 E
Habay 108 58 50N 118 44W
Habiganj 69 24 24N 91 30 E
Hablingbo 49 57 12N 18 16 E
Habo 49 57 55N 14 6 E
Hachenburg 24 50 40N 7 49 E
Hachijō-Jima 74 33 5N 139 45 E
Hachinohe 74 40 30N 141 29 E
Hachiōji 74 35 40N 139 20 E
Hadali 68 32 16N 72 11 E
Hadarba, Ras 86 22 4N 36 51 E
Hadd, Ras al 65 22 35N 59 50 E
Haddington 14 55 57N 2 48W
Hadejia 85 12 30N 10 5 E
Hadejia → 85 12 50N 10 51 E
Haden 99 27 13 S 151 54 E
Hadera 62 32 27N 34 55 E
Hadera, N. → 62 32 28N 34 52 E
Haderslev 49 55 15N 9 30 E
Hadhra 86 20 10N 41 5 E
Hadhramaut = Hadramawt 63 15 30N 49 30 E
Hadibu 63 12 35N 54 2 E
Hadjeb El Aïoun 83 35 21N 9 32 E
Hadramawt 63 15 30N 49 30 E
Hadrians Wall 12 55 0N 2 30W
Hadsten 49 56 19N 10 3 E
Hadsund 49 56 44N 10 8 E
Haeju 76 38 3N 125 45 E
Haerhpin = Harbin 76 45 48N 126 40 E
Hafar al Batin 64 28 25N 46 0 E
Hafizabad 68 32 5N 73 40 E
Haflong 67 25 10N 93 5 E
Hafnarfjördur 50 64 4N 21 57W
Haft-Gel 64 31 30N 49 32 E
Hafun, Ras 63 10 29N 51 30 E
Hagalil 62 32 53N 35 18 E
Hagari → 70 15 40N 77 0 E
Hagen 24 51 21N 7 29 E
Hagenow 24 53 25N 11 10 E
Hagerman 117 33 5N 104 22W
Hagerstown 114 39 39N 77 46W
Hagetmau 20 43 39N 0 37W
Hagfors 48 60 3N 13 45 E
Häggenås 48 63 24N 14 55 E
Hagi, Iceland 50 65 28N 23 25W
Hagi, Japan 74 34 30N 131 22 E
Hagolan 62 33 0N 35 45 E
Hags Hd. 15 52 57N 9 30W
Hague, C. de la 18 49 44N 1 56W
Hague, The = s'-Gravenhage 16 52 7N 4 17 E
Haguenau 19 48 49N 7 47 E
Hai □ 90 3 10 S 37 10 E
Haicheng 76 40 50N 122 45 E
Haifeng 77 22 58N 115 10 E

* Renamed Gweru

Haiger 24 50 44N 8 12 E
Haikang 77 20 52N 110 8 E
Haikou 75 20 1N 110 16 E
Ḥā'il 64 27 28N 41 45 E
Hailar 75 49 10N 119 38 E
Hailar He → 76 49 30N 117 50 E
Hailey 118 43 30N 114 15W
Haileybury 106 47 30N 79 38W
Hailin 76 44 37N 129 30 E
Hailing Dao 77 21 35N 111 47 E
Hailong 76 42 32N 125 40 E
Hailun 75 47 28N 126 50 E
Hailuoto 50 65 3N 24 45 E
Haimen 77 31 52N 121 10 E
Hainan 77 19 0N 110 0 E
Hainan Dao 75 19 0N 109 30 E
Hainaut □ 16 50 30N 4 0 E
Hainburg 27 48 9N 16 56 E
Haines 118 44 51N 117 59W
Haines City 115 28 6N 81 35W
Haines Junction 108 60 45N 137 30W
Hainfeld 26 48 3N 15 48 E
Haining 77 30 28N 120 40 E
Haiphong 71 20 47N 106 41 E
Haiti ■ 121 19 0N 72 30W
Haiya Junction 86 18 20N 36 21 E
Haiyan 77 30 28N 120 58 E
Haiyang 76 36 47N 121 9 E
Haiyuan 76 36 35N 105 52 E
Haja 73 3 19 S 129 37 E
Hajar Bangar 81 10 40N 22 45 E
Hajar, Jabal 64 26 5N 39 10 E
Hajdú-Bihar □ 27 47 30N 21 30 E
Hajdúböszörmény 27 47 40N 21 30 E
Hajdúdurog 27 47 48N 21 30 E
Hajdúhadház 27 47 40N 21 40 E
Hajdúnánás 27 47 50N 21 26 E
Hajdúsámson 27 47 37N 21 42 E
Hajdúszobaszló 27 47 27N 21 22 E
Hajipur 69 25 45N 85 13 E
Hajówka 28 52 47N 23 35 E
Hajr 65 24 0N 56 34 E
Hakansson, Mts. 91 8 40 S 25 45 E
Håkantorp 49 58 18N 12 55 E
Hakken-Zan 74 34 10N 135 54 E
Hakodate 74 41 45N 140 44 E
Ḥalab = Aleppo 64 36 10N 37 15 E
Ḥalabjah 64 35 10N 45 58 E
Halaib 86 22 12N 36 30 E
Halbe 86 19 40N 42 15 E
Halberstadt 24 51 53N 11 2 E
Halcombe 101 40 8 S 175 30 E
Halcyon, Mt. 73 13 0N 121 30 E
Halden 47 59 9N 11 23 E
Haldensleben 24 52 17N 11 30 E
Haldia 67 22 5N 88 3 E
Haldwani-cum-Kathgodam 69 29 31N 79 30 E
Haleakala Crater 110 20 43N 156 12W
Haleyville 115 34 15N 87 40W
Half Assini 84 5 1N 2 50W
Halfway 118 44 56N 117 8W
Halfway → 108 56 12N 121 32W
Ḥalḥul 62 31 35N 35 7 E
Hali, Si. Arab. 86 18 40N 41 15 E
Hali, Yemen 63 18 30N 41 30 E
Haliburton 106 45 3N 78 30W
Halicarnassus 45 37 3N 27 30 E
Halifax, Austral. 98 18 32 S 146 22 E
Halifax, Can. 107 44 38N 63 35W
Halifax, U.K. 12 53 43N 1 51W
Halifax B. 97 18 50 S 147 0 E
Halifax I. 92 26 38 S 15 4 E
Halīl Rūd → 65 27 40N 58 30 E
Hall 26 47 17N 11 30 E
Hall Beach 105 68 46N 81 12W
Hallabro 49 56 22N 15 5 E
Hallands län □ 49 56 50N 12 50 E
Hallands Väderö 49 56 27N 12 34 E
Hallandsås 49 56 22N 13 0 E
Halle, Belg. 16 50 44N 4 13 E
Halle, Halle, Ger. 24 51 29N 12 0 E
Halle, Nordrhein-Westfalen, Ger. 24 52 4N 8 20 E
Halle □ 24 51 28N 11 58 E
Hällefors 48 59 47N 14 31 E
Hallefors 49 59 46N 14 30 E
Hallein 26 47 40N 13 5 E
Hällekis 49 58 38N 13 27 E
Hallett 99 33 25 S 138 55 E
Hallettsville 117 29 28N 96 57W
Hällevadsholm 49 58 35N 11 33 E
Halley Bay 5 75 31 S 26 36W
Hallia → 70 16 55N 79 20 E
Halliday 116 47 20N 102 25W
Halliday L. 109 61 21N 108 56W
Hallingskeid 47 60 40N 7 17 E
Hällnäs 50 64 19N 19 36 E
Hallock 109 48 47N 97 0W
Halls Creek 96 18 16 S 127 38 E
Hallsberg 48 59 5N 15 7 E
Hallstahammar 48 59 38N 16 15 E
Hallstatt 26 47 33N 13 38 E
Hallstavik 48 60 5N 18 37 E
Hallstead 113 41 56N 75 45W
Halmahera 73 0 40N 128 0 E
Halmeu 46 47 57N 23 2 E
Halmstad 49 56 41N 12 52 E
Halq el Oued 83 36 53N 10 18 E
Hals 49 56 59N 10 18 E
Halsa 47 63 3N 8 14 E
Halsafjorden 47 63 5N 8 10 E
Hälsingborg = Helsingborg 49 56 3N 12 42 E
Halstad 116 47 21N 96 50W
Haltdalen 47 62 56N 11 8 E
Haltern 24 51 44N 7 10 E
Halul 65 25 40N 52 40 E
Ham 19 49 45N 3 4 E
Hamab 92 28 7 S 19 16 E
Hamad 87 15 20N 33 32 E
Hamada 74 34 56N 132 4 E
Hamadān 64 34 52N 48 32 E
Hamadān □ 64 35 0N 49 0 E
Hamadia 82 35 28N 1 57 E
Hamāh 64 35 5N 36 40 E
Hamamatsu 74 34 45N 137 45 E
Hamar 47 60 48N 11 7 E
Hamarøy 50 68 5N 15 38 E
Hamâta, Gebel 86 24 17N 35 0 E
Hamber Prov. Park 108 52 20N 118 0W
Hamburg, Ger. 24 53 32N 9 59 E
Hamburg, Ark., U.S.A. 117 33 15N 91 47W
Hamburg, Iowa, U.S.A. 116 40 37N 95 38W
Hamburg, N.Y., U.S.A. 112 42 44N 78 50W
Hamburg, Pa., U.S.A. 113 40 33N 76 0W
Hamburg □ 24 53 30N 10 0 E
Hamden 113 41 21N 72 56W
Hamdh, W. → 86 24 55N 36 20 E
Hämeen lääni □ 51 61 24N 24 10 E
Hämeenlinna 50 61 0N 24 28 E
Hamélé 84 10 56N 2 45W
Hameln 24 52 7N 9 24 E
Hamer Koke 87 5 15N 36 45 E
Hamersley Ra. 96 22 0 S 117 45 E
Hamhung 76 39 54N 127 30 E
Hami 75 42 55N 93 25 E
Hamilton, Austral. 97 37 45 S 142 2 E
Hamilton, Berm. 121 32 15N 64 45W
Hamilton, Can. 106 43 15N 79 50W
Hamilton, N.Z. 101 37 47 S 175 19 E
Hamilton, U.K. 14 55 47N 4 2W
Hamilton, Mo., U.S.A. 116 39 45N 93 59W
Hamilton, Mont., U.S.A. 118 46 20N 114 6W
Hamilton, N.Y., U.S.A. 114 42 49N 75 31W
Hamilton, Ohio, U.S.A. 114 39 20N 84 35W
Hamilton, Tex., U.S.A. 117 31 40N 98 5W
Hamilton → 98 23 30 S 139 47 E
Hamilton Hotel 98 22 45 S 140 40 E
Hamilton Inlet 107 54 0N 57 30W
Hamiota 109 50 11N 100 38W
Hamlet 115 34 56N 79 40W
Hamley Bridge 99 34 17 S 138 35 E
Hamlin, N.Y., U.S.A. 112 43 17N 77 55W
Hamlin, Tex., U.S.A. 117 32 58N 100 8W
Hamm 24 51 40N 7 49 E
Hammam Bouhadjar 82 35 23N 0 58W
Hammamet 83 36 24N 10 38 E
Hammamet, G. de 83 36 10N 10 48 E
Hammarstrand 48 63 7N 16 20 E
Hammel 49 56 16N 9 52 E
Hammelburg 25 50 7N 9 54 E
Hammeren 49 55 18N 14 47 E
Hammerfest 50 70 39N 23 41 E
Hammond, Ind., U.S.A. 114 41 40N 87 30W
Hammond, La., U.S.A. 117 30 32N 90 30W
Hammonton 114 39 40N 74 47W
Hamneda 49 56 41N 13 51 E
Hamoyet, Jebel 86 17 33N 38 2 E
Hampden 101 45 18 S 170 50 E
Hampshire □ 13 51 3N 1 20W
Hampshire Downs 13 51 10N 1 10W
Hampton, Ark., U.S.A. 117 33 35N 92 29W
Hampton, Iowa, U.S.A. 116 42 42N 93 12W
Hampton, N.H., U.S.A. 113 42 56N 70 48W
Hampton, S.C., U.S.A. 115 32 52N 81 2W
Hampton, Va., U.S.A. 114 37 4N 76 18W
Hampton Harbour 96 20 30 S 116 30 E
Hampton Tableland 96 32 0 S 127 0 E
Hamrat esh Sheykh 87 14 38N 27 55 E
Han Jiang → 77 23 25N 116 40 E
Han Shui → 77 30 35N 114 18 E
Hana 110 20 45N 155 59W
Hanak 86 25 32N 37 0 E
Hanang 90 4 30 S 35 25 E
Hanau 25 50 8N 8 56 E
Hancheng 76 35 31N 110 25 E
Hancock, Mich., U.S.A. 116 47 10N 88 40W
Hancock, Minn., U.S.A. 116 45 26N 95 46W
Hancock, Pa., U.S.A. 113 41 57N 75 19W
Handa, Japan 74 34 53N 137 0 E
Handa, Somalia 63 10 37N 51 2 E
Handan 76 36 35N 114 28 E
Handen 48 59 12N 18 12 E
Handeni 90 5 25 S 38 2 E
Handeni □ 90 5 30 S 38 0 E
Handlová 27 48 45N 18 35 E
Handub 86 19 15N 37 16 E
Hanegev 62 30 50N 35 0 E
Haney 108 49 12N 122 40W
Hanford 119 36 23N 119 39W
Hangang → 76 37 50N 126 30 E
Hangayn Nuruu 75 47 30N 100 0 E
Hangchou = Hangzhou 75 30 18N 120 11 E
Hanggin Houqi 76 40 58N 107 4 E
Hangklip, K. 92 34 26 S 18 48 E
Hangö 51 59 50N 22 57 E
Hangu 76 39 18N 117 53 E
Hangzhou 75 30 18N 120 11 E
Hangzhou Wan 75 30 15N 120 45 E
Ḥanish J. 63 13 45N 42 46 E
Haniska 27 48 37N 21 15 E
Hanita 62 33 5N 35 10 E
Hankinson 116 46 9N 96 58W
Hanko 51 59 59N 22 57 E
Hankou 77 30 35N 114 30 E
Hanksville 119 38 19N 110 45W
Hanmer 101 42 32 S 172 50 E
Hann, Mt. 96 16 0 S 126 0 E
Hanna 108 51 40N 111 54W
Hannaford 116 47 23N 98 11W
Hannah 116 48 58N 98 42W
Hannah B. 106 51 40N 80 0W
Hannibal 116 39 42N 91 22W
Hannik 86 18 12N 32 20 E
Hannover 24 52 23N 9 43 E
Hanö 49 56 2N 14 50 E
Hanöbukten 49 55 35N 14 30 E
Hanoi 71 21 5N 105 55 E
Hanover, Can. 112 44 9N 81 2W
Hanover, S. Afr. 92 31 4 S 24 29 E
Hanover, N.H., U.S.A. 114 43 43N 72 17W
Hanover, Ohio, U.S.A. 112 40 5N 82 17W
Hanover, Pa., U.S.A. 114 39 46N 76 59W
Hanover = Hannover 24 52 23N 9 43 E
Hanover, I. 128 51 0 S 74 50W
Hansi 68 29 10N 75 57 E
Hansjö 48 61 10N 14 40 E
Hanson Range 96 27 0 S 136 30 E
Hanwood 100 34 22 S 146 2 E
Hanyang 77 30 35N 114 2 E
Hanyin 77 32 54N 108 28 E
Hanzhong 75 33 10N 107 1 E
Hanzhuang 77 34 33N 117 23 E
Haparanda 50 65 52N 24 8 E
Happy 117 34 47N 101 50W
Happy Camp 118 41 52N 123 22W
Happy Valley 107 53 15N 60 20W
Hapur 68 28 45N 77 45 E
Ḥaql 86 29 10N 35 0 E
Har 73 5 16 S 133 14 E
Har Hu 75 38 20N 97 38 E
Har Us Nuur 75 48 0N 92 0 E
Har Yehuda 62 31 35N 34 57 E
Ḥaraḍ 64 24 22N 49 0 E
Haraisan Plateau 64 23 0N 47 40 E
Haramsøya 47 62 39N 6 12 E
Harardera 63 4 33N 47 38 E
Harat 87 16 5N 39 26 E
Harazé, Chad 81 14 20N 19 12 E
Harazé, Chad 81 9 57N 20 48 E
Harbin 76 45 48N 126 40 E
Harbøør 49 56 38N 8 10 E
Harbor Beach 114 43 50N 82 38W
Harbor Springs 114 45 28N 85 0W
Harbour Breton 107 47 29N 55 50W
Harbour Grace 107 47 40N 53 22W
Harburg 24 53 27N 9 58 E
Hårby 49 55 13N 10 7 E
Harcourt 98 24 17 S 149 55 E
Harda 68 22 27N 77 5 E
Hardangerfjorden 47 60 15N 6 0 E
Hardangerjøkulen 47 60 30N 7 0 E
Hardangervidda 47 60 20N 7 20 E
Hardap Dam 92 24 32 S 17 50 E
Hardenberg 16 52 34N 6 37 E
Harderwijk 16 52 21N 5 38 E
Hardin 118 45 44N 107 35W
Harding 93 30 35 S 29 55 E
Hardisty 108 52 40N 111 18W
Hardman 118 45 12N 119 40W
Hardoi 69 27 26N 80 6 E
Hardwar 68 29 58N 78 9 E
Hardwick 113 44 30N 72 20W
Hardy 117 36 20N 91 30W
Hardy, Pen. 128 55 30 S 68 20W
Hare B. 107 51 15N 55 45W
Hare Gilboa 62 32 31N 35 25 E
Hare Meron 62 32 59N 35 24 E
Haren 24 52 47N 7 18 E
Harer 87 9 20N 42 8 E
Harer □ 87 7 12N 42 0 E
Hareto 87 9 23N 37 6 E
Harfleur 18 49 30N 0 10 E
Hargeisa 63 9 30N 44 2 E
Harghita □ 46 46 30N 25 30 E
Harghita, Mţii 46 46 25N 25 35 E
Hargshamn 48 60 12N 18 30 E
Hari → 72 1 16 S 104 5 E
Haricha, Hamada el 82 22 40N 3 15W
Harihar 70 14 32N 75 44 E
Haringhata → 69 22 0N 89 58 E
Haripad 70 9 14N 76 28 E
Harīrūd 65 35 0N 61 0 E
Harīrūd → 65 34 20N 62 30 E
Harkat 86 20 25N 39 40 E
Harlan, Iowa, U.S.A. 116 41 37N 95 20W
Harlan, Tenn., U.S.A. 115 36 50N 83 20W
Harlech 12 52 52N 4 7W
Harlem 118 48 29N 108 47W
Harlingen, Neth. 16 53 11N 5 25 E
Harlingen, U.S.A. 117 26 20N 97 50W
Harlowton 118 46 30N 109 54W
Harmånger 48 61 55N 17 20 E
Harmil 87 16 30N 40 10 E
Harney Basin 118 43 30N 119 0W
Harney L. 118 43 0N 119 0W
Harney Pk. 116 43 52N 103 33W
Härnön 48 62 36N 18 0 E
Härnösand 48 62 38N 18 0 E
Haro 32 42 35N 2 55W
Haro, C. 120 27 50N 110 55W
Harp L. 107 55 5N 61 50W
Harpanahalli 70 14 47N 76 2 E
Harpe, La 116 40 30N 91 0W
Harper 84 4 25N 7 43W
Harplinge 49 56 45N 12 45 E
Harrand 68 29 28N 70 3 E
Ḥarrat al Kishb 64 22 30N 40 15 E
Harrat al 'Uwairidh 64 26 50N 38 0 E
Harrat Khaibar 86 25 45N 40 0 E
Harrat Nawāsīf 86 21 30N 42 0 E
Harriman 115 36 0N 84 35W
Harrington Harbour 107 50 31N 59 30W
Harris 14 57 50N 6 55W
Harris L. 96 31 10 S 135 10 E
Harris, Sd. of 14 57 44N 7 6W
Harrisburg, Ill., U.S.A. 117 37 42N 88 30W
Harrisburg, Nebr., U.S.A. 116 41 36N 103 46W
Harrisburg, Oreg., U.S.A. 118 44 16N 123 10W
Harrisburg, Pa., U.S.A. 114 40 18N 76 52W
Harrismith 93 28 15 S 29 8 E
Harrison, Ark., U.S.A. 117 36 10N 93 4W
Harrison, Idaho, U.S.A. 118 47 30N 116 51W
Harrison, Nebr., U.S.A. 116 42 42N 103 52W
Harrison B. 104 70 25N 151 30W
Harrison, C. 107 54 55N 57 55W
Harrison L. 108 49 33N 121 50W
Harrisonburg 114 38 28N 78 52W
Harrisonville 116 38 39N 94 21W
Harriston 106 43 57N 80 53W
Harrisville 106 44 40N 83 19W
Harrogate 12 53 59N 1 32W
Harrow, Can. 112 42 2N 82 55W
Harrow, U.K. 13 51 35N 0 15W
Harsefeld 24 53 26N 9 30 E
Harstad 50 68 48N 16 30 E
Hart 114 43 42N 86 21W
Hartbees → 92 28 45 S 20 32 E
Hartberg 26 47 17N 15 58 E
Hartford, Conn., U.S.A. 114 41 47N 72 41W
Hartford, Ky., U.S.A. 114 37 26N 86 50W
Hartford, S.D., U.S.A. 116 43 40N 96 58W
Hartford, Wis., U.S.A. 116 43 18N 88 25W
Hartford City 114 40 22N 85 20W
Hartland 107 46 20N 67 32W
Hartland Pt. 13 51 2N 4 32W
Hartlepool 12 54 42N 1 11W
Hartley 91 18 10 S 30 14 E
Hartley Bay 108 53 25N 129 15W
Hartmannberge 92 17 0 S 13 0 E
Hartney 109 49 30N 100 35W
Hartselle 115 34 25N 86 55W
Hartshorne 117 34 51N 95 30W
Hartsville 115 34 23N 80 2W
Hartwell 115 34 21N 82 52W
Harunabad 68 29 35N 73 8 E
Harur 70 12 3N 78 29 E
Harvey, Ill., U.S.A. 114 41 40N 87 40W
Harvey, N.D., U.S.A. 116 47 50N 99 58W
Harwich 13 51 56N 1 18 E
Haryana □ 68 29 0N 76 10 E
Harz 24 51 40N 10 40 E
Harzgerode 24 51 38N 11 8 E
Hasa 64 26 0N 49 0 E
Hasaheisa 87 14 44N 33 20 E
Hasani 86 25 0N 37 8 E
Hasanpur 68 28 43N 78 17 E
Haselünne 24 52 40N 7 30 E
Hasharon 62 32 12N 34 49 E
Hashefela 62 31 30N 34 43 E
Håsjö 48 63 1N 16 5 E
Haskell, Okla., U.S.A. 117 35 51N 95 40W
Haskell, Tex., U.S.A. 117 33 10N 99 45W
Haslach 25 48 16N 8 7 E
Hasle 49 55 11N 14 44 E
Haslev 49 55 18N 11 57 E
Hasparren 20 43 24N 1 18W
Hasselt 16 50 56N 5 21 E
Hassene, Ad. 82 21 0N 4 0 E
Hassfurt 25 50 2N 10 30 E
Hassi Berrekrem 83 33 45N 5 16 E
Hassi bou Khelala 82 30 17N 0 18W
Hassi Daoula 83 33 4N 5 38 E
Hassi Djafou 82 30 55N 3 35 E
Hassi el Abiod 82 31 47N 3 37 E
Hassi el Biod 83 28 30N 6 0 E
Hassi el Gassi 83 30 52N 6 5 E
Hassi el Hadjar 83 31 28N 4 45 E
Hassi er Rmel 82 32 56N 3 17 E
Hassi Imoulaye 83 29 54N 9 10 E
Hassi Inifel 82 29 50N 3 41 E
Hassi Marroket 82 30 10N 3 0 E
Hassi Messaoud 83 31 43N 6 8 E
Hassi Rhénami 83 31 50N 5 58 E
Hassi Tartrat 83 30 5N 6 28 E
Hassi Zerzour 82 30 51N 3 56W
Hastings, Can. 112 44 18N 77 57W
Hastings, N.Z. 101 39 39 S 176 52 E
Hastings, U.K. 13 50 51N 0 36 E
Hastings, Mich., U.S.A. 114 42 40N 85 20W
Hastings, Minn., U.S.A. 116 44 41N 92 51W
Hastings, Nebr., U.S.A. 116 40 34N 98 22W
Hastings Ra. 99 31 15 S 152 14 E
Hästveda 49 56 17N 13 55 E
Hat Nhao 71 14 46N 106 32 E
Hatch 119 32 45N 107 8W
Hatches Creek 96 20 56 S 135 12 E
Hatchet L. 109 58 36N 103 40W
Haţeg 46 45 36N 22 55 E
Haţeg, Mţii. 46 45 25N 23 0 E
Hatfield P.O. 99 33 54 S 143 49 E
Hatgal 75 50 26N 100 9 E
Hathras 68 27 36N 78 6 E
Hattah 99 34 48 S 142 17 E
Hatteras, C. 115 35 10N 75 30W
Hattiesburg 117 31 20N 89 20W
Hatvan 27 47 40N 19 45 E
Hau Bon = Cheo Reo 71 13 25N 108 28 E
Haug 47 60 23N 10 26 E
Haugastøl 47 60 30N 7 50 E
Haugesund 47 59 23N 5 13 E
Haultain → 109 55 51N 106 46W
Hauraki Gulf 101 36 35 S 175 5 E
Hauran 62 32 50N 36 15 E
Hausruck 26 48 6N 13 30 E
Haut Atlas 82 32 30N 5 0W
Haut-Rhin □ 19 48 0N 7 15 E
Haut Zaïre □ 90 2 20N 26 0 E
Hautah, Wahāt al 64 23 40N 47 0 E
Haute-Corse □ 21 42 30N 9 30 E
Haute-Garonne □ 20 43 28N 1 30 E
Haute-Loire □ 20 45 5N 3 50 E
Haute-Marne □ 19 48 10N 5 20 E
Haute-Saône □ 19 47 45N 6 10 E
Haute-Savoie □ 21 46 0N 6 20 E
Haute-Vienne □ 20 45 50N 1 10 E
Hauterive 107 49 10N 68 16W
Hautes-Alpes □ 21 44 42N 6 20 E
Hautes-Pyrénées □ 20 43 0N 0 10 E
Hauteville 21 45 58N 5 36 E
Hautmont 19 50 15N 3 55 E
Hauts-de-Seine □ 19 48 52N 2 15 E
Hauts Plateaux 82 34 14N 1 0 E
Hauzenberg 25 48 39N 13 38 E
Havana 116 40 19N 90 3W
Havana = La Habana 121 23 8N 82 22W
Havasu, L. 119 34 18N 114 28W
Havdhem 49 57 10N 18 20 E
Havelange 16 50 23N 5 15 E
Havelock, N.B., Can. 107 46 2N 65 24W
Havelock, Ont., Can. 106 44 26N 77 53W
Havelock, N.Z. 101 41 17 S 173 48 E
Havelock I. 71 11 55N 93 2 E
Haverfordwest 13 51 48N 4 59W
Haverhill 114 42 50N 71 2W
Haveri 70 14 53N 75 24 E
Havering 13 51 33N 0 20 E
Haverstraw 113 41 12N 73 58W
Håverud 49 58 50N 12 28 E

Havîrna	46	48 4N	26 43 E
Havlíčkův Brod	26	49 36N	15 33 E
Havneby	49	55 5N	8 34 E
Havre	118	48 34N	109 40W
Havre-St.-Pierre	107	50 18N	63 33W
Havre-Aubert	107	47 12N	61 56W
Havre, Le	18	49 30N	0 5 E
Havza	64	41 0N	35 35 E
Haw →	115	35 36N	79 3W
Hawaii □	110	20 30N	157 0W
Hawaii	110	20 0N	155 0W
Hawaiian Is.	110	20 30N	156 0W
Hawaiian Ridge	95	24 0N	165 0W
Hawarden, Can.	109	51 25N	106 36W
Hawarden, U.S.A.	116	43 2N	96 28W
Hawea Lake	101	44 28 S	169 19 E
Hawera	101	39 35 S	174 19 E
Hawick	14	55 25N	2 48W
Hawk Junction	106	48 5N	84 38W
Hawke B.	101	39 25 S	177 20 E
Hawke, C.	100	32 13 S	152 34 E
Hawker	97	31 59 S	138 22 E
Hawke's Bay □	101	39 45 S	176 35 E
Hawkesbury	106	45 37N	74 37W
Hawkesbury →	97	33 30 S	151 10 E
Hawkesbury I.	108	53 37N	129 3W
Hawkinsville	115	32 17N	83 30W
Hawkwood	99	25 45 S	150 50 E
Hawley	116	46 58N	96 20W
Hawrān	62	32 45N	36 15 E
Hawthorne	118	38 31N	118 37W
Hawzen	87	13 58N	39 28 E
Haxtun	116	40 40N	102 39W
Hay, Austral.	97	34 30 S	144 51 E
Hay, U.K.	13	52 4N	3 9W
Hay →, Austral.	97	25 14 S	138 0 E
Hay →, Can.	108	60 50N	116 26W
Hay L.	108	58 50N	118 50W
Hay Lakes	108	53 12N	113 2W
Hay River	108	60 51N	115 44W
Hay Springs	116	42 40N	102 38W
Hayange	19	49 20N	6 2 E
Hayden, Ariz., U.S.A.	119	33 2N	110 48W
Hayden, Colo., U.S.A.	118	40 30N	107 22W
Haydon	98	18 0 S	141 30 E
Haye-Descartes, La	18	46 58N	0 42 E
Haye-du-Puits, La	18	49 17N	1 33W
Hayes	116	44 22N	101 1W
Hayes →	109	57 3N	92 12W
Haynesville	117	33 0N	93 7W
Hays, Can.	108	50 6N	111 48W
Hays, U.S.A.	116	38 55N	99 25W
Hayward	116	46 2N	91 30W
Hayward's Heath	13	51 0N	0 5W
Hazard	114	37 18N	83 10W
Hazaribagh	69	23 58N	85 26 E
Hazaribagh Road	69	24 12N	85 57 E
Hazebrouck	19	50 42N	2 31 E
Hazelton, Can.	108	55 20N	127 42W
Hazelton, U.S.A.	116	46 30N	100 15W
Hazen, N.D., U.S.A.	116	47 18N	101 38W
Hazen, Nev., U.S.A.	118	39 37N	119 2W
Hazlehurst, Ga., U.S.A.	115	31 50N	82 35W
Hazlehurst, Miss., U.S.A.	117	31 52N	90 24W
Hazleton	114	40 58N	76 0W
Hazor	62	33 2N	35 32 E
He Xian	77	24 27N	111 30 E
Head of Bight	96	31 30 S	131 25 E
Headlands	91	18 15 S	32 2 E
Healdsburg	118	38 33N	122 51W
Healdton	117	34 16N	97 31W
Healesville	99	37 35 S	145 30 E
Heanor	12	53 1N	1 20W
Heard I.	3	53 0 S	74 0 E
Hearne	117	30 54N	96 35W
Hearne B.	109	60 10N	99 10W
Hearne L.	108	62 20N	113 10W
Hearst	106	49 40N	83 41W
Heart →	116	46 40N	100 51W
Heart's Content	107	47 54N	53 27W
Heath Pt.	107	49 8N	61 40W
Heath Steele	107	47 17N	66 5W
Heavener	117	34 54N	94 36W
Hebbronville	117	27 20N	98 40W
Hebei □	76	39 0N	116 0 E
Hebel	99	28 58 S	147 47 E
Heber Springs	117	35 29N	91 59W
Hebert	109	50 30N	107 10W
Hebgen, L.	118	44 50N	111 15W
Hebi	76	35 57N	114 7 E
Hebrides	14	57 30N	7 0W
Hebrides, Inner Is.	14	57 20N	6 40W
Hebrides, Outer Is.	14	57 30N	7 40W
Hebron, Can.	105	58 5N	62 30W
Hebron, N.D., U.S.A.	116	46 56N	102 2W
Hebron, Nebr., U.S.A.	116	40 15N	97 33W
Hebron = Al Khalil	62	31 32N	35 6 E
Heby	48	59 56N	16 53 E
Hecate Str.	108	53 10N	130 30W
Hechi	75	24 40N	108 2 E
Hechingen	25	48 20N	8 58 E
Hechuan	75	30 2N	106 12 E
Hecla	116	45 56N	98 8W
Hecla I.	109	51 10N	96 43W
Heddal	47	59 36N	9 9 E
Hédé	18	48 18N	1 49W
Hede	48	62 23N	13 30 E
Hedemora	48	60 18N	15 58 E
Hedley	117	34 53N	100 39W
Hedmark fylke □	47	61 17N	11 40 E
Hedrum	47	59 7N	10 5 E
Heemstede	16	52 22N	4 37 E
Heerde	16	52 24N	6 2 E
Heerenveen	16	52 57N	5 55 E
Heerlen	16	50 55N	6 0 E
Hefa	62	32 46N	35 0 E
Hefei	75	31 52N	117 18 E
Hegang	75	47 20N	130 19 E
Hegyalja	27	48 25N	21 25 E
Heide	24	54 10N	9 7 E
Heidelberg, Ger.	25	49 23N	8 41 E
Heidelberg, C. Prov., S. Afr.	92	34 6 S	20 59 E
Heidelberg, Trans., S. Afr.	93	26 30 S	28 23 E
Heidenheim	25	48 40N	10 10 E
Heilbron	93	27 16 S	27 59 E
Heilbronn	25	49 8N	9 13 E
Heiligenblut	26	47 2N	12 51 E
Heiligenhafen	24	54 21N	10 58 E
Heiligenstadt	24	51 22N	10 9 E
Heilongjiang □	75	48 0N	126 0 E
Heilunkiang = Heilongjiang □	75	48 0N	126 0 E
Heim	47	63 26N	9 5 E
Heinola	51	61 13N	26 2 E
Heinze Is.	71	14 25N	97 45 E
Hejaz = Ḥijāz	64	26 0N	37 30 E
Hejian	76	38 25N	116 5 E
Hejiang	77	28 43N	105 46 E
Hekimhan	64	38 50N	38 0 E
Hekla	50	63 56N	19 35W
Hekou	75	22 30N	103 59 E
Hel	28	54 37N	18 47 E
Helagsfjället	48	62 54N	12 25 E
Helan Shan	76	39 0N	105 55 E
Helechosa	31	39 22N	4 53W
Helena, Ark., U.S.A.	117	34 30N	90 35W
Helena, Mont., U.S.A.	118	46 40N	112 0W
Helensburgh, Austral.	100	34 11 S	151 1 E
Helensburgh, U.K.	14	56 0N	4 44W
Helensville	101	36 41 S	174 29 E
Helez	62	31 36N	34 39 E
Helgasjön	49	57 0N	14 50 E
Helgeroa	47	59 0N	9 45 E
Helgoland	24	54 10N	7 51 E
Heligoland = Helgoland	24	54 10N	7 51 E
Heliopolis	86	30 6N	31 17 E
Hell-Ville	93	13 25 S	48 16 E
Hellebæk	49	56 4N	12 32 E
Helleland	47	58 33N	6 7 E
Hellendoorn	16	52 24N	6 27 E
Hellevoetsluis	16	51 50N	4 8 E
Hellin	33	38 31N	1 40W
Helmand □	65	31 20N	64 0 E
Helmand →	66	31 12N	61 34 E
Helmand, Hamun	65	31 15N	61 15 E
Helme →	24	51 40N	11 20 E
Helmond	16	51 29N	5 41 E
Helmsdale	14	58 7N	3 40W
Helmstedt	24	52 16N	11 0 E
Helnæs	49	55 9N	10 0 E
Helper	118	39 44N	110 56W
Helsingborg	49	56 3N	12 42 E
Helsinge	49	56 2N	12 12 E
Helsingfors	51	60 15N	25 3 E
Helsingør	49	56 2N	12 35 E
Helsinki	51	60 15N	25 3 E
Helska, Mierzeja	28	54 45N	18 40 E
Helston	13	50 7N	5 17W
Helvellyn	12	54 31N	3 1W
Helwân	86	29 50N	31 20 E
Hemavati →	70	12 30N	76 20 E
Hemet	119	33 45N	116 59W
Hemingford	116	42 21N	103 4W
Hemphill	117	31 21N	93 49W
Hempstead	117	30 5N	96 5W
Hemse	49	57 15N	18 22 E
Hemsö	48	62 43N	18 5 E
Henan □	75	34 0N	114 0 E
Henares →	32	40 24N	3 30W
Hendaye	20	43 23N	1 47W
Henderson, Argent.	124	36 18 S	61 43W
Henderson, Ky., U.S.A.	114	37 50N	87 38W
Henderson, N.C., U.S.A.	115	36 20N	78 25W
Henderson, Nev., U.S.A.	119	36 2N	115 0W
Henderson, Pa., U.S.A.	115	35 25N	88 40W
Henderson, Tex., U.S.A.	117	32 5N	94 49W
Hendersonville	115	35 21N	82 28W
Hendon	99	28 5 S	151 50 E
Hendorf	46	46 4N	24 55 E
Heng Xian	77	22 40N	109 17 E
Hengdaohezi	76	44 52N	129 0 E
Hengelo	16	52 3N	6 19 E
Hengshan, Hunan, China	77	27 16N	112 45 E
Hengshan, Shaanxi, China	76	37 58N	109 5 E
Hengshui	76	37 41N	115 40 E
Hengyang	75	26 52N	112 33 E
Hénin-Beaumont	19	50 25N	2 58 E
Henlopen, C.	114	38 48N	75 5W
Hennan, L.	48	62 3N	15 46 E
Hennebont	18	47 49N	3 19W
Hennenman	92	27 59 S	27 1 E
Hennessy	117	36 8N	97 53W
Hennigsdorf	24	52 38N	13 13 E
Henrichemont	19	47 20N	2 30 E
Henrietta	117	33 50N	98 15W
Henrietta Maria C.	106	55 9N	82 20W
Henrietta, Ostrov	59	77 6N	156 30 E
Henry	116	41 5N	89 20W
Henryetta	117	35 30N	96 0W
Hensall	112	43 26N	81 30W
Hentiyn Nuruu	75	48 30N	108 30 E
Henty	99	35 30 S	147 0 E
Henzada	67	17 38N	95 26 E
Hephaestia	44	39 55N	25 14 E
Heping	77	24 29N	115 0 E
Heppner	118	45 21N	119 34W
Hepu	77	21 40N	109 12 E
Hepworth	112	44 37N	81 9W
Herad	47	58 8N	6 47 E
Héraðsflói	50	65 42N	14 12W
Héraðsvötn →	50	65 45N	19 25W
Herāt	65	34 20N	62 7 E
Herāt □	65	35 0N	62 0 E
Hérault □	20	43 34N	3 15 E
Hérault →	20	43 17N	3 26 E
Herbault	18	47 36N	1 8 E
Herbert →	98	18 31 S	146 17 E
Herbert Downs	98	23 7 S	139 9 E
Herberton	98	17 20 S	145 25 E
Herbiers, Les	18	46 52N	1 0W
Herbignac	18	47 27N	2 18W
Herborn	24	50 40N	8 19 E
Herby	28	50 45N	18 50 E
Hercegnovi	42	42 30N	18 33 E
Herðubreið	50	65 11N	16 21W
Hereford, U.K.	13	52 4N	2 42W
Hereford, U.S.A.	117	34 50N	102 28W
Hereford and Worcester □	13	52 10N	2 30W
Herefoss	47	58 32N	8 23 E
Herentals	16	51 12N	4 51 E
Herføge	49	55 26N	12 9 E
Herford	24	52 7N	8 40 E
Héricourt	19	47 32N	6 45 E
Herington	116	38 43N	97 0W
Herisau	25	47 22N	9 17 E
Hérisson	20	46 32N	2 42 E
Herkimer	114	43 0N	74 59W
Herm	18	49 30N	2 28W
Hermagor	26	46 38N	13 23 E
Herman	116	45 51N	96 8W
Hermann	116	38 40N	91 25W
Hermannsburg	24	52 49N	10 6 E
Hermanus	92	34 27 S	19 12 E
Herment	20	45 45N	2 24 E
Hermidale	99	31 30 S	146 42 E
Hermiston	118	45 50N	119 16W
Hermitage	101	43 44 S	170 5 E
Hermite, I.	128	55 50 S	68 0W
Hermon, Mt. = Ash Shaykh, J.	64	33 20N	35 51 E
Hermosillo	120	29 10N	111 0W
Hernad →	27	47 56N	21 8 E
Hernandarias	125	25 20 S	54 40W
Hernando, Argent.	124	32 28 S	63 40W
Hernando, U.S.A.	117	34 50N	89 59W
Herne	24	51 33N	7 12 E
Herne Bay	13	51 22N	1 8 E
Herning	49	56 8N	8 58 E
Heroica Nogales = Nogales	120	31 20N	110 56W
Heron Bay	106	48 40N	86 25W
Herowābād	64	38 37N	48 32 E
Herreid	116	45 53N	100 5W
Herrera	31	37 26N	4 55W
Herrera de Alcántar	31	39 39N	7 25W
Herrera de Pisuerga	30	42 35N	4 20W
Herrera del Duque	31	39 10N	5 3W
Herrick	99	41 5 S	147 55 E
Herrin	117	37 50N	89 0W
Herrljunga	49	58 5N	13 1 E
Hersbruck	25	49 30N	11 25 E
Herstal	16	50 40N	5 38 E
Hersvik	47	61 10N	4 53 E
Hertford	13	51 47N	0 4W
Hertford □	13	51 51N	0 5W
's-Hertogenbosch	16	51 42N	5 17 E
Hertzogville	92	28 9 S	25 30 E
Hervás	30	40 16N	5 52W
Hervey B.	97	25 0 S	152 52 E
• Hervey Is.	95	19 30 S	159 0W
Herzberg, Cottbus, Ger.	24	51 40N	13 13 E
Herzberg, Niedersachsen, Ger.	24	51 38N	10 20 E
Herzliyya	62	32 10N	34 50 E
Herzogenburg	26	48 17N	15 41 E
Hesdin	19	50 21N	2 0 E
Hesel	24	53 18N	7 36 E
Heskestad	47	58 28N	6 22 E
Hespeler	112	43 26N	80 19W
Hesse = Hessen	24	50 40N	9 20 E
Hessen □	24	50 40N	9 20 E
Hettinger	116	46 0N	102 38W
Hettstedt	24	51 39N	11 30 E
Hève, C. de la	18	49 30N	0 5 E
Heves □	27	47 50N	20 0 E
Hevron →	62	31 12N	34 42 E
Hewett, C.	105	70 16N	67 45W
Hex River	92	33 30 S	19 35 E
Hexham	12	54 58N	2 7W
Hexigten Qi	76	43 18N	117 30 E
Heyfield	100	37 59 S	146 47 E
Heysham	12	54 5N	2 53W
Heywood	99	38 8 S	141 37 E
Hi-no-Misaki	74	35 26N	132 38 E
Hialeach	115	25 49N	80 17W
Hiawatha, Kans., U.S.A.	116	39 55N	95 33W
Hiawatha, Utah, U.S.A.	118	39 29N	111 1W
Hibbing	116	47 30N	93 0W
Hickman	117	36 35N	89 8W
Hickory	115	35 46N	81 17W
Hicks Pt.	97	37 49 S	149 17 E
Hicksville	113	40 46N	73 30W
Hida	46	47 10N	23 19 E
Hida-Sammyaku	74	36 30N	137 40 E
Hidalgo	120	24 15N	99 26W
Hidalgo del Parral	120	26 58N	105 40W
Hidalgo, Presa M.	120	26 30N	108 35W
Hiddensee	24	54 30N	13 6 E
Hieflau	26	47 36N	14 46 E
Hiendelaencina	32	41 5N	3 0W
Hierro	80	27 44N	18 0 E
Higashiōsaka	74	34 40N	135 37 E
Higgins	117	36 9N	100 1W
High Atlas = Haut Atlas	82	32 30N	5 0W
High I.	107	56 40N	61 10W
High Island	117	29 32N	94 22W
High Level	108	58 31N	117 8W
High Point	115	35 57N	79 58W
High Prairie	108	55 30N	116 30W
High River	108	50 30N	113 50W
High Springs	115	29 50N	82 40W
High Tatra	27	49 30N	20 00 E
High Wycombe	13	51 37N	0 45W
Highbury	98	16 25 S	143 9 E
Highland □	14	57 30N	5 0W
Highland Park	114	42 10N	87 50W
Highmore	116	44 35N	99 26W
Highrock L.	109	57 5N	105 32W
Higley	119	33 27N	111 46W
Hihya	86	30 40N	31 36 E
Hiiumaa	54	58 50N	22 45 E
Hijar	32	41 10N	0 27W
Ḥijārah, Şaḥrā' al	64	30 25N	44 30 E
Hiko	119	37 30N	115 13W
Hikone	74	35 15N	136 10 E
Hildburghhausen	25	50 24N	10 43 E
Hildesheim	24	52 9N	9 55 E
Hill City, Idaho, U.S.A.	118	43 20N	115 2W
Hill City, Kans., U.S.A.	116	39 25N	99 51W
Hill City, Minn., U.S.A.	116	46 57N	93 35W
Hill City, S.D., U.S.A.	116	43 58N	103 35W
Hill Island L.	109	60 30N	109 50W
Hillared	49	57 37N	13 10 E
Hillegom	16	52 18N	4 35 E
Hillerød	49	55 56N	12 19 E
Hillerstorp	49	57 20N	13 52 E
Hillingdon	13	51 33N	0 29W
Hillman	114	45 5N	83 52W
Hillmond	109	53 26N	109 41W
Hillsboro, Kans., U.S.A.	116	38 22N	97 10W
Hillsboro, N. Mex., U.S.A.	119	33 0N	107 35W
Hillsboro, N.D., U.S.A.	116	47 23N	97 9W
Hillsboro, N.H., U.S.A.	114	43 8N	71 56W
Hillsboro, Oreg., U.S.A.	118	45 31N	123 0W
Hillsboro, Tex., U.S.A.	117	32 0N	97 10W
Hillsdale, Mich., U.S.A.	114	41 55N	84 40W
Hillsdale, N.Y., U.S.A.	113	42 11N	73 30W
Hillsport	106	49 27N	85 34W
Hillston	97	33 30 S	145 31 E
Hilo	110	19 44N	155 5W
Hilonghilong	73	9 10N	125 45 E
Hilton	112	43 16N	77 48W
Hilversum	16	52 14N	5 10 E
Himachal Pradesh □	68	31 30N	77 0 E
Himalaya	67	29 0N	84 0 E
Himara	44	40 8N	19 43 E
Himeji	74	34 50N	134 40 E
Himi	74	36 50N	137 0 E
Himmerland	49	56 45N	9 30 E
Ḥimş	64	34 40N	36 45 E
Hinako, Kepulauan	72	0 50N	97 20 E
Hinchinbrook I.	97	18 20 S	146 15 E
Hinckley, U.K.	13	52 33N	1 21W
Hinckley, U.S.A.	118	39 18N	112 41W
Hindås	49	57 42N	12 27 E
Hindaun	68	26 44N	77 5 E
Hindmarsh L.	99	36 5 S	141 55 E
Hindol	69	20 40N	85 10 E
Hindsholm	49	55 30N	10 40 E
Hindu Bagh	68	30 56N	67 50 E
Hindu Kush	65	36 0N	71 0 E
Hindupur	70	13 49N	77 32 E
Hines Creek	108	56 20N	118 40W
Hinganghat	68	20 30N	78 52 E
Hingham	118	48 34N	110 29W
Hingoli	70	19 41N	77 15 E
Hinlopenstretet	4	79 35N	18 40 E
Hinna	85	10 25N	11 35 E
Hinojosa del Duque	31	38 30N	5 9W
Hinsdale	118	48 26N	107 2W
Hinterrhein →	25	46 40N	9 25 E
Hinton, Can.	108	53 26N	117 34W
Hinton, U.S.A.	114	37 40N	80 51W
Hippolytushoef	16	52 54N	4 58 E
Hirakud	69	21 32N	83 51 E
Hirakud Dam	69	21 32N	83 45 E
Hiratsuka	74	35 19N	139 21 E
Hirhafok	83	23 49N	5 45 E
Hîrlău	46	47 23N	27 0 E
Hirosaki	74	40 34N	140 28 E
Hiroshima	74	34 24N	132 30 E
Hiroshima □	74	34 50N	133 0 E
Hirsoholmene	49	57 30N	10 36 E
Hirson	19	49 55N	4 4 E
Hîrşova	46	44 40N	27 59 E
Hirtshals	49	57 36N	9 57 E
Ḥişn Dibā	65	25 45N	56 16 E
Hispaniola	121	19 0N	71 0W
Hissar	68	29 12N	75 45 E
Hita	74	33 20N	130 58 E
Hitachi	74	36 36N	140 39 E
Hitchin	13	51 57N	0 16W
Hitoyoshi	74	32 13N	130 45 E
Hitra	47	63 30N	8 45 E
Hitzacker	24	53 9N	11 1 E
Ḥiyyon, N. →	62	30 25N	35 10 E
Hjalmar L.	109	61 33N	109 25W
Hjälmare kanal	48	59 20N	15 59 E
Hjälmaren	48	59 18N	15 40 E
Hjartdal	47	59 37N	8 41 E
Hjerkinn	47	62 13N	9 33 E
Hjørring	49	57 29N	9 59 E
Hjorted	49	57 37N	16 19 E
Hjortkvarn	49	58 54N	15 26 E
Hlinsko	26	49 45N	15 54 E
Hlohovec	27	48 26N	17 49 E
Hṅak	4	70 40N	52 10W
Ho	85	6 37N	0 27 E
Ho Chi Minh, Phanh Bho	71	10 58N	106 40 E
Hoa Binh	71	20 50N	105 20 E
Hoai Nhon (Bon Son)	71	14 28N	109 1 E
Hoare B.	105	65 17N	62 30W
Hobart, Austral.	97	42 50 S	147 21 E
Hobart, U.S.A.	117	35 0N	99 5W
Hobbs	117	32 40N	103 3W
Hobbs Coast	5	74 50 S	131 0W
Hoboken, Belg.	16	51 11N	4 21 E
Hoboken, U.S.A.	113	40 45N	74 4W
Hobro	49	56 39N	9 46 E
Hoburgen	49	56 55N	18 7 E
Hochatown	117	34 11N	94 39W
Hochschwab	26	47 35N	15 0 E
Höchst	25	50 6N	8 33 E
Höchstadt	25	49 42N	10 48 E
Hockenheim	25	49 18N	8 33 E
Hodgson	109	51 13N	97 36W
Hódmezövásárhely	27	46 28N	20 22 E
Hodna, Chott el	83	35 30N	5 0 E
Hodna, Monts du	83	35 52N	4 42 E
Hodonín	27	48 50N	17 10 E
Hoëdic	18	47 21N	2 52W
Hoek van Holland	16	52 0N	4 7 E
Hoëveld	93	26 30 S	30 0 E
Hof, Ger.	25	50 18N	11 55 E
Hof, Iceland	50	64 33N	14 40W
Höfðakaupstaður	50	65 50N	20 19W
Hofgeismar	24	51 29N	9 23 E
Hofors	48	60 31N	16 15 E
Hofsjökull	50	64 49N	18 48W
Hofsós	50	65 53N	19 26W
Hōfu	74	34 3N	131 34 E
Hogansville	115	33 14N	84 50W

• Renamed Manuae

Hogeland	118	48 51N	108 40W
Hogenakai Falls	70	12 6N	77 50 E
Högfors	48	59 58N	15 3 E
Högsäter	49	58 38N	12 5 E
Högsby	49	57 10N	16 1 E
Högsjö	48	59 4N	15 44 E
Hoh Xil Shan	75	35 0N	89 0 E
Hohe Rhön	25	50 24N	9 58 E
Hohe Tauern	26	47 11N	12 40 E
Hohe Venn	16	50 30N	6 5 E
Hohenau	27	48 36N	16 55 E
Hohenems	26	47 22N	9 42 E
Hohenstein Ernstthal	24	50 48N	12 43 E
Hohenwald	115	35 35N	87 30W
Hohenwestedt	24	54 6N	9 30 E
Hohhot	76	40 52N	111 40 E
Hohoe	85	7 8N	0 32 E
Hoi An	71	15 30N	108 19 E
Hoi Xuan	71	20 25N	105 9 E
Hoisington	116	38 33N	98 50W
Højer	49	54 58N	8 42 E
Hok	49	57 31N	14 16 E
Hökensås	49	58 0N	14 5 E
Hökerum	49	57 51N	13 16 E
Hokianga Harbour	101	35 31 S	173 22 E
Hokitika	101	42 42 S	171 0 E
Hokkaidō □	74	43 30N	143 0 E
Hokksund	47	59 44N	9 59 E
Hol-Hol	87	11 20N	42 50 E
Holbæk	49	55 43N	11 43 E
Holbrook, Austral.	99	35 42 S	147 18 E
Holbrook, U.S.A.	119	35 54N	110 10W
Holden, Can.	108	53 13N	112 11W
Holden, U.S.A.	118	39 0N	112 26W
Holdenville	117	35 5N	96 25W
Holderness	12	53 45N	0 5W
Holdfast	109	50 58N	105 25W
Holdrege	116	40 26N	99 22W
Hole	47	60 6N	10 12 E
Hole-Narsipur	70	12 48N	76 16 E
Holešov	27	49 20N	17 35 E
Holguín	121	20 50N	76 20W
Holíč	27	48 49N	17 10 E
Hollabrunn	26	48 34N	16 5 E
Hollams Bird I.	92	24 40 S	14 30 E
Holland	114	42 47N	86 7W
Hollandia = Jayapura	73	2 28 S	140 38 E
Höllen	47	58 6N	7 49 E
Hollfeld	25	49 56N	11 18 E
Hollick Kenyon Plateau	5	82 0 S	110 0W
Hollidaysburg	114	40 26N	78 25W
Hollis	117	34 45N	99 55W
Hollister, Calif., U.S.A.	119	36 51N	121 24W
Hollister, Idaho, U.S.A.	118	42 21N	114 40W
Holly	116	38 7N	102 7W
Holly Hill	115	29 15N	81 3W
Holly Springs	117	34 45N	89 25W
Hollywood, Calif., U.S.A.	110	34 7N	118 25W
Hollywood, Fla., U.S.A.	115	26 0N	80 9W
Holm	48	62 40N	16 40 E
Holman Island	104	70 42N	117 41W
Hólmavík	50	65 42N	21 40W
Holmedal	47	61 22N	5 11 E
Holmegil	48	59 10N	11 44 E
Holmestrand	47	59 31N	10 14 E
Holmsbu	47	59 32N	10 27 E
Holmsjön	48	62 26N	15 20 E
Holmsland Klit	49	56 0N	8 5 E
Holmsund	50	63 41N	20 20 E
Holod	46	46 49N	22 8 E
Holon	62	32 2N	34 47 E
Holroyd →	97	14 10 S	141 36 E
Holstebro	49	56 22N	8 37 E
Holsworthy	13	50 48N	4 21W
Holt	50	63 33N	19 48W
Holte	49	55 50N	12 29 E
Holton, Can.	107	54 31N	57 12W
Holton, U.S.A.	116	39 28N	95 44W
Holtville	119	32 50N	115 27W
Holum	47	58 6N	7 32 E
Holwerd	16	53 22N	5 54 E
Holy Cross	104	62 10N	159 52W
Holy I., England, U.K.	12	55 42N	1 48W
Holy I., Wales, U.K.	12	53 17N	4 37W
Holyhead	12	53 18N	4 38W
Holyoke, Colo., U.S.A.	116	40 39N	102 18W
Holyoke, Mass., U.S.A.	114	42 14N	72 37W
Holyrood	107	47 27N	53 8W
Holzkirchen	25	47 53N	11 42 E
Holzminden	24	51 49N	9 31 E
Homa Bay	90	0 36 S	34 30 E
* Homa Bay □	90	0 50 S	34 30 E
Homalin	67	24 55N	95 0 E
Homberg	24	51 2N	9 20 E
Hombori	85	15 20N	1 38W
Homburg	25	49 19N	7 21 E
Home B.	105	68 40N	67 10W
Home Hill	97	19 43 S	147 25 E
Homedale	118	43 42N	116 59W
Homer, Alaska, U.S.A.	104	59 40N	151 35W
Homer, La., U.S.A.	117	32 50N	93 4W
Homestead, Austral.	98	20 20 S	145 40 E
Homestead, Fla., U.S.A.	115	25 29N	80 27W
Homestead, Oreg., U.S.A.	118	45 5N	116 57W
Hominy	117	36 26N	96 24W
Homnabad	70	17 45N	77 11 E
Homoine	93	23 55 S	35 8 E
Homoljske Planina	42	44 10N	21 45 E
Homorod	46	46 5N	25 15 E
Homs = Ḥimş	64	34 40N	36 45 E
Hon Chong	71	10 25N	104 30 E
Honan = Henan □	75	34 0N	114 0 E
Honda	126	5 12N	74 45W
Hondeklipbaai	92	30 19 S	17 17 E
Hondo	117	29 22N	99 6W
Hondo →	120	18 25N	88 21W
Honduras ■	121	14 40N	86 30W
Honduras, Golfo de	120	16 50N	87 0W
Honesdale	113	41 34N	75 17W
Honey L.	118	40 13N	120 14W
Honfleur	18	49 25N	0 13 E
Hong Kong ■	75	22 11N	114 14 E
Hong'an	77	31 20N	114 40 E
Hongha →	71	22 0N	104 0 E
Honghai Wan	77	22 40N	115 0 E
Honghu	77	29 50N	113 30 E
Hongjiang	75	27 7N	109 59 E
Hongshui He →	75	23 48N	109 30 E
Hongtong	76	36 16N	111 40 E
Honguedo, Détroit d'	107	49 15N	64 0W
Hongze Hu	75	33 15N	118 35 E
Honiara	94	9 27 S	159 57 E
Honiton	13	50 48N	3 11W
Honkorâb, Ras	86	24 35N	35 10 E
Honolulu	110	21 19N	157 52W
Honshū	74	36 0N	138 0 E
Hontoria del Pinar	32	41 50N	3 10W
Hood Mt.	118	45 24N	121 41W
Hood, Pt.	96	34 23 S	119 34 E
Hood River	118	45 45N	121 31W
Hoodsport	118	47 24N	123 7W
Hooge	24	54 31N	8 36 E
Hoogeveen	16	52 44N	6 30 E
Hoogezand	16	53 11N	6 45 E
Hooghly →	69	21 56N	88 4 E
Hooghly-Chinsura	69	22 53N	88 27 E
Hook Hd.	15	52 8N	6 57W
Hook I.	98	20 4 S	149 0 E
Hook of Holland = Hoek van Holland	16	52 0N	4 7 E
Hooker	117	36 55N	101 10W
Hoopeston	114	40 30N	87 40W
Hoopstad	92	27 50 S	25 55 E
Hoorn	16	52 38N	5 4 E
Hoover Dam	119	36 0N	114 45W
Hooversville	112	40 8N	78 57W
Hop Bottom	113	41 41N	75 47W
Hopà	57	41 28N	41 30 E
Hope, Can.	108	49 25N	121 25 E
Hope, Ark., U.S.A.	117	33 40N	93 36W
Hope, N.D., U.S.A.	116	47 21N	97 42W
Hope Bay	5	65 0 S	55 0W
Hope, L.	99	28 24 S	139 18 E
Hope Pt.	104	68 20N	166 50W
Hope Town	121	26 35N	76 57W
Hopedale	107	55 28N	60 13W
Hopefield	92	33 3 S	18 22 E
Hopei = Hebei □	76	39 0N	116 0 E
Hopelchén	120	19 46N	89 50W
Hopen	47	63 27N	8 2 E
Hopetoun, Vic., Austral.	99	35 42 S	142 22 E
Hopetoun, W. Australia, Austral.	100	33 57 S	120 7 E
Hopetown	92	29 34 S	24 3 E
Hopkins	116	40 31N	94 45W
Hopkins →	100	38 25 S	142 30 E
Hopkinsville	115	36 52N	87 26W
Hopland	118	39 0N	123 7W
Hoptrup	49	55 11N	9 28 E
Hoquiam	118	46 50N	123 55W
Horazdovice	26	49 19N	13 42 E
Horcajo de Santiago	32	39 50N	3 1W
Hordaland fylke □	47	60 25N	6 15 E
Horden Hills	96	20 40 S	130 20 E
Horezu	46	45 6N	24 0 E
Horgen	25	47 15N	8 35 E
Horgoš	42	46 10N	20 0 E
Horice	26	50 21N	15 39 E
Horlick Mts.	5	84 0 S	102 0W
Hormoz	65	27 35N	55 0 E
Hormoz, Jaz. ye	65	27 8N	56 28 E
Hormuz Str.	65	26 30N	56 30 E
Horn, Austria	26	48 39N	15 40 E
Horn, Ísafjarðarsýsla, Iceland	50	66 28N	22 28W
Horn, Suður-Múlasýsla, Iceland	50	65 10N	13 31W
Horn →	108	61 30N	118 1W
Horn, Cape = Hornos, Cabo de	128	55 50 S	67 30W
Horn Head	15	55 13N	8 0W
Horn, I.	115	30 17N	88 40W
Horn Mts.	108	62 15N	119 15W
Hornachuelos	31	37 50N	5 14W
Hornavan	50	66 15N	17 30 E
Hornbæk	49	56 5N	12 26 E
Hornbeck	117	31 22N	93 20W
Hornbrook	118	41 58N	122 37W
Hornburg	24	52 2N	10 36 E
Horncastle	12	53 13N	0 8W
Horndal	48	60 18N	16 23 E
Hornell	114	42 23N	77 41W
Hornell L.	108	62 20N	119 25W
Hornepayne	106	49 14N	84 48W
Hornindal	47	61 58N	6 30 E
Hornnes	47	58 34N	7 45 E
Hornos, Cabo de	128	55 50 S	67 30W
Hornoy	19	49 50N	1 54 E
Hornsby	99	33 42 S	151 2 E
Hornsea	12	53 55N	0 10W
Hornslandet	48	61 35N	17 37 E
Hornslet	49	56 18N	10 19 E
Hörnum	24	54 44N	8 18 E
Horovice	26	49 48N	13 53 E
Horqin Youyi Qianqi	75	46 5N	122 3 E
Horqueta	124	23 15 S	56 55W
Horra, La	30	41 44N	3 53W
Horred	49	57 22N	12 28 E
Horse Cr. →	116	41 57N	103 58W
Horse Is.	107	50 15N	55 50W
Horsefly L.	108	52 25N	121 0W
Horsens	49	55 52N	9 51 E
Horsens Fjord	49	55 50N	10 0 E
Horseshoe Dam	119	33 45N	111 35W
Horsham, Austral.	97	36 44 S	142 13 E
Horsham, U.K.	13	51 4N	0 20W
Horšovský Týn	26	49 31N	12 58 E
Horten	47	59 25N	10 32 E
Hortobágy →	27	47 30N	21 6 E
Horton	116	39 42N	95 30W
Horton →	104	69 56N	126 52W
Hörvik	49	56 2N	14 45 E
Horwood, L.	106	48 5N	82 20W
Hosaina	87	7 30N	37 47 E
Hosdurga	70	13 49N	76 17 E
Hose, Pegunungan	72	2 5N	114 6 E
Hoshangabad	68	22 45N	77 45 E
Hoshiarpur	68	31 30N	75 58 E
Hosmer	116	45 36N	99 29W
Hospet	70	15 15N	76 20 E
Hospitalet de Llobregat	32	41 21N	2 6 E
Hospitalet, L'	20	42 36N	1 47 E
Hoste, I.	128	55 0 S	69 0W
Hostens	20	44 30N	0 40W
Hot	71	18 8N	98 29 E
Hot Creek Ra.	118	39 0N	116 0W
Hot Springs, Ari., U.S.A.	117	34 30N	93 0W
Hot Springs, S.D., U.S.A.	116	43 25N	103 30W
Hotagen	50	63 50N	14 30 E
Hotan	75	37 25N	79 55 E
Hotazel	92	27 17 S	23 00 E
Hotchkiss	119	38 47N	107 47W
Hoting	50	64 8N	16 15 E
Hotolishti	44	41 10N	20 25 E
Hottentotsbaai	92	26 8 S	14 59 E
Houat	18	47 24N	2 58W
Houck	119	35 15N	109 15W
Houdan	19	48 48N	1 35 E
Houffalize	16	50 8N	5 48 E
Houghton	116	47 9N	88 39W
Houghton L.	114	44 20N	84 40W
Houghton-le-Spring	12	54 51N	1 28W
Houhora	101	34 49 S	173 9 E
Houlton	107	46 5N	67 50W
Houma	117	29 35N	90 44W
Houndé	84	11 34N	3 31W
Hourtin	20	45 11N	1 4W
Hourtin, Étang d'	20	45 10N	1 6W
Houston, Can.	108	54 25N	126 39W
Houston, Mo., U.S.A.	117	37 20N	92 0W
Houston, Tex., U.S.A.	117	29 50N	95 20W
Houtman Abrolhos	96	28 43 S	113 48 E
Hov	49	55 55N	10 15 E
Hova	49	58 53N	14 14 E
Høvåg	47	58 10N	8 16 E
Hovd (Jargalant)	75	48 2N	91 37 E
Hovden	47	59 33N	7 22 E
Hove	13	50 50N	0 10W
Hovmantorp	49	56 47N	15 7 E
Hövsgöl Nuur	75	51 0N	100 30 E
Hovsta	48	59 22N	15 15 E
Howakil	87	15 10N	40 16 E
Howar, Wadi →	87	17 30N	27 8 E
Howard, Austral.	99	25 16 S	152 32 E
Howard, Kans., U.S.A.	117	37 30N	96 16W
Howard, Pa., U.S.A.	112	41 0N	77 40W
Howard, S.D., U.S.A.	116	44 2N	97 30W
Howard L.	109	62 15N	105 57W
Howe	118	43 48N	113 0W
Howe, C.	97	37 30 S	150 0 E
Howell	114	42 38N	83 56W
Howick, Can.	113	45 11N	73 51W
Howick, S. Afr.	93	29 28 S	30 14 E
Howick Group	98	14 20 S	145 30 E
Howitt, L.	99	27 40 S	138 40 E
Howley	107	49 12N	57 2W
Howrah	69	22 37N	88 20 E
Howth Hd.	15	53 21N	6 0W
Höxter	24	51 45N	9 26 E
Hoy I.	14	58 50N	3 15W
Hoya	24	52 47N	9 10 E
Hoyerswerda	24	51 26N	14 14 E
Hoyos	30	40 9N	6 45W
Hpungan Pass	67	27 30N	96 55 E
Hrádec Králové	26	50 15N	15 50 E
Hrádek	27	48 46N	16 16 E
Hranice	27	49 34N	17 45 E
Hron →	27	47 49N	18 45 E
Hrubieszów	28	50 49N	23 51 E
Hrubý Nizký Jeseník	27	50 7N	17 10 E
Hrvatska	39	45 20N	16 0 E
Hrvatska □	42	45 20N	18 0 E
Hsenwi	67	23 22N	97 55 E
Hsiamen = Xiamen	75	24 25N	118 4 E
Hsian = Xi'an	77	34 15N	109 0 E
Hsinhailien = Lianyungang	77	34 40N	119 11 E
Hsüchou = Xuzhou	77	34 18N	117 18 E
Hua Hin	71	12 34N	99 58 E
Hua Xian, Henan, China	77	35 30N	114 30 E
Hua Xian, Shaanxi, China	77	34 30N	109 48 E
Huacheng	77	24 4N	115 37 E
Huacho	126	11 10 S	77 35W
Huachón	126	10 35 S	76 0W
Huachuan	76	46 50N	130 21 E
Huade	76	41 55N	113 59 E
Huadian	76	43 0N	126 40 E
Huai He →	75	33 0N	118 30 E
Huai'an	77	33 30N	119 10 E
Huaide	76	43 30N	124 40 E
Huainan	75	32 38N	116 58 E
Huaiyang	77	33 40N	114 52 E
Huaiyuan	77	24 31N	108 22 E
Huajianzi	76	41 23N	125 20 E
Huajuapan de Leon	120	17 50N	97 48W
Hualian	77	23 59N	121 37 E
Huallaga →	126	5 0 S	75 30W
Hualpai Pk.	119	35 8N	113 58W
Huambo	89	12 42 S	15 54 E
Huan Jiang →	76	34 28N	109 0 E
Huan Xian	76	36 33N	107 7 E
Huancabamba	126	5 10 S	79 15W
Huancane	126	15 10 S	69 44W
Huancapi	126	13 40 S	74 0W
Huancavelica	126	12 50 S	75 5W
Huancayo	126	12 5 S	75 12W
Huang He	75	37 55N	118 50 E
Huangchuan	77	32 15N	115 10 E
Huangliu	75	18 20N	108 50 E
Huanglong	76	35 30N	109 59 E
Huangshi	75	30 10N	115 3 E
Huangyan	77	28 38N	121 19 E
Huánuco	126	9 55 S	76 15W
Huaraz	126	9 30 S	77 32W
Huarmey	126	10 5 S	78 5W
Huascarán	126	9 8 S	77 36W
Huasco	124	28 30 S	71 15W
Huasco →	124	28 27 S	71 13W
Huatabampo	120	26 50N	109 50W
Huay Namota	120	21 56N	104 30W
Huayllay	126	11 03 S	76 21W
Hubbard	117	31 50N	96 50W
Hubbart Pt.	109	59 21N	94 41W
Hubei □	75	31 0N	112 0 E
Hubli	70	15 22N	75 15 E
Hückelhoven-Ratheim	24	51 6N	6 13 E
Huczwa →	28	50 49N	23 58 E
Huddersfield	12	53 38N	1 49W
Hudi	86	17 43N	34 18 E
Hudiksvall	48	61 43N	17 10 E
Hudson, Can.	109	50 6N	92 09W
Hudson, Mass., U.S.A.	113	42 23N	71 35W
Hudson, Mich., U.S.A.	114	41 50N	84 20W
Hudson, N.Y., U.S.A.	114	42 15N	73 46W
Hudson, Wis., U.S.A.	116	44 57N	92 45W
Hudson, Wyo., U.S.A.	118	42 54N	108 37W
Hudson →	114	40 42N	74 2W
Hudson Bay, Can.	105	60 0N	86 0W
Hudson Bay, Sask., Can.	109	52 51N	102 23W
Hudson Falls	114	43 18N	73 34W
Hudson Hope	108	56 0N	121 54W
Hudson Mts.	5	74 32 S	99 20W
Hudson Str.	105	62 0N	70 0W
Hue	71	16 30N	107 35 E
Huebra →	30	41 2N	6 48W
Huedin	46	46 52N	23 2 E
Huelgoat	18	48 22N	3 46W
Huelma	33	37 39N	3 28W
Huelva	31	37 18N	6 57W
Huelva □	31	37 40N	7 0W
Huelva →	31	37 27N	6 0W
Huentelauquén	124	31 38 S	71 33W
Huércal Overa	33	37 23N	1 57W
Huerta, Sa. de la	124	31 10 S	67 30W
Huertas, C. de las	33	38 21N	0 24W
Huerva →	32	41 39N	0 52W
Huesca	32	42 8N	0 25W
Huesca □	32	42 20N	0 1 E
Huéscar	33	37 44N	2 35W
Huetamo	120	18 36N	100 54W
Huete	32	40 10N	2 43W
Hugh →	96	25 1 S	134 1 E
Hughenden	97	20 52 S	144 10 E
Hughes	104	66 0N	154 20W
Hugo	116	39 12N	103 27W
Hugoton	117	37 11N	101 22W
Hui Xian	76	35 27N	113 12 E
Hui'an	77	25 1N	118 43 E
Huichang	77	25 32N	115 45 E
Huichapán	120	20 24N	99 40W
Huihe	76	48 12N	119 17 E
Huila, Nevado del	126	3 0N	76 0W
Huilai	77	23 0N	116 18 E
Huimin	76	37 27N	117 28 E
Huinan	76	42 40N	126 2 E
Huinca Renancó	124	34 51 S	64 22W
Huining	76	35 38N	105 0 E
Huinong	76	39 5N	106 35 E
Huisne →	18	47 59N	0 11 E
Huize	75	26 24N	103 15 E
Huizhou	77	23 0N	114 23 E
Hukawng Valley	67	26 30N	96 30 E
Hukou	77	29 45N	116 21 E
Hukuntsi	92	23 58 S	21 45 E
Hula	87	6 33N	38 30 E
Hulan	75	46 1N	126 37 E
Ḥulayfā'	64	25 58N	40 45 E
Huld	75	45 5N	105 30 E
Ḥulda	62	31 50N	34 51 E
Hulin	76	45 48N	132 59 E
Hull, Can.	106	45 25N	75 44W
Hull, U.K.	12	53 45N	0 20W
Hull →	12	53 43N	0 25W
Hulst	16	51 17N	4 2 E
Hultsfred	49	57 30N	15 52 E
Hulun Nur	75	49 0N	117 30 E
Huma	76	51 43N	126 38 E
Huma He →	76	51 42N	126 42 E
Humahuaca	124	23 10 S	65 25W
Humaitá, Brazil	126	7 35 S	63 1W
Humaitá, Parag.	124	27 2 S	58 31W
Humansdorp	92	34 2 S	24 46 E
Humbe	92	16 40 S	14 55 E
Humber →	12	53 40N	0 10W
Humberside □	12	53 50N	0 30W
Humble	117	29 59N	93 18W
Humboldt, Can.	109	52 15N	105 9W
Humboldt, Iowa, U.S.A.	116	42 42N	94 15W
Humboldt, Tenn., U.S.A.	117	35 50N	88 55W
Humboldt →	118	40 2N	118 31W
Humboldt Gletscher	4	79 30N	62 0W
Hume, L.	97	36 0 S	147 0 E
Humenné	27	48 55N	21 50 E
Humphreys Pk.	119	35 24N	111 38W
Humpolec	26	49 31N	15 20 E
Hūn	83	29 2N	16 0 E
Húnaflói	50	65 50N	20 50W
Hunan □	75	27 30N	112 0 E
Hunchun	76	42 52N	130 28 E
Hundested	49	55 58N	11 52 E
Hundred Mile House	108	51 38N	121 18W
Hunedoara	46	45 40N	22 50 E
Hunedoara □	46	45 50N	22 54 E
Hünfeld	24	50 40N	9 47 E
Hungary ■	27	47 20N	19 20 E
Hungary, Plain of	9	47 0N	20 0 E
Hungerford	99	28 58 S	144 24 E
Hüngnam	76	39 49N	127 45 E
Huni Valley	84	5 33N	1 56W
Hunsberge	92	27 45 S	17 12 E
Hunsrück	25	49 30N	7 0 E
Hunstanton	12	52 57N	0 30 E
Hunsur	70	12 16N	76 16 E
Hunte →	24	52 30N	8 19 E
Hunter, N.D., U.S.A.	116	47 12N	97 17W
Hunter, N.Y., U.S.A.	113	42 13N	74 13W
Hunter →	100	32 52 S	151 46 E
Hunter I., Austral.	97	40 30 S	144 45 E
Hunter I., Can.	108	51 55N	128 0W
Hunter Ra.	99	32 45 S	150 15 E
Hunters Road	91	19 9 S	29 49 E
Hunterton	99	26 12 S	148 30 E
Hunterville	101	39 56 S	175 35 E

* Renamed South Nyanza

Huntingburg **114** 38 20N 86 58W
Huntingdon, Can. **106** 45 6N 74 10W
Huntingdon, U.K. **13** 52 20N 0 11W
Huntingdon, U.S.A. **114** 40 28N 78 1W
Huntington, Ind., U.S.A. **114** 40 52N 85 30W
Huntington, N.Y., U.S.A. **113** 40 52N 73 25W
Huntington, Oreg., U.S.A. **118** 44 22N 117 21W
Huntington, Ut., U.S.A. **118** 39 24N 111 1W
Huntington, W. Va., U.S.A. **114** 38 20N 82 30W
Huntington Beach **119** 33 40N 118 0W
Huntington Park **119** 33 58N 118 15W
Huntly, N.Z. **101** 37 34 S 175 11 E
Huntly, U.K. **14** 57 27N 2 48W
Huntsville, Can. **106** 45 20N 79 14W
Huntsville, Ala., U.S.A. **115** 34 45N 86 35W
Huntsville, Tex., U.S.A. **117** 30 45N 95 35W
Hunyani → **91** 15 57 S 30 39 E
Huo Xian **76** 36 36N 111 42 E
Huon, G. **98** 7 0 S 147 30 E
Huonville **97** 43 0 S 147 5 E
Huoqiu **77** 32 20N 116 12 E
Huoshao Dao **77** 22 40N 121 30 E
Hupeh □ = Hubei □ **75** 31 0N 112 0 E
Hurbanovo **27** 47 51N 18 11 E
Hure Qi **76** 42 45N 121 45 E
Hurezani **46** 44 49N 23 40 E
Hurghada **86** 27 15N 33 50 E
Hurley, N. Mex., U.S.A. **119** 32 45N 108 7W
Hurley, Wis., U.S.A. **116** 46 26N 90 10W
Huron, Ohio, U.S.A. **112** 41 22N 82 34W
Huron, S.D., U.S.A. **116** 44 22N 98 12W
Huron, L. **112** 45 0N 83 0W
Hurricane **119** 37 10N 113 12W
Hurso **87** 9 35N 41 33 E
Hurum, Buskerud, Norway **47** 59 36N 10 23 E
Hurum, Oppland, Norway **47** 61 9N 8 46 E
Hurunui → **101** 42 54 S 173 18 E
Hurup **49** 56 46N 8 25 E
Húsavík **50** 66 3N 17 21W
Huşi **46** 46 41N 28 7 E
Huskvarna **49** 57 47N 14 15 E
Husøy **47** 61 3N 4 44 E
Hussar **108** 51 3N 112 41W
Hustopéce **27** 48 57N 16 43 E
Husum, Ger. **24** 54 27N 9 3 E
Husum, Sweden **48** 63 21N 19 12 E
Hutchinson, Kans., U.S.A. **117** 38 3N 97 59W
Hutchinson, Minn., U.S.A. **116** 44 50N 94 22W
Hutou **76** 45 58N 133 38 E
Huttenberg **26** 46 56N 14 33 E
Hüttental **24** 50 52N 8 1 E
Huttig **117** 33 5N 92 10W
Hutton, Mt. **99** 25 51 S 148 20 E
Huwun **87** 4 23N 40 6 E
Ḩuwwārah **62** 32 9N 35 15 E
Huy **16** 50 31N 5 15 E
Hvaler **47** 59 4N 11 1 E
Hvammur **50** 65 13N 21 49W
Hvar **39** 43 11N 16 28 E
Hvarski Kanal **39** 43 15N 16 35 E
Hvítá **50** 64 40N 21 5W
Hvítá → **50** 64 0N 20 58W
Hvítárvatn **50** 64 37N 19 50W
Hvitsten **47** 59 35N 10 42 E
Hwang Ho = Huang He → **76** 37 50N 118 50 E
Hyannis **116** 42 0N 101 45W
Hyargas Nuur **75** 49 0N 93 0 E
Hyatts **114** 38 59N 76 55W
Hybo **48** 61 49N 16 15 E
Hyderabad, India **70** 17 22N 78 29 E
Hyderabad, Pak. **68** 25 23N 68 24 E
* Hyderabad □ **68** 25 3N 68 24 E
Hyères **21** 43 8N 6 9 E
Hyères, Îles d' **21** 43 0N 6 28 E
Hyesan **76** 41 20N 128 10 E
Hyland → **108** 59 52N 128 12W
Hylestad **47** 59 6N 7 29 E
Hyltebruk **49** 56 59N 13 15 E
Hyndman Pk. **118** 43 50N 114 10W
Hyōgo □ **74** 35 15N 135 0 E
Hyrum **118** 41 35N 111 56W
Hysham **118** 46 21N 107 11W
Hythe **13** 51 4N 1 5 E
Hyvinkää **51** 60 38N 24 50 E

I

I-n-Azaoua **83** 20 45N 7 31 E
I-n-Échaï **82** 20 10N 2 5W
I-n-Gall **85** 16 51N 7 1 E
I-n-Tabedog **82** 19 48N 1 11 E
Iabès, Erg **82** 27 30N 2 2W
Iaco → **126** 9 3 S 68 34W
Iacobeni **46** 47 25N 25 20 E
Iakora **93** 23 6 S 46 40 E
Ialomiţa □ **46** 44 30N 27 30 E
Ialomiţa → **46** 44 42N 27 51 E
Ianca **46** 45 6N 27 29 E
Iara **46** 46 31N 23 35 E
Iaşi **46** 47 20N 27 0 E
Iba **73** 15 22N 120 0 E
Ibadan **85** 7 22N 3 58 E
Ibagué **126** 4 20N 75 20W
Iballja **44** 42 12N 20 0 E
Ibăneşti **46** 46 45N 24 50 E
Ibar → **42** 43 43N 20 45 E
Ibaraki □ **74** 36 10N 140 10 E
Ibarra **126** 0 21N 78 7W
Ibba **87** 4 49N 29 2 E
Ibba, Bahr el **87** 5 30N 28 55 E
Ibbenbüren **24** 52 16N 7 41 E
Ibembo **90** 2 35N 23 35 E
Ibera, Laguna **124** 28 30 S 57 9W
Iberian Peninsula **8** 40 0N 5 0W
Iberville **106** 45 19N 73 17W
Iberville, Lac d' **106** 55 55N 73 15W
Ibi **85** 8 15N 9 44 E
Ibiá **127** 19 30 S 46 30W
Ibicuy **124** 33 55 S 59 10W
Ibioapaba, Sa. da **127** 4 0 S 41 30W
Ibiza **33** 38 54N 1 26 E
Íblei, Monti **41** 37 15N 14 45 E
Ibo **91** 12 22 S 40 40 E
Ibonma **73** 3 29 S 133 31 E
Ibotirama **127** 12 13 S 43 12W
İbriktepe **44** 41 2N 26 33 E
Ibshawâi **86** 29 21N 30 40 E
Ibu **73** 1 35N 127 33 E
Iburg **24** 52 10N 8 3 E
Icá **126** 14 0 S 75 48W
Iça → **126** 2 55 S 67 58W
Içana **126** 0 21N 67 19W
Iceland ■ **50** 65 0N 19 0W
Icha **59** 55 30N 156 0 E
Ich'ang = Yichang **75** 30 40N 111 20 E
Ichchapuram **70** 19 10N 84 40 E
Ichihara **74** 35 28N 140 5 E
Ichihawa **74** 35 44N 139 55 E
Ichilo → **126** 15 57 S 64 50W
Ichinomiya **74** 35 18N 136 48 E
Ichnya **54** 50 52N 32 24 E
Icht **82** 29 6N 8 54W
Icy Str. **108** 58 20N 135 30W
Ida Grove **116** 42 20N 95 25W
Idabel **117** 33 53N 94 50W
Idaga Hamus **87** 14 13N 39 48 E
Idah **85** 7 5N 6 40 E
Idaho □ **118** 44 10N 114 0W
Idaho City **118** 43 50N 115 52W
Idaho Falls **118** 43 30N 112 1W
Idaho Springs **118** 39 49N 105 30W
Idanha-a-Nova **30** 39 50N 7 15W
Idar-Oberstein **25** 49 43N 7 19 E
Idd el Ghanam **81** 11 30N 24 19 E
Iddan **63** 6 10N 48 55 E
Idehan **83** 27 10N 11 30 E
Idehan Marzūq **83** 24 50N 13 51 E
Idelès **83** 23 50N 5 53 E
Idfû **86** 25 0N 32 49 E
Ídhi Óros **45** 35 15N 24 45 E
Ídhra **45** 37 20N 23 28 E
Idi **72** 5 2N 97 37 E
Idi Amin Dada, L. = Edward, L. **90** 0 25 S 29 40 E
Idiofa **88** 4 55 S 19 42 E
Idkerberget **48** 60 22N 15 15 E
Idku, Bahra el **86** 31 18N 30 18 E
Idlip **64** 35 55N 36 38 E
Idna **62** 31 34N 34 58 E
Idrija **39** 46 0N 14 5 E
Idritsa **54** 56 25N 28 30 E
Idstein **25** 50 13N 8 17 E
Idutywa **93** 32 8 S 28 18 E
Ieper **16** 50 51N 2 53 E
Ierápetra **45** 35 0N 25 44 E
Ierissós **44** 40 22N 23 52 E
Ierissóu Kólpos **44** 40 27N 23 57 E
Ierzu **40** 39 48N 9 32 E
Iesi **39** 43 32N 13 12 E
Ifach, Punta **33** 38 38N 0 5 E
Ifanadiana **93** 21 19 S 47 39 E
Ife **85** 7 30N 4 31 E
Iférouâne **85** 19 5N 8 24 E
Iffley **98** 18 53 S 141 12 E
Ifni **82** 29 29N 10 12W
Ifon **85** 6 58N 5 40 E
Iforas, Adrar des **85** 19 40N 1 40 E
Ifrane **82** 33 33N 5 7W
Iganga **90** 0 37N 33 28 E
Igarapava **127** 20 3 S 47 47W
Igarapé Açu **127** 1 4 S 47 33W
Igarka **59** 67 30N 86 33 E
Igatimi **125** 24 5 S 55 40W
Igatpuri **70** 19 40N 73 35 E
Igbetti **85** 8 44N 4 8 E
Igbo-Ora **85** 7 29N 3 15 E
Igboho **85** 8 53N 3 50 E
Iggesund **48** 61 39N 17 10 E
Ighil Izane **82** 35 44N 0 31 E
Iglene **82** 22 57N 4 58 E
Iglésias **40** 39 19N 8 27 E
Igli **82** 30 25N 2 19W
Igloolik **105** 69 20N 81 49W
Igma **82** 29 9N 6 24W
Igma, Gebel el **86** 28 55N 34 0 E
Ignace **106** 49 30N 91 40W
Igoshevo **55** 59 25N 42 35 E
Igoumenítsa **44** 39 32N 20 18 E
Iguaçu → **125** 25 36 S 54 36W
Iguaçu, Cat. del **125** 25 41 S 54 26W
Iguala **120** 18 20N 99 40W
Igualada **32** 41 37N 1 37 E
Iguassu = Iguaçu **125** 25 41N 54 26W
Iguatu **127** 6 20 S 39 18W
Iguéla **88** 2 0 S 9 16 E
Igunga □ **90** 4 20 S 33 45 E
Ihiala **85** 5 51N 6 55 E
Ihosy **93** 22 24 S 46 8 E
Ihotry, L. **93** 21 56 S 43 41 E
Ii **50** 65 19N 25 22 E
Iida **74** 35 35N 137 50 E
Iijoki → **50** 65 20N 25 20 E
Iisalmi **50** 63 32N 27 10 E
Iizuka **74** 33 38N 130 42 E
Ijebu-Igbo **85** 6 56N 4 1 E
Ijebu-Ode **85** 6 47N 3 58 E
IJmuiden **16** 52 28N 4 35 E
IJssel → **16** 52 35N 5 50 E
IJsselmeer **16** 52 45N 5 20 E
Ijuí → **125** 27 58 S 55 20W
Ikale **85** 7 40N 5 37 E
Ikare **85** 7 32N 5 40 E
Ikaría **45** 37 35N 26 10 E
Ikast **49** 56 8N 9 10 E
Ikeja **85** 6 36N 3 23 E
Ikela **88** 1 6 S 23 6 E
Ikerre-Ekiti **85** 7 25N 5 19 E
Ikhtiman **43** 42 27N 23 48 E
Iki **74** 33 45N 129 42 E
Ikimba L. **90** 1 30 S 31 20 E
Ikire **85** 7 23N 4 15 E
Ikom **85** 6 0N 8 42 E
Ikopa → **93** 16 45 S 46 40 E
Ikot Ekpene **85** 5 12N 7 40 E
Ikungu **90** 1 33 S 33 42 E
Ikurun **85** 7 54N 4 40 E
Ila **85** 8 0N 4 39 E
Ilagan **73** 17 7N 121 53 E
Ilam **69** 26 58N 87 58 E
Ilanskiy **59** 56 14N 96 3 E
Ilaro **85** 6 53N 3 3 E
Iława **28** 53 36N 19 34 E
Ilayangudi **70** 9 34N 78 37 E
Ilbilbie **98** 21 45 S 149 20 E
Île-à-la Crosse **109** 55 27N 107 53W
Île-à-la-Crosse, Lac **109** 55 40N 107 45W
Île-Bouchard, L' **18** 47 7N 0 26 E
Île-de-France **19** 49 0N 2 20 E
Île-sur-le-Doubs, L' **19** 47 26N 6 34 E
Ilebo **88** 4 17 S 20 55 E
Ileje □ **91** 9 30 S 33 25 E
Ilek **58** 51 32N 53 21 E
Ilek → **52** 51 30N 53 22 E
Ilero **85** 8 0N 3 20 E
Ilesha, Oyo, Nigeria **85** 7 37N 4 40 E
Ilesha, Oyo, Nigeria **85** 8 57N 3 28 E
Ilford **109** 56 4N 95 35W
Ilfov □ **46** 44 20N 26 0 E
Ilfracombe, Austral. **97** 23 30 S 144 30 E
Ilfracombe, U.K. **13** 51 13N 4 8W
Ílhavo **30** 40 33N 8 43W
Ilhéus **127** 14 49 S 39 2W
Ilia **46** 45 57N 22 40 E
Ilia □ **45** 37 45N 21 35 E
Ilich **58** 40 50N 68 27 E
Iliff **116** 40 50N 103 3W
Iligan **73** 8 12N 124 13 E
Ilíkí, L. **45** 38 24N 23 15 E
Iliodhrómia **44** 39 12N 23 50 E
Ilion **114** 43 0N 75 3W
Ilirska-Bistrica **39** 45 34N 14 14 E
Ilkal **70** 15 57N 76 8 E
Ilkeston **12** 52 59N 1 19W
Illana B. **73** 7 35N 123 45 E
Illapel **124** 32 0 S 71 10W
'Illār **62** 32 23N 35 7 E
Ille **20** 42 40N 2 37 E
Ille-et-Vilaine □ **18** 48 10N 1 30W
Iller → **25** 48 23N 9 58 E
Illescas **30** 40 8N 3 51W
Illiers **18** 48 18N 1 15 E
Illimani **126** 16 30 S 67 50W
Illinois □ **111** 40 15N 89 30W
Illinois → **111** 38 55N 90 28W
Illium = Troy **44** 39 57N 26 12 E
Illizi **83** 26 31N 8 32 E
Illora **31** 37 17N 3 53W
Ilm → **24** 51 7N 11 45 E
Ilmen, Oz. **54** 58 15N 31 10 E
Ilmenau **24** 50 41N 10 55 E
Ilo **126** 17 40 S 71 20W
Ilobu **85** 7 45N 4 25 E
Iloilo **73** 10 45N 122 33 E
Ilok **42** 45 15N 19 20 E
Ilora **85** 7 45N 3 50 E
Ilorin **85** 8 30N 4 35 E
Iloulya **57** 49 15N 44 2 E
Ilovatka **55** 50 30N 45 50 E
Ilovlya → **57** 49 14N 43 54 E
Iłowa **28** 51 30N 15 10 E
Ilubabor □ **87** 7 25N 35 0 E
Ilukste **54** 55 55N 26 20 E
Ilva Mică **46** 47 17N 24 40 E
Ilwaki **73** 7 55 S 126 30 E
Ilyichevsk **56** 46 10N 30 35 E
Iłża **28** 51 10N 21 15 E
Iłżanka → **28** 51 14N 21 48 E
Imabari **74** 34 4N 133 0 E
Imaloto → **93** 23 27 S 45 13 E
Imandra, Oz. **52** 67 30N 33 0 E
Imari **74** 33 15N 129 52 E
Imasa **86** 18 0N 36 12 E
Imathía □ **44** 40 30N 22 15 E
Imbâbah **86** 30 5N 31 12 E
Imbler **118** 45 31N 118 0W
Imdahane **82** 32 8N 7 0W
imeni 26 Bakinskikh Komissarov (Neft-chala) **53** 39 19N 49 12 E
imeni 26 Bakinskikh Komissarov (Vyshzha) **53** 39 22N 54 10 E
Imeni Poliny Osipenko **59** 52 30N 136 29 E
Imeri, Serra **126** 0 50N 65 25W
Imerimandroso **93** 17 26 S 48 35 E
Imi (Hinna) **87** 6 28N 42 10 E
Imishly **57** 39 49N 48 4 E
Imitek **82** 29 43N 8 10W
Imlay **118** 40 45N 118 9W
Imlay City **112** 43 0N 83 2W
Immenstadt **25** 47 34N 10 13 E
Immingham **12** 53 37N 0 12W
Immokalee **115** 26 25N 81 26W
Imo □ **85** 5 15N 7 20 E
Imola **39** 44 20N 11 42 E
Imotski **42** 43 27N 17 12 E
Imperatriz **127** 5 30 S 47 29W
Impéria **38** 43 52N 8 0 E
Imperial, Can. **109** 51 21N 105 28W
Imperial, Calif., U.S.A. **119** 32 52N 115 34W
Imperial, Nebr., U.S.A. **116** 40 38N 101 39W
Imperial Dam **119** 32 50N 114 30W
Impfondo **88** 1 40N 18 0 E
Imphal **67** 24 48N 93 56 E
Imphy **19** 46 56N 3 15 E
İmroz = Gökçeada **44** 40 10N 25 50 E
Imst **26** 47 15N 10 44 E
Imuruan B. **73** 10 40N 119 10 E
In Belbel **82** 27 55N 1 12 E
In Delimane **85** 15 52N 1 31 E
In Rhar **82** 27 10N 1 59 E
In Salah **82** 27 10N 2 32 E
In Tallak **85** 16 19N 3 15 E
Ina **74** 35 50N 138 0 E
Ina-Bonchi **74** 35 45N 137 58 E
Inangahua Junc. **101** 41 52 S 171 59 E
Inanwatan **73** 2 10 S 132 14 E
Iñapari **126** 11 0 S 69 40W
Inari **50** 68 54N 27 5 E
Inarijärvi **50** 69 0N 28 0 E
Inawashiro-Ko **74** 37 29N 140 6 E
Inca **32** 39 43N 2 54 E
Incaguasi **124** 29 12 S 71 5W
İnce-Burnu **56** 42 7N 34 56 E
Inchon **76** 37 27N 126 40 E
Incio **30** 42 39N 7 21W
Incomáti → **93** 25 46 S 32 43 E
Incudine, L' **21** 41 50N 9 12 E
Inda Silase **87** 14 10N 38 15 E
Indalsälven → **48** 62 36N 17 30 E
Indaw **67** 24 15N 96 5 E
Indbir **87** 8 7N 37 52 E
Independence, Calif., U.S.A. **119** 36 51N 118 14W
Independence, Iowa, U.S.A. **116** 42 27N 91 52W
Independence, Kans., U.S.A. **117** 37 10N 95 43W
Independence, Mo., U.S.A. **116** 39 3N 94 25W
Independence, Oreg., U.S.A. **118** 44 53N 123 12W
Independence Fjord **4** 82 10N 29 0W
Independence Mts. **118** 41 30N 116 2W
Independenţa **46** 45 25N 27 42 E
Inderborskiy **57** 48 30N 51 42 E
India ■ **3** 20 0N 78 0 E
Indian → **115** 27 59N 80 34W
Indian-Antarctic Ridge **94** 49 0 S 120 0 E
Indian Cabins **108** 59 52N 117 40W
Indian Harbour **107** 54 27N 57 13W
Indian Head **109** 50 30N 103 41W
Indian Ocean **3** 5 0 S 75 0 E
Indiana **114** 40 38N 79 9W
Indiana □ **114** 40 0N 86 0W
Indianapolis **114** 39 42N 86 10W
Indianola, Iowa, U.S.A. **116** 41 20N 93 32W
Indianola, Miss., U.S.A. **117** 33 27N 90 40W
Indiga **52** 67 50N 48 50 E
Indigirka → **59** 70 48N 148 54 E
Inđija **42** 45 6N 20 7 E
Indio **119** 33 46N 116 15W
Indonesia ■ **72** 5 0 S 115 0 E
Indore **68** 22 42N 75 53 E
Indramayu **73** 6 21 S 108 20 E
Indramayu, Tg. **73** 6 20 S 108 20 E
Indravati → **70** 19 20N 80 20 E
Indre □ **19** 46 50N 1 39 E
Indre → **18** 47 16N 0 19 E
Indre-et-Loire □ **18** 47 12N 0 40 E
Indus → **68** 24 20N 67 47 E
Indus, Mouth of the **68** 24 00N 68 00 E
İnebolu **64** 41 55N 33 40 E
İnegöl **64** 40 5N 29 31 E
Ineu **42** 46 26N 21 51 E
Inezgane **82** 30 25N 9 29W
Infante, Kaap **92** 34 27 S 20 51 E
Infantes **33** 38 43N 3 1W
Infiernillo, Presa del **120** 18 9N 102 0W
Infiesto **30** 43 21N 5 21W
Ingende **88** 0 12 S 18 57 E
Ingenio Santa Ana **124** 27 25 S 65 40W
Ingersoll **112** 43 4N 80 55W
Ingham **97** 18 43 S 146 10 E
Ingleborough **12** 54 11N 2 23W
Inglewood, Queensland, Austral. **99** 28 25 S 151 2 E
Inglewood, Vic., Austral. **99** 36 29 S 143 53 E
Inglewood, N.Z. **101** 39 9 S 174 14 E
Inglewood, U.S.A. **119** 33 58N 118 21W
Ingólfshöfði **50** 63 48N 16 39W
Ingolstadt **25** 48 45N 11 26 E
Ingomar **118** 46 35N 107 21W
Ingonish **107** 46 42N 60 18W
Ingore **84** 12 24N 15 48W
Ingrid Christensen Coast **5** 69 30 S 76 00 E
Ingul → **56** 46 50N 32 15 E
Ingulec **56** 47 42N 33 14 E
Ingulets → **56** 46 41N 32 48 E
Inguri →, U.S.S.R. **57** 42 38N 41 35 E
Inguri →, U.S.S.R. **57** 42 15N 41 48 E
Inhaca, I. **93** 26 1 S 32 57 E
Inhafenga **93** 20 36 S 33 53 E
Inhambane **93** 23 54 S 35 30 E
Inhambane □ **93** 22 30 S 34 20 E
Inhaminga **91** 18 26 S 35 0 E
Inharrime **93** 24 30 S 35 0 E
Inharrime → **93** 24 30 S 35 0 E
Iniesta **33** 39 27N 1 45W
Ining = Yining **75** 43 58N 81 10 E
Inírida → **126** 3 55N 67 52W
Inishbofin **15** 53 35N 10 12W
Inishmore **15** 53 8N 9 45W
Inishowen **15** 55 14N 7 15W
Injune **97** 25 53 S 148 32 E
Inklin **108** 58 56N 133 5W
Inklin → **108** 58 50N 133 10W
Inkom **118** 42 51N 112 15W
Inle L. **67** 20 30N 96 58 E
Inn → **25** 48 35N 13 28 E
Innamincka **99** 27 44 S 140 46 E
Inner Hebrides **14** 57 0N 6 30W
Inner Mongolia = Nei Monggol Zizhiqu □ **76** 42 0N 112 0 E
Inner Sound **14** 57 30N 5 55W
Innerkip **112** 43 13N 80 42W
Innerste → **24** 52 45N 9 40 E
Innetalling I. **106** 56 0N 79 0W
Innisfail, Austral. **97** 17 33 S 146 5 E
Innisfail, Can. **108** 52 0N 113 57W
Innsbruck **26** 47 16N 11 23 E
Inny → **15** 53 30N 7 50W
Inongo **88** 1 55 S 18 30 E
Inoucdjouac (Port Harrison) **105** 58 25N 78 15W
Inowrocław **28** 52 50N 18 12 E
Inquisivi **126** 16 50 S 67 10W
Insein **67** 16 50N 96 5 E
Însurăţei **46** 44 50N 27 40 E
Inta **52** 66 5N 60 8 E
Intendente Alvear **124** 35 12 S 63 32W
Interior **116** 43 46N 101 59W
Interlaken **25** 46 41N 7 50 E
International Falls **116** 48 36N 93 25W
Interview I. **71** 12 55N 92 42 E
Inthanon, Doi **71** 18 35N 98 29 E

* *Now part of Sind* □

Intiyaco **124** 28 43 S 60 5W
Inútil, B. **128** 53 30 S 70 15W
Inuvik **104** 68 16N 133 40W
Inveraray **14** 56 13N 5 5W
Inverbervie **14** 56 50N 2 17W
Invercargill **101** 46 24 S 168 24 E
Inverell **97** 29 45 S 151 8 E
Invergordon **14** 57 41N 4 10W
Invermere **108** 50 30N 116 2W
Inverness, Can. **107** 46 15N 61 19W
Inverness, U.K. **14** 57 29N 4 12W
Inverness, U.S.A. **115** 28 50N 82 20W
Inverurie **14** 57 15N 2 21W
Investigator Group **96** 34 45 S 134 20 E
Investigator Str. **97** 35 30 S 137 0 E
Invona **112** 40 46N 78 35W
Inya **58** 50 28N 86 37 E
Inyanga **91** 18 12 S 32 40 E
Inyangani **91** 18 5 S 32 50 E
Inyantue **91** 18 30 S 26 40 E
Inyazura **91** 18 40 S 32 16 E
Inyo Range **119** 37 0N 118 0W
Inyokern **119** 35 38N 117 48W
Inza **55** 53 55N 46 25 E
Inzhavino **55** 52 22N 42 30 E
Ioánnina **44** 39 42N 20 47 E
Ioánnina (Janinà) □ **44** 39 39N 20 57 E
Iola **117** 38 0N 95 20W
Ion Corvin **46** 44 7N 27 50 E
Iona **14** 56 20N 6 25W
Ione, Calif., U.S.A. **118** 38 20N 120 56W
Ione, Wash., U.S.A. **118** 48 44N 117 29W
Ionia **114** 42 59N 85 7W
Ionian Is. = Iónioi Nísoi **45** 38 40N 20 0 E
Ionian Sea **35** 37 30N 17 30 E
Iónioi Nísoi **45** 38 40N 20 0 E
Iori → **57** 41 3N 46 17 E
Íos **45** 36 41N 25 20 E
Iowa □ **116** 42 18N 93 30W
Iowa City **116** 41 40N 91 35W
Iowa Falls **116** 42 30N 93 15W
Ipala **90** 4 30 S 32 52 E
Ipameri **127** 17 44 S 48 9W
Ipáti **45** 38 52N 22 14 E
Ipatovo **57** 45 45N 42 50 E
Ipel → **27** 48 10N 19 35 E
Ipiales **126** 0 50N 77 37W
Ipin = Yibin **75** 28 45N 104 32 E
Ipiros □ **44** 39 30N 20 30 E
Ipixuna **126** 7 0 S 71 40W
Ipoh **71** 4 35N 101 5 E
Ippy **88** 6 5N 21 7 E
İpsala **44** 40 55N 26 23 E
Ipsárion Óros **44** 40 40N 24 40 E
Ipswich, Austral. **97** 27 35 S 152 40 E
Ipswich, U.K. **13** 52 4N 1 9 E
Ipswich, Mass., U.S.A. **113** 42 40N 70 50W
Ipswich, S.D., U.S.A. **116** 45 28N 99 1W
Ipu **127** 4 23 S 40 44W
Iput → **54** 52 26N 31 2 E
Iquique **126** 20 19 S 70 5W
Iquitos **126** 3 45 S 73 10W
Iracoubo **127** 5 30N 53 10W
Iráklia **45** 36 50N 25 28 E
Iráklion **45** 35 20N 25 12 E
Iráklion □ **45** 35 10N 25 10 E
Irala **125** 25 55 S 54 35W
Iramba □ **90** 4 30 S 34 30 E
Iran ■ **65** 33 0N 53 0 E
Iran, Pegunungan **72** 2 20N 114 50 E
Iranamadu Tank **70** 9 23N 80 29 E
Īrānshahr **65** 27 15N 60 40 E
Irapuato **120** 20 40N 101 30W
Iraq ■ **64** 33 0N 44 0 E
Irarrar, O. → **82** 20 0N 1 30 E
Irati **125** 25 25 S 50 38W
Irbid **62** 32 35N 35 48 E
Irebu **88** 0 40 S 17 46 E
Iregua → **32** 42 27N 2 24 E
Ireland ■ **15** 53 0N 8 0W
Ireland I. **121** 32 16N 64 50W
Ireland's Eye **15** 53 25N 6 4W
Irele **85** 7 40N 5 40 E
Iret **59** 60 3N 154 20 E
Irgiz, Bol. **55** 52 10N 49 10 E
Irhârharene **83** 27 37N 7 30 E
Irharrhar, O. → **83** 28 3N 6 15 E
Irherm **82** 30 7N 8 18W
Irhil Mgoun **82** 31 30N 6 28W
Irian Jaya □ **73** 4 0 S 137 0 E
Irié **84** 8 15N 9 10W
Iringa **90** 7 48 S 35 43 E
Iringa □ **90** 7 48 S 35 43 E
Irinjalakuda **70** 10 21N 76 14 E
Iriri → **127** 3 52 S 52 37W
Irish Sea **12** 54 0N 5 0W
Irkineyeva **59** 58 30N 96 49 E
Irkutsk **59** 52 18N 104 20 E
Irma **109** 52 55N 111 14W
Iroise, Mer d' **18** 48 15N 4 45W
Iron Baron **99** 32 58 S 137 11 E
Iron Gate = Portile de Fier **46** 44 42N 22 30 E
Iron Knob **97** 32 46 S 137 8 E
Iron Mountain **114** 45 49N 88 4W
Iron River **116** 46 6N 88 40W
Ironbridge **13** 52 38N 2 29W
Ironstone Kopje **92** 25 17 S 24 5 E
Ironton, Mo., U.S.A. **117** 37 40N 90 40W
Ironton, Ohio, U.S.A. **114** 38 35N 82 40W
Ironwood **116** 46 30N 90 10W
Iroquois Falls **106** 48 46N 80 41W
Irpen **54** 50 30N 30 15 E
Irrara Cr. → **99** 29 35 S 145 31 E
Irrawaddy □ **67** 17 0N 95 0 E
Irrawaddy → **67** 15 50N 95 6 E
Irsina **41** 40 45N 16 15 E
Irtysh → **58** 61 4N 68 52 E
Irumu **90** 1 32N 29 53 E
Irún **32** 43 20N 1 52W
Irurzun **32** 42 55N 1 50W
Irvine, Can. **109** 49 57N 110 16W
Irvine, U.K. **14** 55 37N 4 40W
Irvine, U.S.A. **114** 37 42N 83 58W
Irvinestown **15** 54 28N 7 38W
Irymple **99** 34 14 S 142 8 E
Is-sur-Tille **19** 47 30N 5 10 E
Isa **85** 13 14N 6 24 E
Isaac → **97** 22 55 S 149 20 E
Isabel **116** 45 27N 101 22W
Isabela, I. **120** 21 51N 105 55W
Isabella, Cord. **121** 13 30N 85 25W
Ísafjarðardjúp **50** 66 10N 23 0W
Ísafjörður **50** 66 5N 23 9W
Isagarh **68** 24 48N 77 51 E
Isaka **90** 3 56 S 32 59 E
Isangi **88** 0 52N 24 10 E
Isar → **25** 48 49N 12 58 E
Isarco → **39** 46 57N 11 18 E
Ísari **45** 37 22N 22 0 E
Isbergues **19** 50 36N 2 24 E
Isbiceni **46** 43 45N 24 40 E
Íschia **40** 40 45N 13 51 E
Ise **74** 34 25N 136 45 E
Ise-Wan **74** 34 43N 136 43 E
Isefjord **49** 55 53N 11 50 E
Iseo **38** 45 40N 10 3 E
Iseo, L. d' **38** 45 45N 10 3 E
Iseramagazi **90** 4 37 S 32 10 E
Isère □ **21** 45 15N 5 40 E
Isère → **21** 44 59N 4 51 E
Iserlohn **24** 51 22N 7 40 E
Isérnia **41** 41 35N 14 12 E
Iseyin **85** 8 0N 3 36 E
Ishikari-Wan (Otaru-Wan) **74** 43 25N 141 1 E
Ishikawa □ **74** 36 30N 136 30 E
Ishim **58** 56 10N 69 30 E
Ishim → **58** 57 45N 71 10 E
Ishinomaki **74** 38 32N 141 20 E
Ishmi **44** 41 33N 19 34 E
Ishpeming **114** 46 30N 87 40W
Isigny-sur-Mer **18** 49 19N 1 6W
Isil Kul **58** 54 55N 71 16 E
Isiolo **90** 0 24N 37 33 E
Isiolo □ **90** 2 30N 37 30 E
Isipingo Beach **93** 30 00 S 30 57 E
Isiro **90** 2 53N 27 40 E
Isisford **98** 24 15 S 144 21 E
İskenderun **64** 36 32N 36 10 E
İskilip **56** 40 50N 34 20 E
Iskŭr → **43** 43 45N 24 25 E
Iskŭr, Yazovir **43** 42 23N 23 30 E
Iskut → **108** 56 45N 131 49W
Isla → **14** 56 32N 3 20W
Isla Cristina **31** 37 13N 7 17W
Islamabad **66** 33 40N 73 10 E
Islamkot **68** 24 42N 70 13 E
Islampur **70** 17 2N 74 20 E
Island → **108** 60 25N 121 12W
Island Falls, Can. **106** 49 35N 81 20W
Island Falls, U.S.A. **107** 46 0N 68 16W
Island L. **109** 53 47N 94 25W
Island Pond **114** 44 50N 71 50W
Islands, B. of, Can. **107** 49 11N 58 15W
Islands, B. of, N.Z. **101** 35 20 S 174 20 E
Islay **14** 55 46N 6 10W
Isle → **20** 44 55N 0 15W
Isle-Adam, L' **19** 49 6N 2 14 E
Isle aux Morts **107** 47 35N 59 0W
Isle-Jourdain, L', Gers, France **20** 43 36N 1 5 E
Isle-Jourdain, L', Vienne, France **20** 46 13N 0 31 E
Isle of Wight □ **13** 50 40N 1 20W
Isle Royale **116** 48 0N 88 50W
Isleta **119** 34 58N 106 46W
Ismail **56** 45 22N 28 46 E
Ismâ'ilîya **86** 30 37N 32 18 E
Ismaning **25** 48 14N 11 41 E
Ismay **116** 46 33N 104 44W
Isna **86** 25 17N 32 30 E
Ísola del Gran Sasso d'Italia **39** 42 30N 13 40 E
Ísola del Liri **40** 41 39N 13 32 E
Ísola della Scala **38** 45 16N 11 0 E
Ísola di Capo Rizzuto **41** 38 56N 17 5 E
İsparta **64** 37 47N 30 30 E
Isperikh **43** 43 43N 26 50 E
Íspica **41** 36 47N 14 53 E
İspir **57** 40 40N 40 50 E
Israel ■ **62** 32 0N 34 50 E
Issia **84** 6 33N 6 33W
Issoire **20** 45 32N 3 15 E
Issoudun **19** 46 57N 2 0 E
Issyk-Kul, Ozero **58** 42 25N 77 15 E
Ist **39** 44 17N 14 47 E
İstanbul **64** 41 0N 29 0 E
Istiaía **45** 38 57N 23 9 E
Istok **42** 42 45N 20 24 E
Istokpoga, L. **115** 27 22N 81 14W
Istra, U.S.S.R. **55** 55 55N 36 50 E
Istra, Yugo. **39** 45 10N 14 0 E
Istranca Dağları **43** 41 48N 27 30 E
Istres **21** 43 31N 4 59 E
Istria = Istra **39** 45 10N 14 0 E
Itá **124** 25 29 S 57 21W
Itabaiana **127** 7 18 S 35 19W
Itaberaba **127** 12 32 S 40 18W
Itabira **127** 19 37 S 43 13W
Itabirito **125** 20 15 S 43 48W
Itabuna **127** 14 48 S 39 16W
Itaituba **127** 4 10 S 55 50W
Itajaí **125** 27 50 S 48 39W
Itajubá **125** 22 24 S 45 30W
Itaka **91** 8 50 S 32 49 E
Italy ■ **36** 42 0N 13 0 E
Itampolo **93** 24 41 S 43 57 E
Itapecuru-Mirim **127** 3 24 S 44 20W
Itaperuna **127** 21 10 S 41 54W
Itapetininga **125** 23 36 S 48 7W
Itapeva **125** 23 59 S 48 59W
Itapicuru →, Bahia, Brazil **127** 11 47 S 37 32W
Itapicuru →, Maranhão, Brazil **127** 2 52 S 44 12W
Itapuá □ **125** 26 40 S 55 40W
Itaquari **125** 20 20 S 40 25W
Itaquatiara **126** 2 58 S 58 30W
Itaquí **124** 29 8 S 56 30W
Itararé **125** 24 6 S 49 23W
Itarsi **68** 22 36N 77 51 E
Itatí **124** 27 16 S 58 15W
Itatuba **126** 5 46 S 63 20W
Itchen → **13** 50 57N 1 20W
Itéa **45** 38 25N 22 25 E
Ithaca **114** 42 25N 76 30W
Ithaca = Itháki **45** 38 25N 20 43 E
Itháki **45** 38 25N 20 40 E
Ito **74** 34 58N 139 5 E
Itoman **77** 26 7N 127 40 E
Iton → **18** 49 9N 1 12 E
Itonamas → **126** 12 28 S 64 24W
Itsa **86** 29 15N 30 47 E
Íttiri **40** 40 38N 8 32 E
Itu, Brazil **125** 23 17 S 47 15W
Itu, Nigeria **85** 5 10N 7 58 E
Ituaçu **127** 13 50 S 41 18W
Ituiutaba **127** 19 0 S 49 25W
Itumbiara **127** 18 20 S 49 10W
Ituna **109** 51 10N 103 24W
Itunge Port **91** 9 40 S 33 55 E
Iturbe **124** 23 0 S 65 25W
Ituri → **90** 1 40N 27 1 E
Iturup, Ostrov **59** 45 0N 148 0 E
Ituyuro → **124** 22 40 S 63 50W
Itzehoe **24** 53 56N 9 31 E
Ivaí → **125** 23 18 S 53 42W
Ivalo **50** 68 38N 27 35 E
Ivalojoki → **50** 68 40N 27 40 E
Ivangorod **54** 59 37N 28 40 E
Ivangrad **42** 42 51N 19 52 E
Ivanhoe **97** 32 56 S 144 20 E
Ivanhoe L. **109** 60 25N 106 30W
Ivanić Grad **39** 45 41N 16 25 E
Ivanjica **42** 43 35N 20 12 E
Ivanjšcice **39** 46 12N 16 13 E
Ivankoyskoye Vdkhr. **55** 56 37N 36 32 E
Ivano-Frankovsk **56** 48 56N 24 43 E
Ivano-Frankovsk (Stanislav) **54** 48 40N 24 40 E
Ivanovo, Byelorussia, U.S.S.R. **54** 52 7N 25 29 E
Ivanovo, R.S.F.S.R., U.S.S.R. **55** 57 5N 41 0 E
Ivato **93** 20 37 S 47 10 E
Ivaylovgrad **43** 41 32N 26 8 E
Ivdel **52** 60 42N 60 24 E
Ivinheima → **125** 23 14 S 53 42W
Iviza = Ibiza **33** 39 0N 1 30 E
Ivohibe **93** 22 31 S 46 57 E
Ivory Coast ■ **84** 7 30N 5 0W
Ivösjön **49** 56 8N 14 25 E
Ivrea **38** 45 30N 7 52 E
Ivugivik, (N.D. d'Ivugivic) **105** 62 24N 77 55W
Iwahig **72** 8 35N 117 32 E
Iwaki **74** 37 3N 140 55 E
Iwakuni **74** 34 15N 132 8 E
Iwata **74** 34 42N 137 51 E
Iwate □ **74** 39 30N 141 30 E
Iwate-San **74** 39 51N 141 0 E
Iwo **85** 7 39N 4 9 E
IwoniczZdrój **27** 49 37N 21 47 E
Ixiamas **126** 13 50 S 68 5W
Ixopo **93** 30 11 S 30 5 E
Ixtepec **120** 16 32N 95 10W
Ixtlán de Juárez **120** 17 23N 96 28W
Ixtlán del Río **120** 21 5N 104 21W
Izabel, L. de **120** 15 30N 89 10W
Izamal **120** 20 56N 89 1W
Izberbash **57** 42 35N 47 52 E
Izbica **28** 50 53N 23 10 E
Izbica Kujawska **28** 52 25N 18 30 E
Izegem **16** 50 55N 3 12 E
Izgrev **43** 43 36N 26 58 E
*Izhevsk **52** 56 51N 53 14 E
İzmir (Smyrna) **53** 38 25N 27 8 E
İzmit **64** 40 45N 29 50 E
Iznajar **31** 37 15N 4 19W
Iznalloz **33** 37 24N 3 30W
Izobil'nyy **57** 45 25N 41 44 E
Izola **39** 45 32N 13 39 E
Izra **62** 32 51N 36 15 E
Izra' **62** 32 52N 36 5 E
Iztochni Rodopi **43** 41 45N 25 30 E
Izumi-sano **74** 34 23N 135 18 E
Izumo **74** 35 20N 132 46 E
Izyaslav **54** 50 5N 26 50 E
Izyum **56** 49 12N 37 19 E

J

Jaba **87** 6 20N 35 7 E
Jaba' **62** 32 20N 35 13 E
Jabal el Awlîya **87** 15 10N 32 31 E
Jabalón → **31** 38 53N 4 5W
Jabalpur **69** 23 9N 79 58 E
Jabālyah **62** 31 32N 34 27 E
Jablah **64** 35 20N 36 0 E
Jablanac **39** 44 42N 14 56 E
Jablonec **26** 50 43N 15 10 E
Jablonica **27** 48 37N 17 26 E
Jabłonowo **28** 53 23N 19 10 E
Jaboticabal **125** 21 15 S 48 17W
Jabukovac **42** 44 22N 22 21 E
Jaburu **126** 5 30 S 64 0W
Jaca **32** 42 35N 0 33W
Jacareí **125** 23 20 S 46 0W
Jacarèzinho **125** 23 5 S 50 0W
Jáchymov **26** 50 22N 12 55 E
Jackman **107** 45 35N 70 17W
Jacksboro **117** 33 14N 98 15W
Jackson, Austral. **99** 26 39 S 149 39 E
Jackson, Ala., U.S.A. **115** 31 32N 87 53W
Jackson, Calif., U.S.A. **118** 38 19N 120 47W
Jackson, Ky., U.S.A. **114** 37 35N 83 22W
Jackson, Mich., U.S.A. **114** 42 18N 84 25W
Jackson, Minn., U.S.A. **116** 43 35N 95 0W
Jackson, Miss., U.S.A. **117** 32 20N 90 10W
Jackson, Mo., U.S.A. **117** 37 25N 89 42W
Jackson, Ohio, U.S.A. **114** 39 0N 82 40W
Jackson, Tenn., U.S.A. **115** 35 40N 88 50W
Jackson, Wyo., U.S.A. **118** 43 30N 110 49W
Jackson Bay **101** 43 58 S 168 42 E
Jackson, L. **118** 43 55N 110 40W
Jacksons **101** 42 46 S 171 32 E
Jacksonville, Ala., U.S.A. **115** 33 49N 85 45W
Jacksonville, Fla., U.S.A. **115** 30 15N 81 38W
Jacksonville, Ill., U.S.A. **116** 39 42N 90 15W
Jacksonville, N.C., U.S.A. **115** 34 50N 77 29W
Jacksonville, Oreg., U.S.A. **118** 42 19N 122 56W
Jacksonville, Tex., U.S.A. **117** 31 58N 95 19W
Jacksonville Beach **115** 30 19N 81 26W
Jacmel **121** 18 14N 72 32W
Jacob Lake **119** 36 45N 112 12W
Jacobabad **68** 28 20N 68 29 E
Jacobina **127** 11 11 S 40 30W
Jacob's Well **62** 32 13N 35 13 E
Jacques-Cartier, Mt. **107** 48 57N 66 0W
Jacqueville **84** 5 12N 4 25W
Jacuí → **125** 30 2 S 51 15W
Jacundá → **127** 1 57 S 50 26W
Jade **24** 53 22N 8 14 E
Jadebusen **24** 53 30N 8 15 E
Jadotville = Likasi **91** 10 55 S 26 48 E
Jadovnik **42** 43 20N 19 45 E
Jadów **28** 52 28N 21 38 E
Jadraque **32** 40 55N 2 55W
Jādū **83** 32 0N 12 0 E
Jaén, Peru **126** 5 25 S 78 40W
Jaén, Spain **31** 37 44N 3 43W
Jaén □ **31** 37 50N 3 30W
Jaerens Rev **47** 58 45N 5 45 E
Jafène **82** 20 35N 5 30W
Jaffa = Tel Aviv-Yafo **62** 32 4N 34 48 E
Jaffa, C. **99** 36 58 S 139 40 E
Jaffna **70** 9 45N 80 2 E
Jagadhri **68** 30 10N 77 20 E
Jagadishpur **69** 25 30N 84 21 E
Jagdalpur **70** 19 3N 82 0 E
Jagersfontein **92** 29 44 S 25 27 E
Jagst → **25** 49 14N 9 11 E
Jagtial **70** 18 50N 79 0 E
Jaguariaíva **125** 24 10 S 49 50W
Jaguaribe → **127** 4 25 S 37 45W
Jagüey Grande **121** 22 35N 81 7W
Jahangirabad **68** 28 19N 78 4 E
Jahrom **65** 28 30N 53 31 E
Jailolo **73** 1 5N 127 30 E
Jailolo, Selat **73** 0 5N 129 5 E
Jainti **69** 26 45N 89 40 E
Jaipur **68** 27 0N 75 50 E
Jajce **42** 44 19N 17 17 E
Jajpur **69** 20 53N 86 22 E
Jakarta **73** 6 9 S 106 49 E
Jakobstad (Pietarsaari) **50** 63 40N 22 43 E
Jakupica **42** 41 45N 21 22 E
Jal **117** 32 8N 103 8W
Jalai Nur **76** 49 27N 117 42 E
Jalalabad, Afghan. **66** 34 30N 70 29 E
Jalalabad, India **69** 27 41N 79 42 E
Jalalpur Jattan **68** 32 38N 74 11 E
Jalapa, Guat. **120** 14 39N 89 59W
Jalapa, Mexico **120** 19 30N 96 56W
Jalas, Jabal al **64** 27 30N 36 30 E
Jalaun **69** 26 8N 79 25 E
Jaleswar **69** 26 38N 85 48 E
Jalgaon, Maharashtra, India **68** 21 0N 75 42 E
Jalgaon, Maharashtra, India **68** 21 2N 76 31 E
Jalingo **85** 8 55N 11 25 E
Jalisco □ **120** 20 0N 104 0W
Jallas → **30** 42 54N 9 8W
Jalna **70** 19 48N 75 38 E
Jalón → **32** 41 47N 1 4W
Jalpa **120** 21 38N 102 58W
Jalpaiguri **69** 26 32N 88 46 E
Jalq **65** 27 35N 62 46 E
Jaluit I. **94** 6 0N 169 30 E
Jamaari **85** 11 44N 9 53 E
Jamaica ■ **121** 18 10N 77 30W
Jamalpur, Bangla. **69** 24 52N 89 56 E
Jamalpur, India **69** 25 18N 86 28 E
Jamalpurganj **69** 23 2N 88 1 E
Jamanxim → **127** 4 43 S 56 18W
Jambe **73** 1 15 S 132 10 E
Jambi **72** 1 38 S 103 30 E
Jambi □ **72** 1 30 S 102 30 E
Jambusar **68** 22 3N 72 51 E
James → **116** 42 52N 97 18W
James B. **106** 51 30N 80 0W
James Range **96** 24 10 S 132 30 E
James Ross I. **5** 63 58 S 57 50W
Jamestown, Austral. **97** 33 10 S 138 32 E
Jamestown, S. Afr. **92** 31 6 S 26 45 E
Jamestown, Ky., U.S.A. **114** 37 0N 85 5W
Jamestown, N.D., U.S.A. **116** 46 54N 98 42W
Jamestown, N.Y., U.S.A. **114** 42 5N 79 18W
Jamestown, Pa., U.S.A. **112** 41 32N 80 27W
Jamestown, Tenn., U.S.A. **115** 36 25N 85 0W
Jamkhaudi **70** 16 30N 75 15 E
Jammā'īn **62** 32 8N 35 12 E
Jammalamadugu **70** 14 51N 78 25 E
Jammerbugt **49** 57 15N 9 20 E
Jammu **68** 32 43N 74 54 E
Jammu & Kashmir □ **66** 34 25N 77 0 E
Jamnagar **68** 22 30N 70 6 E
Jamner **68** 20 45N 75 52 E
Jampur **68** 29 39N 70 40 E
Jamrud Fort **66** 33 59N 71 24 E
Jamshedpur **69** 22 44N 86 12 E
Jamtara **69** 23 59N 86 49 E
Jämtlands län □ **48** 62 40N 13 50 E
Jan Kemp **92** 27 55 S 24 51 E
Jan L. **109** 54 56N 102 55W
Jan Mayen Is. **4** 71 0N 9 0W
Jand **66** 33 30N 72 6 E
Janda, Laguna de la **31** 36 15N 5 45W
Jandaq **65** 34 3N 54 22 E
Jandola **68** 32 20N 70 9 E
Jandowae **99** 26 45 S 151 7 E
Jándula → **31** 38 3N 4 6W
Janesville **116** 42 39N 89 1W
Janga **85** 10 5N 1 0W
Jangaon **70** 17 44N 79 5 E
Jangeru **72** 2 20 S 116 29 E
Janikowo **28** 52 45N 18 7 E

*Renamed Ustinov

Janīn 62 32 28N 35 18 E
Janja 42 44 40N 19 17 E
Janjevo 42 42 35N 21 19 E
Janjina 42 42 58N 17 25 E
Jánoshalma 27 46 18N 19 21 E
Jánosháza 27 47 8N 17 12 E
Jánossomorja 27 47 47N 17 11 E
Janów 28 50 44N 19 27 E
Janów Lubelski 28 50 48N 22 23 E
Janów Podlaski 28 52 11N 23 11 E
Janowiec Wielkopolski 28 52 45N 17 30 E
Januária 127 15 25 S 44 25W
Janub Dârfûr □ 87 11 0N 25 0 E
Janub Kordofân □ 87 12 0N 30 0 E
Janville 19 48 10N 1 50 E
Janzé 18 47 55N 1 28W
Jaora 68 23 40N 75 10 E
Japan ■ 74 36 0N 136 0 E
Japan, Sea of 74 40 0N 135 0 E
Japan Trench 94 32 0N 142 0 E
Japara 73 6 30 S 110 40 E
Japen = Yapen 73 1 50 S 136 0 E
Japurá → 126 3 8 S 64 46W
Jaque 126 7 27N 78 8W
Jara, La 119 37 16N 106 0W
Jaraicejo 31 39 40N 5 49W
Jaraiz 30 40 4N 5 45W
Jarales 119 34 39N 106 51W
Jarama → 32 40 2N 3 39W
Jarandilla 30 40 8N 5 39W
Jaranwala 68 31 15N 73 26 E
Jarash 62 32 17N 35 54 E
Jarbidge 118 41 56N 115 27W
Jardim 124 21 28 S 56 2W
Jardín → 33 38 50N 2 10W
Jardines de la Reina, Is. 121 20 50N 78 50W
Jargalant (Kobdo) 75 48 2N 91 37 E
Jargeau 19 47 50N 2 1 E
Jarmen 24 53 56N 13 20 E
Jarnac 20 45 40N 0 11W
Jarny 19 49 9N 5 53 E
Jarocin 28 51 59N 17 29 E
Jaroměr 26 50 22N 15 52 E
Jarosław 27 50 2N 22 42 E
Järpås 49 58 23N 12 57 E
Järpen 48 63 21N 13 26 E
Jarso 87 5 15N 37 30 E
Jarvis 112 42 53N 80 6W
Jarvis I. 95 0 15 S 159 55W
Jarvornik 27 50 23N 17 2 E
Jarwa 69 27 38N 82 30 E
Jaša Tomić 42 45 26N 20 50 E
Jasien 28 51 46N 15 0 E
Jasin 71 2 20N 102 26 E
Jäsk 65 25 38N 57 45 E
Jasło 27 49 45N 21 30 E
Jasper, Alta., Can. 108 52 55N 118 5W
Jasper, Ont., Can. 113 44 52N 75 57W
Jasper, Ala., U.S.A. 115 33 48N 87 16W
Jasper, Fla., U.S.A. 115 30 31N 82 58W
Jasper, Minn., U.S.A. 116 43 52N 96 22W
Jasper, Tex., U.S.A. 117 30 59N 93 58W
Jasper Nat. Park 108 52 50N 118 8W
Jassy = Iaşi 46 47 10N 27 40 E
Jastrebarsko 39 45 41N 15 39 E
Jastrowie 28 53 26N 16 49 E
Jastrzębie Zdrój 27 49 57N 18 35 E
Jászapáti 27 47 32N 20 10 E
Jászárokszállás 27 47 39N 20 1 E
Jászberény 27 47 30N 19 55 E
Jászkiser 27 47 27N 20 20 E
Jászladány 27 47 23N 20 10 E
Jataí 127 17 58 S 51 48W
Jati 68 24 20N 68 19 E
Jatibarang 73 6 28 S 108 18 E
Jatinegara 73 6 13 S 106 52 E
Játiva 33 39 0N 0 32W
Jatobal 127 4 35 S 49 33W
Jatt 62 32 24N 35 2 E
Jaú 125 22 10 S 48 30W
Jauja 126 11 45 S 75 15W
Jaunjelgava 54 56 35N 25 0 E
Jaunpur 69 25 46N 82 44 E
Java = Jawa 73 7 0 S 110 0 E
Java Sea 72 4 35 S 107 15 E
Java Trench 94 10 0 S 110 0W
Javadi Hills 70 12 40N 78 40 E
Jávea 33 38 48N 0 10 E
Javhlant = Ulyasutay 75 47 56N 97 28 E
Javla 70 17 18N 75 9 E
Javron 18 48 25N 0 25W
Jawa 73 7 0 S 110 0 E
Jawor 28 51 4N 16 11 E
Jaworzno 27 50 13N 19 11 E
Jay 117 36 25N 94 46W
Jaya, Puncak 73 3 57 S 137 17 E
Jayapura 73 2 28 S 140 38 E
Jayawijaya, Pegunungan 73 5 0 S 139 0 E
Jayton 117 33 17N 100 35W
Jean 119 35 47N 115 20W
Jean Marie River 104 61 32N 120 38W
Jean Rabel 121 19 50N 73 5W
Jeanerette 117 29 52N 91 38W
Jeanette, Ostrov 59 76 43N 158 0 E
Jeannette 112 40 20N 79 36W
Jebba, Moroc. 82 35 11N 4 43W
Jebba, Nigeria 85 9 9N 4 48 E
Jebel, Bahr el → 81 15 38N 32 31 E
Jebel Qerri 87 16 16N 32 50 E
Jedburgh 14 55 28N 2 33W
Jedlicze 27 49 43N 21 40 E
Jedlnia-Letnisko 28 51 25N 21 19 E
Jędrzejów 28 50 35N 20 15 E
Jedwabne 28 53 17N 22 18 E
Jedway 108 52 17N 131 14W
Jeetze → 24 53 9N 11 6 E
Jefferson, Iowa, U.S.A. 116 42 3N 94 25W
Jefferson, Ohio, U.S.A. 112 41 40N 80 46W
Jefferson, Tex., U.S.A. 117 32 45N 94 23W
Jefferson, Wis., U.S.A. 116 43 0N 88 49W
Jefferson City, Mo., U.S.A. 116 38 34N 92 10W
Jefferson City, Tenn., U.S.A. 115 36 8N 83 30W
Jefferson, Mt., Nev., U.S.A. 118 38 51N 117 0W
Jefferson, Mt., Oreg., U.S.A. 118 44 45N 121 50W
Jeffersonville 114 38 20N 85 42W
Jega 85 12 15N 4 23 E
Jekabpils 54 56 29N 25 57 E
Jelenia Góra 28 50 50N 15 45 E
Jelenia Góra □ 28 51 0N 15 30 E
Jelgava 54 56 41N 23 49 E
Jelica 42 43 50N 20 17 E
Jelli 87 5 25N 31 45 E
Jellicoe 106 49 40N 87 30W
Jelšava 27 48 37N 20 15 E
Jemaja 72 3 5N 105 45 E
Jember 73 8 11 S 113 41 E
Jembongan 72 6 45N 117 20 E
Jemeppe 16 50 37N 5 30 E
Jemnice 26 49 1N 15 34 E
Jena, Ger. 24 50 56N 11 33 E
Jena, U.S.A. 117 31 41N 92 7W
Jenbach 26 47 24N 11 47 E
Jendouba 83 36 29N 8 47 E
Jenkins 114 37 13N 82 41W
Jennings 117 30 10N 92 45W
Jennings → 108 59 38N 132 5W
Jenny 49 57 47N 16 35 E
Jeparit 99 36 8 S 142 1 E
Jequié 127 13 51 S 40 5W
Jequitinhonha 127 16 30 S 41 0W
Jequitinhonha → 127 15 51 S 38 53W
Jerada 82 34 17N 2 10W
Jerantut 71 3 56N 102 22 E
Jérémie 121 18 40N 74 10W
Jerez de García Salinas 120 22 39N 103 0W
Jerez de la Frontera 31 36 41N 6 7W
Jerez de los Caballeros 31 38 20N 6 45W
Jerez, Punta 120 22 58N 97 40W
Jericho 98 23 38 S 146 6 E
Jericho = El Arīhā 62 31 52N 35 27 E
Jerichow 24 52 30N 12 2 E
Jerilderie 99 35 20 S 145 41 E
Jermyn 113 41 31N 75 31W
Jerome 119 34 50N 112 0W
Jerrobert 109 51 56N 109 8W
Jersey City 114 40 41N 74 8W
Jersey, I. 18 49 13N 2 7W
Jersey Shore 114 41 17N 77 18W
Jerseyville 116 39 5N 90 20W
Jerusalem 62 31 47N 35 10 E
Jervis B. 97 35 8 S 150 46 E
Jesenice 39 46 28N 14 3 E
Jeseník 27 50 0N 17 8 E
Jesenske 27 48 20N 20 10 E
Jesselton = Kota Kinabalu 72 6 0N 116 4 E
Jessnitz 24 51 42N 12 19 E
Jessore 69 23 10N 89 10 E
Jesup 115 31 36N 81 54W
Jesús María 124 30 59 S 64 5W
Jetmore 117 38 10N 99 57W
Jetpur 68 21 45N 70 10 E
Jevnaker 47 60 15N 10 26 E
Jewett, Ohio, U.S.A. 112 40 22N 81 2W
Jewett, Tex., U.S.A. 117 31 20N 96 8W
Jewett City 113 41 36N 72 0W
Jeypore 70 18 50N 82 38 E
Jeziorak, Jezioro 28 53 40N 19 35 E
Jeziorany 28 53 58N 20 46 E
Jeziorka → 28 51 59N 20 57 E
Jhajjar 68 28 37N 76 42 E
Jhal Jhao 66 26 20N 65 35 E
Jhalawar 68 24 40N 76 10 E
Jhang Maghiana 68 31 15N 72 22 E
Jhansi 68 25 30N 78 36 E
Jharia 69 23 45N 86 26 E
Jharsuguda 69 21 56N 84 5 E
Jhelum 68 33 0N 73 45 E
Jhelum → 68 31 20N 72 10 E
Jhunjhunu 68 28 10N 75 30 E
Ji Xian 76 36 7N 110 40 E
Jia Xian 76 38 12N 110 28 E
Jiamusi 75 46 40N 130 26 E
Ji'an 75 27 6N 114 59 E
Jianchuan 75 26 38N 99 55 E
Jiande 77 29 23N 119 15 E
Jiangbei 77 29 40N 106 34 E
Jiange 77 32 4N 105 32 E
Jiangjin 77 29 14N 106 14 E
Jiangling 75 30 25N 112 12 E
Jiangmen 75 22 32N 113 0 E
Jiangshan 77 28 40N 118 37 E
Jiangsu □ 75 33 0N 120 0 E
Jiangxi □ 75 27 30N 116 0 E
Jiangyin 77 31 54N 120 17 E
Jiangyong 77 25 20N 111 22 E
Jiangyou 77 31 44N 104 43 E
Jianning 77 26 50N 116 50 E
Jian'ou 75 27 3N 118 17 E
Jianshi 77 30 37N 109 38 E
Jianshui 75 23 36N 102 43 E
Jianyang 77 27 20N 118 5 E
Jiao Xian 76 36 18N 120 1 E
Jiaohe 76 38 2N 116 20 E
Jiaozhou Wan 76 36 5N 120 10 E
Jiaozuo 77 35 16N 113 12 E
Jiawang 77 34 28N 117 26 E
Jiaxing 75 30 49N 120 45 E
Jiayi 75 23 30N 120 24 E
Jibāl 63 22 10N 56 8 E
Jibiya 85 13 5N 7 12 E
Jibou 46 47 15N 23 17 E
Jibuti = Djibouti ■ 63 12 0N 43 0 E
Jičín 26 50 25N 15 28 E
Jiddah 64 21 29N 39 10 E
Jido 67 29 2N 94 58 E
Jifnā 62 31 58N 35 13 E
Jihlava 26 49 28N 15 35 E
Jihlava → 26 48 55N 16 36 E
Jihočeský □ 26 49 8N 14 35 E
Jihomoravský □ 27 49 5N 16 30 E
Jijel 83 36 52N 5 50 E
Jijiga 63 9 20N 42 50 E
Jijona 33 38 34N 0 30W
Jikamshi 85 12 12N 7 45 E
Jilin 76 43 44N 126 30 E
Jilin □ 76 44 0N 124 0 E
Jiloca → 32 41 21N 1 39W
Jilong 75 25 8N 121 42 E
Jílové 26 49 52N 14 29 E
Jima 87 7 40N 36 47 E
Jimbolia 42 45 47N 20 43 E
Jimena de la Frontera 31 36 27N 5 24W
Jiménez 120 27 10N 104 54W
Jimo 76 36 23N 120 30 E
Jin Xian 76 38 55N 121 42 E
Jinan 76 36 38N 117 1 E
Jincheng 76 35 29N 112 50 E
Jind 68 29 19N 76 22 E
Jindabyne 99 36 25 S 148 35 E
Jindabyne L. 100 36 20 S 148 38 E
Jindrichuv Hradeç 26 49 10N 15 2 E
Jing He → 77 34 27N 109 4 E
Jing Xian 77 26 33N 109 40 E
Jingchuan 76 35 20N 107 20 E
Jingdezhen 75 29 20N 117 11 E
Jinggu 75 23 35N 100 41 E
Jinghai 76 38 55N 116 55 E
Jingle 76 38 20N 111 55 E
Jingmen 77 31 0N 112 10 E
Jingning 76 35 30N 105 43 E
Jingshan 77 31 1N 113 7 E
Jingtai 76 37 10N 104 6 E
Jingxi 75 23 8N 106 27 E
Jingyu 76 42 25N 126 45 E
Jingyuan 76 36 30N 104 40 E
Jingziguan 77 33 15N 111 0 E
Jinhe 76 51 18N 121 32 E
Jinhua 75 29 8N 119 38 E
Jining, Nei Mongol Zizhiqu, China 76 41 5N 113 0 E
Jining, Shandong, China 77 35 22N 116 34 E
Jinja 90 0 25N 33 12 E
Jinjini 84 7 26N 3 42W
Jinmen Dao 77 24 25N 118 25 E
Jinnah Barrage 65 32 58N 71 33 E
Jinotega 121 13 6N 85 59W
Jinotepe 121 11 50N 86 10W
Jinshi 75 29 40N 111 50 E
Jinxiang 77 35 5N 116 22 E
Jinzhou 76 41 5N 121 3 E
Jiparaná (Machado) → 126 8 3 S 62 52W
Jipijapa 126 1 0 S 80 40W
Jiquilpan 120 19 57N 102 42W
Jishou 77 28 21N 109 43 E
Jisr al Ḥusayn (Allenby) Br. 62 31 53N 35 33 E
Jisr ash Shughūr 64 35 49N 36 18 E
Jitra 71 6 16N 100 25 E
Jiu → 46 44 40N 23 25 E
Jiudengkou 76 39 56N 106 40 E
Jiujiang 75 29 42N 115 58 E
Jiuling Shan 77 28 40N 114 40 E
Jiuquan 75 39 50N 98 20 E
Jixi 76 45 20N 130 50 E
Jizera → 26 50 10N 14 43 E
Jizl Wadi 86 25 30N 38 30 E
Joaçaba 125 27 5 S 51 31W
João Pessoa 127 7 10 S 34 52W
Joaquín V. González 124 25 10 S 64 0W
Jobourg, Nez de 18 49 41N 1 57W
Jódar 33 37 50N 3 21W
Jodhpur 68 26 23N 73 8 E
Joensuu 52 62 37N 29 49 E
Jœuf 19 49 12N 6 1 E
Joggins 107 45 42N 64 27W
Jogjakarta = Yogyakarta 73 7 49 S 110 22 E
Johannesburg 93 26 10 S 28 2 E
Johansfors 49 56 42N 15 32 E
John Day 118 44 25N 118 57W
John Day → 118 45 44N 120 39W
John H. Kerr Res. 115 36 20N 78 30W
John o' Groats 14 58 39N 3 3W
Johnson 117 37 35N 101 48W
Johnson City, N.Y., U.S.A. 114 42 7N 75 57W
Johnson City, Tenn., U.S.A. 115 36 18N 82 21W
Johnson City, Tex., U.S.A. 117 30 15N 98 24W
Johnsonburg 112 41 30N 78 40W
Johnson's Crossing 108 60 29N 133 18W
Johnston Falls = Mambilima Falls 91 10 31 S 28 45 E
Johnston I. 95 17 10N 169 8W
Johnstone Str. 108 50 28N 126 0W
Johnstown, N.Y., U.S.A. 114 43 1N 74 20W
Johnstown, Pa., U.S.A. 114 40 19N 78 53W
Johor □ 71 2 5N 103 20 E
Joigny 19 48 0N 3 20 E
Joinvile 125 26 15 S 48 55 E
Joinville 19 48 27N 5 10 E
Joinville I. 5 65 0 S 55 30W
Jokkmokk 50 66 35N 19 50 E
Jökulsá á Brú → 50 65 40N 14 16W
Jökulsá Fjöllum → 50 66 10N 16 30W
Joliet 114 41 30N 88 0W
Joliette 106 46 3N 73 24W
Jolo 73 6 0N 121 0 E
Jombang 73 7 33 S 112 14 E
Jome 73 1 16 S 127 30 E
Jomfruland 49 58 52N 9 36 E
Jönåker 49 58 44N 16 40 E
Jonava 54 55 8N 24 12 E
Jones Sound 4 76 0N 85 0W
Jonesboro, Ark., U.S.A. 117 35 50N 90 45W
Jonesboro, Ill., U.S.A. 117 37 26N 89 18W
Jonesboro, La., U.S.A. 117 32 15N 92 41W
Jonesport 107 44 32N 67 38W
Jonglei 87 6 25N 30 50 E
Joniskis 54 56 13N 23 35 E
Jönköping 49 57 45N 14 10 E
Jönköpings län □ 49 57 30N 14 30 E
Jonquière 107 48 27N 71 14W
Jonsberg 49 58 30N 16 48 E
Jonsered 49 57 45N 12 10 E
Jonzac 20 45 27N 0 28W
Joplin 117 37 0N 94 31W
Jordan, Phil. 73 10 41N 122 38 E
Jordan, U.S.A. 118 47 25N 106 58W
Jordan ■ 64 31 0N 36 0 E
Jordan → 62 31 48N 35 32 E
Jordan Valley 118 43 0N 117 2W
Jordanów 27 49 41N 19 49 E
Jorhat 67 26 45N 94 12 E
Jorm 65 36 50N 70 52 E
Jörn 50 65 4N 20 1 E
Jørpeland 47 59 3N 6 1 E
Jorquera → 124 28 3 S 69 58W
Jos 85 9 53N 8 51 E
Jošanička Banja 42 43 24N 20 47 E
José Batlle y Ordóñez 125 33 20 S 55 10W
Joseni 46 46 42N 25 29 E
Joseph 118 45 27N 117 13W
Joseph Bonaparte G. 96 14 35 S 128 50 E
Joseph City 119 35 0N 110 16W
Joseph, L., Newf., Can. 107 52 45N 65 18W
Joseph, L., Ont., Can. 112 45 10N 79 44W
Josselin 18 47 57N 2 33W
Jostedal 47 61 35N 7 15 E
Jotunheimen 47 61 35N 8 25 E
Jourdanton 117 28 54N 98 32W
Joussard 108 55 22N 115 50W
Jovellanos 121 22 40N 81 10W
Jowzjān □ 65 36 10N 66 0 E
Joyeuse 21 44 29N 4 16 E
Józefów 28 52 10N 21 11 E
Ju Xian 76 36 35N 118 20 E
Juan Aldama 120 24 20N 103 23W
Juan Bautista 119 36 55N 121 33W
Juan Bautista Alberdi 124 34 26 S 61 48W
Juan de Fuca Str. 118 48 15N 124 0W
Juan de Nova 93 17 3 S 43 45 E
Juan Fernández, Arch. de 95 33 50 S 80 0W
Juan José Castelli 124 25 27 S 60 57W
Juan L. Lacaze 124 34 26 S 57 25W
Juárez 124 37 40 S 59 43W
Juárez, Sierra de 120 32 0N 116 0W
Juàzeiro 127 9 30 S 40 30W
Juàzeiro do Norte 127 7 10 S 39 18W
Jubbulpore = Jabalpur 69 23 9N 79 58 E
Jübek 24 54 31N 9 24 E
Jubga 57 44 19N 38 48 E
Juby, C. 80 28 0N 12 59W
Júcar → 33 39 5N 0 10W
Juchitán 120 16 27N 95 5W
Judaea = Yehuda 62 31 35N 34 57 E
Judenburg 26 47 12N 14 38 E
Judith → 118 47 44N 109 38W
Judith Gap 118 46 40N 109 46W
Judith Pt. 113 41 20N 71 30W
Jugoslavia = Yugoslavia ■ 37 44 0N 20 0 E
Juigalpa 121 12 6N 85 26W
Juillac 20 45 20N 1 19 E
Juist 24 53 40N 7 0 E
Juiz de Fora 127 21 43 S 43 19W
Jujuy □ 124 23 20 S 65 40W
Julesberg 116 41 0N 102 20W
Juli 126 16 10 S 69 25W
Julia Cr. → 98 20 0 S 141 11 E
Julia Creek 97 20 39 S 141 44 E
Juliaca 126 15 25 S 70 10W
Julian 119 33 4N 116 38W
Julian Alps = Julijske Alpe 39 46 15N 14 1 E
Julianehåb 4 60 43N 46 0W
Jülich 24 50 55N 6 20 E
Julijske Alpe 39 46 15N 14 1 E
Jullundur 68 31 20N 75 40 E
Julu 76 37 15N 115 2 E
Jumbo 91 17 30 S 30 58 E
Jumentos Cays 121 23 0N 75 40 E
Jumet 16 50 27N 4 25 E
Jumilla 33 38 28N 1 19W
Jumla 69 29 15N 82 13 E
Jumna = Yamuna → 68 25 30N 81 53 E
Junagadh 68 21 30N 70 30 E
Junction, Tex., U.S.A. 117 30 29N 99 48W
Junction, Utah, U.S.A. 119 38 10N 112 15W
Junction B. 96 11 52 S 133 55 E
Junction City, Kans., U.S.A. 116 39 4N 96 55W
Junction City, Oreg., U.S.A. 118 44 14N 123 12W
Jundah 97 24 46 S 143 2 E
Jundiaí 125 24 30 S 47 0W
Juneau 104 58 20N 134 20W
Junee 97 34 53 S 147 35 E
Jungfrau 25 46 32N 7 58 E
Junggar Pendi 75 44 30N 86 0 E
Jungshahi 68 24 52N 67 44 E
Juniata → 112 40 30N 77 40W
Junín 124 34 33 S 60 57W
Junín de los Andes 128 39 45 S 71 0W
Jūniyah 64 33 59N 35 38 E
Junnar 70 19 12N 73 58 E
Junquera, La 32 42 25N 2 53 E
Junta, La 117 38 0N 103 30W
Juntura 118 43 44N 118 4W
Jupiter → 107 49 29N 63 37W
Jur, Nahr el → 87 8 45N 29 15 E
Jura, France 19 46 35N 6 5 E
Jura, U.K. 14 56 0N 5 50W
Jura □ 19 46 47N 5 45 E
Jura, Sd. of 14 55 57N 5 45W
Jura Suisse 25 47 10N 7 0 E
Jurado 126 7 7N 77 46W
Jurien B. 96 30 17 S 115 0 E
Jurilovca 46 44 46N 28 52 E
Juruá → 126 2 37 S 65 44W
Juruena → 126 7 20 S 58 3W
Juruti 127 2 9 S 56 4W
Jussey 19 47 50N 5 55 E
Justo Daract 124 33 52 S 65 12W
Jüterbog 24 52 0N 13 6 E
Juticalpa 121 14 40N 86 12W
Jutland = Jylland 8 56 25N 9 30 E
Juvigny-sous-Andaine 18 48 32N 0 30W
Juvisy 19 48 43N 2 23 E
Juwain 65 31 45N 61 30 E
Juzennecourt 19 48 10N 4 48 E
Jylland 8 56 25N 9 30 E
Jyväskylä 72 62 14N 25 50 E

K

K2 **66** 35 58N 76 32 E
Kaalasin **71** 16 26N 103 30 E
Kaap die Goeie Hoop **92** 34 24 S 18 30 E
Kaap Plato **92** 28 30 S 24 0 E
Kaapkruis **92** 21 43 S 14 0 E
Kaapstad = Cape Town **92** 33 55 S 18 22 E
Kabaena **73** 5 15 S 122 0 E
Kabala **84** 9 38N 11 37W
Kabale **90** 1 15 S 30 0 E
Kabalo **90** 6 0 S 27 0 E
Kabambare **90** 4 41 S 27 39 E
Kabango **91** 8 35 S 28 30 E
Kabanjahe **72** 3 6N 98 30 E
Kabara **84** 16 40N 2 50W
Kabardinka **56** 44 40N 37 57 E
Kabardino-Balkar-A.S.S.R. □ **57** 43 30N 43 30 E
Kabare **73** 0 4 S 130 58 E
Kabarega Falls **90** 2 15N 31 30 E
Kabasalan **73** 7 47N 122 44 E
Kabba **85** 7 50N 6 3 E
Kabi **85** 13 30N 12 35 E
Kabinakagami L. **106** 48 54N 84 25W
Kabīr Kūh **64** 33 0N 47 30 E
Kabīr, Zab al **64** 36 0N 43 0 E
Kabkabīyah **81** 13 50N 24 0 E
Kabna **86** 19 6N 32 40 E
Kabompo **91** 13 36 S 24 14 E
Kabompo → **89** 14 10 S 23 11 E
Kabondo **91** 8 58 S 25 40 E
Kabongo **90** 7 22 S 25 33 E
Kabou **85** 9 28N 0 55 E
Kaboudia, Rass **83** 35 13N 11 10 E
Kabra **98** 23 25 S 150 25 E
Kabūd Gonbad **65** 37 5N 59 45 E
Kabul **66** 34 28N 69 11 E
Kabúl □ **65** 34 30N 69 0 E
Kabul → **66** 33 55N 72 14 E
Kabunga **90** 1 38 S 28 3 E
Kaburuang **73** 3 50N 126 30 E
Kabushiya **87** 16 54N 33 41 E
Kabwe **91** 14 30 S 28 29 E
Kačanik **42** 42 13N 21 12 E
Kachanovo **54** 57 25N 27 38 E
Kachebera **91** 13 50 S 32 50 E
Kachin □ **67** 26 0N 97 30 E
Kachira, L. **90** 0 40 S 31 7 E
Kachiry **58** 53 10N 75 50 E
Kachisi **87** 9 40N 37 50 E
Kackar **57** 40 45N 41 10 E
Kadan Kyun **72** 12 30N 98 20 E
Kadarkút **27** 46 13N 17 39 E
Kadayanallur **70** 9 3N 77 22 E
Kade **85** 6 7N 0 56W
Kadi **68** 23 18N 72 23 E
Kadina **97** 34 0 S 137 43 E
Kadiri **70** 14 12N 78 13 E
Kadirli **64** 37 23N 36 5 E
Kadiyevka **57** 48 35N 38 40 E
Kadoka **116** 43 50N 101 31W
Kadom **55** 54 37N 42 30 E
Kâdugli **81** 11 0N 29 45 E
Kaduna **85** 10 30N 7 21 E
Kaduna □ **85** 11 0N 7 30 E
Kaédi **84** 16 9N 13 28W
Kaelé **85** 10 7N 14 27 E
Kaesŏng **76** 37 58N 126 35 E
Kāf **64** 31 25N 37 29 E
Kafakumba **88** 9 38 S 23 46 E
Kafan **53** 39 18N 46 15 E
Kafanchan **85** 9 40N 8 20 E
Kafareti **85** 10 25N 11 12 E
Kaffrine **84** 14 8N 15 36W
Kafia Kingi **81** 9 20N 24 25 E
Kafinda **91** 12 32 S 30 20 E
Kafirévs, Ákra **45** 38 9N 24 38 E
Kafr 'Ayn **62** 32 3N 35 7 E
Kafr el Dauwâr **86** 31 8N 30 8 E
Kafr el Sheikh **86** 31 15N 30 50 E
Kafr Kammā **62** 32 44N 35 26 E
Kafr Kannā **62** 32 45N 35 20 E
Kafr Mālik **62** 32 0N 35 18 E
Kafr Mandā **62** 32 49N 35 15 E
Kafr Quaddūm **62** 32 14N 35 7 E
Kafr Rā'ī **62** 32 23N 35 9 E
Kafr Şīr **62** 33 19N 35 23 E
Kafr Yāsīf **62** 32 58N 35 10 E
Kafue **91** 15 46 S 28 9 E
Kafue Flats **91** 15 40 S 27 25 E
Kafulwe **91** 9 0 S 29 1 E
Kaga Bandoro **88** 7 0N 19 10 E
Kagan **58** 39 43N 64 33 E
Kagawa □ **74** 34 15N 134 0 E
Kagera → **90** 0 57 S 31 47 E
Kağizman **64** 40 5N 43 10 E
Kagoshima **74** 31 35N 130 33 E
Kagoshima □ **74** 31 30N 130 30 E
Kagoshima-Wan **74** 31 25N 130 40 E
Kagul **56** 45 50N 28 15 E
Kahajan → **72** 3 40 S 114 0 E
Kahama **90** 4 8 S 32 30 E
Kahama □ **90** 3 50 S 32 0 E
Kahe **90** 3 30 S 37 25 E
Kahemba **88** 7 18 S 18 55 E
Kahil, Djebel bou **83** 34 26N 4 0 E
Kahniah → **108** 58 15N 120 55W
Kahnūj **65** 27 55N 57 40 E
Kahoka **116** 40 25N 91 42W
Kahoolawe **110** 20 33N 156 35W
Kai Besar **73** 5 35 S 133 0 E
Kai Kai **92** 19 52 S 21 15 E
Kai, Kepulauan **73** 5 55 S 132 45W
Kai-Ketjil **73** 5 45 S 132 40 E
Kaiama **85** 9 36N 4 1 E
Kaiapoi **101** 42 24 S 172 40 E
Kaieteur Falls **126** 5 1N 59 10W
Kaifeng **77** 34 48N 114 21 E
Kaihua **77** 29 12N 118 20 E
Kaiingveld **92** 30 0 S 22 0 E
Kaikohe **101** 35 25 S 173 49 E
Kaikoura **101** 42 25 S 173 43 E
Kaikoura Pen. **101** 42 25 S 173 43 E
Kaikoura Ra. **101** 41 59 S 173 41 E
Kailahun **84** 8 18N 10 39W
Kaili **77** 26 33N 107 59 E
Kailu **76** 43 38N 121 18 E
Kailua **110** 19 39N 156 0W
Kaimana **73** 3 39 S 133 45 E
Kaimanawa Mts. **101** 39 15 S 175 56 E
Kaimganj **69** 27 33N 79 24 E
Kaimur Hill **69** 24 30N 82 0 E
Kainantu **98** 6 18 S 145 52 E
Kaingaroa Forest **101** 38 24 S 176 30 E
Kainji Res. **85** 10 1N 4 40 E
Kaipara Harbour **101** 36 25 S 174 14 E
Kaiping **77** 22 23N 112 42 E
Kaipokok B. **107** 54 54N 59 47W
Kairana **68** 29 24N 77 15 E
Kaironi **73** 0 47 S 133 40 E
Kairouan **83** 35 45N 10 5 E
Kairuku **98** 8 51 S 146 35 E
Kaiserslautern **25** 49 30N 7 43 E
Kaitaia **101** 35 8 S 173 17 E
Kaitangata **101** 46 17 S 169 51 E
Kaithal **68** 29 48N 76 26 E
Kaiwi Channel **110** 21 13N 157 30W
Kaiyuan **76** 42 28N 124 1 E
Kajaani **50** 64 17N 27 46 E
Kajabbi **97** 20 0 S 140 1 E
Kajan → **72** 2 55N 117 35 E
Kajang **71** 2 59N 101 48 E
Kajiado **90** 1 53 S 36 48 E
Kajiado □ **90** 2 0 S 36 30 E
Kajo Kaji **87** 3 58N 31 40 E
Kajoa **73** 0 1N 127 28 E
Kaka **81** 10 38N 32 10 E
Kakabeka Falls **106** 48 24N 89 37W
Kakamega **90** 0 20N 34 46 E
Kakamega □ **90** 0 20N 34 46 E
Kakanj **42** 44 9N 18 7 E
Kakanui Mts. **101** 45 10 S 170 30 E
Kakegawa **74** 34 45N 138 1 E
Kakhib **57** 42 28N 46 34 E
Kakhovka **56** 46 40N 33 15 E
Kakhovskoye Vdkhr. **56** 47 5N 34 16 E
Kakinada (Cocanada) **70** 16 57N 82 11 E
Kakisa → **108** 61 3N 118 10W
Kakisa L. **108** 60 56N 117 43W
Kakwa → **108** 54 37N 118 28W
Kala **85** 12 2N 14 40 E
Kala Oya → **70** 8 20N 79 45 E
Kalaa-Kebira **83** 35 59N 10 32 E
Kalabagh **68** 33 0N 71 28 E
Kalabahi **73** 8 13 S 124 31 E
Kalabáka **44** 39 42N 21 39 E
Kalabo **89** 14 58 S 22 40 E
Kalach **55** 50 22N 41 0 E
Kalach na Donu **57** 48 43N 43 32 E
Kaladan → **67** 20 20N 93 5 E
Kaladar **112** 44 37N 77 5W
Kalahari **92** 24 0 S 21 30 E
Kalahari Gemsbok Nat. Park **92** 25 30 S 20 30 E
Kalahasti **70** 13 45N 79 44 E
Kalakamati **93** 20 40 S 27 25 E
Kalakan **59** 55 15N 116 45 E
Kalama, U.S.A. **118** 46 0N 122 55W
Kalama, Zaïre **90** 2 52 S 28 35 E
Kalamariá **44** 40 33N 22 55 E
Kalamata **45** 37 3N 22 10 E
Kalamazoo **114** 42 20N 85 35W
Kalamazoo → **114** 42 40N 86 12W
Kalamb **70** 18 3N 74 48 E
Kalambo Falls **91** 8 37 S 31 35 E
Kálamos, Greece **45** 38 37N 20 55 E
Kálamos, Greece **45** 38 17N 23 52 E
Kalamoti **45** 38 15N 26 4 E
Kalan **64** 39 7N 39 32 E
Kalao **73** 7 21 S 121 0 E
Kalaotoa **73** 7 20 S 121 50 E
Kälarne **48** 62 59N 16 8 E
Kalárovo **27** 47 54N 18 0 E
Kalasin **71** 16 26N 103 30 E
Kalat **66** 29 8N 66 31 E
• Kalat □ **68** 27 30N 66 0 E
Kálathos (Calato) **45** 36 9N 28 8 E
Kalaus → **57** 45 40N 44 7 E
Kalávrita **45** 38 3N 22 8 E
Kalecik **56** 40 4N 33 26 E
Kalegauk Kyun **67** 15 33N 97 35 E
Kalehe **90** 2 6 S 28 50 E
Kalema **90** 1 12 S 31 55 E
Kalemie **90** 5 55 S 29 9 E
Kalety **28** 50 35N 18 52 E
Kalewa **67** 23 10N 94 15 E
Kálfafellsstaður **50** 64 11N 15 53W
Kalgan = Zhangjiakou **76** 40 48N 114 55 E
Kalgoorlie **96** 30 40 S 121 22 E
Kaliakra, Nos **43** 43 21N 28 30 E
Kalianda **72** 5 50 S 105 45 E
Kalibo **73** 11 43N 122 22 E
Kaliganj Town **69** 22 25N 89 8 E
Kalima **90** 2 33 S 26 32 E
Kalimantan Barat □ **72** 0 0 110 30 E
Kalimantan Selatan □ **72** 2 30 S 115 30 E
Kalimantan Tengah □ **72** 2 0 S 113 30 E
Kalimantan Timur □ **72** 1 30N 116 30 E
Kálimnos **45** 37 0N 27 0 E
Kalimpong **69** 27 4N 88 35 E
Kalinadi → **70** 14 50N 74 7 E
Kalinin **55** 56 55N 35 55 E
Kaliningrad **54** 54 42N 20 32 E
Kalinkovichi **54** 52 12N 29 20 E
Kalinovik **42** 43 31N 18 29 E
Kalipetrovo (Stančevo) **43** 44 5N 27 14 E
Kaliro **90** 0 56N 33 30 E
Kalirrákhi **44** 40 40N 24 35 E
Kalispell **118** 48 10N 114 22W
Kalisz **28** 51 45N 18 8 E
Kalisz □ **28** 51 30N 18 0 E
Kalisz Pomorski **28** 53 17N 15 55 E
Kaliua **90** 5 5 S 31 48 E
Kaliveli Tank **70** 12 5N 79 50 E

• * *Now part of Baluchistan* □

Kalix, → **50** 65 50N 23 11 E
Kalka **68** 30 46N 76 57 E
Kalkaska **106** 44 44N 85 11W
Kalkfeld **92** 20 57 S 16 14 E
Kalkfontein **92** 22 4 S 20 57 E
Kalkrand **92** 24 1 S 17 35 E
Kallakurichi **70** 11 44N 79 1 E
Kållandsö **49** 58 40N 13 5 E
Kallia **62** 31 46N 35 30 E
Kallidaikurichi **70** 8 38N 77 31 E
Kallinge **49** 56 15N 15 18 E
Kallithéa **45** 37 55N 23 41 E
Kallmeti **44** 41 51N 19 41 E
Kallonís, Kólpos **45** 39 10N 26 10 E
Kallsjön **50** 63 38N 13 0 E
Kalmalo **85** 13 40N 5 20 E
Kalmar **49** 56 40N 16 20 E
Kalmar län □ **49** 57 25N 16 0 E
Kalmar sund **49** 56 40N 16 25 E
Kalmyk A.S.S.R. □ **57** 46 5N 46 1 E
Kalmykovo **57** 49 0N 51 47 E
Kalna **69** 23 13N 88 25 E
Kalo **98** 10 1 S 147 48 E
Kalocsa **27** 46 32N 19 0 E
Kalofer **43** 42 37N 24 59 E
Kaloko **90** 6 47 S 25 48 E
Kalol, Gujarat, India **68** 23 15N 72 33 E
Kalol, Gujarat, India **68** 22 37N 73 31 E
Kalolímnos **45** 37 4N 27 8 E
Kalomo **91** 17 0 S 26 30 E
Kaloneròn **45** 37 20N 21 38 E
Kalpi **69** 26 8N 79 47 E
Kalrayan Hills **70** 11 45N 78 40 E
Kalsubai **70** 19 35N 73 45 E
Kaltungo **85** 9 48N 11 19 E
Kalu **68** 25 5N 67 39 E
Kaluga **55** 54 35N 36 10 E
Kalulushi **91** 12 50 S 28 3 E
Kalundborg **49** 55 41N 11 5 E
Kalush **54** 49 3N 24 23 E
Kałuszyn **28** 52 13N 21 52 E
Kalutara **70** 6 35N 80 0 E
Kalwaria **27** 49 53N 19 41 E
Kalya **52** 60 15N 59 59 E
Kalyan **68** 20 30N 74 3 E
Kalyazin **55** 57 15N 37 55 E
Kam Keut **71** 18 20N 104 48 E
Kama **90** 3 30 S 27 5 E
Kama → **52** 55 45N 52 0 E
Kamachumu **90** 1 37 S 31 37 E
Kamaishi **74** 39 20N 142 0 E
Kamalia **68** 30 44N 72 42 E
Kamandorskiye Ostrava **59** 55 0N 167 0 E
Kamapanda **91** 12 5 S 24 0 E
Kamaran **63** 15 21N 42 35 E
Kamativi **91** 18 15 S 27 27 E
Kamba **85** 11 50N 3 45 E
Kambam **70** 9 45N 77 16 E
Kambar **68** 27 37N 68 1 E
Kambarka **52** 56 15N 54 11 E
Kambia **84** 9 3N 12 53W
Kambolé **91** 8 47 S 30 48 E
Kambove **91** 10 51 S 26 33 E
Kamchatka, P-ov. **59** 57 0N 160 0 E
Kamen **58** 53 50N 81 30 E
Kamen Kashirskiy **54** 51 39N 24 56 E
Kamenica, Srbija, Yugo. **42** 44 25N 19 40 E
Kamenica, Srbija, Yugo. **42** 43 27N 22 27 E
Kamenice **26** 49 18N 15 2 E
Kamenjak, Rt **39** 44 47N 13 55 E
Kamenka, R.S.F.S.R., U.S.S.R. **52** 65 58N 44 0 E
Kamenka, R.S.F.S.R., U.S.S.R. **55** 50 47N 39 20 E
Kamenka, R.S.F.S.R., U.S.S.R. **55** 53 10N 44 5 E
Kamenka, Ukraine S.S.R., U.S.S.R. **56** 49 3N 32 6 E
Kamenka Bugskaya **54** 50 8N 24 16 E
Kamenka Dneprovskaya **56** 47 29N 34 14 E
Kameno **43** 42 34N 27 18 E
Kamenolomini **57** 47 40N 40 14 E
Kamensk-Shakhtinskiy **57** 48 23N 40 20 E
Kamensk Uralskiy **58** 56 25N 62 2 E
Kamenskiy, R.S.F.S.R., U.S.S.R. **55** 50 48N 45 25 E
Kamenskiy, R.S.F.S.R., U.S.S.R. **57** 49 20N 41 15 E
Kamenskoye **59** 62 45N 165 30 E
Kamenyak **43** 43 24N 26 57 E
Kamenz **24** 51 17N 14 7 E
Kami **44** 42 17N 20 18 E
Kamiah **118** 46 12N 116 2W
Kamień Krajeński **28** 53 32N 17 32 E
Kamień Pomorski **28** 53 57N 14 43 E
Kamienna → **28** 51 6N 21 47 E
Kamienna Góra **28** 50 47N 16 2 E
Kamieńsk **28** 51 12N 19 29 E
Kamilukuak, L. **109** 62 22N 101 40W
Kamina **91** 8 45 S 25 0 E
Kaminak L. **109** 62 10N 95 0W
Kamituga **90** 3 2 S 28 10 E
Kamloops **108** 50 40N 120 20W
Kamloops L. **108** 50 45N 120 40W
Kamnik **39** 46 14N 14 37 E
Kamo **57** 40 21N 45 7 E
Kamoke **68** 32 4N 74 4 E
Kamp → **26** 48 23N 15 42 E
Kampala **90** 0 20N 32 30 E
Kampar **71** 4 18N 101 9 E
Kampar → **72** 0 30N 103 8 E
Kampen **16** 52 33N 5 53 E
Kampolombo, L. **91** 11 37 S 29 42 E
Kampot **71** 10 36N 104 10 E
Kamptee **68** 21 9N 79 19 E
Kampti **84** 10 7N 3 25W
Kampuchea = Cambodia ■ **71** 13 0N 105 0 E
Kampung → **73** 5 44 S 138 24 E
Kampungbaru = Tolitoli **73** 1 5N 120 50 E
Kamrau, Teluk **73** 3 30 S 133 36 E
Kamsack **109** 51 34N 101 54W
Kamskoye Ustye **55** 55 10N 49 20 E
Kamskoye Vdkhr. **52** 58 0N 56 0 E
Kamuchawie L. **109** 56 18N 101 59W
Kamyshin **55** 50 10N 45 24 E
Kamyzyak **57** 46 4N 48 10 E
Kanaaupscow **106** 54 2N 76 30W
Kanab **119** 37 3N 112 29W
Kanab Creek **119** 37 0N 112 40W
Kanagawa □ **74** 35 20N 139 20 E
Kanairiktok → **107** 55 2N 60 18W
Kanakapura **70** 12 33N 77 28 E
Kanália **44** 39 30N 22 53 E
Kananga **88** 5 55 S 22 18 E
Kanarraville **119** 37 34N 113 12W
Kanash **55** 55 30N 47 32 E
Kanastraíon, Ákra **44** 39 57N 23 45 E
Kanawha → **114** 38 50N 82 8W
Kanazawa **74** 36 30N 136 38 E
Kanchanaburi **71** 14 2N 99 31 E
Kanchenjunga **69** 27 50N 88 10 E
Kanchipuram (Conjeeveram) **70** 12 52N 79 45 E
Kańczuga **27** 49 59N 22 25 E
Kanda Kanda **88** 6 52 S 23 48 E
Kandahar **65** 31 32N 65 30 E
Kandalaksha **52** 67 9N 32 30 E
Kandalakshkiy Zaliv **52** 66 0N 35 0 E
Kandangan **72** 2 50 S 115 20 E
Kandanos **45** 35 19N 23 44 E
Kandhila **45** 37 46N 22 22 E
Kandhkot **68** 28 16N 69 8 E
Kandhla **68** 29 18N 77 19 E
Kandi, Benin **85** 11 7N 2 55 E
Kandi, India **69** 23 58N 88 5 E
Kandla **68** 23 0N 70 10 E
Kandos **99** 32 45 S 149 58 E
Kandukur **70** 15 12N 79 57 E
Kandy **70** 7 18N 80 43 E
Kane **114** 41 39N 78 53W
Kane Bassin **4** 79 30N 68 0W
Kanevskaya **57** 46 3N 39 3 E
Kanfanar **39** 45 7N 13 50 E
Kangaba **84** 11 56N 8 25W
Kangar **71** 6 27N 100 12 E
Kangaroo I. **97** 35 45 S 137 0 E
Kangaroo Mts. **98** 23 25 S 142 0 E
Kangavar **64** 34 40N 48 0 E
Kangean, Kepulauan **72** 6 55 S 115 23 E
Kangerdlugsuak **4** 68 10N 32 20W
Kanggyee **76** 41 0N 126 35 E
Kangnŭng **76** 37 45N 128 54 E
Kango **88** 0 11N 10 5 E
Kangto **67** 27 50N 92 35 E
Kanhangad **70** 12 21N 74 58 E
Kanheri **70** 19 13N 72 50 E
Kani **84** 8 29N 6 36W
Kaniama **90** 7 30 S 24 12 E
Kaniapiskau → **107** 56 40N 69 30W
Kaniapiskau L. **107** 54 10N 69 55W
Kanin Nos, Mys **52** 68 45N 43 20 E
Kanin, P-ov. **52** 68 0N 45 0 E
Kanina **44** 40 23N 19 30 E
Kaniva **99** 36 22 S 141 18 E
Kanjiža **42** 46 3N 20 4 E
Kankakee **114** 41 6N 87 50W
Kankakee → **114** 41 23N 88 16W
Kankan **84** 10 23N 9 15W
Kanker **70** 20 10N 81 40 E
Kankunskiy **59** 57 37N 126 8 E
Kannapolis **115** 35 32N 80 37W
Kannauj **69** 27 3N 79 56 E
Kano **85** 12 2N 8 30 E
Kano □ **85** 11 45N 9 0 E
Kanoroba **84** 9 7N 6 8W
Kanowit **72** 2 14N 112 20 E
Kanowna **96** 30 32 S 121 31 E
Kanoya **74** 31 25N 130 50 E
Kanpetlet **67** 21 10N 93 59 E
Kanpur **69** 26 28N 80 20 E
Kansas □ **116** 38 40N 98 0W
Kansas → **116** 39 7N 94 36W
Kansas City, Kans., U.S.A. **116** 39 0N 94 40W
Kansas City, Mo., U.S.A. **116** 39 0N 94 30W
Kansenia **91** 10 20 S 26 0 E
Kansk **59** 56 20N 95 37 E
Kansu = Gansu □ **75** 37 0N 103 0 E
Kantang **71** 7 25N 99 31 E
Kantché **85** 13 31N 8 30 E
Kanté **85** 9 57N 1 3 E
Kantemirovka **57** 49 43N 39 55 E
Kanturk **15** 52 10N 8 55W
Kanuma **74** 36 34N 139 42 E
Kanus **92** 27 50 S 18 39 E
Kanye **92** 25 0 S 25 28 E
Kanyu **92** 20 7 S 24 37 E
Kanzenze **91** 10 30 S 25 12 E
Kanzi, Ras **90** 7 1 S 39 33 E
Kaohsiung = Gaoxiong **75** 22 38N 120 18 E
Kaokoveld **92** 18 20 S 13 37 E
Kaolack **84** 14 5N 16 8W
Kapadvanj **68** 23 5N 73 0 E
Kapanga **88** 8 30 S 22 40 E
Kapchagai **58** 43 50N 77 10 E
Kapéllo, Ákra **45** 36 9N 23 3 E
Kapema **91** 10 45 S 28 22 E
Kapfenberg **26** 47 26N 15 18 E
Kapiri Mposhi **91** 13 59 S 28 43 E
Kapisa □ **65** 35 0N 69 20 E
Kapiskau → **106** 52 47N 81 55W
Kapit **72** 2 0N 112 55 E
Kapiti I. **101** 40 50 S 174 56 E
Kaplice **26** 48 42N 14 30 E
Kapoeta **87** 4 50N 33 35 E
Kápolnásnyék **27** 47 16N 18 41 E
Kapos → **27** 46 44N 18 30 E
Kaposvár **27** 46 25N 17 47 E
Kappeln **24** 54 37N 9 56 E
Kapps **92** 22 32 S 17 18 E
Kaprije **39** 43 42N 15 43 E
Kapsukas **54** 54 33N 23 19 E
Kapuas → **72** 0 25 S 109 20 E
Kapuas Hulu, Pegunungan **72** 1 30N 113 30 E
Kapulo **91** 8 18 S 29 15 E
Kapunda **99** 34 20 S 138 56 E
Kapurthala **68** 31 23N 75 25 E
Kapuskasing **106** 49 25N 82 30W
Kapuskasing → **106** 49 49N 82 0W
Kapustin Yar **57** 48 37N 45 40 E
Kaputir **90** 2 5N 35 28 E

Kapuvár **27** 47 36N 17 1 E
Kara, Turkey **45** 36 58N 27 30 E
Kara, U.S.S.R. **58** 69 10N 65 0 E
Kara Bogaz Gol, Zaliv **53** 41 0N 53 30 E
Kara Burun **45** 38 41N 26 28 E
Kara Kalpak A.S.S.R. □ **58** 43 0N 60 0 E
Kara Sea **58** 75 0N 70 0 E
Kara, Wadi **86** 20 0N 41 25 E
Karabük **64** 41 12N 32 37 E
Karaburuni **44** 40 25N 19 20 E
Karabutak **58** 49 59N 60 14 E
Karachala **57** 39 45N 48 53 E
Karachayevsk **57** 43 50N 42 0 E
Karachev **54** 53 10N 35 5 E
Karachi **68** 24 53N 67 0 E
Karachi □ **68** 25 30N 67 0 E
Karád **27** 46 41N 17 51 E
Karad **70** 17 15N 74 10 E
Karadeniz Boğazı **64** 41 10N 29 10 E
Karaga **85** 9 58N 0 28W
Karaganda **58** 49 50N 73 10 E
Karagayly **58** 49 26N 76 0 E
Karaginskiy, Ostrov **59** 58 45N 164 0 E
Karagiye Depression **53** 43 27N 51 45 E
Karagwe □ **90** 2 0S 31 0 E
Karaikkudi **70** 10 0N 78 45 E
Karaitivu I. **70** 9 45N 79 52 E
Karaitivu, I. **70** 8 22N 79 47 E
Karaj **65** 35 48N 51 0 E
Karakas **58** 48 20N 83 30 E
Karakitang **73** 3 14N 125 28 E
Karakoram Pass **66** 35 33N 77 50 E
Karakoram Ra. **66** 35 30N 77 0 E
Karakum, Peski **58** 39 30N 60 0 E
Karalon **59** 57 5N 115 50 E
Karaman **64** 37 14N 33 13 E
Karamay **75** 45 30N 84 58 E
Karambu **72** 3 53S 116 6 E
Karamea Bight **101** 41 22S 171 40 E
Karamoja □ **90** 3 0N 34 15 E
Karamsad **68** 22 35N 72 50 E
Karanganjar **73** 7 38S 109 37 E
Karanja **68** 20 29N 77 31 E
Karasburg **92** 28 0S 18 44 E
Karasino **58** 66 50N 86 50 E
Karasjok **50** 69 27N 25 30 E
Karasuk **58** 53 44N 78 2 E
Karatau **58** 43 10N 70 28 E
Karatau, Khrebet **58** 43 30N 69 30 E
Karauli **68** 26 30N 77 4 E
Karávi **45** 36 49N 23 37 E
Karawanken **26** 46 30N 14 40 E
Karazhal **58** 48 2N 70 49 E
Karbalā **64** 32 36N 44 3 E
Kårböle **48** 61 59N 15 22 E
Karcag **27** 47 19N 20 57 E
Karda **59** 55 0N 103 16 E
Kardhámila **45** 38 35N 26 5 E
Kardhítsa **44** 39 23N 21 54 E
Kardhítsa □ **44** 39 15N 21 50 E
Kärdla **54** 58 50N 22 40 E
Kareeberge **92** 30 50S 22 0 E
Kareima **86** 18 30N 31 49 E
Karelian A.S.S.R. □ **52** 65 30N 32 30 E
Karen **71** 12 49N 92 53 E
Kargānrūd **64** 37 55N 49 0 E
Kargasok **58** 59 3N 80 53 E
Kargat **58** 55 10N 80 15 E
Kargı **56** 41 11N 34 30 E
Kargil **69** 34 32N 76 12 E
Kargopol **52** 61 30N 38 58 E
Kargowa **28** 52 5N 15 51 E
Karguéri **85** 13 27N 10 30 E
Karia ba Mohammed **82** 34 22N 5 12W
Kariaí **44** 40 14N 24 19 E
Kariba **91** 16 28S 28 50 E
Kariba Gorge **91** 16 30S 28 50 E
Kariba Lake **91** 16 40S 28 25 E
Karibib **92** 21 0S 15 56 E
Karikal **70** 10 59N 79 50 E
Karimata, Kepulauan **72** 1 25S 109 0 E
Karimata, Selat **72** 2 0S 108 40 E
Karimnagar **70** 18 26N 79 10 E
Karimunjawa, Kepulauan **72** 5 50S 110 30 E
Karin **63** 10 50N 45 52 E
Káristos **45** 38 1N 24 29 E
Kariya **74** 34 58N 137 1 E
Karkal **70** 13 15N 74 56 E
Karkar I. **98** 4 40S 146 0 E
Karkaralinsk **58** 49 26N 75 30 E
Karkinitskiy Zaliv **56** 45 56N 33 0 E
Karkur **62** 32 29N 34 57 E
Karkur Tohl **86** 22 5N 25 5 E
Karl Libknekht **54** 51 40N 35 35 E
Karl-Marx-Stadt **24** 50 50N 12 55 E
Karl-Marx-Stadt □ **24** 50 45N 13 0 E
Karla, L. = Voiviïs, L. **44** 39 30N 22 45 E
Karlino **28** 54 3N 15 53 E
Karlobag **39** 44 32N 15 5 E
Karlovac **39** 45 31N 15 36 E
Karlovka **56** 49 29N 35 8 E
Karlovy Vary **26** 50 13N 12 51 E
Karlsborg **49** 58 33N 14 33 E
Karlshamn **49** 56 10N 14 51 E
Karlskoga **48** 59 22N 14 33 E
Karlskrona **49** 56 10N 15 35 E
Karlsruhe **25** 49 3N 8 23 E
Karlstad, Sweden **48** 59 23N 13 30 E
Karlstad, U.S.A. **116** 48 38N 96 30W
Karlstadt **25** 49 57N 9 46 E
Karmøy **47** 59 15N 5 15 E
Karnal **68** 29 42N 77 2 E
Karnali → **69** 29 0N 83 20 E
Karnaphuli Res. **67** 22 40N 92 20 E
Karnataka □ **70** 14 15N 76 0 E
Karnes City **117** 28 53N 97 53W
Karnische Alpen **26** 46 36N 13 0 E
Kärnten □ **26** 46 52N 13 30 E
Karo **84** 12 16N 3 18W
Karoi **91** 16 48S 29 45 E
Karonga **91** 9 57S 33 55 E
Karoonda **99** 35 1S 139 59 E
Káros **45** 36 54N 25 40 E
Karousádhes **44** 39 47N 19 45 E
Kárpathos **45** 35 37N 27 10 E
Karpáthos, Stenón **45** 36 0N 27 30 E
Karpinsk **52** 59 45N 60 1 E
Karpogory **52** 63 59N 44 27 E
Karrebæk **49** 55 12N 11 39 E
Kars, Turkey **64** 40 40N 43 5 E
Kars, U.S.S.R. **56** 40 36N 43 5 E
Karsakpay **58** 47 55N 66 40 E
Karsha **57** 49 45N 51 35 E
Karshi **58** 38 53N 65 48 E
Karst **39** 45 35N 14 0 E
Karsun **55** 54 14N 46 57 E
Kartál Óros **44** 41 15N 25 13 E
Kartaly **58** 53 3N 60 40 E
Kartapur **68** 31 27N 75 32 E
Karthaus **112** 41 8N 78 9W
Kartuzy **28** 54 22N 18 10 E
Karufa **73** 3 50S 133 20 E
Karumba **98** 17 31S 140 50 E
Karumo **90** 2 25S 32 50 E
Karumwa **90** 3 12S 32 38 E
Karungu **90** 0 50S 34 10 E
Karup **49** 56 19N 9 10 E
Karur **70** 10 59N 78 2 E
Karviná **27** 49 53N 18 25 E
Karwi **69** 25 12N 80 57 E
Kas Kong **71** 11 27N 102 12 E
Kasache **91** 13 25S 34 20 E
Kasai → **88** 3 30S 16 10 E
Kasai Oriental □ **90** 5 0S 24 30 E
Kasaji **91** 10 25S 23 27 E
Kasama **91** 10 16S 31 9 E
Kasane **92** 17 34S 24 50 E
Kasanga **91** 8 30S 31 10 E
Kasangulu **88** 4 33S 15 15 E
Kasaragod **70** 12 30N 74 58 E
Kasba L. **109** 60 20N 102 10W
Kasba Tadla **82** 32 36N 6 17W
Kasempa **91** 13 30S 25 44 E
Kasenga **91** 10 20S 28 45 E
Kasese **90** 0 13N 30 3 E
Kasewa **91** 14 28S 28 53 E
Kasganj **68** 27 48N 78 42 E
Kashabowie **106** 48 40N 90 26W
Kāshān **65** 34 5N 51 30 E
Kashi **75** 39 30N 76 2 E
Kashimbo **91** 11 12S 26 19 E
Kashin **55** 57 20N 37 36 E
Kashipur, Orissa, India **70** 19 16N 83 3 E
Kashipur, Ut. P., India **68** 29 15N 79 0 E
Kashira **55** 54 45N 38 10 E
Kāshmar **65** 35 16N 58 26 E
Kashmir **69** 34 0N 76 0 E
Kashmor **68** 28 28N 69 32 E
Kashpirovka **55** 53 0N 48 30 E
Kashun Noerh = Gaxun Nur **75** 42 22N 100 30 E
Kasimov **55** 54 55N 41 20 E
Kasinge **90** 6 15S 26 58 E
Kasiruta **73** 0 25S 127 12 E
Kaskaskia → **116** 37 58N 89 57W
Kaskattama → **109** 57 3N 90 4W
Kaskinen **50** 62 22N 21 15 E
Kaskö **50** 62 22N 21 15 E
Kaslo **108** 49 55N 116 55W
Kasmere L. **109** 59 34N 101 10W
Kasongo **90** 4 30S 26 33 E
Kasongo Lunda **88** 6 35S 16 49 E
Kásos **45** 35 20N 26 55 E
Kasos, Stenón **45** 35 30N 26 30 E
Kaspi **57** 41 54N 44 17 E
Kaspichan **43** 43 18N 27 11 E
Kaspiysk **57** 42 52N 47 40 E
Kaspiyskiy **57** 45 22N 47 23 E
Kassab ed Doleib **87** 13 30N 33 35 E
Kassaba **86** 22 40N 29 55 E
Kassala **87** 16 0N 36 0 E
Kassalâ □ **87** 15 20N 36 26 E
Kassándra **44** 40 0N 23 30 E
Kassel **24** 51 19N 9 32 E
Kassinga **89** 15 5S 16 4 E
Kassinger **86** 18 46N 31 51 E
Kassue **73** 6 58S 139 21 E
Kastamonu **64** 41 25N 33 43 E
Kastav **39** 45 22N 14 20 E
Kastélli **45** 35 29N 23 38 E
Kastéllion **45** 35 12N 25 20 E
Kastellorizon = Megiste **35** 36 8N 29 34 E
Kastellou, Ákra **45** 35 30N 27 15 E
Kastlösa **49** 56 26N 16 25 E
Kastóri **45** 37 10N 22 17 E
Kastoría **44** 40 30N 21 19 E
Kastoría □ **44** 40 30N 21 15 E
Kastorías, L. **44** 40 30N 21 20 E
Kastornoye **55** 51 55N 38 2 E
Kastós **45** 38 35N 20 55 E
Kástron **44** 39 50N 25 2 E
Kastrosikiá **45** 39 6N 20 36 E
Kasulu **90** 4 37S 30 5 E
Kasulu □ **90** 4 37S 30 5 E
Kasumkent **57** 41 47N 48 15 E
Kasungu **91** 13 0S 33 29 E
Kasur **68** 31 5N 74 25 E
Kata **59** 58 46N 102 40 E
Kataba **91** 16 5S 25 10 E
Katako Kombe **90** 3 25S 24 20 E
Katákolon **45** 37 38N 21 19 E
Katale **90** 4 52S 31 7 E
Katamatite **99** 36 6S 145 41 E
Katanda, Zaïre **90** 0 55S 29 21 E
Katanda, Zaïre **90** 7 52S 24 13 E
Katangi **69** 21 56N 79 50 E
Katangli **59** 51 42N 143 14 E
Katanning **96** 33 40S 117 33 E
Katastári **45** 37 50N 20 45 E
Katavi Swamp **90** 6 50S 31 10 E
Katerini **44** 40 18N 22 37 E
Katha **67** 24 10N 96 30 E
Katherîna, Gebel **86** 28 30N 33 57 E
Katherine **96** 14 27S 132 20 E
Kathiawar **68** 22 20N 71 0 E
Kati **84** 12 41N 8 4W
Katiet **72** 2 21S 99 54 E
Katihar **69** 25 34N 87 36 E
Katima Mulilo **92** 17 28S 24 13 E
Katimbira **91** 12 40S 34 0 E
Katiola **84** 8 10N 5 10W
Katkopberg **92** 30 0S 20 0 E
Katlanovo **42** 41 52N 21 40 E
Katmandu **69** 27 45N 85 20 E
Kato Akhaïa **45** 38 8N 21 33 E
Káto Stavros **44** 40 39N 23 43 E
Katol **68** 21 17N 78 38 E
Katompe **90** 6 2S 26 23 E
Katonga → **90** 0 34N 31 50 E
Katoomba **97** 33 41S 150 19 E
Katowice **28** 50 17N 19 5 E
Katowice □ **28** 50 10N 19 0 E
Katrine, L. **14** 56 15N 4 30W
Katrineholm **48** 59 9N 16 12 E
Katsepe **93** 15 45S 46 15 E
Katsina Ala → **85** 7 10N 9 20 E
Katsuura **74** 35 10N 140 20 E
Kattawaz-Urgun □ **65** 32 10N 68 20 E
Kattegatt **49** 57 0N 11 20 E
Katumba **90** 7 40S 25 17 E
Katungu **90** 2 55S 40 3 E
Katwa **69** 23 30N 88 5 E
Katwijk-aan-Zee **16** 52 12N 4 24 E
Katy **28** 51 2N 16 45 E
Kauai **110** 22 0N 159 30W
Kauai Chan. **110** 21 45N 158 50W
Kaub **25** 50 5N 7 46 E
Kaufbeuren **25** 47 50N 10 37 E
Kaufman **117** 32 35N 96 20W
Kaukauna **114** 44 20N 88 13W
Kaukauveld **92** 20 0S 20 15 E
Kaukonen **50** 67 31N 24 53 E
Kauliranta **50** 66 27N 23 41 E
Kaunas **54** 54 54N 23 54 E
Kaura Namoda **85** 12 37N 6 33 E
Kautokeino **50** 69 0N 23 4 E
Kavacha **59** 60 16N 169 51 E
Kavadarci **42** 41 26N 22 3 E
Kavaja **44** 41 11N 19 33 E
Kavali **70** 14 55N 80 1 E
Kavála **44** 40 57N 24 28 E
Kavála □ **44** 41 5N 24 30 E
Kavála Kólpos **44** 40 50N 24 25 E
Kavarna **43** 43 26N 28 22 E
Kavieng **98** 2 36S 150 51 E
Kavkaz, Bolshoi **57** 42 50N 44 0 E
Kavoúsi **45** 35 7N 25 51 E
Kaw = Caux **127** 4 30N 52 15W
Kawa **87** 13 42N 32 34 E
Kawagama L. **112** 45 18N 78 45W
Kawagoe **74** 35 55N 139 29 E
Kawaguchi **74** 35 52N 139 45 E
Kawaihae **110** 20 3N 155 50W
Kawambwa **91** 9 48S 29 3 E
Kawardha **69** 22 0N 81 17 E
Kawasaki **74** 35 35N 139 42 E
Kawene **106** 48 45N 91 15W
Kawerau **101** 38 7S 176 42 E
Kawhia Harbour **101** 38 5S 174 51 E
Kawio, Kepulauan **73** 4 30N 125 30 E
Kawnro **67** 22 48N 99 8 E
Kawthaung **71** 10 5N 98 36 E
Kawthoolei □ = Kawthule **67** 18 0N 97 30 E
Kawthule □ **67** 18 0N 97 30 E
Kaya **85** 13 4N 1 10W
Kayah □ **67** 19 15N 97 15 E
Kayangulam **70** 9 10N 76 33 E
Kaycee **118** 43 45N 106 46W
Kayeli **73** 3 20S 127 10 E
Kayenta **119** 36 46N 110 15W
Kayes **84** 14 25N 11 30W
Kayima **84** 8 54N 11 15W
Kayomba **91** 13 11S 24 2 E
Kayoro **85** 11 0N 1 28W
Kayrunnera **99** 30 40S 142 30 E
Kaysatskoye **57** 49 47N 46 49 E
Kayseri **64** 38 45N 35 30 E
Kaysville **118** 41 2N 111 58W
Kayuagung **72** 3 24S 104 50 E
Kazachinskoye **59** 56 16N 107 36 E
Kazachye **59** 70 52N 135 58 E
Kazakh S.S.R. □ **58** 50 0N 70 0 E
Kazan **55** 55 48N 49 3 E
Kazanlŭk **43** 42 38N 25 20 E
Kazanskaya **57** 49 50N 41 10 E
Kazatin **56** 49 45N 28 50 E
Kazbek **57** 42 42N 44 30 E
Kāzerūn **65** 29 38N 51 40 E
Kazi Magomed **57** 40 3N 49 0 E
Kazimierz Dolny **28** 51 19N 21 57 E
Kazimierza Wielka **28** 50 15N 20 30 E
Kazincbarcika **27** 48 17N 20 36 E
Kaztalovka **57** 49 47N 48 43 E
Kazumba **88** 6 25S 22 5 E
Kazym → **58** 63 54N 65 50 E
Kcynia **28** 53 0N 17 30 E
Ké-Macina **84** 13 58N 5 22W
Kéa **45** 37 35N 24 22 E
Kea **45** 37 30N 24 22 E
Keams Canyon **119** 35 53N 110 9W
Kearney **116** 40 45N 99 3W
Keban **64** 38 50N 38 50 E
Kébi **84** 9 18N 6 37W
Kebili **83** 33 47N 9 0 E
Kebnekaise **50** 67 53N 18 33 E
Kebri Dehar **63** 6 45N 44 17 E
Kebumen **73** 7 42S 109 40 E
Kecel **27** 46 31N 19 16 E
Kechika → **108** 59 41N 127 12W
Kecskemét **27** 46 57N 19 42 E
Kedada **87** 5 25N 35 58 E
Kedah □ **71** 5 50N 100 40 E
Kedainiai **54** 55 15N 24 2 E
Kedgwick **107** 47 40N 67 20W
Kedia Hill **92** 21 28S 24 37 E
Kediri **73** 7 51S 112 1 E
Kédougou **84** 12 35N 12 10W
Kedzierzyn **28** 50 20N 18 12 E
Keefers **108** 50 0N 121 40W
Keeley L. **109** 54 54N 108 8W
Keeling Is. = Cocos Is. **94** 12 12S 96 55 E
Keene **114** 42 57N 72 17W
Keeper Hill **15** 52 46N 8 17W
Keer-Weer, C. **97** 14 0S 141 32 E
Keeseville **113** 44 29N 73 30W
Keetmanshoop **92** 26 35S 18 8 E
Keewatin **116** 47 23N 93 0W
Keewatin □ **109** 63 20N 95 0W
Keewatin → **109** 56 29N 100 46W
Kefa □ **87** 6 55N 36 30 E
Kefallinía **45** 38 20N 20 30 E
Kefamenanu **73** 9 28S 124 29 E
Kefar 'Eqron **62** 31 52N 34 49 E
Kefar Hasīdim **62** 32 47N 35 5 E
Kefar Nahum **62** 32 54N 35 34 E
Kefar Sava **62** 32 11N 34 54 E
Kefar Szold **62** 33 11N 35 39 E
Kefar Vitkin **62** 32 22N 34 53 E
Kefar Yehezqel **62** 32 34N 35 22 E
Kefar Yona **62** 32 20N 34 54 E
Kefar Zekharya **62** 31 43N 34 57 E
Kefar Zetim **62** 32 48N 35 27 E
Keffi **85** 8 55N 7 43 E
Keflavík **50** 64 2N 22 35W
Keg River **108** 57 54N 117 55W
Kegahka **107** 50 9N 61 18W
Kegalla **70** 7 15N 80 21 E
Kehl **25** 48 34N 7 50 E
Keighley **12** 53 52N 1 54W
Keimoes **92** 28 41S 21 0 E
Keita **85** 14 46N 5 56 E
Keith, Austral. **99** 36 6S 140 20 E
Keith, U.K. **14** 57 33N 2 58W
Keith Arm **104** 64 20N 122 15W
Kekri **68** 26 0N 75 10 E
Kël **59** 69 30N 124 10 E
Kelamet **87** 16 0N 38 30 E
Kelan **76** 38 43N 111 31 E
Kelang **71** 3 2N 101 26 E
Kelani Ganga → **70** 6 58N 79 50 E
Kelantan □ **71** 5 10N 102 0 E
Kelantan → **71** 6 13N 102 14 E
Këlcyra **44** 40 22N 20 12 E
Kelheim **25** 48 58N 11 57 E
Kelibia **83** 36 50N 11 3 E
Kellé **88** 0 8S 14 38 E
Keller **118** 48 2N 118 44W
Kellerberrin **96** 31 36S 117 38 E
Kellett C. **4** 72 0N 126 0W
Kelleys I. **112** 41 35N 82 42W
Kellogg **118** 47 30N 116 5W
Kelloselkä **50** 66 56N 28 53 E
Kells = Ceanannus Mor **15** 53 42N 6 53W
Kélo **81** 9 10N 15 45 E
Kelowna **108** 49 50N 119 25W
Kelsey Bay **108** 50 25N 126 0W
Kelso, N.Z. **101** 45 54S 169 15 E
Kelso, U.K. **14** 55 36N 2 27W
Kelso, U.S.A. **118** 46 10N 122 57W
Keluang **71** 2 3N 103 18 E
Kelvington **109** 52 10N 103 30W
Kem **52** 65 0N 34 38 E
Kem → **52** 64 57N 34 41 E
Kem-Kem **82** 30 40N 4 30W
Kema **73** 1 22N 125 8 E
Kemah **64** 39 32N 39 5 E
Kemano **108** 53 35N 128 0W
Kembolcha **87** 11 2N 39 42 E
Kemenets-Podolskiy **56** 48 40N 26 40 E
Kemerovo **58** 55 20N 86 5 E
Kemi **50** 65 44N 24 34 E
Kemi älv = Kemijoki → **50** 65 47N 24 32 E
Kemijärvi **50** 66 43N 27 22 E
Kemijoki → **50** 65 47N 24 32 E
Kemmerer **118** 41 52N 110 30W
Kemp Coast **5** 69 0S 55 0 E
Kemp L. **117** 33 45N 99 15W
Kempsey **97** 31 1S 152 50 E
Kempt, L. **106** 47 25N 74 22W
Kempten **25** 47 42N 10 18 E
Kemptville **106** 45 0N 75 38W
Kenadsa **82** 31 48N 2 26W
Kendal, Indon. **72** 6 56S 110 14 E
Kendal, U.K. **12** 54 19N 2 44W
Kendall **99** 31 35S 152 44 E
Kendall → **98** 14 4S 141 35 E
Kendallville **114** 41 25N 85 15W
Kendari **73** 3 50S 122 30 E
Kendawangan **72** 2 32S 110 17 E
Kende **85** 11 30N 4 12 E
Kendervicĕs, m. e. **44** 40 15N 19 52 E
Kendrapara **69** 20 35N 86 30 E
Kendrick **118** 46 43N 116 41W
Kenedy **117** 28 49N 97 51W
Kenema **84** 7 50N 11 14W
Keng Tung **67** 21 0N 99 30 E
Kenge **88** 4 50S 17 4 E
Kengeja **90** 5 26S 39 45 E
Kenhardt **92** 29 19S 21 12 E
Kénitra (Port Lyautey) **82** 34 15N 6 40W
Kenmare, Ireland **15** 51 52N 9 35W
Kenmare, U.S.A. **116** 48 40N 102 4W
Kenmare → **15** 51 40N 10 0W
Kenmore **100** 34 44S 149 45 E
Kenn Reef **97** 21 12S 155 46 E
Kennebec **116** 43 56N 99 54W
Kennedy **91** 18 52S 27 10 E
Kennedy Taungdeik **67** 23 15N 93 45 E
Kennet → **13** 51 24N 0 58W
Kennett **117** 36 7N 90 0W
Kennewick **118** 46 11N 119 2W
Kénogami **107** 48 25N 71 15W
Kenogami → **106** 51 6N 84 28W
Kenora **109** 49 47N 94 29W
Kenosha **114** 42 33N 87 48W
Kensington, Can. **107** 46 28N 63 34W
Kensington, U.S.A. **116** 39 48N 99 2W
Kensington Downs **98** 22 31S 144 19 E
Kent, Ohio, U.S.A. **114** 41 8N 81 20W

Kent, Oreg., U.S.A. **118** 45 11N 120 45W
Kent, Tex., U.S.A. **117** 31 5N 104 12W
Kent □ **13** 51 12N 0 40 E
Kent Group **99** 39 30 S 147 20 E
Kent Pen. **104** 68 30N 107 0W
Kentau **58** 43 32N 68 36 E
Kentland **114** 40 45N 87 25W
Kenton **114** 40 40N 83 35W
Kentucky □ **114** 37 20N 85 0W
Kentucky → **114** 38 41N 85 11W
Kentucky Dam **114** 37 2N 88 15W
Kentucky L. **115** 36 25N 88 0W
Kentville **107** 45 6N 64 29W
Kentwood **117** 31 0N 90 30W
Kenya ■ **90** 1 0N 38 0 E
Kenya, Mt. **90** 0 10 S 37 18 E
Keokuk **116** 40 25N 91 24W
Kep-i-Gjuhës **44** 40 28N 19 15 E
Kepi **73** 6 32 S 139 19 E
Kepice **28** 54 16N 16 51 E
Kępno **28** 51 18N 17 58 E
Keppel B. **97** 23 21 S 150 55 E
Kepsut **64** 39 40N 28 9 E
Kerala □ **70** 11 0N 76 15 E
Kerang **97** 35 40 S 143 55 E
Keratéa **45** 37 48N 23 58 E
Keraudren, C. **99** 19 58 S 119 45 E
Keray **65** 26 15N 57 30 E
Kerch **56** 45 20N 36 20 E
Kerchenskiy Proliv **56** 45 10N 36 30 E
Kerchoual **85** 17 12N 0 20 E
Kerem Maharal **62** 32 39N 34 59 E
Kerema **98** 7 58 S 145 50 E
Keren **87** 15 45N 38 28 E
Kerewan **84** 13 29N 16 10W
Kerguelen **3** 48 15 S 69 10 E
Keri **45** 37 40N 20 49 E
Keri Kera **87** 12 21N 32 42 E
Kericho **90** 0 22 S 35 15 E
Kericho □ **90** 0 30 S 35 15 E
Kerinci **72** 1 40 S 101 15 E
Kerkenna, Iles **83** 34 48N 11 11 E
Kerki **58** 37 50N 65 12 E
Kerkinítis, Límni **44** 41 12N 23 10 E
Kérkira **44** 39 38N 19 50 E
Kerkrade **16** 50 53N 6 4 E
Kerma **86** 19 33N 30 32 E
Kermadec Is. **94** 30 0 S 178 15W
Kermadec Trench **94** 30 30 S 176 0W
Kermān **65** 30 15N 57 1 E
Kermān □ **65** 30 0N 57 0 E
** Kermānshāh **64** 34 23N 47 0 E
Kermānshāhān □ **64** 34 0N 46 30 E
Kerme Körfezi **45** 36 55N 27 50 E
Kermen **43** 42 30N 26 16 E
Kermit **117** 31 56N 103 3W
Kern → **119** 35 16N 119 18W
Kerrobert **109** 52 0N 109 11W
Kerrville **117** 30 1N 99 8W
Kerry □ **15** 52 7N 9 35W
Kerry Hd. **15** 52 26N 9 56W
Kersa **87** 9 28N 41 48 E
Kerteminde **49** 55 28N 10 39 E
Kertosono **73** 7 38 S 112 9 E
Kerulen → **75** 48 48N 117 0 E
Kerzaz **82** 29 29N 1 37W
Kesagami → **106** 51 40N 79 45W
Kesagami L. **106** 50 23N 80 15W
Keşan **44** 40 49N 26 38 E
Keski-Suomen lääni □ **50** 62 0N 25 30 E
Kestell **93** 28 17 S 28 42 E
Kestenga **52** 66 0N 31 50 E
Keswick **12** 54 35N 3 9W
Keszthely **27** 46 50N 17 15 E
Ket → **58** 58 55N 81 32 E
Keta **85** 5 49N 1 0 E
Ketapang **72** 1 55 S 110 0 E
Ketchikan **104** 55 25N 131 40W
Ketchum **118** 43 41N 114 27W
Kete Krachi **85** 7 46N 0 1W
Ketef, Khalîg Umm el **86** 23 40N 35 35 E
Keti Bandar **68** 24 8N 67 27 E
Ketri **68** 28 1N 75 50 E
Kętrzyn **28** 54 7N 21 22 E
Kettering **13** 52 24N 0 44W
Kettle → **109** 56 40N 89 34W
Kettle Falls **118** 48 41N 118 2W
Kety **27** 49 51N 19 16 E
Kevin **118** 48 45N 111 58W
Kewanee **116** 41 18N 89 55W
Kewaunee **114** 44 27N 87 30W
Keweenaw B. **114** 46 56N 88 23W
Keweenaw Pen. **114** 47 30N 88 0W
Keweenaw Pt. **114** 47 26N 87 40W
Key Harbour **106** 45 50N 80 45W
Key West **121** 24 33N 82 0W
Keyport **113** 40 26N 74 12W
Keyser **114** 39 26N 79 0W
Keystone, S.D., U.S.A. **116** 43 54N 103 27W
Keystone, W. Va., U.S.A. **114** 37 30N 81 30W
Kezhma **59** 58 59N 101 9 E
Kežmarok **27** 49 10N 20 28 E
Khabarovo **58** 69 30N 60 30 E
Khabarovsk **59** 48 30N 135 5 E
Khābūr → **64** 35 0N 40 30 E
Khachmas **57** 41 31N 48 42 E
Khachraud **68** 23 25N 75 20 E
Khadari, W. el → **87** 10 29N 27 15 E
Khadro **68** 26 11N 68 50 E
Khadyzhensk **57** 44 26N 39 32 E
Khagaria **69** 25 30N 86 32 E
Khaibar **86** 25 49N 39 16 E
Khaipur, Bahawalpur, Pak. **68** 29 34N 72 17 E
Khaipur, Hyderabad, Pak. **68** 27 32N 68 49 E
Khair **68** 27 57N 77 46 E
Khairabad **69** 27 33N 80 47 E
Khairagarh Raj **69** 21 27N 81 2 E
* Khairpur □ **68** 27 20N 69 8 E
Khakhea **92** 24 48 S 23 22 E
Khalfallah **82** 34 20N 0 16 E
Khalij-e-Fars □ **65** 28 20N 51 45 E
Khalilabad **69** 26 48N 83 5 E

* *Now part of Sind □*
** *Renamed Bakhtāran*

Khálki **44** 39 36N 22 30 E
Khalkidhikí □ **44** 40 25N 23 20 E
Khalkís **45** 38 27N 23 42 E
Khalmer-Sede = Tazovskiy **58** 67 30N 78 30 E
Khalmer Yu **58** 67 58N 65 1 E
Khalturin **55** 58 40N 48 50 E
Khamaria **69** 23 10N 80 52 E
Khamas Country **92** 21 45 S 26 30 E
Khambhalia **68** 22 14N 69 41 E
Khamgaon **68** 20 42N 76 37 E
Khamilonision **45** 35 50N 26 15 E
Khamir **63** 16 0N 44 0 E
Khammam **70** 17 11N 80 6 E
Khān Yūnis **62** 31 21N 34 18 E
Khānābād **65** 36 45N 69 5 E
Khānaqīn **64** 34 23N 45 25 E
Khandrá **45** 35 3N 26 8 E
Khandwa **68** 21 49N 76 22 E
Khandyga **59** 62 42N 135 35 E
Khanewal **68** 30 20N 71 55 E
* Khanh Hung **71** 9 37N 105 50 E
Khaniá **45** 35 30N 24 4 E
Khaniá □ **45** 35 30N 24 0 E
Khanion Kólpos **45** 35 33N 23 55 E
Khanka, Oz. **59** 45 0N 132 30 E
Khanna **68** 30 42N 76 16 E
Khanpur **68** 28 42N 70 35 E
Khanty-Mansiysk **58** 61 0N 69 0 E
Khapcheranga **59** 49 42N 112 24 E
Kharagpur **69** 22 20N 87 25 E
Kharaij **86** 21 25N 41 0 E
Kharan Kalat **66** 28 34N 65 21 E
Kharānaq **65** 32 20N 54 45 E
Kharda **70** 18 40N 75 34 E
Khârga, El Wâhât el **86** 25 10N 30 35 E
Khargon **68** 21 45N 75 40 E
Kharit, Wadi el → **86** 24 26N 33 3 E
Khārk, Jazireh **64** 29 15N 50 28 E
Kharkov **56** 49 58N 36 20 E
Kharmanli **43** 41 55N 25 55 E
Kharovsk **55** 59 56N 40 13 E
Kharsānīya **64** 27 10N 49 10 E
Khartoum = El Khartûm **87** 15 31N 32 35 E
Khasab **65** 26 14N 56 15 E
Khasavyurt **57** 43 16N 46 40 E
Khasebake **92** 20 42 S 24 29 E
Khāsh **65** 28 15N 61 15 E
Khashm el Girba **87** 14 59N 35 58 E
Khashuri **57** 41 58N 43 35 E
Khasi Hills **69** 25 30N 91 30 E
Khaskovo **43** 41 56N 25 30 E
Khatanga **59** 72 0N 102 20 E
Khatanga → **59** 72 55N 106 0 E
Khatangskiy, Saliv **4** 66 0N 112 0 E
Khatauli **68** 29 17N 77 43 E
Khatyrka **59** 62 3N 175 15 E
Khavār □ **64** 37 20N 47 0 E
Khaybar, Harrat **64** 25 45N 40 0 E
Khazzān Jabal el Awliyā **87** 15 24N 32 20 E
Khed, Maharashtra, India **70** 17 43N 73 27 E
Khed, Maharashtra, India **70** 18 51N 73 56 E
Khekra **68** 28 52N 77 20 E
Khemelnik **56** 49 33N 27 58 E
Khemis Miliana **82** 36 11N 2 14 E
Khemissèt **82** 33 50N 6 1W
Khemmarat **71** 16 10N 105 15 E
Khenchela **83** 35 28N 7 11 E
Khenifra **82** 32 58N 5 46W
Kherrata **83** 36 27N 5 13 E
Khérson **44** 41 5N 22 47 E
Kherson **56** 46 35N 32 35 E
Khersónisos Akrotiri **45** 35 30N 24 10 E
Kheta → **59** 71 54N 102 6 E
Khiliomódhion **45** 37 48N 22 51 E
Khilok **59** 51 30N 110 45 E
Khimki **55** 55 50N 37 20 E
Khíos **45** 38 27N 26 9 E
Khisar-Momina Banya **43** 42 30N 24 44 E
Khiuma = Hiiumaa **54** 58 50N 22 45 E
Khiva **58** 41 30N 60 18 E
Khīyāv **64** 38 30N 47 45 E
Khlebarovo **43** 43 37N 26 15 E
Khlong → **71** 15 30N 98 50 E
Khmelnitskiy **56** 49 23N 27 0 E
Khmer Rep. = Cambodia ■ **71** 12 15N 105 0 E
Khojak P. **65** 30 55N 66 30 E
Khokholskiy **55** 51 35N 38 40 E
Kholm, Afghan. **65** 36 45N 67 40 E
Kholm, U.S.S.R. **54** 57 10N 31 15 E
Kholmsk **59** 47 40N 142 5 E
Khomas Hochland **92** 22 40 S 16 0 E
Khomeyn **64** 33 40N 50 7 E
Khomo **92** 21 7 S 24 35 E
Khon Kaen **71** 16 30N 102 47 E
Khong **71** 14 5N 105 56 E
Khong → **71** 15 0N 106 50 E
Khonu **59** 66 30N 143 12 E
Khoper → **55** 49 30N 42 20 E
Khor el 'Atash **87** 13 20N 34 15 E
Khóra **45** 37 3N 21 42 E
Khóra Sfakion **45** 35 15N 24 9 E
Khorāsān □ **65** 34 0N 58 0 E
Khorat = Nakhon Ratchasima **71** 14 59N 102 12 E
Khorat, Cao Nguyen **71** 15 30N 102 50 E
Khorb el Ethel **82** 28 30N 6 17W
Khorixas **92** 20 16 S 14 59 E
Khorog **58** 37 30N 71 36 E
Khorol **56** 49 48N 33 15 E
Khorramābād **64** 33 30N 48 25 E
Khorramshahr **64** 30 29N 48 15 E
Khotin **56** 48 31N 26 27 E
Khouribga **82** 32 58N 6 57W
Khowai **67** 24 5N 91 40 E
Khoyniki **54** 51 54N 29 55 E
Khrami → **57** 41 30N 45 0 E
Khrenovoye **55** 51 4N 40 16 E
Khristianá **45** 36 14N 25 13 E
Khtapodhiá **45** 37 24N 25 34 E
Khu Khan **71** 14 42N 104 12 E
Khulna **69** 22 45N 89 34 E
Khulo **57** 41 33N 42 19 E
Khumago **92** 20 26 S 24 32 E

* *Renamed Soc Trang*

Khunzakh **57** 42 35N 46 42 E
Khūr **65** 32 55N 58 18 E
Khurai **68** 24 3N 78 23 E
Khurayṣ **64** 24 55N 48 5 E
Khurja **68** 28 15N 77 58 E
Khūryān Mūryān, Jazā 'ir **63** 17 30N 55 58 E
Khushab **68** 32 20N 72 20 E
Khuzdar **66** 27 52N 66 30 E
Khūzestān □ **64** 31 0N 50 0 E
Khvalynsk **55** 52 30N 48 2 E
Khvatovka **55** 52 24N 46 32 E
Khvor **65** 33 45N 55 0 E
Khvormūj **65** 28 40N 51 30 E
Khvoy **64** 38 35N 45 0 E
Khvoynaya **54** 58 58N 34 28 E
Khyber Pass **66** 34 10N 71 8 E
Kiabukwa **91** 8 40 S 24 48 E
Kiadho → **70** 19 37N 77 40 E
Kiama **99** 34 40 S 150 50 E
Kiamba **73** 6 2N 124 46 E
Kiambi **90** 7 15 S 28 0 E
Kiambu **90** 1 8 S 36 50 E
Kiangsi = Jiangxi □ **75** 27 30N 116 0 E
Kiangsu = Jiangsu □ **75** 33 0N 120 0 E
Kiáton **45** 38 2N 22 43 E
Kibæk **49** 56 2N 8 51 E
Kibanga Port **90** 0 10N 32 58 E
Kibangou **88** 3 26 S 12 22 E
Kibara **90** 2 8 S 33 30 E
Kibare, Mts. **90** 8 25 S 27 10 E
Kibombo **90** 3 57 S 25 53 E
Kibondo **90** 3 35 S 30 45 E
Kibondo □ **90** 4 0 S 30 55 E
Kibumbu **90** 3 32 S 29 45 E
Kibungu **90** 2 10 S 30 32 E
Kibuye, Burundi **90** 3 39 S 29 59 E
Kibuye, Rwanda **90** 2 3 S 29 21 E
Kibwesa **90** 6 30 S 29 58 E
Kibwezi **90** 2 27 S 37 57 E
Kičevo **42** 41 34N 20 59 E
Kichiga **59** 59 50N 163 5 E
Kicking Horse Pass **108** 51 28N 116 16W
Kidal **85** 18 26N 1 22 E
Kidderminster **13** 52 24N 2 13W
Kidete **90** 6 25 S 37 17 E
Kidira **84** 14 28N 12 13W
Kidnappers, C. **101** 39 38 S 177 5 E
Kidston **98** 18 52 S 144 8 E
Kidugallo **90** 6 49 S 38 15 E
Kiel **24** 54 16N 10 8 E
Kiel Kanal = Nord-Ostee-Kanal **24** 54 15N 9 40 E
Kielce **28** 50 52N 20 42 E
Kielce □ **28** 50 40N 20 40 E
Kieler Bucht **24** 54 30N 10 30 E
Kienge **91** 10 30 S 27 30 E
Kiessé **85** 13 29N 4 1 E
Kiev = Kiyev **54** 50 30N 30 28 E
Kifār 'Aşyūn **62** 31 39N 35 7 E
Kiffa **84** 16 37N 11 24W
Kifisiá **45** 38 4N 23 49 E
Kifissós → **45** 38 35N 23 20 E
Kifrī **64** 34 45N 45 0 E
Kigali **90** 1 59 S 30 4 E
Kigarama **90** 1 1 S 31 50 E
Kigoma □ **90** 5 0 S 30 0 E
Kigoma-Ujiji **90** 4 55 S 29 36 E
Kigomasha, Ras **90** 4 58 S 38 58 E
Kihee **99** 27 23 S 142 37 E
Kii-Suidō **74** 33 40N 135 0 E
Kikinda **42** 45 50N 20 30 E
Kikládhes **45** 37 20N 24 30 E
Kikládhes □ **45** 37 0N 25 0 E
Kikori **98** 7 25 S 144 15 E
Kikori → **98** 7 38 S 144 20 E
Kikwit **88** 5 5 S 18 45 E
Kilafors **48** 61 14N 16 36 E
Kilakarai **70** 9 12N 78 47 E
Kilalki **45** 36 15N 27 35 E
Kilauea Crater **110** 19 24N 155 17W
Kilcoy **99** 26 59 S 152 30 E
Kildare **15** 53 10N 6 50W
Kildare □ **15** 53 10N 6 50W
Kilgore **117** 32 22N 94 55W
Kilifi **90** 3 40 S 39 48 E
Kilifi □ **90** 3 30 S 39 40 E
Kilimanjaro **90** 3 7 S 37 20 E
Kilimanjaro □ **90** 4 0 S 38 0 E
Kilindini **90** 4 4 S 39 40 E
Kilis **64** 36 50N 37 10 E
Kiliya **56** 45 28N 29 16 E
Kilju **76** 40 57N 129 25 E
Kilkee **15** 52 41N 9 40W
Kilkenny **15** 52 40N 7 17W
Kilkenny □ **15** 52 35N 7 15W
Kilkieran B. **15** 53 18N 9 45W
Kilkís **44** 40 58N 22 57 E
Kilkís □ **44** 41 5N 22 50 E
Killala **15** 54 13N 9 12W
Killala B. **15** 54 20N 9 12W
Killaloe **15** 52 48N 8 28W
Killaloe Sta. **112** 45 33N 77 25W
Killam **108** 52 47N 111 51W
Killarney, Can. **106** 45 55N 81 30W
Killarney, Ireland **15** 52 2N 9 30W
Killarney, Lakes of **15** 52 0N 9 30W
Killary Harbour **15** 53 38N 9 52W
Killdeer, Can. **109** 49 6N 106 22W
Killdeer, U.S.A. **116** 47 26N 102 48W
Killeen **117** 31 7N 97 45W
Killiecrankie, Pass of **14** 56 44N 3 46W
Killin **14** 56 28N 4 20W
Killíni, Ilía, Greece **45** 37 55N 21 8 E
Killíni, Korinthía, Greece **45** 37 54N 22 25 E
Killybegs **15** 54 38N 8 26W
Kilmarnock **14** 55 36N 4 30W
Kilmez **55** 56 58N 50 55 E
Kilmez → **55** 56 58N 50 28 E
Kilmore **99** 37 25 S 144 53 E
Kilondo **91** 9 45 S 34 20 E
Kilosa **90** 6 48 S 37 0 E
Kilosa □ **90** 6 48 S 37 0 E
Kilrush **15** 52 39N 9 30W
Kilsmo **48** 59 6N 15 35 E
Kilwa □ **91** 9 0 S 39 0 E
Kilwa Kisiwani **91** 8 58 S 39 32 E
Kilwa Kivinje **91** 8 45 S 39 25 E
Kilwa Masoko **91** 8 55 S 39 30 E
Kim **117** 37 18N 103 20W
Kimaam **73** 7 58 S 138 53 E
Kimamba **90** 6 45 S 37 10 E
Kimba **97** 33 8 S 136 23 E
Kimball, Nebr., U.S.A. **116** 41 17N 103 40W
Kimball, S.D., U.S.A. **116** 43 47N 98 57W
Kimbe **98** 5 33 S 150 11 E
Kimbe B. **98** 5 15 S 150 30 E
Kimberley, Austral. **96** 16 20 S 127 0 E
Kimberley, Can. **108** 49 40N 115 59W
Kimberley, S. Afr. **92** 28 43 S 24 46 E
Kimberly **118** 42 33N 114 25W
Kimchaek **76** 40 40N 129 10 E
Kimchŏn **76** 36 11N 128 4 E
Kími **45** 38 38N 24 6 E
Kímolos **45** 36 48N 24 37 E
Kimovsk **55** 54 0N 38 29 E
Kimparana **84** 12 48N 5 0W
Kimry **55** 56 55N 37 15 E
Kimsquit **108** 52 45N 126 57W
Kimstad **49** 58 35N 15 58 E
Kinabalu **72** 6 0N 116 0 E
Kínaros **45** 36 59N 26 15 E
Kinaskan L. **108** 57 38N 130 8W
Kincaid **109** 49 40N 107 0W
Kincardine **106** 44 10N 81 40W
Kinda **91** 9 18 S 25 4 E
Kindersley **109** 51 30N 109 10W
Kindia **84** 10 0N 12 52W
Kindu **90** 2 55 S 25 50 E
Kinel **55** 53 15N 50 40 E
Kineshma **55** 57 30N 42 5 E
Kinesi **90** 1 25 S 33 50 E
King City **119** 36 11N 121 8W
King Cr. → **98** 24 35 S 139 30 E
King Frederick VI Land = Kong Frederik VI.s. Kyst **4** 63 0N 43 0W
King George B. **128** 51 30 S 60 30W
King George I. **5** 60 0 S 60 0W
King George Is. **105** 57 20N 80 30W
King George Sd. **96** 35 5 S 118 0 E
King I., Austral. **97** 39 50 S 144 0 E
King I., Can. **108** 52 10N 127 40W
King I. = Kadah Kyun **71** 12 30N 98 20 E
King Leopold Ranges **96** 17 30 S 125 45 E
King, Mt. **99** 25 10 S 147 30 E
King Sd. **96** 16 50 S 123 20 E
King William I. **104** 69 10N 97 25W
King William's Town **92** 32 51 S 27 22 E
Kingaroy **97** 26 32 S 151 51 E
Kingfisher **117** 35 50N 97 55W
Kingisepp **54** 59 25N 28 40 E
Kingisepp (Kuressaare) **54** 58 15N 22 30 E
Kingman, Ariz., U.S.A. **119** 35 12N 114 2W
Kingman, Kans., U.S.A. **117** 37 41N 98 9W
Kings → **119** 36 10N 119 50W
Kings Canyon National Park **119** 37 0N 118 35W
King's Lynn **12** 52 45N 0 25 E
Kings Mountain **115** 35 13N 81 20W
King's Peak **118** 40 46N 110 27W
Kingsbridge **13** 50 17N 3 46W
Kingsburg **119** 36 35N 119 36W
Kingscote **99** 35 40 S 137 38 E
Kingscourt **15** 53 55N 6 48W
Kingsley **116** 42 37N 95 58W
Kingsley Dam **116** 41 20N 101 40W
Kingsport **115** 36 33N 82 36W
Kingston, Can. **106** 44 14N 76 30W
Kingston, Jamaica **121** 18 0N 76 50W
Kingston, N.Z. **101** 45 20 S 168 43 E
Kingston, N.Y., U.S.A. **114** 41 55N 74 0W
Kingston, Pa., U.S.A. **114** 41 19N 75 58W
Kingston, R.I., U.S.A. **113** 41 29N 71 30W
Kingston South East **97** 36 51 S 139 55 E
Kingston-upon-Thames **13** 51 23N 0 20W
Kingstown **121** 13 10N 61 10W
Kingstree **115** 33 40N 79 48W
Kingsville, Can. **106** 42 2N 82 45W
Kingsville, U.S.A. **117** 27 30N 97 53W
Kingussie **14** 57 5N 4 2W
Kinistino **109** 52 57N 105 2W
Kinkala **88** 4 18 S 14 49 E
Kinleith **101** 38 20 S 175 56 E
Kinmount **112** 44 48N 78 45W
Kinn **47** 61 34N 4 45 E
Kinna **49** 57 32N 12 42 E
Kinnaird **108** 49 17N 117 39W
Kinnairds Hd. **14** 57 40N 2 0W
Kinnared **49** 57 2N 13 7 E
Kinneret **62** 32 44N 35 34 E
Kinneret, Yam **62** 32 45N 35 35 E
Kinoje → **106** 52 8N 81 25W
Kinoni **90** 0 41 S 30 28 E
Kinross **14** 56 13N 3 25W
Kinsale **15** 51 42N 8 31W
Kinsale, Old Hd. of **15** 51 37N 8 32W
Kinsarvik **47** 60 22N 6 43 E
Kinshasa **88** 4 20 S 15 15 E
Kinsley **117** 37 57N 99 30W
Kinston **115** 35 18N 77 35W
Kintampo **85** 8 5N 1 41W
Kintap **72** 3 51 S 115 13 E
Kintyre **14** 55 30N 5 35W
Kintyre, Mull of **14** 55 17N 5 55W
Kinushseo → **106** 55 15N 83 45W
Kinuso **108** 55 20N 115 25W
Kinyangiri **90** 4 25 S 34 37 E
Kinzig → **25** 48 37N 7 49 E
Kinzua **112** 41 52N 78 58W
Kinzua Dam **112** 41 53N 79 0W
Kióni **45** 38 27N 20 41 E
Kiosk **106** 46 6N 78 53W
Kiowa, Kans., U.S.A. **117** 37 3N 98 30W
Kiowa, Okla., U.S.A. **117** 34 45N 95 50W
Kipahigan L. **109** 55 20N 101 55W
Kipanga **90** 6 15 S 35 20 E
Kiparissía **45** 37 15N 21 40 E

Kiparissiakós Kólpos	**45**	37 25N	21 25 E
Kipembawe	**90**	7 38 S	33 27 E
Kipengere Ra.	**91**	9 12 S	34 15 E
Kipili	**90**	7 28 S	30 32 E
Kipini	**90**	2 30 S	40 32 E
Kipling	**109**	50 6N	102 38W
Kippure	**15**	53 11N	6 23W
Kipushi	**91**	11 48 S	27 12 E
Kirandul	**70**	18 33N	81 10 E
Kiratpur	**68**	29 32N	78 12 E
Kirchhain	**24**	50 49N	8 54 E
Kirchheim	**25**	48 38N	9 20 E
Kirchheim-Bolanden	**25**	49 40N	8 0 E
Kirchschlag	**27**	47 30N	16 19 E
Kirensk	**59**	57 50N	107 55 E
Kirgiz S.S.R. □	**58**	42 0N	75 0 E
Kirgiziya Steppe	**53**	50 0N	55 0 E
Kiri	**88**	1 29 S	19 0 E
Kiribati ■	**94**	1 0N	176 0 E
Kiriburu	**69**	22 0N	85 0 E
Kırıkkale	**64**	39 51N	33 32 E
Kirillov	**55**	59 51N	38 14 E
Kirin = Jilin	**76**	43 55N	126 30 E
Kirin = Jilin □	**76**	44 0N	126 0 E
Kirindi ⤳	**70**	6 15N	81 20 E
Kirishi	**54**	59 28N	31 59 E
Kirkcaldy	**14**	56 7N	3 10W
Kirkcudbright	**14**	54 50N	4 3W
Kirkee	**70**	18 34N	73 56 E
Kirkenær	**47**	60 27N	12 3 E
Kirkenes	**50**	69 40N	30 5 E
Kirkintilloch	**14**	55 57N	4 10W
Kirkjubæjarklaustur	**50**	63 47N	18 4W
Kirkland	**119**	34 29N	112 46W
Kirkland Lake	**106**	48 9N	80 2W
Kırklareli	**43**	41 44N	27 15 E
Kirksville	**116**	40 8N	92 35W
Kirkūk	**64**	35 30N	44 21 E
Kirkwall	**14**	58 59N	2 59W
Kirkwood	**92**	33 22 S	25 15 E
Kirlampudi	**70**	17 12N	82 12 E
Kirn	**25**	49 46N	7 29 E
Kirov, R.S.F.S.R., U.S.S.R.	**54**	54 3N	34 20 E
Kirov, R.S.F.S.R., U.S.S.R.	**58**	58 35N	49 40 E
Kirovabad	**57**	40 45N	46 20 E
Kirovakan	**57**	40 48N	44 30 E
Kirovo-Chepetsk	**55**	58 28N	50 0 E
Kirovograd	**56**	48 35N	32 20 E
Kirovsk, R.S.F.S.R., U.S.S.R.	**52**	67 48N	33 50 E
Kirovsk, Turkmen S.S.R., U.S.S.R.	**58**	37 42N	60 23 E
Kirovsk, Ukraine S.S.R., U.S.S.R.	**57**	48 35N	38 30 E
Kirovski	**57**	45 51N	48 11 E
Kirovskiy	**59**	54 27N	155 42 E
Kirriemuir, Can.	**109**	51 56N	110 20W
Kirriemuir, U.K.	**14**	56 41N	3 0W
Kirsanov	**55**	52 35N	42 40 E
Kırşehir	**64**	39 14N	34 5 E
Kirstonia	**92**	25 30 S	23 45 E
Kirtachi	**85**	12 52N	2 30 E
Kīrteh	**65**	32 15N	63 0 E
Kirthar Range	**68**	27 0N	67 0 E
Kiruna	**50**	67 52N	20 15 E
Kirundu	**90**	0 50 S	25 35 E
Kirya	**55**	55 5N	46 45 E
Kiryū	**74**	36 24N	139 20 E
Kisa	**49**	58 0N	15 39 E
Kisaga	**90**	4 30 S	34 23 E
Kisámou, Kólpos	**45**	35 30N	23 38 E
Kisanga	**90**	2 30N	26 35 E
Kisangani	**90**	0 35N	25 15 E
Kisar	**73**	8 5 S	127 10 E
Kisaran	**72**	3 0N	99 37 E
Kisarawe	**90**	6 53 S	39 0 E
Kisarawe □	**90**	7 3 S	39 0 E
Kisarazu	**74**	35 23N	139 55 E
Kisbér	**27**	47 30N	18 0 E
Kiselevsk	**58**	54 5N	86 39 E
Kishanganj	**69**	26 3N	88 14 E
Kishangarh	**68**	27 50N	70 30 E
Kishi	**85**	9 1N	3 52 E
Kishinev	**56**	47 0N	28 50 E
Kishiwada	**74**	34 28N	135 22 E
Kishon	**62**	32 49N	35 2 E
Kishorganj	**69**	24 26N	90 40 E
Kishtwar	**69**	33 20N	75 48 E
Kisii	**90**	0 40 S	34 45 E
Kisii □	**90**	0 40 S	34 45 E
Kisiju	**90**	7 23 S	39 19 E
Kısır, Dağ	**57**	41 0N	43 5 E
Kisizi	**90**	1 0 S	29 58 E
Kiska I.	**104**	52 0N	177 30 E
Kiskatinaw ⤳	**108**	56 8N	120 10W
Kiskittogisu L.	**109**	54 13N	98 20W
Kiskomárom = Zalakomár	**27**	46 33N	17 10 E
Kiskörös	**27**	46 37N	19 20 E
Kiskundorozsma	**27**	46 16N	20 5 E
Kiskunfelégyháza	**27**	46 42N	19 53 E
Kiskunhalas	**27**	46 28N	19 37 E
Kiskunmajsa	**27**	46 30N	19 48 E
Kislovodsk	**57**	43 50N	42 45 E
Kiso-Sammyaku	**74**	35 45N	137 45 E
Kisoro	**90**	1 17 S	29 48 E
Kispest	**27**	47 27N	19 9 E
Kissidougou	**84**	9 5N	10 0W
Kissimmee	**115**	28 18N	81 22W
Kissimmee ⤳	**115**	27 20N	80 55W
Kississing L.	**109**	55 10N	101 20W
Kistanje	**39**	43 58N	15 55 E
Kisterenye	**27**	48 3N	19 50 E
Kisújszállás	**27**	47 12N	20 50 E
Kisumu	**90**	0 3 S	34 45 E
Kisvárda	**27**	48 14N	22 4 E
Kiswani	**90**	4 5 S	37 57 E
Kiswere	**91**	9 27 S	39 30 E
Kit Carson	**116**	38 48N	102 45W
Kita	**84**	13 5N	9 25W
Kitab	**58**	39 7N	66 52 E
Kitaibaraki	**74**	36 50N	140 45 E
Kitakami-Gawa ⤳	**74**	38 25N	141 19 E
Kitakyūshū	**74**	33 50N	130 50 E
Kitale	**90**	1 0N	35 0 E
Kitangiri, L.	**90**	4 5 S	34 20 E
Kitaya	**91**	10 38 S	40 8 E
Kitchener	**106**	43 27N	80 29W
Kitega = Citega	**90**	3 30 S	29 58 E
Kitengo	**90**	7 26 S	24 8 E
Kiteto □	**90**	5 0 S	37 0 E
Kitgum	**90**	3 17N	32 52 E
Kíthira	**45**	36 9N	23 0 E
Kíthnos	**45**	37 26N	24 27 E
Kitimat	**108**	54 3N	128 38W
Kitinen ⤳	**50**	67 34N	26 40 E
Kitiyab	**87**	17 13N	33 35 E
Kítros	**44**	40 22N	22 34 E
Kittakittaooloo, L.	**99**	28 3 S	138 14 E
Kittanning	**114**	40 49N	79 30W
Kittatinny Mts.	**113**	41 0N	75 0W
Kittery	**114**	43 7N	70 42W
Kitui	**90**	1 17 S	38 0 E
Kitui □	**90**	1 30 S	38 25 E
Kitwe	**91**	12 54 S	28 13 E
Kitzbühel	**26**	47 27N	12 24 E
Kitzingen	**25**	49 44N	10 9 E
Kivalo	**50**	66 18N	26 0 E
Kivarli	**68**	24 33N	72 46 E
Kivotós	**44**	40 13N	21 26 E
Kivu □	**90**	3 10 S	27 0 E
Kivu, L.	**90**	1 48 S	29 0 E
Kiyev	**54**	50 30N	30 28 E
Kiyevskoye Vdkhr.	**54**	51 0N	30 0 E
Kizel	**52**	59 3N	57 40 E
Kiziguru	**90**	1 46 S	30 23 E
Kızıl Irmak ⤳	**56**	39 15N	36 0 E
Kizil Yurt	**57**	43 13N	46 54 E
Kızılcahamam	**56**	40 30N	32 30 E
Kizimkazi	**90**	6 28 S	39 30 E
Kizlyar	**57**	43 51N	46 40 E
Kizyl-Arvat	**58**	38 58N	56 15 E
Kjellerup	**49**	56 17N	9 25 E
Kladanj	**42**	44 14N	18 42 E
Kladnica	**42**	43 23N	20 2 E
Kladno	**26**	50 10N	14 7 E
Kladovo	**42**	44 36N	22 33 E
Klagenfurt	**26**	46 38N	14 20 E
Klagshamn	**49**	55 32N	12 53 E
Klagstorp	**49**	55 22N	13 23 E
Klaipeda	**54**	55 43N	21 10 E
Klamath ⤳	**118**	41 40N	124 4W
Klamath Falls	**118**	42 20N	121 50W
Klamath Mts.	**118**	41 20N	123 0W
Klanjec	**39**	46 3N	15 45 E
Klappan ⤳	**108**	58 0N	129 43W
Klaten	**73**	7 43 S	110 36 E
Klatovy	**26**	49 23N	13 18 E
Klawak	**108**	55 35N	133 0W
Klawer	**92**	31 44 S	18 36 E
Kłecko	**28**	52 38N	17 25 E
Kleczew	**28**	52 22N	18 9 E
Kleena Kleene	**108**	52 0N	124 59W
Klein	**118**	46 26N	108 31W
Klein-Karas	**92**	27 33 S	18 7 E
Klein Karoo	**92**	33 45 S	21 30 E
Klekovača	**39**	44 25N	16 32 E
Klemtu	**108**	52 35N	128 55W
Klenovec, Czech.	**27**	48 36N	19 54 E
Klenovec, Yugo.	**42**	41 32N	20 49 E
Klerksdorp	**92**	26 51 S	26 38 E
Kleszczele	**28**	52 35N	23 19 E
Kletnya	**54**	53 23N	33 12 E
Kletsk	**54**	53 5N	26 45 E
Kletskiy	**57**	49 20N	43 0 E
Kleve	**24**	51 46N	6 10 E
Klickitat	**118**	45 50N	121 10W
Klimovichi	**54**	53 36N	32 0 E
Klin	**55**	56 20N	36 48 E
Klinaklini ⤳	**108**	51 21N	125 40W
Klintsey	**54**	52 50N	32 10 E
Klipplaat	**92**	33 0 S	24 22 E
Klisura	**43**	42 40N	24 28 E
Klitmøller	**49**	57 3N	8 30 E
Kljajićevo	**42**	45 45N	19 17 E
Ključ	**39**	44 32N	16 48 E
Kłobuck	**28**	50 55N	18 55 E
Kłodawa	**28**	52 15N	18 55 E
Kłodzko	**28**	50 28N	16 38 E
Klondike	**104**	64 0N	139 26W
Klosi	**44**	41 28N	20 10 E
Klosterneuburg	**27**	48 18N	16 19 E
Klosters	**25**	46 52N	9 52 E
Klötze	**24**	52 38N	11 9 E
Klouto	**85**	6 57N	0 44 E
Kluane L.	**104**	61 15N	138 40W
Kluczbork	**28**	50 58N	18 12 E
Klyuchevskaya, Guba	**59**	55 50N	160 30 E
Knaresborough	**12**	54 1N	1 29W
Knee L., Man., Can.	**109**	55 3N	94 45W
Knee L., Sask., Can.	**109**	55 51N	107 0W
Kneïss, I.	**83**	34 22N	10 18 E
Knezha	**43**	43 30N	24 5 E
Knić	**42**	43 53N	20 45 E
Knight Inlet	**108**	50 45N	125 40W
Knighton	**13**	52 21N	3 2W
Knight's Landing	**118**	38 50N	121 43W
Knin	**39**	44 1N	16 17 E
Knittelfeld	**26**	47 13N	14 51 E
Knjaževac	**42**	43 35N	22 18 E
Knob, C.	**96**	34 32 S	119 16 E
Knockmealdown Mts.	**15**	52 16N	8 0W
Knokke	**16**	51 20N	3 17 E
Knossos	**45**	35 16N	25 10 E
Knox	**114**	41 18N	86 36W
Knox, C.	**108**	54 11N	133 5W
Knox City	**117**	33 26N	99 49W
Knox Coast	**5**	66 30 S	108 0 E
Knoxville, Iowa, U.S.A.	**116**	41 20N	93 5W
Knoxville, Tenn., U.S.A.	**115**	35 58N	83 57W
Knurów	**27**	50 13N	18 38 E
Knutshø	**47**	62 18N	9 41 E
Knysna	**92**	34 2 S	23 2 E
Knyszyn	**28**	53 20N	22 56 E
Ko Chang	**71**	12 0N	102 20 E
Ko Kut	**71**	11 40N	102 32 E
Ko Phra Thong	**71**	9 6N	98 15 E
Ko Tao	**71**	10 6N	99 48 E
Koartac (Notre Dame de Koartac)	**105**	60 55N	69 40W
Koba, Aru, Indon.	**73**	6 37 S	134 37 E
Koba, Bangka, Indon.	**72**	2 26 S	106 14 E
Kobarid	**39**	46 15N	13 30 E
Kobayashi	**74**	31 56N	130 59 E
Kobdo = Hovd	**75**	48 2N	91 37 E
Kōbe	**74**	34 45N	135 10 E
Kobelyaki	**56**	49 11N	34 9 E
København	**49**	55 41N	12 34 E
Koblenz	**25**	50 21N	7 36 E
Kobo	**87**	12 2N	39 56 E
Kobrin	**54**	52 15N	24 22 E
Kobroor, Kepulauan	**73**	6 10 S	134 30 E
Kobuleti	**57**	41 55N	41 45 E
Kobylin	**28**	51 43N	17 12 E
Kobyłka	**28**	52 21N	21 10 E
Kobylkino	**55**	54 8N	43 56 E
Kobylnik	**54**	54 58N	26 39 E
Kočane	**42**	43 12N	21 52 E
Kočani	**42**	41 55N	22 25 E
Koçarlı	**45**	37 45N	27 43 E
Koceljevo	**42**	44 28N	19 50 E
Kočevje	**39**	45 39N	14 50 E
Kochas	**69**	25 15N	83 56 E
Kocher ⤳	**25**	49 14N	9 12 E
Kocheya	**59**	52 32N	120 42 E
Kōchi	**74**	33 30N	133 35 E
Kōchi □	**74**	33 40N	133 30 E
Kochiu = Gejiu	**75**	23 20N	103 10 E
Kock	**28**	51 38N	22 27 E
Koddiyar Bay	**70**	8 33N	81 15 E
Kodiak	**104**	57 30N	152 45W
Kodiak I.	**104**	57 30N	152 45W
Kodiang	**71**	6 21N	100 18 E
Kodinar	**68**	20 46N	70 46 E
Kodori ⤳	**57**	42 47N	41 10 E
Koes	**92**	26 0 S	19 15 E
Kofiau	**73**	1 11 S	129 50 E
Köflach	**26**	47 4N	15 5 E
Koforidua	**85**	6 3N	0 17W
Kōfu	**74**	35 40N	138 30 E
Kogaluk ⤳	**107**	56 12N	61 44W
Kogin Baba	**85**	7 55N	11 35 E
Koh-i-Bābā	**65**	34 30N	67 0 E
Kohat	**66**	33 40N	71 29 E
Kohima	**67**	25 35N	94 10 E
Kohler Ra.	**5**	77 0 S	110 0W
Kohtla Järve	**54**	59 20N	27 20 E
Kojetin	**27**	49 21N	17 20 E
Koka	**86**	20 5N	30 35 E
Kokand	**58**	40 30N	70 57 E
Kokanee Glacier Prov. Park	**108**	49 47N	117 10W
Kokas	**73**	2 42 S	132 26 E
Kokava	**27**	48 35N	19 50 E
Kokchetav	**58**	53 20N	69 25 E
Kokemäenjoki ⤳	**51**	61 32N	21 44 E
Kokhma	**55**	56 55N	41 18 E
Kokkola (Gamlakarleby)	**50**	63 50N	23 8 E
Koko	**85**	11 28N	4 29 E
Koko Kyunzu	**71**	14 10N	93 25 E
Kokoda	**98**	8 54 S	147 47 E
Kokolopozo	**84**	5 8N	6 5W
Kokomo	**114**	40 30N	86 6W
Kokonau	**73**	4 43 S	136 26 E
Kokopo	**98**	4 22 S	152 19 E
Kokoro	**85**	14 12N	0 55 E
Koksoak ⤳	**105**	58 30N	68 10W
Kokstad	**93**	30 32 S	29 29 E
Kokuora	**59**	71 35N	144 50 E
Kola, Indon.	**73**	5 35 S	134 30 E
Kola, U.S.S.R.	**52**	68 45N	33 8 E
Kola Pen. = Kolskiy P-ov.	**52**	67 30N	38 0 E
Kolahun	**84**	8 15N	10 4W
Kolaka	**73**	4 3 S	121 46 E
Kolar	**70**	13 12N	78 15 E
Kolar Gold Fields	**70**	12 58N	78 16 E
Kolari	**50**	67 20N	23 48 E
Kolarovgrad	**43**	43 18N	26 55 E
Kolašin	**42**	42 50N	19 31 E
Kolby Kås	**49**	55 48N	10 32 E
Kolchugino	**55**	56 17N	39 22 E
Kolda	**84**	12 55N	14 57W
Kolding	**49**	55 30N	9 29 E
Kole	**88**	3 16 S	22 42 E
Koléa	**82**	36 38N	2 46 E
* Kolepom, Pulau	**73**	8 0 S	138 30 E
Kolguyev, Ostrov	**52**	69 20N	48 30 E
Kolhapur	**70**	16 43N	74 15 E
Kolia	**84**	9 46N	6 28W
Kolín	**26**	50 2N	15 9 E
Kolind	**49**	56 21N	10 34 E
Kölleda	**24**	51 11N	11 14 E
Kollegal	**70**	12 9N	77 9 E
Kolleru L.	**70**	16 40N	81 10 E
Kolmanskop	**92**	26 45 S	15 14 E
Köln	**24**	50 56N	6 58 E
Kolno	**28**	53 25N	21 56 E
Koło	**28**	52 14N	18 40 E
Kołobrzeg	**28**	54 10N	15 35 E
Kologriv	**55**	58 48N	44 25 E
Kolokani	**84**	13 35N	7 45W
Kolomna	**55**	55 8N	38 45 E
Kolomyya	**56**	48 31N	25 2 E
Kolondiéba	**84**	11 5N	6 54W
Kolonodale	**73**	2 3 S	121 25 E
Kolosib	**67**	24 15N	92 45 E
Kolpashevo	**58**	58 20N	83 5 E
Kolpino	**54**	59 44N	30 39 E
Kolpny	**55**	52 12N	37 10 E
Kolskiy Poluostrov	**52**	67 30N	38 0 E
Kolskiy Zaliv	**52**	69 23N	34 0 E
Kolubara ⤳	**42**	44 35N	20 15 E
Kolumna	**28**	51 36N	19 14 E
Koluszki	**28**	51 45N	19 46 E
Kolwezi	**91**	10 40 S	25 25 E
Kolyberovo	**55**	55 15N	38 40 E
Kolyma ⤳	**59**	69 30N	161 0 E
Kolymskoye, Okhotsko	**59**	63 0N	157 0 E
Kôm Ombo	**86**	24 25N	32 52 E
Komárno	**27**	47 49N	18 5 E
Komárom	**27**	47 43N	18 7 E
Komárom □	**27**	47 35N	18 20 E
Komarovo	**54**	58 38N	33 40 E
Komatipoort	**93**	25 25 S	31 55 E
Kombissiri	**85**	12 4N	1 20W
Kombori	**84**	13 26N	3 56W
Kombóti	**45**	39 6N	21 5 E
Komen	**39**	45 49N	13 45 E
Komenda	**85**	5 4N	1 28W
Komi A.S.S.R. □	**52**	64 0N	55 0 E
Komiža	**39**	43 3N	16 11 E
Komló	**27**	46 15N	18 16 E
Kommamur Canal	**70**	16 0N	80 25 E
Kommunarsk	**57**	48 30N	38 45 E
Kommunizma, Pik	**58**	39 0N	72 2 E
Komnes	**47**	59 30N	9 55 E
Komodo	**73**	8 37 S	119 20 E
Komoé	**84**	5 12N	3 44W
Komono	**88**	3 10 S	13 20 E
Komoran, Pulau	**73**	8 18 S	138 45 E
Komotini	**44**	41 9N	25 26 E
Komovi	**42**	42 41N	19 39 E
Kompong Cham	**71**	12 0N	105 30 E
Kompong Chhnang	**71**	12 20N	104 35 E
Kompong Speu	**71**	11 26N	104 32 E
Kompong Thom	**71**	12 35N	104 51 E
Komrat	**56**	46 18N	28 40 E
Komsberge	**92**	32 40 S	20 45 E
Komsomolets, Ostrov	**59**	80 30N	95 0 E
Komsomolsk, R.S.F.S.R., U.S.S.R.	**55**	57 2N	40 20 E
Komsomolsk, R.S.F.S.R., U.S.S.R.	**59**	50 30N	137 0 E
Komsomolskaya	**5**	66 33 S	93 1 E
Komsomolskiy	**55**	53 30N	49 30 E
Konakovo	**55**	56 52N	36 45 E
Konarhá □	**65**	35 30N	71 3 E
Konawa	**117**	34 59N	96 46W
Kondagaon	**70**	19 35N	81 35 E
Kondakovo	**59**	69 36N	152 0 E
Konde	**90**	4 57 S	39 45 E
Kondiá	**44**	39 49N	25 10 E
Kondoa	**90**	4 55 S	35 50 E
Kondoa □	**90**	5 0 S	36 0 E
Kondopaga	**52**	62 12N	34 17 E
Kondratyevo	**59**	57 22N	98 15 E
Konduga	**85**	11 35N	13 26 E
Konevo	**52**	62 8N	39 20 E
Kong	**84**	8 54N	4 36W
Kong Christian IX.s Land	**4**	68 0N	36 0W
Kong Christian X.s Land	**4**	74 0N	29 0W
Kong Franz Joseph Fd.	**4**	73 20N	24 30W
Kong Frederik IX.s Land	**4**	67 0N	52 0W
Kong Frederik VI.s Kyst	**4**	63 0N	43 0W
Kong Frederik VIII.s Land	**4**	78 30N	26 0W
Kong, Koh	**71**	11 20N	103 0 E
Kong Oscar Fjord	**4**	72 20N	24 0W
Konga	**49**	56 30N	15 6 E
Kongeå	**49**	55 24N	9 39 E
Kongju	**76**	36 30N	127 0 E
Konglu	**67**	27 13N	97 57 E
Kongolo, Kasai Or., Zaïre	**90**	5 26 S	24 49 E
Kongolo, Shaba, Zaïre	**90**	5 22 S	27 0 E
Kongor	**81**	7 1N	31 27 E
Kongoussi	**85**	13 19N	1 32W
Kongsberg	**47**	59 39N	9 39 E
Kongsvinger	**47**	60 12N	12 2 E
Kongwa	**90**	6 11 S	36 26 E
Koni	**91**	10 40 S	27 11 E
Koni, Mts.	**91**	10 36 S	27 10 E
Koniecpol	**28**	50 46N	19 40 E
Königsberg = Kaliningrad	**54**	54 42N	20 32 E
Königshofen	**25**	50 18N	10 29 E
Königslutter	**24**	52 14N	10 50 E
Königswusterhausen	**24**	52 19N	13 38 E
Konin	**28**	52 12N	18 15 E
Konin □	**28**	52 15N	18 30 E
Konispoli	**44**	39 42N	20 10 E
Kónitsa	**44**	40 5N	20 48 E
Konjic	**42**	43 42N	17 58 E
Konjice	**39**	46 20N	15 28 E
Konkouré ⤳	**84**	9 50N	13 42W
Könnern	**24**	51 40N	11 45 E
Konnur	**70**	16 14N	74 49 E
Kono	**84**	8 30N	11 5W
Konongo	**85**	6 40N	1 15W
Konosha	**52**	61 0N	40 5 E
Konotop	**54**	51 12N	33 7 E
Konqi He ⤳	**75**	40 45N	90 10 E
Końskie	**28**	51 15N	20 23 E
Konsmo	**47**	58 16N	7 23 E
Konstantinovka	**56**	48 32N	37 39 E
Konstantinovski	**57**	47 33N	41 10 E
Konstantynów Łódźki	**28**	51 45N	19 20 E
Konstanz	**25**	47 39N	9 10 E
Kontagora	**85**	10 23N	5 27 E
Kontum	**71**	14 24N	108 0 E
Konya	**64**	37 52N	32 35 E
Konya Ovasi	**64**	38 30N	33 0 E
Konz	**25**	49 41N	6 36 E
Konza	**90**	1 45 S	37 7 E
Koo-wee-rup	**100**	38 13 S	145 28 E
Koolan I.	**96**	16 0 S	123 45 E
Kooloonong	**99**	34 48 S	143 10 E
Koondrook	**99**	35 33 S	144 8 E
Koorawatha	**99**	34 2 S	148 33 E
Kooskia	**118**	46 9N	115 59W
Koostatak	**109**	51 26N	97 26W
Kootenai ⤳	**118**	49 15N	117 39W
Kootenay L.	**108**	49 45N	116 50W
Kootenay Nat. Park	**108**	51 0N	116 0W
Kopanovka	**57**	47 28N	46 50 E
Kopaonik Planina	**42**	43 10N	21 50 E
Kopargaon	**70**	19 51N	74 28 E
Kópavogur	**50**	64 6N	21 55W
Koper	**39**	45 31N	13 44 E
Kopervik	**47**	59 17N	5 17 E
Kopeysk	**58**	55 7N	61 37 E
Köping	**48**	59 31N	16 3 E
Kopiste	**39**	42 48N	16 42 E
Kopliku	**44**	42 15N	19 25 E

* Renamed Yos Sudarso, P.

Köpmanholmen	**48**	63 10N	18 35 E
Koppal	**70**	15 23N	76 5 E
Koppang	**47**	61 34N	11 3 E
Kopparbergs län □	**48**	61 20N	14 15 E
Koppeh Dāgh	**65**	38 0N	58 0 E
Kopperå	**47**	63 24N	11 50 E
Koppom	**48**	59 43N	12 10 E
Koprivlen	**43**	41 36N	23 53 E
Koprivnica	**39**	46 12N	16 45 E
Koprivshtitsa	**43**	42 40N	24 19 E
Kopychintsy	**54**	49 7N	25 58 E
Kopys	**54**	54 20N	30 17 E
Korab	**42**	41 44N	20 40 E
Korakiána	**44**	39 42N	19 45 E
Koraput	**70**	18 50N	82 40 E
Korba	**69**	22 20N	82 45 E
Korbach	**24**	51 17N	8 50 E
Korça	**44**	40 37N	20 50 E
Korça □	**44**	40 40N	20 50 E
Korčula	**39**	42 57N	17 8 E
Korčulanski Kanal	**39**	43 3N	16 40 E
Kordestan	**64**	35 30N	42 0 E
Kordestān □	**64**	36 0N	47 0 E
Korea Bay	**76**	39 0N	124 0 E
Koregaon	**70**	17 40N	74 10 E
Korenevo	**54**	51 27N	34 55 E
Korenovsk	**57**	45 30N	39 22 E
Korets	**54**	50 40N	27 5 E
Korgus	**86**	19 16N	33 29 E
Korhogo	**84**	9 29N	5 28W
Koribundu	**84**	7 41N	11 46W
Korim	**73**	0 58 S	136 10 E
Korinthía □	**45**	37 50N	22 35 E
Korinthiakós Kólpos	**45**	38 16N	22 30 E
Kórinthos	**45**	37 56N	22 55 E
Korioumé	**84**	16 35N	3 0W
Kōriyama	**74**	37 24N	140 23 E
Körmend	**27**	47 5N	16 35 E
Kornat	**39**	43 50N	15 20 E
Korneshty	**56**	47 21N	28 1 E
Korneuburg	**27**	48 20N	16 20 E
Kornsjø	**47**	58 57N	11 39 E
Kornstad	**47**	62 59N	7 27 E
Koro, Fiji	**101**	17 19 S	179 23 E
Koro, Ivory C.	**84**	8 32N	7 30W
Koro, Mali	**84**	14 1N	2 58W
Koro Sea	**101**	17 30 S	179 45W
Korocha	**55**	50 55N	37 30 E
Korogwe	**90**	5 5 S	38 25 E
Korogwe □	**90**	5 0 S	38 20 E
Koroit	**99**	38 18 S	142 24 E
Koróni	**45**	36 48N	21 57 E
Korónia, Limni	**44**	40 47N	23 37 E
Koronís	**45**	37 12N	25 35 E
Koronowo	**28**	53 19N	17 55 E
Koror	**73**	7 20N	134 28 E
Körös ⤳	**27**	46 43N	20 12 E
Köröstarcsa	**27**	46 53N	21 3 E
Korosten	**54**	50 57N	28 25 E
Korotoyak	**55**	51 1N	39 2 E
Korraraika, Helodranon' i	**93**	17 45 S	43 57 E
Korsakov	**59**	46 36N	142 42 E
Korshunovo	**59**	58 37N	110 10 E
Korsun Shevchenkovskiy	**56**	49 26N	31 16 E
Korsze	**28**	54 11N	21 9 E
Korti	**86**	18 6N	31 33 E
Kortrijk	**16**	50 50N	3 17 E
Korwai	**68**	24 7N	78 5 E
Koryakskiy Khrebet	**59**	61 0N	171 0 E
Kos	**45**	36 50N	27 15 E
Kosa	**87**	7 50N	36 50 E
Kosaya Gora	**55**	54 10N	37 30 E
Koschagyl	**53**	46 40N	54 0 E
Kościan	**28**	52 5N	16 40 E
Kościerzyna	**28**	54 8N	17 59 E
Kosciusko	**117**	33 3N	89 34W
Kosciusko I.	**108**	56 0N	133 40W
Kosciusko, Mt.	**97**	36 27 S	148 16 E
Kösély ⤳	**27**	47 25N	21 5 E
Kosgi	**70**	16 58N	77 43 E
Kosha	**86**	20 50N	30 30 E
K'oshih = Kashi	**75**	39 30N	76 2 E
Koshk-e Kohneh	**65**	34 55N	62 30 E
Kosi	**68**	27 48N	77 29 E
Kosi-meer	**93**	27 0 S	32 50 E
Košice	**27**	48 42N	21 15 E
Kosjerić	**42**	44 0N	19 55 E
Koslan	**52**	63 28N	48 52 E
Kosŏng	**76**	38 40N	128 22 E
Kosovo, Pokrajina	**42**	42 40N	21 5 E
Kosovo, Soc. Aut. Pokrajina □	**42**	42 30N	21 0 E
Kosovska-Mitrovica	**42**	42 54N	20 52 E
Kostajnica	**39**	45 17N	16 30 E
Kostamuksa	**52**	62 34N	32 44 E
Kostanjevica	**39**	45 51N	15 27 E
Kostelec	**27**	50 14N	16 35 E
Kostenets	**43**	42 15N	23 52 E
Koster	**92**	25 52 S	26 54 E
Kôstî	**87**	13 8N	32 43 E
Kostolac	**42**	44 37N	21 15 E
Kostopol	**54**	50 51N	26 22 E
Kostroma	**55**	57 50N	40 58 E
Kostromskoye Vdkhr.	**55**	57 52N	40 49 E
Kostrzyn, Poland	**28**	52 24N	17 14 E
Kostrzyn, Poland	**28**	52 35N	14 39 E
Kostyukovichi	**54**	53 20N	32 4 E
Koszalin	**28**	53 50N	16 8 E
Koszalin □	**28**	53 40N	16 10 E
Köszeg	**27**	47 23N	16 33 E
Kot Adu	**68**	30 30N	71 0 E
Kot Moman	**68**	32 13N	73 0 E
Kota	**68**	25 14N	75 49 E
Kota Baharu	**71**	6 7N	102 14 E
Kota Belud	**72**	6 21N	116 26 E
Kota Kinabalu	**72**	6 0N	116 4 E
Kota Tinggi	**71**	1 44N	103 53 E
Kotaagung	**72**	5 38 S	104 29 E
Kotabaru	**72**	3 20 S	116 20 E
Kotabumi	**72**	4 49 S	104 54 E
Kotagede	**73**	7 54 S	110 26 E
Kotamobagu	**73**	0 57N	124 31 E
Kotaneelee ⤳	**108**	60 11N	123 42W
Kotawaringin	**72**	2 28 S	111 27 E
Kotcho L.	**108**	59 7N	121 12W
Kotel	**43**	42 52N	26 26 E
Kotelnich	**55**	58 20N	48 10 E
Kotelnikovo	**57**	47 38N	43 8 E
Kotelnyy, Ostrov	**59**	75 10N	139 0 E
Kothagudam	**70**	17 30N	80 40 E
Kothapet	**70**	19 21N	79 28 E
Köthen	**24**	51 44N	11 59 E
Kothi	**69**	24 45N	80 40 E
Kotiro	**68**	26 17N	67 13 E
Kotka	**51**	60 28N	26 58 E
Kotlas	**52**	61 15N	47 0 E
Kotlenska Planina	**43**	42 56N	26 30 E
Kotli	**66**	33 30N	73 55 E
Kotonkoro	**85**	11 3N	5 58 E
Kotor	**42**	42 25N	18 47 E
Kotor Varoš	**42**	44 38N	17 22 E
Kotoriba	**39**	46 23N	16 48 E
Kotovo	**55**	50 22N	44 45 E
Kotovsk	**56**	47 45N	29 35 E
Kotputli	**68**	27 43N	76 12 E
Kotri	**68**	25 22N	68 22 E
Kotri ⤳	**70**	19 15N	80 35 E
Kótronas	**45**	36 38N	22 29 E
Kötschach-Mauthen	**26**	46 41N	13 1 E
Kottayam	**70**	9 35N	76 33 E
Kottur	**70**	10 34N	76 56 E
Kotuy ⤳	**59**	71 54N	102 6 E
Kotzebue	**104**	66 50N	162 40W
Kouango	**88**	5 0N	20 10 E
Koudougou	**84**	12 10N	2 20W
Koufonísi	**45**	34 56N	26 8 E
Koufonísia	**45**	36 57N	25 35 E
Kougaberge	**92**	33 48 S	23 50 E
Kouibli	**84**	7 15N	7 14W
Kouilou ⤳	**88**	4 10 S	12 5 E
Kouki	**88**	7 22N	17 3 E
Koula Moutou	**88**	1 15 S	12 25 E
Koulen	**71**	13 50N	104 40 E
Koulikoro	**84**	12 40N	7 50W
Koumala	**98**	21 38 S	149 15 E
Koumankou	**84**	11 58N	6 6W
Koumbia, Guin.	**84**	11 48N	13 29W
Koumbia, Upp. Vol.	**84**	11 10N	3 50W
Koumboum	**84**	10 25N	13 0W
Koumpenntoum	**84**	13 59N	14 34W
Koumra	**81**	8 50N	17 35 E
Koundara	**84**	12 29N	13 18W
Kounradskiy	**58**	46 59N	75 0 E
Kountze	**117**	30 20N	94 22W
Koupéla	**85**	12 11N	0 21W
Kourizo, Passe de	**83**	22 28N	15 27 E
Kouroussa	**84**	10 45N	9 45W
Koussané	**84**	14 53N	11 14W
Kousseri	**81**	12 0N	14 55 E
Koutiala	**84**	12 25N	5 23W
Kouto	**84**	9 53N	6 25W
Kouvé	**85**	6 25N	1 25 E
Kovačica	**42**	45 5N	20 38 E
Kovdor	**52**	67 34N	30 24 E
Kovel	**54**	51 10N	24 20 E
Kovilpatti	**70**	9 10N	77 50 E
Kovin	**42**	44 44N	20 59 E
Kovrov	**55**	56 25N	41 25 E
Kovur, Andhra Pradesh, India	**70**	17 3N	81 39 E
Kovur, Andhra Pradesh, India	**70**	14 30N	80 1 E
Kowal	**28**	52 32N	19 7 E
Kowalewo Pomorskie	**28**	53 10N	18 52 E
Kowkash	**106**	50 20N	87 12W
Kowloon	**75**	22 20N	114 15 E
Koyabuti	**73**	2 36 S	140 37 E
Koyan, Pegunungan	**72**	3 15N	114 30 E
Koyuk	**104**	64 55N	161 20W
Koyukuk ⤳	**104**	64 56N	157 30W
Koyulhisar	**56**	40 20N	37 52 E
Koza	**77**	26 19N	127 46 E
Kozan	**64**	37 35N	35 50 E
Kozáni	**44**	40 19N	21 47 E
Kozáni □	**44**	40 18N	21 45 E
Kozara	**39**	45 0N	17 0 E
Kozarac	**39**	44 58N	16 48 E
Kozelsk	**54**	54 2N	35 48 E
Kozhikode = Calicut	**70**	11 15N	75 43 E
Kozhva	**52**	65 10N	57 0 E
Koziegłowy	**28**	50 37N	19 8 E
Kozienice	**28**	51 35N	21 34 E
Kozje	**39**	46 5N	15 35 E
Kozle	**28**	50 20N	18 8 E
Kozloduy	**43**	43 45N	23 42 E
Kozlovets	**43**	43 30N	25 20 E
Koźmin	**28**	51 48N	17 27 E
Kozmodemyansk	**55**	56 20N	46 36 E
Kozuchów	**28**	51 45N	15 31 E
Kpabia	**85**	9 10N	0 20W
Kpalimé	**85**	6 57N	0 44 E
Kpandae	**85**	8 30N	0 2W
Kpessi	**85**	8 4N	1 16 E
Kra Buri	**71**	10 22N	98 46 E
Kra, Isthmus of = Kra, Kho Khot	**71**	10 15N	99 30 E
Kra, Kho Khot	**71**	10 15N	99 30 E
Kragan	**73**	6 43 S	111 38 E
Kragerø	**47**	58 52N	9 25 E
Kragujevac	**42**	44 2N	20 56 E
Krajenka	**28**	53 18N	16 59 E
Krakatau = Rakata, Pulau	**72**	6 10 S	105 20 E
Kraków	**27**	50 4N	19 57 E
Kraków □	**27**	50 0N	20 0 E
Kraksaan	**73**	7 43 S	113 23 E
Kråkstad	**47**	59 39N	10 55 E
Králiky	**27**	50 6N	16 45 E
Kraljevo	**42**	43 44N	20 41 E
Kralovice	**26**	49 59N	13 29 E
Královský Chlmec	**27**	48 27N	22 0 E
Kralupy	**26**	50 13N	14 20 E
Kramatorsk	**56**	48 50N	37 30 E
Kramer	**119**	35 0N	117 38W
Kramfors	**48**	62 55N	17 48 E
Kramis, C.	**82**	36 26N	0 45 E
Krångede	**48**	63 9N	16 10 E
Kraniá	**44**	39 53N	21 18 E
Kranídhion	**45**	37 20N	23 10 E
Kranj	**39**	46 16N	14 22 E
Kranjska Gora	**39**	46 29N	13 48 E
Krapina	**39**	46 10N	15 52 E
Krapina ⤳	**39**	45 50N	15 50 E
Krapivna	**55**	53 58N	37 10 E
Krapkowice	**28**	50 29N	17 56 E
Krasavino	**52**	60 58N	46 29 E
Kraskino	**59**	42 44N	130 48 E
Kraslice	**26**	50 19N	12 31 E
Krasnaya Gorbatka	**55**	55 52N	41 45 E
Krasnaya Polyana	**57**	43 40N	40 13 E
Kraśnik	**28**	50 55N	22 5 E
Kraśnik Fabryczny	**28**	50 58N	22 11 E
Krasnoarmeisk	**56**	48 18N	37 11 E
Krasnoarmeysk, R.S.F.S.R., U.S.S.R.	**55**	51 0N	45 42 E
Krasnoarmeysk, R.S.F.S.R., U.S.S.R.	**57**	48 30N	44 25 E
Krasnodar	**57**	45 5N	39 0 E
Krasnodon	**57**	48 17N	39 44 E
Krasnodonetskaya	**57**	48 5N	40 50 E
Krasnogorskiy	**55**	56 10N	48 28 E
Krasnograd	**56**	49 27N	35 27 E
Krasnogvardeyskoye	**57**	45 52N	41 33 E
Krasnogvardyesk	**56**	45 32N	34 16 E
Krasnokamsk	**52**	58 4N	55 48 E
Krasnokutsk	**54**	50 10N	34 50 E
Krasnoperekopsk	**56**	46 0N	33 54 E
Krasnoselkupsk	**58**	65 20N	82 10 E
Krasnoslobodsk, R.S.F.S.R., U.S.S.R.	**55**	54 25N	43 45 E
Krasnoslobodsk, R.S.F.S.R., U.S.S.R.	**57**	48 42N	44 33 E
Krasnoturinsk	**58**	59 46N	60 12 E
Krasnoufimsk	**52**	56 57N	57 46 E
Krasnouralsk	**52**	58 21N	60 3 E
Krasnovishersk	**52**	60 23N	57 3 E
Krasnovodsk	**53**	40 0N	52 52 E
Krasnoyarsk	**59**	56 8N	93 0 E
Krasnoye, Kalmyk A.S.S.R., U.S.S.R.	**57**	46 16N	45 0 E
Krasnoye, R.S.F.S.R., U.S.S.R.	**55**	59 15N	47 40 E
Krasnoye = Krasnyy	**54**	54 25N	31 30 E
Krasnozavodsk	**55**	56 27N	38 25 E
Krasny Liman	**56**	48 58N	37 50 E
Krasny Sulin	**57**	47 52N	40 8 E
Krasnystaw	**28**	50 57N	23 5 E
Krasnyy	**54**	54 25N	31 30 E
Krasnyy Kholm	**55**	58 10N	37 10 E
Krasnyy Kut	**55**	50 50N	47 0 E
Krasnyy Luch	**57**	48 13N	39 0 E
Krasnyy Profintern	**55**	57 45N	40 27 E
Krasnyy Yar, Kalmyk A.S.S.R., U.S.S.R.	**57**	46 43N	48 23 E
Krasnyy Yar, R.S.F.S.R., U.S.S.R.	**55**	53 30N	50 22 E
Krasnyy Yar, R.S.F.S.R., U.S.S.R.	**55**	50 42N	44 45 E
Krasnyye Baki	**55**	57 8N	45 10 E
Krasnyyoskolskoye Vdkhr.	**56**	49 30N	37 30 E
Kraszna ⤳	**27**	48 0N	22 20 E
Kratie	**71**	12 32N	106 10 E
Kratovo	**42**	42 6N	22 10 E
Krau	**73**	3 19 S	140 5 E
Kravanh, Chuor Phnum	**71**	12 0N	103 32 E
Krawang	**73**	6 19N	107 18 E
Krefeld	**24**	51 20N	6 32 E
Krémaston, Límni	**45**	38 52N	21 30 E
Kremenchug	**56**	49 5N	33 25 E
Kremenchugskoye Vdkhr.	**56**	49 20N	32 30 E
Kremenets	**56**	50 8N	25 43 E
Kremenica	**42**	40 55N	21 25 E
Kremennaya	**56**	49 1N	38 10 E
Kremges = Svetlovodsk	**56**	49 5N	33 15 E
Kremikovtsi	**43**	42 46N	23 28 E
Kremmen	**24**	52 45N	13 1 E
Kremmling	**118**	40 10N	106 30W
Kremnica	**27**	48 45N	18 50 E
Krems	**26**	48 25N	15 36 E
Kremsmünster	**26**	48 3N	14 8 E
Kretinga	**54**	55 53N	21 15 E
Krettamia	**82**	28 47N	3 27W
Krettsy	**54**	58 15N	32 30 E
Kreuzberg	**25**	50 22N	9 58 E
Kribi	**88**	2 57N	9 56 E
Krichem	**43**	42 8N	24 28 E
Krichev	**54**	53 45N	31 50 E
Krim	**39**	45 53N	14 30 E
Krionéri	**45**	38 20N	21 35 E
Krishna ⤳	**70**	15 57N	80 59 E
Krishnagiri	**70**	12 32N	78 16 E
Krishnanagar	**69**	23 24N	88 33 E
Krishnaraja Sagara	**70**	12 20N	76 30 E
Kristiansand	**47**	58 9N	8 1 E
Kristianstad	**49**	56 2N	14 9 E
Kristiansund	**47**	63 7N	7 45 E
Kristiinankaupunki	**50**	62 16N	21 21 E
Kristinehamn	**48**	59 18N	14 13 E
Kristinestad	**50**	62 16N	21 21 E
Kríti	**45**	35 15N	25 0 E
Kritsá	**45**	35 10N	25 41 E
Kriva ⤳	**42**	42 5N	21 47 E
Kriva Palanka	**42**	42 11N	22 19 E
Krivaja ⤳	**42**	44 27N	18 9 E
Krivelj	**42**	44 8N	22 5 E
Krivoy Rog	**56**	47 51N	33 20 E
Križevci	**39**	46 3N	16 32 E
Krk	**39**	45 8N	14 40 E
Krka ⤳	**39**	45 50N	15 30 E
Krkonoše	**26**	50 50N	15 35 E
Krnov	**27**	50 5N	17 40 E
Krobia	**28**	51 47N	16 59 E
Kročehlavy	**26**	50 8N	14 9 E
Krøderen	**47**	60 9N	9 49 E
Krokawo	**28**	54 47N	18 9 E
Krokeaí	**45**	36 53N	22 32 E
Krokom	**48**	63 20N	14 30 E
Krolevets	**54**	51 35N	33 20 E
Kroměříz	**27**	49 18N	17 21 E
Krompachy	**27**	48 54N	20 52 E
Kromy	**54**	52 40N	35 48 E
Kronach	**25**	50 14N	11 19 E
Kronobergs län □	**49**	56 45N	14 30 E
Kronprins Olav Kyst	**5**	69 0 S	42 0 E
Kronprinsesse Märtha Kyst	**5**	73 30 S	10 0 E
Kronshtadt	**54**	60 5N	29 45 E
Kroonstad	**92**	27 43 S	27 19 E
Kröpelin	**24**	54 4N	11 48 E
Kropotkin, R.S.F.S.R., U.S.S.R.	**57**	45 28N	40 28 E
Kropotkin, R.S.F.S.R., U.S.S.R.	**59**	59 0N	115 30 E
Kropp	**24**	54 24N	9 32 E
Krościenko	**27**	49 29N	20 25 E
Krośniewice	**28**	52 15N	19 11 E
Krosno	**27**	49 42N	21 46 E
Krosno □	**27**	49 35N	22 0 E
Krosno Odrzańskie	**28**	52 3N	15 7 E
Krotoszyn	**28**	51 42N	17 23 E
Krraba	**44**	41 13N	20 0 E
Krško	**39**	45 57N	15 30 E
Krstača	**42**	42 57N	20 8 E
Kruger Nat. Park	**93**	24 0 S	31 40 E
Krugersdorp	**93**	26 5 S	27 46 E
Kruis, Kaap	**92**	21 55 S	13 57 E
Kruja	**44**	41 32N	19 46 E
Krulevshchina	**54**	55 5N	27 45 E
Kruma	**44**	42 14N	20 28 E
Krumbach	**25**	48 15N	10 22 E
Krumovgrad	**43**	41 29N	25 38 E
Krung Thep	**71**	13 45N	100 35 E
Krupanj	**42**	44 25N	19 22 E
Krupina	**27**	48 22N	19 5 E
Krupinica ⤳	**27**	48 15N	18 52 E
Kruševac	**42**	43 35N	21 28 E
Kruševo	**42**	41 23N	21 19 E
Kruszwica	**28**	52 40N	18 20 E
Kruzof I.	**108**	57 10N	135 40W
Krylbo	**48**	60 7N	16 15 E
Krymsk Abinsk	**56**	44 50N	38 0 E
Krymskiy P-ov.	**56**	45 0N	34 0 E
Krynica	**27**	49 25N	20 57 E
Krynica Morska	**28**	54 23N	19 28 E
Krynki	**28**	53 17N	23 43 E
Krzepice	**28**	50 58N	18 50 E
Krzeszów	**28**	50 24N	22 21 E
Krzeszowice	**27**	50 8N	19 37 E
Krzna ⤳	**28**	51 59N	22 47 E
Krzywiń	**28**	51 58N	16 50 E
Krzyz	**28**	52 52N	16 0 E
Ksabi	**82**	32 51N	4 13W
Ksar Chellala	**82**	35 13N	2 19 E
Ksar el Boukhari	**82**	35 51N	2 52 E
Ksar el Kebir	**82**	35 0N	6 0W
Ksar es Souk = Ar Rachidiya	**82**	31 58N	4 20W
Ksar Rhilane	**83**	33 0N	9 39 E
Ksiba, El	**82**	32 46N	6 0W
Ksour, Mts. des	**82**	32 45N	0 30W
Kstovo	**55**	56 12N	44 13 E
Kuala	**72**	2 55N	105 47 E
Kuala Kangsar	**71**	4 46N	100 56 E
Kuala Kerai	**71**	5 30N	102 12 E
Kuala Kubu Baharu	**71**	3 34N	101 39 E
Kuala Lipis	**71**	4 10N	102 3 E
Kuala Lumpur	**71**	3 9N	101 41 E
Kuala Sedili Besar	**71**	1 55N	104 5 E
Kuala Terengganu	**72**	5 20N	103 8 E
Kualakapuas	**72**	2 55 S	114 20 E
Kualakurun	**72**	1 10 S	113 50 E
Kualapembuang	**72**	3 14 S	112 38 E
Kualasimpang	**72**	4 17N	98 3 E
Kuandang	**73**	0 56N	123 1 E
Kuandian	**76**	40 45N	124 45 E
Kuangchou = Guangzhou	**75**	23 5N	113 10 E
Kuantan	**71**	3 49N	103 20 E
Kuba	**57**	41 21N	48 32 E
Kubak	**66**	27 10N	63 10 E
Kuban ⤳	**56**	45 20N	37 30 E
Kubenskoye, Oz.	**55**	59 40N	39 25 E
Kuberle	**57**	47 0N	42 20 E
Kubrat	**43**	43 49N	26 31 E
Kučevo	**42**	44 30N	21 40 E
Kuchaman	**68**	27 13N	74 47 E
Kuchenspitze	**26**	47 7N	10 12 E
Kuching	**72**	1 33N	110 25 E
Kuçove = Qytet Stalin	**44**	40 47N	19 57 E
Kücük Kuyu	**44**	39 35N	26 27 E
Kudalier ⤳	**70**	18 35N	79 48 E
Kudat	**72**	6 55N	116 55 E
Kudremukh, Mt.	**70**	13 15N	75 20 E
Kudus	**73**	6 48 S	110 51 E
Kudymkar	**58**	59 1N	54 39 E
Kueiyang = Guiyang	**75**	26 32N	106 40 E
Kufrinjah	**62**	32 20N	35 41 E
Kufstein	**26**	47 35N	12 11 E
Kugong I.	**106**	56 18N	79 50W
Kūh-e 'Alijūq	**65**	31 30N	51 41 E
Kūh-e Dīnār	**65**	30 40N	51 0 E
Kūh-e-Hazārān	**65**	29 35N	57 20 E
Kūh-e-Jebāl Bārez	**65**	29 0N	58 0 E
Kūh-e Sorkh	**65**	35 30N	58 45 E
Kūh-e Taftān	**65**	28 40N	61 0 E
Kūhak	**65**	27 12N	63 10 E
Kūhhā-ye-Bashākerd	**65**	26 45N	59 0 E
Kūhhā-ye Sabalān	**64**	38 15N	47 45 E
Kuhnsdorf	**26**	46 37N	14 38 E
Kūhpāyeh	**65**	32 44N	52 20 E
Kuile He ⤳	**76**	49 32N	124 42 E
Kuito	**89**	12 22 S	16 55 E
Kukavica	**42**	42 48N	21 57 E
Kukawa	**85**	12 58N	13 27 E
Kukësi	**44**	42 5N	20 20 E
Kukësi □	**44**	42 25N	20 15 E
Kukmor	**55**	56 11N	50 54 E
Kukvidze	**55**	50 40N	43 15 E
Kula, Bulg.	**42**	43 52N	22 36 E
Kula, Yugo.	**42**	45 37N	19 32 E
Kulai	**71**	1 44N	103 35 E
Kulal, Mt.	**90**	2 42N	36 57 E
Kulaly, O.	**57**	45 0N	50 0 E
Kulasekharapattanam	**70**	8 20N	78 0 E
Kuldiga	**54**	56 58N	21 59 E
Kuldja = Yining	**75**	43 58N	81 10 E
Kuldu	**87**	12 50N	28 30 E
Kulebaki	**55**	55 22N	42 25 E
Kulen Vakuf	**39**	44 35N	16 2 E

Kuli **57** 42 2N 47 12 E
Küllük **45** 37 12N 27 36 E
Kulm **116** 46 22N 98 58W
Kulmbach **25** 50 6N 11 27 E
Kulsary **58** 46 59N 54 1 E
Kultay **57** 45 5N 51 40 E
Kulti **69** 23 43N 86 50 E
Kulunda **58** 52 35N 78 57 E
Kulwin **99** 35 0S 142 42 E
Kulyab **58** 37 55N 69 50 E
Kum Tekei **58** 43 10N 79 30 E
Kuma → **57** 44 55N 47 0 E
Kumaganum **85** 13 8N 10 38 E
Kumagaya **74** 36 9N 139 22 E
Kumai **72** 2 44S 111 43 E
Kumamba, Kepulauan **73** 1 36S 138 45 E
Kumamoto **74** 32 45N 130 45 E
Kumamoto □ **74** 32 55N 130 55 E
Kumanovo **42** 42 9N 21 42 E
Kumara **101** 42 37S 171 12 E
Kumasi **84** 6 41N 1 38W
Kumba **88** 4 36N 9 24 E
Kumbakonam **70** 10 58N 79 25 E
Kumbarilla **99** 27 15S 150 55 E
Kumbo **85** 6 15N 10 36 E
Kumbukkan Oya → **70** 6 35N 81 40 E
Kumeny **55** 58 10N 49 47 E
Kumertau **52** 52 46N 55 47 E
Kumi **90** 1 30N 33 58 E
Kumkale **44** 40 0N 26 13 E
Kumla **48** 59 8N 15 10 E
Kummerower See **24** 53 47N 12 52 E
Kumo **85** 10 1N 11 12 E
Kumon Bum **67** 26 30N 97 15 E
Kumta **70** 14 29N 74 25 E
Kumtorkala **57** 43 2N 46 50 E
Kumylzhenskaya **57** 49 51N 42 38 E
Kunágota **27** 46 26N 21 3 E
Kunama **99** 35 35S 148 4 E
Kunashir, Ostrov **59** 44 0N 146 0 E
Kunch **68** 26 0N 79 10 E
Kunda **54** 59 30N 26 34 E
Kundiawa **98** 6 2S 145 1 E
Kundla **68** 21 21N 71 25 E
Kungala **99** 29 58S 153 7 E
Kungälv **49** 57 53N 11 59 E
Kunghit I. **108** 52 6N 131 3W
Kungrad **58** 43 6N 58 54 E
Kungsbacka **49** 57 30N 12 5 E
Kungur **52** 57 25N 56 57 E
Kungurri **98** 21 3S 148 46 E
Kunhegyes **27** 47 22N 20 36 E
Kuningan **73** 6 59S 108 29 E
Kunlong **67** 23 20N 98 50 E
Kunlun Shan **75** 36 0N 85 0 E
Kunmadaras **27** 47 28N 20 45 E
Kunming **75** 25 1N 102 41 E
Kunnamkulam **70** 10 38N 76 7 E
Kunsan **76** 35 59N 126 45 E
Kunshan **77** 31 22N 120 58 E
Kunszentmárton **27** 46 50N 20 20 E
Kununurra **96** 15 40S 128 50 E
Kunwarara **98** 22 55S 150 9 E
Kunya-Urgenoh **58** 42 19N 59 10 E
Künzelsau **25** 49 17N 9 41 E
Kuopio **50** 62 53N 27 35 E
Kuopion lääni □ **50** 63 25N 27 10 E
Kupa → **39** 45 28N 16 24 E
Kupang **73** 10 19S 123 39 E
Kupres **42** 44 1N 17 15 E
Kupyansk **56** 49 52N 37 35 E
Kupyansk-Uzlovoi **56** 49 45N 37 34 E
Kuqa **75** 41 35N 82 30 E
Kura → **57** 39 50N 49 20 E
Kuranda **98** 16 48S 145 35 E
Kurashiki **74** 34 40N 133 50 E
Kurayoshi **74** 35 26N 133 50 E
Kurduvadi **70** 18 8N 75 29 E
Kŭrdzhali **43** 41 38N 25 21 E
Kure **74** 34 14N 132 32 E
Kuressaare = Kingisepp **54** 58 15N 22 15 E
Kurgaldzhino **58** 50 35N 70 20 E
Kurgan **58** 55 26N 65 18 E
Kurganinsk **57** 44 54N 40 34 E
Kurgannaya = Kurganinsk **57** 44 54N 40 34 E
Kuria Maria I. = Khūryān Mūryān, Jazā 'ir **63** 17 30N 55 58 E
Kurichchi **70** 11 36N 77 35 E
Kuridala P.O **98** 21 16S 140 29 E
Kuril Is. = Kurilskiye Os. **59** 45 0N 150 0 E
Kuril Trench **94** 44 0N 153 0 E
Kurilsk **59** 45 14N 147 53 E
Kurilskiye Ostrova **59** 45 0N 150 0 E
Kuring Kuru **92** 17 42S 18 32 E
Kurkur **86** 23 50N 32 0 E
Kurkūrah **83** 31 30N 20 1 E
Kurla **70** 19 5N 72 52 E
Kurlovskiy **55** 55 25N 40 40 E
Kurmuk **87** 10 33N 34 21 E
Kurnool **70** 15 45N 78 0 E
Kurovskoye **55** 55 35N 38 55 E
Kurow **101** 44 44S 170 29 E
Kurów **28** 51 23N 22 12 E
Kurrajong **99** 33 33S 150 42 E
Kurri Kurri **99** 32 50S 151 28 E
Kursavka **57** 44 29N 42 32 E
Kuršenai **54** 56 1N 23 3 E
Kurseong **69** 26 56N 88 18 E
Kursk **55** 51 42N 36 11 E
Kuršumlija **42** 43 9N 21 19 E
Kuršumlijska Banja **42** 43 3N 21 11 E
Kuru (Chel), Bahr el **87** 8 10N 26 50 E
Kuruktag **75** 41 0N 89 0 E
Kuruman **92** 27 28S 23 28 E
Kurume **74** 33 15N 130 30 E
Kurunegala **70** 7 30N 80 23 E
Kurya **59** 61 15N 108 10 E
Kuşada Körfezı **45** 37 56N 27 0 E
Kuşadası **45** 37 52N 27 15 E
Kusawa L. **108** 60 20N 136 13W
Kusel **25** 49 31N 7 25 E
Kushchevskaya **57** 46 33N 39 35 E
Kushiro **74** 43 0N 144 25 E
Kushiro → **74** 42 59N 144 23 E
Kushka **58** 35 20N 62 18 E
Kushtia **69** 23 55N 89 5 E
Kushum → **57** 49 0N 50 20 E
Kushva **52** 58 18N 59 45 E
Kuskokwim → **104** 60 17N 162 27W
Kuskokwim Bay **104** 59 50N 162 56W
Kussharo-Ko **74** 43 38N 144 21 E
Kustanay **58** 53 10N 63 35 E
Kütahya **64** 39 30N 30 2 E
Kutaisi **57** 42 19N 42 40 E
Kutaraja = Banda Aceh **72** 5 35N 95 20 E
Kutch, G. of **68** 22 50N 69 15 E
Kutch, Rann of **68** 24 0N 70 0 E
Kutina **39** 45 29N 16 48 E
Kutiyana **68** 21 36N 70 2 E
Kutjevo **42** 45 23N 17 55 E
Kutkashen **57** 40 58N 47 47 E
Kutná Hora **26** 49 57N 15 16 E
Kutno **28** 52 15N 19 23 E
Kuttabul **98** 21 5S 148 48 E
Kutu **88** 2 40S 18 11 E
Kutum **87** 14 10N 24 40 E
Kúty **27** 48 40N 17 3 E
Kuvshinovo **54** 57 2N 34 11 E
Kuwait = Al Kuwayt **64** 29 30N 47 30 E
Kuwait ■ **64** 29 30N 47 30 E
Kuwana **74** 35 0N 136 43 E
Kuybyshev **58** 55 27N 78 19 E
Kuybyshev **58** 53 8N 50 6 E
Kuybyshevskoye Vdkhr. **55** 55 2N 49 30 E
Kūysanjaq **64** 36 5N 44 38 E
Kuyto, Oz. **52** 64 40N 31 0 E
Kuyumba **59** 60 58N 96 59 E
Kuzey Anadolu Dağlari **64** 41 30N 35 0 E
Kuzhithura **70** 8 18N 77 11 E
Kuzmin **42** 45 2N 19 25 E
Kuznetsk **55** 53 12N 46 40 E
Kuzomen **52** 66 22N 36 50 E
Kvænangen **50** 70 5N 21 15 E
Kvam **47** 61 40N 9 42 E
Kvamsøy **47** 61 7N 6 28 E
Kvareli **57** 41 27N 45 47 E
Kvarner **39** 44 50N 14 10 E
Kvarnerič **39** 44 43N 14 37 E
Kvernes **47** 63 1N 7 44 E
Kvillsfors **49** 57 24N 15 29 E
Kvine → **47** 58 17N 6 56 E
Kvinesdal **47** 58 19N 6 57 E
Kviteseid **47** 59 24N 8 29 E
Kwabhaga **93** 30 51S 29 0 E
Kwadacha → **108** 57 28N 125 38W
Kwakhanai **92** 21 39S 21 16 E
Kwakoegron **127** 5 12N 55 25W
Kwale, Kenya **90** 4 15S 39 31 E
Kwale, Nigeria **85** 5 46N 6 26 E
Kwale □ **90** 4 15S 39 10 E
Kwamouth **88** 3 9S 16 12 E
Kwando → **92** 18 27S 23 32 E
Kwangsi-Chuang = Guangxi Zhuangzu □ **75** 24 0N 109 0 E
Kwangtung = Guangdong □ **75** 23 0N 113 0 E
Kwara □ **85** 8 0N 5 0 E
Kwataboahegan → **106** 51 9N 80 50W
Kwatisore **73** 3 18S 134 50 E
Kweichow = Guizhou □ **75** 27 0N 107 0 E
Kwidzyn **28** 53 44N 18 55 E
Kwiguk **104** 63 45N 164 35W
Kwimba □ **90** 3 0S 33 0 E
Kwinana **96** 32 15S 115 47 E
Kwisa → **28** 51 34N 15 24 E
Kwoka **73** 0 31S 132 27 E
Kyabé **81** 9 30N 19 0 E
Kyabra Cr. → **99** 25 36S 142 55 E
Kyabram **99** 36 19S 145 4 E
Kyaikto **71** 17 20N 97 3 E
Kyakhta **59** 50 30N 106 25 E
Kyangin **67** 18 20N 95 20 E
Kyaukpadaung **67** 20 52N 95 8 E
Kyaukpyu **67** 19 28N 93 30 E
Kyaukse **67** 21 36N 96 10 E
Kyenjojo **90** 0 40N 30 37 E
Kyle Dam **91** 20 15S 31 0 E
Kyle of Lochalsh **14** 57 17N 5 43W
Kyll → **25** 49 48N 6 42 E
Kyllburg **25** 50 2N 6 35 E
Kyneton **99** 37 10S 144 29 E
Kynuna **98** 21 37S 141 55 E
Kyō-ga-Saki **74** 35 45N 135 15 E
Kyoga, L. **90** 1 35N 33 0 E
Kyogle **99** 28 40S 153 0 E
Kyongju **76** 35 51N 129 14 E
Kyongpyaw **67** 17 12N 95 10 E
Kyōto **74** 35 0N 135 45 E
Kyōto □ **74** 35 15N 135 45 E
Kyren **59** 51 45N 101 45 E
Kyrenia **64** 35 20N 33 20 E
Kyritz **24** 52 57N 12 25 E
Kystatyam **59** 67 20N 123 10 E
Kytal Ktakh **59** 65 30N 123 40 E
Kyulyunken **59** 64 10N 137 5 E
Kyunhla **67** 23 25N 95 15 E
Kyuquot **108** 50 3N 127 25W
Kyurdamir **57** 40 25N 48 3 E
Kyūshū **74** 33 0N 131 0 E
Kyūshū-Sanchi **74** 32 35N 131 17 E
Kyustendil **42** 42 16N 22 41 E
Kyusyur **59** 70 39N 127 15 E
Kywong **99** 34 58S 146 44 E
Kyzyl **59** 51 50N 94 30 E
Kyzyl-Kiya **58** 40 16N 72 8 E
Kyzylkum, Peski **58** 42 30N 65 0 E
Kzyl-Orda **58** 44 48N 65 28 E

L

Laa **27** 48 43N 16 23 E
Laaber → **25** 49 0N 12 3 E
Laage **24** 53 55N 12 21 E
Laasphe **24** 50 56N 8 23 E
Laba → **57** 45 11N 39 42 E
Labastide **20** 43 28N 2 39 E
Labastide-Murat **20** 44 39N 1 33 E
Labbézenga **85** 15 2N 0 48 E
Labdah = Leptis Magna **83** 32 40N 14 12 E
Labé **84** 11 24N 12 16W
Labe = Elbe → **26** 50 50N 14 12 E
Laberec → **27** 48 37N 21 58 E
Laberge, L. **108** 61 11N 135 12W
Labin **39** 45 5N 14 8 E
Labinsk **57** 44 40N 40 48 E
Labis **71** 2 22N 103 2 E
Labiszyn **28** 52 57N 17 54 E
Laboe **24** 54 25N 10 13 E
Labouheyre **20** 44 13N 0 55W
Laboulaye **124** 34 10S 63 30W
Labra, Peña **30** 43 3N 4 26W
Labrador City **107** 52 57N 66 55W
Labrador, Coast of □ **105** 53 20N 61 0W
Lábrea **126** 7 15S 64 51W
Labrède **20** 44 41N 0 32W
Labuan **72** 5 21N 115 13 E
Labuha **73** 0 30S 127 30 E
Labuhan **73** 6 26S 105 50 E
Labuhanbajo **73** 8 28S 120 1 E
Labuk, Telok **72** 6 10N 117 50 E
Labytnangi **58** 66 39N 66 21 E
Łabźenica **28** 53 18N 17 15 E
Lac Allard **107** 50 33N 63 24W
Lac Bouchette **107** 48 16N 72 11W
Lac du Flambeau **116** 46 1N 89 51W
Lac Édouard **106** 47 40N 72 16W
Lac la Biche **108** 54 45N 111 58W
Lac la Martre **104** 63 8N 117 16W
Lac-Mégantic **107** 45 35N 70 53W
Lac Seul **109** 50 28N 92 0W
Lacanau, Étang de **20** 44 58N 1 7W
Lacanau-Médoc **20** 44 59N 1 5W
Lacantúm → **120** 16 36N 90 40W
Lacara → **31** 38 55N 6 25W
Lacaune **20** 43 43N 2 40 E
Lacaune, Mts. de **20** 43 43N 2 50 E
Laccadive Is. = Lakshadweep Is. **60** 10 0N 72 30 E
Lacepede B. **99** 36 40S 139 40 E
Lacepede Is. **96** 16 55S 122 0 E
Lacerdónia **91** 18 3S 35 35 E
Lachine **106** 45 30N 73 40W
Lachlan → **97** 34 22S 143 55 E
Lachmangarh **68** 27 50N 75 4 E
Lachute **106** 45 39N 74 21W
Lackawanna **114** 42 49N 78 50W
Lacolle **113** 45 5N 73 22W
Lacombe **108** 52 30N 113 44W
Lacona **113** 43 37N 76 5W
Láconi **40** 39 54N 9 4 E
Laconia **114** 43 32N 71 30W
Lacq **20** 43 25N 0 35W
Lacrosse **118** 46 51N 117 58W
Ladakh Ra. **69** 34 0N 78 0 E
Lądekzdrój **28** 50 21N 16 53 E
Ládhon → **45** 37 40N 21 50 E
Ladik **56** 40 57N 35 58 E
Ladismith **92** 33 28S 21 15 E
Lādīz **65** 28 55N 61 15 E
Ladnun **68** 27 38N 74 25 E
Ladoga, L. = Ladozhskoye Oz. **52** 61 15N 30 30 E
Ladon **19** 48 0N 2 30 E
Ladozhskoye Ozero **52** 61 15N 30 30 E
Lady Grey **92** 30 43S 27 13 E
Ladybrand **92** 29 9S 27 29 E
Ladysmith, Can. **108** 49 0N 123 49W
Ladysmith, S. Afr. **93** 28 32S 29 46 E
Ladysmith, U.S.A. **116** 45 27N 91 4W
Lae **94** 6 40S 147 2 E
Læsø **49** 57 15N 10 53 E
Læsø Rende **49** 57 20N 10 45 E
Lafayette, Colo., U.S.A. **116** 40 0N 105 2W
Lafayette, Ga., U.S.A. **115** 34 44N 85 15W
Lafayette, La., U.S.A. **117** 30 18N 92 0W
Lafayette, Tenn., U.S.A. **115** 36 35N 86 0W
Laferte → **108** 61 53N 117 44W
Lafia **85** 8 30N 8 34 E
Lafiagi **85** 8 52N 5 20 E
Lafleche **109** 49 45N 106 40W
Lafon **87** 5 5N 32 29 E
Laforsen **48** 61 56N 15 3 E
Lagan →, Sweden **49** 56 56N 13 58 E
Lagan →, U.K. **15** 54 35N 5 55W
Lagarfljót → **50** 65 40N 14 18W
Lage, Ger. **24** 52 0N 8 47 E
Lage, Spain **30** 43 13N 9 0W
Lågen →, Oppland, Norway **47** 61 8N 10 25 E
Lågen →, Vestfold, Norway **47** 59 3N 10 5 E
Lägerdorf **24** 53 53N 9 35 E
Laggers Pt. **99** 30 52S 153 4 E
Laghán □ **65** 34 20N 70 0 E
Laghouat **82** 33 50N 2 59 E
Lagnieu **21** 45 55N 5 20 E
Lagny **19** 48 52N 2 40 E
Lago **41** 39 9N 16 8 E
Lagôa **31** 37 8N 8 27W
Lagoaça **30** 41 11N 6 44W
Lagodekhi **57** 41 50N 46 22 E
Lagónegro **41** 40 8N 15 45 E
Lagonoy Gulf **73** 13 50N 123 50 E
Lagos, Nigeria **85** 6 25N 3 27 E
Lagos, Port. **31** 37 5N 8 41W
Lagos de Moreno **120** 21 21N 101 55W
Lagrange **96** 18 45S 121 43 E
Laguardia **32** 42 33N 2 35W
Laguépie **20** 44 8N 1 57 E
Laguna, Brazil **125** 28 30S 48 50W
Laguna, U.S.A. **119** 35 3N 107 28W
Laguna Beach **119** 33 31N 117 52W
Laguna Dam **119** 32 55N 114 30W
Laguna de la Janda **31** 36 15N 5 45W
Laguna Limpia **124** 26 32S 59 45W
Laguna Madre **120** 27 0N 97 20W
Lagunas, Chile **124** 21 0S 69 45W
Lagunas, Peru **126** 5 10S 75 35W
Laha **76** 48 12N 124 35 E
Lahad Datu **73** 5 0N 118 20 E
Laharpur **69** 27 43N 80 56 E
Lahat **72** 3 45S 103 30 E
Lahewa **72** 1 22N 97 12 E
Lahijan **64** 37 10N 50 6 E
Lahn → **25** 50 52N 8 35 E
Laholm **49** 56 30N 13 2 E
Laholmsbukten **49** 56 30N 12 45 E
Lahontan Res. **118** 39 28N 118 58W
Lahore **68** 31 32N 74 22 E
Lahore □ **68** 31 55N 74 5 E
* Lahr **25** 48 20N 7 52 E
Lahti **51** 60 58N 25 40 E
Laï **81** 9 25N 16 18 E
Lai Chau **71** 22 5N 103 3 E
Laibin **75** 23 42N 109 14 E
Laidley **99** 27 39S 152 20 E
Laifeng **77** 29 27N 109 20 E
Laignes **19** 47 50N 4 20 E
Laikipia □ **90** 0 30N 36 30 E
Laingsburg **92** 33 9S 20 52 E
Lairg **14** 58 1N 4 24W
Lais **72** 3 35S 102 0 E
Laiyang **76** 36 59N 120 45 E
Laizhou Wan **76** 37 30N 119 30 E
Laja → **120** 20 55N 100 46W
Lajere **85** 11 58N 11 25 E
Lajes **125** 27 48S 50 20W
Lajkovac **42** 44 27N 20 14 E
Lajosmizse **27** 47 3N 19 32 E
Lakaband **68** 31 2N 69 15 E
Lakar **73** 8 15S 128 17 E
Lake Andes **116** 43 10N 98 32W
Lake Anse **114** 46 42N 88 25W
Lake Arthur **117** 30 8N 92 40W
Lake Cargelligo **97** 33 15S 146 22 E
Lake Charles **117** 30 15N 93 10W
Lake City, Colo, U.S.A. **119** 38 3N 107 27W
Lake City, Fla., U.S.A. **115** 30 10N 82 40W
Lake City, Iowa, U.S.A. **116** 42 12N 94 42W
Lake City, Mich., U.S.A. **114** 44 20N 85 10W
Lake City, Minn., U.S.A. **116** 44 28N 92 21W
Lake City, Pa., U.S.A. **112** 42 2N 80 20W
Lake City, S.C., U.S.A. **115** 33 51N 79 44W
Lake George **113** 43 25N 73 43W
Lake Harbour **105** 62 50N 69 50W
Lake Havasu City **119** 34 25N 114 29W
Lake Lenore **109** 52 24N 104 59W
Lake Louise **108** 51 30N 116 10W
Lake Mead Nat. Rec. Area **119** 36 0N 114 30W
Lake Mills **116** 43 23N 93 33W
Lake Nash **98** 20 57S 138 0 E
Lake Providence **117** 32 49N 91 12W
Lake River **106** 54 30N 82 31W
Lake Superior Prov. Park **106** 47 45N 84 45W
Lake Village **117** 33 20N 91 19W
Lake Wales **115** 27 55N 81 32W
Lake Worth **115** 26 36N 80 3W
Lakefield **106** 44 25N 78 16W
Lakeland **115** 28 0N 82 0W
Lakemba **101** 18 13S 178 47W
Lakes Entrance **99** 37 50S 148 0 E
Lakeside, Ariz., U.S.A. **119** 34 12N 109 59W
Lakeside, Nebr., U.S.A. **116** 42 5N 102 24W
Lakeview **118** 42 15N 120 22W
Lakewood, N.J., U.S.A. **114** 40 5N 74 13W
Lakewood, Ohio, U.S.A. **114** 41 28N 81 50W
Lakhaniá **45** 35 58N 27 54 E
Lákhi **45** 35 24N 23 57 E
Lakhpat **68** 23 48N 68 47 E
Laki **50** 64 4N 18 14W
Lakin **117** 37 58N 101 18W
Lakitusaki → **106** 54 21N 82 25W
Lakonía □ **45** 36 55N 22 30 E
Lakonikós Kólpos **45** 36 40N 22 40 E
Lakota, Ivory C. **84** 5 50N 5 30W
Lakota, U.S.A. **116** 48 0N 98 22W
Laksefjorden **50** 70 45N 26 50 E
Lakselv **50** 70 2N 24 56 E
Lakshmi Kantapur **69** 22 5N 88 20 E
Lala Ghat **67** 24 30N 92 40 E
Lala Musa **68** 32 40N 73 57 E
Lalago **90** 3 28S 33 58 E
Lalapanzi **91** 19 20S 30 15 E
Lalganj **69** 25 52N 85 13 E
Lalibela **87** 12 2N 39 2 E
Lalin **76** 45 12N 127 0 E
Lalín **30** 42 40N 8 5W
Lalinde **20** 44 50N 0 44 E
Lalitpur **68** 24 42N 78 28 E
Lama Kara **85** 9 30N 1 15 E
Lamaing **67** 15 25N 97 53 E
Lamar, Colo., U.S.A. **116** 38 9N 102 35W
Lamar, Mo., U.S.A. **117** 37 30N 94 20W
Lamas **126** 6 28S 76 31W
Lamastre **21** 44 59N 4 35 E
Lambach **26** 48 6N 13 51 E
Lamballe **18** 48 29N 2 31W
Lambaréné **88** 0 41S 10 12 E
Lambasa **101** 16 30S 179 10 E
Lambay I. **15** 53 30N 6 0W
Lambert **116** 47 44N 104 39W
Lambert Glacier **5** 71 0S 70 0 E
Lambesc **21** 43 39N 5 16 E
Lambi Kyun (Sullivan I.) **71** 10 50N 98 20 E
Lámbia **45** 37 52N 21 53 E
Lambro → **38** 45 8N 9 32 E
Lame **85** 45 35N 106 40W
Lame Deer **118** 45 45N 106 40W
Lamego **30** 41 5N 7 52W
Lamèque **107** 47 45N 64 38W
Lameroo **99** 35 19S 140 33 E
Lamesa **117** 32 45N 101 57W
Lamía **45** 38 55N 22 26 E
† Lamitan **73** 6 40N 122 10 E
Lammermuir Hills **14** 55 50N 2 40W
Lamoille **118** 40 47N 115 31W
Lamon Bay **73** 14 30N 122 20 E
Lamont **108** 53 46N 112 50W
Lampa **126** 15 22S 70 22W
Lampang, Thai. **71** 18 18N 99 31 E
Lampang, Thai. **71** 18 16N 99 32 E

* *Now part of Punjab □*

† *Renamed Isabela*

Lampasas 117 31 5N 98 10W
Lampaul 18 48 28N 5 7W
Lampazos de Naranjo 120 27 2N 100 32W
Lampedusa 36 35 36N 12 40 E
Lampeter 13 52 6N 4 6W
Lampione 83 35 33N 12 20 E
Lampman 109 49 25N 102 50W
Lamprechtshausen 26 48 0N 12 58 E
Lamprey 109 58 33N 94 8W
Lampung □ 72 5 30 S 104 30 E
Lamu 90 2 16 S 40 55 E
Lamu □ 90 2 0 S 40 45 E
Lamut, Tg. 72 3 50 S 105 58 E
Lamy 119 35 30N 105 58W
Lan Xian 76 38 15N 111 35 E
Lan Yu 77 22 5N 121 35 E
Lanai I. 110 20 50N 156 55W
Lanak La 69 34 27N 79 32 E
Lanak'o Shank'ou = Lanak La 69 34 27N 79 32 E
Lanao, L. 73 7 52N 124 15 E
Lanark, Can. 113 45 1N 76 22W
Lanark, U.K. 14 55 40N 3 48W
Lancashire □ 12 53 40N 2 30W
Lancaster, Can. 113 45 10N 74 30W
Lancaster, U.K. 12 54 3N 2 48W
Lancaster, Calif., U.S.A. 119 34 47N 118 8W
Lancaster, Ky., U.S.A. 114 37 40N 84 40W
Lancaster, N.H., U.S.A. 114 44 27N 71 33W
Lancaster, N.Y., U.S.A. 112 42 53N 78 43W
Lancaster, Pa., U.S.A. 114 40 4N 76 19W
Lancaster, S.C., U.S.A. 115 34 45N 80 47W
Lancaster, Wis., U.S.A. 116 42 48N 90 43W
Lancaster Sd. 4 74 13N 84 0W
Lancer 109 50 48N 108 53W
Lanchow = Lanzhou 76 36 1N 103 52 E
Lanciano 39 42 15N 14 22 E
Łancut 27 50 10N 22 13 E
Lándana 88 5 11 S 12 5 E
Landau, Bayern, Ger. 25 48 41N 12 41 E
Landau, Rhld-Pfz., Ger. 25 49 12N 8 7 E
Landeck 26 47 9N 10 34 E
Landen 16 50 45N 5 5 E
Lander 118 42 50N 108 49W
Landerneau 18 48 28N 4 17W
Landeryd 49 57 7N 13 15 E
Landes □ 20 43 57N 0 48W
Landes, Les 20 44 20N 1 0W
Landete 32 39 56N 1 25W
Landi Kotal 66 34 7N 71 6 E
Landivisiau 18 48 31N 4 6W
Landquart 25 46 58N 9 32 E
Landrecies 19 50 7N 3 40 E
Land's End 13 50 4N 5 43W
Landsberg 25 48 3N 10 52 E
Landsborough Cr. → 98 22 28 S 144 35 E
Landsbro 49 57 24N 14 56 E
Landshut 25 48 31N 12 10 E
Landskrona 49 55 53N 12 50 E
Landstuhl 25 49 25N 7 34 E
Landvetter 49 57 41N 12 17 E
Lanesboro 113 41 57N 75 34W
Lanett 115 33 0N 85 15W
Lang Bay 108 49 45N 124 21W
Lang Shan 76 41 0N 106 30 E
Lang Son 71 21 52N 106 42 E
La'nga Co 67 30 45N 81 15 E
Lángadhás 44 40 46N 23 2 E
Langádhia 45 37 43N 22 1 E
Långan → 48 63 19N 14 44 E
Langara I. 108 54 14N 133 1W
Langdon 116 48 47N 98 24W
Langeac 20 45 7N 3 29 E
Langeais 18 47 20N 0 24 E
Langeb Baraka → 86 17 28N 36 50 E
Langeberge, C. Prov., S. Afr. 92 33 55 S 21 40 E
Langeberge, C. Prov., S. Afr. 92 28 15 S 22 33 E
Langeland 49 54 56N 10 48 E
Langen 25 49 59N 8 40 E
Langenburg 109 50 51N 101 43W
Langeness 24 54 34N 8 35 E
Langenlois 26 48 29N 15 40 E
Langeoog 24 53 44N 7 33 E
Langeskov 49 55 22N 10 35 E
Langesund 47 59 0N 9 45 E
Långhem 49 57 36N 13 14 E
Langhirano 38 44 39N 10 16 E
Langholm 14 55 9N 2 59W
Langjökull 50 64 39N 20 12W
Langkawi, P. 71 6 25N 99 45 E
Langkon 72 6 30N 116 40 E
Langlade 107 46 50N 56 20W
Langlois 118 42 54N 124 26W
Langnau 25 46 56N 7 47 E
Langogne 20 44 43N 3 50 E
Langon 20 44 33N 0 16W
Langøya 50 68 45N 14 50 E
Langpran, Gunong 72 1 0N 114 23 E
Langres 19 47 52N 5 20 E
Langres, Plateau de 19 47 45N 5 3 E
Langsa 72 4 30N 97 57 E
Långsele 48 63 12N 17 4 E
Långshyttan 48 60 27N 16 2 E
Langtry 117 29 50N 101 33W
Languedoc 20 43 58N 4 0 E
Langxiangzhen 76 39 43N 116 8 E
Langzhong 75 31 38N 105 58 E
Lanigan 109 51 51N 105 2W
Lankao 77 34 48N 114 50 E
Lannemezan 20 43 8N 0 23 E
Lannilis 18 48 35N 4 32W
Lannion 18 48 46N 3 29W
Lanouaille 20 45 24N 1 9 E
Lansdale 113 40 14N 75 18W
Lansdowne, Austral. 99 31 48 S 152 30 E
Lansdowne, Can. 113 44 24N 76 1W
Lansdowne House 106 52 14N 87 53W
Lansford 113 40 48N 75 55W
Lansing 114 42 47N 84 40W
Lanslebourg 21 45 17N 6 52 E
Lant, Pulau 72 4 10 S 116 0 E
Lanus 124 34 44 S 58 27W
Lanusei 40 39 53N 9 31 E
Lanxi 77 29 13N 119 28 E
Lanzarote 80 29 0N 13 40W
Lanzhou 76 36 1N 103 52 E
Lanzo Torinese 38 45 16N 7 29 E
Lao → 41 39 45N 15 45 E
Lao Cai 71 22 30N 103 57 E
Laoag 73 18 7N 120 34 E
Laoang 73 12 32N 125 8 E
Laoha He → 76 43 25N 120 35 E
Laois □ 15 53 0N 7 20W
Laon 19 49 33N 3 35 E
Laona 114 45 32N 88 41W
Laos ■ 71 17 45N 105 0 E
Lapa 125 25 46 S 49 44W
Lapalisse 20 46 15N 3 38 E
Laparan Cap 73 6 0N 120 0 E
Lapeer 114 43 3N 83 20W
Lapi □ 50 67 0N 27 0 E
Lapland = Lappland 50 68 7N 24 0 E
Laporte 113 41 27N 76 30W
Lapovo 42 44 10N 21 2 E
Lappland 50 68 7N 24 0 E
Laprairie 113 45 20N 73 30W
Laprida 124 37 34 S 60 45W
Laptev Sea 59 76 0N 125 0 E
Lapuş, Munţii 46 47 20N 23 50 E
Lapush 118 47 56N 124 33W
Lăpusul → 46 47 25N 23 40 E
Łapy 28 52 59N 22 52 E
Lâr 65 27 40N 54 14 E
Larabanga 84 9 16N 1 56W
Laracha 30 43 15N 8 35W
Larache 82 35 10N 6 5W
Laragne-Monteglin 21 44 18N 5 49 E
Laramie 116 41 20N 105 38W
Laramie Mts. 116 42 0N 105 30W
Laranjeiras do Sul 125 25 23 S 52 23W
Larantuka 73 8 21 S 122 55 E
Larap 73 14 18N 122 39 E
Larat 73 7 0 S 132 0 E
Lårdal 47 59 25N 8 10 E
Larde 91 16 28 S 39 43 E
Larder Lake 106 48 5N 79 40W
Lárdhos, Ákra 45 36 4N 28 10 E
Laredo, Spain 32 43 26N 3 28W
Laredo, U.S.A. 117 27 34N 99 29W
Laredo Sd. 108 52 30N 128 53W
Largentière 21 44 34N 4 18 E
Largs 14 55 48N 4 51W
Lari 38 43 34N 10 35 E
Lariang 73 1 26 S 119 17 E
Larimore 116 47 55N 97 35W
Larino 41 41 48N 14 54 E
Lárisa 44 39 49N 22 28 E
Lárisa □ 44 39 39N 22 24 E
Larkana 68 27 32N 68 18 E
Larkollen 47 59 20N 10 41 E
Larnaca 64 35 0N 33 35 E
Larne 15 54 52N 5 50W
Larned 116 38 15N 99 10W
Larrimah 96 15 35 S 133 12 E
Larsen Ice Shelf 5 67 0 S 62 0W
Larvik 47 59 4N 10 0 E
Laryak 58 61 15N 80 0 E
Larzac, Causse du 20 44 0N 3 17 E
Las Animas 117 38 8N 103 18W
Las Anod 63 8 26N 47 19 E
Las Blancos 33 37 38N 0 49W
Las Brenãs 124 27 5 S 61 7W
Las Cabezas de San Juan 31 37 0N 5 58W
Las Cascadas 120 9 5N 79 41W
Las Cruces 119 32 18N 106 50W
Las Flores 124 36 10 S 59 7W
Las Heras 124 32 51 S 68 49W
Las Khoreh 63 11 10N 48 20 E
Las Lajas 128 38 30 S 70 25W
Las Lomitas 124 24 43 S 60 35W
Las Marismas 31 37 5N 6 20W
Las Navas de la Concepción 31 37 56N 5 30W
Las Navas de Tolosa 31 38 18N 3 38W
Las Palmas, Argent. 124 27 8 S 58 45W
Las Palmas, Canary Is. 80 28 7N 15 26W
Las Palmas □ 80 28 10N 15 28W
Las Piedras 125 34 44 S 56 14W
Las Pipinas 124 35 30 S 57 19W
Las Plumas 128 43 40 S 67 15W
Las Rosas 124 32 30 S 61 35W
Las Tablas 121 7 49N 80 14W
Las Termas 124 27 29 S 64 52W
Las Varillas 124 31 50 S 62 50W
Las Vegas, N. Mex., U.S.A. 119 35 35N 105 10W
Las Vegas, Nev., U.S.A. 119 36 10N 115 5W
Lascano 125 33 35 S 54 12W
Lascaux 20 45 5N 1 10 E
Lashburn 109 53 10N 109 40W
Lashio 67 22 56N 97 45 E
Lashkar 68 26 10N 78 10 E
Łasin 28 53 30N 19 2 E
Lasíthi □ 45 35 5N 25 50 E
Lask 28 51 34N 19 8 E
Łaskarzew 28 51 48N 21 36 E
Laško 39 46 10N 15 16 E
Lassay 18 48 27N 0 30W
Lassen Pk. 118 40 29N 121 31W
Last Mountain L. 109 51 5N 105 14W
Lastoursville 88 0 55 S 12 38 E
Lastovo 39 42 46N 16 55 E
Lastovski Kanal 39 42 50N 17 0 E
Latacunga 126 0 50 S 78 35W
Latakia = Al Lādhiqīyah 64 35 30N 35 45 E
Latchford 106 47 20N 79 50W
Laterza 41 40 38N 16 47 E
Lathen 24 52 51N 7 21 E
Latiano 41 40 33N 17 43 E
Latina 40 41 26N 12 53 E
Latisana 39 45 47N 13 1 E
Latium = Lazio 39 42 10N 12 30 E
Latorica → 27 48 28N 21 50 E
Latouche Treville, C. 96 18 27 S 121 49 E
Latrobe 112 40 19N 79 21W
Latrónico 41 40 5N 16 0 E
Latrun 62 31 50N 34 58 E
Latur 70 18 25N 76 40 E
Latvian S.S.R. □ 54 56 50N 24 0 E
Lau (Eastern) Group 101 17 0 S 178 30W
Lauchhammer 24 51 35N 13 48 E
Laudal 47 58 15N 7 30 E
Lauenburg 24 53 23N 10 33 E
Lauffen 25 49 4N 9 9 E
Laugarbakki 50 65 20N 20 55W
Laujar 33 37 0N 2 54W
Launceston, Austral. 97 41 24 S 147 8 E
Launceston, U.K. 13 50 38N 4 21W
Laune → 15 52 5N 9 40W
Launglon Bok 71 13 50N 97 54 E
Laupheim 25 48 13N 9 53 E
Laura 97 15 32 S 144 32 E
Laureana di Borrello 41 38 28N 16 5 E
Laurel, Miss., U.S.A. 117 31 41N 89 9W
Laurel, Mont., U.S.A. 118 45 46N 108 49W
Laurencekirk 14 56 50N 2 30W
Laurens 115 34 32N 82 2W
Laurentian Plat. 107 52 0N 70 0W
Laurentides, Parc Prov. des 107 47 45N 71 15W
Lauria 41 40 3N 15 50 E
Laurie I. 5 60 44 S 44 37W
Laurie L. 109 56 35N 101 57W
Laurinburg 115 34 50N 79 25W
Laurium 114 47 14N 88 26W
Lausanne 25 46 32N 6 38 E
Laut, Kepulauan 72 4 45N 108 0 E
Laut Ketil, Kepulauan 72 4 45 S 115 40 E
Lauterbach 24 50 39N 9 23 E
Lauterecken 25 49 38N 7 35 E
Lautoka 101 17 37 S 177 27 E
Lauzon 107 46 48N 71 10W
Lava Hot Springs 118 42 38N 112 1W
Lavadores 30 42 14N 8 41W
Lavagna 38 44 18N 9 22 E
Laval 18 48 4N 0 48W
Lavalle 124 28 15 S 65 15W
Lavandou, Le 21 43 8N 6 22 E
Lávara 44 41 19N 26 22 E
Lavardac 20 44 12N 0 20 E
Lavaur 20 43 30N 1 49 E
Lavaveix 20 46 5N 2 8 E
Lavelanet 20 42 57N 1 51 E
Lavello 41 41 4N 15 47 E
Laverendrye Prov. Park 106 46 15N 17 15W
Laverne 117 36 43N 99 58W
Laverton 96 28 44 S 122 29 E
Lavi 62 32 47N 35 25 E
Lavik 47 61 6N 5 25 E
Lávkos 45 39 9N 23 14 E
Lavos 30 40 6N 8 49W
Lavras 125 21 20 S 45 0W
Lavre 31 38 46N 8 22W
Lavrentiya 59 65 35N 171 0W
Lávrion 45 37 40N 24 4 E
Lavumisa 93 27 20 S 31 55 E
Lawas 72 4 55N 115 25 E
Lawele 73 5 16 S 123 3 E
Lawn Hill 98 18 36 S 138 33 E
Lawng Pit 67 25 30N 97 25 E
Lawra 84 10 39N 2 51W
Lawrence, Kans., U.S.A. 116 39 0N 95 10W
Lawrence, Mass., U.S.A. 114 42 40N 71 9W
Lawrenceburg, Ind., U.S.A. 114 39 5N 84 50W
Lawrenceburg, Tenn., U.S.A. 115 35 12N 87 19W
Lawrenceville 115 33 55N 83 59W
Lawton 117 34 33N 98 25W
Lawu 73 7 40 S 111 13 E
Laxford, L. 14 58 25N 5 10W
Laxmeshwar 70 15 9N 75 28 E
Laylá 64 22 10N 46 40 E
Layon → 18 47 20N 0 45W
Laysan I. 95 25 30N 167 0W
Laytonville 118 39 44N 123 29W
Lazarevac 42 44 23N 20 17 E
Lazio □ 39 42 10N 12 30 E
Łazy 28 50 27N 19 24 E
Lea → 13 51 30N 0 10W
Lead 116 44 20N 103 40W
Leader 109 50 50N 109 30W
Leadhills 14 55 25N 3 47W
Leadville 119 39 17N 106 23W
Leaf → 117 31 0N 88 45W
Leakey 117 29 45N 99 45W
Leamington, Can. 106 42 3N 82 36W
Leamington, U.K. 13 52 18N 1 32W
Leamington, U.S.A. 118 39 37N 112 17W
Leandro Norte Alem 125 27 34 S 55 15W
Learmonth 96 22 13 S 114 10 E
Leask 109 53 5N 106 45W
Leavenworth, Mo., U.S.A. 116 39 25N 95 0W
Leavenworth, Wash., U.S.A. 118 47 44N 120 37W
Łeba 28 54 45N 17 32 E
Łeba → 28 54 46N 17 33 E
Lebak 73 6 32N 124 5 E
Lebane 42 42 56N 21 44 E
Lebanon, Ind., U.S.A. 114 40 3N 86 28W
Lebanon, Kans., U.S.A. 116 39 50N 98 35W
Lebanon, Ky., U.S.A. 114 37 35N 85 15W
Lebanon, Mo., U.S.A. 117 37 40N 92 40W
Lebanon, Oreg., U.S.A. 118 44 31N 122 57W
Lebanon, Pa., U.S.A. 114 40 20N 76 28W
Lebanon, Tenn., U.S.A. 115 36 15N 86 20W
Lebanon ■ 64 34 0N 36 0 E
Lebec 119 34 50N 118 59W
Lebedin 54 50 35N 34 30 E
Lebedyan 55 53 0N 39 10 E
Lebombo-berge 93 24 30 S 32 0 E
Lębork 28 54 33N 17 46 E
Lebrija 31 36 53N 6 5W
Łebsko, Jezioro 28 54 40N 17 25 E
Lebu 124 37 40 S 73 47W
Lecce 41 40 20N 18 10 E
Lecco 38 45 50N 9 27 E
Lecco, L. di. 38 45 51N 9 22 E
Lécera 32 41 13N 0 43W
Lech 26 47 13N 10 9 E
Lech → 25 48 44N 10 56 E
Lechang 77 25 10N 113 20 E
Lechtaler Alpen 26 47 15N 10 30 E
Lectoure 20 43 56N 0 38 E
Łeczna 28 51 18N 22 53 E
Łeczyca 28 52 5N 19 15 E
Ledbury 13 52 3N 2 25W
Ledeč 26 49 41N 15 18 E
Ledesma 30 41 6N 5 59W
Ledong 77 18 41N 109 5 E
Leduc 108 53 15N 113 30W
Ledyczek 28 53 33N 16 59 E
Lee, Mass., U.S.A. 113 42 17N 73 18W
Lee, Nev., U.S.A. 118 40 35N 115 36W
Lee → 15 51 50N 8 30W
Leech L. 116 47 9N 94 23W
Leedey 117 35 53N 99 24W
Leeds, U.K. 12 53 48N 1 34W
Leeds, U.S.A. 115 33 32N 86 30W
Leek 12 53 7N 2 2W
Leer 24 53 13N 7 29 E
Leesburg 115 28 47N 81 52W
Leesville 117 31 12N 93 15W
Leeton 97 34 33 S 146 23 E
Leetonia 112 40 53N 80 45W
Leeuwarden 16 53 15N 5 48 E
Leeuwin, C. 96 34 20 S 115 9 E
Leeward Is., Atl. Oc. 121 16 30N 63 30W
Leeward Is., Pac. Oc. 95 16 0 S 147 0W
Lefors 117 35 30N 100 50W
Lefroy, L. 96 31 21 S 121 40 E
Łeg → 28 50 42N 21 50 E
Legal 108 53 55N 113 35W
Legazpi 73 13 10N 123 45 E
Leghorn = Livorno 38 43 32N 10 18 E
Legion 91 21 25 S 28 30 E
Legionowo 28 52 25N 20 50 E
Legnago 39 45 10N 11 19 E
Legnano 38 45 35N 8 55 E
Legnica 28 51 12N 16 10 E
Legnica □ 28 51 30N 16 0 E
Legrad 39 46 17N 16 51 E
Legume 99 28 20 S 152 19 E
Leh 69 34 9N 77 35 E
Lehi 118 40 20N 111 51W
Lehighton 113 40 50N 75 44W
Lehliu 46 44 29N 26 20 E
Lehrte 24 52 22N 9 58 E
Lehututu 92 23 54 S 21 55 E
Leiah 68 30 58N 70 58 E
Leibnitz 26 46 47N 15 34 E
Leicester 13 52 39N 1 9W
Leicester □ 13 52 40N 1 10W
Leichhardt → 97 17 35 S 139 48 E
Leichhardt Ra. 98 20 46 S 147 40 E
Leiden 16 52 9N 4 30 E
Leie → 16 51 2N 3 45 E
Leigh Creek 97 30 28 S 138 24 E
Leikanger 47 61 10N 6 52 E
Leine → 24 52 20N 9 50 E
Leinster □ 15 53 0N 7 10W
Leinster, Mt. 15 52 38N 6 47W
Leipzig 24 51 20N 12 23 E
Leipzig □ 24 51 20N 12 30 E
Leiria 31 39 46N 8 53W
Leiria □ 31 39 46N 8 53W
Leith 14 55 59N 3 10W
Leith Hill 13 51 10N 0 23W
Leitha → 27 48 0N 16 35 E
Leitrim 15 54 0N 8 5W
Leitrim □ 15 54 8N 8 0W
Leiyang 77 26 27N 112 45 E
Leiza 32 43 5N 1 55W
Leizhou Bandao 77 21 0N 110 0 E
Leizhou Wan 77 20 50N 110 20 E
Lek → 16 52 0N 6 0 E
Lekáni 44 41 10N 24 35 E
Lekhainá 45 37 57N 21 16 E
Leksula 73 3 46 S 126 31 E
Leland 117 33 25N 90 52W
Leland Lakes 109 60 0N 110 59W
Leleque 128 42 28 S 71 0W
Lelystad 16 52 30N 5 25 E
Lema 85 12 58N 4 13 E
Léman, Lac 25 46 26N 6 30 E
Lemera 90 3 0 S 28 55 E
Lemery 73 13 51N 120 56 E
Lemgo 24 52 2N 8 52 E
Lemhi Ra. 118 44 30N 113 30W
Lemmer 16 52 51N 5 43 E
Lemmon 116 45 59N 102 10W
Lemoore 119 36 23N 119 46W
Lempdes 20 45 22N 3 17 E
Lemvig 49 56 33N 8 20 E
Lena → 59 72 52N 126 40 E
Lenartovce 27 48 18N 20 19 E
Lencloître 18 46 50N 0 20 E
Lendinara 39 45 4N 11 37 E
Lengau de Vaca, Pta. 124 30 14 S 71 38W
Lengerich 24 52 12N 7 50 E
Lenggong 71 5 6N 100 58 E
Lenggries 25 47 41N 11 34 E
Lengyeltóti 27 46 40N 17 40 E
Lenhovda 49 57 0N 15 16 E
Lenin 57 48 20N 40 56 E
Leninabad 58 40 17N 69 37 E
Leninakan 57 40 47N 43 50 E
Leningrad 54 59 55N 30 20 E
Lenino 56 45 17N 35 46 E
Leninogorsk 58 50 20N 83 30 E
Leninsk, R.S.F.S.R., U.S.S.R. 57 48 40N 45 15 E
Leninsk, R.S.F.S.R., U.S.S.R. 57 46 10N 43 46 E
Leninsk-Kuznetskiy 58 54 44N 86 10 E
Leninskaya Sloboda 55 56 7N 44 29 E
Leninskoye, R.S.F.S.R., U.S.S.R. 55 58 23N 47 3 E
Leninskoye, R.S.F.S.R., U.S.S.R. 59 47 56N 132 38 E
Lenk 25 46 27N 7 28 E
Lenkoran 53 39 45N 48 50 E
Lenmalu 73 1 45 S 130 15 E
Lenne → 24 51 25N 7 30 E
Lennoxville 113 45 22N 71 51W
Leno 38 45 24N 10 14 E
Lenoir 115 35 55N 81 36W
Lenoir City 115 35 40N 84 20W
Lenora 116 39 39N 100 1W

Lenore L. 109 52 30N 104 59W
Lenox 113 42 20N 73 18W
Lens 19 50 26N 2 50 E
Lensk (Mukhtuya) 59 60 48N 114 55 E
Lenskoye 56 45 3N 34 1 E
Lenti 27 46 37N 16 33 E
Lentini 41 37 18N 15 0 E
Lentvaric 54 54 39N 25 3 E
Lenzen 24 53 6N 11 26 E
Léo 84 11 3N 2 2W
Leoben 26 47 22N 15 5 E
Leola 116 45 47N 98 58W
Leominster, U.K. 13 52 15N 2 43W
Leominster, U.S.A. 114 42 32N 71 45W
Léon 20 43 53N 1 18W
León, Mexico 120 21 7N 101 30W
León, Nic. 121 12 20N 86 51W
León, Spain 30 42 38N 5 34W
Leon 116 40 40N 93 40W
León □ 30 42 40N 5 55W
León, Montañas de 30 42 30N 6 18W
Leonardtown 114 38 19N 76 39W
Leonforte 41 37 39N 14 22 E
Leongatha 99 38 30 S 145 58 E
Leonidhion 45 37 9N 22 52 E
Leonora 96 28 49 S 121 19 E
Léopold II, Lac = Mai-Ndombe 88 2 0 S 18 20 E
Leopoldina 125 21 28 S 42 40W
Leopoldsburg 16 51 7N 5 13 E
Léopoldville = Kinshasa 88 4 20 S 15 15 E
Leoti 116 38 31N 101 19W
Leoville 109 53 39N 107 33W
Lépa, L. do 92 17 0 S 19 0 E
Lepe 31 37 15N 7 12W
Lepel 54 54 50N 28 40 E
Lepikha 59 64 45N 125 55 E
Leping 77 28 47N 117 7 E
Lepontino, Alpi 38 46 22N 8 27 E
Lepsény 27 47 0N 18 15 E
Leptis Magna 83 32 40N 14 12 E
Lequeitio 32 43 20N 2 32W
Lercara Friddi 40 37 42N 13 36 E
Léré 81 9 39N 14 13 E
Lere 85 9 43N 9 18 E
Leribe 93 28 51 S 28 3 E
Lérici 38 44 4N 9 58 E
Lérida 32 41 37N 0 39 E
Lérida □ 32 42 6N 1 0 E
Lérins, Is. de 21 43 31N 7 3 E
Lerma 30 42 0N 3 47W
Léros 45 37 10N 26 50 E
Lérouville 19 48 50N 5 30 E
Lerwick 14 60 10N 1 10W
Les 46 46 58N 21 50 E
Lesbos, I. = Lésvos 45 39 10N 26 20 E
Leshukonskoye 52 64 54N 45 46 E
Lésina, L. di 39 41 53N 15 25 E
Lesja 47 62 7N 8 51 E
Lesjaverk 47 62 12N 8 34 E
Lesko 27 49 30N 22 23 E
Leskov I. 5 56 0 S 28 0W
Leskovac 42 43 0N 21 58 E
Leskoviku 44 40 10N 20 34 E
Leslie 117 35 50N 92 35W
Lesna 28 51 0N 15 15 E
Lesneven 18 48 35N 4 20W
Lešnica 42 44 39N 19 20 E
Lesnoye 54 58 15N 35 18 E
Lesotho ■ 93 29 40 S 28 0 E
Lesozavodsk 59 45 30N 133 29 E
Lesparre-Médoc 20 45 18N 0 57W
Lessay 18 49 14N 1 30W
Lesse ⤳ 16 50 15N 4 54 E
Lesser Antilles 121 15 0N 61 0W
Lesser Slave L. 108 55 30N 115 25W
Lessines 16 50 42N 3 50 E
Lestock 109 51 19N 103 59W
Lésvos 45 39 10N 26 20 E
Leszno 28 51 50N 16 30 E
Leszno □ 28 51 45N 16 30 E
Letchworth 13 51 58N 0 13W
Letea, Ostrov 46 45 18N 29 20 E
Lethbridge 108 49 45N 112 45W
Leti 73 8 10 S 127 40 E
Leti, Kepulauan 73 8 10 S 128 0 E
Letiahau ⤳ 92 21 16 S 24 0 E
Leticia 126 4 9 S 70 0W
Leting 76 39 23N 118 55 E
Letlhakeng 92 24 0 S 24 59 E
Letpadan 67 17 45N 95 45 E
Letpan 67 19 28N 94 10 E
Letsôk-aw Kyun (Domel I.) 71 11 30N 98 25 E
Letterkenny 15 54 57N 7 42W
Leu 46 44 10N 24 0 E
Leucate 20 42 56N 3 3 E
Leucate, Étang de 20 42 50N 3 0 E
Leuk 25 46 19N 7 37 E
Leuser, G. 72 3 46N 97 12 E
Leutkirch 25 47 49N 10 1 E
Leuven (Louvain) 16 50 52N 4 42 E
Leuze, Hainaut, Belg. 16 50 36N 3 37 E
Leuze, Namur, Belg. 16 50 33N 4 54 E
Lev Tolstoy 55 53 13N 39 29 E
Levádhia 45 38 27N 22 54 E
Levan 118 39 37N 111 52W
Levanger 47 63 45N 11 19 E
Levani 44 40 40N 19 28 E
Levant, I. du 21 43 3N 6 28 E
Lévanto 38 44 10N 9 37 E
Levanzo 40 38 0N 12 19 E
Levelland 117 33 38N 102 23W
Leven 14 56 12N 3 0W
Leven, L. 14 56 12N 3 22W
Leven, Toraka 93 12 30 S 47 45 E
Levens 21 43 50N 7 12 E
Leveque C. 96 16 20 S 123 0 E
Leverano 41 40 16N 18 0 E
Leverkusen 24 51 2N 6 59 E
Levet 19 46 56N 2 22 E
Levice 27 48 13N 18 35 E
Levick, Mt. 5 75 0 S 164 0 E
Levico 39 46 0N 11 18 E
Levie 21 41 40N 9 7 E
Levier 19 46 58N 6 8 E
Levin 101 40 37 S 175 18 E
Lévis 107 46 48N 71 9W
Levis, L. 108 62 37N 117 58W
Levítha 45 37 0N 26 28 E
Levittown, N.Y., U.S.A. 113 40 41N 73 31W
Levittown, Pa., U.S.A. 113 40 10N 74 51W
Levka 43 41 52N 26 15 E
Lévka 45 35 18N 24 3 E
Levkás 45 38 48N 20 43 E
Levkimmi 44 39 25N 20 3 E
Levkôsia = Nicosia 64 35 10N 33 25 E
Levoča 27 49 2N 20 35 E
Levroux 19 47 0N 1 38 E
Levski 43 43 21N 25 10 E
Levskigrad 43 42 38N 24 47 E
Lewellen 116 41 22N 102 5W
Lewes, U.K. 13 50 53N 0 2 E
Lewes, U.S.A. 114 38 45N 75 8W
Lewin Brzeski 28 50 45N 17 37 E
Lewis 14 58 10N 6 40W
Lewis, Butt of 14 58 30N 6 12W
Lewis Ra. 118 48 0N 113 15W
Lewisburg, Pa., U.S.A. 112 40 57N 76 57W
Lewisburg, Tenn., U.S.A. 115 35 29N 86 46W
Lewisporte 107 49 15N 55 3W
Lewiston, Idaho, U.S.A. 118 46 25N 117 0W
Lewiston, Utah, U.S.A. 118 41 58N 111 56W
Lewistown, Mont., U.S.A. 118 47 0N 109 25W
Lewistown, Pa., U.S.A. 114 40 37N 77 33W
Lexington, Ill., U.S.A. 116 40 37N 88 47W
Lexington, Ky., U.S.A. 114 38 6N 84 30W
Lexington, Miss., U.S.A. 117 33 8N 90 2W
Lexington, Mo., U.S.A. 116 39 7N 93 55W
Lexington, N.C., U.S.A. 115 35 50N 80 13W
Lexington, Nebr., U.S.A. 116 40 48N 99 45W
Lexington, Ohio, U.S.A. 112 40 39N 82 35W
Lexington, Oreg., U.S.A. 118 45 29N 119 46W
Lexington, Tenn., U.S.A. 115 35 38N 88 25W
Lexington Park 114 38 16N 76 27W
Leyre ⤳ 20 44 39N 1 1W
Leyte 73 11 0N 125 0 E
Lezajsk 28 50 16N 22 25 E
Lezay 20 46 17N 0 0 E
Lezha 44 41 47N 19 42 E
Lézignan-Corbières 20 43 13N 2 43 E
Lezoux 20 45 49N 3 21 E
Lgov 54 51 42N 35 16 E
Lhasa 75 29 25N 90 58 E
Lhazê 75 29 5N 87 38 E
Lhokseumawe 72 5 10N 97 10 E
Lhuntsi Dzong 67 27 39N 91 10 E
Li Shui ⤳ 77 29 24N 112 1 E
Li Xian, Gansu, China 77 34 10N 105 5 E
Li Xian, Hunan, China 77 29 36N 111 42 E
Liádhoi 45 36 50N 26 11 E
Lianga 73 8 38N 126 6 E
Liangdang 77 33 56N 106 18 E
Lianhua 77 27 3N 113 54 E
Lianjiang 77 26 12N 119 27 E
Lianping 77 24 26N 114 30 E
Lianshanguan 76 40 53N 123 43 E
Lianyungang 77 34 40N 119 11 E
Liao He ⤳ 76 41 0N 121 50 E
Liaocheng 76 36 28N 115 58 E
Liaodong Bandao 76 40 0N 122 30 E
Liaodong Wan 76 40 20N 121 10 E
Liaoning □ 76 42 0N 122 0 E
Liaoyang 76 41 15N 122 58 E
Liaoyuan 76 42 58N 125 2 E
Liaozhong 76 41 23N 122 50 E
Liapádhes 44 39 42N 19 40 E
Liard ⤳ 108 61 51N 121 18W
Libau = Liepaja 54 56 30N 21 0 E
Libby 118 48 20N 115 33W
Libenge 88 3 40N 18 55 E
Liberal, Kans., U.S.A. 117 37 4N 101 0W
Liberal, Mo., U.S.A. 117 37 35N 94 30W
Liberec 26 50 47N 15 7 E
Liberia 121 10 40N 85 30W
Liberia ■ 84 6 30N 9 30W
Liberty, Mo., U.S.A. 116 39 15N 94 24W
Liberty, Tex., U.S.A. 117 30 5N 94 50W
Libiaz 27 50 7N 19 21 E
Libo 77 25 22N 107 53 E
Libobo, Tanjung 73 0 54 S 128 28 E
Libohava 44 40 3N 20 10 E
Libonda 89 14 28 S 23 12 E
Libourne 20 44 55N 0 14W
Libramont 16 49 55N 5 23 E
Librazhdi 44 41 12N 20 22 E
Libreville 88 0 25N 9 26 E
Libya ■ 81 27 0N 17 0 E
Libyan Plateau = Ed-Déffa 86 30 40N 26 30 E
Licantén 124 35 55 S 72 0W
Licata 40 37 6N 13 55 E
Lichfield 12 52 40N 1 50W
Lichinga 91 13 13 S 35 11 E
Lichtenburg 92 26 8 S 26 8 E
Lichtenfels 25 50 7N 11 4 E
Lichuan 77 30 18N 108 57 E
Licosa, Punta 41 40 15N 14 53 E
Lida, U.S.A. 119 37 30N 117 30W
Lida, U.S.S.R. 54 53 53N 25 15 E
Lidhult 49 56 50N 13 27 E
Lidingö 48 59 22N 18 8 E
Lidköping 49 58 31N 13 14 E
Lido, Italy 39 45 25N 12 23 E
Lido, Niger 85 12 54N 3 44 E
Lido di Ostia 40 41 44N 12 14 E
Lidzbark 28 53 15N 19 49 E
Lidzbark Warminski 28 54 7N 20 34 E
Liebenwalde 24 52 51N 13 23 E
Lieberose 24 51 59N 14 18 E
Liebling 42 45 36N 21 20 E
Liechtenstein ■ 25 47 8N 9 35 E
Liège 16 50 38N 5 35 E
Liège □ 16 50 32N 5 35 E
Liegnitz = Legnica 28 51 12N 16 10 E
Lienart 90 3 3N 25 31 E
Lienyünchiangshih = Lianyungang 77 34 40N 119 11 E
Lienz 26 46 50N 12 46 E
Liepaja 54 56 30N 21 0 E
Lier 16 51 7N 4 34 E
Lieşta 46 45 38N 27 34 E
Liévin 19 50 24N 2 47 E
Lièvre ⤳ 106 45 31N 75 26W
Liezen 26 47 34N 14 15 E
Liffey ⤳ 15 53 21N 6 20W
Lifford 15 54 50N 7 30W
Liffré 18 48 12N 1 30W
Lifjell 47 59 27N 8 45 E
Lightning Ridge 99 29 22 S 148 0 E
Lignano 39 45 42N 13 8 E
Ligny-en-Barrois 19 48 36N 5 20 E
Ligny-le-Châtel 19 47 54N 3 45 E
Ligoúrion 45 37 37N 23 2 E
Ligua, La 124 32 30 S 71 16W
Ligueil 18 47 2N 0 49 E
Liguria □ 38 44 30N 9 0 E
Ligurian Sea 38 43 20N 9 0 E
Lihir Group 98 3 0 S 152 35 E
Lihou Reefs and Cays 97 17 25 S 151 40 E
Lihue 110 21 59N 159 24W
Lijiang 75 26 55N 100 20 E
Likasi 91 10 55 S 26 48 E
Likati 88 3 20N 24 0 E
Likhoslavl 54 57 12N 35 30 E
Likhovski 57 48 10N 40 10 E
Likoma I. 91 12 3 S 34 45 E
Likumburu 91 9 43 S 35 8 E
Liling 77 27 42N 113 29 E
Lille 19 50 38N 3 3 E
Lille Bælt 49 55 20N 9 45 E
Lillebonne 18 49 30N 0 32 E
Lillehammer 47 61 8N 10 30 E
Lillers 19 50 35N 2 28 E
Lillesand 47 58 15N 8 23 E
Lilleshall 13 52 45N 2 22W
Lillestrøm 47 59 58N 11 5 E
Lillo 32 39 45N 3 20W
Lillooet ⤳ 108 49 15N 121 57W
Lilongwe 91 14 0 S 33 48 E
Liloy 73 8 4N 122 39 E
Lim ⤳ 42 43 0N 19 40 E
Lima, Indon. 73 3 37 S 128 4 E
Lima, Peru 126 12 0 S 77 0W
Lima, Sweden 48 60 55N 13 20 E
Lima, Mont., U.S.A. 118 44 41N 112 38W
Lima, Ohio, U.S.A. 114 40 42N 84 5W
Lima ⤳ 30 41 41N 8 50W
Limages 113 45 20N 75 16W
Liman 57 45 45N 47 12 E
Limanowa 27 49 42N 20 22 E
Limassol 64 34 42N 33 1 E
Limavady 15 55 3N 6 58W
Limavady □ 15 55 0N 6 55W
Limay ⤳ 128 39 0 S 68 0W
Limay Mahuida 124 37 10 S 66 45W
Limbang 72 4 42N 115 6 E
Limbara, Monti 40 40 50N 9 10 E
Limbdi 68 22 34N 71 51 E
Limbri 99 31 3 S 151 5 E
Limburg 25 50 22N 8 4 E
Limburg □, Belg. 16 51 2N 5 25 E
Limburg □, Neth. 16 51 20N 5 55 E
Limedsforsen 48 60 52N 13 25 E
Limeira 125 22 35 S 47 28W
Limenária 44 40 38N 24 32 E
Limerick 15 52 40N 8 38W
Limerick □ 15 52 30N 8 50W
Limestone 112 42 2N 78 39W
Limestone ⤳ 109 56 31N 94 7W
Limfjorden 49 56 55N 9 0 E
Limia ⤳ 30 41 41N 8 50W
Limmared 49 57 34N 13 20 E
Limmen Bight 96 14 40 S 135 35 E
Límni 45 38 43N 23 18 E
Límnos 44 39 50N 25 5 E
Limoeiro do Norte 127 5 5 S 38 0W
Limoges 20 45 50N 1 15 E
Limón 121 10 0N 83 2W
Limon, Panama 120 9 17N 79 45W
Limon, U.S.A. 116 39 18N 103 38W
Limon B. 120 9 22N 79 56W
Limone Piemonte 38 44 12N 7 32 E
Limousin 20 46 0N 1 0 E
Limousin, Plateaux du 20 46 0N 1 0 E
Limoux 20 43 4N 2 12 E
Limpopo ⤳ 93 25 15 S 33 30 E
Limuru 90 1 2 S 36 35 E
Linares, Chile 124 35 50 S 71 40W
Linares, Mexico 120 24 50N 99 40W
Linares, Spain 33 38 10N 3 40W
Linares □ 124 36 0 S 71 0W
Linas Mte. 40 39 25N 8 38 E
Lincheng 76 37 25N 114 30 E
Linchuan 75 27 57N 116 15 E
Lincoln, Argent. 124 34 55 S 61 30W
Lincoln, N.Z. 101 43 38 S 172 30 E
Lincoln, U.K. 12 53 14N 0 32W
Lincoln, Ill., U.S.A. 116 40 10N 89 20W
Lincoln, Kans., U.S.A. 116 39 6N 98 9W
Lincoln, Maine, U.S.A. 107 45 27N 68 29W
Lincoln, N. Mex., U.S.A. 119 33 30N 105 26W
Lincoln, N.H., U.S.A. 113 44 3N 71 40W
Lincoln, Nebr., U.S.A. 116 40 50N 96 42W
Lincoln □ 12 53 14N 0 32W
Lincoln Sea 4 84 0N 55 0W
Lincoln Wolds 12 53 20N 0 5W
Lincolnton 115 35 30N 81 15W
Lind 118 47 0N 118 33W
Lindås, Norway 47 60 44N 5 9 E
Lindås, Sweden 49 56 38N 15 35 E
Lindau 25 47 33N 9 41 E
Linden, Guyana 126 6 0N 58 10W
Linden, U.S.A. 117 33 0N 94 20W
Linderöd 49 55 56N 13 47 E
Linderödsåsen 49 55 53N 13 53 E
Lindesberg 48 59 36N 15 15 E
Lindesnes 47 57 58N 7 3 E
Lindi 91 9 58 S 39 38 E
Lindi □ 91 9 40 S 38 30 E
Lindi ⤳ 90 0 33N 25 5 E
Lindian 76 47 11N 124 52 E
Lindoso 30 41 52N 8 11W
Lindow 24 52 58N 12 58 E
Lindsay, Can. 106 44 22N 78 43W
Lindsay, Calif., U.S.A. 119 36 14N 119 6W
Lindsay, Okla., U.S.A. 117 34 51N 97 37W
Lindsborg 116 38 35N 97 40W
Línea de la Concepción, La 31 36 15N 5 23W
Linfen 76 36 3N 111 30 E
Ling Xian 76 37 22N 116 30 E
Lingao 77 19 56N 109 42 E
Lingayen 73 16 1N 120 14 E
Lingayen G. 73 16 10N 120 15 E
Lingchuan 77 25 26N 110 21 E
Lingen 24 52 32N 7 21 E
Lingga 72 0 12 S 104 37 E
Lingga, Kepulauan 72 0 10 S 104 30 E
Linghed 48 60 48N 15 55 E
Lingle 116 42 10N 104 18W
Lingling 77 26 17N 111 37 E
Lingshan 77 22 25N 109 18 E
Lingshi 76 36 48N 111 48 E
Lingshui 77 18 27N 110 0 E
Lingtai 77 35 0N 107 40 E
Linguéré 84 15 25N 15 5W
Lingyuan 76 41 10N 119 15 E
Lingyun 75 25 2N 106 35 E
Linh Cam 71 18 31N 105 31 E
Linhai 75 28 50N 121 8 E
Linhe 76 40 48N 107 20 E
Linjiang 76 41 50N 127 0 E
Linköping 49 58 28N 15 36 E
Linkou 76 45 15N 130 18 E
Linlithgow 14 55 58N 3 38W
Linn, Mt. 118 40 0N 123 0W
Linnhe, L. 14 56 36N 5 25W
Linosa, I. 83 35 51N 12 50 E
Linqing 76 36 50N 115 42 E
Lins 125 21 40 S 49 44W
Lintao 76 35 18N 103 52 E
Linth ⤳ 25 47 7N 9 7W
Linthal 25 46 54N 9 0 E
Lintlaw 109 52 4N 103 14W
Linton, Can. 107 47 15N 72 16W
Linton, Ind., U.S.A. 114 39 0N 87 10W
Linton, N. Dak., U.S.A. 116 46 21N 100 12W
Linville 99 26 50 S 152 11 E
Linwood 112 43 35N 80 43W
Linwu 77 25 19N 112 31 E
Linxe 20 43 56N 1 13W
Linxi 76 43 36N 118 2 E
Linxia 75 35 36N 103 10 E
Linyanti ⤳ 92 17 50 S 25 5 E
Linyi 77 35 5N 118 21 E
Linz, Austria 26 48 18N 14 18 E
Linz, Ger. 24 50 33N 7 18 E
Lion-d'Angers, Le 18 47 37N 0 43W
Lion, G. du 20 43 0N 4 0 E
Lioni 41 40 52N 15 10 E
Lion's Den 91 17 15 S 30 5 E
Lion's Head 106 44 58N 81 15W
Liozno 54 55 0N 30 50 E
Lipali 91 15 50 S 35 50 E
Lipari 41 38 26N 14 58 E
Lipari, Is. 41 38 30N 14 50 E
Lipetsk 55 52 37N 39 35 E
Lipiany 28 53 2N 14 58 E
Liping 77 26 15N 109 7 E
Lipkany 56 48 14N 26 48 E
Lipljan 42 42 31N 21 7 E
Lipnik 27 49 32N 17 36 E
Lipno 28 52 49N 19 15 E
Lipova 42 46 8N 21 42 E
Lipovets 56 49 12N 29 1 E
Lippe ⤳ 24 51 39N 6 38 E
Lippstadt 24 51 40N 8 19 E
Lipscomb 117 36 16N 100 16W
Lipsko 28 51 9N 21 40 E
Lipsói 45 37 19N 26 50 E
Liptovsky Svaty Milkulaš 27 49 6N 19 35 E
Liptrap C. 99 38 50 S 145 55 E
Lira 90 2 17N 32 57 E
Liri ⤳ 40 41 25N 13 52 E
Liria 32 39 37N 0 35W
Lisala 88 2 12N 21 38 E
Lisboa 31 38 42N 9 10W
Lisboa □ 31 39 0N 9 12W
Lisbon, N. Dak., U.S.A. 116 46 30N 97 46W
Lisbon, N.H., U.S.A. 113 44 13N 71 52W
Lisbon, Ohio, U.S.A. 112 40 45N 80 42W
Lisbon = Lisboa 31 38 42N 9 10W
Lisburn 15 54 30N 6 9W
Lisburne, C. 104 68 50N 166 0W
Liscannor, B. 15 52 57N 9 24W
Liscia ⤳ 40 41 11N 9 9 E
Lishi 76 37 31N 111 8 E
Lishui 75 28 28N 119 54 E
Lisianski I. 94 26 2N 174 0W
Lisichansk 56 48 55N 38 30 E
Lisieux 18 49 10N 0 12 E
Lisle-sur-Tarn 20 43 52N 1 49 E
Lismore, Austral. 97 28 44 S 153 21 E
Lismore, Ireland 15 52 8N 7 58W
Lisse 16 52 16N 4 33 E
List 24 55 1N 8 26 E
Lista 47 58 7N 6 39 E
Lister, Mt. 5 78 0 S 162 0 E
Liston 99 28 39 S 152 6 E
Listowel, Can. 106 43 44N 80 58W
Listowel, Ireland 15 52 27N 9 30W
Lit-et-Mixe 20 44 2N 1 15W
Litang, China 77 23 12N 109 8 E
Litang, Malay. 73 5 27N 118 31 E
Litani ⤳, Leb. 62 33 20N 35 14 E
Litani ⤳, Surinam 62 3 40N 54 0W
Litchfield, Conn., U.S.A. 113 41 44N 73 12W
Litchfield, Ill., U.S.A. 116 39 10N 89 40W
Litchfield, Minn., U.S.A. 116 45 5N 94 31W
Liteni 46 47 32N 26 32 E

Place	Map	Lat.	Long.
Lithgow	**97**	33 25 S	150 8 E
Líthinon, Ákra	**45**	34 55N	24 44 E
Lithuanian S.S.R. □	**54**	55 30N	24 0 E
Litija	**39**	46 3N	14 50 E
Litókhoron	**44**	40 8N	22 34 E
Litoměřice	**26**	50 33N	14 10 E
Litomysl	**27**	49 52N	16 20 E
Litschau	**26**	48 58N	15 4 E
Little Abaco I.	**121**	26 50N	77 30W
Little America	**5**	79 0 S	160 0W
Little Andaman I.	**71**	10 40N	92 15 E
Little Barrier I.	**101**	36 12 S	175 8 E
Little Belt Mts.	**118**	46 50N	111 0W
Little Blue →	**116**	39 41N	96 40W
Little Bushman Land	**92**	29 10 S	18 10 E
Little Cadotte →	**108**	56 41N	117 6W
Little Churchill →	**109**	57 30N	95 22W
Little Colorado →	**119**	36 11N	111 48W
Little Current	**106**	45 55N	82 0W
Little Current →	**106**	50 57N	84 36W
Little Falls, Minn., U.S.A.	**116**	45 58N	94 19W
Little Falls, N.Y., U.S.A.	**114**	43 3N	74 50W
Little Fork →	**116**	48 31N	93 35W
Little Grand Rapids	**109**	52 0N	95 29W
Little Humboldt →	**118**	41 0N	117 43W
Little Inagua I.	**121**	21 40N	73 50W
Little Lake	**119**	35 58N	117 58W
Little Marais	**116**	47 24N	91 8W
Little Minch	**14**	57 35N	6 45W
Little Missouri →	**116**	47 30N	102 25W
Little Namaqualand	**92**	29 0 S	17 9 E
Little Ouse →	**13**	52 25N	0 50 E
Little Rann of Kutch	**68**	23 25N	71 25 E
Little Red →	**117**	35 11N	91 27W
Little River	**101**	43 45 S	172 49 E
Little Rock	**117**	34 41N	92 10W
Little Ruaha →	**90**	7 57 S	37 53 E
Little Sable Pt.	**114**	43 40N	86 32W
Little Sioux →	**116**	41 49N	96 4W
Little Smoky →	**108**	54 44N	117 11W
Little Snake →	**118**	40 27N	108 26W
Little Valley	**112**	42 15N	78 48W
Little Wabash →	**114**	37 54N	88 5W
Littlefield	**117**	33 57N	102 17W
Littlefork	**116**	48 24N	93 35W
Littlehampton	**13**	50 48N	0 32W
Littleton	**114**	44 19N	71 47W
Liuba	**77**	33 38N	106 55 E
Liucheng	**77**	24 38N	109 14 E
Liukang Tenggaja	**73**	6 45 S	118 50 E
Liuli	**91**	11 3 S	34 38 E
Liuwa Plain	**89**	14 20 S	22 30 E
Liuyang	**77**	28 10N	113 37 E
Liuzhou	**75**	24 22N	109 22 E
Livada	**46**	47 52N	23 5 E
Livadherón	**44**	40 2N	21 57 E
Livarot	**18**	49 0N	0 9 E
Live Oak	**115**	30 17N	83 0W
Livermore, Mt.	**117**	30 45N	104 8W
Liverpool, Austral.	**97**	33 54 S	150 58 E
Liverpool, Can.	**107**	44 5N	64 41W
Liverpool, U.K.	**12**	53 25N	3 0W
Liverpool Plains	**97**	31 15 S	150 15 E
Liverpool Ra.	**97**	31 50 S	150 30 E
Livingston, Guat.	**120**	15 50N	88 50W
Livingston, U.S.A.	**118**	45 40N	110 40W
Livingstone, U.S.A.	**117**	30 44N	94 54W
Livingstone, Zambia	**91**	17 46 S	25 52 E
Livingstone I.	**5**	63 0 S	60 15W
Livingstone Memorial	**91**	12 20 S	30 18 E
Livingstone Mts.	**91**	9 40 S	34 20 E
Livingstonia	**91**	10 38 S	34 5 E
Livno	**42**	43 50N	17 0 E
Livny	**55**	52 30N	37 30 E
Livorno	**38**	43 32N	10 18 E
Livramento	**125**	30 55 S	55 30W
Livron-sur-Drôme	**21**	44 46N	4 51 E
Liwale	**91**	9 48 S	37 58 E
Liwale □	**91**	9 0 S	38 0 E
Liwiec →	**28**	52 36N	21 34 E
Lixoúrion	**45**	38 14N	20 24 E
Lizard I.	**98**	14 42 S	145 30 E
Lizard Pt.	**13**	49 57N	5 11W
Lizzano	**41**	40 23N	17 25 E
Ljig	**42**	44 13N	20 18 E
Ljubija	**39**	44 55N	16 35 E
Ljubinje	**42**	42 58N	18 5 E
Ljubljana	**39**	46 4N	14 33 E
Ljubno	**39**	46 25N	14 46 E
Ljubovija	**42**	44 11N	19 22 E
Ljubuški	**42**	43 12N	17 34 E
Ljung	**49**	58 1N	13 3 E
Ljungan →	**48**	62 18N	17 23 E
Ljungaverk	**48**	62 30N	16 5 E
Ljungby	**49**	56 49N	13 55 E
Ljusdal	**48**	61 46N	16 3 E
Ljusnan →	**48**	61 12N	17 8 E
Ljusne	**48**	61 13N	17 7 E
Ljutomer	**39**	46 31N	16 11 E
Llagostera	**32**	41 50N	2 54 E
Llancanelo, Salina	**124**	35 40 S	69 8W
Llandeilo	**13**	51 53N	4 0W
Llandovery	**13**	51 59N	3 49W
Llandrindod Wells	**13**	52 15N	3 23W
Llandudno	**12**	53 19N	3 51W
Llanelli	**13**	51 41N	4 11W
Llanes	**30**	43 25N	4 50W
Llangollen	**12**	52 58N	3 10W
Llanidloes	**13**	52 28N	3 31W
Llano	**117**	30 45N	98 41W
Llano →	**117**	30 50N	98 25W
Llano Estacado	**117**	34 0N	103 0W
Llanos	**126**	5 0N	71 35W
Llera	**120**	23 19N	99 1W
Llerena	**31**	38 17N	6 0W
Llico	**124**	34 46 S	72 5W
Llobregat →	**32**	41 19N	2 9 E
Lloret de Mar	**32**	41 41N	2 53 E
Lloyd B.	**98**	12 45 S	143 27 E
Lloyd L.	**109**	57 22N	108 57W
Lloydminster	**109**	53 17N	110 0W
Lluchmayor	**33**	39 29N	2 53 E
Llullaillaco, volcán	**124**	24 43 S	68 30W
Loa	**119**	38 18N	111 40W
Loa →	**124**	21 26 S	70 41W
Loano	**38**	44 8N	8 14 E
Lobatse	**92**	25 12 S	25 40 E
Löbau	**24**	51 5N	14 42 E
Lobenstein	**24**	50 25N	11 39 E
Lobería	**124**	38 10 S	58 40W
Łobez	**28**	53 38N	15 39 E
Lobito	**89**	12 18 S	13 35 E
Lobón, Canal de	**31**	38 50N	6 55W
Lobos	**124**	35 10 S	59 0W
Lobos, I.	**120**	27 15N	110 30W
Lobos, Is.	**122**	6 57 S	80 45W
Lobstick L.	**107**	54 0N	65 0W
Loc Binh	**71**	21 46N	106 54 E
Loc Ninh	**71**	11 50N	106 34 E
Locarno	**25**	46 10N	8 47 E
Lochaber	**14**	56 55N	5 0W
Lochcarron	**14**	57 25N	5 30W
Loche, La	**109**	56 29N	109 26W
Lochem	**16**	52 9N	6 26 E
Loches	**18**	47 7N	1 0 E
Lochgelly	**14**	56 7N	3 18W
Lochgilphead	**14**	56 2N	5 37W
Lochinver	**14**	58 9N	5 15W
Lochnagar, Austral.	**98**	23 33 S	145 38 E
Lochnagar, U.K.	**14**	56 57N	3 14W
Łochów	**28**	52 33N	21 42 E
Lochy →	**14**	56 52N	5 3W
Lock	**99**	33 34 S	135 46 E
Lock Haven	**114**	41 7N	77 31W
Lockeport	**107**	43 47N	65 4W
Lockerbie	**14**	55 7N	3 21W
Lockhart, Austral.	**99**	35 14 S	146 40 E
Lockhart, U.S.A.	**117**	29 55N	97 40W
Lockney	**117**	34 7N	101 27W
Lockport	**114**	43 12N	78 42W
Locle, Le	**25**	47 3N	6 44 E
Locminé	**18**	47 54N	2 51W
Locri	**41**	38 14N	16 14 E
Locronan	**18**	48 7N	4 15W
Loctudy	**18**	47 50N	4 12W
Lod	**62**	31 57N	34 54 E
Lodalskåpa	**47**	61 47N	7 13 E
Loddon →	**100**	35 31 S	143 51 E
Lodeinoye Pole	**52**	60 44N	33 33 E
Lodève	**20**	43 44N	3 19 E
Lodge Grass	**118**	45 21N	107 20W
Lodgepole	**116**	41 12N	102 40W
Lodgepole Cr. →	**116**	41 20N	104 30W
Lodhran	**68**	29 32N	71 30 E
Lodi, Italy	**38**	45 19N	9 30 E
Lodi, U.S.A.	**118**	38 12N	121 16W
Lodja	**90**	3 30 S	23 23 E
Lodosa	**32**	42 25N	2 4W
Lödöse	**49**	58 2N	12 9 E
Lodwar	**90**	3 10N	35 40 E
Łódź	**28**	51 45N	19 27 E
Łódź □	**28**	51 45N	19 27 E
Loengo	**90**	4 48 S	26 30 E
Lofer	**26**	47 35N	12 41 E
Lofoten	**50**	68 30N	15 0 E
Lofsdalen	**48**	62 10N	13 20 E
Lofsen →	**48**	62 7N	13 57 E
Loftahammar	**49**	57 54N	16 41 E
Logan, Kans., U.S.A.	**116**	39 40N	99 35W
Logan, Ohio, U.S.A.	**114**	39 25N	82 22W
Logan, Utah, U.S.A.	**118**	41 45N	111 50W
Logan, W. Va., U.S.A.	**114**	37 51N	81 59W
Logan, Mt .	**104**	60 31N	140 22W
Logan Pass	**108**	48 41N	113 44W
Logansport, Ind., U.S.A.	**114**	40 45N	86 21W
Logansport, La., U.S.A.	**117**	31 58N	93 58W
Logar □	**65**	34 0N	69 0 E
Logo	**87**	5 20N	30 18 E
Logroño	**32**	42 28N	2 27W
* Logroño □	**32**	42 28N	2 27W
Logrosán	**31**	39 20N	5 32W
Løgstør	**49**	56 58N	9 14 E
Lohardaga	**69**	23 27N	84 45 E
Lohja	**51**	60 12N	24 5 E
Lohr	**25**	50 0N	9 35 E
Loi-kaw	**67**	19 40N	97 17 E
Loimaa	**51**	60 50N	23 5 E
Loir →	**18**	47 33N	0 32W
Loir-et-Cher □	**18**	47 40N	1 20 E
Loire □	**21**	45 40N	4 5 E
Loire →	**18**	47 16N	2 10W
Loire-Atlantique □	**18**	47 25N	1 40W
Loiret □	**19**	47 58N	2 10 E
Loitz	**24**	53 58N	13 8 E
Loja, Ecuador	**126**	3 59 S	79 16W
Loja, Spain	**31**	37 10N	4 10W
Loji	**73**	1 38 S	127 28 E
Loka	**87**	4 13N	31 0 E
Lokandu	**90**	2 30 S	25 45 E
Løken	**47**	59 48N	11 29 E
Lokeren	**16**	51 6N	3 59 E
Lokhvitsa	**54**	50 25N	33 18 E
Lokichokio	**90**	4 19N	34 13 E
Lokitaung	**90**	4 12N	35 48 E
Lokka	**50**	67 49N	27 45 E
Løkken	**49**	57 22N	9 41 E
Løkkenverk	**47**	63 8N	9 45 E
Loknya	**54**	56 49N	30 4 E
Lokoja	**85**	7 47N	6 45 E
Lokolama	**88**	2 35 S	19 50 E
Lokwei	**77**	19 5N	110 31 E
Lol →	**87**	9 13N	26 30 E
Lola	**84**	7 52N	8 29W
Lolibai, Gebel	**87**	3 50N	33 0 E
Lolimi	**87**	4 35N	34 0 E
Loliondo	**90**	2 2 S	35 39 E
Lolland	**49**	54 45N	11 30 E
Lollar	**24**	50 39N	8 43 E
Lolo	**118**	46 50N	114 8W
Lolodorf	**85**	3 16N	10 49 E
Lom	**43**	43 48N	23 12 E
Lom →	**42**	43 45N	23 15 E
Loma	**118**	47 59N	110 29W
Lomami →	**90**	0 46N	24 16 E
Lomas de Zamóra	**124**	34 45 S	58 25W
Lombard	**118**	46 7N	111 28W
Lombardia □	**38**	45 35N	9 45 E
Lombardy = Lombardia	**38**	45 35N	9 45 E
Lombez	**20**	43 29N	0 55 E
Lomblen	**73**	8 30 S	123 32 E
Lombok	**72**	8 45 S	116 30 E
Lomé	**85**	6 9N	1 20 E
Lomela	**88**	2 19 S	23 15 E
Lomela →	**88**	1 30 S	22 50 E
Lomello	**38**	45 5N	8 46 E
Lometa	**117**	31 15N	98 25W
Lomié	**88**	3 13N	13 38 E
Lomma	**49**	55 43N	13 6 E
Lomond	**108**	50 24N	112 36W
Lomond, L.	**14**	56 8N	4 38W
Lomonosov	**54**	59 57N	29 53 E
Lompobatang	**73**	5 24 S	119 56 E
Lompoc	**119**	34 41N	120 32W
Lomsegga	**47**	61 49N	8 21 E
Łomza	**28**	53 10N	22 2 E
Łomza □	**28**	53 0N	22 30 E
Lonavla	**70**	18 46N	73 29 E
Loncoche	**128**	39 20 S	72 50W
Londa	**70**	15 30N	74 30 E
Londe, La	**21**	43 8N	6 14 E
Londiani	**90**	0 10 S	35 33 E
Londinières	**18**	49 50N	1 25 E
London, Can.	**106**	42 59N	81 15W
London, U.K.	**13**	51 30N	0 5W
London, Ky., U.S.A.	**114**	37 11N	84 5W
London, Ohio, U.S.A.	**114**	39 54N	83 28W
London, Greater □	**13**	51 30N	0 5W
Londonderry	**15**	55 0N	7 20W
Londonderry □	**15**	55 0N	7 20W
Londonderry, C.	**96**	13 45 S	126 55 E
Londonderry, I.	**128**	55 0 S	71 0W
Londrina	**125**	23 18 S	51 10W
Lone Pine	**119**	36 35N	118 2W
Long Beach, Calif., U.S.A.	**119**	33 46N	118 12W
Long Beach, N.Y., U.S.A.	**113**	40 35N	73 40W
Long Beach, Wash., U.S.A.	**118**	46 20N	124 1W
Long Branch	**114**	40 19N	74 0W
Long Creek	**118**	44 43N	119 6W
Long Eaton	**12**	52 54N	1 16W
Long I., Austral.	**98**	22 8 S	149 53 E
Long I., Bahamas	**121**	23 20N	75 10W
Long I., P.N.G.	**98**	5 20 S	147 5 E
Long I., U.S.A.	**114**	40 50N	73 20W
Long I. Sd.	**113**	41 10N	73 0W
Long L.	**106**	49 30N	86 50W
Long Lake	**113**	43 57N	74 25W
Long Pine	**116**	42 33N	99 41W
Long Pt., Newf., Can.	**107**	48 47N	58 46W
Long Pt., Ont., Can.	**112**	42 35N	80 2W
Long Point B.	**112**	42 40N	80 10W
Long Range Mts.	**107**	49 30N	57 30W
Long Str.	**4**	70 0N	175 0 E
Long Xian	**77**	34 55N	106 55 E
Long Xuyen	**71**	10 19N	105 28 E
Longá	**45**	36 53N	21 55 E
Long'an	**77**	23 10N	107 40 E
Longarone	**39**	46 15N	12 18 E
Longchuan	**77**	24 5N	115 17 E
Longde	**76**	35 30N	106 20 E
Longeau	**19**	47 47N	5 20 E
Longford, Austral.	**99**	41 32 S	147 3 E
Longford, Ireland	**15**	53 43N	7 50W
Longford □	**15**	53 42N	7 45W
Longhua	**76**	41 18N	117 45 E
Longido	**90**	2 43 S	36 42 E
Longiram	**72**	0 5 S	115 45 E
Longjiang	**76**	47 20N	123 12 E
Longkou	**76**	37 40N	120 18 E
Longlac	**106**	49 45N	86 25W
Longlin	**77**	24 47N	105 20 E
Longmen	**77**	23 40N	114 18 E
Longmont	**116**	40 10N	105 4W
Longnan	**77**	24 55N	114 47 E
Longnawan	**72**	1 51N	114 55 E
Longobucco	**41**	39 27N	16 37 E
Longone →	**81**	10 0N	15 40 E
Longquan	**77**	28 7N	119 10 E
Longreach	**97**	23 28 S	144 14 E
Longs Peak	**118**	40 20N	105 37W
Longshan	**77**	29 29N	109 25 E
Longsheng	**77**	25 48N	110 0 E
Longton	**98**	20 58 S	145 55 E
Longtown	**13**	51 58N	2 59W
Longué	**18**	47 22N	0 8W
Longueau	**19**	49 52N	2 21 E
Longueuil	**113**	45 32N	73 28W
Longuyon	**19**	49 27N	5 35 E
Longview, Can.	**108**	50 32N	114 10W
Longview, Tex., U.S.A.	**117**	32 30N	94 45W
Longview, Wash., U.S.A.	**118**	46 9N	122 58W
Longwy	**19**	49 30N	5 45 E
Longxi	**76**	34 53N	104 40 E
Longzhou	**77**	22 22N	106 50 E
Lonigo	**39**	45 23N	11 22 E
Löningen	**24**	52 43N	7 44 E
Lonja →	**39**	45 30N	16 40 E
Lonoke	**117**	34 48N	91 57W
Lons-le-Saunier	**19**	46 40N	5 31 E
Lønstrup	**49**	57 29N	9 47 E
Looc	**73**	12 20N	112 5 E
Lookout, C., Can.	**106**	55 18N	83 56W
Lookout, C., U.S.A.	**115**	34 30N	76 30W
Loolmalasin	**90**	3 0 S	35 53 E
Loon →, Alta., Can.	**108**	57 8N	115 3W
Loon →, Man., Can.	**109**	55 53N	101 59W
Loon Lake	**109**	54 2N	109 10W
Loop Hd.	**15**	52 34N	9 55W
Lop Nor = Lop Nur	**75**	40 20N	90 10 E
Lop Nur	**75**	40 20N	90 10 E
Lopare	**42**	44 39N	18 46 E
Lopatin	**57**	43 50N	47 35 E
Lopatina, G.	**59**	50 47N	143 10 E
Lopaye	**87**	6 37N	33 40 E
Lopera	**31**	37 56N	4 14W
Lopez, C.	**88**	0 47 S	8 40 E
Lopphavet	**50**	70 27N	21 15 E
Lora →, Afghan.	**65**	32 0N	67 15 E
Lora →, Norway	**47**	62 8N	8 42 E
Lora del Río	**31**	37 39N	5 33W
Lora, Hamun-i-	**66**	29 38N	64 58 E
Lora, La	**30**	42 45N	4 0W
Lorain	**114**	41 28N	82 55W
Loralai	**68**	30 20N	68 41 E
Lorca	**33**	37 41N	1 42W
Lord Howe I.	**94**	31 33 S	159 6 E
Lord Howe Ridge	**94**	30 0 S	162 30 E
Lordsburg	**119**	32 22N	108 45W
Lorengau	**98**	2 1 S	147 15 E
Loreto, Brazil	**127**	7 5 S	45 10W
Loreto, Italy	**39**	43 26N	13 36 E
Loreto Aprutina	**39**	42 24N	13 59 E
Lorgues	**21**	43 28N	6 22 E
Lorient	**18**	47 45N	3 23W
Loristān □	**64**	33 20N	47 0 E
Lorn	**14**	56 26N	5 10W
Lorn, Firth of	**14**	56 20N	5 40W
Lorne	**99**	38 33 S	143 59 E
Lörrach	**25**	47 36N	7 38 E
Lorraine	**19**	49 0N	6 0 E
Lorrainville	**106**	47 21N	79 23W
Los Alamos	**119**	35 57N	106 17W
Los Andes	**124**	32 50 S	70 40W
Los Angeles, Chile	**124**	37 28 S	72 23W
Los Angeles, U.S.A.	**119**	34 0N	118 10W
Los Angeles Aqueduct	**119**	35 25N	118 0W
Los Banos	**119**	37 8N	120 56W
Los Barrios	**31**	36 11N	5 30W
Los Blancos	**124**	23 40 S	62 30W
Los Gatos	**119**	37 15N	121 59W
Los Hermanos	**126**	11 45N	84 25W
Los, Îles de	**84**	9 30N	13 50W
Los Lamentos	**120**	30 36N	105 50W
Los Lunas	**119**	34 48N	106 47W
Los Mochis	**120**	25 45N	109 5W
Los Monegros	**32**	41 29N	0 13W
Los Olivos	**119**	34 40N	120 7W
Los Palacios y Villafranca	**31**	37 10N	5 55W
Los Roques	**126**	11 50N	66 45W
Los Santos de Maimona	**31**	38 27N	6 22W
Los Testigos	**126**	11 23N	63 6W
Los Vilos	**124**	32 10 S	71 30W
Los Yébenes	**31**	39 36N	3 55W
Loshkalakh	**59**	62 45N	147 20 E
Łosice	**28**	52 13N	22 43 E
Lošinj	**39**	44 30N	14 30 E
Lossiemouth	**14**	57 43N	3 17W
Losuia	**98**	8 30 S	151 4 E
Lot □	**20**	44 39N	1 40 E
Lot →	**20**	44 18N	0 20 E
Lot-et-Garonne □	**20**	44 22N	0 30 E
Lota	**124**	37 5 S	73 10W
Løten	**47**	60 51N	11 21 E
Lothian □	**14**	55 50N	3 0W
Lothiers	**19**	46 42N	1 33 E
Lotschbergtunnel	**25**	46 26N	7 43 E
Lottefors	**48**	61 25N	16 24 E
Loubomo	**88**	4 9 S	12 47 E
Loudéac	**18**	48 11N	2 47W
Loudon	**115**	35 35N	84 22W
Loudonville	**112**	40 40N	82 15W
Loudun	**18**	47 0N	0 5 E
Loué	**18**	47 59N	0 9W
Loue →	**19**	47 1N	5 27 E
Louga	**84**	15 45N	16 5W
Loughborough	**12**	52 46N	1 11W
Loughrea	**15**	53 11N	8 33W
Loughros More B.	**15**	54 48N	8 30W
Louhans	**21**	46 38N	5 12 E
Louis Trichardt	**93**	23 0 S	29 43 E
Louis XIV, Pte.	**106**	54 37N	79 45W
Louisa	**114**	38 5N	82 40W
Louisbourg	**107**	45 55N	60 0W
Louise I.	**108**	52 55N	131 50W
Louiseville	**106**	46 20N	72 56W
Louisiade Arch.	**94**	11 10 S	153 0 E
Louisiana	**116**	39 25N	91 0W
Louisiana □	**117**	30 50N	92 0W
Louisville, Ky., U.S.A.	**114**	38 15N	85 45W
Louisville, Miss., U.S.A.	**117**	33 7N	89 3W
Loulay	**20**	46 3N	0 30W
Loulé	**31**	37 9N	8 0W
Lount L.	**109**	50 10N	94 20W
Louny	**26**	50 20N	13 48 E
Loup City	**116**	41 19N	98 57W
Loupe, La	**18**	48 29N	1 1 E
Lourdes	**20**	43 6N	0 3W
Lourdes-du-Blanc-Sablon	**107**	51 24N	57 12W
Lourenço-Marques = Maputo	**93**	25 58 S	32 32 E
Loures	**31**	38 50N	9 9W
Lourinhã	**31**	39 14N	9 17W
Louroux-Béconnais, Le	**18**	47 30N	0 55W
Lousã	**30**	40 7N	8 14W
Louth, Austral.	**99**	30 30 S	145 8 E
Louth, Ireland	**15**	53 47N	6 33W
Louth, U.K.	**12**	53 23N	0 0W
Louth □	**15**	53 55N	6 30W
Loutrá Aidhipsoú	**45**	38 54N	23 2 E
Loutráki	**45**	38 0N	22 57 E
Louvière, La	**16**	50 27N	4 10 E
Louviers	**18**	49 12N	1 10 E
Lovat →	**54**	58 14N	30 28 E
Lovćen	**42**	42 23N	18 51 E
Love	**109**	53 29N	104 10W
Lovech	**43**	43 8N	24 42 E
Loveland	**116**	40 27N	105 4W
Lovell	**118**	44 51N	108 20W
Lovelock	**118**	40 17N	118 25W
Lóvere	**38**	45 50N	10 4 E
Loviisa	**51**	60 28N	26 12 E
Loving	**117**	32 17N	104 4W
Lovington	**117**	33 0N	103 20W
Lovios	**30**	41 55N	8 4W
Lovisa	**51**	60 28N	26 12 E
Lovosice	**26**	50 30N	14 2 E
Lovran	**39**	45 18N	14 15 E
Lovrin	**42**	45 58N	20 48 E
Lövstabukten	**48**	60 35N	17 45 E
Low Rocky Pt.	**97**	42 59 S	145 29 E

* *Renamed La Rioja* □

Lowa	90	1 25S	25 47E
Lowa →	90	1 24S	25 51E
Lowell	114	42 38N	71 19W
Lower Arrow L.	108	49 40N	118 5W
Lower Austria = Niederösterreich □	26	48 25N	15 40E
Lower Hutt	101	41 10S	174 55E
Lower L.	118	41 17N	120 3W
Lower Lake	118	38 56N	122 36W
Lower Neguac	107	47 20N	65 10W
Lower Post	108	59 58N	128 30W
Lower Red L.	116	47 58N	95 0W
Lower Saxony = Niedersachsen □	24	52 45N	9 0E
Lowestoft	13	52 29N	1 44E
Łowicz	28	52 6N	19 55E
Lowville	114	43 48N	75 30W
Loxton	97	34 28S	140 31E
Loyalty Is. = Loyauté, Is.	94	21 0S	167 30E
Loyang = Luoyang	77	34 40N	112 26E
Loyev, U.S.S.R.	54	51 55N	30 40E
Loyev, U.S.S.R.	54	51 56N	30 46E
Loyoro	90	3 22N	34 14E
Lož	39	45 43N	30 14E
Lozère □	20	44 35N	3 30E
Loznica	42	44 32N	19 14E
Lozovaya	56	49 0N	36 20E
Luachimo	88	7 23S	20 48E
Luacono	88	11 15S	21 37E
Lualaba →	90	0 26N	25 20E
Luampa	91	15 4S	24 20E
Lu'an	77	31 45N	116 29E
Luan Chau	71	21 38N	103 24E
Luan Xian	76	39 40N	118 40E
Luanda	88	8 50S	13 15E
Luang Prabang	71	19 52N	102 10E
Luangwa Valley	91	13 30S	31 30E
Luanping	76	40 53N	117 23E
Luanshya	91	13 3S	28 28E
Luapula □	91	11 0S	29 0E
Luapula →	91	9 26S	28 33E
Luarca	30	43 32N	6 32W
Luashi	91	10 50S	23 36E
Luau	88	10 40S	22 10E
Lubaczów	28	50 10N	23 8E
Lubalo	88	9 10S	19 15E
Lubań	28	51 5N	15 15E
Lubana, Ozero	54	56 45N	27 0E
Lubang Is.	73	13 50N	120 12E
Lubartów	28	51 28N	22 42E
Lubawa	28	53 30N	19 48E
Lübben	24	51 56N	13 54E
Lübbenau	24	51 49N	13 59E
Lubbock	117	33 40N	101 53W
Lübeck	24	53 52N	10 41E
Lübecker Bucht	24	54 3N	11 0E
Lubefu	90	4 47S	24 27E
Lubefu →	90	4 10S	23 0E
Lubero = Luofu	90	0 1S	29 15E
Lubicon L.	108	56 23N	115 56W
Lubień Kujawski	28	52 23N	19 9E
Lubin	28	51 24N	16 11E
Lublin	28	51 12N	22 38E
Lublin □	28	51 5N	22 30E
Lubliniec	28	50 43N	18 45E
Lubny	54	50 3N	32 58E
Lubok Antu	72	1 3N	111 50E
Lubon	28	52 21N	16 51E
Lubongola	90	2 35S	27 50E
Lubotin	27	49 17N	20 53E
Lubran	64	34 0N	36 0E
Lubraniec	28	52 33N	18 50E
Lubsko	28	51 45N	14 57E
Lübtheen	24	53 18N	11 4E
Lubuagan	73	17 21N	121 10E
Lubudi →	91	9 0S	25 35E
Lubuklinggau	72	3 15S	102 55E
Lubuksikaping	72	0 10N	100 15E
Lubumbashi	91	11 40S	27 28E
Lubunda	90	5 12S	26 41E
Lubungu	91	14 35S	26 24E
Lubutu	90	0 45S	26 30E
Luc-en-Diois	21	44 36N	5 28E
Luc, Le	21	43 23N	6 21E
Lucan	112	43 11N	81 24W
Lucca	38	43 50N	10 30E
Luce Bay	14	54 45N	4 48W
Lucea	121	18 25N	78 10W
Lucedale	115	30 55N	88 34W
Lucena, Phil.	73	13 56N	121 37E
Lucena, Spain	31	37 27N	4 31W
Lucena del Cid	32	40 9N	0 17W
Lučenec	27	48 18N	19 42E
Lucera	41	41 30N	15 20E
Lucerne = Luzern	25	47 3N	8 18E
Luchena →	33	37 44N	1 50W
Lucheringo →	91	11 43S	36 17E
Lüchow	24	52 58N	11 8E
Lucira	89	14 0S	12 35E
Luckau	24	51 50N	13 43E
Luckenwalde	24	52 5N	13 11E
Lucknow	69	26 50N	81 0E
Luçon	20	46 28N	1 10W
Lüda	76	38 50N	121 40E
Luda Kamchiya →	43	43 3N	27 29E
Ludbreg	39	46 15N	16 38E
Lüdenscheid	24	51 13N	7 37E
Lüderitz	92	26 41S	15 8E
Ludewe □	91	10 0S	34 50E
Ludhiana	68	30 57N	75 56E
Lüdinghausen	24	51 46N	7 28E
Ludington	114	43 58N	86 27W
Ludlow, U.K.	13	52 23N	2 42W
Ludlow, Calif., U.S.A.	119	34 43N	116 10W
Ludlow, Vt., U.S.A.	113	43 25N	72 40W
Ludus	46	46 29N	24 5E
Ludvika	48	60 8N	15 14E
Ludwigsburg	25	48 53N	9 11E
Ludwigshafen	25	49 27N	8 27E
Ludwigslust	24	53 19N	11 28E
Ludza	54	56 32N	27 43E
Luebo	88	5 21S	21 23E
Lueki	90	3 20S	25 48E
Luena, Zaïre	91	9 28S	25 43E
Luena, Zambia	91	10 40S	30 25E
Lüeyang	77	33 22N	106 10E
Lufeng	77	22 57N	115 38E
Lufkin	117	31 25N	94 40W
Lufupa	91	10 37S	24 56E
Luga	54	58 40N	29 55E
Luga →	54	59 40N	28 18E
Lugang	77	24 4N	120 23E
Lugano	25	46 0N	8 57E
Lugano, L. di	25	46 0N	9 0E
Lugansk = Voroshilovgrad	57	48 35N	39 20E
Lugard's Falls	90	3 6S	38 41E
Lugela	91	16 25S	36 43E
Lugenda →	91	11 25S	38 33E
Lugh Ganana	63	3 48N	42 34E
Lugnaquilla	15	52 58N	6 28W
Lugnvik	48	62 56N	17 55E
Lugo, Italy	39	44 25N	11 53E
Lugo, Spain	30	43 2N	7 35W
Lugo □	30	43 0N	7 30W
Lugoj	42	45 42N	21 57E
Lugones	30	43 26N	5 50W
Lugovoy	58	42 54N	72 45E
Luhe →	24	53 18N	10 11E
Luiana	92	17 25S	22 59E
Luino	38	46 0N	8 42E
Luís Correia	127	3 0S	41 35W
Luitpold Coast	5	78 30S	32 0W
Luize	88	7 40S	22 30E
Luizi	90	6 0S	27 25E
Luján	124	34 45S	59 5W
Lukanga Swamps	91	14 30S	27 40E
Lukenie →	88	3 0S	18 50E
Lukhisaral	69	25 11N	86 5E
Lŭki	43	41 50N	24 43E
Lukolela, Equateur, Zaïre	88	1 10S	17 12E
Lukolela, Kasai Or., Zaïre	90	5 23S	24 32E
Lukosi	91	18 30S	26 30E
Lukovit	43	43 13N	24 11E
Łuków	28	51 55N	22 23E
Lukoyanov	55	55 2N	44 29E
Lule älv →	50	65 35N	22 10E
Luleå	50	65 35N	22 10E
Lüleburgaz	43	41 23N	27 22E
Luling	117	29 45N	97 40W
Lulong	76	39 53N	118 51E
Lulonga →	88	1 0N	19 0E
Lulua →	88	6 30S	22 50E
Luluabourg = Kananga	88	5 55S	22 26E
Lumai	89	13 13S	21 25E
Lumajang	73	8 8S	113 16E
Lumbala	89	14 18S	21 18E
Lumberton, Miss., U.S.A.	117	31 4N	89 28W
Lumberton, N. Mex., U.S.A.	119	36 58N	106 57W
Lumberton, N.C., U.S.A.	115	34 37N	78 59W
Lumbres	19	50 40N	2 5E
Lumbwa	90	0 12S	35 28E
Lumby	108	50 10N	118 50W
Lumsden	101	45 44S	168 27E
Lumut	71	4 13N	100 37E
Lunavada	68	23 8N	73 37E
Lunca	46	47 22N	25 1E
Lund, Sweden	49	55 44N	13 12E
Lund, U.S.A.	118	38 53N	115 0W
Lundazi	91	12 20S	33 7E
Lunde	47	59 17N	9 5E
Lunderskov	49	55 29N	9 19E
Lundi →	91	21 43S	32 34E
Lundu	72	1 40N	109 50E
Lundy	13	51 10N	4 41W
Lune →	12	54 0N	2 51W
Lüneburg	24	53 15N	10 23E
Lüneburg Heath = Lüneburger Heide	24	53 0N	10 0E
Lüneburger Heide	24	53 0N	10 0E
Lunel	21	43 39N	4 9E
Lünen	24	51 36N	7 31E
Lunenburg	107	44 22N	64 18W
Lunéville	19	48 36N	6 30E
Lunga →	91	14 34S	26 25E
Lungi Airport	84	8 40N	13 17W
Lungleh	67	22 55N	92 45E
Luni	68	26 0N	73 6E
Lūni →	68	24 41N	71 14E
Luninets	54	52 15N	26 50E
Luning	118	38 30N	118 10W
Lunino	55	53 35N	45 6E
Lunner	47	60 19N	10 35E
Lunsemfwa →	91	14 54S	30 12E
Lunsemfwa Falls	91	14 30S	29 6E
Luo He →	77	34 35N	110 20E
Luobei	76	47 35N	130 50E
Luocheng	77	24 48N	108 53E
Luochuan	76	35 45N	109 26E
Luoding	77	22 45N	111 40E
Luodong	77	24 41N	121 46E
Luofu	90	0 10S	29 15E
Luoning	77	34 35N	111 40E
Luoyang	77	34 40N	112 26E
Luoyuan	77	26 28N	119 30E
Luozi	88	4 54S	14 0E
Lupeni	46	45 21N	23 13E
Łupków	27	49 15N	22 4E
Luque, Parag.	124	25 19S	57 25W
Luque, Spain	31	37 35N	4 16W
Luray	114	38 39N	78 26W
Lure	19	47 40N	6 30E
Luremo	88	8 30S	17 50E
Lurgan	15	54 28N	6 20W
Lusaka	91	15 28S	28 16E
Lusambo	90	4 58S	23 28E
Lusangaye	90	4 54S	26 0E
Luseland	109	52 5N	109 24W
Lushan	77	33 45N	112 55E
Lushih	77	34 3N	111 3E
Lushnja	44	40 55N	19 41E
Lushoto	90	4 47S	38 20E
Lushoto □	90	4 45S	38 20E
Lüshun	76	38 45N	121 15E
Lusignan	20	46 26N	0 8E
Lusigny-sur-Barse	19	48 16N	4 15E
Lusk	116	42 47N	104 27W
Lussac-les-Châteaux	20	46 24N	0 43E
Luta = Lüda	76	38 50N	121 40E
Luton	13	51 53N	0 24W
Lutong	72	4 30N	114 0E
Lutsk	54	50 50N	25 15E
Lützow Holmbukta	5	69 10S	37 30E
Luverne	116	43 35N	96 12W
Luvua	91	8 48S	25 17E
Luwegu →	91	8 31S	37 23E
Luwuk	73	0 56S	122 47E
Luxembourg	16	49 37N	6 9E
Luxembourg ■	16	50 0N	6 0E
Luxembourg □	16	49 58N	5 30E
Luxeuil-les-Bains	19	47 49N	6 24E
Luxi	77	28 20N	110 7E
Luxor = El Uqsur	86	25 41N	32 38E
Luy →	20	43 39N	1 9W
Luy-de-Béarn →	20	43 39N	0 48W
Luy-de-France →	20	43 39N	0 48W
Luz-St-Sauveur	20	42 53N	0 1E
Luza	52	60 39N	47 10E
Luzern	25	47 3N	8 18E
Luzern □	25	47 2N	7 55E
Luzhai	77	24 29N	109 42E
Luzhou	75	28 52N	105 20E
Luziânia	127	16 20S	48 0W
Luzon	73	16 0N	121 0E
Luzy	19	46 47N	3 58E
Luzzi	41	39 28N	16 17E
Lvov	54	49 50N	24 0E
Lwówek	28	52 28N	16 10E
Lwówek Śląski	28	51 7N	15 38E
Lyakhovichi	54	53 2N	26 32E
Lyakhovskiye, Ostrova	59	73 40N	141 0E
Lyaki	57	40 34N	47 22E
Lyallpur = Faisalabad	68	31 30N	73 5E
Lyaskovets	43	43 6N	25 44E
Lychen	24	53 13N	13 20E
Lyckeby	49	56 12N	15 37E
Lycksele	50	64 38N	18 40E
Lycosura	45	37 20N	22 3E
Lydda = Lod	62	31 57N	34 54E
Lydenburg	93	25 10S	30 29E
Lyell	101	41 48S	172 4E
Lyell I.	108	52 40N	131 35W
Lyell Range	101	41 38S	172 20E
Lygnern	49	57 30N	12 15E
Lykling	47	59 42N	5 12E
Lyman	118	41 24N	110 15W
Lyme Regis	13	50 44N	2 57W
Lymington	13	50 46N	1 32W
Łyńa →	28	54 37N	21 14E
Lynchburg	114	37 23N	79 10W
Lynd →	98	16 28S	143 18E
Lynd Ra.	99	25 30S	149 20E
Lynden, Can.	112	43 14N	80 9W
Lynden, U.S.A.	118	48 56N	122 32W
Lyndhurst	99	30 15S	138 18E
Lyndonville, N.Y., U.S.A.	112	43 19N	78 25W
Lyndonville, Vt., U.S.A.	113	44 32N	72 1W
Lyngdal, Aust-Agder, Norway	47	58 8N	7 7E
Lyngdal, Buskerud, Norway	47	59 54N	9 32E
Lynn	114	42 28N	70 57W
Lynn Canal	108	58 50N	135 20W
Lynn Lake	109	56 51N	101 3W
Lynton	13	51 14N	3 50W
Lyntupy	54	55 4N	26 23E
Lynx L.	109	62 25N	106 15W
Lyø	49	55 3N	10 9E
Lyon	21	45 46N	4 50E
Lyonnais	21	45 45N	4 15E
Lyons, Colo., U.S.A.	116	40 17N	105 15W
Lyons, Ga., U.S.A.	115	32 10N	82 15W
Lyons, Kans., U.S.A.	116	38 24N	98 13W
Lyons, N.Y., U.S.A.	114	43 3N	77 0W
Lyons = Lyon	21	45 46N	4 50E
Lyrestad	49	58 48N	14 4E
Lys →	19	50 39N	2 24E
Lysá	26	50 11N	14 51E
Lysekil	49	58 17N	11 26E
Lyskovo	55	56 0N	45 3E
Lysva	52	58 07N	57 49E
Lysvik	48	60 1N	13 9E
Lytle	117	29 14N	98 46W
Lyttelton	101	43 35S	172 44E
Lytton	108	50 13N	121 31W
Lyuban	54	59 16N	31 18E
Lyubcha	54	53 46N	26 1E
Lyubertsy	55	55 39N	37 50E
Lyubim	55	58 20N	40 39E
Lyubimets	43	41 50N	26 5E
Lyuboml, U.S.S.R.	54	51 10N	24 2E
Lyuboml, U.S.S.R.	54	51 11N	24 4E
Lyubotin	56	50 0N	36 0E
Lyubytino	54	58 50N	33 16E
Lyudinovo	54	53 52N	34 28E

M

Mā'ad	62	32 37N	35 36E
Ma'alah	64	26 31N	47 20E
Maamba	92	17 17S	26 28E
Ma'ânn	64	30 12N	35 44E
Ma'anshan	77	31 44N	118 29E
Ma'arrat un Nu'man	64	35 38N	36 40E
Maas →	16	51 45N	4 32E
Maaseik	16	51 6N	5 45E
Maassluis	16	51 56N	4 16E
Maastricht	16	50 50N	5 40E
Maave	93	21 4S	34 47E
Mabel L.	108	50 35N	118 43W
Mabenge	90	4 15N	24 12E
Mablethorpe	12	53 21N	0 14E
Maboma	90	2 30N	28 10E
Mabrouk	85	19 29N	1 15W
Mabton	118	46 15N	120 12W
Mac Nutt	109	51 5N	101 36W
Mac Tier	112	45 9N	79 46W
Macachín	124	37 10S	63 43W
Macaé	125	22 20S	41 43W
McAlester	117	34 57N	95 46W
McAllen	117	26 12N	98 15W
Macallister →	100	38 2S	146 59E
Macamic	106	48 45N	79 0W
Macão	31	39 35N	7 59W
Macao = Macau ■	75	22 16N	113 35E
Macapá	127	0 5N	51 4W
McArthur →	97	15 54S	136 40E
McArthur River	97	16 27S	136 7E
Macau	127	5 0S	36 40W
Macau ■	75	22 16N	113 35E
McBride	108	53 20N	120 19W
McCall	118	44 55N	116 6W
McCamey	117	31 8N	102 15W
McCammon	118	42 41N	112 11W
McCauley I.	108	53 40N	130 15W
Macclesfield	12	53 16N	2 9W
McClintock	109	57 50N	94 10W
McCloud	118	41 14N	122 5W
McClure	112	40 42N	77 20W
McClure Str.	4	75 0N	119 0W
McClusky	116	47 30N	100 31W
McComb	117	31 13N	90 30W
McCook	116	40 15N	100 35W
McCusker →	109	55 32N	108 39W
McDame	108	59 44N	128 59W
McDermitt	118	42 0N	117 45W
Macdonald →	100	33 22S	151 0E
McDonald Is.	3	54 0S	73 0E
Macdonald L.	96	23 30S	129 0E
Macdonnell Ranges	96	23 40S	133 0E
Macdougall L.	104	66 0N	98 27W
MacDowell L.	106	52 15N	92 45W
Macduff	14	57 40N	2 30W
Maceda	30	42 16N	7 39W
* Macedo de Cavaleiros	88	11 25S	16 45E
Macedonia = Makedhonía	44	40 39N	22 0E
Macedonia = Makedonija	42	41 53N	21 40E
Maceió	127	9 40S	35 41W
Maceira	31	39 41N	8 55W
Macenta	84	8 35N	9 32W
Macerata	39	43 19N	13 28E
McFarlane →	109	59 12N	107 58W
Macfarlane, L.	97	32 0S	136 40E
McGehee	117	33 40N	91 25W
McGill	118	39 27N	114 50W
Macgillycuddy's Reeks	15	52 2N	9 45W
MacGregor	109	49 57N	98 48W
McGregor, Iowa, U.S.A.	116	42 58N	91 15W
McGregor, Minn., U.S.A.	116	46 37N	93 17W
McGregor →	108	55 10N	122 0W
McGregor Ra.	99	27 0S	142 45E
Mach	66	29 50N	67 20E
Machado = Jiparana →	126	8 3S	62 52W
Machagai	124	26 56S	60 2W
Machakos	90	1 30S	37 15E
Machakos □	90	1 30S	37 15E
Machala	126	3 20S	79 57W
Machanga	93	20 59S	35 0E
Machattie, L.	97	24 50S	139 48E
Machava	93	25 54S	32 28E
Machece	91	19 15S	35 32E
Machecoul	18	47 0N	1 49W
Macheng	77	31 12N	115 2E
Machevna	59	61 20N	172 20E
Machezo	31	39 21N	4 20W
Machias	107	44 40N	67 28W
Machichaco, Cabo	32	43 28N	2 47W
Machichi →	109	57 3N	92 6W
Machilipatnam	70	16 12N	81 8E
Machine, La	19	46 54N	3 27E
Machiques	126	10 4N	72 34W
Machupicchu	126	13 8S	72 30W
Machynlleth	13	52 36N	3 51W
** Macias Nguema Biyoga	85	3 30N	8 40E
Maciejowice	28	51 36N	21 26E
McIlwraith Ra.	97	13 50S	143 20E
Măcin	46	45 16N	28 8E
Macina	84	14 50N	5 0W
McIntosh	116	45 57N	101 20W
McIntosh L.	109	55 45N	105 0W
Macintyre →	97	28 37S	150 47E
Macizo Galaico	30	42 30N	7 30W
Mackay, Austral.	97	21 8S	149 11E
Mackay, U.S.A.	118	43 58N	113 37W
Mackay →	108	57 10N	111 38W
Mackay, L.	96	22 30S	129 0E
McKees Rock	112	40 27N	80 3W
McKeesport	114	40 21N	79 50W
Mackenzie	108	55 20N	123 05W
McKenzie	115	36 10N	88 31W
† Mackenzie □	104	61 30N	115 0W
Mackenzie →, Austral.	97	23 38S	149 46E
Mackenzie →, Can.	104	69 10N	134 20W
McKenzie →	118	44 2N	123 6W
Mackenzie City = Linden	126	6 0N	58 10W
Mackenzie Highway	108	58 0N	117 15W
Mackenzie Mts.	104	64 0N	130 0W
Mackinaw City	114	45 47N	84 44W
McKinlay	98	21 16S	141 18E
McKinlay →	98	20 50S	141 28E
McKinley, Mt.	104	63 2N	151 0W
McKinley Sea	4	84 0N	10 0W
McKinney	117	33 10N	96 40W
Mackinnon Road	90	3 40S	39 1E
McKittrick	119	35 18N	119 39W
Macksville	99	30 40S	152 56E
McLaughlin	116	45 50N	100 50W
Maclean	97	29 26S	153 16E
McLean	117	35 15N	100 35W
McLeansboro	116	38 5N	88 30W
Maclear	93	31 2S	28 23E
Macleay →	97	30 56S	153 0E
McLennan	108	55 42N	116 50W
MacLeod, B.	109	62 53N	110 0W
McLeod L.	96	24 9S	113 47E
MacLeod Lake	108	54 58N	123 0W
M'Clintock Chan.	104	72 0N	102 0W
McLoughlin, Mt.	118	42 10N	122 19W
McLure	108	51 2N	120 13W

* *Renamed Andulo*

** *Renamed Bioko*

† *Now part of Fort Smith and Inuvik* □

McMechen **112** 39 57N 80 44W
McMillan L. **117** 32 40N 104 20W
McMinnville, Oreg., U.S.A. **118** 45 16N 123 11W
McMinnville, Tenn., U.S.A. **115** 35 43N 85 45W
McMorran **109** 51 19N 108 42W
McMurdo Sd. **5** 77 0S 170 0E
McMurray = Fort McMurray **108** 56 45N 111 27W
McNary **119** 34 4N 109 53W
McNaughton L. **108** 52 0N 118 10W
Macodoene **93** 23 32S 35 5E
Macomb **116** 40 25N 90 40W
Macomer **40** 40 16N 8 48E
Mâcon **21** 46 19N 4 50E
Macon, Ga., U.S.A. **115** 32 50N 83 37W
Macon, Miss., U.S.A. **115** 33 7N 88 31W
Macon, Mo., U.S.A. **116** 39 40N 92 26W
Macondo **89** 12 37S 23 46E
Macossa **91** 17 55S 33 56E
Macoun L. **109** 56 32N 103 40W
Macovane **93** 21 30S 35 0E
McPherson **116** 38 25N 97 40W
Macpherson Ra. **99** 28 15S 153 15E
Macquarie → **97** 30 5S 147 30E
Macquarie Harbour **97** 42 15S 145 23E
Macquarie Is. **94** 54 36S 158 55E
Macquarie, L. **100** 33 4S 151 36E
MacRobertson Coast **5** 68 30S 63 0E
Macroom **15** 51 54N 8 57W
Macubela **91** 16 53S 37 49E
Macugnaga **38** 45 57N 7 58E
Macuiza **91** 18 7S 34 29E
Macuse **91** 17 45S 37 10E
Macuspana **120** 17 46N 92 36W
Macusse **92** 17 48S 20 23E
Mácuzari, Presa **120** 27 10N 109 10W
McVille **116** 47 46N 98 11W
Madā 'in Salih **86** 26 51N 37 58E
Madagali **85** 10 56N 13 33E
Madagascar ■ **93** 20 0S 47 0E
Madā'in Sālih **64** 26 46N 37 57E
Madama **83** 22 0N 13 40E
Madame I. **107** 45 30N 60 58W
Madan **43** 41 30N 24 57E
Madanapalle **70** 13 33N 78 28E
Madang **94** 5 12S 145 49E
Madaoua **85** 14 5N 6 27E
Madara **85** 11 45N 10 35E
Madaripur **69** 23 19N 90 15E
Madauk **67** 17 56N 96 52E
Madawaska **112** 45 30N 77 55W
Madawaska → **106** 45 27N 76 21W
Madaya **67** 22 12N 96 10E
Madbar **87** 6 17N 30 45E
Maddalena **40** 41 15N 9 23E
Maddalena, La **40** 41 13N 9 25E
Maddaloni **41** 41 4N 14 23E
Madden Dam **120** 9 13N 79 37W
Madden Lake **120** 9 20N 79 37W
Madeira **80** 32 50N 17 0W
Madeira → **126** 3 22S 58 45W
Madeleine, Îs. de la **107** 47 30N 61 40W
Madera **119** 37 0N 120 1W
Madha **70** 18 0N 75 30E
Madhubani **69** 26 21N 86 7E
Madhya Pradesh □ **68** 21 50N 81 0E
Madill **117** 34 5N 96 49W
Madimba **88** 5 0S 15 0E
Madīnat ash Sha'b **63** 12 50N 45 0E
Madingou **88** 4 10S 13 33E
Madirovalo **93** 16 26S 46 32E
Madison, Fla., U.S.A. **115** 30 29N 83 39W
Madison, Ind., U.S.A. **114** 38 42N 85 20W
Madison, Nebr., U.S.A. **116** 41 53N 97 25W
Madison, Ohio, U.S.A. **112** 41 45N 81 4W
Madison, S.D., U.S.A. **116** 44 0N 97 8W
Madison, Wis., U.S.A. **116** 43 5N 89 25W
Madison → **118** 45 56N 111 30W
Madison Junc. **118** 44 42N 110 56W
Madisonville, Ky., U.S.A. **114** 37 20N 87 30W
Madisonville, Tex., U.S.A. **117** 30 57N 95 55W
Madista **92** 21 15S 25 6E
Madiun **73** 7 38S 111 32E
Madley **13** 52 3N 2 51W
Madol **87** 9 3N 27 45E
Madon → **19** 48 36N 6 6E
Madona **54** 56 53N 26 5E
Madonie, Le **40** 37 50N 13 50E
Madras, India **70** 13 8N 80 19E
Madras, U.S.A. **118** 44 40N 121 10W
Madras = Tamil Nadu □ **70** 11 0N 77 0E
Madre de Dios → **126** 10 59S 66 8W
Madre de Dios, I. **128** 50 20S 75 10W
Madre del Sur, Sierra **120** 17 30N 100 0W
Madre, Laguna, Mexico **120** 25 0N 97 30W
Madre, Laguna, U.S.A. **117** 25 0N 97 40W
Madre Occidental, Sierra **120** 27 0N 107 0W
Madre Oriental, Sierra **120** 25 0N 100 0W
Madre, Sierra, Mexico **120** 16 0N 93 0W
Madre, Sierra, Phil. **73** 17 0N 122 0E
Madri **68** 24 16N 73 32E
Madrid **30** 40 25N 3 45W
Madrid □ **30** 40 30N 3 45W
Madridejos **31** 39 28N 3 33W
Madrigal de las Altas Torres **30** 41 5N 5 0W
Madrona, Sierra **31** 38 27N 4 16W
Madroñera **31** 39 26N 5 42W
Madu **87** 14 37N 26 4E
Madura, Selat **73** 7 30S 113 20E
Madurai **70** 9 55N 78 10E
Madurantakam **70** 12 30N 79 50E
Madzhalis **57** 42 9N 47 47E
Mae Hong Son **71** 19 16N 98 1E
Mae Sot **71** 16 43N 98 34E
Maebashi **74** 36 24N 139 4E
Maella **32** 41 8N 0 7E
Măeruş **46** 45 53N 25 31E
Maesteg **13** 51 36N 3 40W
Maestra, Sierra **121** 20 15N 77 0W
Maestrazgo, Mts. del **32** 40 30N 0 25W
Maevatanana **93** 16 56N 46 49E
Ma'fan **83** 25 56N 14 29E
Mafeking, Can. **109** 52 40N 101 10W
* Mafeking, S. Afr. **92** 25 50S 25 38E
Maféré **84** 5 30N 3 2W
Mafeteng **92** 29 51S 27 15E
Maffra **99** 37 53S 146 58E
Mafia **90** 7 45S 39 50E
Mafra, Brazil **125** 26 10S 50 0W
Mafra, Port. **31** 38 55N 9 20W
Mafungabusi Plateau **91** 18 30S 29 8E
Magadan **59** 59 38N 150 50E
Magadi **90** 1 54S 36 19E
Magadi, L. **90** 1 54S 36 19E
Magaliesburg **93** 26 1S 27 32E
Magallanes, Estrecho de **128** 52 30S 75 0W
Magangué **126** 9 14N 74 45W
Magaria **85** 13 4N 9 5E
Magburaka **84** 8 47N 12 0W
Magdalena, Argent. **124** 35 5S 57 30W
Magdalena, Boliv. **126** 13 13S 63 57W
Magdalena, Malay. **72** 4 25N 117 55E
Magdalena, Mexico **120** 30 50N 112 0W
Magdalena, U.S.A. **119** 34 10N 107 20W
Magdalena →, Colomb. **126** 11 6N 74 51W
Magdalena →, Mexico **120** 30 40N 112 25W
Magdalena, B. **120** 24 30N 112 10W
Magdalena, I. **120** 24 40N 112 15W
Magdalena, Llano de la **120** 25 0N 111 30W
Magdeburg **24** 52 8N 11 36E
Magdeburg □ **24** 52 20N 11 30E
Magdi'el **62** 32 10N 34 54E
Magdub **87** 13 42N 25 5E
Magee **117** 31 53N 89 45W
Magee, I. **15** 54 48N 5 44W
Magelang **73** 7 29S 110 13E
Magellan's Str. = Magallanes, Est. de **128** 52 30S 75 0W
Magenta **38** 45 28N 8 53E
Maggia → **25** 46 18N 8 36E
Maggiorasca, Mte. **38** 44 33N 9 29E
Maggiore, L. **38** 46 0N 8 35E
Maghama **84** 15 32N 12 57W
Maghār **62** 32 54N 35 24E
Magherafelt **15** 54 44N 6 37W
Maghnia **82** 34 50N 1 43W
Magione **39** 43 10N 12 12E
Maglaj **42** 44 33N 18 7E
Magliano in Toscana **39** 42 36N 11 18E
Máglie **41** 40 8N 18 17E
Magnac-Laval **20** 46 13N 1 11E
Magnetic Pole, 1976 (North) **4** 76 12N 100 12W
Magnetic Pole, 1976 (South) **5** 68 48S 139 30E
Magnisía □ **44** 39 15N 22 45E
Magnitogorsk **52** 53 27N 59 4E
Magnolia, Ark., U.S.A. **117** 33 18N 93 12W
Magnolia, Miss., U.S.A. **117** 31 8N 90 28W
Magnor **47** 59 56N 12 15E
Magny-en-Vexin **19** 49 9N 1 47E
Magog **107** 45 18N 72 9W
Magoro **90** 1 45N 34 12E
Magosa = Famagusta **64** 35 8N 33 55E
Magoye **91** 16 1S 27 30E
Magpie L. **107** 51 0N 64 41W
Magrath **108** 49 25N 112 50W
Magro → **33** 39 11N 0 25W
Magrur, Wadi → **87** 16 5N 26 30E
Magu □ **90** 2 31S 33 28E
Maguarinho, C. **127** 0 15S 48 30W
Maguse L. **109** 61 40N 95 10W
Maguse Pt. **109** 61 20N 93 50W
Magwe **67** 20 10N 95 0E
Mahābād **64** 36 50N 45 45E
Mahabaleshwar **70** 17 58N 73 43E
Mahabharat Lekh **69** 28 30N 82 0E
Mahabo **93** 20 23S 44 40E
Mahad **70** 18 6N 73 29E
Mahadeo Hills **68** 22 20N 78 30E
Mahadeopur **70** 18 48N 80 0E
Mahagi **90** 2 20N 31 0E
Mahajamba → **93** 15 33S 47 8E
Mahajamba, Helodranon' i **93** 15 24S 47 5E
Mahajan **68** 28 48N 73 56E
Mahajanga □ **93** 17 0S 47 0E
Mahajilo → **93** 19 42S 45 22E
Mahakam → **72** 0 35S 117 17E
Mahalapye **92** 23 1S 26 51E
Maḩallāt **65** 33 55N 50 30E
Mahanadi → **69** 20 20N 86 25E
Mahanoro **93** 19 54S 48 48E
Mahanoy City **113** 40 48N 76 10W
Maharashtra □ **70** 20 30N 75 30E
Maharès **83** 34 32N 10 29E
Mahari Mts. **90** 6 20S 30 0E
Mahasolo **93** 19 7S 46 22E
Mahaweli → Ganga **70** 8 30N 81 15E
Mahboobabad **70** 17 42N 80 2E
Mahbubnagar **70** 16 45N 77 59E
Mahdia **83** 35 28N 11 0E
Mahé **70** 11 42N 75 34E
Mahendra Giri **70** 8 20N 77 30E
Mahenge **91** 8 45S 36 41E
Maheno **101** 45 10S 170 50E
Mahia Pen. **101** 39 9S 177 55E
Mahirija **82** 34 0N 3 16W
Mahmiya **87** 17 12N 33 43E
Mahmud Kot **68** 30 16N 71 0E
Mahmudia **46** 45 5N 29 5E
Mahnomen **116** 47 22N 95 57W
Mahoba **69** 25 15N 79 55E
Mahón **32** 39 53N 4 16E
Mahone Bay **107** 44 30N 64 20W
Mahuta **85** 11 32N 4 58E
Mai-Ndombe, L. **88** 2 0S 18 20E
Maîche **19** 47 16N 6 48E
Maicurú → **127** 2 14S 54 17W
Máida **41** 38 51N 16 21E
Maidenhead **13** 51 31N 0 42W
Maidi **87** 16 20N 42 45E
Maidstone, Can. **109** 53 5N 109 20W
Maidstone, U.K. **13** 51 16N 0 31E
Maiduguri **85** 12 0N 13 20E
Maignelay **19** 49 32N 2 30E
Maigudo **87** 7 30N 37 8E
Maijdi **69** 22 48N 91 10E

* *Renamed Mafikeng*

Maikala Ra. **69** 22 0N 81 0E
Mailly-le-Camp **19** 48 41N 4 12E
Mailsi **68** 29 48N 72 15E
Main →, Ger. **25** 50 0N 8 18E
Main →, U.K. **15** 54 49N 6 20W
Main Centre **109** 50 35N 107 21W
Mainburg **25** 48 37N 11 49E
Maine **18** 48 0N 0 0E
Maine □ **107** 45 20N 69 0W
Maine → **15** 52 10N 9 40W
Maine-et-Loire □ **18** 47 31N 0 30W
Maïne-Soroa **85** 13 13N 12 2E
Maingkwan **67** 26 15N 96 37E
Mainit, L. **73** 9 31N 125 30E
Mainland, Orkney, U.K. **14** 59 0N 3 10W
Mainland, Shetland, U.K. **14** 60 15N 1 22W
Mainpuri **68** 27 18N 79 4E
Maintenon **19** 48 35N 1 35E
Maintirano **93** 18 3S 44 1E
Mainz **25** 50 0N 8 17E
Maipú **124** 36 52S 57 50W
Maiquetía **126** 10 36N 66 57W
Maira → **38** 44 49N 7 38E
Mairabari **67** 26 30N 92 22E
Maisi, Pta. de **121** 20 10N 74 10W
Maisse **19** 48 24N 2 21E
Maitland, N.S.W., Austral. **97** 32 33S 151 36E
Maitland, S. Australia, Austral. **99** 34 23S 137 40E
Maitland → **112** 43 45N 81 33W
Maiyema **85** 12 5N 4 25E
Maizuru **74** 35 25N 135 22E
Majalengka **73** 6 55S 108 14E
Majd el Kurūm **62** 32 56N 35 15E
Majene **73** 3 38S 118 57E
Majevica Planina **42** 44 45N 18 50E
Maji **87** 6 12N 35 30E
Major **109** 51 52N 109 37W
Majorca, I. = Mallorca **32** 39 30N 3 0E
Maka **84** 13 40N 14 10W
Makak **85** 3 36N 11 0E
Makale **73** 3 6S 119 51E
Makamba **90** 4 8S 29 49E
Makari **88** 12 35N 14 28E
Makarikari = Makgadikgadi Salt Pans **92** 20 40S 25 45E
Makarovo **59** 57 40N 107 45E
Makarska **42** 43 20N 17 2E
Makaryev **55** 57 52N 43 50E
Makasar = Ujung Pandang **73** 5 10S 119 20E
Makasar, Selat **73** 1 0S 118 20E
Makat **58** 47 39N 53 19E
Makedhonia □ **44** 40 39N 22 0E
Makedonija □ **42** 41 53N 21 40E
Makena **110** 20 39N 156 27W
Makeni **84** 8 55N 12 5W
Makeyevka **56** 48 0N 38 0E
Makgadikgadi Salt Pans **92** 20 40S 25 45E
Makhachkala **57** 43 0N 47 30E
Makhambet, U.S.S.R. **57** 47 43N 51 40E
Makhambet, U.S.S.R. **57** 47 40N 51 35E
Makharadze **57** 41 55N 42 2E
Makian **73** 0 20N 127 20E
** Makin **94** 3 30N 174 0E
Makindu **90** 2 18S 37 50E
Makinsk **58** 52 37N 70 26E
Makkah **86** 21 30N 39 54E
Makkovik **107** 55 10N 59 10W
† Maklakovo **59** 58 16N 92 29E
Makó **27** 46 14N 20 33E
Makokou **88** 0 40N 12 50E
Makongo **90** 3 25N 26 17E
Makoro **90** 3 10N 29 59E
Makoua **88** 0 5S 15 50E
Maków Mazowiecki **28** 52 52N 21 6E
Maków Podhal **27** 49 43N 19 45E
Makrá **45** 36 15N 25 54E
Makran **65** 26 13N 61 30E
Makran Coast Range **66** 25 40N 64 0E
Makrana **68** 27 2N 74 46E
Mákri **44** 40 52N 25 40E
Maksimkin Yar **58** 58 42N 86 50E
Maktar **83** 35 48N 9 12E
Mākū **64** 39 15N 44 31E
Makumbi **88** 5 50S 20 43E
Makunda **92** 22 30S 20 7E
Makurazaki **74** 31 15N 130 20E
Makurdi **85** 7 43N 8 35E
Makwassie **92** 27 17S 26 0E
Mal B. **15** 52 50N 9 30W
Mal i Gjalicës së Lumës **44** 42 2N 20 25E
Mal i Gribës **44** 40 17N 19 45E
Mal i Nemërçkës **44** 40 15N 20 15E
Mal i Tomorit **44** 40 42N 20 11E
Mala Kapela **39** 44 45N 15 30E
Mala, Pta. **121** 7 28N 80 2W
Malabang **73** 7 36N 124 3E
Malabar Coast **70** 11 0N 75 0E
Malacca, Str. of **71** 3 0N 101 0E
Malacky **27** 48 27N 17 0E
Malad City **118** 42 10N 112 20E
Málaga **31** 36 43N 4 23W
Malaga **117** 32 12N 104 2W
Málaga □ **31** 36 38N 4 58W
Malagarasi **90** 5 5S 30 50E
Malagarasi → **90** 5 12S 29 47E
Malagón **31** 39 11N 3 52W
Malagón → **31** 37 35N 7 29W
Malaimbandy **93** 20 20S 45 36E
Malakâl **87** 9 33N 31 40E
Malakand **66** 34 40N 71 55E
Malakoff **117** 32 10N 95 55W
Malamyzh **59** 50 0N 136 50E
Malang **73** 7 59S 112 45E
Malanje **88** 9 36S 16 17E
Mälaren **48** 59 30N 17 10E
Malargüe **124** 35 32S 69 30W
Malartic **106** 48 9N 78 9W
Malatya **64** 38 25N 38 20E
Malawi ■ **91** 13 0S 34 0E
Malawi, L. **91** 12 30S 34 30E
Malay Pen. **71** 7 25N 100 0E
* Malaya □ **71** 4 0N 102 0E

* *Renamed Peninsular Malaysia*

† *Renamed Lesosibirsk*

** *Renamed Butaritari*

Malaya Belozërka **56** 47 12N 34 56E
Malaya Vishera **54** 58 55N 32 25E
Malaya Viska **56** 48 39N 31 36E
Malaybalay **73** 8 5N 125 7E
Malāyer **64** 34 19N 48 51E
Malaysia ■ **72** 5 0N 110 0E
Malazgirt **64** 39 10N 42 33E
Malbaie, La **107** 47 40N 70 10W
Malbon **98** 21 5S 140 17E
Malbork **28** 54 3N 19 1E
Malcésine **38** 45 46N 10 48E
Malchin **24** 53 43N 12 44E
Malchow **24** 53 29N 12 25E
Malcolm **96** 28 51S 121 25E
Malczyce **28** 51 14N 16 29E
Maldegem **16** 51 14N 3 26E
Malden, Mass., U.S.A. **113** 42 26N 71 5W
Malden, Mo., U.S.A. **117** 36 35N 90 0W
Malden I. **95** 4 3S 155 1W
Maldives ■ **60** 7 0N 73 0E
Maldonado **125** 35 0S 55 0W
Maldonado, Punta **120** 16 19N 98 35W
Malé **38** 46 20N 10 55E
Malé Karpaty **27** 48 30N 17 20E
Maléa, Ákra **45** 36 28N 23 7E
Malegaon **68** 20 30N 74 38E
Malei **91** 17 12S 36 58E
Malela **90** 4 22S 26 8E
Målerås **49** 56 54N 15 34E
Malerkotla **68** 30 32N 75 58E
Máles **45** 35 6N 25 35E
Malesherbes **19** 48 15N 2 24E
Maleshevska Planina **42** 41 38N 23 7E
Malestroit **18** 47 49N 2 25W
Malfa **41** 38 35N 14 50E
Malgobek **57** 43 30N 44 34E
Malgomaj **50** 64 40N 16 30E
Malgrat **32** 41 39N 2 46E
Malha **81** 15 8N 25 10E
Malheur → **118** 44 3N 116 59W
Malheur L. **118** 43 19N 118 42W
Mali **84** 12 10N 12 20W
Mali ■ **85** 15 0N 2 0W
Mali → **67** 25 40N 97 40E
Mali Kanal **42** 45 36N 19 24E
Mali Kyun **71** 13 0N 98 20E
Malih → **62** 32 20N 35 34E
Malik **73** 0 39S 123 16E
Malili **73** 2 42S 121 6E
Malimba, Mts. **90** 7 30S 29 30E
Malin **54** 50 46N 29 3E
Malin Hd. **15** 55 18N 7 24W
Malinau **72** 3 35N 116 40E
Malindi **90** 3 12S 40 5E
Maling **73** 1 0N 121 0E
Malingping **73** 6 45S 106 2E
Malinyi **91** 8 56S 36 0E
Maliqi **44** 40 45N 20 48E
Malita **73** 6 19N 125 39E
Maljenik **42** 43 59N 21 55E
Malkapur, Maharashtra, India **68** 20 53N 73 58E
Malkapur, Maharashtra, India **70** 16 57N 73 58E
Małkinia Górna **28** 52 42N 22 5E
Malko Tŭrnovo **43** 41 59N 27 31E
Mallacoota **100** 37 40S 149 40E
Mallacoota Inlet **97** 37 34S 149 40E
Mallaig **14** 57 0N 5 50W
Mallawan **69** 27 4N 80 12E
Mallawi **86** 27 44N 30 44E
Mallemort **21** 43 44N 5 11E
Málles Venosta **38** 46 42N 10 32E
Mállia **45** 35 17N 25 27E
Mallorca **32** 39 30N 3 0E
Mallorytown **113** 44 29N 75 53W
Mallow **15** 52 8N 8 40W
Malmbäck **49** 57 34N 14 28E
Malmberget **50** 67 11N 20 40E
Malmédy **16** 50 25N 6 2E
Malmesbury **92** 33 28S 18 41E
Malmö **49** 55 36N 12 59E
Malmöhus län □ **49** 55 45N 13 30E
Malmslätt **49** 58 27N 15 33E
Malmyzh **55** 56 35N 50 41E
Malnaş **46** 46 2N 25 49E
Malo Konare **43** 42 12N 24 24E
Maloarkhangelsk **55** 52 28N 36 30E
Malolos **73** 14 50N 120 49E
Malombe L. **91** 14 40S 35 15E
Malomir **43** 42 16N 26 30E
Malone **114** 44 50N 74 19W
Malorad **43** 43 28N 23 41E
Malorita **54** 51 50N 24 3E
Maloyaroslovets **55** 55 2N 36 20E
Malozemelskaya Tundra **52** 67 0N 50 0E
Malpartida **31** 39 26N 6 30W
Malpelo **126** 4 3N 81 35W
Malpica **30** 43 19N 8 50W
Malprabha → **70** 16 20N 76 5E
Malta, Idaho, U.S.A. **118** 42 15N 113 30W
Malta, Mont., U.S.A. **118** 48 20N 107 55W
Malta ■ **36** 35 50N 14 30E
Malta Channel **40** 36 40N 14 0E
Malton, Can. **112** 43 42N 79 38W
Malton, U.K. **12** 54 9N 0 48W
Maluku **73** 1 0S 127 0E
Maluku □ **73** 3 0S 128 0E
Maluku, Kepulauan **73** 3 0S 128 0E
Malumfashi **85** 11 48N 7 39E
Malung **48** 60 42N 13 44E
Malvalli **70** 12 28N 77 8E
Malvan **70** 16 2N 73 30E
Malvern, U.K. **13** 52 7N 2 19W
Malvern, U.S.A. **117** 34 22N 92 50W
Malvern Hills **13** 52 0N 2 19W
Malvérnia **93** 22 6S 31 42E
Malvik **47** 63 25N 10 40E
Malvinas, Is. = Falkland Is. **128** 51 30S 59 0W
Malya **90** 3 5S 33 38E
Malyy Lyakhovskiy, Ostrov **59** 74 7N 140 36E
Mama **59** 58 18N 112 54E
Mamadysh **55** 55 44N 51 23E
Mamahatun **64** 39 50N 40 23E

Mamaia	**46**	44 18N	28 37 E
Mamanguape	**127**	6 50 S	35 4W
Mamasa	**73**	2 55 S	119 20 E
Mambasa	**90**	1 22N	29 3 E
Mamberamo →	**73**	2 0 S	137 50 E
Mambilima	**91**	10 31 S	28 45 E
Mambirima	**91**	11 25 S	27 33 E
Mambo	**90**	4 52 S	38 22 E
Mambrui	**90**	3 5 S	40 5 E
Mamburao	**73**	13 13N	120 39 E
Mameigwess L.	**106**	52 35N	87 50W
Mamers	**18**	48 21N	0 22 E
Mamfe	**85**	5 50N	9 15 E
Mámmola	**41**	38 23N	16 13 E
Mammoth	**119**	32 46N	110 43W
Mamoré →	**126**	10 23 S	65 53W
Mamou	**84**	10 15N	12 0W
Mampatá	**84**	11 54N	14 53W
Mampawah	**72**	0 30N	109 5 E
Mampong	**85**	7 6N	1 26W
Mamry, Jezioro	**28**	54 5N	21 50 E
Mamuju	**73**	2 41 S	118 50 E
Man	**84**	7 30N	7 40W
Man →	**70**	17 31N	75 32 E
Man, I. of	**12**	54 15N	4 30W
Man Na	**67**	23 27N	97 19 E
Mana	**127**	5 45N	53 55W
Måna →	**47**	59 55N	8 50 E
Manaar, Gulf of	**70**	8 30N	79 0 E
Manacapuru	**126**	3 16 S	60 37W
Manacor	**32**	39 34N	3 13 E
Manado	**73**	1 29N	124 51 E
Managua	**121**	12 6N	86 20W
Managua, L.	**121**	12 20N	86 30W
Manakara	**93**	22 8 S	48 1 E
Manam I.	**98**	4 5 S	145 0 E
Manamāh, Al	**65**	26 11N	50 35 E
Manambao →	**93**	17 35 S	44 0 E
Manambato	**93**	13 43 S	49 7 E
Manambolo →	**93**	19 18 S	44 22 E
Manambolosy	**93**	16 2 S	49 40 E
Mananara	**93**	16 10 S	49 46 E
Mananara →	**93**	23 21 S	47 42 E
Mananjary	**93**	21 13 S	48 20 E
Manantenina	**93**	24 17 S	47 19 E
Manaos = Manaus	**126**	3 0 S	60 0W
Manapouri	**101**	45 34 S	167 39 E
Manapouri, L.	**101**	45 32 S	167 32 E
Manar →	**70**	18 50N	77 20 E
Manas	**75**	44 17N	85 56 E
Manasir	**65**	24 30N	51 10 E
Manaslu, Mt.	**69**	28 33N	84 33 E
Manasquan	**113**	40 7N	74 3W
Manassa	**119**	37 12N	105 58W
Manaung	**67**	18 45N	93 40 E
Manaus	**126**	3 0 S	60 0W
Manawan L.	**109**	55 24N	103 14W
Manay	**73**	7 17N	126 33 E
Mancelona	**114**	44 54N	85 5W
Mancha, La	**33**	39 10N	2 54W
Mancha Real	**31**	37 48N	3 39W
Manche □	**18**	49 10N	1 20W
Manchegorsk	**52**	67 40N	32 40 E
Manchester, U.K.	**12**	53 30N	2 15W
Manchester, Conn., U.S.A.	**114**	41 47N	72 30W
Manchester, Ga., U.S.A.	**115**	32 53N	84 32W
Manchester, Iowa, U.S.A.	**116**	42 28N	91 27W
Manchester, Ky., U.S.A.	**114**	37 9N	83 45W
Manchester, N.H., U.S.A.	**114**	42 58N	71 29W
Manchester, N.Y., U.S.A.	**112**	42 56N	77 16W
Manchester, Vt., U.S.A.	**113**	43 10N	73 5W
Manchester L.	**109**	61 28N	107 29W
Manciano	**39**	42 35N	11 30 E
Mancifa	**87**	6 53N	41 50 E
Mand →	**65**	28 20N	52 30 E
Manda, Chunya, Tanz.	**90**	6 51 S	32 29 E
Manda, Ludewe, Tanz.	**91**	10 30 S	34 40 E
Mandaguari	**125**	23 32 S	51 42W
Mandal	**47**	58 2N	7 25 E
Mandalay	**67**	22 0N	96 4 E
Mandale = Mandalay	**67**	22 0N	96 4 E
Mandalī	**64**	33 43N	45 28 E
Mandalya Körfezi	**45**	37 15N	27 20 E
Mandan	**116**	46 50N	101 0W
Mandapeta	**70**	16 47N	81 56 E
Mandar, Teluk	**73**	3 35 S	119 15 E
Mandas	**40**	39 40N	9 8 E
Mandasaur	**68**	24 3N	75 8 E
Mandasor = Mandasaur	**68**	24 3N	75 8 E
Mandawai (Katingan) →	**72**	3 30 S	113 0 E
Mandelieu-la-Napoule	**21**	43 34N	6 57 E
Mandera	**90**	3 55N	41 53 E
Mandera □	**90**	3 30N	41 0 E
Mandi	**68**	31 39N	76 58 E
Mandioli	**73**	0 40 S	127 20 E
Mandla	**69**	22 39N	80 30 E
Mandø	**49**	55 18N	8 33 E
Mandoto	**93**	19 34 S	46 17 E
Mandoúdhion	**45**	38 48N	23 29 E
Mandráki	**45**	36 36N	27 11 E
Mandrare →	**93**	25 10 S	46 30 E
Mandritsara	**93**	15 50 S	48 49 E
Mandúria	**41**	40 25N	17 38 E
Mandvi	**68**	22 51N	69 22 E
Mandya	**70**	12 30N	77 0 E
Mandzai	**68**	30 55N	67 6 E
Mané	**85**	12 59N	1 21W
Manengouba, Mts.	**85**	5 0N	9 50 E
Maner →	**70**	18 30N	79 40 E
Maneroo	**98**	23 22 S	143 53 E
Maneroo Cr. →	**98**	23 21 S	143 53 E
Manfalût	**86**	27 20N	30 52 E
Manfred	**99**	33 19 S	143 45 E
Manfredónia	**41**	41 40N	15 55 E
Manfredónia, G. di	**41**	41 30N	16 10 E
Manga, Niger	**85**	15 0N	14 0 E
Manga, Upp. Vol.	**85**	11 40N	1 4W
Mangaia	**101**	21 55 S	157 55W
Mangalagiri	**70**	16 26N	80 36 E
Mangalia	**46**	43 50N	28 35 E
Mangalore	**70**	12 55N	74 47 E
Manganeses	**30**	41 45N	5 43W
Mangaon	**70**	18 15N	73 20 E
Manger	**47**	60 38N	5 3 E
Manggar	**72**	2 50 S	108 10 E
Manggawitu	**73**	4 8 S	133 32 E
Mangkalihat, Tanjung	**73**	1 2N	118 59 E
Manglaur	**68**	29 44N	77 49 E
Mangnai	**75**	37 52N	91 43 E
Mango	**85**	10 20N	0 30 E
Mangoky →	**93**	21 29 S	43 41 E
Mangole	**73**	1 50 S	125 55 E
Mangombe	**90**	1 20 S	26 48 E
Mangonui	**101**	35 1 S	173 32 E
Mangualde	**30**	40 38N	7 48W
Mangueigne	**81**	10 30N	21 15 E
Mangueira, Lagoa da	**125**	33 0 S	52 50W
Manguéni, Hamada	**83**	22 35N	12 40 E
Mangum	**117**	34 50N	99 30W
Mangyshlak P-ov.	**57**	44 30N	52 30 E
Mangyshlakskiy Zaliv	**57**	44 40N	50 50 E
Manhattan, Kans., U.S.A.	**116**	39 10N	96 40W
Manhattan, Nev., U.S.A.	**119**	38 31N	117 3W
Manhiça	**93**	25 23 S	32 49 E
Manhuaçu	**127**	20 15 S	42 2W
Mania →	**93**	19 42 S	45 22 E
Maniago	**39**	46 11N	12 40 E
Manica e Sofala □	**93**	19 10 S	33 45 E
Manicaland □	**91**	19 0 S	32 30 E
Manicoré	**126**	5 48 S	61 16W
Manicouagan →	**107**	49 30N	68 30W
Manicouagan L.	**107**	51 25N	68 15W
Manīfah	**64**	27 44N	49 0 E
Manigotagan	**109**	51 6N	96 18W
Manigotagan L.	**109**	50 52N	95 37W
Manihiki	**95**	10 24 S	161 1W
Manika, Plat. de la	**91**	10 0 S	25 5 E
Manila, Phil.	**73**	14 40N	121 3 E
Manila, U.S.A.	**118**	41 0N	109 44W
Manila B.	**73**	14 0N	120 0 E
Manilla	**99**	30 45 S	150 43 E
Manimpé	**84**	14 11N	5 28W
Manipur □	**67**	25 0N	94 0 E
Manipur →	**67**	23 45N	94 20 E
Manisa	**64**	38 38N	27 30 E
Manistee	**114**	44 15N	86 20W
Manistee →	**114**	44 15N	86 21W
Manistique	**114**	45 59N	86 18W
Manito L.	**109**	52 43N	109 43W
Manitoba □	**109**	55 30N	97 0W
Manitoba, L.	**109**	51 0N	98 45W
Manitou	**109**	49 15N	98 32W
Manitou I.	**106**	47 22N	87 30W
Manitou Is.	**114**	45 8N	86 0W
Manitou L., Ont., Can.	**109**	49 15N	93 0W
Manitou L., Qué., Can.	**107**	50 55N	65 17W
Manitou Springs	**116**	38 52N	104 55W
Manitoulin I.	**106**	45 40N	82 30W
Manitowaning	**106**	45 46N	81 49W
Manitowoc	**114**	44 8N	87 40W
Manizales	**126**	5 5N	75 32W
Manja	**93**	21 26 S	44 20 E
Manjakandriana	**93**	18 55 S	47 47 E
Manjeri	**70**	11 7N	76 11 E
Manjhand	**68**	25 50N	68 10 E
Manjil	**64**	36 46N	49 30 E
Manjimup	**96**	34 15 S	116 6 E
Manjra →	**70**	18 49N	77 52 E
Mankato, Kans., U.S.A.	**116**	39 49N	98 11W
Mankato, Minn., U.S.A.	**116**	44 8N	93 59W
Mankayana	**93**	26 38 S	31 6 E
Mankono	**84**	8 1N	6 10W
Mankota	**109**	49 25N	107 5W
Manlleu	**32**	42 2N	2 17 E
Manly	**99**	33 48 S	151 17 E
Manmad	**70**	20 18N	74 28 E
Manna	**72**	4 25 S	102 55 E
Mannahill	**99**	32 25 S	140 0 E
Mannar	**70**	9 1N	79 54 E
Mannar, G. of	**70**	8 30N	79 0 E
Mannar I.	**70**	9 5N	79 45 E
Mannargudi	**70**	10 45N	79 51 E
Mannheim	**25**	49 28N	8 29 E
Manning, Can.	**108**	56 53N	117 39W
Manning, U.S.A.	**115**	33 40N	80 9W
Manning →	**100**	31 52 S	152 43 E
Manning Prov. Park	**108**	49 5N	120 45W
Mannington	**114**	39 35N	80 25W
Mannu →	**40**	39 15N	9 32 E
Mannu, C.	**40**	40 2N	8 24 E
Mannum	**99**	34 50 S	139 20 E
Mano	**84**	8 3N	12 2W
Manokwari	**73**	0 54 S	134 0 E
Manolás	**45**	38 4N	21 21 E
Manombo	**93**	22 57 S	43 28 E
Manono	**90**	7 15 S	27 25 E
Manosque	**21**	43 49N	5 47 E
Manouane L.	**107**	50 45N	70 45W
Manresa	**32**	41 48N	1 50 E
Mans, Le	**18**	48 0N	0 10 E
Mansa, Gujarat, India	**68**	23 27N	72 45 E
Mansa, Punjab, India	**68**	30 0N	75 27 E
Mansa, Zambia	**91**	11 13 S	28 55 E
Mansel I.	**105**	62 0N	80 0W
Mansfield, Austral.	**100**	37 4 S	146 6 E
Mansfield, U.K.	**12**	53 8N	1 12W
Mansfield, La., U.S.A.	**117**	32 2N	93 40W
Mansfield, Mass., U.S.A.	**113**	42 2N	71 12W
Mansfield, Ohio, U.S.A.	**114**	40 45N	82 30W
Mansfield, Pa., U.S.A.	**112**	41 48N	77 4W
Mansfield, Wash., U.S.A.	**118**	47 51N	119 44W
Mansilla de las Mulas	**30**	42 30N	5 25W
Mansle	**20**	45 52N	0 9 E
Mansoa	**84**	12 0N	15 20W
Manson Creek	**108**	55 37N	124 32W
Mansoura	**83**	36 1N	4 31 E
Manta	**126**	1 0 S	80 40W
Mantalingajan, Mt.	**72**	8 55N	117 45 E
Mantare	**90**	2 42 S	33 13 E
Manteca	**119**	37 50N	121 12W
Manteo	**115**	35 55N	75 41W
Mantes-la-Jolie	**19**	49 0N	1 41 E
Manthani	**70**	18 40N	79 35 E
Manthelan	**18**	47 9N	0 47 E
Manti	**118**	39 23N	111 32W
Mantiqueira, Serra da	**125**	22 0 S	44 0W
Manton	**114**	44 23N	85 25W
Mantorp	**49**	58 21N	15 20 E
Mántova	**38**	45 20N	10 42 E
Mänttä	**50**	62 0N	24 40 E
Mantua = Mántova	**38**	45 20N	10 42 E
Manturovo	**55**	58 30N	44 30 E
Manu	**126**	12 10 S	70 51W
Manua Is.	**101**	14 13 S	169 35W
Manuel Alves →	**127**	11 19 S	48 28W
Manui	**73**	3 35 S	123 5 E
Manukan	**73**	8 14N	123 3 E
Manus I.	**98**	2 0 S	147 0 E
Manvi	**70**	15 57N	76 59 E
Manville	**116**	42 48N	104 36W
Manwath	**70**	19 19N	76 32 E
Many	**117**	31 36N	93 28W
Manyane	**92**	23 21 S	21 42 E
Manyara, L.	**90**	3 40 S	35 50 E
Manych →	**57**	47 15N	40 0 E
Manych-Gudilo, Oz.	**57**	46 24N	42 38 E
Manyonga →	**90**	4 10 S	34 15 E
Manyoni	**90**	5 45 S	34 55 E
Manyoni □	**90**	6 30 S	34 30 E
Manzai	**68**	32 12N	70 15 E
Manzala, Bahra el	**86**	31 10N	31 56 E
Manzanares	**33**	39 0N	3 22W
Manzaneda, Cabeza de	**30**	42 12N	7 15W
Manzanillo, Cuba	**121**	20 20N	77 31W
Manzanillo, Mexico	**120**	19 0N	104 20W
Manzanillo, Pta.	**121**	9 30N	79 40W
Manzano Mts.	**119**	34 30N	106 45W
Manzhouli	**75**	49 35N	117 25 E
Manzini	**93**	26 30 S	31 25 E
Mao	**81**	14 4N	15 19 E
Maoke, Pegunungan	**73**	3 40 S	137 30 E
Maoming	**75**	21 50N	110 54 E
Mapam Yumco	**75**	30 45N	81 28 E
Mapia, Kepulauan	**73**	0 50N	134 20 E
Mapimí	**120**	25 50N	103 50W
Mapimí, Bolsón de	**120**	27 30N	104 15W
Mapinga	**90**	6 40 S	39 12 E
Mapinhane	**93**	22 20 S	35 0 E
Maple Creek	**109**	49 55N	109 29W
Mapleton	**118**	44 4N	123 58W
Maplewood	**116**	38 33N	90 18W
Maprik	**98**	3 44 S	143 3 E
Mapuca	**70**	15 36N	73 46 E
Mapuera →	**126**	1 5 S	57 2W
Maputo	**93**	25 58 S	32 32 E
Maputo, B. de	**93**	25 50 S	32 45 E
Maqnā	**64**	28 25N	34 50 E
Maquela do Zombo	**88**	6 0 S	15 15 E
Maquinchao	**128**	41 15 S	68 50W
Maquoketa	**116**	42 4N	90 40W
Mår →	**47**	59 59N	8 46 E
Mar Chiquita, L.	**124**	30 40 S	62 50W
Mar del Plata	**124**	38 0 S	57 30W
Mar Menor, L.	**33**	37 40N	0 45W
Mar, Serra do	**125**	25 30 S	49 0W
Mara	**90**	1 30 S	34 32 E
Mara □	**90**	1 45 S	34 20 E
Maraã	**126**	1 52 S	65 25W
Marabá	**127**	5 20 S	49 5W
Maracá, I. de	**127**	2 10N	50 30W
Maracaibo	**126**	10 40N	71 37W
Maracaibo, Lago de	**126**	9 40N	71 30W
Maracaju	**125**	21 38 S	55 9W
Maracay	**126**	10 15N	67 28W
Marādah	**83**	29 15N	19 15 E
Maradi	**85**	13 29N	8 10 E
Maradun	**85**	12 35N	6 18 E
Marāgheh	**64**	37 30N	46 12 E
Marāh	**64**	25 0N	45 35 E
Marajó, Ilha de	**127**	1 0 S	49 30W
Maralal	**90**	1 0N	36 38 E
Maralinga	**96**	30 13 S	131 32 E
Marama	**99**	35 10 S	140 10 E
Marampa	**84**	8 45N	12 28W
Maramureş □	**46**	47 45N	24 0 E
Marana	**119**	32 30N	111 9W
Maranchón	**32**	41 6N	2 15W
Marand	**64**	38 30N	45 45 E
Marandellas	**91**	18 5 S	31 42 E
Maranguape	**127**	3 55 S	38 50W
Maranhão = São Luis	**127**	2 39 S	44 15W
Maranhão □	**127**	5 0 S	46 0W
Marano, L. di	**39**	45 42N	13 13 E
Maranoa →	**97**	27 50 S	148 37 E
Marañón →	**126**	4 30 S	73 35W
Maraş	**64**	37 37N	36 53 E
Mărăşeşti	**46**	45 52N	27 14 E
Maratea	**41**	39 59N	15 43 E
Marateca	**31**	38 34N	8 40W
Marathókambos	**45**	37 43N	26 42 E
Marathon, Austral.	**98**	20 51 S	143 32 E
Marathon, Can.	**106**	48 44N	86 23W
Marathón	**45**	38 11N	23 58 E
Marathon, N.Y., U.S.A.	**113**	42 25N	76 3W
Marathon, Tex., U.S.A.	**117**	30 15N	103 15W
Maratua	**73**	2 10N	118 35 E
Marbella	**31**	36 30N	4 57W
Marble Bar	**96**	21 9 S	119 44 E
Marble Falls	**117**	30 30N	98 15W
Marblehead	**113**	42 29N	70 51W
Marburg	**24**	50 49N	8 36 E
Marby	**48**	63 7N	14 18 E
Marcal →	**27**	47 41N	17 32 E
Marcali	**27**	46 35N	17 25 E
Marcaria	**38**	45 7N	10 34 E
March	**13**	52 33N	0 5 E
Marchand = Rommani	**82**	33 20N	6 40W
Marché	**20**	46 0N	1 20 E
Marche □	**39**	43 22N	13 10 E
Marche-en-Famenne	**16**	50 14N	5 19 E
Marchena	**31**	37 18N	5 23W
Marches = Marche	**39**	43 22N	13 10 E
Marciana Marina	**38**	42 44N	10 12 E
Marcianise	**41**	41 3N	14 16 E
Marcigny	**21**	46 17N	4 2 E
Marcillac-Vallon	**20**	44 29N	2 27 E
Marcillat	**20**	46 12N	2 38 E
Marck	**19**	50 57N	1 57 E
Marckolsheim	**19**	48 10N	7 30 E
Marcos Juárez	**124**	32 42 S	62 5W
Marcus	**94**	24 0N	153 45 E
Marcus Necker Ridge	**94**	20 0N	175 0 E
Marcy Mt.	**113**	44 7N	73 55W
Mardin	**64**	37 20N	40 43 E
Maree L.	**14**	57 40N	5 30W
Mareeba	**97**	16 59 S	145 28 E
Marek	**73**	4 41 S	120 24 E
Marek = Stanke Dimitrov	**42**	42 17N	23 9 E
Maremma	**38**	42 45N	11 15 E
Maréna	**84**	14 0N	7 20W
Marenberg	**39**	46 38N	15 13 E
Marengo	**116**	41 42N	92 5W
Marennes	**20**	45 49N	1 7W
Marenyi	**90**	4 22 S	39 8 E
Marerano	**93**	21 23 S	44 52 E
Maréttimo	**40**	37 58N	12 5 E
Mareuil-sur-Lay	**20**	46 32N	1 14W
Marfa	**117**	30 15N	104 0W
Marganets	**56**	47 40N	34 40 E
Margao	**70**	15 12N	73 58 E
Margaret Bay	**108**	51 20N	126 35W
Margaret L.	**108**	58 56N	115 25W
Margarita	**120**	9 20N	79 55W
Margarita, Isla de	**126**	11 0N	64 0W
Margarítion	**44**	39 22N	20 26 E
Margate, S. Afr.	**93**	30 50 S	30 20 E
Margate, U.K.	**13**	51 23N	1 24 E
Margeride, Mts. de la	**20**	44 43N	3 38 E
Margherita di Savola	**41**	41 25N	16 5 E
Marghita	**46**	47 22N	22 22 E
Margonin	**28**	52 58N	17 5 E
Marguerite	**108**	52 30N	122 25W
Marhoum	**82**	34 27N	0 11W
Mari, A.S.S.R. □	**55**	56 30N	48 0 E
María Elena	**124**	22 18 S	69 40W
María Grande	**124**	31 45 S	59 55W
Maria I.	**96**	14 52 S	135 45 E
Maria van Diemen, C.	**101**	34 29 S	172 40 E
Mariager	**49**	56 40N	10 0 E
Mariager Fjord	**49**	56 42N	10 19 E
Mariakani	**90**	3 50 S	39 27 E
Marian L.	**108**	63 0N	116 15W
Mariana Is.	**94**	17 0N	145 0 E
Mariana Trench	**94**	13 0N	145 0 E
Marianao	**121**	23 8N	82 24W
Marianna, Ark., U.S.A.	**117**	34 48N	90 48W
Marianna, Fla., U.S.A.	**115**	30 45N	85 15W
Mariannelund	**49**	57 37N	15 35 E
Mariánské Lázně	**26**	49 48N	12 41 E
Marias →	**118**	47 56N	110 30W
Mariato, Punta	**121**	7 12N	80 52W
Mariazell	**26**	47 47N	15 19 E
Ma'rib	**63**	15 25N	45 30 E
Maribo	**49**	54 48N	11 30 E
Maribor	**39**	46 36N	15 40 E
Marico →	**92**	23 35 S	26 57 E
Maricopa, Ariz., U.S.A.	**119**	33 5N	112 2W
Maricopa, Calif., U.S.A.	**119**	35 7N	119 27W
Marîdî	**87**	4 55N	29 25 E
Maridi, Wadi →	**87**	6 15N	29 21 E
Marie-Galante	**121**	15 56N	61 16W
Mariecourt	**105**	61 30N	72 0W
Mariefred	**48**	59 15N	17 12 E
Mariehamn	**51**	60 5N	19 55 E
Marienberg, Ger.	**24**	50 40N	13 10 E
Marienberg, Neth.	**16**	52 30N	6 35 E
Marienbourg	**16**	50 6N	4 31 E
Mariental	**92**	24 36 S	18 0 E
Marienville	**112**	41 27N	79 8W
Mariestad	**49**	58 43N	13 50 E
Marietta, Ga., U.S.A.	**115**	34 0N	84 30W
Marietta, Ohio, U.S.A.	**114**	39 27N	81 27W
Marieville	**113**	45 26N	73 10W
Marignane	**21**	43 25N	5 13 E
Mariinsk	**58**	56 10N	87 20 E
Mariinskiy Posad	**55**	56 10N	47 45 E
Marília	**125**	22 13 S	50 0W
Marín	**30**	42 23N	8 42W
Marina di Cirò	**41**	39 22N	17 8 E
Mariña, La	**30**	43 30N	7 40W
Marina Plains	**98**	14 37 S	143 57 E
Marinduque	**73**	13 25N	122 0 E
Marine City	**114**	42 45N	82 29W
Marinel, Le	**91**	10 25 S	25 17 E
Marineo	**40**	37 57N	13 23 E
Marinette, Ariz., U.S.A.	**119**	33 41N	112 16W
Marinette, Wis., U.S.A.	**114**	45 4N	87 40W
Maringá	**125**	23 26 S	52 2W
Marinha Grande	**31**	39 45N	8 56W
Marion, Ala., U.S.A.	**115**	32 33N	87 20W
Marion, Ill., U.S.A.	**117**	37 45N	88 55W
Marion, Ind., U.S.A.	**114**	40 35N	85 40W
Marion, Iowa, U.S.A.	**116**	42 2N	91 36W
Marion, Kans., U.S.A.	**116**	38 25N	97 2W
Marion, Mich., U.S.A.	**114**	44 7N	85 8W
Marion, N.C., U.S.A.	**115**	35 42N	82 0W
Marion, Ohio, U.S.A.	**114**	40 38N	83 8W
Marion, S.C., U.S.A.	**115**	34 11N	79 22W
Marion, Va., U.S.A.	**115**	36 51N	81 29W
Marion, L.	**115**	33 30N	80 15W
Marion Reef	**97**	19 10 S	152 17 E
Mariposa	**119**	37 31N	119 59W
Mariscal Estigarribia	**124**	22 3 S	60 40W
Maritime Alps = Alpes Maritimes	**38**	44 10N	7 10 E
Maritsa	**43**	42 1N	25 50 E
Maritsá	**45**	36 22N	28 10 E
Maritsa →	**43**	42 15N	24 0 E
Mariyampole = Kapsukas	**54**	54 33N	23 19 E
Marka	**86**	18 14N	41 19 E
Markapur	**70**	15 44N	79 19 E
Markaryd	**49**	56 28N	13 35 E
Markdale	**112**	44 19N	80 39W
Marked Tree	**117**	35 35N	90 24W
Markelsdorfer Huk	**24**	54 33N	11 0 E
Marken	**16**	52 26N	5 12 E
Market Drayton	**12**	52 55N	2 30W
Market Harborough	**13**	52 29N	0 55W

Markham **112** 43 52N 79 16W
Markham → **98** 6 41 S 147 2 E
Markham I. **4** 84 0N 0 45W
Markham L. **109** 62 30N 102 35W
Markham Mt. **5** 83 0 S 164 0 E
Marki **28** 52 20N 21 2 E
Markoupoulon **45** 37 53N 23 57 E
Markovac **42** 44 14N 21 7 E
Markovo **59** 64 40N 169 40 E
Markoye **85** 14 39N 0 2 E
Marks **55** 51 45N 46 50 E
Marksville **117** 31 10N 92 2W
Markt Schwaben **25** 48 14N 11 49 E
Marktredwitz **25** 50 1N 12 2 E
Marlboro **113** 42 19N 71 33W
Marlborough **98** 22 46 S 149 52 E
Marlborough □ **101** 41 45 S 173 33 E
Marlborough Downs **13** 51 25N 1 55W
Marle **19** 49 43N 3 47 E
Marlin **117** 31 25N 96 50W
Marlow, Ger. **24** 54 8N 12 34 E
Marlow, U.S.A. **117** 34 40N 97 58W
Marmagao **70** 15 25N 73 56 E
Marmande **20** 44 30N 0 10 E
Marmara **56** 40 35N 27 38 E
Marmara Denizi **64** 40 45N 28 15 E
Marmara, Sea of = Marmara Denizi **64** 40 45N 28 15 E
Marmaris **64** 36 50N 28 14 E
Marmarth **116** 46 21N 103 52W
Marmion L. **106** 48 55N 91 20W
Marmolada, Mte. **39** 46 25N 11 55 E
Marmolejo **31** 38 3N 4 13W
Marmora **106** 44 28N 77 41W
Marnay **19** 47 20N 5 48 E
Marne **24** 53 57N 9 1 E
Marne □ **19** 49 0N 4 10 E
Marne → **19** 8 23N 18 36 E
Marnoo **100** 36 40 S 142 54 E
Marnueli **57** 41 30N 44 48 E
Maroala **93** 15 23 S 47 59 E
Maroantsetra **93** 15 26 S 49 44 E
Maromandia **93** 14 13 S 48 5 E
Maroni → **127** 4 0N 52 0W
Marónia **44** 40 53N 25 24 E
Maroochydore **99** 26 29 S 153 5 E
Maroona **99** 37 27 S 142 54 E
Maros → **27** 46 15N 20 13 E
Marosakoa **93** 15 26 S 46 38 E
Marostica **39** 45 44N 11 40 E
Maroua **85** 10 40N 14 20 E
Marovoay **93** 16 6 S 46 39 E
Marquard **92** 28 40 S 27 28 E
Marqueira **31** 38 41N 9 9W
Marquesas Is. **95** 9 30 S 140 0W
Marquette **114** 46 30N 87 21W
Marquise **19** 50 50N 1 40 E
Marra, Gebel **87** 7 20N 27 35 E
Marradi **39** 44 5N 11 37 E
Marrakech **82** 31 9N 8 0W
Marrawah **99** 40 55 S 144 42 E
Marree **97** 29 39 S 138 1 E
Marrimane **93** 22 58 S 33 34 E
Marronne → **20** 45 4N 1 56 E
Marroquí, Punta **31** 36 0N 5 37W
Marrowie Creek **99** 33 23 S 145 40 E
Marrubane **91** 18 0 S 37 0 E
Marrupa **91** 13 8 S 37 30 E
Mars, Le **116** 43 0N 96 0W
Marsa Brega **83** 30 24N 19 37 E
Marsá Susah **81** 32 52N 21 59 E
Marsabit **90** 2 18N 38 0 E
Marsabit □ **90** 2 45N 37 45 E
Marsala **40** 37 48N 12 25 E
Marsaxlokk (Medport) **36** 35 47N 14 32 E
Marsciano **39** 42 54N 12 20 E
Marsden **99** 33 47 S 147 32 E
Marseillan **20** 43 23N 3 31 E
Marseille **21** 43 18N 5 23 E
Marseilles = Marseille **21** 43 18N 5 23 E
Marsh I. **117** 29 35N 91 50W
Marsh L. **116** 45 5N 96 0W
Marshall, Liberia **84** 6 8N 10 22W
Marshall, Ark., U.S.A. **117** 35 58N 92 40W
Marshall, Mich., U.S.A. **114** 42 17N 84 59W
Marshall, Minn., U.S.A. **116** 44 25N 95 45W
Marshall, Mo., U.S.A. **116** 39 8N 93 15W
Marshall, Tex., U.S.A. **117** 32 29N 94 20W
Marshall Is. **94** 9 0N 171 0 E
Marshalltown **116** 42 5N 92 56W
Marshfield, Mo., U.S.A. **117** 37 20N 92 58W
Marshfield, Wis., U.S.A. **116** 44 42N 90 10W
Mársico Nuovo **41** 40 26N 15 43 E
Märsta **48** 59 37N 17 52 E
Marstal **49** 54 51N 10 30 E
Marstrand **49** 57 53N 11 35 E
Mart **117** 31 34N 96 51W
Marta → **39** 42 14N 11 42 E
Martaban **67** 16 30N 97 35 E
Martaban, G. of **67** 16 5N 96 30 E
Martagne **18** 46 59N 0 57W
Martano **41** 40 14N 18 18 E
Martapura, Kalimantan, Indon. **72** 3 22 S 114 47 E
Martapura, Sumatera, Indon. **72** 4 19 S 104 22 E
Marte **85** 12 23N 13 46 E
Martel **20** 44 57N 1 37 E
Martelange **16** 49 49N 5 43 E
Martés, Sierra **33** 39 20N 1 0W
Marthaguy Creek → **99** 30 16 S 147 35 E
Martha's Vineyard **114** 41 25N 70 35W
Martigné-Ferchaud **18** 47 50N 1 20W
Martigny **25** 46 6N 7 3 E
Martigues **21** 43 24N 5 4 E
Martil **82** 35 36N 5 15W
Martin, Czech. **27** 49 6N 18 48 E
Martin, S.D., U.S.A. **116** 43 11N 101 45W
Martin, Tenn., U.S.A. **117** 36 23N 88 51W
Martín → **32** 41 18N 0 19W
Martin, L. **115** 32 45N 85 50W
Martina Franca **41** 40 42N 17 20 E
Martinborough **101** 41 14 S 175 29 E
Martinique **121** 14 40N 61 0W
Martinique Passage **121** 15 15N 61 0W
Martínon **45** 38 35N 23 15 E
Martinópolis **125** 22 11 S 51 12W
Martins Ferry **113** 40 5N 80 46W
Martinsberg **26** 48 22N 15 9 E
Martinsburg, Pa., U.S.A. **112** 40 18N 78 21W
Martinsburg, W. Va., U.S.A. **114** 39 30N 77 57W
Martinsville, Ind., U.S.A. **114** 39 29N 86 23W
Martinsville, Va., U.S.A. **115** 36 41N 79 52W
Marton **101** 40 4 S 175 23 E
Martorell **32** 41 28N 1 56 E
Martos **31** 37 44N 3 58W
Martuni **57** 40 9N 45 10 E
Maru **85** 12 22N 6 22 E
Marudi **72** 4 10N 114 19 E
Ma'ruf **65** 31 30N 67 6 E
Marugame **74** 34 15N 133 40 E
Marúggio **41** 40 20N 17 33 E
Marulan **99** 34 43 S 150 3 E
Marunga **92** 17 28 S 20 2 E
Marungu, Mts. **90** 7 30 S 30 0 E
Mårvatn **47** 60 8N 8 14 E
Marvejols **20** 44 33N 3 19 E
Marwar **68** 25 43N 73 45 E
Mary **58** 37 40N 61 50 E
Mary Frances L. **109** 63 19N 106 13W
Mary Kathleen **97** 20 44 S 139 48 E
Maryborough, Queens., Austral. **97** 25 31 S 152 37 E
Maryborough, Vic., Austral. **97** 37 0 S 143 44 E
Maryfield **109** 49 50N 101 35W
Maryland □ **114** 39 10N 76 40W
Maryland Jc. **91** 17 45 S 30 31 E
Maryport **12** 54 43N 3 30W
Mary's Harbour **107** 52 18N 55 51W
Marystown **107** 47 10N 55 10W
Marysvale **119** 38 25N 112 17W
Marysville, Can. **108** 49 35N 116 0W
Marysville, Calif., U.S.A. **118** 39 14N 121 40W
Marysville, Kans., U.S.A. **116** 39 50N 96 49W
Marysville, Mich., U.S.A. **112** 42 55N 82 29W
Marysville, Ohio, U.S.A. **114** 40 15N 83 20W
Maryvale **99** 28 4 S 152 12 E
Maryville **115** 35 50N 84 0W
Marzūq **83** 25 53N 13 57 E
Masada = Mesada **62** 31 20N 35 19 E
Masahunga **90** 2 6 S 33 18 E
Masai Steppe **90** 4 30 S 36 30 E
Masaka **90** 0 21 S 31 45 E
Masalembo, Kepulauan **72** 5 35 S 114 30 E
Masalima, Kepulauan **72** 5 4 S 117 5 E
Masamba **73** 2 30 S 120 15 E
Masan **76** 35 11N 128 32 E
Masanasa **33** 39 25N 0 25W
Masandam, Ras **65** 26 30N 56 30 E
Masasi **91** 10 45 S 38 52 E
Masasi □ **91** 10 45 S 38 50 E
Masaya **121** 12 0N 86 7W
Masba **85** 10 35N 13 1 E
Masbate **73** 12 21N 123 36 E
Mascara **82** 35 26N 0 6 E
Mascota **120** 20 30N 104 50W
Masela **73** 8 9 S 129 51 E
Maseru **92** 29 18 S 27 30 E
Mashaba **91** 20 2 S 30 29 E
Mashābih **64** 25 35N 36 30 E
Mashan **77** 23 40N 108 11 E
Mashhad **65** 36 20N 59 35 E
Mashi **85** 13 0N 7 54 E
Mashike **74** 43 31N 141 30 E
Mashkel, Hamun-i- **66** 28 30N 63 0 E
Mashki Chah **66** 29 5N 62 30 E
Mashtaga **57** 40 35N 50 0 E
Masi **50** 69 26N 23 40 E
Masi Manimba **88** 4 40 S 17 54 E
Masindi **90** 1 40N 31 43 E
Masindi Port **90** 1 43N 32 2 E
Masisea **126** 8 35 S 74 22W
Masisi **90** 1 23 S 28 49 E
Masjed Soleyman **64** 31 55N 49 18 E
Mask, L. **15** 53 36N 9 24W
Maski **70** 15 56N 76 46 E
Maslen Nos **43** 42 18N 27 48 E
Maslinica **39** 43 24N 16 13 E
Masnou **32** 41 28N 2 20 E
Masoala, Tanjon' i **93** 15 59 S 50 13 E
Masoarivo **93** 19 3 S 44 19 E
Masohi **73** 3 2 S 128 15 E
Masomeloka **93** 20 17 S 48 37 E
Mason, S.D., U.S.A. **116** 45 12N 103 27W
Mason, Tex., U.S.A. **117** 30 45N 99 15W
Mason City, Iowa, U.S.A. **116** 43 9N 93 12W
Mason City, Wash., U.S.A. **118** 48 0N 119 0W
Masqat **65** 23 37N 58 36 E
Massa **38** 44 2N 10 7 E
Massa Maríttima **38** 43 3N 10 52 E
Massa, O. → **82** 30 2N 9 40W
Massachusetts □ **114** 42 25N 72 0W
Massachusetts B. **113** 42 30N 70 0W
Massada **62** 33 41N 35 36 E
Massafra **41** 40 35N 17 8 E
Massaguet **81** 12 28N 15 26 E
Massakory **81** 13 0N 15 49 E
Massangena **93** 21 34 S 33 0 E
Massarosa **38** 43 53N 10 17 E
Massat **20** 42 53N 1 21 E
Massawa = Mitsiwa **87** 15 35N 39 25 E
Massena **114** 44 52N 74 55W
Massénya **81** 11 21N 16 9 E
Masset **108** 54 2N 132 10W
Massiac **20** 45 15N 3 11 E
Massif Central **20** 45 30N 2 21 E
Massillon **114** 40 47N 81 30W
Massinga **93** 23 46 S 32 4 E
Masson **113** 45 32N 75 25W
Masson I. **5** 66 10 S 93 20 E
Mastaba **86** 20 52N 39 30 E
Mastanli = Momchilgrad **43** 41 33N 25 23 E
Masterton **101** 40 56 S 175 39 E
Mástikho, Ákra **45** 38 10N 26 2 E
Mastuj **69** 36 20N 72 36 E
Mastung **66** 29 50N 66 56 E
Mastura **86** 23 7N 38 52 E
Masuda **74** 34 40N 131 51 E
Maswa □ **90** 3 30 S 34 0 E
Matabeleland North □ **91** 19 0 S 28 0 E
Matabeleland South □ **91** 21 0 S 29 0 E
Mataboor **73** 1 41 S 138 3 E
Matachel → **31** 38 50N 6 17W
Matachewan **106** 47 56N 80 39W
Matad **75** 47 11N 115 27 E
Matadi **88** 5 52 S 13 31 E
Matagalpa **121** 13 0N 85 58W
Matagami **106** 49 45N 77 34W
Matagami, L. **106** 49 50N 77 40W
Matagorda **117** 28 43N 96 0W
Matagorda B. **117** 28 30N 96 15W
Matagorda I. **117** 28 10N 96 40W
Matak, P. **72** 3 18N 106 16 E
Matakana **99** 32 59 S 145 54 E
Matale **70** 7 30N 80 37 E
Matam **84** 15 34N 13 17W
Matameye **85** 13 26N 8 28 E
Matamoros, Coahuila, Mexico **120** 25 33N 103 15W
Matamoros, Puebla, Mexico **120** 18 2N 98 17W
Matamoros, Tamaulipas, Mexico **120** 25 50N 97 30W
Ma'ṭan as Sarra **81** 21 45N 22 0 E
Matandu → **91** 8 45 S 34 19 E
Matane **107** 48 50N 67 33W
Matankari **85** 13 46N 4 1 E
Matanuska **104** 61 39N 149 19W
Matanzas **121** 23 0N 81 40W
Matapan, C. = Taínaron, Akra **45** 36 22N 22 27 E
Matapédia **107** 48 0N 66 59W
Matara **70** 5 58N 80 30 E
Mataram **72** 8 41 S 116 10 E
Matarani **126** 77 0 S 72 10W
Mataranka **96** 14 55 S 133 4 E
Mataró **32** 41 32N 2 29 E
Matarraña → **32** 41 14N 0 22 E
Mataruška Banja **42** 43 40N 20 45 E
Matatiele **93** 30 20 S 28 49 E
Mataura **101** 46 11 S 168 51 E
Matehuala **120** 23 40N 100 40W
Mateke Hills **91** 21 48 S 31 0 E
Matélica **39** 43 15N 13 0 E
Matera **41** 40 40N 16 37 E
Mátészalka **27** 47 58N 22 20 E
Matetsi **91** 18 12 S 26 0 E
Mateur **83** 37 0N 9 40 E
Matfors **48** 62 21N 17 2 E
Matha **20** 45 52N 0 20W
Matheson Island **109** 51 45N 96 56W
Mathis **117** 28 4N 97 48W
Mathura **68** 27 30N 77 40 E
Mati **73** 6 55N 126 15 E
Mati → **44** 41 40N 20 0 E
Matías Romero **120** 16 53N 95 2W
Matibane **91** 14 49 S 40 45 E
Matima **92** 20 15 S 24 26 E
Matlock **12** 53 8N 1 32W
Matmata **83** 33 37N 9 59 E
Matna **87** 13 49N 35 10 E
Mato Grosso □ **127** 14 0 S 55 0W
Mato Grosso, Planalto do **127** 15 0 S 59 57W
Matochkin Shar **58** 73 10N 56 40 E
Matopo Hills **91** 20 36 S 28 20 E
Matopos **91** 20 20 S 28 29 E
Matosinhos **30** 41 11N 8 42W
Matour **21** 46 19N 4 29 E
Matrah **65** 23 37N 58 30 E
Matrûh **86** 31 19N 27 9 E
Matsena **85** 13 5N 10 5 E
Matsesta **57** 43 34N 39 51 E
Matsue **74** 35 25N 133 10 E
Matsumoto **74** 36 15N 138 0 E
Matsuyama **74** 33 45N 132 45 E
Mattagami → **106** 50 43N 81 29W
Mattancheri **70** 9 50N 76 15 E
Mattawa **106** 46 20N 78 45W
Mattawamkeag **107** 45 30N 68 21W
Matterhorn **25** 45 58N 7 39 E
Mattersburg **27** 47 44N 16 24 E
Matthew Town **121** 20 57N 73 40W
Matthew's Ridge **126** 7 37N 60 10W
Mattice **106** 49 40N 83 20W
Mattituck **113** 40 58N 72 32W
Mattmar **48** 63 18N 13 45 E
Matua **72** 2 58 S 110 46 E
Matuba **93** 24 28 S 32 49 E
Matucana **126** 11 55 S 76 25W
Matun **66** 33 22N 69 58 E
Maturín **126** 9 45N 63 11W
Matveyev Kurgan **57** 47 35N 38 47 E
Mau-é-ele **93** 24 18 S 34 2 E
Mau Escarpment **90** 0 40 S 36 0 E
Mau Ranipur **68** 25 16N 79 8 E
Maubeuge **19** 50 17N 3 57 E
Maubourguet **20** 43 29N 0 1 E
Maude **99** 34 29 S 144 18 E
Maudheim **5** 71 5 S 11 0W
Maudin Sun **67** 16 0N 94 30 E
Maués **126** 3 20 S 57 45W
Maui **110** 20 45N 156 20 E
Mauke **101** 20 09 S 157 20W
Maule □ **124** 36 5 S 72 30W
Mauléon-Licharre **20** 43 14N 0 54W
Maumee **114** 41 35N 83 40W
Maumee → **114** 41 42N 83 28W
Maumere **73** 8 38 S 122 13 E
Maun **92** 20 0 S 23 26 E
Mauna Kea **110** 19 50N 155 28W
Mauna Loa **110** 21 8N 157 10W
Maunath Bhanjan **69** 25 56N 83 33 E
Maungmagan Kyunzu **71** 14 0N 97 48 E
Maupin **118** 45 12N 121 9W
Maure-de-Bretagne **18** 47 53N 2 0W
Maurepas L. **117** 30 18N 90 35W
Maures **21** 43 15N 6 15 E
Mauriac **20** 45 13N 2 19 E
Maurice L. **96** 29 30 S 131 0 E
Mauritania ■ **80** 20 50N 10 0W
Mauritius ■ **3** 20 0 S 57 0 E
Mauron **18** 48 9N 2 18W
Maurs **20** 44 43N 2 12 E
Mauston **116** 43 48N 90 5W
Mauterndorf **26** 47 9N 13 40 E
Mauvezin **20** 43 44N 0 53 E
Mauzé-sur-le-Mignon **20** 46 12N 0 41W
Mavelikara **70** 9 14N 76 32 E
Mavinga **89** 15 50 S 20 21 E
Mavli **68** 24 45N 73 55 E
Mavqi'im **62** 31 38N 34 32 E
Mavrova **44** 40 26N 19 32 E
Mavuradonha Mts. **91** 16 30 S 31 30 E
Mawa **90** 2 45N 26 40 E
Mawana **68** 29 6N 77 58 E
Mawand **68** 29 33N 68 38 E
Mawk Mai **67** 20 14N 97 37 E
Mawson Base **5** 67 30 S 62 53 E
Max **116** 47 50N 101 20W
Maxcanú **120** 20 40N 92 0W
Maxhamish L. **108** 59 50N 123 17W
Maxixe **93** 23 54 S 35 17 E
Maxville **113** 45 17N 74 51W
Maxwelton **98** 20 43 S 142 41 E
May Downs **98** 22 38 S 148 55 E
May Glacier Tongue **5** 66 08 S 130 35 E
May Pen **121** 17 58N 77 15W
Maya **32** 43 12N 1 29W
Maya → **59** 54 31N 134 41 E
Maya Mts. **120** 16 30N 89 0W
Mayaguana **121** 22 30N 72 44W
Mayagüez **121** 18 12N 67 9W
Mayahi **85** 13 58N 7 40 E
Mayals **32** 41 22N 0 30 E
Mayarí **121** 20 40N 75 41W
Mayavaram = Mayuram **70** 11 3N 79 42 E
Maybell **118** 40 30N 108 4W
Maychew **87** 12 50N 39 31 E
Maydena **99** 42 45 S 146 30 E
Maydos **44** 40 13N 26 20 E
Mayen **25** 50 18N 7 10 E
Mayenne **18** 48 20N 0 38W
Mayenne □ **18** 48 10N 0 40W
Mayenne → **18** 47 30N 0 32W
Mayer **119** 34 28N 112 17W
Mayerthorpe **108** 53 57N 115 8W
Mayfield **115** 36 45N 88 40W
Mayhill **119** 32 58N 105 30W
Maykop **57** 44 35N 40 25 E
Maymyo **71** 22 2N 96 28 E
Maynooth **15** 53 22N 6 38W
Mayo **104** 63 38N 135 57W
Mayo □ **15** 53 47N 9 7W
Mayo → **120** 26 45N 109 47W
Mayo L. **104** 63 45N 135 0W
Mayon, Mt. **73** 13 15N 123 42 E
Mayor I. **101** 37 16 S 176 17 E
Mayorga **30** 42 10N 5 16W
Mayskiy **57** 43 47N 44 2 E
Mayson L. **109** 57 55N 107 10W
Maysville **114** 38 39N 83 46W
Maythalūn **62** 32 21N 35 16 E
Mayu **73** 1 30N 126 30 E
Mayuram **70** 11 3N 79 42 E
Mayville, N.D., U.S.A. **116** 47 30N 97 23W
Mayville, N.Y., U.S.A. **112** 42 14N 79 31W
Mayya **59** 61 44N 130 18 E
Mazabuka **91** 15 52 S 27 44 E
Mazagán = El Jadida **82** 33 11N 8 17W
Mazagão **127** 0 7 S 51 16W
Mazamet **20** 43 30N 2 20 E
Mazán **126** 3 30 S 73 0W
Mazan Deran □ **65** 36 30N 52 0 E
Mazar-e Sharīf **65** 36 41N 67 0 E
Mazar, O. → **82** 31 50N 1 36 E
Mazara del Vallo **40** 37 40N 12 34 E
Mazarredo **128** 47 10 S 66 50W
Mazarrón **33** 37 38N 1 19W
Mazarrón, Golfo de **33** 37 27N 1 19W
Mazaruni → **126** 6 25N 58 35W
Mazatenango **120** 14 35N 91 30W
Mazatlán **120** 23 10N 106 30W
Mažeikiai **54** 56 20N 22 20 E
Māzhān **65** 32 30N 59 0 E
Mazīnān **65** 36 19N 56 56 E
Mazoe, Mozam. **91** 16 42 S 33 7 E
Mazoe, Zimb. **91** 17 28 S 30 58 E
Mazrûb **87** 14 0N 29 20 E
Mazu Dao **77** 26 10N 119 55 E
Mazurian Lakes = Mazurski, Pojezierze **28** 53 50N 21 0 E
Mazurski, Pojezierze **28** 53 50N 21 0 E
Mazzarino **41** 37 19N 14 12 E
Mbaba **84** 14 59N 16 44W
Mbabane **93** 26 18 S 31 6 E
Mbagne **84** 16 6N 14 47W
M'bahiakro **84** 7 33N 4 19W
Mbaïki **88** 3 53N 18 1 E
Mbala **91** 8 46 S 31 24 E
Mbale **90** 1 8N 34 12 E
Mbalmayo **88** 3 33N 11 33 E
Mbamba Bay **91** 11 13 S 34 49 E
Mbandaka **88** 0 1N 18 18 E
Mbanga **85** 4 30N 9 33 E
Mbanza Congo **88** 6 18 S 14 16 E
Mbanza Ngungu **88** 5 12 S 14 53 E
Mbarara **90** 0 35 S 30 40 E
Mbatto **84** 6 28N 4 22W
Mbenkuru → **91** 9 25 S 39 50 E
Mberubu **85** 6 10N 7 38 E
Mbesuma **91** 10 0 S 32 2 E
Mbeya **91** 8 54 S 33 29 E
Mbeya □ **90** 8 15 S 33 30 E
Mbinga **91** 10 50 S 35 0 E
Mbinga □ **91** 10 50 S 35 0 E
Mbini = Rio Muni □ **88** 1 30N 10 0 E
Mbokì **87** 5 19N 25 58 E
Mboro **84** 15 9N 16 54W
Mboune **84** 14 42N 13 34W
Mbour **84** 14 22N 16 54W
Mbout **84** 16 1N 12 38W
Mbozi □ **91** 9 0 S 32 50 E
Mbuji-Mayi **90** 6 9 S 23 40 E
Mbulu **90** 3 45 S 35 30 E
Mbulu □ **90** 3 52 S 35 33 E

Mburucuyá **124** 28 1 S 58 14W
Mcherrah **82** 27 0N 4 30W
Mchinja **91** 9 44 S 39 45 E
Mchinji **91** 13 47 S 32 58 E
Mdennah **82** 24 37N 6 0W
Mdina **36** 35 51N 14 25 E
Mead, L. **119** 36 1N 114 44W
Meade **117** 37 18N 100 25W
Meadow Lake **109** 54 10N 108 26W
Meadow Lake Prov. Park **109** 54 27N 109 0W
Meadow Valley Wash ⤳ **119** 36 39N 114 35W
Meadville **114** 41 39N 80 9W
Meaford **106** 44 36N 80 35W
Mealhada **30** 40 22N 8 27W
Mealy Mts. **107** 53 10N 58 0W
Meander River **108** 59 2N 117 42W
Meares, C. **118** 45 37N 124 0W
Mearim ⤳ **127** 3 4 S 44 35W
Meath □ **15** 53 32N 6 40W
Meath Park **109** 53 27N 105 22W
Meaulne **20** 46 36N 2 36 E
Meaux **19** 48 58N 2 50 E
Mecanhelas **91** 15 12 S 35 54 E
Mecca **119** 33 37N 116 3W
Mecca = Makkah **86** 21 30N 39 54 E
Mechanicsburg **112** 40 12N 77 0W
Mechanicville **113** 42 54N 73 41W
Mechara **87** 8 36N 40 20 E
Mechelen **16** 51 2N 4 29 E
Mecheria **82** 33 35N 0 18W
Mechernich **24** 50 35N 6 39 E
Mechetinskaya **57** 46 45N 40 32 E
Mechra Benâbbou **82** 32 39N 7 48W
Mecidiye **44** 40 38N 26 32 E
Mecitözü **56** 40 32N 35 17 E
Meconta **91** 14 59 S 39 50 E
Meda **30** 40 57N 7 18W
Meda ⤳ **96** 17 20 S 123 50 E
Medak **70** 18 1N 78 15 E
Medan **72** 3 40N 98 38 E
Medanosa, Pta. **128** 48 8 S 66 0W
Medawachchiya **70** 8 30N 80 30 E
Medéa **82** 36 12N 2 50 E
Mededa **42** 43 44N 19 15 E
Medellín **126** 6 15N 75 35W
Medemblik **16** 52 46N 5 8 E
Médenine **83** 33 21N 10 30 E
Mederdra **84** 17 0N 15 38W
Medford, Oreg., U.S.A. **118** 42 20N 122 52W
Medford, Wis., U.S.A. **116** 45 9N 90 21W
Medgidia **46** 44 15N 28 19 E
Medi **87** 5 4N 30 42 E
Media Agua **124** 31 58 S 68 25W
Media Luna **124** 34 45 S 66 44W
Mediaş **46** 46 9N 24 22 E
Medical Lake **118** 47 35N 117 42W
Medicina **39** 44 29N 11 38 E
Medicine Bow **118** 41 56N 106 11W
Medicine Bow Pk. **118** 41 21N 106 19W
Medicine Bow Ra. **118** 41 10N 106 25W
Medicine Hat **109** 50 0N 110 45W
Medicine Lake **116** 48 30N 104 30W
Medicine Lodge **117** 37 20N 98 37W
Medina, N.D., U.S.A. **116** 46 57N 99 20W
Medina, N.Y., U.S.A. **114** 43 15N 78 27W
Medina, Ohio, U.S.A. **114** 41 9N 81 50W
Medina = Al Madīnah **64** 24 35N 39 35 E
Medina ⤳ **117** 29 10N 98 20W
Medina de Ríoseco **30** 41 53N 5 3W
Medina del Campo **30** 41 18N 4 55W
Medina L. **117** 29 35N 98 58W
Medina-Sidonia **31** 36 28N 5 57W
Medinaceli **32** 41 12N 2 30W
Mediterranean Sea **34** 35 0N 15 0 E
Medjerda, O. ⤳ **83** 37 7N 10 13 E
Medley **109** 54 25N 110 16W
Médoc **20** 45 10N 0 56W
Medstead **109** 53 19N 108 5W
Medulin **39** 44 49N 13 55 E
Medveda **42** 42 50N 21 32 E
Medveditsa ⤳, R.S.F.S.R., U.S.S.R. **55** 49 35N 42 41 E
Medveditsa ⤳, R.S.F.S.R., U.S.S.R. **55** 57 5N 37 30 E
Medvedok **55** 57 20N 50 1 E
Medvezhi, Ostrava **59** 71 0N 161 0 E
Medvezhyegorsk **52** 63 0N 34 25 E
Medway ⤳ **13** 51 28N 0 45 E
Medyn **55** 54 58N 35 52 E
Medzev **27** 48 43N 20 55 E
Medzilaborce **27** 49 17N 21 52 E
Meekatharra **96** 26 32 S 118 29 E
Meeker **118** 40 1N 107 58W
Meerane **24** 50 51N 12 30 E
Meersburg **25** 47 42N 9 16 E
Meerut **68** 29 1N 77 42 E
Meeteetse **118** 44 10N 108 56W
Mega **87** 3 57N 38 19 E
Megálo Khorío **45** 36 27N 27 24 E
Megálo Petalí **45** 38 0N 24 15 E
Megalópolis **45** 37 25N 22 7 E
Meganísi **45** 38 39N 20 48 E
Mégara **45** 37 58N 23 22 E
Megarine **83** 33 14N 6 2 E
Megdhova ⤳ **45** 39 10N 21 45 E
Mégève **21** 45 51N 6 37 E
Meghezez, Mt. **87** 9 18N 39 26 E
Meghna ⤳ **69** 22 50N 90 50 E
Megiddo **62** 32 36N 35 11 E
Mégiscane, L. **106** 48 35N 75 55W
Megiste **35** 36 8N 29 34 E
Mehadia **46** 44 56N 22 23 E
Mehaïguene, O. ⤳ **82** 32 15N 2 59 E
Meharry, Mt. **96** 22 59 S 118 35 E
Mehedinţi □ **46** 44 40N 22 45 E
Meheisa **86** 19 38N 32 57 E
Mehndawal **69** 26 58N 83 5 E
Mehsana **68** 23 39N 72 26 E
Mehun-sur-Yèvre **19** 47 10N 2 13 E
Mei Jiang ⤳ **77** 24 25N 116 35 E
Mei Xian **75** 24 16N 116 6 E
Meiganga **88** 6 30N 14 25 E
Meiktila **67** 20 53N 95 54 E
Meiningen **24** 50 32N 10 25 E
Me'ir Shefeya **62** 32 35N 34 58 E
Meira, Sierra de **30** 43 15N 7 15W
Meiringen **25** 46 43N 8 12 E
Meissen **24** 51 10N 13 29 E
Meissner **24** 51 13N 9 51 E
Meitan **77** 27 45N 107 29 E
Méjean, Causse **20** 44 15N 3 30 E
Mejillones **124** 23 10 S 70 30W
Mékambo **88** 1 2N 13 50 E
Mekdela **87** 11 24N 39 10 E
Mekele **87** 13 33N 39 30 E
Meklong = Samut Songkhram **71** 13 24N 100 1 E
Meknès **82** 33 57N 5 33W
Meko **85** 7 27N 2 52 E
Mekong ⤳ **71** 9 30N 106 15 E
Mekongga **73** 3 39 S 121 15 E
Melagiri Hills **70** 12 20N 77 30 E
Melah, Sebkhet el **82** 29 20N 1 30W
Melaka **71** 2 15N 102 15 E
Melaka □ **71** 2 20N 102 15 E
Melalap **72** 5 10N 116 5 E
Mélambes **45** 35 8N 24 40 E
Melanesia **94** 4 0 S 155 0 E
Melapalaiyam **70** 8 39N 77 44 E
Melbourne, Austral. **97** 37 50 S 145 0 E
Melbourne, U.S.A. **115** 28 4N 80 35W
Melchor Múzquiz **120** 27 50N 101 30W
Melchor Ocampo (San Pedro Ocampo) **120** 24 52N 101 40W
Méldola **39** 44 7N 12 3 E
Meldorf **24** 54 5N 9 5 E
Mêle-sur-Sarthe, Le **18** 48 31N 0 22 E
Melegnano **38** 45 21N 9 20 E
Melenci **42** 45 32N 20 20 E
Melenki **55** 55 20N 41 37 E
Mélèzes ⤳ **105** 57 30N 71 0W
Melfi, Chad **81** 11 0N 17 59 E
Melfi, Italy **41** 41 0N 15 33 E
Melfort, Can. **109** 52 50N 104 37W
Melfort, Zimb. **91** 18 0 S 31 25 E
Melgaço **30** 42 7N 8 15W
Melgar de Fernamental **30** 42 27N 4 17W
Melhus **47** 63 17N 10 18 E
Meligalá **45** 37 15N 21 59 E
Melilla **82** 35 21N 2 57W
Melilot **62** 31 22N 34 37 E
Melipilla **124** 33 42 S 71 15W
Mélissa Óros **45** 37 32N 26 4 E
Melita **109** 49 15N 101 0W
Mélito di Porto Salvo **41** 37 55N 15 47 E
Melitopol **56** 46 50N 35 22 E
Melk **26** 48 13N 15 20 E
Mellan-Fryken **48** 59 45N 13 10 E
Mellansel **50** 63 25N 18 17 E
Melle, France **20** 46 14N 0 10W
Melle, Ger. **24** 52 12N 8 20 E
Mellégue, O. ⤳ **83** 36 32N 8 51 E
Mellen **116** 46 19N 90 36W
Mellerud **49** 58 41N 12 28 E
Mellette **116** 45 11N 98 29W
Mellid **30** 42 55N 8 1W
Mellish Reef **97** 17 25 S 155 50 E
Mellit **87** 14 7N 25 34 E
Mellrichstadt **25** 50 26N 10 19 E
Melnik **43** 41 30N 23 25 E
Mělník **26** 50 22N 14 23 E
Melo **125** 32 20 S 54 10W
Melolo **73** 9 53 S 120 40 E
Melovoye **57** 49 25N 40 5 E
Melrhir, Chott **83** 34 25N 6 24 E
Melrose, Austral. **99** 32 42 S 146 57 E
Melrose, U.K. **14** 53 35N 2 44W
Melrose, U.S.A. **117** 34 27N 103 33W
Melstone **118** 46 36N 107 50W
Melsungen **24** 51 8N 9 34 E
Melton Mowbray **12** 52 46N 0 52W
Melun **19** 48 32N 2 39 E
Melur **70** 10 2N 78 23 E
Melut **87** 10 30N 32 13 E
Melville **109** 50 55N 102 50W
Melville B. **97** 12 0 S 136 45 E
Melville, C. **97** 14 11 S 144 30 E
Melville I., Austral. **96** 11 30 S 131 0 E
Melville I., Can. **4** 75 30N 112 0W
Melville, L. **107** 53 30N 60 0W
Melville Pen. **105** 68 0N 84 0W
Melvin ⤳ **108** 59 11N 117 31W
Mélykút **27** 46 11N 19 25 E
Memaliaj **44** 40 25N 19 58 E
Memba **91** 14 11 S 40 30 E
Memboro **73** 9 30 S 119 30 E
Membrilla **33** 38 59N 3 21W
Memel **93** 27 38 S 29 36 E
Memel = Klaipeda **54** 55 43N 21 10 E
Memmingen **25** 47 59N 10 12 E
Memphis, Tenn., U.S.A. **117** 35 7N 90 0W
Memphis, Tex., U.S.A. **117** 34 45N 100 30W
Mena **117** 34 40N 94 15W
Mena ⤳ **87** 5 40N 40 50 E
Menai Strait **12** 53 14N 4 10W
Ménaka **85** 15 59N 2 18 E
Menan = Chao Phraya ⤳ **71** 13 32N 100 36 E
Menarandra ⤳ **93** 25 17 S 44 30 E
Menard **117** 30 57N 99 48W
Menasha **114** 44 13N 88 27W
Menate **72** 0 12 S 113 3 E
Mendawai ⤳ **72** 3 17 S 113 21 E
Mende **20** 44 31N 3 30 E
Mendebo Mts. **87** 7 0N 39 22 E
Menderes ⤳ **64** 37 25N 28 45 E
Mendi, Ethiopia **87** 9 47N 35 4 E
Mendi, P.N.G. **98** 6 11 S 143 39 E
Mendip Hills **13** 51 17N 2 40W
Mendocino **118** 39 26N 123 50W
Mendocino Seascarp **95** 41 0N 140 0W
Mendota, Calif., U.S.A. **119** 36 46N 120 24W
Mendota, Ill., U.S.A. **116** 41 35N 89 5W
Mendoza **124** 32 50 S 68 52W
Mendoza □ **124** 33 0 S 69 0W
Mene Grande **126** 9 49N 70 56W
Menemen **64** 38 34N 27 3 E
Menen **16** 50 47N 3 7 E
Menfi **40** 37 36N 12 57 E
Mengcheng **77** 33 18N 116 31 E
Mengeš **39** 46 24N 14 35 E
Menggala **72** 4 30 S 105 15 E
Mengíbar **31** 37 58N 3 48W
Mengoub **82** 29 49N 5 26W
Mengshan **77** 24 14N 110 55 E
Mengzi **75** 23 20N 103 22 E
Menihek L. **107** 54 0N 67 0W
Menin = Menen **16** 50 47N 3 7 E
Menindee **97** 32 20 S 142 25 E
Menindee, L. **99** 32 20 S 142 25 E
Meningie **99** 35 35 S 139 0 E
Menominee **114** 45 9N 87 39W
Menominee ⤳ **114** 45 5N 87 36W
Menomonie **116** 44 50N 91 54W
Menongue **89** 14 48 S 17 52 E
Menorca **32** 40 0N 4 0 E
Mentawai, Kepulauan **72** 2 0 S 99 0 E
Menton **21** 43 50N 7 29 E
Mentor **112** 41 40N 81 24W
Menzel-Bourguiba **83** 39 9N 9 49 E
Menzel Chaker **83** 35 0N 10 26 E
Menzel-Temime **83** 36 46N 11 0 E
Menzelinsk **52** 55 53N 53 1 E
Menzies **96** 29 40 S 120 58 E
Me'ona (Tarshiha) **62** 33 1N 35 15 E
Mepaco **91** 15 57 S 30 48 E
Meppel **16** 52 42N 6 12 E
Meppen **24** 52 41N 7 20 E
Mequinenza **32** 41 22N 0 17 E
Mer Rouge **117** 32 47N 91 48W
Merabéllou, Kólpos **45** 35 10N 25 50 E
Merak **73** 5 56 S 106 0 E
Meran = Merano **39** 46 40N 11 10 E
Merano **39** 46 40N 11 10 E
Merate **38** 45 42N 9 23 E
Merauke **73** 8 29 S 140 24 E
Merbabu **73** 7 30 S 110 40 E
Merbein **99** 34 10 S 142 2 E
Merca **63** 1 48N 44 50 E
Mercadal **32** 39 59N 4 5 E
Mercara **70** 12 30N 75 45 E
Mercato Saraceno **39** 43 57N 12 11 E
Merced **119** 37 18N 120 30W
Mercedes, Buenos Aires, Argent. **124** 34 40 S 59 30W
Mercedes, Corrientes, Argent. **124** 29 10 S 58 5W
Mercedes, San Luis, Argent. **124** 33 40 S 65 21W
Mercedes, Uruguay **124** 33 12 S 58 0W
Merceditas **124** 28 20 S 70 35W
Mercer, N.Z. **101** 37 16 S 175 5 E
Mercer, U.S.A. **112** 41 14N 80 13W
Mercy C. **105** 65 0N 63 30W
Merdrignac **18** 48 11N 2 27W
Meredith C. **128** 52 15 S 60 40W
Meredith, L. **117** 35 30N 101 35W
Merei **46** 45 7N 26 43 E
Méréville **19** 48 20N 2 5 E
Mergenevsky **57** 49 59N 51 15 E
Mergui Arch. = Myeik Kyunzu **71** 11 30N 97 30 E
Mérida, Mexico **120** 20 9N 89 40W
Mérida, Spain **31** 38 55N 6 25W
Mérida, Venez. **126** 8 24N 71 8W
Meriden **114** 41 33N 72 47W
Meridian, Idaho, U.S.A. **118** 43 41N 116 25W
Meridian, Miss., U.S.A. **115** 32 20N 88 42W
Meridian, Tex., U.S.A. **117** 31 55N 97 37W
Mering **25** 48 15N 11 0 E
Meringur **100** 34 20 S 141 19 E
Meriruma **127** 1 15N 54 50W
Merkel **117** 32 30N 100 0W
Merksem **16** 51 16N 4 25 E
Merlebach **19** 49 5N 6 52 E
Merlerault, Le **18** 48 41N 0 16 E
Mern **49** 55 3N 12 3 E
Merowe **86** 18 29N 31 46 E
Merredin **96** 31 28 S 118 18 E
Merrick **14** 55 8N 4 30W
Merrickville **113** 44 55N 75 50W
Merrill, Oregon, U.S.A. **118** 42 2N 121 37W
Merrill, Wis., U.S.A. **116** 45 11N 89 41W
Merriman **116** 42 55N 101 42W
Merritt **108** 50 10N 120 45W
Merriwa **99** 32 6 S 150 22 E
Merriwagga **99** 33 47 S 145 43 E
Merry I. **106** 55 29N 77 31W
Merrygoen **99** 31 51 S 149 12 E
Merryville **117** 30 47N 93 31W
Mersa Fatma **87** 14 57N 40 17 E
Mersch **16** 49 44N 6 7 E
Merseburg **24** 51 20N 12 0 E
Mersey ⤳ **12** 53 20N 2 56W
Merseyside □ **12** 53 25N 2 55W
Mersin **64** 36 51N 34 36 E
Mersing **71** 2 25N 103 50 E
Merta **68** 26 39N 74 4 E
Merthyr Tydfil **13** 51 45N 3 23W
Mértola **31** 37 40N 7 40 E
Mertzon **117** 31 17N 100 48W
Méru **19** 49 13N 2 8 E
Meru, Kenya **90** 0 3N 37 40 E
Meru, Tanz. **90** 3 15 S 36 46 E
Meru □ **90** 0 3N 37 46 E
Merville **19** 50 38N 2 38 E
Méry-sur-Seine **19** 48 31N 3 54 E
Merzifon **56** 40 53N 35 32 E
Merzig **25** 49 26N 6 37 E
Merzouga, Erg Tin **83** 24 0N 11 4 E
Mesa **119** 33 20N 111 56W
Mesa, La, Calif., U.S.A. **119** 32 48N 117 5W
Mesa, La, N. Mex., U.S.A. **119** 32 6N 106 48W
Mesach Mellet **83** 24 30N 11 30 E
Mesada **62** 31 20N 35 19 E
Mesagne **41** 40 34N 17 48 E
Mesaras, Kólpos **45** 35 6N 24 47 E
Meschede **24** 51 20N 8 17 E
Mesfinto **87** 13 20N 37 22 E
Mesgouez, L. **106** 51 20N 75 0W
Meshchovsk **54** 54 22N 35 17 E
Meshed = Mashhad **65** 36 20N 59 35 E
Meshoppen **113** 41 36N 76 3W
Meshra er Req **81** 8 25N 29 18 E
Mesick **114** 44 24N 85 42W
Mesilinka ⤳ **108** 56 6N 124 30W
Mesilla **119** 32 20N 106 50W
Meslay-du-Maine **18** 47 58N 0 33W
Mesocco **25** 46 23N 9 12 E
Mesolóngion **43** 38 21N 21 28 E
Mesopotamia = Al Jazirah **64** 33 30N 44 0 E
Mesoraca **41** 39 5N 16 47 E
Mésou Volímais **45** 37 53N 20 35 E
Mess Cr. ⤳ **108** 57 55N 131 14W
Messac **18** 47 49N 1 50W
Messad **82** 34 8N 3 30 E
Messalo ⤳ **91** 12 25 S 39 15 E
Méssaména **85** 3 48N 12 49 E
Messeix **20** 45 37N 2 33 E
Messeue **45** 37 12N 21 58 E
Messina, Italy **41** 38 10N 15 32 E
Messina, S. Afr. **93** 22 20 S 30 0 E
Messina, Str. di **41** 38 5N 15 35 E
Messíni **45** 37 4N 22 1 E
Messínia □ **45** 37 10N 22 0 E
Messiniakós, Kólpos **45** 36 45N 22 5 E
Messkirch **25** 47 59N 9 7 E
Mesta ⤳ **43** 41 30N 24 0 E
Mestà, Ákra **45** 38 16N 25 53 E
Mestanza **31** 38 35N 4 4W
Město Teplá **26** 49 59N 12 52 E
Mestre **39** 45 30N 12 13 E
Městys Zelezná Ruda **26** 49 8N 13 15 E
Meta ⤳ **126** 6 12N 67 28W
Metairie **117** 29 59N 90 9W
Metalici, Munţii **42** 46 15N 22 50 E
Metaline Falls **118** 48 52N 117 22W
Metán **124** 25 30 S 65 0W
Metauro ⤳ **39** 43 50N 13 3 E
Metema **87** 12 56N 36 13 E
Metengobalame **91** 14 49 S 34 30 E
Méthana **45** 37 35N 23 23 E
Methóni **45** 36 49N 21 42 E
Methven **101** 43 38 S 171 40 E
Methy L. **109** 56 28N 109 30W
Metkovets **43** 43 37N 23 10 E
Metković **42** 43 6N 17 39 E
Metlakatla **108** 55 10N 131 33W
Metlaoui **83** 34 24N 8 24 E
Metlika **39** 45 40N 15 20 E
Metropolis **117** 37 10N 88 47W
Métsovon **44** 39 48N 21 12 E
Mettuppalaiyam **70** 11 18N 76 59 E
Mettur **70** 11 48N 77 47 E
Mettur Dam **70** 11 45N 77 45 E
Metulla **62** 33 17N 35 34 E
Metz **19** 49 8N 6 10 E
Meulaboh **72** 4 11N 96 3 E
Meulan **19** 49 0N 1 52 E
Meung-sur-Loire **19** 47 50N 1 40 E
Meureudu **72** 5 19N 96 10 E
Meurthe ⤳ **19** 48 47N 6 9 E
Meurthe-et-Moselle □ **19** 48 52N 6 0 E
Meuse □ **19** 49 8N 5 25 E
Meuse ⤳ **16** 50 45N 5 41 E
Meuselwitz **24** 51 3N 12 18 E
Mexborough **12** 53 29N 1 18W
Mexia **117** 31 38N 96 32W
Mexiana, I. **127** 0 0 49 30W
Mexicali **120** 32 40N 115 30W
México **120** 19 20N 99 10W
Mexico, Me., U.S.A. **113** 44 35N 70 30W
Mexico, Mo., U.S.A. **116** 39 10N 91 55W
Mexico ■ **120** 20 0N 100 0W
México □ **120** 19 20N 99 10W
Mexico, G. of **120** 25 0N 90 0W
Meyenburg **24** 53 19N 12 15 E
Meymac **20** 45 32N 2 10 E
Meymaneh **65** 35 53N 64 38 E
Meyrargues **21** 43 38N 5 32 E
Meyrueis **20** 44 12N 3 27 E
Meyssac **20** 45 3N 1 40 E
Mezdra **43** 43 12N 23 42 E
Mèze **20** 43 27N 3 36 E
Mezen **52** 65 50N 44 20 E
Mézenc **21** 44 55N 4 11 E
Mezeş, Munţii **46** 47 5N 23 5 E
Mezha ⤳ **54** 55 50N 31 45 E
Mézidon **18** 49 5N 0 1W
Mézilhac **21** 44 49N 4 21 E
Mézin **20** 44 4N 0 16 E
Mezöberény **27** 46 49N 21 3 E
Mezöfalva **27** 46 55N 18 49 E
Mezöhegyes **27** 46 19N 20 49 E
Mezökövácsháza **27** 46 25N 20 57 E
Mezökövesd **27** 47 49N 20 35 E
Mézos **20** 44 5N 1 10W
Mezötúr **27** 47 0N 20 41 E
Mezquital **120** 23 29N 104 23W
Mezzolombardo **38** 46 13N 11 5 E
Mgeta **91** 8 22 S 36 6 E
Mglin **54** 53 2N 32 50 E
Mhlaba Hills **91** 18 30 S 30 30 E
Mhow **68** 22 33N 75 50 E
Miahuatlán **120** 16 21N 96 36W
Miajadas **31** 39 9N 5 54W
Mialar **68** 26 15N 70 20 E
Miallo **98** 16 28 S 145 22 E
Miami, Ariz., U.S.A. **119** 33 25N 110 54W
Miami, Fla., U.S.A. **115** 25 45N 80 15W
Miami, Tex., U.S.A. **117** 35 44N 100 38W
Miami ⤳ **114** 39 20N 84 40W
Miami Beach **115** 25 49N 80 6W
Miamisburg **114** 39 40N 84 11W
Mian Xian **77** 33 10N 106 32 E
Mianchi **77** 34 48N 111 48 E
Mīāndow āb **64** 37 0N 46 5 E
Miandrivazo **93** 19 31 S 45 29 E
Mīāneh **64** 37 30N 47 40 E
Mianwali **68** 32 38N 71 28 E
Mianyang, Hubei, China **77** 30 25N 113 25 E
Mianyang, Sichuan, China **77** 31 22N 104 47 E
Miaoli **75** 24 37N 120 49 E
Miarinarivo **93** 18 57 S 46 55 E

Miass 52 54 59N 60 6 E
Miasteczko Kraj 28 53 7N 17 1 E
Miastko 28 54 0N 16 58 E
Micăsasa 46 46 7N 24 7 E
Michalovce 27 48 47N 21 58 E
Michelstadt 25 49 40N 9 0 E
Michigan □ 111 44 40N 85 40W
Michigan City 114 41 42N 86 56W
Michigan, L. 114 44 0N 87 0W
Michipicoten 106 47 55N 84 55W
Michipicoten I. 106 47 40N 85 40W
Michoacan □ 120 19 0N 102 0W
Michurin 43 42 9N 27 51 E
Michurinsk 55 52 58N 40 27 E
Miclere 98 22 34 S 147 32 E
Mico, Pta. 121 12 0N 83 30W
Micronesia 94 11 0N 160 0 E
Mid Glamorgan □ 13 51 40N 3 25W
Mid-Indian Ridge 94 40 0 S 75 0 E
Mid-Oceanic Ridge 94 42 0 S 90 0 E
Midai, P. 72 3 0N 107 47 E
Midale 109 49 25N 103 20W
Midas 118 41 14N 116 48W
Middagsfjället 48 63 27N 12 19 E
Middelburg, Neth. 16 51 30N 3 36 E
Middelburg, C. Prov., S. Afr. 92 31 30 S 25 0 E
Middelburg, Trans., S. Afr. 93 25 49 S 29 28 E
Middelfart 49 55 30N 9 43 E
Middle Alkali L. 118 41 30N 120 3W
Middle Andaman I. 71 12 30N 92 30 E
Middle Loup → 116 41 17N 98 23W
Middleboro 113 41 56N 70 52W
Middleburg, N.Y., U.S.A. 113 42 36N 74 19W
Middleburg, Pa., U.S.A. 112 40 46N 77 5W
Middlebury 113 44 0N 73 9W
Middleport 114 39 0N 82 5W
Middlesboro 115 36 36N 83 43W
Middlesbrough 12 54 35N 1 14W
Middlesex 113 40 36N 74 30W
Middleton 107 44 57N 65 4W
Middleton Cr. → 98 22 35 S 141 51 E
Middleton P.O. 98 22 22 S 141 32 E
Middletown, Conn., U.S.A. 114 41 37N 72 40W
Middletown, N.Y., U.S.A. 114 41 28N 74 28W
Middletown, Ohio, U.S.A. 114 39 29N 84 25W
Middletown, Pa., U.S.A. 113 40 12N 76 44W
Midelt 82 32 46N 4 44W
Midi, Canal du 20 43 45N 1 21 E
Midi d'Ossau 32 42 50N 0 25W
Midland, Austral. 96 31 54 S 115 59 E
Midland, Can. 106 44 45N 79 50W
Midland, Mich., U.S.A. 114 43 37N 84 17W
Midland, Pa., U.S.A. 112 40 39N 80 27W
Midland, Tex., U.S.A. 117 32 0N 102 3W
Midlands □ 91 19 40 S 29 0 E
Midleton 15 51 52N 8 12W
Midlothian 117 32 30N 97 0W
Midnapore 69 22 25N 87 21 E
Midongy Atsimo 93 23 35 S 47 1 E
Midongy, Tangorombohitr' i 93 23 30 S 47 0 E
Midour → 20 43 54N 0 30W
Midouze → 20 43 48N 0 51W
Midvale 118 40 39N 111 58W
Midway Is. 94 28 13N 177 22W
Midwest 118 43 27N 106 19W
Midyat 64 37 25N 41 23 E
Midzur 42 43 24N 22 40 E
Mie □ 74 34 30N 136 10 E
Miechów 28 50 21N 20 5 E
Miedwie, Jezioro 28 53 17N 14 54 E
Międzybód 28 51 25N 17 34 E
Międzychód 28 52 35N 15 53 E
Międzylesie 28 50 8N 16 40 E
Międzyrzec Podlaski 28 51 58N 22 45 E
Międzyrzecz 28 52 26N 15 35 E
Międzyzdroje 28 53 56N 14 26 E
Miejska 28 51 39N 16 58 E
Miélan 20 43 27N 0 19 E
Mielec 28 50 15N 21 25 E
Mienga 92 17 12 S 19 48 E
Miercurea Ciuc 46 46 21N 25 48 E
Mieres 30 43 18N 5 48W
Mieroszów 28 50 40N 16 11 E
Mieso 87 9 15N 40 43 E
Mieszkowice 28 52 47N 14 30 E
Migdāl 62 32 51N 35 30 E
Migdal Afeq 62 32 5N 34 58 E
Migennes 19 47 58N 3 31 E
Migliarino 39 44 45N 11 56 E
Miguel Alemán, Presa 120 18 15N 96 40W
Miguel Alves 127 4 11 S 42 55W
Mihara 74 34 24N 133 5 E
Mijares → 32 39 55N 0 1W
Mijas 31 36 36N 4 40W
Mikese 90 6 48 S 37 55 E
Mikha-Tskhakaya 57 42 15N 42 7 E
Mikhailovka 56 47 36N 35 16 E
Mikhaylov 55 54 14N 39 0 E
Mikhaylovgrad 43 43 27N 23 16 E
Mikhaylovka, Azerbaijan, U.S.S.R. 57 41 31N 48 52 E
Mikhaylovka, R.S.F.S.R., U.S.S.R. 55 50 3N 43 5 E
Mikhnevo 55 55 4N 37 59 E
Mikínai 45 37 43N 22 46 E
Mikindani 91 10 15 S 40 2 E
Mikkeli 51 61 43N 27 15 E
Mikkeli □ 50 62 0N 28 0 E
Mikkwa → 108 58 25N 114 46W
Mikniya 87 17 0N 33 45 E
Mikołajki 28 53 49N 21 37 E
Mikołów 27 50 10N 18 50 E
Míkonos 45 37 30N 25 25 E
Mikrí Préspa, Límni 44 40 47N 21 3 E
Mikrón Dhérion 44 41 19N 26 6 E
Mikstat 28 51 32N 17 59 E
Mikulov 27 48 48N 16 39 E
Mikumi 90 7 26 S 37 0 E
Mikun 52 62 20N 50 0 E
Mikura-Jima 74 33 52N 139 36 E
Milaca 116 45 45N 93 40W
Milagro 126 2 11 S 79 36W
Milan, Mo., U.S.A. 116 40 10N 93 5W
Milan, Tenn., U.S.A. 115 35 55N 88 45W
Milan = Milano 38 45 28N 9 10 E
Milange 91 16 3 S 35 45 E
Milano 38 45 28N 9 10 E
Milâs 64 37 20N 27 50 E
Milazzo 41 38 13N 15 13 E
Milbank 116 45 17N 96 38W
Milden 109 51 29N 107 32W
Mildmay 112 44 3N 81 7W
Mildura 97 34 13 S 142 9 E
Miléai 44 39 20N 23 9 E
Miles, Austral. 97 26 40 S 150 9 E
Miles, U.S.A. 117 31 39N 100 11W
Miles City 116 46 24N 105 50W
Milestone 109 49 59N 104 31W
Mileto 41 38 37N 16 3 E
Miletto, Mte. 41 41 26N 14 23 E
Miletus 45 37 20N 27 33 E
Milevsko 26 49 27N 14 21 E
Milford, Conn., U.S.A. 113 41 13N 73 4W
Milford, Del., U.S.A. 114 38 52N 75 27W
Milford, Mass., U.S.A. 113 42 8N 71 30W
Milford, Pa., U.S.A. 113 41 20N 74 47W
Milford, Utah, U.S.A. 119 38 20N 113 0W
Milford Haven 13 51 43N 5 2W
Milford Haven, B. 13 51 40N 5 10W
Milford Sd. 101 44 41 S 167 47 E
Milh, Bahr al 64 32 40N 43 35 E
Milh, Ras al 81 31 54N 25 6 E
Miliana, Aïn Salah, Alg. 82 27 20N 2 32 E
Miliana, Médéa, Alg. 82 36 20N 2 15 E
Milicz 28 51 31N 17 19 E
Militello in Val di Catánia 41 37 16N 14 46 E
Milk → 118 48 5N 106 15W
Milk River 108 49 10N 112 5W
Milk, Wadi el → 86 17 55N 30 20 E
Mill City 118 44 45N 122 28W
Mill I. 5 66 0 S 101 30 E
Millau 20 44 8N 3 4 E
Millbridge 112 44 41N 77 36W
Millbrook 112 44 10N 78 29W
Mille 115 33 7N 83 15W
Mille Lacs, L. 116 46 10N 93 30W
Mille Lacs, L. des 106 48 45N 90 35W
Millen 115 32 50N 81 57W
Miller 116 44 35N 98 59W
Millerovo 57 48 57N 40 28 E
Millersburg, Ohio, U.S.A. 112 40 32N 81 52W
Millersburg, Pa., U.S.A. 112 40 32N 76 58W
Millerton 113 41 57N 73 32W
Millevaches, Plateau de 20 45 45N 2 0 E
Millicent 97 37 34 S 140 21 E
Millinocket 107 45 45N 68 45W
Millmerran 99 27 53 S 151 16 E
Mills L. 108 61 30N 118 20W
Millsboro 112 40 0N 80 0W
Milltown Malbay 15 52 51N 9 25W
Millville 114 39 22N 75 0W
Millwood Res. 117 33 45N 94 0W
Milly 19 48 24N 2 28 E
Milna 39 43 20N 16 28 E
Milne Inlet 105 72 30N 80 0W
Milnor 116 46 19N 97 29W
Milo 108 50 34N 112 53W
Mílos 45 36 44N 24 25 E
Miloševo 42 45 42N 20 20 E
Miłosław 28 52 12N 17 32 E
Milparinka P.O. 99 29 46 S 141 57 E
Miltenberg 25 49 41N 9 13 E
Milton, Can. 112 43 33N 79 53W
Milton, N.Z. 101 46 7 S 169 59 E
Milton, U.K. 14 57 18N 4 32W
Milton, Fla., U.S.A. 115 30 38N 87 0W
Milton, Pa., U.S.A. 114 41 0N 76 53W
Milton-Freewater 118 45 57N 118 24W
Milton Keynes 13 52 3N 0 42W
Miltou 81 10 14N 17 26 E
Milverton 112 43 34N 80 55W
Milwaukee 114 43 9N 87 58W
Milwaukie 118 45 27N 122 39W
Mim 84 6 57N 2 33W
Mimizan 20 44 12N 1 13W
Mimon 26 50 38N 14 43 E
Min Jiang →, Fujian, China 75 26 0N 119 35 E
Min Jiang →, Sichuan, China 75 28 45N 104 40 E
Min Xian 77 34 25N 104 0 E
Mina 119 38 21N 118 9W
Mina Pirquitas 124 22 40 S 66 30W
Mīnā Su'ud 64 28 45N 48 28 E
Mīnā'al Ahmadī 64 29 5N 48 10 E
Mīnāb 65 27 10N 57 1 E
Minago → 109 54 33N 98 59W
Minaki 109 49 59N 94 40W
Minamata 74 32 10N 130 30 E
Minas 125 34 20 S 55 10W
Minas Basin 107 45 20N 64 12W
Minas de Rio Tinto 31 37 42N 6 35W
Minas de San Quintín 31 38 49N 4 23W
Minas Gerais □ 127 18 50 S 46 0W
Minas, Sierra de las 120 15 9N 89 31W
Minatitlán 120 17 58N 94 35W
Minbu 67 20 10N 94 52 E
Mincio → 38 45 4N 10 59 E
Mindanao 73 8 0N 125 0 E
* Mindanao Sea 73 9 0N 124 0 E
Mindanao Trench 73 8 0N 128 0 E
Mindel → 25 48 31N 10 23 E
Mindelheim 25 48 4N 10 30 E
Minden, Can. 112 44 55N 78 43W
Minden, Ger. 24 52 18N 8 45 E
Minden, U.S.A. 117 32 40N 93 20W
Mindiptana 73 5 55 S 140 22 E
Mindona, L. 100 33 6 S 142 6 E
Mindoro 73 13 0N 121 0 E
Mindoro Strait 73 12 30N 120 30 E
Mindouli 88 4 12 S 14 28 E
Minehead 13 51 12N 3 29W
Mineoia 117 32 40N 95 30W
Mineral Wells 117 32 50N 98 5W
Mineralnyye Vody 57 44 2N 43 8 E
Minersville, Pa., U.S.A. 113 40 11N 76 17W
Minersville, Utah, U.S.A. 119 38 14N 112 58W
Minerva 112 40 43N 81 8W
Minervino Murge 41 41 6N 16 4 E
Minetto 113 43 24N 76 28W
Mingan 107 50 20N 64 0W
Mingechaur 57 40 45N 47 0 E
Mingechaurskoye Vdkhr. 57 40 56N 47 20 E
Mingela 98 19 52 S 146 38 E
Mingera Cr. → 98 20 38 S 138 10 E
Minggang 77 32 24N 114 3 E
Mingin 67 22 50N 94 30 E
Minglanilla 32 39 34N 1 38W
Mingorria 30 40 45N 4 40W
Mingxi 77 26 18N 117 12 E
Minićevo 42 43 42N 22 18 E
Minidoka 118 42 47N 113 34W
Minigwal L. 96 29 31 S 123 14 E
Minipi, L. 107 52 25N 60 45W
Mink L. 108 61 54N 117 40W
Minna 85 9 37N 6 30 E
Minneapolis, Kans., U.S.A. 116 39 11N 97 40W
Minneapolis, Minn., U.S.A. 116 44 58N 93 20W
Minnedosa 109 50 14N 99 50W
Minnesota □ 116 46 40N 94 0W
Minnesund 47 60 23N 11 14 E
Minnitaki L. 106 49 57N 92 10W
Miño → 30 41 52N 8 40W
Minoa 45 35 6N 25 45 E
Minorca = Menorca 32 40 0N 4 0 E
Minore 99 32 14 S 148 27 E
Minot 116 48 10N 101 15W
Minqing 77 26 15N 118 50 E
Minquiers, Les 18 48 58N 2 8W
Minsen 24 53 43N 7 58 E
Minsk 54 53 52N 27 30 E
Mińsk Mazowiecki 28 52 10N 21 33 E
Mintaka Pass 69 37 0N 74 58 E
Minto 104 64 55N 149 20W
Minton 109 49 10N 104 35W
Minturn 118 39 35N 106 25W
Minturno 40 41 15N 13 43 E
Minûf 86 30 26N 30 52 E
Minusinsk 59 53 50N 91 20 E
Minutang 67 28 15N 96 30 E
Minvoul 88 2 9N 12 8 E
Minya el Qamh 86 30 31N 31 21 E
Mionica 42 44 14N 20 6 E
Mir 85 14 5N 11 59 E
Mir-Bashir 57 40 20N 46 58 E
Mira, Italy 39 45 26N 12 9 E
Mira, Port. 30 40 26N 8 44W
Mira → 31 37 43N 8 47W
Mirabella Eclano 41 41 3N 14 59 E
Miraflores Locks 120 8 59N 79 36W
Miraj 70 16 50N 74 45 E
Miram 98 21 15 S 148 55 E
Miramar, Argent. 124 38 15 S 57 50W
Miramar, Mozam. 93 23 50 S 35 35 E
Miramas 21 43 33N 4 59 E
Mirambeau 20 45 23N 0 35W
Miramichi B. 107 47 15N 65 0W
Miramont-de-Guyenne 20 44 37N 0 21 E
Miranda 127 20 10 S 56 15W
Miranda de Ebro 32 42 41N 2 57W
Miranda do Corvo 30 40 6N 8 20W
Miranda do Douro 30 41 30N 6 16W
Mirande 20 43 31N 0 25 E
Mirandela 30 41 32N 7 10W
Mirando City 117 27 28N 98 59W
Mirandola 38 44 53N 11 2 E
Mirandópolis 125 21 9 S 51 6W
Mirango 91 13 32 S 34 58 E
Mirano 39 45 29N 12 6 E
Mirassol 125 20 46 S 49 28W
Mirbāţ 63 17 0N 54 45 E
Mirear 86 23 15N 35 41 E
Mirebeau, Côte-d'or, France 19 47 25N 5 20 E
Mirebeau, Vienne, France 18 46 49N 0 10 E
Mirecourt 19 48 20N 6 10 E
Mirgorod 54 49 58N 33 37 E
Miri 72 4 18N 114 0 E
Miriam Vale 98 24 20 S 151 33 E
Mirim, Lagoa 125 32 45 S 52 50W
Mirnyy, Antarct. 5 66 33 S 93 1 E
Mirnyy, U.S.S.R. 59 62 33N 113 53 E
Miroč 42 44 32N 22 16 E
Mirond L. 109 55 6N 102 47W
Mirosławiec 28 53 20N 16 5 E
Mirpur Bibiwari 68 28 33N 67 44 E
Mirpur Khas 68 25 30N 69 0 E
Mirpur Sakro 68 24 33N 67 41 E
Mirria 85 13 43N 9 7 E
Mirror 108 52 30N 113 7W
Mîrşani 46 44 1N 23 59 E
Mirsk 28 50 58N 15 23 E
Miryang 76 35 31N 128 44 E
Mirzaani 57 41 24N 46 5 E
Mirzapur-cum-Vindhyachal 69 25 10N 82 34 E
Miscou I. 107 47 57N 64 31W
Mish'āb, Ra'as al 64 28 15N 48 43 E
Mishan 75 45 37N 131 48 E
Mishawaka 114 41 40N 86 8W
Mishbih, Gebel 86 22 38N 34 44 E
Mishima 74 35 10N 138 52 E
Mishmar Ayyalon 62 31 52N 34 57 E
Mishmar Ha' Emeq 62 32 37N 35 7 E
Mishmar Ha Negev 62 31 22N 34 48 E
Mishmar Ha Yarden 62 33 0N 35 36 E
Misilmeri 40 38 2N 13 25 E
Misima I. 98 10 40 S 152 45 E
Misiones □, Argent. 125 27 0 S 55 0W
Misiones □, Parag. 124 27 0 S 56 0W
Miskīn 65 23 44N 56 52 E
Miskitos, Cayos 121 14 26N 82 50W
Miskolc 27 48 7N 20 50 E
Misoke 90 0 42 S 28 2 E
Misool 73 1 52 S 130 10 E
Misrātah 83 32 24N 15 3 E
Misrātah □ 83 29 0N 16 0 E
Misriç 64 37 55N 41 40 E
Missanabie 106 48 20N 84 6W
Missinaibi → 106 50 43N 81 29W
Missinaibi L. 106 48 23N 83 40W
Mission, S.D., U.S.A. 116 43 21N 100 36W
Mission, Tex., U.S.A. 117 26 15N 98 20W
Mission City 108 49 10N 122 15W
Missisa L. 106 52 20N 85 7W
Mississagi → 106 46 15N 83 9W
Mississippi → 117 29 0N 89 15W
Mississippi, Delta of the 117 29 15N 90 30W
Mississippi L. 113 45 5N 76 10W
Mississippi □ 117 33 25N 89 0W
Missoula 118 46 52N 114 0W
Missouri □ 116 38 25N 92 30W
Missouri → 116 38 50N 90 8W
Missouri Valley 116 41 33N 95 53W
Mistake B. 109 62 8N 93 0W
Mistassini → 107 48 42N 72 20W
Mistassini L. 106 51 0N 73 30W
Mistastin L. 107 55 57N 63 20W
Mistatim 109 52 52N 103 22W
Mistelbach 27 48 34N 16 34 E
Misterbianco 41 37 32N 15 0 E
Mistretta 41 37 56N 14 20 E
Misty L. 109 58 53N 101 40W
Mît Ghamr 86 30 42N 31 12 E
Mitatib 87 15 59N 36 12 E
Mitchell, Austral. 97 26 29 S 147 58 E
Mitchell, Can. 112 43 28N 81 12W
Mitchell, Ind., U.S.A. 114 38 42N 86 25W
Mitchell, Nebr., U.S.A. 116 41 58N 103 45W
Mitchell, Oreg., U.S.A. 118 44 31N 120 8W
Mitchell, S.D., U.S.A. 116 43 40N 98 0W
Mitchell → 97 15 12 S 141 35 E
Mitchell, Mt. 115 35 40N 82 20W
Mitchelstown 15 52 16N 8 18W
Mitha Tiwana 68 32 13N 72 6 E
Míthimna 44 39 20N 26 12 E
Mitiaro, I. 101 19 49 S 157 43W
Mitilini 45 39 6N 26 35 E
Mitilinoí 45 37 42N 26 56 E
Mitla 120 16 55N 96 24W
Mito 74 36 20N 140 30 E
Mitsinjo 93 16 1 S 45 52 E
Mitsiwa 87 15 35N 39 25 E
Mitsiwa Channel 87 15 30N 40 0 E
Mitta Mitta → 100 36 14 S 147 10 E
Mittagong 99 34 28 S 150 29 E
Mittelland Kanal 24 52 23N 7 45 E
Mittenwalde 24 52 16N 13 33 E
Mitterteich 25 49 57N 12 15 E
Mittweida 24 50 59N 13 0 E
Mitú 126 1 8N 70 3W
Mitumba 90 7 8 S 31 2 E
Mitumba, Chaîne des 90 6 0 S 29 0 E
Mitwaba 91 8 2 S 27 17 E
Mityana 90 0 23N 32 2 E
Mitzic 88 0 45N 11 40 E
Mixteco → 120 18 11N 98 30W
Miyagi □ 74 38 15N 140 45 E
Miyâh, W. el → 86 25 0N 33 23 E
Miyake-Jima 74 34 0N 139 30 E
Miyako 74 39 40N 141 59 E
Miyakonojō 74 31 40N 131 5 E
Miyazaki 74 31 56N 131 30 E
Miyazaki □ 74 32 30N 131 30 E
Miyazu 74 35 35N 135 10 E
Miyet, Bahr el 64 31 30N 35 30 E
Miyun 76 40 28N 116 50 E
Mizal 64 23 59N 45 11 E
Mizamis = Ozamiz 73 8 15N 123 50 E
Mizdah 83 31 30N 13 0 E
Mizen Hd., Cork, Ireland 15 51 27N 9 50W
Mizen Hd., Wicklow, Ireland 15 52 52N 6 4W
Mizhi 76 37 47N 110 12 E
Mizil 46 44 59N 26 29 E
Mizoram □ 67 23 30N 92 40 E
Mizpe Ramon 62 30 34N 34 49 E
Mjöbäck 49 57 28N 12 53 E
Mjölby 49 58 20N 15 10 E
Mjømna 47 60 55N 4 55 E
Mjörn 49 57 55N 12 25 E
Mjøsa 47 60 48N 11 0 E
Mkata 90 5 45 S 38 20 E
Mkokotoni 90 5 55 S 39 15 E
Mkomazi 90 4 40 S 38 7 E
Mkulwe 91 8 37 S 32 20 E
Mkumbi, Ras 90 7 38 S 39 55 E
Mkushi 91 14 25 S 29 15 E
Mkushi River 91 13 32 S 29 45 E
Mkuze → 93 27 45 S 32 30 E
Mladá Boleslav 26 50 27N 14 53 E
Mladenovac 42 44 28N 20 44 E
Mlala Hills 90 6 50 S 31 40 E
Mlange 91 16 2 S 35 33 E
Mlava → 42 44 45N 21 13 E
Mława 28 53 9N 20 25 E
Mlinište 39 44 15N 16 50 E
Mljet 42 42 43N 17 30 E
Mljetski Kanal 42 42 48N 17 35 E
Młynary 28 54 12N 19 46 E
Mlynary 28 54 12N 19 43 E
Mme 85 6 18N 10 14 E
Mo 47 59 28N 7 50 E
Mo i Rana 50 66 15N 14 7 E
Moa 73 8 0 S 128 0 E
Moa → 84 6 59N 11 36 E
Moab 119 38 40N 109 35W
Moabi 88 2 24 S 10 59 E
Moala 101 18 36 S 179 53 E
Moalie Park 99 29 42 S 143 3 E
Moaña 30 42 18N 8 43W
Moapa 119 36 45N 114 37W
Moba 90 7 0 S 29 48 E
Mobaye 88 4 25N 21 5 E
Mobayi 88 4 15N 21 8 E
Moberley 116 39 25N 92 25W
Moberly → 108 56 12N 120 55W
Mobile 115 30 41N 88 3W
Mobile B. 115 30 30N 88 0W
Mobile, Pt. 115 30 15N 88 0W
Mobridge 116 45 31N 100 28W
Mobutu Sese Seko, L. 90 1 30N 31 0 E

* Renamed Bohol Sea

Place	Map	Lat.	Long.
Mocabe Kasari	**91**	9 58 S	26 12 E
Moçambique	**91**	15 3 S	40 42 E
Moçambique □	**91**	14 45 S	38 30 E
* Moçâmedes	**89**	15 7 S	12 11 E
* Moçâmedes □	**92**	16 35 S	12 30 E
Mochudi	**92**	24 27 S	26 7 E
Mocimboa da Praia	**91**	11 25 S	40 20 E
Mociu	**46**	46 46N	24 3 E
Möckeln	**49**	56 40N	14 15 E
Moclips	**118**	47 14N	124 10W
Mocoa	**126**	1 7N	76 35W
Mococa	**125**	21 28 S	47 0W
Mocorito	**120**	25 30N	107 53W
Moctezuma	**120**	29 50N	109 0W
Moctezuma →	**120**	21 59N	98 34W
Mocuba	**91**	16 54 S	36 57 E
Modalen	**47**	60 49N	5 48 E
Modane	**21**	45 12N	6 40 E
Modasa	**68**	23 30N	73 21 E
Modder →	**92**	29 2 S	24 37 E
Modderrivier	**92**	29 2 S	24 38 E
Módena	**38**	44 39N	10 55 E
Modena	**119**	37 55N	113 56W
Modesto	**119**	37 43N	121 0W
Módica	**41**	36 52N	14 45 E
Modigliana	**39**	44 9N	11 48 E
Modlin	**28**	52 24N	20 41 E
Mödling	**27**	48 5N	16 17 E
Modo	**87**	5 31N	30 33 E
Modra	**27**	48 19N	17 20 E
Modriča	**42**	44 57N	18 17 E
Moe	**97**	38 12 S	146 19 E
Moebase	**91**	17 3 S	38 41 E
Moei →	**71**	17 25N	98 10 E
Moëlan-sur-Mer	**18**	47 49N	3 38W
Moengo	**127**	5 45N	54 20W
Moffat	**14**	55 20N	3 27W
Moga	**68**	30 48N	75 8 E
Mogadishu = Muqdisho	**63**	2 2N	45 25 E
Mogador = Essaouira	**82**	31 32N	9 48W
Mogadouro	**30**	41 22N	6 47W
Mogami →	**74**	38 45N	140 0 E
Mogaung	**67**	25 20N	97 0 E
Møgeltønder	**49**	54 57N	8 48 E
Mogente	**33**	38 52N	0 45W
Mogho	**87**	4 54N	40 16 E
Mogi das Cruzes	**125**	23 31 S	46 11W
Mogi-Guaçu →	**125**	20 53 S	48 10W
Mogi-Mirim	**125**	22 29 S	47 0W
Mogielnica	**28**	51 42N	20 41 E
Mogilev	**54**	53 55N	30 18 E
Mogilev-Podolskiy	**56**	48 20N	27 40 E
Mogilno	**28**	52 39N	17 55 E
Mogincual	**91**	15 35 S	40 25 E
Mogliano Véneto	**39**	45 33N	12 15 E
Mogocha	**59**	53 40N	119 50 E
Mogoi	**73**	1 55 S	133 10 E
Mogok	**67**	23 0N	96 40 E
Mogollon	**119**	33 25N	108 48W
Mogollon Mesa	**119**	35 0N	111 0W
Moguer	**31**	37 15N	6 52W
Mohács	**27**	45 58N	18 41 E
Mohall	**116**	48 46N	101 30W
Moḩammadābād	**65**	37 52N	59 5 E
Mohammadia	**82**	35 33N	0 3 E
Mohammedia	**82**	33 44N	7 21W
Mohawk	**119**	32 45N	113 50W
Mohawk →	**113**	42 47N	73 42W
Mohe	**76**	53 28N	122 17 E
Moheda	**49**	57 1N	14 35 E
Möhne →	**24**	51 29N	7 57 E
Moholm	**49**	58 37N	14 5 E
Mohon	**19**	49 45N	4 44 E
Mohoro	**90**	8 6 S	39 8 E
Moia	**87**	5 3N	28 2 E
Moidart, L.	**14**	56 47N	5 40W
Moinabad	**70**	17 44N	77 16 E
Moineşti	**46**	46 28N	26 31 E
Mointy	**58**	47 10N	73 18 E
Moirans	**21**	45 20N	5 33 E
Moirans-en-Montagne	**21**	46 26N	5 43 E
Moíres	**45**	35 4N	24 56 E
Moisakula	**54**	58 3N	25 12 E
Moisie	**107**	50 12N	66 1W
Moisie →	**107**	50 14N	66 5W
Moissac	**20**	44 7N	1 5 E
Moïssala	**81**	8 21N	17 46 E
Moita	**31**	38 38N	8 58W
Mojácar	**33**	37 6N	1 55W
Mojados	**30**	41 26N	4 40W
Mojave	**119**	35 8N	118 8W
Mojave Desert	**119**	35 0N	116 30W
Mojo, Boliv.	**124**	21 48 S	65 33W
Mojo, Ethiopia	**87**	8 35N	39 5 E
Mojo, Indon.	**72**	8 10 S	117 40 E
Mojokerto	**73**	7 29 S	112 25 E
Mokai	**101**	38 32 S	175 56 E
Mokambo	**91**	12 25 S	28 20 E
Mokameh	**69**	25 24N	85 55 E
Mokhós	**45**	35 16N	25 27 E
Mokhotlong	**93**	29 22 S	29 2 E
Moknine	**83**	35 35N	10 58 E
Mokokchung	**67**	26 15N	94 30 E
Mokra Gora	**42**	42 50N	20 30 E
Mokronog	**39**	45 57N	15 9 E
Moksha →	**55**	54 45N	41 53 E
Mokshan	**55**	53 25N	44 35 E
Mol	**16**	51 11N	5 5 E
Mola, C. de la	**32**	39 40N	4 20 E
Mola di Bari	**41**	41 3N	17 5 E
Moláoi	**45**	36 49N	22 56 E
Molat	**39**	44 15N	14 50 E
Molchanovo	**58**	57 40N	83 50 E
Mold	**12**	53 10N	3 10W
Moldava nad Bodvou	**27**	48 38N	21 0 E
Moldavia = Moldova	**46**	46 30N	27 0 E
Moldavian S.S.R. □	**56**	47 0N	28 0 E
Molde	**47**	62 45N	7 9 E
Moldova	**46**	46 30N	27 0 E
Moldova Nouă	**42**	44 45N	21 41 E
Moldoveanu	**43**	45 36N	24 45 E
Molepolole	**92**	24 28 S	25 28 E
Molfetta	**41**	41 12N	16 35 E
Molina de Aragón	**32**	40 46N	1 52W
Moline	**116**	41 30N	90 30W
Molinella	**39**	44 38N	11 40 E
Molinos	**124**	25 28 S	66 15W
Moliro	**90**	8 12 S	30 30 E
Molise □	**39**	41 45N	14 30 E
Moliterno	**41**	40 14N	15 50 E
Mollahat	**69**	22 56N	89 48 E
Mölle	**49**	56 17N	12 31 E
Molledo	**30**	43 8N	4 6W
Mollendo	**126**	17 0 S	72 0W
Mollerusa	**32**	41 37N	0 54 E
Mollina	**31**	37 8N	4 38W
Mölln	**24**	53 37N	10 41 E
Mölltorp	**49**	58 30N	14 26 E
Mölndal	**49**	57 40N	12 3 E
Molochansk	**56**	47 15N	35 35 E
Molochnaya →	**56**	47 0N	35 30 E
Molodechno	**54**	54 20N	26 50 E
Molokai	**110**	21 8N	157 0W
Moloma →	**55**	58 20N	48 15 E
Molong	**99**	33 5 S	148 54 E
Molopo →	**92**	28 30 S	20 13 E
Mólos	**45**	38 47N	22 37 E
Moloundou	**88**	2 8N	15 15 E
Molsheim	**19**	48 33N	7 29 E
Molson L.	**109**	54 22N	96 40W
Molteno	**92**	31 22 S	26 22 E
Molu	**73**	6 45 S	131 40 E
Molucca Sea	**73**	4 0 S	124 0 E
Moluccas = Maluku	**73**	1 0 S	127 0 E
Molusi	**92**	20 21 S	24 29 E
Moma, Mozam.	**91**	16 47 S	39 4 E
Moma, Zaïre	**90**	1 35 S	23 52 E
Momanga	**92**	18 7 S	21 41 E
Mombasa	**90**	4 2 S	39 43 E
Mombuey	**30**	42 3N	6 20W
Momchilgrad	**43**	41 33N	25 23 E
Momi	**90**	1 42 S	27 0 E
Mompós	**126**	9 14N	74 26W
Møn	**49**	54 57N	12 15 E
Mon →	**67**	20 25N	94 30 E
Mona, Canal de la	**121**	18 30N	67 45W
Mona, I.	**121**	18 5N	67 54W
Mona, Pta.	**121**	9 37N	82 36W
Mona, Punta	**31**	36 43N	3 45W
Monach Is.	**14**	57 32N	7 40W
Monaco ■	**21**	43 46N	7 23 E
Monadhliath Mts.	**14**	57 10N	4 4W
Monaghan	**15**	54 15N	6 58W
Monaghan □	**15**	54 10N	7 0W
Monahans	**117**	31 35N	102 50W
Monapo	**91**	14 56 S	40 19 E
Monarch Mt.	**108**	51 55N	125 57W
Monastier-sur-Gazeille, Le	**20**	44 57N	3 59 E
Monastir	**83**	35 50N	10 49 E
Monastyriska	**54**	49 8N	25 14 E
Moncada	**32**	39 30N	0 24W
Moncalieri	**38**	45 0N	7 40 E
Moncalvo	**38**	45 3N	8 15 E
Moncão	**30**	42 4N	8 27W
Moncarapacho	**31**	37 5N	7 46W
Moncayo, Sierra del	**32**	41 48N	1 50W
Mönchengladbach	**24**	51 12N	6 23 E
Monchique	**31**	37 19N	8 38W
Monclova	**120**	26 50N	101 30W
Moncontour	**18**	48 22N	2 38W
Moncoutant	**18**	46 43N	0 35W
Moncton	**107**	46 7N	64 51W
Mondego →	**30**	40 9N	8 52W
Mondego, Cabo	**30**	40 11N	8 54W
Mondeodo	**73**	3 34 S	122 9 E
Mondolfo	**39**	43 45N	13 8 E
Mondoñedo	**30**	43 25N	7 23W
Mondoví	**38**	44 23N	7 49 E
Mondovi	**116**	44 37N	91 40W
Mondragon	**21**	44 13N	4 44 E
Mondragone	**40**	41 8N	13 52 E
Monduli □	**90**	3 0 S	36 0 E
Monemvasía	**45**	36 41N	23 3 E
Monessen	**114**	40 9N	79 50W
Monesterio	**31**	38 6N	6 15W
Monestier-de-Clermont	**21**	44 55N	5 38 E
Monêtier-les-Bains, Le	**21**	44 58N	6 30 E
Monett	**117**	36 55N	93 56W
Monfalcone	**39**	45 49N	13 32 E
Monflanquin	**20**	44 32N	0 47 E
Monforte	**31**	39 6N	7 25W
Monforte de Lemos	**30**	42 31N	7 33W
Mong Cai	**71**	21 27N	107 54 E
Mong Hsu	**67**	21 54N	98 30 E
Mong Kung	**67**	21 35N	97 35 E
Mong Lang	**71**	21 29N	97 52 E
Mong Nai	**67**	20 32N	97 46 E
Mong Pawk	**67**	22 4N	99 16 E
Mong Ton	**67**	20 17N	98 45 E
Mong Wa	**67**	21 26N	100 27 E
Mong Yai	**67**	22 21N	98 3 E
Mongalla	**87**	5 8N	31 42 E
Mongers, L.	**96**	29 25 S	117 5 E
Monghyr	**69**	25 23N	86 30 E
Mongla	**69**	22 8N	89 35 E
Mongo	**81**	12 14N	18 43 E
Mongolia ■	**75**	47 0N	103 0 E
Mongonu	**85**	12 40N	13 32 E
Mongororo	**81**	12 3N	22 26 E
Mongu	**89**	15 16 S	23 12 E
Môngua	**92**	16 43 S	15 20 E
Monistrol	**20**	45 57N	3 38 E
Monistrol-St-Loire	**21**	45 17N	4 11 E
Monkey Bay	**91**	14 7 S	35 1 E
Mońki	**28**	53 23N	22 48 E
Monkira	**98**	24 46 S	140 30 E
Monkoto	**88**	1 38 S	20 35 E
Monmouth, U.K.	**13**	51 48N	2 43W
Monmouth, U.S.A.	**116**	40 50N	90 40W
Mono, L.	**119**	38 0N	119 9W
Monongahela	**112**	40 12N	79 56W
Monópoli	**41**	40 57N	17 18 E
Monor	**27**	47 21N	19 27 E
Monóvar	**33**	38 28N	0 53W
Monqoumba	**88**	3 33N	18 40 E
Monreal del Campo	**32**	40 47N	1 20W
Monreale	**40**	38 6N	13 16 E
Monroe, Ga., U.S.A.	**115**	33 47N	83 43W
Monroe, La., U.S.A.	**117**	32 32N	92 4W
Monroe, Mich., U.S.A.	**114**	41 55N	83 26W
Monroe, N.C., U.S.A.	**115**	35 2N	80 37W
Monroe, N.Y., U.S.A.	**113**	41 19N	74 11W
Monroe, Utah, U.S.A.	**119**	38 45N	112 5W
Monroe, Wis., U.S.A.	**116**	42 38N	89 40W
Monroe City	**116**	39 40N	91 40W
Monroeville	**115**	31 33N	87 15W
Monrovia, Liberia	**84**	6 18N	10 47W
Monrovia, U.S.A.	**119**	34 7N	118 1W
Mons	**16**	50 27N	3 58 E
Monsaraz	**31**	38 28N	7 22W
Monse	**73**	4 0 S	123 10 E
Monségur	**20**	44 38N	0 4 E
Monsélice	**39**	45 16N	11 46 E
Mont-de-Marsan	**20**	43 54N	0 31W
Mont d'Or, Tunnel	**19**	46 45N	6 18 E
Mont-Dore, Le	**20**	45 35N	2 50 E
Mont-Joli	**107**	48 37N	68 10W
Mont Laurier	**106**	46 35N	75 30W
Mont-sous-Vaudrey	**19**	46 58N	5 36 E
Mont-St-Michel, Le	**18**	48 40N	1 30W
Mont Tremblant Prov. Park	**106**	46 30N	74 30W
Montabaur	**24**	50 26N	7 49 E
Montagnac	**20**	43 29N	3 28 E
Montagnana	**39**	45 13N	11 29 E
Montagu	**92**	33 45 S	20 8 E
Montagu I.	**5**	58 25 S	26 20W
Montague, Can.	**107**	46 10N	62 39W
Montague, Calif., U.S.A.	**118**	41 47N	122 30W
Montague, Mass., U.S.A.	**113**	42 31N	72 33W
Montague, I.	**120**	31 40N	114 56W
Montague I.	**104**	60 0N	147 0W
Montague Sd.	**96**	14 28 S	125 20 E
Montaigu	**18**	46 59N	1 18W
Montalbán	**32**	40 50N	0 45W
Montalbano di Elicona	**41**	38 1N	15 0 E
Montalbano Iónico	**41**	40 17N	16 33 E
Montalbo	**32**	39 53N	2 42W
Montalcino	**39**	43 4N	11 30 E
Montalegre	**30**	41 49N	7 47W
Montalto di Castro	**39**	42 20N	11 36 E
Montalto Uffugo	**41**	39 25N	16 9 E
Montamarta	**30**	41 39N	5 49W
Montaña	**126**	6 0 S	73 0W
Montana □	**110**	47 0N	110 0W
Montánchez	**31**	39 15N	6 8W
Montargis	**19**	48 0N	2 43 E
Montauban	**20**	44 0N	1 21 E
Montauk	**114**	41 3N	71 57W
Montauk Pt.	**113**	41 4N	71 52W
Montbard	**19**	47 38N	4 20 E
Montbéliard	**19**	47 31N	6 48 E
Montblanch	**32**	41 23N	1 4 E
Montbrison	**21**	45 36N	4 3 E
Montcalm, Pic de	**20**	42 40N	1 25 E
Montceau-les-Mines	**19**	46 40N	4 23 E
Montchanin	**38**	46 47N	4 30 E
Montclair	**113**	40 53N	74 13W
Montcornet	**19**	49 40N	4 0 E
Montcuq	**20**	44 21N	1 13 E
Montdidier	**19**	49 38N	2 35 E
Monte Alegre	**127**	2 0 S	54 0W
Monte Azul	**127**	15 9 S	42 53W
Monte Bello Is.	**96**	20 30 S	115 45 E
Monte-Carlo	**21**	43 46N	7 23 E
Monte Caseros	**124**	30 10 S	57 50W
Monte Comán	**124**	34 40 S	67 53W
Monte Lindo →	**124**	23 56 S	57 12W
Monte Quemado	**124**	25 53 S	62 41W
Monte Redondo	**30**	39 53N	8 50W
Monte San Giovanni	**40**	41 39N	13 33 E
Monte San Savino	**39**	43 20N	11 42 E
Monte Sant' Ángelo	**41**	41 42N	15 59 E
Monte Santu, C. di	**40**	40 5N	9 42 E
Monte Vista	**119**	37 40N	106 8W
Monteagudo	**125**	27 14 S	54 8W
Montealegre	**33**	38 48N	1 17W
Montebello	**106**	45 40N	74 55W
Montebelluna	**39**	45 47N	12 3 E
Montebourg	**18**	49 30N	1 20W
Montecastrilli	**39**	42 40N	12 30 E
Montecatini Terme	**38**	43 55N	10 48 E
Montecristi	**126**	1 0 S	80 40W
Montecristo	**38**	42 20N	10 20 E
Montefalco	**39**	42 53N	12 38 E
Montefiascone	**39**	42 31N	12 2 E
Montefrío	**31**	37 20N	4 0W
Montego Bay	**121**	18 30N	78 0W
Montegranaro	**39**	43 13N	13 38 E
Montehanin	**19**	46 46N	4 44 E
Montejicar	**33**	37 33N	3 30W
Montélimar	**21**	44 33N	4 45 E
Montella	**41**	40 50N	15 0 E
Montellano	**31**	36 59N	5 36W
Montello	**116**	43 49N	89 21W
Montelupo Fiorentino	**38**	43 44N	11 2 E
Montemor-o-Novo	**31**	38 40N	8 12W
Montemor-o-Velho	**30**	40 11N	8 40W
Montemorelos	**120**	25 11N	99 42W
Montendre	**20**	45 16N	0 26W
Montenegro	**125**	29 39 S	51 29W
Montenegro = Crna Gora □	**42**	42 40N	19 20 E
Montenero di Bisaccia	**39**	42 0N	14 47 E
Montepuez	**91**	13 8 S	38 59 E
Montepuez →	**91**	12 32 S	40 27 E
Montepulciano	**39**	43 5N	11 46 E
Montereale	**39**	42 31N	13 13 E
Montereau	**19**	48 22N	2 57 E
Monterey	**119**	36 35N	121 57W
Montería	**126**	8 46N	75 53W
Monteros	**124**	27 11 S	65 30W
Monterotondo	**39**	42 3N	12 36 E
Monterrey	**120**	25 40N	100 30W
Montes Claros	**127**	16 30 S	43 50W
Montesano	**118**	47 0N	123 39W
Montesárchio	**41**	41 5N	14 37 E
Montescaglioso	**41**	40 34N	16 40 E
Montesilvano	**39**	42 30N	14 8 E
Montevarchi	**39**	43 30N	11 32 E
Montevideo	**125**	34 50 S	56 11W
Montezuma	**116**	41 32N	92 35W
Montfaucon, Haute-Loire, France	**21**	45 11N	4 20 E
Montfaucon, Meuse, France	**19**	49 16N	5 8 E
Montfort-l'Amaury	**19**	48 47N	1 49 E
Montfort-sur-Meu	**18**	48 8N	1 58W
Montgenèvre	**21**	44 56N	6 42 E
Montgomery, U.K.	**13**	52 34N	3 9W
Montgomery, Ala., U.S.A.	**115**	32 20N	86 20W
Montgomery, W. Va., U.S.A.	**114**	38 9N	81 21W
Montgomery = Sahiwal	**68**	30 45N	73 8 E
Montguyon	**20**	45 12N	0 12W
Monthey	**25**	46 15N	6 56 E
Monticelli d'Ongina	**38**	45 3N	9 56 E
Monticello, Ark., U.S.A.	**117**	33 40N	91 48W
Monticello, Fla., U.S.A.	**115**	30 35N	83 50W
Monticello, Ind., U.S.A.	**114**	40 40N	86 45W
Monticello, Iowa, U.S.A.	**116**	42 18N	91 12W
Monticello, Ky., U.S.A.	**115**	36 52N	84 50W
Monticello, Minn., U.S.A.	**116**	45 17N	93 52W
Monticello, Miss., U.S.A.	**117**	31 35N	90 8W
Monticello, N.Y., U.S.A.	**113**	41 37N	74 42W
Monticello, Utah, U.S.A.	**119**	37 55N	109 27W
Montichiari	**38**	45 28N	10 29 E
Montier	**19**	48 30N	4 45 E
Montignac	**20**	45 4N	1 10 E
Montigny-les-Metz	**19**	49 7N	6 10 E
Montigny-sur-Aube	**19**	47 57N	4 45 E
Montijo	**31**	38 52N	6 39W
Montijo, Presa de	**31**	38 55N	6 26W
Montilla	**31**	37 36N	4 40W
Montivideo	**116**	44 55N	95 40W
Montlhéry	**19**	48 39N	2 15 E
Montluçon	**20**	46 22N	2 36 E
Montmagny	**107**	46 58N	70 34W
Montmarault	**20**	46 19N	2 57 E
Montmartre	**109**	50 14N	103 27W
Montmédy	**19**	49 30N	5 20 E
Montmélian	**21**	45 30N	6 4 E
Montmirail	**19**	48 51N	3 30 E
Montmoreau-St-Cybard	**20**	45 23N	0 8 E
Montmorency	**107**	46 53N	71 11W
Montmorillon	**20**	46 26N	0 50 E
Montmort	**19**	48 55N	3 49 E
Monto	**97**	24 52 S	151 6 E
Montoire	**18**	47 45N	0 52 E
Montório al Vomano	**39**	42 35N	13 38 E
Montoro	**31**	38 1N	4 27W
Montour Falls	**112**	42 20N	76 51W
Montpelier, Idaho, U.S.A.	**118**	42 15N	111 20W
Montpelier, Ohio, U.S.A.	**114**	41 34N	84 40W
Montpelier, Vt., U.S.A.	**114**	44 15N	72 38W
Montpellier	**20**	43 37N	3 52 E
Montpezat-de-Quercy	**20**	44 15N	1 30 E
Montpon	**20**	45 2N	0 11 E
Montréal, Can.	**106**	45 31N	73 34W
Montréal, France	**20**	43 13N	2 8 E
Montreal L.	**109**	54 20N	105 45W
Montreal Lake	**109**	54 3N	105 46W
Montredon-Labessonniè	**20**	43 45N	2 18 E
Montréjeau	**20**	43 6N	0 35 E
Montrésor	**18**	47 10N	1 10 E
Montreuil	**19**	50 27N	1 45 E
Montreuil-Bellay	**18**	47 8N	0 9W
Montreux	**25**	46 26N	6 55 E
Montrevault	**18**	47 17N	1 2W
Montrevel-en-Bresse	**21**	46 21N	5 8 E
Montrichard	**18**	47 20N	1 10 E
Montrose, U.K.	**14**	56 43N	2 28W
Montrose, Col., U.S.A.	**119**	38 30N	107 52W
Montrose, Pa., U.S.A.	**113**	41 50N	75 55W
Monts, Pte des	**107**	49 20N	67 12W
Monts-sur-Guesnes	**18**	46 55N	0 13 E
Montsalvy	**20**	44 41N	2 30 E
Montsant, Sierra de	**32**	41 17N	1 0 E
Montsauche	**19**	47 13N	4 0 E
Montsech, Sierra del	**32**	42 0N	0 45 E
Montseny	**32**	41 55N	2 25W
Montserrat, Spain	**32**	41 36N	1 49 E
Montserrat, W. Indies	**121**	16 40N	62 10W
Montuenga	**30**	41 3N	4 38W
Montuiri	**32**	39 34N	2 59 E
Monveda	**88**	2 52N	21 30 E
Monywa	**67**	22 7N	95 11 E
Monza	**38**	45 35N	9 15 E
Monze	**91**	16 17 S	27 29 E
Monze, C.	**66**	24 47N	66 37 E
Monzón	**32**	41 52N	0 10 E
Moolawatana	**99**	29 55 S	139 45 E
Moonah →	**98**	22 3 S	138 33 E
Moonbeam	**106**	49 20N	82 10W
Moonie	**99**	27 46 S	150 20 E
Moonie →	**97**	29 19 S	148 43 E
Moonta	**99**	34 6 S	137 32 E
Mooraberree	**99**	25 13 S	140 54 E
Moorcroft	**116**	44 17N	104 58W
Moore, L.	**96**	29 50 S	117 35 E
Moorefield	**114**	39 5N	78 59W
Moores Res.	**113**	44 45N	71 50W
Mooresville	**115**	35 36N	80 45W
Moorfoot Hills	**14**	55 44N	3 8W
Moorhead	**116**	46 51N	96 44W
Mooroopna	**99**	36 25 S	145 22 E
Moorreesburg	**92**	33 6 S	18 38 E
Moosburg	**25**	48 28N	11 57 E
Moose →	**106**	51 20N	80 25W
Moose Factory	**106**	51 16N	80 32W
Moose I.	**109**	51 42N	97 10W
Moose Jaw	**109**	50 24N	105 30W
Moose Jaw Cr. →	**109**	50 34N	105 18W
Moose Lake, Can.	**109**	53 43N	100 20W
Moose Lake, U.S.A.	**116**	46 27N	92 48W
Moose Mountain Cr. →	**109**	49 13N	102 12W
Moose Mountain Prov. Park	**109**	49 48N	102 25W
Moose River	**106**	50 48N	81 17W
Moosehead L.	**107**	45 34N	69 40W
Moosomin	**109**	50 9N	101 40W
Moosonee	**106**	51 17N	80 39W
Moosup	**113**	41 44N	71 52W

* *Renamed Namibe*

Mopipi 92 21 6S 24 55 E
Mopoi 90 5 6N 26 54 E
Mopti 84 14 30N 4 0W
Moqatta 87 14 38N 35 50 E
Moquegua 126 17 15S 70 46W
Mór 27 47 25N 18 12 E
Móra 31 38 55N 8 10W
Mora, Sweden 48 61 2N 14 38 E
Mora, Minn., U.S.A. 116 45 52N 93 19W
Mora, N. Mex., U.S.A. 119 35 58N 105 21W
Mora de Ebro 32 41 6N 0 38 E
Mora de Rubielos 32 40 15N 0 45W
Mora la Nueva 32 41 7N 0 39 E
Morača ~ 42 42 20N 19 9 E
Moradabad 68 28 50N 78 50 E
Morafenobe 93 17 50S 44 53 E
Morąg 28 53 55N 19 56 E
Moral de Calatrava 33 38 51N 3 33W
Moraleja 30 40 6N 6 43W
Moran, Kans., U.S.A. 117 37 53N 94 35W
Moran, Wyo., U.S.A. 118 43 53N 110 37W
Morano Cálabro 41 39 51N 16 8 E
Morant Cays 121 17 22N 76 0W
Morant Pt. 121 17 55N 76 12W
Morar L. 14 56 57N 5 40W
Moratalla 33 38 14N 1 49W
Moratuwa 70 6 45N 79 55 E
Morava ~ 27 48 10N 16 59 E
Moravia 116 40 50N 92 50W
Moravian Hts. = Ceskemoravská V. 26 49 30N 15 40 E
Moravica ~ 42 43 52N 20 8 E
Moravice ~ 27 49 50N 17 43 E
Moraviţa 42 45 17N 21 14 E
Moravská Třebová 27 49 45N 16 40 E
Moravské Budějovice 26 49 4N 15 49 E
Morawhanna 126 8 30N 59 40W
Moray Firth 14 57 50N 3 30W
Morbach 25 49 48N 7 7 E
Morbegno 38 46 8N 9 34 E
Morbihan □ 18 47 55N 2 50W
Morcenx 20 44 0N 0 55W
Mordelles 18 48 5N 1 52W
Morden 109 49 15N 98 10W
Mordialloc 100 38 1S 145 6 E
Mordovian A.S.S.R. □ 55 54 20N 44 30 E
Mordovo 55 52 6N 40 50 E
Mordy 28 52 13N 22 31 E
Møre og Romsdal fylke □ 47 62 30N 8 0 E
Morea 9 37 45N 22 10 E
Moreau ~ 116 45 15N 100 43W
Morecambe 12 54 5N 2 52W
Morecambe B. 12 54 7N 3 0W
Moree 97 29 28S 149 54 E
Morehead 114 38 12N 83 22W
Morehead City 115 34 46N 76 44W
Morelia 120 19 40N 101 11W
Morella, Austral. 98 23 0S 143 52 E
Morella, Spain 32 40 35N 0 5W
Morelos □ 120 18 40N 99 10W
Morena, Sierra 31 38 20N 4 0W
Morenci 119 33 7N 109 20W
Moreni 46 44 59N 25 36 E
Moresby I. 108 52 30N 131 40W
Morestel 21 45 40N 5 28 E
Moret 19 48 22N 2 58 E
Moreton 98 12 22S 142 30 E
Moreton B. 97 27 10S 153 10 E
Moreton I. 97 27 10S 153 25 E
Moreuil 19 49 46N 2 30 E
Morez 21 46 31N 6 2 E
Morgan, Austral. 99 34 0S 139 35 E
Morgan, U.S.A. 118 41 3N 111 44W
Morgan City 117 29 40N 91 15W
Morganfield 114 37 40N 87 55W
Morganton 115 35 46N 81 48W
Morgantown 114 39 39N 79 58W
Morganville 99 25 10S 151 50 E
Morgat 18 48 15N 4 32W
Morgenzon 93 26 45S 29 36 E
Morges 25 46 31N 6 29 E
Morhange 19 48 55N 6 38 E
Mori 38 45 51N 10 59 E
Moriarty 119 35 3N 106 2W
Morice L. 108 53 50N 127 40W
Moriki 85 12 52N 6 30 E
Morinville 108 53 49N 113 41W
Morioka 74 39 45N 141 8 E
Morkalla 99 34 23S 141 10 E
Morlaàs 20 43 21N 0 18W
Morlaix 18 48 36N 3 52W
Mormanno 41 39 53N 15 59 E
Mormant 19 48 37N 2 52 E
Mornington 99 38 15S 145 5 E
Mornington I. 97 16 30S 139 30 E
Mornington, I. 128 49 50S 75 30W
Mórnos ~ 45 38 30N 22 0 E
Moro 87 10 50N 30 9 E
Moro G. 73 6 30N 123 0 E
Morobe 98 7 49S 147 38 E
Morocco ■ 82 32 0N 5 50W
Morococha 126 11 40S 76 5W
Morogoro 90 6 50S 37 40 E
Morogoro □ 90 8 0S 37 0 E
Moroleón 120 20 8N 101 32W
Morombe 93 21 45S 43 22 E
Moron 124 34 39S 58 37W
Morón 121 22 8N 78 39W
Mörön ~ 75 47 14N 110 37 E
Morón de Almazán 32 41 29N 2 27W
Morón de la Frontera 31 37 6N 5 28W
Morondava 93 20 17S 44 17 E
Morondo 84 8 57N 6 47W
Moronou 84 6 16N 4 59W
Morotai 73 2 10N 128 30 E
Moroto 90 2 28N 34 42 E
Moroto Summit 90 2 30N 34 43 E
Morozov (Bratan) 43 42 30N 25 10 E
Morozovsk 57 48 25N 41 50 E
Morpeth 12 55 11N 1 41W
Morphou 64 35 12N 32 59 E
Morrilton 117 35 10N 92 45W
Morrinhos 127 17 45S 49 10W
Morrinsville 101 37 40S 175 32 E
Morris, Can. 109 49 25N 97 22W
Morris, Ill., U.S.A. 114 41 20N 88 20W
Morris, Minn., U.S.A. 116 45 33N 95 56W
Morrisburg 106 44 55N 75 7W
Morrison 116 41 47N 90 0W
Morristown, Ariz., U.S.A. 119 33 54N 112 35W
Morristown, N.J., U.S.A. 113 40 48N 74 30W
Morristown, S.D., U.S.A. 116 45 57N 101 44W
Morristown, Tenn., U.S.A. 115 36 18N 83 20W
Morro Bay 119 35 27N 120 54W
Morro, Pta. 124 27 6S 71 0W
Morrosquillo, Golfo de 121 9 35N 75 40W
Mörrum 49 56 12N 14 45 E
Mors 49 56 50N 8 45 E
Morshansk 55 53 28N 41 50 E
Mörsil 48 63 19N 13 40 E
Mortagne 20 45 28N 0 49W
Mortagne ~ 19 48 33N 6 27 E
Mortagne-au-Perche 18 48 31N 0 33 E
Mortain 18 48 40N 0 57W
Mortara 38 45 15N 8 43 E
Morteau 19 47 3N 6 35 E
Morteros 124 30 50S 62 0W
Mortes, R. das ~ 127 11 45S 50 44W
Mortlake 99 38 5S 142 50 E
Morton, Tex., U.S.A. 117 33 39N 102 49W
Morton, Wash., U.S.A. 118 46 33N 122 17W
Morundah 99 34 57S 146 19 E
Moruya 99 35 58S 150 3 E
Morvan, Mts. du 19 47 5N 4 0 E
Morven 99 26 22S 147 5 E
Morvern 14 56 38N 5 44W
Morvi 68 22 50N 70 42 E
Morwell 97 38 10S 146 22 E
Moryn 28 52 51N 14 22 E
Morzhovets, Ostrov 52 66 44N 42 35 E
Mosalsk 54 54 30N 34 55 E
Mosbach 25 49 21N 9 9 E
Moščenice 39 45 17N 14 16 E
Mosciano Sant' Ángelo 39 42 42N 13 52 E
Moscos Is. 72 14 0N 97 30 E
Moscow 118 46 45N 116 59W
Moscow = Moskva 55 55 45N 37 35 E
Mosel ~ 16 50 22N 7 36 E
Moselle = Mosel ~ 16 50 22N 7 36 E
Moselle □ 19 48 59N 6 33 E
Moses Lake 118 47 9N 119 17W
Mosgiel 101 45 53S 170 21 E
Moshi 90 3 22S 37 18 E
Moshi □ 90 3 22S 37 18 E
Moshupa 92 24 46S 25 29 E
Mošina 28 52 15N 16 50 E
Mosjøen 50 65 51N 13 12 E
Moskenesøya 50 67 58N 13 0 E
Moskenstraumen 50 67 47N 12 45 E
Moskva 55 55 45N 37 35 E
Moskva ~ 55 55 5N 38 51 E
Moslavačka Gora 39 45 40N 16 37 E
Mosomane (Artesia) 92 24 2S 26 19 E
Mosonmagyaróvár 27 47 52N 17 18 E
Mošorin 42 45 19N 20 4 E
Mospino 56 47 52N 38 0 E
Mosquera 126 2 35N 78 24W
Mosquero 117 35 48N 103 57W
Mosqueruela 32 40 21N 0 27W
Mosquitos, Golfo de los 121 9 15N 81 10W
Moss 47 59 27N 10 40 E
Moss Vale 99 34 32S 150 25 E
Mossaka 88 1 15S 16 45 E
Mossbank 109 49 56N 105 56W
Mossburn 101 45 41S 168 15 E
Mosselbaai 92 34 11S 22 8 E
Mossendjo 88 2 55S 12 42 E
Mossgiel 99 33 15S 144 5 E
Mossman 97 16 21S 145 15 E
Mossoró 127 5 10S 37 15W
Møsstrand 47 59 51N 8 4 E
Mossuril 91 14 58S 40 42 E
Mossy ~ 109 54 5N 102 58W
Most 26 50 31N 13 38 E
Mostaganem 82 35 54N 0 5 E
Mostar 42 43 22N 17 50 E
Mostardas 125 31 2S 50 51W
Mostefa, Rass 83 36 55N 11 3 E
Mosterøy 47 59 5N 5 37 E
Mostiska 54 49 48N 23 4 E
Mosty 54 53 27N 24 38 E
Mosul = Al Mawşil 64 36 20N 43 5 E
Mosvatn 47 59 52N 8 5 E
Mota del Cuervo 32 39 30N 2 52W
Mota del Marqués 30 41 38N 5 11W
Motagua ~ 120 15 44N 88 14W
Motala 49 58 32N 15 1 E
Mothe-Achard, La 18 46 37N 1 40W
Motherwell 14 55 48N 4 0W
Motihari 69 26 30N 84 55 E
Motilla del Palancar 32 39 34N 1 55W
Motnik 39 46 14N 14 54 E
Motovun 39 45 20N 13 50 E
Motozintla de Mendoza 120 15 21N 92 14W
Motril 33 36 31N 3 37W
Motru ~ 46 44 44N 22 59 E
Mott 116 46 25N 102 29W
Motte-Chalançon, La 21 44 30N 5 21 E
Motte, La 21 44 20N 6 3 E
Móttola 41 40 38N 17 0 E
Motueka 101 41 7S 173 1 E
Motul 120 21 0N 89 20W
Mouanda 88 1 28S 13 7 E
Mouchalagane ~ 107 50 56N 68 41W
Moucontant 18 46 43N 0 36W
Moúdhros 44 39 50N 25 18 E
Moudjeria 84 17 50N 12 28W
Moudon 25 46 40N 6 49 E
Mouila 88 1 50S 11 0 E
Moulamein 99 35 3S 144 1 E
Moule 121 16 20N 61 22W
Moulins 20 46 35N 3 19 E
Moulmein 67 16 30N 97 40 E
Moulouya, O. ~ 82 35 5N 2 25W
Moulton 117 29 35N 97 8W
Moultrie 115 31 11N 83 47W
Moultrie, L. 115 33 25N 80 10W
Mound City, Mo., U.S.A. 116 40 2N 95 25W
Mound City, S.D., U.S.A. 116 45 46N 100 3W
Moúnda, Ákra 45 38 5N 20 45 E
Moundou 81 8 40N 16 10 E
Moundsville 114 39 53N 80 43W
Mount Airy 115 36 31N 80 37W
Mount Albert 112 44 8N 79 19W
Mount Angel 118 45 4N 122 46W
Mount Barker, S.A., Austral. 99 35 5S 138 52 E
Mount Barker, W.A., Austral. 96 34 38S 117 40 E
Mount Carmel, Ill., U.S.A. 114 38 20N 87 48W
Mount Carmel, Pa., U.S.A. 114 40 46N 76 25W
Mount Clemens 106 42 35N 82 50W
Mount Coolon 98 21 25S 147 25 E
Mount Darwin 91 16 45S 31 33 E
Mount Desert I. 107 44 15N 68 25W
Mount Dora 115 28 49N 81 32W
Mount Douglas 98 21 35S 146 50 E
Mount Edgecumbe 108 57 8N 135 22W
Mount Enid 96 21 42S 116 26 E
Mount Forest 106 43 59N 80 43W
Mount Gambier 97 37 50S 140 46 E
Mount Garnet 98 17 37S 145 6 E
Mount Hope 114 37 52N 81 9W
Mount Horeb 116 43 0N 89 42W
Mount Howitt 99 26 31S 142 16 E
Mount Isa 97 20 42S 139 26 E
Mount Larcom 98 23 48S 150 59 E
Mount Lofty Ra. 97 34 35S 139 5 E
Mount McKinley Nat. Park 104 64 0N 150 0W
Mount Magnet 96 28 2S 117 47 E
Mount Margaret 99 26 54S 143 21 E
Mount Maunganui 101 37 40S 176 14 E
Mount Morgan 97 23 40S 150 25 E
Mount Morris 114 42 43N 77 50W
Mount Mulligan 98 16 45S 144 47 E
Mount Nicholas 96 22 54S 120 27 E
Mount Oxide Mine 98 19 30S 139 29 E
Mount Pearl 107 47 31N 52 47W
Mount Perry 99 25 13S 151 42 E
Mount Pleasant, Iowa, U.S.A. 116 41 0N 91 35W
Mount Pleasant, Mich., U.S.A. 114 43 35N 84 47W
Mount Pleasant, Pa., U.S.A. 112 40 9N 79 31W
Mount Pleasant, S.C., U.S.A. 115 32 45N 79 48W
Mount Pleasant, Tenn., U.S.A. 115 35 31N 87 11W
Mount Pleasant, Tex., U.S.A. 117 33 5N 95 0W
Mount Pleasant, Ut., U.S.A. 118 39 40N 111 29W
Mount Pocono 113 41 8N 75 21W
Mount Rainier Nat. Park 118 46 50N 121 43W
Mount Revelstoke Nat. Park 108 51 5N 118 30W
Mount Robson 108 52 56N 119 15W
Mount Robson Prov. Park 108 53 0N 119 0W
Mount Shasta 118 41 20N 122 18W
Mount Sterling, Ill., U.S.A. 116 40 0N 90 40W
Mount Sterling, Ky., U.S.A. 114 38 0N 84 0W
Mount Surprise 98 18 10S 144 17 E
Mount Union 112 40 22N 77 51W
Mount Vernon, Ind., U.S.A. 116 38 17N 88 57W
Mount Vernon, N.Y., U.S.A. 114 40 57N 73 49W
Mount Vernon, Ohio, U.S.A. 114 40 20N 82 30W
Mount Vernon, Wash., U.S.A. 108 48 25N 122 20W
Mount Whaleback 96 23 18S 119 44 E
Mountain City, Nev., U.S.A. 118 41 54N 116 0W
Mountain City, Tenn., U.S.A. 115 36 30N 81 50W
Mountain Grove 117 37 5N 92 20W
Mountain Home, Ark., U.S.A. 117 36 20N 92 25W
Mountain Home, Idaho, U.S.A. 118 43 11N 115 45W
Mountain Iron 116 47 30N 92 37W
Mountain Park. 108 52 50N 117 15W
Mountain View, Ark., U.S.A. 117 35 52N 92 10W
Mountain View, Calif., U.S.A. 117 37 26N 122 5W
Mountainair 119 34 35N 106 15W
Mountmellick 15 53 7N 7 20W
Moura, Austral. 98 24 35S 149 58 E
Moura, Brazil 126 1 32S 61 38W
Moura, Port. 31 38 7N 7 30W
Mourão 31 38 22N 7 22W
Mourdi Depression 81 18 10N 23 0 E
Mourdiah 84 14 35N 7 25W
Moure, La 116 46 27N 98 17W
Mourenx 20 43 23N 0 36W
Mouri 85 5 6N 1 14W
Mourilyan 98 17 35S 146 3 E
Mourmelon-le-Grand 19 49 8N 4 22 E
Mourne ~ 15 54 45N 7 39W
Mourne Mts. 15 54 10N 6 0W
Mouscron 16 50 45N 3 12 E
Moussoro 81 13 41N 16 35 E
Mouthe 19 46 44N 6 12 E
Moutier 25 47 16N 7 21 E
Moûtiers 21 45 29N 6 31 E
Moutong 73 0 28N 121 13 E
Mouy 19 49 18N 2 20 E
Mouzáki 44 39 25N 21 37 E
Moville 15 55 11N 7 3W
Moy ~ 15 54 5N 8 50W
Moyale, Ethiopia 87 3 34N 39 4 E
Moyale, Kenya 90 3 30N 39 0 E
Moyamba 84 8 4N 12 30W
Moyen Atlas 80 32 0N 5 0W
Moyle □ 15 55 10N 6 15W
Moyobamba 126 6 0S 77 0W
Moyyero ~ 59 68 44N 103 42 E
Mozambique = Moçambique 91 15 3S 40 42 E
Mozambique ■ 91 19 0S 35 0 E
Mozambique Chan. 93 20 0S 39 0 E
Mozdok 57 43 45N 44 48 E
Mozhaysk 55 55 30N 36 2 E
Mozhga 55 56 26N 52 15 E
Mozirje 39 46 22N 14 58 E
Mozyr 54 52 0N 29 15 E
Mpanda 90 6 23S 31 1 E
Mpanda □ 90 6 23S 31 40 E
Mpésoba 84 12 31N 5 39W
Mpika 91 11 51S 31 25 E
Mpulungu 91 8 51S 31 5 E
Mpwapwa 90 6 23S 36 30 E
Mpwapwa □ 90 6 30S 36 20 E
Mrągowo 28 53 52N 21 18 E
Mramor 42 43 20N 21 45 E
Mrimina 82 29 50N 7 9W
Mrkonjić Grad 42 44 26N 17 4 E
Mrkopalj 39 45 21N 14 52 E
Mrocza 28 53 16N 17 35 E
Msab, Oued en ~ 83 32 25N 5 20 E
Msaken 83 35 49N 10 33 E
Msambansovu 91 15 50S 30 3 E
M'sila 83 35 46N 4 30 E
Msta ~ 54 58 25N 31 20 E
Mstislavl 54 54 0N 31 50 E
Mszana Dolna 27 49 41N 20 5 E
Mszczonów 28 51 58N 20 33 E
Mtama 91 10 17S 39 21 E
Mtilikwe ~ 91 21 9S 31 30 E
Mtsensk 55 53 25N 36 30 E
Mtskheta 57 41 52N 44 45 E
Mtwara-Mikindani 91 10 20S 40 20 E
Mu Us Shamo 76 39 0N 109 0 E
Muaná 127 1 25S 49 15W
Muang Chiang Rai 71 19 52N 99 50 E
Muang Lamphun 71 18 40N 99 2 E
Muang Phichit 71 16 29N 100 21 E
Muar 71 2 3N 102 34 E
Muar ~ 71 2 15N 102 48 E
Muarabungo 72 1 28S 102 52 E
Muaradjuloi 72 0 12S 114 3 E
Muaraenim 72 3 40S 103 50 E
Muarakaman 72 0 2S 116 45 E
Muaratebo 72 1 30S 102 26 E
Muaratembesi 72 1 42S 103 8 E
Muaratewe 72 0 58S 114 52 E
Mubarakpur 69 26 6N 83 18 E
Mubende 90 0 33N 31 22 E
Mubi 85 10 18N 13 16 E
Mücheln 24 51 18N 11 49 E
Muchinga Mts. 91 11 30S 31 30 E
Muchkapskiy 55 51 52N 42 28 E
Muck 14 56 50N 6 15W
Muckadilla 99 26 35S 148 23 E
Mucuri 127 18 0S 39 36W
Mucusso 92 18 1S 21 25 E
Mudanjiang 76 44 38N 129 30 E
Mudanya 56 40 25N 28 50 E
Muddy ~ 119 38 0N 110 22W
Mudgee 97 32 32S 149 31 E
Mudjatik ~ 109 56 1N 107 36W
Muecate 91 14 55S 39 40 E
Muêda 91 11 36S 39 28 E
Muela, La 32 41 36N 1 7W
Muerto, Mar 120 16 10N 94 10W
Muertos, Punta de los 33 36 57N 1 54W
Mufindi □ 91 8 30S 35 20 E
Mufulira 91 12 32S 28 15 E
Mufumbiro Range 90 1 25S 29 30 E
Mugardos 30 43 27N 8 15W
Muge 31 39 3N 8 40W
Muge ~ 31 39 8N 8 44W
Múggia 39 45 36N 13 47 E
Mugia 30 43 3N 9 10W
Mugila, Mts. 90 7 0S 28 50 E
Muğla 64 37 15N 28 22 E
Müglizh 43 42 37N 25 32 E
Mugshin 63 19 35N 54 40 E
Mugu 69 29 45N 82 30 E
Muhammad Qol 86 20 53N 37 9 E
Muhammad Râs 86 27 42N 34 13 E
Muhammadabad 69 26 4N 83 25 E
Muharraqa = Sa'ad 62 31 28N 34 33 E
Muhesi ~ 90 7 0S 35 20 E
Muheza □ 90 5 0S 39 0 E
Mühldorf 25 48 14N 12 33 E
Mühlhausen 24 51 12N 10 29 E
Mühlig Hofmann fjella 5 72 30S 5 0 E
Muhutwe 90 1 35S 31 45 E
Mui Bai Bung 71 8 35N 104 42 E
Mui Ron 71 18 7N 106 27 E
Muikamachi 74 37 15N 138 50 E
Muine Bheag 15 52 42N 6 57W
Muiños 30 41 58N 7 59W
Mukachevo 54 48 27N 22 45 E
Mukah 72 2 55N 112 5 E
Mukawwa, Geziret 86 23 55N 35 53 E
Mukden = Shenyang 76 41 48N 123 27 E
Mukhtolovo 55 55 29N 43 15 E
Mukishi 91 8 30S 24 44 E
Mukomuko 72 2 30S 101 10 E
Mukomwenze 90 6 49S 27 15 E
Muktsar 68 30 30N 74 30 E
Mukur 66 32 50N 67 42 E
Mukutawa ~ 109 53 10N 97 24W
Mukwela 91 17 0S 26 40 E
Mula 33 38 3N 1 33W
Mula ~ 70 18 34N 74 21 E
Mulange 90 3 40S 27 10 E
* Mulatas, Arch. de las 121 9 50N 78 31W
Mulchén 124 37 45S 72 20W
Mulde ~ 24 51 10N 12 48 E
Mule Creek 116 43 19N 104 8W
Muleba 90 1 50S 31 37 E
Muleba □ 90 2 0S 31 30 E
Muleshoe 117 34 17N 102 42W
Mulgrave 107 45 38N 61 31W
Mulgrave I. 98 10 5S 142 10 E
Mulhacén 33 37 4N 3 20W
Mülheim 24 51 26N 6 53 E
Mulhouse 19 47 40N 7 20 E
Muling He ~ 76 45 53N 133 30 E
Mull 14 56 27N 6 0W
Mullaittvu 70 9 15N 80 49 E
Mullen 116 42 5N 101 0W
Mullengudgery 99 31 43S 147 23 E
Mullens 114 37 34N 81 22W
Muller, Pegunungan 72 0 30N 113 30 E
Mullet Pen. 15 54 10N 10 2W
Mullewa 96 28 29S 115 30 E
Müllheim 25 47 48N 7 37 E
Mulligan ~ 98 26 40S 139 0 E
Mullin 117 31 33N 98 38W
Mullingar 15 53 31N 7 20W
Mullins 115 34 12N 79 15W
Mullsjö 49 57 56N 13 55 E

* *Renamed San Blas, Arch. de*

Mullumbimby 99 28 30 S 153 30 E
Mulobezi 91 16 45 S 25 7 E
Mulshi L. 70 18 30N 73 48 E
Multai 68 21 50N 78 21 E
Multan 68 30 15N 71 36 E
* Multan □ 68 30 29N 72 29 E
Multrå 48 63 10N 17 24 E
Mulumbe, Mts. 91 8 40 S 27 30 E
Mulungushi Dam 91 14 48 S 28 48 E
Mulvane 117 37 30N 97 15W
Mulwad 86 18 45N 30 39 E
Mulwala 100 35 59 S 146 0 E
Mumra 57 45 45N 47 41 E
Mun → 71 15 17N 103 0 E
Muna 73 5 0 S 122 30 E
Munamagi 54 57 43N 27 4 E
Münchberg 25 50 11N 11 48 E
Muncheberg 24 52 30N 14 9 E
München 25 48 8N 11 33 E
Munchen-Gladbach = Mönchengladbach 24 51 12N 6 23 E
Muncho Lake 108 59 0N 125 50W
Muncie 114 40 10N 85 20W
Mundakayam 70 9 30N 76 50 E
Mundala, Puncak 73 4 30 S 141 0 E
Mundare 108 53 35N 112 20W
Munday 117 33 26N 99 39W
Münden 24 51 25N 9 42 E
Mundo → 33 38 30N 2 15W
Mundo Novo 127 11 50 S 40 29W
Mundra 68 22 54N 69 48 E
Munera 33 39 2N 2 29W
Muneru → 70 16 45N 80 3 E
Mungallala 99 26 28 S 147 34 E
Mungallala Cr. → 99 28 53 S 147 5 E
Mungana 98 17 8 S 144 27 E
Mungaoli 68 24 24N 78 7 E
Mungari 91 17 12 S 33 30 E
Mungbere 90 2 36N 28 28 E
Mungindi 97 28 58 S 149 1 E
Munhango 89 12 10 S 18 38 E
Munich = München 25 48 8N 11 33 E
Munising 114 46 25N 86 39W
Munjiye 86 18 47N 41 20 E
Munka-Ljungby 49 56 16N 12 58 E
Munkedal 49 58 28N 11 40 E
Munkfors 48 59 50N 13 30 E
Munku-Sardyk 59 51 45N 100 20 E
Münnerstadt 25 50 15N 10 11 E
Muñoz Gamero, Pen. 128 52 30 S 73 5 E
Munroe L. 109 59 13N 98 35W
Munster, France 19 48 2N 7 8 E
Munster, Ger. 24 52 59N 10 5 E
Münster 24 51 58N 7 37 E
Munster □ 15 52 20N 8 40W
Muntele Mare 46 46 30N 23 12 E
Muntok 72 2 5 S 105 10 E
Munyak 58 43 30N 59 15 E
Munyama 91 16 5 S 28 31 E
Muon Pak Beng 71 19 51N 101 4 E
Muonio 50 67 57N 23 40 E
Mupa 89 16 5 S 15 50 E
Muping 76 37 22N 121 36 E
Muqaddam, Wadi → 86 18 4N 31 30 E
Muqdisho 63 2 2N 45 25 E
Mur → 26 46 18N 16 53 E
Mur-de-Bretagne 18 48 12N 3 0W
Mura → 39 46 18N 16 53 E
Murallón, Cuerro 128 49 48 S 73 30W
Muranda 90 1 52 S 29 20 E
Murang'a 90 0 45 S 37 9 E
Murashi 55 59 30N 49 0 E
Murat 20 45 7N 2 53 E
Murau 26 47 6N 14 10 E
Muravera 40 39 25N 9 35 E
Murça 30 41 24N 7 28W
Murchison → 96 27 45 S 114 0 E
Murchison Falls = Kabarega Falls 90 2 15N 31 38 E
Murchison Ra. 96 20 0 S 134 10 E
Murchison Rapids 91 15 55 S 34 35 E
Murcia 33 38 20N 1 10W
Murcia □ 33 37 50N 1 30W
Murdo 116 43 56N 100 43W
Murdoch Pt. 98 14 37 S 144 55 E
Mure, La 21 44 55N 5 48 E
Mureş □ 46 46 45N 24 40 E
Mureş (Mureşul) → 46 46 15N 20 13 E
Muret 20 43 30N 1 20 E
Murfatlar 46 44 10N 28 26 E
Murfreesboro 115 35 50N 86 21W
Murg → 25 48 55N 8 10 E
Murgab 58 38 10N 74 2 E
Murgeni 46 46 12N 28 1 E
Murgon 97 26 15 S 151 54 E
Muriaé 125 21 8 S 42 23W
Murias de Paredes 30 42 52N 6 11W
Muriel Mine 91 17 14 S 30 40 E
Müritz see 24 53 25N 12 40 E
Murka 90 3 27 S 38 0 E
Murmansk 52 68 57N 33 10 E
Murnau 25 47 40N 11 11 E
Muro, France 21 42 34N 8 54 E
Muro, Spain 32 39 44N 3 3 E
Muro, C. de 21 41 44N 8 37 E
Muro Lucano 41 40 45N 15 30 E
Murom 55 55 35N 42 3 E
Muroran 74 42 25N 141 0 E
Muros 30 42 45N 9 5W
Muros y de Noya, Ría de 30 42 45N 9 0W
Muroto-Misaki 74 33 15N 134 10 E
Murowana Goślina 28 52 35N 17 0 E
Murphy 118 43 11N 116 33W
Murphysboro 117 37 50N 89 20W
Murrat 86 18 51N 29 33 E
Murray, Ky., U.S.A. 115 36 40N 88 20W
Murray, Utah, U.S.A. 118 40 41N 111 58W
Murray →, Austral. 97 35 20 S 139 22 E
Murray →, Can. 108 56 11N 120 45W
Murray Bridge 97 35 6 S 139 14 E
Murray Harbour 107 46 0N 62 28W
Murray, L., P.N.G. 98 7 0 S 141 35 E

* *Now part of Punjab* □

Murray, L., U.S.A. 115 34 8N 81 30W
Murray Seascarp 95 30 0N 135 0W
Murraysburg 92 31 58 S 23 47 E
Murrayville 100 35 16 S 141 11 E
Murree 66 33 56N 73 28 E
Murrumbidgee → 97 34 43 S 143 12 E
Murrumburrah 99 34 32 S 148 22 E
Murrurundi 99 31 42 S 150 51 E
Mursala 72 1 41N 98 28 E
Murshid 86 21 40N 31 10 E
Murshidabad 69 24 11N 88 19 E
Murska Sobota 39 46 39N 16 12 E
Murtazapur 68 20 40N 77 25 E
Murtle L. 108 52 8N 119 38W
Murtoa 99 36 35 S 142 28 E
Murtosa 30 40 44N 8 40W
Murungu 90 4 12 S 31 10 E
Murwara 69 23 46N 80 28 E
Murwillumbah 97 28 18 S 153 27 E
Muryo 73 6 36 S 110 53 E
Mürz → 26 47 30N 15 25 E
Mürzzuschlag 26 47 36N 15 41 E
Muş 64 38 45N 41 30 E
Musa Khel Bazar 68 30 59N 69 52 E
Mūsá Qal'eh 65 32 20N 64 50 E
Musairik, Wadi → 86 19 30N 43 10 E
Musala 43 42 13N 23 37 E
Musan, Kor., N. 76 42 12N 129 12 E
Musan, Kor., N. 76 42 12N 129 12 E
Musangu 91 10 28 S 23 55 E
Musasa 90 3 25 S 31 30 E
Musay'īd 65 25 0N 51 33 E
Muscat = Masqat 65 23 37N 58 36 E
Muscat & Oman = Oman ■ 63 23 0N 58 0 E
Muscatine 116 41 25N 91 5W
Musel 30 43 34N 5 42W
Musgrave Ras. 96 26 0 S 132 0 E
Mushie 88 2 56 S 16 55 E
Mushin 85 6 32N 3 21 E
Musi →, India 70 16 41N 79 40 E
Musi →, Indon. 72 2 20 S 104 56 E
Muskeg → 108 60 20N 123 20W
Muskegon 114 43 15N 86 17W
Muskegon → 114 43 25N 86 0W
Muskegon Hts. 114 43 12N 86 17W
Muskogee 117 35 50N 95 25W
Muskwa → 108 58 47N 122 48W
Musmar 86 18 13N 35 40 E
Musofu 91 13 30 S 29 0 E
Musoma 90 1 30 S 33 48 E
Musoma □ 90 1 50 S 34 30 E
Musquaro, L. 107 50 38N 61 5W
Musquodoboit Harbour 107 44 50N 63 9W
Musselburgh 14 55 57N 3 3W
Musselshell → 118 47 21N 107 58W
Mussidan 20 45 2N 0 22 E
Mussomeli 40 37 35N 13 43 E
Mussooree 68 30 27N 78 6 E
Mussuco 92 17 2 S 19 3 E
Mustang 69 29 10N 83 55 E
Musters, L. 128 45 20 S 69 25W
Muswellbrook 97 32 16 S 150 56 E
Muszyna 27 49 22N 20 55 E
Mût 86 25 28N 28 58 E
Mut 64 36 40N 33 28 E
Mutanda, Mozam. 93 21 0 S 33 34 E
Mutanda, Zambia 91 12 24 S 26 13 E
Mutaray 59 60 56N 101 0 E
Muting 73 7 23 S 140 20 E
Mutshatsha 91 10 35 S 24 20 E
Muttaburra 97 22 38 S 144 29 E
Mutuáli 91 14 55 S 37 0 E
Muvatupusha 70 9 53N 76 35 E
Muxima 88 9 33 S 13 58 E
Muy, Le 21 43 28N 6 34 E
Muya 59 56 27N 115 50 E
Muyinga 90 3 14 S 30 33 E
Muzaffarabad 69 34 25N 73 30 E
Muzaffargarh 68 30 5N 71 14 E
Muzaffarnagar 68 29 26N 77 40 E
Muzaffarpur 69 26 7N 85 23 E
Muzhi 58 65 25N 64 40 E
Muzillac 18 47 35N 2 30W
Muzon C. 108 54 40N 132 40W
Muztag 75 36 20N 87 28 E
Mvôlô 87 6 2N 29 53 E
Mwadui 90 3 26 S 33 32 E
Mwambo 91 10 30 S 40 22 E
Mwandi 91 17 30 S 24 51 E
Mwanza, Tanz. 90 2 30 S 32 58 E
Mwanza, Zaïre 90 7 55 S 26 43 E
Mwanza, Zambia 91 16 58 S 24 28 E
Mwanza □ 90 2 0 S 33 0 E
Mwaya 91 9 32 S 33 55 E
Mweelrea 15 53 37N 9 48W
Mweka 88 4 50 S 21 34 E
Mwenga 90 3 1 S 28 28 E
Mweru, L. 91 9 0 S 28 40 E
Mweza Range 91 21 0 S 30 0 E
Mwilambwe 90 8 7 S 25 0 E
Mwimbi 91 8 38 S 31 39 E
Mwinilunga 91 11 43 S 24 25 E
My Tho 71 10 29N 106 23 E
Mya, O. → 83 30 46N 4 54 E
Myall → 100 32 30 S 152 15 E
Myanaung 67 18 18N 95 22 E
Myaungmya 67 16 30N 94 40 E
Mycenae = Mikínai 45 37 43N 22 46 E
Myeik Kyunzu 71 11 30N 97 30 E
Myerstown 113 40 22N 76 18W
Myitkyina 67 25 24N 97 26 E
Myjava 27 48 41N 17 37 E
Mymensingh 69 24 45N 90 24 E
Myndus 45 37 3N 27 14 E
Mynydd ddu 13 51 45N 3 45W
Myrdal 47 60 43N 7 10 E
Mýrdalsjökull 50 63 40N 19 6W
Myrtle Beach 115 33 43N 78 50W
Myrtle Creek 118 43 0N 123 9W
Myrtle Point 118 43 0N 124 4W
Myrtleford 100 36 34 S 146 44 E
Mysen 47 59 33N 11 20 E

Myslenice 27 49 51N 19 57 E
Myślibórz 28 52 55N 14 50 E
Mysłowice 27 50 15N 19 12 E
Mysore 70 12 17N 76 41 E
Mysore □ = Karnataka 70 13 15N 77 0 E
Mystic 113 41 21N 71 58W
Mystishchi 55 55 50N 37 50 E
Myszków 28 50 45N 19 22 E
Myszyniec 28 53 23N 21 21 E
Myton 118 40 10N 110 2W
Mývatn 50 65 36N 17 0W
Mze → 26 49 46N 13 24 E
Mzimba 91 11 55 S 33 39 E
Mzimvubu → 93 31 38 S 29 33 E
Mzuzu 91 11 30 S 33 55 E

N

N' Dioum 84 16 31N 14 39W
Naab → 25 49 1N 12 2 E
Na'am 87 9 42N 28 27 E
Na'an 62 31 53N 34 52 E
Naantali 51 60 29N 22 2 E
Naas 15 53 12N 6 40W
Nababiep 92 29 36 S 17 46 E
Nabadwip 69 23 34N 88 20 E
Nabas 73 11 47N 122 6 E
Nabburg 25 49 27N 12 11 E
* Nabereznyje Celny 58 55 42N 52 19 E
Nabeul 83 36 30N 10 44 E
Nabha 68 30 26N 76 14 E
Nabire 73 3 15 S 135 26 E
Nabisar 68 25 8N 69 40 E
Nabisipi → 107 50 14N 62 13W
Nabiswera 90 1 27N 32 15 E
Nablus = Nābulus 62 32 14N 35 15 E
Naboomspruit 93 24 32 S 28 40 E
Nābulus 62 32 14N 35 15 E
Nacala-Velha 91 14 32 S 40 34 E
Nacaroa 91 14 22 S 39 56 E
Naches 118 46 48N 120 42W
Nachingwea 91 10 23 S 38 49 E
Nachingwea □ 91 10 30 S 38 30 E
Nachna 68 27 34N 71 41 E
Náchod 27 50 25N 16 8 E
Nacka 48 59 17N 18 12 E
Nackara 99 32 48 S 139 12 E
Naco 119 31 24N 109 58W
Nacogdoches 117 31 33N 94 39W
Nacozari 120 30 24N 109 39W
Nadi 86 18 40N 33 41 E
Nadiad 68 22 41N 72 56 E
Nădlac 42 46 10N 20 50 E
Nador 82 35 14N 2 58W
Nadūshan 65 32 2N 53 35 E
Nadvoitsy 52 63 52N 34 14 E
Nadvornaya 56 48 37N 24 30 E
Nadym 58 65 35N 72 42 E
Nadym → 58 66 12N 72 0 E
Nærbø 47 58 40N 5 39 E
Næstved 49 55 13N 11 44 E
Nafada 85 11 8N 11 20 E
Naft-e Shāh 64 34 0N 45 30 E
Nafūd ad Dahy 64 22 0N 45 0 E
Nafūsah, Jabal 83 32 12N 12 30 E
Nag Hammâdi 86 26 2N 32 18 E
Naga 73 13 38N 123 15 E
Naga, Kreb en 82 24 12N 6 0W
Nagagami → 106 49 40N 84 40W
Nagaland □ 67 26 0N 94 30 E
Nagano 74 36 40N 138 10 E
Nagano □ 74 36 15N 138 0 E
Nagaoka 74 37 27N 138 50 E
Nagappattinam 70 10 46N 79 51 E
Nagar Parkar 68 24 28N 70 46 E
Nagari Hills 70 13 3N 79 45 E
Nagarjuna Sagar 70 16 35N 79 17 E
Nagasaki 74 32 47N 129 50 E
Nagasaki □ 74 32 50N 129 40 E
Nagaur 68 27 15N 73 45 E
Nagbhil 70 20 34N 79 55 E
Nagercoil 70 8 12N 77 26 E
Nagina 68 29 30N 78 30 E
Nagīneh 65 34 20N 57 15 E
Nago 77 26 36N 128 0 E
Nagold 25 34 14N 57 2 E
Nagold → 25 48 52N 8 42 E
Nagoorin 98 24 17 S 151 15 E
Nagornyy 59 55 58N 124 57 E
Nagorsk 55 59 18N 50 48 E
Nagoya 74 35 10N 136 50 E
Nagpur 68 21 8N 79 10 E
Nagyatád 27 46 14N 17 22 E
Nagyecsed 27 47 53N 22 24 E
Nagykanizsa 27 46 28N 17 0 E
Nagykörös 27 47 5N 19 48 E
Nagyléta 27 47 23N 21 55 E
Naha 77 26 13N 127 42 E
Nahalal 62 32 41N 35 12 E
Nahanni Butte 108 61 2N 123 31W
Nahanni Nat. Park 108 61 15N 125 0W
Nahariyya 62 33 1N 35 5 E
Nahāvand 64 34 10N 48 22 E
Nahe → 25 49 58N 7 57 E
Nahf 62 32 56N 35 18 E
Nahîya, Wadi → 86 28 55N 31 0 E
Nahlin 108 58 55N 131 38W
Nahud 86 18 12N 41 40 E
Naicam 109 52 30N 104 30W
Nā'ifah 63 19 59N 50 46 E
Naila 25 50 19N 11 43 E
Nain 107 56 34N 61 40W
Nā'īn 65 32 54N 53 0 E
Naini Tal 69 29 30N 79 30 E
Naintré 18 46 46N 0 29 E
Naipu 46 44 12N 25 47 E
Naira 73 4 28 S 130 0 E
Nairn 14 57 35N 3 54W
Nairobi 90 1 17 S 36 48 E
Naivasha 90 0 40 S 36 30 E

* *Renamed Brezhnev*

Naivasha L. 90 0 48 S 36 20 E
Najac 20 44 14N 1 58 E
Najafābād 65 32 40N 51 15 E
Najd 64 26 30N 42 0 E
Nájera 32 42 26N 2 48W
Najerilla → 32 42 32N 2 48W
Najibabad 68 29 40N 78 20 E
Najin 76 42 12N 130 15 E
Nakalagba 90 2 50N 27 58 E
Nakamura 74 33 0N 133 0 E
Nakfa 87 16 40N 38 32 E
Nakhichevan A.S.S.R. □ 53 39 14N 45 30 E
Nakhl 86 29 55N 33 43 E
Nakhodka 59 42 53N 132 54 E
Nakhon Phanom 71 17 23N 104 43 E
Nakhon Ratchasima (Khorat) 71 14 59N 102 12 E
Nakhon Sawan 71 15 35N 100 10 E
Nakhon Si Thammarat 71 8 29N 100 0 E
Nakina, B.C., Can. 108 59 12N 132 52W
Nakina, Ont., Can. 106 50 10N 86 40W
Nakło nad Noteçią 28 53 9N 17 38 E
Nakodar 68 31 8N 75 31 E
Nakskov 49 54 50N 11 8 E
Näkten 48 62 48N 14 38 E
Naktong → 76 35 7N 128 57 E
Nakuru 90 0 15 S 36 4 E
Nakuru □ 90 0 15 S 35 5 E
Nakuru, L. 90 0 23 S 36 5 E
Nakusp 108 50 20N 117 45W
Nal → 66 25 20N 65 30 E
Nalchik 57 43 30N 43 33 E
Nälden 48 63 21N 14 14 E
Näldsjön 48 63 25N 14 15 E
Nalerigu 85 10 35N 0 25W
Nalgonda 70 17 6N 79 15 E
Nalhati 69 24 17N 87 52 E
Nallamalai Hills 70 15 30N 78 50 E
Nalón → 30 43 32N 6 4W
Nālūt 83 31 54N 11 0 E
Nam Co 75 30 30N 90 45 E
Nam Dinh 71 20 25N 106 5 E
Nam-Phan 72 10 30N 106 0 E
Nam Phong 71 16 42N 102 52 E
Nam Tha 71 20 58N 101 30 E
Nama unde 92 17 18 S 15 50 E
Namak, Daryácheh-ye 65 34 30N 52 0 E
Namak, Kavir-e 65 34 30N 57 30 E
Namakkal 70 11 13N 78 13 E
Namaland 92 24 30 S 17 0 E
Namangan 58 41 0N 71 40 E
Namapa 91 13 43 S 39 50 E
Namaqualand 92 30 0 S 18 0 E
Namasagali 90 1 2N 33 0 E
Namatanai 98 3 40 S 152 29 E
Namber 73 1 2 S 134 49 E
Nambour 97 26 32 S 152 58 E
Nambucca Heads 99 30 37 S 153 0 E
Namche Bazar 69 27 51N 86 47 E
Namecunda 91 14 54 S 37 37 E
Nameh 72 2 34N 116 21 E
Nameponda 91 15 50 S 39 50 E
Náměšt' nad Oslavou 27 49 12N 16 10 E
Námestovo 27 49 24N 19 25 E
Nametil 91 15 40 S 39 21 E
Namew L. 109 54 14N 101 56W
Namib Desert = Namib Woestyn 92 22 30 S 15 0 E
Namib-Woestyn 92 22 30 S 15 0 E
Namibia ■ 92 22 0 S 18 9 E
Namlea 73 3 18 S 127 5 E
Namoi → 99 30 12 S 149 30 E
Namous, O. en → 82 31 0N 0 15W
Nampa 118 43 34N 116 34W
Nampula 91 15 6N 39 15 E
Namrole 73 3 46 S 126 46 E
Namse Shankou 67 30 0N 82 25 E
Namsen → 50 64 27N 11 42 E
Namsos 50 64 29N 11 30 E
Namtay 59 62 43N 129 37 E
Namtu 67 23 5N 97 28 E
Namtumbo 91 10 30 S 36 4 E
Namu 108 51 52N 127 50W
Namucha Shank'ou 69 30 0N 82 28 E
Namur 16 50 27N 4 52 E
Namur □ 16 50 17N 5 0 E
Namutoni 92 18 49 S 16 55 E
Namwala 91 15 44 S 26 30 E
Namysłów 28 51 6N 17 42 E
Nan 71 18 52N 100 42 E
Nana 46 44 17N 26 34 E
Nanaimo 108 49 10N 124 0W
Nanam 76 41 44N 129 40 E
Nanan 77 24 59N 118 21 E
Nanango 97 26 40 S 152 0 E
Nan'ao 77 23 28N 117 5 E
Nanao 74 37 0N 137 0 E
Nanbu 77 31 18N 106 3 E
Nanchang 75 28 42N 115 55 E
Nancheng 77 27 33N 116 35 E
Nanching = Nanjing 75 32 2N 118 47 E
Nanchong 75 30 43N 106 2 E
Nanchuan 77 29 9N 107 6 E
Nancy 19 48 42N 6 12 E
Nanda Devi 69 30 23N 79 59 E
Nandan 77 24 58N 107 29 E
Nander 70 19 10N 77 20 E
Nandewar Ra. 99 30 15 S 150 35 E
Nandi 101 17 42 S 177 20 E
Nandi □ 90 0 15N 35 0 E
Nandikotkur 70 15 52N 78 18 E
Nandura 68 20 52N 76 25 E
Nandurbar 68 21 20N 74 15 E
Nandyal 70 15 30N 78 30 E
Nanga-Eboko 88 4 41N 12 22 E
Nanga Parbat 69 35 10N 74 35 E
Nangade 91 11 5 S 39 36 E
Nangapinoh 72 0 20 S 11 44 E
Nangarhár □ 65 34 20N 70 0 E
Nangatayap 72 1 32 S 110 34 E
Nangeya Mts. 90 3 30N 33 30 E
Nangis 19 48 33N 3 0 E
Nanjangud 70 12 6N 76 43 E
Nanjeko 91 15 31 S 23 30 E

Nanjiang	**77**	32 28N	106 51 E
Nanjing	**75**	32 2N	118 47 E
Nanjirinji	**91**	9 41 S	39 5 E
Nankana Sahib	**68**	31 27N	73 38 E
Nankang	**77**	25 40N	114 45 E
Nanking = Nanjing	**75**	32 2N	118 47 E
Nannine	**96**	26 51 S	118 18 E
Nanning	**75**	22 48N	108 20 E
Nanpara	**69**	27 52N	81 33 E
Nanpi	**76**	38 2N	116 45 E
Nanping	**75**	26 38N	118 10 E
Nanripe	**91**	13 52 S	38 52 E
Nansei-Shotō	**74**	26 0N	128 0 E
Nansen Sd.	**4**	81 0N	91 0W
Nansio	**90**	2 3 S	33 4 E
Nant	**20**	44 1N	3 18 E
Nantes	**18**	47 12N	1 33W
Nanteuil-le-Haudouin	**19**	49 9N	2 48 E
Nantiat	**20**	46 1N	1 11 E
Nanticoke	**114**	41 12N	76 1W
Nanton	**108**	50 21N	113 46W
Nantong	**77**	32 1N	120 52 E
Nantua	**21**	46 10N	5 35 E
Nantucket I.	**102**	41 16N	70 3W
Nanuque	**127**	17 50 S	40 21W
Nanxiong	**77**	25 6N	114 15 E
Nanyang	**75**	33 11N	112 30 E
Nanyuan	**76**	39 44N	116 22 E
Nanyuki	**90**	0 2N	37 4 E
Nanzhang	**77**	31 45N	111 50 E
Náo, C. de la	**33**	38 44N	0 14 E
Naococane L.	**107**	52 50N	70 45W
Naoetsu	**74**	37 12N	138 10 E
Naogaon	**69**	24 52N	88 52 E
Naoli He →	**76**	47 18N	134 9 E
Náousa	**44**	40 42N	22 9 E
Napa	**118**	38 18N	122 17W
Napanee	**106**	44 15N	77 0W
Napanoch	**113**	41 44N	74 22W
Napier	**101**	39 30 S	176 56 E
Naples	**115**	26 10N	81 45W
Naples = Nápoli	**41**	40 50N	14 17 E
Napo →	**126**	3 20 S	72 40W
Napoleon, N. Dak., U.S.A.	**116**	46 32N	99 49W
Napoleon, Ohio, U.S.A.	**114**	41 24N	84 7W
Nápoli	**41**	40 50N	14 17 E
Nápoli, G. di	**41**	40 40N	14 10 E
Napopo	**90**	4 15N	28 0 E
Nappa Merrie	**99**	27 36 S	141 7 E
Naqâda	**86**	25 53N	32 42 E
Nara, Japan	**74**	34 40N	135 49 E
Nara, Mali	**84**	15 10N	7 20W
Nara □	**74**	34 30N	136 0 E
Nara, Canal	**68**	24 30N	69 20 E
Nara Visa	**117**	35 39N	103 10W
Naracoorte	**97**	36 58 S	140 45 E
Naradhan	**99**	33 34 S	146 17 E
Narasapur	**70**	16 26N	81 40 E
Narasaropet	**70**	16 14N	80 4 E
Narathiwat	**71**	6 30N	101 48 E
Narayanganj	**69**	23 40N	90 33 E
Narayanpet	**70**	16 45N	77 30 E
Narbonne	**20**	43 11N	3 0 E
Narcea →	**30**	43 33N	6 44W
Nardò	**41**	40 10N	18 0 E
Narew	**28**	52 55N	23 31 E
Narew →	**28**	52 26N	20 41 E
Nari →	**68**	29 40N	68 0 E
Narindra, Helodranon' i	**93**	14 55 S	47 30 E
Narmada →	**68**	21 38N	72 36 E
Narnaul	**68**	28 5N	76 11 E
Narni	**39**	42 30N	12 30 E
Naro, Ghana	**84**	10 22N	2 27W
Naro, Italy	**40**	37 18N	13 48 E
Naro Fominsk	**55**	55 23N	36 43 E
Narodnaya, G.	**52**	65 5N	60 0 E
Narok	**90**	1 55 S	33 52 E
Narok □	**90**	1 20 S	36 30 E
Narón	**30**	43 32N	8 9W
Narooma	**99**	36 14 S	150 4 E
Narowal	**68**	32 6N	74 52 E
Narrabri	**97**	30 19 S	149 46 E
Narran →	**99**	28 37 S	148 12 E
Narrandera	**97**	34 42 S	146 31 E
Narraway →	**108**	55 44N	119 55W
Narrogin	**96**	32 58 S	117 14 E
Narromine	**97**	32 12 S	148 12 E
Narsampet	**70**	17 57N	79 58 E
Narsimhapur	**68**	22 54N	79 14 E
Nartkala	**57**	43 33N	43 51 E
Narva	**54**	59 23N	28 12 E
Narva →	**54**	59 27N	28 2 E
Narvik	**50**	68 28N	17 26 E
Narvskoye Vdkhr.	**54**	59 18N	28 14 E
Narwana	**68**	29 39N	76 6 E
Naryan-Mar	**52**	68 0N	53 0 E
Naryilco	**99**	28 37 S	141 53 E
Narym	**58**	59 0N	81 30 E
Narymskoye	**58**	49 10N	84 15 E
Naryn	**58**	41 26N	75 58 E
Nasa	**50**	66 29N	15 23 E
Nasarawa	**85**	8 32N	7 41 E
Năsăud	**46**	47 19N	24 29 E
Naseby	**101**	45 1 S	170 10 E
Naser, Buheirat en	**86**	23 0N	32 30 E
Nashua, Iowa, U.S.A.	**116**	42 55N	92 34W
Nashua, Mont., U.S.A.	**118**	48 10N	106 25W
Nashua, N.H., U.S.A.	**114**	42 50N	71 25W
Nashville, Ark., U.S.A.	**117**	33 56N	93 50W
Nashville, Ga., U.S.A.	**115**	31 3N	83 15W
Nashville, Tenn., U.S.A.	**115**	36 12N	86 46W
Našice	**42**	45 32N	18 4 E
Nasielsk	**28**	52 35N	20 50 E
Nasik	**70**	19 58N	73 50 E
Nasirabad	**68**	26 15N	74 45 E
Naskaupi →	**107**	53 47N	60 51W
Naso	**41**	38 8N	14 46 E
Nass →	**108**	55 0N	129 40W
Nassau, Bahamas	**121**	25 0N	77 20W
Nassau, U.S.A.	**113**	42 30N	73 34W
Nassau, Bahía	**128**	55 20 S	68 0W
Nasser City = Kôm Ombo	**86**	24 25N	32 52 E
Nasser, L. = Naser, Buheiret en	**86**	23 0N	32 30 E
Nassian	**84**	8 28N	3 28W
Nässjö	**49**	57 39N	14 42 E
Nastopoka Is.	**106**	57 0N	77 0W
Näsum	**49**	56 10N	14 29 E
Näsviken	**48**	61 46N	16 52 E
Nat Kyizin	**71**	14 57N	97 59 E
Nata	**92**	20 12 S	26 12 E
Natagaima	**126**	3 37N	75 6W
Natal, Brazil	**127**	5 47 S	35 13W
Natal, Can.	**108**	49 43N	114 51W
Natal, Indon.	**72**	0 35N	99 7 E
Natal □	**93**	28 30 S	30 30 E
Natalinci	**42**	44 15N	20 49 E
Naţanz	**65**	33 30N	51 55 E
Natashquan	**107**	50 14N	61 46W
Natashquan →	**107**	50 7N	61 50W
Natchez	**117**	31 35N	91 25W
Natchitoches	**117**	31 47N	93 4W
Nathalia	**99**	36 1 S	145 13 E
Nathdwara	**68**	24 55N	73 50 E
Natick	**113**	42 16N	71 19W
Natih	**65**	22 25N	56 30 E
Natimuk	**99**	36 42 S	142 0 E
Nation →	**108**	55 30N	123 32W
National City	**119**	32 39N	117 7W
Natitingou	**85**	10 20N	1 26 E
Natividad, I.	**120**	27 50N	115 10W
Natoma	**116**	39 14N	99 0W
Natron, L.	**90**	2 20 S	36 0 E
Natrona	**112**	40 39N	79 43W
Natrûn, W. el. →	**86**	30 25N	30 13 E
Natuna Besar, Kepulauan	**72**	4 0N	108 15 E
Natuna Selatan, Kepulauan	**72**	2 45N	109 0 E
Natural Bridge	**113**	44 5N	75 30W
Naturaliste, C.	**96**	33 32 S	115 0 E
Naturaliste C.	**99**	40 50 S	148 15 E
Naturaliste Channel	**96**	25 20 S	113 0 E
Naubinway	**106**	46 7N	85 27W
Naucelle	**20**	44 13N	2 20 E
Nauders	**26**	46 54N	10 30 E
Nauen	**24**	52 36N	12 52 E
Naugatuck	**113**	41 28N	73 4W
Naujoji Vilnia	**54**	54 48N	25 27 E
Naumburg	**24**	51 10N	11 48 E
Nauru	**94**	1 0 S	166 0 E
Nauru Is.	**94**	0 32 S	166 55 E
Nauta	**126**	4 31 S	73 35W
Nautla	**120**	20 20N	96 50W
Nava del Rey	**30**	41 22N	5 6W
Navacerrada, Puerto de	**30**	40 47N	4 0W
Navahermosa	**31**	39 41N	4 28W
Navajo Res.	**119**	36 55N	107 30W
Navalcarnero	**30**	40 17N	4 5W
Navalmoral de la Mata	**30**	39 52N	5 33W
Navalvillar de Pela	**31**	39 9N	5 24W
Navan = An Uaimh	**15**	53 39N	6 40W
Navare	**20**	43 20N	1 20W
Navarino, I.	**128**	55 0 S	67 40W
Navarra □	**32**	42 40N	1 40W
Navarre, France	**20**	43 15N	1 20W
Navarre, U.S.A.	**112**	40 43N	81 31W
Navarrenx	**20**	43 20N	0 45W
Navas del Marqués, Las	**30**	40 36N	4 20W
Navasota	**117**	30 20N	96 5W
Navassa	**121**	18 30N	75 0W
Nave	**38**	45 35N	10 17 E
Naver →	**14**	58 34N	4 15W
Navia	**30**	43 35N	6 42W
Navia →	**30**	43 15N	6 50W
Navia de Suarna	**30**	42 58N	6 59W
Navidad	**124**	33 57 S	71 50W
Navlya	**54**	52 53N	34 30 E
Navoi	**58**	40 9N	65 22 E
Navojoa	**120**	27 0N	109 30W
Navolok	**52**	62 33N	39 57 E
Návpaktos	**45**	38 23N	21 50 E
Návplion	**45**	37 33N	22 50 E
Navrongo	**85**	10 51N	1 3W
Navsari	**68**	20 57N	72 59 E
Nawa Kot	**68**	28 21N	71 24 E
Nawabganj, Bangla.	**69**	24 35N	88 14 E
Nawabganj, India	**69**	26 56N	81 14 E
Nawabganj, Bareilly	**69**	28 32N	79 40 E
Nawabshah	**68**	26 15N	68 25 E
Nawada	**69**	24 50N	85 33 E
Nawakot	**69**	27 55N	85 10 E
Nawalgarh	**68**	27 50N	75 15 E
Nawapara	**69**	20 46N	82 33 E
Nawāsīf, Harrat	**64**	21 20N	42 10 E
Nawi	**86**	18 32N	30 50 E
Náxos	**45**	37 8N	25 25 E
Nay	**20**	43 10N	0 18W
Nāy Band	**65**	27 20N	52 40 E
Nayakhan	**59**	61 56N	159 0 E
Nayarit □	**120**	22 0N	105 0W
Nayé	**84**	14 28N	12 12W
Nazaré	**31**	39 36N	9 4W
Nazas	**120**	25 10N	104 6W
Nazas →	**120**	25 35N	103 25W
Naze, The	**13**	51 53N	1 19 E
Nazerat	**62**	32 42N	35 17 E
Nazir Hat	**67**	22 35N	91 49 E
Nazko	**108**	53 1N	123 37W
Nazko →	**108**	53 7N	123 34W
Nazret	**87**	8 32N	39 22 E
Nchanga	**91**	12 30 S	27 49 E
Ncheu	**91**	14 50 S	34 47 E
Ndala	**90**	4 45 S	33 15 E
Ndalatando	**88**	9 12 S	14 48 E
Ndali	**85**	9 50N	2 46 E
Ndareda	**90**	4 12 S	35 30 E
Ndélé	**81**	8 25N	20 36 E
Ndendé	**88**	2 22 S	11 23 E
Ndjamena	**81**	12 10N	14 59 E
Ndjolé	**88**	0 10 S	10 45 E
Ndola	**91**	13 0 S	28 34 E
Ndoto Mts.	**90**	2 0N	37 0 E
Nduguti	**90**	4 18 S	34 41 E
Nea →	**47**	63 15N	11 0 E
Néa Epídhavros	**45**	37 40N	23 7 E
Néa Flippiás	**44**	39 12N	20 53 E
Néa Kallikrátia	**44**	40 21N	23 1 E
Néa Víssi	**44**	41 34N	26 33 E
Neagh, Lough	**15**	54 35N	6 25W
Neah Bay	**118**	48 25N	124 40W
Neamţ □	**46**	47 0N	26 20 E
Neápolis, Kozan, Greece	**44**	40 20N	21 24 E
Neápolis, Lakonia, Greece	**45**	36 27N	23 8 E
Near Is.	**104**	53 0N	172 0 E
Neath	**13**	51 39N	3 49W
Nebbou	**85**	11 9N	1 51W
Nebine Cr. →	**99**	29 27 S	146 56 E
Nebit Dag	**58**	39 30N	54 22 E
Nebolchy, U.S.S.R.	**54**	59 12N	32 58 E
Nebolchy, U.S.S.R.	**54**	59 8N	33 18 E
Nebraska □	**116**	41 30N	100 0W
Nebraska City	**116**	40 40N	95 52W
Nébrodi, Monti	**40**	37 55N	14 50 E
Necedah	**116**	44 2N	90 7W
Nechako →	**108**	53 30N	122 44W
Neches →	**117**	29 55N	93 52W
Neckar →	**25**	49 31N	8 26 E
Necochea	**124**	38 30 S	58 50W
Nedelišće	**39**	46 23N	16 22 E
Nédha →	**45**	37 25N	21 45 E
Nedroma	**82**	35 1N	1 45W
Nedstrand	**47**	59 21N	5 49 E
Needles	**119**	34 50N	114 35W
Needles, The	**13**	50 39N	1 35W
Ñeembucú □	**124**	27 0 S	58 0W
Neemuch (Nimach)	**68**	24 30N	74 56 E
Neenah	**114**	44 10N	88 30W
Neepawa	**109**	50 15N	99 30W
Nefta	**83**	33 53N	7 50 E
Neftah Sidi Boubekeur	**82**	35 1N	0 4 E
Neftegorsk	**57**	44 25N	39 45 E
Neftyannyye Kamni	**53**	40 20N	50 55 E
Negapatam = Nagappattinam	**70**	10 46N	79 50 E
Negaunee	**114**	46 30N	87 36W
Negba	**62**	31 40N	34 41 E
Negele	**87**	5 20N	39 36 E
Negeri Sembilan □	**71**	2 50N	102 10 E
Negev = Hanegev	**62**	30 50N	35 0 E
Negoiu	**46**	45 35N	24 32 E
Negombo	**70**	7 12N	79 50 E
Negotin	**42**	44 16N	22 37 E
Negotino	**42**	41 29N	22 9 E
Negra, La	**124**	23 46 S	70 18W
Negra, Peña	**30**	42 11N	6 30W
Negra Pt.	**73**	18 40N	120 50 E
Negreira	**30**	42 54N	8 45W
Negreşti	**46**	46 50N	27 30 E
Négrine	**83**	34 30N	7 30 E
Negro →, Argent.	**128**	41 2 S	62 47W
Negro →, Brazil	**126**	3 0 S	60 0W
Negro →, Uruguay	**125**	33 24 S	58 22W
Negros	**73**	10 0N	123 0 E
Negru Vodă	**46**	43 47N	28 21 E
Nehbandān	**65**	31 35N	60 5 E
Neheim-Hüsten	**24**	51 27N	7 58 E
Nehoiaşu	**46**	45 24N	26 20 E
Nei Monggol Zizhiqu □	**76**	42 0N	112 0 E
Neidpath	**109**	50 12N	107 20W
Neihart	**118**	47 0N	110 44W
Neijiang	**75**	29 35N	104 55 E
Neilton	**118**	17 24N	123 52W
Neira de Jusá	**30**	42 53N	7 14W
Neisse →	**24**	52 4N	14 46 E
Neiva	**126**	2 56N	75 18W
Neixiang	**77**	33 10N	111 52 E
Nejanilini L.	**109**	59 33N	97 48W
Nejo	**87**	9 30N	35 28 E
Nekemte	**87**	9 4N	36 30 E
Nêkheb	**86**	25 10N	32 48 E
Neksø	**49**	55 4N	15 8 E
Nelas	**30**	40 32N	7 52W
Nelaug	**47**	58 39N	8 40 E
Nelia	**98**	20 39 S	142 12 E
Nelidovo	**54**	56 13N	32 49 E
Neligh	**116**	42 11N	98 2W
Nelkan	**59**	57 40N	136 4 E
Nellikuppam	**70**	11 46N	79 43 E
Nellore	**70**	14 27N	79 59 E
Nelma	**59**	47 39N	139 0 E
Nelson, Austral.	**100**	38 3 S	141 2 E
Nelson, Can.	**108**	49 30N	117 20W
Nelson, N.Z.	**101**	41 18 S	173 16 E
Nelson, U.K.	**12**	53 50N	2 14W
Nelson, Ariz., U.S.A.	**119**	35 35N	113 16W
Nelson, Nev., U.S.A.	**119**	35 46N	114 48W
Nelson □	**101**	42 11 S	172 15 E
Nelson →	**109**	54 33N	98 2W
Nelson, C., Austral.	**99**	38 26 S	141 32 E
Nelson, C., P.N.G.	**98**	9 0 S	149 20 E
Nelson, Estrecho	**128**	51 30 S	75 0W
Nelson Forks	**108**	59 30N	124 0W
Nelson House	**109**	55 47N	98 51W
Nelson L.	**109**	55 48N	100 7W
Nelspruit	**93**	25 29 S	30 59 E
Néma	**84**	16 40N	7 15W
Neman (Nemunas) →	**54**	55 25N	21 10 E
Neméa	**45**	37 49N	22 40 E
Nemeiben L.	**109**	55 20N	105 20W
Nemira	**46**	46 17N	26 19 E
Nemours	**19**	48 16N	2 40 E
Nemunas = Neman →	**54**	55 25N	21 10 E
Nemuro	**74**	43 20N	145 35 E
Nemuro-Kaikyō	**74**	43 30N	145 30 E
Nemuy	**59**	55 40N	136 9 E
Nen Jiang →	**76**	45 28N	124 30 E
Nenagh	**15**	52 52N	8 11W
Nenana	**104**	64 30N	149 20W
Nene →	**12**	52 38N	0 13 E
Nenjiang	**75**	49 10N	125 10 E
Neno	**91**	15 25 S	34 40 E
Nenusa, Kepulauan	**73**	4 45N	127 1 E
Neodesha	**117**	37 30N	95 37W
Néon Petrítsi	**44**	41 16N	23 15 E
Neosho	**117**	36 56N	94 28W
Neosho →	**117**	35 59N	95 10W
Nepal ■	**69**	28 0N	84 30 E
Nepalganj	**69**	28 5N	81 40 E
Nephi	**118**	39 43N	111 52W
Nephin	**15**	54 1N	9 21W
Nepomuk	**26**	49 29N	13 35 E
Neptune City	**113**	40 13N	74 4W
Néra →	**42**	44 48N	21 25 E
Nérac	**20**	44 8N	0 21 E
Nerchinsk	**59**	52 0N	116 39 E
Nerchinskiy Zavod	**59**	51 20N	119 40 E
Nereju	**46**	45 43N	26 43 E
Nerekhta	**55**	57 26N	40 38 E
Néret L.	**107**	54 45N	70 44W
Neretva →	**42**	43 1N	17 27 E
Neretvanski Kanal	**42**	43 7N	17 10 E
Neringa	**54**	55 30N	21 5 E
Nerja	**31**	36 43N	3 55W
Nerl →	**55**	56 11N	40 34 E
Nerokoúrou	**45**	35 29N	24 3 E
Nerpio	**33**	38 11N	2 16W
Nerva	**31**	37 42N	6 30W
Nes	**50**	65 53N	17 24W
Nes Ziyyona	**62**	31 56N	34 48W
Nesbyen	**47**	60 34N	9 35 E
Nesebŭr	**43**	42 41N	27 46 E
Nesflaten	**47**	59 38N	6 48 E
Neskaupstaður	**50**	65 9N	13 42W
Nesland	**47**	59 31N	7 59 E
Neslandsvatn	**47**	58 57N	9 10 E
Nesle	**19**	49 45N	2 53 E
Nesodden	**47**	59 48N	10 40 E
Nesque →	**21**	43 59N	4 59 E
Ness, Loch	**14**	57 15N	4 30W
Nestórion Óros	**44**	40 24N	21 5 E
Néstos →	**44**	41 20N	24 35 E
Nesttun	**47**	60 19N	5 21 E
Nesvizh	**54**	53 14N	26 38 E
Netanya	**62**	32 20N	34 51 E
Nète →	**16**	51 7N	4 14 E
Nether Stowey	**13**	51 0N	3 10W
Netherbury	**13**	50 46N	2 45W
Netherdale	**97**	21 10 S	148 33 E
Netherlands ■	**16**	52 0N	5 30 E
Netherlands Antilles □	**121**	12 30N	68 0W
Netherlands Guiana = Surinam ■	**127**	4 0N	56 0W
Neto →	**41**	39 13N	17 8 E
Netrakona	**69**	24 53N	90 47 E
Nettancourt	**19**	48 51N	4 57 E
Nettilling L.	**105**	66 30N	71 0W
Nettuno	**40**	41 29N	12 40 E
Netzahualcoyotl, Presa	**120**	17 10N	93 30W
Neu-Isenburg	**25**	50 3N	8 42 E
Neu-Ulm	**25**	48 23N	10 2 E
Neubrandenburg	**24**	53 33N	13 17 E
Neubrandenburg □	**24**	53 30N	13 20 E
Neubukow	**24**	54 1N	11 40 E
Neuburg	**25**	48 43N	11 11 E
Neuchâtel	**25**	47 0N	6 55 E
Neuchâtel □	**25**	47 0N	6 55 E
Neuchâtel, Lac de	**25**	46 53N	6 50 E
Neudau	**26**	47 11N	16 6 E
Neuenhaus	**24**	52 30N	6 55 E
Neuf-Brisach	**19**	48 0N	7 30 E
Neufahrn	**25**	48 44N	12 11 E
Neufchâteau, Belg.	**16**	49 50N	5 25 E
Neufchâteau, France	**19**	48 21N	5 40 E
Neufchâtel	**19**	49 43N	1 30 E
Neufchâtel-sur-Aisne	**19**	49 26N	4 0 E
Neuhaus	**24**	53 16N	10 54 E
Neuillé-Pont-Pierre	**18**	47 33N	0 33 E
Neuilly-St-Front	**19**	49 10N	3 15 E
Neukalen	**24**	53 49N	12 48 E
Neumarkt	**25**	49 16N	11 28 E
Neumarkt-Sankt Veit	**25**	48 22N	12 30 E
Neumünster	**24**	54 4N	9 58 E
Neung-sur-Beuvron	**19**	47 30N	1 50 E
Neunkirchen, Austria	**26**	47 43N	16 4 E
Neunkirchen, Ger.	**25**	49 23N	7 12 E
Neuquén	**128**	38 55 S	68 0 E
Neuquén □	**124**	38 0 S	69 50W
Neuruppin	**24**	52 56N	12 48 E
Neuse →	**115**	35 5N	76 30W
Neusiedl	**27**	47 57N	16 50 E
Neusiedler See	**27**	47 50N	16 47 E
Neuss	**24**	51 12N	6 39 E
Neussargues-Moissac	**20**	45 9N	3 1 E
Neustadt, Baden-W., Ger.	**25**	47 54N	8 13 E
Neustadt, Bayern, Ger.	**25**	50 23N	11 0 E
Neustadt, Bayern, Ger.	**25**	49 42N	12 10 E
Neustadt, Bayern, Ger.	**25**	48 48N	11 47 E
Neustadt, Bayern, Ger.	**25**	49 34N	10 37 E
Neustadt, Gera, Ger.	**24**	50 45N	11 43 E
Neustadt, Hessen, Ger.	**24**	50 51N	9 9 E
Neustadt, Niedersachsen, Ger.	**24**	52 30N	9 30 E
Neustadt, Potsdam, Ger.	**24**	52 50N	12 27 E
Neustadt, Rhld-Pfz., Ger.	**25**	49 21N	8 10 E
Neustadt, Schleswig-Holstein, Ger.	**24**	54 6N	10 49 E
Neustrelitz	**24**	53 22N	13 4 E
Neuvic	**20**	45 23N	2 16 E
Neuville, Rhône, France	**21**	45 52N	4 51 E
Neuville, Vienne, France	**18**	46 41N	0 15 E
Neuville-aux-Bois	**19**	48 4N	2 3 E
Neuvy-le-Roi	**18**	47 36N	0 36 E
Neuvy-St-Sépulchure	**20**	46 35N	1 48 E
Neuvy-sur-Barangeon	**19**	47 20N	2 15 E
Neuwerk	**24**	53 55N	8 30 E
Neuwied	**24**	50 26N	7 29 E
Neva →	**52**	59 50N	30 30 E
Nevada	**117**	37 51N	94 22W
Nevada □	**118**	39 20N	117 0W
Nevada City	**118**	39 20N	121 0W
Nevada de Sta. Marta, Sa.	**126**	10 55N	73 50W
Nevada, Sierra, Spain	**33**	37 3N	3 15W
Nevada, Sierra, U.S.A.	**118**	39 0N	120 30W
Nevado, Cerro	**124**	35 30 S	68 32W
Nevanka	**59**	56 31N	98 55 E
Nevasa	**70**	19 34N	75 0 E
Nevel	**54**	56 0N	29 55 E
Nevers	**19**	47 0N	3 9 E
Nevertire	**99**	31 50 S	147 44 E
Nevesinje	**42**	43 14N	18 6 E
Neville	**109**	49 58N	107 39W
Nevinnomyssk	**57**	44 40N	42 0 E
Nevis	**121**	17 0N	62 30W

Nevlunghavn 47 55 58N 9 52 E
Nevrokop = Gotse Delchev 43 41 33N 23 46 E
Nevşehir 64 38 33N 34 40 E
Nevyansk 52 57 30N 60 13 E
New Albany, Ind., U.S.A. 114 38 20N 85 50W
New Albany, Miss., U.S.A. 117 34 30N 89 0W
New Albany, Pa., U.S.A. 113 41 35N 76 28W
New Amsterdam 126 6 15N 57 36W
New Bedford 114 41 40N 70 52W
New Bern 115 35 8N 77 3W
New Bethlehem 112 41 0N 79 22W
New Bloomfield 112 40 24N 77 12W
New Boston 117 33 27N 94 21W
New Braunfels 117 29 43N 98 9W
New Brighton, N.Z. 101 43 29 S 172 43 E
New Brighton, U.S.A. 112 40 42N 80 19W
New Britain, P.N.G. 94 5 50 S 150 20 E
New Britain, U.S.A. 114 41 41N 72 47W
New Brunswick 114 40 30N 74 28W
New Brunswick □ 107 46 50N 66 30W
New Bussa 85 9 53N 4 31 E
New Byrd 5 80 0 S 120 0W
New Caledonia = Nouvelle-Calédonie 94 21 0 S 165 0 E
New Castile = Castilla La Neuva 31 39 45N 3 20W
New Castle, Ind., U.S.A. 114 39 55N 85 23W
New Castle, Pa., U.S.A. 114 41 0N 80 20W
New City 113 41 8N 74 0W
New Cristóbal 120 9 22N 79 40W
New Cumberland 112 40 30N 80 36W
New Delhi 68 28 37N 77 13 E
New Denver 108 50 0N 117 25W
New England 116 46 36N 102 47W
New England Ra. 97 30 20 S 151 45 E
New Forest 13 50 53N 1 40W
New Glasgow 107 45 35N 62 36W
New Guinea 94 4 0 S 136 0 E
New Hamburg 112 43 23N 80 42W
New Hampshire □ 114 43 40N 71 40W
New Hampton 116 43 2N 92 20W
New Hanover, P.N.G. 98 2 30 S 150 10 E
New Hanover, S. Afr. 93 29 22 S 30 31 E
New Haven, Conn., U.S.A. 114 41 20N 72 54W
New Haven, Mich., U.S.A. 112 42 44N 82 46W
New Hazelton 108 55 20N 127 30W
* New Hebrides 94 15 0 S 168 0 E
New Iberia 117 30 2N 91 54W
New Ireland 94 3 20 S 151 50 E
New Jersey □ 114 40 30N 74 10W
New Kensington 114 40 36N 79 43W
New Lexington 114 39 40N 82 15W
New Liskeard 106 47 31N 79 41W
New London, Conn., U.S.A. 114 41 23N 72 8W
New London, Minn., U.S.A. 116 45 17N 94 55W
New London, Ohio, U.S.A. 112 41 4N 82 25W
New London, Wis., U.S.A. 116 44 23N 88 43W
New Madrid 117 36 40N 89 30W
New Meadows 118 45 0N 116 32W
New Mexico □ 110 34 30N 106 0W
New Milford, Conn., U.S.A. 113 41 35N 73 25W
New Milford, Pa., U.S.A. 113 41 50N 75 45W
New Norfolk 97 42 46 S 147 2 E
New Orleans 117 30 0N 90 5W
New Philadelphia 114 40 29N 81 25W
New Plymouth, N.Z. 101 39 4 S 174 5 E
New Plymouth, U.S.A. 118 43 58N 116 49W
New Providence 121 25 25N 78 35W
New Radnor 13 52 15N 3 10W
New Richmond 116 45 6N 92 34W
New Roads 117 30 43N 91 30W
New Rochelle 113 40 55N 73 46W
New Rockford 116 47 44N 99 7W
New Ross 15 52 24N 6 58W
New Salem 116 46 51N 101 25W
New Siberian Is. = Novosibirskiye Os. 59 75 0N 142 0 E
New Smyrna Beach 115 29 0N 80 50W
New South Wales □ 97 33 0 S 146 0 E
New Town 116 47 59N 102 30W
New Ulm 116 44 15N 94 30W
New Waterford 107 46 13N 60 4W
New Westminster 108 49 13N 122 55W
New York □ 114 42 40N 76 0W
New York City 114 40 45N 74 0W
New Zealand ■ 94 40 0 S 176 0 E
Newala 91 10 58 S 39 18 E
Newala □ 91 10 46 S 39 20 E
Newark, Del., U.S.A. 114 39 42N 75 45W
Newark, N.J., U.S.A. 114 40 41N 74 12W
Newark, N.Y., U.S.A. 114 43 2N 77 10W
Newark, Ohio, U.S.A. 114 40 5N 82 24W
Newark-on-Trent 12 53 6N 0 48W
Newaygo 114 43 25N 85 48W
Newberg 118 45 22N 123 0W
Newberry, Mich., U.S.A. 114 46 20N 85 32W
Newberry, S.C., U.S.A. 115 34 17N 81 37W
Newbrook 108 54 24N 112 57W
Newburgh 114 41 30N 74 1W
Newbury, U.K. 13 51 24N 1 19W
Newbury, U.S.A. 113 44 7N 72 6W
Newburyport 114 42 48N 70 50W
Newcastle, Austral. 97 33 0 S 151 46 E
Newcastle, Can. 107 47 1N 65 38W
Newcastle, S. Afr. 93 27 45 S 29 58 E
Newcastle, U.K. 15 54 13N 5 54W
Newcastle, U.S.A. 116 43 50N 104 12W
Newcastle Emlyn 13 52 2N 4 29W
Newcastle Ra. 97 15 45 S 130 15 E
Newcastle-under-Lyme 12 53 2N 2 15W
Newcastle-upon-Tyne 12 54 59N 1 37W
Newcastle Waters 96 17 30 S 133 28 E
Newdegate 96 33 6 S 119 0 E
Newe Etan 62 32 30N 35 32 E
Newe Sha'anan 62 32 47N 34 59 E
Newe Zohar 62 31 9N 35 21 E
Newell 116 44 48N 103 25W
Newenham, C. 104 58 40N 162 15W
Newfoundland 107 48 30N 56 0W
Newfoundland □ 107 53 0N 58 0W
Newhalem 108 48 41N 121 16W
Newham 13 51 31N 0 2 E
Newhaven 13 50 47N 0 4 E
Newkirk 117 36 52N 97 3W
Newman, Mt. 96 23 20 S 119 34 E
Newmarket, Can. 112 44 3N 79 28W
Newmarket, Ireland 15 52 13N 9 0W
Newmarket, U.K. 13 52 15N 0 23 E
Newmarket, U.S.A. 113 43 4N 70 57W
Newnan 115 33 22N 84 48W
Newnes 99 33 9 S 150 16 E
Newport, Gwent, U.K. 13 51 35N 3 0W
Newport, I. of W., U.K. 13 50 42N 1 18W
Newport, Salop, U.K. 13 52 47N 2 22W
Newport, Ark., U.S.A. 117 35 38N 91 15W
Newport, Ky., U.S.A. 114 39 5N 84 23W
Newport, N.H., U.S.A. 114 43 23N 72 8W
Newport, Oreg., U.S.A. 118 44 41N 124 2W
Newport, Pa., U.S.A. 112 40 28N 77 8W
Newport, R.I., U.S.A. 114 41 13N 71 19W
Newport, Tenn., U.S.A. 115 35 59N 83 12W
Newport, Vt., U.S.A. 114 44 57N 72 17W
Newport, Wash., U.S.A. 118 48 11N 117 2W
Newport Beach 119 33 40N 117 58W
Newport News 114 37 2N 76 30W
Newquay 13 50 24N 5 6W
Newry 15 54 10N 6 20W
Newry & Mourne □ 15 54 10N 6 15W
Newton, Iowa, U.S.A. 116 41 40N 93 3W
Newton, Mass., U.S.A. 114 42 21N 71 10W
Newton, Miss., U.S.A. 117 32 19N 89 10W
Newton, N.C., U.S.A. 115 35 42N 81 10W
Newton, N.J., U.S.A. 114 41 3N 74 46W
Newton, Texas, U.S.A. 117 30 54N 93 42W
Newton Abbot 13 50 32N 3 37W
Newton Boyd 99 29 45 S 152 16 E
Newton Stewart 14 54 57N 4 30W
Newtonmore 14 57 4N 4 7W
Newtown 13 52 31N 3 19W
Newtownabbey 15 54 40N 5 55W
Newtownabbey □ 15 54 45N 6 0W
Newtownards 15 54 37N 5 40W
Newville 112 40 10N 77 24W
Nexon 20 45 41N 1 11 E
Neya 55 58 21N 43 49 E
Neyrīz 65 29 15N 54 19 E
Neyshābūr 65 36 10N 58 50 E
Neyyattinkara 70 8 26N 77 5 E
Nezhin 54 51 5N 31 55 E
Nezperce 118 46 13N 116 15W
Ngabang 72 0 23N 109 55 E
Ngabordamlu, Tanjung 73 6 56 S 134 11 E
Ngambé 85 5 48N 11 29 E
Ngami Depression 92 20 30 S 22 46 E
Ngamo 91 19 3 S 27 32 E
Nganglong Kangri 67 33 0N 81 0 E
Nganjuk 73 7 32 S 111 55 E
Ngaoundéré 88 7 15N 13 35 E
Ngapara 101 44 57 S 170 46 E
Ngara 90 2 29 S 30 40 E
Ngara □ 90 2 29 S 30 40 E
Ngau 101 18 2 S 179 18 E
Ngawi 73 7 24 S 111 26 E
Ngha Lo 71 21 33N 104 28 E
Ngiva 92 16 48 S 15 50 E
Ngoma 91 13 8 S 33 45 E
Ngomahura 91 20 26 S 30 43 E
Ngomba 91 8 20 S 32 53 E
Ngop 87 6 17N 30 9 E
Ngoring Hu 75 34 55N 97 5 E
Ngorkou 84 15 40N 3 41W
Ngorongoro 90 3 11 S 35 32 E
Ngozi 90 2 54 S 29 50 E
Ngudu 90 2 58 S 33 25 E
Nguigmi 81 14 20N 13 20 E
Ngunga 90 3 37 S 33 37 E
Ngunza 88 11 10 S 13 48 E
Nguru 85 12 56N 10 29 E
Nguru Mts. 90 6 0 S 37 30 E
Nha Trang 71 12 16N 109 10 E
Nhacoongo 93 24 18 S 35 14 E
Nhangutazi, L. 93 24 0 S 34 30 E
Nhill 99 36 18 S 141 40 E
Nia-nia 90 1 30N 27 40 E
Niafounké 84 16 0N 4 5W
Niagara 114 45 45N 88 0W
Niagara Falls, Can. 106 43 7N 79 5W
Niagara Falls, U.S.A. 114 43 5N 79 0W
Niagara-on-the-Lake 112 43 15N 79 4W
Niah 72 3 58N 113 46 E
Nialia, L. 100 33 20 S 141 42 E
Niamey 85 13 27N 2 6 E
Nianforando 84 9 37N 10 36W
Nianfors 48 61 36N 16 46 E
Niangara 90 3 42N 27 50 E
Nianzishan 76 47 31N 122 53 E
Nias 72 1 0N 97 30 E
Niassa □ 91 13 30 S 36 0 E
Nibbiano 38 44 54N 9 20 E
Nibe 49 56 59N 9 38 E
Nibong Tebal 71 5 10N 100 29 E
Nicaragua ■ 121 11 40N 85 30W
Nicaragua, Lago de 121 12 0N 85 30W
Nicastro 41 39 0N 16 18 E
Nice 21 43 42N 7 14 E
Niceville 115 30 30N 86 30W
Nichinan 74 31 38N 131 23 E
Nicholás, Canal 121 23 30N 80 5W
Nicholasville 114 37 54N 84 31W
Nichols 113 42 1N 76 22W
Nicholson 113 41 37N 75 47W
Nicobar Is. 60 9 0N 93 0 E
Nicola 108 50 12N 120 40W
Nicolet 106 46 17N 72 35W
Nicolls Town 121 25 8N 78 0W
Nicopolis 45 39 2N 20 37 E
Nicosia, Cyprus 64 35 10N 33 25 E
Nicosia, Italy 41 37 45N 14 22 E
Nicótera 41 38 33N 15 57 E
Nicoya, G. de 121 10 0N 85 0W
Nicoya, Pen. de 121 9 45N 85 40W
Nidd → 12 54 1N 1 32W
Nidda 24 50 24N 9 2 E
Nidda → 25 50 6N 8 34 E
Nidzica 28 53 25N 20 28 E
Niebüll 24 54 47N 8 49 E
Nied → 19 49 23N 6 40 E
Niederaula 24 50 48N 9 37 E
Niederbronn 19 48 57N 7 39 E
Niedere Tauern 26 47 20N 14 0 E
Niedermarsberg 24 51 28N 8 52 E
Niederösterreich □ 26 48 25N 15 40 E
Niedersachsen □ 24 52 45N 9 0 E
Niellé 84 10 5N 5 38W
Niemba 90 5 58 S 28 24 E
Niemcza 28 50 42N 16 47 E
Niemodlin 28 50 38N 17 38 E
Niemur 100 35 17 S 144 9 E
Nienburg 24 52 38N 9 15 E
Niepołomice 27 50 3N 20 13 E
Niers → 24 51 45N 5 58 E
Niesky 24 51 18N 14 48 E
Nieszawa 28 52 52N 18 50 E
Nieuw Amsterdam 127 5 53N 55 5W
Nieuw Nickerie 127 6 0N 56 59W
Nieuwpoort 16 51 8N 2 45 E
Nieves 30 42 7N 8 26W
Nièvre □ 19 47 10N 3 40 E
Niğde 64 38 0N 34 40 E
Nigel 93 26 27 S 28 25 E
Niger ■ 85 13 30N 10 0 E
Niger □ 85 10 0N 5 0 E
Niger → 85 5 33N 6 33 E
Nigeria ■ 85 8 30N 8 0 E
Nightcaps 101 45 57 S 168 2 E
Nigrita 44 40 56N 23 29 E
Nihtaur 69 29 20N 78 23 E
Nii-Jima 74 34 20N 139 15 E
Niigata 74 37 58N 139 0 E
Niigata □ 74 37 15N 138 45 E
Niihama 74 33 55N 133 16 E
Niihau 110 21 55N 160 10W
Nijar 33 36 53N 2 15W
Nijkerk 16 52 13N 5 30 E
Nijmegen 16 51 50N 5 52 E
Nijverdal 16 52 22N 6 28 E
Nike 85 6 26N 7 29 E
Nikel 50 69 24N 30 12 E
Nikiniki 73 9 49 S 124 30 E
Nikitas 44 40 13N 23 34 E
Nikki 85 9 58N 3 12 E
Nikkō 74 36 45N 139 35 E
Nikolayev 56 46 58N 32 0 E
Nikolayevsk 55 50 0N 45 35 E
Nikolayevsk-na-Amur 59 53 8N 140 44 E
Nikolsk 55 59 30N 45 28 E
Nikolskoye 59 55 12N 166 0 E
Nikopol, Bulg. 43 43 43N 24 54 E
Nikopol, U.S.S.R. 56 47 35N 34 25 E
Niksar 56 40 31N 37 2 E
Nīkshahr 65 26 15N 60 10 E
Nikšić 42 42 50N 18 57 E
Nîl el Abyad → 87 15 38N 32 31 E
Nîl el Azraq → 87 15 38N 32 31 E
Nîl, Nahr en → 86 30 10N 31 6 E
Niland 119 33 16N 115 30W
Nile = Nîl, Nahr en → 86 30 10N 31 6 E
Nile □ 90 2 0N 31 30 E
Nile Delta 86 31 40N 31 0 E
Niles 114 41 8N 80 40W
Nilgiri Hills 70 11 30N 76 30 E
Nimach = Neemuch 68 24 30N 74 56 E
Nimbahera 68 24 37N 74 45 E
Nîmes 21 43 50N 4 23 E
Nimfaíon, Ákra- 44 40 5N 24 20 E
Nimingarra 96 20 31 S 119 55 E
Nimmitabel 99 36 29 S 149 15 E
Nimneryskiy 59 57 50N 125 10 E
Nimrod Glacier 5 82 27 S 161 0 E
Nimule 87 3 32N 32 3 E
Nin 39 44 16N 15 12 E
Nindigully 99 28 21 S 148 50 E
Ninemile 108 56 0N 130 7W
Ninety Mile Beach, The 97 38 15 S 147 24 E
Nineveh = Nīnawá 64 36 25N 43 10 E
Ning'an 76 44 22N 129 20 E
Ningbo 75 29 51N 121 28 E
Ningde 75 26 38N 119 23 E
Ningdu 77 26 25N 115 59 E
Ningjin 76 37 35N 114 57 E
Ningming 77 22 8N 107 4 E
Ningpo = Ningbo 75 29 51N 121 28 E
Ningqiang 77 32 47N 106 15 E
Ningshan 77 33 21N 108 21 E
Ningsia Hui A.R. = Ningxia Huizu Zizhiqu □ 76 38 0N 106 0 E
Ningwu 76 39 0N 112 18 E
Ningxia Huizu Zizhiqu □ 76 38 0N 106 0 E
Ningxiang 77 28 15N 112 30 E
Ningyuan 77 25 37N 111 57 E
Ninh Binh 71 20 15N 105 55 E
Ninove 16 50 51N 4 2 E
Nioaque 125 21 5 S 55 50W
Niobrara 116 42 48N 97 59W
Niobrara → 116 42 45N 98 0W
Niono 84 14 15N 6 0W
Nioro du Rip 84 13 40N 15 50W
Nioro du Sahel 84 15 15N 9 30W
Niort 20 46 19N 0 29W
Nipani 70 16 20N 74 25 E
Nipawin 109 53 20N 104 0W
Nipawin Prov. Park 109 54 0N 104 37W
Nipigon 106 49 0N 88 17W
Nipigon, L. 106 49 50N 88 30W
Nipin → 109 55 46N 108 35W
Nipishish L. 107 54 12N 60 45W
Nipissing L. 106 46 20N 80 0W
Nipomo 119 35 4N 120 29W
Niquelândia 127 14 33 S 48 23W
Nira → 70 17 58N 75 8 E
Nirmal 70 19 3N 78 20 E
Nirmali 69 26 20N 86 35 E
Niš 42 43 19N 21 58 E
Nisa 31 39 30N 7 41W
Nişāb 63 14 25N 46 29 E
Nišava → 42 43 20N 21 46 E
Niscemi 41 37 8N 14 21 E
Nishinomiya 74 34 45N 135 20 E
Nísíros 45 36 35N 27 12 E
Niskibi → 106 56 29N 88 9W
Nisko 28 50 35N 22 7 E
Nisporeny 46 47 4N 28 10 E
Nissafors 49 57 25N 13 37 E
Nissan → 49 56 40N 12 51 E
Nissedal 47 59 10N 8 30 E
Nisser 47 59 7N 8 28 E
Nissum Fjord 49 56 20N 8 11 E
Nisutlin → 108 60 14N 132 34W
Niţă' 64 27 15N 48 35 E
Nitchequon 107 53 10N 70 58W
Niterói 125 22 52 S 43 0W
Nith → 14 55 20N 3 5W
Nitra 27 48 19N 18 4 E
Nitra → 27 47 46N 18 10 E
Nittedal 47 60 1N 10 57 E
Nittendau 25 49 12N 12 16 E
Niuafo'ou 101 15 30 S 175 58W
Niue I. (Savage I.) 95 19 2 S 169 54W
Niut 72 0 55N 110 6 E
Nivelles 16 50 35N 4 20 E
Nivernais 19 47 0N 3 40 E
Nixon, Nev., U.S.A. 118 39 54N 119 22W
Nixon, Tex., U.S.A. 117 29 17N 97 45W
Nizam Sagar 70 18 10N 77 58 E
Nizamabad 70 18 45N 78 7 E
Nizamghat 67 28 20N 95 45 E
Nizhne Kolymsk 59 68 34N 160 55 E
Nizhne-Vartovskoye 58 60 56N 76 38 E
Nizhneangarsk 59 55 47N 109 30 E
Nizhnegorskiy 56 45 27N 34 38 E
Nizhneudinsk 59 54 54N 99 3 E
Nizhneyansk 59 71 26N 136 4 E
Nizhniy Lomov 55 53 34N 43 38 E
Nizhniy Novgorod = Gorkiy 55 56 20N 44 0 E
Nizhniy Tagil 52 57 55N 59 57 E
Nizhnyaya Tunguska → 59 64 20N 93 0 E
Nizip 64 37 5N 37 50 E
Nizké Tatry 27 48 55N 20 0 E
Nizza Monferrato 38 44 46N 8 22 E
Njakwa 91 11 1 S 33 56 E
Njanji 91 14 25 S 31 46 E
Njinjo 91 8 48 S 38 54 E
Njombe 91 9 20 S 34 50 E
Njombe □ 91 9 20 S 34 49 E
Njombe → 90 6 56 S 35 6 E
Nkambe 85 6 35N 10 40 E
Nkana 91 12 50 S 28 8 E
Nkawkaw 85 6 36N 0 49W
Nkhota Kota 91 12 56 S 34 15 E
Nkongsamba 88 4 55N 9 55 E
Nkwanta 84 6 10N 2 10W
Noatak 104 67 32N 162 59W
Nobel 112 45 25N 80 6W
Nobeoka 74 32 36N 131 41 E
Noblejas 32 39 58N 3 26W
Noblesville 114 40 1N 85 59W
Noce → 38 46 9N 11 4 E
Nocera Inferiore 41 40 45N 14 37 E
Nocera Terinese 41 39 2N 16 9 E
Nocera Umbra 39 43 8N 12 47 E
Noci 41 40 47N 17 7 E
Nockatunga 99 27 42 S 142 42 E
Nocona 117 33 48N 97 45W
Nocrich 46 45 55N 24 26 E
Noel 117 36 36N 94 29W
Nogales, Mexico 120 31 20N 110 56W
Nogales, U.S.A. 119 31 33N 110 56W
Nogat → 28 54 17N 19 17 E
Nōgata 74 33 48N 130 44 E
Nogent-en-Bassigny 19 48 0N 5 20 E
Nogent-le-Rotrou 18 48 20N 0 50 E
Nogent-sur-Seine 19 48 30N 3 30 E
Noginsk, Moskva, U.S.S.R. 55 55 50N 38 25 E
Noginsk, Sib., U.S.S.R. 59 64 30N 90 50 E
Nogoa → 97 23 40 S 147 55 E
Nogoyá 124 32 24 S 59 48W
Nógrád □ 27 48 0N 19 30 E
Nogueira de Ramuin 30 42 21N 7 43W
Noguera Pallaresa → 32 42 15N 1 0 E
Noguera Ribagorzana → 32 41 40N 0 43 E
Nohar 68 29 11N 74 49 E
Noi → 71 14 50N 100 15 E
Noire, Mt. 18 48 11N 3 40W
Noirétable 20 45 48N 3 46 E
Noirmoutier 18 47 0N 2 15W
Noirmoutier, Î. de 18 46 58N 2 10W
Nojane 92 23 15 S 20 14 E
Nok Kundi 66 28 50N 62 45 E
Nokaneng 92 19 40 S 22 17 E
Nokhtuysk 59 60 0N 117 45 E
Nokomis 109 51 35N 105 0W
Nokomis L. 109 57 0N 103 0W
Nol 49 57 56N 12 5 E
Nola, C. Afr. Rep. 88 3 35N 16 4 E
Nola, Italy 41 40 54N 14 29 E
Nolay 19 46 58N 4 35 E
Noli, C. di 38 44 12N 8 26 E
Nolinsk 55 57 28N 49 57 E
Noma Omuramba → 92 18 52 S 20 53 E
Noman L. 109 62 15N 108 55W
Nome 104 64 30N 165 24W
Nonacho L. 109 61 42N 109 40W
Nonancourt 18 48 47N 1 11 E
Nonant-le-Pin 18 48 42N 0 12 E
Nonda 98 20 40 S 142 28 E
Nong Khae 71 14 29N 100 53 E
Nong Khai 71 17 50N 102 46 E
Nong'an 76 44 25N 125 5 E
Nonoava 120 27 28N 106 44W
Nontron 20 45 31N 0 40 E
Noonan 116 48 51N 102 59W
Noondoo 99 28 35 S 148 30 E
Noord Brabant □ 16 51 40N 5 0 E
Noord Holland □ 16 52 30N 4 45 E
Noordbeveland 16 51 35N 3 50 E
Noordoostpolder 16 52 45N 5 45 E
Noordwijk aan Zee 16 52 14N 4 26 E
Nootka 108 49 38N 126 38W
Nootka I. 108 49 32N 126 42W

* *Renamed Vanuatu* ■

Nóqui 88 5 55S 13 30 E
Nora, Ethiopia 87 16 6N 40 4 E
Nora, Sweden 48 59 32N 15 2 E
Noranda 106 48 20N 79 0W
Norberg 48 60 4N 15 56 E
Nórcia 39 42 50N 13 5 E
Nord □ 19 50 15N 3 30 E
Nord-Ostee Kanal 24 54 15N 9 40 E
Nord-Süd Kanal 24 53 0N 10 32 E
Nord-Trøndelag fylke □ 50 64 20N 12 0 E
Nordagutu 47 59 25N 9 20 E
Nordaustlandet 4 79 14N 23 0 E
Nordborg 49 55 5N 9 50 E
Nordby, Arhus, Denmark 49 55 58N 10 32 E
Nordby, Ribe, Denmark 49 55 27N 8 24 E
Norddal 47 62 15N 7 14 E
Norddalsfjord 47 61 39N 5 23 E
Norddeich 24 53 37N 7 10 E
Nordegg 108 52 29N 116 5W
Norden 24 53 35N 7 12 E
Nordenham 24 53 29N 8 28 E
Norderhov 47 60 7N 10 17 E
Norderney 24 53 42N 7 15 E
Nordfjord 47 61 55N 5 30 E
Nordfriesische Inseln 24 54 40N 8 20 E
Nordhausen 24 51 29N 10 47 E
Nordhorn 24 52 27N 7 4 E
Nordjyllands Amtskommune □ 49 57 0N 10 0 E
Nordkapp, Norway 50 71 10N 25 44 E
Nordkapp, Svalb. 4 80 31N 20 0 E
Nordkinn 9 71 8N 27 40 E
Nordland fylke □ 50 65 40N 13 0 E
Nördlingen 25 48 50N 10 30 E
Nordrhein-Westfalen □ 24 51 45N 7 30 E
Nordstrand 24 54 27N 8 50 E
Nordvik 59 74 2N 111 32 E
Nore 47 60 10N 9 0 E
Nore → 15 52 40N 7 20W
Norefjell 47 60 16N 9 29 E
Norembega 106 48 59N 80 43W
Noresund 47 60 11N 9 37 E
Norfolk, Nebr., U.S.A. 116 42 3N 97 25W
Norfolk, Va., U.S.A. 114 36 40N 76 15W
Norfolk □ 12 52 39N 1 0 E
Norfolk Broads 12 52 30N 1 15 E
Norfolk I. 94 28 58S 168 3 E
Norfork Res. 117 36 13N 92 15W
Norilsk 59 69 20N 88 6 E
Norley 99 27 45S 143 48 E
Norma, Mt. 98 20 55S 140 42 E
Normal 116 40 30N 89 0W
Norman 117 35 12N 97 30W
Norman → 97 17 28S 140 49 E
Norman Wells 104 65 17N 126 51W
Normanby → 97 14 23S 144 10 E
Normanby I. 98 10 55S 151 5 E
Normandie 18 48 45N 0 10 E
Normandie, Collines de 18 48 55N 0 45W
Normandin 106 48 49N 72 31W
Normandy = Normandie 18 48 45N 0 10 E
Normanton 97 17 40S 141 10 E
Norquay 109 51 53N 102 5W
Norquinco 128 41 51S 70 55W
Norrahammar 49 57 43N 14 7 E
Norrbotten □ 50 66 30N 22 30 E
Norrby 50 64 55N 18 15 E
Nørre Åby 49 55 27N 9 52 E
Nørre Nebel 49 55 47N 8 17 E
Nørresundby 49 57 5N 9 52 E
Norris 118 45 40N 111 40W
Norristown 114 40 9N 75 21W
Norrköping 49 58 37N 16 11 E
Norrland □ 50 66 50N 18 0 E
Norrtälje 48 59 46N 18 42 E
Norsholm 49 58 31N 15 59 E
Norsk 59 52 30N 130 0 E
North Adams 114 42 42N 73 6W
North America 102 40 0N 100 0W
North Andaman I. 71 13 15N 92 40 E
North Atlantic Ocean 6 30 0N 50 0W
North Battleford 109 52 50N 108 17W
North Bay 106 46 20N 79 30W
North Belcher Is. 106 56 50N 79 50W
North Bend, Can. 108 49 50N 121 27W
North Bend, Oreg., U.S.A. 118 43 28N 124 14W
North Bend, Pa., U.S.A. 112 41 20N 77 42W
North Berwick, U.K. 14 56 4N 2 44W
North Berwick, U.S.A. 113 43 18N 70 43W
North Buganda □ 90 1 0N 32 0 E
North Canadian → 117 35 17N 95 31W
North C., Antarct. 5 71 0S 166 0 E
North C., Can. 107 47 2N 60 20W
North C., N.Z. 101 34 23S 173 4 E
North Caribou L. 106 52 50N 90 40W
North Carolina □ 115 35 30N 80 0W
North Channel, Br. Is. 14 55 0N 5 30W
North Channel, Can. 106 46 0N 83 0W
North Chicago 114 42 19N 87 50W
North Dakota □ 116 47 30N 100 0W
North Down □ 15 54 40N 5 45W
North Downs 13 51 17N 0 30 E
North East 112 42 17N 79 50W
North East Frontier Agency = Arunachal Pradesh □ 67 28 0N 95 0 E
North East Providence Chan. 121 26 0N 76 0W
North Eastern □ 90 1 30N 40 0 E
North Esk → 14 56 44N 2 25W
North European Plain 9 55 0N 20 0 E
North Foreland 13 51 22N 1 28 E
North Frisian Is. = Nordfr'sche Inseln 24 54 50N 8 20 E
North Henik L. 109 61 45N 97 40W
North Horr 90 3 20N 37 8 E
North I., Kenya 90 4 5N 36 5 E
North I., N.Z. 101 38 0S 175 0 E
North Kingsville 112 41 53N 80 42W
North Knife → 109 58 53N 94 45W
North Koel → 69 24 45N 83 50 E
North Korea ■ 76 40 0N 127 0 E
North Lakhimpur 67 27 14N 94 7 E
North Las Vegas 119 36 15N 115 6W
North Loup → 116 41 17N 98 23W
North Mashonaland □ 91 16 30S 30 0 E
North Minch 14 58 5N 5 55W
North Nahanni → 108 62 15N 123 20W
North Ossetian A.S.S.R. □ 57 43 30N 44 30 E
North Palisade 119 37 6N 118 32W
North Platte 116 41 10N 100 50W
North Platte → 116 41 15N 100 45W
North Pt. 107 47 5N 64 0W
North Pole 4 90 0N 0 0 E
North Portal 109 49 0N 102 33W
North Powder 118 45 2N 117 59W
North Ronaldsay 14 59 20N 2 30W
North Sea 8 56 0N 4 0 E
North Sentinel I. 71 11 35N 92 15 E
North Sporades = Voríai Sporádhes 45 39 15N 23 30 E
North Stradbroke I. 97 27 35S 153 28 E
North Sydney 107 46 12N 60 15W
North Thompson → 108 50 40N 120 20W
North Tonawanda 114 43 5N 78 50W
North Troy 113 44 59N 72 24W
North Truchas Pk. 119 36 0N 105 30W
North Twin I. 106 53 20N 80 0W
North Tyne → 12 54 59N 2 7W
North Uist 14 57 40N 7 15W
North Vancouver 108 49 25N 123 3W
North Vernon 114 39 0N 85 35W
North Village 121 32 15N 64 45W
North Wabiskaw L. 108 56 0N 113 55W
North Walsham 12 52 49N 1 22 E
North West Basin 96 25 45S 115 0 E
North West C. 96 21 45S 114 9 E
North West Christmas I. Ridge 95 6 30N 165 0W
North West Highlands 14 57 35N 5 2W
North West Providence Channel 121 26 0N 78 0W
North West River 107 53 30N 60 10W
North Western □ 91 13 30S 25 30 E
North York Moors 12 54 25N 0 50W
North Yorkshire □ 12 54 15N 1 25W
Northallerton 12 54 20N 1 26W
Northam 96 31 35S 116 42 E
Northampton, Austral. 96 28 27S 114 33 E
Northampton, U.K. 13 52 14N 0 54W
Northampton, Mass., U.S.A. 114 42 22N 72 31W
Northampton, Pa., U.S.A. 113 40 38N 75 24W
Northampton □ 13 52 16N 0 55W
Northampton Downs 98 24 35S 145 48 E
Northbridge 113 42 12N 71 40W
Northeim 24 51 42N 10 0 E
Northern □, Malawi 91 11 0S 34 0 E
Northern □, Uganda 90 3 5N 32 30 E
Northern □, Zambia 91 10 30S 31 0 E
Northern Circars 70 17 30N 82 30 E
Northern Group 101 10 00S 160 00W
Northern Indian L. 109 57 20N 97 20W
Northern Ireland □ 15 54 45N 7 0W
Northern Light, L. 106 48 15N 90 39W
Northern Province □ 84 9 15N 11 30W
Northern Territory □ 96 16 0S 133 0 E
Northfield 116 44 30N 93 10W
Northome 116 47 53N 94 15W
Northport, Ala., U.S.A. 115 33 15N 87 35W
Northport, Mich., U.S.A. 114 45 8N 85 39W
Northport, Wash., U.S.A. 118 48 55N 117 48W
Northumberland □ 12 55 12N 2 0W
Northumberland, C. 97 38 5S 140 40 E
Northumberland Is. 98 21 30S 149 50 E
Northumberland Str. 107 46 20N 64 0W
Northwest Territories □ 104 65 0N 100 0W
Northwich 12 53 16N 2 30W
Northwood, Iowa, U.S.A. 116 43 27N 93 0W
Northwood, N.D., U.S.A. 116 47 44N 97 30W
Norton, U.S.A. 116 39 50N 99 53W
Norton, Zimb. 91 17 52S 30 40 E
Norton Sd. 104 64 0N 164 0W
Nortorf 24 54 14N 9 47 E
Norwalk, Conn., U.S.A. 114 41 9N 73 25W
Norwalk, Ohio, U.S.A. 114 41 13N 82 38W
Norway 114 45 46N 87 57W
Norway House 109 53 59N 97 50W
Norwegian Dependency 5 66 0S 15 0 E
Norwegian Sea 6 66 0N 1 0 E
Norwich, Can. 112 42 59N 80 36W
Norwich, U.K. 12 52 38N 1 17 E
Norwich, Conn., U.S.A. 113 41 33N 72 5W
Norwich, N.Y., U.S.A. 114 42 32N 75 30W
Norwood, Can. 112 44 23N 77 59W
Norwood, U.S.A. 113 42 10N 71 10W
Nosok 58 70 10N 82 20 E
Nosovka 54 50 50N 31 37 E
Noşratābād 65 29 55N 60 0 E
Noss Hd. 14 58 29N 3 4W
Nossebro 49 58 12N 12 43 E
Nossob → 92 26 55S 20 37 E
Nosy Boraha 93 16 50S 49 55 E
Nosy Varika 93 20 35S 48 32 E
Noteć → 28 52 44N 15 26 E
Notigi Dam 109 56 40N 99 10W
Notikewin → 108 57 2N 117 38W
Notios Evvoïkos Kólpos 45 38 20N 24 0 E
Noto 41 36 52N 15 4 E
Noto, G. di 41 36 50N 15 10 E
Noto-Hanto 74 37 0N 137 0 E
Notodden 47 59 35N 9 17 E
Notre-Dame 107 46 18N 64 46W
Notre Dame B. 107 49 45N 55 30W
Notre Dame de Koartac 105 60 55N 69 40W
Notsé 85 7 0N 1 17 E
Nottaway → 106 51 22N 78 55W
Nøtterøy 47 59 14N 10 24 E
Nottingham 12 52 57N 1 10W
Nottingham □ 12 53 10N 1 0W
Nottoway → 114 36 33N 76 55W
Notwani → 92 23 35S 26 58 E
Nouâdhibou 80 20 54N 17 0W
Nouâdhibou, Ras 80 20 50N 17 0W
Nouakchott 84 18 9N 15 58W
Nouméa 94 22 17S 166 30 E
Noupoort 92 31 10S 24 57 E
Nouveau Comptoir (Paint Hills) 106 53 0N 78 49W
Nouvelle Calédonie 94 21 0S 165 0 E
Nouzonville 19 49 48N 4 44 E
Nová Baňa 27 48 28N 18 39 E
Nová Bystřice 26 49 2N 15 8 E
† Nova Chaves 88 10 31S 21 15 E
Nova Cruz 127 6 28S 35 25W
Nova Esperança 125 23 8S 52 24W
Nova Friburgo 125 22 16S 42 30W
Nova Gaia 88 10 10S 17 35 E
Nova Gradiška 42 45 17N 17 28 E
Nova Iguaçu 125 22 45S 43 28W
Nova Iorque 127 7 0S 44 5W
Nova Lamego 84 12 19N 14 11W
Nova Lima 125 19 59S 43 51W
Nova Lisboa = Huambo 89 12 42S 15 44 E
Nova Lusitânia 91 19 50S 34 34 E
Nova Mambone 93 21 0S 35 3 E
Nova Mesto 39 45 47N 15 12 E
Nova Paka 26 50 29N 15 30 E
Nova Scotia □ 107 45 10N 63 0W
Nova Sofala 93 20 7S 34 42 E
Nova Varoš 42 43 29N 19 48 E
Nova Venécia 127 18 45S 40 24W
Nova Zagora 43 42 32N 25 59 E
Novaci, Romania 46 45 10N 23 42 E
Novaci, Yugo. 42 41 5N 21 29 E
Noval Iorque 127 6 48S 44 0W
Novaleksandrovskaya 57 45 29N 41 17 E
Novannenskiy 55 50 32N 42 39 E
Novara 38 45 27N 8 36 E
Novaya Kakhovka 56 46 42N 33 27 E
Novaya Ladoga 52 60 7N 32 16 E
Novaya Lyalya 58 59 10N 60 35 E
Novaya Sibir, O. 59 75 10N 150 0 E
Novaya Zemlya 58 75 0N 56 0 E
Nové Mêsto 27 48 45N 17 50 E
Nové Zámky 27 48 0N 18 8 E
Novelda 33 38 24N 0 45W
Novellara 38 44 50N 10 43 E
Noventa Vicentina 39 45 18N 11 30 E
Novgorod 54 58 30N 31 25 E
Novgorod-Severskiy 54 52 2N 33 10 E
Novi Bečej 42 45 36N 20 10 E
Novi Grad 39 45 19N 13 33 E
Novi Kneževa 42 46 4N 20 8 E
* Novi Krichim 43 42 8N 24 31 E
Novi Lígure 38 44 45N 8 47 E
Novi Pazar, Bulg. 43 43 25N 27 15 E
Novi Pazar, Yugo. 42 43 12N 20 28 E
Novi Sad 42 45 18N 19 52 E
Novi Vinodolski 39 45 10N 14 48 E
Novigrad 39 44 10N 15 32 E
Nôvo Hamburgo 125 29 37S 51 7W
Novo-Zavidovskiy 55 56 32N 36 29 E
Novoakrainka 56 48 25N 31 30 E
Novoaltaysk 58 53 30N 84 0 E
Novoazovsk 56 47 15N 38 4 E
Novobelitsa 54 52 27N 31 2 E
Novobogatinskoye 57 47 20N 51 11 E
Novocherkassk 57 47 27N 40 5 E
Novodevichye 55 53 37N 48 50 E
Novograd-Volynskiy 54 50 34N 27 35 E
Novogrudok 54 53 40N 25 50 E
Novokayakent 57 42 30N 47 52 E
Novokazalinsk 58 45 48N 62 6 E
Novokhopersk 55 51 5N 41 39 E
Novokuybyshevsk 55 53 7N 49 58 E
Novokuznetsk 58 53 45N 87 10 E
Novomirgorod 56 48 45N 31 33 E
Novomoskovsk, R.S.F.S.R., U.S.S.R. 55 54 5N 38 15 E
Novomoskovsk, Ukraine, U.S.S.R. 56 48 33N 35 17 E
Novopolotsk 54 55 32N 28 37 E
Novorossiysk 56 44 43N 37 46 E
Novorybnoye 59 72 50N 105 50 E
Novorzhev 54 57 3N 29 25 E
Novoselitsa 56 48 14N 26 15 E
Novoshakhtinsk 57 47 46N 39 58 E
Novosibirsk 58 55 0N 83 5 E
Novosibirskiye Ostrava 59 75 0N 142 0 E
Novosil 55 52 58N 36 58 E
Novosokolniki 54 56 33N 30 5 E
Novotroitsk 52 51 10N 58 15 E
Novotulskiy 55 54 10N 37 43 E
Novouzensk 55 50 32N 48 17 E
Novovolynsk 54 50 45N 24 4 E
Novovyatsk 55 58 29N 49 44 E
Novozybkov 54 52 30N 32 0 E
Novska 42 45 19N 17 0 E
Novvy Port 58 67 40N 72 30 E
Novy Bug 56 47 34N 32 29 E
Nový Bydzov 26 50 14N 15 29 E
Nowy Dwór Mazowiecki 28 52 26N 20 44 E
Nový Jičín 27 49 30N 18 0 E
Novyy Afon 57 43 7N 40 50 E
Novyy Oskol 55 50 44N 37 55 E
Now Shahr 65 36 40N 51 30 E
Nowa Deba 28 50 26N 21 41 E
Nowa Huta 27 50 5N 20 30 E
Nowa Ruda 28 50 35N 16 30 E
Nowa Skalmierzyce 28 51 43N 18 0 E
Nowa Sól 28 51 48N 15 44 E
Nowe 28 53 41N 18 44 E
Nowe Miasteczko 28 51 42N 15 42 E
Nowe Miasto 28 51 38N 20 34 E
Nowe Miasto Lubawskie 28 53 27N 19 33 E
Nowe Warpno 28 53 42N 14 18 E
Nowgong 67 26 20N 92 50 E
Nowingi 100 34 33S 142 15 E
Nowogard 28 53 41N 15 10 E
Nowogród 28 53 14N 21 53 E
Nowra 97 34 53S 150 35 E
Nowy Dwór, Białystok, Poland 28 53 40N 23 30 E
Nowy Dwór, Gdansk, Poland 28 54 13N 19 7 E
Nowy Korczyn 28 50 19N 20 48 E
Nowy Sącz 27 49 40N 20 41 E
Nowy Sącz □ 27 49 30N 20 30 E
Nowy Staw 28 54 13N 19 2 E
Nowy Tomyśl 28 52 19N 16 10 E
Noxen 113 41 25N 76 4W
Noxon 118 48 0N 115 43W
Noya 30 42 48N 8 53W
Noyant 18 47 30N 0 6 E
Noyers 19 47 40N 4 0 E
Noyes I. 108 55 30N 133 40W
Noyon 19 49 34N 3 0 E
Nozay 18 47 34N 1 38W
Nsa, O. en → 83 32 28N 5 24 E
Nsanje 91 16 55S 35 12 E
Nsawam 85 5 50N 0 24W
Nsomba 91 10 45S 29 51 E
Nsukka 85 6 51N 7 29 E
Nuanetsi → 91 22 40S 31 50 E
Nuba Mts. = Nubah, Jibalan 87 12 0N 31 0 E
Nubah, Jibalan 87 12 0N 31 0 E
Nûbîya, Es Sahrâ En 86 21 30N 33 30 E
Ñuble □ 124 37 0S 72 0W
Nuboai 73 2 10S 136 30 E
Nueces → 117 27 50N 97 30W
Nueima → 62 31 54N 35 25 E
Nueltin L. 109 60 30N 99 30W
Nueva Gerona 121 21 53N 82 49W
Nueva Imperial 128 38 45S 72 58W
Nueva Palmira 124 33 52S 58 20W
Nueva Rosita 120 28 0N 101 11W
Nueva San Salvador 120 13 40N 89 18W
Nuéve de Julio 124 35 30S 61 0W
Nuevitas 121 21 30N 77 20W
Nuevo, Golfo 128 43 0S 64 30W
Nuevo Laredo 120 27 30N 99 30W
Nuevo León □ 120 25 0N 100 0W
Nugget Pt. 101 46 27S 169 50 E
Nugrus, Gebel 86 24 47N 34 35 E
Nuhaka 101 39 3S 177 45 E
Nuits 19 47 44N 4 12 E
Nuits-St-Georges 19 47 10N 4 56 E
Nukheila (Merga) 86 19 1N 26 21 E
Nuku'alofa 101 21 10S 174 0W
Nukus 58 42 20N 59 7 E
Nulato 104 64 40N 158 10W
Nules 32 39 51N 0 9W
Nullagine 96 21 53S 120 6 E
Nullarbor Plain 96 30 45S 129 0 E
Numalla, L. 99 28 43S 144 20 E
Numan 85 9 29N 12 3 E
Numata 74 36 45N 139 4 E
Numatinna → 87 7 38N 27 20 E
Numazu 74 35 7N 138 51 E
Numfoor 73 1 0S 134 50 E
Numurkah 99 36 5S 145 26 E
Nunaksaluk I. 107 55 49N 60 20W
Nuneaton 13 52 32N 1 29W
Nungo 91 13 23S 37 43 E
Nungwe 90 2 48S 32 2 E
Nunivak 104 60 0N 166 0W
Nunkun 69 33 57N 76 2 E
Nunspeet 16 52 21N 5 45 E
Nuomin He → 76 46 45N 126 55 E
Nuoro 40 40 20N 9 20 E
Nuqayy, Jabal 83 23 11N 19 30 E
Nure → 38 45 3N 9 49 E
Nuremburg = Nürnberg 25 49 26N 11 5 E
Nuriootpa 99 34 27S 139 0 E
Nurlat 55 54 29N 50 45 E
Nürnberg 25 49 26N 11 5 E
Nurran, L. = Terewah, L. 99 29 52S 147 35 E
Nurri 40 39 43N 9 13 E
Nurzec → 28 52 37N 22 25 E
Nusa Barung 73 8 22S 113 20 E
Nusa Kambangan 73 7 47S 109 0 E
Nusa Tenggara Barat □ 72 8 50S 117 30 E
Nusa Tenggara Timur □ 73 9 30S 122 0 E
Nushki 66 29 35N 66 0 E
Nutak 105 57 28N 61 59W
Nuwakot 69 28 10N 83 55 E
Nuwara Eliya 70 6 58N 80 48 E
Nuweiba' 86 28 58N 34 40 E
Nuweveldberge 92 32 10S 21 45 E
Nuyts Arch. 96 32 35S 133 20 E
Nuyts, Pt. 96 35 4S 116 38 E
Nuzvid 70 16 47N 80 53 E
Nxau-Nxau 92 18 57S 21 4 E
Nyaake (Webo) 84 4 52N 7 37W
Nyabing 96 33 30S 118 7 E
Nyack 113 41 5N 73 57W
Nyadal 48 62 48N 17 59 E
Nyah West 100 35 16S 143 21 E
Nyahanga 90 2 20S 33 37 E
Nyahua 90 5 25S 33 23 E
Nyahururu 90 0 2N 36 27 E
Nyainqentanglha Shan 75 30 0N 90 0 E
Nyakanazi 90 3 2S 31 10 E
Nyakrom 85 5 40N 0 50W
Nyâlâ 87 12 2N 24 58 E
Nyamandhlovu 91 19 55S 28 16 E
Nyambiti 90 2 48S 33 27 E
Nyamwaga 90 1 27S 34 33 E
Nyandekwa 90 3 57S 32 32 E
Nyanding →, 87 8 40N 32 41 E
Nyandoma 52 61 40N 40 12 E
Nyangana 92 18 0S 20 40 E
Nyanguge 90 2 30S 33 12 E
Nyankpala 85 9 21N 0 58W
Nyanza, Burundi 90 4 21S 29 36 E
Nyanza, Rwanda 90 2 20S 29 42 E
Nyanza □ 90 0 10S 34 15 E
Nyarling → 108 60 41N 113 23W
Nyasa, L. = Malawi, L. 91 12 0S 34 30 E
Nyazepetrovsk 52 56 3N 59 36 E
Nyazwidzi → 91 20 0S 31 17 E
Nyborg 49 55 18N 10 47 E
Nybro 49 56 44N 15 55 E
Nyda 58 66 40N 72 58 E
Nyeri 90 0 23S 36 56 E
Nyerol 87 8 41N 32 1 E
Nyhem 48 62 54N 15 37 E
Nyiel 87 6 9N 31 13 E
Nyinahin 84 6 43N 2 3W
Nyirbátor 27 47 49N 22 9 E
Nyíregyháza 27 47 58N 21 47 E
Nykarleby 50 63 22N 22 31 E
Nykøbing, Sjælland, Denmark 49 55 55N 11 40 E
Nykøbing, Storstrøm, Denmark 49 54 56N 11 52 E
Nykøbing, Viborg, Denmark 49 56 48N 8 51 E
Nyköping 49 58 45N 17 0 E

* Renamed Stamboliyski

† Renamed Muconda

Nykroppa **48** 59 37N 14 18 E
Nykvarn **48** 59 11N 17 25 E
Nyland **48** 63 1N 17 45 E
Nylstroom **93** 24 42 S 28 22 E
Nymagee **99** 32 7 S 146 20 E
Nymburk **26** 50 10N 15 1 E
Nynäshamn **48** 58 54N 17 57 E
Nyngan **99** 31 30 S 147 8 E
Nyon **25** 46 23N 6 14 E
Nyong → **85** 3 17N 9 54 E
Nyons **21** 44 22N 5 10 E
Nyord **49** 55 4N 12 13 E
Nyou **85** 12 42N 2 1W
Nysa **28** 50 30N 17 22 E
Nysa →, Poland/Poland **28** 52 4N 14 46 E
Nysa →, Poland **28** 50 49N 17 40 E
Nyssa **118** 43 56N 117 2W
Nysted **49** 54 40N 11 44 E
Nyunzu **90** 5 57 S 27 58 E
Nyurba **59** 63 17N 118 28 E
Nzega **90** 4 10 S 33 12 E
Nzega □ **90** 4 10 S 33 10 E
N'Zérékoré **84** 7 49N 8 48W
Nzeto **88** 7 10 S 12 52 E
Nzilo, Chutes de **91** 10 18 S 25 27 E
Nzubuka **90** 4 45 S 32 50 E

O

Oacoma **116** 43 50N 99 26W
Oahe **116** 44 33N 100 29W
Oahe Dam **116** 44 28N 100 25W
Oahe Res. **116** 45 30N 100 25W
Oahu **110** 21 30N 158 0W
Oak Creek **118** 40 15N 106 59W
Oak Harb. **118** 48 20N 122 38W
Oak Hill **114** 38 0N 81 7W
Oak Park **114** 41 55N 87 45W
Oak Ridge **115** 36 1N 84 12W
Oakbank **99** 33 4 S 140 33 E
Oakdale, Calif., U.S.A. **119** 46 14N 98 4W
Oakdale, La., U.S.A. **117** 30 50N 92 38W
Oakengates **12** 52 42N 2 29W
Oakes **116** 46 14N 98 4W
Oakesdale **118** 47 11N 117 15W
Oakey **99** 27 25 S 151 43 E
Oakham **12** 52 40N 0 43W
Oakland, Calif., U.S.A. **119** 37 50N 122 18W
Oakland, Oreg., U.S.A. **118** 43 23N 123 18W
Oakland City **114** 38 20N 87 20W
Oakleigh **100** 37 54 S 145 6 E
Oakley, Id., U.S.A. **118** 42 14N 113 55W
Oakley, Kans., U.S.A. **116** 39 8N 100 51W
Oakridge **118** 43 47N 122 31W
Oakwood **117** 31 35N 94 45W
Oamaru **101** 45 5 S 170 59 E
Oates Coast **5** 69 0 S 160 0 E
Oatman **119** 35 1N 114 19W
Oaxaca **120** 17 2N 96 40W
Oaxaca □ **120** 17 0N 97 0W
Ob → **58** 66 45N 69 30 E
Oba **106** 49 4N 84 7W
Obala **85** 4 9N 11 32 E
Oban, N.Z. **101** 46 55 S 168 10 E
Oban, U.K. **14** 56 25N 5 30W
Obbia **63** 5 25N 48 30 E
Obed **108** 53 30N 117 10W
Obera **125** 27 21 S 55 2W
Oberammergau **25** 47 35N 11 3 E
Oberdrauburg **26** 46 44N 12 58 E
Oberengadin **25** 46 35N 9 55 E
Oberhausen **24** 51 28N 6 50 E
Oberkirch **25** 48 31N 8 5 E
Oberlin, Kans., U.S.A. **116** 39 52N 100 31W
Oberlin, La., U.S.A. **117** 30 42N 92 42W
Oberlin, Ohio, U.S.A. **112** 41 15N 82 10W
Obernai **19** 48 28N 7 30 E
Oberndorf **25** 48 17N 8 35 E
Oberon **99** 33 45 S 149 52 E
Oberösterreich □ **26** 48 10N 14 0 E
Oberpfälzer Wald **25** 49 30N 12 25 E
Oberstdorf **25** 47 25N 10 16 E
Obi, Kepulauan **73** 1 23 S 127 45 E
Obiaruku **85** 5 51N 6 9 E
Óbidos, Brazil **127** 1 50 S 55 30W
Óbidos, Port. **31** 39 19N 9 10W
Obihiro **74** 42 56N 143 12 E
Obilatu **73** 1 25 S 127 20 E
Obilnoye **57** 47 32N 44 30 E
Obing **25** 48 0N 12 25 E
Obisfelde **24** 52 27N 10 57 E
Objat **20** 45 16N 1 24 E
Obluchye **59** 49 1N 131 4 E
Obninsk **55** 55 8N 36 37 E
Obo, C. Afr. Rep. **90** 5 20N 26 32 E
Obo, Ethiopia **87** 3 46N 38 52 E
Oboa, Mt. **90** 1 45N 34 45 E
Obock **87** 12 0N 43 20 E
Oborniki **28** 52 39N 16 50 E
Oborniki Śląskie **28** 51 17N 16 53 E
Oboyan **55** 51 13N 36 37 E
Obrenovac **42** 44 40N 20 11 E
Obrovac **39** 44 11N 15 41 E
Observatory Inlet **108** 55 10N 129 54W
Obshchi Syrt **9** 52 0N 53 0 E
Obskaya Guba **58** 69 0N 73 0 E
Obuasi **85** 6 17N 1 40W
Obubra **85** 6 8N 8 20 E
Obzor **43** 42 50N 27 52 E
Ocala **115** 29 11N 82 5W
Ocampo **120** 28 9N 108 24W
Ocaña **32** 39 55N 3 30W
Ocanomowoc **116** 43 7N 88 30W
Ocate **117** 36 12N 104 59W
Occidental, Cordillera **126** 5 0N 76 0W
Ocean City **114** 39 18N 74 34W
Ocean, I. = Banaba **94** 0 52 S 169 35 E
Ocean Park **118** 46 30N 124 2W
Oceanlake **118** 45 0N 124 0W
Oceanport **113** 40 20N 74 3W
Oceanside **119** 33 13N 117 26W
Ochagavia **32** 42 55N 1 5W
Ochamchire **57** 42 46N 41 32 E
Ochil Hills **14** 56 14N 3 40W
Ochre River **109** 51 4N 99 47W
Ochsenfurt **25** 49 38N 10 3 E
Ochsenhausen **25** 48 4N 9 57 E
Ocilla **115** 31 35N 83 12W
Ockelbo **48** 60 54N 16 45 E
Ocmulgee → **115** 31 58N 82 32W
Ocna Mureş **46** 46 23N 23 55 E
Ocna Sibiului **46** 45 52N 24 2 E
Ocnele Mari **46** 45 8N 24 18 E
Oconee → **115** 31 58N 82 32W
Oconto **114** 44 52N 87 53W
Oconto Falls **114** 44 52N 88 10W
Ocotal **121** 13 41N 86 31W
Ocotlán **120** 20 21N 102 42W
Ocreza → **31** 39 32N 7 50W
Ócsa **27** 47 17N 19 15 E
Octave **119** 34 10N 112 43W
Octeville **18** 49 38N 1 40W
Ocumare del Tuy **126** 10 7N 66 46W
Ocussi **73** 9 20 S 124 23 E
Oda **85** 5 50N 0 51W
Oda, Jebel **86** 20 21N 36 39 E
Ódáðahraun **50** 65 5N 17 0W
Ödåkra **49** 56 7N 12 45 E
Odawara **74** 35 20N 139 6 E
Odda **47** 60 3N 6 35 E
Odder **49** 55 58N 10 10 E
Oddur **63** 4 11N 43 52 E
Ödeborg **49** 58 32N 11 58 E
Odei → **109** 56 6N 96 54W
Odemira **31** 37 35N 8 40W
Ödemiş **64** 38 15N 28 0 E
Odendaalsrus **92** 27 48 S 26 45 E
Odense **49** 55 22N 10 23 E
Odenwald **25** 49 40N 9 0 E
Oder → **24** 53 33N 14 38 E
Oderzo **39** 45 47N 12 29 E
Odessa, Can. **113** 44 17N 76 43W
Odessa, Tex., U.S.A. **117** 31 51N 102 23W
Odessa, Wash., U.S.A. **118** 47 19N 118 35W
Odessa, U.S.S.R. **56** 46 30N 30 45 E
Odiakwe **92** 20 12 S 25 17 E
Odiel → **31** 37 10N 6 55W
Odienné **84** 9 30N 7 34W
Odobeşti **46** 45 43N 27 4 E
Odolanów **28** 51 34N 17 40 E
O'Donnell **117** 33 0N 101 48W
Odorheiul Secuiesc **46** 46 21N 25 21 E
Odoyevo **55** 53 56N 36 42 E
Odra →, Poland **28** 53 33N 14 38 E
Odra →, Spain **30** 42 14N 4 17W
Odžaci **42** 45 30N 19 17 E
Odžak **42** 45 3N 18 18 E
Oeiras, Brazil **127** 7 0 S 42 8W
Oeiras, Port. **31** 38 41N 9 18W
Oelrichs **116** 43 11N 103 14W
Oelsnitz **24** 50 24N 12 11 E
Oelwein **116** 42 41N 91 55W
Ofanto → **41** 41 22N 16 13 E
Offa **85** 8 13N 4 42 E
Offaly □ **15** 53 15N 7 30W
Offenbach **25** 50 6N 8 46 E
Offenburg **25** 48 29N 7 56 E
Offerdal **48** 63 28N 14 0 E
Offida **39** 42 56N 13 40 E
Offranville **18** 49 52N 1 0 E
Ofidhousa **45** 36 33N 26 8 E
Ofotfjorden **50** 68 27N 16 40 E
Oga-Hantō **74** 39 58N 139 47 E
Ogahalla **106** 50 6N 85 51W
Ōgaki **74** 35 21N 136 37 E
Ogallala **116** 41 12N 101 40W
Ogbomosho **85** 8 1N 4 11 E
Ogden, Iowa, U.S.A. **116** 42 3N 94 0W
Ogden, Utah, U.S.A. **118** 41 13N 112 1W
Ogdensburg **114** 44 40N 75 27W
Ogeechee → **115** 31 51N 81 6W
Oglio → **38** 45 2N 10 39 E
Ogmore **98** 22 37 S 149 35 E
Ogna **47** 58 31N 5 48 E
Ognon → **19** 47 16N 5 28 E
Ogoja **85** 6 38N 8 39 E
Ogoki → **106** 51 38N 85 57W
Ogoki L. **106** 50 50N 87 10W
Ogoki Res. **106** 50 45N 88 15W
Ogooué → **88** 1 0 S 10 0 E
Ogosta → **43** 43 48N 23 55 E
Ogowe = Ogooué → **88** 1 0 S 10 0 E
Ograźden **42** 41 30N 22 50 E
Ogrein **86** 17 55N 34 50 E
Ogulin **39** 45 16N 15 16 E
Ogun □ **85** 7 0N 3 0 E
Oguta **85** 5 44N 6 44 E
Ogwashi-Uku **85** 6 15N 6 30 E
Ogwe **85** 5 0N 7 14 E
Ohai **101** 44 55 S 168 0 E
Ohakune **101** 39 24 S 175 24 E
Ohau, L. **101** 44 15 S 169 53 E
Ohey **16** 50 26N 5 8 E
O'Higgins □ **124** 34 15 S 70 45W
Ohio □ **114** 40 20N 14 10 E
Ohio → **114** 38 0N 86 0W
Ohre →, Czech. **26** 50 30N 14 10 E
Ohre →, Ger. **24** 52 18N 11 47 E
Ohrid **42** 41 8N 20 52 E
Ohridsko, Jezero **42** 41 8N 20 52 E
Ohrigstad **93** 24 19 S 30 36 E
Öhringen **25** 49 11N 9 31 E
Oil City **114** 41 26N 79 40W
Oinousa **45** 38 33N 26 14 E
Oise □ **19** 49 28N 2 30 E
Oise → **19** 49 0N 2 4 E
Ōita **74** 33 14N 131 36 E
Ōita □ **74** 33 15N 131 30 E
Oiticica **127** 5 3 S 41 5W
Ojai **119** 34 28N 119 16W
Ojinaga **120** 29 34N 104 25W
Ojos del Salado, Cerro **124** 27 0 S 68 40W
Oka → **55** 56 20N 43 59 E
Okaba **73** 8 6 S 139 42 E
Okahandja **92** 22 0 S 16 59 E
Okahukura **94** 38 48 S 175 14 E
Okanagan L. **108** 50 0N 119 30W
Okandja **88** 0 35 S 13 45 E
Okanogan **118** 48 6N 119 43W
Okanogan → **118** 48 6N 119 43W
Okány **27** 46 52N 21 21 E
Okaputa **92** 20 5 S 17 0 E
Okara **68** 30 50N 73 31 E
Okarito **101** 43 15 S 170 9 E
Okavango Swamps **92** 18 45 S 22 45 E
Okaya **74** 36 0N 138 10 E
Okayama **74** 34 40N 133 54 E
Okayama □ **74** 35 0N 133 50 E
Okazaki **74** 34 57N 137 10 E
Oke-Iho **85** 8 1N 3 18 E
Okeechobee **115** 27 16N 80 46W
Okeechobee L. **115** 27 0N 80 50W
Okefenokee Swamp **115** 30 50N 82 15W
Okehampton **13** 50 44N 4 1W
Okene **85** 7 32N 6 11 E
Oker → **24** 52 30N 10 22 E
Okha **59** 53 40N 143 0 E
Ókhi Óros **45** 38 5N 24 25 E
Okhotsk **59** 59 20N 143 10 E
Okhotsk, Sea of **59** 55 0N 145 0 E
Okhotskiy Perevoz **59** 61 52N 135 35 E
Okhotsko Kolymskoye **59** 63 0N 157 0 E
Oki-Shotō **74** 36 5N 133 15 E
Okiep **92** 29 39 S 17 53 E
Okigwi **85** 5 52N 7 20 E
Okija **85** 5 54N 6 55 E
Okinawa □ **77** 26 40N 128 0 E
Okitipupa **85** 6 31N 4 50 E
Oklahoma □ **117** 35 20N 97 30W
Oklahoma City **117** 35 25N 97 30W
Okmulgee **117** 35 38N 96 0W
Oknitsa **56** 48 25N 27 30 E
Okolo **90** 2 37N 31 8 E
Okolona **117** 34 0N 88 45W
Okondeka **92** 21 38 S 15 37 E
Okonek **28** 53 32N 16 51 E
Okrika **85** 4 40N 7 10 E
Oktabrsk **58** 49 28N 57 25 E
Oktyabrsk **55** 53 11N 48 40 E
Oktyabrskiy, Byelorussia, U.S.S.R. **54** 52 38N 28 53 E
Oktyabrskiy, R.S.F.S.R., U.S.S.R. **52** 54 28N 53 28 E
Oktyabrskoy Revolyutsii, Os. **59** 79 30N 97 0 E
Oktyabrskoye **58** 62 28N 66 3 E
Oktyabrskoye = Zhovtnevoye **56** 47 54N 32 2 E
Okulovka **54** 58 25N 33 19 E
Okuru **101** 43 55 S 168 55 E
Okushiri-Tō **74** 42 15N 139 30 E
Okuta **85** 9 14N 3 12 E
Okwa → **92** 22 30 S 23 0 E
Ola **117** 35 2N 93 10W
Ólafsfjörður **50** 66 4N 18 39W
Ólafsvík **50** 64 53N 23 43W
Olancha **119** 36 15N 118 1W
Olanchito **121** 15 30N 86 30W
Öland **49** 56 45N 16 38 E
Olargues **20** 43 34N 2 53 E
Olary **99** 32 18 S 140 19 E
Olascoaga **124** 35 15 S 60 39W
Olathe **116** 38 50N 94 50W
Olavarría **124** 36 55 S 60 20W
Oława **28** 50 57N 17 20 E
Ólbia **40** 40 55N 9 30 E
Ólbia, G. di **40** 40 55N 9 35 E
Old Bahama Chan. = Bahama, Canal Viejo de **121** 22 10N 77 30W
Old Castile = Castilla la Vieja □ **30** 41 55N 4 0W
Old Castle **15** 53 46N 7 10W
Old Cork **98** 22 57 S 141 52 E
Old Crow **104** 67 30N 140 5 E
Old Dongola **86** 18 11N 30 44 E
Old Forge, N.Y., U.S.A. **113** 43 43N 74 58W
Old Forge, Pa., U.S.A. **113** 41 20N 75 46W
Old Fort → **109** 58 36N 110 24W
Old Shinyanga **90** 3 33 S 33 27 E
Old Speckle, Mt. **113** 44 35N 70 57W
Old Town **107** 45 0N 68 41W
Old Wives L. **109** 50 5N 106 0W
Oldbury **13** 51 38N 2 30W
Oldeani **90** 3 22 S 35 35 E
Oldenburg, Niedersachsen, Ger. **24** 53 10N 8 10 E
Oldenburg, Schleswig-Holstein, Ger. **24** 54 16N 10 53 E
Oldenzaal **16** 52 19N 6 53 E
Oldham **12** 53 33N 2 8W
Oldman → **108** 49 57N 111 42W
Olds **108** 51 50N 114 10W
Olean **114** 42 8N 78 25W
Olecko **28** 54 2N 22 31 E
Oléggio **38** 45 36N 8 38 E
Oleiros **30** 39 56N 7 56W
Olekma → **59** 60 22N 120 42 E
Olekminsk **59** 60 25N 120 30 E
Olenegorsk **52** 68 9N 33 18 E
Olenek **59** 68 28N 112 18 E
Olenek → **59** 73 0N 120 10 E
Olenino **54** 56 15N 33 30 E
Oléron, Île d' **20** 45 55N 1 15W
Oleśnica **28** 51 13N 17 22 E
Olesno **28** 50 51N 18 26 E
Olevsk **54** 51 12N 27 39 E
Olga **59** 43 50N 135 14 E
Olga, L. **106** 49 47N 77 15W
Olga, Mt. **96** 25 20 S 130 50 E
Olgastretet **4** 78 35N 25 0 E
Ølgod **49** 55 49N 8 36 E
Olhão **31** 37 3N 7 48W
Olib **39** 44 23N 14 44 E
Olib, I. **39** 44 23N 14 44 E
Oliena **40** 40 18N 9 22 E
Oliete **32** 41 1N 0 41W
Olifants → **93** 24 5 S 31 20 E
Olifantshoek **92** 27 57 S 22 42 E
Ólimbos **45** 35 44N 27 11 E
Ólimbos, Óros **44** 40 6N 22 23 E
Olímpia **125** 20 44 S 48 54W
Olimpo□ **124** 20 30 S 58 45W
Olite **32** 42 29N 1 40W
Oliva, Argent. **124** 32 0 S 63 38W
Oliva, Spain **33** 38 58N 0 9W
Oliva de la Frontera **31** 38 17N 6 54W
Oliva, Punta del **30** 43 37N 5 28W
Olivares **32** 39 46N 2 20W
Oliveira **127** 20 39 S 44 50W
Oliveira de Azemeis **30** 40 49N 8 29W
Olivença **91** 11 47 S 35 13 E
Olivenza **31** 38 41N 7 9W
Oliver **108** 49 13N 119 37W
Oliver L. **109** 56 56N 103 22W
Olkhovka **57** 49 48N 44 32 E
Olkusz **28** 50 18N 19 33 E
Ollagüe **124** 21 15 S 68 10W
Olmedo **30** 41 20N 4 43W
Olney, Ill., U.S.A. **114** 38 40N 88 0W
Olney, Tex., U.S.A. **117** 33 25N 98 45W
Olofström **49** 56 17N 14 32 E
Oloma **85** 3 29N 11 19 E
Olomane → **107** 50 14N 60 37W
Olomouc **27** 49 38N 17 12 E
Olonets **52** 61 10N 33 0 E
Olongapo **73** 14 50N 120 18 E
Oloron, Gave d' **20** 43 33N 1 5W
Oloron-Ste-Marie **20** 43 11N 0 38W
Olot **32** 42 11N 2 30 E
Olovo **42** 44 8N 18 35 E
Olovyannaya **59** 50 58N 115 35 E
Oloy → **59** 66 29N 159 29 E
Olpe **24** 51 2N 7 50 E
Olshanka **56** 48 16N 30 58 E
Olshany **56** 50 3N 35 53 E
Olsztyn **28** 53 48N 20 29 E
Olsztyn □ **28** 54 0N 21 0 E
Olsztynek **28** 53 34N 20 19 E
Olt □ **46** 44 20N 24 30 E
Olt → **46** 43 50N 24 40 E
Olten **25** 47 21N 7 53 E
Olteniţa **46** 44 7N 26 42 E
Olton **117** 34 16N 102 7W
Oltu **64** 40 35N 41 58 E
Olvega **32** 41 47N 2 0W
Olvera **31** 36 55N 5 18W
Olympia, Greece **45** 37 39N 21 39 E
Olympia, U.S.A. **118** 47 0N 122 58W
Olympic Mts. **118** 47 50N 123 45W
Olympic Nat. Park **118** 47 48N 123 30W
Olympus, Mt. **118** 47 52N 123 40W
Olympus, Mt. = Ólimbos, Óros **44** 40 6N 22 23 E
Olyphant **113** 41 27N 75 36W
Om → **58** 54 59N 73 22 E
Om Hajer **87** 14 20N 36 41 E
Ōmachi **74** 36 30N 137 50 E
Omagh **15** 54 36N 7 20W
Omagh □ **15** 54 35N 7 15W
Omaha **116** 41 15N 96 0W
Omak **118** 48 24N 119 31W
Oman ■ **63** 23 0N 58 0 E
Oman, G. of **65** 24 30N 58 30 E
Omaruru **92** 21 26 S 16 0 E
Omaruru → **92** 22 7 S 14 15 E
Omate **126** 16 45 S 71 0W
Ombai, Selat **73** 8 30 S 124 50 E
Ombo **47** 59 18N 6 0 E
Omboué **88** 1 35 S 9 15 E
Ombrone → **38** 42 39N 11 0 E
Omchi **83** 21 22N 17 53 E
Omdurmân **87** 15 40N 32 28 E
Omegna **38** 45 52N 8 23 E
Omeonga **90** 3 40 S 24 22 E
Ometepe, Isla de **121** 11 32N 85 35W
Ometepec **120** 16 39N 98 23W
Omez **62** 32 22N 35 0 E
Omineca → **108** 56 3N 124 16W
Omiš **39** 43 28N 16 40 E
Omisalj **39** 45 13N 14 32 E
Omitara **92** 22 16 S 18 2 E
Ōmiya **74** 35 54N 139 38 E
Omme Å → **49** 55 56N 8 32 E
Ommen **16** 52 31N 6 26 E
Omo → **81** 6 25N 36 10 E
Omolon → **59** 68 42N 158 36 E
Omsk **58** 55 0N 73 12 E
Omsukchan **59** 62 32N 155 48 E
Omul, Vf. **46** 45 27N 25 29 E
Omulew → **28** 53 5N 21 33 E
Ōmura **74** 32 56N 130 0 E
Omurtag **43** 43 8N 26 26 E
Ōmuta **74** 33 0N 130 26 E
Omutninsk **55** 58 45N 52 4 E
Oña **32** 42 43N 3 25W
Onaga **116** 39 32N 96 12W
Onalaska **116** 43 53N 91 14W
Onamia **116** 46 4N 93 38W
Onancock **114** 37 42N 75 49W
Onang **73** 3 2 S 118 49 E
Onaping L. **106** 47 3N 81 30W
Onarheim **47** 59 57N 5 35 E
Oñate **32** 43 3N 2 25W
Onavas **120** 28 28N 109 30W
Onawa **116** 42 2N 96 2W
Onaway **114** 45 21N 84 11W
Oncesti **46** 43 56N 25 52 E
Oncócua **92** 16 30 S 13 25 E
Onda **32** 39 55N 0 17W
Ondangua **92** 17 57 S 16 4 E
Ondárroa **32** 43 19N 2 25W
Ondava → **27** 48 27N 21 48 E
Ondo **85** 7 4N 4 47 E
Ondo □ **85** 7 0N 5 0 E
Öndörhaan **75** 47 19N 110 39 E
Öndverðarnes **50** 64 52N 24 0W
Onega **52** 64 0N 38 10 E
Onega → **52** 63 58N 37 55 E
Onega, G. of = Onezhskaya G. **52** 64 30N 37 0 E
Onega, L. = Onezhskoye Oz. **52** 62 0N 35 30 E
Onehunga **101** 36 55 S 174 48 E

Oneida 114 43 5N 75 40W
Oneida L. 114 43 12N 76 0W
O'Neill 116 42 30N 98 38W
Onekotan, Ostrov 59 49 25N 154 45 E
Onema 90 4 35 S 24 30 E
Oneonta, Ala., U.S.A. 115 33 58N 86 29W
Oneonta, N.Y., U.S.A. 114 42 26N 75 5W
Onezhskaya Guba 52 64 30N 37 0 E
Onezhskoye Ozero 52 62 0N 35 30 E
Ongarue 101 38 42 S 175 19 E
Ongniud Qi 76 43 0N 118 38 E
Ongoka 90 1 20 S 26 0 E
Ongole 70 15 33N 80 2 E
Onguren 59 53 38N 107 36 E
Oni 57 42 33N 43 26 E
Onida 116 44 42N 100 5W
Onilahy ~ 93 23 34 S 43 45 E
Onitsha 85 6 6N 6 42 E
Onoda 74 34 2N 131 25 E
Ons, Islas d' 30 42 23N 8 55W
Onsala 49 57 26N 12 0 E
Onslow 96 21 40 S 115 12 E
Onslow B. 115 34 20N 77 20W
Onstwedde 16 53 2N 7 4 E
Ontake-San 74 35 53N 137 29 E
Ontaneda 30 43 12N 3 57W
Ontario, Calif., U.S.A. 119 34 2N 117 40W
Ontario, Oreg., U.S.A. 118 44 1N 117 1W
Ontario □ 106 52 0N 88 10W
Ontario, L. 106 43 40N 78 0 E
Onteniente 33 38 50N 0 35W
Ontonagon 116 46 52N 89 19W
Ontur 33 38 38N 1 29W
Oodnadatta 96 27 33 S 135 30 E
Ooldea 96 30 27 S 131 50 E
Oona River 108 53 57N 130 16W
Oorindi 98 20 40 S 141 1 E
Oost-Vlaanderen □ 16 51 5N 3 50 E
Oostende 16 51 15N 2 50 E
Oosterhout 16 51 39N 4 47 E
Oosterschelde 16 51 33N 4 0 E
Ootacamund 70 11 30N 76 44 E
Ootsa L. 108 53 50N 126 2W
Ootsi 92 25 2 S 25 45 E
Opaka 43 43 28N 26 10 E
Opala, U.S.S.R. 59 51 58N 156 30 E
Opala, Zaïre 88 0 40 S 24 20 E
Opalenica 28 52 18N 16 24 E
Opan 43 42 13N 25 41 E
Opanake 70 6 35N 80 40 E
Opasatika 106 49 30N 82 50W
Opasquia 109 53 16N 93 34W
Opatija 39 45 21N 14 17 E
Opatów 28 50 50N 21 27 E
Opava 27 49 57N 17 58 E
Opelousas 117 30 35N 92 7W
Opémisca L. 106 50 0N 75 0W
Opheim 118 48 52N 106 30W
Ophir 104 63 10N 156 40W
Ophthalmia Ra. 96 23 15 S 119 30 E
Opi 85 6 36N 7 2 E
Opinaca ~ 106 52 15N 78 2W
Opinaca L. 106 52 39N 76 20W
Opiskotish, L. 107 53 10N 67 50W
Opobo 85 4 35N 7 34 E
Opochka 54 56 42N 28 45 E
Opoczno 28 51 22N 20 18 E
Opole 28 50 42N 17 58 E
Opole □ 28 50 40N 17 56 E
Oporto = Porto 30 41 8N 8 40W
Opotiki 101 38 1 S 177 19 E
Opp 115 31 19N 86 13W
Oppegård 47 59 48N 10 48 E
Oppenheim 25 49 50N 8 22 E
Óppido Mamertina 41 38 16N 15 59 E
Oppland fylke □ 47 61 15N 9 40 E
Oppstad 47 60 17N 11 40 E
Oprtalj 39 45 23N 13 50 E
Opua 101 35 19 S 174 9 E
Opunake 101 39 26 S 173 52 E
Opuzen 42 43 1N 17 34 E
Or Yehuda 62 32 2N 34 50 E
Ora, Israel 62 30 55N 35 1 E
Ora, Italy 39 46 20N 11 19 E
Oracle 119 32 36N 110 46W
Oradea 46 47 2N 21 58 E
Öræfajökull 50 64 2N 16 39W
Orahovac 42 42 24N 20 40 E
Orahovica 42 45 35N 17 52 E
Orai 69 25 58N 79 30 E
Oraison 21 43 55N 5 55 E
Oran, Alg. 82 35 45N 0 39W
Oran, Argent. 124 23 10 S 64 20W
Orange, Austral. 97 33 15 S 149 7 E
Orange, France 21 44 8N 4 47 E
Orange, Mass., U.S.A. 113 42 35N 72 15W
Orange, Tex., U.S.A. 117 30 10N 93 50W
Orange, Va., U.S.A. 114 38 17N 78 5W
Orange, C. 127 4 20N 51 30W
Orange Free State = Oranje Vrystaat □ 92 28 30 S 27 0 E
Orange Grove 117 27 57N 97 57W
Orange Walk 120 18 6N 88 33W
Orangeburg 115 33 35N 80 53W
Orangeville 106 43 55N 80 5W
Oranienburg 24 52 45N 13 15 E
Oranje ~ 92 28 41 S 16 28 E
Oranje Vrystaat □ 92 28 30 S 27 0 E
Oranjemund 92 28 38 S 16 29 E
Or'Aquiva 62 32 30N 34 54 E
Oras 73 12 9N 125 28 E
Orašje 42 45 1N 18 42 E
Orăştie 46 45 50N 23 10 E
Oraşul Stalin = Braşov 46 45 38N 25 35 E
Orava ~ 27 49 24N 19 20 E
Oravita 42 45 2N 21 43 E
Orb ~ 20 43 17N 3 17 E
Orba ~ 38 44 53N 8 37 E
Ørbæk 49 55 17N 10 39 E
Orbe 25 46 43N 6 32 E
Orbec 18 49 1N 0 23 E
Orbetello 39 42 26N 11 11 E

Órbigo ~ 30 42 5N 5 42W
Orbost 97 37 40 S 148 29 E
Örbyhus 48 60 15N 17 43 E
Orce 33 37 44N 2 28W
Orce ~ 33 37 44N 2 28W
Orchies 19 50 28N 3 14 E
Orchila, Isla 126 11 48N 66 10W
Orco ~ 38 45 10N 7 52 E
Ord ~ 96 15 33 S 138 15 E
Ord, Mt. 96 17 20 S 125 34 E
Ordenes 30 43 5N 8 29W
Orderville 119 37 18N 112 43W
Ordos = Mu Us Shamo 76 39 0N 109 0 E
Ordu 64 40 55N 37 53 E
Orduña, Álava, Spain 32 42 58N 2 58 E
Orduña, Granada, Spain 33 37 20N 3 30W
Ordway 116 38 15N 103 42W
Ordzhonikidze, R.S.F.S.R., U.S.S.R. 57 43 0N 44 43 E
Ordzhonikidze, Ukraine S.S.R., U.S.S.R. 56 47 39N 34 3 E
Ore, Sweden 48 61 8N 15 10 E
Ore, Zaïre 90 3 17N 29 30 E
Ore Mts. = Erzgebirge 24 50 25N 13 0 E
Orebić 42 43 0N 17 11 E
Örebro 48 59 20N 15 18 E
Örebro län □ 48 59 27N 15 0 E
Oregon 116 42 1N 89 20W
Oregon □ 118 44 0N 121 0W
Oregon City 118 45 21N 122 35W
Öregrund 48 60 21N 18 30 E
Öregrundsgrepen 48 60 25N 18 15 E
Orekhov 56 47 30N 35 48 E
Orekhovo-Zuyevo 55 55 50N 38 55 E
Orel 55 52 57N 36 3 E
Orel ~ 56 48 30N 34 54 E
Orellana, Canal de 31 39 2N 6 0W
Orellana la Vieja 31 39 1N 5 32W
Orellana, Pantano de 31 39 5N 5 10W
Orem 118 40 20N 111 45W
Oren 45 37 3N 27 57 E
Orenburg 52 51 45N 55 6 E
Orense 30 42 19N 7 55W
Orense □ 30 42 15N 7 51W
Orepuki 101 46 19 S 167 46 E
Orestiás 44 41 30N 26 33 E
Øresund 49 55 45N 12 45 E
Orford Ness 13 52 6N 1 31 E
Organá 32 42 13N 1 20 E
Orgaz 31 39 39N 3 53 E
Orgeyev 56 47 24N 28 50 E
Orgon 21 43 47N 5 3 E
Orgūn 65 32 55N 69 12 E
Orhon Gol ~ 75 49 30N 106 0 E
Oria 41 40 30N 17 38 E
Orient 99 28 7 S 142 50 E
Oriental, Cordillera 126 6 0N 73 0W
Oriente 124 38 44 S 60 37W
Origny-Ste-Benoîte 19 49 50N 3 30 E
Orihuela 33 38 7N 0 55W
Orihuela del Tremedal 32 40 33N 1 39W
Oriku 44 40 20N 19 30 E
Orinoco ~ 126 9 15N 61 30W
Orissa □ 69 20 0N 84 0 E
Oristano 40 39 54N 8 35 E
Oristano, Golfo di 40 39 50N 8 22 E
Orizaba 120 18 50N 97 10W
Orizare 43 42 44N 27 39 E
Ørje 47 59 29N 11 39 E
Orjen 42 42 35N 18 34 E
Orjiva 33 36 53N 3 24W
Orkanger 47 63 18N 9 52 E
Orkelljunga 49 56 17N 13 17 E
Örkény 27 47 9N 19 26 E
Orkla ~ 47 63 18N 9 51 E
Orkney 92 26 58 S 26 40 E
Orkney □ 14 59 0N 3 0W
Orkney Is. 14 59 0N 3 0W
Orla 28 52 42N 23 20 E
Orland 118 39 46N 122 12W
Orlando 115 28 30N 81 25W
Orlando, C. d' 41 38 10N 14 43 E
Orléanais 19 48 0N 2 0 E
Orléans 19 47 54N 1 52 E
Orleans 113 44 49N 72 10W
Orléans, Î. d' 107 46 54N 70 58W
Orlice ~ 26 50 5N 16 10 E
Orlické Hory 27 50 15N 16 30 E
Orlik 59 52 30N 99 55 E
Orlov 27 49 17N 20 51 E
Orlov Gay 55 50 56N 48 19 E
Orlovat 42 45 14N 20 33 E
Ormara 66 25 16N 64 33 E
Ormea 38 44 9N 7 54 E
Ormília 44 40 16N 23 39 E
Ormoc 73 11 0N 124 37 E
Ormond, N.Z. 101 38 33 S 177 56 E
Ormond, U.S.A. 115 29 13N 81 5W
Ormož 39 46 25N 16 10 E
Ormstown 113 45 8N 74 0W
Ornans 19 47 7N 6 10 E
Orne □ 18 48 40N 0 5 E
Orne ~ 18 49 18N 0 15W
Orneta 28 54 8N 20 9 E
Ørnhøj 49 56 13N 8 14 E
Ornö 48 59 4N 18 24 E
Örnsköldsvik 48 63 17N 18 40 E
Oro ~ 120 25 35N 105 2W
Orocué 126 4 48N 71 20W
Orodo 85 5 34N 7 4 E
Orogrande 119 32 20N 106 4W
Orol 30 43 34N 7 39W
Oromocto 107 45 54N 66 29W
Oron 85 4 48N 8 14 E
Orono 112 43 59N 78 37W
Oropesa 30 39 57N 5 10W
Oroqen Zizhiqi 76 50 34N 123 43 E
Oroquieta 73 8 32N 123 44 E
Orós 127 6 15 S 38 55W
Orosei, G. di 40 40 15N 9 40 E
Orosháza 27 46 32N 20 42 E
Orotukan 59 62 16N 151 42 E

Oroville, Calif., U.S.A. 118 39 31N 121 30W
Oroville, Wash., U.S.A. 118 48 58N 119 30W
Orrefors 49 56 50N 15 45 E
Ororoo 99 32 43 S 138 38 E
Orrville 112 40 50N 81 46W
Orsa 48 61 7N 14 37 E
Orsara di Púglia 41 41 17N 15 16 E
Orsasjön 48 61 7N 14 37 E
Orsha 54 54 30N 30 25 E
Orsk 52 51 12N 58 34 E
Orsogna 39 42 13N 14 17 E
Orsova 46 44 41N 22 25 E
Ørsted 49 56 30N 10 20 E
Orta, L. d' 38 45 48N 8 21 E
Orta Nova 41 41 20N 15 40 E
Orte 39 42 28N 12 23 E
Ortegal, C. 30 43 43N 7 52W
Orthez 20 43 29N 0 48W
Ortigueira 30 43 40N 7 50W
Ortles 38 46 31N 10 33 E
Ortón ~ 126 10 50 S 67 0W
Ortona 39 42 21N 14 24 E
Orune 40 40 25N 9 20 E
Oruro 126 18 0 S 67 9W
Orust 49 58 10N 11 40 E
Orūzgān □ 65 33 30N 66 0 E
Orvault 18 47 17N 1 38W
Orvieto 39 42 43N 12 8 E
Orwell 112 41 32N 80 52W
Orwell ~ 13 52 2N 1 12 E
Oryakhovo 43 43 40N 23 57 E
Orzinuovi 38 45 24N 9 55 E
Orzyc ~ 28 52 46N 21 14 E
Orzysz 28 53 50N 21 58 E
Os 47 60 9N 5 30 E
Osa 52 57 17N 55 26 E
Osa ~ 28 53 33N 18 46 E
Osa, Pen. de 121 8 0N 84 0W
Osage, Iowa, U.S.A. 116 43 15N 92 50W
Osage, Wyo., U.S.A. 116 43 59N 104 25W
Osage ~ 116 38 35N 91 57W
Osage City 116 38 43N 95 51W
Ōsaka 74 34 40N 135 30 E
Ōsaka □ 74 34 30N 135 30 E
Osawatomie 116 38 30N 94 55W
Osborne 116 39 30N 98 45W
Osby 49 56 23N 13 59 E
Osceola, Ark., U.S.A. 117 35 40N 90 0W
Osceola, Iowa, U.S.A. 116 41 0N 93 20W
Oschatz 24 51 17N 13 8 E
Oschersleben 24 52 2N 11 13 E
Óschiri 40 40 43N 9 7 E
Oscoda 114 44 26N 83 20W
Oscoda-Au-Sable 112 44 26N 83 20W
Osečina 42 44 23N 19 34 E
Ösel = Saaremaa 54 58 30N 22 30 E
Osëry 55 54 52N 38 28 E
Osh 58 40 37N 72 49 E
Oshawa 106 43 50N 78 50W
Ō-Shima 74 34 44N 139 24 E
Oshkosh, Nebr., U.S.A. 116 41 27N 102 20W
Oshkosh, Wis., U.S.A. 116 44 3N 88 35W
Oshmyany 54 54 26N 25 52 E
Oshogbo 85 7 48N 4 37 E
Oshwe 88 3 25 S 19 28 E
Osica de Jos 46 44 14N 24 20 E
Osieczna 28 51 55N 16 40 E
Osijek 42 45 34N 18 41 E
Ósilo 40 40 45N 8 41 E
Osimo 39 43 28N 13 30 E
Osintorf 54 54 40N 30 39 E
Osipenko = Berdyansk 56 46 45N 36 50 E
Osipovichi 54 53 19N 28 33 E
Oskaloosa 116 41 18N 92 40W
Oskarshamn 49 57 15N 16 27 E
Oskélanéo 106 48 5N 75 15W
Oskol ~ 55 49 6N 37 25 E
Oslo 47 59 55N 10 45 E
Oslob 73 9 31N 123 26 E
Oslofjorden 47 59 20N 10 35 E
Osmanabad 70 18 5N 76 10 E
Osmancık 56 40 45N 34 47 E
Osmaniye 64 37 5N 36 10 E
Ösmo 48 58 58N 17 55 E
Osnabrück 24 52 16N 8 2 E
Ośno Lubuskie 28 52 28N 14 51 E
Osobláha 27 50 17N 17 44 E
Osogovska Planina 42 42 10N 22 30 E
Osor 38 44 42N 14 24 E
Osorio 125 29 53 S 50 17W
Osorno, Chile 128 40 25 S 73 0W
Osorno, Spain 30 42 24N 4 22W
Osoyoos 108 49 0N 119 30W
Ospika ~ 108 56 20N 124 0W
Osprey Reef 97 13 52 S 146 36 E
Oss 16 51 46N 5 32 E
Ossa de Montiel 33 38 58N 2 45W
Ossa, Mt. 97 41 52 S 146 3 E
Óssa, Oros 44 39 47N 22 42 E
Ossabaw I. 115 31 45N 81 8W
Osse ~ 20 44 7N 0 17 E
Ossining 114 41 9N 73 50W
Ossipee 113 43 41N 71 9W
Ossokmanuan L. 107 53 25N 65 0W
Ossora 59 59 20N 163 13 E
Ostashkov 54 57 4N 33 2 E
Oste ~ 24 53 30N 9 12 E
Ostend = Oostende 16 51 15N 2 50 E
Oster 54 50 57N 30 53 E
Osterburg 24 52 47N 11 44 E
Osterburken 25 49 26N 9 25 E
Österbybruk 48 60 13N 17 55 E
Österbymo 49 57 49N 15 15 E
Österdalälven 48 61 30N 13 45 E
Österfärnebo 48 60 13N 16 50 E
Österforse 48 63 10N 17 0 E
Östergötlands län □ 49 58 35N 15 45 E
Osterholz-Scharmbeck 24 53 14N 8 48 E
Osterild 49 57 2N 8 51 E
Österkorsberga 49 57 18N 15 6 E
Österøya 47 60 32N 5 30 E
Östersund 48 63 10N 14 38 E
Østfold fylke □ 47 59 25N 11 25 E
Ostfriesland 24 53 20N 7 30 E

Ostfriesische Inseln 24 53 45N 7 15 E
Ostia, Lido di (Lido di Roma) 40 41 43N 12 17 E
Ostiglia 39 45 4N 11 9 E
Ostra 39 43 40N 13 5 E
Ostrava 27 49 51N 18 18 E
Ostróda 28 53 42N 19 58 E
Ostrog 54 50 20N 26 30 E
Ostrogozhsk 55 50 55N 39 7 E
Ostrołęka 28 53 4N 21 32 E
Ostrołęka □ 28 53 0N 21 30 E
Ostrov, Bulg. 43 43 40N 24 9 E
Ostrov, Romania 46 44 6N 27 24 E
Ostrov, U.S.S.R. 54 57 25N 28 20 E
Ostrów Lubelski 28 51 29N 22 51 E
Ostrów Mazowiecka 28 52 50N 21 51 E
Ostrów Wielkopolski 28 51 36N 17 44 E
Ostrowiec-Świętokrzyski 28 50 55N 21 22 E
Ostrozac 42 43 43N 17 49 E
Ostrzeszów 28 51 25N 17 52 E
Ostseebad-Kühlungsborn 24 54 10N 11 40 E
Ostuni 41 40 44N 17 34 E
Osum ~ 43 43 40N 24 50 E
Osumi ~ 44 40 40N 20 10 E
Ōsumi-Kaikyō 74 30 55N 131 0 E
Osuna 31 37 14N 5 8W
Oswego 114 43 29N 76 30W
Oswestry 12 52 52N 3 3W
Oświęcim 27 50 2N 19 11 E
Otago □ 101 44 44 S 169 10 E
Otago Harb. 101 45 47 S 170 42 E
Ōtake 74 34 12N 132 13 E
Otaki 101 40 45 S 175 10 E
Otaru 74 43 10N 141 0 E
Otavalo 126 0 13N 78 20W
Otavi 92 19 40 S 17 24 E
Otchinjau 92 16 30 S 13 56 E
Otelec 42 45 36N 20 50 E
Otero de Rey 30 43 6N 7 36W
Othello 118 46 53N 119 8W
Othonoí 44 39 52N 19 22 E
Óthris, Óros 45 39 4N 22 42 E
Otira Gorge 101 42 53 S 171 33 E
Otis 116 40 12N 102 58W
Otjiwarongo 92 20 30 S 16 33 E
Otmuchów 28 50 28N 17 10 E
Otočac 39 44 53N 15 12 E
Otorohanga 101 38 12 S 175 14 E
Otoskwin ~ 106 52 13N 88 6W
Otosquen 109 53 17N 102 1W
Otra ~ 47 58 8N 8 1 E
Otranto 41 40 9N 18 28 E
Otranto, C. d' 41 40 7N 18 30 E
Otranto, Str. of 41 40 15N 18 40 E
Ōtsu 74 35 0N 135 50 E
Otta 47 61 46N 9 32 E
Otta ~ 47 61 46N 9 31 E
Ottapalam 70 10 46N 76 23 E
Ottawa, Can. 106 45 27N 75 42W
Ottawa, Ill., U.S.A. 116 41 20N 88 55W
Ottawa, Kans., U.S.A. 116 38 40N 95 6W
Ottawa = Outaouais ~ 106 45 27N 74 8W
Ottawa Is. 105 59 35N 80 10W
Ottenby 49 56 15N 16 24 E
Otter L. 109 55 35N 104 39W
Otter Rapids, Ont., Can. 106 50 11N 81 39W
Otter Rapids, Sask., Can. 109 55 38N 104 44W
Otterberg 25 49 30N 7 46 E
Otterndorf 24 53 47N 8 52 E
Ottersheim 26 48 21N 14 12 E
Otterup 49 55 30N 10 22 E
Otterville 112 42 55N 80 36W
Otto Beit Bridge 91 15 59 S 28 56 E
Ottosdal 92 26 46 S 25 59 E
Ottoshoop 92 25 45 S 25 58 E
Ottsjö 48 63 13N 13 2 E
Ottumwa 116 41 0N 92 25W
Otu 85 8 14N 3 22 E
Otukpa (Al Owuho) 85 7 9N 7 41 E
Oturkpo 85 7 16N 8 8 E
Otway, Bahía 128 53 30 S 74 0W
Otway, C. 97 38 52 S 143 30 E
Otwock 28 52 5N 21 20 E
Ötz 26 47 13N 10 53 E
Ötz ~ 26 47 14N 10 50 E
Ötztaler Alpen 26 46 45N 11 0 E
Ou ~ 71 20 4N 102 13 E
Ou-Sammyaku 74 39 20N 140 35 E
Ouachita ~ 117 31 38N 91 49W
Ouachita, L. 117 34 40N 93 25W
Ouachita Mts. 117 34 50N 94 30W
Ouadâne 80 20 50N 11 40W
Ouadda 81 8 15N 22 20 E
Ouagadougou 85 12 25N 1 30W
Ouahigouya 84 13 31N 2 25W
Ouahila 82 27 50N 5 0W
Ouahran = Oran 82 35 49N 0 39W
Oualâta 84 17 20N 6 55W
Ouallene 82 24 41N 1 11 E
Ouanda Djallé 81 8 55N 22 53 E
Ouango 88 4 19N 22 30 E
Ouargla 83 31 59N 5 16 E
Ouarkziz, Djebel 82 28 50N 8 0W
Ouarzazate 82 30 55N 6 50W
Ouatagouna 85 15 11N 0 43 E
Oubangi ~ 88 1 0N 17 50 E
Oubarakai, O. ~ 83 27 20N 9 0 E
Ouche ~ 19 47 6N 5 16 E
Ouddorp 16 51 50N 3 57 E
Oude Rijn ~ 16 52 12N 4 24 E
Oudenaarde 16 50 50N 3 37 E
Oudon 18 47 22N 1 19W
Oudtshoorn 92 33 35 S 22 14 E
Oued Zem 82 32 52N 6 34W
Ouellé 84 7 26N 4 1W
Ouenza 83 35 57N 8 4 E
Ouessa 84 11 4N 2 47W
Ouessant, Île d' 18 48 28N 5 6W
Ouesso 88 1 37N 16 5 E

Ouest, Pte. 107 49 52N 64 40W
Ouezzane 82 34 51N 5 35W
Ouidah 85 6 25N 2 0 E
Ouistreham 18 49 17N 0 18W
Oujda 82 34 41N 1 55W
Oujeft 80 20 2N 13 0W
Ould Yenjé 84 15 38N 12 16W
Ouled Djellal 83 34 28N 5 2 E
Ouled Naïl, Mts. des 82 34 30N 3 30 E
Oulmès 82 33 17N 6 0W
Oulu 50 65 1N 25 29 E
Oulu □ 50 65 10N 27 20 E
Oulujärvi 50 64 25N 27 15 E
Oulujoki → 50 65 1N 25 30 E
Oulx 38 45 2N 6 49 E
Oum Chalouba 81 15 48N 20 46 E
Oum-el-Bouaghi 83 35 55N 7 6 E
Oum el Ksi 82 29 4N 6 59W
Oum-er-Rbia, O. → 82 33 19N 8 21W
Oumè 84 6 21N 5 27W
Ounane, Dj. 83 25 4N 7 19 E
Ounguati 92 21 54 S 15 46 E
Ounianga-Kébir 81 19 4N 20 29 E
Ounianga Sérir 81 18 54N 19 51 E
Our → 16 49 55N 6 5 E
Ouray 119 38 3N 107 40W
Ourcq → 19 49 1N 3 1 E
Oureg, Oued el → 82 32 34N 2 10 E
Ouricuri 127 7 53 S 40 5W
Ourinhos 125 23 0 S 49 54W
Ourique 31 37 38N 8 16W
Ouro Fino 125 22 16 S 46 25W
Ouro Prêto 125 20 20 S 43 30W
Ouro Sogui 84 15 36N 13 19W
Oursi 85 14 41N 0 27W
Ourthe → 16 50 29N 5 35 E
Ouse 99 42 38 S 146 42 E
Ouse →, Sussex, U.K. 13 50 43N 0 3 E
Ouse →, Yorks., U.K. 12 54 3N 0 7 E
Oust 20 42 52N 1 13 E
Oust → 18 47 35N 2 6W
Outaouais → 106 45 27N 74 8W
Outardes → 107 49 24N 69 30W
Outat Oulad el Haj 82 33 22N 3 42W
Outer Hebrides 14 57 30N 7 40W
Outer I. 107 51 10N 58 35W
Outes 30 42 52N 8 55W
Outjo 92 20 5 S 16 7 E
Outlook, Can. 109 51 30N 107 0W
Outlook, U.S.A. 116 48 53N 104 46W
Outreau 19 50 40N 1 36 E
Ouvèze → 21 43 59N 4 51 E
Ouyen 97 35 1 S 142 22 E
Ouzouer-le-Marché 18 47 54N 1 32 E
Ovada 38 44 39N 8 40 E
Ovalau 101 17 40 S 178 48 E
Ovalle 124 30 33 S 71 18W
Ovar 30 40 51N 8 40W
Ovens → 100 36 2 S 146 12 E
Over Flakkee 16 51 45N 4 5 E
Overijssel □ 16 52 25N 6 35 E
Overpelt 16 51 12N 5 20 E
Overton 119 36 32N 114 31W
Övertorneå 50 66 23N 23 38 E
Overum 49 58 0N 16 20 E
Ovid 116 41 0N 102 17W
Ovidiopol 56 46 15N 30 30 E
Oviedo 30 43 25N 5 50W
Oviedo □ 30 43 20N 6 0W
Oviken 48 63 0N 14 23 E
Oviksfjällen 48 63 0N 13 49 E
Ovoro 85 5 26N 7 16 E
Övre Sirdal 47 58 48N 6 43 E
Ovruch 54 51 25N 28 45 E
Owaka 101 46 27 S 169 40 E
Owambo 92 17 20 S 16 30 E
Owase 74 34 7N 136 12 E
Owatonna 116 44 3N 93 10W
Owbeh 65 34 28N 63 10 E
Owego 114 42 6N 76 17W
Owen Falls 90 0 30N 33 5 E
Owen Sound 106 44 35N 80 55W
Owen Stanley Range 98 8 30 S 147 0 E
Owendo 88 0 17N 9 30 E
Owens L. 119 36 20N 118 0W
Owensboro 114 37 40N 87 5W
Owensville 116 38 20N 91 30W
Owerri 85 5 29N 7 0 E
Owl → 109 57 51N 92 44W
Owo 85 7 10N 5 39 E
Owosso 114 43 0N 84 10W
Owyhee 118 42 0N 116 3W
Owyhee → 118 43 46N 117 2W
Owyhee Res. 118 43 40N 117 16W
Ox Mts. 15 54 6N 9 0W
Oxberg 48 61 7N 14 11 E
Oxelösund 49 58 43N 17 15 E
Oxford, N.Z. 101 43 18 S 172 11 E
Oxford, U.K. 13 51 45N 1 15W
Oxford, Miss., U.S.A. 117 34 22N 89 30W
Oxford, N.C., U.S.A. 115 36 19N 78 36W
Oxford, Ohio, U.S.A. 114 39 30N 84 40W
Oxford □ 13 51 45N 1 15W
Oxford L. 109 54 51N 95 37W
Oxia 45 38 16N 21 5 E
Oxílithos 45 38 35N 24 7 E
Oxley 99 34 11 S 144 6 E
Oxnard 119 34 10N 119 14W
Oya 72 2 55N 111 55 E
Oyem 88 1 34N 11 31 E
Oyen 109 51 22N 110 28W
Öyeren 47 59 50N 11 15 E
Oykel → 14 57 55N 4 26W
Oymyakon 59 63 25N 142 44 E
Oyo 85 7 46N 3 56 E
Oyo □ 85 8 0N 3 30 E
Oyonnax 21 46 16N 5 40 E
Oyster B. 113 40 52N 73 32W
Øystese 47 60 22N 6 9 E
Ozamis (Mizamis) 73 8 15N 123 50 E
Ozark, Ala., U.S.A. 115 31 29N 85 39W
Ozark, Ark., U.S.A. 117 35 30N 93 50W
Ozark, Mo., U.S.A. 117 37 0N 93 15W
Ozark Plateau 117 37 20N 91 40W
Ozarks, L. of 116 38 10N 92 40W
Ózd 27 48 14N 20 15 E
Ozieri 40 40 35N 9 0 E
Ozimek 28 50 41N 18 11 E
Ozona 117 30 43N 101 11W
Ozorków 28 51 57N 19 16 E
Ozren 42 43 55N 18 29 E
Ozuluama 120 21 40N 97 50W
Ozun 46 45 47N 25 50 E

P

Pa 84 11 33N 3 19W
Pa-an 67 16 51N 97 40 E
Pa Sak → 71 15 30N 101 0 E
Paar → 25 48 13N 10 59 E
Paarl 92 33 45 S 18 56 E
Paatsi → 50 68 55N 29 0 E
Paauilo 110 20 3N 155 22W
Pab Hills 66 26 30N 66 45 E
Pabianice 28 51 40N 19 20 E
Pabna 69 24 1N 89 18 E
Pabo 90 3 1N 32 10 E
Pacaja → 127 1 56 S 50 50W
Pacaraima, Sierra 126 4 0N 62 30W
Pacasmayo 126 7 20 S 79 35W
Pacaudière, La 20 46 11N 3 52 E
Paceco 40 37 59N 12 32 E
Pachhar 68 24 40N 77 42 E
Pachino 41 36 43N 15 4 E
Pachora 68 20 38N 75 29 E
Pachuca 120 20 10N 98 40W
Pacific 108 54 48N 128 28W
Pacific-Antarctic Basin 95 46 0 S 95 0W
Pacific-Antarctic Ridge 95 43 0 S 115 0W
Pacific Grove 119 36 38N 121 58W
Pacific Ocean 94 10 0N 140 0W
Pacitan 73 8 12 S 111 7 E
Pacofi 108 53 0N 132 30W
Pacov 26 49 27N 15 0 E
Pacsa 27 46 44N 17 2 E
Paczków 28 50 28N 17 0 E
Padaido, Kepulauan 73 1 5 S 138 0 E
Padalarang 73 7 50 S 107 30 E
Padang 72 1 0 S 100 20 E
Padangpanjang 72 0 40 S 100 20 E
Padangsidempuan 72 1 30N 99 15 E
Padborg 49 54 49N 9 21 E
Paddockwood 109 53 30N 105 30W
Paderborn 24 51 42N 8 44 E
Padeşul 46 45 40N 22 22 E
Padina 46 44 50N 27 8 E
Padloping Island 105 67 0N 62 50W
Padmanabhapuram 70 8 16N 77 17 E
Pádova 39 45 24N 11 52 E
Padra 68 22 15N 73 7 E
Padrauna 69 26 54N 83 59 E
Padre I. 117 27 0N 97 20W
Padrón 30 42 41N 8 39W
Padstow 12 50 33N 4 57W
Padua = Pádova 39 45 24N 11 52 E
Paducah, Ky., U.S.A. 114 37 0N 88 40W
Paducah, Tex., U.S.A. 117 34 3N 100 16W
Padul 31 37 1N 3 38W
Padula 41 40 20N 15 40 E
Padwa 70 18 27N 82 47 E
Paeroa 101 37 23 S 175 41 E
Paesana 38 44 40N 7 18 E
Pag 39 44 30N 14 50 E
Paga 85 11 1N 1 8W
Pagadian 73 7 55N 123 30 E
Pagai Selatan 72 3 0 S 100 15W
Pagai Utara 72 2 35 S 100 0 E
Pagalu = Annobón 79 1 25 S 5 36 E
Pagastikós Kólpos 44 39 15N 23 0 E
Pagatan 72 3 33 S 115 59 E
Page, Ariz., U.S.A. 119 36 57N 111 27W
Page, N.D., U.S.A. 116 47 11N 97 37W
Paglieta 39 42 10N 14 30 E
Pagny-sur-Moselle 19 48 59N 6 2 E
Pago Pago 101 14 16 S 170 43W
Pagosa Springs 119 37 16N 107 4W
Pagwa River 106 50 2N 85 14W
Pahala 110 19 12N 155 25W
Pahang □ 71 3 40N 102 20 E
Pahang → 71 3 30N 103 9 E
Pahiatua 101 40 27 S 175 50 E
Pahokee 115 26 50N 80 40W
Pahrump 119 36 15N 116 0W
Paia 110 20 54N 156 22W
Paide 54 58 57N 25 31 E
Paignton 13 50 26N 3 33W
Päijänne, L. 51 61 30N 25 30 E
Pailin 71 12 46N 102 36 E
Paimbœuf 18 47 17N 2 0W
Paimpol 18 48 48N 3 4W
Painan 72 1 21 S 100 34 E
Painesville 114 41 42N 81 18W
Paint I. 109 55 28N 97 57W
Paint Rock 117 31 30N 99 56W
Painted Desert 119 36 0N 111 30W
Paintsville 114 37 50N 82 50W
Paisley, Can. 112 44 18N 81 16W
Paisley, U.K. 14 55 51N 4 27W
Paisley, U.S.A. 118 42 43N 120 40W
Paita 126 5 11 S 81 9W
Paiva → 30 41 4N 8 16W
Pajares 30 43 1N 5 46W
Pajares, Puerto de 30 43 0N 5 46W
Pajeczno 28 51 10N 19 0 E
Pak Lay 71 18 15N 101 27 E
Pakala 70 13 29N 79 8 E
Pakanbaru 72 0 30N 101 15 E
Pakaraima Mts. 126 6 0N 60 0W
Pakistan ■ 66 30 0N 70 0 E
Pakistan, East = Bangladesh ■ 67 24 0N 90 0 E
Pakokku 67 21 20N 95 0 E
Pakosc 28 52 48N 18 6 E
Pakpattan 68 30 25N 73 27 E
Pakrac 42 45 27N 17 12 E
Paks 27 46 38N 18 55 E
Pakse 71 15 5N 105 52 E
Paktīā □ 65 33 0N 69 15 E
Pakwach 90 2 28N 31 27 E
Pala, Chad 81 9 25N 15 5 E
Pala, Zaïre 90 6 45 S 29 30 E
Palabek 90 3 22N 32 33 E
Palacios 117 28 44N 96 12W
Palafrugell 32 41 55N 3 10 E
Palagiano 41 40 35N 17 0 E
Palagonía 41 37 20N 14 43 E
Palagruža 39 42 24N 16 15 E
Palaiokastron 45 35 12N 26 18 E
Palaiokhóra 45 35 16N 23 39 E
Pálairos 45 38 45N 20 51 E
Palais, Le 18 47 20N 3 10W
Palakol 70 16 31N 81 46 E
Palam 70 19 0N 77 0 E
Palamás 44 39 26N 22 4 E
Palamós 32 41 50N 3 10 E
Palampur 68 32 10N 76 30 E
Palana, Austral. 99 39 45 S 147 55 E
Palana, U.S.S.R. 59 59 10N 159 59 E
Palanan 73 17 8N 122 29 E
Palanan Pt. 73 17 17N 122 30 E
Palangkaraya 72 2 16 S 113 56 E
Palanpur 68 24 10N 72 25 E
Palapye 92 22 30 S 27 7 E
Palar → 70 12 27N 80 13 E
Palatka, U.S.A. 115 29 40N 81 40W
Palatka, U.S.S.R. 59 60 6N 150 54 E
* Palau Is. 94 7 30N 134 30 E
Palauig 73 15 26N 119 54 E
Palauk 71 13 10N 98 40 E
Palavas 20 43 32N 3 56 E
Palawan 72 9 30N 118 30 E
Palayancottai 70 8 45N 77 45 E
Palazzo San Gervásio 41 40 53N 15 58 E
Palazzolo Acreide 41 37 4N 14 54 E
Paldiski 54 59 23N 24 9 E
Pale 42 43 50N 18 38 E
Paleleh 73 1 10N 121 50 E
Palembang 72 3 0 S 104 50 E
Palencia 30 42 1N 4 34W
Palencia □ 30 42 31N 4 33W
Palermo, Italy 40 38 8N 13 20 E
Palermo, U.S.A. 118 39 30N 121 37W
Palestine, Asia 62 32 0N 35 0 E
Palestine, U.S.A. 117 31 42N 95 35W
Palestrina 40 41 50N 12 52 E
Paletwa 67 21 10N 92 50 E
Palghat 70 10 46N 76 42 E
Pali 68 25 50N 73 20 E
Palinuro, C. 41 40 1N 15 14 E
Palisade 116 40 21N 101 10W
Palitana 68 21 32N 71 49 E
Palizada 120 18 18N 92 8W
Palizzi 41 37 58N 15 59 E
Palk Bay 70 9 30N 79 15 E
Palk Strait 70 10 0N 79 45 E
Palkonda 70 18 36N 83 48 E
Palkonda Ra. 70 13 50N 79 20 E
Pallanza = Verbánia 38 45 50N 8 55 E
Pallasovka 55 50 4N 47 0 E
Palleru → 70 16 45N 80 2 E
Pallisa 90 1 12N 33 43 E
Pallu 68 28 59N 74 14 E
Palm Beach 115 26 46N 80 0W
Palm Is. 97 18 40 S 146 35 E
Palm Springs 119 33 51N 116 35W
Palma, Canary Is. 8 28 40N 17 50W
Palma, Mozam. 91 10 46 S 40 29 E
Palma → 127 12 33 S 47 52W
Palma, B. de 33 39 30N 2 39 E
Palma de Mallorca 32 39 35N 2 39 E
Palma del Río 31 37 43N 5 17W
Palma di Montechiaro 40 37 12N 13 46 E
Palma, La, Canary Is. 80 28 40N 17 50W
Palma, La, Panama 121 8 15N 78 0W
Palma, La, Spain 31 37 21N 6 38W
Palma Soriano 121 20 15N 76 0W
Palmahim 62 31 56N 34 44 E
Palmanova 39 45 54N 13 18 E
Palmares 127 8 41 S 35 28W
Palmarola 40 40 57N 12 50 E
Palmas 125 26 29 S 52 0W
Palmas, C. 84 4 27N 7 46W
Pálmas, G. di 40 39 0N 8 30 E
Palmdale 119 34 36N 118 7W
Palmeira dos Índios 127 9 25 S 36 37W
Palmeirinhas, Pta. das 88 9 2 S 12 57 E
Palmela 31 38 32N 8 57W
Palmer, Alaska, U.S.A. 104 61 35N 149 10W
Palmer, Mass., U.S.A. 113 42 9N 72 21W
Palmer →, N. Terr., Austral. 96 24 46 S 133 25 E
Palmer →, Queens., Austral. 98 15 34 S 142 26 E
Palmer Arch 5 64 15 S 65 0W
Palmer Lake 116 39 10N 104 52W
Palmer Land 5 73 0 S 60 0W
Palmerston 112 43 50N 80 51W
Palmerston, C. 97 21 32 S 149 29 E
Palmerston North 101 40 21 S 175 39 E
Palmerton 113 40 47N 75 36W
Palmetto 115 27 33N 82 33W
Palmi 41 38 21N 15 51 E
Palmira, Argent. 124 32 59 S 68 34W
Palmira, Colomb. 126 3 32N 76 16W
Palms 112 43 37N 82 47W
Palmyra, Mo., U.S.A. 116 39 45N 91 30W
Palmyra, N.Y., U.S.A. 112 42 5N 77 18W
Palmyra = Tudmur 64 34 30N 37 17 E
Palmyra Is. 95 5 52N 162 6W
Palni 70 10 30N 77 30 E
Palni Hills 70 10 14N 77 33 E
Palo Alto 119 37 25N 122 8W
Palo del Colle 41 41 4N 16 43 E
Paloma, La 124 30 35 S 71 0W
Palombara Sabina 39 42 4N 12 45 E
Palopo 73 3 0 S 120 16 E
Palos, Cabo de 33 37 38N 0 40W

* *Renamed Belau*

Palouse 118 46 59N 117 5W
Palparara 98 24 47 S 141 28 E
Pålsboda 49 59 3N 15 22 E
Palu, Indon. 73 1 0 S 119 52 E
Palu, Turkey 64 38 45N 40 0 E
Paluan 73 13 26N 120 29 E
Palwal 68 28 8N 77 19 E
Pama 85 11 19N 0 44 E
Pamamaroo, L. 100 32 17 S 142 28 E
Pamanukan 73 6 16 S 107 49 E
Pamban I. 70 9 15N 79 20 E
Pamekasan 73 7 10 S 113 29 E
Pameungpeuk 73 7 38 S 107 44 E
Pamiers 20 43 7N 1 39 E
Pamir 58 37 40N 73 0 E
Pamlico → 115 35 25N 76 30W
Pamlico Sd. 115 35 20N 76 0W
Pampa 117 35 35N 100 58W
Pampa de las Salinas 124 32 1 S 66 58W
Pampa, La □ 124 36 50 S 66 0W
Pampanua 73 4 16 S 120 8 E
Pamparato 38 44 16N 7 54 E
Pampas, Argent. 124 35 0 S 63 0W
Pampas, Peru 126 12 20 S 74 50W
Pamplona, Colomb. 126 7 23N 72 39W
Pamplona, Spain 32 42 48N 1 38W
Pampoenpoort 92 31 3 S 22 40 E
Pana 116 39 25N 89 10W
Panaca 119 37 51N 114 23W
Panagyurishte 43 42 30N 24 15 E
Panaitan 73 6 35 S 105 10 E
Panaji (Panjim) 70 15 25N 73 50 E
Panamá 121 9 0N 79 25W
Panama ■ 121 8 48N 79 55W
Panama Canal 121 9 10N 79 37W
Panama City 115 30 10N 85 41W
Panamá, Golfo de 121 8 4N 79 20W
Panamint Mts. 119 36 30N 117 20W
Panão 126 9 55 S 75 55W
Panarea 41 38 38N 15 3 E
Panaro → 38 44 55N 11 25 E
Panarukan 73 7 40 S 113 52 E
Panay 73 11 10N 122 30 E
Panay, G. 73 11 0N 122 30 E
Pancake Ra. 119 38 30N 116 0W
Pančevo 42 44 52N 20 41 E
Panciu 46 45 54N 27 8 E
Panco 73 8 42 S 118 40 E
Pancorbo, Paso 32 42 32N 3 5W
Pandan 73 11 45N 122 10 E
Pandeglang 73 6 25 S 106 0 E
Pandharpur 70 17 41N 75 20 E
Pandhurna 68 21 36N 78 35 E
Pandilla 32 41 32N 3 43W
Pando 125 34 44 S 56 0W
Pando, L. = Hope L. 99 28 24 S 139 18 E
Panevezys 54 55 42N 24 25 E
Panfilov 58 44 10N 80 0 E
Panfilovo 55 50 25N 42 46 E
Pang-Long 67 23 11N 98 45 E
Pang-Yang 67 22 7N 98 48 E
Panga 90 1 52N 26 18 E
Pangaíon Óros 44 40 50N 24 0 E
Pangalanes, Canal des 93 22 48 S 47 50 E
Pangani 90 5 25 S 38 58 E
Pangani □ 90 5 25 S 39 0 E
Pangani → 90 5 26 S 38 58 E
Pangfou = Bengbu 77 32 56N 117 20 E
Pangil 90 3 10 S 26 35 E
Pangkah, Tanjung 73 6 51 S 112 33 E
Pangkalanberandan 72 4 1N 98 20 E
Pangkalanbuun 72 2 41 S 111 37 E
Pangkalansusu 72 4 2N 98 13 E
Pangkoh 72 3 5 S 114 8 E
Pangnirtung 105 66 8N 65 54W
Pangrango 73 6 46 S 107 1 E
Panguitch 119 37 52N 112 30W
Pangutaran Group 73 6 18N 120 34 E
Panhandle 117 35 23N 101 23W
Pani Mines 68 22 29N 73 50 E
Pania-Mutombo 90 5 11 S 23 51 E
Panipat 68 29 25N 77 2 E
Panjal Range 68 32 30N 76 50 E
Panjgur 66 27 0N 64 5 E
Panjim = Panaji 70 15 25N 73 50 E
Panjinad Barrage 65 29 22N 71 15 E
Pankajene 73 4 46 S 119 34 E
Pankalpinang 72 2 0 S 106 0 E
Pankshin 85 9 16N 9 25 E
Panna 69 24 40N 80 15 E
Panna Hills 69 24 40N 81 15 E
Pannuru 70 16 5N 80 34 E
Panorama 125 21 21 S 51 51W
Panruti 70 11 46N 79 35 E
Panshan 76 41 3N 122 2 E
Panshi 76 42 58N 126 5 E
Pantano 119 32 0N 110 32W
Pantar 73 8 28 S 124 10 E
Pantelleria 40 36 52N 12 0 E
Pantón 30 42 31N 7 37W
Pánuco 120 22 0N 98 15W
Panyam 85 9 27N 9 8 E
Panyu 77 22 51N 113 20 E
Páola 41 39 21N 16 2 E
Paola 116 38 36N 94 50W
Paonia 119 38 56N 107 37W
Paoting = Baoding 76 38 50N 115 28 E
Paot'ou = Baotou 76 40 32N 110 2 E
Paoua 88 7 9N 16 20 E
Papá 27 47 22N 17 30 E
Papagayo → 120 16 36N 99 43W
Papagayo, Golfo de 121 10 30N 85 50W
Papagni → 70 15 35N 77 45 E
Papakura 101 37 4 S 174 59 E
Papantla 120 20 30N 97 30W
Papar 72 5 45N 116 0 E
Pápas, Ákra 45 38 13N 21 20 E
Papenburg 24 53 7N 7 25 E
Papigochic → 120 29 9N 109 40W
Paposo 124 25 0 S 70 30W
Papua, Gulf of 98 9 0 S 144 50 E
Papua New Guinea ■ 94 8 0 S 145 0 E

Papuča	39	44 22N	15 30 E
Papudo	124	32 29 S	71 27W
Papuk	42	45 30N	17 30 E
Papun	67	18 0N	97 30 E
Pará = Belém	127	1 20 S	48 30W
Pará □	127	3 20 S	52 0W
Parábita	41	40 3N	18 8 E
Paraburdoo	96	23 14 S	117 32 E
Paracatu	127	17 10 S	46 50W
Parachilna	99	31 10 S	138 21 E
Parachinar	66	33 55N	70 5 E
Paraćin	42	43 54N	21 27 E
Paradas	31	37 18N	5 29W
Paradela	30	42 44N	7 37W
Paradip	69	20 15N	86 35 E
Paradise	118	47 27N	114 17W
Paradise →	107	53 27N	57 19W
Paradise Valley	118	41 30N	117 28W
Parado	73	8 42 S	118 30 E
Paradyz	28	51 19N	20 2 E
Paragould	117	36 5N	90 30W
Paragua →	126	6 55N	62 55W
Paragua, La	126	6 50N	63 20W
Paraguaçu →	127	12 45 S	38 54W
Paraguaçu Paulista	125	22 22 S	50 35W
Paraguaná, Pen. de	126	12 0N	70 0W
Paraguarí	124	25 36 S	57 0W
Paraguarí □	124	26 0 S	57 10W
Paraguay ■	124	23 0 S	57 0W
Paraguay →	124	27 18 S	58 38W
Paraíba = João Pessoa	127	7 10 S	35 0W
Paraíba □	127	7 0 S	36 0W
Paraíba do Sul →	125	21 37 S	41 3W
Parainen	51	60 18N	22 18 E
Parakhino Paddubye	54	58 26N	33 10 E
Parakou	85	9 25N	2 40 E
Parálion-Astrous	45	37 25N	22 45 E
Paramagudi	70	9 31N	78 39 E
Paramaribo	127	5 50N	55 10W
Paramithiá	44	39 30N	20 35 E
Paramushir, Ostrov	59	50 24N	156 0 E
Paran →	62	30 20N	35 10 E
Paraná	124	31 45 S	60 30W
Paranã	127	12 30 S	47 48W
Paraná □	125	24 30 S	51 0W
Paraná →	124	33 43 S	59 15W
Paranaguá	125	25 30 S	48 30W
Paranaíba →	127	20 6 S	51 4W
Paranapanema →	125	22 40 S	53 9W
Paranapiacaba, Serra do	125	24 31 S	48 35W
Paranavaí	125	23 4 S	52 56W
Parang, Jolo, Phil.	73	5 55N	120 54 E
Parang, Mindanao, Phil.	73	7 23N	124 16 E
Parapóla	45	36 55N	23 27 E
Paraspóri, Ákra	45	35 55N	27 15 E
Paratinga	127	12 40 S	43 10W
Paratoo	99	32 42 S	139 40 E
Parattah	99	42 22 S	147 23 E
Paray-le-Monial	21	46 27N	4 7 E
Parbati →	68	25 50N	76 30 E
Parbhani	68	19 8N	76 52 E
Parchim	24	53 25N	11 50 E
Parczew	28	51 40N	22 52 E
Pardes Hanna	62	32 28N	34 57 E
Pardilla	30	41 33N	3 43W
Pardo →, Bahia, Brazil	127	15 40 S	39 0W
Pardo →, Mato Grosso, Brazil	125	21 46 S	52 9W
Pardo →, São Paulo, Brazil	127	20 10 S	48 38W
Pardubice	26	50 3N	15 45 E
Pare	73	7 43 S	112 12 E
Pare □	90	4 10 S	38 0 E
Pare Mts.	90	4 0 S	37 45 E
Parecis, Serra dos	126	13 0 S	60 0W
Paredes de Nava	30	42 9N	4 42W
Paren	59	62 30N	163 15 E
Parent	106	47 55N	74 35W
Parent, Lac.	106	48 31N	77 1W
Parentis-en-Born	20	44 21N	1 4W
Parepare	73	4 0 S	119 40 E
Parfino	54	57 59N	31 34 E
Parfuri	93	22 28 S	31 17 E
Parguba	52	62 20N	34 27 E
Parham	113	44 39N	76 43W
Pariaguán	126	8 51N	64 34W
Pariaman	72	0 47 S	100 11 E
Paricutín, Cerro	120	19 28N	102 15W
Parigi, Java, Indon.	73	7 42 S	108 29 E
Parigi, Sulawesi, Indon.	73	0 50 S	120 5 E
Parika	126	6 50N	58 20W
Parima, Serra	126	2 30N	64 0W
Parinari	126	4 35 S	74 25W
Parincea	46	46 27N	27 9 E
Parîng	46	45 20N	23 37 E
Parintins	127	2 40 S	56 50W
Pariparit Kyun	67	14 55 S	93 45 E
Paris, Can.	106	43 12N	80 25W
Paris, France	19	48 50N	2 20 E
Paris, Idaho, U.S.A.	118	42 13N	111 30W
Paris, Ky., U.S.A.	114	38 12N	84 12W
Paris, Tenn., U.S.A.	115	36 20N	88 20W
Paris, Tex., U.S.A.	117	33 40N	95 30W
Paris, Ville de □	19	48 50N	2 20 E
Parish	113	43 24N	76 9W
Pariti	73	10 15 S	123 45 E
Park City	118	40 42N	111 35W
Park Falls	116	45 58N	90 27W
Park Range	118	40 0N	106 30W
Park Rapids	116	46 56N	95 0W
Park River	116	48 25N	97 43W
Park Rynie	93	30 25 S	30 45 E
Park View	119	36 45N	106 37W
Parker, Ariz., U.S.A.	119	34 8N	114 16W
Parker, S.D., U.S.A.	116	43 25N	97 7W
Parker Dam	119	34 13N	114 5W
Parkersburg	114	39 18N	81 31W
Parkerview	109	51 21N	103 18W
Parkes, A.C.T., Austral.	97	35 18 S	149 8 E
Parkes, N.S.W., Austral.	97	33 9 S	148 11 E
Parkside	109	53 10N	106 33W
Parkston	116	43 25N	98 0W
Parksville	108	49 20N	124 21W
Parlakimedi	70	18 45N	84 5 E
Parma, Italy	38	44 50N	10 20 E
Parma, Idaho, U.S.A.	118	43 49N	116 59W
Parma, Ohio, U.S.A.	112	41 25N	81 42W
Parma →	38	44 56N	10 26 E
Parnaguá	127	10 10 S	44 38W
Parnaíba, Piauí, Brazil	127	2 54 S	41 47W
Parnaíba, São Paulo, Brazil	127	19 34 S	51 14W
Parnaíba →	127	3 0 S	41 50W
Parnassós	45	38 35N	22 30 E
Párnis	45	38 14N	23 45 E
Párnon Óros	45	37 15N	22 45 E
Pärnu	54	58 28N	24 33 E
Parola	68	20 47N	75 7 E
Paroo →	97	31 28 S	143 32 E
Paroo Chan.	97	30 50 S	143 35 E
Páros, Greece	45	37 5N	25 9 E
Páros, Greece	45	37 5N	25 12 E
Parowan	119	37 54N	112 56W
Parpaillon	21	44 30N	6 40 E
Parral	124	36 10 S	71 52W
Parramatta	99	33 48 S	151 1 E
Parras	120	25 30N	102 20W
Parrett →	13	51 7N	2 58W
Parris I.	115	32 20N	80 30W
Parrsboro	107	45 30N	64 25W
Parry Is.	4	77 0N	110 0W
Parry Sound	106	45 20N	80 0W
Parsberg	25	49 10N	11 43 E
Parseta →	28	54 11N	15 34 E
Parshall	116	47 56N	102 11W
Parsnip →	108	55 10N	123 2W
Parsons	117	37 20N	95 17W
Partabpur	70	20 0N	80 42 E
Partanna	40	37 43N	12 51 E
Partapgarh	68	24 2N	74 40 E
Parthenay	18	46 38N	0 16W
Partinico	40	38 3N	13 6 E
Partur	70	19 40N	76 14 E
Paru →	127	1 33 S	52 38W
Parur	70	10 13N	76 14 E
Paruro	126	13 45 S	71 50W
Parván □	65	35 0N	69 0 E
Parvatipuram	70	18 50N	83 25 E
Parys	92	26 52 S	27 29 E
Pas-de-Calais □	19	50 30N	2 30 E
Pasadena, Calif., U.S.A.	119	34 5N	118 9W
Pasadena, Tex., U.S.A.	117	29 45N	95 14W
Pasaje	126	3 23 S	79 50W
Pasaje →	124	25 39 S	63 56W
Pascagoula	117	30 21N	88 30W
Pascagoula →	117	30 21N	88 35W
Paşcani	46	47 14N	26 45 E
Pasco	118	46 10N	119 0W
Pasco, Cerro de	126	10 45 S	76 10W
Pasewalk	24	53 30N	14 0 E
Pasfield L.	109	58 24N	105 20W
Pasha →	54	60 29N	32 55 E
Pashmakli = Smolyan	43	41 36N	24 38 E
Pasing	25	48 9N	11 27 E
Pasir Mas	71	6 2N	102 8 E
Pasir Puteh	71	5 50N	102 24 E
Pasirian	73	8 13 S	113 8 E
Pasłeka →	28	54 26N	19 46 E
Pasley, C.	96	33 52 S	123 35 E
Pašman	39	43 58N	15 20 E
Pasni	66	25 15N	63 27 E
Paso de Indios	128	43 55 S	69 0W
Paso de los Libres	124	29 44 S	57 10W
Paso de los Toros	124	32 45 S	56 30W
Paso Robles	119	35 40N	120 45W
Paspébiac	107	48 3N	65 17W
Pasrur	68	32 16N	74 43 E
Passage West	15	51 52N	8 20W
Passaic	113	40 50N	74 8W
Passau	25	48 34N	13 27 E
Passero, C.	41	36 42N	15 8 E
Passo Fundo	125	28 10 S	52 20W
Passos	127	20 45 S	46 37W
Passow	24	53 13N	14 10 E
Passy	21	45 55N	6 41 E
Pastaza →	126	4 50 S	76 52W
Pastęk	28	54 3N	19 41 E
Pasto	126	1 13N	77 17W
Pastrana	32	40 27N	2 53W
Pasuruan	73	7 40 S	112 44 E
Pasym	28	53 48N	20 49 E
Pásztó	27	47 52N	19 43 E
Patagonia, Argent.	128	45 0 S	69 0W
Patagonia, U.S.A.	119	31 35N	110 45W
Patan, Gujarat, India	70	17 22N	73 57 E
Patan, Maharashtra, India	68	23 54N	72 14 E
Patani	73	0 20N	128 50 E
Pataudi	68	28 18N	76 48 E
Patay	19	48 2N	1 40 E
Patchewollock	99	35 22 S	142 12 E
Patchogue	114	40 46N	73 1W
Patea	101	39 45 S	174 30 E
Pategi	85	8 50N	5 45 E
Patensie	92	33 46 S	24 49 E
Paternò	41	37 34N	14 53 E
Paternoster, Kepulauan	72	7 5 S	118 15 E
Pateros	118	48 4N	119 58W
Paterson, Austral.	100	32 37 S	151 39 E
Paterson, U.S.A.	114	40 55N	74 10W
Pathankot	68	32 18N	75 45 E
Pathfinder Res.	118	42 30N	107 0W
Pati	73	6 45 S	111 3 E
Patiala	68	30 23N	76 26 E
Patine Kouka	84	12 45N	13 45W
Patkai Bum	67	27 0N	95 30 E
Pátmos	45	37 21N	26 36 E
Patna	69	25 35N	85 12 E
Patonga	90	2 45N	33 15 E
Patos de Minas	127	18 35 S	46 32W
Patos, Lag. dos	125	31 20 S	51 0 E
Patosi	44	40 42N	19 38 E
Patquía	124	25 30N	102 11W
Pátrai	45	38 14N	21 47 E
Pátraikós, Kólpos	45	38 17N	21 30 E
Patrocínio	127	18 57 S	47 0W
Patta	90	2 10 S	41 0 E
Pattada	40	40 35N	9 7 E
Pattanapuram	70	9 6N	76 50 E
Pattani	71	6 48N	101 15 E
Patten	107	45 59N	68 28W
Patterson, Calif., U.S.A.	119	37 30N	121 9W
Patterson, La., U.S.A.	117	29 44N	91 20W
Patti, India	68	31 17N	74 54 E
Patti, Italy	41	38 8N	14 57 E
Pattoki	68	31 5N	73 52 E
Patton	112	40 38N	78 40W
Pattukkottai	70	10 25N	79 20 E
Patuakhali	69	22 20N	90 25 E
Patuca →	121	15 50N	84 18W
Patuca, Punta	121	15 49N	84 14W
Pátzcuaro	120	19 30N	101 40W
Pau	20	43 19N	0 25W
Pau, Gave de	20	43 33N	1 12W
Pauillac	20	45 11N	0 46W
Pauini →	126	1 42 S	62 50W
Pauk	67	21 27N	94 30 E
Paul I.	107	56 30N	61 20W
Paulhan	20	43 33N	3 28 E
Paulis = Isiro	90	2 47N	27 37 E
Paulistana	127	8 9 S	41 9W
Paullina	116	42 55N	95 40W
Paulo Afonso	127	9 21 S	38 15W
Paulpietersburg	93	27 23 S	30 50 E
Pauls Valley	117	34 40N	97 17W
Pauni	69	20 48N	79 40 E
Pavelets	55	53 49N	39 14 E
Pavia	38	45 10N	9 10 E
Pavlikeni	43	43 14N	25 20 E
Pavlodar	58	52 33N	77 0 E
Pavlograd	56	48 30N	35 52 E
Pavlovo, Gorkiy, U.S.S.R.	55	55 58N	43 5 E
Pavlovo, Yakut A.S.S.R., U.S.S.R.	59	63 5N	115 25 E
Pavlovsk	55	50 26N	40 5 E
Pavlovskaya	57	46 17N	39 47 E
Pavlovskiy-Posad	55	55 47N	38 42 E
Pavullo nel Frignano	38	44 20N	10 50 E
Pawhuska	117	36 40N	96 25W
Pawling	113	41 35N	73 37W
Pawnee	117	36 24N	96 50W
Pawnee City	116	40 8N	96 10W
Pawtucket	114	41 51N	71 22W
Paximádhia	45	35 0N	24 35 E
Paxoí	44	39 14N	20 12 E
Paxton, Ill., U.S.A.	114	40 25N	88 7W
Paxton, Nebr., U.S.A.	116	41 12N	101 27W
Paya Bakri	71	2 3N	102 44 E
Payakumbah	72	0 20 S	100 35 E
Payerne	25	46 49N	6 56 E
Payette	118	44 0N	117 0W
Paymogo	31	37 44N	7 21W
Payne L.	105	59 30N	74 30W
Paynesville, Liberia	84	6 20N	10 45W
Paynesville, U.S.A.	116	45 21N	94 44W
Pays Basque	20	43 15N	1 0W
Paysandú	124	32 19 S	58 8W
Payson, Ariz., U.S.A.	119	34 17N	111 15W
Payson, Utah, U.S.A.	118	40 8N	111 41W
Paz →	120	13 44N	90 10W
Paz, Bahía de la	120	24 15N	110 25W
Paz, La, Entre Ríos, Argent.	124	30 50 S	59 45W
Paz, La, San Luis, Argent.	124	33 30 S	67 20W
Paz, La, Boliv.	126	16 20 S	68 10W
Paz, La, Hond.	120	14 20N	87 47W
Paz, La, Mexico	120	24 10N	110 20W
Pazar	64	41 10N	40 50 E
Pazardzhik	43	42 12N	24 20 E
Pazin	39	45 14N	13 56 E
Pčinja →	42	41 50N	21 45 E
Pe Ell	118	46 30N	123 18W
Peabody	113	42 31N	70 56W
Peace →	108	59 0N	111 25W
Peace Point	108	59 7N	112 27W
Peace River	108	56 15N	117 18W
Peach Springs	119	35 36N	113 30W
Peak Downs	98	22 14 S	148 0 E
Peak Hill	99	32 47 S	148 11 E
Peak Range	97	22 50 S	148 20 E
Peak, The	12	53 24N	1 53W
Peake	99	35 25 S	140 0 E
Peale Mt.	119	38 25N	109 12W
Pearce	119	31 57N	109 56W
Pearl →	117	30 23N	89 45W
Pearl Banks	70	8 45N	79 45 E
Pearl City	110	21 24N	158 0W
Pearsall	117	28 55N	99 8W
Pearse I.	108	54 52N	130 14W
Peary Land	4	82 40N	33 0W
Pease →	117	34 12N	99 7W
Pebane	91	17 10 S	38 8 E
Pebas	126	3 10 S	71 46W
Peč	42	42 40N	20 17 E
Péccioli	38	43 32N	10 43 E
Pechea	46	45 36N	27 49 E
Pechenezhin	56	48 30N	24 48 E
Pechenga	52	69 30N	31 25 E
Pechnezhskoye Vdkhr.	55	50 0N	37 10 E
Pechora →	52	68 13N	54 15 E
Pechorskaya Guba	52	68 40N	54 0 E
Pechory	54	57 48N	27 40 E
Pecica	42	46 10N	21 3 E
Pećka	42	44 18N	19 33 E
Pécora, C.	40	39 28N	8 23 E
Pecos	117	31 25N	103 35W
Pecos →	117	29 42N	102 30W
Pécs	27	46 5N	18 15 E
Peddapalli	70	18 40N	79 24 E
Peddapuram	70	17 6N	8 13 E
Pedra Azul	127	16 2 S	41 17W
Pedreiras	127	4 32 S	44 40W
Pedrera, La	126	1 18 S	69 43W
Pedro Afonso	127	9 0 S	48 10W
Pedro Cays	121	17 5N	77 48W
Pedro de Valdivia	124	22 55 S	69 38W
Pedro Juan Caballero	125	22 30 S	55 40W
Pedro Miguel Locks	120	9 1N	79 36W
Pedro Muñoz	33	39 25N	2 56W
Pedrógão Grande	30	39 55N	8 9W
Peduyim	62	31 20N	34 37 E
Peebinga	99	34 52 S	140 57 E
Peebles	14	55 40N	3 12W
Peekskill	114	41 18N	73 57W
Peel	12	54 14N	4 40W
Peel →, Austral.	99	30 50 S	150 29 E
Peel →, Can.	104	67 0N	135 0W
Peene →	24	54 9N	13 46 E
Peera Peera Poolanna L.	99	26 30 S	138 0 E
Peers	108	53 40N	116 0W
Pegasus Bay	101	43 20 S	173 10 E
Peggau	26	47 12N	15 21 E
Pegnitz	25	49 45N	11 33 E
Pegnitz →	25	49 29N	10 59 E
Pego	33	38 51N	0 8W
Pegu Yoma	67	19 0N	96 0 E
Pehčevo	42	41 41N	22 55 E
Pehuajó	124	35 45 S	62 0W
Peine, Chile	124	23 45 S	68 8W
Peine, Ger.	24	52 19N	10 12 E
Peip'ing = Beijing	76	39 55N	116 20 E
Peiss	25	47 58N	11 47 E
Peissenberg	25	47 48N	11 4 E
Peitz	24	51 50N	14 23 E
Peixe	127	12 0 S	48 40W
Pek →	42	44 45N	21 29 E
Pekalongan	73	6 53 S	109 40 E
Pekan	71	3 30N	103 25 E
Pekin	116	40 35N	89 40W
Peking = Beijing	76	39 55N	116 20 E
Pelabuhan Ratu, Teluk	73	7 5 S	106 30 E
Pelabuhanratu	73	7 0 S	106 32 E
Pélagos	44	39 17N	24 4 E
Pelaihari	72	3 55 S	114 45 E
Pelat, Mont	21	44 16N	6 42 E
Pełczyce	28	53 3N	15 16 E
Peleaga	46	45 22N	22 55 E
Pelee I.	106	41 47N	82 40W
Pelée, Mt.	121	14 48N	61 0W
Pelee, Pt.	106	41 54N	82 31W
Pelekech, mt.	90	3 52N	35 8 E
Peleng	73	1 20 S	123 30 E
Pelham	115	31 5N	84 6W
Pelhřimov	26	49 24N	15 12 E
Pelican L.	109	52 28N	100 20W
Pelican Narrows	109	55 10N	102 56W
Pelican Portage	108	55 51N	112 35W
Pelican Rapids	109	52 45N	100 42W
Peljesac	42	42 55N	17 25 E
Pelkosenniemi	50	67 6N	27 28 E
Pella, Greece	44	40 46N	22 23 E
Pella, U.S.A.	116	41 30N	93 0W
Pélla □	44	40 52N	22 0 E
Pëllaro	41	38 1N	15 40 E
Pellworm	24	54 30N	8 40 E
Pelly →	104	62 47N	137 19W
Pelly Bay	105	68 38N	89 50W
Pelly L.	104	66 0N	102 0W
Peloponnes = Pelóponnisos □	45	37 10N	22 0 E
Pelopónnisos □	45	37 10N	22 0 E
Peloritani, Monti	41	38 2N	15 25 E
Peloro, C.	41	38 15N	15 40 E
Pelorus Sound	101	40 59 S	173 59 E
Pelotas	125	31 42 S	52 23W
Pelòvo	43	43 26N	24 17 E
Pelvoux, Massif de	21	44 52N	6 20 E
Pemalang	73	6 53 S	109 23 E
Pematang	72	0 12 S	102 4 E
Pematangsiantar	72	2 57N	99 5 E
Pemba, Mozam.	91	12 58 S	40 30 E
Pemba, Tanz.	90	5 0 S	39 45 E
Pemba, Zambia	91	16 30 S	27 28 E
Pemba Channel	90	5 0 S	39 37 E
Pemberton, Austral.	96	34 30 S	116 0 E
Pemberton, Can.	108	50 25N	122 50W
Pembina	109	48 58N	97 15W
Pembina →	109	49 0N	98 12W
Pembine	114	45 38N	87 59W
Pembino	116	48 58N	97 15W
Pembroke, Can.	106	45 50N	77 7W
Pembroke, U.K.	13	51 41N	4 57W
Pembroke, U.S.A.	115	32 5N	81 32W
Pen-y-Ghent	12	54 10N	2 15W
Peña de Francia, Sierra de	30	40 32N	6 10W
Peña, Sierra de la	32	42 32N	0 45W
Penafiel	30	41 12N	8 17W
Peñafiel	30	41 35N	4 7W
Peñaflor	31	37 43N	5 21W
Peñalara, Pico	30	40 51N	3 57W
Penamacôr	30	40 10N	7 10W
Penang = Pinang	71	5 25N	100 15 E
Penápolis	125	21 30 S	50 0W
Peñaranda de Bracamonte	30	40 53N	5 13W
Peñarroya-Pueblonuevo	31	38 19N	5 16W
Peñas, C. de	30	43 42N	5 52W
Peñas de San Pedro	33	38 44N	2 0W
Penas, G. de	128	47 0 S	75 0W
Peñausende	30	41 17N	5 52W
Pench'i = Benxi	76	41 20N	123 48 E
Pend Oreille →	118	49 4N	117 37W
Pend Oreille, L.	118	48 0N	116 30W
Pendálofon	44	40 14N	21 12 E
Pendelikón	45	38 10N	23 53 E
Pendembu	84	9 7N	12 14W
Pendleton	118	45 35N	118 50W
Penedo	127	10 15 S	36 36W
Penetanguishene	106	44 50N	79 55W
Pengalengan	73	7 9 S	107 30 E
Penge, Kasai Oriental, Congo	90	5 30 S	24 33 E
Penge, Kivu, Congo	90	4 27 S	28 25 E
Penglai	76	37 48N	120 42 E
Pengshui	77	29 17N	108 12 E
Penguin	99	41 8 S	146 6 E
Penhalonga	91	18 52 S	32 40 E
Peniche	31	39 19N	9 22W
Penicuik	14	55 50N	3 14W
Penida	72	8 45 S	115 30 E
Peñíscola	32	40 22N	0 24 E
Penmarch	18	47 49N	4 21W
Penmarch, Pte. de	18	47 48N	4 22W
Pennabilli	39	43 50N	12 17 E
Pennant	109	50 32N	108 14W
Penne	39	42 28N	13 56 E

Pennel Glacier 5 69 20S 157 27E
Penner → 70 14 35N 80 10E
Pennine, Alpi 38 46 4N 7 30E
Pennines 12 54 50N 2 20W
Pennino, Mte. 39 43 6N 12 54E
Pennsylvania □ 114 40 50N 78 0W
Penny 108 53 51N 121 20W
Pennyan 114 42 39N 77 7W
Peno 54 57 2N 32 49E
Penola 97 37 25S 140 21E
Penong 96 31 59S 133 5E
Penonomé 121 8 31N 80 21W
Penrhyn Is. 95 9 0S 158 30W
Penrith, Austral. 97 33 43S 150 38E
Penrith, U.K. 12 54 40N 2 45W
Pensacola 115 30 30N 87 10W
Pensacola Mts. 5 84 0S 40 0W
Pense 109 50 25N 104 59W
Penshurst 99 37 49S 142 20E
Penticton 108 49 30N 119 38W
Pentland 97 20 32S 145 25E
Pentland Firth 14 58 43N 3 10W
Pentland Hills 14 55 48N 3 25W
Penukonda 70 14 5N 77 38E
Penylan L. 109 61 50N 106 20W
Penza 55 53 15N 45 5E
Penzance 13 50 7N 5 32W
Penzberg 25 47 46N 11 23E
Penzhino 59 63 30N 167 55E
Penzhinskaya Guba 59 61 30N 163 0E
Penzlin 24 53 32N 13 6E
Peoria, Ariz., U.S.A. 119 33 40N 112 15W
Peoria, Ill., U.S.A. 116 40 40N 89 40W
Pepperwood 118 40 23N 124 0W
Peqini 44 41 4N 19 44E
Pera Hd. 98 12 55S 141 37E
Perabumilih 72 3 27S 104 15E
Perak → 71 5 10N 101 4E
Perakhóra 45 38 2N 22 56E
Perales de Alfambra 32 40 38N 1 0W
Perales del Puerto 30 40 10N 6 40W
Peralta 32 42 21N 1 49W
Pérama 45 35 20N 24 40E
Perast 42 42 31N 18 47E
Percé 107 48 31N 64 13W
Perche 18 48 31N 1 1E
Perche, Collines du 18 48 30N 0 40E
Percy 18 48 55N 1 11W
Percy Is. 98 21 39S 150 16E
Pereira 126 4 49N 75 43W
Perekerten 99 34 55S 143 40E
Perekop 56 46 10N 33 42E
Pereslavl-Zalesskiy 55 56 45N 38 50E
Pereyaslav Khmelnitskiy 54 50 3N 31 28E
Pérez, I. 120 22 24N 89 42W
Perg 26 48 15N 14 38E
Pergamino 124 33 52S 60 30W
Pérgine Valsugano 39 46 4N 11 15E
Pérgola 39 43 35N 12 50E
Perham 116 46 36N 95 36W
Perhentian, Kepulauan 71 5 54N 102 42E
Periam 42 46 2N 20 59E
Péribonca → 107 48 45N 72 5W
Péribonca, L. 107 50 1N 71 10W
Perico 124 24 20S 65 5W
Pericos 120 25 3N 107 42W
Périers 18 49 11N 1 25W
Périgord 20 45 0N 0 40E
Périgueux 20 45 10N 0 42E
Perijá, Sierra de 126 9 30N 73 3W
Peristéra 45 39 15N 23 58E
Periyakulam 70 10 5N 77 30E
Periyar → 70 10 15N 76 10E
Periyar, L. 70 9 25N 77 10E
Perkam, Tg. 73 1 35S 137 50E
Perković 39 43 41N 16 10E
Perlas, Arch. de las 121 8 41N 79 7W
Perlas, Punta de 121 12 30N 83 30W
Perleberg 24 53 5N 11 50E
Perlevka 55 51 48N 38 57E
Perlez 42 45 11N 20 22E
Perlis □ 71 6 30N 100 15E
Perm (Molotov) 52 58 0N 57 10E
Përmeti 44 40 15N 20 21E
Pernambuco = Recife 127 8 0S 35 0W
Pernambuco □ 127 8 0S 37 0W
Pernik 42 42 35N 23 2E
Péronne 19 49 55N 2 57E
Perosa Argentina 38 44 57N 7 11E
Perow 108 54 35N 126 10W
Perpendicular Pt. 99 31 37S 152 52E
Perpignan 20 42 42N 2 53E
Perros-Guirec 18 48 49N 3 28W
Perry, Fla., U.S.A. 115 30 9N 83 40W
Perry, Ga., U.S.A. 115 32 25N 83 41W
Perry, Iowa, U.S.A. 116 41 48N 94 5W
Perry, Maine, U.S.A. 115 44 59N 67 20W
Perry, Okla., U.S.A. 117 36 20N 97 20W
Perryton 117 36 28N 100 48W
Perryville 117 37 42N 89 50W
Persberg 48 59 47N 14 15E
Persepolis 65 29 55N 52 50E
Persia = Iran ■ 65 35 0N 50 0E
Persian Gulf 65 27 0N 50 0E
Perstorp 49 56 10N 13 25E
Perth, Austral. 96 31 57S 115 52E
Perth, Can. 106 44 55N 76 15W
Perth, U.K. 14 56 24N 3 27W
Perth Amboy 114 40 31N 74 16W
Perthus, Le 20 42 30N 2 53E
Pertuis 21 43 42N 5 30E
Peru, Ill., U.S.A. 116 41 18N 89 12W
Peru, Ind., U.S.A. 114 40 42N 86 0W
Peru ■ 126 8 0S 75 0W
Peru-Chile Trench 95 20 0S 72 0W
Perúgia 39 43 6N 12 24E
Perušić 39 44 40N 15 22E
Pervomaysk, R.S.F.S.R., U.S.S.R. 55 54 56N 43 58E
Pervomaysk, Ukraine S.S.R., U.S.S.R. 56 48 10N 30 46E
Pervouralsk 52 56 55N 60 0E
Pésaro 39 43 55N 12 53E
Pescara 39 42 28N 14 13E
Pescara → 39 42 28N 14 13E
Peschanokopskoye 57 46 14N 41 4E
Péscia 38 43 54N 10 40E
Pescina 39 42 0N 13 39E
Peshawar 66 34 2N 71 37E
* Peshawar □ 66 33 30N 71 20E
Peshkopia 44 41 41N 20 25E
Peshtera 43 42 2N 24 18E
Peshtigo 114 45 4N 87 46W
Peski 55 51 14N 42 29E
Peskovka 55 59 23N 52 20E
Pêso da Régua 30 41 10N 7 47W
Pesqueira 127 8 20S 36 42W
Pesqueira → 120 25 54N 99 11W
Pessac 20 44 48N 0 37W
Pest □ 27 47 29N 19 5E
Pestovo 54 58 33N 35 42E
Pestravka 55 52 28N 49 57E
Péta 45 39 10N 21 2E
Petah Tiqwa 62 32 6N 34 53E
Petalidhion 45 36 57N 21 55E
Petaling Jaya 71 3 4N 101 42E
Petaluma 118 38 13N 122 39W
Petange 16 49 33N 5 55E
Petatlán 120 17 31N 101 16W
Petauke 91 14 14S 31 20E
Petawawa 106 45 54N 77 17W
Petén Itzá, Lago 120 16 58N 89 50W
Peter 1st, I. 5 69 0S 91 0W
Peter Pond L. 109 55 55N 108 44W
Peterbell 106 48 36N 83 21W
Peterborough, Austral. 97 32 58S 138 51E
Peterborough, Can. 112 44 20N 78 20W
Peterborough, U.K. 13 52 35N 0 14W
Peterborough, U.S.A. 113 42 55N 71 59W
Peterhead 14 57 30N 1 49W
Petersburg, Alas., U.S.A. 108 56 50N 133 0W
Petersburg, Ind., U.S.A. 114 38 30N 87 15W
Petersburg, Va., U.S.A. 114 37 17N 77 26W
Petersburg, W. Va., U.S.A. 114 38 59N 79 10W
Petford 98 17 20S 144 58E
Petília Policastro 41 39 7N 16 48E
Petit Bois I. 115 30 16N 88 25W
Petit-Cap 107 48 3N 64 30W
Petit Goâve 121 18 27N 72 51W
Petit-Quevilly, Le 18 49 26N 1 0E
Petit Saint Bernard, Col du 38 45 40N 6 52E
Petitcodiac 107 45 57N 65 11W
Petite Baleine → 106 55 50N 77 0W
Petite Saguenay 107 48 15N 70 4W
Petitsikapau, L. 107 54 37N 66 25W
Petlad 68 22 30N 72 45E
Peto 120 20 10N 88 53W
Petone 101 41 13S 174 53E
Petoskey 106 45 22N 84 57W
Petra, Jordan 62 30 20N 35 22E
Petra, Spain 32 39 37N 3 6E
Petra, Ostrova 4 76 15N 118 30E
Petralia 41 37 49N 14 4E
Petrel 33 38 30N 0 46W
Petrich 43 41 24N 23 13E
Petrijanec 39 46 23N 16 17E
Petrikov 54 52 11N 28 29E
Petrila 46 45 29N 23 29E
Petrinja 39 45 28N 16 18E
Petrolândia 127 9 5S 38 20W
Petrolia 106 42 54N 82 9W
Petrolina 127 9 24S 40 30W
Petromagoúla 45 38 31N 23 0E
Petropavlovsk 58 54 53N 69 13E
Petropavlovsk-Kamchatskiy 59 53 3N 158 43E
Petrópolis 125 22 33S 43 9W
Petroşeni 46 45 28N 23 20E
Petroskey 114 45 22N 84 57W
Petrova Gora 39 45 15N 15 45E
Petrovac, Crna Gora, Yugo. 42 42 13N 18 57E
Petrovac, Srbija, Yugo. 42 44 22N 21 26E
Petrovaradin 42 45 16N 19 55E
Petrovsk 55 52 22N 45 19E
Petrovsk-Zabaykalskiy 59 51 20N 108 55E
Petrovskoye = Svetlograd 57 45 25N 42 58E
Petrozavodsk 52 61 41N 34 20E
Petrus Steyn 93 27 38S 28 8E
Petrusburg 92 29 4S 25 26E
Petukhovka 54 53 42N 30 54E
Peumo 124 34 21S 71 12W
Peureulak 72 4 48N 97 45E
Pevek 59 69 41N 171 19E
Peveragno 38 44 20N 7 37E
Peyrehorade 20 43 34N 1 7W
Peyruis 21 44 1N 5 56E
Pézenas 20 43 28N 3 24E
Pezinok 27 48 17N 17 17E
Pfaffenhofen 25 48 31N 11 31E
Pfarrkirchen 25 48 25N 12 57E
Pfeffenhausen 25 48 40N 11 58E
Pforzheim 25 48 53N 8 43E
Pfullendorf 25 47 55N 9 15E
Pfungstadt 25 49 47N 8 36E
Phala 92 23 45S 26 50E
Phalodi 68 27 12N 72 24E
Phalsbourg 19 48 46N 7 15E
Phan Rang 71 11 34N 109 0E
Phan Thiet 71 11 1N 108 9E
Phanae 45 38 8N 25 57E
Phangan, Ko 71 9 45N 100 0E
Phangnga 71 8 28N 98 30E
Phanh Bho Ho Chi Minh 71 10 58N 106 40E
Pharenda 69 27 5N 83 17E
Phatthalung 71 7 39N 100 6E
Phelps, N.Y., U.S.A. 112 42 57N 77 5W
Phelps, Wis., U.S.A. 116 46 2N 89 2W
Phelps L. 109 59 15N 103 15W
Phenix City 115 32 30N 85 0W
Phetchabun 71 16 25N 101 8E
Phetchabun, Thiu Khao 71 16 0N 101 20E
Phetchaburi 71 13 1N 99 55E
Phichai 71 17 22N 100 10E
Philadelphia, Miss., U.S.A. 117 32 47N 89 5W
Philadelphia, N.Y., U.S.A. 113 44 9N 75 40W

* Now part of North West Frontier □

Philadelphia, Pa., U.S.A. 114 40 0N 75 10W
Philip 116 44 4N 101 42W
Philippeville 16 50 12N 4 33E
Philippi 44 41 1N 24 16E
Philippi L. 98 24 20S 138 55E
Philippines ■ 73 12 0N 123 0E
Philippolis 92 30 15S 25 16E
Philippopolis = Plovdiv 43 42 8N 24 44E
Philipsburg, Mont., U.S.A. 118 46 20N 113 21W
Philipsburg, Pa., U.S.A. 112 40 53N 78 10W
Philipstown 92 30 28S 24 30E
Phillip 97 38 30S 145 12E
Phillips, Texas, U.S.A. 117 35 48N 101 17W
Phillips, Wis., U.S.A. 116 45 41N 90 22W
Phillipsburg, Kans., U.S.A. 116 39 48N 99 20W
Phillipsburg, Pa., U.S.A. 113 40 43N 75 12W
Phillott 99 27 53S 145 50E
Philmont 113 42 14N 73 37W
Philomath 118 44 28N 123 21W
Phitsanulok 71 16 50N 100 12E
Phnom Dangrek 71 14 20N 104 0E
Phnom Penh 71 11 33N 104 55E
Phnom Thbeng 71 13 50N 104 56E
Phoenix, Ariz., U.S.A. 119 33 30N 112 10W
Phoenix, N.Y., U.S.A. 113 43 13N 76 18W
Phoenix Is. 94 3 30S 172 0W
Phoenixville 113 40 12N 75 29W
Phong Saly 71 21 42N 102 9E
Phra Chedi Sam Ong 71 15 16N 98 23E
Phra Nakhon Si Ayutthaya 71 14 25N 100 30E
Phrae 71 18 7N 100 9E
Phrao 71 19 23N 99 15E
Phu Doan 71 21 40N 105 10E
Phu Loi 71 20 14N 103 14E
Phu Ly 71 20 35N 105 50E
Phu Qui 71 19 20N 105 20E
Phuket 71 7 52N 98 22E
Phulera (Phalera) 68 26 52N 75 16E
† Phuoc Le 71 10 30N 107 10E
Piacenza 38 45 2N 9 42E
Piádena 38 45 8N 10 22E
Pialba 97 25 20S 152 45E
Pian Cr. → 99 30 2S 148 12E
Piana 21 42 15N 8 34E
Pianella 39 42 24N 14 5E
Pianoro 39 44 20N 11 20E
Pianosa, Puglia, Italy 39 42 12N 15 44E
Pianosa, Toscana, Italy 38 42 36N 10 4E
Piapot 109 49 59N 109 8W
Piare → 39 45 32N 12 44E
Pias 31 38 1N 7 29W
Piaseczno 28 52 5N 21 2E
Piaski 28 51 8N 22 52E
Piastów 28 52 12N 20 48E
Piatra 46 43 51N 25 9E
Piatra Neamţ 46 46 56N 26 21E
Piatra Olt 46 44 22N 24 16E
Piauí □ 127 7 0S 43 0W
Piave → 39 45 32N 12 44E
Piazza Ármerina 41 37 21N 14 20E
Pibor → 87 7 35N 33 0E
Pibor Post 87 6 47N 33 3E
Pica 126 20 35S 69 25W
Picardie 19 50 0N 2 15E
Picardie, Plaine de 19 50 0N 2 0E
Picardy = Picardie 19 50 0N 2 15E
Picayune 117 30 31N 89 40W
Picerno 41 40 40N 15 37E
Pichilemu 124 34 22S 72 0W
Pickerel L. 106 48 40N 91 25W
Pickle Lake 106 51 30N 90 12W
Pico 8 38 28N 28 18W
Pico Truncado 128 46 40S 68 0W
Picos Ancares, Sierra de 30 42 51N 6 52W
Picquigny 19 49 56N 2 10E
Picton, Austral. 99 34 12S 150 34E
Picton, Can. 106 44 1N 77 9W
Picton, N.Z. 101 41 18S 174 3E
Pictou 107 45 41N 62 42W
Picture Butte 108 49 55N 112 45W
Picún Leufú 128 39 30S 69 5W
Pidurutalagala 70 7 10N 80 50E
Piedad, La 120 20 20N 102 1W
Piedicavallo 38 45 41N 7 57E
Piedmont 115 33 55N 85 39W
Piedmont = Piemonte 38 45 0N 7 30E
Piedmont Plat. 115 34 0N 81 30W
Piedmonte d'Alife 41 41 22N 14 22E
Piedra → 32 41 18N 1 47W
Piedrabuena 31 39 0N 4 10W
Piedrahita 30 40 28N 5 23W
Piedras Blancas Pt. 119 35 45N 121 18W
Piedras Negras 120 28 35N 100 35W
Piedras, R. de las → 126 12 30S 69 15W
Piemonte □ 38 45 0N 7 30E
Piensk 28 51 16N 15 2E
Pierce 118 46 29N 115 53W
Piercefield 113 44 13N 74 35W
Pieria □ 44 40 13N 22 25E
Pierre, France 19 46 54N 5 13E
Pierre, U.S.A. 116 44 23N 100 20W
Pierre Benite, Barrage 21 45 42N 4 49E
Pierrefeu 21 43 8N 6 9E
Pierrefonds 19 49 20N 3 0E
Pierrefontaine 19 47 14N 6 32E
Pierrefort 20 44 55N 2 50E
Pierrelatte 21 44 23N 4 43E
Pieštany 27 48 38N 17 55E
Piesting → 27 48 6N 16 40E
Pieszyce 28 50 43N 16 33E
Piet Retief 93 27 1S 30 50E
Pietarsaari 50 63 40N 22 43E
Pietermaritzburg 93 29 35S 30 25E
Pietersburg 93 23 54S 29 25E
Pietraperzia 41 37 26N 14 8E
Pietrasanta 38 43 57N 10 12E
Pietrosu 46 47 12N 25 8E
Pietrosul 46 47 35N 24 43E
Pieve di Cadore 39 46 25N 12 22E
Pieve di Teco 38 44 3N 7 54E
Pievepélago 38 44 12N 10 35E
Pigádhia 45 35 30N 27 12E

† Renamed Ba Ria

Pigadhítsa 44 39 59N 21 23E
Pigeon 114 43 50N 83 17W
Pigeon I. 70 14 2N 74 20E
Piggott 117 36 20N 90 10W
Pigna 38 43 57N 7 40E
Pigüe 124 37 36S 62 25W
Pihani 69 27 36N 80 15E
Pikalevo 54 59 37N 34 0E
Pikes Peak 116 38 50N 105 10W
Piketberg 92 32 55S 18 40E
Pikeville 114 37 30N 82 30W
Pikwitonei 109 55 35N 97 9W
Piła 28 53 10N 16 48E
Pila 33 38 16N 1 11W
Piła □ 28 53 0N 17 0E
Pilaía 44 40 32N 22 59E
Pilani 68 28 22N 75 33E
Pilar, Brazil 127 9 36S 35 56W
Pilar, Parag. 124 26 50S 58 20W
Pilas 73 6 39N 121 37E
Pilawa 28 51 57N 21 32E
Pilbara 96 21 15S 118 16E
Pilcomayo → 124 25 21S 57 42W
Píli 45 36 50N 27 15E
Pilibhit 69 28 40N 79 50E
Pilica → 28 51 52N 21 17E
Pilion 44 39 27N 23 7E
Pilis 27 47 17N 19 35E
Pilisvörösvár 27 47 38N 18 56E
Pilkhawa 68 28 43N 77 42E
Pílos 45 36 55N 21 42E
Pilot Mound 109 49 15N 98 54W
Pilot Point 117 33 26N 97 0W
Pilot Rock 118 45 30N 118 50W
Pilsen = Plzen 26 49 45N 13 22E
Pilštanj 39 46 8N 15 39E
Pilzno 27 50 0N 21 16E
Pima 119 32 54N 109 50W
Pimba 97 31 18S 136 46E
Pimenta Bueno 126 11 35S 61 10W
Pimentel 126 6 45S 79 55W
Pina 32 41 29N 0 33W
Pinang 71 5 25N 100 15E
Pinar del Río 121 22 26N 83 40W
Pinaroo 97 35 17S 140 53E
Pincehely 27 46 41N 18 27E
Pincher Creek 108 49 30N 113 57W
Pinchi L. 108 54 38N 124 30W
Pinckneyville 116 38 5N 89 20W
Pîncota 42 46 20N 21 45E
Pińczów 28 50 32N 20 32E
Pind Dadan Khan 68 32 36N 73 7E
Pindiga 85 9 58N 10 53E
Pindos Óros 44 40 0N 21 0E
Pindus Mts. = Pindos Óros 44 40 0N 21 0E
Pine 119 34 27N 111 30W
Pine → 109 58 50N 105 38W
Pine Bluff 117 34 10N 92 0W
Pine, C. 107 46 37N 53 32W
Pine City 116 45 46N 93 0W
Pine Creek 96 13 50S 132 10E
Pine Falls 109 50 34N 96 11W
Pine, La 118 43 40N 121 30W
Pine Pass 108 55 25N 122 42W
Pine Point 108 60 50N 114 28W
Pine Ridge 116 43 0N 102 35W
Pine River, Can. 109 51 45N 100 30W
Pine River, U.S.A. 116 46 43N 94 24W
Pinedale 119 34 23N 110 16W
Pinega → 52 64 8N 46 54E
Pinehill 98 23 38S 146 57E
Pinerolo 38 44 47N 7 21E
Pineto 39 42 36N 14 4E
Pinetop 119 34 10N 109 57W
Pinetown 93 29 48S 30 54E
Pinetree 118 43 42N 105 52W
Pineville, Ky., U.S.A. 115 36 42N 83 42W
Pineville, La., U.S.A. 117 31 22N 92 30W
Piney 19 48 22N 4 21E
Ping → 71 15 42N 100 9E
Pingding 76 37 47N 113 38E
Pingdingshan 77 33 43N 113 27E
Pingdong 75 22 39N 120 30E
Pingdu 76 36 42N 119 59E
Pingguo 77 23 19N 107 36E
Pinghe 77 24 17N 117 21E
Pingjiang 77 28 45N 113 36E
Pingle 77 24 40N 110 40E
Pingliang 76 35 35N 106 31E
Pingluo 76 38 52N 106 30E
Pingnan 77 23 33N 110 22E
Pingtan Dao 77 25 29N 119 47E
Pingwu 75 32 25N 104 30E
Pingxiang, Guangxi Zhuangzu, China 75 22 6N 106 46E
Pingxiang, Jiangxi, China 77 27 43N 113 48E
Pingyao 76 37 12N 112 10E
Pinhal 125 22 10S 46 46W
Pinhel 30 40 50N 7 1W
Pini 72 0 10N 98 40E
Piniós →, Ilia, Greece 45 37 48N 21 20E
Piniós →, Trikkala, Greece 44 39 55N 22 10E
Pinjarra 96 32 37S 115 52E
Pink → 109 56 50N 103 50W
Pinkafeld 27 47 22N 16 9E
Pinneberg 24 53 39N 9 48E
Pinos 120 22 20N 101 40W
Pinos, I. de 121 21 40N 82 40W
Pinos Pt. 119 36 38N 121 57W
Pinos Puente 31 37 15N 3 45W
Pinrang 73 3 46S 119 41E
Pinsk 54 52 10N 26 1E
Pintados 126 20 35S 69 40W
Pinyang 77 27 42N 120 31E
Pinyug 52 60 5N 48 0E
Pinzolo 38 46 9N 10 45E
Pioche 119 38 0N 114 35W
Piombino 38 42 54N 10 30E
Piombino, Canale di 38 42 50N 10 25E
Pioner, Os. 59 79 50N 92 0E
Pionki 28 51 29N 21 28E
Piorini, L. 126 3 15S 62 35W

Piotrków Trybunalski 28 51 23N 19 43 E
Piotrków Trybunalski □ 28 51 30N 19 45 E
Piove di Sacco 39 45 18N 12 1 E
Pip 65 26 45N 60 10 E
Pipar 68 26 25N 73 31 E
Pipariya 68 22 45N 78 23 E
Pipéri 44 39 20N 24 19 E
Pipestone 116 44 0N 96 20W
Pipestone → 106 52 53N 89 23W
Pipestone Cr. → 109 49 42N 100 45W
Pipmuacan, Rés. 107 49 45N 70 30W
Pipriac 18 47 49N 1 58W
Piqua 114 40 10N 84 10W
Piquiri → 125 24 3 S 54 14W
Piracicaba 125 22 45 S 47 40W
Piracuruca 127 3 50 S 41 50W
Piræus = Piraiévs 45 37 57N 23 42 E
Piraiévs 45 37 57N 23 42 E
Piraiévs □ 45 37 0N 23 30 E
Piráino 41 38 10N 14 52 E
Pirajuí 125 21 59 S 49 29W
Piran (Pirano) 39 45 31N 13 33 E
Pirané 124 25 42 S 59 6W
Pirapora 127 17 20 S 44 56W
Pirdop 43 42 40N 24 10 E
Pirganj 69 25 51N 88 24 E
Pírgos, Ilía, Greece 45 37 40N 21 27 E
Pírgos, Messinia, Greece 45 36 50N 22 16 E
Pirgovo 43 43 44N 25 43 E
Piriac-sur-Mer 18 47 22N 2 33W
Piribebuy 124 25 26 S 57 2W
Pirin Planina 43 41 40N 23 30 E
Pirineos 32 42 40N 1 0 E
Piripiri 127 4 15 S 41 46W
Pirmasens 25 49 12N 7 30 E
Pirna 24 50 57N 13 57 E
Pirojpur 69 22 35N 90 1 E
Pirot 42 43 9N 22 39 E
Pirtleville 119 31 25N 109 35W
Piru 73 3 4 S 128 12 E
Piryatin 54 50 15N 32 25 E
Piryí 45 38 13N 25 59 E
Pisa 38 43 43N 10 23 E
Pisa → 28 53 14N 21 52 E
Pisagua 126 19 40 S 70 15W
Pisarovina 39 45 35N 15 50 E
Pisciotta 41 40 7N 15 12 E
Pisco 126 13 50 S 76 12W
Piscu 46 45 30N 27 43 E
Písek 26 49 19N 14 10 E
Pishan 75 37 30N 78 33 E
Pising 73 5 8 S 121 53 E
Pissos 20 44 19N 0 49W
Pisticci 41 40 24N 16 33 E
Pistóia 38 43 57N 10 53 E
Pistol B. 109 62 25N 92 37W
Pisuerga → 30 41 33N 4 52W
Pisz 28 53 38N 21 49 E
Pitarpunga, L. 99 34 24 S 143 30 E
Pitcairn I. 95 25 5 S 130 5W
Pite älv → 50 65 20N 21 25 E
Piteå 50 65 20N 21 25 E
Piterka 55 50 41N 47 29 E
Piteşti 46 44 52N 24 54 E
Pithapuram 70 17 10N 82 15 E
Pithion 44 41 24N 26 40 E
Pithiviers 19 48 10N 2 13 E
Pitigliano 39 42 38N 11 40 E
Pitlochry 14 56 43N 3 43W
Pitt I. 108 53 30N 129 50W
Pittsburg, Calif., U.S.A. 118 38 1N 121 50W
Pittsburg, Kans., U.S.A. 117 37 21N 94 43W
Pittsburg, Tex., U.S.A. 117 32 59N 94 58W
Pittsburgh 114 40 25N 79 55W
Pittsfield, Ill., U.S.A. 116 39 35N 90 46W
Pittsfield, Mass., U.S.A. 114 42 28N 73 17W
Pittsfield, N.H., U.S.A. 113 43 17N 71 18W
Pittston 114 41 19N 75 50W
Pittsworth 99 27 41 S 151 37 E
Pituri → 98 22 35 S 138 30 E
Piura 126 5 15 S 80 38W
Piva → 42 43 20N 18 50 E
Piwniczna 27 49 27N 20 42 E
Piyai 44 39 17N 21 25 E
Pizzo 41 38 44N 16 10 E
Placentia 107 47 20N 54 0W
Placentia B. 107 47 0N 54 40W
Placerville 118 38 47N 120 51W
Placetas 121 22 15N 79 44W
Plačkovica 42 41 45N 22 30 E
Plain Dealing 117 32 56N 93 41W
Plainfield 114 40 37N 74 28W
Plains, Kans., U.S.A. 117 37 20N 100 35W
Plains, Mont., U.S.A. 118 47 27N 114 57W
Plains, Tex., U.S.A. 117 33 11N 102 50W
Plainview, Nebr., U.S.A. 116 42 25N 97 48W
Plainview, Tex., U.S.A. 117 34 10N 101 40W
Plainville 116 39 18N 99 19W
Plainwell 114 42 28N 85 40W
Plaisance 20 43 36N 0 3 E
Pláka 44 40 0N 25 24 E
Plakenska Planina 42 41 14N 21 2 E
Plakhino 58 67 45N 86 5 E
Planá 26 49 50N 12 44 E
Plancoët 18 48 32N 2 13W
Plandište 42 45 16N 21 10 E
Planina, Slovenija, Yugo. 39 46 10N 15 20 E
Planina, Slovenija, Yugo. 39 45 47N 14 19 E
Plankinton 116 43 45N 98 27W
Plano 117 33 0N 96 45W
Plant City 115 28 0N 82 8W
Plant, La 116 45 11N 100 40W
Plaquemine 117 30 20N 91 15W
Plasencia 30 40 3N 6 8W
Plaški 39 45 4N 15 22 E
Plassen 48 61 9N 12 30 E
Plaster Rock 107 46 53N 67 22W
Plata, La 124 35 0 S 57 55W
Plata, Río de la 124 34 45 S 57 30W
Platani → 40 37 23N 13 16 E
Plateau 5 79 55 S 40 0 E
Plateau □ 85 8 0N 8 30 E
Plateau du Coteau du Missouri 116 47 9N 101 5W
Platí, Ákra- 44 40 27N 24 0 E
Plato 126 9 47N 74 47W
Platte 116 43 28N 98 50W
Platte → 116 39 16N 94 50W
Platteville 116 40 18N 104 47W
Plattling 25 48 46N 12 53 E
Plattsburg 114 44 41N 73 30W
Plattsmouth 116 41 0N 95 50W
Plau 24 53 27N 12 16 E
Plauen 24 50 29N 12 9 E
Plav 42 42 38N 19 57 E
Plavinas 54 56 35N 25 46 E
Plavnica 42 42 20N 19 13 E
Plavsk 55 53 40N 37 18 E
Playgreen L. 109 54 0N 98 15W
Pleasant Bay 107 46 51N 60 48W
Pleasant Hill 116 38 48N 94 14W
Pleasanton 117 29 0N 98 30W
Pleasantville 114 39 25N 74 30W
Pléaux 20 45 8N 2 13 E
Pleiku (Gia Lai) 71 13 57N 108 0 E
Plélan-le-Grand 18 48 0N 2 7W
Plémet 18 48 11N 2 36W
Pléneuf-Val-André 18 48 35N 2 32W
Pleniţa 46 44 14N 23 10 E
Plenty, Bay of 101 37 45 S 177 0 E
Plentywood 116 48 45N 104 35W
Plesetsk 52 62 40N 40 10 E
Plessisville 107 46 14N 71 47W
Plestin-les-Grèves 18 48 40N 3 39W
Pleszew 28 51 53N 17 47 E
Pleternica 42 45 17N 17 48 E
Pletipi L. 107 51 44N 70 6W
Pleven 43 43 26N 24 37 E
Plevlja 42 43 21N 19 21 E
Ploče 42 43 4N 17 26 E
Płock 28 52 32N 19 40 E
Płock □ 28 52 30N 19 45 E
Plöcken Passo 39 46 37N 12 57 E
Ploëmeur 18 47 44N 3 26W
Ploërmel 18 47 55N 2 26W
Ploieşti 46 44 57N 26 5 E
Plomárion 45 38 58N 26 24 E
Plomb du Cantal 20 45 2N 2 48 E
Plombières 19 47 59N 6 27 E
Plomin 39 45 8N 14 10 E
Plön 24 54 8N 10 22 E
Plöner See 24 45 10N 10 22 E
Plonge, Lac La 109 55 8N 107 20W
Płońsk 28 52 37N 20 21 E
Płoty 28 53 48N 15 18 E
Plouaret 18 48 37N 3 28W
Plouay 18 47 55N 3 21W
Ploučnice → 26 50 46N 14 13 E
Ploudalmézeau 18 48 34N 4 41W
Plougasnou 18 48 42N 3 49W
Plouha 18 48 41N 2 57W
Plouhinec 18 48 0N 4 29W
Plovdiv 43 42 8N 24 44 E
Plum I. 113 41 10N 72 12W
Plummer 118 47 21N 116 59W
Plumtree 91 20 27 S 27 55 E
Plunge 54 55 53N 21 59 E
Pluvigner 18 47 46N 3 1W
Plymouth, U.K. 13 50 23N 4 9W
Plymouth, Ind., U.S.A. 114 41 20N 86 19W
Plymouth, Mass., U.S.A. 113 41 58N 70 40W
Plymouth, N.C., U.S.A. 115 35 54N 76 46W
Plymouth, N.H., U.S.A. 113 43 44N 71 41W
Plymouth, Pa., U.S.A. 113 41 17N 76 0W
Plymouth, Wis., U.S.A. 114 43 42N 87 58W
Plymouth Sd. 13 50 20N 4 10W
Plynlimon = Pumlumon Fawr 13 52 29N 3 47W
Plyussa 54 58 40N 29 20 E
Plyussa → 54 58 40N 29 0 E
Plzen 26 49 45N 13 22 E
Pniewy 28 52 31N 16 16 E
Pô 85 11 14N 1 5W
Po → 38 44 57N 12 4 E
Po, Foci del 39 44 55N 12 30 E
Po Hai = Bo Hai 76 39 0N 120 0 E
Pobé 85 7 0N 2 56 E
Pobeda 59 65 12N 146 12 E
Pobedino 59 49 51N 142 49 E
Pobedy Pik 58 40 45N 79 58 E
Pobiedziska 28 52 29N 17 11 E
Pobla de Lillet, La 32 42 16N 1 59 E
Pobla de Segur 32 42 15N 0 58 E
Pobladura de Valle 30 42 6N 5 44W
Pocahontas, Arkansas, U.S.A. 117 36 18N 91 0W
Pocahontas, Iowa, U.S.A. 116 42 41N 94 42W
Pocatello 118 42 50N 112 25W
Počátky 26 49 15N 15 14 E
Pochep 54 52 58N 33 29 E
Pochinki 55 54 41N 44 59 E
Pochinok 54 54 28N 32 29 E
Pöchlarn 26 48 12N 15 12 E
Pochontas 108 53 10N 117 51W
Pochutla 120 15 50N 96 31W
Pocomoke City 114 38 4N 75 32W
Poços de Caldas 125 21 50 S 46 33W
Poddebice 28 51 54N 18 58 E
Poděbrady 26 50 9N 15 8 E
Podensac 20 44 40N 0 22W
Podgorač 42 45 27N 18 13 E
Podgorica = Titograd 42 42 30N 19 19 E
Podkamennaya Tunguska → 59 61 50N 90 13 E
Podlapac 39 44 37N 15 47 E
Podmokly 26 50 48N 14 10 E
Podoleni 46 46 46N 26 39 E
Podolínec 27 49 16N 20 31 E
Podolsk 55 55 25N 37 30 E
Podor 84 16 40N 15 2W
Podporozhy 52 60 55N 34 2 E
Podravska Slatina 42 45 42N 17 45 E
Podu Turcului 46 46 11N 27 25 E
Podujevo 42 42 54N 21 10 E
Poel 24 54 0N 11 25 E
Pofadder 92 29 10 S 19 22 E
Pogamasing 106 46 55N 81 50W
Poggiardo 41 40 3N 18 21 E
Poggibonsi 39 43 27N 11 8 E
Pogoanele 46 44 55N 27 0 E
Pogorzela 28 51 50N 17 12 E
Pogradeci 44 40 57N 20 37 E
Poh 73 0 46 S 122 51 E
Pohang 76 36 1N 129 23 E
Pohorelá 27 48 50N 20 2 E
Pohořelice 27 48 59N 16 31 E
Pohorje 39 46 30N 15 20 E
Poiana Mare 46 43 57N 23 5 E
Poiana Ruscăi, Munţii 46 45 45N 22 25 E
Poinsett, C. 5 65 42 S 113 18 E
Point Edward 106 43 0N 82 30W
Point Pedro 70 9 50N 80 15 E
Point Pleasant, U.S.A. 113 40 5N 74 4W
Point Pleasant, W. Va., U.S.A. 114 38 50N 82 7W
Pointe-à-la Hache 117 29 35N 89 55W
Pointe-à-Pitre 121 16 10N 61 30W
Pointe Noire 88 4 48 S 11 53 E
Poirino 38 44 55N 7 50 E
Poissy 19 48 55N 2 0 E
Poitiers 18 46 35N 0 20 E
Poitou, Plaines et Seuil du 20 46 30N 0 1W
Poix 19 49 47N 2 0 E
Poix-Terron 19 49 38N 4 38 E
Pojoaque 119 35 55N 106 0W
Pokataroo 99 29 30 S 148 36 E
Poko, Sudan 87 5 41N 31 55 E
Poko, Zaïre 90 3 7N 26 52 E
Pokrov 55 55 55N 39 7 E
Pokrovsk 59 61 29N 126 12 E
Pol 30 43 9N 7 20W
Pola de Allande 30 43 16N 6 37W
Pola de Gordón, La 30 42 51N 5 41W
Pola de Lena 30 43 10N 5 49W
Pola de Siero 30 43 24N 5 39W
Pola de Somiedo 30 43 5N 6 15W
Polacca 119 35 52N 110 25W
Polan 65 25 30N 61 10 E
Poland ■ 28 52 0N 20 0 E
Polanów 28 54 7N 16 41 E
Polar Sub-Glacial Basin 5 85 0 S 110 0 E
Polcura 124 37 17 S 71 43W
Połczyn Zdrój 28 53 47N 16 5 E
Polden Hills 13 51 7N 2 50W
Polessk 54 54 50N 21 8 E
Polevskoy 52 56 26N 60 11 E
Polewali, Sulawesi, Indon. 73 4 8 S 119 43 E
Polewali, Sulawesi, Indon. 73 3 21 S 119 23 E
Polgar 27 47 54N 21 6 E
Poli 88 8 34N 13 15 E
Poliaigos 45 36 45N 24 38 E
Policastro, Golfo di 41 39 55N 15 35 E
Police 28 53 33N 14 33 E
Polička 27 49 43N 16 15 E
Polignano a Mare 41 41 0N 17 12 E
Poligny 19 46 50N 5 42 E
Políkhnitas 45 39 4N 26 10 E
Polillo Is. 73 14 56N 122 0 E
Polistena 41 38 25N 16 4 E
Políyiros 44 40 23N 23 25 E
Polk 112 41 22N 79 57W
Polkowice 28 51 29N 16 3 E
Polla 41 40 31N 15 27 E
Pollachi 70 10 35N 77 0 E
Pollensa 32 39 54N 3 1 E
Pollensa, B. de 32 39 53N 3 8 E
Póllica 41 40 13N 15 3 E
Pollino, Mte. 41 39 54N 16 13 E
Pollock 116 45 58N 100 18W
Polna 54 58 31N 28 0 E
Polnovat 58 63 50N 65 54 E
Polo 116 42 0N 89 38W
Pologi 56 47 29N 36 15 E
Polonnoye 54 50 6N 27 30 E
Polotsk 54 55 30N 28 50 E
Polski Trŭmbesh 43 43 20N 25 38 E
Polsko Kosovo 43 43 23N 25 38 E
Polson 118 47 45N 114 12W
Poltava 56 49 35N 34 35 E
Polunochnoye 52 60 52N 60 25 E
Polur 70 12 32N 79 11 E
Polyanovgrad 43 42 39N 26 59 E
Polyarny 52 69 8N 33 20 E
Polynesia 95 10 0 S 162 0W
Pomarance 38 43 18N 10 51 E
Pomarico 41 40 31N 16 33 E
Pombal, Brazil 127 6 45 S 37 50W
Pombal, Port. 30 39 55N 8 40W
Pómbia 45 35 0N 24 51 E
Pomeroy, Ohio, U.S.A. 114 39 0N 82 0W
Pomeroy, Wash., U.S.A. 118 46 30N 117 33W
Pomona 119 34 2N 117 49W
Pomorie 43 42 32N 27 41 E
Pomoshnaya 56 48 13N 31 36 E
Pompano Beach 115 26 12N 80 6W
Pompei 41 40 45N 14 30 E
Pompey 19 48 50N 6 2 E
Pompeys Pillar 118 46 0N 108 0W
Ponape 94 6 55N 158 10 E
Ponask, L. 106 54 0N 92 41W
Ponass L. 109 52 16N 103 58W
Ponca 116 42 38N 96 41W
Ponca City 117 36 40N 97 5W
Ponce 121 18 1N 66 37W
Ponchatoula 117 30 27N 90 25W
Poncheville, L. 106 50 10N 76 55W
Poncin 21 46 6N 5 25 E
Pond Inlet 105 72 40N 77 0W
Pondicherry 70 11 59N 79 50 E
Pondoland 93 31 10 S 29 30 E
Ponds, I. of 107 53 27N 55 52W
Ponferrada 30 42 32N 6 35W
Pongo, Wadi → 87 8 42N 27 40 E
Poniatowa 28 51 11N 22 3 E
Poniec 28 51 48N 16 50 E
Ponikva 39 46 16N 15 26 E
Ponnaiyar → 70 11 50N 79 45 E
Ponnani 70 10 45N 75 59 E
Ponneri 70 13 20N 80 15 E
Ponnyadaung 67 22 0N 94 10 E
Ponoi 52 67 0N 41 0 E
Ponoi → 52 66 59N 41 17 E
Ponoka 108 52 42N 113 40W
Ponorogo 73 7 52 S 111 29 E
Pons, France 20 45 35N 0 34W
Pons, Spain 32 41 55N 1 12 E
Ponsul → 31 39 40N 7 31W
Pont-à-Mousson 19 48 54N 6 1 E
Pont-Audemer 18 49 21N 0 30 E
Pont-Aven 18 47 51N 3 47W
Pont Canavese 38 45 24N 7 33 E
Pont-de-Roide 19 47 23N 6 45 E
Pont-de-Salars 20 44 18N 2 44 E
Pont-de-Vaux 19 46 26N 4 56 E
Pont-de-Veyle 21 46 17N 4 53 E
Pont-l'Abbé 18 47 52N 4 15W
Pont-l'Évêque 18 49 18N 0 11 E
Pont-St-Esprit 21 44 16N 4 40 E
Pont-sur-Yonne 19 48 18N 3 10 E
Ponta Grossa 125 25 7 S 50 10W
Ponta Pora 125 22 20 S 55 35W
Pontacq 20 43 11N 0 8W
Pontailler 19 47 18N 5 24 E
Pontarlier 19 46 54N 6 20 E
Pontassieve 39 43 47N 11 25 E
Pontaubault 18 48 40N 1 20W
Pontaumur 20 45 52N 2 40 E
Pontcharra 21 45 26N 6 1 E
Pontchartrain, L. 117 30 12N 90 0W
Pontchâteau 18 47 25N 2 5W
Ponte da Barca 30 41 48N 8 25W
Ponte de Sor 31 39 17N 7 57W
Ponte dell 'Olio 38 44 52N 9 39 E
Ponte di Legno 38 46 15N 10 30 E
Ponte do Lima 30 41 46N 8 35W
Ponte do Pungué 91 19 30 S 34 33 E
Ponte Leccia 21 42 28N 9 13 E
Ponte Macassar 73 9 30 S 123 58 E
Ponte nell' Alpi 39 46 10N 12 18 E
Ponte Nova 125 20 25 S 42 54W
Ponte San Martino 38 45 36N 7 47 E
Ponte San Pietro 38 45 42N 9 35 E
Pontebba 39 46 30N 13 17 E
Pontecorvo 40 41 28N 13 40 E
Pontedera 38 43 40N 10 37 E
Pontefract 12 53 42N 1 19W
Ponteix 109 49 46N 107 29W
Pontelandolfo 41 41 17N 14 41 E
Pontevedra 30 42 26N 8 40W
Pontevedra □ 30 42 25N 8 39W
Pontevedra, R. de → 30 42 22N 8 45W
Pontevico 38 45 16N 10 6 E
Pontiac, Ill., U.S.A. 116 40 50N 88 40W
Pontiac, Mich., U.S.A. 114 42 40N 83 20W
Pontian Kechil 71 1 29N 103 23 E
Pontianak 72 0 3 S 109 15 E
Pontine Is. = Ponziane, Isole 40 40 55N 13 0 E
Pontine Mts. = Karadeniz D. 64 41 30N 35 0 E
Pontínia 40 41 25N 13 2 E
Pontivy 18 48 5N 3 0W
Pontoise 19 49 3N 2 5 E
Ponton → 108 58 27N 116 11W
Pontorson 18 48 34N 1 30W
Pontrémoli 38 44 22N 9 52 E
Pontrieux 18 48 42N 3 10W
Ponts-de-Cé, Les 18 47 25N 0 30W
Pontypool, Can. 112 44 6N 78 38W
Pontypool, U.K. 13 51 42N 3 1W
Pontypridd 13 51 36N 3 21W
Ponza 40 40 55N 12 57 E
Ponziane, Isole 40 40 55N 13 0 E
Poole 13 50 42N 1 58W
Pooley I. 108 52 45N 128 15W
Poona = Pune 70 18 29N 73 57 E
Poonamallee 70 13 3N 80 10 E
Pooncarie 99 33 22 S 142 31 E
Poopelloe, L. 99 31 40 S 144 0 E
Poopó, Lago de 126 18 30 S 67 35W
Popayán 126 2 27N 76 36W
Poperinge 16 50 51N 2 42 E
Popigay 59 72 1N 110 39 E
Popilta, L. 99 33 10 S 141 42 E
Popina 43 44 7N 26 57 E
Popio, L. 99 33 10 S 141 52 E
Poplar 116 48 3N 105 9W
Poplar →, Man., Can. 109 53 0N 97 19W
Poplar →, N.W.T., Can. 108 61 22N 121 52W
Poplar Bluff 117 36 45N 90 22W
Poplarville 117 30 55N 89 30W
Popocatepetl 120 19 10N 98 40W
Popokabaka 88 5 41 S 16 40 E
Pópoli 39 42 12N 13 50 E
Popondetta 98 8 48 S 148 17 E
Popovača 39 45 30N 16 41 E
Popovo 43 43 21N 26 18 E
Poprád 27 49 3N 20 18 E
Poprád → 27 49 38N 20 42 E
Porbandar 68 21 44N 69 43 E
Porcher I. 108 53 50N 130 30W
Porcuna 31 37 52N 4 11W
Porcupine →, Can. 109 59 11N 104 46W
Porcupine →, U.S.A. 104 66 35N 145 15W
Pordenone 39 45 58N 12 40 E
Pordim 43 43 23N 24 51 E
Poreč 39 45 14N 13 36 E
Poretskoye 55 55 9N 46 21 E
Pori 51 61 29N 21 48 E
Porí 45 35 58N 23 13 E
Porjus 50 66 57N 19 50 E
Porkhov 54 57 45N 29 38 E
Porkkala 51 59 59N 24 26 E
Porlamar 126 10 57N 63 51W
Porlezza 38 46 2N 9 8 E
Porma → 30 42 49N 5 28W
Pornic 18 47 7N 2 5W
Poronaysk 59 49 13N 143 0 E
Póros 45 37 30N 23 30 E
Poroshiri-Dake 74 42 41N 142 52 E
Poroszló 27 47 39N 20 40 E
Poroto Mts. 91 9 0 S 33 30 E
Porquerolles, Îles de 21 43 0N 6 13 E
Porrentruy 25 47 25N 7 6 E
Porreras 32 39 31N 3 2 E

Porretta, Passo di 38 44 2N 10 56 E
Porsangen 50 70 40N 25 40 E
Porsgrunn 47 59 10N 9 40 E
Port 19 47 43N 6 4 E
Port Adelaide 99 34 46S 138 30 E
Port Alberni 108 49 40N 124 50W
Port Albert 100 38 42S 146 42 E
Port Albert Victor 68 21 0N 71 30 E
Port Alfred, Can. 107 48 18N 70 53W
Port Alfred, S. Afr. 92 33 36S 26 55 E
Port Alice 108 50 20N 127 25W
Port Allegany 114 41 49N 78 17W
Port Allen 117 30 30N 91 15W
Port Alma 98 23 38S 150 53 E
Port Angeles 118 48 7N 123 30W
Port Antonio 121 18 10N 76 30W
Port Aransas 117 27 49N 97 4W
Port Arthur, Austral. 97 43 7S 147 50 E
Port Arthur, U.S.A. 117 30 0N 94 0W
Port au Port B. 107 48 40N 58 50W
Port-au-Prince 121 18 40N 72 20W
Port Augusta 97 32 30S 137 50 E
Port Augusta West 97 32 29S 137 29 E
Port Austin 106 44 3N 82 59W
Port Bell 90 0 18N 32 35 E
Port Bergé Vaovao 93 15 33S 47 40 E
Port Blair 71 11 40N 92 30 E
Port Blandford 107 48 20N 54 10W
Port Bolivar 117 29 20N 94 40W
Port Bou 32 42 25N 3 9 E
Port Bouët 84 5 16N 3 57W
Port Bradshaw 97 12 30S 137 20 E
Port Broughton 99 33 37S 137 56 E
Port Burwell 106 42 40N 80 48W
Port-Cartier 107 50 2N 66 50W
Port Chalmers 101 45 49S 170 30 E
Port Chester 114 41 0N 73 41W
Port Clements 108 53 40N 132 10W
Port Clinton 114 41 30N 82 58W
Port Colborne 106 42 50N 79 10W
Port Coquitlam 108 49 15N 122 45W
Port Credit 112 43 33N 79 35W
Port Dalhousie 112 43 13N 79 16W
Port Darwin, Austral. 96 12 24S 130 45 E
Port Darwin, Falk. Is. 128 51 50S 59 0W
Port Davey 97 43 16S 145 55 E
Port-de-Bouc 21 43 24N 4 59 E
Port-de-Paix 121 19 50N 72 50W
Port Dickson 71 2 30N 101 49 E
Port Douglas 98 16 30S 145 30 E
Port Dover 112 42 47N 80 12W
Port Edward 108 54 12N 130 10W
Port Elgin 106 44 25N 81 25W
Port Elizabeth 92 33 58S 25 40 E
Port Ellen 14 55 38N 6 10W
Port-en-Bessin 18 49 21N 0 45W
Port Erin 12 54 5N 4 45W
Port Etienne = Nouâdhibou 80 20 54N 17 0W
Port Fairy 97 38 22S 142 12 E
Port Fouâd = Bûr Fuad 86 31 15N 32 20 E
Port-Gentil 88 0 40S 8 50 E
Port Gibson 117 31 57N 91 0W
Port Glasgow 14 55 57N 4 40W
Port Harcourt 85 4 40N 7 10 E
Port Hardy 108 50 41N 127 30W
Port Harrison 105 58 25N 78 15W
Port Hawkesbury 107 45 36N 61 22W
Port Hedland 96 20 25S 118 35 E
Port Henry 114 44 0N 73 30W
Port Hood 107 46 0N 61 32W
Port Hope 106 43 56N 78 20W
Port Huron 114 43 0N 82 28W
Port Isabel 117 26 4N 97 9W
Port Jackson 97 33 50S 151 18 E
Port Jefferson 114 40 58N 73 5W
Port Jervis 113 41 22N 74 42W
Port-Joinville 18 46 45N 2 23W
Port Katon 57 46 52N 38 46 E
Port Kelang 71 3 0N 101 23 E
Port Kembla 99 34 52S 150 49 E
Port-la-Nouvelle 20 43 1N 3 3 E
Port Laoise 15 53 2N 7 20W
Port Lavaca 117 28 38N 96 38W
Port-Leucate-Barcarès 20 42 53N 3 3 E
Port Lincoln 96 34 42S 135 52 E
Port Loko 84 8 48N 12 46W
Port Louis 18 47 42N 3 22W
Port Lyautey = Kenitra 82 34 15N 6 40W
Port Macdonnell 99 38 0S 140 48 E
Port Macquarie 97 31 25S 152 25 E
Port Maria 121 18 25N 77 5W
Port Mellon 108 49 32N 123 31W
Port-Menier 107 49 51N 64 15W
Port Moresby 94 9 24S 147 8 E
Port Mouton 107 43 58N 64 50W
Port Musgrave 97 11 55S 141 50 E
Port-Navalo 18 47 34N 2 54W
Port Nelson 109 57 3N 92 36W
Port Nolloth 92 29 17S 16 52 E
Port Nouveau-Québec (George River) 105 58 30N 65 59W
Port O'Connor 117 28 26N 96 24W
Port of Spain 121 10 40N 61 31W
Port Orchard 118 47 31N 122 38W
Port Oxford 118 42 45N 124 28W
Port Pegasus 101 47 12S 167 41 E
Port Perry 106 44 6N 78 56W
Port Phillip B. 97 38 10S 144 50 E
Port Pirie 97 33 10S 138 1 E
Port Pólnocny 28 54 25N 18 42 E
Port Radium = Echo Bay 104 66 10N 117 40W
Port Renfrew 108 48 30N 124 20W
Port Rowan 106 42 40N 80 30W
Port Safaga = Bûr Safâga 86 26 43N 33 57 E
Port Said = Bûr Sa'îd 86 31 16N 32 18 E
Port St. Joe 115 29 49N 85 20W
Port St. Louis 93 13 7S 48 48 E
Port-St-Louis-du-Rhône 21 43 23N 4 49 E
Port Sanilac 106 43 26N 82 33W
Port Saunders 107 50 40N 57 18W
Port Severn 112 44 48N 79 43W
Port Shepstone 93 30 44S 30 28 E
Port Simpson 108 54 30N 130 20W
Port Stanley 106 42 40N 81 10W
Port Stephens 97 32 38S 152 12 E
Port Sudan = Bûr Sûdân 86 19 32N 37 9 E
Port Talbot 13 51 35N 3 48W
Port Taufiq = Bûr Taufiq 86 29 54N 32 32 E
Port Townsend 118 48 7N 122 50W
Port-Vendres 20 42 32N 3 8 E
Port Vladimir 52 69 25N 33 6 E
Port Washington 114 43 25N 87 52W
Port Weld 71 4 50N 100 38 E
Portachuelo 126 17 10S 63 20W
Portadown 15 54 27N 6 26W
Portage 116 43 31N 89 25W
Portage La Prairie 109 49 58N 98 18W
Portageville 117 36 25N 89 40W
Portalegre 31 39 19N 7 25W
Portalegre □ 31 39 20N 7 40W
Portales 117 34 12N 103 25W
Portarlington 15 53 10N 7 10W
Porte, La 114 41 36N 86 43W
Portel 31 38 19N 7 41W
Porter L., N.W.T., Can. 109 61 41N 108 5W
Porter L., Sask., Can. 109 56 20N 107 20W
Porterville, S. Afr. 92 33 0S 18 57 E
Porterville, U.S.A. 119 36 5N 119 0W
Porthcawl 13 51 28N 3 42W
Porthill 118 49 0N 116 30W
Portile de Fier 46 44 42N 22 30 E
Portimão 31 37 8N 8 32W
Portland, N.S.W., Austral. 99 33 20S 150 0 E
Portland, Victoria, Austral. 97 38 20S 141 35 E
Portland, Can. 113 44 42N 76 12W
Portland, Conn., U.S.A. 113 41 34N 72 39W
Portland, Me., U.S.A. 107 43 40N 70 15W
Portland, Mich., U.S.A. 114 42 52N 84 58W
Portland, Oreg., U.S.A. 118 45 35N 122 40W
Portland B. 99 38 15S 141 45 E
Portland, Bill of 13 50 31N 2 27W
Portland, C. 97 40 46S 148 0 E
Portland, I. of 13 50 32N 2 25W
Portland Prom. 105 58 40N 78 33W
Portneuf 107 46 43N 71 55W
Porto 30 41 8N 8 40W
Porto □ 30 41 8N 8 20W
Pôrto Alegre 125 30 5S 51 10W
Porto Alexandre 92 15 55S 11 55 E
Porto Amboim = Gunza 88 10 50S 13 50 E
Porto Argentera 38 44 15N 7 27 E
Porto Azzurro 38 42 46N 10 24 E
Porto Botte 40 39 3N 8 33 E
Porto Civitanova 39 43 19N 13 44 E
Pôrto de Móz 127 1 41S 52 13W
Porto Empêdocle 40 37 18N 13 30 E
Pôrto Esperança 126 19 37S 57 29W
Pôrto Franco 127 6 20S 47 24W
Porto Garibaldi 39 44 41N 12 14 E
Porto, G. de 21 42 17N 8 34 E
Pórto Lágo 44 40 58N 25 6 E
Porto Mendes 125 24 30S 54 15W
Pôrto Murtinho 126 21 45S 57 55W
Pôrto Nacional 127 10 40S 48 30W
Porto Novo, Benin 85 6 23N 2 42 E
Porto Novo, India 70 11 30N 79 38 E
Porto Recanati 39 43 26N 13 40 E
Porto San Giórgio 39 43 11N 13 49 E
Porto Santo 80 33 45N 16 25W
Porto Santo Stefano 38 42 26N 11 7 E
Pôrto São José 125 22 43S 53 10W
Pôrto Seguro 127 16 26S 39 5W
Porto Tolle 39 44 57N 12 20 E
Porto Tôrres 40 40 50N 8 23 E
Pôrto União 125 26 10S 51 10W
Pôrto Válter 126 8 15S 72 40W
Porto-Vecchio 21 41 35N 9 16 E
Pôrto Velho 126 8 46S 63 54W
Portoferráio 38 42 50N 10 20 E
Portogruaro 39 45 47N 12 50 E
Portola 118 39 49N 120 28W
Portomaggiore 39 44 41N 11 47 E
Portoscuso 40 39 12N 8 22 E
Portovénere 38 44 2N 9 50 E
Portoviejo 126 1 7S 80 28W
Portpatrick 14 54 50N 5 7W
Portree 14 57 25N 6 11W
Portrush 15 55 13N 6 40W
Portsall 18 48 37N 4 45W
Portsmouth, Domin. 121 15 34N 61 27W
Portsmouth, U.K. 13 50 48N 1 6W
Portsmouth, N.H., U.S.A. 114 43 5N 70 45W
Portsmouth, Ohio, U.S.A. 114 38 45N 83 0W
Portsmouth, R.I., U.S.A. 113 41 35N 71 15W
Portsmouth, Va., U.S.A. 114 36 50N 76 20W
Portsoy 14 57 41N 2 41W
Porttipahta 50 68 5N 26 40 E
Portugal ■ 30 40 0N 7 0W
Portugalete 32 43 19N 3 4W
Portuguese-Guinea = Guinea-Bissau ■ 84 12 0N 15 0W
Portuguese Timor □ = Timor 73 8 0S 126 30 E
Portumna 15 53 5N 8 12W
Portville 112 42 3N 78 21W
Porvenir 128 53 10S 70 16W
Porvoo 51 60 24N 25 40 E
Porzuna 31 39 9N 4 9W
Posada → 40 40 40N 9 45 E
Posadas, Argent. 125 27 30S 55 50W
Posadas, Spain 31 37 47N 5 11W
Poschiavo 25 46 19N 10 4 E
Posets 32 42 39N 0 25 E
Poshan = Boshan 76 36 28N 117 49 E
Posídhion, Ákra 44 39 57N 23 30 E
Posidium 45 35 30N 27 10 E
Poso 73 1 20S 120 55 E
Posse 127 14 4S 46 18W
Possel 88 5 5N 19 10 E
Possession I. 5 72 4S 172 0 E
Pössneck 24 50 42N 11 34 E
Post 117 33 13N 101 21W
Post Falls 118 47 46N 116 59W
Postavy 54 55 4N 26 50 E
Poste Maurice Cortier (Bidon 5) 82 22 14N 1 2 E
Postmasburg 92 28 18S 23 5 E
Postojna 39 45 46N 14 12 E
Potamós, Andikíthira, Greece 45 36 18N 22 58 E
Potamós, Kíthira, Greece 45 36 15N 22 58 E
Potchefstroom 92 26 41S 27 7 E
Potcoava 46 44 30N 24 39 E
Poteau 117 35 5N 94 37W
Poteet 117 29 4N 98 35W
Potelu, Lacul 46 43 44N 24 20 E
Potenza 41 40 40N 15 50 E
Potenza → 39 43 27N 13 38 E
Potenza Picena 39 43 22N 13 37 E
Poteriteri, L. 101 46 5S 167 10 E
Potes 30 43 15N 4 42W
Potgietersrus 93 24 10S 28 55 E
Poti 57 42 10N 41 38 E
Potiskum 85 11 39N 11 2 E
Potlogi 46 44 34N 25 34 E
Potomac → 114 38 0N 76 23W
Potosí 126 19 38S 65 50W
Pototan 73 10 54N 122 38 E
Potrerillos 124 26 30S 69 30W
Potsdam, Ger. 24 52 23N 13 4 E
Potsdam, U.S.A. 114 44 40N 74 59W
Potsdam □ 24 52 40N 12 50 E
Pottenstein 25 49 46N 11 25 E
Potter 116 41 15N 103 20W
Pottery Hill = Abu Ballas 86 24 26N 27 36 E
Pottstown 114 40 17N 75 40W
Pottsville 114 40 39N 76 12W
Pouancé 18 47 44N 1 10W
Pouce Coupé 108 55 40N 120 10W
Poughkeepsie 114 41 40N 73 57W
Pouilly 19 47 18N 2 57 E
Poulaphouca Res. 15 53 8N 6 30W
Pouldu, Le 18 47 41N 3 36W
Poulsbo 118 47 45N 122 39W
Pourri, Mont 21 45 32N 6 52 E
Pouso Alegre, Mato Grosso, Brazil 127 11 46S 57 16W
Pouso Alegre, Minas Gerais, Brazil 125 22 14S 45 57W
Pouzages 20 46 40N 0 50W
Pouzauges 18 46 47N 0 50W
Povenets 52 62 50N 34 50 E
Poverty Bay 101 38 43S 178 2 E
Povlen 42 44 9N 19 44 E
Póvoa de Lanhosa 30 41 33N 8 15W
Póvoa de Varzim 30 41 25N 8 46W
Povorino 55 51 12N 42 5 E
Powassan 106 46 5N 79 25W
Powder → 116 46 47N 105 12W
Powder River 118 43 5N 107 0W
Powell 118 44 45N 108 45W
Powell Creek 96 18 6S 133 46 E
Powell, L. 119 37 25N 110 45W
Powell River 108 49 50N 124 35W
Powers, Mich., U.S.A. 114 45 40N 87 32W
Powers, Oreg., U.S.A. 118 42 53N 124 2W
Powers Lake 116 48 37N 102 38W
Powys □ 13 52 20N 3 20W
Poyang Hu 75 29 5N 116 20 E
Poyarkovo 59 49 36N 128 41 E
Poysdorf 27 48 40N 16 37 E
Poza de la Sal 32 42 35N 3 31W
Poza Rica 120 20 33N 97 27W
Požarevac 42 44 35N 21 18 E
Požega 42 43 53N 20 2 E
Poznań 28 52 25N 16 55 E
Poznań □ 28 52 50N 17 0 E
Pozo Alcón 33 37 42N 2 56W
Pozo Almonte 126 20 10S 69 50W
Pozo Colorado 124 23 30S 58 45W
Pozoblanco 31 38 23N 4 51W
Pozzallo 41 36 44N 14 52 E
Pozzuoli 41 40 46N 14 6 E
Pra → 85 5 1N 1 37W
Prabuty 28 53 47N 19 15 E
Prača 42 43 47N 18 43 E
Prachatice 26 49 1N 14 0 E
Prachin Buri 71 14 0N 101 25 E
Prachuap Khiri Khan 71 11 49N 99 48 E
Pradelles 20 44 46N 3 52 E
Prades 20 42 38N 2 23 E
Prado 127 17 20S 39 13W
Prado del Rey 31 36 48N 5 33W
Præstø 49 55 8N 12 2 E
Pragersko 39 46 27N 15 42 E
Prague = Praha 26 50 5N 14 22 E
Praha 26 50 5N 14 22 E
Prahecq 20 46 19N 0 26W
Prahita → 70 19 0N 79 55 E
Prahova □ 46 45 10N 26 0 E
Prahova → 46 44 50N 25 50 E
Prahovo 42 44 18N 22 39 E
Praid 46 46 32N 25 10 E
Prainha, Amazonas, Brazil 126 7 10S 60 30W
Prainha, Pará, Brazil 127 1 45S 53 30W
Prairie 98 20 50S 144 35 E
Prairie → 117 34 30N 99 23W
Prairie City 118 44 27N 118 44W
Prairie du Chien 116 43 1N 91 9W
Praja 72 8 39S 116 17 E
Pramánda 44 39 32N 21 8 E
Prang 85 8 1N 0 56W
Prapat 72 2 41N 98 58 E
Praszka 28 51 5N 18 31 E
Prata 127 19 25S 48 54W
Prática di Mare 40 41 40N 12 26 E
Prato 38 43 53N 11 5 E
Prátola Peligna 39 42 7N 13 51 E
Pratovécchio 39 43 44N 11 43 E
Prats-de-Mollo 20 42 25N 2 27 E
Pratt 117 37 40N 98 45W
Prattville 115 32 30N 86 28W
Pravara → 70 19 35N 74 45 E
Pravdinsk 55 56 29N 43 28 E
Pravia 30 43 30N 6 12W
Pré-en-Pail 18 48 28N 0 12W
Pré St. Didier 38 45 45N 7 0 E
Precordillera 124 30 0S 69 1W
Predáppio 39 44 7N 11 58 E
Predazzo 39 46 19N 11 37 E
Predejane 42 42 51N 22 9 E
Preeceville 109 51 57N 102 40W
Préfailles 18 47 9N 2 11W
Pregrada 39 46 11N 15 45 E
Preko 39 44 7N 15 14 E
Prelate 109 50 51N 109 24W
Prelog 39 46 18N 16 32 E
Premier 108 56 4N 129 56W
Premier Downs 96 30 30S 126 30 E
Premont 117 27 19N 98 8W
Premuda 39 44 20N 14 36 E
Prenj 42 43 33N 17 53 E
Prenjasi 44 41 6N 20 32 E
Prentice 116 45 31N 90 19W
Prenzlau 24 53 19N 13 51 E
Prepansko Jezero 44 40 55N 21 0 E
Preparis North Channel 71 15 12N 93 40 E
Preparis South Channel 71 14 36N 93 40 E
Přerov 27 49 28N 17 27 E
Presanella 38 46 13N 10 40 E
Prescott, Can. 106 44 45N 75 30W
Prescott, Ariz., U.S.A. 119 34 35N 112 30W
Prescott, Ark., U.S.A. 117 33 49N 93 22W
Preservation Inlet 101 46 8S 166 35 E
Preševo 42 42 19N 21 39 E
Presho 116 43 56N 100 4W
Presicce 41 39 53N 18 13 E
Presidencia de la Plaza 124 27 0S 29 50W
Presidencia Roque Saenz Peña 124 26 45S 60 30W
Presidente Epitácio 127 21 56S 52 6W
Presidente Hayes □ 124 24 0S 59 0W
Presidente Hermes 126 11 17S 61 55W
Presidente Prudente 125 22 5S 51 25W
Presidio 117 29 30N 104 20W
Preslav 43 43 10N 26 52 E
Preslavska Planina 43 43 10N 26 45 E
Prešov 27 49 0N 21 15 E
Prespa 43 41 44N 24 55 E
Prespa, L. = Prepansko Jezero 44 40 55N 21 0 E
Presque Isle 107 46 40N 68 0W
Presseger See 26 46 37N 13 26 E
Prestbury 13 51 54N 2 2W
Prestea 84 5 22N 2 7W
Presteigne 13 52 17N 3 0W
Přeštice 26 49 34N 13 20 E
Preston, Can. 112 43 23N 80 21W
Preston, U.K. 12 53 46N 2 42W
Preston, Idaho, U.S.A. 118 42 10N 111 55W
Preston, Minn., U.S.A. 116 43 39N 92 3W
Preston, Nev., U.S.A. 118 38 59N 115 2W
Preston, C. 96 20 51S 116 12 E
Prestonpans 14 55 58N 3 0W
Prestwick 14 55 30N 4 38W
Pretoria 93 25 44S 28 12 E
Preuilly-sur-Claise 18 46 51N 0 56 E
Préveza 45 38 57N 20 47 E
Préveza □ 44 39 20N 20 40 E
Prey-Veng 71 11 35N 105 29 E
Priazovskoye 56 46 44N 35 40 E
Pribilof Is. 4 56 0N 170 0W
Priboj 42 43 35N 19 32 E
Pribram 26 49 41N 14 2 E
Price 118 39 40N 110 48W
Price I. 108 52 23N 128 41W
Prichalnaya 57 48 57N 44 33 E
Priego 32 40 26N 2 21W
Priego de Córdoba 31 37 27N 4 12W
Priekule 54 57 27N 21 45 E
Prien 25 47 52N 12 20 E
Prieska 92 29 40S 22 42 E
Priest L. 118 48 30N 116 55W
Priest River 118 48 11N 116 55W
Priestly 108 54 8N 125 20W
Prievidza 27 48 46N 18 36 E
Prijedor 39 44 58N 16 41 E
Prijepolje 42 43 27N 19 40 E
Prikaspiyskaya Nizmennost 57 47 0N 48 0 E
Prikumsk 56 44 50N 44 10 E
Prilep 42 41 21N 21 37 E
Priluki 58 50 30N 32 24 E
Primorsko 43 42 15N 27 44 E
Primorsko-Akhtarsk 56 46 2N 38 10 E
Primorskoye 56 47 10N 37 38 E
Primrose L. 109 54 55N 109 45W
Prince Albert 109 53 15N 105 50W
Prince Albert Mts. 5 76 0S 161 30 E
Prince Albert Nat. Park 109 54 0N 106 25W
Prince Albert Pen. 104 72 30N 116 0W
Prince Albert Sd. 104 70 25N 115 0W
Prince Alfred C. 4 74 20N 124 40W
Prince Charles I. 105 67 47N 76 12W
Prince Charles Mts. 5 72 0S 67 0 E
Prince Edward I. □ 107 46 20N 63 20W
Prince Edward Is. 3 45 15S 39 0 E
Prince George 108 53 55N 122 50W
Prince of Wales I. 104 55 30N 133 0W
Prince of Wales Is. 97 10 40S 142 10 E
Prince Patrick I. 4 77 0N 120 0W
Prince Regent Inlet 4 73 0N 90 0W
Prince Rupert 108 54 20N 130 20W
Princess Charlotte B. 97 14 25S 144 0 E
Princess Royal I. 108 53 0N 128 40W
Princeton, Can. 108 49 27N 120 30W
Princeton, Ill., U.S.A. 116 41 25N 89 25W
Princeton, Ind., U.S.A. 114 38 20N 87 35W
Princeton, Ky., U.S.A. 114 37 6N 87 55W
Princeton, Mo., U.S.A. 116 40 23N 93 35W
Princeton, N.J., U.S.A. 114 40 18N 74 40W
Princeton, W. Va., U.S.A. 114 37 21N 81 8W
Principe Chan. 108 53 28N 130 0W
Principe da Beira 126 12 20S 64 30W
Principe, I. de 79 1 37N 7 27 E
Prineville 118 44 17N 120 50W
Prins Albert 92 33 12S 22 2 E
Prins Harald Kyst 5 70 0S 35 1 E
Prinsesse Astrid Kyst 5 70 45S 12 30 E
Prinsesse Ragnhild Kyst 5 70 15S 27 30 E
Prior, C. 30 43 34N 8 17W
Priozersk 52 61 2N 30 7 E
Pripet = Pripyat → 54 51 20N 30 9 E
Pripet Marshes = Polesye 54 52 0N 28 10 E

Pripyat → 54 51 20N 30 9 E
Prislop, Pasul 46 47 37N 25 15 E
Pristen 55 51 15N 36 44 E
Priština 42 42 40N 21 13 E
Pritchard 115 30 47N 88 5W
Pritzwalk 24 53 10N 12 11 E
Privas 21 44 45N 4 37 E
Priverno 40 41 29N 13 10 E
Privolzhsk 55 57 23N 41 16 E
Privolzhskaya Vozvyshennost 55 51 0N 46 0 E
Privolzhskiy 55 51 25N 46 3 E
Privolzhye 55 52 52N 48 33 E
Priyutnoye 57 46 12N 43 40 E
Prizren 42 42 13N 20 45 E
Prizzi 40 37 44N 13 24 E
Prnjavor 42 44 52N 17 43 E
Probolinggo 73 7 46 S 113 13 E
Prochowice 28 51 17N 16 20 E
Procida 40 40 46N 14 0 E
Proddatur 70 14 45N 78 30 E
Proença-a-Nova 31 39 45N 7 54W
Progreso 120 21 20N 89 40W
Prokhladnyy 57 43 50N 44 2 E
Prokletije 44 42 30N 19 45 E
Prokopyevsk 58 54 0N 86 45 E
Prokuplje 42 43 16N 21 36 E
Proletarskaya 57 46 42N 41 50 E
Prome = Pyè 67 18 45N 95 30 E
Prophet → 108 58 48N 122 40W
Propriá 127 10 13 S 36 51W
Propriano 21 41 41N 8 52 E
Proserpine 97 20 21 S 148 36 E
Prosna 28 51 1N 18 30 E
Prosser 118 46 11N 119 52W
Prostějov 27 49 30N 17 9 E
Prostki 28 53 42N 22 25 E
Proston 99 26 8 S 151 32 E
Proszowice 27 50 13N 20 16 E
Protection 117 37 16N 99 30W
Próti 45 37 5N 21 32 E
Provadiya 43 43 12N 27 30 E
Provence 21 43 40N 5 46 E
Providence, Ky., U.S.A. 114 37 25N 87 46W
Providence, R.I., U.S.A. 114 41 50N 71 28W
Providence Bay 106 45 41N 82 15W
Providence Mts. 119 35 0N 115 30W
Providencia, I. de 121 13 25N 81 26W
Provideniya 59 64 23N 173 18W
Provins 19 48 33N 3 15 E
Provo 118 40 16N 111 37W
Provost 109 52 25N 110 20W
Prozor 42 43 50N 17 34 E
Prud'homme 109 52 20N 105 54W
Prudnik 28 50 20N 17 38 E
Prüm 25 50 14N 6 22 E
Pruszcz Gd. 28 54 17N 18 40 E
Pruszków 28 52 9N 20 49 E
Prut → 46 46 3N 28 10 E
Pruzhany 54 52 33N 24 28 E
Prvič 39 44 55N 14 47 E
Prydz B. 5 69 0 S 74 0 E
Pryor 117 36 17N 95 20W
Przasnysz 28 53 2N 20 45 E
Przedbórz 28 51 6N 19 53 E
Przedecz 28 52 20N 18 53 E
Przemyśl 27 49 50N 22 45 E
Przeworsk 27 50 6N 22 32 E
Przewóz 28 51 28N 14 57 E
Przhevalsk 58 42 30N 78 20 E
Przysuchla 28 51 22N 20 38 E
Psakhná 45 38 34N 23 35 E
Psará 45 38 37N 25 38 E
Psathoúra 44 39 30N 24 12 E
Psel → 56 49 5N 33 20 E
Pserimos 45 36 56N 27 12 E
Pskov 54 57 50N 28 25 E
Psunj 42 45 25N 17 19 E
Pszczyna 27 49 59N 18 58 E
Pteleón 45 39 3N 22 57 E
Ptich → 54 52 9N 28 52 E
Ptolemaís 44 40 30N 21 43 E
Ptuj 39 46 28N 15 50 E
Ptujska Gora 39 46 23N 15 47 E
Puán 124 37 30 S 62 45W
Pucallpa 126 8 25 S 74 30W
Pucheng 77 27 59N 118 31 E
Pucheni 46 45 12N 25 17 E
Pučišće 39 43 22N 16 43 E
Puck 28 54 45N 18 23 E
Pucka, Zatoka 28 54 30N 18 40 E
Pudozh 52 61 48N 36 32 E
Pudukkottai 70 10 28N 78 47 E
Puebla 120 19 0N 98 10W
Puebla □ 120 18 30N 98 0W
Puebla de Alcocer 31 38 59N 5 14W
Puebla de Cazalla, La 31 37 10N 5 20W
Puebla de Don Fadrique 33 37 58N 2 25W
Puebla de Don Rodrigo 31 39 5N 4 37W
Puebla de Guzmán 31 37 37N 7 15W
Puebla de los Infantes, La 31 37 47N 5 24W
Puebla de Montalbán, La 30 39 52N 4 22W
Puebla de Sanabria 30 42 4N 6 38W
Puebla de Trives 30 42 20N 7 10W
Puebla del Caramiñal 30 42 37N 8 56W
Puebla, La 32 39 46N 3 1 E
Pueblo 116 38 20N 104 40W
Pueblo Bonito 119 36 4N 107 57W
Pueblo Hundido 124 26 20 S 70 5W
Puelches 124 38 5 S 65 51W
Puelén 124 37 32 S 67 38W
Puente Alto 124 33 32 S 70 35W
Puente del Arzobispo 30 39 48N 5 10W
Puente-Genil 31 37 22N 4 47W
Puente la Reina 32 42 40N 1 49W
Puenteareas 30 42 10N 8 28W
Puentedeume 30 43 24N 8 10W
Puentes de Garcia Rodriguez 30 43 27N 7 50W
Puerco → 119 34 22N 107 50W
Puerta, La 33 38 22N 2 45W
Puerto Aisén 128 45 27 S 73 0W
Puerto Armuelles 121 8 20N 82 51W
Puerto Ayacucho 126 5 40N 67 35W
Puerto Barrios 120 15 40N 88 32W
Puerto Bermejo 124 26 55 S 58 34W
Puerto Bermúdez 126 10 20 S 75 0W
Puerto Bolívar 126 3 19 S 79 55W
Puerto Cabello 126 10 28N 68 1W
Puerto Cabezas 121 14 0N 83 30W
Puerto Capaz = Jebba 82 35 11N 4 43W
Puerto Carreño 126 6 12N 67 22W
Puerto Castilla 121 16 0N 86 0W
Puerto Chicama 126 7 45 S 79 20W
Puerto Coig 128 50 54 S 69 15W
Puerto Cortes 121 8 55N 84 0W
Puerto Cortés 120 15 51N 88 0W
Puerto Cumarebo 126 11 29N 69 30W
Puerto de Santa María 31 36 36N 6 13W
Puerto del Rosario 80 28 30N 13 52W
Puerto Deseado 128 47 55 S 66 0W
Puerto Heath 126 12 34 S 68 39W
Puerto Juárez 120 21 11N 86 49W
Puerto La Cruz 126 10 13N 64 38W
Puerto Leguízamo 126 0 12 S 74 46W
Puerto Libertad 120 29 55N 112 41W
Puerto Lobos 128 42 0 S 65 3W
Puerto Lumbreras 33 37 34N 1 48W
Puerto Madryn 128 42 48 S 65 4W
Puerto Maldonado 126 12 30 S 69 10W
Puerto Mazarrón 33 37 34N 1 15W
Puerto Montt 128 41 28 S 73 0W
Puerto Morelos 120 20 49N 86 52W
Puerto Natales 128 51 45 S 72 15W
Puerto Padre 121 21 13N 76 35W
Puerto Páez 126 6 13N 67 28W
Puerto Peñasco 120 31 20N 113 33W
Puerto Pinasco 124 22 36 S 57 50W
Puerto Pirámides 128 42 35 S 64 20W
Puerto Plata 121 19 48N 70 45W
Puerto Princesa 73 9 46N 118 45 E
Puerto Quellón 128 43 7 S 73 37W
Puerto Quepos 121 9 29N 84 6W
Puerto Real 31 36 33N 6 12W
Puerto Rico ■ 121 18 15N 66 45W
Puerto Sastre 124 22 2 S 57 55W
Puerto Suárez 126 18 58 S 57 52W
Puerto Vallarta 120 20 36N 105 15W
Puerto Wilches 126 7 21N 73 54W
Puertollano 31 38 43N 4 7W
Puertomarin 30 42 48N 7 36W
Pueyrredón, L. 128 47 20 S 72 0W
Pugachev 55 52 0N 48 49 E
Puge 90 4 45 S 33 11 E
Puget Sd. 118 47 15N 122 30W
Puget-Théniers 21 43 58N 6 53 E
Púglia □ 41 41 0N 16 30 E
Pugu 90 6 55 S 39 4 E
Pui 46 45 30N 23 4 E
Puieşti 46 46 25N 27 33 E
Puig Mayor, Mte. 32 39 48N 2 47 E
Puigcerdá 32 42 24N 1 50 E
Puigmal 32 42 23N 2 7 E
Puisaye, Collines de 19 47 34N 3 18 E
Puiseaux 19 48 11N 2 30 E
Puka 44 42 2N 19 53 E
Pukaki L. 101 44 4 S 170 1 E
Pukatawagan 109 55 45N 101 20W
Pukekohe 101 37 12 S 174 55 E
Pukou 77 32 7N 118 38 E
Pula 40 39 0N 9 0 E
Pula (Pola) 39 44 54N 13 57 E
Pulaski, N.Y., U.S.A. 114 43 32N 76 9W
Pulaski, Tenn., U.S.A. 115 35 10N 87 0W
Pulaski, Va., U.S.A. 114 37 4N 80 49W
Pulawy 28 51 23N 21 59 E
Pulgaon 68 20 44N 78 21 E
Pulicat, L. 70 13 40N 80 15 E
Puliyangudi 70 9 11N 77 24 E
Pullman 118 46 49N 117 10W
Pulog, Mt. 73 16 40N 120 50 E
Puloraja 72 4 55N 95 24 E
Pułtusk 28 52 43N 21 6 E
Pumlumon Fawr 13 52 29N 3 47W
Puna 126 19 45 S 65 28W
Puná, I. 126 2 55 S 80 5W
Punakha 69 27 42N 89 52 E
Punalur 70 9 0N 76 56 E
Punasar 68 27 6N 73 6 E
Punata 126 17 32 S 65 50W
Punch 69 33 48N 74 4 E
Pune 70 18 29N 73 57 E
Pungue, Ponte de 91 19 0 S 34 0 E
Puning 77 23 20N 116 12 E
Punjab □ 68 31 0N 76 0 E
Puno 126 15 55 S 70 3W
Punta Alta 128 38 53 S 62 4W
Punta Arenas 128 53 10 S 71 0W
Punta de Díaz 124 28 0 S 70 45W
Punta Gorda, Belize 120 16 10N 88 45W
Punta Gorda, U.S.A. 115 26 55N 82 0W
Puntarenas 121 10 0N 84 50W
Punto Fijo 126 11 50N 70 13W
Punxsutawney 114 40 56N 79 0W
Puqi 77 29 40N 113 50 E
Puquio 126 14 45 S 74 10W
Pur → 58 67 31N 77 55 E
Purace, Vol. 126 2 21N 76 23W
Puračić 42 44 33N 18 28 E
Purari → 98 7 49 S 145 0 E
Purbeck, Isle of 13 50 40N 2 5W
Purcell 117 35 0N 97 25W
Purchena Tetica 33 37 21N 2 21W
Puri 69 19 50N 85 58 E
Purli 68 18 50N 76 35 E
Purmerend 16 52 30N 4 58 E
Purna → 70 19 6N 77 2 E
Purnea 69 25 45N 87 31 E
Pursat 71 12 34N 103 50 E
Purukcahu 72 0 35 S 114 35 E
Purulia 69 23 17N 86 24 E
Purus → 126 3 42 S 61 28W
Pūrvomay 43 42 8N 25 17 E
Purwakarta 73 6 35 S 107 29 E
Purwodadi, Jawa, Indon. 73 7 51 S 110 0 E
Purwodadi, Jawa, Indon. 73 7 7 S 110 55 E
Purwokerto 73 7 25 S 109 14 E
Purworedjo 73 7 43 S 110 2 E
Pus → 70 19 55N 77 55 E
Pusad 70 19 56N 77 36 E
Pusan 76 35 5N 129 0 E
Pushchino 59 54 10N 158 0 E
Pushkin 54 59 45N 30 25 E
Pushkino, R.S.F.S.R., U.S.S.R. 55 51 16N 47 0 E
Pushkino, R.S.F.S.R., U.S.S.R. 55 56 2N 37 49 E
Püspökladány 27 47 19N 21 6 E
Pustoshka 54 56 20N 29 30 E
Puszczykowo 28 52 18N 16 49 E
Putahow L. 109 59 54N 100 40W
Putao 67 27 28N 97 30 E
Putaruru 101 38 2 S 175 50 E
Putbus 24 54 19N 13 29 E
Puţeni 46 45 49N 27 42 E
Puthein Myit → 67 15 56N 94 18 E
Putian 77 25 23N 119 0 E
Putignano 41 40 50N 17 5 E
Puting, Tanjung 72 3 31 S 111 46 E
Putlitz 24 53 15N 12 3 E
Putna 46 47 50N 25 33 E
Putna → 46 45 42N 27 26 E
Putnam 113 41 55N 71 55W
Putnok 27 48 18N 20 26 E
Putorana, Gory 59 69 0N 95 0 E
Puttalam Lagoon 70 8 15N 79 45 E
Putten 16 52 16N 5 36 E
Puttgarden 24 54 28N 11 15 E
Puttur 70 12 46N 75 12 E
Putumayo → 126 3 7 S 67 58W
Putussibau 72 0 50N 112 56 E
Puy-de-Dôme 20 45 46N 2 57 E
Puy-de-Dôme □ 20 45 47N 3 0 E
Puy-de-Sancy 20 45 32N 2 48 E
Puy-Guillaume 20 45 57N 3 29 E
Puy, Le 20 45 3N 3 52 E
Puy l'Évêque 20 44 31N 1 9 E
Puyallup 118 47 10N 122 22W
Puyang 76 35 40N 115 1 E
Puylaurens 20 43 35N 2 0 E
Puyôo 20 43 33N 0 56W
Pwani □ 90 7 0 S 39 0 E
Pweto 91 8 25 S 28 51 E
Pwllheli 12 52 54N 4 26W
Pya-ozero 52 66 5N 30 58 E
Pyana → 55 55 30N 46 0 E
Pyapon 67 16 20N 95 40 E
Pyasina → 59 73 30N 87 0 E
Pyatigorsk 57 44 2N 43 6 E
Pyatikhatki 56 48 28N 33 38 E
Pydna 44 40 20N 22 34 E
Pyinmana 67 19 45N 96 12 E
Pyŏngyang 76 39 0N 125 30 E
Pyote 117 31 34N 103 5W
Pyramid L. 118 40 0N 119 30W
Pyramids 86 29 58N 31 9 E
Pyrénées 20 42 45N 0 18 E
Pyrenees = Pyrénées 20 42 45N 0 18 E
Pyrénées-Atlantiques □ 20 43 15N 1 0W
Pyrénées-Orientales □ 20 42 35N 2 26 E
Pyrzyce 28 53 10N 14 55 E
Pyshchug 55 58 57N 45 47 E
Pytalovo 54 57 5N 27 55 E
Pyttegga 47 62 13N 7 42 E
Pyu 67 18 30N 96 28 E
Pyzdry 28 52 11N 17 42 E

Q

Qabalān 62 32 8N 35 17 E
Qabātiyah 62 32 25N 35 16 E
Qaidam Pendi 75 37 0N 95 0 E
Qa'iya 64 24 33N 43 15 E
Qal' at Shajwa 86 25 2N 38 57 E
Qala-i-Jadid (Spin Baldak) 68 31 1N 66 25 E
Qalāt 65 32 15N 66 58 E
Qal'at al Akhḑar 64 28 0N 37 10 E
Qal'at al Mu'azzam 64 27 45N 37 31 E
Qal'at Saura 86 26 10N 38 40 E
Qal'eh-ye Now 65 35 0N 63 5 E
Qalqīlya 62 32 12N 34 58 E
Qalyūb 86 30 12N 31 11 E
Qam 62 32 36N 35 43 E
Qamar, Ghubbat al 63 16 20N 52 30 E
Qamruddin Karez 68 31 45N 68 20 E
Qāna 62 33 12N 35 17 E
Qâra 86 29 38N 26 30 E
Qarachuk 64 37 0N 42 2 E
Qārah 64 29 55N 40 3 E
Qardud 87 10 20N 29 56 E
Qarqan 75 38 5N 85 20 E
Qarqan He → 75 39 30N 88 30 E
Qarrasa 87 14 38N 32 5 E
Qasim 64 26 0N 43 0 E
Qāsim 62 32 59N 36 2 E
Qaşr Bū Hadi 83 31 1N 16 45 E
Qaşr-e Qand 65 26 15N 60 45 E
Qasr Farâfra 86 27 0N 28 1 E
Qatar ■ 65 25 30N 51 15 E
Qattâra 86 30 12N 27 3 E
Qattâra Depression = Qattâra, Munkhafed el 86 29 30N 27 30 E
Qattâra, Munkhafed el 86 29 30N 27 30 E
Qāyen 65 33 40N 59 10 E
Qazvin 64 36 15N 50 0 E
Qena 86 26 10N 32 43 E
Qena, Wadi → 86 26 12N 32 44 E
Qeshm 65 26 55N 56 10 E
Qezi'ot 62 30 52N 34 26 E
Qian Xian 77 34 31N 108 15 E
Qianshan 77 30 37N 116 35 E
Qianxi 77 27 3N 106 3 E
Qianyang 77 27 18N 110 10 E
Qijiang 77 28 57N 106 35 E
Qila Safed 66 29 0N 61 30 E
Qila Saifulla 68 30 45N 68 17 E
Qilian Shan 75 38 30N 96 0 E
Qin Ling = Qinling Shandi 77 33 50N 108 10 E
Qin'an 77 34 48N 105 40 E
Qingdao 76 36 5N 120 20 E
Qinghai □ 75 36 0N 98 0 E
Qinghai Hu 75 36 40N 100 10 E
Qingjiang, Jiangsu, China 77 33 30N 119 2 E
Qingjiang, Jiangxi, China 77 28 4N 115 29 E
Qingliu 77 26 11N 116 48 E
Qingshuihe 76 39 55N 111 35 E
Qingyang 76 36 2N 107 55 E
Qingyuan 77 23 40N 112 59 E
Qinhuangdao 76 39 56N 119 30 E
Qinling Shandi 77 33 50N 108 10 E
Qinyang 77 35 7N 112 57 E
Qinyuan 76 36 29N 112 20 E
Qinzhou 75 21 58N 108 38 E
Qiongshan 77 19 51N 110 26 E
Qiongzhou Haixia 77 20 10N 110 15 E
Qiqihar 75 47 26N 124 0 E
Qiryat 'Anavim 62 31 49N 35 7 E
Qiryat Ata 62 32 47N 35 6 E
Qiryat Bialik 62 32 50N 35 5 E
Qiryat Gat 62 31 32N 34 46 E
Qiryat Hayyim 62 32 49N 35 4 E
Qiryat Mal'akhi 62 31 44N 34 44 E
Qiryat Shemona 62 33 13N 35 35 E
Qiryat Yam 62 32 51N 35 4 E
Qishan 77 22 52N 120 25 E
Qishon → 62 32 49N 35 2 E
Qishrān 86 20 14N 40 2 E
Qitai 75 44 2N 89 35 E
Qiyahe 76 53 0N 120 35 E
Qiyang 77 26 35N 111 50 E
Qizan 87 16 57N 42 34 E
Qizān 63 17 0N 42 20 E
Qom 65 34 40N 51 0 E
Qomolangma Feng (Mt. Everest) 75 28 0N 86 45 E
Qondūz 65 36 50N 68 50 E
Qondūz □ 65 36 50N 68 50 E
Qu Jiang → 77 30 1N 106 24 E
Qu Xian, Sichuan, China 77 30 48N 106 58 E
Qu Xian, Zhejiang, China 75 28 57N 118 54 E
Quackenbrück 24 52 40N 7 59 E
Quakertown 113 40 27N 75 20W
Quambatook 99 35 49 S 143 34 E
Quambone 99 30 57 S 147 53 E
Quan Long = Ca Mau 71 9 7N 105 8 E
Quanan 117 34 20N 99 45W
Quandialla 99 34 1 S 147 47 E
Quang Ngai 71 15 13N 108 58 E
Quang Yen 71 20 56N 106 52 E
Quantock Hills 13 51 8N 3 10W
Quanzhou, Fujian, China 75 24 55N 118 34 E
Quanzhou, Guangxi Zhuangzu, China 77 25 57N 111 5 E
Quaraí 124 30 15 S 56 20W
Quarré-les-Tombes 19 47 21N 4 0 E
Quartu Sant' Elena 40 39 15N 9 10 E
Quartzsite 119 33 44N 114 16W
Quatsino 108 50 30N 127 40W
Quatsino Sd. 108 50 25N 127 58W
Qubab = Mishmar Ayyalon 62 31 52N 34 57 E
Qūchān 65 37 10N 58 27 E
Que Que † 91 18 58 S 29 48 E
Queanbeyan 97 35 17 S 149 14 E
Québec 107 46 52N 71 13W
Québec □ 107 50 0N 70 0W
Quedlinburg 24 51 47N 11 9 E
Queen Alexandra Ra. 5 85 0 S 170 0 E
Queen Charlotte 108 53 15N 132 2W
Queen Charlotte Is. 108 53 20N 132 10W
Queen Charlotte Str. 108 51 0N 128 0W
Queen Elizabeth Is. 102 76 0N 95 0W
Queen Elizabeth Nat. Park 90 0 0 S 30 0 E
Queen Mary Coast 5 70 0 S 95 0 E
Queen Maud G. 104 68 15N 102 30W
Queen Maud Ra. 5 86 0 S 160 0W
Queens Chan. 96 15 0 S 129 30 E
Queenscliff 97 38 16 S 144 39 E
Queensland □ 97 22 0 S 142 0 E
Queenstown, Austral. 97 42 4 S 145 35 E
Queenstown, N.Z. 101 45 1 S 168 40 E
Queenstown, S. Afr. 92 31 52 S 26 52 E
Queguay Grande → 124 32 9 S 58 9W
Queimadas 127 11 0 S 39 38W
Quela 88 9 10 S 16 56 E
Quelimane 91 17 53 S 36 58 E
Quelpart = Cheju Do 77 33 29N 126 34 E
Quemado, N. Mex., U.S.A. 119 34 17N 108 28W
Quemado, Tex., U.S.A. 117 28 58N 100 35W
Quemú-Quemú 124 36 3 S 63 36W
Quequén 124 38 30 S 58 30W
Querétaro 120 20 40N 100 23W
Querétaro □ 120 20 30N 100 0W
Querfurt 24 51 22N 11 33 E
Querqueville 18 49 40N 1 42W
Quesada 33 37 51N 3 4W
Queshan 77 32 55N 114 2 E
Quesnel 108 53 0N 122 30W
Quesnel → 108 52 58N 122 29W
Quesnel L. 108 52 30N 121 20W
Quesnoy, Le 19 50 15N 3 38 E
Questa 119 36 45N 105 35W
Questembert 18 47 40N 2 28W
Quetico Prov. Park 106 48 30N 91 45W
Quetta 66 30 15N 66 55 E
Quetta □ * 66 30 15N 66 55 E
Quezaltenango 120 14 50N 91 30W
Quezon City 73 14 38N 121 0 E
Qui Nhon 71 13 40N 109 13 E
Quiaca, La 124 22 5 S 65 35W
Quibaxe 88 8 24 S 14 27 E
Quibdo 126 5 42N 76 40W
Quiberon 18 47 29N 3 9W
Quick 108 54 36N 126 54W
Quickborn 24 53 42N 9 52 E
Quiet L. 108 61 5N 133 5W
Quiindy 124 25 58 S 57 14W
Quilán, C. 128 43 15 S 74 30W
Quilengues 89 14 12 S 14 12 E
Quilimarí 124 32 5 S 71 30W
Quilino 124 30 14 S 64 29W
Quillabamba 126 12 50 S 72 50W

* *Now part of Baluchistan □*

† *Renamed Kwekwe*

Quillagua 124 21 40 S 69 40W
Quillaicillo 124 31 17 S 71 40W
Quillan 20 42 53N 2 10 E
Quillebeuf 18 49 28N 0 30 E
Quillota 124 32 54 S 71 16W
Quilmes 124 34 43 S 58 15W
Quilon 70 8 50N 76 38 E
Quilpie 97 26 35 S 144 11 E
Quilpué 124 33 5 S 71 33W
Quilua 91 16 17 S 39 54 E
Quimilí 124 27 40 S 62 30W
Quimper 18 48 0N 4 9W
Quimperlé 18 47 53N 3 33W
Quincy, Calif., U.S.A. 118 39 56N 121 0W
Quincy, Fla., U.S.A. 115 30 34N 84 34W
Quincy, Ill., U.S.A. 116 39 55N 91 20W
Quincy, Mass., U.S.A. 114 42 14N 71 0W
Quincy, Wash., U.S.A. 118 47 22N 119 56W
Quines 124 32 13 S 65 48W
Quinga 91 15 49 S 40 15 E
Quingey 19 47 7N 5 52 E
Quintana de la Serena 31 38 45N 5 40W
Quintana Roo □ 120 19 0N 88 0W
Quintanar de la Orden 32 39 36N 3 5W
Quintanar de la Sierra 32 41 57N 2 55W
Quintanar del Rey 33 39 21N 1 56W
Quintero 124 32 45 S 71 30W
Quintin 18 48 26N 2 56W
Quinto 32 41 25N 0 32W
Quinyambie 99 30 15 S 141 0 E
Quípar → 33 38 15N 1 40W
Quirihue 124 36 15 S 72 35W
Quirindi 99 31 28 S 150 40 E
Quiroga 30 42 28N 7 18W
Quissac 21 43 55N 4 0 E
Quissanga 91 12 24 S 40 28 E
Quitilipi 124 26 50 S 60 13W
Quitman, Ga., U.S.A. 115 30 49N 83 35W
Quitman, Miss., U.S.A. 115 32 2N 88 42W
Quitman, Tex., U.S.A. 117 32 48N 95 25W
Quito 126 0 15 S 78 35W
Quixadá 127 4 55 S 39 0W
Quixaxe 91 15 17 S 40 4 E
Qul'ân, Jazâ'ir 86 24 22N 35 31 E
Qumrān 62 31 43N 35 27 E
Quneitra 62 33 7N 35 48 E
Quoin Pt. 92 34 46 S 19 37 E
Quondong 99 33 6 S 140 18 E
Quorn 97 32 25 S 138 0 E
Qurein 87 13 30N 34 50 E
Qûs 86 25 55N 32 50 E
Quseir 86 26 7N 34 16 E
Qusrah 62 32 5N 35 20 E
Quthing 93 30 25 S 27 36 E
Qytet Stalin (Kuçove) 44 40 47N 19 57 E

R

Råå 49 56 0N 12 45 E
Raab 26 48 21N 13 39 E
Raahe 50 64 40N 24 28 E
Ra'ananna 62 32 12N 34 52 E
Raasay 14 57 25N 6 4W
Raasay, Sd. of 14 57 30N 6 8W
Rab 39 44 45N 14 45 E
Raba 73 8 36 S 118 55 E
Rába → 27 47 38N 17 38 E
Raba → 27 50 8N 20 30 E
Rabaçal → 30 41 30N 7 12W
Rabah 85 13 5N 5 30 E
Rabai 90 3 50 S 39 31 E
Rabastens, Hautes-Pyrénées, France 20 43 25N 0 10 E
Rabastens, Tarn, France 20 43 50N 1 43 E
Rabat, Malta 36 35 53N 14 25 E
Rabat, Moroc. 82 34 2N 6 48W
Rabaul 94 4 24 S 152 18 E
Rabbit → 108 59 41N 127 12W
Rabbit Lake 109 53 8N 107 46W
Rabbitskin → 108 61 47N 120 42W
Rābigh 64 22 50N 39 5 E
Rabka 27 49 37N 19 59 E
Rača 42 44 14N 21 0 E
Rácale 41 39 57N 18 6 E
Racalmuto 40 37 25N 13 41 E
Răcăşdia 42 44 59N 21 36 E
Racconigi 38 44 47N 7 41 E
Race, C. 107 46 40N 53 5W
Rach Gia 71 10 5N 105 5 E
Raciąż 28 52 46N 20 10 E
Racibórz 27 50 7N 18 18 E
Racine 114 42 41N 87 51W
Radama, Nosy 93 14 0 S 47 47 E
Radama, Saikanosy 93 14 16 S 47 53 E
Radan 42 42 59N 21 29 E
Rădăuţi 46 47 50N 25 59 E
Radbuza → 26 49 35N 13 5 E
Räde 47 59 21N 10 53 E
Radeburg 24 51 6N 13 55 E
Radeče 39 46 5N 15 14 E
Radekhov 54 50 25N 24 32 E
Radew → 28 54 2N 15 52 E
Radford 114 37 8N 80 32W
Radhanpur 68 23 50N 71 38 E
Radhwa, Jabal 64 24 34N 38 18 E
Radiska → 42 41 38N 20 37 E
Radisson 109 52 30N 107 20W
Radium Hill 97 32 30 S 140 42 E
Radium Hot Springs 108 50 35N 116 2W
Radja, Kepulauan 73 0 30 S 130 00 E
Radków 28 50 30N 16 24 E
Radlin 27 50 3N 18 29 E
Radna 42 46 7N 21 41 E
Radnevo 43 42 17N 25 58 E
Radnice 26 49 51N 13 35 E
Radnor Forest 13 52 17N 3 10W
Radolfzell 25 47 44N 8 58 E
Radom 28 51 23N 21 12 E
Radom □ 28 51 30N 21 0 E
Radomir 42 42 37N 23 4 E
Radomka → 28 51 31N 21 11 E
Radomsko 28 51 5N 19 28 E
Radomyshl 54 50 30N 29 12 E
Radomysl Wielki 27 50 14N 21 15 E
Radoszyce 28 51 4N 20 15 E
Radoviš 42 41 38N 22 28 E
Radovljica 39 46 22N 14 12 E
Radstadt 26 47 24N 13 28 E
Radstock 13 51 17N 2 25W
Răducăneni 46 46 58N 27 54 E
Raduša 42 42 7N 21 15 E
Radviliškis 54 55 49N 23 33 E
Radville 109 49 30N 104 15W
Radymno 27 49 59N 22 52 E
Radzanów 28 52 56N 20 8 E
Radziejów 28 52 40N 18 30 E
Radzymin 28 52 25N 21 11 E
Radzyń Chełmiński 28 53 23N 18 55 E
Radzyń Podlaski 28 51 47N 22 37 E
Rae 108 62 50N 116 3W
Rae Bareli 69 26 18N 81 20 E
Rae Isthmus 105 66 40N 87 30W
Raeren 16 50 41N 6 7 E
Raeside, L. 96 29 20 S 122 0 E
Raetihi 101 39 25 S 175 17 E
Rafaela 124 31 10 S 61 30W
Rafah 86 31 18N 34 14 E
Rafai 90 4 59N 23 58 E
Raffadali 40 37 23N 13 29 E
Rafḥā 64 29 35N 43 35 E
Rafsanjān 65 30 30N 56 5 E
Ragag 87 10 59N 24 40 E
Raglan, Austral. 98 23 42 S 150 49 E
Raglan, N.Z. 101 37 55 S 174 55 E
Ragunda 48 63 6N 16 23 E
Ragusa 41 36 56N 14 42 E
Raha 73 4 55 S 123 0 E
Rahad al Bardī 81 11 20N 23 40 E
Rahad, Nahr ed → 87 14 28N 33 31 E
Rahden 24 52 26N 8 36 E
Raheita 87 12 46N 43 4 E
Rahimyar Khan 68 28 30N 70 25 E
Raichur 70 16 10N 77 20 E
Raiganj 69 25 37N 88 10 E
Raigarh, Madhya Pradesh, India 69 21 56N 83 25 E
Raigarh, Orissa, India 70 19 51N 82 6 E
Raiis 64 23 33N 38 43 E
Raijua 73 10 37 S 121 36 E
Railton 99 41 25 S 146 28 E
Rainbow Lake 108 58 30N 119 23W
Rainier 118 46 4N 123 0W
Rainier, Mt. 118 46 50N 121 50W
Rainy L. 109 48 42N 93 10W
Rainy River 109 48 43N 94 29W
Raipur 69 21 17N 81 45 E
Raja, Kepulauan 73 0 30 S 129 40 E
Raja, Ujung 72 3 40N 96 25 E
Rajahmundry 70 17 1N 81 48 E
Rajang → 72 2 30N 112 0 E
Rajapalaiyam 70 9 25N 77 35 E
Rajasthan □ 68 26 45N 73 30 E
Rajasthan Canal 68 28 0N 72 0 E
Rajbari 69 23 47N 89 41 E
Rajgarh, Mad. P., India 68 24 2N 76 45 E
Rajgarh, Raj., India 68 28 40N 75 25 E
Rajgród 28 53 42N 22 42 E
Rajhenburg 39 46 1N 15 29 E
Rajkot 68 22 15N 70 56 E
Rajmahal Hills 69 24 30N 87 30 E
Rajnandgaon 69 21 5N 81 5 E
Rajojooseppi 50 68 25N 28 30 E
Rajpipla 68 21 50N 73 30 E
Rajpura 68 30 25N 76 32 E
Rajshahi 69 24 22N 88 39 E
Rajshahi □ 69 25 0N 89 0 E
Rakaia 101 43 45 S 172 1 E
Rakaia → 101 43 36 S 172 15 E
Rakan, Ra's 65 26 10N 51 20 E
Rakaposhi 69 36 10N 74 25 E
Rakha 86 18 25N 41 30 E
Rakhni 68 30 4N 69 56 E
Rakitovo 43 41 59N 24 5 E
Rakkestad 47 59 25N 11 21 E
Rakoniewice 28 52 10N 16 16 E
Rakops 92 21 1 S 24 28 E
Rákospalota 27 47 30N 19 5 E
Rakov 54 53 58N 26 59 E
Rakovica 39 44 59N 15 38 E
Rakovník 26 50 6N 13 42 E
Rakovski 43 42 21N 24 57 E
Rakvere 54 59 30N 26 25 E
Raleigh 115 35 47N 78 39W
Raleigh B. 115 34 50N 76 15W
Ralja 42 44 33N 20 34 E
Ralls 117 33 40N 101 20W
Ram → 108 62 1N 123 41W
Rām Allāh 62 31 55N 35 10 E
Rama 62 32 56N 35 21 E
Ramacca 41 37 24N 14 40 E
Ramachandrapuram 70 16 50N 82 4 E
Ramales de la Victoria 32 43 15N 3 28W
Ramanathapuram 70 9 25N 78 55 E
Ramanetaka, B. de 93 14 13 S 47 52 E
Ramas C. 70 15 5N 73 55 E
Ramat Gan 62 32 4N 34 48 E
Ramat HaSharon 62 32 7N 34 50 E
Ramatlhabama 92 25 37 S 25 33 E
Rambervillers 19 48 20N 6 38 E
Rambipuji 73 8 12 S 113 37 E
Rambla, La 31 37 37N 4 45W
Rambouillet 19 48 40N 1 48 E
Ramdurg 70 15 58N 75 22 E
Rame Hd. 99 37 47 S 149 30 E
Ramea 107 47 28N 57 4W
Ramechhap 69 27 25N 86 10 E
Ramelau 73 8 55 S 126 22 E
Ramenskoye 55 55 32N 38 15 E
Ramgarh, Bihar, India 69 23 40N 85 35 E
Ramgarh, Rajasthan, India 68 27 16N 75 14 E
Ramgarh, Rajasthan, India 68 27 30N 70 36 E
Rāmhormoz 64 31 15N 49 35 E
Ramla 62 31 55N 34 52 E
Ramlat Zalṭan 83 28 30N 19 30 E
Ramlu 87 13 32N 41 40 E
Ramme 49 56 30N 8 11 E
Rammūn 62 31 55N 35 17 E
Ramnad = Ramanathapuram 70 9 25N 78 55 E
Ramnäs 48 59 46N 16 12 E
Ramon 55 51 55N 39 21 E
Ramon, Har 62 30 30N 34 38 E
Ramona 119 33 1N 116 56W
Ramore 106 48 30N 80 25W
Ramos → 120 25 35N 105 3W
Ramoutsa 92 24 50 S 25 52 E
Rampart 104 65 0N 150 15W
Rampur, H.P., India 68 31 26N 77 43 E
Rampur, Mad. P., India 68 23 25N 73 53 E
Rampur, Orissa, India 69 21 48N 83 58 E
Rampur, U.P., India 68 28 50N 79 5 E
Rampura 68 24 30N 75 27 E
Rampurhat 69 24 10N 87 50 E
Ramree Kyun 67 19 0N 94 0 E
Ramsey, Can. 106 47 25N 82 20W
Ramsey, U.K. 12 54 20N 4 21W
Ramsgate 13 51 20N 1 25 E
Ramsjö 48 62 11N 15 37 E
Ramtek 69 21 20N 79 15 E
Ramu → 98 4 0 S 144 41 E
Ramvik 48 62 49N 17 51 E
Ranaghat 69 23 15N 88 35 E
Ranahu 68 25 55N 69 45 E
Ranau 72 6 2N 116 40 E
Rancagua 124 34 10 S 70 50W
Rance → 18 48 34N 1 59W
Rance, Barrage de la 18 48 30N 2 3W
Rancheria → 108 60 13N 129 7W
Ranchester 118 44 57N 107 12W
Ranchi 69 23 19N 85 27 E
Rancu 46 44 32N 24 15 E
Rand 100 35 33 S 146 32 E
Randan 20 46 2N 3 21 E
Randazzo 41 37 53N 14 56 E
Randers 49 56 29N 10 1 E
Randers Fjord 49 56 37N 10 20 E
Randfontein 93 26 8 S 27 45 E
Randolph, Mass., U.S.A. 113 42 10N 71 3W
Randolph, N.Y., U.S.A. 112 42 10N 78 59W
Randolph, Utah, U.S.A. 118 41 43N 111 10W
Randolph, Vt., U.S.A. 113 43 55N 72 39W
Randsburg 119 35 22N 117 44W
Randsfjorden 47 60 15N 10 25 E
Råne älv → 50 65 50N 22 20 E
Rangaunu B. 101 34 51 S 173 15 E
Rångedala 49 57 47N 13 9 E
Rangeley 114 44 58N 70 33W
Rangely 118 40 3N 108 53W
Ranger 117 32 30N 98 42W
Rangia 67 26 28N 91 38 E
Rangiora 101 43 19 S 172 36 E
Rangitaiki → 101 37 54 S 176 49 E
Rangitata → 101 43 45 S 171 15 E
Rangkasbitung 73 6 22 S 106 16 E
Rangon → 67 16 28N 96 40 E
Rangoon 67 16 45N 96 20 E
Ranibennur 70 14 35N 75 30 E
Raniganj 69 23 40N 87 5 E
Ranipet 70 12 56N 79 23 E
Rankin 117 31 16N 101 56W
Rankin Inlet 104 62 30N 93 0W
Rankins Springs 99 33 49 S 146 14 E
Rannoch, L. 14 56 41N 4 20W
Rannoch Moor 14 56 38N 4 48W
Ranobe, Helodranon' i 93 23 3 S 43 33 E
Ranohira 93 22 29 S 45 24 E
Ranomafana, Tamatave, Madag. 93 18 57 S 48 50 E
Ranomafana, Tuléar, Madag. 93 24 34 S 47 0 E
Ranong 71 9 56N 98 40 E
Ransiki 73 1 30 S 134 10 E
Rantau 72 2 56 S 115 9 E
Rantauprapat 72 2 15N 99 50 E
Rantemario 73 3 15 S 119 57 E
Rantīs 62 32 4N 35 3 E
Rantoul 114 40 18N 88 10W
Ranum 49 56 54N 9 14 E
Ranwanlenau 92 19 37 S 22 49 E
Raohe 76 46 47N 134 0 E
Raon l'Étape 19 48 24N 6 50 E
Raoui, Erg er 82 29 0N 2 0W
Rapa Iti 95 27 35 S 144 20W
Rapallo 38 44 21N 9 12 E
Rapang 73 3 45 S 119 55 E
Rāpch 65 25 40N 59 15 E
Rapid → 108 59 15N 129 5W
Rapid City 116 44 0N 103 0W
Rapid River 114 45 55N 87 0W
Rapides des Joachims 106 46 13N 77 43W
Rapla 54 59 1N 24 52 E
Rarotonga 95 21 30 S 160 0W
Ra's al Khaymah 65 25 50N 56 5 E
Ra's al-Unuf 83 30 25N 18 15 E
Ras Bânâs 81 23 57N 35 59 E
Ras Dashen 87 13 8N 38 26 E
Ras el Ma 82 34 26N 0 50W
Ras Mallap 86 29 18N 32 50 E
Ra's Tannūrah 64 26 40N 50 10 E
Râs Timirist 84 19 21N 16 30W
Rasa, Punta 128 40 50 S 62 15W
Raseiniai 54 55 25N 23 5 E
Rashad 87 11 55N 31 0 E
Rashîd 86 31 21N 30 22 E
Rashîd, Masabb 86 31 22N 30 17 E
Rasht 64 37 20N 49 40 E
Rasipuram 70 11 30N 78 15 E
Raška 42 43 19N 20 39 E
Rason, L. 96 28 45 S 124 25 E
Raşova 46 44 15N 27 55 E
Rasovo 43 43 42N 23 17 E
Rasra 69 25 50N 83 50 E
Rass el Oued 83 35 57N 5 2 E
Rasskazovo 55 52 35N 41 50 E
Rastatt 25 48 50N 8 12 E
Rastu 46 43 53N 23 16 E
Raszków 28 51 43N 17 40 E
Rat Buri 71 13 30N 99 54 E
Rat Is. 104 51 50N 178 15 E
Rat River 108 61 7N 112 36W
Ratangarh 68 28 5N 74 35 E
Rath 69 25 36N 79 37 E
Rath Luirc (Charleville) 15 52 21N 8 40W
Rathdrum, Ireland 15 52 57N 6 13W
Rathdrum, U.S.A. 118 47 50N 116 58W
Rathenow 24 52 38N 12 23 E
Rathkeale 15 52 32N 8 57W
Rathlin I. 15 55 18N 6 14W
Rathlin O'Birne I. 15 54 40N 8 50W
Ratibor = Racibórz 27 50 7N 18 18 E
Rätikon 26 47 0N 9 55 E
Ratlam 68 23 20N 75 0 E
Ratnagiri 70 16 57N 73 18 E
Ratnapura 70 6 40N 80 20 E
Raton 117 37 0N 104 30W
Ratten 26 47 28N 15 44 E
Rattray Hd. 14 57 38N 1 50W
Rättvik 48 60 52N 15 7 E
Ratz, Mt. 108 57 23N 132 12W
Ratzeburg 24 53 41N 10 46 E
Raub 71 3 47N 101 52 E
Rauch 124 36 45 S 59 5W
Raufarhöfn 50 66 27N 15 57W
Raufoss 47 60 44N 10 37 E
Raukumara Ra. 101 38 5 S 177 55 E
Rauland 47 59 43N 8 0 E
Rauma 51 61 10N 21 30 E
Rauma → 47 62 34N 7 43 E
Raundal 47 60 40N 6 37 E
Raung 73 8 8 S 114 4 E
Raurkela 69 22 14N 84 50 E
Rava Russkaya 54 50 15N 23 42 E
Ravanusa 40 37 16N 13 58 E
Rāvar 65 31 20N 56 51 E
Ravena 113 42 28N 73 49W
Ravenna, Italy 39 44 28N 12 15 E
Ravenna, Nebr., U.S.A. 116 41 3N 98 58W
Ravenna, Ohio, U.S.A. 112 41 11N 81 15W
Ravensburg 25 47 48N 9 38 E
Ravenshoe 97 17 37 S 145 29 E
Ravensthorpe 96 33 35 S 120 2 E
Ravenswood, Austral. 98 20 6 S 146 54 E
Ravenswood, U.S.A. 114 38 58N 81 47W
Ravi → 68 30 35N 71 49 E
Ravna Gora 39 45 24N 14 50 E
Ravna Reka 42 43 59N 21 35 E
Rawa Mazowiecka 28 51 46N 20 12 E
Rawalpindi 66 33 38N 73 8 E
Rawāndūz 64 36 40N 44 30 E
Rawang 71 3 20N 101 35 E
Rawdon 106 46 3N 73 40W
Rawene 101 35 25 S 173 32 E
Rawicz 28 51 36N 16 52 E
Rawka → 28 52 9N 20 8 E
Rawlinna 96 30 58 S 125 28 E
Rawlins 118 41 50N 107 20W
Rawlinson Range 96 24 40 S 128 30 E
Rawson 128 43 15 S 65 0W
Ray 116 48 21N 103 6W
Ray, C. 107 47 33N 59 15W
Rayachoti 70 14 4N 78 50 E
Rayadrug 70 14 40N 76 50 E
Rayagada 70 19 15N 83 20 E
Raychikhinsk 59 49 46N 129 25 E
Raymond, Can. 108 49 30N 112 35W
Raymond, U.S.A. 118 46 45N 123 48W
Raymondville 117 26 30N 97 50W
Raymore 109 51 25N 104 31W
Rayne 117 30 16N 92 16W
Rayong 71 12 40N 101 20 E
Rayville 117 32 30N 91 45W
Raz, Pte. du 18 48 2N 4 47W
Ražana 42 44 6N 19 55 E
Ražanj 42 43 40N 21 31 E
Razdelna 43 43 13N 27 41 E
Razdel'naya 56 46 50N 30 2 E
Razdolnoye 56 45 46N 33 29 E
Razelm, Lacul 46 44 50N 29 0 E
Razgrad 43 43 33N 26 34 E
Razlog 43 41 53N 23 28 E
Razmak 68 32 45N 69 50 E
Razole 70 16 36N 81 48 E
Ré, Île de 20 46 12N 1 30W
Reading, U.K. 13 51 27N 0 57W
Reading, U.S.A. 114 40 20N 75 53W
Realicó 124 35 0 S 64 15W
Réalmont 20 43 48N 2 10 E
Ream 71 10 34N 103 39 E
Rebais 19 48 50N 3 10 E
Rebi 73 6 23 S 134 7 E
Rebiana 81 24 12N 22 10 E
Rebun-Tō 74 45 23N 141 2 E
Recanati 39 43 24N 13 32 E
Recaş 42 45 46N 21 30 E
Recherche, Arch. of the 96 34 15 S 122 50 E
Rechitsa 54 52 13N 30 15 E
Recife 127 8 0 S 35 0W
Recklinghausen 24 51 36N 7 10 E
Reconquista 124 29 10 S 59 45W
Recreo 124 29 25 S 65 10W
Recz 28 53 16N 15 31 E
Red →, Can. 109 50 24N 96 48W
Red →, Minn., U.S.A. 116 48 10N 97 0W
Red →, Tex., U.S.A. 117 31 0N 91 40W
Red Bank 113 40 21N 74 4W
Red Bay 107 51 44N 56 25W
Red Bluff 118 40 11N 122 11W
Red Bluff L. 117 31 59N 103 58W
Red Cloud 116 40 8N 98 33W
Red Deer 108 52 20N 113 50W
Red Deer →, Alta., Can. 109 50 58N 110 0W
Red Deer →, Man., Can. 109 52 53N 101 1W
Red Deer L. 109 52 55N 101 20W
Red Indian L. 107 48 35N 57 0W
Red Lake 109 51 3N 93 49W
Red Lake Falls 116 47 54N 96 15W
Red Lodge 118 45 10N 109 10W
Red Oak 116 41 0N 95 10W
Red Rock 106 48 55N 88 15W
Red Rock, L. 116 41 30N 93 15W

Red Sea 63 25 0N 36 0 E
Red Sucker L 109 54 9N 93 40W
Red Tower Pass = Turnu Rosu P. 46 45 33N 24 17 E
Red Wing 116 44 32N 92 35W
Reda 28 54 40N 18 19 E
Redbridge 13 51 35N 0 7 E
Redcar 12 54 37N 1 4W
Redcliff 109 50 10N 110 50W
Redcliffe 99 27 12 S 153 0 E
Reddersburg 92 29 41 S 26 10 E
Redding 118 40 30N 122 25W
Redditch 13 52 18N 1 57W
Redfield 116 45 0N 98 30W
Redknife → 108 61 14N 119 22W
Redlands 119 34 0N 117 11W
Redmond 118 44 19N 121 11W
Redon 18 47 40N 2 6W
Redonda 121 16 58N 62 19W
Redondela 30 42 15N 8 38W
Redondo 31 38 39N 7 37W
Redondo Beach 119 33 52N 118 26W
Redrock Pt. 108 62 11N 115 2W
Redruth 13 50 14N 5 14W
Redvers 109 49 35N 101 40W
Redwater 108 53 55N 113 6W
Redwood 113 44 18N 75 48W
Redwood City 119 37 30N 122 15W
Redwood Falls 116 44 30N 95 2W
Ree, L. 15 53 35N 8 0W
Reed City 114 43 52N 85 30W
Reed, L 109 54 38N 100 30W
Reeder 116 46 7N 102 52W
Reedley 119 36 36N 119 27W
Reedsburg 116 43 34N 90 5W
Reedsport 118 43 45N 124 4W
Reefton 101 42 6 S 171 51 E
Reftele 49 57 11N 13 35 E
Refugio 117 28 18N 97 17W
Rega → 28 54 10N 15 18 E
Regalbuto 41 37 40N 14 38 E
Regavim 62 32 32N 35 2 E
Regen 25 48 58N 13 9 E
Regen → 25 49 2N 12 6 E
Regensburg 25 49 1N 12 7 E
Réggio di Calábria 41 38 7N 15 38 E
Réggio nell' Emilia 38 44 42N 10 38 E
Regina 109 50 27N 104 35W
Registro 125 24 29 S 47 49W
Reguengos de Monsaraz 31 38 25N 7 32W
Rehar → 69 23 55N 82 40 E
Rehoboth 92 23 15 S 17 4 E
Rehovot 62 31 54N 34 48 E
Rei-Bouba 81 8 40N 14 15 E
Reichenbach 24 50 36N 12 19 E
Reid River 98 19 40 S 146 48 E
Reidsville 115 36 21N 79 40W
Reigate 13 51 14N 0 11W
Reillo 32 39 54N 1 53W
Reims 19 49 15N 4 0 E
Reina 62 32 43N 35 18 E
Reina Adelaida, Arch. 128 52 20 S 74 0W
Reinbeck 116 42 18N 92 0W
Reindeer → 109 55 36N 103 11W
Reindeer I. 109 52 30N 98 0W
Reindeer L. 109 57 15N 102 15W
Reine, La 32 48 50N 79 30W
Reinga, C. 101 34 25 S 172 43 E
Reinosa 30 43 2N 4 15W
Reinosa, Paso 30 42 56N 4 10W
Reitz 93 27 48 S 28 29 E
Reivilo 92 27 36 S 24 8 E
Rejmyra 49 58 50N 15 55 E
Rejowiec Fabryczny 28 51 5N 23 17 E
Reka → 39 45 40N 14 0 E
Rekinniki 59 60 51N 163 40 E
Rekovac 42 43 51N 21 3 E
Reliance 109 63 0N 109 20W
Remad, Oued → 82 33 28N 1 20W
Rémalard 18 48 26N 0 47 E
Remanso 127 9 41 S 42 4W
Remarkable, Mt. 99 32 48 S 138 10 E
Rembang 73 6 42 S 111 21 E
Remchi 82 35 2N 1 26W
Remeshk 65 26 55N 58 50 E
Remetea 46 46 45N 25 29 E
Remich 16 49 32N 6 22 E
Remiremont 19 48 0N 6 36 E
Remo 87 6 48N 41 20 E
Remontnoye 57 46 34N 43 37 E
Remoulins 21 43 55N 4 35 E
Remscheid 24 51 11N 7 12 E
Rena 47 61 8N 11 20 E
Rena → 47 61 8N 11 23 E
Rende 41 39 19N 16 11 E
Rendina 45 39 4N 21 58 E
Rendsburg 24 54 18N 9 41 E
Rene 59 66 2N 179 25W
Renfrew, Can. 106 45 30N 76 40W
Renfrew, U.K. 14 55 52N 4 24W
Rengat 72 0 30 S 102 45 E
Rengo 124 34 24 S 70 50W
Renhuai 77 27 48N 106 24 E
Reni 56 45 28N 28 15 E
Renigunta 70 13 38N 79 30 E
Renk 81 11 50N 32 50 E
Renkum 16 51 58N 5 43 E
Renmark 97 34 11 S 140 43 E
Rennell Sd. 108 53 23N 132 35W
Renner Springs T.O. 96 18 20 S 133 47 E
Rennes 18 48 7N 1 41W
Rennes, Bassin de 18 48 12N 1 33W
Rennesøy 47 59 6N 5 43 E
Reno 118 39 30N 119 50W
Reno → 39 44 37N 12 17 E
Renovo 114 41 20N 77 47W
Rensselaer, Ind., U.S.A. 114 40 57N 87 10W
Rensselaer, N.Y., U.S.A. 113 42 38N 73 41W
Rentería 32 43 19N 1 54W
Renton 118 47 30N 122 9W
Réo 84 12 28N 2 35W
Réole, La 20 44 35N 0 1W
Reotipur 69 25 33N 83 45 E
Repalle 70 16 2N 80 45 E
Répcelak 27 47 24N 17 1 E
Republic, Mich., U.S.A. 114 46 25N 87 59W
Republic, Wash., U.S.A. 118 48 38N 118 42W
Republican → 116 39 3N 96 48W
Republican City 116 40 9N 99 20W
Repulse B., Antarct. 5 64 30 S 99 30 E
Repulse B., Austral. 97 20 31 S 148 45 E
Repulse Bay 105 66 30N 86 30W
Requena, Peru 126 5 5 S 73 52W
Requena, Spain 33 39 30N 1 4W
Resele 48 63 20N 17 5 E
Resen 42 41 5N 21 0 E
Reserve, Can. 109 52 28N 102 39W
Reserve, U.S.A. 119 33 50N 108 54W
Resht = Rasht 64 37 20N 49 40 E
Resistencia 124 27 30 S 59 0W
Reşiţa 42 45 18N 21 53 E
Resko 28 53 47N 15 25 E
Resolution I., Can. 105 61 30N 65 0W
Resolution I., N.Z. 101 45 40 S 166 40 E
Ressano Garcia 93 25 25 S 32 0 E
Reston 109 49 33N 101 6W
Reszel 28 54 4N 21 10 E
Retalhuleu 120 14 33N 91 46W
Reteag 46 47 10N 24 0 E
Retenue, Lac de 91 11 0 S 27 0 E
Rethel 19 49 30N 4 20 E
Rethem 24 52 47N 9 25 E
Réthimnon 45 35 18N 24 30 E
Réthimnon □ 45 35 23N 24 28 E
Rétiers 18 47 55N 1 25W
Retortillo 30 40 48N 6 21W
Rétság 27 47 58N 19 10 E
Réunion 3 22 0 S 56 0 E
Reus 32 41 10N 1 5 E
Reuss → 25 47 16N 8 24 E
Reuterstadt Stavenhagen 24 53 41N 12 54 E
Reutlingen 25 48 28N 9 13 E
Reutte 26 47 29N 10 42 E
Reval = Tallinn 54 59 29N 24 58 E
Revda 52 56 48N 59 57 E
Revel 20 43 28N 2 0 E
Revelganj 69 25 50N 84 40 E
Revelstoke 108 51 0N 118 10W
Reventazón 126 6 10 S 81 0W
Revigny 19 48 50N 5 0 E
Revilla Gigedo, Is. 95 18 40N 112 0W
Revillagigedo I. 108 55 50N 131 20W
Revin 19 49 55N 4 39 E
Revuè → 91 19 50 S 34 0 E
Rewa 69 24 33N 81 25 E
Rewari 68 28 15N 76 40 E
Rexburg 118 43 55N 111 50W
Rey Malabo 88 3 45N 8 50 E
Rey, Rio del → 85 4 30N 8 48 E
Reykjahlíð 50 65 40N 16 55W
Reykjanes 50 63 48N 22 40W
Reykjavík 50 64 10N 21 57 E
Reynolds 109 49 40N 95 55W
Reynolds Ra. 96 22 30 S 133 0 E
Reynoldsville 112 41 5N 78 58W
Reynosa 120 26 5N 98 18W
Rezā'īyeh 64 37 40N 45 0 E
Rezā'īyeh, Daryācheh-ye 64 37 50N 45 30 E
Rezekne 54 56 30N 27 17 E
Rezovo 43 42 0N 28 0 E
Rgotina 42 44 1N 22 17 E
Rhamnus 45 38 12N 24 3 E
Rharis, O. → 83 26 0N 5 4 E
Rhayader 13 52 19N 3 30W
Rheden 16 52 0N 6 3 E
Rhein 109 51 25N 102 15W
Rhein → 24 51 52N 6 20 E
Rhein-Main-Donau-Kanal 25 49 1N 11 27 E
Rheinbach 24 50 38N 6 54 E
Rheine 24 52 17N 7 25 E
Rheinland-Pfalz □ 25 50 0N 7 0 E
Rheinsberg 24 53 6N 12 52 E
Rheriss, Oued → 82 30 50N 4 34W
Rheydt 24 51 10N 6 24 E
Rhin = Rhein → 24 51 52N 6 20 E
Rhinau 19 48 19N 7 43 E
Rhine = Rhein → 24 51 52N 6 20 E
Rhinelander 116 45 38N 89 29W
Rhino Camp 90 3 0N 31 22 E
Rhir, Cap 82 30 38N 9 54W
Rho 38 45 31N 9 2 E
Rhode Island □ 114 41 38N 71 37W
Rhodes = Ródhos 45 36 15N 28 10 E
Rhodes' Tomb 91 20 30 S 28 30 E
Rhodesia = Zimbabwe ■ 91 20 0 S 30 0 E
Rhodope Mts. = Rhodopi Planina 43 41 40N 24 20 E
Rhodopi Planina 43 41 40N 24 20 E
Rhondda 13 51 39N 3 30W
Rhône □ 21 45 54N 4 35 E
Rhône → 21 43 28N 4 42 E
Rhum 14 57 0N 6 20W
Rhumney 13 51 32N 3 7W
Rhyl 12 53 19N 3 29W
Ri-Aba 85 3 28N 8 40 E
Riachão 127 7 20 S 46 37W
Riaño 30 42 59N 5 0W
Rians 21 43 37N 5 44 E
Riansares → 32 39 32N 3 18W
Riasi 69 33 10N 74 50 E
Riau □ 72 0 0 102 35 E
Riau, Kepulauan 72 0 30N 104 20 E
Riaza 32 41 18N 3 30W
Riaza → 32 41 42N 3 55W
Riba de Saelices 32 40 55N 2 17W
Ribadavia 30 42 17N 8 8W
Ribadeo 30 43 35N 7 5W
Ribadesella 30 43 30N 5 7W
Ribas 32 42 19N 2 15 E
Ribble → 12 54 13N 2 20W
Ribe 49 55 19N 8 44 E
Ribeauvillé 19 48 10N 7 20 E
Ribécourt 19 49 30N 2 55 E
Ribeira 30 42 36N 8 58W
Ribeirão Prêto 125 21 10 S 47 50W
Ribemont 19 49 47N 3 27 E
Ribera 40 37 30N 13 13 E
Ribérac 20 45 15N 0 20 E
Riberalta 126 11 0 S 66 0W
Ribnica 39 45 45N 14 45 E
Ribnitz-Damgarten 24 54 14N 12 24 E
Ričany 26 50 0N 14 40 E
Riccarton 101 43 32 S 172 37 E
Riccia 41 41 30N 14 50 E
Riccione 39 44 0N 12 39 E
Rice L. 112 44 12N 78 10W
Rice Lake 116 45 30N 91 42W
Riceys, Les 19 47 59N 4 22 E
Rich 82 32 16N 4 30W
Rich Hill 117 38 5N 94 22W
Richards Bay 93 28 48 S 32 6 E
Richards L. 109 59 10N 107 10W
Richardson → 109 58 25N 111 14W
Richardton 116 46 56N 102 22W
Richelieu 18 47 0N 0 20 E
Richey 116 47 42N 105 5W
Richfield, Idaho, U.S.A. 118 43 2N 114 5W
Richfield, Utah, U.S.A. 119 38 50N 112 0W
Richford 113 45 0N 72 40W
Richibucto 107 46 42N 64 54W
Richland, Ga., U.S.A. 115 32 7N 84 40W
Richland, Oreg., U.S.A. 118 44 49N 117 9W
Richland, Wash., U.S.A. 118 46 15N 119 15W
Richland Center 116 43 21N 90 22W
Richlands 114 37 7N 81 49W
Richmond, N.S.W., Austral. 100 33 35 S 150 42 E
Richmond, Queens., Austral. 97 20 43 S 143 8 E
Richmond, N.Z. 101 41 20 S 173 12 E
Richmond, S. Afr. 93 29 51 S 30 18 E
Richmond, N. Yorks., U.K. 12 54 24N 1 43W
Richmond, Surrey, U.K. 13 51 28N 0 18W
Richmond, Calif., U.S.A. 118 37 58N 122 21W
Richmond, Ind., U.S.A. 114 39 50N 84 50W
Richmond, Ky., U.S.A. 114 37 40N 84 20W
Richmond, Mich., U.S.A. 112 42 47N 82 45W
Richmond, Mo., U.S.A. 116 39 15N 93 58W
Richmond, Tex., U.S.A. 117 29 32N 95 42W
Richmond, Utah, U.S.A. 118 41 55N 111 48W
Richmond, Va., U.S.A. 114 37 33N 77 27W
Richmond, Ra. 99 29 0 S 152 45 E
Richton 115 31 23N 88 58W
Richwood 114 38 17N 80 32W
Ricla 32 41 31N 1 24W
Riddarhyttan 48 59 49N 15 33 E
Ridgedale 109 53 0N 104 10W
Ridgeland 115 32 30N 80 58W
Ridgelands 98 23 16 S 150 17 E
Ridgetown 106 42 26N 81 52W
Ridgewood 113 40 59N 74 7W
Ridgway 114 41 25N 78 43W
Riding Mt. Nat. Park 109 50 50N 100 0W
Ried 26 48 14N 13 30 E
Riedlingen 25 48 9N 9 28 E
Rienza → 39 46 49N 11 47 E
Riesa 24 51 19N 13 19 E
Riesi 41 37 16N 14 4 E
Rieti 39 42 23N 12 50 E
Rieupeyroux 20 44 19N 2 12 E
Riez 21 43 49N 6 6 E
Rifle 118 39 40N 107 50W
Rifstangi 50 66 32N 16 12W
Rift Valley □ 90 0 20N 36 0 E
Rig Rig 81 14 13N 14 25 E
Riga 54 56 53N 24 8 E
Riga, G. of = Rīgas Jūras Līcis 54 57 40N 23 45 E
Rīgas Jūras Līcis 54 57 40N 23 45 E
Rigaud 113 45 29N 74 18W
Rigby 118 43 41N 111 58W
Rīgestān □ 65 30 15N 65 0 E
Riggins 118 45 29N 116 26W
Rignac 20 44 25N 2 16 E
Rigolet 107 54 10N 58 23W
Riihimäki 51 60 45N 24 48 E
Riiser-Larsen-halvøya 5 68 0 S 35 0 E
Rijau 85 11 8N 5 17 E
Rijeka 39 45 20N 14 21 E
Rijeka Crnojevica 42 42 24N 19 1 E
Rijn → 16 52 12N 4 21 E
Rijssen 16 52 19N 6 30 E
Rijswijk 16 52 4N 4 22 E
Rike 87 10 50N 39 53 E
Rila 43 42 7N 23 7 E
Rila Planina 42 42 10N 23 0 E
Riley 118 43 35N 119 33W
Rilly 19 49 11N 4 3 E
Rima → 85 13 4N 5 10 E
Rimah, Wadi ar → 64 26 5N 41 30 E
Rimavská Sobota 27 48 22N 20 2 E
Rimbey 108 52 35N 114 15W
Rimbo 48 59 44N 18 21 E
Rimforsa 49 58 6N 15 43 E
Rimi 85 12 58N 7 43 E
Rimini 39 44 3N 12 33 E
Rîmna → 46 45 36N 27 3 E
Rîmnicu Sărat 46 45 26N 27 3 E
Rîmnicu Vîlcea 46 45 9N 24 21 E
Rimouski 107 48 27N 68 30W
Rinca 73 8 45 S 119 35 E
Rinconada 124 22 26 S 66 10W
Rineanna 15 52 42N 85 7W
Ringarum 49 58 21N 16 26 E
Ringe 49 55 13N 10 28 E
Ringim 85 12 13N 9 10 E
Ringkøbing 49 56 5N 8 15 E
Ringling 118 46 16N 110 56W
Ringsaker 47 60 54N 10 45 E
Ringsjön 49 55 55N 13 30 E
Ringsted 49 55 25N 11 46 E
Ringvassøy 50 69 56N 19 15 E
Rinía 45 37 23N 25 13 E
Rinjani 72 8 24 S 116 28 E
Rinteln 24 52 11N 9 3 E
Rio Branco 126 9 58 S 67 49W
Río Branco 125 32 40 S 53 40W
Rio Brilhante 125 21 48 S 54 33W
Rio Claro, Brazil 125 22 19 S 47 35W
Rio Claro, Trin. 121 10 20N 61 25W
Río Colorado 128 39 0 S 64 0W
Río Cuarto 124 33 10 S 64 25W
Rio das Pedras 93 23 8 S 35 28 E
Rio de Janeiro 125 23 0 S 43 12W
Rio de Janeiro □ 125 22 50 S 43 0W
Rio do Sul 125 27 13 S 49 37W
Río Gallegos 128 51 35 S 69 15W
Río Grande 128 53 50 S 67 45W
Rio Grande 125 32 0 S 52 20W
Rio Grande → 117 25 57N 97 9W
Rio Grande City 117 26 23N 98 49W
Río Grande del Norte → 110 26 0N 97 0W
Rio Grande do Norte □ 127 5 40 S 36 0W
Rio Grande do Sul □ 125 30 0 S 53 0W
Rio Largo 127 9 28 S 35 50W
Rio Maior 31 39 19N 8 57W
Rio Marina 38 42 48N 10 25 E
Río Mulatos 126 19 40 S 66 50W
Río Muni □ 88 1 30N 10 0 E
Rio Negro 125 26 0 S 50 0W
Rio Pardo 125 30 0 S 52 30W
Río, Punta del 33 36 49N 2 24W
Río Segundo 124 31 40 S 63 59W
Río Tercero 124 32 15 S 64 8W
Rio Tinto 30 41 11N 8 34W
Rio Verde 127 17 50 S 51 0W
Río Verde 120 21 56N 99 59W
Rio Vista 118 38 11N 121 44W
Riobamba 126 1 50 S 78 45W
Ríohacha 126 11 33N 72 55W
Rioja, La, Argent. 124 29 20 S 67 0W
Rioja, La, Spain 32 42 20N 2 20W
Rioja, La □ 124 29 30 S 67 0W
Riom 20 45 54N 3 7 E
Riom-ès-Montagnes 20 45 17N 2 39 E
Rion-des-Landes 20 43 55N 0 56W
Rionero in Vúlture 41 40 55N 15 40 E
Rioni → 57 42 5N 41 50 E
Rios 30 41 58N 7 16W
Riosucio 126 5 30N 75 40W
Ríosucio 126 7 27N 77 7W
Riou L. 109 59 7N 106 25W
Rioz 19 47 25N 6 04 E
Riparia, Dora → 38 45 7N 7 24 E
Ripatransone 39 43 0N 13 45 E
Ripley, Can. 112 44 4N 81 35W
Ripley, N.Y., U.S.A. 112 42 16N 79 44W
Ripley, Tenn., U.S.A. 117 35 43N 89 34W
Ripoll 32 42 15N 2 13 E
Ripon, U.K. 12 54 8N 1 31W
Ripon, U.S.A. 114 43 51N 88 50W
Riposto 41 37 44N 15 12 E
Risan 42 42 32N 18 42 E
Riscle 20 43 39N 0 5W
Rishiri-Tō, Japan 74 45 11N 141 15 E
Rishiri-Tō, Japan 74 45 11N 141 15 E
Rishon le Ziyyon 62 31 58N 34 48 E
Rishpon 62 32 12N 34 49 E
Risle → 18 49 26N 0 23 E
Rîsnov 46 45 35N 25 27 E
Rison 117 33 57N 92 11W
Risør 47 58 43N 9 13 E
Ritchies Archipelago 71 12 5N 94 0 E
Riti 85 7 57N 9 41 E
Rittman 112 40 57N 81 48W
Ritzville 118 47 10N 118 21W
Riva Bella 18 49 17N 0 18W
Riva del Garda 38 45 53N 10 50 E
Rivadavia, Buenos Aires, Argent. 124 35 29 S 62 59W
Rivadavia, Mendoza, Argent. 124 33 13 S 68 30W
Rivadavia, Salta, Argent. 124 24 5 S 62 54W
Rivadavia, Chile 124 29 57 S 70 35W
Rivarolo Canavese 38 45 20N 7 42 E
Rivas 121 11 30N 85 50W
Rive-de-Gier 21 45 32N 4 37 E
River Cess 84 5 30N 9 32W
Rivera 125 31 0 S 55 50W
Riverdsale 92 34 7 S 21 15 E
Riverhead 114 40 53N 72 40W
Riverhurst 109 50 55N 106 50W
Riverina 97 35 30 S 145 20 E
Rivers 109 50 2N 100 14W
Rivers □ 85 5 0N 6 30 E
Rivers Inl. 108 51 40N 127 20W
Rivers, L. of the 109 49 49N 105 44W
Riverside, Calif., U.S.A. 119 34 0N 117 22W
Riverside, Wyo., U.S.A. 118 41 12N 106 57W
Riversleigh 98 19 5 S 138 40 E
Riverton, Austral. 99 34 10 S 138 46 E
Riverton, Can. 109 51 1N 97 0W
Riverton, N.Z. 101 46 21 S 168 0 E
Riverton, U.S.A. 118 43 1N 108 27W
Rives 21 45 21N 5 31 E
Rivesaltes 20 42 47N 2 50 E
Riviera 38 44 0N 8 30 E
Riviera di Levante 36 44 23N 9 15 E
Riviera di Ponente 36 43 50N 7 58 E
Rivière-à-Pierre 107 46 59N 72 11W
Rivière-au-Renard 107 48 59N 64 23W
Rivière-du-Loup 107 47 50N 69 30W
Rivière-Pentecôte 107 49 57N 67 1W
Rívoli 38 45 3N 7 31 E
Rivoli B. 99 37 32 S 140 3 E
Riyadh = Ar Riyāḍ 64 24 41N 46 42 E
Rize 64 41 0N 40 30 E
Rizhao 77 35 25N 119 30 E
Rizzuto, C. 41 38 54N 17 5 E
Rjukan 47 59 54N 8 33 E
Rjuven 47 59 9N 7 8 E
Roa, Norway 47 60 17N 10 37 E
Roa, Spain 30 41 41N 3 56W
Roag, L. 14 58 10N 6 55W
Roanne 21 46 3N 4 4 E
Roanoke, Ala., U.S.A. 115 33 9N 85 23W
Roanoke, Va., U.S.A. 114 37 19N 79 55W
Roanoke → 115 35 56N 76 43W
Roanoke I. 115 35 55N 75 40W
Roanoke Rapids 115 36 28N 77 42W
Roatán 121 16 18N 86 35W
Robbins I. 99 40 42 S 145 0 E
Robe → 15 53 38N 9 10W
Robe, Mt. 100 31 40 S 141 20 E
Röbel 24 53 24N 12 37 E

Robert Lee 117 31 55N 100 26W
Roberts 118 43 44N 112 8W
Robertsganj 69 24 44N 83 4 E
Robertson 92 33 46 S 19 50 E
Robertson I. 5 65 15 S 59 30W
Robertsport 84 6 45N 11 26W
Robertstown 99 33 58 S 139 5 E
Roberval 107 48 32N 72 15W
Robeson Ch. 4 82 0N 61 30W
Robinson Crusoe I. 95 33 38 S 78 52W
Robinson Ranges 96 25 40 S 119 0 E
Robinvale 99 34 40 S 142 45 E
Robla, La 30 42 50N 5 41W
Roblin 109 51 14N 101 21W
Roboré 126 18 10 S 59 45W
Robson, Mt. 108 53 10N 119 10W
Robstown 117 27 47N 97 40W
Roc, Pointe du 18 48 50N 1 37W
Roca, C. da 31 38 40N 9 31W
Rocas, I. 127 4 0 S 34 1W
Rocca d'Aspidé 41 40 27N 15 10 E
Rocca San Casciano 39 44 3N 11 45 E
Roccalbegna 39 42 47N 11 30 E
Roccastrada 39 43 0N 11 10 E
Roccella Iónica 41 38 20N 16 24 E
Rocha 125 34 30 S 54 25W
Rochdale 12 53 36N 2 10W
Roche-Bernard, La 18 47 31N 2 19W
Roche-Canillac, La 20 45 12N 1 57 E
Roche, La 21 46 4N 6 19 E
Roche-sur-Yon, La 18 46 40N 1 25W
Rochechouart 20 45 50N 0 49 E
Rochefort, Belg. 16 50 9N 5 12 E
Rochefort, France 20 45 56N 0 57W
Rochefort-en-Terre 18 47 42N 2 22W
Rochefoucauld, La 20 45 44N 0 24 E
Rochelle 116 41 55N 89 5W
Rochelle, La 20 46 10N 1 9W
Rocher River 108 61 23N 112 44W
Rocheservière 18 46 57N 1 30W
Rochester, Austral. 100 36 22 S 144 41 E
Rochester, Can. 108 54 22N 113 27W
Rochester, U.K. 13 51 22N 0 30 E
Rochester, Ind., U.S.A. 114 41 5N 86 15W
Rochester, Minn., U.S.A. 116 44 1N 92 28W
Rochester, N.H., U.S.A. 114 43 19N 70 57W
Rochester, N.Y., U.S.A. 114 43 10N 77 40W
Rochester, Pa., U.S.A. 112 40 41N 80 17W
Rociana 31 37 19N 6 35W
Rociu 46 44 43N 25 2 E
Rock → 108 60 7N 127 7W
Rock Hill 115 34 55N 81 2W
Rock Island 116 41 30N 90 35W
Rock Port 116 40 26N 95 30W
Rock Rapids 116 43 25N 96 10W
Rock River 118 41 49N 106 0W
Rock Sound 121 24 54N 76 12W
Rock Sprs., Ariz., U.S.A. 119 34 2N 112 11W
Rock Sprs., Mont., U.S.A. 118 46 55N 106 11W
Rock Sprs., Tex., U.S.A. 117 30 2N 100 11W
Rock Sprs., Wyo., U.S.A. 118 41 40N 109 10W
Rock Valley 116 43 10N 96 17W
Rockall 8 57 37N 13 42W
Rockdale 117 30 40N 97 0W
Rockefeller Plat. 5 80 0 S 140 0W
Rockford 116 42 20N 89 0W
Rockglen 109 49 11N 105 57W
Rockhampton 97 23 22 S 150 32 E
Rockingham B. 98 18 5 S 146 10 E
Rockingham Forest 13 52 28N 0 42W
Rocklake 116 48 50N 99 13W
Rockland, Can. 113 45 33N 75 17W
Rockland, Idaho, U.S.A. 118 42 37N 112 57W
Rockland, Me., U.S.A. 107 44 6N 69 6W
Rockland, Mich., U.S.A. 116 46 40N 89 10W
Rocklands Reservoir 100 37 15 S 142 5 E
Rockmart 115 34 1N 85 2W
Rockport 117 28 2N 97 3W
Rockville, Conn., U.S.A. 113 41 51N 72 27W
Rockville, Md., U.S.A. 114 39 7N 77 10W
Rockwall 117 32 55N 96 30W
Rockwell City 116 42 20N 94 35W
Rockwood 115 35 52N 84 40W
Rocky Ford 116 38 7N 103 45W
Rocky Lane 108 58 31N 116 22W
Rocky Mount 115 35 55N 77 48W
Rocky Mountain House 108 52 22N 114 55W
Rocky Mts. 108 55 0N 121 0W
Rocky Pt. 96 33 30 S 123 57 E
Rocky River 112 41 30N 81 40W
Rockyford 108 51 14N 113 10W
Rocroi 19 49 55N 4 30 E
Rod 66 28 10N 63 5 E
Roda, La, Albacete, Spain 33 39 13N 2 15W
Roda, La, Sevilla, Spain 31 37 12N 4 46W
Rødberg 47 60 17N 8 56 E
Rødby 49 54 41N 11 23 E
Rødbyhavn 49 54 39N 11 22 E
Roddickton 107 50 51N 56 8W
Rødding 49 55 23N 9 3 E
Rødekro 49 55 4N 9 20 E
Rødenes 47 59 35N 11 34 E
Rodenkirchen 24 53 24N 8 26 E
Roderick I. 108 52 38N 128 22W
Rodez 20 44 21N 2 33 E
Rodholívas 44 40 55N 24 0 E
Rodhópi □ 44 41 5N 25 30 E
Ródhos 45 36 15N 28 10 E
Rodi Garganico 41 41 55N 15 53 E
Rodna 46 47 25N 24 50 E
Rodnei, Munţii 46 47 35N 24 35 E
Rodney 112 42 34N 81 41W
Rodney, C. 101 36 17 S 174 50 E
Rodniki 55 57 7N 41 47 E
Rodriguez 3 19 45 S 63 20 E
Rodstock, C. 96 33 12 S 134 20 E
Roe → 15 55 10N 6 59W
Roebling 113 40 7N 74 45W
Roebourne 96 20 44 S 117 9 E
Roebuck B. 96 18 5 S 122 20 E
Roermond 16 51 12N 6 0 E
Roes Welcome Sd. 105 65 0N 87 0W
Roeselare 16 50 57N 3 7 E
Rogachev 54 53 8N 30 5 E
Rogaçica 42 44 4N 19 40 E
Rogagua, L. 126 13 43 S 66 50W
Rogaland fylke □ 47 59 12N 6 20 E
Rogaška Slatina 39 46 15N 15 42 E
Rogatec 39 46 15N 15 46 E
Rogatica 42 43 47N 19 0 E
Rogatin 54 49 24N 24 36 E
Rogers 117 36 20N 94 5W
Rogers City 114 45 25N 83 49W
Rogerson 118 42 10N 114 40W
Rogersville 115 36 27N 83 1W
Roggan 106 54 25N 79 32W
Roggeveldberge 92 32 10 S 20 10 E
Roggiano Gravina 41 39 37N 16 9 E
Rogliano, France 21 42 57N 9 30 E
Rogliano, Italy 41 39 11N 16 20 E
Rogoaguado, L. 126 13 0 S 65 30W
Rogowo 28 52 43N 17 38 E
Rogozno 28 52 45N 16 59 E
Rogue → 118 42 30N 124 0W
Rohan 18 48 4N 2 45W
Rohrbach 19 49 3N 7 15 E
Rohri 68 27 45N 68 51 E
Rohri Canal 68 26 15N 68 27 E
Rohtak 68 28 55N 76 43 E
Roi Et 71 16 4N 103 40 E
Roisel 19 49 58N 3 6 E
Rojas 124 34 10 S 60 45W
Rojo, C. 120 21 33N 97 20W
Rokan → 72 2 0N 100 50 E
Rokeby 98 13 39 S 142 40 E
Rokiskis 54 55 55N 25 35 E
Rokitno 54 50 57N 35 56 E
Rokycany 26 49 43N 13 35 E
Rolândia 125 23 18 S 51 23W
Røldal 47 59 47N 6 50 E
Rolette 116 48 42N 99 50W
Rolla, Kansas, U.S.A. 117 37 10N 101 40W
Rolla, Mo., U.S.A. 117 37 56N 91 42W
Rolla, N. Dak., U.S.A. 116 48 50N 99 36W
Rollag 47 60 2N 9 18 E
Rolleston 98 24 28 S 148 35 E
Rollingstone 98 19 2 S 146 24 E
Rom 87 9 54N 32 16 E
Roma, Austral. 97 26 32 S 148 49 E
Roma, Italy 40 41 54N 12 30 E
Roman, Bulg. 43 43 8N 23 54 E
Roman, Romania 46 46 57N 26 55 E
Roman, U.S.S.R. 59 66 4N 112 14 E
Roman-Kosh, Gora 56 44 37N 34 15 E
Romana, La 121 18 27N 68 57W
Romanche → 21 45 5N 5 43 E
Romang 73 7 30 S 127 20 E
Români 86 30 59N 32 38 E
Romania ■ 46 46 0N 25 0 E
Romanija Planina 42 43 50N 18 45 E
Romano, Cayo 121 22 0N 77 30W
Romano di Lombardia 38 45 32N 9 45 E
Romanovka = Bessarabka 56 46 21N 28 58 E
Romans 21 45 3N 5 3 E
Romanshorn 25 47 33N 9 22 E
Romblon 73 12 33N 122 17 E
Rombo □ 90 3 10 S 37 30 E
Rome, Ga., U.S.A. 115 34 20N 85 0W
Rome, N.Y., U.S.A. 114 43 14N 75 29W
Rome = Roma 40 41 54N 12 30 E
Romeleåsen 49 55 34N 13 33 E
Romenay 21 46 30N 5 1 E
Romerike 47 60 7N 11 10 E
Romilly 19 48 31N 3 44 E
Romîni 46 44 59N 24 11 E
Rommani 82 33 31N 6 40W
Romney 114 39 21N 78 45W
Romney Marsh 13 51 0N 1 0 E
Romny 54 50 48N 33 28 E
Rømø 49 55 10N 8 30 E
Romodan 54 50 0N 33 15 E
Romodanovo 55 54 26N 45 23 E
Romont 25 46 42N 6 54 E
Romorantin-Lanthenay 19 47 21N 1 45 E
Romsdalen 47 62 25N 8 0 E
Rona 14 57 33N 6 0W
Ronan 118 47 30N 114 6W
Roncador, Cayos 121 13 32N 80 4W
Roncador, Serra do 127 12 30 S 52 30W
Roncesvalles, Paso 32 43 1N 1 19W
Ronceverte 114 37 45N 80 28W
Ronciglione 39 42 18N 12 12 E
Ronco → 39 44 24N 12 12 E
Ronda 31 36 46N 5 12W
Ronda, Serrania de 31 36 44N 5 3W
Rondane 47 61 57N 9 50 E
Rondônia □ 126 11 0 S 63 0W
Rondonópolis 127 16 28 S 54 38W
Rong, Koh 71 10 45N 103 15 E
Rong Xian 77 29 23N 104 22 E
Rong'an 77 25 14N 109 22 E
Ronge, L. la 109 55 6N 105 17W
Ronge, La 109 55 5N 105 20W
Rongshui 77 25 5N 109 12 E
Ronne Land 5 83 0 S 70 0W
Ronneby 49 56 12N 15 17 E
Ronse 16 50 45N 3 35 E
Roof Butte 119 36 29N 109 5W
Roorkee 68 29 52N 77 59 E
Roosendaal 16 51 32N 4 29 E
Roosevelt, Minn., U.S.A. 116 48 51N 95 2W
Roosevelt, Utah, U.S.A. 118 40 19N 110 1W
Roosevelt I. 5 79 30 S 162 0W
Roosevelt, Mt. 108 58 26N 125 20W
Roosevelt Res. 119 33 46N 111 0W
Ropczyce 27 50 4N 21 38 E
Roper → 96 14 43 S 135 27 E
Ropesville 117 33 25N 102 10W
Roque Pérez 124 35 25 S 59 24W
Roquebrou, La 20 44 58N 2 12 E
Roquefort 20 44 2N 0 20W
Roquefort-sur-Soulzon 20 43 58N 2 59 E
Roquemaure 21 44 3N 4 48 E
Roquetas 32 40 50N 0 30 E
Roquevaire 21 43 20N 5 36 E
Roraima □ 126 2 0N 61 30W
Roraima, Mt. 126 5 10N 60 40W
Rorketon 109 51 24N 99 35W
Røros 47 62 35N 11 23 E
Rorschach 25 47 28N 9 30 E
Rosa 91 9 33 S 31 15 E
Rosa, C. 83 37 0N 8 16 E
Rosa, Monte 25 45 57N 7 53 E
Rosal 30 41 57N 8 51W
Rosal de la Frontera 31 37 59N 7 13W
Rosalia 118 47 14N 117 25W
Rosans 21 44 24N 5 29 E
Rosario 124 33 0 S 60 40W
Rosário 127 3 0 S 44 15W
Rosario, Baja Calif. N., Mexico 120 30 0N 115 50W
Rosario, Durango, Mexico 120 26 30N 105 35W
Rosario, Sinaloa, Mexico 120 23 0N 105 52W
Rosario, Parag. 124 24 30 S 57 35W
Rosario de la Frontera 124 25 50 S 65 0W
Rosario de Lerma 124 24 59 S 65 35W
Rosario del Tala 124 32 20 S 59 10W
Rosário do Sul 125 30 15 S 54 55W
Rosarno 41 38 29N 15 59 E
Rosas 32 42 19N 3 10 E
Roscoe 116 45 27N 99 20W
Roscoff 18 48 44N 4 0W
Roscommon, Ireland 15 53 38N 8 11W
Roscommon, U.S.A. 114 44 27N 84 35W
Roscommon □ 15 53 40N 8 15W
Roscrea 15 52 58N 7 50W
Rose Blanche 107 47 38N 58 45W
Rose Harbour 108 52 15N 131 10W
Rose Pt. 108 54 11N 131 39W
Rose Valley 109 52 19N 103 49W
Roseau, Domin. 121 15 20N 61 24W
Roseau, U.S.A. 116 48 51N 95 46W
Rosebery 99 41 46 S 145 33 E
Rosebud, Austral. 100 38 21 S 144 54 E
Rosebud, U.S.A. 117 31 5N 97 0W
Roseburg 118 43 10N 123 20W
Rosedale, Austral. 98 24 38 S 151 53 E
Rosedale, U.S.A. 117 33 51N 91 0W
Rosemary 108 50 46N 112 5W
Rosenberg 117 29 30N 95 48W
Rosendaël 19 51 3N 2 24 E
Rosenheim 25 47 51N 12 9 E
Roseto degli Abruzzi 39 42 40N 14 2 E
Rosetown 109 51 35N 107 59W
Rosetta = Rashîd 86 31 21N 30 22 E
Roseville 118 38 46N 121 17W
Rosewood 99 27 38 S 152 36 E
Rosh Haniqra, Kefar 62 33 5N 35 5 E
Rosh Pinna 62 32 58N 35 32 E
Rosières 19 49 49N 2 43 E
Rosignano Marittimo 38 43 23N 10 28 E
Rosignol 126 6 15N 57 30W
Roşiori de Vede 46 44 9N 25 0 E
Rositsa 43 43 57N 27 57 E
Rositsa → 43 43 10N 25 30 E
Roskilde 49 55 38N 12 3 E
Roskilde Amtskommune □ 49 55 35N 12 5 E
Roskilde Fjord 49 55 50N 12 2 E
Roslavl 54 53 57N 32 55 E
Roslyn 99 34 29 S 149 37 E
Rosmaninhal 31 39 44N 7 5W
Røsnæs 49 55 44N 10 55 E
Rosolini 41 36 49N 14 58 E
Rosporden 18 47 57N 3 50W
Ross, Austral. 99 42 2 S 147 30 E
Ross, N.Z. 101 42 53 S 170 49 E
Ross Dependency □ 5 70 0 S 170 5W
Ross I. 5 77 30 S 168 0 E
Ross Ice Shelf 5 80 0 S 180 0W
Ross L. 118 48 50N 121 5W
Ross on Wye 13 51 55N 2 34W
Ross Sea 5 74 0 S 178 0 E
Rossan Pt. 15 54 42N 8 47W
Rossano Cálabro 41 39 36N 16 39 E
Rossburn 109 50 40N 100 49W
Rosseau 112 45 16N 79 39W
Rossignol, L., N.S., Can. 107 44 12N 65 10W
Rossignol, L., Qué., Can. 106 52 43N 73 40W
Rossland 108 49 6N 117 50W
Rosslare 15 52 17N 6 23W
Rosslau 24 51 52N 12 15 E
Rosso 84 16 40N 15 45W
Rossosh 57 50 15N 39 28 E
Rossport 106 48 50N 87 30W
Røssvatnet 50 65 45N 14 5 E
Rossville 98 15 48 S 145 15 E
Rosthern 109 52 40N 106 20W
Rostock 24 54 4N 12 9 E
Rostock □ 24 54 10N 12 30 E
Rostov, Don, U.S.S.R. 57 47 15N 39 45 E
Rostov, Moskva, U.S.S.R. 55 57 14N 39 25 E
Rostrenen 18 48 14N 3 21W
Roswell 117 33 26N 104 32W
Rosyth 14 56 2N 3 26W
Rota 31 36 37N 6 20W
Rotälven → 48 61 15N 14 3 E
Rotan 117 32 52N 100 30W
Rotenburg 24 53 6N 9 24 E
Roth 25 49 15N 11 6 E
Rothaargebirge 22 51 0N 8 20 E
Rothenburg ob der Tauber 25 49 21N 10 11 E
Rother → 13 50 59N 0 40 E
Rotherham 12 53 26N 1 21W
Rothes 14 57 31N 3 12W
Rothesay, Can. 107 45 23N 66 0W
Rothesay, U.K. 14 55 50N 5 3W
Roti 73 10 50 S 123 0 E
Roto 97 33 0 S 145 30 E
Rotondella 41 40 10N 16 30 E
Rotoroa, L. 101 41 55 S 172 39 E
Rotorua 101 38 9 S 176 16 E
Rotorua, L. 101 38 5 S 176 18 E
Rott → 25 48 26N 13 26 E
Rottenburg 25 48 28N 8 56 E
Rottenmann 26 47 31N 14 22 E
Rotterdam 16 51 55N 4 30 E
Rottumeroog 16 53 33N 6 34 E
Rottweil 25 48 9N 8 38 E
Rotuma 94 12 25 S 177 5 E
Roubaix 19 50 40N 3 10 E
Roudnice 26 50 25N 14 15 E
Rouen 18 49 27N 1 4 E
Rouillac 20 45 47N 0 4W
Rouleau 109 50 10N 104 56W
Round Mt. 97 30 26 S 152 16 E
Round Mountain 118 38 46N 117 3W
Roundup 118 46 25N 108 35W
Rousay 14 59 10N 3 2W
Rouses Point 113 44 58N 73 22W
Rousse, L'Île 21 42 37N 8 57 E
Roussillon, Isère, France 21 45 24N 4 49 E
Roussillon, Pyrénées-Or., France 20 42 30N 2 35 E
Rouxville 92 30 25 S 26 50 E
Rouyn 106 48 20N 79 0W
Rovaniemi 50 66 29N 25 41 E
Rovato 38 45 34N 10 0 E
Rovenki 57 48 5N 39 21 E
Rovereto 38 45 53N 11 3 E
Rovigo 39 45 4N 11 48 E
Rovinari 46 44 56N 23 10 E
Rovinj 39 45 5N 13 40 E
Rovno 54 50 40N 26 10 E
Rovnoye 55 50 52N 46 3 E
Rovuma → 91 10 29 S 40 28 E
Rowena 99 29 48 S 148 55 E
Rowley Shoals 96 17 30 S 119 0 E
Roxa 84 11 15N 15 45W
Roxas 73 11 36N 122 49 E
Roxboro 115 36 24N 78 59W
Roxborough Downs 98 22 30 S 138 45 E
Roxburgh 101 45 33 S 169 19 E
Roxen 49 58 30N 15 40 E
Roy, Mont., U.S.A. 118 47 17N 109 0W
Roy, N. Mex., U.S.A. 117 35 57N 104 8W
Roy, Le 117 38 8N 95 35W
Roya, Peña 32 40 25N 0 40W
Royal Oak 114 42 30N 83 5W
Royan 20 45 37N 1 2W
Roye 19 49 42N 2 48 E
Røyken 47 59 45N 10 23 E
Rožaj 42 42 50N 20 15 E
Rózan 28 52 52N 21 25 E
Rozay 19 48 40N 2 56 E
Rozhishche 54 50 54N 25 15 E
Rozier, Le 20 44 13N 3 12 E
Rŏžnava 27 48 37N 20 35 E
Rozogi 28 53 48N 21 9 E
Rozoy-sur-Serre 19 49 40N 4 8 E
Rozwadów 28 50 37N 22 2 E
Rrësheni 44 41 47N 19 49 E
Rrogozhino 44 41 2N 19 50 E
Rtanj 42 43 45N 21 50 E
Rtishchevo 55 55 16N 43 50 E
Rúa 30 42 24N 7 6W
Ruacaná 92 17 20 S 14 12 E
Ruahine Ra. 101 39 55 S 176 2 E
Ruapehu 101 39 17 S 175 35 E
Ruapuke I. 101 46 46 S 168 31 E
Ruaus, Wadi → 83 30 26N 15 24 E
Rubeho Mts. 90 6 50 S 36 25 E
Rubezhnoye 56 49 6N 38 25 E
Rubh' a' Mhail 14 55 55N 6 10W
Rubha Hunish 14 57 42N 6 20W
Rubicone → 39 44 8N 12 28 E
Rubino 84 6 4N 4 18W
Rubio 126 7 43N 72 22W
Rubtsovsk 58 51 30N 81 10 E
Ruby 104 64 40N 155 35W
Ruby L. 118 40 10N 115 28W
Ruby Mts. 118 40 30N 115 30W
Rubyvale 98 23 25 S 147 45 E
Rucava 54 56 9N 21 12 E
Ruciane-Nida 28 53 40N 21 32 E
Rud 47 60 1N 10 1 E
Ruda 49 57 6N 16 7 E
Ruda Śląska 28 50 16N 18 50 E
Ruden 24 54 13N 13 47 E
Rüdersdorf 24 52 28N 13 48 E
Rudewa 91 10 7 S 34 40 E
Rudkøbing 49 54 56N 10 41 E
Rudna 28 51 30N 16 17 E
Rudnichnyy 52 59 38N 52 26 E
Rudnik, Bulg. 43 42 36N 27 30 E
Rudnik, Poland 28 50 26N 22 15 E
Rudnik, Yugo. 42 44 8N 20 30 E
Rudnik, Yugo. 43 44 7N 20 35 E
Rudnogorsk 59 57 15N 103 42 E
Rudnya 54 54 55N 31 7 E
Rudnyy 58 52 57N 63 7 E
Rudo 42 43 41N 19 23 E
Rudolf, Ostrov 58 81 45N 58 30 E
Rudolstadt 24 50 44N 11 20 E
Rudozem 43 41 29N 24 51 E
Rudyard 114 46 14N 84 35W
Rue 19 50 15N 1 40 E
Ruelle 20 45 41N 0 14 E
Rufa'a 87 14 44N 33 22 E
Ruffec-Charente 20 46 2N 0 12 E
Rufiji □ 90 8 0 S 38 30 E
Rufiji → 90 7 50 S 39 15 E
Rufino 124 34 20 S 62 50W
Rufisque 84 14 40N 17 15W
Rufunsa 91 15 4 S 29 34 E
Rugao 77 32 23N 120 31 E
Rugby, U.K. 13 52 23N 1 16W
Rugby, U.S.A. 116 48 21N 100 0W
Rügen 24 54 22N 13 25 E
Rugles 18 48 50N 0 40 E
Ruhama 62 31 31N 34 43 E
Ruhengeri 90 1 30 S 29 36 E
Ruhla 24 50 53N 10 21 E
Ruhland 24 51 27N 13 52 E
Ruhr → 24 51 25N 6 44 E
Ruhuhu → 91 10 31 S 34 34 E
Rui'an 77 27 47N 120 40 E
Ruidosa 117 29 59N 104 39W
Ruidoso 119 33 19N 105 39W
Ruj 42 42 52N 22 42 E
Rujen 42 42 9N 22 30 E

Place	Page	Lat.	Long.
Ruk	**68**	27 50N	68 42 E
Rukwa □	**90**	7 0 S	31 30 E
Rukwa L.	**90**	8 0 S	32 20 E
Rum Cay	**121**	23 40N	74 58W
Rum Jungle	**96**	13 0 S	130 59 E
Ruma	**42**	45 0N	19 50 E
Rumāḩ	**64**	25 29N	47 10 E
Rumania = Romania ■	**46**	46 0N	25 0 E
Rumbêk	**87**	6 54N	29 37 E
Rumburk	**26**	50 57N	14 32 E
Rumford	**114**	44 30N	70 30W
Rumia	**28**	54 37N	18 25 E
Rumilly	**21**	45 53N	5 56 E
Rumoi	**74**	43 56N	141 39W
Rumonge	**90**	3 59 S	29 26 E
Rumsey	**108**	51 51N	112 48W
Rumula	**98**	16 35 S	145 20 E
Rumuruti	**90**	0 17N	36 32 E
Runan	**77**	33 0N	114 30 E
Runanga	**101**	42 25 S	171 15 E
Runaway, C.	**101**	37 32 S	178 2 E
Runcorn	**12**	53 20N	2 44W
Rungwa	**90**	6 55 S	33 32 E
Rungwa →	**90**	7 36 S	31 50 E
Rungwe	**91**	9 11 S	33 32 E
Rungwe □	**91**	9 25 S	33 32 E
Runka	**85**	12 28N	7 20 E
Runn	**48**	60 30N	15 40 E
Ruoqiang	**75**	38 55N	88 10 E
Rupa	**67**	27 15N	92 21 E
Rupar	**68**	31 2N	76 38 E
Rupat	**72**	1 45N	101 40 E
Rupea	**46**	46 2N	25 13 E
Rupert →	**106**	51 29N	78 45W
Rupert House = Fort Rupert	**106**	51 30N	78 40W
Rupsa	**69**	21 44N	89 30 E
Rur →	**24**	51 20N	6 0 E
Rurrenabaque	**126**	14 30 S	67 32W
Rus →	**33**	39 30N	2 30W
Rusambo	**91**	16 30 S	32 4 E
Rusape	**91**	18 35 S	32 8 E
Ruschuk = Ruse	**43**	43 48N	25 59 E
Ruse	**43**	43 48N	25 59 E
Ruşeţu	**46**	44 57N	27 14 E
Rushden	**13**	52 17N	0 37W
Rushford	**116**	43 48N	91 46W
Rushville, Ill., U.S.A.	**116**	40 6N	90 35W
Rushville, Ind., U.S.A.	**114**	39 38N	85 22W
Rushville, Nebr., U.S.A.	**116**	42 43N	102 28W
Rushworth	**100**	36 32 S	145 1 E
Rusken	**49**	57 15N	14 20 E
Russas	**127**	4 55 S	37 50W
Russell, Can.	**109**	50 50N	101 20W
Russell, N.Z.	**101**	35 16 S	174 10 E
Russell, U.S.A.	**116**	38 56N	98 55W
Russell L., Man., Can.	**109**	56 15N	101 30W
Russell L., N.W.T., Can.	**108**	63 5N	115 44W
Russellkonda	**69**	19 57N	84 42 E
Russellville, Ala., U.S.A.	**115**	34 30N	87 44W
Russellville, Ark., U.S.A.	**117**	35 15N	93 8W
Russellville, Ky., U.S.A.	**115**	36 50N	86 50W
Russi	**39**	44 21N	12 1 E
Russian S.F.S.R. □	**59**	62 0N	105 0 E
Russkaya Polyana	**58**	53 47N	73 53 E
Russkoye Ustie	**4**	71 0N	149 0 E
Rust	**27**	47 49N	16 42 E
Rustavi	**57**	41 30N	45 0 E
Rustenburg	**92**	25 41 S	27 14 E
Ruston	**117**	32 30N	92 58W
Rutana	**90**	3 55 S	30 0 E
Rute	**31**	37 19N	4 23W
Ruteng	**73**	8 35 S	120 30 E
Ruth, Mich., U.S.A.	**112**	43 42N	82 45W
Ruth, Nev., U.S.A.	**118**	39 15N	115 1W
Rutherglen, Austral.	**100**	36 5 S	146 29 E
Rutherglen, U.K.	**14**	55 50N	4 11W
Rutigliano	**41**	41 1N	17 0 E
Rutland I.	**71**	11 25N	92 40 E
Rutland Plains	**98**	15 38 S	141 43 E
Rutledge →	**109**	61 4N	112 0W
Rutledge L.	**109**	61 33N	110 47W
Rutshuru	**90**	1 13 S	29 25 E
Ruurlo	**16**	52 5N	6 24 E
Ruvo di Púglia	**41**	41 7N	16 27 E
Ruvu	**90**	6 49 S	38 43 E
Ruvu →	**90**	6 23 S	38 52 E
Ruvuma □	**91**	10 20 S	36 0 E
Ruwenzori	**90**	0 30N	29 55 E
Ruyigi	**90**	3 29 S	30 15 E
Ruzayevka	**55**	54 4N	45 0 E
Růzhevo Konare	**43**	42 23N	24 46 E
Ružomberok	**27**	49 3N	19 17 E
Rwanda ■	**90**	2 0 S	30 0 E
Ry	**49**	56 5N	9 45 E
Ryakhovo	**43**	44 0N	26 18 E
Ryan, L.	**14**	55 0N	5 2W
Ryazan	**55**	54 40N	39 40 E
Ryazhsk	**55**	53 45N	40 3 E
Rybache	**58**	46 40N	81 20 E
Rybachiy Poluostrov	**52**	69 43N	32 0 E
*Rybinsk	**55**	58 5N	38 50 E
Rybinskoye Vdkhr.	**55**	58 30N	38 25 E
Rybnik	**27**	50 6N	18 32 E
Rybnitsa	**56**	47 45N	29 0 E
Rybnoye	**55**	54 45N	39 30 E
Rychwał	**28**	52 4N	18 10 E
Ryd	**49**	56 27N	14 42 E
Ryde	**13**	50 44N	1 9W
Rydöbruk	**49**	56 58N	13 7 E
Rydsnäs	**49**	57 47N	15 9 E
Rydułtowy	**27**	50 4N	18 23 E
Rydzyna	**28**	51 47N	16 39 E
Rye	**13**	50 57N	0 46 E
Rye →	**12**	54 12N	0 53W
Rye Patch Res.	**118**	40 38N	118 20W
Ryegate	**118**	46 21N	109 15W
Ryki	**28**	51 38N	21 56 E
Rylsk	**54**	51 36N	34 43 E
Rylstone	**99**	32 46 S	149 58 E
Rymanów	**27**	49 35N	21 51 E
Ryn	**28**	53 57N	21 34 E
Rypin	**28**	53 3N	19 25 E
Ryūkyū Is. = Nansei-Shotō	**74**	26 0N	128 0 E
Rzepin	**28**	52 20N	14 49 E
Rzeszów	**27**	50 5N	21 58 E
Rzeszów □	**27**	50 0N	22 0 E
Rzhev	**54**	56 20N	34 20 E

S

Place	Page	Lat.	Long.
Sa Dec	**71**	10 20N	105 46 E
Sa'ad (Muharraqa)	**62**	31 28N	34 33 E
Sa'ādatābād	**65**	30 10N	53 5 E
Saale →	**24**	51 57N	11 56 E
Saaler Bodden	**24**	54 20N	12 25 E
Saalfeld	**24**	50 39N	11 21 E
Saalfelden	**26**	47 25N	12 51 E
Saane →	**25**	46 23N	7 18 E
Saar (Sarre) →	**19**	49 42N	6 34 E
Saarbrücken	**25**	49 15N	6 58 E
Saarburg	**25**	49 36N	6 32 E
Saaremaa	**54**	58 30N	22 30 E
Saariselkä	**50**	68 16N	28 15 E
Saarland □	**25**	49 15N	7 0 E
Saarlouis	**25**	49 19N	6 45 E
Saba	**121**	17 42N	63 26W
Šabac	**42**	44 48N	19 42 E
Sabadell	**32**	41 28N	2 7 E
Sabagalet	**72**	1 36 S	98 40 E
Sabah □	**72**	6 0N	117 0 E
Sábana de la Mar	**121**	19 7N	69 24W
Sábanalarga	**126**	10 38N	74 55W
Sabang	**72**	5 50N	95 15 E
Sabará	**127**	19 55 S	43 46W
Sabarania	**73**	2 5 S	138 18 E
Sabari →	**70**	17 35N	81 16 E
Sabasţiyah	**62**	32 17N	35 12 E
Sabattis	**113**	44 6N	74 40W
Sabáudia	**40**	41 17N	13 2 E
Sabhah	**83**	27 9N	14 29 E
Sabhah □	**83**	26 0N	14 0 E
Sabie	**93**	25 10 S	30 48 E
Sabinal, Mexico	**120**	30 58N	107 25W
Sabinal, U.S.A.	**117**	29 20N	99 27W
Sabinal, Punta del	**33**	36 43N	2 44W
Sabinas	**120**	27 50N	101 10W
Sabinas Hidalgo	**120**	26 33N	100 10W
Sabine	**117**	29 42N	93 54W
Sabine →	**117**	30 0N	93 35W
Sabine L.	**117**	29 50N	93 50W
Sabinov	**27**	49 6N	21 5 E
Sabirabad	**57**	40 5N	48 30 E
Sabkhat Tāwurghā'	**83**	31 48N	15 30 E
Sablayan	**73**	12 50N	120 50 E
Sable, C., Can.	**107**	43 29N	65 38W
Sable, C., U.S.A.	**121**	25 13N	81 0W
Sable I.	**107**	44 0N	60 0W
Sablé-sur-Sarthe	**18**	47 50N	0 20W
Sables-d'Olonne, Les	**20**	46 30N	1 45W
Sabolev	**59**	54 20N	155 30 E
Sabor →	**30**	41 10N	7 7W
Sabou	**84**	12 1N	2 15W
Sabrātah	**83**	32 47N	12 29 E
Sabria	**83**	33 22N	8 45 E
Sabrina Coast	**5**	68 0 S	120 0 E
Sabugal	**30**	40 20N	7 5W
Sabzevār	**65**	36 15N	57 40 E
Sabzvārān	**65**	28 45N	57 50 E
Sac City	**116**	42 26N	95 0W
Sacedón	**32**	40 29N	2 41W
Sachigo →	**106**	55 6N	88 58W
Sachigo, L.	**106**	53 50N	92 12W
Sachkhere	**57**	42 25N	43 28 E
Sacile	**39**	45 58N	12 30 E
Sackets Harbor	**113**	43 56N	76 7W
Säckingen	**25**	47 34N	7 56 E
Saco, Me., U.S.A.	**115**	43 30N	70 27W
Saco, Mont., U.S.A.	**118**	48 28N	107 19W
Sacramento	**118**	38 33N	121 30 E
Sacramento →	**118**	38 3N	121 56W
Sacramento Mts.	**119**	32 30N	105 30W
Sacratif, Cabo	**33**	36 42N	3 28W
Săcueni	**46**	47 20N	22 5 E
Sada	**30**	43 22N	8 15W
Sádaba	**32**	42 19N	1 12W
Sadani	**90**	5 58 S	38 35 E
Sadao	**71**	6 38N	100 26 E
Sadasivpet	**70**	17 38N	77 59 E
Sadd el Aali	**86**	23 54N	32 54 E
Sade	**85**	11 22N	10 45 E
Sadimi	**91**	9 25 S	23 32 E
Sado	**74**	38 0N	138 25 E
Sado →	**31**	38 29N	8 55W
Sado, Shima	**74**	38 15N	138 30 E
Sadon, Burma	**67**	25 28N	98 0 E
Sadon, U.S.S.R.	**57**	42 52N	43 58 E
Sæby	**49**	57 21N	10 30 E
Saegerstown	**112**	41 42N	80 10W
Saelices	**32**	39 55N	2 49W
Safaga	**86**	26 42N	34 0 E
Safaha	**86**	26 25N	39 0 E
Šafárikovo	**27**	48 25N	20 20 E
Säffle	**48**	59 8N	12 55 E
Safford	**119**	32 50N	109 43W
Saffron Walden	**13**	52 2N	0 15 E
Safi	**82**	32 18N	9 20W
Safīd Kūh	**65**	34 45N	63 0 E
Safonovo	**54**	55 4N	33 16 E
Safranbolu	**56**	41 15N	32 41 E
Sag Harbor	**113**	40 59N	72 17W
Saga	**73**	2 40 S	132 55 E
Saga □	**74**	33 15N	130 20 E
Sagala	**84**	14 9N	6 38W
Sagara	**70**	14 14N	75 6 E
Sagara, L.	**90**	5 20 S	31 0 E
Saghīr, Zab al	**64**	35 10N	43 20 E
Sagil	**75**	50 15N	91 15 E
Saginaw	**114**	43 26N	83 55W
Saginaw B.	**106**	43 50N	83 40W
Sagleipie	**84**	7 0N	8 52W
Saglouc (Sugluk)	**105**	62 10N	74 40W
Sagone	**21**	42 7N	8 42 E
Sagone, G. de	**21**	42 4N	8 40 E
Sagra, La>	**33**	37 57N	2 35W
Sagres	**31**	37 0N	8 58W
Sagua la Grande	**121**	22 50N	80 10W
Saguache	**119**	38 10N	106 10W
Saguenay →	**107**	48 22N	71 0W
Sagunto	**32**	39 42N	0 18W
Sahaba	**86**	18 57N	30 25 E
Sahagún	**30**	42 18N	5 2W
Saham	**62**	32 42N	35 46 E
Saḩam al Jawlān	**62**	32 45N	35 55 E
Sahand, Kūh-e	**64**	37 44N	46 27 E
Sahara	**82**	23 0N	5 0 E
Saharanpur	**68**	29 58N	77 33 E
Saharien Atlas	**82**	33 30N	1 0 E
Sahasinaka	**93**	21 49 S	47 49 E
Sahaswan	**68**	28 5N	78 45 E
Sahel, Canal du	**84**	14 20N	6 0W
Sahibganj	**69**	25 12N	87 40 E
Sahiwal	**68**	30 45N	73 8 E
Sahtaneh →	**108**	59 2N	122 28W
Sahuaripa	**120**	29 0N	109 13W
Sahuarita	**119**	31 58N	110 59W
Sahuayo	**120**	20 4N	102 43W
Sahy	**27**	48 4N	18 55 E
Saibai I.	**98**	9 25 S	142 40 E
Sa'id Bundas	**81**	8 24N	24 48 E
Saïda	**82**	34 50N	0 11 E
Saīdābād	**65**	29 30N	55 45 E
Saïdia	**82**	35 5N	2 14W
Saidu	**69**	34 43N	72 24 E
Saignes	**20**	45 20N	2 31 E
Saigon = Thanh Bho Ho Chi Minh	**71**	10 46N	106 40 E
Saih-al-Malih	**65**	23 37N	58 31 E
Saijō	**74**	33 55N	133 11 E
Saikhoa Ghat	**67**	27 50N	95 40 E
Saiki	**74**	32 58N	131 51 E
Saillans	**21**	44 42N	5 12 E
Sailolof	**73**	1 7 S	130 46 E
St. Abb's Head	**14**	55 55N	2 10W
St. Aegyd	**26**	47 52N	15 33 E
St-Affrique	**20**	43 57N	2 53 E
St-Agrève	**21**	45 0N	4 23 E
St-Aignan	**18**	47 16N	1 22 E
St. Alban's	**107**	47 51N	55 50W
St. Albans, U.K.	**13**	51 44N	0 19W
St. Albans, Vt., U.S.A.	**114**	44 49N	73 7W
St. Albans, W. Va., U.S.A.	**114**	38 21N	81 50W
St. Alban's Head	**13**	50 34N	2 3W
St. Albert	**108**	53 37N	113 32W
St-Amand	**19**	50 25N	3 26 E
St-Amand-en-Puisaye	**19**	47 32N	3 5 E
St-Amand-Mont-Rond	**20**	46 43N	2 30 E
St-Amarin	**19**	47 54N	7 0 E
St-Amour	**21**	46 26N	5 21 E
St-André-de-Cubzac	**20**	44 59N	0 26W
St-André-de-l'Eure	**18**	48 54N	1 16 E
St-André-les-Alpes	**21**	43 58N	6 30 E
St. André, Tanjona	**93**	16 11 S	44 27 E
St. Andrew's	**107**	47 45N	59 15W
St. Andrews	**14**	56 20N	2 48W
St-Anicet	**113**	45 8N	74 22W
St. Ann B.	**107**	46 22N	60 25W
St. Anne	**18**	49 43N	2 11W
St. Anthony, Can.	**107**	51 22N	55 35W
St. Anthony, U.S.A.	**118**	44 0N	111 40W
St-Antonin-Noble-Val	**20**	44 10N	1 45 E
St. Arnaud	**99**	36 40 S	143 16 E
St. Arthur	**107**	47 33N	67 46W
St. Asaph	**12**	53 15N	3 27W
St-Astier	**20**	45 8N	0 31 E
St-Aubin-du-Cormier	**18**	48 15N	1 26W
St. Augustin	**93**	23 33 S	43 46 E
St-Augustin-Saguenay	**107**	51 13N	58 38W
St. Augustine	**115**	29 52N	81 20W
St. Austell	**13**	50 20N	4 48W
St-Avold	**19**	49 6N	6 43 E
St.-Barthélemy, I.	**121**	17 50N	62 50W
St. Bee's Hd.	**12**	54 30N	3 38 E
St-Benoît-du-Sault	**20**	46 26N	1 24 E
St. Bernard, Col du Grand	**25**	45 53N	7 11 E
St. Boniface	**109**	49 53N	97 5W
St-Bonnet	**21**	44 40N	6 5 E
St-Brévin-les-Pins	**18**	47 14N	2 10W
St-Brice-en-Coglès	**18**	48 25N	1 22W
St. Bride's	**107**	46 56N	54 10W
St. Bride's B.	**13**	51 48N	5 15W
St-Brieuc	**18**	48 30N	2 46W
St-Calais	**18**	47 55N	0 45 E
St-Cast	**18**	48 37N	2 18W
St. Catharines	**106**	43 10N	79 15W
St. Catherines I.	**115**	31 35N	81 10W
St. Catherine's Pt.	**13**	50 34N	1 18W
St-Céré	**20**	44 51N	1 54 E
St.-Cergue	**25**	46 27N	6 10 E
St-Cernin	**20**	45 5N	2 25 E
St-Chamond	**21**	45 28N	4 31 E
St. Charles, Ill., U.S.A.	**114**	41 55N	88 21W
St. Charles, Mo., U.S.A.	**116**	38 46N	90 30W
St-Chély-d'Apcher	**20**	44 48N	3 17 E
St-Chinian	**20**	43 25N	2 56 E
St. Christopher (St. Kitts)	**121**	17 20N	62 40W
St-Ciers-sur-Gironde	**20**	45 17N	0 37W
St. Clair, Mich, U.S.A.	**112**	42 47N	82 27W
St. Clair, Pa., U.S.A.	**113**	40 42N	76 12W
St. Clair, L.	**106**	42 30N	82 45W
St. Clairsville	**112**	40 5N	80 53W
St-Claud	**20**	45 54N	0 28 E
St. Claude	**109**	49 40N	98 20W
St-Claude	**21**	46 22N	5 52 E
St-Cloud	**18**	48 51N	2 12 E
St. Cloud, Fla., U.S.A.	**115**	28 15N	81 15W
St. Cloud, Minn., U.S.A.	**116**	45 30N	94 11W
St-Coeur de Marie	**107**	48 39N	71 43W
St. Croix	**121**	17 45N	64 45W
St. Croix →	**116**	44 45N	92 50W
St. Croix Falls	**116**	45 18N	92 22W
St-Cyprien	**20**	42 37N	3 0 E
St-Cyr	**21**	43 11N	5 43 E
St. David's, Can.	**107**	48 12N	58 52W
St. David's, U.K.	**13**	51 54N	5 16W
St. David's Head	**13**	51 55N	5 16W
St-Denis	**19**	48 56N	2 22 E
St-Denis-d'Orques	**18**	48 2N	0 17W
St-Dié	**19**	48 17N	6 56 E
St-Dizier	**19**	48 40N	5 0 E
St-Egrève	**21**	45 14N	5 41 E
St. Elias, Mt.	**104**	60 14N	140 50W
St Elias Mts.	**108**	60 33N	139 28W
St-Éloy-les-Mines	**20**	46 10N	2 51 E
St-Émilion	**20**	44 53N	0 9W
St-Étienne	**21**	45 27N	4 22 E
St-Étienne-de-Tinée	**21**	44 16N	6 56 E
St. Eugène	**113**	45 30N	74 28W
St. Eustatius	**121**	17 20N	63 0W
St-Félicien	**106**	48 40N	72 25W
St-Florent	**21**	42 41N	9 18 E
St-Florent-sur-Cher	**19**	46 59N	2 15 E
St-Florentin	**19**	48 0N	3 45 E
St-Flour	**20**	45 2N	3 6 E
St-Fons	**21**	45 42N	4 52 E
St. Francis	**116**	39 48N	101 47W
St. Francis →	**117**	34 38N	90 36W
St. Francis, C.	**92**	34 14 S	24 49 E
St-Francis, L.	**113**	45 10N	74 22W
St. Francisville	**117**	30 48N	91 22W
St-Fulgent	**18**	46 50N	1 10W
St-Gabriel-de-Brandon	**106**	46 17N	73 24W
St-Gaudens	**20**	43 6N	0 44 E
St-Gengoux-le-National	**21**	46 37N	4 40 E
St-Geniez-d'Olt	**20**	44 27N	2 58 E
St. George, Austral.	**97**	28 1 S	148 30 E
St. George, Berm.	**121**	32 24N	64 42W
St. George, Can.	**107**	45 11N	66 50W
St. George, S.C., U.S.A.	**115**	33 13N	80 37W
St. George, Utah, U.S.A.	**119**	37 10N	113 35W
St. George, C., Can.	**107**	48 30N	59 16W
St. George, C., U.S.A.	**115**	29 36N	85 2W
St-Georges	**16**	50 37N	5 20 E
St. George's	**107**	48 26N	58 31W
St. Georges	**106**	46 42N	72 35W
St-Georges	**107**	46 8N	70 40W
St. Georges	**127**	4 0N	52 0W
St. George's	**121**	12 5N	61 43W
St. George's B.	**107**	48 24N	58 53W
Saint George's Channel	**98**	4 10 S	152 20 E
St. George's Channel	**11**	52 0N	6 0W
St-Georges-de-Didonne	**20**	45 36N	1 0W
St. Georges Head	**100**	35 12 S	150 42 E
St-Germain	**19**	48 53N	2 5 E
St-Germain-Lembron	**20**	45 27N	3 14 E
St-Germain-de-Calberte	**20**	44 13N	3 48 E
St-Germain-des-Fossés	**20**	46 12N	3 26 E
St-Germain-du-Plain	**19**	46 42N	4 58 E
St-Germain-Laval	**21**	45 50N	4 1 E
St-Gers	**20**	45 18N	0 37W
St-Gervais, Haute Savoie, France	**21**	45 53N	6 42 E
St-Gervais, Puy de Dôme, France	**20**	46 4N	2 50 E
St-Gildas, Pte. de	**18**	47 8N	2 14W
St-Gilles-Croix-de-Vie	**18**	46 41N	1 55W
St-Gilles-du-Gard	**21**	43 40N	4 26 E
St-Girons	**20**	42 59N	1 8 E
St. Goar	**25**	50 12N	7 43 E
St-Gualtier	**18**	46 39N	1 26 E
St-Guénolé	**18**	47 49N	4 23W
St. Helena, Atl. Oc.	**7**	15 55 S	5 44W
St. Helena, U.S.A.	**118**	38 29N	122 30W
St. Helenabaai	**92**	32 40 S	18 10 E
St. Helens, U.K.	**12**	53 28N	2 44W
St. Helens, U.S.A.	**118**	45 55N	122 50W
St. Helier	**18**	49 11N	2 6W
St-Hilaire	**18**	48 35N	1 7W
St-Hippolyte	**19**	47 20N	6 50 E
St-Hippolyte-du-Fort	**20**	43 58N	3 52 E
St-Honoré	**19**	46 54N	3 50 E
St-Hubert	**16**	50 2N	5 23 E
St-Hyacinthe	**106**	45 40N	72 58W
St. Ignace	**114**	45 53N	84 43W
St. Ignace I.	**106**	48 45N	88 0W
St. Ignatius	**118**	47 19N	114 8W
St-Imier	**25**	47 9N	6 58 E
St. Ives, Cambs., U.K.	**13**	52 20N	0 5W
St. Ives, Cornwall, U.K.	**13**	50 13N	5 29W
St-James	**18**	48 31N	1 20W
St. James	**116**	43 57N	94 40W
St. Jean	**106**	45 20N	73 20W
St-Jean	**21**	45 30N	5 10 E
St-Jean →	**107**	50 17N	64 20W
St. Jean Baptiste	**109**	49 15N	97 20W
St-Jean-d'Angély	**20**	45 57N	0 31W
St-Jean-de-Maurienne	**21**	45 16N	6 21 E
St-Jean-de-Luz	**20**	43 23N	1 39W
St-Jean-de-Monts	**18**	46 47N	2 4W
St-Jean-du-Gard	**20**	44 7N	3 52 E
St-Jean-en-Royans	**21**	45 1N	5 18 E
St-Jean, L.	**107**	48 40N	72 0W
St-Jean-Port-Joli	**107**	47 15N	70 13W
St-Jérôme, Qué., Can.	**106**	45 47N	74 0W
St-Jérôme, Qué., Can.	**107**	48 26N	71 53W
St. John, Can.	**107**	45 20N	66 8W
St. John, Kans., U.S.A.	**117**	37 59N	98 45W
St. John, N.D., U.S.A.	**116**	48 58N	99 40W
St. John →	**107**	45 15N	66 4W
St. John, C.	**107**	50 0N	55 32W
St. John's, Antigua	**121**	17 6N	61 51W
St. John's, Can.	**107**	47 35N	52 40W
St. Johns, Ariz., U.S.A.	**119**	34 31N	109 26W
St. Johns, Mich., U.S.A.	**114**	43 0N	84 31W
St. John's →	**115**	30 20N	81 30W
St. Johnsbury	**114**	44 25N	72 1W
St. Johnsville	**113**	43 0N	74 43W
St. Joseph, La., U.S.A.	**117**	31 55N	91 15W
St. Joseph, Mich., U.S.A.	**114**	42 5N	86 30W
St. Joseph, Mo., U.S.A.	**116**	39 46N	94 50W
St. Joseph →	**114**	42 7N	86 30W
St. Joseph, I.	**106**	46 12N	83 58W
St. Joseph, L.	**106**	51 10N	90 35W
St-Jovite	**106**	46 8N	74 38W
St-Juéry	**20**	43 55N	2 12 E
St-Julien	**21**	46 8N	6 5 E
St-Julien-Chapteuil	**21**	45 2N	4 4 E
St-Julien-du-Sault	**19**	48 1N	3 17 E
St-Junien	**20**	45 53N	0 55 E

*Renamed Andropov

St-Just-en-Chaussée **19** 49 30N 2 25 E
St-Just-en-Chevalet **20** 45 55N 3 50 E
St-Justin **20** 43 59N 0 14W
St. Kilda, N.Z. **101** 45 53 S 170 31 E
St. Kilda, U.K. **8** 57 9N 8 34W
St. Kitts-Nevis ■ **121** 17 20N 62 40W
St. Laurent **109** 50 25N 97 58W
St-Laurent **127** 5 29N 54 3W
St-Laurent-du-Pont **21** 45 23N 5 45 E
St-Laurent-en-Grandvaux **21** 46 35N 5 58 E
St. Lawrence **107** 46 54N 55 23W
St. Lawrence → **107** 49 30N 66 0W
St. Lawrence, Gulf of **107** 48 25N 62 0W
St. Lawrence I. **104** 63 0N 170 0W
St. Leonard **107** 47 12N 67 58W
St-Léonard-de-Noblat **20** 45 49N 1 29 E
St. Lewis → **107** 52 26N 56 11W
St-Lô **18** 49 7N 1 5W
St-Louis **84** 16 8N 16 27W
St. Louis, Mich., U.S.A. **114** 43 27N 84 38W
St. Louis, Mo., U.S.A. **116** 38 40N 90 12W
St. Louis → **116** 47 15N 92 45W
St-Loup-sur-Semouse **19** 47 53N 6 16 E
St. Lucia ■ **121** 14 0N 60 50W
St. Lucia, C. **93** 28 32 S 32 29 E
St. Lucia Channel **121** 14 15N 61 0W
St. Lucia, Lake **93** 28 5 S 32 30 E
St. Lunaire-Griquet **107** 51 31N 55 28W
St. Maarten **121** 18 0N 63 5W
St-Maixent-l'École **20** 46 24N 0 12W
St-Malo **18** 48 39N 2 1W
St-Malo, G. de **18** 48 50N 2 30W
St-Mandrier **21** 43 4N 5 56 E
St-Marc **121** 19 10N 72 41W
St-Marcellin **21** 45 9N 5 20 E
St-Marcouf, Îs. **18** 49 30N 1 10W
St. Maries **118** 47 17N 116 34W
St-Martin, Charente-M., France **20** 46 12N 1 22W
St-Martin, Pas-de-Calais, France **19** 50 42N 1 38 E
St-Martin, I. **121** 18 0N 63 0W
St. Martin L. **109** 51 40N 98 30W
St-Martin-Vésubie **21** 44 4N 7 15 E
St. Martins **107** 45 22N 65 34W
St. Martinsville **117** 30 10N 91 50W
St-Martory **20** 43 9N 0 56 E
St. Mary B. **107** 46 50N 53 50W
St. Mary Is. **70** 13 20N 74 35 E
St. Mary Pk. **97** 31 32 S 138 34 E
St. Marys, Austral. **97** 41 35 S 148 11 E
St. Marys, Can. **112** 43 20N 81 10W
St. Mary's, U.K. **13** 49 55N 6 17W
St. Mary's, U.S.A. **114** 40 33N 84 20W
St. Marys **114** 41 27N 78 33W
St. Marys Bay **107** 44 25N 66 10W
St. Mary's, C. **107** 46 50N 54 12W
St. Mathews I. = Zadetkyi Kyun **71** 10 0N 98 25 E
St-Mathieu, Pte. de **18** 48 20N 4 45W
St-Maur-des-Fossés **19** 48 48N 2 30 E
St-Maurice → **106** 46 21N 72 31W
St-Médard-de-Guizières **20** 45 1N 0 4W
St-Méen-le-Grand **18** 48 11N 2 12W
St. Michaels **119** 35 38N 109 5W
St. Michael's Mt. **13** 50 7N 5 30W
St-Michel **21** 45 15N 6 29 E
St-Mihiel **19** 48 54N 5 30 E
St-Nazaire **18** 47 17N 2 12W
St. Neots **13** 52 14N 0 16W
St-Nicolas-de-Port **19** 48 38N 6 18 E
St-Omer **19** 50 45N 2 15 E
St. Ouen **19** 48 50N 2 20 E
St-Ouen **19** 50 2N 2 7 E
St-Pacome **107** 47 24N 69 58W
St-Palais **20** 45 40N 1 8W
St-Pamphile **107** 46 58N 69 48W
St-Pardoux-la-Rivière **20** 45 29N 0 45 E
St. Pascal **107** 47 32N 69 48W
St. Paul, Can. **108** 54 0N 111 17W
St. Paul, Ind. Oc. **3** 30 40 S 77 34 E
St. Paul, Minn., U.S.A. **116** 44 54N 93 5W
St. Paul, Nebr., U.S.A. **116** 41 15N 98 30W
St-Paul-de-Fenouillet **20** 42 50N 2 28 E
St. Paul, I. **107** 47 12N 60 9W
St-Péray **21** 44 57N 4 50 E
St-Père-en-Retz **18** 47 11N 2 2W
St. Peter **116** 44 21N 93 57W
St. Peter Port **18** 49 27N 2 31W
St. Peters, N.S., Can. **107** 45 40N 60 53W
St. Peters, P.E.I., Can. **107** 46 25N 62 35W
St. Petersburg **115** 27 45N 82 40W
St-Philbert-de-Grand-Lieu **18** 47 2N 1 39W
St Pierre **107** 46 46N 56 12W
St-Pierre-d'Oléron **20** 45 57N 1 19W
St-Pierre-Église **18** 49 40N 1 24W
St-Pierre-en-Port **18** 49 48N 0 30 E
St-Pierre et Miquelon □ **107** 46 55N 56 10W
St-Pierre, L. **106** 46 12N 72 52W
St-Pierre-le-Moûtier **19** 46 47N 3 7 E
St.-Pierre-sur-Dives **18** 49 2N 0 1W
St.-Pol **19** 50 21N 2 20 E
St-Pol-de-Léon **18** 48 41N 4 0W
St-Pol-sur-Mer **19** 51 1N 2 20 E
St-Pons **20** 43 30N 2 45 E
St-Pourçain-sur-Sioule **20** 46 18N 3 18 E
St-Quay-Portrieux **18** 48 39N 2 51W
St-Quentin **19** 49 50N 3 16 E
St-Rambert-d'Albon **21** 45 17N 4 49 E
St-Raphaël **21** 43 25N 6 46 E
St. Regis, Mont., U.S.A. **118** 47 20N 115 3W
St. Regis, N.Y., U.S.A. **113** 44 39N 74 34W
St-Rémy-de-Provence **21** 43 48N 4 50 E
St-Renan **18** 48 26N 4 37W
St-Saëns **18** 49 41N 1 16 E
St-Sauveur-en-Puisaye **19** 47 37N 3 12 E
St-Sauveur-le-Vicomte **18** 49 23N 1 32W
St-Savin **20** 46 34N 0 50 E
St-Savinien **20** 45 53N 0 42W
St. Sebastien, Tanjon' i **93** 12 26 S 48 44 E
St-Seine-l'Abbaye **19** 47 26N 4 47 E
St-Sernin **20** 43 54N 2 35 E
St-Servan-sur-Mer **18** 48 38N 2 0W
St-Sever **20** 43 46N 0 34W
St-Sever-Calvados **18** 48 50N 1 3W
St-Siméon **107** 47 51N 69 54W
St. Stephen **107** 45 16N 67 17W
St-Sulpice-Laurière **20** 46 3N 1 29 E
St-Sulpice-la-Pointe **20** 43 46N 1 41 E
St-Thégonnec **18** 48 31N 3 57W
St. Thomas, Can. **106** 42 45N 81 10W
St. Thomas, W. Indies **121** 18 21N 64 55W
St-Tite **106** 46 45N 72 34W
St-Tropez **21** 43 17N 6 38 E
St. Troud = Sint Truiden **16** 50 48N 5 10 E
St-Vaast-la-Hougue **18** 49 35N 1 17W
St-Valéry **19** 50 10N 1 38 E
St-Valéry-en-Caux **18** 49 52N 0 43 E
St-Vallier **21** 45 11N 4 50 E
St-Vallier-de-Thiey **21** 43 42N 6 51 E
St-Varent **18** 46 53N 0 13W
St. Vincent **6** 18 0N 26 1W
St. Vincent ■ **121** 13 10N 61 10W
St-Vincent-de-Tyrosse **20** 43 39N 1 18W
St. Vincent, G. **97** 35 0 S 138 0 E
St. Vincent Passage **121** 13 30N 61 0W
St. Vincent, Tanjona **93** 21 58 S 43 20 E
St-Vith **16** 50 17N 6 9 E
St-Yrieux-la-Perche **20** 45 31N 1 12 E
Ste-Adresse **18** 49 31N 0 5 E
Ste-Agathe-des-Monts **106** 46 3N 74 17W
Ste Anne de Beaupré **107** 47 2N 70 58W
Ste-Anne-des-Monts **107** 49 8N 66 30W
Ste-Énimie **20** 44 22N 3 26 E
Ste-Foy-la-Grande **20** 44 50N 0 13 E
Ste. Genevieve **116** 37 59N 90 2W
Ste-Hermine **20** 46 32N 1 4W
Ste-Livrade-sur-Lot **20** 44 24N 0 36 E
Ste-Marguerite → **107** 50 9N 66 36W
Ste Marie **121** 14 48N 61 1W
Ste-Marie-aux-Mines **19** 48 10N 7 12 E
Ste-Marie de la Madeleine **107** 46 26N 71 0W
Ste-Maure-de-Touraine **18** 47 7N 0 37 E
Ste-Maxime **21** 43 19N 6 39 E
Ste-Menehould **19** 49 5N 4 54 E
Ste-Mère-Église **18** 49 24N 1 19W
Ste-Rose **121** 16 20N 61 45W
Ste.-Rose du lac **109** 51 4N 99 30W
Saintes **20** 45 45N 0 37W
Saintes, Île des **121** 15 50N 61 35W
Saintes-Maries-de-la-Mer **21** 43 26N 4 26 E
Saintonge **20** 45 40N 0 50W
Sairang **67** 23 50N 92 45 E
Sairecábur, Cerro **124** 22 43 S 67 54W
Saitama □ **74** 36 25N 139 30 E
Sajama **126** 18 7 S 69 0W
Sajan **42** 45 50N 20 20 E
Sajószentpéter **27** 48 12N 20 44 E
Sakai **74** 34 30N 135 30 E
Sakākah **64** 30 0N 40 8 E
Sakami, L. **106** 53 15N 77 0W
Sâkâne, 'Erg i-n **82** 20 30N 1 30W
Sakania **91** 12 43 S 28 30 E
Sakarya → **56** 41 7N 30 39 E
Sakata **74** 38 55N 139 50 E
Sakeny → **93** 20 0 S 45 25 E
Sakété **85** 6 40N 2 45 E
Sakhalin, Ostrov **59** 51 0N 143 0 E
Sakhi Gopal **69** 19 58N 85 50 E
Sakhnīn **62** 32 52N 35 12 E
Saki **56** 45 9N 33 34 E
Sakiai **54** 54 59N 23 0 E
Sakołow Małopolski **28** 50 10N 22 9 E
Sakon Nakhon **71** 17 10N 104 9 E
Sakrand **68** 26 10N 68 15 E
Sakri **68** 21 2N 74 20 E
Sakskøbing **49** 54 49N 11 39 E
Sal → **57** 47 31N 40 45 E
Šal'a **27** 48 10N 17 50 E
Sala **48** 59 58N 16 35 E
Sala Consilina **41** 40 23N 15 35 E
Sala-y-Gómez **95** 26 28 S 105 28W
Salaberry-de-Valleyfield **106** 45 15N 74 8W
Saladas **124** 28 15 S 58 40W
Saladillo **124** 35 40 S 59 55W
Salado →, Buenos Aires, Argent. **124** 35 44 S 57 22W
Salado →, La Pampa, Argent. **128** 37 30 S 67 0W
Salado →, Santa Fe, Argent. **124** 31 40 S 60 41W
Salado →, Mexico **120** 26 52N 99 19W
Salaga **85** 8 31N 0 31W
Sălaj □ **46** 47 15N 23 0 E
Salala, Liberia **84** 6 42N 10 7W
Salala, Sudan **86** 21 17N 36 16 E
Salālah **63** 16 56N 53 59 E
Salamanca, Chile **124** 31 46 S 70 59W
Salamanca, Spain **30** 40 58N 5 39W
Salamanca, U.S.A. **114** 42 10N 78 42W
Salamanca □ **30** 40 57N 5 40W
Salamis **45** 37 56N 23 30 E
Salar de Atacama **124** 23 30 S 68 25W
Salar de Uyuni **126** 20 30 S 67 45W
Sălard **46** 47 12N 22 3 E
Salas **30** 43 25N 6 15W
Salas de los Infantes **32** 42 2N 3 17W
Salatiga **73** 7 19 S 110 30 E
Salavat **52** 53 21N 55 55 E
Salaverry **126** 8 15 S 79 0W
Salawati **73** 1 7 S 130 52 E
Salayar **73** 6 7 S 120 30 E
Salazar → **32** 42 40N 1 20W
Salbris **19** 47 25N 2 3 E
Salcia **46** 43 56N 24 55 E
Salcombe **13** 50 14N 3 47W
Saldaña **30** 42 32N 4 48W
Saldanha **92** 33 0 S 17 58 E
Saldanhabaai **92** 33 6 S 18 0 E
Saldus **54** 56 38N 22 30 E
Sale **97** 38 6 S 147 6 E
Salé **82** 34 3N 6 48W
Sale **12** 53 26N 2 19W
Salebabu **73** 3 55N 126 40 E
Salekhard **58** 66 30N 66 35 E
Salem, India **70** 11 40N 78 11 E
Salem, Ind., U.S.A. **114** 38 38N 86 6W
Salem, Mass., U.S.A. **114** 42 29N 70 53W
Salem, Mo., U.S.A. **117** 37 40N 91 30W
Salem, N.J., U.S.A. **114** 39 34N 75 29W
Salem, Ohio, U.S.A. **114** 40 52N 80 50W
Salem, Oreg., U.S.A. **118** 45 0N 123 0W
Salem, S.D., U.S.A. **116** 43 44N 97 23W
Salem, Va., U.S.A. **114** 37 19N 80 8W
Salemi **40** 37 49N 12 47 E
Salernes **21** 43 34N 6 15 E
Salerno **41** 40 40N 14 44 E
Salerno, G. di **41** 40 35N 14 45 E
Salfīt **62** 32 5N 35 11 E
Salford **12** 53 30N 2 17W
Salgir → **56** 45 38N 35 1 E
Salgótarján **27** 48 5N 19 47 E
Salies-de-Béarn **20** 43 28N 0 56W
Salina, Italy **41** 38 35N 14 50 E
Salina, U.S.A. **116** 38 50N 97 40W
Salina Cruz **120** 16 10N 95 10W
Salinas, Brazil **127** 16 10 S 42 10W
Salinas, Chile **124** 23 31 S 69 29W
Salinas, Ecuador **126** 2 10 S 80 58W
Salinas, U.S.A. **119** 36 40N 121 41W
Salinas →, Mexico **120** 16 28N 90 31W
Salinas →, U.S.A. **119** 36 45N 121 48W
Salinas Ambargasta **124** 29 0 S 65 0W
Salinas, B. de **121** 11 4N 85 45W
Salinas, C. de **33** 39 16N 3 4 E
Salinas (de Hidalgo) **120** 22 30N 101 40W
Salinas Grandes **124** 30 0 S 65 0W
Salinas, Pampa de las **124** 31 58 S 66 42W
Saline →, Ark., U.S.A. **117** 33 10N 92 8W
Saline →, Kans., U.S.A. **116** 38 51N 97 30W
Salinópolis **127** 0 40 S 47 20W
Salins **19** 46 57N 5 53 E
Salins-les-Bains **19** 46 58N 5 52 E
Salir **31** 37 14N 8 2W
Salisbury, Austral. **99** 34 46 S 138 40 E
Salisbury, U.K. **13** 51 4N 1 48W
Salisbury, Md., U.S.A. **114** 38 20N 75 38W
Salisbury, N.C., U.S.A. **115** 35 20N 80 29W
* Salisbury, Zimb. **91** 17 43 S 31 2 E
Salisbury Plain **13** 51 13N 1 50W
Săliște **46** 45 45N 23 56 E
Salka **85** 10 20N 4 58 E
Salle, La **116** 41 20N 89 6W
Sallent **32** 41 49N 1 54 E
Salles-Curan **20** 44 11N 2 48 E
Salling **49** 56 40N 8 55 E
Sallisaw **117** 35 26N 94 45W
Sallom Junction **86** 19 17N 37 6 E
Salmerón **32** 40 33N 2 29W
Salmo **108** 49 10N 117 20W
Salmon **118** 45 12N 113 56W
Salmon →, Can. **108** 54 3N 122 40W
Salmon →, U.S.A. **118** 45 51N 116 46W
Salmon Arm **108** 50 40N 119 15W
Salmon Falls **118** 42 48N 114 59W
Salmon Res. **107** 48 05N 56 00W
Salmon River Mts. **118** 45 0N 114 30W
Salo **51** 60 22N 23 10 E
Salò **38** 45 37N 10 32 E
Salobreña **31** 36 44N 3 35W
Salome **119** 33 51N 113 37W
Salon-de-Provence **21** 43 39N 5 6 E
Salonica = Thessaloníki **44** 40 38N 22 58 E
Salonta **46** 46 49N 21 42 E
Salop = Shropshire □ **13** 52 36N 2 45W
Salor → **31** 39 39N 7 3W
Salou, Cabo **32** 41 3N 1 10 E
Salsacate **124** 31 20 S 65 5W
Salses **20** 42 50N 2 55 E
Salsette I. **70** 19 5N 72 50 E
Salsk **57** 46 28N 41 30 E
Salso → **41** 37 6N 13 55 E
Salsomaggiore **38** 44 48N 9 59 E
Salt →, Can. **108** 60 0N 112 25W
Salt →, U.S.A. **119** 33 23N 112 18W
Salt Creek **99** 36 8 S 139 38 E
Salt Fork → **117** 36 37N 97 7W
Salt Lake City **118** 40 45N 111 58W
Salt Range **68** 32 30N 72 25 E
Salta **124** 24 57 S 65 25W
Salta □ **124** 24 48 S 65 30W
Saltcoats **14** 55 38N 4 47W
Saltee Is. **15** 52 7N 6 37W
Saltfjorden **50** 67 15N 14 10 E
Saltholm **49** 55 38N 12 43 E
Salthólmavík **50** 65 24N 21 57W
Saltillo **120** 25 30N 100 57W
Salto, Argent. **124** 34 20 S 60 15W
Salto, Uruguay **124** 31 27 S 57 50W
Salton Sea **119** 33 20N 115 50W
Saltpond **85** 5 15N 1 3W
Saltsjöbaden **49** 59 15N 18 20 E
Saltspring **108** 48 54N 123 37W
Saltville **114** 36 53N 81 46W
Saluda → **115** 34 0N 81 4W
Salûm **86** 31 31N 25 7 E
Salûm, Khâlig el **86** 31 30N 25 9 E
Salur **70** 18 27N 83 18 E
Saluzzo **38** 44 39N 7 29 E
Salvador, Brazil **127** 13 0 S 38 30W
Salvador, Can. **109** 52 10N 109 32W
Salvador, L. **117** 29 46N 90 16W
Salvaterra de Magos **31** 39 1N 8 47W
Sálvora, Isla **30** 42 30N 8 58W
Salwa **65** 24 45N 50 55 E
Salween → **67** 16 31N 97 37 E
Salyany **53** 39 10N 48 50 E
Salyersville **114** 37 45N 83 4W
Salza → **26** 47 40N 14 43 E
Salzach → **26** 48 12N 12 56 E
Salzburg **26** 47 48N 13 2 E
Salzburg □ **26** 47 15N 13 0 E
Salzgitter **24** 52 13N 10 22 E
Salzwedel **24** 52 50N 11 11 E
Sam Neua **71** 20 29N 104 0 E
Sam Ngao **71** 17 18N 99 0 E
Sam Rayburn Res. **117** 31 15N 94 20W
Sama **58** 60 12N 60 22 E
Sama de Langreo **30** 43 18N 5 40W
Samagaltai **59** 50 36N 95 3 E
Samales Group **73** 6 0N 122 0 E
Samalkot **70** 17 3N 82 13 E
Samâlût **86** 28 20N 30 42 E
Samana **68** 30 10N 76 13 E
Samanga **91** 8 20 S 39 13 E
Samangán □ **65** 36 15N 68 3 E
Samangwa **90** 4 23 S 24 10 E
Samar **73** 12 0N 125 0 E
Samarai **98** 10 39 S 150 41 E
Samaria = Shōmrōn **62** 32 15N 35 13 E
Samarinda **72** 0 30 S 117 9 E
Samarkand **58** 39 40N 66 55 E
Sāmarrā" **64** 34 16N 43 55 E
Samastipur **69** 25 50N 85 50 E
Samatan **20** 43 29N 0 55 E
Samba **90** 4 38 S 26 22 E
Sambalpur **69** 21 28N 84 4 E
Sambar, Tanjung **72** 2 59 S 110 19 E
Sambas **72** 1 20N 109 20 E
Sambava **93** 14 16 S 50 10 E
Sambawizi **91** 18 24 S 26 13 E
Sambhal **68** 28 35N 78 37 E
Sambhar **68** 26 52N 75 6 E
Sambiase **41** 38 58N 16 16 E
Sambonifacio **38** 45 24N 11 16 E
Sambor, Camb. **71** 12 46N 106 0 E
Sambor, U.S.S.R. **54** 49 30N 23 10 E
Sambre → **16** 50 27N 4 52 E
Sambuca di Sicilia **40** 37 39N 13 6 E
Samburu □ **90** 1 10N 37 0 E
Samchŏk **76** 37 30N 129 10 E
Same **90** 4 2 S 37 38 E
Samer **19** 50 38N 1 44 E
Samfya **91** 11 22 S 29 31 E
Sámi **45** 38 15N 20 39 E
Samna **86** 25 12N 37 17 E
Samnū **83** 27 15N 14 55 E
Samo Alto **124** 30 22 S 71 0W
Samobor **39** 45 47N 15 44 E
Samoëns **21** 46 5N 6 45 E
Samokov **43** 42 18N 23 35 E
Samoorombón, Bahía **124** 36 5 S 57 20W
Samorogouan **84** 11 21N 4 57W
Sámos **45** 37 45N 26 50 E
Samos **30** 42 44N 7 20W
Samoš **42** 45 13N 20 49 E
Samotharáki **44** 39 48N 19 31 E
Samothráki **44** 40 28N 25 28 E
Samoylovka **55** 51 12N 43 43 E
Sampa **84** 8 0N 2 36W
Sampacho **124** 33 20 S 64 50W
Sampang **73** 7 11 S 113 13 E
Samper de Calanda **32** 41 11N 0 28W
Sampit **72** 2 34 S 113 0 E
Sampit, Teluk **72** 3 5 S 113 3 E
Samra **64** 25 35N 41 0 E
Samsø **49** 55 50N 10 35 E
Samsø Bælt **49** 55 45N 10 45 E
Samsun **64** 41 15N 36 22 E
Samsun Dağı **45** 37 45N 27 10 E
Samtredia **57** 42 7N 42 24 E
Samui, Ko **71** 9 30N 100 0 E
Samur → **57** 41 53N 48 32 E
Samusole **91** 10 2 S 24 0 E
Samut Prakan **71** 13 32N 100 40 E
Samut Sakhon **71** 13 31N 100 13 E
Samut Songkhram (Mekong) **71** 13 24N 100 1 E
Samwari **68** 28 30N 66 46 E
San **84** 13 15N 4 57W
San → **27** 50 45N 21 51 E
San Adrián, C. de **30** 43 21N 8 50W
San Agustin, C. **73** 6 20N 126 13 E
San Agustín de Valle Fértil **124** 30 35 S 67 30W
San Ambrosio **95** 26 28 S 79 53W
San Andreas **118** 38 0N 120 39W
San Andrés, I. de **121** 12 42N 81 46W
San Andres Mts. **119** 33 0N 106 45W
San Andrés Tuxtla **120** 18 30N 95 20W
San Angelo **117** 31 30N 100 30W
San Antonio, Chile **124** 33 40 S 71 40W
San Antonio, N. Mex., U.S.A. **119** 33 58N 106 57W
San Antonio, Tex., U.S.A. **117** 29 30N 98 30W
San Antonio → **117** 28 30N 96 50W
San Antonio Abad **33** 38 59N 1 19 E
San Antonio, C., Argent. **124** 36 15 S 56 40W
San Antonio, C., Cuba **121** 21 50N 84 57W
San Antonio, C. de **33** 38 48N 0 12 E
San Antonio de los Baños **121** 22 54N 82 31W
San Antonio de los Cobres **124** 24 10 S 66 17W
San Antonio Oeste **128** 40 40 S 65 0W
San Augustine **117** 31 30N 94 7W
San Bartolomeo in Galdo **41** 41 23N 15 2 E
San Benedetto **38** 45 2N 10 57 E
San Benedetto del Tronto **39** 42 57N 13 52 E
San Benito **117** 26 5N 97 39W
San Bernardino **119** 34 7N 117 18W
San Bernardino Str. **73** 13 0N 125 0 E
San Bernardo **124** 33 40 S 70 50W
San Bernardo, I. de **126** 9 45N 75 50W
San Blas **120** 26 4N 108 46W
San Blas, C. **115** 29 40N 85 12W
San Borja **126** 14 50 S 66 52W
San Buenaventura **120** 27 5N 101 32W
San Carlos, Argent. **124** 33 50 S 69 0W
San Carlos, Chile **124** 36 10 S 72 0W
San Carlos, Mexico **120** 29 0N 100 54W
San Carlos, Nic. **121** 11 12N 84 50W
San Carlos, Phil. **73** 10 29N 123 25 E
San Carlos, Uruguay **125** 34 46 S 54 58W
San Carlos, U.S.A. **119** 33 24N 110 27W
San Carlos, Amazonas, Venez. **126** 1 55N 67 4W
San Carlos, Cojedes, Venez. **126** 9 40N 68 36W
San Carlos = Butuku-Luba **85** 3 29N 8 33 E
San Carlos de Bariloche **128** 41 10 S 71 25W
San Carlos de la Rápita **32** 40 37N 0 35 E
San Carlos del Zulia **126** 9 1N 71 55W
San Carlos L. **119** 33 15N 110 25W
San Cataldo **40** 37 30N 13 58 E
San Celoni **32** 41 42N 2 30 E
San Clemente, Chile **124** 35 30 S 71 29W
San Clemente, Spain **33** 39 24N 2 25W
San Clemente, U.S.A. **119** 33 29N 117 36W
San Clemente I. **119** 32 53N 118 30W
San Constanzo **39** 43 46N 13 5 E

* *Renamed Harare*

San Cristóbal, Argent. **124** 30 20 S 61 10W
San Cristóbal, Dom. Rep. **121** 18 25N 70 6W
San Cristóbal, Venez. **126** 16 50N 92 40W
San Cristóbal de las Casas **120** 16 50N 92 33W
San Damiano d'Asti **38** 44 51N 8 4 E
San Daniele del Friuli **39** 46 10N 13 0 E
San Demétrio Corone **41** 39 34N 16 22 E
San Diego, Calif., U.S.A. **119** 32 43N 117 10W
San Diego, Tex., U.S.A. **117** 27 47N 98 15W
San Diego, C. **128** 54 40 S 65 10W
San Donà di Piave **39** 45 38N 12 34 E
San Elpídio a Mare **39** 43 16N 13 41 E
San Estanislao **124** 24 39 S 56 26W
San Esteban de Gormaz **32** 41 34N 3 13W
San Felice sul Panaro **38** 44 51N 11 9 E
San Felipe, Chile **124** 32 43 S 70 42W
San Felipe, Mexico **120** 31 0N 114 52W
San Felipe, Venez. **126** 10 20N 68 44W
San Feliu de Guixols **32** 41 45N 3 1 E
San Feliu de Llobregat **32** 41 23N 2 2 E
San Félix **95** 26 23 S 80 0W
San Fernando, Chile **124** 34 30 S 71 0W
San Fernando, Mexico **120** 30 0N 115 10W
San Fernando, Luzon, Phil. **73** 16 40N 120 23 E
San Fernando, Luzon, Phil. **73** 15 5N 120 37 E
San Fernando, Spain **31** 36 28N 6 17W
San Fernando, Trin. **121** 10 20N 61 30W
San Fernando, U.S.A. **119** 34 15N 118 29W
San Fernando → **120** 24 55N 98 10W
San Fernando de Apure **126** 7 54N 67 15W
San Fernando de Atabapo **126** 4 3N 67 42W
San Fernando di Púglia **41** 41 18N 16 5 E
San Francisco, Argent. **124** 31 30 S 62 5W
San Francisco, U.S.A. **119** 37 47N 122 30W
San Francisco → **119** 32 59N 109 22W
San Francisco de Macorîs **121** 19 19N 70 15W
San Francisco del Monte de Oro **124** 32 36 S 66 8W
San Francisco del Oro **120** 26 52N 105 50W
San Francisco Javier **33** 38 42N 1 26 E
San Francisco, Paso de **124** 27 0 S 68 0W
San Fratello **41** 38 1N 14 33 E
San Gavino Monreale **40** 39 33N 8 47 E
San Gil **126** 6 33N 73 8W
San Gimignano **38** 43 28N 11 3 E
San Giórgio di Nogaro **39** 45 50N 13 13 E
San Giórgio Iónico **41** 40 27N 17 23 E
San Giovanni Bianco **38** 45 52N 9 40 E
San Giovanni in Fiore **41** 39 16N 16 42 E
San Giovanni in Persiceto **39** 44 39N 11 12 E
San Giovanni Rotondo **41** 41 41N 15 42 E
San Giovanni Valdarno **39** 43 32N 11 30 E
San Giuliano Terme **38** 43 45N 10 26 E
San Gottardo, Paso del **25** 46 33N 8 33 E
San Grcángelo **40** 40 14N 16 14 E
San Gregorio **125** 32 37 S 55 40W
San Guiseppe Iato **40** 37 57N 13 11 E
San Ignacio, Boliv. **126** 16 20 S 60 55W
San Ignacio, Parag. **124** 26 52 S 57 3W
San Ignacio, Laguna **120** 26 50N 113 11W
San Ildefonso, C. **73** 16 0N 122 1 E
San Isidro **124** 34 29 S 58 31W
San Javier, Misiones, Argent. **125** 27 55 S 55 5W
San Javier, Santa Fe, Argent. **124** 30 40 S 59 55W
San Javier, Boliv. **126** 16 18 S 62 30W
San Javier, Chile **124** 35 40 S 71 45W
San Javier, Spain **33** 37 49N 0 50W
San Joaquin → **119** 37 4N 121 51W
San Jorge **124** 31 54 S 61 50W
San Jorge, Bahía de **120** 31 20N 113 20W
San Jorge, Golfo **128** 46 0 S 66 0W
San Jorge, G. de **32** 40 50N 0 55W
San José, Boliv. **126** 17 53 S 60 50W
San José, C. Rica **121** 10 0N 84 2W
San José, Guat. **120** 14 0N 90 50W
San José, Mexico **120** 25 0N 110 50W
San Jose, Luzon, Phil. **73** 15 45N 120 55 E
San Jose, Mindoro, Phil. **73** 12 27N 121 4 E
San Jose, Panay, Phil. **73** 10 50N 122 5 E
San José **33** 38 55N 1 18 E
San Jose, Calif., U.S.A. **119** 37 20N 121 53W
San Jose, N. Mex., U.S.A. **119** 35 26N 105 30W
San Jose → **119** 34 58N 106 7W
San José de Feliciano **124** 30 26 S 58 46W
San José de Jáchal **124** 30 15 S 68 46W
San José de Mayo **124** 34 27 S 56 40W
San José de Ocune **126** 4 15N 70 20W
San José del Cabo **120** 23 0N 109 40W
San José del Guaviare **126** 2 35N 72 38W
San Juan, Argent. **124** 31 30 S 68 30W
San Juan, Dom. Rep. **121** 18 45N 72 45W
San Juan, Mexico **120** 21 20N 102 50W
San Juan, Phil. **73** 8 25N 126 20 E
San Juan, Pto. Rico **121** 18 28N 66 8W
San Juan □ **124** 31 9 S 69 0W
San Juan →, Argent. **124** 32 20 S 67 25W
San Juan →, Nic. **121** 10 56N 83 42W
San Juan →, U.S.A. **119** 37 20N 110 20W
San Juan Bautista, Parag. **124** 26 37 S 57 6W
San Juan Bautista, Spain **33** 39 5N 1 31 E
San Juan, C. **88** 1 5N 9 20 E
San Juan Capistrano **119** 33 29N 117 40W
San Juan de los Morros **126** 9 55N 67 21W
San Juan del Norte, B. de **121** 11 0N 83 40W
San Juan del Puerto **31** 37 20N 6 50W
San Juan del Río **120** 20 25N 100 0W
San Juan del Sur **121** 11 20N 85 51W
San Juan Mts. **119** 38 30N 108 30W
San Julián **128** 49 15 S 67 45W
San Just, Sierra de **32** 40 45N 0 49W
San Justo **124** 30 47 S 60 30W
San Lázaro, C. **120** 24 50N 112 18W
San Lázaro, Sa. de **120** 23 25N 110 0W
San Leandro **119** 37 40N 122 6W
San Leonardo **32** 41 51N 3 5W
San Lorenzo, Argent. **124** 32 45 S 60 45W
San Lorenzo, Ecuador **126** 1 15N 78 50W
San Lorenzo, Parag. **124** 25 20 S 57 32W
San Lorenzo → **120** 24 15N 107 24W
San Lorenzo de la Parrilla **32** 39 51N 2 22W
San Lorenzo de Morunys **32** 42 8N 1 35 E
San Lorenzo, I., Mexico **120** 28 35N 112 50W
San Lorenzo, I., Peru **126** 12 7 S 77 15W
San Lorenzo, Mt. **128** 47 40 S 72 20W
San Lucas, Boliv. **126** 20 5 S 65 7W
San Lucas, Mexico **120** 27 10N 112 14W
San Lucas, C. de **120** 22 50N 110 0W
San Lúcido **41** 39 18N 16 3 E
San Luis, Argent. **124** 33 20 S 66 20W
San Luis, U.S.A. **119** 37 3N 105 26W
San Luis □ **124** 34 0 S 66 0W
San Luis de la Paz **120** 21 19N 100 32W
San Luis, I. **120** 29 58N 114 26W
San Luis Obispo **119** 35 21N 120 38W
San Luis Potosí **120** 22 9N 100 59W
San Luis Potosí □ **120** 22 10N 101 0W
San Luis Río Colorado **120** 32 29N 114 58W
San Luis, Sierra de **124** 32 30 S 66 10W
San Marco Argentano **41** 39 34N 16 8 E
San Marco dei Cavoti **41** 41 20N 14 50 E
San Marco in Lámis **41** 41 43N 15 38 E
San Marcos, Guat. **120** 14 59N 91 52W
San Marcos, Mexico **120** 27 13N 112 6W
San Marcos, U.S.A. **117** 29 53N 98 0W
San Marino **39** 43 56N 12 25 E
San Marino ■ **39** 43 56N 12 25 E
San Martín **124** 33 5 S 68 28W
San Martín de Valdeiglesias **30** 40 21N 4 24W
San Martín, L. **128** 48 50 S 72 50W
San Martino de Calvi **38** 45 57N 9 41 E
San Mateo, Spain **32** 40 28N 0 10 E
San Mateo, U.S.A. **119** 37 32N 122 19W
San Matías **126** 16 25 S 58 20W
San Matías, Golfo **128** 41 30 S 64 0W
San Matías, G. of **122** 41 30 S 64 0W
San Miguel, El Sal. **120** 13 30N 88 12W
San Miguel, Spain **33** 39 3N 1 26 E
San Miguel, U.S.A. **119** 35 45N 120 42W
San Miguel → **126** 13 52 S 63 56W
San Miguel de Salinas **33** 37 59N 0 47W
San Miguel de Tucumán **124** 26 50 S 65 20W
San Miguel del Monte **124** 35 23 S 58 50W
San Miniato **38** 43 40N 10 50 E
San Narciso **73** 15 2N 120 3 E
San Nicolás de los Arroyas **124** 33 25 S 60 10W
San Nicolas I. **119** 33 16N 119 30W
San Pablo **124** 21 43 S 66 38W
San Paolo di Civitate **41** 41 44N 15 16 E
San Pedro, Buenos Aires, Argent. **125** 26 30 S 54 10W
San Pedro, Jujuy, Argent. **124** 24 12 S 64 55W
San-Pédro **84** 4 50N 6 33W
San Pedro □ **124** 24 0 S 57 0W
San Pedro →, Chihuahua, Mexico **120** 28 20N 106 10W
San Pedro →, Nayarit, Mexico **120** 21 45N 105 30W
San Pedro →, U.S.A. **119** 33 0N 110 50W
San Pedro de Atacama **124** 22 55 S 68 15W
San Pedro de Jujuy **124** 24 12 S 64 55W
San Pedro de las Colonias **120** 25 50N 102 59W
San Pedro de Lloc **126** 7 15 S 79 28W
San Pedro de Macorís **121** 18 30N 69 18W
San Pedro del Paraná **124** 26 43 S 56 13W
San Pedro del Pinatar **33** 37 50N 0 50W
San Pedro Mártir, Sierra **120** 31 0N 115 30W
San Pedro Mixtepec **120** 16 2N 97 7W
San Pedro Ocampo = Melchor Ocampo **120** 24 52N 101 40W
San Pedro, Pta. **124** 25 30 S 70 38W
San Pedro, Sierra de **31** 39 18N 6 40W
San Pedro Sula **120** 15 30N 88 0W
San Pedro,Pta. **124** 25 30 S 70 38W
San Pietro, I. **40** 39 9N 8 17 E
San Pietro Vernótico **41** 40 28N 18 0 E
San Quintín **73** 16 1N 120 56 E
San Rafael, Argent. **124** 34 40 S 68 21W
San Rafael, Calif., U.S.A. **118** 37 59N 122 32W
San Rafael, N. Mex., U.S.A. **119** 35 6N 107 58W
San Ramón de la Nueva Orán **124** 23 10 S 64 20W
San Remo **38** 43 48N 7 47 E
San Roque, Argent. **124** 28 25 S 58 45W
San Roque, Spain **31** 36 17N 5 21W
San Rosendo **124** 37 16 S 72 43W
San Saba **117** 31 12N 98 45W
San Salvador **120** 13 40N 89 10W
San Salvador de Jujuy **124** 24 10 S 64 48W
San Salvador I. **121** 24 0N 74 32W
San Sebastián, Argent. **128** 53 10 S 68 30W
San Sebastián, Spain **32** 43 17N 1 58W
San Serverino Marche **39** 43 13N 13 10 E
San Simon **119** 32 14N 109 16W
San Stéfano di Cadore **39** 46 34N 12 33 E
San Valentin, Mte. **128** 46 30 S 73 30W
San Vicente de Alcántara **31** 39 22N 7 8W
San Vicente de la Barquera **30** 43 23N 4 29W
San Vincenzo **38** 43 6N 10 29 E
San Vito **40** 39 26N 9 32 E
San Vito al Tagliamento **39** 45 55N 12 50 E
San Vito, C. **40** 38 11N 12 41 E
San Vito Chietino **39** 42 19N 14 27 E
San Vito dei Normanni **41** 40 40N 17 40 E
San Ygnacio **117** 27 6N 99 24W
Sana' **63** 15 27N 44 12 E
Sana → **39** 45 3N 16 23 E
Sanaba **84** 12 25N 3 47W
Sanabria, La **30** 42 0N 6 30W
Sanâfir **86** 27 55N 34 37 E
Sanaga → **88** 3 35N 9 38 E
Sanak I. **104** 53 30N 162 30W
Sanana **73** 2 5 S 125 59 E
Sanand **68** 22 59N 72 25 E
Sanandaj **64** 35 18N 47 1 E
Sanandita **124** 21 40 S 63 45W
Sanary **21** 43 7N 5 48 E
Sanawad **68** 22 11N 76 5 E
Sancergues **19** 47 10N 2 54 E
Sancerre **19** 47 20N 2 50 E
Sancerrois, Coll. du **19** 47 20N 2 40 E
Sancha He → **77** 26 48N 106 7 E
Sanchor **68** 24 45N 71 55 E
Sanco, Pt. **73** 8 15N 126 24 E
Sancoins **19** 46 47N 2 55 E
Sancti-Spíritus **121** 21 52N 79 33W
Sand → **93** 22 25 S 30 5 E
Sand Springs **117** 36 12N 96 5W
Sandah **86** 20 35N 39 32 E
Sandakan **72** 5 53N 118 4 E
Sandan **71** 12 46N 106 0 E
Sandanski **43** 41 35N 23 16 E
Sandaré **84** 14 40N 10 15W
Sanday **14** 59 15N 2 30W
Sande, Möre og Romsdal, Norway **47** 62 15N 5 27 E
Sande, Sogn og Fjordane, Norway **47** 61 20N 5 47 E
Sandefjord **47** 59 10N 10 15 E
Sandeid **47** 59 33N 5 52 E
Sanders **119** 35 12N 109 25W
Sanderson **117** 30 5N 102 30W
Sandfly L. **109** 55 43N 106 6W
Sandgate **99** 27 18 S 153 3 E
Sandía **126** 14 10 S 69 30W
Sandıklı **64** 38 30N 30 20 E
Sandnes **47** 58 50N 5 45 E
Sandness **14** 60 18N 1 38W
Sandoa **88** 9 41 S 23 0 E
Sandomierz **28** 50 40N 21 43 E
Sandover → **97** 21 43 S 136 32 E
Sandoway **67** 18 20N 94 30 E
Sandpoint **118** 48 20N 116 34W
Sandringham **12** 52 50N 0 30 E
Sandslån **48** 63 2N 17 49 E
Sandspit **108** 53 14N 131 49W
Sandstone **96** 27 59 S 119 16 E
Sandusky, Mich., U.S.A. **106** 43 26N 82 50W
Sandusky, Ohio, U.S.A. **114** 41 25N 82 40W
Sandvig **49** 55 18N 14 48 E
Sandviken **48** 60 38N 16 46 E
Sandwich B., Can. **107** 53 40N 57 15W
Sandwich B., S. Afr. **92** 23 25 S 14 20 E
Sandwich, C. **98** 18 14 S 146 18 E
Sandwich Group **5** 57 0 S 27 0W
Sandwip Chan. **67** 22 35N 91 35 E
Sandy C., Queens., Austral. **97** 24 42 S 153 15 E
Sandy C., Tas., Austral. **97** 41 25 S 144 45 E
Sandy Cr. → **118** 41 15N 109 47W
Sandy L. **106** 53 2N 93 0W
Sandy Lake **106** 53 0N 93 15W
Sandy Narrows **109** 55 5N 103 4W
Sanford, Fla., U.S.A. **115** 28 45N 81 20W
Sanford, Me., U.S.A. **113** 43 28N 70 47W
Sanford, N.C., U.S.A. **115** 35 30N 79 10W
Sanford → **96** 27 22 S 115 53 E
Sanford Mt. **104** 62 30N 143 0W
Sanga **91** 12 22 S 35 21 E
Sanga → **88** 1 5 S 17 0 E
Sanga-Tolon **59** 61 50N 149 40 E
Sangamner **70** 19 37N 74 15 E
Sangar **59** 64 2N 127 31 E
Sangasanga **72** 0 36 S 117 13 E
Sange **90** 6 58 S 28 21 E
Sangeang **73** 8 12 S 119 6 E
Sanger **119** 36 41N 119 35W
Sangerhausen **24** 51 28N 11 18 E
Sanggan He → **76** 38 12N 117 15 E
Sanggau **72** 0 5N 110 30 E
Sangihe, Kepulauan **73** 3 0N 126 0 E
Sangihe, P. **73** 3 45N 125 30 E
Sangkapura **72** 5 52 S 112 40 E
Sangli **70** 16 55N 74 33 E
Sangmélina **88** 2 57N 12 1 E
Sangonera → **33** 37 59N 1 4W
Sangre de Cristo Mts. **117** 37 0N 105 0W
Sangro → **39** 42 14N 14 32 E
Sangudo **108** 53 50N 114 54W
Sangüesa **32** 42 37N 1 17W
Sanguinaires, Îs. **21** 41 51N 8 36 E
Sangzhi **77** 29 25N 110 12 E
Sanhala **84** 10 3N 6 51W
Sanish **116** 48 0N 102 30W
Sanje **90** 0 49 S 31 30 E
Sanjiang **77** 25 48N 109 37 E
Sankaranayinarkovil **70** 9 10N 77 35 E
Sankeshwar **70** 16 23N 74 32 E
Sankt Andra **26** 46 46N 14 50 E
Sankt Blasien **25** 47 47N 8 7 E
Sankt Gallen **25** 47 26N 9 22 E
Sankt Gallen □ **25** 47 25N 9 22 E
Sankt Gotthard P. = San Gottardo, Paso del **25** 46 33N 8 33 E
Sankt Ingbert **25** 49 16N 7 6 E
Sankt Johann, Salzburg, Austria **26** 47 22N 13 12 E
Sankt Johann, Tirol, Austria **26** 47 30N 12 25 E
Sankt Moritz **25** 46 30N 9 50 E
Sankt Olof **49** 55 37N 14 8 E
Sankt Pölten **26** 48 12N 15 38 E
Sankt Valentin **26** 48 11N 14 33 E
Sankt Veit **26** 46 54N 14 22 E
Sankt Wendel **25** 49 27N 7 9 E
Sankt Wolfgang **26** 47 43N 13 27 E
Sankuru → **88** 4 17 S 20 25 E
Sanlúcar de Barrameda **31** 36 46N 6 21W
Sanlúcar la Mayor **31** 37 26N 6 18W
Sanluri **40** 39 35N 8 55 E
Sanmenxia **77** 34 47N 111 12 E
Sannaspos **92** 29 6 S 26 34 E
Sannicandro Gargánico **41** 41 50N 15 34 E
Sannidal **47** 58 55N 9 15 E
Sannieshof **92** 26 30 S 25 47 E
Sanok **27** 49 35N 22 10 E
Sanquhar **14** 55 21N 3 56W
Sansanding Dam **84** 13 48N 6 0W
Sansepolcro **39** 43 34N 12 8 E
Sanshui **75** 23 10N 112 56 E
Sanski Most **39** 44 46N 16 40 E
Sant' Ágata de Goti **41** 41 6N 14 30 E
Sant' Ágata di Militello **41** 38 2N 14 8 E
Santa Ana, Boliv. **126** 13 50 S 65 40W
Santa Ana, Ecuador **126** 1 16 S 80 20W
Santa Ana, El Sal. **120** 14 0N 89 31W
Santa Ana, Mexico **120** 30 31N 111 8W
Santa Ana, U.S.A. **119** 33 48N 117 55W
Sant' Ángelo Lodigiano **38** 45 14N 9 25 E
Sant' Antioco **40** 39 2N 8 30 E
Sant' Arcángelo di Romagna **39** 44 4N 12 26 E
Santa Bárbara, Mexico **120** 26 48N 105 50W
Santa Bárbara, Spain **32** 40 42N 0 29 E
Santa Barbara **119** 34 25N 119 40W
Santa Bárbara, Mt. **33** 37 23N 2 50W
Santa Catalina **120** 25 40N 110 50W
Santa Catalina, G. of **119** 33 0N 118 0W
Santa Catalina I. **119** 33 20N 118 30W
Santa Catarina □ **125** 27 25 S 48 30W
Santa Catarina, I. de **125** 27 30 S 48 40W
Santa Caterina Villarmosa **41** 37 37N 14 1 E
Santa Cecília **125** 26 56 S 50 18W
Santa Clara, Cuba **121** 22 20N 80 0W
Santa Clara, Calif., U.S.A. **119** 37 21N 122 0W
Santa Clara, Utah, U.S.A. **119** 37 10N 113 38W
Santa Clara de Olimar **125** 32 50 S 54 54W
Santa Clara Pk. **119** 35 58N 106 45W
Santa Clotilde **126** 2 33 S 73 45W
Santa Coloma de Farnés **32** 41 50N 2 39 E
Santa Coloma de Gramanet **32** 41 27N 2 13 E
Santa Comba **30** 43 2N 8 49W
Santa Croce Camerina **41** 36 50N 14 30 E
Santa Croce di Magliano **41** 41 43N 14 59 E
Santa Cruz, Argent. **128** 50 0 S 68 32W
Santa Cruz, Boliv. **126** 17 43 S 63 10W
Santa Cruz, Chile **124** 34 38 S 71 27W
Santa Cruz, C. Rica **121** 10 15N 85 35W
Santa Cruz, Phil. **73** 14 20N 121 24 E
Santa Cruz, Calif., U.S.A. **119** 36 55N 122 1W
Santa Cruz, N. Mexico, U.S.A. **119** 35 59N 106 1W
Santa Cruz □ **126** 17 43 S 63 10W
Santa Cruz → **128** 50 10 S 68 20W
Santa Cruz de Mudela **33** 38 39N 3 28W
Sta. Cruz de Tenerife **80** 28 28N 16 15W
Santa Cruz del Retamar **30** 40 8N 4 14W
Santa Cruz del Sur **121** 20 44N 78 0W
Santa Cruz do Rio Pardo **125** 22 54 S 49 37W
Santa Cruz do Sul **125** 29 42 S 52 25W
Santa Cruz I. **119** 34 0N 119 45W
Santa Cruz, Is. **94** 10 30 S 166 0 E
Santa Domingo, Cay **121** 21 25N 75 15W
Santa Elena, Argent. **124** 30 58 S 59 47W
Santa Elena, Ecuador **126** 2 16 S 80 52W
Santa Elena, C. **121** 10 54N 85 56W
Sant' Eufémia, Golfo di **41** 38 50N 16 10 E
Santa Eulalia **33** 38 59N 1 32 E
Santa Fe, Argent. **124** 31 35 S 60 41W
Santa Fe, Spain **31** 37 11N 3 43W
Santa Fe, U.S.A. **119** 35 40N 106 0W
Santa Fé □ **124** 31 50 S 60 55W
Santa Filomena **127** 9 6 S 45 50W
Santa Genoveva **120** 23 18N 109 52W
Santa Inés **31** 38 32N 5 37W
Santa Inés, I. **128** 54 0 S 73 0W
Santa Isabel, Argent. **124** 36 10 S 66 54W
Santa Isabel, Brazil **127** 11 45 S 51 30W
Santa Isabel = Rey Malabo **85** 3 45N 8 50 E
Santa Isabel, Pico **85** 3 36N 8 49 E
Santa Lucía, Corrientes, Argent. **124** 28 58 S 59 5W
Santa Lucía, San Juan, Argent. **124** 31 30 S 68 30W
Santa Lucía, Spain **33** 37 35N 0 58W
Santa Lucia **124** 34 27 S 56 24W
Santa Lucia Range **119** 36 0N 121 20W
Santa Margarita, Argent. **124** 38 28 S 61 35W
Santa Margarita, Mexico **120** 24 30N 111 50W
Santa Margherita **38** 44 20N 9 11 E
Santa Maria **124** 26 40 S 66 0W
Santa Maria, Brazil **125** 29 40 S 53 48W
Santa Maria, Spain **32** 39 38N 2 47 E
Santa Maria, U.S.A. **119** 34 58N 120 29W
Santa Maria, Zambia **91** 11 5 S 29 58 E
Santa Maria → **120** 31 0N 107 14W
Santa María, Bahía de **120** 25 10N 108 40W
Santa Maria, Cabo de **31** 36 58N 7 53W
Santa Maria Capua Vetere **41** 41 3N 14 15 E
Santa Maria da Vitória **127** 13 24 S 44 12W
Santa María del Oro **120** 25 58N 105 20W
Santa Maria di Leuca, C. **41** 39 48N 18 20 E
Santa María la Real de Nieva **30** 41 4N 4 24W
Santa Marta, Colomb. **126** 11 15N 74 13W
Santa Marta, Spain **31** 38 37N 6 39W
Santa Marta Grande, C. **125** 28 43 S 48 50W
Santa Marta, Ría de **30** 43 44N 7 45W
Santa Marta, Sierra Nevada de **126** 10 55N 73 50W
Santa Maura = Levkás **45** 38 40N 20 43 E
Santa Monica **119** 34 0N 118 30W
Santa Olalla, Huelva, Spain **31** 37 54N 6 14W
Santa Olalla, Toledo, Spain **30** 40 2N 4 25W
Sant' Onofrio **41** 38 42N 16 10 E
Santa Paula **119** 34 20N 119 2W
Santa Pola **33** 38 13N 0 35W
Santa Rita **119** 32 50N 108 0W
Santa Rosa, La Pampa, Argent. **124** 36 40 S 64 17W
Santa Rosa, San Luis, Argent. **124** 32 21 S 65 10W
Santa Rosa, Boliv. **126** 10 36 S 67 20W
Santa Rosa, Brazil **125** 27 52 S 54 29W
Santa Rosa, Calif., U.S.A. **118** 38 26N 122 43W
Santa Rosa, N. Mexico, U.S.A. **117** 34 58N 104 40W
Santa Rosa de Copán **120** 14 47N 88 46W
Santa Rosa de Río Primero **124** 31 8 S 63 20W
Santa Rosa I., Calif., U.S.A. **119** 34 0N 120 6W
Santa Rosa I., Fla., U.S.A. **115** 30 23N 87 0W
Santa Rosa Mts. **118** 41 45N 117 30W
Santa Rosalía **120** 27 20N 112 20W
Santa Sofia **39** 43 57N 11 55 E
Santa Sylvina **124** 27 50 S 61 10W
Santa Tecla = Nueva San Salvador **120** 13 40N 89 25W
Santa Teresa **124** 33 25 S 60 47W
Santa Teresa di Riva **41** 37 58N 15 21 E
Santa Teresa Gallura **40** 41 14N 9 12 E
Santa Vitória do Palmar **125** 33 32 S 53 25W
Santadi **40** 39 5N 8 42 E
Santai **75** 31 5N 104 58 E
Santana, Coxilha de **125** 30 50 S 55 35W
Santana do Livramento **125** 30 55 S 55 30W
Santanayi **33** 39 20N 3 5 E
Santander **30** 43 27N 3 51W
Santander □ **30** 43 25N 4 0W
Santander Jiménez **120** 24 11N 98 29W
Santaquin **118** 40 0N 111 51W
Santarém, Brazil **127** 2 25 S 54 42W
Santarém, Port. **31** 39 12N 8 42W
Santarém □ **31** 39 10N 8 40W
Santaren Channel **121** 24 0N 79 30W
Santéramo in Colle **41** 40 48N 16 45 E

Santerno →	**39**	44 10N	11 38 E
Santhia	**38**	45 20N	8 10 E
Santiago, Brazil	**125**	29 11 S	54 52W
Santiago, Chile	**124**	33 24 S	70 40W
Santiago, Panama	**121**	8 0N	81 0W
Santiago □	**124**	33 30 S	70 50W
Santiago de Compostela	**30**	42 52N	8 37W
Santiago de Cuba	**121**	20 0N	75 49W
Santiago de los Cabelleros	**121**	19 30N	70 40W
Santiago del Estero	**124**	27 50 S	64 15W
Santiago del Estero □	**124**	27 40 S	63 15W
Santiago do Cacém	**31**	38 1N	8 42W
Santiago Ixcuintla	**120**	21 50N	105 11W
Santiago Papasquiaro	**120**	25 0N	105 20W
Santiago, Punta de	**85**	3 12N	8 40 E
Santiaguillo, L. de	**120**	24 50N	104 50W
Santillana del Mar	**30**	43 24N	4 6W
Santipur	**69**	23 17N	88 25 E
Santisteban del Puerto	**33**	38 17N	3 15W
Santo Amaro	**127**	12 30 S	38 43W
Santo Anastácio	**125**	21 58 S	51 39W
Santo André	**125**	23 39 S	46 29W
Santo Ângelo	**125**	28 15 S	54 15W
Santo Antonio	**127**	15 50 S	56 0W
Santo Corazón	**126**	18 0 S	58 45W
Santo Domingo, Dom. Rep.	**121**	18 30N	64 54W
Santo Domingo, Baja Calif. N., Mexico	**120**	30 43N	116 2W
Santo Domingo, Baja Calif. S., Mexico	**120**	25 32N	112 2W
Santo Domingo, Nic.	**121**	12 14N	84 59W
Santo Domingo de la Calzada	**32**	42 26N	2 57W
Santo Stéfano di Camastro	**41**	38 1N	14 22 E
Santo Stino di Livenza	**39**	45 45N	12 40 E
Santo Tirso	**30**	41 21N	8 28W
Santo Tomás	**126**	14 26 S	72 8W
Santo Tomé	**125**	28 40 S	56 5W
Santo Tomé de Guayana	**126**	8 22N	62 40W
Santoña	**30**	43 29N	3 27W
Santos	**125**	24 0 S	46 20W
Santos Dumont	**125**	22 55 S	43 10W
Santos, Sierra de los	**31**	38 7N	5 12W
Şãnūr	**62**	32 22N	35 15 E
Sanvignes-les-Mines	**19**	46 40N	4 18 E
Sanyuan	**77**	34 35N	108 58 E
Sanza Pombo	**88**	7 18 S	15 56 E
São Anastácio	**125**	22 0 S	51 40W
São Bartolomeu de Messines	**31**	37 15N	8 17W
São Borja	**125**	28 39 S	56 0W
São Bras d'Alportel	**31**	37 8N	7 37W
São Carlos	**125**	22 0 S	47 50W
São Cristóvão	**127**	11 1 S	37 15W
São Domingos	**127**	13 25 S	46 19W
São Francisco	**127**	16 0 S	44 50W
São Francisco →	**127**	10 30 S	36 24W
São Francisco do Sul	**125**	26 15 S	48 36W
São Gabriel	**125**	30 20 S	54 20W
São Gonçalo	**125**	22 48 S	43 5W
Sao Hill	**91**	8 20 S	35 12 E
São João da Boa Vista	**125**	22 0 S	46 52W
São João da Pesqueira	**30**	41 8N	7 24W
São João del Rei	**125**	21 8 S	44 15W
São João do Araguaia	**127**	5 23 S	48 46W
São João do Piauí	**127**	8 21 S	42 15W
São José do Rio Prêto	**125**	20 50 S	49 20W
São José dos Campos	**125**	23 7 S	45 52W
São Leopoldo	**125**	29 50 S	51 10W
São Lourenço	**125**	22 7 S	45 3W
São Lourenço →	**127**	17 53 S	57 27W
São Luís Gonzaga	**125**	28 25 S	55 0W
São Luís (Maranhão)	**127**	2 39 S	44 15W
São Marcos →	**127**	18 15 S	47 37W
São Marcos, B. de	**127**	2 0 S	44 0W
São Martinho	**30**	40 18N	8 8W
São Mateus	**127**	18 44 S	39 50W
São Miguel	**8**	37 33N	25 27W
São Paulo	**125**	23 32 S	46 37W
São Paulo □	**125**	22 0 S	49 0W
Sao Paulo, I.	**6**	0 50N	31 40W
São Pedro do Sul	**30**	40 46N	8 4W
São Roque, C. de	**127**	5 30 S	35 16W
São Sebastião do Paraíso	**125**	20 54 S	46 59W
São Sebastião, I. de	**125**	23 50 S	45 18W
São Teotónio	**31**	37 30N	8 42W
São Tomé	**79**	0 10N	6 39 E
São Tomé, C. de	**125**	22 0 S	40 59W
São Vicente	**125**	23 57 S	46 23W
São Vicente, Cabo de	**31**	37 0N	9 0W
Saona, I.	**121**	18 10N	68 40W
Saône →	**19**	45 44N	4 50 E
Saône-et-Loire □	**19**	46 25N	4 50 E
Saonek	**73**	0 22 S	130 55 E
Saoura, O. →	**82**	29 0N	0 55W
Sápai	**44**	41 2N	25 43 E
Saparua	**73**	3 33 S	128 40 E
Sapele	**85**	5 50N	5 40 E
Sapelo I.	**115**	31 28N	81 15W
Sapiéntza	**45**	36 45N	21 43 E
Sapone	**85**	12 3N	1 35W
Saposoa	**126**	6 55 S	76 45W
Sapozhok	**55**	53 59N	40 41 E
Sapphire Mts.	**118**	46 20N	113 45W
Sapporo	**74**	43 0N	141 21 E
Sapri	**41**	40 5N	15 37 E
Sapudi	**73**	7 2 S	114 17 E
Sapulpa	**117**	36 0N	96 0W
Saqqez	**64**	36 15N	46 20 E
Sar-e Pol	**65**	36 10N	66 0 E
Sar Planina	**42**	42 10N	21 0 E
Sara	**84**	11 40N	3 53W
Sarāb	**64**	38 0N	47 30 E
Saragossa = Zaragoza	**32**	41 39N	0 53W
Saraguro	**126**	3 35 S	79 16W
Saraipalli	**69**	21 20N	82 59 E
Sarajevo	**42**	43 52N	18 26 E
Saralu	**46**	44 43N	28 10 E
Saran	**86**	19 35N	40 30 E
Saran, G.	**72**	0 30 S	111 25 E
Saranac Lake	**114**	44 20N	74 10W
Saranda, Alb.	**44**	39 52N	19 55 E
Saranda, Tanz.	**90**	5 45 S	34 59 E
Sarandí del Yi	**125**	33 18 S	55 38W
Sarandí Grande	**124**	33 44 S	56 20W
Sarangani B.	**73**	6 0N	125 13 E
Sarangani Is.	**73**	5 25N	125 25 E
Sarangarh	**69**	21 30N	83 5 E
Saransk	**55**	54 10N	45 10 E
Sarapul	**52**	56 28N	53 48 E
Sarasota	**115**	27 20N	82 30W
Saratoga	**118**	41 30N	106 48W
Saratoga Springs	**114**	43 5N	73 47W
Saratov	**55**	51 30N	46 2 E
Saravane	**71**	15 43N	106 25 E
Sarawak □	**72**	2 0N	113 0 E
Saraya	**84**	12 50N	11 45W
Sarbāz	**65**	26 38N	61 19 E
Sarbīsheh	**65**	32 30N	59 40 E
Sârbogârd	**27**	46 50N	18 40 E
Sarca →	**38**	45 52N	10 52 E
Sardalas	**83**	25 50N	10 34 E
Sardarshahr	**68**	28 30N	74 29 E
Sardegna	**40**	39 57N	9 0 E
Sardhana	**68**	29 9N	77 39 E
Sardinia = Sardegna	**40**	39 57N	9 0 E
Šarengrad	**42**	45 14N	19 16 E
Saréyamou	**84**	16 7N	3 10W
Sargasso Sea	**6**	27 0N	72 0W
Sargent	**116**	41 42N	99 24W
Sargodha	**68**	32 10N	72 40 E
* Sargodha □	**68**	31 50N	72 0 E
Sarh	**81**	9 5N	18 23 E
Sarhro, Djebel	**82**	31 6N	5 0W
Sārī	**65**	36 30N	53 4 E
Sária	**45**	35 54N	27 17 E
Sarida →	**62**	32 4N	34 45 E
Sarikamiş	**64**	40 22N	42 35 E
Sarikei	**72**	2 8N	111 30 E
Sarina	**97**	21 22 S	149 13 E
Sariñena	**32**	41 47N	0 10W
Sarīr Tibasti	**83**	22 50N	18 30 E
Sarita	**117**	27 14N	97 49W
Sariyer	**43**	41 10N	29 3 E
Sark	**18**	49 25N	2 20W
Sarkad	**27**	46 47N	21 23 E
Sarlat-la-Canéda	**20**	44 54N	1 13 E
Sarles	**116**	48 58N	99 0W
Sărmaşu	**46**	46 45N	24 13 E
Sarmi	**73**	1 49 S	138 44 E
Sarmiento	**128**	45 35 S	69 5W
Särna	**48**	61 41N	13 8 E
Sarnano	**39**	43 2N	13 17 E
Sarnen	**25**	46 53N	8 13 E
Sarnia	**106**	42 58N	82 23W
Sarno	**41**	40 48N	14 35 E
Sarnowa	**28**	51 39N	16 53 E
Sarny	**54**	51 17N	26 40 E
Särö	**49**	57 31N	11 57 E
Sarolangun	**72**	2 19 S	102 42 E
Saronikós Kólpos	**45**	37 45N	23 45 E
Saronno	**38**	45 38N	9 2 E
Saros Körfezi	**44**	40 30N	26 15 E
Sárospatak	**27**	48 18N	21 33 E
Sarosul Românesc	**42**	45 34N	21 43 E
Sarova	**55**	54 55N	43 19 E
Sarpsborg	**47**	59 16N	11 12 E
Sarracín	**32**	42 15N	3 45W
Sarralbe	**19**	48 55N	7 1 E
Sarre = Saar →	**19**	49 7N	7 4 E
Sarre, La	**106**	48 45N	79 15W
Sarre-Union	**19**	48 55N	7 4 E
Sarrebourg	**19**	48 43N	7 3 E
Sarreguemines	**19**	49 1N	7 4 E
Sarriá	**30**	42 49N	7 29W
Sarrión	**32**	40 9N	0 49W
Sarro	**84**	13 40N	5 15W
Sarstedt	**24**	52 13N	9 50 E
Sartène	**21**	41 38N	8 58 E
Sarthe □	**18**	47 58N	0 10 E
Sarthe →	**18**	47 33N	0 31W
Sartilly	**18**	48 45N	1 28W
Sartynya	**58**	63 22N	63 11 E
Sarum	**86**	21 11N	39 10 E
Sarūr	**65**	23 17N	58 4 E
Sárvár	**27**	47 15N	16 56 E
Sarvestān	**65**	29 20N	53 10 E
Särvfjället	**48**	62 42N	13 30 E
Sárviz →	**27**	46 24N	18 41 E
Sary-Tash	**58**	39 44N	73 15 E
Sarych, Mys.	**56**	44 25N	33 45 E
Saryshagan	**58**	46 12N	73 38 E
Sarzana	**38**	44 5N	9 59 E
Sarzeau	**18**	47 31N	2 48W
Sasa	**62**	33 2N	35 23 E
Sasabeneh	**63**	7 59N	44 43 E
Sasaram	**69**	24 57N	84 5 E
Sasca Montană	**42**	44 50N	21 45 E
Sasebo	**74**	33 10N	129 43 E
Saser Mt.	**69**	34 50N	77 50 E
Saskatchewan □	**109**	54 40N	106 0W
Saskatchewan →	**109**	53 37N	100 40W
Saskatoon	**109**	52 10N	106 38W
Saskylakh	**59**	71 55N	114 1 E
Sasnovka	**55**	56 20N	51 4 E
Sasolburg	**93**	26 46 S	27 49 E
Sasovo	**55**	54 25N	41 55 E
Sassandra	**84**	5 0N	6 8W
Sassandra →	**84**	4 58N	6 5W
Sássari	**40**	40 44N	8 33 E
Sassnitz	**24**	54 29N	13 39 E
Sasso Marconi	**39**	44 22N	11 12 E
Sassocorvaro	**39**	43 47N	12 30 E
Sassoferrato	**39**	43 26N	12 51 E
Sassuolo	**38**	44 31N	10 47 E
Sástago	**32**	41 19N	0 21W
Sastown	**84**	4 45N	8 27W
Sasumua Dam	**90**	0 45 S	36 40 E
Sasyk, Ozero	**46**	45 45N	30 0 E
Sata-Misaki	**74**	30 59N	130 40 E
Satadougou	**84**	12 25N	11 25W
Satanta	**117**	37 30N	101 0W
Satara	**70**	17 44N	73 58 E
Satilla →	**115**	30 59N	81 28W
Satka	**52**	55 3N	59 1 E
Satkhira	**69**	22 43N	89 8 E
Satmala Hills	**70**	20 15N	74 40 E
Satna	**69**	24 35N	80 50 E
Sator	**39**	44 11N	16 37 E
Sátoraljaújhely	**27**	48 25N	21 41 E
Satpura Ra.	**68**	21 25N	76 10 E
Satrup	**24**	54 39N	9 38 E
Sattenapalle	**70**	16 25N	80 6 E
Satu Mare	**46**	47 46N	22 55 E
Satui	**72**	3 50 S	115 27 E
Satumare □	**46**	47 45N	23 0 E
Satun	**71**	6 43N	100 2 E
Saturnina →	**126**	12 15 S	58 10W
Sauce	**124**	30 5 S	58 46W
Saucillo	**120**	28 1N	105 17W
Sauda	**47**	59 40N	6 20 E
Sauðarkrókur	**50**	65 45N	19 40W
Saudi Arabia ■	**64**	26 0N	44 0 E
Sauerland	**24**	51 0N	8 0 E
Saugeen →	**112**	44 30N	81 22W
Saugerties	**114**	42 4N	73 58W
Saugues	**20**	44 58N	3 32 E
Sauherad	**47**	59 25N	9 15 E
Saujon	**20**	45 41N	0 55W
Sauk Center	**116**	45 42N	94 56W
Sauk Rapids	**116**	45 35N	94 10W
Saulgau	**25**	48 4N	9 32 E
Saulieu	**19**	47 17N	4 14 E
Sault	**21**	44 6N	5 24 E
Sault Ste. Marie, Can.	**106**	46 30N	84 20W
Sault Ste. Marie, U.S.A.	**114**	46 27N	84 22W
Saumlaki	**73**	7 55 S	131 20 E
Saumur	**18**	47 15N	0 5W
Saunders C.	**101**	45 53 S	170 45 E
Saunders I.	**5**	57 48 S	26 28W
Saurbær, Borgarfjarðarsýsla, Iceland	**50**	64 24N	21 35W
Saurbær, Eyjafjarðarsýsla, Iceland	**50**	65 27N	18 13W
Sauri	**85**	11 42N	6 44 E
Saurimo	**88**	9 40 S	20 12 E
Sauveterre	**20**	43 25N	0 57W
Sauzé-Vaussais	**20**	46 8N	0 8 E
Sava	**39**	40 28N	17 32 E
Sava →	**39**	44 50N	20 26 E
Savage	**116**	47 27N	104 20W
Savai'i	**101**	13 28 S	172 24W
Savalou	**85**	7 57N	1 58 E
Savane	**91**	19 37 S	35 8 E
Savanna	**116**	42 5N	90 10W
Savanna la Mar	**121**	18 10N	78 10W
Savannah, Ga., U.S.A.	**115**	32 4N	81 4W
Savannah, Mo., U.S.A.	**116**	39 55N	94 46W
Savannah, Tenn., U.S.A.	**115**	35 12N	88 18W
Savannah →	**115**	32 2N	80 53W
Savannakhet	**71**	16 30N	104 49 E
Savant L.	**106**	50 16N	90 44W
Savant Lake	**106**	50 14N	90 40W
Savantvadi	**70**	15 55N	73 54 E
Savanur	**70**	14 59N	75 21 E
Savda	**68**	21 9N	75 56 E
Savé	**85**	8 2N	2 29 E
Save →	**20**	43 47N	1 17 E
Sāveh	**64**	35 2N	50 20 E
Savelugu	**85**	9 38N	0 54W
Savenay	**18**	47 20N	1 55W
Saverdun	**20**	43 14N	1 34 E
Saverne	**19**	48 39N	7 20 E
Savigliano	**38**	44 39N	7 40 E
Savigny-sur-Braye	**18**	47 53N	0 49 E
Saviñao	**30**	42 35N	7 38W
Savio →	**39**	44 19N	12 20 E
Šavnik	**42**	42 59N	19 10 E
Savoie □	**21**	45 26N	6 35 E
Savona	**38**	44 19N	8 29 E
Savonlinna	**52**	61 52N	28 53 E
Sävsjö	**49**	57 20N	14 40 E
Sävsjøström	**49**	57 1N	15 25 E
Sawahlunto	**72**	0 40 S	100 52 E
Sawai	**73**	3 0 S	129 5 E
Sawai Madhopur	**68**	26 0N	76 25 E
Sawara	**74**	35 55N	140 30 E
Sawatch Mts.	**119**	38 30N	106 30W
Sawdā, Jabal as	**83**	28 51N	15 12 E
Sawel, Mt.	**15**	54 48N	7 5W
Sawfajjin, W.	**83**	31 46N	14 30 E
Sawknah	**81**	29 4N	15 47 E
Sawmills	**91**	19 30 S	28 2 E
Sawu	**73**	10 35 S	121 50 E
Sawu Sea	**73**	9 30 S	121 50 E
Sawyerville	**113**	45 20N	71 34W
Saxby →	**98**	18 25 S	140 53 E
Saxony, Lower = Niedersachsen □	**24**	52 45N	9 0 E
Saxton	**112**	40 12N	78 18W
Say	**85**	13 8N	2 22 E
Saya	**85**	9 30N	3 18 E
Sayabec	**107**	48 35N	67 41W
Sayán	**126**	11 8 S	77 12W
Sayan, Vostochnyy	**59**	54 0N	96 0 E
Sayan, Zapadnyy	**59**	52 30N	94 0 E
Sayasan	**57**	42 56N	46 15 E
Saydā	**64**	33 35N	35 25 E
Şayghān	**65**	35 10N	67 55 E
Sayḫut	**63**	15 12N	51 10 E
Saynshand	**75**	44 55N	110 11 E
Sayre, Okla., U.S.A.	**117**	35 20N	99 40W
Sayre, Pa., U.S.A.	**114**	42 0N	76 30W
Sayula	**120**	19 50N	103 40W
Sayville	**113**	40 45N	73 7W
Sazan	**44**	40 30N	19 20 E
Săzava →	**26**	49 53N	14 24 E
Sazin	**69**	35 35N	73 30 E
Sazlika →	**43**	41 59N	25 50 E
Sbeïtla	**83**	35 12N	9 7 E
Scaër	**18**	48 2N	3 42W
Scafell Pikes	**12**	54 26N	3 14W
Scalea	**41**	39 49N	15 47 E
Scalpay	**14**	57 51N	6 40W
Scandia	**108**	50 20N	112 0W
Scandiano	**38**	44 36N	10 40 E
Scandinavia	**9**	64 0N	12 0 E
Scansano	**39**	42 40N	11 20 E
Scapa Flow	**14**	58 52N	3 6W
Scarborough, Trin.	**121**	11 11N	60 42W
Scarborough, U.K.	**12**	54 17N	0 24W
Scarpe →	**19**	50 31N	3 27 E
Śćedro	**39**	43 6N	16 43 E
Scenic	**116**	43 49N	102 32W
Schaal See	**24**	53 40N	10 57 E
Schaffhausen □	**25**	47 42N	8 36 E
Schagen	**16**	52 49N	4 48 E
Schärding	**26**	48 27N	13 27 E
Scharhörn	**24**	53 58N	8 24 E
Scharnitz	**26**	47 23N	11 15 E
Scheessel	**24**	53 10N	9 33 E
Schefferville	**107**	54 48N	66 50W
Scheibbs	**26**	48 1N	15 9 E
Schelde →	**16**	51 15N	4 16 E
Schenectady	**114**	42 50N	73 58W
Scherfede	**24**	51 32N	9 2 E
Schesslitz	**25**	49 59N	11 2 E
Scheveningen	**16**	52 6N	4 16 E
Schiedam	**16**	51 55N	4 25 E
Schiermonnikoog	**16**	53 30N	6 15 E
Schifferstadt	**25**	49 22N	8 23 E
Schiltigheim	**19**	48 35N	7 45 E
Schio	**39**	45 42N	11 21 E
Schirmeck	**19**	48 29N	7 12 E
Schladming	**26**	47 23N	13 41 E
Schlei →	**24**	54 45N	9 52 E
Schleiden	**24**	50 32N	6 26 E
Schleiz	**24**	50 35N	11 49 E
Schleswig	**24**	54 32N	9 34 E
Schleswig-Holstein □	**24**	54 10N	9 40 E
Schlüchtern	**25**	50 20N	9 32 E
Schmalkalden	**24**	50 43N	10 28 E
Schmölin	**24**	50 54N	12 22 E
Schmölln	**24**	53 15N	14 6 E
Schneeberg, Austria	**26**	47 47N	15 48 E
Schneeberg, Ger.	**24**	50 35N	12 39 E
Schofield	**116**	44 54N	89 39W
Schönberg, Rostock, Ger.	**24**	53 50N	10 55 E
Schönberg, Schleswig-Holstein, Ger.	**24**	54 23N	10 20 E
Schönebeck	**24**	52 2N	11 42 E
Schongau	**25**	47 49N	10 54 E
Schöningen	**24**	52 8N	10 57 E
Schortens	**24**	53 37N	7 51 E
Schouten I.	**99**	42 20 S	148 20 E
Schouten, Kepulauan	**73**	1 0 S	136 0 E
Schouwen	**16**	51 43N	3 45 E
Schramberg	**25**	48 12N	8 24 E
Schrankogl	**26**	47 3N	11 7 E
Schreiber	**106**	48 45N	87 20W
Schrobenhausen	**25**	48 33N	11 16 E
Schruns	**26**	47 5N	9 56 E
Schuler	**109**	50 20N	110 6W
Schumacher	**106**	48 30N	81 16W
Schurz	**118**	38 57N	118 48W
Schuyler	**116**	41 30N	97 3W
Schuylkill Haven	**113**	40 37N	76 11W
Schwabach	**25**	49 19N	11 3 E
Schwäbisch Gmünd	**25**	48 49N	9 48 E
Schwäbisch Hall	**25**	49 7N	9 45 E
Schwäbische Alb	**25**	48 30N	9 30 E
Schwabmünchen	**25**	48 11N	10 45 E
Schwandorf	**25**	49 20N	12 7 E
Schwarmstedt	**24**	52 41N	9 37 E
Schwarzach →	**26**	46 56N	12 35 E
Schwärze	**24**	52 50N	13 49 E
Schwarzenberg	**24**	50 31N	12 49 E
Schwarzwald	**25**	48 0N	8 0 E
Schwaz	**26**	47 20N	11 44 E
Schwedt	**24**	53 4N	14 18 E
Schweinfurt	**25**	50 3N	10 12 E
Schweizer Reneke	**92**	27 11 S	25 18 E
Schwerin	**24**	53 37N	11 22 E
Schwerin □	**24**	53 35N	11 20 E
Schweriner See	**24**	53 45N	11 26 E
Schwetzingen	**25**	49 22N	8 35 E
Schwyz	**25**	47 2N	8 39 E
Schwyz □	**25**	47 2N	8 39 E
Sciacca	**40**	37 30N	13 3 E
Scicli	**41**	36 48N	14 41 E
Scie, La	**107**	49 57N	55 36W
Scilla	**41**	38 18N	15 44 E
Scilly, Isles of	**13**	49 55N	6 15W
Ścinawa	**28**	51 25N	16 26 E
Scione	**44**	39 57N	23 36 E
Scioto →	**114**	38 44N	83 0W
Scobey	**116**	48 47N	105 30W
Scone, Austral.	**99**	32 5 S	150 52 E
Scone, U.K.	**14**	56 25N	3 26W
Scordia	**41**	37 19N	14 50 E
Scoresbysund	**4**	70 20N	23 0W
Scorno, Punta dello	**40**	41 7N	8 23 E
Scotia, Calif., U.S.A.	**118**	40 36N	124 4W
Scotia, N.Y., U.S.A.	**113**	42 50N	73 58W
Scotia Sea	**5**	56 5 S	56 0W
Scotland	**116**	43 10N	97 45W
Scotland □	**13**	57 0N	4 0W
Scotland Neck	**115**	36 6N	77 32W
Scott	**5**	77 0 S	165 0 E
Scott, C.	**5**	71 30 S	168 0 E
Scott City	**116**	38 30N	100 52W
Scott Glacier	**5**	66 15 S	100 5 E
Scott I.	**5**	67 0 S	179 0 E
Scott Inlet	**105**	71 0N	71 0W
Scott Is.	**108**	50 48N	128 40W
Scott L.	**109**	59 55N	106 18W
Scott Reef	**96**	14 0 S	121 50 E
Scottburgh	**93**	30 15 S	30 47 E
Scottdale	**112**	40 8N	79 35W
Scottsbluff	**116**	41 55N	103 35W
Scottsboro	**115**	34 40N	86 0W
Scottsburg	**114**	38 40N	85 46W
Scottsdale	**97**	41 9 S	147 31 E
Scottsville, Ky., U.S.A.	**115**	36 48N	86 10W
Scottsville, N.Y., U.S.A.	**112**	43 2N	77 47W
Scottville, Austral.	**98**	20 33 S	147 49 E
Scottville, U.S.A.	**114**	43 57N	86 18W
Scranton	**114**	41 22N	75 41W
Scugog, L.	**112**	44 10N	78 55W
Scunthorpe	**12**	53 35N	0 38W

* *Now part of Punjab* □

Scusciuban 63 10 18N 50 12 E
Sea Breeze 112 43 12N 77 32W
Seaford, Austral. 100 38 10S 145 11 E
Seaford, U.S.A. 114 38 37N 75 36W
Seaforth 106 43 35N 81 25W
Seagraves 117 32 56N 102 30W
Seal → 109 58 50N 97 30W
Seal Cove 107 49 57N 56 22W
Seal L. 107 54 20N 61 30W
Sealy 117 29 46N 96 9W
Searchlight 119 35 31N 114 55W
Searcy 117 35 15N 91 45W
Searles L. 119 35 47N 117 17W
Seaside 118 45 59N 123 55W
Seaspray 99 38 25S 147 15 E
Seattle 118 47 41N 122 15W
Seaview Ra. 97 18 40S 145 45 E
Sebastián Vizcaíno, Bahía 120 28 0N 114 30W
Sebastopol 118 38 24N 122 49W
Sebastopol = Sevastopol 56 44 35N 33 30 E
Sebderat 87 15 26N 36 42 E
Sebdou 82 34 38N 1 19W
Sebeş 46 45 58N 23 34 E
Sebeşului, Munţii 46 45 36N 23 40 E
Sebewaing 114 43 45N 83 27W
Sebezh 54 56 14N 28 22 E
Sébi 84 15 50N 4 12W
Şebinkarahisar 56 40 22N 38 28 E
Sebiş 46 46 23N 22 13 E
Sebkhet Te-n-Dghâmcha 84 18 30N 15 55W
Sebkra Azzel Mati 82 26 10N 0 43 E
Sebkra Mekerghene 82 26 21N 1 30 E
Sebnitz 24 50 58N 14 17 E
Sebou, Oued → 82 34 16N 6 40W
Sebring, Fla., U.S.A. 115 27 30N 81 26W
Sebring, Ohio, U.S.A. 112 40 55N 81 2W
Sebringville 112 43 24N 81 4W
Sebta = Ceuta 82 35 52N 5 19W
Sebuku 72 3 30S 116 25 E
Sebuku, Teluk 72 4 0N 118 10 E
Sečanj 42 45 25N 20 47 E
Secchia → 38 44 4N 11 0 E
Sechelt 108 49 25N 123 42W
Sechura, Desierto de 126 6 0S 80 30W
Seclin 19 50 33N 3 2 E
Secondigny 18 46 37N 0 26W
Sečovce 27 48 42N 21 40 E
Secretary I. 101 45 15S 166 56 E
Secunderabad 70 17 28N 78 30 E
Sedalia 116 38 40N 93 18W
Sedan, Austral. 99 34 34S 139 19 E
Sedan, France 19 49 43N 4 57 E
Sedan, U.S.A. 117 37 10N 96 11W
Sedano 32 42 43N 3 49W
Seddon 101 41 40S 174 7 E
Seddonville 101 41 33S 172 1 E
Sede Ya'aqov 62 32 43N 35 7 E
Sedgewick 108 52 48N 111 41W
Sedhiou 84 12 44N 15 30W
Sedičany 26 49 40N 14 25 E
Sedico 39 46 8N 12 6 E
Sedienie 43 42 16N 24 33 E
Sedley 109 50 10N 104 0W
Sedom 62 31 5N 35 20 E
Sedova, Pik 58 73 29N 54 58 E
Sedrata 83 36 7N 7 31 E
Sedro Woolley 118 48 30N 122 15W
Seduva 54 55 45N 23 45 E
Sedziszów Małapolski 27 50 5N 21 45 E
Seebad Ahlbeck 24 53 56N 14 10 E
Seefeld 26 47 19N 11 13 E
Seehausen 24 52 52N 11 43 E
Seeheim 92 26 50S 17 45 E
Seekoe → 92 30 18S 25 1 E
Seelaw 24 52 32N 14 22 E
Se'elim, Nahal 62 31 21N 35 24 E
Sées 18 48 38N 0 10 E
Seesen 24 51 53N 10 10 E
Sefadu 84 8 35N 10 58W
Séfeto 84 14 8N 9 49W
Sefrou 82 33 52N 4 52W
Sefwi Bekwai 84 6 10N 2 25W
Seg-ozero 54 63 0N 33 10 E
Segamat 71 2 30N 102 50 E
Segarcea 46 44 6N 23 43 E
Segbwema 84 8 0N 11 0W
Seget 73 1 24S 130 58 E
Segezha 52 63 44N 34 19 E
Seggueur, O. → 82 32 4N 2 4 E
Segid 87 16 55N 42 0 E
Segonzac 20 45 36N 0 14W
Segorbe 32 39 50N 0 30W
Ségou 84 13 30N 6 16W
Segovia 30 40 57N 4 10W
Segovia = Coco → 121 15 0N 83 8W
Segovia □ 30 40 55N 4 10W
Segré 18 47 40N 0 52W
Segre → 32 41 40N 0 43 E
Séguéla 84 7 55N 6 40W
Seguin 117 29 34N 97 58W
Segundo 117 37 12N 104 50W
Segundo → 124 30 53S 62 44W
Segura → 33 38 6N 0 54W
Segura, Sierra de 33 38 5N 2 45W
Sehore 68 23 10N 77 5 E
Sehwan 68 26 28N 67 53 E
Şeica Mare 46 46 1N 24 7 E
Seiland 50 70 25N 23 15 E
Seiling 117 36 10N 98 56W
Seille →, Moselle, France 19 49 7N 6 11 E
Seille →, Saône-et-Loire, France 21 46 31N 4 57 E
Sein, Î. de 18 48 2N 4 52W
Seinäjoki → 50 62 40N 22 45 E
Seine → 18 49 26N 0 26 E
Seine, B. de la 18 49 40N 0 40W
Seine-et-Marne □ 19 48 45N 3 0 E
Seine-Maritime □ 18 49 40N 1 0 E
Seine-Saint-Denis □ 19 48 58N 2 24 E
Seini 46 47 44N 23 21 E
Seistan 65 30 50N 61 0 E
Seistan-Balūchestān □ 65 27 0N 62 0 E
Sejerø 49 55 54N 11 9 E
Sejerø Bugt 49 55 53N 11 15 E
Sejny 28 54 6N 23 21 E
Seka 87 8 10N 36 52 E
Sekayu 72 2 51S 103 51 E
Seke 90 3 20S 33 31 E
Sekenke 90 4 18S 34 11 E
Sekiu 118 48 16N 124 18W
Sekken Veøy 47 62 45N 7 30 E
Sekondi-Takoradi 84 4 58N 1 45W
Sekuma 92 24 36S 23 50 E
Selah 118 46 44N 120 30W
Selama 71 5 12N 100 42 E
Selangor □ 71 3 20N 101 30 E
Selárgius 40 39 14N 9 14 E
Selaru 73 8 9S 131 0 E
Selb 25 50 9N 12 9 E
Selby, U.K. 12 53 47N 1 5W
Selby, U.S.A. 116 45 34N 100 2W
Selca 39 43 20N 16 50 E
Selden 116 39 33N 100 39W
Seldovia 104 59 30N 151 45W
Sele → 41 40 27N 14 58 E
Selemdzha → 59 51 42N 128 53 E
Selenge → 75 49 25N 103 59 E
Selenica 44 40 33N 19 39 E
Selenter See 24 54 19N 10 26 E
Sélestat 19 48 16N 7 26 E
Seletan, Tg. 72 4 10S 114 40 E
Seletin 46 47 50N 25 12 E
Selevac 42 44 28N 20 52 E
Selfridge 116 46 3N 100 57W
Sélibabi 84 15 10N 12 15W
Seliger, Oz. 54 57 15N 33 0 E
Seligman 119 35 17N 112 56W
Şelim 57 40 30N 42 46 E
Selîma, El Wâhât el 86 21 22N 29 19 E
Selinda Spillway 92 18 35S 23 10 E
Selinoús 45 37 35N 21 37 E
Selizharovo 54 56 51N 33 27 E
Selje 47 62 3N 5 22 E
Seljord 47 59 30N 8 40 E
Selkirk, Can. 109 50 10N 96 55W
Selkirk, U.K. 14 55 33N 2 50W
Selkirk I. 109 53 20N 99 6W
Selkirk Mts. 108 51 15N 117 40W
Selles-sur-Cher 19 47 16N 1 33 E
Sellières 19 46 50N 5 32 E
Sells 119 31 57N 111 57W
Sellye 27 45 52N 17 51 E
Selma, Ala., U.S.A. 115 32 30N 87 0W
Selma, Calif., U.S.A. 119 36 39N 119 39W
Selma, N.C., U.S.A. 115 35 32N 78 15W
Selmer 115 35 9N 88 36W
Selo 44 41 10N 25 53 E
Selongey 19 47 36N 5 10 E
Selowandoma Falls 91 21 15S 31 50 E
Selpele 73 0 1S 130 5 E
Selsey Bill 13 50 44N 0 47W
Seltz 19 48 48N 8 4 E
Selu 73 7 32S 130 55 E
Selukwe 91 19 40S 30 0 E
Sélune → 18 48 38N 1 22W
Selva, Argent. 124 29 50S 62 0W
Selva, Italy 39 46 33N 11 46 E
Selva, Spain 32 41 13N 1 8 E
Selva, La 32 42 0N 2 45 E
Selvas 126 6 30S 67 0W
Selwyn L. 109 60 0N 104 30W
Selwyn P.O. 97 21 32S 140 30 E
Selwyn Ra. 97 21 10S 140 0 E
Seman → 44 40 45N 19 50 E
Semara 82 26 48N 11 41W
Semarang 73 7 0S 110 26 E
Semau 73 10 13S 123 22 E
Sembabule 90 0 4S 31 25 E
Sémé 84 15 4N 13 41W
Semeih 87 12 43N 30 53 E
Semenov 55 56 43N 44 30 E
Semenovka, Ukraine S.S.R., U.S.S.R. 54 52 8N 32 36 E
Semenovka, Ukraine S.S.R., U.S.S.R. 56 49 37N 33 10 E
Semeru 73 8 4S 112 55 E
Semiluki 55 51 41N 39 2 E
Seminoe Res. 118 42 0N 107 0W
Seminole, Okla., U.S.A. 117 35 15N 96 45W
Seminole, Tex., U.S.A. 117 32 41N 102 38W
Semiozernoye 58 52 22N 64 8 E
Semipalatinsk 58 50 30N 80 10 E
Semirara Is. 73 12 0N 121 20 E
Semisopochnoi 104 52 0N 179 40W
Semitau 72 0 29N 111 57 E
Semiyarskoye 58 50 55N 78 23 E
Semmering Pass 26 47 41N 15 45 E
Semnān 65 35 55N 53 25 E
Semnān □ 65 36 0N 54 0 E
Semois → 16 49 53N 4 44 E
Semporna 73 4 30N 118 33 E
Semuda 72 2 51S 112 58 E
Semur-en-Auxois 19 47 30N 4 20 E
Sen → 71 13 45N 105 12 E
Sena 91 17 25S 35 0 E
Sena Madureira 126 9 5S 68 45W
Senador Pompeu 127 5 40S 39 20W
Senai 71 1 38N 103 38 E
Senaja 72 6 45N 117 3 E
Senanga 92 16 2S 23 14 E
Senatobia 117 34 38N 89 57W
Sendafa 87 9 11N 39 3 E
Sendai, Kagoshima, Japan 74 31 50N 130 20 E
Sendai, Miyagi, Japan 74 38 15N 140 53 E
Sendamangalam 70 11 17N 78 17 E
Sendeling's Drift 92 28 12S 16 52 E
Sendenhorst 24 51 50N 7 49 E
Sendurjana 68 21 32N 78 17 E
Senec 27 48 12N 17 23 E
Seneca, Oreg., U.S.A. 118 44 10N 119 2W
Seneca, S.C., U.S.A. 115 34 43N 82 59W
Seneca Falls 114 42 55N 76 50W
Seneca L. 114 42 40N 76 58W
Senegal ■ 84 14 30N 14 30W
Senegal → 84 15 48N 16 32W
Senekal 93 28 30S 27 36 E
Senftenberg 24 51 30N 14 1 E
Senga Hill 91 9 19S 31 11 E
Senge Khambab (Indus) → 68 28 40N 70 10 E
Sengerema □ 90 2 10S 32 20 E
Sengiley 55 53 58N 48 46 E
Sengkang 73 4 8S 120 1 E
Sengua → 91 17 7S 28 5 E
Senhor-do-Bonfim 127 10 30S 40 10W
Senica 27 48 41N 17 25 E
Senigállia 39 43 42N 13 12 E
Senio → 39 44 35N 12 15 E
Senise 40 40 6N 16 15 E
Senj 39 45 0N 14 58 E
Senja 50 69 25N 17 30 E
Senlis 19 49 13N 2 35 E
Senmonorom 71 12 27N 107 12 E
Sennâr 87 13 30N 33 35 E
Senneterre 106 48 25N 77 15W
Senniquelle 84 7 19N 8 38W
Senno 54 54 45N 29 43 E
Sennori 40 40 49N 8 36 E
Senonches 18 48 34N 1 2 E
Senorbì 40 39 33N 9 8 E
Senožeče 39 45 43N 14 3 E
Sens 19 48 11N 3 15 E
Senta 42 45 55N 20 3 E
Sentein 20 42 53N 0 58 E
Sentery 90 5 17S 25 42 E
Sentinel 119 32 45N 113 13W
Sentolo 73 7 55S 110 13 E
Senya Beraku 85 5 28N 0 31W
Seo de Urgel 32 42 22N 1 23 E
Seohara 68 29 15N 78 33 E
Seoni 69 22 5N 79 30 E
Seoriuarayan 69 21 45N 82 34 E
Seoul = Sŏul 76 37 31N 127 6 E
Separation Point 107 53 37N 57 25W
Sepik → 98 3 49S 144 30 E
Sępólno Krajeńskie 28 53 26N 17 30 E
Sepone 71 16 45N 106 13 E
Sepopa 92 18 49S 22 12 E
Sepopol 28 54 16N 21 2 E
Sept-Îles 107 50 13N 66 22W
Septemvri 43 42 13N 24 6 E
Septimus 98 21 13S 148 47 E
Sepúlveda 30 41 18N 3 45W
Sequeros 30 40 31N 6 2W
Sequim 118 48 3N 123 9W
Sequoia Nat. Park 119 36 30N 118 30W
Serafimovich 57 49 36N 42 43 E
Seraing 16 50 35N 5 32 E
Seram 73 3 10S 129 0 E
Seram Sea 73 2 30S 128 30 E
Serampore 69 22 44N 88 21 E
Serang 73 6 8S 106 10 E
Serasan 72 2 29N 109 4 E
Seravezza 38 43 59N 10 13 E
Serbia = Srbija 42 43 30N 21 0 E
Sercaia 46 45 49N 25 9 E
Serdo 87 11 56N 41 14 E
Serdobsk 55 52 28N 44 10 E
Seredka 54 58 12N 28 10 E
Seregno 38 45 40N 9 12 E
Seremban 71 2 43N 101 53 E
Serena, La, Chile 124 29 55S 71 10W
Serena, La, Spain 31 38 45N 5 40W
Serengeti □ 90 2 0S 34 30 E
Serengeti Plain 90 2 40S 35 0 E
Sereth = Siret → 46 47 58N 26 5 E
Sergach 55 55 30N 45 30 E
Serge → 32 41 54N 0 50 E
Sergino 58 62 30N 65 38 E
Sergipe □ 127 10 30S 37 30W
Seria 72 4 37N 114 23 E
Serian 72 1 10N 110 31 E
Seriate 38 45 42N 9 43 E
Seribu, Kepulauan 72 5 36S 106 33 E
Sérifontaine 19 49 20N 1 45 E
Sérifos 45 37 9N 24 30 E
Sérignan 20 43 17N 3 17 E
Sermaize-les-Bains 19 48 47N 4 54 E
Sermata 73 8 15S 128 50 E
Sérmide 39 45 0N 11 17 E
Sernovodsk 55 53 54N 51 16 E
Serny Zavod 58 39 59N 58 50 E
Serock 28 52 31N 21 4 E
Serón 33 37 20N 2 29W
Serós 32 41 27N 0 24 E
Serov 58 59 29N 60 35 E
Serowe 92 22 25S 26 43 E
Serpa 31 37 57N 7 38 E
Serpeddi, Punta 40 39 19N 9 18 E
Serpentara 40 39 8N 9 38 E
Serpis → 33 38 59N 0 9W
Serpukhov 55 54 55N 37 28 E
Serra San Bruno 41 38 31N 16 23 E
Serracapriola 41 41 47N 15 12 E
Serradilla 30 39 50N 6 9W
Sérrai 44 41 5N 23 31 E
Sérrai □ 44 41 5N 23 37 E
Serramanna 40 39 26N 8 56 E
Serrat, C. 83 37 14N 9 10 E
Serre-Poncon, Barrage de 21 44 22N 6 20 E
Serres 21 44 26N 5 43 E
Serrezuela 124 30 40S 65 20W
Serrinha 127 11 39S 39 0W
Sersale 41 39 1N 16 44 E
Sertã 30 39 48N 8 6W
Sertânia 127 8 5S 37 20W
Sertanópolis 125 23 4S 51 2W
Serua 73 6 18S 130 1 E
Serui 73 1 53S 136 10 E
Serule 92 21 57S 27 20 E
Sérvia 44 40 9N 21 58 E
Sese Is. 90 0 20S 32 20 E
Sesepe 73 1 30S 127 59 E
Sesfontein 92 19 7S 13 39 E
Sesheke 92 17 29S 24 13 E
Sesia → 38 45 5N 8 37 E
Sesimbra 31 38 28N 9 6W
Sessa Aurunca 40 41 14N 13 55 E
Sestao 32 43 18N 3 0W
Sesto S. Giovanni 38 45 32N 9 14 E
Sestos 44 40 16N 26 23 E
Sestri Levante 38 44 17N 9 22 E
Sestrières 38 44 58N 6 56 E
Sestrunj 39 44 10N 15 0 E
Sestu 40 39 18N 9 6 E
Sète 20 43 25N 3 42 E
Sete Lagôas 127 19 27S 44 16W
Sétif 83 36 9N 5 26 E
Setonaikai 74 34 20N 133 30 E
Settat 82 33 0N 7 40W
Setté-Cama 88 2 32S 9 45 E
Séttimo Tor 38 45 9N 7 46 E
Setting L. 109 55 0N 98 38W
Settle 12 54 5N 2 18W
Settlement Pt. 115 26 40N 79 0W
Setto Calende 38 45 44N 8 37 E
Setúbal 31 38 30N 8 58W
Setúbal □ 31 38 25N 8 35W
Setúbal, B. de 31 38 40N 8 56W
Seugne → 20 45 42N 0 32W
Seul, Lac-Rés. 106 50 25N 92 30W
Seulimeum 72 5 27N 95 15 E
Sevan 57 40 33N 44 56 E
Sevan, Ozero 57 40 30N 45 20 E
Sevastopol 56 44 35N 33 30 E
Seven Sisters 108 54 56N 128 10W
Sever → 31 39 40N 7 32W
Sévérac-le-Château 20 44 20N 3 5 E
Severn →, Can. 106 56 2N 87 36W
Severn →, U.K. 13 51 35N 2 38W
Severn L. 106 53 54N 90 48W
Severnaya Zemlya 59 79 0N 100 0 E
Severnyye Uvaly 52 58 0N 48 0 E
Severo-Kurilsk 59 50 40N 156 8 E
Severo-Yeniseyskiy 59 60 22N 93 1 E
Severočeský □ 26 50 30N 14 0 E
Severodinsk 52 64 27N 39 58 E
Severodonetsk 57 48 58N 38 30 E
Severomoravský □ 27 49 38N 17 40 E
Severomorsk 52 69 5N 33 27 E
Severouralsk 52 60 9N 59 57 E
Sevier 119 38 39N 112 11W
Sevier → 119 39 10N 113 6W
Sevier L. 118 39 0N 113 20W
Sevilla 31 37 23N 6 0W
Sevilla □ 31 37 25N 5 30W
Seville = Sevilla 31 37 23N 6 0W
Sevlievo 43 43 2N 25 3 E
Sevnica 39 46 2N 15 19 E
Sèvre-Nantaise → 18 47 12N 1 33W
Sèvre-Niortaise → 20 46 18N 1 8W
Sevsk 54 52 10N 34 30 E
Seward, Alaska, U.S.A. 104 60 6N 149 26W
Seward, Nebr., U.S.A. 116 40 55N 97 6W
Seward Pen. 104 65 0N 164 0W
Sewell 124 34 10S 70 23W
Sewer 73 5 53S 134 40 E
Sewickley 112 40 33N 80 12W
Sexsmith 108 55 21N 118 47W
Seychelles ■ 3 5 0S 56 0 E
Seyðisfjörður 50 65 16N 14 0W
Seym → 54 51 27N 32 34 E
Seymchan 59 62 54N 152 30 E
Seymour, Austral. 99 37 0S 145 10 E
Seymour, Conn., U.S.A. 113 41 23N 73 5W
Seymour, Ind., U.S.A. 114 39 0N 85 50W
Seymour, Tex., U.S.A. 117 33 35N 99 18W
Seymour, Wis., U.S.A. 114 44 30N 88 20W
Seyne 21 44 21N 6 22 E
Seyne-sur-Mer, La 21 43 7N 5 52 E
Seyssel 21 45 57N 5 50 E
Sežana 39 45 43N 13 41 E
Sézanne 19 48 40N 3 40 E
Sezze 40 41 30N 13 3 E
Sfax 83 34 49N 10 48 E
Sfîntu Gheorghe 46 45 52N 25 48 E
Sha Xian 77 26 23N 117 45 E
Shaanxi □ 77 35 0N 109 0 E
Shaba 90 8 0S 25 0 E
† Shabani 91 20 17S 30 2 E
Shabla 43 43 31N 28 32 E
Shabunda 90 2 40S 27 16 E
Shache 75 38 20N 77 10 E
Shackleton 5 78 30S 36 1W
Shackleton Ice Shelf 5 66 0S 100 0 E
Shackleton Inlet 5 83 0S 160 0 E
Shaddad 86 21 25N 40 2 E
Shadrinsk 58 56 5N 63 32 E
Shaffa 85 10 30N 12 6 E
Shafter, Calif., U.S.A. 119 35 32N 119 14W
Shafter, Tex., U.S.A. 117 29 49N 104 18W
Shaftesbury 13 51 0N 2 12W
Shagamu 85 6 51N 3 39 E
Shah Bunder 68 24 13N 67 56 E
* Shah Faisalabad 68 31 30N 73 5 E
Shahabad, Andhra Pradesh, India 70 17 10N 76 54 E
Shahabad, Punjab, India 68 30 10N 76 55 E
Shahabad, Raj., India 68 25 15N 77 11 E
Shahabad, Ut. P., India 69 27 36N 79 56 E
Shāhābād, Kermanshāhān, Iran 64 34 10N 46 30 E
Shāhābād, Khorāsān, Iran 65 37 40N 56 50 E
Shahada 68 21 33N 74 30 E
Shahadpur 68 25 55N 68 35 E
Shahapur 70 15 50N 74 34 E
Shahdād 65 30 30N 57 40 E
Shahdadkot 68 27 50N 67 55 E
Shahganj 69 26 3N 82 44 E
Shaḩḩāt 81 32 48N 21 54 E
Shāhī 65 36 30N 52 55 E
Shahjahanpur 69 27 54N 79 57 E
Shahpur, Mad. P., India 68 22 12N 77 58 E
Shahpur, Mysore, India 70 16 40N 76 48 E
Shahpūr 64 38 12N 44 45 E
Shahpur 68 28 46N 68 27 E
Shahpura 69 23 10N 80 45 E
Shahr Kord 65 32 15N 50 55 E
Shahrezā 65 32 0N 51 55 E
Shahrig 68 30 15N 67 40 E
Shāhrūd 65 36 30N 55 0 E

* *Renamed Faisalabad*

† *Renamed Zvishavane*

Shahsād, Namakzār-e 65 30 20N 58 20 E
Shahsavār 65 36 45N 51 12 E
Shaibara 86 25 26N 36 47 E
Shaikhabad 66 34 2N 68 45 E
Shajapur 68 23 27N 76 21 E
Shakargarh 68 32 17N 75 10 E
Shakawe 92 18 28 S 21 49 E
Shaker Heights 112 41 29N 81 36W
Shakhty 57 47 40N 40 16 E
Shakhunya 55 57 40N 46 46 E
Shaki 85 8 41N 3 21 E
Shakopee 116 44 45N 93 30W
Shala, L. 87 7 30N 38 30 E
Shallow Lake 112 44 36N 81 5W
Sham, J. ash 65 23 10N 57 5 E
Shamâl Dârfûr □ 87 15 0N 25 0 E
Shamâl Kordofân □ 87 15 0N 30 0 E
Shamattawa 109 55 51N 92 5W
Shamattawa → 106 55 1N 85 23W
Shambe 87 7 8N 30 46 E
Shambu 87 9 32N 37 3 E
Shamgong Dzong 69 27 13N 90 35 E
Shamīl 65 27 30N 56 55 E
Shamkhor 57 40 50N 46 0 E
Shamli 68 29 32N 77 18 E
Shammar, Jabal 64 27 40N 41 0 E
Shamo, L. 87 5 45N 37 30 E
Shamokin 114 40 47N 76 33W
Shamrock 117 35 15N 100 15W
Shan □ 67 21 30N 98 30 E
Shanan → 87 8 0N 40 20 E
Shanchengzhen 76 42 20N 125 20 E
Shandong □ 76 36 0N 118 0 E
Shang Xian 77 33 50N 109 58 E
Shangalowe 91 10 50 S 26 30 E
Shangani 91 19 41 S 29 20 E
Shangani → 91 18 41 S 27 10 E
Shangbancheng 76 40 50N 118 1 E
Shangcheng 77 31 47N 115 26 E
Shangchuan Dao 77 21 40N 112 50 E
Shangdu 76 41 30N 113 30 E
Shanggao 77 28 17N 114 55 E
Shanghai 75 31 15N 121 26 E
Shangqiu 77 34 26N 115 36 E
Shangrao 75 28 25N 117 59 E
Shangshui 77 33 42N 114 35 E
Shangsi 77 22 8N 107 58 E
Shangyou 77 25 48N 114 32 E
Shangzhi 76 45 22N 127 56 E
Shani 85 10 14N 12 2 E
Shaniko 118 45 0N 120 50W
Shannon, Greenl. 4 75 10N 18 30W
Shannon, N.Z. 101 40 33 S 175 25 E
Shannon → 15 52 35N 9 30W
Shansi = Shanxi □ 76 37 0N 112 0 E
Shantar, Ostrov Bolshoy 59 55 9N 137 40 E
Shantou 75 23 18N 116 40 E
Shantung = Shandong □ 76 36 0N 118 0 E
Shanxi □ 76 37 0N 112 0 E
Shanyang 77 33 31N 109 55 E
Shaoguan 75 24 48N 113 35 E
Shaowu 75 27 22N 117 28 E
Shaoxing 75 30 0N 120 35 E
Shaoyang 75 27 14N 111 25 E
Shapinsay 14 59 2N 2 50W
Shaqrā', Si. Arab. 64 25 15N 45 16 E
Shaqrā', Yemen, S. 63 13 22N 45 44 E
Sharafa (Ogr) 87 11 59N 27 7 E
Sharavati → 70 14 20N 74 25 E
Sharbot Lake 113 44 46N 76 41W
Shark B. 96 25 55 S 113 32 E
Sharm el Sheikh 86 27 53N 34 15 E
Sharon, Mass., U.S.A. 113 42 5N 71 11W
Sharon, Pa., U.S.A. 114 41 18N 80 30W
Sharon, Plain of = Hasharon 62 32 12N 34 49 E
Sharon Springs 116 38 54N 101 45W
Sharp Pt. 98 10 58 S 142 43 E
Sharpe L. 109 54 5N 93 40W
Sharpsville 112 41 16N 80 28W
Shary 64 27 14N 43 29 E
Sharya 55 58 22N 45 20 E
Shasha 87 6 29N 35 59 E
Shashemene 87 7 13N 38 33 E
Shashi 75 30 25N 112 14 E
Shashi → 91 21 14 S 29 20 E
Shasta, Mt. 118 41 30N 122 12W
Shasta Res. 118 40 50N 122 15W
Shatsk 55 54 0N 41 45 E
Shattuck 117 36 17N 99 55W
Shatura 55 55 34N 39 31 E
Shaumyani 57 41 22N 41 45 E
Shaunavon 109 49 35N 108 25W
Shaw → 96 20 21 S 119 17 E
Shaw I. 98 20 30 S 149 2 E
Shawan 75 44 34N 85 50 E
Shawanaga 112 45 31N 80 17W
Shawano 114 44 45N 88 38W
Shawinigan 106 46 35N 72 50W
Shawnee 117 35 15N 97 0W
Shayib el Banat, Gebel 86 26 59N 33 29 E
Shchekino 55 54 1N 37 34 E
Shcherbakov = Rybinsk 55 58 5N 38 50 E
Shchigri 55 51 55N 36 58 E
Shchors 54 51 48N 31 56 E
Shchuchiosk 58 52 56N 70 12 E
She Xian 77 29 50N 118 25 E
Shebekino 55 50 28N 36 54 E
Shebele, Wabi → 87 2 0N 44 0 E
Sheboygan 114 43 46N 87 45W
Shechem 62 32 13N 35 21 E
Shediac 107 46 14N 64 32W
Sheelin, Lough 15 53 48N 7 20W
Sheep Haven 15 55 12N 7 55W
Sheerness 13 51 26N 0 47 E
Sheet Harbour 107 44 56N 62 31W
Shefar'am 62 32 48N 35 10 E
Sheffield, U.K. 12 53 23N 1 28W
Sheffield, Ala., U.S.A. 115 34 45N 87 42W
Sheffield, Mass., U.S.A. 113 42 6N 73 23W
Sheffield, Pa., U.S.A. 112 41 42N 79 3W
Sheffield, Tex., U.S.A. 117 30 42N 101 49W
Shegaon 68 20 48N 76 47 E
Sheho 109 51 35N 103 13W
Shehojele 87 10 40N 35 9 E
Sheikhpura 69 25 9N 85 53 E
Shek Hasan 87 12 5N 35 58 E
Shekhupura 68 31 42N 73 58 E
Sheki 57 41 10N 47 5 E
Sheksna → 55 59 0N 38 30 E
Shelburne, N.S., Can. 107 43 47N 65 20W
Shelburne, Ont., Can. 106 44 4N 80 15W
Shelburne, U.S.A. 113 44 23N 73 15W
Shelburne B. 97 11 50 S 142 50 E
Shelburne Falls 113 42 36N 72 45W
Shelby, Mich., U.S.A. 114 43 34N 86 27W
Shelby, Mont., U.S.A. 118 48 30N 111 52W
Shelby, N.C., U.S.A. 115 35 18N 81 34W
Shelby, Ohio, U.S.A. 112 40 52N 82 40W
Shelbyville, Ill., U.S.A. 116 39 25N 88 45W
Shelbyville, Ind., U.S.A. 114 39 30N 85 42W
Shelbyville, Tenn., U.S.A. 115 35 30N 86 25W
Sheldon 116 43 6N 95 40W
Sheldrake 107 50 20N 64 51W
Shelikhova, Zaliv 59 59 30N 157 0 E
Shell Creek Ra. 118 39 15N 114 30W
Shell Lake 109 53 19N 107 2W
Shellbrook 109 53 13N 106 24W
Shellharbour 97 34 31 S 150 51 E
Shelling Rocks 15 51 45N 10 35W
Shelon → 54 58 10N 30 30 E
Shelton, Conn., U.S.A. 113 41 18N 73 7W
Shelton, Wash., U.S.A. 118 47 15N 123 6W
Shemakha 57 40 38N 48 37 E
Shenandoah, Iowa, U.S.A. 116 40 50N 95 25W
Shenandoah, Pa., U.S.A. 114 40 49N 76 13W
Shenandoah, Va., U.S.A. 114 38 30N 78 38W
Shenandoah → 114 39 19N 77 44W
Shenchi 76 39 8N 112 10 E
Shencottah 70 8 59N 77 18 E
Shendam 85 8 49N 9 30 E
Shendî 87 16 46N 33 22 E
Shendurni 70 20 39N 75 36 E
Sheng Xian 77 29 35N 120 50 E
Shëngjergji 44 41 17N 20 10 E
Shëngjini 44 41 50N 19 35 E
Shenmëria 44 42 7N 20 13 E
Shenmu 76 38 50N 110 29 E
Shenqiucheng 77 33 24N 115 2 E
Shensi = Shaanxi □ 77 35 0N 109 0 E
Shenyang 76 41 48N 123 27 E
Shepetovka 54 50 10N 27 10 E
Shephelah = Hashefela 62 31 30N 34 43 E
Shepparton 97 36 23 S 145 26 E
Sheqi 77 33 12N 112 57 E
Sherada 87 7 18N 36 30 E
Sherborne 13 50 56N 2 31W
Sherbro I. 84 7 30N 12 40W
Sherbrooke 107 45 28N 71 57W
Sherda 83 20 7N 16 46 E
Shereik 86 18 44N 33 47 E
Sheridan, Ark., U.S.A. 117 34 20N 92 25W
Sheridan, Col., U.S.A. 116 39 44N 105 3W
Sheridan, Wyo., U.S.A. 118 44 50N 107 0W
Sherkot 68 29 22N 78 35 E
Sherman 117 33 40N 96 35W
Sherpur 69 25 0N 90 0 E
Sherridon 109 55 8N 101 5W
Sherwood, N.D., U.S.A. 116 48 59N 101 36W
Sherwood, Tex., U.S.A. 117 31 18N 100 45W
Sherwood Forest 12 53 5N 1 5W
Sheslay 108 58 17N 131 52W
Sheslay → 108 58 48N 132 5W
Shethanei L. 109 58 48N 97 50W
Shetland □ 14 60 30N 1 30W
Shetland Is. 14 60 30N 1 30W
Shevaroy Hills 70 11 58N 78 12 E
Shewa □ 87 9 33N 38 10 E
Shewa Gimira 87 7 4N 35 51 E
Sheyenne 116 47 52N 99 8W
Sheyenne → 116 47 5N 96 50W
Shibām 63 16 0N 48 36 E
Shibîn El Kôm 86 30 31N 30 55 E
Shibîn el Qanâtir 86 30 19N 31 19 E
Shibogama L. 106 53 35N 88 15W
Shibushi 74 31 25N 131 8 E
Shidao 76 36 50N 122 25 E
Shiel, L. 14 56 48N 5 32W
Shiga □ 74 35 20N 136 0 E
Shigaib 81 15 5N 23 35 E
Shiguaigou 76 40 52N 110 15 E
Shihchiachuangi = Shijiazhuang 76 38 2N 114 28 E
Shijaku 44 41 21N 19 33 E
Shijiazhuang 76 38 2N 114 28 E
Shikarpur, India 68 28 17N 78 7 E
Shikarpur, Pak. 68 27 57N 68 39 E
Shikoku 74 33 30N 133 30 E
Shikoku □ 74 33 30N 133 30 E
Shikoku-Sanchi 74 33 30N 133 30 E
Shilabo 63 6 22N 44 32 E
Shilka 59 52 0N 115 55 E
Shilka → 59 53 20N 121 26 E
Shillelagh 15 52 46N 6 32W
Shillong 67 25 35N 91 53 E
Shilo 62 32 4N 35 18 E
Shilong 75 23 5N 113 52 E
Shilovo 55 54 25N 40 57 E
Shimabara 74 32 48N 130 20 E
Shimada 74 34 49N 138 10 E
Shimane □ 74 35 0N 132 30 E
Shimanovsk 59 52 15N 127 30 E
Shimizu 74 35 0N 138 30 E
Shimodate 74 36 20N 139 55 E
Shimoga 70 13 57N 75 32 E
Shimoni 90 4 38 S 39 20 E
Shimonoseki 74 33 58N 131 0 E
Shimpuru Rapids 92 17 45 S 19 55 E
Shimsha → 70 13 15N 77 10 E
Shimsk 54 58 15N 30 50 E
Shin, L. 14 58 7N 4 30W
Shin-Tone → 74 35 44N 140 51 E
Shinano → 74 36 50N 138 30 E
Shīndand 65 33 12N 62 8 E
Shingleton 106 46 25N 86 33W
Shingū 74 33 40N 135 55 E
Shinkafe 85 13 8N 6 29 E
Shinyanga 90 3 45 S 33 27 E
Shinyanga □ 90 3 50 S 34 0 E
Shio-no-Misaki 74 33 25N 135 45 E
Ship I. 117 30 16N 88 55W
Shipehenski Prokhod 43 42 45N 25 15 E
Shippegan 107 47 45N 64 45W
Shippensburg 114 40 4N 77 32W
Shiprock 119 36 51N 108 45W
Shiqian 77 27 32N 108 13 E
Shiqma, N. → 62 31 37N 34 30 E
Shiquan 77 33 5N 108 15 E
Shīr Kūh 65 31 39N 54 3 E
Shīrāz 65 29 42N 52 30 E
Shirbin 86 31 11N 31 32 E
Shire → 91 17 42 S 35 19 E
Shiretoko-Misaki 74 44 21N 145 20 E
Shiringushi 55 53 51N 42 46 E
Shiriya-Zaki 74 41 25N 141 30 E
Shirol 70 16 47N 74 41 E
Shirpur 68 21 21N 74 57 E
Shīrvān 65 37 30N 57 50 E
Shishmanova 43 42 58N 23 12 E
Shisur 63 17 30N 54 0 E
Shitai 77 30 12N 117 25 E
Shivali (Sirkali) 70 11 15N 79 41 E
Shivpuri 68 25 26N 77 42 E
Shivta 62 30 53N 34 40 E
Shiwei 76 51 19N 119 55 E
Shixing 77 24 46N 114 5 E
Shiyata 86 29 25N 25 7 E
Shizuishan 76 39 15N 106 50 E
Shizuoka 74 35 0N 138 24 E
Shizuoka □ 74 35 15N 138 40 E
Shklov 54 54 16N 30 15 E
Shkoder = Shkodra 44 42 6N 19 1 E
Shkodra 44 42 6N 19 20 E
Shkodra □ 44 42 25N 19 20 E
Shkumbini → 44 41 5N 19 50 E
Shmidt, O. 59 81 0N 91 0 E
Shoal Lake 109 50 30N 100 35W
Shoalhaven → 100 34 54 S 150 42 E
Shoeburyness 13 51 31N 0 49 E
Sholapur 70 17 43N 75 56 E
Shologontsy 59 66 13N 114 0 E
Shomera 62 33 4N 35 17 E
Shōmrōn 62 32 15N 35 13 E
Shongopovi 119 35 49N 110 37W
Shoranur 70 10 46N 76 19 E
Shorapur 70 16 31N 76 48 E
Shoshone 118 43 0N 114 27W
Shoshone L. 118 44 30N 110 40W
Shoshone Mts. 118 39 30N 117 30W
Shoshong 92 22 56 S 26 31 E
Shoshoni 118 43 13N 108 5W
Shostka 54 51 57N 33 32 E
Shouyang 76 37 54N 113 8 E
Show Low 119 34 16N 110 0W
Shpola 56 49 1N 31 30 E
Shreveport 117 32 30N 93 50W
Shrewsbury 12 52 42N 2 45W
Shrivardhan 70 18 4N 73 3 E
Shropshire □ 13 52 36N 2 45W
Shuangcheng 76 45 20N 126 15 E
Shuangliao 76 43 29N 123 30 E
Shuangyashan 75 46 28N 131 5 E
Shucheng 77 31 28N 116 57 E
Shu'eib, Wadi 62 31 54N 35 38 E
Shuguri Falls 91 8 33 S 37 22 E
Shujalpur 68 23 18N 76 46 E
Shulan 76 44 28N 127 0 E
Shule 75 39 25N 76 3 E
Shumagin Is. 104 55 0N 159 0W
Shumerlya 55 55 30N 46 25 E
Shumikha 58 55 10N 63 15 E
Shunchang 77 26 54N 117 48 E
Shunde 77 22 42N 113 14 E
Shungay 57 48 30N 46 45 E
Shungnak 104 66 55N 157 10W
Shuo Xian 76 39 20N 112 33 E
Shūr → 65 28 30N 55 0 E
Shurma 55 56 58N 50 21 E
Shūsf 65 31 50N 60 5 E
Shūshtar 64 32 0N 48 50 E
Shuswap L. 108 50 55N 119 3W
Shuwaykah 62 32 20N 35 1 E
Shuya 55 56 50N 41 28 E
Shwebo 67 22 30N 95 45 E
Shwegu 67 24 15N 96 26 E
Shweli → 67 23 45N 96 45 E
Shyok 69 34 15N 78 12 E
Shyok → 69 35 13N 75 53 E
Si Kiang = Xi Jiang → 75 22 5N 113 20 E
Si Racha 71 13 10N 100 48 E
Siah 64 22 0N 47 0 E
Siahan Range 66 27 30N 64 40 E
Siaksrinderapura 72 0 51N 102 0 E
Sialkot 68 32 32N 74 30 E
Siam = Thailand ■ 71 16 0N 102 0 E
Siam, G. of 71 11 30N 101 0 E
Sian = Xi'an 77 34 15N 109 0 E
Siantan, P. 72 3 10N 106 15 E
Sīāreh 65 28 5N 60 14 E
Siargao 73 9 52N 126 3 E
Siasi 73 5 34N 120 50 E
Siátista 44 40 15N 21 33 E
Siau 73 2 50N 125 25 E
Siauliai 54 55 56N 23 15 E
Siaya □ 90 0 0N 34 20 E
Siazan 57 41 3N 49 10 E
Sibâi, Gebel el 86 25 45N 34 10 E
Sibari 41 39 47N 16 27 E
Sibay 52 52 42N 58 39 E
Sibaya, L. 93 27 20 S 32 45 E
Šibenik 39 43 48N 15 54 E
Siberia 60 60 0N 100 0 E
Siberut 72 1 30 S 99 0 E
Sibi 68 29 30N 67 54 E
Sibil 73 4 59 S 140 35 E
Sibiti 88 3 38 S 13 19 E
Sibiu 46 45 45N 24 9 E
Sibiu □ 46 45 50N 24 15 E
Sibley, Iowa, U.S.A. 116 43 21N 95 43W
Sibley, La., U.S.A. 117 32 34N 93 16W
Sibolga 72 1 42N 98 45 E
Sibsagar 67 27 0N 94 36 E
Sibu 72 2 18N 111 49 E
Sibuco 73 7 20N 122 10 E
Sibuguey B. 73 7 50N 122 45 E
Sibutu 73 4 45N 119 30 E
Sibutu Passage 73 4 50N 120 0 E
Sibuyan 73 12 25N 122 40 E
Sibuyan Sea 73 12 30N 122 20 E
Sicamous 108 50 49N 119 0W
Siccus → 99 31 42 S 139 25 E
Sichuan □ 75 31 0N 104 0 E
Sicilia 41 37 30N 14 30 E
Sicilia, Canale di 40 37 25N 12 30 E
Sicilian Channel = Sicilia, Canale di 40 37 25N 12 30 E
Sicily = Sicilia 41 37 30N 14 30 E
Sicuani 126 14 21 S 71 10W
Siculiana 40 37 20N 13 23 E
Šid 42 45 8N 19 14 E
Sidamo □ 87 5 0N 37 50 E
Sidaouet 85 18 34N 8 3 E
Siddipet 70 18 0N 78 51 E
Sidéradougou 84 10 42N 4 12W
Siderno Marina 41 38 16N 16 17 E
Sidheros, Ákra 45 35 19N 26 19 E
Sidhirókastron 44 41 13N 23 24 E
Sidhpur 68 23 56N 72 25 E
Sîdi Abd el Rahmân 86 30 55N 29 44 E
Sîdi Barrâni 86 31 38N 25 58 E
Sidi-bel-Abbès 82 35 13N 0 39W
Sidi Bennour 82 32 40N 8 25W
Sidi Haneish 86 31 10N 27 35 E
Sidi Kacem 82 34 11N 5 49W
Sidi Moussa, O. → 82 26 58N 3 54 E
Sidi Omar 86 31 24N 24 57 E
Sidi Slimane 82 34 16N 5 56W
Sidi Smaïl 82 32 50N 8 31W
Sidlaw Hills 14 56 32N 3 10W
Sidley, Mt. 5 77 2 S 126 2W
Sidmouth 13 50 40N 3 13W
Sidmouth, C. 98 13 25 S 143 36 E
Sidney, Can. 108 48 39N 123 24W
Sidney, Mont., U.S.A. 116 47 42N 104 7W
Sidney, N.Y., U.S.A. 114 42 18N 75 20W
Sidney, Ohio, U.S.A. 114 40 18N 84 6W
Sidoarjo 73 7 30 S 112 46 E
Sidra, G. of = Khalīj Surt 35 31 40N 18 30 E
Siedlce 28 52 10N 22 20 E
Siedlce □ 28 52 0N 22 0 E
Sieg → 24 50 46N 7 7 E
Siegburg 24 50 48N 7 12 E
Siegen 24 50 52N 8 2 E
Siem Reap 71 13 20N 103 52 E
Siena 39 43 20N 11 20 E
Sieniawa 27 50 11N 22 38 E
Sieradź 28 51 37N 18 41 E
Sieraków 28 52 39N 16 2 E
Sierck-les-Bains 19 49 26N 6 20 E
Sierpc 28 52 55N 19 43 E
Sierra Blanca, N. Mex., U.S.A. 119 33 20N 105 54W
Sierra Blanca, Tex., U.S.A. 119 31 11N 105 17W
Sierra City 118 39 34N 120 42W
Sierra Colorada 128 40 35 S 67 50W
Sierra de Yeguas 31 37 7N 4 52W
Sierra Gorda 124 22 50 S 69 15W
Sierra Leone ■ 84 9 0N 12 0W
Sierra Mojada 120 27 19N 103 42W
Sierre 25 46 17N 7 31 E
Sif Fatima 83 31 6N 8 41 E
Sifnos 45 37 0N 24 45 E
Sifton 109 51 21N 100 8W
Sifton Pass 108 57 52N 126 15W
Sig 82 35 32N 0 12W
Sigdal 47 60 4N 9 38 E
Sigean 20 43 2N 2 58 E
Sighetul Marmatiei 46 47 57N 23 52 E
Sighişoara 46 46 12N 24 50 E
Sigli 72 5 25N 96 0 E
Siglufjörður 50 66 12N 18 55W
Sigma 73 11 29N 122 40 E
Sigmaringen 25 48 5N 9 13 E
Signakhi 57 41 40N 45 57 E
Signy I. 5 60 45 S 45 56W
Signy-l'Abbaye 19 49 40N 4 25 E
Sigsig 126 3 0 S 78 50W
Sigtuna 48 59 36N 17 44 E
Sigüenza 32 41 3N 2 40W
Siguiri 84 11 31N 9 10W
Sigulda 54 57 10N 24 55 E
Sigurd 119 38 49N 112 0W
Sihanoukville = Kompong Som 71 10 40N 103 30 E
Sihui 77 23 20N 112 40 E
Si'ir 62 31 35N 35 9 E
Siirt 64 37 57N 41 55 E
Sijarira Ra. 91 17 36 S 27 45 E
Sikar 68 27 33N 75 10 E
Sikasso 84 11 18N 5 35W
Sikeston 117 36 52N 89 35W
Sikhote Alin, Khrebet 59 46 0N 136 0 E
Sikiá. 44 40 2N 23 56 E
Síkinos 45 36 40N 25 8 E
Sikkani Chief → 108 57 47N 122 15W
Sikkim □ 69 27 50N 88 30 E
Siklós 27 45 50N 18 19 E
Sil → 30 42 27N 7 43W
Sila, La 41 39 15N 16 35 E
Silandro 38 46 38N 10 48 E
Sīlat az Ẓahr 62 32 19N 35 11 E
Silba 39 44 24N 14 41 E
Silchar 67 24 49N 92 48 E
Silcox 109 57 12N 94 10W
Siler City 115 35 44N 79 30W
Sileru → 70 17 49N 81 24 E
Silesia = Slask 22 51 0N 16 30 E
Silet 82 22 44N 4 37 E
Silgarhi Doti 69 29 15N 81 0 E
Silghat 67 26 35N 93 0 E
Silifke 64 36 22N 33 58 E
Siliguri 69 26 45N 88 25 E

Siling Co 75 31 50N 89 20 E
Siliqua 40 39 20N 8 49 E
Silistra 43 44 6N 27 19 E
Siljan, L. 48 60 55N 14 45 E
Silkeborg 49 56 10N 9 32 E
Sillajhuay, Cordillera 126 19 46 S 68 40W
Sillé-le-Guillaume 18 48 10N 0 8W
Siloam Springs 117 36 15N 94 31W
Silogui 72 1 10 S 9 0 E
Silsbee 117 30 20N 94 8W
Silute 54 55 21N 21 33 E
Silva Porto = Bié 89 12 22 S 16 55 E
Silver City, Panama 120 9 19N 79 53W
Silver City, N. Mex., U.S.A. 119 32 50N 108 18W
Silver City, Nev., U.S.A. 118 39 15N 119 48W
Silver Cr. ⇝ 118 43 16N 119 13W
Silver Creek 114 42 33N 79 9W
Silver Lake 118 43 9N 121 4W
Silverton, Austral. 100 31 52 S 141 10 E
Silverton, Colo., U.S.A. 119 37 51N 107 45W
Silverton, Tex., U.S.A. 117 34 30N 101 16W
Silves 31 37 11N 8 26W
Silvi 39 42 32N 14 5 E
Silvies ⇝ 118 43 22N 118 48W
Silvretta Gruppe 25 46 50N 10 6 E
Silwa Bahari 86 24 45N 32 55 E
Silwâd 62 31 59N 35 15 E
Silz 26 47 16N 10 56 E
Sim, C. 82 31 26N 9 51W
Simanggang 72 1 15N 111 32 E
Simard, L. 106 47 40N 78 40W
Sîmărtin 46 46 19N 25 58 E
Simba 90 2 10 S 37 36 E
Simbach 25 48 16N 13 3 E
Simbo 90 4 51 S 29 41 E
Simcoe 106 42 50N 80 20W
Simcoe, L. 106 44 25N 79 20W
Simenga 59 62 42N 108 25 E
Simeto ⇝ 41 37 25N 15 10 E
Simeulue 72 2 45N 95 45 E
Simferopol 56 44 55N 34 3 E
Sími 45 36 35N 27 50 E
Simikot 69 30 0N 81 50 E
Simitli 42 41 52N 23 7 E
Simla 68 31 2N 77 9 E
Şimleu-Silvaniei 46 47 17N 22 50 E
Simmern 25 49 59N 7 32 E
Simmie 109 49 56N 108 6W
Simojärvi 50 66 5N 27 3 E
Simojoki ⇝ 50 65 35N 25 1 E
Simonette ⇝ 108 55 9N 118 15W
Simonstown 92 34 14 S 18 26 E
Simontornya 27 46 45N 18 33 E
Simpang, Indon. 72 1 16 S 104 5 E
Simpang, Malay. 71 4 50N 100 40 E
Simplon Pass 25 46 15N 8 0 E
Simplon Tunnel 25 46 15N 8 7 E
Simpson Des. 97 25 0 S 137 0 E
Simrishamn 49 55 33N 14 22 E
Simunjan 72 1 25N 110 45 E
Simushir, Ostrov 59 46 50N 152 30 E
Sina ⇝ 70 17 30N 75 55 E
Sinabang 72 2 30N 96 24 E
Sinadogo 63 5 50N 47 0 E
Sinai = Es Sînâ' 86 29 0N 34 0 E
Sinai, Mt. = Mûsa, G. 86 28 32N 33 59 E
Sinaia 46 45 21N 25 38 E
Sinaloa 120 25 50N 108 20W
Sinaloa □ 120 25 0N 107 30W
Sinalunga 39 43 12N 11 43 E
Sinan 77 27 56N 108 13 E
Sînandrei 46 45 52N 21 13 E
Sînâwan 83 31 0N 10 37 E
Sincelejo 126 9 18N 75 24W
Sinclair 118 41 47N 107 10W
Sinclair Mills 108 54 5N 121 40W
Sincorá, Serra do 127 13 30 S 41 0W
Sind 68 26 0N 68 30 E
Sind Sagar Doab 68 32 0N 71 30 E
Sindal 49 57 28N 10 10 E
Sindangan 73 8 10N 123 5 E
Sindangbarang 73 7 27 S 107 1 E
Sinde 91 17 28 S 25 51 E
Sinegorski 57 48 0N 40 52 E
Sinelnikovo 56 48 25N 35 30 E
Sines 31 37 56N 8 51W
Sines, Cabo de 31 37 58N 8 53W
Sineu 32 39 38N 3 1 E
Sinfra 84 6 35N 5 56W
Singa 87 13 10N 33 57 E
Singanallur 70 11 2N 77 1 E
Singaparna 73 7 23 S 108 4 E
Singapore ■ 71 1 17N 103 51 E
Singapore, Straits of 71 1 15N 104 0 E
Singaraja 72 8 6 S 115 10 E
Singen 25 47 45N 8 50 E
Singida 90 4 49 S 34 48 E
Singida □ 90 6 0 S 34 30 E
Singitikós Kólpos 44 40 6N 24 0 E
Singkaling Hkamti 67 26 0N 95 39 E
Singkawang 72 1 0N 108 57 E
Singkep 72 0 30 S 104 20 E
Singleton 97 32 33 S 151 0 E
Singleton, Mt. 96 29 27 S 117 15 E
Singö 48 60 12N 18 45 E
Singoli 68 25 0N 75 22 E
Siniátsikon, Óros 44 40 25N 21 35 E
Siniscóla 40 40 35N 9 40 E
Sinj 39 43 42N 16 39 E
Sinjai 73 5 7 S 120 20 E
Sinjajevina, Planina 42 42 57N 19 22 E
Sinjār 64 36 19N 41 52 E
Sinjil 62 32 3N 35 15 E
Sinkat 86 18 55N 36 49 E
Sinkiang Uighur = Xinjiang Uygur □ 75 42 0N 86 0 E
Sinnai 40 39 18N 9 13 E
Sinnar 70 19 48N 74 0 E
Sinni ⇝ 41 40 9N 16 42 E
Sînnicolau Maré 42 46 5N 20 39 E
Sinnuris 86 29 26N 30 31 E
Sinoe, L. 46 44 35N 28 50 E
Sinoia 91 17 20 S 30 8 E
Sinop 64 42 1N 35 11 E
Sinskoye 59 61 8N 126 48 E
Sint Maarten 121 18 0N 63 5W
Sint Niklaas 16 51 10N 4 9 E
Sint Truiden 16 50 48N 5 10 E
Sîntana 46 46 20N 21 30 E
Sintang 72 0 5N 111 35 E
Sinton 117 28 1N 97 30W
Sintra 31 38 47N 9 25W
Sinŭiju 76 40 5N 124 24 E
Sinyukha ⇝ 56 48 3N 30 51 E
Siocon 73 7 40N 122 10 E
Siófok 27 16 39 S 23 36 E
Sioma 92 16 25 S 23 28 E
Sion 25 46 14N 7 20 E
Sioux City 116 42 32N 96 25W
Sioux Falls 116 43 35N 96 40W
Sioux Lookout 106 50 10N 91 50W
Šipan 42 42 45N 17 52 E
Siping 76 43 8N 124 21 E
Sipiwesk L. 109 55 5N 97 35W
Sipora 72 2 18 S 99 40 E
Siquia ⇝ 121 12 10N 84 20W
Siquijor 73 9 12N 123 35 E
Sir Edward Pellew Group 97 15 40 S 137 10 E
Sira 70 13 41N 76 49 E
Siracusa 41 37 4N 15 17 E
Sirajganj 69 24 25N 89 47 E
Sirakoro 84 12 41N 9 14W
Sirasso 84 9 16N 6 6W
Siret 46 47 55N 26 5 E
Siret ⇝ 46 47 58N 26 5 E
Şiria 42 46 16N 21 38 E
Sirino, Monte 41 40 7N 15 50 E
Sirkali (Shivali) 70 11 15N 79 41 E
Sírna. 45 36 22N 26 42 E
Sirohi 68 24 52N 72 53 E
Široki Brijeg 42 43 21N 17 36 E
Sironj 68 24 5N 77 39 E
Síros 45 37 28N 24 57 E
Sirsa 68 29 33N 75 4 E
Sirsi 70 14 40N 74 49 E
Siruela 31 38 58N 5 3W
Sisak 39 45 30N 16 21 E
Sisaket 71 15 8N 104 23 E
Sisante 33 39 25N 2 12W
Sisargas, Islas 30 43 21N 8 50W
Sishen 92 27 47 S 22 59 E
Sishui 77 34 48N 113 15 E
Sisipuk L. 109 55 45N 101 50W
Sisophon 71 13 38N 102 59 E
Sisseton 116 45 43N 97 3W
Sissonne 19 49 34N 3 51 E
Sistema Central 30 40 40N 5 55W
Sistema Iberico 32 41 0N 2 10W
Sisteron 21 44 12N 5 57 E
Sisters 118 44 21N 121 32W
Sitamarhi 69 26 37N 85 30 E
Sitapur 69 27 38N 80 45 E
Siteki 93 26 32 S 31 58 E
Sitges 32 41 17N 1 47 E
Sithoniá 44 40 0N 23 45 E
Sitía 45 35 13N 26 6 E
Sitka 104 57 9N 135 20W
Sitoti 92 23 15 S 23 40 E
Sitra 86 28 40N 26 53 E
Sittang ⇝ 67 17 10N 96 58 E
Sittang Myit ⇝ 67 17 20N 96 45 E
Sittard 16 51 0N 5 52 E
Sittensen 24 53 17N 9 32 E
Sittona 87 14 25N 37 23 E
Situbondo 73 7 45 S 114 0 E
Sivaganga 70 9 50N 78 28 E
Sivagiri 70 9 16N 77 26 E
Sivakasi 70 9 24N 77 47 E
Sivana 68 28 37N 78 6 E
Sivand 65 30 5N 52 55 E
Sivas 64 39 43N 36 58 E
Siverek 64 37 50N 39 19 E
Sivomaskinskiy 52 66 40N 62 35 E
Sivrihisar 64 39 30N 31 35 E
Sîwa 86 29 11N 25 31 E
Sîwa, El Wâhât es 86 29 10N 25 30 E
Siwalik Range 69 28 0N 83 0 E
Siwan 69 26 13N 84 21 E
Siyâl, Jazâ'ir 86 22 49N 36 12 E
Sizewell 13 52 13N 1 38 E
Sjælland 49 55 30N 11 30 E
Sjællands Odde 49 56 0N 11 15 E
Själevad 48 63 18N 18 36 E
Sjarinska Banja 42 42 45N 21 38 E
Sjenica 42 43 16N 20 0 E
Sjoa 47 61 41N 9 33 E
Sjöbo 49 55 37N 13 45 E
Sjösa 49 58 47N 17 4 E
Skadarsko Jezero 42 42 10N 19 20 E
Skadovsk 56 46 17N 32 52 E
Skagafjörður 50 65 54N 19 35W
Skagastølstindane 47 61 28N 7 52 E
Skagen 49 57 43N 10 35 E
Skagern 48 59 0N 14 20 E
Skagerrak 49 57 30N 9 0 E
Skagway 104 59 23N 135 20W
Skaidi 50 70 26N 24 30 E
Skala Podolskaya 56 48 50N 26 15 E
Skalat 54 49 23N 25 55 E
Skalbmierz 28 50 20N 20 25 E
Skalica 27 48 50N 17 15 E
Skalni Dol = Kamenyak 43 43 24N 26 57 E
Skals 49 56 34N 9 24 E
Skanderborg 49 56 2N 9 55 E
Skånevik 47 59 43N 5 53 E
Skänninge 49 58 24N 15 5 E
Skanör 49 55 24N 12 50 E
Skantzoúra 45 39 5N 24 6 E
Skara 49 58 25N 13 30 E
Skaraborgs län □ 49 58 20N 13 30 E
Skardu 69 35 20N 75 44 E
Skarrild 49 55 58N 8 53 E
Skarszewy 28 54 4N 18 25 E
Skaryszew 28 51 19N 21 15 E
Skarzysko Kamienna 28 51 7N 20 52 E
Skattungbyn 48 61 10N 14 56 E
Skebokvarn 48 59 7N 16 45 E
Skeena ⇝ 108 54 9N 130 5W
Skeena Mts. 108 56 40N 128 30W
Skegness 12 53 9N 0 20 E
Skeldon 126 5 55N 57 20W
Skellefte älv ⇝ 50 64 45N 21 10 E
Skellefteå 50 64 45N 20 58 E
Skelleftehamn 50 64 47N 20 59 E
Skender Vakuf 42 44 29N 17 22 E
Skene 49 57 30N 12 37 E
Skerries, The 12 53 27N 4 40W
Skhíza 45 36 41N 21 40 E
Skhoinoúsa 45 36 53N 25 31 E
Skhwaner, Pegunungan 72 1 0 S 112 30 E
Ski 47 59 43N 10 52 E
Skíathos 45 39 12N 23 30 E
Skibbereen 15 51 33N 9 16W
Skiddaw 12 54 39N 3 9W
Skien 47 59 12N 9 35 E
Skierniewice 28 51 58N 20 10 E
Skierniewice □ 28 52 0N 20 10 E
Skikda 83 36 50N 6 58 E
Skillingaryd 49 57 27N 14 5 E
Skillinge 49 55 30N 14 16 E
Skillingmark 48 59 48N 12 1 E
Skinári, Ákra 45 37 56N 20 40 E
Skipton, Austral. 99 37 39 S 143 40 E
Skipton, U.K. 12 53 57N 2 1W
Skiropoúla 45 38 50N 24 21 E
Skíros 45 38 55N 24 34 E
Skivarp 49 55 26N 13 34 E
Skive 49 56 33N 9 2 E
Skjåk 47 61 52N 8 22 E
Skjálfandafljót ⇝ 50 65 59N 17 25W
Skjálfandi 50 66 5N 17 30W
Skjeberg 47 59 12N 11 12 E
Skjern 49 55 57N 8 30 E
Skoczów 27 49 49N 18 45 E
Skodje 47 62 30N 6 43 E
Škofja Loka 39 46 9N 14 19 E
Skoghall 48 59 20N 13 30 E
Skoki 28 52 40N 17 11 E
Skole 54 49 3N 23 30 E
Skópelos 45 39 9N 23 47 E
Skopin 55 53 55N 39 32 E
Skopje 42 42 1N 21 32 E
Skórcz 28 53 47N 18 30 E
Skottfoss 47 59 12N 9 30 E
Skovorodino 59 54 0N 125 0 E
Skowhegan 107 44 49N 69 40W
Skownan 109 51 58N 99 35W
Skradin 39 43 52N 15 53 E
Skreanäs 49 56 52N 12 35 E
Skrwa ⇝ 28 52 35N 19 32 E
Skull 15 51 32N 9 40W
Skultorp 49 58 24N 13 51 E
Skunk ⇝ 116 40 42N 91 7W
Skuodas 54 56 21N 21 45 E
Skurup 49 55 28N 13 30 E
Skutskär 49 60 37N 17 25 E
Skvira 56 49 44N 29 40 E
Skwierzyna 28 52 33N 15 30 E
Skye 14 57 15N 6 10W
Skykomish 118 47 43N 121 16W
Skyros = Skíros 45 38 52N 24 37 E
Slagelse 49 55 23N 11 19 E
Slamet, G. 72 7 16 S 109 8 E
Slaney ⇝ 15 52 52N 6 45W
Slangerup 49 55 50N 12 11 E
Slănic 46 45 14N 25 58 E
Slankamen 42 45 8N 20 15 E
Slano 42 42 48N 17 53 E
Slantsy 54 59 7N 28 5 E
Slany 26 50 13N 14 6 E
Slask 22 51 0N 16 30 E
Slate Is. 106 48 40N 87 0W
Slatina 46 44 28N 24 22 E
Slaton 117 33 27N 101 38W
Slave ⇝ 108 61 18N 113 39W
Slave Coast 85 6 0N 2 30 E
Slave Lake 108 55 17N 114 43W
Slave Pt. 108 61 11N 115 56W
Slavgorod 58 53 1N 78 37 E
Slavinja 42 43 9N 22 50 E
Slavkov (Austerlitz) 27 49 10N 16 52 E
Slavnoye 54 54 24N 29 15 E
Slavonska Požega 42 45 20N 17 40 E
Slavonski Brod 42 45 11N 18 0 E
Slavuta 54 50 15N 27 2 E
Slavyansk 56 48 55N 37 36 E
Slavyansk-na-Kubani 56 45 15N 38 11 E
Sława 28 51 52N 16 2 E
Sławno 28 54 20N 16 41 E
Sławoborze 28 53 55N 15 42 E
Sleaford 12 53 0N 0 22W
Sleat, Sd. of 14 57 5N 5 47W
Sleeper Is. 105 58 30N 81 0W
Sleepy Eye 116 44 15N 94 45W
Sleman 73 7 40 S 110 20 E
Slemon L. 108 63 13N 116 4W
Ślesin 28 52 22N 18 14 E
Slidell 117 30 20N 89 48W
Sliedrecht 16 51 50N 4 45 E
Slieve Aughty 15 53 4N 8 30W
Slieve Bloom 15 53 4N 7 40W
Slieve Donard 15 54 10N 5 57W
Slieve Gullion 15 54 8N 6 26W
Slieve Mish 15 52 12N 9 50W
Slievenamon 15 52 25N 7 37W
Sligo 15 54 17N 8 28W
Sligo □ 15 54 10N 8 35W
Sligo B. 15 54 20N 8 40W
Slite 51 57 42N 18 48 E
Sliven 43 42 42N 26 19 E
Slivnitsa 42 42 50N 23 0 E
Sljeme 39 45 57N 15 58 E
Sloansville 113 42 45N 74 22W
Slobodskoy 52 58 40N 50 6 E
Slobozia, Ialomiţa, Romania 46 44 34N 27 23 E
Slobozia, Valahia, Romania 46 44 30N 25 14 E
Slocan 108 49 48N 117 28W
Slochteren 16 53 12N 6 48 E
Slöinge 49 56 51N 12 42 E
Słomniki 28 50 16N 20 4 E
Slonim 54 53 4N 25 19 E
Slough 13 51 30N 0 35W
Slovakia = Slovensko 27 48 30N 19 0 E
Slovakian Ore Mts. = Slovenské Rudohorie 27 48 45N 20 0 E
Slovenia = Slovenija 39 45 58N 14 30 E
Slovenija □ 39 45 58N 14 30 E
Slovenj Gradec 39 46 31N 15 5 E
Slovenska Bistrica 39 46 24N 15 35 E
Slovenská Socialisticka Republika □ 27 48 30N 10 0 E
Slovenské Rudohorie 27 48 45N 20 0 E
Slovensko □ 27 48 30N 19 0 E
Słubice 28 52 22N 14 35 E
Sluch ⇝ 54 51 37N 26 38 E
Sluis 16 51 18N 3 23 E
Slunchev Bryag 43 42 40N 27 41 E
Slunj 39 45 6N 15 33 E
Słupca 28 52 15N 17 52 E
Słupia ⇝ 28 54 35N 16 51 E
Słupsk 28 54 30N 17 3 E
Słupsk □ 28 54 15N 17 30 E
Slurry 92 25 49 S 25 42 E
Slutsk 54 53 2N 27 31 E
Slyne Hd. 15 53 25N 10 10W
Slyudyanka 59 51 40N 103 40 E
Smålandsfarvandet 49 55 10N 11 20 E
Smalandsstenar 49 57 9N 13 24 E
Smalltree L. 109 61 0N 105 0W
Smallwood Reservoir 107 54 20N 63 10W
Smarje 39 46 15N 15 34 E
Smart Syndicate Dam 92 30 45 S 23 10 E
Smeaton 109 53 30N 104 49W
Smederevo 42 44 40N 20 57 E
Smederevska Palanka 42 44 22N 20 58 E
Smela 56 49 15N 31 58 E
Smethport 112 41 50N 78 28W
Smidovich 59 48 36N 133 49 E
Smigiel 28 52 1N 16 32 E
Smiley 109 51 38N 109 29W
Smilyan 43 41 29N 24 46 E
Smith 108 55 10N 114 0W
Smith ⇝ 108 59 34N 126 30W
Smith Arm 104 66 15N 123 0W
Smith Center 116 39 50N 98 50W
Smith Sund 4 78 30N 74 0W
Smithburne ⇝ 98 17 3 S 140 57 E
Smithers 108 54 45N 127 10W
Smithfield, Madag. 93 30 9 S 26 30 E
Smithfield, N.C., U.S.A. 115 35 31N 78 16W
Smithfield, Utah, U.S.A. 118 41 50N 111 50W
Smiths Falls 106 44 55N 76 0W
Smithton 99 40 53 S 145 6 E
Smithtown 99 30 58 S 152 48 E
Smithville, Can. 112 43 6N 79 33W
Smithville, U.S.A. 117 30 2N 97 12W
Smoky ⇝ 108 56 10N 117 21W
Smoky Falls 106 50 4N 82 10W
Smoky Hill ⇝ 116 39 3N 96 48W
Smoky Lake 108 54 10N 112 30W
Smøla 47 63 23N 8 3 E
Smolensk 54 54 45N 32 0 E
Smolikas, Óros 44 40 9N 20 58 E
Smolnik 27 48 43N 20 44 E
Smolyan 43 41 36N 24 38 E
Smooth Rock Falls 106 49 17N 81 37W
Smoothstone L. 109 54 40N 106 50W
Smorgon 54 54 20N 26 24 E
Smulţi 46 45 57N 27 44 E
Smyadovo 43 43 2N 27 1 E
Smyrna = İzmir 64 38 25N 27 8 E
Snaefell 12 54 18N 4 26W
Snaefellsjökull 50 64 45N 23 46W
Snake ⇝ 118 46 12N 119 2W
Snake I. 99 38 47 S 146 33 E
Snake L. 109 55 32N 106 35W
Snake Ra. 118 39 0N 114 30W
Snake River 118 44 10N 110 42W
Snake River Plain 118 43 13N 113 0W
Snarum 47 60 1N 9 54 E
Snedsted 49 56 55N 8 32 E
Sneek 16 53 2N 5 40 E
Snejbjerg 49 56 8N 8 54 E
Snezhnoye 57 48 0N 38 58 E
Sněžka 26 50 41N 15 50 E
Snežnik 39 45 36N 14 35 E
Sniadowo 28 53 2N 22 0 E
Sniardwy, Jezioro 28 53 48N 21 50 E
Snigirevka 56 47 2N 32 49 E
Snina 27 49 0N 22 9 E
Snizort, L. 14 57 33N 6 28W
Snøhetta 47 62 19N 9 16 E
Snohomish 118 47 53N 122 6W
Snonuten 47 59 31N 6 50 E
Snow Hill 114 38 10N 75 21W
Snow Lake 109 54 52N 100 3W
Snowbird L. 109 60 45N 103 0W
Snowdon 12 53 4N 4 8W
Snowdrift 109 62 24N 110 44W
Snowdrift ⇝ 109 62 24N 110 44W
Snowflake 119 34 30N 110 4W
Snowshoe Pk. 118 48 13N 115 41W
Snowtown 99 33 46 S 138 14 E
Snowville 118 41 59N 112 47W
Snowy ⇝ 97 37 46 S 148 30 E
Snowy Mts. 99 36 30 S 148 20 E
Snyatyn 56 48 30N 25 50 E
Snyder, Okla., U.S.A. 117 34 40N 99 0W
Snyder, Tex., U.S.A. 117 32 45N 100 57W
Soahanina 93 18 42 S 44 13 E
Soalala 93 16 6 S 45 20 E
Soanierana-Ivongo 93 16 55 S 49 35 E
Soap Lake 118 47 23N 119 31W
Sobat, Nahr ⇝ 87 9 22N 31 33 E
Soběslav 26 49 16N 14 45 E
Sobhapur 68 22 47N 78 17 E
Sobinka 55 56 0N 40 0 E
Sobótka 28 50 54N 16 44 E

Sobrado **30** 43 2N 8 2W
Sobral **127** 3 50 S 40 20W
Sobreira Formosa **31** 39 46N 7 51W
Soča → **39** 46 20N 13 40 E
Sochaczew **28** 52 15N 20 13 E
Soch'e = Shache **75** 38 20N 77 10 E
Sochi **57** 43 35N 39 40 E
Société, Is. de la **95** 17 0 S 151 0W
Society Is. = Société, Is. de la **95** 17 0 S 151 0W
Socompa, Portezuelo de **124** 24 27 S 68 18W
Socorro, Colomb. **126** 6 29N 73 16W
Socorro, U.S.A. **119** 34 4N 106 54W
Socotra **63** 12 30N 54 0 E
Socúellmos **33** 39 16N 2 47W
Soda L. **119** 35 7N 116 2W
Soda Plains **69** 35 30N 79 0 E
Soda Springs **118** 42 40N 111 40W
Söderfors **48** 60 23N 17 25 E
Söderhamn **48** 61 18N 17 10 E
Söderköping **48** 58 31N 16 20 E
Södermanlands län □ **48** 59 10N 16 30 E
Södertälje **48** 59 12N 17 39 E
Sodiri **81** 14 27N 29 0 E
Sodo **87** 7 0N 37 41 E
Södra Vi **49** 57 45N 15 45 E
Sodražica **39** 45 45N 14 39 E
Sodus **112** 43 13N 77 5W
Soekmekaar **93** 23 30 S 29 55 E
Soest, Ger. **24** 51 34N 8 7 E
Soest, Neth. **16** 52 9N 5 19 E
Sofádhes **44** 39 20N 22 4 E
Sofara **84** 13 59N 4 9W
Sofia = Sofiya **43** 42 45N 23 20 E
Sofia → **93** 15 27 S 47 23 E
Sofievka **56** 48 6N 33 55 E
Sofiiski **59** 52 15N 133 59 E
Sofikón **45** 37 47N 23 3 E
Sofiya **43** 42 45N 23 20 E
Sogad **73** 10 30N 125 0 E
Sogakofe **85** 6 2N 0 39 E
Sogamoso **126** 5 43N 72 56W
Sögel **24** 52 50N 7 32 E
Sogn og Fjordane fylke □ **47** 61 40N 6 0 E
Sognefjorden **47** 61 10N 5 50 E
Sohâg **86** 26 33N 31 43 E
Soignies **16** 50 35N 4 5 E
Soira, Mt. **87** 14 45N 39 30 E
Soissons **19** 49 25N 3 19 E
Sōja **74** 34 40N 133 45 E
Sojat **68** 25 55N 73 45 E
Sok → **55** 53 24N 50 8 E
Sokal **54** 50 31N 24 15 E
Söke **45** 37 48N 27 28 E
Sokelo **91** 9 55 S 24 36 E
Sokhós **44** 40 48N 23 22 E
Sokki, Oued In → **82** 29 30N 3 42 E
Sokna **47** 60 16N 9 50 E
Soknedal **47** 62 57N 10 13 E
Soko Banja **42** 43 40N 21 51 E
Sokodé **85** 9 0N 1 11 E
Sokol **55** 59 30N 40 5 E
Sokolac **42** 43 56N 18 48 E
Sokółka **28** 53 25N 23 30 E
Sokolo **84** 14 53N 6 8W
Sokolov **26** 50 12N 12 40 E
Sokołów Małpolski **27** 50 12N 22 7 E
Sokołów Podlaski **28** 52 25N 22 15 E
Sokoły **28** 52 59N 22 42 E
Sokoto **85** 13 2N 5 16 E
Sokoto □ **85** 12 30N 5 0 E
Sokoto → **85** 11 20N 4 10 E
Sol Iletsk **52** 51 10N 55 0 E
Sola **47** 58 53N 5 36 E
Sola → **27** 50 4N 19 15 E
Solai **90** 0 2N 36 12 E
Solana, La **33** 38 59N 3 14W
Solano **73** 16 31N 121 15 E
Solares **30** 43 23N 3 43W
Solberga **49** 57 45N 14 43 E
Solca **46** 47 40N 25 50 E
Solec Kujawski **28** 53 5N 18 14 E
Soledad, U.S.A. **119** 36 27N 121 16W
Soledad, Venez. **126** 8 10N 63 34W
Solent, The **13** 50 45N 1 25W
Solenzara **21** 41 53N 9 23 E
Solesmes **19** 50 10N 3 30 E
Solfonn **47** 60 2N 6 57 E
Soligalich **55** 59 5N 42 10 E
Soligorsk **54** 52 51N 27 27 E
Solikamsk **58** 59 38N 56 50 E
Solila **93** 21 25 S 46 37 E
Solimões → = Amazonas → **126** 2 15 S 66 30W
Solingen **24** 51 10N 7 4 E
Sollebrunn **49** 58 8N 12 32 E
Sollefteå **48** 63 12N 17 20 E
Sollentuna **48** 59 26N 17 56 E
Sóller **32** 39 46N 2 43 E
Solling **24** 51 44N 9 36 E
Solna **48** 59 22N 18 1 E
Solnechnogorsk **55** 56 10N 36 57 E
Sologne **19** 47 40N 2 0 E
Solok **72** 0 45 S 100 40 E
Sololá **120** 14 49N 91 10 E
Solomon Is. ■ **94** 6 0 S 155 0 E
Solomon, N. Fork → **116** 39 29N 98 26W
Solomon Sea **98** 7 0 S 150 0 E
Solomon, S. Fork → **116** 39 25N 99 12W
Solomon's Pools = Birak Sulaymān **62** 31 42N 35 7 E
Solon **75** 46 32N 121 10 E
Solon Springs **116** 46 19N 91 47W
Solor **73** 8 27 S 123 0 E
Solotcha **55** 54 48N 39 53 E
Solothurn **25** 47 13N 7 32 E
Solothurn □ **25** 47 18N 7 40 E
Solsona **32** 42 0N 1 31 E
Solt **27** 46 45N 19 1 E
Solta **39** 43 24N 16 15 E
Solţānābād **65** 36 29N 58 5 E
Solţāniyeh **64** 36 20N 48 55 E
Soltau **24** 52 59N 9 50 E
Soltsy **54** 58 10N 30 30 E
Solund **47** 61 5N 4 50 E
Solunska Glava **42** 41 44N 21 31 E
Solvay **114** 43 5N 76 17W
Sölvesborg **49** 56 5N 14 35 E
Solvychegodsk **52** 61 21N 46 56 E
Solway Firth **12** 54 45N 3 38W
Solwezi **91** 12 11 S 26 21 E
Somali Rep. ■ **63** 7 0N 47 0 E
Sombe Dzong **69** 27 13N 89 8 E
Sombernon **19** 47 20N 4 40 E
Sombor **42** 45 46N 19 9 E
Sombra **112** 42 43N 82 29W
Sombrerete **120** 23 40N 103 40W
Sombrero **121** 18 37N 63 30W
Somers **118** 48 4N 114 18W
Somerset, Berm. **121** 32 16N 64 55W
Somerset, Can. **109** 49 25N 98 39W
Somerset, Colo., U.S.A. **119** 38 55N 107 30W
Somerset, Ky., U.S.A. **114** 37 5N 84 40W
Somerset, Mass., U.S.A. **113** 41 45N 71 10W
Somerset, Pa., U.S.A. **112** 40 1N 79 4W
Somerset □ **13** 51 9N 3 0W
Somerset East **92** 32 42 S 25 35 E
Somerset I. **104** 73 30N 93 0W
Somerset West **92** 34 8 S 18 50 E
Somersworth **113** 43 15N 70 51W
Somerton **119** 32 35N 114 47W
Somerville **113** 40 34N 74 36W
Someş → **46** 47 15N 23 45 E
Someşul Mare → **46** 47 18N 24 30 E
Somma Lombardo **38** 45 41N 8 42 E
Somma Vesuviana **41** 40 52N 14 23 E
Sommariva **99** 26 24 S 146 36 E
Sommatino **40** 37 20N 14 0 E
Somme □ **19** 50 0N 2 20 E
Somme, B. de la **18** 50 14N 1 33 E
Sommen **49** 58 12N 15 0 E
Sommen, L. **49** 58 0N 15 15 E
Sommepy-Tahure **19** 49 15N 4 31 E
Sömmerda **24** 51 10N 11 8 E
Sommesous **19** 48 44N 4 12 E
Sommières **21** 43 47N 4 6 E
Somogy □ **27** 46 19N 17 30 E
Somogyszob **27** 46 18N 17 20 E
Sompolno **28** 52 26N 18 30 E
Somport, Paso **32** 42 48N 0 31W
Somport, Puerto de **32** 42 48N 0 31W
Son, Norway **47** 59 32N 10 42 E
Son, Spain **30** 42 43N 8 58W
Son La **71** 21 20N 103 50 E
Sonamukhi **69** 23 18N 87 27 E
Soncino **38** 45 24N 9 52 E
Sondags → **92** 33 44 S 25 51 E
Sóndalo **38** 46 20N 10 20 E
Sønder Omme **49** 55 50N 8 54 E
Sønder Ternby **49** 57 31N 9 58 E
Sønderborg **49** 54 55N 9 49 E
Sonderjyllands Amtskommune □ **49** 55 10N 9 10 E
Sondershausen **24** 51 22N 10 50 E
Sóndrio **38** 46 10N 9 53 E
Sone **91** 17 23 S 34 55 E
Sonepat **68** 29 0N 77 5 E
Sonepur **69** 20 55N 83 50 E
Song Cau **71** 13 27N 109 18 E
Song Xian **77** 34 12N 112 8 E
Songea **91** 10 40 S 35 40 E
Songea □ **91** 10 30 S 36 0 E
Songeons **19** 49 32N 1 50 E
Songhua Hu **76** 43 35N 126 50 E
Songhua Jiang → **75** 47 45N 132 30 E
Songjiang **77** 31 1N 121 12 E
Songkhla **71** 7 13N 100 37 E
Songling **76** 48 2N 121 9 E
Songpan **75** 32 40N 103 30 E
Songtao **77** 28 11N 109 10 E
Songwe **90** 3 20 S 26 16 E
Songwe → **91** 9 44 S 33 58 E
Songzi **77** 30 12N 111 45 E
Sonkovo **55** 57 50N 37 5 E
Sonmiani **66** 25 25N 66 40 E
Sonnino **40** 41 25N 13 13 E
Sono → **127** 9 58 S 48 11W
Sonora, Calif., U.S.A. **119** 37 59N 120 27W
Sonora, Texas, U.S.A. **117** 30 33N 100 37W
Sonora □ **120** 29 0N 111 0W
Sonora → **120** 28 50N 111 33W
Sonora P. **118** 38 17N 119 35W
Sonsomate **120** 13 43N 89 44W
Sonthofen **25** 47 31N 10 16 E
Soo Junction **114** 46 20N 85 14W
Soochow = Suzhou **75** 31 19N 120 38 E
Sopi **73** 2 34N 128 28 E
Sopo, Nahr → **87** 8 40N 26 30 E
Sopot, Poland **28** 54 27N 18 31 E
Sopot, Yugo. **42** 44 29N 20 30 E
Sopotnica **42** 41 23N 21 13 E
Sopron **27** 47 45N 16 32 E
Sop's Arm **107** 49 46N 56 56W
Sør-Rondane **5** 72 0 S 25 0 E
Sør-Trøndelag fylke □ **47** 63 0N 10 0 E
Sora **40** 41 45N 13 36 E
Sorada **70** 19 45N 84 26 E
Sorah **68** 27 13N 68 56 E
Söråker **48** 62 30N 17 32 E
Sorano **39** 42 40N 11 42 E
Sorata **126** 15 50 S 68 40W
Sorbas **33** 37 6N 2 7W
Sorel **106** 46 0N 73 10W
Sorento **99** 38 22 S 144 47 E
Soreq, N. → **62** 31 57N 34 43 E
Soresina **38** 45 17N 9 51 E
Sorgono **40** 40 01N 9 06 E
Sorgues **21** 44 1N 4 53 E
Soria **32** 41 43N 2 32W
Soria □ **32** 41 46N 2 28W
Soriano **124** 33 24 S 58 19W
Soriano nel Cimino **39** 42 25N 12 14 E
Sorkh, Kuh-e **65** 35 40N 58 30 E
Sorø **49** 55 26N 11 32 E
Soro **84** 10 9N 9 48W
Sorocaba **125** 23 31 S 47 27W
Sorochinsk **52** 52 26N 53 10 E
Soroki **56** 48 8N 28 12 E
Soroksár **27** 47 24N 19 9 E
Soron **68** 27 55N 78 45 E
Sorong **73** 0 55 S 131 15 E
Soroti **90** 1 43N 33 35 E
Sørøya **50** 70 40N 22 30 E
Sørøyane **47** 62 25N 5 32 E
Sørøysundet **50** 70 25N 23 0 E
Sorraia → **31** 38 55N 8 53W
Sorrento **41** 40 38N 14 23 E
Sorris Sorris **92** 21 0 S 14 46 E
Sorsele **50** 65 31N 17 30 E
Sorso **40** 40 50N 8 34 E
Sorsogon **73** 13 0N 124 0 E
Sortavala **52** 61 42N 30 41 E
Sortino **41** 37 9N 15 1 E
Sorvizhi **55** 57 52N 48 32 E
Sos **32** 42 30N 1 13W
Soscumica, L. **106** 50 15N 77 27W
Sosna → **55** 52 42N 38 55 E
Sosnogorsk **52** 63 37N 53 51 E
Sosnovka, R.S.F.S.R., U.S.S.R. **55** 53 13N 41 24 E
Sosnovka, R.S.F.S.R., U.S.S.R. **59** 54 9N 109 35 E
Sosnowiec **28** 50 20N 19 10 E
Sospel **21** 43 52N 7 27 E
Sostanj **39** 46 23N 15 4 E
Sosva **52** 59 10N 61 50 E
Soto la Marina → **120** 23 40N 97 40W
Soto y Amío **30** 42 46N 5 53W
Sotteville-lès-Rouen **18** 49 24N 1 5 E
Sotuta **120** 20 29N 89 43W
Souanké **88** 2 10N 14 3 E
Soúdhas, Kólpos **45** 35 25N 24 10 E
Souflíon **44** 41 12N 26 18 E
Souillac **20** 44 53N 1 29 E
Souk-Ahras **83** 36 23N 7 57 E
Souk el Arba du Rharb **82** 34 43N 5 59W
Sŏul **76** 37 31N 126 58 E
Soulac-sur-Mer **20** 45 30N 1 7W
Soultz **19** 48 57N 7 52 E
Soúnion, Ákra **45** 37 37N 24 1 E
Sour el Ghozlane **83** 36 10N 3 45 E
Sources, Mt. aux **93** 28 45 S 28 50 E
Sourdeval **18** 48 43N 0 55W
Soure, Brazil **127** 0 35 S 48 30W
Soure, Port. **30** 40 4N 8 38W
Souris, Man., Can. **109** 49 40N 100 20W
Souris, P.E.I., Can. **107** 46 21N 62 15W
Souris → **109** 49 40N 99 34W
Soúrpi **45** 39 6N 22 54 E
Sousa **127** 6 45 S 38 10W
Sousel, Brazil **127** 2 38 S 52 29W
Sousel, Port. **31** 38 57N 7 40W
Souss, O. → **82** 30 27N 9 31W
Sousse **83** 35 50N 10 38 E
Soustons **20** 43 45N 1 19W
Souterraine, La **20** 46 15N 1 30 E
South Africa, Rep. of, ■ **89** 32 0 S 17 0 E
South America **122** 10 0 S 60 0W
South Atlantic Ocean **7** 20 0 S 10 0W
South Aulatsivik I. **107** 56 45N 61 30W
South Australia □ **96** 32 0 S 139 0 E
South Baldy, Mt. **119** 34 6N 107 27W
South Bend, Ind., U.S.A. **114** 41 38N 86 20W
South Bend, Wash., U.S.A. **118** 46 44N 123 52W
South Boston **115** 36 42N 78 58W
South Branch **107** 47 55N 59 2W
South Brook **107** 49 26N 56 5W
South Buganda □ **90** 0 15 S 31 30 E
South Carolina □ **115** 33 45N 81 0W
South Charleston **114** 38 20N 81 40W
South China Sea **71** 10 0N 113 0 E
South Dakota □ **116** 45 0N 100 0W
South Downs **13** 50 53N 0 10W
South East C. **97** 43 40 S 146 50 E
South-East Indian Rise **94** 43 0 S 80 0 E
South Esk → **14** 56 44N 3 3W
South Foreland **13** 51 7N 1 23 E
South Fork → **118** 47 54N 113 15W
South Gamboa **120** 9 4N 79 40W
South Georgia **5** 54 30 S 37 0W
South Glamorgan □ **13** 51 30N 3 20W
South Grafton **99** 29 41 S 152 57 E
South Haven **114** 42 22N 86 20W
South Henik, L. **109** 61 30N 97 30W
South Honshu Ridge **94** 23 0N 143 0 E
South Horr **90** 2 12N 36 56 E
South I., Kenya **90** 2 35N 36 35 E
South I., N.Z. **101** 44 0 S 170 0 E
South Invercargill **101** 46 26 S 168 23 E
South Knife → **109** 58 55N 94 37W
South Korea ■ **76** 36 0N 128 0 E
South Loup → **116** 41 4N 98 40W
South Mashonaland □ **91** 18 0 S 31 30 E
South Milwaukee **114** 42 50N 87 52W
South Molton **13** 51 1N 3 50W
South Nahanni → **108** 61 3N 123 21W
South Negril Pt. **121** 18 14N 78 30W
South Orkney Is. **5** 63 0 S 45 0W
South Pass **118** 42 20N 108 58W
South Passage **96** 26 07 S 113 09 E
South Pines **115** 35 10N 79 25W
South Pittsburg **115** 35 1N 85 42W
South Platte → **116** 41 7N 100 42W
South Pole **5** 90 0 S 0 0 E
South Porcupine **106** 48 30N 81 12W
South River, Can. **106** 45 52N 79 23W
South River, U.S.A. **113** 40 27N 74 23W
South Ronaldsay **14** 58 46N 2 58W
South Sandwich Is. **7** 57 0 S 27 0W
South Saskatchewan → **109** 53 15N 105 5W
South Seal → **109** 58 48N 98 8W
South Sentinel I. **71** 11 1N 92 16 E
South Shetland Is. **5** 62 0 S 59 0W
South Shields **12** 54 59N 1 26W
South Sioux City **116** 42 30N 96 24W
South Taranaki Bight **101** 39 40 S 174 5 E
South Thompson → **108** 50 40N 120 20W
South Twin I. **106** 53 7N 79 52W
South Tyne → **12** 54 46N 2 25W
South Uist **14** 57 20N 7 15W
South West Africa = Namibia ■ **92** 22 0 S 18 9 E
South West C. **99** 43 34 S 146 3 E
South Yemen ■ **63** 15 0N 48 0 E
South Yorkshire □ **12** 53 30N 1 20W
Southampton, Can. **106** 44 30N 81 25W
Southampton, U.K. **13** 50 54N 1 23W
Southampton, U.S.A. **114** 40 54N 72 22W
Southampton I. **105** 64 30N 84 0W
Southbridge, N.Z. **101** 43 48 S 172 16 E
Southbridge, U.S.A. **113** 42 4N 72 2W
Southeast Pacific Basin **95** 16 30 S 92 0W
Southend **109** 56 19N 103 22W
Southend-on-Sea **13** 51 32N 0 42 E
Southern □, Malawi **91** 15 0 S 35 0 E
Southern □, S. Leone **84** 8 0N 12 30W
Southern □, Zambia **91** 16 20 S 26 20 E
Southern Alps **101** 43 41 S 170 11 E
Southern Cross **96** 31 12 S 119 15 E
Southern Indian L. **109** 57 10N 98 30W
Southern Ocean **5** 62 0 S 60 0 E
Southern Uplands **14** 55 30N 3 3W
Southington **113** 41 37N 72 53W
Southold **113** 41 4N 72 26W
Southport, Austral. **97** 27 58 S 153 25 E
Southport, U.K. **12** 53 38N 3 1W
Southport, U.S.A. **115** 33 55N 78 0W
Southwestern Pacific Basin **94** 42 0 S 170 0W
Southwold **13** 52 19N 1 41 E
Soutpansberge **93** 23 0 S 29 30 E
Souvigny **20** 46 33N 3 10 E
Sovata **46** 46 35N 25 3 E
Sovetsk, Lithuania, U.S.S.R. **54** 55 6N 21 50 E
Sovetsk, R.S.F.S.R., U.S.S.R. **55** 57 38N 48 53 E
Sovetskaya **57** 49 1N 42 7 E
Sovetskaya Gavan **59** 48 50N 140 0 E
Sovicille **39** 43 16N 11 12 E
Sovra **42** 42 44N 17 34 E
Sōya-Misaki **74** 45 30N 142 0 E
Soyo **88** 6 13 S 12 20 E
Sozh → **54** 51 57N 30 48 E
Sozopol **43** 42 23N 27 42 E
Spa **16** 50 29N 5 53 E
Spain ■ **29** 40 0N 5 0W
Spalding, Austral. **99** 33 30 S 138 37 E
Spalding, U.K. **12** 52 47N 0 9W
Spalding, U.S.A. **116** 41 45N 98 27W
Spangereid **47** 58 3N 7 9 E
Spangler **112** 40 39N 78 48W
Spaniard's Bay **107** 47 38N 53 20W
Spanish **106** 46 12N 82 20W
Spanish Fork **118** 40 10N 111 37W
Spanish Town **121** 18 0N 76 57W
Sparks **118** 39 30N 119 45W
Sparta, Ga., U.S.A. **115** 33 18N 82 59W
Sparta, Wis., U.S.A. **116** 43 55N 90 47W
Sparta = Spárti **45** 37 5N 22 25 E
Spartanburg **115** 35 0N 82 0W
Spartansburg **112** 41 48N 79 43W
Spartel, C. **82** 35 47N 5 56W
Spárti **45** 37 5N 22 25 E
Spartivento, C., Calabria, Italy **41** 37 56N 16 4 E
Spartivento, C., Sard., Italy **40** 38 52N 8 50 E
Spas-Demensk **54** 54 20N 34 0 E
Spas-Klepiki **55** 55 10N 40 10 E
Spassk-Dalniy **59** 44 40N 132 48 E
Spassk-Ryazanskiy **55** 54 24N 40 25 E
Spátha, Akra **45** 35 42N 23 43 E
Spatsizi → **108** 57 42N 128 7W
Spearfish **116** 44 32N 103 52W
Spearman **117** 36 15N 101 10W
Speers **109** 52 43N 107 34W
Speightstown **121** 13 15N 59 39W
Speke Gulf **90** 2 20 S 32 50 E
Spenard **104** 61 11N 149 50W
Spence Bay **104** 69 32N 93 32W
Spencer, Idaho, U.S.A. **118** 44 18N 112 8W
Spencer, Iowa, U.S.A. **116** 43 5N 95 19W
Spencer, N.Y., U.S.A. **113** 42 14N 76 30W
Spencer, Nebr., U.S.A. **116** 42 52N 98 43W
Spencer, W. Va., U.S.A. **114** 38 47N 81 24W
Spencer B. **92** 25 30 S 14 47 E
Spencer, C. **97** 35 20 S 136 53 E
Spencer G. **97** 34 0 S 137 20 E
Spencerville **113** 44 51N 75 33W
Spences Bridge **108** 50 25N 121 20W
Spenser Mts. **101** 42 15 S 172 45 E
Sperkhiós → **45** 38 57N 22 3 E
Sperrin Mts. **15** 54 50N 7 0W
Spessart **25** 50 10N 9 20 E
Spétsai **45** 37 15N 23 10 E
Spey → **14** 57 26N 3 25W
Speyer **25** 49 19N 8 26 E
Speyer → **25** 49 19N 8 27 E
Spézia, La **38** 44 8N 9 50 E
Spezzano Albanese **41** 39 41N 16 19 E
Spiekeroog **24** 53 45N 7 42 E
Spielfeld **39** 46 43N 15 38 E
Spiez **25** 46 40N 7 40 E
Spíli **45** 35 13N 24 31 E
Spilimbergo **39** 46 7N 12 53 E
Spinazzola **41** 40 58N 16 5 E
Spind **47** 58 6N 6 53 E
Spineni **46** 44 43N 24 37 E
Spirit Lake **118** 47 56N 116 56W
Spirit River **108** 55 45N 118 50W
Spiritwood **109** 53 24N 107 33W
Spišská Nová Ves **27** 48 58N 20 34 E
Spišské Podhradie **27** 49 0N 20 48 E
Spital **26** 47 42N 14 18 E
Spithead **13** 50 43N 1 5W
Spittal **26** 46 48N 13 31 E
Spitzbergen = Svalbard **4** 78 0N 17 0 E
Split **39** 43 31N 16 26 E
Split L. **109** 56 8N 96 15W
Splitski Kanal **39** 43 31N 16 20 E
Splügenpass **25** 46 30N 9 20 E
Spoffard **117** 29 10N 100 27W
Spokane **118** 47 45N 117 25W
Spoleto **39** 42 46N 12 47 E
Spooner **116** 45 49N 91 51W
Sporádhes **45** 39 0N 24 30 E
Sporyy Navolok, Mys **58** 75 50N 68 40 E
Spragge **106** 46 15N 82 40W

Sprague	118	47 18N	117 59W	Stanley, Falk. Is.	128	51 40 S	59 51W	Stewart, B.C., Can.	108	55 56N	129 57W	Strasbourg, Can.	109	51 4N	104 55W
Sprague River	118	42 28N	121 31W	Stanley, Idaho, U.S.A.	118	44 10N	114 59W	Stewart, N.W.T., Can.	104	63 19N	139 26W	Strasbourg, France	19	48 35N	7 42 E
Spratly, I.	72	8 20N	112 0 E	Stanley, N.D., U.S.A.	116	48 20N	102 23W	Stewart, I.	128	54 50 S	71 15W	Strasburg, Ger.	24	53 30N	13 44 E
Spray	118	44 50N	119 46W	Stanley, N.Y., U.S.A.	112	42 48N	77 6W	Stewart I.	101	46 58 S	167 54 E	Strasburg, U.S.A.	116	46 12N	100 9W
Spree ~	24	52 32N	13 13 E	Stanley, Wis., U.S.A.	116	44 57N	91 0W	Stewiacke	107	45 9N	63 22W	Stratford, Austral.	100	37 59 S	147 7 E
Spring City	118	39 31N	111 28W	Stanley Res.	70	11 50N	77 40 E	Steynsburg	92	31 15 S	25 49 E	Stratford, Can.	106	43 23N	81 0W
Spring Mts.	119	36 20N	115 43W	Stann Creek	120	17 0N	88 13W	Steyr	26	48 3N	14 25 E	Stratford, N.Z.	101	39 20 S	174 19 E
Spring Valley, Minn., U.S.A.	116	43 40N	92 23W	Stanovoy Khrebet	59	55 0N	130 0 E	Steyr ~	26	48 17N	14 15 E	Stratford, Calif., U.S.A.	119	36 10N	119 49W
Spring Valley, N.Y., U.S.A.	113	41 7N	74 4W	Stanthorpe	97	28 36 S	151 59 E	Steytlerville	92	33 17 S	24 19 E	Stratford, Conn., U.S.A.	113	41 13N	73 8W
Springbok	92	29 42 S	17 54 E	Stanton	117	32 8N	101 45W	Stia	39	43 48N	11 41 E	Stratford, Tex., U.S.A.	117	36 20N	102 3W
Springburn	101	43 40 S	171 32 E	Staples	116	46 21N	94 48W	Stigler	117	35 19N	95 6W	Stratford-on-Avon	13	52 12N	1 42W
Springdale, Can.	107	49 30N	56 6W	Stapleton	116	41 30N	100 31W	Stigliano	41	40 24N	16 13 E	Strath Spey	14	57 15N	3 40W
Springdale, Ark., U.S.A.	117	36 10N	94 5W	Staporków	28	51 9N	20 31 E	Stigsnæs	49	55 13N	11 18 E	Strathalbyn	99	35 13 S	138 53 E
Springdale, Wash., U.S.A.	118	48 1N	117 50W	Star City	109	52 50N	104 20W	Stigtomta	49	58 47N	16 48 E	Strathclyde □	14	56 0N	4 50W
Springe	24	52 12N	9 35 E	Stara-minskaya	57	46 33N	39 0 E	Stikine ~	104	56 40N	132 30W	Strathcona Prov. Park	108	49 38N	125 40W
Springer	117	36 22N	104 36W	Stara Moravica	42	45 50N	19 30 E	Stilfontein	92	26 50 S	26 50 E	Strathmore, Austral.	98	17 50 S	142 35 E
Springerville	119	34 10N	109 16W	Stara Pazova	42	45 0N	20 10 E	Stilis	45	38 55N	22 47 E	Strathmore, Can.	108	51 5N	113 18W
Springfield, Can.	112	42 50N	80 56W	Stara Planina	43	43 15N	23 0 E	Stillwater, Minn., U.S.A.	116	45 3N	92 47W	Strathmore, U.K.	14	56 40N	3 4W
Springfield, N.Z.	101	43 19N	171 56 E	Stara Zagora	43	42 26N	25 39 E	Stillwater, N.Y., U.S.A.	113	42 55N	73 41W	Strathnaver	108	53 20N	122 33W
Springfield, Colo., U.S.A.	117	37 26N	102 40W	Starachowice	28	51 3N	21 2 E	Stillwater, Okla., U.S.A.	117	36 5N	97 3W	Strathpeffer	14	57 35N	4 32W
Springfield, Ill., U.S.A.	116	39 48N	89 40W	Starashcherbinovskaya	57	46 40N	38 53 E	Stillwater Mts.	118	39 45N	118 6W	Strathroy	106	42 58N	81 38W
Springfield, Mass., U.S.A.	114	42 8N	72 37W	Staraya Russa	54	57 58N	31 23 E	Stilwell	117	35 52N	94 36W	Strathy Pt.	14	58 35N	4 0W
Springfield, Mo., U.S.A.	117	37 15N	93 20W	Starbuck I.	95	5 37 S	155 55W	Stimfalias, L.	45	37 51N	22 27 E	Stratton, U.S.A.	116	39 20N	102 36W
Springfield, Ohio, U.S.A.	114	39 58N	83 48W	Stargard	24	53 29N	13 19 E	Štip	42	41 42N	22 10 E	Stratton, U.K.	12	51 41N	1 45W
Springfield, Oreg., U.S.A.	118	44 2N	123 0W	Stargard Szczeciński	28	53 20N	15 0 E	Stira	45	38 9N	24 14 E	Straubing	25	48 53N	12 35 E
Springfield, Tenn., U.S.A.	115	36 35N	86 55W	Stari Bar	42	42 7N	19 13 E	Stirling, Austral.	98	17 12 S	141 35 E	Straumnes	50	66 26N	23 8W
Springfield, Vt., U.S.A.	113	43 20N	72 30W	Stari Trg	39	45 29N	15 7 E	Stirling, Can.	108	49 30N	112 30W	Strausberg	24	52 40N	13 52 E
Springfontein	92	30 15 S	25 40 E	Staritsa	54	56 33N	35 0 E	Stirling, U.K.	14	56 7N	3 57W	Strawberry Res.	118	40 10N	111 7W
Springhouse	108	51 56N	122 7W	Starke	115	30 0N	82 10W	Stirling Ra.	96	34 23 S	118 0 E	Strawn	117	32 36N	98 30W
Springhurst	99	36 10 S	146 31 E	Starkville, Colo., U.S.A.	117	37 10N	104 31W	Stittsville	113	45 15N	75 55W	Strážnice	27	48 54N	17 19 E
Springs	93	26 13 S	28 25 E	Starkville, Miss., U.S.A.	115	33 26N	88 48W	Stockach	25	47 51N	9 1 E	Streaky Bay	96	32 48 S	134 13 E
Springsure	97	24 8 S	148 6 E	Starnberg	25	48 0N	11 20 E	Stockaryd	49	57 19N	14 36 E	Streator	116	41 9N	88 52W
Springvale, Austral.	98	23 33 S	140 42 E	Starnberger See	25	47 55N	11 20 E	Stockerau	27	48 24N	16 12 E	Středočeský □	26	49 55N	14 30 E
Springvale, U.S.A.	113	43 28N	70 48W	Starobelsk	57	49 16N	39 0 E	Stockett	118	47 23N	111 7W	Středoslovenský □	27	48 30N	19 15 E
Springville, N.Y., U.S.A.	114	42 31N	78 41W	Starodub	54	52 30N	32 50 E	Stockholm	48	59 20N	18 3 E	Streeter	116	46 39N	99 21W
Springville, Utah, U.S.A.	118	40 14N	111 35W	Starogard	28	53 59N	18 30 E	Stockholms län □	48	59 30N	18 20 E	Streetsville	112	43 35N	79 42W
Springwater	109	51 58N	108 23W	Starokonstantinov	56	49 48N	27 10 E	Stockinbingal	100	34 30 S	147 53 E	Strehaia	46	44 37N	23 10 E
Spruce-Creek	112	40 36N	78 9W	Starosielce	28	53 8N	23 5 E	Stockport	12	53 25N	2 11W	Strelcha	43	42 25N	24 19 E
Spur	117	33 28N	100 50W	Start Pt.	13	50 13N	3 38W	Stockton, Austral.	100	32 50 S	151 47 E	Strelka	59	58 5N	93 3 E
Spurn Hd.	12	53 34N	0 8 E	Stary Sącz	27	49 33N	20 35 E	Stockton, Calif., U.S.A.	119	38 0N	121 20W	Stresa	38	45 52N	8 28 E
Spuž	42	42 32N	19 10 E	Staryy Biryuzyak	57	44 46N	46 50 E	Stockton, Kans., U.S.A.	116	39 30N	99 20W	Strezhevoy	58	60 42N	77 34 E
Spuzzum	108	49 37N	121 23W	Staryy Chartoriysk	54	51 15N	25 54 E	Stockton, Mo., U.S.A.	117	37 40N	93 48W	Stříbro	26	49 44N	13 0 E
Squam L.	113	43 45N	71 32W	Staryy Kheydzhan	59	60 0N	144 50 E	Stockton-on-Tees	12	54 34N	1 20W	Strickland ~	98	7 35 S	141 36 E
Squamish	108	49 45N	123 10W	Staryy Krym	56	45 3N	35 8 E	Stockvik	48	62 17N	17 23 E	Strimón ~	44	40 46N	23 51 E
Square Islands	107	52 47N	55 47W	Staryy Oskol	55	51 19N	37 55 E	Stoczek Łukowski	28	51 58N	22 0 E	Strimonikós Kólpos	44	40 33N	24 0 E
Squillace, Golfo di	41	38 43N	16 35 E	Stassfurt	24	51 51N	11 34 E	Stöde	48	62 28N	16 35 E	Strofádhes	45	37 15N	21 0 E
Squinzano	41	40 27N	18 1 E	Staszów	28	50 33N	21 10 E	Stogovo	42	41 31N	20 38 E	Stromboli	41	38 48N	15 12 E
Sragen	73	7 28 S	110 59 E	State College	114	40 47N	77 49W	Stoke-on-Trent	12	53 1N	2 11W	Strömeferry	14	57 20N	5 33W
Srbac	42	45 7N	17 30 E	Staten I.	113	40 35N	74 10W	Stokes Bay	106	45 0N	81 28W	Stromness	14	58 58N	3 18W
Srbija □	42	43 30N	21 0 E	Staten, I. = Los Estados, I. de	128	54 40 S	64 30W	Stokes Pt.	99	40 10 S	143 56 E	Ströms vattudal	50	64 15N	14 55 E
Srbobran	42	45 32N	19 48 E	Statesboro	115	32 26N	81 46W	Stokkseyri	50	63 50N	21 2W	Strömsnäsbruk	49	56 35N	13 45 E
Sre Umbell	71	11 8N	103 46 E	Statesville	115	35 48N	80 51W	Stokksnes	50	64 14N	14 58W	Strömstad	48	58 55N	11 15 E
Srebrnica	42	44 10N	19 18 E	Staunton, Ill., U.S.A.	116	39 0N	89 49W	Stolac	42	43 5N	17 59 E	Strömsund	50	63 51N	15 33 E
Sredinnyy Khrebet	59	57 0N	160 0 E	Staunton, Va., U.S.A.	114	38 7N	79 4W	Stolberg	24	50 48N	6 13 E	Stróngoli	41	39 16N	17 2 E
Središče	39	46 24N	16 17 E	Stavanger	47	58 57N	5 40 E	Stolbovaya, R.S.F.S.R., U.S.S.R.	55	55 10N	37 32 E	Stronsay	14	59 8N	2 38W
Sredna Gora	43	42 40N	24 20 E	Stavelot	16	50 23N	5 55 E	Stolbovaya, R.S.F.S.R., U.S.S.R.	59	64 50N	153 50 E	Stronsburg	116	41 7N	97 36W
Sredne Tambovskoye	59	50 55N	137 45 E	Staveren	16	52 53N	5 22 E	Stolbovoy, Ostrov	59	56 44N	163 14 E	Stropkov	27	49 13N	21 39 E
Srednekolymsk	59	67 27N	153 40 E	Stavern	47	59 0N	10 1 E	Stolbtsy	54	53 30N	26 43 E	Stroud	13	51 44N	2 12W
Srednevilyuysk	59	63 50N	123 5 E	Stavre	48	62 51N	15 19 E	Stolin	54	51 53N	26 50 E	Stroud Road	99	32 18 S	151 57 E
Sredni Rodopi	43	41 40N	24 45 E	Stavropol	57	45 5N	42 0 E	Stolnici	46	44 31N	24 48 E	Stroudsberg	113	40 59N	75 15W
Šrem	28	52 6N	17 2 E	Stavroúpolis	44	41 12N	24 45 E	Ston	42	42 51N	17 43 E	Struer	49	56 30N	8 35 E
Sremska Mitrovica	42	44 59N	19 33 E	Stawell	97	37 5 S	142 47 E	Stonehaven	14	56 58N	2 11W	Struga	42	41 13N	20 44 E
Sremski Karlovci	42	45 12N	19 56 E	Stawell ~	98	20 20 S	142 55 E	Stonehenge	98	24 22 S	143 17 E	Strugi Krasnyye	54	58 21N	29 1 E
Sretensk	59	52 10N	117 40 E	Stawiski	28	53 22N	22 9 E	Stonewall	109	50 10N	97 19W	Strumica	42	41 28N	22 41 E
Sri Lanka ■	70	7 30N	80 50 E	Stawiszyn	28	51 56N	18 4 E	Stonington I.	5	68 11 S	67 0W	Strumica ~	42	41 20N	22 22 E
Sriharikota, I.	70	13 40N	80 20 E	Stayner	112	44 25N	80 5W	Stony L., Man., Can.	109	58 51N	98 40W	Struthers, Can.	106	48 41N	85 51W
Srikakulam	70	18 14N	83 58 E	Steamboat Springs	118	40 30N	106 50W	Stony L., Ont., Can.	112	44 30N	78 0W	Struthers, U.S.A.	114	41 6N	80 38W
Srinagar	66	34 5N	74 50 E	Stębark	28	53 30N	20 10 E	Stony Rapids	109	59 16N	105 50W	Stryama	43	42 16N	24 54 E
Sripur	69	24 14N	90 30 E	Stebleva	44	41 18N	20 33 E	Stony Tunguska = Tunguska, Nizhnyaya ~	59	65 48N	88 4 E	Stryi	54	49 16N	23 48 E
Srirangam	70	10 54N	78 42 E	Steele	116	46 56N	99 52W	Stopnica	28	50 27N	20 57 E	Stryker	108	48 40N	114 44W
Srirangapatnam	70	12 26N	76 43 E	Steelton	114	40 17N	76 50W	Stora Gla	48	59 30N	12 30 E	Stryków	28	51 55N	19 33 E
Srivilliputtur	70	9 31N	77 40 E	Steelville	117	37 57N	91 21W	Stora Karlsö	49	57 17N	17 59 E	Strzegom	28	50 58N	16 20 E
Środa Śląska	28	51 10N	16 36 E	Steen River	108	59 40N	117 12W	Stora Lulevatten	50	67 10N	19 30 E	Strzelce Krajeńskie	28	52 52N	15 33 E
Środa Wielkopolski	28	52 15N	17 19 E	Steenvoorde	19	50 48N	2 33 E	Stora Sjöfallet	50	67 29N	18 40 E	Strzelce Opolskie	28	50 31N	18 18 E
Srokowo	28	54 13N	21 31 E	Steenwijk	16	52 47N	6 7 E	Storavan	50	65 45N	18 10 E	Strzelecki Cr. ~	97	29 37 S	139 59 E
Srpska Crnja	42	45 38N	20 44 E	Steep Pt.	96	26 08 S	113 8 E	Størdal	47	63 3N	10 56 E	Strzelin	28	50 46N	17 2 E
Srpska Itabej	42	45 35N	20 44 E	Steep Rock	109	51 30N	98 48W	Store Bælt	49	55 20N	11 0 E	Strzelno	28	52 35N	18 9 E
Staaten ~	98	16 24 S	141 17 E	Ştefăneşti	46	47 44N	27 15 E	Store Creek	99	32 54 S	149 6 E	Strzybnica	27	50 28N	18 48 E
Staberhuk	24	54 23N	11 18 E	Stefanie L. = Chew Bahir	87	4 40N	36 50 E	Store Heddinge	49	55 18N	12 23 E	Strzyżów	27	49 52N	21 47 E
Stade	24	53 35N	9 31 E	Stefansson Bay	5	67 20 S	59 8 E	Støren	47	63 3N	10 18 E	Stuart, Fla., U.S.A.	115	27 11N	80 12W
Staðarhólskirkja	50	65 23N	21 58W	Stege	49	55 0N	12 18 E	Storfjorden	47	62 25N	6 30 E	Stuart, Nebr., U.S.A.	116	42 39N	99 8W
Städjan	48	61 56N	12 52 E	Steiermark □	26	47 26N	15 0 E	Storm B.	97	43 10 S	147 30 E	Stuart ~	108	54 0N	123 35W
Stadlandet	47	62 10N	5 10 E	Steigerwald	25	49 45N	10 30 E	Storm Lake	116	42 35N	95 11W	Stuart L.	108	54 30N	124 30W
Stadskanaal	16	53 4N	6 55 E	Steinbach	109	49 32N	96 40W	Stormberg	92	31 16 S	26 17 E	Stuart Range	96	29 10 S	134 56 E
Stadthagen	24	52 20N	9 14 E	Steinfort	16	49 39N	5 55 E	Stormsrivier	92	33 59 S	23 52 E	Stuart Town	100	32 44 S	149 4 E
Stadtlohn	24	52 0N	6 52 E	Steinheim	24	51 50N	9 6 E	Stornoway	14	58 12N	6 23W	Stubbekøbing	49	54 53N	12 9 E
Stadtroda	24	50 51N	11 44 E	Steinhuder Meer	24	52 48N	9 20 E	Storozhinets	56	48 14N	25 45 E	Stuben	26	47 10N	10 8 E
Stafafell	50	64 25N	14 52W	Steinkjer	50	63 59N	11 31 E	Storsjö	48	62 49N	13 5 E	Studen Kladenets, Yazovir	43	41 37N	25 30 E
Staffa	14	56 26N	6 21W	Stellaland	92	26 45 S	24 50 E	Storsjöen, Hedmark, Norway	47	60 20N	11 40 E	Stugun	48	63 10N	15 40 E
Stafford, U.K.	12	52 49N	2 9W	Stellarton	107	45 32N	62 30W	Storsjöen, Hedmark, Norway	47	61 30N	11 14 E	Stühlingen	25	47 44N	8 26 E
Stafford, U.S.A.	117	38 0N	98 35W	Stellenbosch	92	33 58 S	18 50 E	Storsjön, Gävleborg, Sweden	48	60 35N	16 45 E	Stull, L.	109	54 24N	92 34W
Stafford □	12	52 53N	2 10W	Stemshaug	47	63 19N	8 44 E	Storsjön, Jämtland, Sweden	48	62 50N	13 8 E	Stung Treng	71	13 31N	105 58 E
Stafford Springs	113	41 58N	72 20W	Stendal	24	52 36N	11 50 E	Storstrøms Amt. □	49	54 50N	11 45 E	Stupart ~	109	56 0N	93 25W
Stagnone	40	37 50N	12 28 E	Stensele	50	65 3N	17 8 E	Storuman	50	65 5N	17 10 E	Stupino	55	54 57N	38 2 E
Staines	13	51 26N	0 30W	Stenstorp	49	58 17N	13 45 E	Storuman,sjö	50	65 13N	16 50 E	Sturgeon B.	109	52 0N	97 50W
Stainz	26	46 53N	15 17 E	Stepanakert	53	39 40N	46 25 E	Storvik	48	60 35N	16 33 E	Sturgeon Bay	114	44 52N	87 20W
Stalač	42	43 43N	21 28 E	Stephan	116	48 30N	96 53W	Stoughton	109	49 40N	103 0W	Sturgeon Falls	106	46 25N	79 57W
Stalingrad = Volgograd	57	48 40N	44 25 E	Stephens Creek	99	31 50 S	141 30 E	Stour ~, Dorset, U.K.	13	50 48N	2 7W	Sturgeon L., Alta., Can.	108	55 6N	117 32W
Staliniri = Tskhinvali	57	42 14N	44 1 E	Stephens I.	108	54 10N	130 45W	Stour ~, Here. & Worcs., U.K.	13	52 25N	2 13W	Sturgeon L., Ont., Can.	106	50 0N	90 45W
Stalino = Donetsk	56	48 0N	37 45 E	Stephenville, Can.	107	48 31N	58 35W	Stour ~, Suffolk, U.K.	13	51 55N	1 5 E	Sturgeon L., Ont., Can.	112	44 28N	78 43W
Stalinogorsk = Novomoskovsk	55	54 5N	38 15 E	Stephenville, U.S.A.	117	32 12N	98 12W	Stour (Gt. Stour) ~	13	51 15N	1 20 E	Sturgis, Mich., U.S.A.	114	41 50N	85 25W
Stalowa Wola	28	50 34N	22 3 E	Stepnica	28	53 38N	14 36 E	Stourbridge	13	52 28N	2 8W	Sturgis, S.D., U.S.A.	116	44 25N	103 30W
Stalybridge	12	53 29N	2 4W	Stepnoi = Elista	57	46 16N	44 14 E	Stout, L.	109	52 0N	94 40W	Sturkö	49	56 5N	15 42 E
Stamford, Austral.	98	21 15 S	143 46 E	Stepnyak	58	52 50N	70 50 E	Stowmarket	13	52 11N	1 0 E	Sturt Cr. ~	96	20 8 S	127 24 E
Stamford, U.K.	13	52 39N	0 29W	Steppe	60	50 0N	50 0 E	Strabane	15	54 50N	7 28W	Štúrovo	27	47 48N	18 41 E
Stamford, Conn., U.S.A.	114	41 5N	73 30W	Stereá Ellas □	45	38 50N	22 0 E	Strabane □	15	54 45N	7 25W	Su Xian	77	33 41N	116 59 E
Stamford, Tex., U.S.A.	117	32 58N	99 50W	Sterkstroom	92	31 32 S	26 32 E	Stracin	42	42 13N	22 2 E	Suakin	86	19 8N	37 20 E
Stamps	117	33 22N	93 30W	Sterling, Colo., U.S.A.	116	40 40N	103 15W	Stradella	38	45 4N	9 20 E	Suaqui	120	29 12N	109 41W
Stanberry	116	40 12N	94 32W	Sterling, Ill., U.S.A.	116	41 45N	89 45W	Strahan	97	42 9 S	145 20 E	Subi	72	2 58N	108 50 E
Standerton	93	26 55 S	29 7 E	Sterling, Kans., U.S.A.	116	38 17N	98 13W	Strakonice	26	49 15N	13 53 E	Subiaco	39	41 56N	13 5 E
Standish	114	43 58N	83 57W	Sterling City	117	31 50N	100 59W	Straldzha	43	42 35N	26 40 E	Subotica	42	46 6N	19 49 E
Stanford	118	47 11N	110 10W	Sterling Run	112	41 25N	78 12W	Stralsund	24	54 17N	13 5 E	Success	109	50 28N	108 6W
Stange	47	60 43N	11 5 E	Sterlitamak	52	53 40N	56 0 E	Strand, Norway	47	61 17N	11 19 E	Suceava	46	47 38N	26 16 E
Stanger	93	29 27 S	31 14 E	Sternberg	24	53 42N	11 48 E	Strand, S. Afr.	92	34 9 S	18 48 E				
Stanišić	42	45 56N	19 10 E	Šternberk	27	49 45N	17 15 E	Stranda	47	60 17N	6 0 E				
Stanislav = Ivano-Frankovsk	54	49 0N	24 40 E	Stettin = Szczecin	28	53 27N	14 27 E	Strandebarm	47	60 17N	6 0 E				
Stanisławów	28	52 18N	21 33 E	Stettiner Haff	24	53 50N	14 25 E	Strandvik	47	60 9N	5 41 E				
Stanke Dimitrov	42	42 17N	23 9 E	Stettler	108	52 19N	112 40W	Strangford, L.	15	54 30N	5 37W				
Stanley, Austral.	99	40 46 S	145 19 E	Steubenville	114	40 21N	80 39W	Strängnäs	48	59 23N	17 2 E				
Stanley, N.B., Can.	107	46 20N	66 44W	Stevens Port	116	44 30N	89 34W	Stranraer	14	54 54N	5 0W				
Stanley, Sask., Can.	109	55 24N	104 22W	Stevenson L.	109	53 55N	96 0W								
				Stevns Klint	49	55 17N	12 28 E								

Suceava □ **46** 47 37N 25 40 E
Suceava → **46** 47 38N 26 16 E
Sucha-Beskidzka **27** 49 44N 19 35 E
Suchan **28** 53 18N 15 18 E
Suchedniów **28** 51 3N 20 49 E
Suchitoto **120** 13 56N 89 0W
Suchou = Suzhou **75** 31 18N 120 36 E
Süchow = Xuzhou **77** 34 18N 117 10 E
Suchowola **28** 53 33N 23 3 E
Suck → **15** 53 17N 8 18W
Suckling, Mt. **98** 9 49 S 148 53 E
Sucre **126** 19 0 S 65 15W
Sućuraj **39** 43 10N 17 8 E
Sud-Ouest, Pte. du **107** 49 23N 63 36W
Sud, Pte. **107** 49 3N 62 14W
Suda → **55** 59 0N 37 40 E
Sudair **64** 26 0N 45 0 E
Sudak **56** 44 51N 34 57 E
Sudan **117** 34 4N 102 32W
Sudan ■ **81** 15 0N 30 0 E
Suday **55** 59 0N 43 0 E
Sudbury **106** 46 30N 81 0W
Sûdd **87** 8 20N 30 0 E
Süderbrarup **24** 54 38N 9 47 E
Süderlügum **24** 54 50N 8 55 E
Süderoog-Sand **24** 54 27N 8 30 E
Sudetan Mts. = Sudety **27** 50 20N 16 45 E
Sudety **27** 50 20N 16 45 E
Sudi **91** 10 11 S 39 57 E
Sudirman, Pegunungan **73** 4 30 S 137 0 E
Sudiţi **46** 44 35N 27 38 E
Sudogda **55** 55 55N 40 50 E
Sudr **86** 29 40N 32 42 E
Sudzha **54** 51 14N 35 17 E
Sueca **33** 39 12N 0 21W
Suedala **49** 55 30N 13 15 E
Sueur, Le **116** 44 25N 93 52W
Suez = El Suweis **86** 28 40N 33 0 E
Suez Canal = Suweis, Qanâl es **86** 31 0N 33 20 E
Sūf **62** 32 19N 35 49 E
Şufaynah **64** 23 6N 40 33 E
Suffield **109** 50 12N 111 10W
Suffolk **114** 36 47N 76 33W
Suffolk □ **13** 52 16N 1 0 E
Sufuk **65** 23 50N 51 50 E
Şugag **46** 45 47N 23 37 E
Sugar City **116** 38 18N 103 38W
Sugluk = Sagloue **105** 62 30N 74 15W
Suhaia, L. **46** 43 45N 25 15 E
Suhār **65** 24 20N 56 40 E
Suhbaatar **75** 50 17N 106 10 E
Suhl **24** 50 35N 10 40 E
Suhl □ **24** 50 37N 10 43 E
Sui Xian, Henan, China **77** 34 25N 115 2 E
Sui Xian, Henan, China **77** 31 42N 113 24 E
Suichang **77** 28 29N 119 15 E
Suichuan **77** 26 20N 114 32 E
Suide **76** 37 30N 110 12 E
Suifenhe **76** 44 25N 131 10 E
Suihua **75** 46 32N 126 55 E
Suining, Hunan, China **77** 26 35N 110 10 E
Suining, Sichuan, China **77** 30 26N 105 35 E
Suiping **77** 33 10N 113 59 E
Suippes **19** 49 8N 4 30 E
Suir → **15** 52 15N 7 10W
Suixi **77** 21 19N 110 18 E
Suizhong **76** 40 21N 120 20 E
Sujangarh **68** 27 42N 74 31 E
Sujica **42** 43 52N 17 11 E
Sukabumi **73** 6 56 S 106 50 E
Sukadana, Kalimantan, Indon. **72** 1 10 S 110 0 E
Sukadana, Sumatera, Indon. **72** 5 5 S 105 33 E
Sukaradja **72** 2 28 S 110 25 E
Sukarnapura = Jayapura **73** 2 37 S 140 38 E
Sukhindol **43** 43 11N 25 10 E
Sukhinichi **54** 54 8N 35 10 E
Sukhona → **52** 60 30N 45 0 E
Sukhumi **57** 43 0N 41 0 E
Sukkur **68** 27 42N 68 54 E
Sukkur Barrage **68** 27 40N 68 50 E
Sukma **70** 18 24N 81 45 E
Sukovo **42** 43 4N 22 37 E
Sukunka → **108** 55 45N 121 15W
Sula → **54** 49 40N 32 41 E
Sula, Kepulauan **73** 1 45 S 125 0 E
Sulaiman Range **68** 30 30N 69 50 E
Sulak → **57** 43 20N 47 34 E
Sulam Tsor **62** 33 4N 35 6 E
Sulawesi □ **73** 2 0 S 120 0 E
Sulechów **28** 52 5N 15 40 E
Sulęcin **28** 52 26N 15 10 E
Sulejów **28** 51 26N 19 53 E
Sulejówek **28** 52 13N 21 17 E
Sulima **84** 6 58N 11 32W
Sulina **46** 45 10N 29 40 E
Sulingen **24** 52 41N 8 47 E
Suliţa **46** 47 39N 26 59 E
Sulitälma **50** 67 17N 17 28 E
Sulitjelma **50** 67 9N 16 3 E
Sułkowice **27** 49 50N 19 49 E
Sullana **126** 4 52 S 80 39W
Sullivan, Ill., U.S.A. **116** 39 40N 88 40W
Sullivan, Ind., U.S.A. **114** 39 5N 87 26W
Sullivan, Mo., U.S.A. **116** 38 10N 91 10W
Sullivan Bay **108** 50 55N 126 50W
Sully-sur-Loire **19** 47 45N 2 20 E
Sulmierzyce **28** 51 37N 17 32 E
Sulmona **39** 42 3N 13 55 E
Sulphur, La., U.S.A. **117** 30 13N 93 22W
Sulphur, Okla., U.S.A. **117** 34 35N 97 0W
Sulphur Pt. **108** 60 56N 114 48W
Sulphur Springs **117** 33 5N 95 36W
Sulphur Springs, Cr. → **117** 32 12N 101 36W
Sultan **106** 47 36N 82 47W
Sultanpur **69** 26 18N 82 4 E
Sultsa **52** 63 27N 46 2 E
Sulu Arch. **73** 6 0N 121 0 E
Sulu Sea **73** 8 0N 120 0 E
Sululta **87** 9 10N 38 43 E
Suluq **83** 31 44N 20 14 E
Sulzbach **25** 49 18N 7 4 E
Sulzbach-Rosenberg **25** 49 30N 11 46 E
Sumalata **73** 1 0N 122 31 E
Sumampa **124** 29 25 S 63 29W
Sumatera □ **72** 0 40N 100 20 E
Sumatera Barat □ **72** 1 0 S 100 0 E
Sumatera Selatan □ **72** 3 30 S 104 0 E
Sumatera Utara □ **72** 2 0N 99 0 E
Sumatra **118** 46 38N 107 31W
Sumatra = Sumatera □ **72** 0 40N 100 20 E
Sumba **73** 9 45 S 119 35 E
Sumba, Selat **73** 9 0 S 118 40 E
Sumbawa **72** 8 26 S 117 30 E
Sumbawa Besar **72** 8 30 S 117 26 E
Sumbawanga □ **90** 8 0 S 31 30 E
Sumbing **73** 7 19 S 110 3 E
Sumburgh Hd. **14** 59 52N 1 17W
Sumedang **73** 6 49 S 107 56 E
Sümeg **27** 46 59N 17 20 E
Sumenep **73** 7 3 S 113 51 E
Sumgait **57** 40 34N 49 38 E
Summer L. **118** 42 50N 120 50W
Summerland **108** 49 32N 119 41W
Summerside **107** 46 24N 63 47W
Summerville, Ga., U.S.A. **115** 34 30N 85 20W
Summerville, S.C., U.S.A. **115** 33 2N 80 11W
Summit Lake **108** 54 20N 122 40W
Summit Pk. **119** 37 20N 106 48W
Sumner **116** 42 49N 92 7W
Sumperk **27** 49 59N 17 0 E
Sumter **115** 33 55N 80 22W
Sumy **54** 50 57N 34 50 E
Sunart, L. **14** 56 42N 5 43W
Sunburst **118** 48 56N 111 59W
Sunbury, Austral. **99** 37 35 S 144 44 E
Sunbury, U.S.A. **114** 40 50N 76 46W
Sunchales **124** 30 58 S 61 35W
Suncho Corral **124** 27 55 S 63 27W
Sunchon **77** 34 52N 127 31 E
Suncook **113** 43 8N 71 27W
Sunda Is. **94** 5 0 S 105 0 E
Sunda Kecil, Kepulauan **72** 7 30 S 117 0 E
Sunda, Selat **72** 6 20 S 105 30 E
Sundance **116** 44 27N 104 27W
Sundarbans, The **69** 22 0N 89 0 E
Sundargarh **69** 22 4N 84 5 E
Sundays = Sondags → **92** 33 44 S 25 51 E
Sundbyberg **48** 59 22N 17 58 E
Sunderland, Can. **112** 44 16N 79 4W
Sunderland, U.K. **12** 54 54N 1 22W
Sunderland, U.S.A. **113** 42 27N 72 36W
Sundre **108** 51 49N 114 38W
Sundridge **106** 45 45N 79 25W
Sunds **49** 56 13N 9 1 E
Sundsjö **48** 62 59N 15 9 E
Sundsvall **48** 62 23N 17 17 E
Sungaigerong **72** 2 59 S 104 52 E
Sungailiat **72** 1 51 S 106 8 E
Sungaipakning **72** 1 19N 102 0 E
Sungaipenuh **72** 2 1 S 101 20 E
Sungaitiram **72** 0 45 S 117 8 E
Sungari = Songhua Jiang → **76** 47 45N 132 30 E
Sungei Patani **71** 5 38N 100 29 E
Sungei Siput **71** 4 51N 101 6 E
Sungguminasa **73** 5 17 S 119 30 E
Sunghua Chiang = Songhua Jiang → **76** 47 45N 132 30 E
Sungikai **87** 12 20N 29 51 E
Sungtao Hu **77** 19 20N 109 35 E
Sungurlu **56** 40 12N 34 21 E
Sunja **39** 45 21N 16 35 E
Sunndalsøra **47** 62 40N 8 33 E
Sunne **48** 59 52N 13 5 E
Sunnfjord **47** 61 25N 5 18 E
Sunnyside, Utah, U.S.A. **118** 39 34N 110 24W
Sunnyside, Wash., U.S.A. **118** 46 24N 120 2W
Sunray **117** 36 1N 101 47W
Sunshine **100** 37 48 S 144 52 E
Suntar **59** 62 15N 117 30 E
Sunyani **84** 7 21N 2 22W
Suoyarvi **52** 62 12N 32 23 E
Supai **119** 36 14N 112 44W
Supaul **69** 26 10N 86 40 E
Superior, Ariz., U.S.A. **119** 33 19N 111 9W
Superior, Mont., U.S.A. **118** 47 15N 114 57W
Superior, Nebr., U.S.A. **116** 40 3N 98 2W
Superior, Wis., U.S.A. **116** 46 45N 92 5W
Superior, L. **111** 47 40N 87 0W
Supetar **39** 43 25N 16 32 E
Suphan Buri **71** 14 14N 100 10 E
Suphan Dağı **64** 38 54N 42 48 E
Supraśl **28** 53 13N 23 19 E
Suq al Jum'ah **83** 32 58N 13 12 E
Sūq ash Shūyukh **64** 30 53N 46 28 E
Suqian **77** 33 54N 118 8 E
Sūr, Leb. **62** 33 19N 35 16 E
Sūr, Oman **65** 22 34N 59 32 E
Sur, Pt. **119** 36 18N 121 54W
Sura → **55** 56 6N 46 0 E
Surabaja = Surabaya **73** 7 17 S 112 45 E
Surabaya **73** 7 17 S 112 45 E
Surahammar **48** 59 43N 16 13 E
Suraia **46** 45 40N 27 25 E
Surakarta **73** 7 35 S 110 48 E
Surakhany **57** 40 25N 50 1 E
Surandai **70** 8 58N 77 26 E
Šurany **27** 48 6N 18 10 E
Surat, Austral. **99** 27 10 S 149 6 E
Surat, India **68** 21 12N 72 55 E
Surat Thani **71** 9 6N 99 20 E
Suratgarh **68** 29 18N 73 55 E
Suraz **28** 52 57N 22 57 E
Surazh, Byelorussia, U.S.S.R. **54** 55 25N 30 44 E
Surazh, R.S.F.S.R., U.S.S.R. **54** 53 5N 32 27 E
Surduc **46** 47 15N 23 25 E
Surduc Pasul **46** 45 21N 23 23 E
Surdulica **42** 42 41N 22 11 E
Sûre → **16** 49 44N 6 31 E
Surendranagar **68** 22 45N 71 40 E
Surgères **20** 46 7N 0 47W
Surgut **58** 61 14N 73 20 E
Suri **69** 23 50N 87 34 E
Surianu **46** 45 33N 23 31 E
Suriapet **70** 17 10N 79 40 E
Şūrīf **62** 31 40N 35 4 E
Surigao **73** 9 47N 125 29 E
Surin **71** 14 50N 103 34 E
Surinam ■ **127** 4 0N 56 0W
Suriname → **127** 5 50N 55 15W
Surmene **57** 41 0N 40 1 E
Surovikino **57** 48 32N 42 55 E
Surprise L. **108** 59 40N 133 15W
Surrey □ **13** 51 16N 0 30W
Sursee **25** 47 11N 8 6 E
Sursk **55** 53 3N 45 40 E
Surt **83** 31 11N 16 39 E
Surt, Al Hammadah al **83** 30 0N 17 50 E
Surt, Khalīj **83** 31 40N 18 30 E
Surtsey **50** 63 20N 20 30W
Suruga-Wan **74** 34 45N 138 30 E
Susa **38** 45 8N 7 3 E
Suså → **49** 55 20N 11 42 E
Sušac **39** 42 46N 16 30 E
Susak **39** 44 30N 14 18 E
Sūsangerd **64** 31 35N 48 6 E
Susanino **59** 52 50N 140 14 E
Susanville **118** 40 28N 120 40W
Sušice **26** 49 17N 13 30 E
Susquehanna → **114** 39 33N 76 5W
Susquehanna Depot **113** 41 55N 75 36W
Susques **124** 23 35 S 66 25W
Sussex, Can. **107** 45 45N 65 37W
Sussex, U.S.A. **113** 41 12N 74 38W
Sussex, E. □ **13** 51 0N 0 20 E
Sussex, W. □ **13** 51 0N 0 30W
Sustut → **108** 56 20N 127 30W
Susuman **59** 62 47N 148 10 E
Susunu **73** 3 20 S 133 25 E
Susz **28** 53 44N 19 20 E
Şuţeşti **46** 45 13N 27 27 E
Sutherland, S. Afr. **92** 32 33 S 20 40 E
Sutherland, U.S.A. **116** 41 12N 101 11W
Sutherland Falls **101** 44 48 S 167 46 E
Sutherland Pt. **97** 28 15 S 153 35 E
Sutherlin **118** 43 28N 123 16W
Sutivan **39** 43 23N 16 30 E
Sutlej → **68** 29 23N 71 3 E
Sutton, Can. **113** 45 6N 72 37W
Sutton, U.S.A. **116** 40 40N 97 50W
Sutton → **106** 55 15N 83 45W
Sutton-in-Ashfield **12** 53 7N 1 20W
Suttor → **98** 21 36 S 147 2 E
Suva **94** 18 6 S 178 30 E
Suva Gora **42** 41 45N 21 3 E
Suva Planina **42** 43 10N 22 5 E
Suva Reka **42** 42 21N 20 50 E
Suvo Rudïste **42** 43 17N 20 49 E
Suvorov **55** 54 7N 36 30 E
Suvorov Is. = Suwarrow Is. **95** 13 15 S 163 30W
Suvorovo **43** 43 20N 27 35 E
Suwałki **28** 54 8N 22 59 E
Suwałki □ **28** 54 0N 22 30 E
Suwannee → **115** 29 18N 83 9W
Suwanose Jima **74** 29 26N 129 30 E
Suwarrow Is. **95** 15 0 S 163 0W
Suweis, Khalîg el **86** 28 40N 33 0 E
Suweis, Qanâl es **86** 31 0N 32 20 E
Suwŏn **76** 37 17N 127 1 E
Suzdal **55** 56 29N 40 26 E
Suze, La **18** 47 54N 0 2 E
Suzhou **75** 31 19N 120 38 E
Suzu-Misaki **74** 37 31N 137 21 E
Suzuka **74** 34 55N 136 36 E
Suzzara **38** 45 0N 10 45 E
Svalbard **4** 78 0N 17 0 E
Svalbarð **50** 66 12N 15 43W
Svalöv **49** 55 57N 13 8 E
Svanvik **50** 69 25N 30 3 E
Svappavaara **50** 67 40N 21 03 E
Svarstad **47** 59 27N 9 56 E
Svartisen **50** 66 40N 13 50 E
Svartvik **48** 62 19N 17 24 E
Svatovo **56** 49 35N 38 11 E
Svay Rieng **71** 11 9N 105 45 E
Sveio **47** 59 33N 5 23 E
Svendborg **49** 55 4N 10 35 E
Svene **47** 59 45N 9 31 E
Svenljunga **49** 57 29N 13 5 E
Svenstrup **49** 56 58N 9 50 E
Sverdlovsk, R.S.F.S.R., U.S.S.R. **52** 56 50N 60 30 E
Sverdlovsk, Ukraine S.S.R., U.S.S.R. **57** 48 5N 39 37 E
Sverdrup Is. **4** 79 0N 97 0W
Svetac **39** 43 3N 15 43 E
Sveti Ivan Zelina **39** 45 57N 16 16 E
Sveti Jurij **39** 46 14N 15 24 E
Sveti Lenart **39** 46 36N 15 48 E
Sveti Nikola, Prokhad **42** 43 27N 22 6 E
Sveti Nikole **42** 41 51N 21 56 E
Sveti Rok **39** 40 1N 9 6 E
Sveti Trojica **39** 46 37N 15 50 E
Svetlogorsk **54** 52 38N 29 46 E
Svetlograd **57** 45 25N 42 58 E
Svetlovodsk **54** 49 2N 33 13 E
Svetozarevo **42** 44 5N 21 15 E
Svidník **27** 49 20N 21 37 E
Svilaja Pl. **39** 43 49N 16 31 E
Svilajnac **42** 44 15N 21 11 E
Svilengrad **43** 41 49N 26 12 E
Svir → **52** 60 30N 32 48 E
Svishtov **43** 43 36N 25 23 E
Svisloch **54** 53 3N 24 2 E
Svitava → **27** 49 30N 16 37 E
Svitavy **27** 49 47N 16 28 E
Svobodnyy **59** 51 20N 128 0 E
Svoge **43** 42 59N 23 23 E
Svolvær **50** 68 15N 14 34 E
Svratka → **27** 49 11N 16 38 E
Svrljig **42** 43 25N 22 6 E
Swabian Alps = Schäbischer Alb **25** 48 30N 9 30 E
Swain Reefs **97** 21 45 S 152 20 E
Swainsboro **115** 32 38N 82 22W
Swakopmund **92** 22 37 S 14 30 E
Swale → **12** 54 5N 1 20W
Swan → **96** 32 3 S 115 45 E
Swan Hill **97** 35 20 S 143 33 E
Swan Hills **108** 54 42N 115 24W
Swan Islands **121** 17 22N 83 57W
Swan L. **109** 52 30N 100 40W
Swan River **109** 52 10N 101 16W
Swanage **13** 50 36N 1 59W
Swansea, Austral. **99** 33 3 S 151 35 E
Swansea, U.K. **13** 51 37N 3 57W
Swartberge **92** 33 20 S 22 0 E
Swartruggens **92** 25 39 S 26 42 E
Swarzędz **28** 52 25N 17 4 E
Swastika **106** 48 7N 80 6W
Swatow = Shantou **76** 23 18N 116 40 E
Swaziland ■ **93** 26 30 S 31 30 E
Sweden ■ **50** 67 0N 15 0 E
Swedru **85** 5 32N 0 41W
Sweet Home **118** 44 26N 122 25W
Sweetwater **117** 32 30N 100 28W
Sweetwater → **118** 42 31N 107 2W
Swellendam **92** 34 1 S 20 26 E
Swider → **28** 52 6N 21 14 E
Świdnica **28** 50 50N 16 30 E
Świdnik **28** 51 13N 22 39 E
Świdwin **28** 53 47N 15 49 E
Świebodzice **28** 50 51N 16 20 E
Świebodzin **28** 52 15N 15 31 E
Świecie **28** 53 25N 18 30 E
Świętokrzyskie, Góry **28** 51 0N 20 30 E
Swift Current **109** 50 20N 107 45W
Swiftcurrent → **109** 50 38N 107 44W
Swilly, L. **15** 55 12N 7 35W
Swindle, I. **108** 52 30N 128 35W
Swindon **13** 51 33N 1 47W
Swinemünde = Świnoujście **28** 53 54N 14 16 E
Świnoujście **28** 53 54N 14 16 E
Switzerland ■ **25** 46 30N 8 0 E
Swords **15** 53 27N 6 15W
Syasstroy **54** 60 5N 32 15 E
Sychevka **54** 55 59N 34 16 E
Syców **28** 51 19N 17 40 E
Sydney, Austral. **97** 33 53 S 151 10 E
Sydney, Can. **107** 46 7N 60 7W
Sydney, U.S.A. **116** 41 12N 103 0W
Sydney Mines **107** 46 18N 60 15W
Sydprøven **4** 60 30N 45 35W
Sydra G. of = Surt, Khalīj **35** 31 40N 18 30 E
Syke **24** 52 55N 8 50 E
Syktyvkar **52** 61 45N 50 40 E
Sylacauga **115** 33 10N 86 15W
Sylarna **50** 63 2N 12 13 E
Sylhet **67** 24 54N 91 52 E
Sylt **24** 54 50N 8 20 E
Sylvan Lake **108** 52 20N 114 03W
Sylvania **115** 32 45N 81 37W
Sylvester **115** 31 31N 83 50W
Sym **58** 60 20N 88 18 E
Syracuse, Kans., U.S.A. **117** 38 0N 101 46W
Syracuse, N.Y., U.S.A. **114** 43 4N 76 11W
Syrdarya → **58** 46 3N 61 0 E
Syria ■ **64** 35 0N 38 0 E
Syriam **69** 16 44N 96 19 E
Syrian Desert **60** 31 0N 40 0 E
Syul'dzhyukyor **59** 63 14N 113 32 E
Syutkya **43** 41 50N 24 16 E
Syzran **55** 53 12N 48 30 E
Szabolcs-Szatmár □ **27** 48 2N 21 45 E
Szamocin **28** 53 2N 17 7 E
Szamos → **27** 48 7N 22 20 E
Szaraz → **27** 46 28N 20 44 E
Szarvas **27** 46 50N 20 38 E
Szazhalombatta **27** 47 20N 18 58 E
Szczawnica **27** 49 26N 20 30 E
Szczebrzeszyn **28** 50 42N 22 59 E
Szczecin **28** 53 27N 14 27 E
Szczecin □ **28** 53 25N 14 32 E
Szczecinek **28** 53 43N 16 41 E
Szczekocimy **28** 50 38N 19 48 E
Szczucin **28** 50 18N 21 4 E
Szczuczyn **28** 53 36N 22 19 E
Szczytno **28** 53 33N 21 0 E
Szechwan = Sichuan □ **75** 31 0N 104 0 E
Szécsény **27** 48 7N 19 30 E
Szeged **27** 46 16N 20 10 E
Szeghalom **27** 47 1N 21 10 E
Székesfehérvár **27** 47 15N 18 25 E
Szekszárd **27** 46 22N 18 42 E
Szendrö **27** 48 24N 20 41 E
Szentendre **27** 47 39N 19 4 E
Szentes **27** 46 39N 20 21 E
Szentgotthárd **27** 46 58N 16 19 E
Szentlörinc **27** 46 3N 18 1 E
Szerencs **27** 48 10N 21 12 E
Szigetvár **27** 46 3N 17 46 E
Szikszó **27** 48 12N 20 56 E
Szkwa → **28** 53 11N 21 43 E
Szlichtyngowa **28** 51 42N 16 15 E
Szob **27** 47 48N 18 53 E
Szolnok **27** 47 10N 20 15 E
Szolnok □ **27** 47 15N 20 30 E
Szombathely **27** 47 14N 16 38 E
Szprotawa **28** 51 33N 15 35 E
Sztum **28** 53 55N 19 1 E
Sztutowo **28** 54 20N 19 15 E
Szubin **28** 53 1N 17 45 E
Szydłowiec **28** 51 15N 20 51 E
Szypliszki **28** 54 17N 23 2 E

T

Tabacal **124** 23 15 S 64 15W
Tabaco **73** 13 22N 123 44 E
Tabagné **84** 7 59N 3 4W
Ţābah **64** 26 55N 42 38 E
Tabar Is. **98** 2 50 S 152 0 E
Tabarca, Isla de **33** 38 17N 0 30W
Tabarka **83** 36 56N 8 46 E
Ţabas, Khorāsān, Iran **65** 33 35N 56 55 E
Ţabas, Khorāsān, Iran **65** 32 48N 60 12 E
Tabasará, Serranía de **121** 8 35N 81 40W
Tabasco □ **120** 17 45N 93 30W
Tabatinga, Serra da **127** 10 30 S 44 0W

Tabelbala, Kahal de **82** 28 47N 2 0W
Tabelkaza **80** 29 50N 0 55 E
Taber **108** 49 47N 112 8W
Tabernas **33** 37 4N 2 26W
Tabernes de Valldigna **33** 39 5N 0 13W
Tablas **73** 12 25N 122 2 E
Table B. **107** 53 40N 56 25W
Table Mt. **92** 34 0 S 18 22 E
Table Top, Mt. **98** 23 24 S 147 11 E
Tábor **26** 49 25N 14 39 E
Tabor **62** 32 42N 35 24 E
Tabora **90** 5 2 S 32 50 E
Tabora □ **90** 5 0 S 33 0 E
Tabou **84** 4 30N 7 20W
Tabrīz **64** 38 7N 46 20 E
Tabuenca **32** 41 42N 1 33W
Tabūk **64** 28 23N 36 36 E
Tacheng **75** 46 40N 82 58 E
Tach'ing Shan = Daqing Shan **76** 40 40N 111 0 E
Tachov **26** 49 47N 12 39 E
Tácina → **41** 38 57N 16 55 E
Tacloban **73** 11 15N 124 58 E
Tacna **126** 18 0 S 70 20W
Tacoma **118** 47 15N 122 30W
Tacuarembó **125** 31 45 S 56 0W
Tademaït, Plateau du **82** 28 30N 2 30 E
Tadent, O. → **83** 22 25N 6 40 E
Tadjerdjeri, O. → **83** 26 0N 8 0W
Tadjerouna **82** 33 31N 2 3 E
Tadjettaret, O. → **83** 21 20N 7 22 E
Tadjmout, Atlas, Alg. **82** 33 52N 2 30 E
Tadjmout, Sahara, Alg. **82** 25 37N 3 48 E
Tadjoura **87** 11 50N 42 55 E
Tadjoura, Golfe de **87** 11 50N 43 0 E
Tadmor **101** 41 27 S 172 45 E
Tadoule, L. **109** 58 36N 98 20W
Tadoussac **107** 48 11N 69 42W
Tadzhik S.S.R. □ **58** 35 30N 70 0 E
Taegu **76** 35 50N 128 37 E
Taejŏn **76** 36 20N 127 28 E
Tafalla **32** 42 30N 1 41W
Tafar **87** 6 52N 28 15 E
Ţafas **62** 32 44N 36 5 E
Tafassasset, O. → **83** 22 0N 9 57 E
Tafelbaai **92** 33 35 S 18 25 E
Tafelney, C. **82** 31 3N 9 51W
Tafermaar **73** 6 47 S 134 10 E
Taffermit **82** 29 37N 9 15W
Tafí Viejo **124** 26 43 S 65 17W
Tafiré **84** 9 4N 5 4W
Tafnidilt **82** 28 47N 10 58W
Tafraoute **82** 29 50N 8 58W
Taft, Phil. **73** 11 57N 125 30 E
Taft, Calif., U.S.A. **119** 35 9N 119 28W
Taft, Tex., U.S.A. **117** 27 58N 97 23W
Taga Dzong **69** 27 5N 89 55 E
Taganrog **57** 47 12N 38 50 E
Taganrogskiy Zaliv **56** 47 0N 38 30 E
Tagânt **84** 18 20N 11 0W
Tagbilaran **73** 9 39N 123 51 E
Tággia **38** 43 52N 7 50 E
Taghrīfat **83** 29 5N 17 26 E
Taghzout **82** 33 30N 4 49W
Tagish **108** 60 19N 134 16W
Tagish L. **104** 60 10N 134 20W
Tagliacozzo **39** 42 4N 13 13 E
Tagliamento → **39** 45 38N 13 5 E
Táglio di Po **39** 45 0N 12 12 E
Tagomago, I. de **33** 39 2N 1 39 E
Taguatinga **127** 12 16 S 42 26W
Tagula I. **98** 11 30 S 153 30 E
Tagum (Hijo) **73** 7 33N 125 53 E
Tagus = Tajo → **29** 39 44N 5 50W
Tahakopa **101** 46 30 S 169 23 E
Tahala **82** 34 0N 4 28W
Tahan, Gunong **71** 4 34N 102 17 E
Tahat **83** 23 18N 5 33 E
Tāherī **65** 27 43N 52 20 E
Tahiti **95** 17 37 S 149 27W
Tahoe City **118** 39 12N 120 9W
Tahoe, L. **118** 39 0N 120 9W
Tahoua **85** 14 57N 5 16 E
Tahta **86** 26 44N 31 32 E
Tahulandang **73** 2 27N 125 23 E
Tahuna **73** 3 38N 125 30 E
Taï **84** 5 55N 7 30W
Tai Hu **75** 31 5N 120 10 E
Tai Shan **76** 36 25N 117 20 E
Tai'an **76** 36 12N 117 8 E
Taibei **75** 25 4N 121 29 E
Taibus Qi **76** 41 54N 115 22 E
T'aichung = Taizhong **75** 24 10N 120 38 E
Taidong **75** 22 43N 121 9 E
Taieri → **101** 46 3 S 170 12 E
Taiga Madema **83** 23 46N 15 25 E
Taigu **76** 37 28N 112 30 E
Taihang Shan **76** 36 0N 113 30 E
Taihape **101** 39 41 S 175 48 E
Taihe **77** 26 47N 114 52 E
Taihu **77** 30 22N 116 20 E
Taijiang **77** 26 39N 108 21 E
Taikang, Heilongjiang, China **76** 46 50N 124 25 E
Taikang, Henan, China **77** 34 5N 114 50 E
Taikkyi **69** 17 20N 96 0 E
Tailai **76** 46 23N 123 24 E
Tailem Bend **99** 35 12 S 139 29 E
Tailfingen **25** 48 15N 9 1 E
Taimyr = Taymyr **59** 75 0N 100 0 E
Taimyr, Oz. **59** 74 20N 102 0 E
Tain **14** 57 49N 4 4W
Tainan **77** 23 17N 120 18 E
Taínaron, Ákra **45** 36 22N 22 27 E
Taining **77** 26 54N 117 9 E
T'aipei = Taibei **75** 25 4N 121 29 E
Taiping **71** 4 51N 100 44 E
Taishan **77** 22 14N 112 41 E
Taishun **77** 27 30N 119 42 E
Taita □ **90** 4 0 S 38 30 E
Taita Hills **90** 3 25 S 38 15 E
Taitao, Pen. de **128** 46 30 S 75 0W
Taivalkoski **50** 65 33N 28 12 E
Taiwan ■ **75** 24 0N 121 0 E
Taïyetos Óros **45** 37 0N 22 23 E
Taiyib → **62** 31 55N 35 17 E
Taiyiba **62** 32 36N 35 27 E
Taiyuan **76** 37 52N 112 33 E
Taizhong **77** 24 12N 120 35 E
Taizhou **77** 32 28N 119 55 E
Ta'izz **63** 13 35N 44 2 E
Tajarḩī **83** 24 21N 14 28 E
Tajo → **31** 38 40N 9 24W
Tajumulco, Volcán de **120** 15 2N 91 50W
Tājūrā **83** 32 51N 13 21 E
Tak **71** 16 52N 99 8 E
Takada **74** 37 7N 138 15 E
Takaka **101** 40 51 S 172 50 E
Takamatsu **74** 34 20N 134 5 E
Takanabe **74** 32 8N 131 30 E
Takaoka **74** 36 47N 137 0 E
Takapuna **101** 36 47 S 174 47 E
Takasaki **74** 36 20N 139 0 E
Takatsuki **74** 34 51N 135 37 E
Takaungu **90** 3 38 S 39 52 E
Takayama **74** 36 18N 137 11 E
Takefu **74** 35 50N 136 10 E
Takengeun **72** 4 45N 96 50 E
Takeo **71** 10 59N 104 47 E
Tåkern **49** 58 22N 14 45 E
Tākestān **64** 36 0N 49 40 E
Takhar □ **65** 36 40N 70 0 E
Takla L. **108** 55 15N 125 45W
Takla Landing **108** 55 30N 125 50W
Takla Makan **60** 39 0N 83 0 E
Takla Makan = Taklimakan Shamo **75** 38 0N 83 0 E
Taklimakan Shamo **75** 38 0N 83 0 E
Taku → **108** 58 30N 133 50W
Takua Pa **71** 7 18N 9 59 E
Takum **85** 7 18N 9 36 E
Tala **125** 34 21 S 55 46W
Talagante **124** 33 40 S 70 50W
Talaïnt **82** 29 41N 9 40W
Talak **85** 18 0N 5 0 E
Talamanca, Cordillera de **121** 9 20N 83 20W
Talara **126** 4 38 S 81 18 E
Talas **58** 42 30N 72 13 E
Talasea **98** 5 20 S 150 2 E
Talata Mafara **85** 12 38N 6 4 E
Talaud, Kepulauan **73** 4 30N 127 10 E
Talavera de la Reina **30** 39 55N 4 46W
Talayan **73** 6 52N 124 24 E
Talbert, Sillon de **18** 48 53N 3 5W
Talbot, C. **96** 13 48 S 126 43 E
Talbragar → **99** 32 12 S 148 37 E
Talca **124** 35 28 S 71 40W
Talca □ **124** 35 20 S 71 46W
Talcahuano **124** 36 40 S 73 10W
Talcher **69** 21 0N 85 18 E
Talcho **85** 14 44N 3 28 E
Taldy Kurgan **58** 45 10N 78 45 E
Ţalesh, Kūhhā-ye **64** 39 0N 48 30 E
Talfīt **62** 32 5N 35 17 E
Talguharai **86** 18 19N 35 56 E
Tali Post **87** 5 55N 30 44 E
Taliabu **73** 1 45 S 125 0 E
Talibon **73** 10 9N 124 20 E
Talihina **117** 34 45N 95 1W
Talikoti **70** 16 29N 76 17 E
Taling Sung **71** 15 5N 99 11 E
Taliwang **72** 8 50 S 116 55 E
Talkeetna **104** 62 20N 150 9W
Tall **62** 33 0N 35 6 E
Tall 'Afar **64** 36 22N 42 27 E
Tall 'Asūr **62** 31 59N 35 17 E
Talla **86** 28 5N 30 43 E
Talladega **115** 33 28N 86 2W
Tallahassee **115** 30 25N 84 15W
Tallangatta **99** 36 15 S 147 19 E
Tallarook **99** 37 5 S 145 6 E
Tällberg **48** 60 51N 15 2 E
Tallering Pk. **96** 28 6 S 115 37 E
Tallinn **54** 59 22N 24 48 E
Tallulah **117** 32 25N 91 12W
Ţallūzā **62** 32 17N 35 18 E
Tălmaciu **46** 45 38N 24 19 E
Talmest **82** 31 48N 9 21W
Talmont **20** 46 27N 1 37W
Talnoye **56** 48 50N 30 44 E
Taloda **68** 21 34N 74 11 E
Talodi **87** 10 35N 30 22 E
Talovaya **55** 51 6N 40 45 E
Talsi **54** 57 10N 22 30 E
Talsinnt **82** 32 33N 3 27W
Taltal **124** 25 23 S 70 33W
Taltson → **108** 61 24N 112 46W
Taltson L. **109** 61 30N 110 15W
Talwood **99** 28 29 S 149 29 E
Talyawalka Cr. → **99** 32 28 S 142 22 E
Tama **116** 41 56N 92 37W
Tamale **85** 9 22N 0 50W
Taman **56** 45 14N 36 41 E
Tamanar **82** 31 1N 9 46W
Tamano **74** 34 29N 133 59 E
Tamanrasset **83** 22 50N 5 30 E
Tamanrasset, O. → **82** 22 0N 2 0 E
Tamaqua **113** 40 46N 75 58W
Tamar → **13** 50 33N 4 15W
Tamarite de Litera **32** 41 52N 0 25 E
Tamási **27** 46 40N 18 18 E
Tamaské **85** 14 49N 5 43 E
Tamaulipas □ **120** 24 0N 99 0W
Tamaulipas, Sierra de **120** 23 30N 98 20W
Tamazula **120** 24 55N 106 58W
Tamba-Dabatou **84** 11 50N 10 40W
Tambacounda **84** 13 45N 13 40W
Tambelan, Kepulauan **72** 1 0N 107 30 E
Tambo **98** 24 54 S 146 14 E
Tambo de Mora **126** 13 30 S 76 8W
Tambohorano **93** 17 30 S 43 58 E
Tambora **72** 8 12 S 118 5 E
Tambov **55** 52 45N 41 28 E
Tambre → **30** 42 49N 8 53W
Tambuku **73** 7 8 S 113 40 E
Tamburâ **87** 5 40N 27 25 E
Tâmchekket **84** 17 25N 10 40W
Tamega → **30** 41 5N 8 21W
Tamelelt **82** 31 50N 7 32W
Tamenglong **67** 25 0N 93 35 E
Tamerza **83** 34 23N 7 58 E
Tamgak, Mts. **80** 19 12N 8 35 E
Tamiahua, Laguna de **120** 21 30N 97 30W
Tamil Nadu □ **70** 11 0N 77 0 E
Tamluk **69** 22 18N 87 58 E
Tammerfors = Tampere **51** 61 30N 23 50 E
Tammisaari **51** 60 0N 23 26 E
Ţammūn **62** 32 18N 35 23 E
Tämnaren **48** 60 10N 17 25 E
Tamo Abu, Pegunungan **72** 3 10N 115 0 E
Tampa **115** 27 57N 82 38W
Tampa B. **115** 27 40N 82 40W
Tampere **51** 61 30N 23 50 E
Tampico **120** 22 20N 97 50W
Tampin **71** 2 28N 102 13 E
Tamri **82** 30 49N 9 50W
Tamrida = Hadibu **63** 12 35N 54 2 E
Tamsagbulag **75** 47 14N 117 21 E
Tamsalu **54** 59 11N 26 8 E
Tamsweg **26** 47 7N 13 49 E
Tamu **67** 24 13N 94 12 E
Tamuja → **31** 39 38N 6 29W
Tamworth, Austral. **97** 31 7 S 150 58 E
Tamworth, U.K. **13** 52 38N 1 41W
Tan-tan **82** 28 29N 11 1W
Tana **50** 70 26N 28 14 E
Tana →, Kenya **90** 2 32 S 40 31 E
Tana →, Norway **50** 70 30N 28 23 E
Tana, L. **87** 13 5N 37 30 E
Tana River **90** 2 0 S 39 30 E
Tanafjorden **50** 70 45N 28 25 E
Tanagro → **41** 40 35N 15 25 E
Tanahbala **72** 0 30 S 98 30 E
Tanahgrogot **72** 1 55 S 116 15 E
Tanahjampea **73** 7 10 S 120 35 E
Tanahmasa **72** 0 12 S 98 39 E
Tanahmerah **73** 6 5 S 140 16 E
Tanakura **74** 37 10N 140 20 E
Tanami Des. **96** 18 50 S 132 0 E
Tanana **104** 65 10N 152 15W
Tanana → **104** 65 9N 151 55W
Tananarive = Antananarivo **93** 18 55 S 47 35 E
Tanannt **82** 31 54N 6 56W
Tánaro → **38** 45 1N 8 47 E
Tanaunella **40** 40 42N 9 45 E
Tancarville **18** 49 29N 0 28 E
Tanchŏn **76** 40 27N 128 54 E
Tanda, U.P., India **68** 28 57N 78 56 E
Tanda, U.P., India **69** 26 33N 82 35 E
Tanda, Ivory C. **84** 7 48N 3 10W
Tandag **73** 9 4N 126 9 E
Tandaia **91** 9 25 S 34 15 E
Tăndărei **46** 44 39N 27 40 E
Tandaué **92** 16 58 S 18 5 E
Tandil **124** 37 15 S 59 6W
Tandil, Sa. del **124** 37 30 S 59 0W
Tandlianwala **68** 31 3N 73 9 E
Tando Adam **68** 25 45N 68 40 E
Tandou L. **99** 32 40 S 142 5 E
Tandsbyn **48** 63 0N 14 45 E
Tandur **70** 19 11N 79 30 E
Tane-ga-Shima **74** 30 30N 131 0 E
Taneatua **101** 38 4 S 177 1 E
Tanen Tong Dan **67** 16 30N 98 30 E
Tanew → **28** 50 29N 22 16 E
Tanezrouft **82** 23 9N 0 11 E
Tanga **88** 5 5 S 39 2 E
Tanga □ **90** 5 20 S 38 0 E
Tanga Is. **98** 3 20 S 153 15 E
Tangail **69** 24 15N 89 55 E
Tanganyika, L. **90** 6 40 S 30 0 E
Tanger **82** 35 50N 5 49W
Tangerang **73** 6 12 S 106 39 E
Tangerhütte **24** 52 26N 11 50 E
Tangermünde **24** 52 32N 11 57 E
Tanggu **76** 39 2N 117 40 E
Tanggula Shan **75** 32 40N 92 10 E
Tanghe **77** 32 47N 112 50 E
Tangier = Tanger **82** 35 50N 5 49W
Tangkak **71** 2 18N 102 34 E
Tangorin P.O. **98** 21 47 S 144 12 E
Tangshan **76** 39 38N 118 10 E
Tanguiéta **85** 10 35N 1 21 E
Tanimbar, Kepulauan **73** 7 30 S 131 30 E
Taninges **21** 46 7N 6 36 E
Tanjay **73** 9 30N 123 5 E
Tanjore = Thanjavur **70** 10 48N 79 12 E
Tanjung **72** 2 10 S 115 25 E
Tanjungbalai **72** 2 55N 99 44 E
Tanjungbatu **72** 2 23N 118 3 E
Tanjungkarang **72** 5 20 S 105 10 E
Tanjungpandan **72** 2 43 S 107 38 E
Tanjungpinang **72** 1 5N 104 30 E
Tanjungpriok **73** 6 8 S 106 55 E
Tanjungredeb **72** 2 9N 117 29 E
Tanjungselor **72** 2 55N 117 25 E
Tank **68** 32 14N 70 25 E
Tänndalen **48** 62 33N 12 18 E
Tannis Bugt **49** 57 40N 10 15 E
Tannu-Ola **59** 51 0N 94 0 E
Tano → **84** 5 7N 2 56W
Tanout **85** 14 50N 8 55 E
Tanta **86** 30 45N 30 57 E
Tantoyuca **120** 21 21N 98 10W
Tantung = Dandong **76** 40 10N 124 20 E
Tantūra = Dor **62** 32 37N 34 55 E
Tanuku **70** 16 45N 81 44 E
Tanumshede **49** 58 42N 11 20 E
Tanunda **99** 34 30 S 139 0 E
Tanur **70** 11 1N 75 52 E
Tanus **20** 44 8N 2 19 E
Tanzania ■ **90** 6 40 S 34 0 E
Tanzilla → **108** 58 8N 130 43W
Tao'an **76** 45 22N 122 40 E
Taormina **41** 37 52N 15 16 E
Taos **119** 36 28N 105 35W
Taoudenni **82** 22 40N 3 55W
Taoudrart, Adrar **82** 24 25N 2 24 E
Taounate **82** 34 25N 4 41W
Taourirt, Alg. **82** 26 37N 0 20 E
Taourirt, Moroc. **82** 34 25N 2 53W
Taouz **82** 30 53N 4 0W
Taoyuan, China **77** 28 55N 111 16 E
Taoyuan, Taiwan **77** 25 0N 121 13 E
Tapa **54** 59 15N 25 50 E
Tapa Shan = Daba Shan **75** 31 50N 109 20 E
Tapachula **120** 14 54N 92 17W
Tapah **71** 4 12N 101 15 E
Tapajós → **127** 2 24 S 54 41W
Tapaktuan **72** 3 15N 97 10 E
Tapanui **101** 45 56 S 169 18 E
Tapauá → **126** 5 40 S 64 21W
Tapeta **84** 6 29N 8 52W
Tapia **30** 43 34N 6 56W
Tápiószele **27** 47 25N 19 55 E
Tapirapecó, Serra **126** 1 10N 65 0W
Tapolca **27** 46 53N 17 29 E
Tappahannock **114** 37 56N 76 50W
Tapti → **68** 21 8N 72 41 E
Tapuaenuku, Mt. **101** 42 0 S 173 39 E
Tapul Group **73** 5 35N 120 50 E
Taquara **125** 29 36 S 50 46W
Taquari → **126** 19 15 S 57 17W
Tar Island **108** 57 03N 111 40W
Tara, Austral. **99** 27 17 S 150 31 E
Tara, Can. **112** 44 28N 81 9W
Tara, U.S.S.R. **58** 56 55N 74 24 E
Tara, Zambia **91** 16 58 S 26 45 E
Tara →, U.S.S.R. **58** 56 42N 74 36 E
Tara →, Yugo. **42** 43 21N 18 51 E
Tarabagatay, Khrebet **58** 48 0N 83 0 E
Tarābulus, Leb. **64** 34 31N 35 50 E
Tarābulus, Libya **83** 32 49N 13 7 E
Tarahouahout **83** 22 41N 5 59 E
Tarakan **72** 3 20N 117 35 E
Tarakit, Mt. **90** 2 2N 35 10 E
Taralga **99** 34 26 S 149 52 E
Taranagar **68** 28 43N 74 50 E
Taranaki □ **101** 39 5 S 174 51 E
Tarancón **32** 40 1N 3 1W
Taranga **68** 23 56N 72 43 E
Taranga Hill **68** 24 0N 72 40 E
Táranto **41** 40 30N 17 11 E
Táranto, G. di **41** 40 0N 17 15 E
Tarapacá **126** 2 56 S 69 46W
Tarapacá □ **124** 20 45 S 69 30W
Tarare **21** 45 54N 4 26 E
Tararua Range **101** 40 45 S 175 25 E
Tarascon, Ariège, France **20** 42 50N 1 37 E
Tarascon, Bouches-du-Rhône, France **21** 43 48N 4 39 E
Tarashcha **56** 49 30N 30 31 E
Tarat **80** 25 55N 9 3 E
Tarat, Bj. **83** 26 13N 9 18 E
Tarauacá **126** 8 6 S 70 48W
Tarauacá → **126** 6 42 S 69 48W
Taravo → **21** 41 42N 8 49 E
Tarawera **101** 39 2 S 176 36 E
Tarawera L. **101** 38 13 S 176 27 E
Tarazona **32** 41 55N 1 43W
Tarazona de la Mancha **33** 39 16N 1 55W
Tarbat Ness **14** 57 52N 3 48W
Tarbert, Strathclyde, U.K. **14** 55 55N 5 25W
Tarbert, W. Isles, U.K. **14** 57 54N 6 49W
Tarbes **20** 43 15N 0 3 E
Tarboro **115** 35 55N 77 30W
Tarbrax **98** 21 7 S 142 26 E
Tarbū **83** 26 0N 15 5 E
Tarcento **39** 46 12N 13 12 E
Tarcoola **96** 30 44 S 134 36 E
Tarcoon **99** 30 15 S 146 43 E
Tardets-Sorholus **20** 43 8N 0 52W
Tardoire → **20** 45 52N 0 14 E
Taree **97** 31 50 S 152 30 E
Tarentaise **21** 45 30N 6 35 E
Tarf, Ras **82** 35 40N 5 11W
Tarf Shaqq al Abd **86** 26 50N 36 6 E
Tarfa, Wadi el → **86** 28 25N 30 50 E
Tarfaya **80** 27 55N 12 55W
Targon **20** 44 44N 0 16W
Targuist **82** 34 59N 4 14W
Tărhăus **46** 46 40N 26 8 E
Tărhăus, Munţii **46** 46 39N 26 7 E
Tarhbalt **82** 30 39N 5 20W
Tarhit **82** 30 58N 2 0W
Tarhūnah **83** 32 27N 13 36 E
Tarib, Wadi → **86** 18 30N 43 23 E
Tarifa **31** 36 1N 5 36W
Tarija **124** 21 30 S 64 40W
Tarija □ **124** 21 30 S 63 30W
Tariku → **73** 2 55 S 138 26 E
Tarim He → **75** 39 30N 88 30 E
Tarim Pendi **75** 40 0N 84 0 E
Tarime □ **90** 1 15 S 34 0 E
Taritatu → **73** 2 54 S 138 27 E
Tarka → **92** 32 10 S 26 0 E
Tarkastad **92** 32 0 S 26 16 E
Tarkhankut, Mys **56** 45 25N 32 30 E
Tarko Sale **58** 64 55N 77 50 E
Tarkwa **84** 5 20N 2 0W
Tarlac **73** 15 29N 120 35 E
Tarm **49** 55 56N 8 31 E
Tarma **126** 11 25 S 75 45W
Tarn □ **20** 43 49N 2 8 E
Tarn → **20** 44 5N 1 6 E
Tarn-et-Garonne □ **20** 44 8N 1 20 E
Tarna → **27** 47 31N 19 59 E
Tårnby **49** 55 37N 12 36 E
Tarnica **27** 49 4N 22 44 E
Tarnobrzeg **28** 50 35N 21 41 E
Tarnobrzeg □ **28** 50 40N 22 0 E
Tarnogród **28** 50 22N 22 45 E
Tarnów **27** 50 3N 21 0 E
Tarnów □ **27** 50 0N 21 0 E
Tarnowskie Góry **28** 50 27N 18 54 E
Táro → **38** 45 0N 10 15 E
Tarong **99** 26 47 S 151 51 E
Taroom **97** 25 36 S 149 48 E
Taroudannt **82** 30 30N 8 52W
Tarp **24** 54 40N 9 25 E

Tarpon Springs **115** 28 8N 82 42W
Tarquínia **39** 42 15N 11 45 E
Tarqūmiyah **62** 31 35N 35 1 E
Tarragona **32** 41 5N 1 17 E
Tarragona □ **32** 41 0N 1 0 E
Tarrasa **32** 41 34N 2 1 E
Tárrega **32** 41 39N 1 9 E
Tarrytown **113** 41 5N 73 52W
Tarshiha = Me'ona **62** 33 1N 35 15 E
Tarso Emissi **83** 21 27N 18 36 E
Tarso Ourari **83** 21 27N 17 27 E
Tarsus **64** 36 58N 34 55 E
Tartagal **124** 22 30 S 63 50W
Tartas **20** 43 50N 0 49W
Tartna Point **99** 32 54 S 142 24 E
Tartu **54** 58 20N 26 44 E
Tarţūs **64** 34 55N 35 55 E
Tarussa **55** 54 44N 37 10 E
Tarutao, Ko **71** 6 33N 99 40 E
Tarutung **72** 2 0N 98 54 E
Tarvisio **39** 46 31N 13 35 E
Tarz Ulli **83** 25 32N 10 8 E
Tasāwah **83** 26 0N 13 30 E
Taschereau **106** 48 40N 78 40W
Taseko → **108** 52 4N 123 9W
Tasgaon **70** 17 2N 74 39 E
Tash-Kumyr **58** 41 40N 72 10 E
Ta'shan **87** 16 31N 42 33 E
Tashauz **58** 41 49N 59 58 E
Tashi Chho Dzong = Thimphu **69** 27 31N 89 45 E
Tashkent **58** 41 20N 69 10 E
Tashtagol **58** 52 47N 87 53 E
Tasikmalaya **73** 7 18 S 108 12 E
Tåsjön **50** 64 15N 16 0 E
Taskan **59** 62 59N 150 20 E
Taskopru **56** 41 30N 34 15 E
Tasman B. **101** 40 59 S 173 25 E
Tasman Mts. **101** 41 3 S 172 25 E
Tasman Pen. **97** 43 10 S 148 0 E
Tasman Sea **94** 36 0 S 160 0 E
Tasmania □ **97** 42 0 S 146 30 E
Tăşnad **46** 47 30N 22 33 E
Tassil Tin-Rerhoh **82** 20 5N 3 55 E
Tassili n-Ajjer **83** 25 47N 8 1 E
Tassili-Oua-n-Ahaggar **83** 20 41N 5 30 E
Tasu Sd. **108** 52 47N 132 2W
Tata, Hung. **27** 47 37N 18 19 E
Tata, Moroc. **82** 29 46N 7 56W
Tatabánya **27** 47 32N 18 25 E
Tatahouine **83** 32 57N 10 29 E
Tatar A.S.S.R. □ **52** 55 30N 51 30 E
Tatarbunary **56** 45 50N 29 39 E
Tatarsk **58** 55 14N 76 0 E
* Tatarskiy Proliv **59** 54 0N 141 0 E
Tateyama **74** 35 0N 139 50 E
Tathlina L. **108** 60 33N 117 39W
Tathra **99** 36 44 S 149 59 E
Tatinnai L. **109** 60 55N 97 40W
Tatnam, C. **109** 57 16N 91 0W
Tatra = Tatry **27** 49 20N 20 0 E
Tatry **27** 49 20N 20 0 E
Tatta **68** 24 42N 67 55 E
Tatuī **125** 23 25 S 47 53W
Tatum **117** 33 16N 103 16W
Tat'ung = Datong **76** 40 6N 113 12 E
Tatura **100** 36 29 S 145 16 E
Tatvan **64** 38 31N 42 15 E
Taubaté **125** 23 0 S 45 36W
Tauberbischofsheim **25** 49 37N 9 40 E
Taucha **24** 51 22N 12 31 E
Tauern **26** 47 15N 12 40 E
Tauern-tunnel **26** 47 0N 13 12 E
Taufikia **87** 9 24N 31 37 E
Taumarunui **101** 38 53 S 175 15 E
Taumaturgo **126** 8 54 S 72 51W
Taung **92** 27 33 S 24 47 E
Taungdwingyi **67** 20 1N 95 40 E
Taunggyi **67** 20 50N 97 0 E
Taungup **67** 18 51N 94 14 E
Taungup Pass **67** 18 40N 94 45 E
Taunsa Barrage **68** 30 42N 70 50 E
Taunton, U.K. **13** 51 1N 3 7W
Taunton, U.S.A. **114** 41 54N 71 6W
Taunus **25** 50 15N 8 20 E
Taupo **101** 38 41 S 176 7 E
Taupo, L. **101** 38 46 S 175 55 E
Taurage **54** 55 14N 22 16 E
Tauranga **101** 37 42 S 176 11 E
Tauranga Harb. **101** 37 30 S 176 5 E
Taurianova **41** 38 22N 16 1 E
Taurus Mts. = Toros Dağlari **64** 37 0N 35 0 E
Tauste **32** 41 58N 1 18W
Tauz **57** 41 0N 45 40 E
Tavda **58** 58 7N 65 8 E
Tavda → **58** 59 20N 63 28 E
Taverny **19** 49 2N 2 13 E
Taveta **90** 3 23 S 37 37 E
Taveuni **101** 16 51 S 179 58W
Tavignano → **21** 42 7N 9 33 E
Tavira **31** 37 8N 7 40W
Tavistock, Can. **112** 43 19N 80 50W
Tavistock, U.K. **13** 50 33N 4 9W
Tavolara **40** 40 55N 9 40 E
Távora → **30** 41 8N 7 35W
Tavoy **71** 14 2N 98 12 E
Taw → **13** 17 37 S 177 55 E
Tawas City **114** 44 16N 83 31W
Tawau **72** 4 20N 117 55 E
Tawitawi **73** 5 10N 120 0 E
Tāwurgha' **83** 32 1N 15 2 E
Tay → **14** 56 37N 3 38W
Tay, Firth of **14** 56 25N 3 8W
Tay, L. **14** 56 30N 4 10W
Tay Ninh **71** 11 20N 106 5 E
Tayabamba **126** 8 15 S 77 16W
Taylakovy **58** 59 13N 74 0 E
Taylor, Can. **108** 56 13N 120 40W
Taylor, Ariz., U.S.A. **119** 34 28N 110 5W
Taylor, Nebr., U.S.A. **116** 41 46N 99 23W
Taylor, Pa., U.S.A. **113** 41 23N 75 43W
Taylor, Tex., U.S.A. **117** 30 30N 97 30W
Taylor Mt. **119** 35 16N 107 36W
Taylorville **116** 39 32N 89 20W
Taymā' **64** 27 35N 38 45 E
Taymyr, P-ov. **59** 75 0N 100 0 E
Tayport **14** 56 27N 2 52W
Ţayr Zibnā **62** 33 14N 35 23 E
Tayshet **59** 55 58N 98 1 E
Tayside □ **14** 56 25N 3 30W
Taytay **73** 10 45N 119 30 E
Taz → **58** 67 32N 78 40 E
Taza **82** 34 16N 4 6W
Tazenakht **82** 30 35N 7 12W
Tazin → **109** 60 26N 110 45W
Tazin L. **109** 59 44N 108 42W
Tazoult **83** 35 29N 6 11 E
Tazovskiy **58** 67 30N 78 44 E
Tbilisi (Tiflis) **57** 41 43N 44 50 E
Tchad (Chad) ■ **81** 12 30N 17 15 E
Tchad, L. **81** 13 30N 14 30 E
Tch'ang-k'ing = Changqing **75** 29 35N 106 35 E
Tchaourou **85** 8 58N 2 40 E
Tch'eng-tou = Chengdu **75** 30 38N 104 2 E
Tchentlo L. **108** 55 15N 125 0W
Tchibanga **88** 2 45 S 11 0 E
Tchin Tabaraden **85** 15 58N 5 56 E
Tczew **28** 54 8N 18 50 E
Te Anau, L. **101** 45 15 S 167 45 E
Te Aroha **101** 37 32 S 175 44 E
Te Awamutu **101** 38 1 S 175 20 E
Te Kuiti **101** 38 20 S 175 11 E
Te Puke **101** 37 46 S 176 22 E
Te Waewae B. **101** 46 13 S 167 33 E
Teaca **46** 46 55N 24 30 E
Teague **117** 31 40N 96 20W
Teano **41** 41 15N 14 1 E
Teapa **120** 18 35N 92 56W
Teba **31** 36 59N 4 55W
Tebakang **72** 1 6N 110 30 E
Teberda **57** 43 30N 41 46 E
Tébessa **83** 35 22N 8 8 E
Tebicuary → **124** 26 36 S 58 16W
Tebingtinggi, Bengkulu, Indon. **72** 3 38 S 103 9 E
Tebingtinggi, Sumatera Utara, Indon. **72** 3 20N 99 9 E
Tébourba **83** 36 49N 9 51 E
Téboursouk **83** 36 29N 9 10 E
Tebulos **57** 42 36N 45 17 E
Tech → **20** 42 36N 3 3 E
Techiman **84** 7 35N 1 58W
Techirghiol **46** 44 4N 28 32 E
Tecuala **120** 22 23N 105 27W
Tecuci **46** 45 51N 27 27 E
Tecumseh **114** 42 1N 83 59W
Tedzhen **58** 37 23N 60 31 E
Tees → **12** 54 36N 1 25W
Teesside **12** 54 37N 1 13W
Teeswater **112** 43 59N 81 17W
Tefé **126** 3 25 S 64 50W
Tegal **73** 6 52 S 109 8 E
Tegelen **16** 51 20N 6 9 E
Tegernsee **25** 47 43N 11 46 E
Teggiano **41** 40 24N 15 32 E
Teghra **69** 25 30N 85 34 E
Tegid, L. **12** 52 53N 3 38W
Tegina **85** 10 5N 6 11 E
Tegucigalpa **121** 14 5N 87 14W
Tehachapi **119** 35 11N 118 29W
Tehachapi Mts. **119** 35 0N 118 40W
Tehamiyam **86** 18 20N 36 32 E
Tehilla **86** 17 42N 36 6 E
Téhini **84** 9 39N 3 40W
Tehrān **65** 35 44N 51 30 E
Tehrān □ **65** 35 0N 49 30 E
Tehuacán **120** 18 30N 97 30W
Tehuantepec **120** 16 21N 95 13W
Tehuantepec, Golfo de **120** 15 50N 95 0W
Tehuantepec, Istmo de **120** 17 0N 94 30W
Teich, Le **20** 44 38N 0 59W
Teifi → **13** 52 4N 4 14W
Teign → **13** 50 41N 3 42W
Teignmouth **13** 50 33N 3 30W
Teil, Le **21** 44 33N 4 40 E
Teilleul, Le **18** 48 32N 0 53W
Teiuş **46** 46 12N 23 40 E
Teixeira Pinto **84** 12 3N 16 0W
Tejo → **31** 38 40N 9 24W
Tekamah **116** 41 48N 96 22W
Tekapo, L. **101** 43 53 S 170 33 E
Tekax **120** 20 11N 89 18W
Tekeli **58** 44 50N 79 0 E
Tekeze → **87** 14 20N 35 50 E
Tekija **42** 44 42N 22 26 E
Tekirdağ **64** 40 58N 27 30 E
Tekkali **70** 18 37N 84 15 E
Tekoa **118** 47 19N 117 4W
Tekouiât, O. → **82** 22 25N 2 35 E
Tel Adashim **62** 32 30N 35 17 E
Tel Aviv-Yafo **62** 32 4N 34 48 E
Tel Lakhish **62** 31 34N 34 51 E
Tel Megiddo **62** 32 35N 35 11 E
Tel Mond **62** 32 15N 34 56 E
Tela **120** 15 40N 87 28W
Télagh **82** 34 51N 0 32W
Telanaipura = Jambi **72** 1 38 S 103 37 E
Telavi **57** 42 0N 45 30 E
Telciu **46** 47 25N 24 24 E
Telegraph Cr. **108** 58 0N 131 10W
Telekhany **54** 52 30N 25 46 E
Telemark fylke □ **47** 59 25N 8 30 E
Telén **124** 36 15 S 65 31W
Teleneshty **46** 47 35N 28 24 E
Teleño **30** 42 23N 6 22W
Teleorman □ **46** 44 0N 25 0 E
Teleorman → **46** 44 15N 25 20 E
Teles Pires → **126** 7 21 S 58 3W
Telescope Peak **119** 36 6N 117 7W
Teletaye **85** 16 31N 1 30 E
Telford **12** 52 42N 2 31W
Telfs **26** 47 19N 11 4 E
Telgte **24** 51 59N 7 46 E
Télimélé **84** 10 54N 13 2W
Telkwa **108** 54 41N 127 5W
Tell City **114** 38 0N 86 44W
Tellicherry **70** 11 45N 75 30 E
Telluride **119** 37 58N 107 48W
Telok Anson **71** 4 3N 101 0 E
Telom → **71** 4 20N 101 46 E
Telpos Iz **52** 63 35N 57 30 E
Telsen **128** 42 30 S 66 50W
Telšiai **54** 55 59N 22 14 E
Teltow **24** 52 24N 13 15 E
Telukbetung **72** 5 29 S 105 17 E
Telukbutun **72** 4 13N 108 12 E
Telukdalem **72** 0 33N 97 50 E
Tema **85** 5 41N 0 0 E
Temanggung **73** 7 18 S 110 10 E
Temax **120** 21 10N 88 50W
Tembe **90** 0 16 S 28 14 E
Tembeling → **71** 4 20N 102 23 E
Tembleque **32** 39 41N 3 30W
Tembuland **93** 31 35 S 28 0 E
Teme → **13** 52 23N 2 15W
Temecula **119** 33 26N 117 6W
Temerloh **71** 3 27N 102 25 E
Temir **58** 49 21N 57 3 E
Temirtau, Kazakh, U.S.S.R. **58** 50 5N 72 56 E
Temirtau, R.S.F.S.R., U.S.S.R. **58** 53 10N 87 30 E
Témiscaming **106** 46 44N 79 5W
Temma **99** 41 12 S 144 48 E
Temnikov **55** 54 40N 43 11 E
Temo → **40** 40 20N 8 30 E
Temora **99** 34 30 S 147 30 E
Temosachic **120** 28 58N 107 50W
Tempe **119** 33 26N 111 59W
Tempino **72** 1 42 S 103 30 E
Témpio Pausania **40** 40 53N 9 6 E
Temple **117** 31 5N 97 22W
Temple B. **97** 12 15 S 143 3 E
Templemore **15** 52 48N 7 50W
Templeton → **98** 21 0 S 138 40 E
Templin **24** 53 8N 13 31 E
Temryuk **56** 45 15N 37 24 E
Temska → **42** 43 17N 22 33 E
Temuco **128** 38 45 S 72 40W
Temuka **101** 44 14 S 171 17 E
Tenabo **120** 20 2N 90 12W
Tenaha **117** 31 57N 94 25W
Tenali **70** 16 15N 80 35 E
Tenancingo **120** 19 0N 99 33W
Tenango **120** 19 7N 99 33W
Tenasserim **71** 12 6N 99 3 E
Tenasserim □ **71** 14 0N 98 30 E
Tenay **21** 45 55N 5 30 E
Tenby **13** 51 40N 4 42W
Tendaho **87** 11 48N 40 54 E
Tende **21** 44 5N 7 35 E
Tende, Col de **21** 44 9N 7 32 E
Tendelti **87** 13 1N 31 55 E
Tendjedi, Adrar **83** 23 41N 7 32 E
Tendrara **82** 33 3N 1 58W
Teneida **86** 25 30N 29 19 E
Ténéré **85** 19 0N 10 30 E
Tenerife **80** 28 15N 16 35W
Ténès **82** 36 31N 1 14 E
Teng → **71** 20 30N 98 10 E
Teng Xian, Guangxi Zhuangzu, China **77** 23 21N 110 56 E
Teng Xian, Shandong, China **77** 35 5N 117 10 E
Tengah □ **73** 2 0 S 122 0 E
Tengah Kepulauan **72** 7 5 S 118 15 E
Tengchong **75** 25 0N 98 28 E
Tenggara □ **73** 3 0 S 122 0 E
Tenggarong **72** 0 24 S 116 58 E
Tengiz, Ozero **58** 50 30N 69 0 E
Tenille **115** 32 58N 82 50W
Tenkasi **70** 8 55N 77 20 E
Tenke, Congo **91** 11 22 S 26 40 E
Tenke, Zaïre **91** 10 32 S 26 7 E
Tenkodogo **85** 11 54N 0 19W
Tenna → **39** 43 12N 13 47 E
Tennant Creek **96** 19 30 S 134 15 E
Tennessee □ **111** 36 0N 86 30W
Tennessee → **114** 34 30N 86 20W
Tennsift, Oued → **82** 32 3N 9 28W
Tenom **72** 5 4N 115 57 E
Tenosique **120** 17 30N 91 24W
Tenryū-Gawa → **74** 35 39N 137 48 E
Tent L. **109** 62 25N 107 54W
Tenterfield **97** 29 0 S 152 0 E
Teófilo Otoni **127** 17 50 S 41 30W
Teotihuacán **120** 19 44N 98 50W
Tepa **73** 7 52 S 129 31 E
Tepalcatepec → **120** 18 35N 101 59W
Tepelena **44** 40 17N 20 2 E
Tepic **120** 21 30N 104 54W
Teplice **26** 50 40N 13 48 E
Tepoca, C. **120** 30 20N 112 25W
Tequila **120** 20 54N 103 47W
Ter → **32** 42 0N 3 12 E
Ter Apel **16** 52 53N 7 5 E
Téra **85** 14 0N 0 45 E
Tera → **30** 41 54N 5 44W
Téramo **39** 42 40N 13 40 E
Terang **99** 38 15 S 142 55 E
Terazit, Massif de **83** 20 2N 8 30 E
Terceira **8** 38 43N 27 13W
Tercero → **124** 32 58 S 61 47W
Terdal **70** 16 33N 75 3 E
Terebovlya **54** 49 18N 25 44 E
Teregova **46** 45 10N 22 16 E
Terek →, U.S.S.R. **56** 43 55N 47 30 E
Terek →, U.S.S.R. **57** 44 0N 47 30 E
Terembone Cr. → **99** 30 25 S 148 50 E
Terengganu □ **71** 4 55N 103 0 E
Tereshka → **55** 51 48N 46 26 E
Teresina **127** 5 9 S 42 45W
Terespol **28** 52 5N 23 37 E
Terewah L. **99** 29 52 S 147 35 E
Terges → **31** 37 49N 7 41W
Tergnier **19** 49 40N 3 17 E
Terhazza **82** 23 38N 5 22W
Terlizzi **41** 41 8N 16 32 E
Terme **56** 41 11N 37 0 E
Termez **58** 37 15N 67 15 E
Términi Imerese **40** 37 58N 13 42 E
Términos, Laguna de **120** 18 35N 91 30W
Térmoli **39** 42 0N 15 0 E
Ternate **73** 0 45N 127 25 E
Terneuzen **16** 51 20N 3 50 E
Terney **59** 45 3N 136 37 E
Terni **39** 42 34N 12 38 E
Ternitz **26** 47 43N 16 2 E
Ternopol **54** 49 30N 25 40 E
Terra Nova B. **5** 74 50 S 164 40 E
Terrace **108** 54 30N 128 35W
Terrace Bay **106** 48 47N 87 5W
Terracina **40** 41 17N 13 12 E
Terralba **40** 39 42N 8 38 E
Terranuova Bracciolini **39** 43 31N 11 35 E
Terrasini Favarotta **40** 38 10N 13 4 E
Terrasson **20** 45 7N 1 19 E
Terre Haute **114** 39 28N 87 24W
Terrebonne B. **117** 29 15N 90 28W
Terrecht **82** 20 10N 0 10W
Terrell **117** 32 44N 96 19W
Terrenceville **107** 47 40N 54 44W
Terrick Terrick **98** 24 44 S 145 5 E
Terry **116** 46 47N 105 20W
Terschelling **16** 53 25N 5 20 E
Terter → **57** 40 35N 47 22 E
Teruel **32** 40 22N 1 8W
Teruel □ **32** 40 48N 1 0W
Tervel **43** 43 45N 27 28 E
Tervola **50** 66 6N 24 49 E
Teryaweyna L. **99** 32 18 S 143 22 E
Tešanj **42** 44 38N 17 59 E
Teseney **87** 15 5N 36 42 E
Tesha → **55** 55 38N 42 9 E
Teshio-Gawa → **74** 44 53N 141 45 E
Tešica **42** 43 27N 21 45 E
Tesiyn Gol → **75** 50 40N 93 20 E
Teslić **42** 44 37N 17 54 E
Teslin **104** 60 10N 132 43W
Teslin → **108** 61 34N 134 35W
Teslin L. **108** 60 15N 132 57W
Tessalit **85** 20 12N 1 0 E
Tessaoua **85** 13 47N 7 56 E
Tessin **24** 54 2N 12 28 E
Tessit **85** 15 13N 0 18 E
Test → **13** 51 7N 1 30W
Testa del Gargano **41** 41 50N 16 10 E
Teste, La **20** 44 37N 1 8W
Tét **27** 47 30N 17 33 E
Têt → **20** 42 44N 3 2 E
Tetachuck L. **108** 53 18N 125 55W
Tetas, Pta. **124** 23 31 S 70 38W
Tete **91** 16 13 S 33 33 E
Tete □ **91** 15 15 S 32 40 E
Teterev → **54** 51 1N 30 5 E
Teterow **24** 53 45N 12 34 E
Teteven **43** 42 58N 24 17 E
Tethul → **108** 60 35N 112 12W
Tetiyev **56** 49 22N 29 38 E
Teton → **118** 47 58N 111 0W
Tétouan **82** 35 35N 5 21W
Tetovo **42** 42 1N 21 2 E
Tetuán = Tétouan **82** 35 30N 5 25W
Tetyushi **55** 54 55N 48 49 E
Teuco → **124** 25 35 S 60 11W
Teulada **40** 38 59N 8 47 E
Teulon **109** 50 23N 97 16W
Teun **73** 6 59 S 129 8 E
Teutoburger Wald **22** 52 5N 8 20 E
Tevere → **39** 41 44N 12 14 E
Teverya **62** 32 47N 35 32 E
Teviot → **14** 55 21N 2 51W
Tewantin **99** 26 27 S 153 3 E
Tewkesbury **13** 51 59N 2 8W
Texada I. **108** 49 40N 124 25W
Texarkana, Ark., U.S.A. **117** 33 25N 94 0W
Texarkana, Tex., U.S.A. **117** 33 25N 94 3W
Texas **99** 28 49 S 151 9 E
Texas □ **117** 31 40N 98 30W
Texas City **117** 29 20N 94 55W
Texel **16** 53 5N 4 50 E
Texhoma **117** 36 32N 101 47W
Texline **117** 36 26N 103 0W
Texoma L. **117** 34 0N 96 38W
Teykovo **55** 56 55N 40 30 E
Teyvareh **65** 33 30N 64 24 E
Teza → **55** 56 32N 41 53 E
Teziutlán **120** 19 50N 97 22W
Tezpur **67** 26 40N 92 45 E
Tezzeron L. **108** 54 43N 124 30W
Tha-anne → **109** 60 31N 94 37W
Tha Nun **71** 8 12N 98 17 E
Thaba Putsoa **93** 29 45 S 28 0 E
Thabana Ntlenyana **93** 29 30 S 29 16 E
Thabazimbi **93** 24 40 S 27 21 E
Thabor, Mt. **21** 45 7N 6 34 E
Thai Nguyen **71** 21 35N 105 55 E
Thailand (Siam) ■ **71** 16 0N 102 0 E
Thakhek **71** 17 25N 104 45 E
Thal **66** 33 28N 70 33 E
Thal Desert **68** 31 10N 71 30 E
Thala **83** 35 35N 8 40 E
Thala La **67** 28 25N 97 23 E
Thallon **99** 28 39 S 148 49 E
Thalwil **25** 47 17N 8 35 E
Thame → **13** 51 35N 1 8W
Thames **101** 37 7 S 175 34 E
Thames →, Can. **106** 42 20N 82 25W
Thames →, U.K. **13** 51 30N 0 35 E
Thames →, U.S.A. **113** 41 18N 72 9W
Thamesford **112** 43 4N 81 0W
Thamesville **112** 42 33N 81 59W
Thāmit, W. **83** 30 51N 16 14 E
Thana **70** 19 12N 72 59 E
Thanesar **68** 30 1N 76 52 E
Thanet, I. of **13** 51 21N 1 20 E
Thang Binh **71** 15 50N 108 20 E
Thangool **98** 24 38 S 150 42 E
Thanh Hoa **71** 19 48N 105 46 E
Thanjavur (Tanjore) **70** 10 48N 79 12 E
Thanlwin Myit → **67** 20 0N 98 0 E
Thann **19** 47 48N 7 5 E
Thaon **19** 48 15N 6 25 E

* *Renamed Sakhalinskiy Zaliv*

Thar (Great Indian) Desert 68 28 0N 72 0 E
Tharad 68 24 30N 71 44 E
Thargomindah 97 27 58 S 143 46 E
Tharrawaddy 67 17 38N 95 48 E
Thasopoúla 44 40 49N 24 45 E
Thásos, Greece 44 40 50N 24 42 E
Thásos, Greece 44 40 40N 24 40 E
Thatcher, Ariz., U.S.A. 119 32 54N 109 46W
Thatcher, Colo., U.S.A. 117 37 38N 104 6W
Thaton 67 16 55N 97 22 E
Thau, Étang de 20 43 23N 3 36 E
Thaungdut 67 24 30N 94 40 E
Thayer 117 36 34N 91 34W
Thayetmyo 67 19 20N 95 10 E
Thazi 67 21 0N 96 5 E
The Bight 121 24 19N 75 24W
The Dalles 118 45 40N 121 11W
The English Company's Is. 97 11 50 S 136 32 E
The Flatts 121 32 16N 64 45W
The Frome → 99 29 8 S 137 54 E
The Granites 96 20 35 S 130 21 E
The Grenadines, Is. 121 12 40N 61 20W
The Hague = s'-Gravenhage 16 52 7N 4 14 E
The Hamilton → 96 26 40 S 135 19 E
The Johnston Lakes 96 32 25 S 120 30 E
The Macumba → 97 27 52 S 137 12 E
The Pas 109 53 45N 101 15W
The Range 91 19 2 S 31 2 E
The Rock 99 35 15 S 147 2 E
The Salt Lake 99 30 6 S 142 8 E
The Warburton → 99 28 4 S 137 28 E
Thebes 86 25 40N 32 35 E
Thebes = Thivai 45 38 19N 23 19 E
Thedford, Can. 112 43 9N 81 51W
Thedford, U.S.A. 116 41 59N 100 31W
Theebine 99 25 57 S 152 34 E
Theil, Le 18 48 16N 0 42 E
Thekulthili L. 109 61 3N 110 0W
Thelon → 109 62 35N 104 3W
Thénezay 18 46 44N 0 2W
Thenia 83 36 44N 3 33 E
Thenon 20 45 9N 1 4 E
Theodore 97 24 55 S 150 3 E
Thérain → 19 49 15N 2 27 E
Theresa 113 44 13N 75 50W
Thermaïkos Kólpos 44 40 15N 22 45 E
Thermopolis 118 43 35N 108 10W
Thermopylae P. 45 38 48N 22 35 E
Thesprotia □ 44 39 27N 20 22 E
Thessalía □ 44 39 30N 22 0 E
Thessalon 106 46 20N 83 30W
Thessaloníki 44 40 38N 22 58 E
Thessaloníki □ 44 40 45N 23 0 E
Thessaly = Thessalía 44 39 30N 22 0 E
Thetford 13 52 25N 0 44 E
Thetford Mines 107 46 8N 71 18W
Theunissen 92 28 26 S 26 43 E
Thiámis → 44 39 15N 20 6 E
Thiberville 18 49 8N 0 27 E
Thibodaux 117 29 48N 90 49W
Thicket Portage 109 55 19N 97 42W
Thief River Falls 116 48 15N 96 48W
Thiel Mts. 5 85 15 S 91 0W
Thiene 39 45 42N 11 29 E
Thiérache 19 49 51N 3 45 E
Thiers 20 45 52N 3 33 E
Thies 84 14 50N 16 51W
Thiet 87 7 37N 28 49 E
Thika 90 1 1 S 37 5 E
Thikombia 101 15 44 S 179 55W
Thille-Boubacar 84 16 31N 15 5W
Thillot, Le 19 47 53N 6 46 E
Thimphu (Tashi Chho Dzong) 69 27 31N 89 45 E
Þingvallavatn 50 64 11N 21 9W
Thionville 19 49 20N 6 10 E
Thíra 45 36 23N 25 27 E
Thirasía 45 36 26N 25 21 E
Thirsk 12 54 15N 1 20W
Thistle I. 96 35 0 S 136 8 E
Thivai 45 38 19N 23 19 E
Thiviers 20 45 25N 0 54 E
Thizy 21 46 2N 4 18 E
Þjórsá → 50 63 47N 20 48W
Thlewiaza →, Man., Can. 109 59 43N 100 5W
Thlewiaza →, N.W.T., Can. 109 60 29N 94 40W
Thoa → 109 60 31N 109 47W
Thoissey 21 46 12N 4 48 E
Thomas, Okla., U.S.A. 117 35 48N 98 48W
Thomas, W. Va., U.S.A. 114 39 10N 79 30W
Thomas, L. 99 26 4 S 137 58 E
Thomaston 115 32 54N 84 20W
Thomasville, Ala., U.S.A. 115 31 55N 87 42W
Thomasville, Ga., U.S.A. 115 30 50N 84 0W
Thomasville, N.C., U.S.A. 115 35 55N 80 4W
Thompson 109 55 45N 97 52W
Thompson →, Can. 108 50 15N 121 24W
Thompson →, U.S.A. 116 39 46N 93 37W
Thompson Falls 118 47 37N 115 20W
Thompson Landing 109 62 56N 110 40W
Thompson Pk. 118 41 0N 123 3W
Thompsons 119 39 0N 109 50W
Thompsonville 113 42 0N 72 37W
Thomson → 97 25 11 S 142 53 E
Thomson's Falls = Nyahururu 90 0 2N 36 27 E
Thon Buri 71 13 43N 100 29 E
Thônes 21 45 54N 6 18 E
Thonon-les-Bains 21 46 22N 6 29 E
Thorez 57 48 4N 38 34 E
Þórisvatn 50 64 20N 18 55W
Þorlákshöfn 50 63 51N 21 22W
Thornaby on Tees 12 54 36N 1 19W
Thornbury 112 44 34N 80 26W
Thorne Glacier 5 87 30 S 150 0W
Thorold 112 43 7N 79 12W
Þórshöfn 50 66 12N 15 20W
Thouarcé 18 47 17N 0 30W
Thouars 18 46 58N 0 15W
Thrace = Thráki □ 44 41 10N 25 30 E
Thráki □ 44 41 9N 25 30 E
Thrakikón Pélagos 44 40 30N 25 0 E
Three Forks 118 45 55N 111 32W
Three Hills 108 51 43N 113 15W
Three Hummock I. 99 40 25 S 144 55 E
Three Lakes 116 45 48N 89 10W
Three Points, C. 84 4 42N 2 6W
Three Rivers 117 28 30N 98 10W
Three Sisters, Mt. 118 44 10N 121 46W
Throssell Ra. 96 22 3 S 121 43 E
Thrun Pass 26 47 20N 12 25 E
Thubun Lakes 109 61 30N 112 0W
Thuddungra 100 34 8 S 148 8 E
Thueyts 21 44 41N 4 9 E
Thuin 16 50 20N 4 17 E
Thuir 20 42 38N 2 45 E
Thule, Antarct. 5 59 27 S 27 19W
Thule, Greenl. 4 77 40N 69 0W
Thun 25 46 45N 7 38 E
Thunder B. 114 45 0N 83 20W
Thunder Bay 106 48 20N 89 15W
Thunersee 25 46 43N 7 39 E
Thung Song 71 8 10N 99 40 E
Thunkar 69 27 55N 91 0 E
Thur → 25 47 32N 9 10 E
Thurgau □ 25 47 34N 9 10 E
Thüringer Wald 24 50 35N 11 0 E
Thurles 15 52 40N 7 53W
Thurloo Downs 99 29 15 S 143 30 E
Thurn P. 25 47 20N 12 25 E
Thursday I. 97 10 30 S 142 3 E
Thurso, Can. 106 45 36N 75 15W
Thurso, U.K. 14 58 34N 3 31W
Thurston I. 5 72 0 S 100 0W
Thury-Harcourt 18 49 0N 0 30W
Thutade L. 108 57 0N 126 55W
Thyborøn 49 56 42N 8 12 E
Thylungra 99 26 4 S 143 28 E
Thyolo 91 16 7 S 35 5 E
Thysville = Mbanza Ngungu 88 5 12 S 14 53 E
Ti-n-Barraouene, O. → 85 18 40N 4 5 E
Ti-n-Medjerdam, O. → 82 25 45N 1 30 E
Ti-n-Tarabine, O. → 83 21 0N 7 25 E
Ti-n-Zaouatène 82 20 0N 2 55 E
Tia 99 31 10 S 150 34 E
Tian Shan 75 43 0N 84 0 E
Tiandu 77 18 18N 109 36 E
Tian'e 77 25 1N 107 9 E
Tianhe 77 24 48N 108 40 E
Tianjin 76 39 8N 117 10 E
Tiankoura 84 10 47N 3 17W
Tianshui 77 34 32N 105 40 E
Tianyang 77 23 42N 106 53 E
Tianzhen 76 40 24N 114 5 E
Tiaret 82 35 20N 1 21 E
Tiassalé 84 5 58N 4 57W
Tibagi 125 24 30 S 50 24W
Tibagi → 125 22 47 S 51 1W
Tibati 85 6 22N 12 30 E
Tiber = Tevere → 39 41 44N 12 14 E
Tiber Res. 118 48 20N 111 15W
Tiberias, L. = Kinneret, Yam 62 32 45N 35 35 E
Tibesti 83 21 0N 17 30 E
Tibet = Xizang □ 75 32 0N 88 0 E
Tibiri 85 13 34N 7 4 E
Ţibleş 46 47 32N 24 15 E
Tibnīn 62 33 12N 35 24 E
Tibooburra 97 29 26 S 142 1 E
Tibro 49 58 28N 14 10 E
Tiburón 120 29 0N 112 30W
Tīchīt 84 18 21N 9 29W
Ticho 87 7 50N 39 32 E
Ticino □ 25 46 20N 8 45 E
Ticino → 38 45 9N 9 14 E
Ticonderoga 114 43 50N 73 28W
Ticul 120 20 20N 89 31W
Tidaholm 49 58 12N 13 55 E
Tiddim 67 23 28N 93 45 E
Tideridjaouine, Adrar 82 23 0N 2 15 E
Tidikelt 82 26 58N 1 30 E
Tidjikja 84 18 29N 11 35W
Tidore 73 0 40N 127 25 E
Tiébissou 84 7 9N 5 10W
Tiéboro 83 21 20N 17 7 E
Tiel, Neth. 16 51 53N 5 26 E
Tiel, Senegal 84 14 55N 15 5W
Tieling 76 42 20N 123 55 E
Tielt 16 51 0N 3 20 E
Tien Shan = Tian Shan 65 42 0N 80 0 E
Tien-tsin = Tianjin 75 39 8N 117 10 E
T'ienching = Tianjin 76 39 8N 117 10 E
Tienen 16 50 48N 4 57 E
Tiénigbé 84 8 11N 5 43W
Tientsin = Tianjin 76 39 8N 117 10 E
Tierp 48 60 20N 17 30 E
Tierra Amarilla, Chile 124 27 28 S 70 18W
Tierra Amarilla, U.S.A. 119 36 42N 106 33W
Tierra de Barros 31 38 40N 6 30W
Tierra de Campos 30 42 10N 4 50W
Tierra del Fuego, I. Gr. de 128 54 0 S 69 0W
Tiétar → 30 39 50N 6 1W
Tieté → 125 20 40 S 51 35W
Tifarit 82 26 9N 10 33W
Tiffin 114 41 8N 83 10W
Tiflèt 82 33 54N 6 20W
Tiflis = Tbilisi 57 41 43N 44 50 E
Tifrah 62 31 19N 34 42 E
Tifton 115 31 28N 83 32W
Tifu 73 3 39 S 126 24 E
Tigil 59 57 49N 158 40 E
Tignish 107 46 58N 64 2W
Tigre □ 87 13 35N 39 15 E
Tigre → 126 4 30 S 74 10W
Tigris = Dijlah, Nahr → 64 31 0N 47 25 E
Tiguentourine 83 27 52N 9 8 E
Tigveni 46 45 10N 24 31 E
Tigyaing 67 23 45N 96 10 E
Tigzerte, O. → 82 28 10N 9 37W
Tîh, Gebel el 86 29 32N 33 26 E
Tihama 64 22 0N 39 0 E
Tihodaine, Dunes de 83 25 15N 7 15 E
Tijesno 39 43 48N 15 39 E
Tījī 83 32 0N 11 18 E
Tijuana 120 32 30N 117 10W
Tikal 120 17 13N 89 24W
Tikamgarh 68 24 44N 78 50 E
Tikhoretsk 57 45 56N 40 5 E
Tikhvin 54 59 35N 33 30 E
Tikkadouine, Adrar 82 24 28N 1 30 E
Tiko 85 4 4N 9 20 E
Tikrīt 64 34 35N 43 37 E
Tiksi 59 71 40N 128 45 E
Tilamuta 73 0 32N 122 23 E
Tilburg 16 51 31N 5 6 E
Tilbury, Can. 106 42 17N 82 23W
Tilbury, U.K. 13 51 27N 0 24 E
Tilcara 124 23 36 S 65 23W
Tilden, Nebr., U.S.A. 116 42 3N 97 45W
Tilden, Tex., U.S.A. 117 28 28N 98 33W
Tilemses 85 15 37N 4 44 E
Tilemsi, Vallée du 85 17 42N 0 15 E
Tilhar 69 28 0N 79 45 E
Tilia, O. → 82 27 32N 0 55 E
Tilichiki 59 60 27N 166 5 E
Tiligul → 56 47 4N 30 57 E
Tililane 82 27 49N 0 6W
Tilissos 45 35 2N 25 0 E
Till → 12 55 35N 2 3W
Tillabéri 85 14 28N 1 28 E
Tillamook 118 45 29N 123 55W
Tillberga 48 59 52N 16 39 E
Tillia 85 16 8N 4 47 E
Tillsonburg 106 42 53N 80 44W
Tilos 45 36 27N 27 27 E
Tilpa 99 30 57 S 144 24 E
Tilrhemt 82 33 9N 3 22 E
Tilsit = Sovetsk 54 55 6N 21 50 E
Tilt → 14 56 50N 3 50W
Tilton 113 43 25N 71 36W
Timagami L. 106 47 0N 80 10W
Timanskiy Kryazh 52 65 58N 50 5 E
Timaru 101 44 23 S 171 14 E
Timashevsk 57 45 35N 39 0 E
Timau, Italy 39 46 35N 13 0 E
Timau, Kenya 90 0 4N 37 15 E
Timbákion 45 35 4N 24 45 E
Timbedgha 84 16 17N 8 16W
Timber Lake 116 45 29N 101 6W
Timboon 99 38 30 S 142 58 E
Timbuktu = Tombouctou 84 16 50N 3 0W
Timdjaouine 82 21 37N 4 30 E
Timellouline 83 29 22N 8 55 E
Timétrine Montagnes 85 19 25N 1 0W
Timfi Óros 44 39 59N 20 45 E
Timfristós, Óros 45 38 57N 21 50 E
Timhadit 82 33 15N 5 4W
Tîmia 85 18 4N 8 40 E
Timimoun 82 29 14N 0 16 E
Timimoun, Sebkha de 82 28 50N 0 46 E
Timiş □ 42 45 40N 21 30 E
Timiş → 46 45 30N 21 0 E
Timişoara 42 45 43N 21 15 E
Timmins 106 48 28N 81 25W
Timok → 42 44 10N 22 40 E
Timon 127 5 8 S 42 52W
Timor 73 9 0 S 125 0 E
Timor □ 73 9 0 S 125 0 E
Timor Sea 97 10 0 S 127 0 E
Tin Alkoum 83 24 42N 10 17 E
Tin Gornai 85 16 38N 0 38W
Tin Gornaï 85 20 30N 4 35 E
Tîna, Khalîg el 86 31 20N 32 42 E
Tinaca Pt. 73 5 30N 125 25 E
Tinafak, O. → 83 27 10N 7 0 E
Tinca 46 46 46N 21 58 E
Tinchebray 18 48 47N 0 45W
Tindivanam 70 12 15N 79 41 E
Tindouf 82 27 42N 8 10W
Tinee → 21 43 55N 7 11 E
Tineo 30 43 21N 6 27W
Tinerhir 82 31 29N 5 31W
Tinfouchi 82 28 52N 5 49W
Tinglev 49 54 57N 9 13 E
Tingo Maria 126 9 10 S 75 54W
Tingsryd 49 56 31N 15 0 E
Tinjoub 82 29 45N 5 40W
Tinnoset 47 59 55N 9 3 E
Tinnsjø 47 59 55N 8 54 E
Tinogasta 124 28 5 S 67 32W
Tínos 45 37 33N 25 8 E
Tiñoso, C. 33 37 32N 1 6W
Tintina 124 27 2 S 62 45W
Tintinara 99 35 48 S 140 2 E
Tinto → 31 37 12N 6 55W
Tioga 112 41 54N 77 9W
Tioman, Pulau 71 2 50N 104 10 E
Tione di Trento 38 46 3N 10 44 E
Tionesta 112 41 29N 79 28W
Tior 87 6 26N 31 11 E
Tioulilin 82 27 1N 0 2W
Tipongpani 67 27 20N 95 55 E
Tipperary 15 52 28N 8 10W
Tipperary □ 15 52 37N 7 55W
Tipton, U.K. 13 52 32N 2 4W
Tipton, Calif., U.S.A. 119 36 3N 119 19W
Tipton, Ind., U.S.A. 114 40 17N 86 0W
Tipton, Iowa, U.S.A. 116 41 45N 91 12W
Tiptonville 117 36 22N 89 30W
Tiptur 70 13 15N 76 26 E
Tirahart, O. 82 23 45N 3 10 E
Tīrān 65 32 45N 51 8 E
Tīrān 86 27 56N 34 35 E
Tirana 44 41 18N 19 49 E
Tirana-Durrësi □ 44 41 35N 20 0 E
Tirano 38 46 13N 10 11 E
Tiraspol 56 46 55N 29 35 E
Tirat Karmel 62 32 46N 34 58 E
Tirat Yehuda 62 32 1N 34 56 E
Tirat Zevi 62 32 26N 35 31 E
Tiratimine 82 25 56N 3 37 E
Tirdout 85 16 7N 1 5W
Tire 64 38 5N 27 50 E
Tirebolu 64 40 58N 38 45 E
Tiree 14 56 31N 6 55W
Tîrgovişte 46 44 55N 25 27 E
Tîrgu Frumos 46 47 12N 27 2 E
Tîrgu-Jiu 46 45 5N 23 19 E
Tîrgu Mureş 46 46 31N 24 38 E
Tîrgu Neamţ 46 47 12N 26 25 E
Tîrgu Ocna 46 46 16N 26 39 E
Tîrgu Secuiesc 46 46 0N 26 10 E
Tirich Mir 66 36 15N 71 55 E
Tiriola 41 38 57N 16 32 E
Tirna → 70 18 4N 76 57 E
Tîrnava Mare → 46 46 15N 24 30 E
Tîrnava Mică → 46 46 17N 24 30 E
Tîrnăveni 46 46 19N 24 13 E
Tírnavos 44 39 45N 22 18 E
Tirnova 46 45 23N 22 1 E
Tirodi 69 21 40N 79 44 E
Tirol □ 26 47 3N 10 43 E
Tirschenreuth 25 49 51N 12 20 E
Tirso → 40 39 52N 8 33 E
Tirso, L. del 40 40 8N 8 56 E
Tiruchchirappalli 70 10 45N 78 45 E
Tiruchendur 70 8 30N 78 11 E
Tiruchengodu 70 11 23N 77 56 E
Tirumangalam 70 9 49N 77 58 E
Tirunelveli (Tinnevelly) 70 8 45N 77 45 E
Tirupati 70 13 39N 79 25 E
Tiruppattur 70 12 30N 78 30 E
Tiruppur 70 11 5N 77 22 E
Tiruturaipundi 70 10 32N 79 41 E
Tiruvadaimarudur 70 11 2N 79 27 E
Tiruvallar 70 13 9N 79 57 E
Tiruvannamalai 70 12 15N 79 5 E
Tiruvarur 70 10 46N 79 38 E
Tiruvatipuram 70 12 39N 79 33 E
Tiruvottiyur 70 13 10N 80 22 E
Tisa → 42 45 15N 20 17 E
Tisdale 109 52 50N 104 0W
Tishomingo 117 34 14N 96 38W
Tisjön 48 60 56N 13 0 E
Tisnaren 48 58 58N 15 56 E
Tišnov 27 49 21N 16 25 E
Tisovec 27 48 41N 19 56 E
Tissemsilt 82 35 35N 1 50 E
Tissint 82 29 57N 7 16W
Tissø 49 55 35N 11 18 E
Tista → 69 25 23N 89 43 E
Tisza → 27 46 8N 20 2 E
Tiszaföldvár 27 47 0N 20 14 E
Tiszafüred 27 47 38N 20 50 E
Tiszalök 27 48 0N 21 10 E
Tiszavasvári 27 47 58N 21 18 E
Tit, Ahaggar, Alg. 83 23 0N 5 10 E
Tit, Tademait, Alg. 82 27 0N 1 29 E
Tit-Ary 59 71 55N 127 2 E
Titaguas 32 39 53N 1 6W
Titel 42 45 10N 20 18 E
Titicaca, L. 126 15 30 S 69 30W
Titilagarh 70 20 15N 83 11 E
Titiwa 85 12 14N 12 53 E
Titograd 42 42 30N 19 19 E
Titov Veles 42 41 46N 21 47 E
Titova Korenica 39 44 45N 15 41 E
Titovo Užice 42 43 55N 19 50 E
Titule 90 3 15N 25 31 E
Titusville, Fla., U.S.A. 115 28 37N 80 49W
Titusville, Pa., U.S.A. 114 41 35N 79 39W
Tivaouane 84 14 56N 16 45W
Tivat 42 42 28N 18 43 E
Tiveden 49 58 50N 14 30 E
Tiverton 13 50 54N 3 30W
Tivoli 39 41 58N 12 45 E
Tiwī 65 22 45N 59 12 E
Tiyo 87 14 41N 40 15 E
Tizga 82 32 1N 5 9W
Ti'zi N'Isli 82 32 28N 5 47W
Tizi-Ouzou 83 36 42N 4 3 E
Tizimín 120 21 0N 88 1W
Tiznit 82 29 48N 9 45W
Tjeggelvas 50 66 37N 17 45 E
Tjirebon = Cirebon 73 6 45 S 108 32 E
Tjöme 47 59 8N 10 26 E
Tjörn 49 58 0N 11 35 E
Tkibuli 57 42 26N 43 0 E
Tkvarcheli 57 42 47N 41 42 E
Tlahualilo 120 26 20N 103 30W
Tlaxcala 120 19 20N 98 14W
Tlaxcala □ 120 19 30N 98 20W
Tlaxiaco 120 17 18N 97 40W
Tlell 108 53 34N 131 56W
Tlemcen 82 34 52N 1 21W
Tleta Sidi Bouguedra 82 32 16N 9 59W
Tlumach, U.S.S.R. 54 48 46N 25 0 E
Tlumach, U.S.S.R. 56 48 51N 25 0 E
Tłuszcz 28 52 25N 21 25 E
Tlyarata 57 42 9N 46 26 E
Tmassah 83 26 19N 15 51 E
Tnine d'Anglou 82 29 50N 9 50W
Toad → 108 59 25N 124 57W
Toala 73 1 30 S 121 40 E
Toamasina 93 18 10 S 49 25 E
Toamasina □ 93 18 0 S 49 0 E
Toay 124 36 43 S 64 38W
Toba 74 34 30N 136 51 E
Toba, Danau 72 2 40N 98 50 E
Toba Kakar 68 31 30N 69 0 E
Toba Tek Singh 68 30 55N 72 25 E
Tobago 121 11 10N 60 30W
Tobarra 33 38 37N 1 44W
Tobelo 73 1 45N 127 56 E
Tobermorey 98 22 12 S 137 51 E
Tobermory, Can. 106 45 12N 81 40W
Tobermory, U.K. 14 56 37N 6 4W
Tobin L. 109 53 35N 103 30W
Toboali 72 3 0 S 106 25 E
Tobol 58 52 40N 62 39 E
Toboli 73 0 38 S 120 5 E
Tobolsk 58 58 15N 68 10 E
Tobruk = Tubruq 81 32 7N 23 55 E
Tobyhanna 113 41 10N 75 25W
Tocantinópolis 127 6 20 S 47 25W
Tocantins → 127 1 45 S 49 10W
Toccoa 115 34 32N 83 17W
Toce → 38 45 56N 8 29 E
Tochigi 74 36 25N 139 45 E
Tochigi □ 74 36 45N 139 45 E
Tocina 31 37 37N 5 44W

Tocopilla 124 22 5 S 70 10W
Tocumwal 99 35 51 S 145 31 E
Tocuyo → 126 11 3N 68 23W
Todeli 73 1 38 S 124 34 E
Todenyang 90 4 35N 35 56 E
Todi 39 42 47N 12 24 E
Todos os Santos, Baía de 127 12 48 S 38 38W
Todos Santos 120 23 27N 110 13W
Todtnau 25 47 50N 7 56 E
Toecé 85 11 50N 1 16W
Tofield 108 53 25N 112 40W
Tofino 108 49 11N 125 55W
Töfsingdalens nationalpark 48 62 15N 12 44 E
Toftlund 49 55 11N 9 2 E
Tofua 101 19 45 S 175 05W
Togba 84 17 26N 10 12W
Togian, Kepulauan 73 0 20 S 121 50 E
Togliatti 55 53 32N 49 24 E
Togo ■ 85 6 15N 1 35 E
Togtoh 76 40 15N 111 10 E
Toinya 87 6 17N 29 46 E
Tojo 73 1 20 S 121 15 E
Tokaj 27 48 8N 21 27 E
Tōkamachi 74 37 8N 138 43 E
Tokanui 101 46 34 S 168 56 E
Tokar 81 18 27N 37 56 E
Tokara Kaikyō 74 30 0N 130 0 E
Tokarahi 101 44 56 S 170 39 E
Tokat 64 40 22N 36 35 E
Tokelau Is. ■ 94 9 0 S 171 45W
Tokmak 58 42 49N 75 15 E
Toko Ra. 98 23 5 S 138 20 E
Tokong 71 5 27N 100 23 E
Tokushima 74 34 4N 134 34 E
Tokushima □ 74 34 15N 134 0 E
Tokuyama 74 34 3N 131 50 E
Tōkyō 74 35 45N 139 45 E
Tōkyō □ 74 35 40N 139 30 E
Tolbukhin 43 43 37N 27 49 E
Toledo, Spain 30 39 50N 4 2W
Toledo, Ohio, U.S.A. 114 41 37N 83 33W
Toledo, Oreg., U.S.A. 118 44 40N 123 59W
Toledo, Wash., U.S.A. 118 46 29N 122 51W
Toledo, Montes de 31 39 33N 4 20W
Tolentino 39 43 12N 13 17 E
Tolga, Alg. 83 34 40N 5 22 E
Tolga, Norway 47 62 26N 11 1 E
Toliara 93 23 21 S 43 40 E
Toliara □ 93 21 0 S 45 0 E
Tolima, Vol. 126 4 40N 75 19W
Tolitoli 73 1 5N 120 50 E
Tolkmicko 28 54 19N 19 31 E
Tollarp 49 55 55N 13 58 E
Tolleson 119 33 29N 112 10W
Tolmachevo 54 58 56N 29 51 E
Tolmezzo 39 46 23N 13 0 E
Tolmin 39 46 11N 13 45 E
Tolna 27 46 25N 18 48 E
Tolna □ 27 46 30N 18 30 E
Tolo 88 2 55 S 18 34 E
Tolo, Teluk 73 2 20 S 122 10 E
Tolochin 54 54 25N 29 42 E
Tolosa 32 43 8N 2 5W
Tolox 31 36 41N 4 54W
Toluca 120 19 20N 99 40W
Tom Burke 93 23 5 S 28 4 E
Tom Price 96 22 40 S 117 48 E
Tomah 116 43 59N 90 30W
Tomahawk 116 45 28N 89 40W
Tomar 31 39 36N 8 25W
Tómaros Óros 44 39 29N 20 48 E
Tomaszów Mazowiecki 28 51 30N 19 57 E
Tombé 87 5 53N 31 40 E
Tombigbee → 115 31 4N 87 58W
Tombouctou 84 16 50N 3 0W
Tombstone 119 31 40N 110 4W
Tomé 124 36 36 S 72 57W
Tomelilla 49 55 33N 13 58 E
Tomelloso 33 39 10N 3 2W
Tomingley 99 32 6 S 148 16 E
Tomini 73 0 30N 120 30 E
Tomini, Teluk 73 0 10 S 122 0 E
Tominian 84 13 17N 4 35W
Tomiño 30 41 59N 8 46W
Tommot 59 59 4N 126 20 E
Tomnavoulin 14 57 19N 3 18W
Toms River 113 39 59N 74 12W
Tomsk 58 56 30N 85 5 E
Tomtabacken 49 57 30N 14 30 E
Tonalá 120 16 8N 93 41W
Tonale, Passo del 38 46 15N 10 34 E
Tonalea 119 36 17N 110 58W
Tonantins 126 2 45 S 67 45W
Tonasket 118 48 45N 119 30W
Tonawanda 114 43 0N 78 54W
Tonbridge 13 51 12N 0 18 E
Tondano 73 1 35N 124 54 E
Tondela 30 40 31N 8 5W
Tønder 49 54 58N 8 50 E
Tondi 70 9 45N 79 4 E
Tondi Kiwindi 85 14 28N 2 02 E
Tondibi 85 16 39N 0 14W
Tong Xian 76 39 55N 116 35 E
Tonga ■ 101 19 50 S 174 30W
Tonga Trench 94 18 0 S 175 0W
Tongaat 93 29 33 S 31 9 E
Tongaland 93 27 0 S 32 0 E
Tongareva 95 9 0 S 158 0W
Tongatapu 101 21 10 S 174 0W
Tongcheng 77 31 4N 116 56 E
Tongchuan 77 35 6N 109 3 E
Tongdao 77 26 10N 109 42 E
Tongeren 16 50 47N 5 28 E
Tongguan 77 34 40N 110 25 E
Tonghua 76 41 42N 125 58 E
Tongio 99 37 14 S 147 44 E
Tongjiang, Heilongjiang, China 75 47 40N 132 27 E
Tongjiang, Sichuan, China 77 31 58N 107 11 E
Tongking = Tonkin, G. of 71 20 0N 108 0 E
Tongliao 76 43 38N 122 18 E
Tongling 77 30 55N 117 48 E
Tonglu 77 29 45N 119 37 E
Tongnan 77 30 9N 105 50 E
Tongobory 93 23 32 S 44 20 E
Tongoy 124 30 16 S 71 31W
Tongren 75 27 43N 109 11 E
Tongres = Tongeren 16 50 47N 5 28 E
Tongue 14 58 29N 4 25W
Tongue → 116 46 24N 105 52W
Tongyu 76 44 45N 123 4 E
Tongzi 77 28 9N 106 49 E
Tonj 87 7 20N 28 44 E
Tonk 68 26 6N 75 54 E
Tonkawa 117 36 44N 97 22W
Tonkin = Bac-Phan 71 22 0N 105 0 E
Tonlé Sap 71 13 0N 104 0 E
Tonnay-Charente 20 45 56N 0 55W
Tonneins 20 44 23N 0 19 E
Tonnerre 19 47 51N 3 59 E
Tönning 24 54 18N 8 57 E
Tonopah 119 38 4N 117 12W
Tønsberg 47 59 19N 10 25 E
Tonstad 47 58 40N 6 45 E
Tonto Basin 119 33 56N 111 27W
Tooele 118 40 30N 112 20W
Toompine 99 27 15 S 144 19 E
Toonpan 98 19 28 S 146 48 E
Toora 99 38 39 S 146 23 E
Toora-Khem 59 52 28N 96 17 E
Toowoomba 97 27 32 S 151 56 E
Top-ozero 52 65 35N 32 0 E
Topalu 46 44 31N 28 3 E
Topeka 116 39 3N 95 40W
Topki 58 55 20N 85 35 E
Topl'a → 27 48 45N 21 45 E
Topley 108 54 49N 126 18W
Toplica → 42 43 15N 21 49 E
Toplița 46 46 55N 25 20 E
Topocalma, Pta. 124 34 10 S 72 2W
Topock 119 34 46N 114 29W
Topola 42 44 17N 20 41 E
Topolčani 42 41 14N 21 56 E
Topolčany 27 48 35N 18 12 E
Topoli 57 47 59N 51 38 E
Topolnitsa → 43 42 11N 24 18 E
Topolobampo 120 25 40N 109 4W
Topolovgrad 43 42 5N 26 20 E
Topolvătu Mare 42 45 46N 21 41 E
Toppenish 118 46 27N 120 16W
Topusko 39 45 18N 15 59 E
Tor Bay 96 35 5 S 117 50 E
Torá 32 41 49N 1 25 E
Tora Kit 87 11 2N 32 36 E
Toraka Vestale 93 16 20 S 43 58 E
Torata 126 17 23 S 70 1W
Torbat-e Ḥeydārīyeh 65 35 15N 59 12 E
Torbat-e Jām 65 35 16N 60 35 E
Torbay, Can. 107 47 40N 52 42W
Torbay, U.K. 13 50 26N 3 31W
Tørdal 47 59 10N 8 45 E
Tordesillas 30 41 30N 5 0W
Tordoya 30 43 6N 8 36W
Töreboda 49 58 41N 14 7 E
Torey 59 50 33N 104 50 E
Torfajökull 50 63 54N 19 0W
Torgau 24 51 32N 13 0 E
Torgelow 24 53 40N 13 59 E
Torhout 16 51 5N 3 7 E
Tori 87 7 53N 33 35 E
Torigni-sur-Vire 18 49 3N 0 58W
Torija 32 40 44N 3 2W
Torin 120 27 33N 110 15W
Toriñana, C. 30 43 3N 9 17W
Torino 38 45 4N 7 40 E
Torit 87 4 27N 32 31 E
Torkovichi 54 58 51N 30 21 E
Tormac 42 45 30N 21 30 E
Tormentine 107 46 6N 63 46W
Tormes → 30 41 18N 6 29W
Tornado Mt. 108 49 55N 114 40W
Torne älv → 50 65 50N 24 12 E
Torneträsk 50 68 24N 19 15 E
Tornio 50 65 50N 24 12 E
Tornionjoki → 50 65 50N 24 12 E
Tornquist 124 38 8 S 62 15W
Toro 30 41 35N 5 24W
Torö 49 58 48N 17 50 E
Toro, Cerro del 124 29 10 S 69 50W
Toro, Pta. 120 9 22N 79 57W
Törökszentmiklós 27 47 11N 20 27 E
Toronios Kólpos 44 40 5N 23 30 E
Toronto, Austral. 99 33 0 S 151 30 E
Toronto, Can. 106 43 39N 79 20W
Toronto, U.S.A. 114 40 27N 80 36W
Toronto, L. 120 27 40N 105 30W
Toropets 54 56 30N 31 40 E
Tororo 90 0 45N 34 12 E
Toros Dağlari 64 37 0N 35 0 E
Torpshammar 48 62 29N 16 20 E
Torquay, Can. 109 49 9N 103 30W
Torquay, U.K. 13 50 27N 3 31W
Torquemada 30 42 2N 4 19W
Torralba de Calatrava 31 39 1N 3 44W
Torrão 31 38 16N 8 11W
Torre Annunziata 41 40 45N 14 26 E
Tôrre de Moncorvo 30 41 12N 7 8W
Torre del Greco 41 40 47N 14 22 E
Torre del Mar 31 36 44N 4 6W
Torre-Pacheco 33 37 44N 0 57W
Torre Pellice 38 44 49N 7 13 E
Torreblanca 32 40 14N 0 12 E
Torrecampo 31 38 29N 4 41W
Torrecilla en Cameros 32 42 15N 2 38W
Torredembarra 32 41 9N 1 24 E
Torredonjimeno 31 37 46N 3 57W
Torrejoncillo 30 39 54N 6 28W
Torrelaguna 32 40 50N 3 38W
Torrelavega 30 43 20N 4 5W
Torremaggiore 41 41 42N 15 17 E
Torremolinos 31 36 38N 4 30W
Torrens Cr. → 98 22 23 S 145 9 E
Torrens Creek 98 20 48 S 145 3 E
Torrens, L. 97 31 0 S 137 50 E
Torrente 33 39 27N 0 28W
Torrenueva 33 38 38N 3 22W
Torréon 120 25 33N 103 25W
Torreperogil 33 38 2N 3 17W
Torres 120 28 46N 110 47W
Torres Novas 31 39 27N 8 33W
Torres Strait 97 9 50 S 142 20 E
Torres Vedras 31 39 5N 9 15W
Torrevieja 33 37 59N 0 42W
Torrey 119 38 18N 111 25W
Torridge → 13 50 51N 4 10W
Torridon, L. 14 57 35N 5 50W
Torrijos 30 39 59N 4 18W
Torrington, Conn., U.S.A. 114 41 50N 73 9W
Torrington, Wyo., U.S.A. 116 42 5N 104 8W
Torroella de Montgri 32 42 2N 3 8 E
Torrox 31 36 46N 3 57W
Torsås 49 56 24N 16 0 E
Torsby 48 60 7N 13 0 E
Torsö 49 58 48N 13 45 E
Tortola 121 18 19N 65 0W
Tórtoles de Esgueva 30 41 49N 4 2W
Tortona 38 44 53N 8 54 E
Tortoreto 39 42 50N 13 55 E
Tortorici 41 38 2N 14 48 E
Tortosa 32 40 49N 0 31 E
Tortosa, C. 32 40 41N 0 52 E
Tortosendo 30 40 15N 7 31W
Tortue, Î. de la 121 20 5N 72 57W
Tortuga, La 126 11 0N 65 22W
Ţorūd 65 35 25N 55 5 E
Toruń 28 53 0N 18 39 E
Toruń □ 28 53 20N 19 0 E
Torup, Denmark 49 57 5N 9 5 E
Torup, Sweden 49 56 57N 13 5 E
Tory I. 15 55 17N 8 12W
Torysa → 27 48 39N 21 21 E
Torzhok 54 57 5N 34 55 E
Tosa-Wan 74 33 15N 133 30 E
Toscana 38 43 30N 11 5 E
Toscano, Arcipelago 38 42 30N 10 30 E
Tosno 54 59 38N 30 46 E
Tossa 32 41 43N 2 56 E
Tostado 124 29 15 S 61 50W
Tostedt 24 53 17N 9 42 E
Tosya 64 41 1N 34 2 E
Toszek 28 50 27N 18 32 E
Totak 47 59 40N 7 45 E
Totana 33 37 45N 1 30W
Toten 47 60 37N 10 53 E
Toteng 92 20 22 S 22 58 E
Tôtes 18 49 41N 1 3 E
Tótkomlós 27 46 24N 20 45 E
Totma 55 60 0N 42 40 E
Totnes 13 50 26N 3 41W
Totonicapán 120 14 58N 91 12W
Totten Glacier 5 66 45 S 116 10 E
Tottenham, Austral. 99 32 14 S 147 21 E
Tottenham, Can. 112 44 1N 79 49W
Tottori 74 35 30N 134 15 E
Tottori □ 74 35 30N 134 12 E
Touat 82 27 27N 0 30 E
Touba 84 8 22N 7 40W
Toubkal, Djebel 82 31 0N 8 0W
Toucy 19 47 44N 3 15 E
Tougan 84 13 11N 2 58W
Touggourt 83 33 10N 6 0 E
Tougué 84 11 25N 11 50W
Toukmatine 83 24 49N 7 11 E
Toul 19 48 40N 5 53 E
Toulepleu 84 6 32N 8 24W
Toulon 21 43 10N 5 55 E
Toulouse 20 43 37N 1 27 E
Toummo 83 22 45N 14 8 E
Toummo Dhoba 83 22 30N 14 31 E
Toumodi 84 6 32N 5 4W
Tounassine, Hamada 82 28 48N 5 0W
Toungoo 67 19 0N 96 30 E
Touques → 18 49 22N 0 8 E
Touquet-Paris-Plage, Le 19 50 30N 1 36 E
Tour-du-Pin, La 21 45 33N 5 27 E
Touraine 18 47 20N 0 30 E
Tourcoing 19 50 42N 3 10 E
Tournai 16 50 35N 3 25 E
Tournan-en-Brie 19 48 44N 2 46 E
Tournay 20 43 13N 0 13 E
Tournon 21 45 4N 4 50 E
Tournon-St-Martin 18 46 45N 0 58 E
Tournus 21 46 35N 4 54 E
Tours 18 47 22N 0 40 E
Touside, Pic 83 21 1N 16 29 E
Touwsrivier 92 33 20 S 20 0 E
Tovarkovskiy 55 53 40N 38 14 E
Tovdal 47 58 47N 8 10 E
Tovdalselva → 47 58 15N 8 5 E
Towamba 99 37 6 S 149 43 E
Towanda 114 41 46N 76 30W
Towang 67 27 37N 91 50 E
Tower 116 47 49N 92 17W
Towerhill Cr. → 98 22 28 S 144 35 E
Towner 116 48 25N 100 26W
Townsend 118 46 25N 111 32W
Townshend, C. 97 22 18 S 150 30 E
Townshend I. 98 22 10 S 150 31 E
Townsville 97 19 15 S 146 45 E
Towson 114 39 26N 76 34W
Towyn 13 52 36N 4 5W
Toyah 117 31 20N 103 48W
Toyahvale 117 30 58N 103 45W
Toyama 74 36 40N 137 15 E
Toyama □ 74 36 45N 137 30 E
Toyama-Wan 74 37 0N 137 30 E
Toyohashi 74 34 45N 137 25 E
Toyokawa 74 34 48N 137 27 E
Toyonaka 74 34 50N 135 28 E
Toyooka 74 35 35N 134 48 E
Toyota 74 35 3N 137 7 E
Tozeur 83 33 56N 8 8 E
Trabancos → 30 41 36N 5 15W
Traben Trarbach 25 49 57N 7 7 E
Trabzon 64 41 0N 39 45 E
Tracadie 107 47 30N 64 55W
Tracy, Calif., U.S.A. 119 37 46N 121 27W
Tracy, Minn., U.S.A. 116 44 12N 95 38W
Tradate 38 45 43N 8 54 E
Trafalgar 100 38 14 S 146 12 E
Trafalgar, C. 31 36 10N 6 2W
Trăghān 83 26 0N 14 30 E
Traian 46 45 2N 28 15 E
Trail 108 49 5N 117 40W
Trainor L. 108 60 24N 120 17W
Tralee 15 52 16N 9 42W
Tralee B. 15 52 17N 9 55W
Tramore 15 52 10N 7 10W
Tran Ninh, Cao Nguyen 71 19 30N 103 10 E
Tranås 49 58 3N 14 59 E
Trancas 124 26 11 S 65 20W
Tranche, La 20 46 20N 1 26W
Tranche-sur-Mer, La 18 46 20N 1 27W
Trancoso 30 40 49N 7 21W
Tranebjerg 49 55 51N 10 36 E
Tranemo 49 57 30N 13 20 E
Trang 71 7 33N 99 38 E
Trangahy 93 19 7 S 44 31 E
Trangan 73 6 40 S 134 20 E
Trangie 99 32 4 S 148 0 E
Trångsviken 48 63 19N 14 0 E
Trani 41 41 17N 16 24 E
Tranoroa 93 24 42 S 45 4 E
Tranquebar 70 11 1N 79 54 E
Tranqueras 125 31 13 S 55 45W
Trans Nzoia □ 90 1 0N 35 0 E
Transcona 109 49 55N 97 0W
Transilvania 46 46 19N 25 0 E
Transkei □ 93 32 15 S 28 15 E
Transtrand 48 61 6N 13 20 E
Transvaal □ 92 25 0 S 29 0 E
Transylvania = Transilvania 46 46 19N 25 0 E
Transylvanian Alps 46 45 30N 25 0 E
Trápani 40 38 1N 12 30 E
Trapper Peak 118 45 56N 114 29W
Traralgon 97 38 12 S 146 34 E
Traryd 49 56 35N 13 45 E
Trarza □ 84 17 30N 15 0W
Trasacco 39 41 58N 13 30 E
Trăscău, Munţii 46 46 14N 23 14 E
Trasimeno, L. 39 43 10N 12 5 E
Trat 71 12 14N 102 33 E
Traun 26 48 14N 14 15 E
Traunsee 26 47 55N 13 50 E
Traunstein 25 47 52N 12 40 E
Tråvad 49 58 15N 13 5 E
Traveller's L. 99 33 20 S 142 0 E
Travemünde 24 53 58N 10 52 E
Travers, Mt. 101 42 1 S 172 45 E
Traverse City 114 44 45N 85 39W
Traverse Is. 5 57 0 S 28 0W
Travnik 42 44 17N 17 39 E
Trazo 30 43 0N 8 30W
Trbovlje 39 46 12N 15 5 E
Trébbia → 38 45 4N 9 41 E
Trebel → 24 53 55N 13 1 E
Třebíč 26 49 14N 15 55 E
Trebinje 42 42 44N 18 22 E
Trebisacce 41 39 52N 16 32 E
Trebišnica → 42 42 47N 18 8 E
Trebišov 27 48 38N 21 41 E
Trebižat → 42 43 15N 17 30 E
Trebnje 39 45 54N 15 1 E
Třeboň 26 48 59N 14 48 E
Trebujena 31 36 52N 6 11W
Trecate 38 45 26N 8 42 E
Tredegar 13 51 47N 3 16W
Tregaron 13 52 14N 3 56W
Trégastel-Plage 18 48 49N 3 31W
Tregnago 39 45 31N 11 10 E
Tréguier 18 48 47N 3 16W
Trégune 18 47 51N 3 51W
Treherne 109 49 38N 98 42W
Tréia 39 43 20N 13 20 E
Treignac 20 45 32N 1 48 E
Treinta y Tres 125 33 16 S 54 17W
Treis 25 50 9N 7 19 E
Treklyano 42 42 33N 22 36 E
Trekveld 92 30 35 S 19 45 E
Trelde Næs 49 55 38N 9 53 E
Trelew 128 43 10 S 65 20W
Trelissac 20 45 11N 0 47 E
Trelleborg 49 55 20N 13 10 E
Trélon 19 50 5N 4 6 E
Tremblade, La 20 45 46N 1 8W
Tremiti 39 42 8N 15 30 E
Tremonton 118 41 45N 112 10W
Tremp 32 42 10N 0 52 E
Trenary 114 46 12N 86 59W
Trenche → 106 47 46N 72 53W
Trenčín 27 48 52N 18 4 E
Trenggalek 73 8 5 S 111 38 E
Trenque Lauquen 124 36 5 S 62 45W
Trent → 12 53 33N 0 44W
Trentino-Alto Adige □ 38 46 30N 11 0 E
Trento 38 46 5N 11 8 E
Trenton, Can. 106 44 10N 77 34W
Trenton, Mo., U.S.A. 116 40 5N 93 37W
Trenton, N.J., U.S.A. 114 40 15N 74 41W
Trenton, Nebr., U.S.A. 116 40 14N 101 4W
Trenton, Tenn., U.S.A. 117 35 58N 88 57W
Trepassey 107 46 43N 53 25W
Tréport, Le 18 50 3N 1 20 E
Trepuzzi 41 40 26N 18 4 E
Tres Arroyos 124 38 26 S 60 20W
Três Corações 125 21 44 S 45 15W
Três Lagoas 127 20 50 S 51 43W
Tres Marías 120 21 25N 106 28W
Tres Montes, C. 128 46 50 S 75 30W
Três Pontas 125 21 23 S 45 29W
Tres Puentes 124 27 50 S 70 15W
Tres Puntas, C. 128 47 0 S 66 0W
Três Rios 125 22 6 S 43 15W
Treska → 42 42 0N 21 20 E
Treskavika Planina 42 43 40N 18 20 E
Trespaderne 32 42 47N 3 24W
Trets 21 43 27N 5 41 E
Treuchtlingen 25 48 58N 10 55 E
Treuenbrietzen 24 52 6N 12 51 E

Treviglio 38 45 31N 9 35 E
Trevinca, Peña 30 42 15N 6 46W
Treviso 39 45 40N 12 15 E
Trévoux 21 45 57N 4 47 E
Treysa 24 50 55N 9 12 E
Trgovište 42 42 20N 22 10 E
Triabunna 99 42 30 S 147 55 E
Triánda 45 36 25N 28 10 E
Triaucourt-en-Argonne 19 48 59N 5 2 E
Tribsees 24 54 4N 12 46 E
Tribulation, C. 97 16 5 S 145 29 E
Tribune 116 38 30N 101 45W
Tricárico 41 40 37N 16 9 E
Tricase 41 39 56N 18 20 E
Trichinopoly = Tiruchchirappalli 70 10 45N 78 45 E
Trichur 70 10 30N 76 18 E
Trida 99 33 1 S 145 1 E
Trier 25 49 45N 6 37 E
Trieste 39 45 39N 13 45 E
Trieste, G. di 39 45 37N 13 40 E
Trieux → 18 48 50N 3 3W
Triggiano 41 41 4N 16 58 E
Triglav 39 46 21N 13 50 E
Trigno → 39 42 4N 14 48 E
Trigueros 31 37 24N 6 50W
Tríkeri 45 39 6N 23 5 E
Trikhonis, Límni 45 38 34N 21 30 E
Tríkkala 44 39 34N 21 47 E
Trikkala □ 44 39 41N 21 30 E
Trikora, Puncak 73 4 15 S 138 45 E
Trilj 39 43 38N 16 42 E
Trillo 32 40 42N 2 35W
Trim 15 53 34N 6 48W
Trincomalee 70 8 38N 81 15 E
Trindade, I. 7 20 20 S 29 50W
Trinidad, Boliv. 126 14 46 S 64 50W
Trinidad, Colomb. 126 5 25N 71 40W
Trinidad, Cuba 121 21 48N 80 0W
Trinidad, Uruguay 124 33 30 S 56 50W
Trinidad, U.S.A. 117 37 15N 104 30W
Trinidad, W. Indies 121 10 30N 61 15W
Trinidad & Tobago ■ 121 10 30N 61 20W
Trinidad → 120 17 49N 95 9W
Trinidad, I. 128 39 10 S 62 0W
Trinitápoli 41 41 22N 16 5 E
Trinity, Can. 107 48 59N 53 55W
Trinity, U.S.A. 117 30 59N 95 25W
Trinity →, Calif., U.S.A. 118 41 11N 123 42W
Trinity →, Tex., U.S.A. 117 30 30N 95 0W
Trinity B., Austral. 97 16 30 S 146 0 E
Trinity B., Can. 107 48 20N 53 10W
Trinity Mts. 118 40 20N 118 50W
Trinkitat 81 18 45N 37 51 E
Trino 38 45 10N 8 18 E
Trion 115 34 35N 85 18W
Trionto C. 41 39 38N 16 47 E
Triora 38 44 0N 7 46 E
Tripoli = Tarābulus, Leb. 64 34 31N 35 50 E
Tripoli = Tarābulus, Libya 83 32 58N 13 12 E
Trípolis 45 37 31N 22 25 E
Tripp 116 43 16N 97 58W
Tripura □ 67 24 0N 92 0 E
Trischen 24 54 3N 8 32 E
Tristan da Cunha 7 37 6 S 12 20W
Trivandrum 70 8 41N 77 0 E
Trivento 41 41 48N 14 31 E
Trnava 27 48 23N 17 35 E
Trobriand Is. 98 8 30 S 151 0 E
Trochu 108 51 50N 113 13W
Trodely I. 106 52 15N 79 26W
Troezen 45 37 25N 23 15 E
Trogir 39 43 32N 16 15 E
Troglav 39 43 56N 16 36 E
Trøgstad 47 59 37N 11 16 E
Tróia 41 41 22N 15 19 E
Troilus, L. 106 50 50N 74 35W
Troina 41 37 47N 14 34 E
Trois Fourches, Cap des 82 35 26N 2 58W
Trois-Pistoles 107 48 5N 69 10W
Trois-Rivières 106 46 25N 72 34W
Troitsk 58 54 10N 61 35 E
Troitsko Pechorsk 52 62 40N 56 10 E
Trölladyngja 50 64 54N 17 16W
Trollhättan 49 58 17N 12 20 E
Trollheimen 47 62 46N 9 1 E
Troms fylke □ 50 68 56N 19 0 E
Tromsø 50 69 40N 18 56 E
Tronador 128 41 10 S 71 50W
Trondheim 47 63 36N 10 25 E
Trondheimsfjorden 47 63 35N 10 30 E
Trönninge 49 56 37N 12 51 E
Trönö 48 61 22N 16 54 E
Tronto → 39 42 54N 13 55 E
Troon 14 55 33N 4 40W
Tropea 41 38 40N 15 53 E
Tropic 119 37 36N 112 4W
Tropoja 44 42 23N 20 10 E
Trossachs, The 14 56 14N 4 24W
Trostan 15 55 4N 6 10W
Trostberg 25 48 2N 12 33 E
Trostyanets 54 50 33N 34 59 E
Trotternish 14 57 32N 6 15W
Troup 117 32 10N 95 3W
Trout → 108 61 19N 119 51W
Trout L., N.W.T., Can. 108 60 40N 121 40W
Trout L., Ont., Can. 109 51 20N 93 15W
Trout Lake 106 46 10N 85 2W
Trout River 107 49 29N 58 8W
Trouville 18 49 21N 0 5 E
Trowbridge 13 51 18N 2 12W
Troy, Turkey 44 39 57N 26 12 E
Troy, Turkey 64 39 55N 26 20 E
Troy, Ala., U.S.A. 115 31 50N 85 58W
Troy, Idaho, U.S.A. 118 46 44N 116 46W
Troy, Kans., U.S.A. 116 39 47N 95 2W
Troy, Mo., U.S.A. 116 38 56N 90 59W
Troy, Montana, U.S.A. 118 48 30N 115 58W
Troy, N.Y., U.S.A. 114 42 45N 73 39W
Troy, Ohio, U.S.A. 114 40 0N 84 10W
Troyan 43 42 57N 24 43 E
Troyes 19 48 19N 4 3 E
Trpanj 42 43 1N 17 15 E
Trstena 27 49 21N 19 37 E
Trstenik 42 43 36N 21 0 E
Trubchevsk 54 52 33N 33 47 E
Trucial States = United Arab Emirates ■ 65 24 0N 54 30 E
Truckee 118 39 20N 120 11W
Trujillo, Hond. 121 16 0N 86 0W
Trujillo, Peru 126 8 6 S 79 0W
Trujillo, Spain 31 39 28N 5 55W
Trujillo, U.S.A. 117 35 34N 104 44W
Trujillo, Venez. 126 9 22N 70 38W
Truk 94 7 25N 151 46 E
Trumann 117 35 42N 90 32W
Trumbull, Mt. 119 36 25N 113 8W
Trun 42 42 51N 22 38 E
Trun 18 48 50N 0 2 E
Trundle 99 32 53 S 147 35 E
Trung-Phan 72 16 0N 108 0 E
Truro, Can. 107 45 21N 63 14W
Truro, U.K. 13 50 17N 5 2W
Trustrup 49 56 20N 10 46 E
Truth or Consequences 119 33 9N 107 16W
Trutnov 26 50 37N 15 54 E
Truyère → 20 44 38N 2 34 E
Tryavna 43 42 54N 25 25 E
Tryon 115 35 15N 82 16W
Tryonville 112 41 42N 79 48W
Trzcianka 28 53 3N 16 25 E
Trzciel 28 52 23N 15 50 E
Trzcińsko Zdrój 28 52 58N 14 35 E
Trzebiatów 28 54 3N 15 18 E
Trzebiez 28 53 38N 14 31 E
Trzebinia-Siersza 27 50 11N 19 18 E
Trzebnica 28 51 20N 17 1 E
Trzemeszno 28 52 33N 17 48 E
Tržič 39 46 22N 14 18 E
Tsageri 57 42 39N 42 46 E
Tsamandás 44 39 46N 20 21 E
Tsaratanana 93 16 47 S 47 39 E
Tsaratanana, Mt. de 93 14 0 S 49 0 E
Tsarevo = Michurin 43 42 9N 27 51 E
Tsarichanka 56 48 55N 34 30 E
Tsaritsáni 44 39 53N 22 14 E
Tsau 92 20 8 S 22 22 E
Tsebrikovo 56 47 9N 30 10 E
Tselinograd 58 51 10N 71 30 E
Tsetserleg 75 47 36N 101 32 E
Tshabong 92 26 2 S 22 29 E
Tshane 92 24 5 S 21 54 E
Tshela 88 4 57 S 13 4 E
Tshesebe 93 21 51 S 27 32 E
Tshibeke 90 2 40 S 28 35 E
Tshibinda 90 2 23 S 28 43 E
Tshikapa 88 6 28 S 20 48 E
Tshilenge 90 6 17 S 23 48 E
Tshinsenda 91 12 20 S 28 0 E
Tshofa 90 5 13 S 25 16 E
Tshwane 92 22 24 S 22 1 E
Tsigara 92 20 22 S 25 54 E
Tsihombe 93 25 18 S 45 29 E
Tsimlyansk 57 47 40N 42 6 E
Tsimlyanskoye Vdkhr. 57 48 0N 43 0 E
Tsinan = Jinan 76 36 38N 117 1 E
Tsineng 92 27 05 S 23 05 E
Tsinga 44 41 23N 24 44 E
Tsinghai = Qinghai □ 75 36 0N 98 0 E
Tsingtao = Qingdao 76 36 5N 120 20 E
Tsinjomitondraka 93 15 40 S 47 8 E
Tsiroanomandidy 93 18 46 S 46 2 E
Tsivilsk 55 55 50N 47 25 E
Tsivory 93 24 4 S 46 5 E
Tskhinali 53 42 22N 43 52 E
Tskhinvali 57 42 14N 44 1 E
Tsna → 55 54 55N 41 58 E
Tsodilo Hill 92 18 49 S 21 43 E
Tsu 74 34 45N 136 25 E
Tsu L. 108 60 40N 111 52W
Tsuchiura 74 36 5N 140 15 E
Tsugaru-Kaikyō 74 41 35N 141 0 E
Tsumeb 92 19 9 S 17 44 E
Tsumis 92 23 39 S 17 29 E
Tsuruga 74 35 45N 136 2 E
Tsushima 74 34 20N 129 20 E
Tsvetkovo 56 49 8N 31 33 E
Tua → 30 41 13N 7 26W
Tual 73 5 38 S 132 44 E
Tuam 15 53 30N 8 50W
Tuamotu Arch. 95 17 0 S 144 0W
Tuamotu Ridge 95 20 0 S 138 0W
Tuao 73 17 55N 122 22 E
Tuapse 57 44 5N 39 10 E
Tuatapere 101 46 8 S 167 41 E
Tuba City 119 36 8N 111 18W
Tubac 119 31 37N 111 20W
Tuban 73 6 54 S 112 3 E
Tubarão 125 28 30 S 49 0W
Tūbās 62 32 20N 35 22 E
Tubau 72 3 10N 113 40 E
Tübingen 25 48 31N 9 4 E
Tubja, W. → 86 25 27N 38 45 E
Ţubruq 81 32 7N 23 55 E
Tubuai Is. 95 25 0 S 150 0W
Tucacas 126 10 48N 68 19W
Tuchodi → 108 58 17N 123 42W
Tuchola 28 53 33N 17 52 E
Tuchów 27 49 54N 21 1 E
Tucker's Town 121 32 17N 64 43W
Tucson 119 32 14N 110 59W
Tucumán □ 124 26 48 S 66 2W
Tucumcari 117 35 12N 103 45W
Tucupita 126 9 2N 62 3W
Tucuruí 127 3 42 S 49 44W
Tuczno 28 53 13N 16 10 E
Tudela 32 42 4N 1 39W
Tudela de Duero 30 41 37N 4 39W
Tudmur 64 34 36N 38 15 E
Tudor, Lac 107 55 50N 65 25W
Tudora 46 47 31N 26 45 E
Tuella → 30 41 30N 7 12W
Tufi 98 9 8 S 149 19 E
Tuguegarao 73 17 35N 121 42 E
Tugur 59 53 44N 136 45 E
Tukangbesi, Kepulauan 73 6 0 S 124 0 E
Tukarak I. 106 56 15N 78 45W
Tūkh 86 30 21N 31 12 E
Tukobo 84 5 1N 2 47W
Tūkrah 83 32 30N 20 37 E
Tuktoyaktuk 104 69 27N 133 2W
Tukums 54 57 2N 23 10 E
Tukuyu 91 9 17 S 33 35 E
Tula, Hidalgo, Mexico 120 20 0N 99 20W
Tula, Tamaulipas, Mexico 120 23 0N 99 40W
Tula, Nigeria 85 9 51N 11 27 E
Tula, U.S.S.R. 55 54 13N 37 38 E
Tulak 65 33 55N 63 40 E
Tulancingo 120 20 5N 99 22W
Tulare 119 36 15N 119 26W
Tulare Lake 119 36 0N 119 53W
Tularosa 119 33 4N 106 1W
Tulbagh 92 33 16 S 19 6 E
Tulcán 126 0 48N 77 43W
Tulcea 46 45 13N 28 46 E
Tulcea □ 46 45 0N 29 0 E
Tulchin 56 48 41N 28 49 E
Tulemalu L. 109 62 58N 99 25W
Tulgheş 46 46 58N 25 45 E
Tuli, Indon. 73 1 24 S 122 26 E
Tuli, Zimb. 91 21 58 S 29 13 E
Ţūlkarm 62 32 19N 35 2 E
Tulla 117 34 35N 101 44W
Tullahoma 115 35 23N 86 12W
Tullamore, Austral. 99 32 39 S 147 36 E
Tullamore, Ireland 15 53 17N 7 30W
Tulle 20 45 16N 1 46 E
Tullibigeal 99 33 25 S 146 44 E
Tullins 21 45 18N 5 29 E
Tulln 26 48 20N 16 4 E
Tullow 15 52 48N 6 45W
Tullus 87 11 7N 24 31 E
Tully 98 17 56 S 145 55 E
Ţulmaythah 81 32 40N 20 55 E
Tulmur 98 22 40 S 142 20 E
Tulnici 46 45 51N 26 38 E
Tulovo 43 42 33N 25 32 E
Tulsa 117 36 10N 96 0W
Tulsequah 108 58 39N 133 35W
Tulu Milki 87 9 55N 38 20 E
Tulu Welel 87 8 56N 34 47 E
Tulua 126 4 6N 76 11W
Tulun 59 54 32N 100 35 E
Tulungagung 72 8 5 S 111 54 E
Tum 73 3 36 S 130 21 E
Tuma 55 55 10N 40 30 E
Tuma → 121 13 6N 84 35W
Tumaco 126 1 50N 78 45W
Tumatumari 126 5 20N 58 55W
Tumba 48 59 12N 17 48 E
Tumba, L. 88 0 50 S 18 0 E
Tumbarumba 99 35 44 S 148 0 E
Tumbaya 124 23 50 S 65 26W
Túmbes 126 3 37 S 80 27W
Tumbwe 91 11 25 S 27 15 E
Tumen 76 43 0N 129 50 E
Tumen Jiang → 76 42 20N 130 35 E
Tumeremo 126 7 18N 61 30W
Tumkur 70 13 18N 77 6 E
Tummel, L. 14 56 43N 3 55W
Tump 66 26 7N 62 16 E
Tumpat 71 6 11N 102 10 E
Tumsar 69 21 26N 79 45 E
Tumu 84 10 56N 1 56W
Tumucumaque, Serra 127 2 0N 55 0W
Tumut 97 35 16 S 148 13 E
Tumwater 118 47 0N 122 58W
Tunas de Zaza 121 21 39N 79 34W
Tunbridge Wells 13 51 7N 0 16 E
Tuncurry 99 32 17 S 152 29 E
Tunduru 91 11 8 S 37 25 E
Tunduru □ 91 11 5 S 37 22 E
Tundzha → 43 41 40N 26 35 E
Tune 47 59 16N 11 2 E
Tunga → 70 15 0N 75 50 E
Tunga Pass 67 29 0N 94 14 E
Tungabhadra → 70 15 57N 78 15 E
Tungabhadra Dam 70 15 0N 75 50 E
Tungaru 81 10 9N 30 52 E
Tungla 121 13 24N 84 21W
Tungnafellsjökull 50 64 45N 17 55W
Tungsten, Can. 108 61 57N 128 16W
Tungsten, U.S.A. 118 40 50N 118 10W
Tunguska, Nizhnyaya → 59 65 48N 88 4 E
Tunguska, Podkamennaya → 59 61 36N 90 18 E
Tuni 70 17 22N 82 36 E
Tunica 117 34 43N 90 23W
Tunis 83 36 50N 10 11 E
Tunis, Golfe de 83 37 0N 10 30 E
Tunisia ■ 83 33 30N 9 10 E
Tunja 126 5 33N 73 25W
Tunkhannock 113 41 32N 75 46W
Tunliu 76 36 13N 112 52 E
Tunnsjøen 50 64 45N 13 25 E
Tunungayualok I. 107 56 0N 61 0W
Tunuyán 124 33 35 S 69 0W
Tunuyán → 124 33 33 S 67 30W
Tunxi 75 29 42N 118 25 E
Tuolumne 119 37 59N 120 16W
Tuoy-Khaya 59 62 32N 111 25 E
Tupã 125 21 57 S 50 28W
Tupelo 115 34 15N 88 42W
Tupik, U.S.S.R. 54 55 42N 33 22 E
Tupik, U.S.S.R. 59 54 26N 119 57 E
Tupinambaranas 126 3 0 S 58 0W
Tupiza 124 21 30 S 65 40W
Tupižnica 42 43 43N 22 10 E
Tupper 108 55 32N 120 1W
Tupper L. 114 44 18N 74 30W
Tupungato, Cerro 124 33 15 S 69 50W
Tuquan 76 45 18N 121 38 E
Tuque, La 106 47 30N 72 50W
Túquerres 126 1 5N 77 37W
Tura, India 69 25 30N 90 16 E
Tura, U.S.S.R. 59 64 20N 100 17 E
Turaba, Wadi → 86 21 15N 41 32 E
Turabah 64 28 20N 43 15 E
Turaiyur 70 11 9N 78 38 E
Tūrān 65 35 39N 56 42 E
Turan 59 51 55N 95 0 E
Turayf 64 31 41N 38 39 E
Turbacz 27 49 30N 20 8 E
Turbe 42 44 15N 17 35 E
Turda 46 46 34N 23 47 E
Turégano 30 41 9N 4 1W
Turek 28 52 3N 18 30 E
Turfan = Turpan 75 43 58N 89 10 E
Turfan Depression = Turpan Hami 75 42 40N 89 25 E
Tŭrgovishte 43 43 17N 26 38 E
Turgutlu 64 38 30N 27 48 E
Turhal 56 40 24N 36 5 E
Turia → 33 39 27N 0 19W
Turiaçu 127 1 40 S 45 19W
Turiaçu → 127 1 36 S 45 19W
Turiec → 27 49 07N 18 55 E
Turin 108 49 47N 112 24W
Turin = Torino 38 45 3N 7 40 E
Turka 54 49 10N 23 2 E
Turkana □ 90 3 0N 35 30 E
Turkana, L. 90 3 30N 36 5 E
Turkestan 58 43 17N 68 16 E
Túrkeve 27 47 6N 20 44 E
Turkey ■ 64 39 0N 36 0 E
Turki 55 52 0N 43 15 E
Turkmen S.S.R. □ 58 39 0N 59 0 E
Turks Is. 121 21 20N 71 20W
Turks Island Passage 121 21 30N 71 30W
Turku 51 60 30N 22 19 E
Turkwe → 90 3 6N 36 6 E
Turlock 119 37 30N 120 55W
Turnagain → 108 59 12N 127 35W
Turnagain, C. 101 40 28 S 176 38 E
Turneffe Is. 120 17 20N 87 50W
Turner 118 48 52N 108 25W
Turner Valley 108 50 40N 114 17W
Turners Falls 113 42 36N 72 34W
Turnhout 16 51 19N 4 57 E
Türnitz 26 47 55N 15 29 E
Turnor L. 109 56 35N 108 35W
Turnov 26 50 34N 15 10 E
Tŭrnovo 43 43 5N 25 41 E
Turnovo 43 43 5N 25 41 E
Turnu Măgurele 46 43 46N 24 56 E
Turnu Rosu Pasul 46 45 33N 24 17 E
Turnu-Severin 46 44 39N 22 41 E
Turobin 28 50 50N 22 44 E
Turon 117 37 48N 98 27W
Turpan 75 43 58N 89 10 E
Turpan Hami 75 42 40N 89 25 E
Turrës, Kalaja e 44 41 10N 19 28 E
Turriff 14 57 32N 2 28W
Tursha 55 56 55N 47 36 E
Tursi 41 40 15N 16 27 E
Turtle Hd. I. 98 10 56 S 142 37 E
Turtle L., Can. 109 53 36N 108 38W
Turtle L., U.S.A. 116 45 22N 92 10W
Turtle Lake 116 47 30N 100 55W
Turtleford 109 53 23N 108 57W
Turukhansk 59 65 21N 88 5 E
Turun ja Porin lääni □ 51 60 27N 22 15 E
Turzovka 27 49 25N 18 35 E
Tuscaloosa 115 33 13N 87 31W
Tuscánia 39 42 25N 11 53 E
Tuscany = Toscana 38 43 28N 11 15 E
Tuscola, Ill., U.S.A. 114 39 48N 88 15W
Tuscola, Tex., U.S.A. 117 32 15N 99 48W
Tuscumbia 115 34 42N 87 42W
Tuskar Rock 15 52 12N 6 10W
Tuskegee 115 32 24N 85 39W
Tustna 47 63 10N 8 5 E
Tuszyn 28 51 36N 19 33 E
Tutayev 55 57 53N 39 32 E
Tuticorin 70 8 50N 78 12 E
Tutin 42 43 0N 20 20 E
Tutóia 127 2 45 S 42 20W
Tutong 72 4 47N 114 40 E
Tutova → 46 46 20N 27 30 E
Tutrakan 43 44 2N 26 40 E
Tutshi L. 108 59 56N 134 30W
Tuttle 116 47 9N 100 00W
Tuttlingen 25 47 59N 8 50 E
Tutuala 73 8 25 S 127 15 E
Tutuila 101 14 19 S 170 50W
Tuva A.S.S.R. □ 59 51 30N 95 0 E
Tuvalu ■ 94 8 0 S 178 0 E
Tuxpan 120 20 58N 97 23W
Tuxtla Gutiérrez 120 16 50N 93 10W
Tuy 30 42 3N 8 39W
Tuy Hoa 71 13 5N 109 10 E
Tuya L. 108 59 7N 130 35W
Tuyen Hoa 71 17 50N 106 10 E
Tuz Gölü 64 38 45N 33 30 E
Ţūz Khurmātū 64 34 56N 44 38 E
Tuzla 42 44 34N 18 41 E
Tuzlov → 57 47 28N 39 45 E
Tvååker 49 57 4N 12 25 E
Tvedestrand 47 58 38N 8 58 E
Tvŭrditsa 43 42 42N 25 53 E
Twardogóra 28 51 23N 17 28 E
Tweed 112 44 29N 77 19W
Tweed → 14 55 42N 2 10W
Tweedsmuir Prov. Park 108 53 0N 126 20W
Twentynine Palms 119 34 10N 116 4W
Twillingate 107 49 42N 54 45W
Twin Bridges 118 45 33N 112 23W
Twin Falls 118 42 30N 114 30W
Twin Valley 116 47 18N 96 15W
Twisp 118 48 21N 120 5W
Twistringen 24 52 48N 8 38 E
Two Harbors 116 47 1N 91 40W
Two Hills 108 53 43N 111 52W
Two Rivers 114 44 10N 87 31W
Twofold B. 97 37 8 S 149 59 E
Tychy 27 50 9N 18 59 E
Tyczyn 27 49 58N 22 2 E
Tydal 47 63 4N 11 34 E
Tykocin 28 53 13N 22 46 E
Tyldal 47 62 8N 10 48 E

Tyler, Minn., U.S.A.	**116**	44 18N	96 8W
Tyler, Tex., U.S.A.	**117**	32 18N	95 18W
Týn nad Vltavou	**26**	49 13N	14 26 E
Tynda	**59**	55 10N	124 43 E
Tyne & Wear □	**12**	54 55N	1 35W
Tyne →	**12**	54 58N	1 28W
Tynemouth	**12**	55 1N	1 27W
Tynset	**47**	62 17N	10 47 E
Tyre = Sūr	**62**	33 12N	35 11 E
Tyrifjorden	**47**	60 2N	10 8 E
Tyringe	**49**	56 9N	13 35 E
Tyristrand	**47**	60 5N	10 5 E
Tyrnyauz	**57**	43 21N	42 45 E
Tyrol = Tirol	**26**	47 3N	10 43 E
Tyrone	**112**	40 39N	78 10W
Tyrrell →	**100**	35 26 S	142 51 E
Tyrrell Arm	**109**	62 27N	97 30W
Tyrrell, L.	**99**	35 20 S	142 50 E
Tyrrell L.	**109**	63 7N	105 27W
Tyrrhenian Sea	**34**	40 0N	12 30 E
Tysfjorden	**50**	68 7N	16 25 E
Tysnes	**47**	60 1N	5 30 E
Tysnesøy	**47**	60 0N	5 35 E
Tyssedal	**47**	60 7N	6 35 E
Tystberga	**49**	58 51N	17 15 E
Tyub Karagan, M.	**57**	44 40N	50 19 E
Tyuleniy	**57**	44 28N	47 30 E
Tyulgan	**52**	52 22N	56 12 E
Tyumen	**58**	57 11N	65 29 E
Tywi →	**13**	51 48N	4 20W
Tzaneen	**93**	23 47 S	30 9 E
Tzermíadhes Neápolis	**46**	35 11N	25 29 E
Tzoumérka, Óros	**44**	39 30N	21 26 E
Tzukong = Zigong	**75**	29 15N	104 48 E

U

Uad Erni, O. →	**82**	26 45N	10 47W
Uanda	**98**	21 37 S	144 55 E
Uarsciek	**63**	2 28N	45 55 E
Uasin □	**90**	0 30N	35 20 E
Uato-Udo	**73**	9 7 S	125 36 E
Uatumã →	**126**	2 26 S	57 37W
Uaupés	**126**	0 8 S	67 5W
Ub	**42**	44 28N	20 6 E
Ubá	**125**	21 8 S	43 0W
Ubaitaba	**127**	14 18 S	39 20W
Ubangi = Oubangi →	**88**	1 0N	17 50 E
Ubauro	**68**	28 15N	69 45 E
Ubaye →	**21**	44 28N	6 18 E
Ube	**74**	33 56N	131 15 E
Ubeda	**33**	38 3N	3 23W
Uberaba	**127**	19 50 S	47 55W
Uberlândia	**127**	19 0 S	48 20W
Überlingen	**25**	47 46N	9 10 E
Ubiaja	**85**	6 41N	6 22 E
Ubombo	**93**	27 31 S	32 4 E
Ubon Ratchathani	**71**	15 15N	104 50 E
Ubondo	**90**	0 55 S	25 42 E
Ubort →	**54**	52 6N	28 30 E
Ubrique	**31**	36 41N	5 27W
Ubundu	**90**	0 22 S	25 30 E
Ucayali →	**126**	4 30 S	73 30W
Uchi Lake	**109**	51 5N	92 35W
Uchiura-Wan	**74**	42 25N	140 40 E
Uchte	**24**	52 29N	8 52 E
Uchur →	**59**	58 48N	130 35 E
Ucluelet	**108**	48 57N	125 32W
Ucuriş	**46**	46 41N	21 58 E
Uda →	**59**	54 42N	135 14 E
Udaipur	**68**	24 36N	73 44 E
Udaipur Garhi	**69**	27 0N	86 35 E
Udamalpet	**70**	10 35N	77 15 E
Udbina	**39**	44 31N	15 47 E
Uddeholm	**48**	60 1N	13 38 E
Uddevalla	**49**	58 21N	11 55 E
Uddjaur	**50**	65 25N	21 15 E
Udgir	**70**	18 25N	77 5 E
Udi	**85**	6 23N	7 21 E
Údine	**39**	46 5N	13 10 E
Udipi	**70**	13 25N	74 42 E
Udmurt A.S.S.R. □	**52**	57 30N	52 30 E
Udon Thani	**71**	17 29N	102 46 E
Udvoy Balkan	**43**	42 50N	26 50 E
Udzungwa Range	**91**	9 30 S	35 10 E
Ueckermünde	**24**	53 45N	14 1 E
Ueda	**74**	36 24N	138 16 E
Uedineniya, Os.	**4**	78 0N	85 0 E
Uelen	**59**	66 10N	170 0W
Uelzen	**24**	53 0N	10 33 E
Uere →	**88**	3 45N	24 45 E
Ufa	**52**	54 45N	55 55 E
Ufa →	**52**	54 40N	56 0 E
Uffenheim	**25**	49 32N	10 15 E
Ugalla →	**90**	5 8 S	30 42 E
Uganda ■	**90**	2 0N	32 0 E
Ugento	**41**	39 55N	18 10 E
Ugep	**85**	5 53N	8 2 E
Ugie	**93**	31 10 S	28 13 E
Ugijar	**33**	36 58N	3 7W
Ugine	**21**	45 45N	6 25 E
Ugla	**86**	25 40N	37 42 E
Uglegorsk	**59**	49 5N	142 2 E
Uglich	**55**	57 33N	38 20 E
Ugljane	**39**	43 35N	16 46 E
Ugolyak	**59**	64 33N	120 30 E
Ugra →	**54**	54 30N	36 7 E
Ugŭrchin	**43**	43 6N	24 26 E
Uh →	**27**	48 7N	21 25 E
Uherske Hradiště	**27**	49 4N	17 30 E
Uhersky Brod	**27**	49 1N	17 40 E
Úhlava →	**26**	49 45N	13 24 E
Uhrichsville	**114**	40 23N	81 22W
Uíge	**88**	7 30 S	14 40 E
Ŭiju	**76**	40 15N	124 35 E
Uinta Mts.	**118**	40 45N	110 30W
Uitenhage	**92**	33 40 S	25 28 E
Uithuizen	**16**	53 24N	6 41 E
Újfehértó	**27**	47 49N	21 41 E
Ujhani	**68**	28 0N	79 6 E
Ujjain	**68**	23 9N	75 43 E
Újpest	**27**	47 32N	19 6 E
Újszász	**27**	47 19N	20 7 E
Ujung Pandang	**73**	5 10 S	119 20 E
Uka	**59**	57 50N	162 0 E
Ukara I.	**90**	1 50 S	33 0 E
Ukerewe □	**90**	2 0 S	32 30 E
Ukerewe I.	**90**	2 0 S	33 0 E
Ukholovo	**55**	53 47N	40 30 E
Ukhrul	**67**	25 10N	94 25 E
Ukhta	**52**	63 55N	54 0 E
Ukiah	**118**	39 10N	123 9W
Ukmerge	**54**	55 15N	24 45 E
Ukrainian S.S.R. □	**56**	49 0N	32 0 E
Ukwi	**92**	23 29 S	20 30 E
Ulaanbaatar	**75**	47 54N	106 52 E
Ulaangom	**75**	50 0N	92 10 E
Ulamba	**91**	9 3 S	23 38 E
Ulan Bator = Ulaanbaatar	**75**	47 54N	106 52 E
Ulan Ude	**59**	51 45N	107 40 E
Ulanga □	**91**	8 40 S	36 50 E
Ulanów	**28**	50 30N	22 16 E
Ulaya, Morogoro, Tanz.	**90**	7 3 S	36 55 E
Ulaya, Tabora, Tanz.	**90**	4 25 S	33 30 E
Ulcinj	**42**	41 58N	19 10 E
Ulco	**92**	28 21 S	24 15 E
Ulefoss	**47**	59 17N	9 16 E
Ulëza	**44**	41 46N	19 57 E
Ulfborg	**49**	56 16N	8 20 E
Ulhasnagar	**70**	19 15N	73 10 E
Uljma	**42**	45 2N	21 10 E
Ulla →	**30**	42 39N	[illegible] 44W
Ulladulla	**99**	35 21 S	150 29 E
Ullånger	**48**	62 58N	18 10 E
Ullapool	**14**	57 54N	5 10W
Ullared	**49**	57 8N	12 42 E
Ulldecona	**32**	40 36N	0 20 E
Ullswater	**12**	54 35N	2 52W
Ullung-do	**76**	37 30N	130 30 E
Ulm	**25**	48 23N	10 0 E
Ulmarra	**99**	29 37 S	153 4 E
Ulmeni	**46**	45 4N	26 40 E
Ulricehamn	**49**	57 46N	13 26 E
Ulsberg	**47**	62 45N	9 59 E
Ulsteinvik	**47**	62 21N	5 53 E
Ulster □	**15**	54 35N	6 30W
Ulstrem	**43**	42 1N	26 27 E
Ulubaria	**69**	22 31N	88 4 E
Uluguru Mts.	**90**	7 15 S	37 40 E
Ulungur He	**75**	47 1N	87 24 E
Ulutau	**58**	48 39N	67 1 E
Ulverston	**12**	54 13N	3 7W
Ulverstone	**97**	41 11 S	146 11 E
Ulvik	**47**	60 35N	6 54 E
Ulya	**59**	59 10N	142 0 E
Ulyanovsk	**55**	54 20N	48 25 E
Ulyasutay (Javhlant)	**75**	47 56N	97 28 E
Ulysses	**117**	37 39N	101 25W
Umag	**39**	45 26N	13 31 E
Umala	**126**	17 25 S	68 5W
Uman	**56**	48 40N	30 12 E
Umarkhed	**70**	19 37N	77 46 E
Umatilla	**118**	45 58N	119 17W
Umba	**52**	66 50N	34 20 E
Umbertide	**39**	43 18N	12 20 E
Umboi I.	**98**	5 40 S	148 0 E
Umbrella Mts.	**101**	45 35 S	169 5 E
Umbria □	**39**	42 53N	12 30 E
Ume älv →	**50**	63 45N	20 20 E
Umeå	**50**	63 45N	20 20 E
Umera	**73**	0 12 S	129 37 E
Umfuli →	**91**	17 30 S	29 23 E
Umgusa	**91**	19 29 S	27 52 E
Umka	**42**	44 40N	20 19 E
Umkomaas	**93**	30 13 S	30 48 E
Umm al Arānib	**83**	26 10N	14 43 E
Umm al Qaywayn	**65**	25 30N	55 35 E
Umm Arda	**87**	15 17N	32 31 E
Umm az Zamul	**65**	22 42N	55 18 E
Umm Bel	**87**	13 35N	28 0 E
Umm Dubban	**87**	15 23N	32 52 E
Umm el Fahm	**62**	32 31N	35 9 E
Umm Koweika	**87**	13 10N	32 16 E
Umm Lajj	**64**	25 0N	37 23 E
Umm Merwa	**86**	18 4N	32 30 E
Umm Qays	**62**	32 40N	35 41 E
Umm Rumah	**86**	25 50N	36 30 E
Umm Ruwaba	**87**	12 50N	31 20 E
Umm Sidr	**87**	14 29N	25 10 E
Ummanz	**24**	54 29N	13 9 E
Umnak	**104**	53 20N	168 20W
Umniati →	**91**	16 49 S	28 45 E
Umpang	**71**	16 3N	98 54 E
Umpqua →	**118**	43 42N	124 3W
Umrer	**68**	20 51N	79 18 E
Umreth	**68**	22 41N	73 4 E
Umshandige Dam	**91**	20 10 S	30 40 E
* Umtali	**91**	18 58 S	32 38 E
Umtata	**93**	31 36 S	28 49 E
Umuahia	**85**	5 33N	7 29 E
Umvukwe Ra.	**91**	16 45 S	30 45 E
Umvukwes	**91**	17 0 S	30 57 E
Umvuma	**91**	19 16 S	30 30 E
Umzimvubu	**93**	31 38 S	29 33 E
Umzingwane →	**91**	22 12 S	29 56 E
Umzinto	**93**	30 15 S	30 45 E
Una	**68**	20 46N	71 8 E
Una →	**39**	45 16N	16 55 E
Unac →	**39**	44 30N	16 9 E
Unadilla	**113**	42 20N	75 17W
Unalaska	**104**	53 40N	166 40W
Uncastillo	**32**	42 21N	1 8W
Uncía	**126**	18 25 S	66 40W
Uncompahgre Pk.	**119**	38 5N	107 32W
Unden	**49**	58 45N	14 25 E
Underbool	**99**	35 10 S	141 51 E
Undersaker	**48**	63 19N	13 21 E
Undersvik	**48**	61 36N	16 20 E
Undredal	**47**	60 57N	7 6 E
Unecha	**54**	52 50N	32 37 E
Ungarie	**99**	33 38 S	146 56 E

* *Renamed Mutare*

Ungava B.	**105**	59 30N	67 30W
Ungeny	**56**	47 11N	27 51 E
Unggi	**76**	42 16N	130 28 E
Ungwatiri	**87**	16 52N	36 10 E
Uni	**55**	56 44N	51 47 E
União da Vitória	**125**	26 13 S	51 5W
Uniejów	**28**	51 59N	18 46 E
Unije	**39**	44 40N	14 15 E
Unimak	**104**	55 0N	164 0W
Unimak Pass.	**104**	53 30N	165 15W
Union, Miss, U.S.A.	**117**	32 34N	89 14W
Union, Mo., U.S.A.	**116**	38 25N	91 0W
Union, S.C., U.S.A.	**115**	34 43N	81 39W
Union City, N.J., U.S.A.	**113**	40 47N	74 5W
Union City, Ohio, U.S.A.	**114**	40 11N	84 49W
Union City, Pa., U.S.A.	**114**	41 53N	79 50W
Union City, Tenn., U.S.A.	**117**	36 25N	89 0W
Union Gap	**118**	46 38N	120 29W
Unión, La, Chile	**128**	40 10 S	73 0W
Unión, La, El Sal.	**120**	13 20N	87 50W
Unión, La, Spain	**33**	37 38N	0 53W
Union, Mt.	**119**	34 34N	112 21W
Union of Soviet Socialist Republics ■	**59**	60 0N	100 0 E
Union Springs	**115**	32 9N	85 44W
Uniondale	**92**	33 39 S	23 7 E
Uniontown	**114**	39 54N	79 45W
Unionville	**116**	40 29N	93 1W
Unirea	**46**	44 15N	27 35 E
United Arab Emirates ■	**65**	23 50N	54 0 E
United Kingdom ■	**11**	55 0N	3 0W
United States of America ■	**111**	37 0N	96 0W
United States Trust Terr. of the Pacific Is.	**94**	10 0N	160 0 E
Unity	**109**	52 30N	109 5W
Universales, Mtes.	**32**	40 18N	1 33W
Unjha	**68**	23 46N	72 24 E
Unnao	**69**	26 35N	80 30 E
Uno, Ilha	**84**	11 15N	16 13W
Unst	**14**	60 50N	0 55W
Unstrut →	**24**	51 10N	11 48 E
Unuk →	**108**	56 5N	131 3W
Ünye	**56**	41 5N	37 15 E
Unzha	**55**	58 0N	44 0 E
Unzha →	**55**	57 30N	43 40 E
Upa →	**27**	50 35N	16 15 E
Upata	**126**	8 1N	62 24W
Upemba, L.	**91**	8 30 S	26 20 E
Upernavik	**4**	72 49N	56 20W
Upington	**92**	28 25 S	21 15 E
Upleta	**68**	21 46N	70 16 E
Upolu	**101**	13 58 S	172 0W
Upper Alkali Lake	**118**	41 47N	120 8W
Upper Arrow L.	**108**	50 30N	117 50W
Upper Austria = Oberösterreich	**26**	48 10N	14 0 E
Upper Foster L.	**109**	56 47N	105 20W
Upper Hutt	**101**	41 8 S	175 5 E
Upper Klamath L.	**118**	42 16N	121 55W
Upper L. Erne	**15**	54 14N	7 22W
Upper Lake	**118**	39 10N	122 55W
Upper Musquodoboit	**107**	45 10N	62 58W
Upper Red L.	**116**	48 0N	95 0W
Upper Sandusky	**114**	40 50N	83 17W
Upper Taimyr →	**59**	74 15N	99 48 E
*Upper Volta ■	**84**	12 0N	1 0W
Upphärad	**49**	58 9N	12 19 E
Uppsala	**48**	59 53N	17 38 E
Uppsala län □	**48**	60 0N	17 30 E
Upstart, C.	**98**	19 41 S	147 45 E
Upton	**116**	44 8N	104 35W
Ur	**64**	30 55N	46 25 E
Uracara	**126**	2 20 S	57 50W
Urach	**25**	48 29N	9 25 E
Urad Qianqi	**76**	40 40N	108 30 E
Ural →	**58**	47 0N	51 48 E
Ural, Mt.	**99**	33 21 S	146 12 E
Ural Mts. = Uralskie Gory	**52**	60 0N	59 0 E
Uralla	**99**	30 37 S	151 29 E
Uralsk	**52**	51 20N	51 20 E
Uralskie Gory	**52**	60 0N	59 0 E
Urambo	**90**	5 4 S	32 0 E
Urambo □	**90**	5 0 S	32 0 E
Urana	**100**	35 15 S	146 21 E
Urandangie	**97**	21 32 S	138 14 E
Uranium City	**109**	59 34N	108 37W
Uravakonda	**70**	14 57N	77 12 E
Urawa	**74**	35 50N	139 40 E
Uray	**58**	60 5N	65 15 E
Urbana, Ill., U.S.A.	**114**	40 7N	88 12W
Urbana, Ohio, U.S.A.	**114**	40 9N	83 44W
Urbana, La	**126**	7 8N	66 56W
Urbánia	**39**	43 40N	12 31 E
Urbel →	**32**	42 21N	3 40W
Urbino	**39**	43 43N	12 38 E
Urbión, Picos de	**32**	42 1N	2 52W
Urcos	**126**	13 40 S	71 38W
Urda, Spain	**31**	39 25N	3 43W
Urda, U.S.S.R.	**57**	48 52N	47 23 E
Urdinarrain	**124**	32 37 S	58 52W
Urdos	**20**	42 51N	0 35W
Urdzhar	**58**	47 5N	81 38 E
Ure →	**12**	54 20N	1 25W
Uren	**55**	57 35N	45 55 E
Urengoy	**58**	65 58N	28 25 E
Ures	**120**	29 30N	110 30W
Urfa	**64**	37 12N	38 50 E
Urfahr	**26**	48 19N	14 17 E
Urgench	**58**	41 40N	60 41 E
Uri □	**25**	46 43N	8 35 E
Uribia	**126**	11 43N	72 16W
Urim	**62**	31 18N	34 32 E
Uriondo	**124**	21 41 S	64 41W
Urique →	**120**	26 29N	107 58W
Urk	**16**	52 39N	5 36 E
Urla	**64**	38 20N	26 47 E
Urlati	**46**	44 59N	26 15 E
Urmia = Rezā'īyeh	**64**	37 40N	45 0 E
Urmia, L. = Rezā'īyeh, Daryācheh-ye	**64**	37 30N	45 30 E
Uroševac	**42**	42 23N	21 10 E
Urshult	**49**	56 31N	14 50 E
Ursus	**28**	52 12N	20 53 E

**Renamed Burkina Faso*

Uruana	**127**	15 30 S	49 41W
Uruapan	**120**	19 30N	102 0W
Urubamba	**126**	13 20 S	72 10W
Urubamba →	**126**	10 43 S	73 48W
Uruçuí	**127**	7 20 S	44 28W
Uruguai →	**125**	26 0 S	53 30W
Uruguaiana	**124**	29 50 S	57 0W
Uruguay ■	**124**	32 30 S	56 30W
Uruguay →	**124**	34 12 S	58 18W
Urumchi = Ürümqi	**75**	43 45N	87 45 E
Ürümqi	**75**	43 45N	87 45 E
Urup →	**57**	46 0N	41 10 E
Urup, Os.	**59**	46 0N	151 0 E
Uryung-Khaya	**59**	72 48N	113 23 E
Uryupinsk	**55**	50 45N	41 58 E
Urzhum	**55**	57 10N	49 56 E
Urziceni	**46**	44 40N	26 42 E
Usa →	**52**	65 67N	56 55 E
Uşak	**64**	38 43N	29 28 E
Usakos	**92**	22 0 S	15 31 E
Ušće	**42**	43 30N	20 39 E
Usedom	**24**	53 50N	13 55 E
Usfan	**86**	21 58N	39 27 E
Ush-Tobe	**58**	45 16N	78 0 E
Ushakova, O.	**4**	82 0N	80 0 E
Ushant = Ouessant, Île d'	**18**	48 25N	5 5W
Ushashi	**90**	1 59 S	33 57 E
Ushat	**87**	7 59N	29 28 E
Ushuaia	**128**	54 50 S	68 23W
Ushumun	**59**	52 47N	126 32 E
Usk →	**13**	51 37N	2 56W
Uskedal	**47**	59 56N	5 53 E
Üsküdar	**64**	41 0N	29 5 E
Uslar	**24**	51 39N	9 39 E
Usman	**55**	52 5N	39 48 E
Usoke	**90**	5 7 S	32 19 E
Usolye Sibirskoye	**59**	52 48N	103 40 E
Usoro	**85**	5 33N	6 11 E
Uspallata, P. de	**124**	32 37 S	69 22W
Uspenskiy	**58**	48 41N	72 43 E
Ussel	**20**	45 32N	2 18 E
Ussuriysk	**59**	43 48N	131 59 E
Ust-Aldan = Batamay	**59**	63 30N	129 15 E
Ust Amginskoye = Khandyga	**59**	62 42N	135 0 E
Ust-Bolsheretsk	**59**	52 50N	156 15 E
Ust Buzulukskaya	**55**	50 8N	42 11 E
Ust chaun	**59**	68 47N	170 30 E
Ust-Donetskiy	**57**	47 35N	40 55 E
Ust'-Ilga	**59**	55 5N	104 55 E
Ust Ilimpeya = Yukti	**59**	63 20N	105 0 E
Ust-Ilimsk	**59**	58 3N	102 39 E
Ust Ishim	**58**	57 45N	71 10 E
Ust-Kamchatsk	**59**	56 10N	162 28 E
Ust-Kamenogorsk	**58**	50 0N	82 36 E
Ust-Karenga	**59**	54 25N	116 30 E
Ust Khayryuzova	**59**	57 15N	156 45 E
Ust-Kut	**59**	56 50N	105 42 E
Ust Kuyga	**59**	70 1N	135 43 E
Ust-Labinsk	**57**	45 15N	39 41 E
Ust Luga	**54**	59 35N	28 20 E
Ust Maya	**59**	60 30N	134 28 E
Ust-Mil	**59**	59 40N	133 11 E
Ust-Nera	**59**	64 35N	143 15 E
Ust-Nyukzha	**59**	56 34N	121 37 E
Ust Olenek	**59**	73 0N	119 48 E
Ust-Omchug	**59**	61 9N	149 38 E
Ust Port	**58**	69 40N	84 26 E
Ust Tsilma	**52**	65 25N	52 0 E
Ust-Tungir	**59**	55 25N	120 36 E
Ust Urt = Ustyurt, Plato	**58**	44 0N	55 0 E
Ust Usa	**52**	66 0N	56 30 E
Ust Vorkuta	**58**	67 24N	64 0 E
Ustaoset	**47**	60 30N	8 2 E
Ustaritz	**20**	43 24N	1 27W
Uste	**55**	59 35N	39 40 E
Ústí nad Labem	**26**	50 41N	14 3 E
Ústí nad Orlicí	**27**	49 58N	16 24 E
Ustica	**40**	38 42N	13 10 E
Ustka	**28**	54 35N	16 55 E
Ustroń	**27**	49 43N	18 48 E
Ustrzyki Dolne	**27**	49 27N	22 40 E
Ustye	**59**	57 46N	94 37 E
Ustyurt, Plato	**58**	44 0N	55 0 E
Ustyuzhna	**55**	58 50N	36 32 E
Usu	**75**	44 27N	84 40 E
Usuki	**74**	33 8N	131 49 E
Usulután	**120**	13 25N	88 28W
Usumacinta →	**120**	17 0N	91 0W
Usure	**90**	4 40 S	34 22 E
Uta	**73**	4 33 S	136 0 E
Utah □	**118**	39 30N	111 30W
Utah, L.	**118**	40 10N	111 58W
Ute Cr.	**117**	35 21N	103 45W
Utena	**54**	55 27N	25 40 E
Ütersen	**24**	53 40N	9 40 E
Utete	**90**	8 0 S	38 45 E
Uthai Thani	**71**	15 22N	100 3 E
Utiariti	**126**	13 0 S	58 10W
Utica, N.Y., U.S.A.	**114**	43 5N	75 18W
Utica, Ohio, U.S.A.	**112**	40 13N	82 26W
Utiel	**32**	39 37N	1 11W
Utik L.	**109**	55 15N	96 0W
Utikuma L.	**108**	55 50N	115 30W
Utrecht, Neth.	**16**	52 5N	5 8 E
Utrecht, S. Afr.	**93**	27 38 S	30 20 E
Utrecht □	**16**	52 6N	5 7 E
Utrera	**31**	37 12N	5 48W
Utsjoki	**50**	69 51N	26 59 E
Utsunomiya	**74**	36 30N	139 50 E
Uttar Pradesh □	**69**	27 0N	80 0 E
Uttaradit	**71**	17 36N	100 5 E
Uttoxeter	**12**	52 53N	1 50W
Ütze	**24**	52 28N	10 11 E
Uusikaarlepyy	**50**	63 32N	22 31 E
Uusikaupunki	**51**	60 47N	21 25 E
Uva	**52**	56 59N	52 13 E
Uvac →	**42**	43 35N	19 40 E
Uvalde	**117**	29 15N	99 48W
Uvarovo	**55**	51 59N	42 14 E
Uvat	**58**	59 5N	68 50 E
Uvinza	**90**	5 5 S	30 24 E
Uvira	**90**	3 22 S	29 3 E

Uvs Nuur 75 50 20N 92 30 E
Uwajima 74 33 10N 132 35 E
Uweinat, Jebel 86 21 54N 24 58 E
Uxbridge 112 44 6N 79 7W
Uxin Qi 76 38 50N 109 5 E
Uxmal 120 20 22N 89 46W
Uyandi 59 69 19N 141 0 E
Uyo 85 5 1N 7 53 E
Uyuni 126 20 28 S 66 47W
Uzbek S.S.R. □ 58 41 30N 65 0 E
Uzen 53 43 27N 53 10 E
Uzen, Bol. → 55 50 0N 49 30 E
Uzen, Mal. → 55 50 0N 48 30 E
Uzerche 20 45 25N 1 34 E
Uzès 21 44 1N 4 26 E
Uzh → 54 51 15N 30 12 E
Uzhgorod 54 48 36N 22 18 E
Uzlovaya 55 54 0N 38 5 E
Uzunköprü 43 41 16N 26 43 E

V

Vaal → 92 29 4 S 23 38 E
Vaaldam 93 27 0 S 28 14 E
Vaalwater 93 24 15 S 28 8 E
Vaasa 50 63 6N 21 38 E
Vaasan lääni □ 50 63 2N 22 50 E
Vabre 20 43 42N 2 24 E
Vác 27 47 49N 19 10 E
Vacaria 125 28 31 S 50 52W
Vacaville 118 38 21N 122 0W
Vaccarès, Étang de 21 43 32N 4 34 E
Vach → 58 60 45N 76 45 E
Vache, Î.-à- 121 18 2N 73 35W
Väddö 48 59 55N 18 50 E
Vadnagar 68 23 47N 72 40 E
Vado Ligure 38 44 16N 8 26 E
Vadodara 68 22 20N 73 10 E
Vadsø 50 70 3N 29 50 E
Vadstena 49 58 28N 14 54 E
Vaduz 25 47 8N 9 31 E
Værøy 50 67 40N 12 40 E
Vagney 19 48 1N 6 43 E
Vagnhärad 48 58 57N 17 33 E
Vagos 30 40 33N 8 42W
Váh → 27 47 55N 18 0 E
Vahsel B. 5 75 0 S 35 0W
Vaigach 58 70 10N 59 0 E
Vaigai → 70 9 15N 79 10 E
Vaiges 18 48 2N 0 30W
Vaihingen 25 48 55N 8 58 E
Vaijapur 70 19 58N 74 45 E
Vaikam 70 9 45N 76 25 E
Vailly Aisne 19 49 25N 3 30 E
Vaippar → 70 9 0N 78 25 E
Vaison 21 44 14N 5 4 E
Vajpur 68 21 24N 73 17 E
Vakarel 43 42 35N 23 40 E
Vaksdal 47 60 29N 5 45 E
Vál 27 47 22N 18 40 E
Val-d'Ajol, Le 19 47 55N 6 30 E
Val-de-Marne □ 19 48 45N 2 28 E
Val-d'Oise □ 19 49 5N 2 10 E
Val d'Or 106 48 7N 77 47W
Val Marie 109 49 15N 107 45W
Valadares 30 41 5N 8 38W
Valahia 46 44 35N 25 0 E
Valais □ 25 46 12N 7 45 E
Valandovo 42 41 19N 22 34 E
Valašské Meziříčí 27 49 29N 17 59 E
Valáxa 45 38 50N 24 29 E
Vălcani 42 46 0N 20 26 E
Valcheta 128 40 40 S 66 8W
Valdagno 39 45 38N 11 18 E
Valdahon, Le 19 47 8N 6 20 E
Valday 54 57 58N 33 9 E
Valdayskaya Vozvyshennost 54 57 0N 33 30 E
Valdeazogues → 31 38 45N 4 55W
Valdemarsvik 49 58 14N 16 40 E
Valdepeñas, Ciudad Real, Spain 31 38 43N 3 25W
Valdepeñas, Jaén, Spain 31 37 33N 3 47W
Valderaduey → 30 41 31N 5 42W
Valderrobres 32 40 53N 0 9 E
Valdés, Pen. 128 42 30 S 63 45W
Valdez 104 61 14N 76 17W
Valdivia 128 39 50 S 73 14W
Valdobbiádene 39 45 53N 12 0 E
Valdosta 115 30 50N 83 20W
Valdoviño 30 43 36N 8 8W
Valdres 47 60 55N 9 28 E
Vale, U.S.A. 118 44 0N 117 15W
Vale, U.S.S.R. 57 41 30N 42 58 E
Valea lui Mihai 46 47 32N 22 11 E
Valença, Brazil 127 13 20 S 39 5W
Valença, Port. 30 42 1N 8 34W
Valença do Piauí 127 6 20 S 41 45W
Valençay 19 47 9N 1 34 E
Valence 21 44 57N 4 54 E
Valence-d'Agen 20 44 8N 0 54 E
Valencia, Spain 33 39 27N 0 23W
Valencia, Venez. 126 10 11N 68 0W
Valencia □ 33 39 20N 0 40W
Valencia, Albufera de 33 39 20N 0 27W
Valencia de Alcántara 31 39 25N 7 14W
Valencia de Don Juan 30 42 17N 5 31W
Valencia del Ventoso 31 38 15N 6 29W
Valencia, G. de 33 39 30N 0 20 E
Valenciennes 19 50 20N 3 34 E
Văleni 46 44 15N 24 45 E
Valensole 21 43 50N 5 59 E
Valentia Hr. 15 51 56N 10 17W
Valentia I. 15 51 54N 10 22W
Valentim, Sa. do 127 6 0 S 43 30W
Valentine, Nebr., U.S.A. 116 42 50N 100 35W
Valentine, Tex., U.S.A. 117 30 36N 104 28W
Valenza 38 45 2N 8 39 E
Våler 47 60 41N 11 50 E
Valera 126 9 19N 70 37W
Valga 54 57 44N 26 0 E
Valguarnera Caropepe 41 37 30N 14 22 E
Valier 118 48 25N 112 9W
Valinco, G. de 21 41 40N 8 52 E
Valjevo 42 44 18N 19 53 E
Valkenswaard 16 51 21N 5 29 E
Vall de Uxó 32 39 49N 0 15W
Valla 48 59 2N 16 20 E
Valladolid, Mexico 120 20 40N 88 11W
Valladolid, Spain 30 41 38N 4 43W
Valladolid □ 30 41 38N 4 43W
Vallata 41 41 3N 15 16 E
Valldemosa 32 39 43N 2 37 E
Valle 47 59 13N 7 33 E
Valle d'Aosta □ 38 45 45N 7 22 E
Valle de Arán 32 42 50N 0 55 E
Valle de Cabuérniga 30 43 14N 4 18W
Valle de la Pascua 126 9 13N 66 0W
Valle de Santiago 120 20 25N 101 15W
Valle Fértil, Sierra del 124 30 20 S 68 0W
Valle Hermoso 120 25 35N 97 40W
Vallecas 30 40 23N 3 41W
Vallejo 118 38 12N 122 15W
Vallenar 124 28 30 S 70 50W
Valleraugue 20 44 6N 3 39 E
Vallet 18 47 10N 1 15W
Valletta 36 35 54N 14 30 E
Valley City 116 46 57N 98 0W
Valley Falls 118 42 33N 120 16W
Valleyview 108 55 5N 117 17W
Valli di Comácchio 39 44 40N 12 15 E
Vallimanca, Arroyo 124 35 40 S 59 10W
Vallo della Lucánia 41 40 14N 15 16 E
Vallon 21 44 25N 4 23 E
Vallorbe 25 46 42N 6 20 E
Valls 32 41 18N 1 15 E
Vallsta 48 61 31N 16 22 E
Valmaseda 32 43 11N 3 12W
Valmiera 54 57 37N 25 29 E
Valmont 18 49 45N 0 30 E
Valmontone 40 41 48N 12 55 E
Valmy 19 49 5N 4 45 E
Valnera, Mte. 32 43 9N 3 40W
Valognes 18 49 30N 1 28W
Valona = Vlóra 44 40 32N 19 28 E
Valongo 30 41 8N 8 30W
Valpaços 30 41 36N 7 17W
Valparaíso, Chile 124 33 2 S 71 40W
Valparaíso, Mexico 120 22 50N 103 32W
Valparaiso 114 41 27N 87 2W
Valparaíso □ 124 33 2 S 71 40W
Valpovo 42 45 39N 18 25 E
Valréas 21 44 24N 5 0 E
Vals 25 46 39N 9 11 E
Vals → 92 27 23 S 26 30 E
Vals-les-Bains 21 44 42N 4 24 E
Vals, Tanjung 73 8 26 S 137 25 E
Valsbaai 92 34 15 S 18 40 E
Valskog 48 59 27N 15 57 E
Válta 44 40 3N 23 25 E
Valtellina 38 46 9N 9 55 E
Valuyki 55 50 10N 38 5 E
Valverde del Camino 31 37 35N 6 47W
Valverde del Fresno 30 40 15N 6 51W
Vama 46 47 34N 25 42 E
Vámos 45 35 24N 24 13 E
Vamsadhara → 70 18 21N 84 8 E
Van 64 38 30N 43 20 E
Van Alstyne 117 33 25N 96 36W
Van Bruyssel 107 47 56N 72 9W
Van Buren, Can. 107 47 10N 67 55W
Van Buren, Ark., U.S.A. 117 35 28N 94 18W
Van Buren, Me., U.S.A. 115 47 10N 68 1W
Van Buren, Mo., U.S.A. 117 37 0N 91 0W
Van der Kloof Dam 92 30 04 S 24 40 E
Van Diemen, C. 97 16 30 S 139 46 E
Van Diemen G. 96 11 45 S 132 0 E
Van Gölü 64 38 30N 43 0 E
Van Horn 117 31 3N 104 55W
Van Reenen P. 93 28 22 S 29 27 E
Van Rees, Pegunungan 73 2 35 S 138 15 E
Van Tassell 116 42 40N 104 3W
Van Tivu 70 8 51N 78 15 E
Van Wert 114 40 52N 84 31W
Vanavara 59 60 22N 102 16 E
Vancouver, Can. 108 49 15N 123 10W
Vancouver, U.S.A. 118 45 44N 122 41W
Vancouver I. 108 49 50N 126 0W
Vandalia, Ill., U.S.A. 116 38 57N 89 4W
Vandalia, Mo., U.S.A. 116 39 18N 91 30W
Vandeloos Bay 70 8 0N 81 45 E
Vanderbijlpark 93 26 42 S 27 54 E
Vandergrift 114 40 36N 79 33W
Vanderhoof 108 54 0N 124 0W
Vanderlin I. 97 15 44 S 137 2 E
Vandyke 98 24 10 S 147 51 E
Vänern 49 58 47N 13 30 E
Vänersborg 49 58 26N 12 19 E
Vang Vieng 71 18 58N 102 32 E
Vanga 90 4 35 S 39 12 E
Vangaindrano 93 23 21 S 47 36 E
Vanguard 109 49 55N 107 20W
Vanier 106 45 27N 75 40W
Vanimo 98 2 42 S 141 21 E
Vanivilasa Sagara 70 13 45N 76 30 E
Vaniyambadi 70 12 46N 78 44 E
Vankarem 59 67 51N 175 50 E
Vankleek Hill 106 45 32N 74 40W
Vanna 50 70 6N 19 50 E
Vännäs 50 63 58N 19 48 E
Vannes 18 47 40N 2 47W
Vanoise, Massif de la 21 45 25N 6 40 E
Vanrhynsdorp 92 31 36 S 18 44 E
Vanrook 98 16 57 S 141 57 E
Vans, Les 21 44 25N 4 7 E
Vansbro 48 60 32N 14 15 E
Vanse 47 58 6N 6 41 E
Vansittart B. 96 14 3 S 126 17 E
Vanthli 68 21 28N 70 25 E
Vanua Levu 101 16 33 S 179 15 E
Vanua Mbalavu 101 17 40 S 178 57W
Vanwyksvlei 92 30 18 S 21 49 E
Vanylven 47 62 5N 5 33 E
Vapnyarka 56 48 32N 28 45 E
Var □ 21 43 27N 6 18 E
Var → 21 43 39N 7 12 E
Vara 49 58 16N 12 55 E
Varada → 70 15 0N 75 40 E
Varades 18 47 25N 1 1W
Varaita → 38 44 49N 7 36 E
Varaldsøy 47 60 6N 5 59 E
Varallo 38 45 50N 8 13 E
Varanasi (Benares) 69 25 22N 83 0 E
Varangerfjorden 50 70 3N 29 25 E
Varaždin 39 46 20N 16 20 E
Varazze 38 44 21N 8 36 E
Varberg 49 57 6N 12 20 E
Vardar → 42 40 35N 22 50 E
Varde 49 55 38N 8 29 E
Varde Å 49 55 35N 8 19 E
Varel 24 53 23N 8 9 E
Varena 54 54 12N 24 30 E
Varennes-sur-Allier 20 46 19N 3 24 E
Vareš 42 44 12N 18 23 E
Varese 38 45 49N 8 50 E
Varese Ligure 38 44 22N 9 33 E
Vårgårda 49 58 2N 12 49 E
Varginha 125 21 33 S 45 25W
Vargön 49 58 22N 12 20 E
Varhaug 47 58 37N 5 41 E
Variadero 117 35 43N 104 17W
Varillas 124 24 0 S 70 10W
Väring 49 58 30N 14 0 E
Värmeln 48 59 35N 12 54 E
Värmlands län □ 48 60 0N 13 20 E
Varna 43 43 13N 27 56 E
Varna → 70 16 48N 74 32 E
Värnamo 49 57 10N 14 3 E
Varnsdorf 26 50 55N 14 35 E
Värö 49 57 16N 12 11 E
Vars 113 45 21N 75 21W
Varteig 47 59 23N 11 12 E
Varvarin 42 43 43N 21 20 E
Varzaneh 65 32 25N 52 40 E
Varzi 38 44 50N 9 12 E
Varzo 38 46 12N 8 15 E
Varzy 19 47 22N 3 20 E
Vas □ 27 47 10N 16 55 E
Vasa 50 63 6N 21 38 E
Vasa Barris → 127 11 10 S 37 10W
Vásárosnamény 27 48 9N 22 19 E
Vascão → 31 37 31N 7 31W
Vaşcău 46 46 28N 22 30 E
Vascongadas 32 42 50N 2 45W
Väse 48 59 23N 13 52 E
Vasht = Khāsh 65 28 14N 61 14 E
Vasilevichi 54 52 15N 29 50 E
Vasilikón 45 38 25N 23 40 E
Vasilkov 54 50 7N 30 15 E
Vaslui 46 46 38N 27 42 E
Vaslui □ 46 46 30N 27 45 E
Väsman 48 60 9N 15 5 E
Vassar, Can. 109 49 10N 95 55W
Vassar, U.S.A. 114 43 23N 83 33W
Västerås 49 59 37N 16 38 E
Västerbottens län □ 50 64 58N 18 0 E
Västernorrlands län □ 48 63 30N 17 30 E
Västervik 49 57 43N 16 43 E
Västmanlands län □ 48 59 45N 16 20 E
Vasto 39 42 8N 14 40 E
Vasvár 27 47 3N 16 47 E
Vatan 19 47 4N 1 50 E
Vathí, Itháki, Greece 45 38 18N 20 40 E
Vathí, Sámos, Greece 45 37 46N 27 1 E
Váthia 45 36 29N 22 29 E
Vatican City ■ 39 41 54N 12 27 E
Vaticano, C. 40 38 40N 15 48 E
Vatin 42 45 12N 21 20 E
Vatnajökull 50 64 30N 16 48W
Vatnås 47 59 58N 9 37 E
Vatne 47 62 33N 6 38 E
Vatneyri 50 65 35N 24 0W
Vatoa 101 19 50 S 178 13W
Vatoloha, Mt. 93 17 52 S 47 48 E
Vatomandry 93 19 20 S 48 59 E
Vatra-Dornei 46 47 22N 25 22 E
Vättern 49 58 25N 14 30 E
Vaucluse □ 21 44 3N 5 10 E
Vaucouleurs 19 48 37N 5 38 E
Vaud □ 25 46 35N 6 30 E
Vaughan 119 34 37N 105 12W
Vaughn 118 47 37N 111 36W
Vaupés → 126 0 2N 67 16W
Vauvert 21 43 42N 4 17 E
Vauxhall 108 50 5N 112 9W
Vava'u 101 18 36 S 174 0W
Vavincourt 19 48 49N 5 12 E
Vavoua 84 7 23N 6 29W
Vaxholm 48 59 25N 18 20 E
Växjö 49 56 52N 14 50 E
Vaygach, Ostrov 58 70 0N 60 0 E
Vazovgrad 43 42 39N 24 45 E
Vechta 24 52 47N 8 18 E
Vechte → 16 52 34N 6 6 E
Vecilla, La 30 42 51N 5 27W
Vecsés 27 47 26N 19 19 E
Vedaraniam 70 10 25N 79 50 E
Veddige 49 57 17N 12 20 E
Vedea → 46 44 0N 25 20 E
Vedia 124 34 30 S 61 31W
Vedra, I. del 33 38 52N 1 12 E
Veendam 16 53 5N 6 52 E
Veenendaal 16 52 2N 5 34 E
Vefsna → 50 65 48N 13 10 E
Vega, Norway 50 65 40N 11 55 E
Vega, U.S.A. 117 35 18N 102 26W
Vega, La 121 19 20N 70 30W
Vegadeo 30 43 27N 7 4W
Vegafjorden 50 65 37N 12 0 E
Vegesack 24 53 10N 8 38 E
Veggli 47 60 3N 9 9 E
Veghel 16 51 37N 5 32 E
Vegorritis, Límni 44 40 45N 21 45 E
Vegreville 108 53 30N 112 5W
Vegusdal 47 58 32N 8 10 E
Veii 39 42 0N 12 24 E
Vejen 49 55 30N 9 9 E
Vejer de la Frontera 31 36 15N 5 59W
Vejle 49 55 43N 9 30 E
Vejle Fjord 49 55 40N 9 50 E
Vela Luka 39 42 59N 16 44 E
Velanai I. 70 9 45N 79 45 E
Velarde 119 36 11N 106 1W
Velasco 117 29 0N 95 20W
Velasco, Sierra de. 124 29 20 S 67 10W
Velay, Mts. du 20 45 0N 3 40 E
Velddrif 92 32 42 S 18 11 E
Velebit Planina 39 44 50N 15 20 E
Velebitski Kanal 39 44 45N 14 55 E
Veleka → 43 42 4N 27 58 E
Velenje 39 46 23N 15 8 E
Velestínon 44 39 23N 22 43 E
Veleta, La 31 37 1N 3 22W
Vélez 126 6 1N 73 41W
Velež 42 43 19N 18 2 E
Vélez Blanco 33 37 41N 2 5W
Vélez Málaga 31 36 48N 4 5W
Vélez Rubio 33 37 41N 2 5W
Velhas → 127 17 13 S 44 49W
Velika 42 45 27N 17 40 E
Velika Gorica 39 45 44N 16 5 E
Velika Gradište 42 44 46N 21 29 E
Velika Kapela 39 45 10N 15 5 E
Velika Kladuša 39 45 11N 15 48 E
Velika Morava → 42 44 43N 21 3 E
Velika Plana 42 44 20N 21 1 E
Velikaya → 54 57 48N 28 20 E
Velikaya Lepetikha 56 47 2N 33 58 E
Veliké Kapušany 27 48 34N 22 5 E
Velike Lašče 39 45 49N 14 45 E
Veliki Backa Kanal 42 45 45N 19 15 E
Veliki Jastrebac 42 43 25N 21 30 E
Veliki Popović 42 44 8N 21 18 E
Veliki Ustyug 52 60 47N 46 20 E
Velikiye Luki 54 56 25N 30 32 E
Velikonda Range 70 14 45N 79 10 E
Velikoye, Oz. 55 55 15N 40 10 E
Velingrad 43 42 4N 23 58 E
Velino, Mte. 39 42 10N 13 20 E
Velizh 54 55 36N 31 11 E
Velké Karlovice 27 49 20N 18 17 E
Velke Meziřici 26 49 21N 16 1 E
Veľký ostrov Žitný 27 48 5N 17 20 E
Vellar → 70 11 30N 79 36 E
Velletri 40 41 43N 12 43 E
Vellinge 49 55 29N 13 0 E
Vellore 70 12 57N 79 10 E
Velsen-Noord 16 52 27N 4 40 E
Velsk 52 61 10N 42 5 E
Velten 24 52 40N 13 11 E
Velva 116 48 6N 100 56W
Velvendós 44 40 15N 22 6 E
Vembanad Lake 70 9 36N 76 15 E
Veme 47 60 14N 10 7 E
Ven 49 55 55N 12 45 E
Vena 49 57 31N 16 0 E
Venado 120 22 56N 101 10W
Venado Tuerto 124 33 50 S 62 0W
Venafro 41 41 28N 14 3 E
Venarey-les-Laumes 19 47 32N 4 26 E
Venaria 38 45 6N 7 39 E
Venčane 42 44 24N 20 28 E
Vence 21 43 43N 7 6 E
Vendas Novas 31 38 39N 8 27W
Vendée □ 18 46 50N 1 35W
Vendée → 18 46 20N 1 10W
Vendée, Collines de 18 46 35N 0 45W
Vendeuvre-sur-Barse 19 48 14N 4 28 E
Vendôme 18 47 47N 1 3 E
Vendrell 32 41 10N 1 30 E
Vendsyssel 49 57 22N 10 0 E
Véneta, Laguna 39 45 23N 12 25 E
Véneto □ 39 45 40N 12 0 E
Venev 55 54 22N 38 17 E
Venézia 39 45 27N 12 20 E
Venézia, Golfo di 39 45 20N 13 0 E
Venezuela ■ 126 8 0N 65 0W
Venezuela, Golfo de 126 11 30N 71 0W
Vengurla 70 15 53N 73 45 E
Vengurla Rocks 70 15 55N 73 22 E
Venice = Venézia 39 45 27N 12 20 E
Vénissieux 21 45 43N 4 53 E
Venkatagiri 70 14 0N 79 35 E
Venkatapuram 70 18 20N 80 30 E
Venlo 16 51 22N 6 11 E
Vennesla 47 58 15N 8 0 E
Venraij 16 51 31N 6 0 E
Venta de Cardeña 31 38 16N 4 20W
Venta de San Rafael 30 40 42N 4 12W
Ventana, Punta de la 120 24 4N 109 48W
Ventana, Sa. de la 124 38 0 S 62 30W
Ventersburg 92 28 7 S 27 9 E
Ventimíglia 38 43 50N 7 39 E
Ventnor 13 50 35N 1 12W
Ventotene 40 40 48N 13 25 E
Ventoux 21 44 10N 5 17 E
Ventspils 54 57 25N 21 32 E
Ventuari → 126 3 58N 67 2W
Ventura 119 34 16N 119 18W
Vera, Argent. 124 29 30 S 60 20W
Vera, Spain 33 37 15N 1 51W
Veracruz 120 19 10N 96 10W
Veracruz □ 120 19 0N 96 15W
Veraval 68 20 53N 70 27 E
Verbánia 38 45 56N 8 43 E
Verbicaro 41 39 46N 15 54 E
Vercelli 38 45 19N 8 25 E
Verchovchevo 56 48 32N 34 10 E
Verdalsøra 50 63 48N 11 30 E
Verde →, Argent. 128 41 56 S 65 5W
Verde →, Chihuahua, Mexico 120 26 29N 107 58W
Verde →, Oaxaca, Mexico 120 15 59N 97 50W
Verde →, Veracruz, Mexico 120 21 10N 102 50W
Verde →, Parag. 124 23 9 S 57 37W
Verde, Cay 121 23 0N 75 5W
Verden 24 52 58N 9 18 E
Verdhikoúsa 44 39 47N 21 59 E
Verdigre 116 42 38N 98 0W

Verdon → 21 43 43N 5 46 E
Verdon-sur-Mer, Le 20 45 33N 1 4W
Verdun 19 49 12N 5 24 E
Verdun-sur-le Doubs 19 46 54N 5 0 E
Vereeniging 93 26 38 S 27 57 E
Vérendrye, Parc Prov. de la 106 47 20N 76 40W
Verga, C. 84 10 30N 14 10W
Vergara 32 43 9N 2 28W
Vergato 38 44 18N 11 8 E
Vergemont 98 23 33 S 143 1 E
Vergemont Cr. → 98 24 16 S 143 16 E
Vergennes 113 44 9N 73 15W
Vergt 20 45 2N 0 43 E
Verín 30 41 57N 7 27W
Veriña 30 43 32N 5 43W
Verkhnedvinsk 54 55 45N 27 58 E
Verkhnevilyuysk 59 63 27N 120 18 E
Verkhneye Kalinino 59 59 54N 108 8 E
Verkhniy Baskunchak 57 48 14N 46 44 E
Verkhovye 55 52 55N 37 15 E
Verkhoyansk 59 67 35N 133 25 E
Verkhoyanskiy Khrebet 59 66 0N 129 0 E
Verlo 109 50 19N 108 35W
Verma 47 62 21N 8 3 E
Vermenton 19 47 40N 3 42 E
Vermilion 109 53 20N 110 50W
Vermilion →, Alta., Can. 109 53 22N 110 51W
Vermilion →, Qué., Can. 106 47 38N 72 56W
Vermilion, B. 117 29 45N 91 55W
Vermilion Bay 109 49 51N 93 34W
Vermilion Chutes 108 58 22N 114 51W
Vermilion L. 116 47 53N 92 25W
Vermillion 116 42 50N 96 56W
Vermont □ 114 43 40N 72 50W
Vernal 118 40 28N 109 35W
Verner 106 46 25N 80 8W
Verneuil-sur-Avre 18 48 45N 0 55 E
Vernon, Can. 108 50 20N 119 15W
Vernon, France 18 49 5N 1 30 E
Vernon, U.S.A. 117 34 10N 99 20W
Vero Beach 115 27 39N 80 23W
Véroia 44 40 34N 22 12 E
Verolanuova 38 45 20N 10 5 E
Véroli 40 41 43N 13 24 E
Verona 38 45 27N 11 0 E
Veropol 59 65 15N 168 40 E
Versailles 19 48 48N 2 8 E
Vert, C. 84 14 45N 17 30W
Vertou 18 47 10N 1 28W
Vertus 19 48 54N 4 0 E
Verulam 93 29 38 S 31 2 E
Verviers 16 50 37N 5 52 E
Vervins 19 49 50N 3 53 E
Verwood 109 49 30N 105 40W
Verzej 39 46 34N 16 13 E
Veselí nad Lužnicí 26 49 12N 14 43 E
Veseliye 43 42 18N 27 38 E
Veselovskoye Vdkhr. 57 47 0N 41 0 E
Veshenskaya 57 49 35N 41 44 E
Vesle → 19 49 23N 3 38 E
Vesoul 19 47 40N 6 11 E
Vessigebro 49 56 58N 12 40 E
Vest-Agder fylke □ 47 58 30N 7 15 E
Vestby 47 59 37N 10 45 E
Vestfjorden 50 67 55N 14 0 E
Vestfold·fylke □ 47 59 15N 10 0 E
Vestmannaeyjar 50 63 27N 20 15W
Vestmarka 47 59 56N 11 59 E
Vestnes 47 62 39N 7 5 E
Vestone 38 45 43N 10 25 E
Vestsjællands Amtskommune □ 49 55 30N 11 20 E
Vestspitsbergen 4 78 40N 17 0 E
Vestvågøy 50 68 18N 13 50 E
Vesuvio 41 40 50N 14 22 E
Vesuvius, Mt. = Vesuvio 41 40 50N 14 22 E
Vesyegonsk 55 58 40N 37 16 E
Veszprém 27 47 8N 17 57 E
Veszprém □ 27 47 5N 17 55 E
Vésztő 27 46 55N 21 16 E
Vetapalem 70 15 47N 80 18 E
Vetlanda 49 57 24N 15 3 E
Vetluga 55 57 53N 45 45 E
Vetluzhskiy 55 57 17N 45 12 E
Vetovo 43 43 42N 26 16 E
Vetralia 39 42 20N 12 2 E
Vetren 43 42 15N 24 3 E
Vettore, Monte 39 42 49N 13 16 E
Veurne 16 51 5N 2 40 E
Vevey 25 46 28N 6 51 E
Vévi 44 40 47N 21 38 E
Veynes 21 44 32N 5 49 E
Veys 64 31 30N 49 0 E
Vézelise 19 48 30N 6 5 E
Vézère → 20 44 53N 0 53 E
Vezhen 43 42 50N 24 20 E
Viacha 126 16 39 S 68 18W
Viadana 38 44 55N 10 30 E
Viana, Brazil 127 3 13 S 45 0W
Viana, Spain 32 42 31N 2 22W
Viana del Bollo 30 42 11N 7 6W
Viana do Alentejo 31 38 17N 7 59W
Viana do Castelo 30 41 42N 8 50W
Vianna do Castelo □ 30 41 50N 8 30W
Vianópolis 127 16 40 S 48 35W
Viar → 31 37 36N 5 50W
Viaréggio 38 43 52N 10 13 E
Viaur → 20 44 8N 1 58 E
Vibank 109 50 20N 103 56W
Vibo Valéntia 41 38 40N 16 5 E
Viborg 49 56 27N 9 23 E
Vibraye 18 48 3N 0 44 E
Vic-en-Bigorre 20 43 24N 0 3 E
Vic-Fézensac 20 43 47N 0 19 E
Vic-sur-Cère 20 44 59N 2 38 E
Vic-sur-Seille 19 48 45N 6 33 E
Vicenza 39 45 32N 11 31 E
Vich 32 41 58N 2 19 E
Vichuga 55 57 12N 41 55 E
Vichy 20 46 9N 3 26 E
Vicksburg, Mich., U.S.A. 114 42 10N 85 30W
Vicksburg, Miss., U.S.A. 117 32 22N 90 56W
Vico del Gargaro 41 41 54N 15 57 E
Vico, L. di 39 42 20N 12 10 E
Viçosa 127 9 28 S 36 14W
Victor, Colo., U.S.A. 116 38 43N 105 7W
Victor, N.Y., U.S.A. 112 42 58N 77 24W
Victor Harbour 97 35 30 S 138 37 E
Victoria, Argent. 124 32 40 S 60 10W
Victoria, Camer. 88 4 1N 9 10 E
Victoria, Can. 108 48 30N 123 25W
Victoria, Chile 128 38 13 S 72 20W
* Victoria, Guin. 84 10 50N 14 32W
Victoria, H. K. 75 22 16N 114 15 E
Victoria, Malay. 72 5 20N 115 14 E
Victoria, Kans., U.S.A. 116 38 52N 99 8W
Victoria, Tex., U.S.A. 117 28 50N 97 0W
Victoria □, Austral. 97 37 0 S 144 0 E
Victoria □, Zimb. 91 21 0 S 31 30 E
Victoria → 96 15 10 S 129 40 E
Victoria Beach 109 50 40N 96 35W
Victoria de las Tunas 121 20 58N 76 59W
Victoria Falls 91 17 58 S 25 52 E
Victoria, Grand L. 106 47 31N 77 30W
Victoria Harbour 106 44 45N 79 45W
Victoria I. 104 71 0N 111 0W
Victoria, L. 90 1 0 S 33 0 E
Victoria Ld. 5 75 0 S 160 0 E
Victoria, Mt. 98 8 55 S 147 32 E
Victoria Nile → 90 2 14N 31 26 E
Victoria Res. 107 48 20N 57 27W
Victoria River Downs 96 16 25 S 131 0 E
Victoria Taungdeik 67 21 15N 93 55 E
Victoria West 92 31 25 S 23 4 E
Victoriaville 107 46 4N 71 56W
Victorica 124 36 20 S 65 30W
Victorville 119 34 32N 117 18W
Vicuña 124 30 0 S 70 50W
Vicuña Mackenna 124 33 53 S 64 25W
Vidalia 115 32 13N 82 25W
Vidauban 21 43 25N 6 27 E
Vidigueira 31 38 12N 7 48W
Vidin 42 43 59N 22 50 E
Vidio, Cabo 30 43 35N 6 14W
Vidisha (Bhilsa) 68 23 28N 77 53 E
Vidöstern 49 57 5N 14 0 E
Vidra 46 45 56N 26 55 E
Viduša 42 42 55N 18 21 E
Vidzy 54 55 23N 26 37 E
Viechtach 25 49 5N 12 53 E
Viedma 128 40 50 S 63 0W
Viedma, L. 128 49 30 S 72 30W
Vieira 30 41 38N 8 8W
Viella 32 42 43N 0 44 E
Vien Pou Kha 71 20 45N 101 5 E
Vienenburg 24 51 57N 10 35 E
Vienna 117 37 29N 88 54W
Vienna = Wien 27 48 12N 16 22 E
Vienne 21 45 31N 4 53 E
Vienne □ 20 46 30N 0 42 E
Vienne → 18 47 13N 0 5 E
Vientiane 71 17 58N 102 36 E
Vientos, Paso de los 121 20 0N 74 0W
Viersen 24 51 15N 6 23 E
Vierwaldstättersee 25 47 0N 8 30 E
Vierzon 19 47 13N 2 5 E
Vieste 40 41 52N 16 14 E
Vietnam ■ 71 19 0N 106 0 E
Vieux-Boucau-les-Bains 20 43 48N 1 23W
Vif 21 45 5N 5 41 E
Vigan 73 17 35N 120 28 E
Vigan, Le 20 44 0N 3 36 E
Vigévano 38 45 18N 8 50 E
Vigia 127 0 50 S 48 5W
Vignacourt 19 50 1N 2 15 E
Vignemale, Pic du 20 42 47N 0 10W
Vigneulles 19 48 59N 5 40 E
Vignola 38 44 29N 11 0 E
Vigo 30 42 12N 8 41W
Vigo, Ría de 30 42 15N 8 45W
Vihiers 18 47 10N 0 30W
Vijayadurg 70 16 30N 73 25 E
Vijayawada (Bezwada) 70 16 31N 80 39 E
Vikedal 47 59 30N 5 55 E
Viken 49 58 39N 14 20 E
Vikersund 47 59 58N 10 2 E
Viking 108 53 7N 111 50W
Vikna 50 64 55N 10 58 E
Vikramasingapuram 70 8 40N 76 47 E
Viksjö 48 62 45N 17 26 E
Vikulovo 58 56 50N 70 40 E
Vila Aiferes Chamusca 93 24 27 S 33 0 E
Vila Caldas Xavier 91 14 28 S 33 0 E
Vila Coutinho 91 14 37 S 34 19 E
Vila da Maganja 91 17 18 S 37 30 E
Vila de João Belo = Xai-Xai 93 25 6 S 33 31 E
Vila de Junqueiro 91 15 25 S 36 58 E
Vila de Manica 91 18 58 S 32 59 E
Vila de Rei 31 39 41N 8 9W
Vila do Bispo 31 37 5N 8 53W
Vila do Chibuto 93 24 40 S 33 33 E
Vila do Conde 30 41 21N 8 45W
Vila Fontes 91 17 51 S 35 24 E
Vila Franca de Xira 31 38 57N 8 59W
Vila Gamito 91 14 12 S 33 0 E
Vila Gomes da Costa 93 24 20 S 33 37 E
Vila Luisa 93 25 45 S 32 35 E
Vila Machado 91 19 15 S 34 14 E
Vila Mouzinho 91 14 48 S 34 25 E
Vila Nova de Foscôa 30 41 5N 7 9W
Vila Nova de Ourém 31 39 40N 8 35W
Vila Novo de Gaia 30 41 4N 8 40W
Vila Paiva de Andrada 91 18 44 S 34 2 E
Vila Pouca de Aguiar 30 41 30N 7 38W
Vila Real 30 41 17N 7 48W
Vila Real de Santo António 31 37 10N 7 28W
Vila Vasco da Gama 91 14 54 S 32 14 E
Vila Velha 125 20 20 S 40 17W
Vila Veríssimo Sarmento 88 8 7 S 20 38 E
Vila Viçosa 31 38 45N 7 27W
Vilaboa 30 42 21N 8 39W
Vilaine → 18 47 30N 2 27W
Vilanculos 93 22 1 S 35 17 E
Vilar Formosa 30 40 38N 6 45W
Vilareal □ 30 41 36N 7 35W
Vilaseca-Salou 32 41 7N 1 9 E
Vilcea □ 46 45 0N 24 10 E
Vileyka 54 54 30N 26 53 E
Vilhelmina 50 64 35N 16 39 E
Vilhena 126 12 40 S 60 5W
Viliga 59 61 36N 156 56 E
Viliya → 54 55 54N 23 53 E
Viljandi 54 58 28N 25 30 E
Vilkovo 56 45 28N 29 32 E
Villa Abecia 124 21 0 S 68 18W
Villa Ahumada 120 30 38N 106 30W
Villa Ana 124 28 28 S 59 40W
Villa Angela 124 27 34 S 60 45W
Villa Bella 126 10 25 S 65 22W
Villa Bens = Tarfaya 80 27 55N 12 55W
Villa Cañás 124 34 0 S 61 35W
Villa Cisneros = Dakhla 80 23 50N 15 53W
Villa Colón 124 31 38 S 68 20W
Villa Constitución 124 33 15 S 60 20W
Villa de María 124 29 55 S 63 43W
Villa Dolores 124 31 58 S 65 15W
Villa Guillermina 124 28 15 S 59 29W
Villa Hayes 124 25 0 S 57 20W
Villa Iris 124 38 12 S 63 12W
Villa María 124 32 20 S 63 10W
Villa Mazán 124 28 40 S 66 30W
Villa Minozzo 38 44 21N 10 30 E
Villa Montes 124 21 10 S 63 30W
Villa Ocampo 124 28 30 S 59 20W
Villa Ojo de Agua 124 29 30 S 63 44W
Villa San Giovanni 41 38 13N 15 38 E
Villa San José 124 32 12 S 58 15W
Villa San Martín 124 28 15 S 64 9W
Villa Santina 39 46 25N 12 55 E
Villablino 30 42 57N 6 19W
Villacañas 32 39 38N 3 20W
Villacarlos 32 39 53N 4 17 E
Villacarriedo 32 43 14N 3 48W
Villacarrillo 33 38 7N 3 3W
Villacastín 30 40 46N 4 25W
Villach 26 46 37N 13 51 E
Villaciado 40 39 27N 8 45 E
Villada 30 42 15N 4 59W
Villadiego 30 42 31N 4 1W
Villadóssola 38 46 4N 8 16 E
Villafeliche 32 41 10N 1 30W
Villafranca 32 42 17N 1 46W
Villafranca de los Barros 31 38 35N 6 18W
Villafranca de los Caballeros 33 39 26N 3 21W
Villafranca del Bierzo 30 42 38N 6 50W
Villafranca del Cid 32 40 26N 0 16W
Villafranca del Panadés 32 41 21N 1 40 E
Villafranca di Verona 38 45 20N 10 51 E
Villagarcía de Arosa 30 42 34N 8 46W
Villagrán 120 24 29N 99 29W
Villaguay 124 32 0 S 59 0W
Villaharta 31 38 9N 4 54W
Villahermosa, Mexico 120 18 0N 92 50W
Villahermosa, Spain 33 38 46N 2 52W
Villaines-la-Juhel 18 48 21N 0 20W
Villajoyosa 33 38 30N 0 12W
Villalba 30 43 26N 7 40W
Villalba de Guardo 30 42 42N 4 49W
Villalcampo, Pantano de 30 41 31N 6 0W
Villalón de Campos 30 42 5N 5 4W
Villalpando 30 41 51N 5 25W
Villaluenga 30 40 2N 3 54W
Villamanán 30 42 19N 5 35W
Villamartín 31 36 52N 5 38W
Villamayor 32 39 50N 2 59W
Villamblard 20 45 2N 0 32 E
Villanova Monteleone 40 40 30N 8 28 E
Villanueva 119 35 16N 105 23W
Villanueva de Castellón 33 39 5N 0 31W
Villanueva de Córdoba 31 38 20N 4 38W
Villanueva de la Fuente 33 38 42N 2 42W
Villanueva de la Serena 31 38 59N 5 50W
Villanueva de la Sierra 30 40 12N 6 24W
Villanueva de los Castillejos 31 37 30N 7 15W
Villanueva del Arzobispo 33 38 10N 3 0W
Villanueva del Duque 31 38 20N 5 0W
Villanueva del Fresno 31 38 23N 7 10W
Villanueva y Geltrú 32 41 13N 1 40 E
Villaodrid 30 43 20N 7 11W
Villaputzu 40 39 28N 9 33 E
Villar del Arzobispo 32 39 44N 0 50W
Villar del Rey 31 39 7N 6 50W
Villarcayo 32 42 56N 3 34W
Villard-Bonnet 21 45 14N 5 53 E
Villard-de-Lans 21 45 3N 5 33 E
Villarino de los Aires 30 41 18N 6 23W
Villarosa 41 37 36N 14 9 E
Villarramiel 30 42 2N 4 55W
Villarreal 32 39 55N 0 3W
Villarrica, Chile 128 39 15 S 72 15W
Villarrica, Parag. 124 25 40 S 56 30W
Villarrobledo 33 39 18N 2 36W
Villarroya de la Sierra 32 41 27N 1 46W
Villarrubia de los Ojos 33 39 14N 3 36W
Villars 21 46 0N 5 2 E
Villarta de San Juan 33 39 15N 3 25W
Villasayas 32 41 24N 2 39W
Villaseca de los Gamitos 30 41 2N 6 7W
Villastar 32 40 17N 1 9W
Villatobas 32 39 54N 3 20W
Villavicencio, Argent. 124 32 28 S 69 0W
Villavicencio, Colomb. 126 4 9N 73 37W
Villaviciosa 30 43 32N 5 27W
Villazón 124 22 0 S 65 35W
Ville-Marie 106 47 20N 79 30W
Ville Platte 117 30 45N 92 17W
Villedieu 18 48 50N 1 12W
Villefort 20 44 28N 3 56 E
Villefranche 19 47 19N 1 46 E
Villefranche-de-Lauragais 20 43 25N 1 44 E
Villefranche-de-Rouergue 20 44 21N 2 2 E
Villefranche-du-Périgord 20 44 38N 1 5 E
Villefranche-sur-Saône 21 45 59N 4 43 E
Villel 32 40 14N 1 12W
Villemaur 19 48 14N 3 40 E
Villemur-sur-Tarn 20 43 51N 1 31 E
Villena 33 38 39N 0 52W
Villenauxe 19 48 36N 3 30 E
Villenave 20 44 46N 0 33W
Villeneuve, France 19 48 42N 2 25 E
Villeneuve, Italy 38 45 40N 7 10 E
Villeneuve-l'Archevêque 19 48 14N 3 32 E
Villeneuve-lès-Avignon 21 43 57N 4 49 E
Villeneuve-sur-Allier 20 46 40N 3 13 E
Villeneuve-sur-Lot 20 44 24N 0 42 E
Villeréal 20 44 38N 0 45 E
Villers-Bocage 18 49 3N 0 40W
Villers-Bretonneux 19 49 50N 2 30 E
Villers-Cotterêts 19 49 15N 3 4 E
Villers-Outreaux 19 50 2N 3 18 E
Villers-sur-Mer 18 49 21N 0 2W
Villersexel 19 47 33N 6 26 E
Villerupt 19 49 28N 5 55 E
Villerville 18 49 26N 0 5 E
Villiers 93 27 2 S 28 36 E
Villingen 25 48 4N 8 28 E
Villingen-Schwenningen 25 48 3N 8 29 E
Villisca 116 40 55N 94 59W
Villupuram 70 11 59N 79 31 E
Vilna 108 54 7N 111 55W
Vilnius 54 54 38N 25 19 E
Vils 26 47 33N 10 37 E
Vils → 25 48 38N 13 11 E
Vilsbiburg 25 48 27N 12 23 E
Vilshofen 25 48 38N 13 11 E
Vilskutskogo, Proliv 59 78 0N 103 0 E
Vilusi 42 42 44N 18 34 E
Vilvoorde 16 50 56N 4 26 E
Vilyuy → 59 64 24N 126 26 E
Vilyuysk 59 63 40N 121 35 E
Vimercate 38 45 38N 9 25 E
Vimiosa 30 41 35N 6 31W
Vimmerby 49 57 40N 15 55 E
Vimoutiers 18 48 57N 0 10 E
Vimperk 26 49 3N 13 46 E
Viña del Mar 124 33 0 S 71 30W
Vinaroz 32 40 30N 0 27 E
Vincennes 114 38 42N 87 29W
Vinchina 124 28 45 S 68 15W
Vindel älven → 50 63 55N 19 50 E
Vindeln 50 64 12N 19 43 E
Vinderup 49 56 29N 8 45 E
Vindhya Ra. 68 22 50N 77 0 E
Vineland 114 39 30N 75 0W
Vinga 42 46 0N 21 14 E
Vingnes 47 61 7N 10 26 E
Vinh 71 18 45N 105 38 E
Vinhais 30 41 50N 7 0W
Vinica, Hrvatska, Yugo. 39 46 20N 16 9 E
Vinica, Slovenija, Yugo. 39 45 28N 15 16 E
Vinita 117 36 40N 95 12W
Vinkovci 42 45 19N 18 48 E
Vinnitsa 56 49 15N 28 30 E
Vinson Massif 5 78 35 S 85 25W
Vinstra 47 61 37N 9 44 E
Vinton, Iowa, U.S.A. 116 42 8N 92 1W
Vinton, La., U.S.A. 117 30 13N 93 35W
Vințu de Jos 46 46 0N 23 30 E
Viöl 24 54 32N 9 12 E
Vipava 39 45 51N 13 58 E
Vipiteno 39 46 55N 11 25 E
Viqueque 73 8 52 S 126 23 E
Vir 39 44 17N 15 3 E
Virac 73 13 30N 124 20 E
Virago Sd. 108 54 0N 132 30W
Virajpet 70 12 10N 75 50 E
Viramgam 68 23 5N 72 0 E
Virananşehir 64 37 13N 39 45 E
Virarajendrapet = Virajpet 70 12 10N 75 50 E
Viravanallur 70 8 40N 77 30 E
Virden 109 49 50N 100 56W
Vire 18 48 50N 0 53W
Vire → 18 49 20N 1 7W
Virgenes, C. 128 52 19 S 68 21W
Virgin →, Can. 109 57 2N 108 17W
Virgin →, U.S.A. 119 36 50N 114 10W
Virgin Gorda 121 18 30N 64 26W
Virgin Is. 121 18 40N 64 30W
Virginia, S. Afr. 92 28 8 S 26 55 E
Virginia, U.S.A. 116 47 30N 92 32W
Virginia □ 114 37 45N 78 0W
Virginia Beach 114 36 54N 75 58W
Virginia City, Mont., U.S.A. 118 45 18N 111 58W
Virginia City, Nev., U.S.A. 118 39 19N 119 39W
Virginia Falls 108 61 38N 125 42W
Virginiatown 106 48 9N 79 36W
Virieu-le-Grand 21 45 51N 5 39 E
Virje 42 46 4N 16 59 E
Viroqua 116 43 33N 90 57W
Virovitica 42 45 51N 17 21 E
Virpazar 42 42 14N 19 6 E
Virserum 49 57 20N 15 35 E
Virton 16 49 35N 5 32 E
Virtsu 54 58 32N 23 33 E
Virudunagar 70 9 30N 78 0 E
Vis 39 43 0N 16 10 E
Vis Kanal 39 43 4N 16 5 E
Visalia 119 36 25N 119 18W
Visayan Sea 73 11 30N 123 30 E
Visby 49 57 37N 18 18 E
Viscount Melville Sd. 4 74 10N 108 0W
Visé 16 50 44N 5 41 E
Višegrad 42 43 47N 19 17 E
Viseu, Brazil 127 1 10 S 46 5W
Viseu, Port. 30 40 40N 7 55W
Viseu □ 30 40 40N 7 55W
Vișeu de Sus 46 47 45N 24 25 E
Vishakhapatnam 70 17 45N 83 20 E
Vishnupur 69 23 8N 87 20 E
Visikoi I. 5 56 43 S 27 15W
Visingsö 49 58 2N 14 20 E
Viskafors 49 57 37N 12 50 E
Vislanda 49 56 46N 14 30 E
Vislinskil Zaliv (Zalew Wislany) 28 54 20N 19 50 E
Visnagar 68 23 45N 72 32 E
Višnja Gora 39 45 58N 14 45 E
Viso del Marqués 33 38 32N 3 34W
Viso, Mte. 38 44 38N 7 5 E
Visoko 42 43 58N 18 10 E

* Renamed Limbe

Visp	**25**	46 17N	7 52 E
Visselhövede	**24**	52 59N	9 36 E
Vistonikos, Ormos	**44**	41 0N	25 7 E
Vistula = Wisła →	**28**	54 22N	18 55 E
Vit →	**43**	43 30N	24 30 E
Vitanje	**39**	46 25N	15 18 E
Vitebsk	**54**	55 10N	30 15 E
Viterbo	**39**	42 25N	12 8 E
Viti Levu	**101**	17 30 S	177 30 E
Vitiaz Str.	**98**	5 40 S	147 10 E
Vitigudino	**30**	41 1N	6 26W
Vitim	**59**	59 28N	112 35 E
Vitim →	**59**	59 26N	112 34 E
Vitína	**45**	37 40N	22 10 E
Vitina	**42**	43 17N	17 29 E
Vitória	**127**	20 20 S	40 22W
Vitoria	**32**	42 50N	2 41W
Vitória da Conquista	**127**	14 51 S	40 51W
Vitória de São Antão	**127**	8 10 S	35 20W
Vitré	**18**	48 8N	1 12W
Vitry-le-François	**19**	48 43N	4 33 E
Vitsi, Óros	**44**	40 40N	21 25 E
Vitteaux	**19**	47 24N	4 30 E
Vittel	**19**	48 12N	5 57 E
Vittória	**41**	36 58N	14 30 E
Vittório Véneto	**39**	45 59N	12 18 E
Vitu Is.	**98**	4 50 S	149 25 E
Viver	**32**	39 55N	0 36W
Vivero	**30**	43 39N	7 38W
Viviers	**21**	44 30N	4 40 E
Vivonne	**20**	46 25N	0 15 E
Vizcaíno, Desierto de	**120**	27 40N	113 50W
Vizcaíno, Sierra	**120**	27 30N	114 0W
Vizcaya □	**32**	43 15N	2 45W
Vizianagaram	**70**	18 6N	83 30 E
Vizille	**21**	45 5N	5 46 E
Viziñada	**39**	45 20N	13 46 E
Viziru	**46**	45 0N	27 43 E
Vizovice	**27**	49 12N	17 56 E
Vizzini	**41**	37 9N	14 43 E
Vjosa →	**44**	40 37N	19 42 E
Vlaardingen	**16**	51 55N	4 21 E
Vlădeasa	**46**	46 47N	22 50 E
Vladicin Han	**42**	42 42N	22 1 E
Vladimir	**55**	56 15N	40 30 E
Vladimir Volynskiy	**54**	50 50N	24 18 E
Vladimirci	**42**	44 36N	19 45 E
Vladimirovac	**42**	45 1N	20 53 E
Vladimirovka, R.S.F.S.R., U.S.S.R.	**57**	48 27N	46 10 E
Vladimirovka, R.S.F.S.R., U.S.S.R.	**57**	44 45N	44 41 E
Vladimirovo	**43**	43 32N	23 22 E
Vladislavovka	**56**	45 15N	35 15 E
Vladivostok	**59**	43 10N	131 53 E
Vlasenica	**42**	44 11N	18 59 E
Vlašić	**42**	44 19N	17 37 E
Vlašim	**26**	49 40N	14 53 E
Vlasinsko Jezero	**42**	42 44N	22 22 E
Vlasotinci	**42**	42 59N	22 7 E
Vlieland	**16**	53 16N	4 55 E
Vlissingen	**16**	51 26N	3 34 E
Vlóra	**44**	40 32N	19 28 E
Vlóra □	**44**	40 12N	20 0 E
Vlorës, Gjiri i	**44**	40 29N	19 27 E
Vltava →	**26**	50 21N	14 30 E
Vobarno	**38**	45 38N	10 30 E
Voćin	**42**	45 37N	17 33 E
Vöcklabruck	**26**	48 1N	13 39 E
Vodice	**39**	43 47N	15 47 E
Vodňany	**26**	49 9N	14 11 E
Vodnjan	**39**	44 59N	13 52 E
Vogelkop = Doberai, Jazirah	**73**	1 25 S	133 0 E
Vogelsberg	**24**	50 37N	9 15 E
Voghera	**38**	44 59N	9 1 E
Vohibinany	**93**	18 49 S	49 4 E
Vohimarina	**93**	13 25 S	50 0 E
Vohimena, Tanjon' i	**93**	25 36 S	45 8 E
Vohipeno	**93**	22 22 S	47 51 E
Voi	**90**	3 25 S	38 32 E
Void	**19**	48 40N	5 36 E
Voineşti, Iaşi, Romania	**46**	47 5N	27 27 E
Voineşti, Prahova, Romania	**46**	45 5N	25 14 E
Voíotía □	**45**	38 20N	23 0 E
Voiron	**21**	45 22N	5 35 E
Voisey B.	**107**	56 15N	61 50W
Voitsberg	**26**	47 3N	15 9 E
Voiviïs Límni	**44**	39 30N	22 45 E
Vojens	**49**	55 16N	9 18 E
Vojmsjön	**50**	64 55N	16 40 E
Vojnik	**38**	46 18N	15 19 E
Vojnió	**39**	45 19N	15 43 E
Vojvodina, Auton. Pokrajina □	**42**	45 20N	20 0 E
Vokhma	**55**	59 0N	46 45 E
Vokhma →	**55**	56 20N	46 20 E
Vokhtoga	**55**	58 46N	41 8 E
Volary	**26**	48 54N	13 52 E
Volborg	**116**	45 50N	105 44W
Volcano Is.	**94**	25 0N	141 0 E
Volchansk	**55**	50 17N	36 58 E
Volchayevka	**59**	48 40N	134 30 E
Volchya →	**56**	48 0N	37 0 E
Volda	**47**	62 9N	6 5 E
Volga	**55**	57 58N	38 16 E
Volga →	**57**	48 30N	46 0 E
Volga Hts. = Privolzhskaya V. S.	**53**	51 0N	46 0 E
Volgodonsk	**57**	47 33N	42 5 E
Volgograd	**57**	48 40N	44 25 E
Volgogradskoye Vdkhr.	**55**	50 0N	45 20 E
Volgorechensk	**55**	57 28N	41 14 E
Volissós	**45**	38 29N	25 54 E
Volkach	**25**	49 52N	10 14 E
Völkermarkt	**26**	46 39N	14 39 E
Volkhov	**54**	59 55N	32 15 E
Volkhov →	**54**	60 8N	32 20 E
Völklingen	**25**	49 15N	6 50 E
Volkovysk	**54**	53 9N	24 30 E
Volksrust	**93**	27 24 S	29 53 E
Vollenhove	**16**	52 40N	5 58 E
Vol'n'ansk	**56**	47 55N	35 29 E
Volnovakha	**56**	47 35N	37 30 E
Volochanka	**59**	71 0N	94 28 E
Volodarsk	**55**	56 12N	43 15 E
Vologda	**55**	59 10N	40 0 E
Volokolamsk	**55**	56 5N	35 57 E
Volokonovka	**55**	50 33N	37 52 E
Vólos	**44**	39 24N	22 59 E
Volosovo	**54**	59 27N	29 32 E
Volozhin	**54**	54 3N	26 30 E
Volsk	**55**	52 5N	47 22 E
Volta →	**85**	5 46N	0 41 E
Volta, L.	**85**	7 30N	0 15 E
Volta Redonda	**125**	22 31 S	44 5W
Volterra	**38**	43 24N	10 50 E
Voltri	**38**	44 25N	8 43 E
Volturara Áppula	**41**	41 30N	15 2 E
Volturno →	**41**	41 1N	13 55 E
Volubilis	**82**	34 2N	5 33W
Volujak	**42**	43 53N	17 47 E
Vólvi, L.	**44**	40 40N	23 34 E
Volzhsk	**55**	55 57N	48 23 E
Volzhskiy	**57**	48 56N	44 46 E
Vondrozo	**93**	22 49 S	47 20 E
Vónitsa	**45**	38 53N	20 58 E
Voorburg	**16**	52 5N	4 24 E
Vopnafjörður	**50**	65 45N	14 40W
Vorarlberg □	**26**	47 20N	10 0 E
Vóras Óros	**44**	40 57N	21 45 E
Vorbasse	**49**	55 39N	9 6 E
Vorderrhein →	**25**	46 49N	9 25 E
Vordingborg	**49**	55 0N	11 54 E
Voreppe	**21**	45 18N	5 39 E
Voríai Sporádhes	**45**	39 15N	23 30 E
Vórios Evvoïkos Kólpos	**45**	38 45N	23 15 E
Vorkuta	**52**	67 48N	64 20 E
Vorma →	**47**	60 9N	11 27 E
Vorona →	**55**	51 22N	42 3 E
Voronezh, R.S.F.S.R., U.S.S.R.	**55**	51 40N	39 10 E
Voronezh, Ukraine, U.S.S.R.	**54**	51 47N	33 28 E
Voronezh →	**55**	51 56N	37 17 E
Vorontsovo-Aleksandrovskoye = Zelenokumsk	**57**	44 30N	44 1 E
Voroshilovgrad	**57**	48 38N	39 15 E
Vorovskoye	**59**	54 30N	155 50 E
Vorskla →	**56**	48 50N	34 10 E
Vöru	**54**	57 48N	26 54 E
Vorupør	**49**	56 58N	8 22 E
Vosges	**19**	48 20N	7 10 E
Vosges □	**19**	48 12N	6 20 E
Voskopoja	**44**	40 40N	20 33 E
Voskresensk	**55**	55 19N	38 43 E
Voskresenskoye	**55**	56 51N	45 30 E
Voss	**47**	60 38N	6 26 E
Vostochnyy Sayan	**59**	54 0N	96 0 E
Vostok I.	**95**	10 5 S	152 23W
Votice	**26**	49 38N	14 39 E
Votkinsk	**52**	57 0N	53 55 E
Votkinskoye Vdkhr.	**52**	57 30N	55 0 E
Vouga →	**30**	40 41N	8 40W
Vouillé	**18**	46 38N	0 10 E
Voulte-sur-Rhône, La	**21**	44 48N	4 46 E
Vouvray	**18**	47 25N	0 48 E
Voúxa, Ákra	**45**	35 37N	23 32 E
Vouzela	**30**	40 43N	8 7W
Vouziers	**19**	49 22N	4 40 E
Voves	**19**	48 15N	1 38 E
Voxna	**48**	61 20N	15 40 E
Vozhe Oz.	**52**	60 45N	39 0 E
Vozhgaly	**55**	58 9N	50 11 E
Voznesenka	**59**	56 40N	95 3 E
Voznesensk	**56**	47 35N	31 21 E
Voznesenye	**52**	61 0N	35 45 E
Vráble	**27**	48 15N	18 16 E
Vraćevšnica	**42**	44 2N	20 34 E
Vrådal	**47**	59 20N	8 25 E
Vraka	**44**	42 8N	19 28 E
Vrakhnéïka	**45**	38 10N	21 40 E
Vrancea □	**46**	45 50N	26 45 E
Vrancei, Munţii	**46**	46 0N	26 30 E
Vrangelya, Ostrov	**59**	71 0N	180 0 E
Vranica	**42**	43 55N	17 50 E
Vranje	**42**	42 34N	21 54 E
Vranjska Banja	**42**	42 34N	22 1 E
Vranov	**27**	48 53N	21 40 E
Vransko	**39**	46 17N	14 58 E
Vratsa	**43**	43 13N	23 30 E
Vrbas	**42**	45 40N	19 40 E
Vrbas →	**42**	45 8N	17 29 E
Vrbnik	**39**	45 4N	14 40 E
Vrbovec	**39**	45 53N	16 28 E
Vrbovsko	**39**	45 24N	15 5 E
Vrchlabí	**26**	50 38N	15 37 E
Vrede	**93**	27 24 S	29 6 E
Vredefort	**92**	27 0 S	26 22 E
Vredenburg	**92**	32 51 S	18 0 E
Vredendal	**92**	31 41 S	18 35 E
Vrena	**49**	58 54N	16 41 E
Vrgorac	**42**	43 12N	17 20 E
Vrhnika	**39**	45 58N	14 15 E
Vriddhachalam	**70**	11 30N	79 20 E
Vrïdi	**84**	5 15N	4 3W
Vrindaban	**68**	27 37N	77 40 E
Vrnograč	**39**	45 10N	15 57 E
Vrondádhes	**45**	38 25N	26 7 E
Vrpolje	**42**	45 13N	18 24 E
Vršac	**42**	45 8N	21 18 E
Vrsacki Kanal	**42**	45 15N	21 0 E
Vryburg	**92**	26 55 S	24 45 E
Vryheid	**93**	27 45 S	30 47 E
Vsetín	**27**	49 20N	18 0 E
Vucha →	**43**	42 10N	24 26 E
Vučitrn	**42**	42 49N	20 59 E
Vught	**16**	51 38N	5 20 E
Vukovar	**42**	45 21N	18 59 E
Vulcan, Can.	**108**	50 25N	113 15W
Vulcan, Romania	**46**	45 23N	23 17 E
Vulcan, U.S.A.	**114**	45 46N	87 51W
Vulcano	**41**	38 25N	14 58 E
Vŭlchedruma	**43**	43 42N	23 27 E
Vulci	**39**	42 23N	11 37 E
Vulkaneshty	**56**	45 35N	28 30 E
Vunduzi →	**91**	18 56 S	34 1 E
Vung Tau	**71**	10 21N	107 4 E
Vŭrbitsa	**43**	42 59N	26 40 E
Vurshets	**43**	43 15N	23 23 E
Vutcani	**46**	46 26N	27 59 E
Vuyyuru	**70**	16 28N	80 50 E
Vyara	**68**	21 8N	73 28 E
Vyasniki	**55**	56 10N	42 10 E
Vyatka →	**52**	56 30N	51 0 E
Vyatskiye Polyany	**52**	56 5N	51 0 E
Vyazemskiy	**59**	47 32N	134 45 E
Vyazma	**54**	55 10N	34 15 E
Vyborg	**52**	60 43N	28 47 E
Vychegda →	**52**	61 18N	46 36 E
Vychodné Beskydy	**27**	49 30N	22 0 E
Východočeský □	**26**	50 20N	15 45 E
Východoslovenský □	**27**	48 50N	21 0 E
Vyg-ozero	**52**	63 30N	34 0 E
Vyksa	**55**	55 19N	42 11 E
Vypin	**70**	10 10N	76 15 E
Vyrnwy, L.	**12**	52 48N	3 30W
Vyshniy Volochek	**54**	57 30N	34 30 E
Vyškov	**27**	49 17N	17 0 E
Vysoké Mýto	**27**	49 58N	10 10 E
Vysokovsk	**55**	56 22N	36 30 E
Vysotsk	**54**	51 43N	26 32 E
Vyšší Brod	**26**	48 37N	14 19 E
Vytegra	**52**	61 0N	36 27 E
W			
W.A.C. Bennett Dam	**108**	56 2N	122 6W
Wa	**84**	10 7N	2 25W
Waal →	**16**	51 59N	4 30 E
Wabakimi L.	**106**	50 38N	89 45W
Wabana	**107**	47 40N	53 0W
Wabasca	**108**	55 57N	113 56W
Wabash	**114**	40 48N	85 46W
Wabash →	**114**	37 46N	88 2W
Wabeno	**114**	45 25N	88 40W
Wabi →	**87**	7 45N	40 50 E
Wabigoon L.	**109**	49 44N	92 44W
Wabowden	**109**	54 55N	98 38W
Wąbrzeźno	**28**	53 16N	18 57 E
Wabuk Pt.	**106**	55 20N	85 5W
Wabush	**107**	52 55N	66 52W
Wabuska	**118**	39 9N	119 13W
Wächtersbach	**25**	50 16N	9 18 E
Waco	**117**	31 33N	97 5W
Waconichi, L.	**106**	50 8N	74 0W
Wad Ban Naqa	**87**	16 32N	33 9 E
Wad Banda	**87**	13 10N	27 56 E
Wad el Haddad	**87**	13 50N	33 30 E
Wad en Nau	**87**	14 10N	33 34 E
Wad Hamid	**87**	16 30N	32 45 E
Wâd Medanî	**87**	14 28N	33 30 E
Waddān	**83**	29 9N	16 10 E
Waddān, Jabal	**83**	29 0N	16 15 E
Waddeneilanden	**16**	53 25N	5 10 E
Waddenzee	**16**	53 6N	5 10 E
Waddington	**113**	44 51N	75 12W
Waddington, Mt.	**108**	51 23N	125 15W
Waddy Pt.	**99**	24 58 S	153 21 E
Wadena, Can.	**109**	51 57N	103 47W
Wadena, U.S.A.	**116**	46 25N	95 8W
Wädenswil	**25**	47 14N	8 40 E
Wadesboro	**115**	35 2N	80 2W
Wadhams	**108**	51 30N	127 30W
Wādī ash Shāţi'	**83**	27 30N	15 0 E
Wādī Banī Walīd	**83**	31 49N	14 0 E
Wadi Gemâl	**86**	24 35N	35 10 E
Wadi Halfa	**86**	21 53N	31 19 E
Wadi Masila	**63**	16 30N	49 0 E
Wadi Şabāḩ	**64**	23 50N	48 30 E
Wadlew	**28**	51 31N	19 23 E
Wadowice	**27**	49 52N	19 30 E
Wadsworth	**118**	39 38N	119 22W
Wafrah	**64**	28 33N	47 56 E
Wageningen	**16**	51 58N	5 40 E
Wager B.	**105**	65 26N	88 40W
Wager Bay	**105**	65 56N	90 49W
Wagga Wagga	**97**	35 7 S	147 24 E
Waghete	**73**	4 10 S	135 50 E
Wagin	**96**	33 17 S	117 25 E
Wagon Mound	**117**	36 1N	104 44W
Wagoner	**117**	36 0N	95 20W
Wagrowiec	**28**	52 48N	17 11 E
Wahai	**73**	2 48 S	129 35 E
Wahiawa	**110**	21 30N	158 2W
Wahoo	**116**	41 15N	96 35W
Wahpeton	**116**	46 20N	96 35W
Wai	**70**	17 56N	73 57 E
Waiau →	**101**	42 47 S	173 22 E
Waiawe Ganga →	**70**	6 15N	81 0 E
Waibeem	**73**	0 30 S	132 59 E
Waiblingen	**25**	48 49N	9 20 E
Waidhofen, Niederösterreich, Austria	**26**	48 49N	15 17 E
Waidhofen, Niederösterreich, Austria	**26**	47 57N	14 46 E
Waigeo	**73**	0 20 S	130 40 E
Waihi	**101**	37 23 S	175 52 E
Waihou →	**101**	37 15 S	175 40 E
Waika	**90**	2 22 S	25 42 E
Waikabubak	**73**	9 45 S	119 25 E
Waikaremoana	**101**	38 42 S	177 12 E
Waikari	**101**	42 58 S	172 41 E
Waikato →	**101**	37 23 S	174 43 E
Waikerie	**99**	34 9 S	140 0 E
Waikokopu	**101**	39 3 S	177 52 E
Waikouaiti	**101**	45 36 S	170 41 E
Waimate	**101**	44 45 S	171 3 E
Wainganga →	**69**	18 50N	79 55 E
Waingapu	**73**	9 35 S	120 11 E
Wainwright, Can.	**109**	52 50N	110 50W
Wainwright, U.S.A.	**104**	70 39N	160 1W
Waiouru	**101**	39 28 S	175 41 E
Waipara	**101**	43 3 S	172 46 E
Waipawa	**101**	39 56 S	176 38 E
Waipiro	**101**	38 2 S	178 22 E
Waipu	**101**	35 59 S	174 29 E
Waipukurau	**101**	40 1 S	176 33 E
Wairakei	**101**	38 37 S	176 6 E
Wairarapa, L.	**101**	41 14 S	175 15 E
Wairoa	**101**	39 3 S	177 25 E
Waitaki →	**101**	44 56 S	171 7 E
Waitara	**101**	38 59 S	174 15 E
Waitsburg	**118**	46 15N	118 0W
Waiuku	**101**	37 15 S	174 45 E
Wajima	**74**	37 30N	137 0 E
Wajir	**90**	1 42N	40 5 E
Wajir □	**90**	1 42N	40 20 E
Wakasa-Wan	**74**	35 40N	135 30 E
Wakatipu, L.	**101**	45 5 S	168 33 E
Wakaw	**109**	52 39N	105 44W
Wakayama	**74**	34 15N	135 15 E
Wakayama-ken □	**74**	33 50N	135 30 E
Wake Forest	**115**	35 58N	78 30W
Wake I.	**94**	19 18N	166 36 E
Wakefield, N.Z.	**101**	41 24 S	173 5 E
Wakefield, U.K.	**12**	53 41N	1 31W
Wakefield, Mass., U.S.A.	**113**	42 30N	71 3W
Wakefield, Mich., U.S.A.	**116**	46 28N	89 53W
Wakema	**67**	16 30N	95 11 E
Wakkanai	**74**	45 28N	141 35 E
Wakkerstroom	**93**	27 24 S	30 10 E
Wakool	**99**	35 28 S	144 23 E
Wakool →	**99**	35 5 S	143 33 E
Wakre	**73**	0 19 S	131 5 E
Wakuach L.	**107**	55 34N	67 32W
Walamba	**91**	13 30 S	28 42 E
Wałbrzych	**28**	50 45N	16 18 E
Walbury Hill	**13**	51 22N	1 28W
Walcha	**99**	30 55 S	151 31 E
Walcheren	**16**	51 30N	3 35 E
Walcott	**118**	41 50N	106 55W
Wałcz	**28**	53 17N	16 27 E
Wald	**25**	47 17N	8 56 E
Waldbröl	**24**	50 52N	7 36 E
Waldeck	**24**	51 12N	9 4 E
Walden, Colo., U.S.A.	**118**	40 47N	106 20W
Walden, N.Y., U.S.A.	**113**	41 32N	74 13W
Waldport	**118**	44 30N	124 2W
Waldron, Can.	**109**	50 53N	102 35W
Waldron, U.S.A.	**117**	34 52N	94 4W
Waldshut	**25**	47 37N	8 12 E
Walembele	**84**	10 30N	1 58W
Wales □	**11**	52 30N	3 30W
Walewale	**85**	10 21N	0 50W
Walgett	**97**	30 0 S	148 5 E
Walgreen Coast	**5**	75 15 S	105 0W
Walhalla, Austral.	**99**	37 56 S	146 29 E
Walhalla, U.S.A.	**109**	48 55N	97 55W
Walker	**116**	47 4N	94 35W
Walker L., Man., Can.	**109**	54 42N	95 57W
Walker L., Qué., Can.	**107**	50 20N	67 11W
Walker L., U.S.A.	**118**	38 56N	118 46W
Walkerston	**98**	21 11 S	149 8 E
Walkerton	**112**	44 10N	81 10W
Wall	**116**	44 0N	102 14W
Walla Walla	**118**	46 3N	118 25W
Wallabadah	**98**	17 57 S	142 15 E
Wallace, Idaho, U.S.A.	**118**	47 30N	116 0W
Wallace, N.C., U.S.A.	**115**	34 44N	77 59W
Wallace, Nebr., U.S.A.	**116**	40 51N	101 12W
Wallaceburg	**106**	42 34N	82 23W
Wallachia = Valahia	**46**	44 35N	25 0 E
Wallal	**99**	26 32 S	146 7 E
Wallaroo	**97**	33 56 S	137 39 E
Wallasey	**12**	53 26N	3 2W
Walldürn	**25**	49 34N	9 23 E
Wallerawang	**99**	33 25 S	150 4 E
Wallingford, U.K.	**12**	51 40N	1 15W
Wallingford, U.S.A.	**113**	41 27N	72 50W
Wallis Arch.	**94**	13 18 S	176 10W
Wallowa	**118**	45 40N	117 35W
Wallowa, Mts.	**118**	45 20N	117 30W
Wallsend, Austral.	**99**	32 55 S	151 40 E
Wallsend, U.K.	**12**	54 59N	1 30W
Wallula	**118**	46 3N	118 59W
Wallumbilla	**99**	26 33 S	149 9 E
Walmer	**92**	33 57 S	25 35 E
Walmsley, L.	**109**	63 25N	108 36W
Walney, Isle of	**12**	54 5N	3 15W
Walnut Ridge	**117**	36 7N	90 58W
Walsall	**13**	52 36N	1 59W
Walsenburg	**117**	37 42N	104 45W
Walsh	**117**	37 28N	102 15W
Walsh →	**98**	16 31 S	143 42 E
Walsh P.O.	**98**	16 40 S	144 0 E
Walsrode	**24**	52 51N	9 37 E
Waltair	**70**	17 44N	83 23 E
Walterboro	**115**	32 53N	80 40W
Walters	**117**	34 25N	98 20W
Waltershausen	**24**	50 53N	10 33 E
Waltham	**113**	42 22N	71 12W
Waltham Sta.	**106**	45 57N	76 57W
Waltman	**118**	43 8N	107 15W
Walton	**113**	42 12N	75 9W
Walvisbaai	**92**	23 0 S	14 28 E
Wamba, Kenya	**90**	0 58N	37 19 E
Wamba, Zaîre	**90**	2 10N	27 57 E
Wamego	**116**	39 14N	96 22W
Wamena	**73**	4 4 S	138 57 E
Wampsville	**113**	43 4N	75 42W
Wamsasi	**73**	3 27 S	126 7 E
Wana	**68**	32 20N	69 32 E
Wanaaring	**99**	29 38 S	144 9 E
Wanaka L.	**101**	44 33 S	169 7 E
Wan'an	**77**	26 26N	114 49 E
Wanapiri	**73**	4 30 S	135 59 E
Wanapitei L.	**106**	46 45N	80 40W
Wanbi	**99**	34 46 S	140 17 E
Wanda Shan	**76**	46 0N	132 0 E
Wanderer	**91**	19 36 S	30 1 E
Wandiwash	**70**	12 30N	79 30 E
Wandoan	**97**	26 5 S	149 55 E
Wang Kai (Ghâbat el Arab)	**87**	9 3N	29 23 E
Wang Saphung	**71**	17 18N	101 46 E
Wanga	**90**	2 58N	29 12 E
Wangal	**73**	6 8 S	134 9 E
Wanganella	**99**	35 6 S	144 49 E
Wanganui	**101**	39 56 S	175 3 E
Wangaratta	**97**	36 21 S	146 19 E
Wangdu	**76**	38 40N	115 7 E

Wangerooge 24 53 47N 7 52 E
Wangi 90 1 58 S 40 58 E
Wangiwangi 73 5 22 S 123 37 E
Wangjiang 77 30 10N 116 42 E
Wangqing 76 43 12N 129 42 E
Wankaner 68 22 35N 71 0 E
* Wankie 91 18 18 S 26 30 E
* Wankie Nat. Park 92 19 0 S 26 30 E
Wanless 109 54 11N 101 21W
Wanning 77 18 48N 110 22 E
Wannon → 100 37 38 S 141 25 E
Wanquan 76 40 50N 114 40 E
Wanxian 75 30 42N 108 20 E
Wanyuan 77 32 4N 108 3 E
Wanzai 77 28 7N 114 30 E
Wapakoneta 114 40 35N 84 10W
Wapato 118 46 30N 120 25W
Wapawekka L. 109 54 55N 104 40W
Wappingers Falls 113 41 35N 73 56W
Wapsipinicon → 116 41 44N 90 19W
Waranga Res. 100 36 32 S 145 5 E
Warangal 70 17 58N 79 35 E
Waratah 99 41 30 S 145 30 E
Waratah B. 99 38 54 S 146 5 E
Warburg 24 51 29N 9 10 E
Warburton 99 37 47 S 145 42 E
Warburton → 97 28 4 S 137 28 E
Ward 101 41 49 S 174 11 E
Ward → 99 26 28 S 146 6 E
Ward Cove 108 55 25N 132 43W
Ward Hunt, C. 98 8 2 S 148 10 E
Wardak □ 65 34 0N 68 0 E
Warden 93 27 50 S 29 0 E
Wardha 68 20 45N 78 39 E
Wardlow 108 50 56N 111 31W
Ware, Can. 108 57 26N 125 41W
Ware, U.S.A. 113 42 16N 72 15W
Wareham 113 41 45N 70 44W
Waren 24 53 30N 12 41 E
Warendorf 24 51 57N 8 0 E
Warialda 97 29 29 S 150 33 E
Wariap 73 1 30 S 134 5 E
Warka 28 51 47N 21 12 E
Warkopi 73 1 12 S 134 9 E
Warley 13 52 30N 2 0W
Warm Springs, Mont., U.S.A. 118 46 11N 112 48W
Warm Springs, Nev., U.S.A. 119 38 16N 116 32W
Warman 109 52 19N 106 30W
Warmbad, Namibia 92 28 25 S 18 42 E
Warmbad, S. Afr. 93 24 51 S 28 19 E
Warmeriville 19 49 20N 4 13 E
Warnambool Downs 98 22 48 S 142 52 E
Warnemünde 24 54 9N 12 5 E
Warner 108 49 17N 112 12W
Warner Range, Mts. 118 41 30 S 120 20W
Warner Robins 115 32 41N 83 36W
Warnow → 24 54 6N 12 9 E
Warora 70 20 14N 79 1 E
Warracknabeal 100 36 9 S 142 26 E
Warragul 99 38 10 S 145 58 E
Warrego → 97 30 24 S 145 21 E
Warrego Ra. 97 24 58 S 146 0 E
Warren, Austral. 99 31 42 S 147 51 E
Warren, Ark., U.S.A. 117 33 35N 92 3W
Warren, Minn., U.S.A. 116 48 12N 96 46W
Warren, Ohio, U.S.A. 114 41 18N 80 52W
Warren, Pa., U.S.A. 114 41 52N 79 10W
Warrenpoint 15 54 7N 6 15W
Warrensburg 116 38 45N 93 45W
Warrenton, S. Afr. 92 28 9 S 24 47 E
Warrenton, U.S.A. 118 46 11N 123 59W
Warrenville 99 25 48 S 147 22 E
Warri 85 5 30N 5 41 E
Warrina 96 28 12 S 135 50 E
Warrington, U.K. 12 53 25N 2 38W
Warrington, U.S.A. 115 30 22N 87 16W
Warrnambool 97 38 25 S 142 30 E
Warroad 116 48 54N 95 19W
Warsa 73 0 47 S 135 55 E
Warsaw, Ind., U.S.A. 114 41 14N 85 50W
Warsaw, N.Y., U.S.A. 112 42 46N 78 10W
Warsaw, Ohio, U.S.A. 112 40 20N 82 0W
Warsaw = Warszawa 28 52 13N 21 0 E
Warstein 24 51 26N 8 20 E
Warszawa 28 52 13N 21 0 E
Warszawa □ 28 52 30N 21 0 E
Warta 28 51 43N 18 38 E
Warta → 28 52 35N 14 39 E
Waru 73 3 30 S 130 36 E
Warud 68 21 30N 78 16 E
Warwick, Austral. 97 28 10 S 152 1 E
Warwick, U.K. 13 52 17N 1 36W
Warwick, U.S.A. 114 41 43N 71 25W
Warwick □ 13 52 20N 1 30W
Wasa 108 49 45N 115 50W
Wasaga Beach 112 44 31N 80 1W
Wasatch, Ra. 118 40 30N 111 15W
Wasbank 93 28 15 S 30 9 E
Wasco, Calif., U.S.A. 119 35 37N 119 16W
Wasco, Oreg., U.S.A. 118 45 36N 120 46W
Waseca 116 44 3N 93 31W
Wasekamio L. 109 56 45N 108 45W
Wash, The 12 52 58N 0 20 E
Washago 112 44 45N 79 20W
Washburn, N.D., U.S.A. 116 47 17N 101 0W
Washburn, Wis., U.S.A. 116 46 38N 90 55W
Washington, D.C., U.S.A. 114 38 52N 77 0W
Washington, Ga., U.S.A. 115 33 45N 82 45W
Washington, Ind., U.S.A. 114 38 40N 87 8W
Washington, Iowa, U.S.A. 116 41 20N 91 45W
Washington, Mo, U.S.A. 116 38 35N 91 1W
Washington, N.C., U.S.A. 115 35 35N 77 1W
Washington, N.J., U.S.A. 113 40 45N 74 59W
Washington, Pa., U.S.A. 114 40 10N 80 20W
Washington, Utah, U.S.A. 119 37 10N 113 30W
Washington □ 118 47 45N 120 30W
† Washington I., Pac. Oc. 95 4 43N 160 25W
Washington I., U.S.A. 114 45 24N 86 54W
Washington Mt. 114 44 15N 71 18W
Wasian 73 1 47 S 133 19 E
Wasilków 28 53 12N 23 13 E
Wasior 73 2 43 S 134 30 E
Waskaiowaka, L. 109 56 33N 96 23W
Waskesiu Lake 109 53 55N 106 5W
Wasm 86 18 2N 41 32 E
Wassenaar 16 52 8N 4 24 E
Wasserburg 25 48 4N 12 15 E
Wasserkuppe 24 50 30N 9 56 E
Wassy 19 48 30N 4 58 E
Waswanipi 106 49 40N 76 29W
Waswanipi, L. 106 49 35N 76 40W
Watangpon 73 4 29 S 120 25 E
Water Park Pt. 98 22 56 S 150 47 E
Water Valley 117 34 9N 89 38W
Waterberg, Namibia 92 20 30 S 17 18 E
Waterberg, S. Afr. 93 24 14 S 28 0 E
Waterbury, Conn., U.S.A. 114 41 32N 73 0W
Waterbury, Vt., U.S.A. 113 44 22N 72 44W
Waterbury L. 109 58 10N 104 22W
Waterdown 112 43 20N 79 53W
Waterford, Can. 112 42 56N 80 17W
Waterford, Ireland 15 52 16N 7 8W
Waterford □ 15 52 10N 7 40W
Waterford Harb. 15 52 10N 6 58W
Waterhen L., Man., Can. 109 52 10N 99 40W
Waterhen L., Sask., Can. 109 54 28N 108 25W
Waterloo, Belg. 16 50 43N 4 25 E
Waterloo, Ont., Can. 106 43 30N 80 32W
Waterloo, Qué., Can. 113 45 22N 72 32W
Waterloo, S. Leone 84 8 26N 13 8W
Waterloo, Ill., U.S.A. 116 38 22N 90 6W
Waterloo, Iowa, U.S.A. 116 42 27N 92 20W
Waterloo, N.Y., U.S.A. 112 42 54N 76 53W
Watersmeet 116 46 15N 89 12W
Waterton Lakes Nat. Park 108 49 5N 114 15W
Watertown, Conn., U.S.A. 113 41 36N 73 7W
Watertown, N.Y., U.S.A. 114 43 58N 75 57W
Watertown, S.D., U.S.A. 116 44 57N 97 5W
Watertown, Wis., U.S.A. 116 43 15N 88 45W
Waterval-Boven 93 25 40 S 30 18 E
Waterville, Can. 113 45 16N 71 54W
Waterville, Me., U.S.A. 107 44 35N 69 40W
Waterville, N.Y., U.S.A. 113 42 56N 75 23W
Waterville, Pa., U.S.A. 112 41 19N 77 21W
Waterville, Wash., U.S.A. 118 47 38N 120 1W
Watervliet 114 42 46N 73 43W
Wates 73 7 53 S 110 6 E
Watford, Can. 112 42 57N 81 53W
Watford, U.K. 13 51 38N 0 23W
Watford City 116 47 50N 103 23W
Wathaman → 109 57 16N 102 59W
Watkins Glen 114 42 25N 76 55W
Watling I. = San Salvador 121 24 0N 74 40W
Watonga 117 35 51N 98 24W
Watrous, Can. 109 51 40N 105 25W
Watrous, U.S.A. 117 35 50N 104 55W
Watsa 90 3 4N 29 30 E
Watseka 114 40 45N 87 45W
Watson 109 52 10N 104 30W
Watson Lake 104 60 6N 128 49W
Watsonville 119 36 55N 121 49W
Wattwil 25 47 18N 9 6 E
Watuata = Batuata 73 6 12 S 122 42 E
Watubela, Kepulauan 73 4 28 S 131 35 E
Wau 98 7 21 S 146 47 E
Waubamik 112 45 27N 80 1W
Waubay 116 45 22N 97 17W
Waubra 99 37 21 S 143 39 E
Wauchope 99 31 28 S 152 45 E
Wauchula 115 27 35N 81 50W
Waugh 109 49 40N 95 11W
Waukegan 114 42 22N 87 54W
Waukesha 114 43 0N 88 15W
Waukon 116 43 14N 91 33W
Wauneta 116 40 27N 101 25W
Waupaca 116 44 22N 89 8W
Waupun 116 43 38N 88 44W
Waurika 117 34 12N 98 0W
Wausau 116 44 57N 89 40W
Wautoma 116 44 3N 89 20W
Wauwatosa 114 43 6N 87 59W
Wave Hill 96 17 32 S 131 0 E
Waveney → 13 52 24N 1 20 E
Waverley 101 39 46 S 174 37 E
Waverly, Iowa, U.S.A. 116 42 40N 92 30W
Waverly, N.Y., U.S.A. 114 42 0N 76 33W
Wavre 16 50 43N 4 38 E
Wâw 87 7 45N 28 1 E
Waw al Kabir 81 25 20N 17 20 E
Wâw al Kabīr 83 25 20N 16 43 E
Wâw an Nāmūs 83 24 55N 17 46 E
Wawa, Can. 106 47 59N 84 47W
Wawa, Nigeria 85 9 54N 4 27 E
Wawa, Sudan 86 20 30N 30 22 E
Wawanesa 109 49 36N 99 40W
Wawoi → 98 7 48 S 143 16 E
Waxahachie 117 32 22N 96 53W
Waxweiler 25 50 6N 6 22 E
Wayabula Rau 73 2 29N 128 17 E
Wayatinah 99 42 19 S 146 27 E
Waycross 115 31 12N 82 25W
Wayi 87 5 8N 30 10 E
Wayne, Nebr., U.S.A. 116 42 16N 97 0W
Wayne, W. Va., U.S.A. 114 38 15N 82 27W
Waynesboro, Ga., U.S.A. 115 33 6N 82 1W
Waynesboro, Miss., U.S.A. 115 31 40N 88 39W
Waynesboro, Pa., U.S.A. 114 39 46N 77 32W
Waynesboro, Va., U.S.A. 114 38 4N 78 57W
Waynesburg 114 39 54N 80 12W
Waynesville 115 35 31N 83 0W
Waynoka 117 36 38N 98 53W
Wāzin 83 31 58N 10 40 E
Wazirabad 68 32 30N 74 8 E
Wda → 28 53 25N 18 29 E
We 72 5 51N 95 18 E
Weald, The 13 51 7N 0 9 E
Wear → 12 54 55N 1 22W
Weatherford, Okla., U.S.A. 117 35 30N 98 45W
Weatherford, Tex., U.S.A. 117 32 45N 97 48W
Weaverville 118 40 44N 122 56W
Webb City 117 37 9N 94 30W
Webster, Mass., U.S.A. 113 42 4N 71 54W
Webster, N.Y., U.S.A. 112 43 11N 77 27W
Webster, S.D., U.S.A. 116 45 24N 97 33W
Webster, Wis., U.S.A. 116 45 53N 92 25W
Webster City 116 42 30N 93 50W
Webster Green 116 38 38N 90 20W
Webster Springs 114 38 30N 80 25W
Weda 73 0 21N 127 50 E
Weda, Teluk 73 0 30N 127 50 E
Weddell I. 128 51 50 S 61 0W
Weddell Sea 5 72 30 S 40 0W
Wedderburn 99 36 26 S 143 33 E
Wedge I. 96 30 50 S 115 11 E
Wedgeport 107 43 44N 65 59W
Wedza 91 18 40 S 31 33 E
Wee Waa 99 30 11 S 149 26 E
Weed 118 41 29N 122 22W
Weedsport 113 43 3N 76 35W
Weedville 112 41 17N 78 28W
Weemelah 99 29 2 S 149 15 E
Weenen 93 28 48 S 30 7 E
Weener 24 53 10N 7 23 E
Weert 16 51 15N 5 43 E
Wegierska-Gorka 27 49 36N 19 7 E
Wegliniec 28 51 18N 15 10 E
Węgorzewo 28 54 13N 21 43 E
Węgrów 28 52 24N 22 0 E
Wei He →, Hebei, China 76 36 10N 115 45 E
Wei He →, Shaanxi, China 77 34 38N 110 15 E
Weida 24 50 47N 12 3 E
Weiden 25 49 40N 12 10 E
Weifang 76 36 44N 119 7 E
Weihai 76 37 30N 122 6 E
Weilburg 24 50 28N 8 17 E
Weilheim 25 47 50N 11 9 E
Weimar 24 51 0N 11 20 E
Weinan 77 34 31N 109 29 E
Weingarten 25 47 49N 9 39 E
Weinheim 25 49 33N 8 40 E
Weipa 97 12 40 S 141 50 E
Weir →, Austral. 99 28 20 S 149 50 E
Weir →, Can. 109 56 54N 93 21W
Weir River 109 56 49N 94 6W
Weirton 112 40 23N 80 35W
Weiser 118 44 10N 117 0W
Weishan 77 34 47N 117 5 E
Weissenburg 25 49 2N 10 58 E
Weissenfels 24 51 11N 12 0 E
Weisswasser 24 51 30N 14 36 E
Wéitra 26 48 41N 14 54 E
Weiyuan 76 35 7N 104 10 E
Weiz 26 47 13N 15 39 E
Weizhou Dao 77 21 0N 109 5 E
Wejherowo 28 54 35N 18 12 E
Wekusko 109 54 30N 99 45W
Wekusko L. 109 54 40N 99 50W
Welby 109 50 33N 101 29W
Welch 114 37 29N 81 36W
Weldya 87 11 50N 39 34 E
Welega □ 87 9 25N 34 20 E
Welkite 87 8 15N 37 42 E
Welkom 92 28 0 S 26 50 E
Welland 106 43 0N 79 15W
Welland → 12 52 43N 0 10W
Wellesley Is. 97 16 42 S 139 30 E
Wellin 16 50 5N 5 6 E
Wellingborough 13 52 18N 0 41W
Wellington, Austral. 97 32 35 S 148 59 E
Wellington, Can. 106 43 57N 77 20W
Wellington, N.Z. 101 41 19 S 174 46 E
Wellington, S. Afr. 92 33 38 S 18 57 E
Wellington, U.K. 13 50 58N 3 13W
Wellington, Col., U.S.A. 116 40 43N 105 0W
Wellington, Kans., U.S.A. 117 37 15N 97 25W
Wellington, Nev., U.S.A. 118 38 47N 119 28W
Wellington, Ohio, U.S.A. 112 41 9N 82 12W
Wellington, Tex., U.S.A. 117 34 55N 100 13W
Wellington □ 101 40 8 S 175 36 E
Wellington, I. 128 49 30 S 75 0W
Wellington, L. 99 38 6 S 147 20 E
Wellington (Telford) 12 52 42N 2 31W
Wells, Norfolk, U.K. 12 52 57N 0 51 E
Wells, Somerset, U.K. 13 51 12N 2 39W
Wells, Me., U.S.A. 113 43 18N 70 35W
Wells, Minn., U.S.A. 116 43 44N 93 45W
Wells, Nev., U.S.A. 118 41 8N 115 0W
Wells Gray Prov. Park 108 52 30N 120 15W
Wells L. 96 26 44 S 123 15 E
Wells River 113 44 9N 72 4W
Wellsboro 114 41 45N 77 20W
Wellsburg 112 40 15N 80 36W
Wellsville, Mo., U.S.A. 116 39 4N 91 30W
Wellsville, N.Y., U.S.A. 114 42 9N 77 53W
Wellsville, Ohio, U.S.A. 114 40 36N 80 40W
Wellsville, Utah, U.S.A. 118 41 35N 111 59W
Wellton 119 32 39N 114 6W
Welmel, Wabi → 87 5 38N 40 47 E
Welna → 28 52 46N 17 32 E
Welo □ 87 11 50N 39 48 E
Wels 26 48 9N 14 1 E
Welshpool 13 52 40N 3 9W
Welwyn. 109 50 20N 101 30W
Wem 12 52 52N 2 45W
Wembere → 90 4 10 S 34 15 E
Wen Xian 77 32 43N 104 36 E
Wenatchee 118 47 30N 120 17W
Wenchang 77 19 38N 110 42 E
Wenchi 84 7 46N 2 8W
Wenchow = Wenzhou 75 28 0N 120 38 E
Wendell 118 42 50N 114 42W
Wendeng 76 37 15N 122 5 E
Wendesi 73 2 30 S 134 17 E
Wendo 87 6 40N 38 27 E
Wendover 118 40 49N 114 1W
Wengcheng 77 24 22N 113 50 E
Wenlock 98 13 6 S 142 58 E
Wenlock → 97 12 2 S 141 55 E
Wensu 75 41 15N 80 10 E
Wentworth 97 34 2 S 141 54 E
Wenut 73 3 11 S 133 19 E
Wenxi 77 35 20N 111 10 E
Wenzhou 75 28 0N 120 38 E
Weott 118 40 19N 123 56W
Wepener 92 29 42 S 27 3 E
Werda 92 25 24 S 23 15 E
Werdau 24 50 45N 12 20 E
Werder, Ethiopia 63 6 58N 45 1 E
Werder, Ger. 24 52 23N 12 56 E
Werdohl 24 51 15N 7 47 E
Wereilu 87 10 40N 39 28 E
Weri 73 3 10 S 132 38 E
Werne 24 51 38N 7 38 E
Werneck 25 49 59N 10 6 E
Wernigerode 24 51 49N 10 45 E
Werra → 24 51 26N 9 39 E
Werribee 99 37 54 S 144 40 E
Werrimull 99 34 25 S 141 38 E
Werris Creek 99 31 18 S 150 38 E
Wersar 73 1 30 S 131 55 E
Wertach → 25 48 24N 10 53 E
Wertheim 25 49 44N 9 32 E
Wertingen 25 48 33N 10 41 E
Wesel 24 51 39N 6 34 E
Weser → 24 53 33N 8 30 E
Wesiri 73 7 30 S 126 30 E
Wesleyville, Can. 107 49 8N 53 36W
Wesleyville, U.S.A. 112 42 9N 80 1W
Wessel Is. 97 11 10 S 136 45 E
Wesselburen 24 54 11N 8 53 E
Wessington 116 44 30N 98 40W
Wessington Springs 116 44 10N 98 35W
West 117 31 50N 97 5W
West B. 117 29 5N 89 27W
West Bend 114 43 25N 88 10W
West Bengal □ 69 23 0N 88 0 E
West Branch 114 44 16N 84 13W
West Bromwich 13 52 32N 2 1W
West Chazy 113 44 49N 73 28W
West Chester 114 39 58N 75 36W
West Columbia 117 29 10N 95 38W
West Des Moines 116 41 30N 93 45W
West Falkland 128 51 40 S 60 0W
West Frankfurt 116 37 56N 89 0W
West Germany ■ 24 52 0N 9 0 E
West Glamorgan □ 13 51 40N 3 55W
West Hartford 113 41 45N 72 45W
West Haven 113 41 18N 72 57W
West Helena 117 34 30N 90 40W
West Ice Shelf 5 67 0 S 85 0 E
West Indies 121 15 0N 70 0W
West Looe 13 50 21N 4 29W
West Lorne 112 42 36N 81 36W
West Lunga → 91 13 6 S 24 39 E
West Magpie → 107 51 2N 64 42W
West Memphis 117 35 5N 90 11W
West Midlands □ 13 52 30N 1 55W
West Monroe 117 32 32N 92 7W
West Moors 12 50 49N 1 50W
West Newton 112 40 14N 79 46W
West Nicholson 91 21 2 S 29 20 E
West Palm Beach 115 26 44N 80 3W
West Pittston 113 41 19N 75 49W
West Plains 117 36 45N 91 50W
West Point, Ga., U.S.A. 115 32 54N 85 10W
West Point, Miss., U.S.A. 115 33 36N 88 38W
West Point, Nebr., U.S.A. 116 41 50N 96 43W
West Point, Va., U.S.A. 114 37 35N 76 47W
West Pokot □ 90 1 30N 35 15 E
West Road → 108 53 18N 122 53W
West Rutland 114 43 38N 73 0W
West Schelde → = Westerschelde 16 51 25N 3 25 E
West Siberian Plain 60 62 0N 75 0 E
West Sussex □ 13 50 55N 0 30W
West-Terschelling 16 53 22N 5 13 E
West Virginia □ 114 39 0N 81 0W
West-Vlaanderen □ 16 51 0N 3 0 E
West Wyalong 100 33 56 S 147 10 E
West Yellowstone 118 44 47N 111 4W
West Yorkshire □ 12 53 45N 1 40W
Westbrook, Maine, U.S.A. 115 43 40N 70 22W
Westbrook, Tex., U.S.A. 117 32 25N 101 0W
Westbury 99 41 30 S 146 51 E
Westby 116 48 52N 104 3W
Westerland 24 54 51N 8 20 E
Western □, Kenya 90 0 30N 34 30 E
Western □, Uganda 90 1 45N 31 30 E
Western □, Zambia 91 15 15 S 24 30 E
Western Australia □ 96 25 0 S 118 0 E
Western Ghats 70 14 0N 75 0 E
Western Isles □ 14 57 30N 7 10W
Western Samoa ■ 101 14 0 S 172 0W
Westernport 114 39 30N 79 5W
Westerschelde → 16 51 25N 3 25 E
Westerstede 24 53 15N 7 55 E
Westerwald 24 50 39N 8 0 E
Westfield, Mass., U.S.A. 113 42 9N 72 49W
Westfield, N.Y., U.S.A. 112 42 20N 79 38W
Westfield, Pa., U.S.A. 112 41 54N 77 32W
Westhope 116 48 55N 101 0W
Westland □ 101 43 33 S 169 59 E
Westland Bight 101 42 55 S 170 5 E
Westlock 108 54 9N 113 55W
Westmeath □ 15 53 30N 7 30W
Westminster 114 39 34N 77 1W
Westmorland 119 33 2N 115 42W
Weston, Malay. 72 5 10N 115 35 E
Weston, Oreg., U.S.A. 118 45 50N 118 30W
Weston, W. Va., U.S.A. 114 39 3N 80 29W
Weston I. 106 52 33N 79 36W
Weston-super-Mare 13 51 20N 2 59W
Westport, Can. 113 44 40N 76 25W
Westport, Ireland 15 53 44N 9 31W
Westport, N.Z. 101 41 46 S 171 37 E
Westport, U.S.A. 118 46 48N 124 4W
Westray, Can. 109 53 36N 101 24W
Westray, U.K. 14 59 18N 3 0W
Westree 106 47 26N 81 34W
Westview 108 49 50N 124 31W
Westville, Ill., U.S.A. 114 40 3N 87 36W
Westville, Okla., U.S.A. 117 36 0N 94 33W
Westwood 118 40 26N 121 0W
Wetar 73 7 30 S 126 30 E
Wetaskiwin 108 52 55N 113 24W
Wethersfield 113 41 43N 72 40W
Wetteren 16 51 0N 3 53 E
Wetzlar 24 50 33N 8 30 E

* Renamed Hwange
† Renamed Teraina

Wewak **98** 3 38 S 143 41 E
Wewaka **117** 35 10N 96 35W
Wexford **15** 52 20N 6 28W
Wexford □ **15** 52 20N 6 25W
Wexford Harb. **15** 52 20N 6 25W
Weyburn **109** 49 40N 103 50W
Weyburn L. **108** 63 0N 117 59W
Weyer **26** 47 51N 14 40 E
Weyib → **87** 7 15N 40 15 E
Weymouth, Can. **107** 44 30N 66 1W
Weymouth, U.K. **13** 50 36N 2 28W
Weymouth, U.S.A. **113** 42 13N 70 53W
Weymouth, C. **97** 12 37 S 143 27 E
Whakatane **101** 37 57 S 177 1 E
Whale → **107** 58 15N 67 40W
Whale Cove **104** 62 11N 92 36W
Whales, B. of **5** 78 0 S 165 0W
Whalsay **14** 60 22N 1 0W
Whangamomona **101** 39 8 S 174 44 E
Whangarei **101** 35 43 S 174 21 E
Whangarei Harbour **101** 35 45 S 174 28 E
Wharfe → **12** 53 55N 1 30W
Wharfedale **12** 54 7N 2 4W
Wharton, N.J., U.S.A. **113** 40 53N 74 36W
Wharton, Pa., U.S.A. **112** 41 31N 78 1W
Wharton, Tex., U.S.A. **117** 29 20N 96 6W
Wheatland **116** 42 4N 104 58W
Wheatley **112** 42 6N 82 27W
Wheaton **116** 45 50N 96 29W
Wheeler, Oreg., U.S.A. **118** 45 50N 123 57W
Wheeler, Tex., U.S.A. **117** 35 29N 100 15W
Wheeler → **109** 57 25N 105 30W
Wheeler Pk., N. Mex., U.S.A. **119** 36 34N 105 25W
Wheeler Pk., Nev., U.S.A. **119** 38 57N 114 15W
Wheeling **114** 40 2N 80 41W
Whernside **12** 54 14N 2 24W
Whidbey I. **108** 48 15N 122 40W
Whidbey Is. **96** 34 30 S 135 3 E
Whiskey Gap **108** 49 0N 113 3W
Whiskey Jack L. **109** 58 23N 101 55W
Whistler **115** 30 50N 88 10W
Whitby, Can. **112** 43 52N 78 56W
Whitby, U.K. **12** 54 29N 0 37W
White →, Ark., U.S.A. **117** 33 53N 91 3W
White →, Colo., U.S.A. **118** 40 8N 109 41W
White →, Ind., U.S.A. **114** 38 25N 87 44W
White →, S.D., U.S.A. **116** 43 45N 99 30W
White B. **107** 50 0N 56 35W
White Bear Res. **107** 48 10N 57 5W
White Bird **118** 45 46N 116 21W
White Butte **116** 46 23N 103 19W
White City **116** 38 50N 96 45W
White Cliffs **99** 30 50 S 143 10 E
White Deer **117** 35 30N 101 8W
White Hall **116** 39 25N 90 27W
White Haven **113** 41 3N 75 47W
White I. **101** 37 30 S 177 13 E
White L., Can. **113** 45 18N 76 31W
White L., U.S.A. **117** 29 45N 92 30W
White Mts., Calif., U.S.A. **119** 37 30N 118 15W
White Mts., N.H., U.S.A. **113** 44 15N 71 15W
White Nile = Nîl el Abyad → **87** 15 38N 32 31 E
White Nile Dam **87** 15 24N 32 30 E
White Otter L. **106** 49 5N 91 55W
White Pass **104** 59 40N 135 3W
White Plains **113** 41 2N 73 44W
White River, Can. **106** 48 35N 85 20W
White River, S. Afr. **93** 25 20 S 31 00 E
White River, U.S.A. **116** 43 34N 100 45W
White River Junc. **113** 43 38N 72 20W
White Russia = Byelorussian S.S.R. □ **54** 53 30N 27 0 E
White Sea = Beloye More **52** 66 30N 38 0 E
White Sulphur Springs, Mont., U.S.A. **118** 46 35N 110 54W
White Sulphur Springs, W. Va., U.S.A. **114** 37 50N 80 16W
White Volta (Volta Blanche) → **85** 9 10N 1 15W
Whitecliffs **101** 43 26 S 171 55 E
Whitecourt **108** 54 10N 115 45W
Whiteface **117** 33 35N 102 40W
Whitefield **113** 44 23N 71 37W
Whitefish **118** 48 25N 114 22W
Whitefish L. **109** 62 41N 106 48W
Whitefish Pt. **114** 46 45N 85 0W
Whitegull, L. **107** 55 27N 64 17W
Whitehall, Mich., U.S.A. **114** 43 21N 86 20W
Whitehall, Mont., U.S.A. **118** 45 52N 112 4W
Whitehall, N.Y., U.S.A. **114** 43 32N 73 28W
Whitehall, Wis., U.S.A. **116** 44 20N 91 19W
Whitehaven **12** 54 33N 3 35W
Whitehorse **104** 60 43N 135 3W
Whitehorse, Vale of **13** 51 37N 1 30W
Whiteman Ra. **98** 5 55 S 150 0 E
Whitemark **99** 40 7 S 148 3 E
Whitemouth **109** 49 57N 95 58W
Whiteplains **84** 6 28N 10 40W
Whitesail, L. **108** 53 35N 127 45W
Whitesboro, N.Y., U.S.A. **113** 43 8N 75 20W
Whitesboro, Tex., U.S.A. **117** 33 40N 96 58W
Whiteshell Prov. Park **109** 50 0N 95 40W
Whitetail **116** 48 54N 105 15W
Whiteville **115** 34 20N 78 40W
Whitewater **114** 42 50N 88 45W
Whitewater Baldy, Mt. **119** 33 20N 108 44W
Whitewater L. **106** 50 50N 89 10W
Whitewood, Austral. **98** 21 28 S 143 30 E
Whitewood, Can. **109** 50 20N 102 20W
Whitfield **99** 36 42 S 146 24 E
Whithorn **14** 54 44N 4 25W
Whitianga **101** 36 47 S 175 41 E
Whitman **113** 42 4N 70 55W
Whitmire **115** 34 33N 81 40W
Whitney **106** 45 31N 78 14W
Whitney, Mt. **119** 36 35N 118 14W
Whitney Pt. **113** 42 19N 75 59W
Whitstable **13** 51 21N 1 2 E
Whitsunday I. **97** 20 15 S 149 4 E
Whittier **104** 60 46N 148 48W
Whittlesea **99** 37 27 S 145 9 E
Whitwell **115** 35 15N 85 30W
Wholdaia L. **109** 60 43N 104 20W
Whyalla **97** 33 2 S 137 30 E
Whyjonta **99** 29 41 S 142 28 E
Wiarton **106** 44 40N 81 10W
Wiawso **84** 6 10N 2 25W
Wiazów **28** 50 50N 17 10 E
Wibaux **116** 47 0N 104 13W
Wichita **117** 37 40N 97 20W
Wichita Falls **117** 33 57N 98 30W
Wick **14** 58 26N 3 5W
Wickenburg **119** 33 58N 112 45W
Wickett **117** 31 37N 102 58W
Wickham, C. **99** 39 35 S 143 57 E
Wickliffe **112** 41 36N 81 29W
Wicklow **15** 53 0N 6 2W
Wicklow □ **15** 52 59N 6 25W
Wicklow Hd. **15** 52 59N 6 3W
Wicklow Mts. **15** 53 0N 6 30W
Widawa **28** 51 27N 18 51 E
Widawka **28** 51 7N 19 36 E
Widnes **12** 53 22N 2 44W
Więcbork **28** 53 21N 17 30 E
Wiedenbrück **24** 51 52N 8 15 E
Wiek **24** 54 37N 13 17 E
Wielbark **28** 53 24N 20 55 E
Wieleń **28** 52 53N 16 9 E
Wieliczka **27** 50 0N 20 5 E
Wieluń **28** 51 15N 18 34 E
Wien **27** 48 12N 16 22 E
Wiener Neustadt **27** 47 49N 16 16 E
Wieprz →, Koszalin, Poland **28** 54 26N 16 35 E
Wieprz →, Lublin, Poland **28** 51 34N 21 49 E
Wierden **16** 52 22N 6 35 E
Wieruszów **28** 51 19N 18 9 E
Wiesbaden **25** 50 7N 8 17 E
Wiesental **25** 49 15N 8 30 E
Wigan **12** 53 33N 2 38W
Wiggins, Colo., U.S.A. **116** 40 16N 104 3W
Wiggins, Miss., U.S.A. **117** 30 53N 89 9W
Wight, I. of **13** 50 40N 1 20W
Wigry, Jezioro **28** 54 2N 23 8 E
Wigtown **14** 54 52N 4 27W
Wigtown B. **14** 54 46N 4 15W
Wil **25** 47 28N 9 3 E
Wilamowice **27** 49 55N 19 9 E
Wilber **116** 40 34N 96 59W
Wilberforce **112** 45 2N 78 13W
Wilberforce, C. **97** 11 54 S 136 35 E
Wilburton **117** 34 55N 95 15W
Wilcannia **97** 31 30 S 143 26 E
Wilcox **112** 41 34N 78 43W
Wildbad **25** 48 44N 8 32 E
Wildeshausen **24** 52 54N 8 25 E
Wildon **26** 46 52N 15 31 E
Wildrose **116** 48 36N 103 11W
Wildspitze **26** 46 53N 10 53 E
Wildwood **114** 38 59N 74 46W
Wilga → **28** 51 52N 21 18 E
Wilhelm II Coast **5** 68 0 S 90 0 E
Wilhelm Mt. **98** 5 50 S 145 1 E
Wilhelm-Pieck-Stadt Guben **24** 51 59N 14 48 E
Wilhelmsburg, Austria **26** 48 6N 15 36 E
Wilhelmsburg, Ger. **24** 53 28N 10 1 E
Wilhelmshaven **24** 53 30N 8 9 E
Wilhelmstal **92** 21 58 S 16 21 E
Wilkes Barre **114** 41 15N 75 52W
Wilkes Land **5** 69 0 S 120 0 E
Wilkes Sub-Glacial Basin **5** 75 0 S 130 0 E
Wilkesboro **115** 36 10N 81 9W
Wilkie **109** 52 27N 108 42W
Wilkinsburg **112** 40 26N 79 50W
Willamina **118** 45 9N 123 32W
Willandra Billabong Creek → **99** 33 22 S 145 52 E
Willapa, B. **118** 46 44N 124 0W
Willard, N. Mex., U.S.A. **119** 34 35N 106 1W
Willard, Utah, U.S.A. **118** 41 28N 112 1W
Willcox **119** 32 13N 109 53W
Willemstad **121** 12 5N 69 0W
William → **109** 59 8N 109 19W
Williams **119** 35 16N 112 11W
Williams Lake **108** 52 10N 122 10W
Williamsburg, Ky., U.S.A. **115** 36 45N 84 10W
Williamsburg, Pa., U.S.A. **112** 40 27N 78 14W
Williamsburg, Va., U.S.A. **114** 37 17N 76 44W
Williamson, N.Y., U.S.A. **112** 43 14N 77 15W
Williamson, W. Va., U.S.A. **114** 37 46N 82 17W
Williamsport **114** 41 18N 77 1W
Williamston **115** 35 50N 77 5W
Williamstown, Austral. **99** 37 51 S 144 52 E
Williamstown, Mass., U.S.A. **113** 42 41N 73 12W
Williamstown, N.Y., U.S.A. **113** 43 25N 75 54W
Williamsville **117** 37 0N 90 33W
Willimantic **113** 41 45N 72 12W
Williston, S. Afr. **92** 31 20 S 20 53 E
Williston, Fla., U.S.A. **115** 29 25N 82 28W
Williston, N.D., U.S.A. **116** 48 10N 103 35W
Williston L. **108** 56 0N 124 0W
Willits **118** 39 28N 123 17W
Willmar **116** 45 5N 95 0W
Willoughby **112** 41 38N 81 26W
Willow Bunch **109** 49 20N 105 35W
Willow L. **108** 62 10N 119 8W
Willow Lake **116** 44 40N 97 40W
Willow River **108** 54 6N 122 28W
Willow Springs **117** 37 0N 92 0W
Willowlake → **108** 62 42N 123 8W
Willowmore **92** 33 15 S 23 30 E
Willows, Austral. **98** 23 39 S 147 25 E
Willows, U.S.A. **118** 39 30N 122 10W
Wills Cr. → **98** 22 43 S 140 2 E
Wills Pt. **117** 32 42N 95 57W
Willunga **99** 35 15 S 138 30 E
Wilmette **114** 42 6N 87 44W
Wilmington, Austral. **99** 32 39 S 138 7 E
Wilmington, Del., U.S.A. **114** 39 45N 75 32W
Wilmington, Ill., U.S.A. **114** 41 19N 88 10W
Wilmington, N.C., U.S.A. **115** 34 14N 77 54W
Wilmington, Ohio, U.S.A. **114** 39 27N 83 50W
Wilpena Cr. → **99** 31 25 S 139 29 E
Wilsall **118** 45 59N 110 40W
Wilson **115** 35 44N 77 54W
Wilson → **99** 27 38 S 141 24 E
Wilson, Mt. **119** 37 55N 108 3W
Wilson's Promontory **97** 38 55 S 146 25 E
Wilster **24** 53 55N 9 23 E
Wilton, U.K. **13** 51 5N 1 52W
Wilton, U.S.A. **116** 47 12N 100 47W
Wiltshire □ **13** 51 20N 2 0W
Wiltz **16** 49 57N 5 55 E
Wiluna **96** 26 36 S 120 14 E
Wimereux **19** 50 45N 1 37 E
Wimmera **97** 36 30 S 142 0 E
Wimmera → **99** 36 8 S 141 56 E
Winam G. **90** 0 20 S 34 15 E
Winburg **92** 28 30 S 27 2 E
Winchendon **113** 42 40N 72 3W
Winchester, U.K. **13** 51 4N 1 19W
Winchester, Conn., U.S.A. **113** 41 53N 73 9W
Winchester, Idaho, U.S.A. **118** 46 11N 116 32W
Winchester, Ind., U.S.A. **114** 40 10N 84 56W
Winchester, Ky., U.S.A. **114** 38 0N 84 8W
Winchester, Mass., U.S.A. **113** 42 28N 71 10W
Winchester, N.H., U.S.A. **113** 42 47N 72 22W
Winchester, Tenn., U.S.A. **115** 35 11N 86 8W
Winchester, Va., U.S.A. **114** 39 14N 78 8W
Wind → **118** 43 8N 108 12W
Wind River Range **118** 43 0N 109 30W
Windber **114** 40 14N 78 50W
Windermere, L. **12** 54 20N 2 57W
Windfall **108** 54 12N 116 13W
Windflower L. **108** 62 52N 118 30W
Windhoek **92** 22 35 S 17 4 E
Windischgarsten **26** 47 42N 14 21 E
Windom **116** 43 48N 95 3W
Windorah **97** 25 24 S 142 36 E
Window Rock **119** 35 47N 109 4W
Windrush → **13** 51 48N 1 35W
Windsor, Austral. **99** 33 37 S 150 50 E
Windsor, N.S., Can. **107** 44 59N 64 5W
Windsor, Newf., Can. **107** 48 57N 55 40W
Windsor, Ont., Can. **106** 42 18N 83 0W
Windsor, U.K. **13** 51 28N 0 36W
Windsor, Col., U.S.A. **116** 40 33N 104 45W
Windsor, Conn., U.S.A. **113** 41 50N 72 40W
Windsor, Mo., U.S.A. **116** 38 32N 93 31W
Windsor, N.Y., U.S.A. **113** 42 5N 75 37W
Windsor, Vt., U.S.A. **114** 43 30N 72 25W
Windsorton **92** 28 16 S 24 44 E
Windward Is., Atl. Oc. **121** 13 0N 63 0W
Windward Is., Pac. Oc. **95** 18 0 S 149 0W
Windward Passage = Vientos, Paso de los **121** 20 0N 74 0W
Windy L. **109** 60 20N 100 2W
Winefred L. **109** 55 30N 110 30W
Winejok **87** 9 1N 27 30 E
Winfield **117** 37 15N 97 0W
Wingen **99** 31 54 S 150 54 E
Wingham, Austral. **99** 31 48 S 152 22 E
Wingham, Can. **106** 43 55N 81 20W
Winifred **118** 47 30N 109 28W
Winisk **106** 55 20N 85 15W
Winisk → **106** 55 17N 85 5W
Winisk L. **106** 52 55N 87 22W
Wink **117** 31 49N 103 9W
Winkler **109** 49 10N 97 56W
Winklern **26** 46 52N 12 52 E
Winlock **118** 46 29N 122 56W
Winneba **85** 5 25N 0 36W
Winnebago **116** 43 43N 94 8W
Winnebago L. **114** 44 0N 88 20W
Winnemucca **118** 41 0N 117 45W
Winnemucca, L. **118** 40 25N 119 21W
Winner **116** 43 23N 99 52W
Winnetka **114** 42 8N 87 46W
Winnett **118** 47 2N 108 21W
Winnfield **117** 31 57N 92 38W
Winnibigoshish L. **116** 47 25N 94 12W
Winnipeg **109** 49 54N 97 9W
Winnipeg → **109** 50 38N 96 19W
Winnipeg Beach **109** 50 30N 96 58W
Winnipeg, L. **109** 52 0N 97 0W
Winnipegosis **109** 51 39N 99 55W
Winnipegosis L. **109** 52 30N 100 0W
Winnipesaukee, L. **113** 43 38N 71 21W
Winnsboro, La., U.S.A. **117** 32 10N 91 41W
Winnsboro, S.C., U.S.A. **115** 34 23N 81 5W
Winnsboro, Tex., U.S.A. **117** 32 56N 95 15W
Winokapau, L. **107** 53 15N 62 50W
Winona, Miss., U.S.A. **117** 33 30N 89 42W
Winona, Wis., U.S.A. **116** 44 2N 91 39W
Winooski **114** 44 31N 73 11W
Winschoten **16** 53 9N 7 3 E
Winsen **24** 53 21N 10 11 E
Winslow **119** 35 2N 110 41W
Winsted **113** 41 55N 73 5W
Winston-Salem **115** 36 7N 80 15W
Winter Garden **115** 28 33N 81 35W
Winter Haven **115** 28 0N 81 42W
Winter Park **115** 28 34N 81 19W
Winterberg **24** 51 12N 8 30 E
Winters **117** 31 58N 99 58W
Winterset **116** 41 18N 94 0W
Wintersville **112** 40 22N 80 38W
Winterswijk **16** 51 58N 6 43 E
Winterthur **25** 47 30N 8 44 E
Winthrop, Minn., U.S.A. **116** 44 31N 94 25W
Winthrop, Wash., U.S.A. **118** 48 27N 120 6W
Winton, Austral. **97** 22 24 S 143 3 E
Winton, N.Z. **101** 46 8 S 168 20 E
Winton, N.C., U.S.A. **115** 36 25N 76 58W
Winton, Pa., U.S.A. **113** 41 27N 75 33W
Wintzenheim **19** 48 4N 7 17 E
Wipper → **24** 51 17N 11 10 E
Wirral **12** 53 25N 3 0W
Wisbech **12** 52 39N 0 10 E
Wisconsin □ **116** 44 30N 90 0W
Wisconsin → **116** 43 0N 91 15W
Wisconsin Dells **116** 43 38N 89 45W
Wisconsin Rapids **116** 44 25N 89 50W
Wisdom **118** 45 37N 113 27W
Wishaw **14** 55 46N 3 55W
Wishek **116** 46 20N 99 35W
Wisła **27** 49 38N 18 53 E
Wisła → **28** 54 22N 18 55 E
Wisłok → **27** 50 13N 22 32 E
Wisłoka → **27** 50 27N 21 23 E
Wismar **24** 53 53N 11 23 E
Wisner **116** 42 0N 96 46W
Wissant **19** 50 52N 1 40 E
Wissembourg **19** 49 2N 7 57 E
Wistoka → **27** 49 50N 21 28 E
Wisznice **28** 51 48N 23 13 E
Witbank **93** 25 51 S 29 14 E
Witdraai **92** 26 58 S 20 48 E
Witham → **12** 53 3N 0 8W
Withernsea **12** 53 43N 0 2 E
Witkowo **28** 52 26N 17 45 E
Witney **13** 51 47N 1 29W
Witnossob → **92** 26 55 S 20 37 E
Wittdün **24** 54 38N 8 23 E
Witten **24** 51 26N 7 19 E
Wittenberg **24** 51 51N 12 39 E
Wittenberge **24** 53 0N 11 44 E
Wittenburg **24** 53 30N 11 4 E
Wittenoom **96** 22 15 S 118 20 E
Wittingen **24** 52 43N 10 43 E
Wittlich **25** 50 0N 6 54 E
Wittmund **24** 53 39N 7 45 E
Wittow **24** 54 37N 13 21 E
Wittstock **24** 53 10N 12 30 E
Witzenhausen **24** 51 20N 9 50 E
Wkra → **28** 52 27N 20 44 E
Władysławowo **28** 54 48N 18 25 E
Wlen **28** 51 0N 15 39 E
Wlingi **73** 8 5 S 112 25 E
Włocławek □ **28** 52 50N 19 10 E
Włocławek **28** 52 40N 19 3 E
Włodawa **28** 51 33N 23 31 E
Włoszczowa **28** 50 50N 19 55 E
Woburn **113** 42 31N 71 7W
Wodonga **99** 36 5 S 146 50 E
Wodzisław Śląski **27** 50 1N 18 26 E
Woerth **19** 48 57N 7 45 E
Woëvre, Plaine de la **19** 49 15N 5 45 E
Wokam **73** 5 45 S 134 28 E
Woking **108** 55 35N 118 50W
Wolbrom **28** 50 24N 19 45 E
Wołczyn **28** 51 1N 18 3 E
Woldegk **24** 53 27N 13 35 E
Wolf → **108** 60 17N 132 33W
Wolf Creek **118** 47 1N 112 2W
Wolf L. **108** 60 24N 131 40W
Wolf Point **116** 48 6N 105 40W
Wolfe I. **106** 44 7N 76 20W
Wolfenbüttel **24** 52 10N 10 33 E
Wolfenden **108** 52 0N 119 25W
Wolfsberg **26** 46 50N 14 52 E
Wolfsburg **24** 52 27N 10 49 E
Wolgast **24** 54 3N 13 46 E
Wolhusen **25** 47 4N 8 4 E
Wolin, Poland **28** 53 50N 14 37 E
Wolin, Poland **28** 54 0N 14 40 E
Wollaston, Islas **128** 55 40 S 67 30W
Wollaston L. **109** 58 7N 103 10W
Wollaston Pen. **104** 69 30N 115 0W
Wollondilly → **100** 34 12 S 150 18 E
Wollongong **97** 34 25 S 150 54 E
Wolmaransstad **92** 27 12 S 26 13 E
Wolmirstedt **24** 52 15N 11 35 E
Wołomin **28** 52 19N 21 15 E
Wołów **28** 51 20N 16 38 E
Wolseley, Austral. **99** 36 23 S 140 54 E
Wolseley, Can. **109** 50 25N 103 15W
Wolseley, S. Afr. **92** 33 26 S 19 7 E
Wolstenholme Fjord **4** 76 0N 70 0W
Wolsztyn **28** 52 8N 16 5 E
Wolvega **16** 52 52N 6 0 E
Wolverhampton **13** 52 35N 2 6W
Wondai **97** 26 20 S 151 49 E
Wonder Gorge **91** 14 40 S 29 0 E
Wongalarroo L. **99** 31 32 S 144 0 E
Wŏnju **76** 37 22N 127 58 E
Wonosari **73** 7 58 S 110 36 E
Wŏnsan **76** 39 11N 127 27 E
Wonthaggi **97** 38 37 S 145 37 E
Woocalla **99** 31 42 S 137 12 E
Wood Buffalo Nat. Park **108** 59 0N 113 41W
Wood L. **109** 55 17N 103 17W
Wood Lake **116** 42 38N 100 14W
Woodbridge **112** 43 47N 79 36W
Woodburn **99** 29 6 S 153 23 E
Woodend **99** 37 20 S 144 33 E
Woodland **118** 38 40N 121 50W
Woodlark I. **98** 9 10 S 152 50 E
Woodpecker **108** 53 30N 122 40W
Woodridge **109** 49 20N 96 9W
Woodroffe, Mt. **96** 26 20 S 131 45 E
Woodruff, Ariz., U.S.A. **119** 34 51N 110 1W
Woodruff, Utah, U.S.A. **118** 41 30N 111 4W
Woods, L., Austral. **96** 17 50 S 133 30 E
Woods, L., Can. **107** 54 30N 65 13W
Woods, L. of the **109** 49 15N 94 45W
Woodside **100** 38 31 S 146 52 E
Woodstock, Austral. **98** 19 35 S 146 50 E
Woodstock, N.B., Can. **107** 46 11N 67 37W
Woodstock, Ont., Can. **106** 43 10N 80 45W
Woodstock, U.K. **13** 51 51N 1 20W
Woodstock, Ill., U.S.A. **116** 42 17N 88 30W
Woodstock, Vt., U.S.A. **113** 43 37N 72 31W
Woodsville **114** 44 10N 72 0W
Woodville, N.Z. **101** 40 20 S 175 53 E
Woodville, U.S.A. **117** 30 45N 94 25W
Woodward **117** 36 24N 99 28W
Woolamai, C. **99** 38 30 S 145 23 E
Woombye **99** 26 40 S 152 55 E
Woomera **97** 31 30 S 137 10 E
Woonona **100** 34 21 S 150 54 E
Woonsocket **114** 42 0N 71 30W
Woonsockett **116** 44 5N 98 15W
Wooramel → **96** 25 47 S 114 10 E
Wooster **114** 40 48N 81 55W
Worcester, S. Afr. **92** 33 39 S 19 27 E
Worcester, U.K. **13** 52 12N 2 12W
Worcester, Mass., U.S.A. **114** 42 14N 71 49W
Worcester, N.Y., U.S.A. **113** 42 35N 74 45W
Wörgl **26** 47 29N 12 3 E
Workington **12** 54 39N 3 34W

Worksop **12** 53 19N 1 9W
Workum **16** 52 59N 5 26 E
Worland **118** 44 0N 107 59W
Wormhoudt **19** 50 52N 2 28 E
Worms **25** 49 37N 8 21 E
Wörth **25** 49 1N 12 24 E
Wortham **117** 31 48N 96 27W
Wörther See **26** 46 37N 14 10 E
Worthing **13** 50 49N 0 21W
Worthington **116** 43 35N 95 36W
Wosi **73** 0 15 S 128 0 E
Wou-han = Wuhan **75** 30 31N 114 18 E
Wour **83** 21 14N 16 0 E
Wowoni **73** 4 5 S 123 5 E
Wozniki **28** 50 35N 19 4 E
Wrangell **104** 56 30N 132 25W
Wrangell, I. **108** 56 20N 132 10W
Wrangell Mts. **104** 61 40N 143 30W
Wrath, C. **14** 58 38N 5 0W
Wray **116** 40 8N 102 18W
Wrekin, The **12** 52 41N 2 35W
Wrens **115** 33 13N 82 23W
Wrexham **12** 53 5N 3 0W
Wriezen **24** 52 43N 14 9 E
Wright, Can. **108** 51 52N 121 40W
Wright, Phil. **73** 11 42N 125 2 E
Wrightson, Mt. **119** 31 43N 110 56W
Wrigley **104** 63 16N 123 37W
Wrocław **28** 51 5N 17 5 E
Wrocław □ **28** 51 0N 17 0 E
Wronki **28** 52 41N 16 21 E
Września **28** 52 21N 17 36 E
Wschowa **28** 51 48N 16 20 E
Wu Jiang → **75** 29 40N 107 20 E
Wuchang **76** 44 55N 127 5 E
Wuchuan **77** 28 25N 108 3 E
Wuding He → **76** 37 2N 110 23 E
Wugang **77** 26 44N 110 35 E
Wugong Shan **77** 27 30N 114 0 E
Wuhan **75** 30 31N 114 18 E
Wuhsi = Wuxi **75** 31 33N 120 18 E
Wuhu **75** 31 22N 118 21 E
Wukari **85** 7 51N 9 42 E
Wulehe **85** 8 39N 0 0
Wuliaru **73** 7 27 S 131 0 E
Wulumuchi = Ürümqi **75** 43 45N 87 45 E
Wum **85** 6 24N 10 2 E
Wuning **77** 29 17N 115 5 E
Wunnummin L. **106** 52 55N 89 10W
Wunsiedel **25** 50 2N 12 0 E
Wunstorf **24** 52 26N 9 29 E
Wuntho **67** 23 55N 95 45 E
Wuping **77** 25 5N 116 5 E
Wuppertal, Ger. **24** 51 15N 7 8 E
Wuppertal, S. Afr. **92** 32 13 S 19 12 E
Wuqing **76** 39 23N 117 4 E
Wurung **98** 19 13 S 140 38 E
Würzburg **25** 49 46N 9 55 E
Wurzen **24** 51 21N 12 45 E
Wushan **77** 31 7N 109 54 E
Wustrow **24** 54 4N 11 33 E
Wutach → **25** 47 37N 8 15 E
Wutongqiao **75** 29 22N 103 50 E
Wuwei, Anhui, China **77** 31 18N 117 54 E
Wuwei, Gansu, China **75** 37 57N 102 34 E
Wuxi, Jiangsu, China **75** 31 33N 120 18 E
Wuxi, Sichuan, China **77** 31 23N 109 35 E
Wuxing **77** 30 51N 120 8 E
Wuyi, Hebei, China **76** 37 46N 115 56 E
Wuyi, Zhejiang, China **77** 28 52N 119 50 E
Wuyi Shan **75** 27 0N 117 0 E
Wuying **76** 47 53N 129 56 E
Wuyo **85** 10 23N 11 50 E
Wuyuan **76** 41 2N 108 20 E
Wuzhai **76** 38 54N 111 48 E
Wuzhi Shan **75** 18 45N 109 45 E
Wuzhong **76** 38 2N 106 12 E
Wuzhou **75** 23 30N 111 18 E
Wyaaba Cr. → **98** 16 27 S 141 35 E
Wyalusing **113** 41 40N 76 16W
Wyandotte **114** 42 14N 83 13W
Wyandra **97** 27 12 S 145 56 E
Wyangala Res. **100** 33 54 S 149 0 E
Wyara, L. **99** 28 42 S 144 14 E
Wycheproof **99** 36 0 S 143 17 E
Wye → **13** 51 36N 2 40W
Wyk **24** 54 41N 8 33 E
Wymondham **13** 52 45N 0 42W
Wymore **116** 40 10N 96 40W
Wynberg **92** 34 2 S 18 28 E
Wyndham, Austral. **96** 15 33 S 128 3 E
Wyndham, N.Z. **101** 46 20 S 168 51 E
Wyndmere **116** 46 23N 97 7W
Wynne **117** 35 15N 90 50W
Wynnum **99** 27 27 S 153 9 E
Wynyard **109** 51 45N 104 10W
Wyoming □ **110** 42 48N 109 0W
Wyong **99** 33 14 S 151 24 E
Wyrzysk **28** 53 10N 17 17 E
Wysoka **28** 53 13N 17 2 E
Wysokie **28** 50 55N 22 40 E
Wysokie Mazowieckie **28** 52 55N 22 30 E
Wyszków **28** 52 36N 21 25 E
Wyszogród **28** 52 23N 20 9 E
Wytheville **114** 37 0N 81 3W

X

Xai-Xai **93** 25 6 S 33 31 E
Xainza **75** 30 58N 88 35 E
Xangongo **92** 16 45 S 15 0 E
Xanten **24** 51 40N 6 27 E
Xánthi **44** 41 10N 24 58 E
Xánthi □ **44** 41 10N 24 58 E
Xapuri **126** 10 35 S 68 35W
Xau, L. **92** 21 15 S 24 44 E
Xavantina **125** 21 15 S 52 48W
Xenia **114** 39 42N 83 57W
Xi Jiang → **75** 22 5N 113 20 E
Xi Xian **76** 36 41N 110 58 E
Xiachengzi **76** 44 40N 130 18 E
Xiachuan Dao **77** 21 40N 112 40 E
Xiaguan **75** 25 32N 100 16 E
Xiajiang **77** 27 30N 115 10 E
Xiamen **75** 24 25N 118 4 E
Xi'an **77** 34 15N 109 0 E
Xianfeng **77** 29 40N 109 8 E
Xiang Jiang → **75** 28 55N 112 50 E
Xiangfan **75** 32 2N 112 8 E
Xiangning **76** 35 58N 110 50 E
Xiangtan **75** 27 51N 112 54 E
Xiangxiang **77** 27 43N 112 28 E
Xiangyang **75** 32 1N 112 8 E
Xiangyin **77** 28 38N 112 54 E
Xiangzhou **77** 23 58N 109 40 E
Xianju **77** 28 51N 120 44 E
Xianyang **77** 34 20N 108 40 E
Xiao Hinggan Ling **75** 49 0N 127 0 E
Xiaogan **77** 30 52N 113 55 E
Xiapu **75** 26 54N 119 59 E
Xichang **75** 27 51N 102 19 E
Xichuan **77** 33 0N 111 30 E
Xieng Khouang **71** 19 17N 103 25 E
Xifeng **77** 27 7N 106 42 E
Xigazê **75** 29 5N 88 45 E
Xihe **77** 34 2N 105 20 E
Xiliao He → **76** 43 32N 123 35 E
Xilin **77** 24 30N 105 6 E
Xilókastron **45** 38 4N 22 43 E
Xin Xian **76** 38 22N 112 46 E
Xinavane **93** 25 2 S 32 47 E
Xinbin **76** 41 40N 125 2 E
Xincheng **77** 24 5N 108 39 E
Xinfeng **77** 25 27N 114 58 E
Xing'an **75** 25 38N 110 40 E
Xingan **77** 27 46N 115 20 E
Xingcheng **76** 40 40N 120 45 E
Xingguo **77** 26 21N 115 21 E
Xinghua **77** 32 58N 119 48 E
Xinghua Wan **77** 25 15N 119 20 E
Xingning **77** 24 3N 115 42 E
Xingren **75** 25 24N 105 11 E
Xingshan **77** 31 15N 110 45 E
Xingtai **76** 37 3N 114 32 E
Xingu → **127** 1 30 S 51 53W
Xingyang **77** 34 45N 112 52 E
Xinhua **77** 27 42N 111 13 E
Xiniás, L. **45** 39 2N 22 12 E
Xining **75** 36 34N 101 40 E
Xinjiang **76** 35 34N 111 11 E
Xinjiang Uygur Zizhiqu □ **75** 42 0N 86 0 E
Xinjin **76** 39 25N 121 58 E
Xinle **76** 38 25N 114 40 E
Xinmin **76** 41 59N 122 50 E
Xinning **77** 26 28N 110 50 E
Xinxiang **77** 35 18N 113 50 E
Xinyang **75** 32 6N 114 3 E
Xinzheng **77** 34 20N 113 45 E
Xinzhou **77** 19 43N 109 17 E
Xinzhu **75** 24 49N 120 57 E
Xiongyuecheng **76** 40 12N 122 5 E
Xiping **77** 33 22N 114 0 E
Xique-Xique **127** 10 50 S 42 40W
Xiuyan **76** 40 18N 123 11 E
Xixabangma Feng **67** 28 20N 85 40 E
Xixiang **77** 33 0N 107 44 E
Xizang □ **75** 32 0N 88 0 E
Xuancheng **77** 30 56N 118 43 E
Xuan'en **77** 30 0N 109 30 E
Xuanhan **77** 31 18N 107 38 E
Xuanhua **76** 40 40N 115 2 E
Xuchang **77** 34 2N 113 48 E
Xuguit Qi **76** 49 17N 120 44 E
Xunke **76** 49 35N 128 27 E
Xupu **77** 27 53N 110 32 E
Xuwen **77** 20 20N 110 10 E
Xuyong **77** 28 10N 105 22 E
Xuzhou **77** 34 18N 117 10 E

Y

Ya 'Bad **62** 32 27N 35 10 E
Yaamba **98** 23 8 S 150 22 E
Ya'an **75** 29 58N 103 5 E
Yaapeet **99** 35 45 S 142 3 E
Yabassi **85** 4 30N 9 57 E
Yabelo **87** 4 50N 38 8 E
Yablanitsa **43** 43 2N 24 5 E
Yablonovy Khrebet **59** 53 0N 114 0 E
Yabrīn **64** 23 17N 48 58 E
Yacheng **77** 18 22N 109 6 E
Yacuiba **124** 22 0 S 63 43W
Yadgir **70** 16 45N 77 5 E
Yadkin → **115** 35 23N 80 3W
Yadrin **55** 55 57N 46 12 E
Yagaba **85** 10 14N 1 20W
Yagodnoye **59** 62 33N 149 40 E
Yagoua **88** 10 20N 15 13 E
Yagur **62** 32 45N 35 4 E
Yahila **90** 0 13N 24 28 E
Yahk **108** 49 6N 116 10W
Yahuma **88** 1 0N 23 10 E
Yajua **85** 11 27N 12 49 E
Yakima **118** 46 42N 120 30W
Yakima → **118** 47 0N 120 30W
Yako **84** 12 59N 2 15W
Yakoruda **43** 42 1N 23 39 E
Yakut A.S.S.R. □ **59** 62 0N 130 0 E
Yakutat **104** 59 29N 139 44W
Yakutsk **59** 62 5N 129 50 E
Yala **71** 6 33N 101 18 E
Yalabusha → **117** 33 30N 90 12W
Yalboroo **98** 20 50 S 148 40 E
Yale **112** 43 9N 82 47W
Yalgoo **96** 28 16 S 116 39 E
Yalinga **88** 6 33N 23 10 E
Yalkubul, Punta **120** 21 32N 88 37W
Yalleroi **98** 24 3 S 145 42 E
Yallourn **97** 38 10 S 146 18 E
Yalong Jiang → **75** 26 40N 101 55 E
Yalpukh, Oz. **46** 45 30N 28 41 E
Yalta **56** 44 30N 34 10 E
Yalu Chiang → **76** 41 30N 126 30 E
Yalu He → **76** 46 56N 123 30 E
Yalu Jiang → **76** 40 0N 124 22 E
Yalutorovsk **58** 56 41N 66 12 E
Yam Kinneret **62** 32 45N 35 35 E
Yamagata **74** 38 15N 140 15 E
Yamagata □ **74** 38 30N 140 0 E
Yamaguchi **74** 34 10N 131 32 E
Yamaguchi □ **74** 34 20N 131 40 E
Yamal, Poluostrov **58** 71 0N 70 0 E
Yamama **64** 24 5N 47 30 E
Yamanashi □ **74** 35 40N 138 40 E
Yamantau **52** 54 20N 57 40 E
Yamantau, Gora **52** 54 15N 58 6 E
Yamba **99** 29 26 S 153 23 E
Yâmbiô **87** 4 35N 28 16 E
Yambol **43** 42 30N 26 36 E
Yamdena **73** 7 45 S 131 20 E
Yamil **85** 12 53N 8 4 E
Yamma-Yamma, L. **97** 26 16 S 141 20 E
Yampa → **118** 40 37N 108 59W
Yampi Sd. **96** 16 8 S 123 38 E
Yampol **56** 48 15N 28 15 E
Yamrat **85** 10 11N 9 55 E
Yamrukchal **43** 42 44N 24 52 E
Yamuna (Jumna) → **68** 25 30N 81 53 E
Yamzho Yumco **75** 28 48N 90 35 E
Yan **85** 10 5N 12 11 E
Yan → **70** 9 0N 81 10 E
Yana → **59** 71 30N 136 0 E
Yanac **99** 36 8 S 141 25 E
Yanai **74** 33 58N 132 7 E
Yanam **70** 16 47N 82 15 E
Yan'an **76** 36 35N 109 26 E
Yanaul **52** 56 25N 55 0 E
Yanbu 'al Baḥr **64** 24 0N 38 5 E
Yancannia **99** 30 12 S 142 35 E
Yanchang **76** 36 43N 110 1 E
Yancheng, Henan, China **77** 33 35N 114 0 E
Yancheng, Jiangsu, China **77** 33 23N 120 8 E
Yanchi **76** 37 48N 107 20 E
Yanchuan **76** 36 51N 110 10 E
Yanco **100** 34 38 S 146 27 E
Yandaran **98** 24 43 S 152 6 E
Yanfolila **84** 11 11N 8 9W
Yangambi **90** 0 47N 24 20 E
Yangch'ü = Taiyuan **76** 37 52N 112 33 E
Yangchun **75** 22 11N 111 48 E
Yanggao **76** 40 21N 113 55 E
Yangi-Yer **58** 40 17N 68 48 E
Yangjiang **75** 21 50N 110 59 E
Yangquan **76** 37 58N 113 31 E
Yangshan **77** 24 30N 112 40 E
Yangshuo **77** 24 48N 110 29 E
Yangtze Kiang = Chang Jiang → **75** 31 20N 121 52 E
Yangxin **77** 29 50N 115 12 E
Yangzhou **77** 32 21N 119 26 E
Yanhee Res. **71** 17 30N 98 45 E
Yanji **76** 42 59N 129 30 E
Yankton **116** 42 55N 97 25W
Yanna **99** 26 58 S 146 0 E
Yanonge **90** 0 35N 24 38 E
Yanqi **75** 42 5N 86 35 E
Yanqing **76** 40 30N 115 58 E
Yanshan **77** 28 15N 117 41 E
Yantabulla **99** 29 21 S 145 0 E
Yantai **76** 37 34N 121 22 E
Yanting **77** 31 11N 105 24 E
Yantra → **43** 43 40N 25 37 E
Yanzhou **76** 35 35N 116 49 E
Yao **81** 12 56N 17 33 E
Yaoundé **88** 3 50N 11 35 E
Yap **94** 9 31N 138 6 E
Yapen **73** 1 50 S 136 0 E
Yapen, Selat **73** 1 20 S 136 10 E
Yappar → **98** 18 22 S 141 16 E
Yaqui → **120** 27 37N 110 39W
Yar **55** 58 14N 52 5 E
Yar-Sale **58** 66 50N 70 50 E
Yaraka **97** 24 53 S 144 3 E
Yarangüme **64** 37 35N 29 8 E
Yaransk **55** 57 22N 47 49 E
Yaratishky **54** 54 3N 26 0 E
Yare → **13** 52 36N 1 28 E
Yarensk **52** 61 10N 49 8 E
Yarfa **86** 24 40N 38 35 E
Yarí → **126** 0 20 S 72 20W
Yarkand = Shache **75** 38 20N 77 10 E
Yarker **113** 44 23N 76 46W
Yarkhun → **69** 36 17N 72 30 E
Yarmouth **107** 43 50N 66 7W
Yarmuk → **62** 32 38N 35 34 E
Yarmūk → **62** 32 42N 35 40 E
Yaroslavl **55** 57 35N 39 55 E
Yarra → **100** 37 50 S 144 53 E
Yarram **99** 38 29 S 146 9 E
Yarraman **99** 26 50 S 152 0 E
Yarranvale **99** 26 50 S 145 20 E
Yarras **99** 31 25 S 152 20 E
Yarrawonga **100** 36 0 S 146 0 E
Yartsevo, R.S.F.S.R., U.S.S.R. **54** 55 6N 32 43 E
Yartsevo, R.S.F.S.R., U.S.S.R. **59** 60 20N 90 0 E
Yasawa Group **101** 17 00 S 177 23 E
Yaselda → **54** 52 7N 26 28 E
Yashi **85** 12 23N 7 54 E
Yasinovataya **56** 48 7N 37 57 E
Yasinski, L. **106** 53 16N 77 35W
Yasothon **71** 15 50N 104 10 E
Yass **97** 34 49 S 148 54 E
Yas'ur **62** 32 54N 35 10 E
Yatağn **45** 37 20N 28 10 E
Yates Center **117** 37 53N 95 45W
Yathkyed L. **109** 62 40N 98 0W
Yatsushiro **74** 32 30N 130 40 E
Yatta Plateau **90** 2 0 S 38 0 E
Yaṭṭah **62** 31 27N 35 6 E
Yauyos **126** 12 19 S 75 50W
Yaval **68** 21 10N 75 42 E
Yavari → **126** 4 21 S 70 2W
Yavne **62** 31 52N 34 45 E
Yavorov **54** 49 55N 23 20 E
Yawatahama **74** 33 27N 132 24 E
Yawri B. **84** 8 22N 13 0W
Yazd (Yezd) **65** 31 55N 54 27 E
Yazdān **65** 33 30N 60 50 E
Yazoo → **117** 32 35N 90 50W
Yazoo City **117** 32 48N 90 28W
Ybbs **26** 48 12N 15 4 E
Ye Xian **76** 37 8N 119 57 E
Yebbi-Souma **83** 21 7N 17 54 E
Yebyu **67** 14 15N 98 13 E
Yecla **33** 38 35N 1 5W
Yedintsy **56** 48 9N 27 18 E
Yefremov **55** 53 8N 38 3 E
Yegorlyk → **57** 46 33N 41 40 E
Yegorlykskaya **57** 46 35N 40 35 E
Yegoryevsk **55** 55 27N 38 55 E
Yegros **124** 26 20 S 56 25W
Yehuda, Midbar **62** 31 35N 35 15 E
Yei **87** 4 9N 30 40 E
Yei, Nahr → **87** 6 15N 30 13 E
Yelabuga **52** 55 45N 52 4 E
Yelan **55** 50 55N 43 43 E
Yelan-Kolenovski **55** 51 16N 41 4 E
Yelandur **70** 12 6N 77 0 E
Yelanskoye **59** 61 25N 128 0 E
Yelarbon **99** 28 33 S 150 38 E
Yelatma **55** 55 0N 41 45 E
Yelets **55** 52 40N 38 30 E
Yélimané **84** 15 9N 10 34W
Yell **14** 60 35N 1 5W
Yell Sd. **14** 60 33N 1 15W
Yellamanchilli (Elamanchili) **70** 17 33N 82 50 E
Yellow Mt. **100** 32 31 S 146 52 E
Yellow Sea **76** 35 0N 123 0 E
Yellowhead P. **108** 52 53N 118 25W
Yellowknife **108** 62 27N 114 29W
Yellowknife → **104** 62 31N 114 19W
Yellowstone → **116** 47 58N 103 59W
Yellowstone L. **118** 44 30N 110 20W
Yellowstone National Park **118** 44 35N 110 0W
Yellowtail Res. **118** 45 6N 108 8W
Yelnya **54** 54 35N 33 15 E
Yelsk **54** 51 50N 29 10 E
Yelvertoft **98** 20 13 S 138 45 E
Yelwa **85** 10 49N 4 41 E
Yemen ■ **63** 15 0N 44 0 E
Yenakiyevo **56** 48 15N 38 15 E
Yenangyaung **67** 20 30N 95 0 E
Yenda **99** 34 13 S 146 14 E
Yendéré **84** 10 12N 4 59W
Yendi **85** 9 29N 0 1W
Yenisaía **44** 41 1N 24 57 E
Yenisey → **58** 71 50N 82 40 E
Yeniseysk **59** 58 27N 92 13 E
Yeniseyskiy Zaliv **58** 72 20N 81 0 E
Yenne **21** 45 43N 5 44 E
Yenotayevka **57** 47 15N 47 0 E
Yenyuka **59** 57 57N 121 15 E
Yeo, L. **96** 28 0 S 124 30 E
Yeola **70** 20 0N 74 30 E
Yeotmal **70** 20 20N 78 15 E
Yeovil **13** 50 57N 2 38W
Yepes **32** 39 55N 3 39W
Yeppoon **97** 23 5 S 150 47 E
Yeráki **45** 37 0N 22 42 E
Yerbent **58** 39 30N 58 50 E
Yerbogachen **59** 61 16N 108 0 E
Yerevan **57** 40 10N 44 31 E
Yerla → **70** 16 50N 74 30 E
Yermak **58** 52 2N 76 55 E
Yermakovo **59** 52 25N 126 20 E
Yermo **119** 34 58N 116 50W
Yerofey Pavlovich **59** 54 0N 122 0 E
Yershov **55** 51 22N 48 16 E
Yerushalayim **62** 31 47N 35 10 E
Yerville **18** 49 40N 0 53 E
Yes Tor **13** 50 41N 3 59W
Yesnogorsk **55** 54 32N 37 38 E
Yeso **117** 34 29N 104 37W
Yessentuki **57** 44 0N 42 53 E
Yessey **59** 68 29N 102 10 E
Yeste **33** 38 22N 2 19W
Yeu, I. d' **18** 46 42N 2 20W
Yevlakh **57** 40 39N 47 7 E
Yevpatoriya **56** 45 15N 33 20 E
Yevstratovskiy **55** 50 11N 39 45 E
Yeya → **57** 46 40N 38 40 E
Yeysk **56** 46 40N 38 12 E
Yhati **124** 25 45 S 56 35W
Yhú **125** 25 0 S 56 0W
Yi → **124** 33 7 S 57 8W
Yi Xian **76** 41 30N 121 22 E
Yialí **45** 36 41N 27 11 E
Yi'allaq, G. **86** 30 21N 33 31 E
Yiáltra **45** 38 51N 22 59 E
Yianisádhes **45** 35 20N 26 10 E
Yiannitsa **44** 40 46N 22 24 E
Yibin **75** 28 45N 104 32 E
Yichang **75** 30 40N 111 20 E
Yicheng **76** 35 42N 111 40 E
Yichuan **76** 36 2N 110 10 E
Yichun, Heilongjiang, China **75** 47 44N 128 52 E
Yichun, Jiangxi, China **77** 27 48N 114 22 E
Yidhá **44** 40 35N 22 53 E
Yidu **76** 36 43N 118 28 E
Yihuang **77** 27 30N 116 12 E
Yijun **76** 35 28N 109 8 E
Yilan, China **76** 46 19N 129 34 E
Yilan, Taiwan **75** 24 51N 121 44 E
Yilehuli Shan **76** 51 20N 124 20 E
Yimianpo **76** 45 7N 128 2 E
Yinchuan **76** 38 30N 106 15 E
Ying He → **77** 32 30N 116 30 E
Ying Xian **76** 39 32N 113 10 E
Yingcheng **77** 30 56N 113 35 E
Yingde **77** 24 10N 113 25 E
Yingkou **76** 40 37N 122 18 E
Yingshan **77** 30 41N 115 32 E
Yingshang **77** 32 38N 116 12 E
Yingtan **75** 28 12N 117 0 E
Yining **75** 43 58N 81 10 E

Yinjiang **77** 28 1N 108 21 E
Yinkanie **99** 34 22 S 140 17 E
Yinnietharra **96** 24 39 S 116 12 E
Yioúra, Greece **44** 39 23N 24 10 E
Yioúra, Greece **45** 37 32N 24 40 E
Yipinglang **75** 25 10N 101 52 E
Yirga Alem **87** 6 48N 38 22 E
Yirshi **76** 47 18N 119 49 E
Yishan **75** 24 28N 108 38 E
Yíthion **45** 36 46N 22 34 E
Yitong **76** 43 13N 125 20 E
Yitulihe **76** 50 38N 121 34 E
Yixing **77** 31 21N 119 48 E
Yiyang, Henan, China **77** 34 27N 112 10 E
Yiyang, Hunan, China **75** 28 35N 112 18 E
Yizhang **77** 25 27N 112 57 E
Yizre'el **62** 32 34N 35 19 E
Ylitornio **50** 66 19N 23 39 E
Ylivieska **50** 64 4N 24 28 E
Yngaren **49** 58 50N 16 35 E
Ynykchanskiy **59** 60 15N 137 35 E
Yoakum **117** 29 20N 97 20W
Yog Pt. **73** 14 6N 124 12 E
Yogan **85** 6 23N 1 30 E
Yogyakarta **73** 7 49 S 110 22 E
Yoho Nat. Park **108** 51 25N 116 30W
Yojoa, L. de **120** 14 53N 88 0W
Yokadouma **88** 3 26N 15 6 E
Yokkaichi **74** 35 0N 136 38 E
Yoko **85** 5 32N 12 20 E
Yokohama **74** 35 27N 139 28 E
Yokosuka **74** 35 20N 139 40 E
Yola **85** 9 10N 12 29 E
Yolaina, Cordillera de **121** 11 30N 84 0W
Yonago **74** 35 25N 133 19 E
Yong Peng **71** 2 0N 103 3 E
Yong'an **77** 25 59N 117 25 E
Yongchun **77** 25 16N 118 20 E
Yongding **77** 24 43N 116 45 E
Yongfeng **77** 27 20N 115 22 E
Yongfu **77** 24 59N 109 59 E
Yonghe **76** 36 46N 110 38 E
Yongji **77** 34 52N 110 28 E
Yongshun **77** 29 2N 109 51 E
Yongxin **77** 26 58N 114 15 E
Yongxing **77** 26 9N 113 8 E
Yongxiu **77** 29 2N 115 42 E
Yonibana **84** 8 30N 12 19W
Yonkers **114** 40 57N 73 51W
Yonne □ **19** 47 50N 3 40 E
Yonne ⤳ **19** 48 23N 2 58 E
Yoqne'am **62** 32 40N 35 6 E
York, Austral. **96** 31 52 S 116 47 E
York, U.K. **12** 53 58N 1 7W
York, Ala., U.S.A. **115** 32 30N 88 18W
York, Nebr., U.S.A. **116** 40 55N 97 35W
York, Pa., U.S.A. **114** 39 57N 76 43W
York, C. **97** 10 42 S 142 31 E
York, Kap **4** 75 55N 66 25W
York Sd. **96** 14 50 S 125 5 E
Yorke Pen. **97** 34 50 S 137 40 E
Yorkshire Wolds **12** 54 0N 0 30W
Yorkton **109** 51 11N 102 28W
Yorktown **117** 29 0N 97 29W
Yosemite National Park **119** 38 0N 119 30W
Yoshkar Ola **55** 56 38N 47 55 E
Yŏsu **77** 34 47N 127 45 E
Yotvata **62** 29 55N 35 2 E
You Jiang ⤳ **75** 23 22N 110 3 E
Youbou **108** 48 53N 124 13W
Youghal **15** 51 58N 7 51W
Youghal B. **15** 51 55N 7 50W
Youkounkoun **84** 12 35N 13 11W
Young, Austral. **97** 34 19 S 148 18 E
Young, Can. **109** 51 47N 105 45W
Young, Uruguay **124** 32 44 S 57 36W
Young, U.S.A. **119** 34 9N 110 56W
Younghusband Pen. **99** 36 0 S 139 25 E
Youngstown, Can. **109** 51 35N 111 10W
Youngstown, N.Y., U.S.A. **112** 43 16N 79 2W
Youngstown, Ohio, U.S.A. **114** 41 7N 80 41W
Youngsville **112** 41 51N 79 21W
Youssoufia **82** 32 16N 8 31W
Youyang **77** 28 47N 108 42 E
Youyu **76** 40 10N 112 20 E
Yozgat **64** 39 51N 34 47 E
Ypané ⤳ **124** 23 29 S 57 19W
Yport **18** 49 45N 0 15 E
Ypres = Ieper **16** 50 51N 2 53 E
Ypsilanti **114** 42 18N 83 40W
Yreka **118** 41 44N 122 40W
Ysleta **119** 31 45N 106 24W
Yssingeaux **21** 45 9N 4 8 E
Ystad **49** 55 26N 13 50 E
Ythan ⤳ **14** 57 26N 2 12W
Ytterhogdal **48** 62 12N 14 56 E
Ytyk-Kel **59** 62 30N 133 45 E
Yu Shan **75** 23 30N 120 58 E
Yu Xian, Hebei, China **76** 39 50N 114 35 E
Yu Xian, Henan, China **77** 34 10N 113 28 E
Yuan Jiang ⤳ **75** 28 55N 111 50 E
Yuanling **75** 28 29N 110 22 E
Yuanyang **75** 23 10N 102 43 E
Yuba City **118** 39 12N 121 37W
Yucatán □ **120** 21 30N 86 30W
Yucatán, Canal de **121** 22 0N 86 30W
Yucca **119** 34 56N 114 6W
Yucheng **76** 36 55N 116 32 E
Yuci **76** 37 42N 112 46 E
Yudino, R.S.F.S.R., U.S.S.R. **55** 55 51N 48 55 E
Yudino, R.S.F.S.R., U.S.S.R. **58** 55 10N 67 55 E
Yudu **77** 25 59N 115 30 E
Yueqing **77** 28 9N 120 59 E
Yueyang **77** 29 21N 113 5 E
Yugan **77** 28 43N 116 37 E
Yugoslavia ■ **37** 44 0N 20 0 E
Yuhuan **77** 28 9N 121 12 E
Yujiang **77** 28 10N 116 43 E
Yukhnov **54** 54 44N 35 15 E
Yukon Territory □ **104** 63 0N 135 0W
Yukti **59** 63 26N 105 42 E
Yule ⤳ **96** 20 41 S 118 17 E
Yuli **85** 9 44N 10 12 E
Yülin **77** 18 10N 109 31 E
Yulin, Guangxi Zhuangzu, China **77** 22 40N 110 8 E
Yulin, Shaanxi, China **76** 38 20N 109 30 E
Yuma, Ariz., U.S.A. **119** 32 45N 114 37W
Yuma, Colo., U.S.A. **116** 40 10N 102 43W
Yuma, B. de **121** 18 20N 68 35W
Yumbe **90** 3 28N 31 15 E
Yumbi **90** 1 12 S 26 15 E
Yumen **75** 39 50N 97 30 E
Yun Xian **75** 32 50N 110 46 E
Yungas **126** 17 0 S 66 0W
Yungay **124** 37 10 S 72 5W
Yunhe **77** 28 8N 119 33 E
Yunlin **77** 23 42N 120 30 E
Yunnan □ **75** 25 0N 102 0 E
Yunquera de Henares **32** 40 47N 3 11W
Yunta **99** 32 34 S 139 36 E
Yunxiao **77** 23 59N 117 18 E
Yur **59** 59 52N 137 41 E
Yurgao **58** 55 42N 84 51 E
Yuribei **58** 71 8N 76 58 E
Yurimaguas **126** 5 55 S 76 7W
Yurya **55** 59 1N 49 13 E
Yuryev-Polskiy **55** 56 30N 39 40 E
Yuryevets **55** 57 25N 43 2 E
Yuscarán **121** 13 58N 86 45W
Yushu, Jilin, China **76** 44 43N 126 38 E
Yushu, Qinghai, China **75** 33 5N 96 55 E
Yuyao **77** 30 3N 121 10 E
Yuzha **55** 56 34N 42 1 E
Yuzhno-Sakhalinsk **59** 46 58N 142 45 E
Yvelines □ **19** 48 40N 1 45 E
Yverdon **25** 46 47N 6 39 E
Yvetot **18** 49 37N 0 44 E

Z

Zaandam **16** 52 26N 4 49 E
Zab, Monts du **83** 34 55N 5 0 E
Žabalj **42** 45 21N 20 5 E
Žabari **42** 44 22N 21 15 E
Zabarjad **86** 23 40N 36 12 E
Zabaykalskiy **59** 49 40N 117 25 E
Zabid **63** 14 0N 43 10 E
Ząbkowice Śląskie **28** 50 35N 16 50 E
Žabljak **42** 43 18N 19 7 E
Zabłudów **28** 53 0N 23 19 E
Żabno **27** 50 9N 20 53 E
Zābol **65** 31 0N 61 32 E
Zābolī **65** 27 10N 61 35 E
Zabré **85** 11 12N 0 36W
Zabrze **28** 50 18N 18 50 E
Zabul □ **65** 32 0N 67 0 E
Zacapa **120** 14 59N 89 31W
Zacatecas **120** 22 49N 102 34W
Zacatecas □ **120** 23 30N 103 0W
Zacatecoluca **120** 13 29N 88 51W
Zacoalco **120** 20 14N 103 33W
Zadar **39** 44 8N 15 14 E
Zadawa **85** 11 33N 10 19 E
Zadetkyi Kyun **72** 10 0N 98 25 E
Zadonsk **55** 52 25N 38 56 E
Zafora **45** 36 5N 26 24 E
Zafra **31** 38 26N 6 30W
Zafriya **62** 31 59N 34 51 E
Żagań **28** 51 39N 15 22 E
Zagazig **86** 30 40N 31 30 E
Zaghouan **83** 36 23N 10 10 E
Zaglivérion **44** 40 36N 23 15 E
Zaglou **82** 27 17N 0 3W
Zagnanado **85** 7 18N 2 28 E
Zagorá **44** 39 27N 23 6 E
Zagora **82** 30 22N 5 51W
Zagórów **28** 52 10N 17 54 E
Zagorsk **55** 56 20N 38 10 E
Zagórz **27** 49 30N 22 14 E
Zagreb **39** 45 50N 16 0 E
Zāgros, Kudhā-ye **65** 33 45N 47 0 E
Žagubica **42** 44 15N 21 47 E
Zaguinaso **84** 10 1N 6 14W
Zagyva ⤳ **27** 47 5N 20 4 E
Zāhedān **65** 29 30N 60 50 E
Zahirabad **70** 17 43N 77 37 E
Zahlah **64** 33 52N 35 50 E
Zahna **24** 51 54N 12 47 E
Zahrez Chergui **82** 35 0N 3 30 E
Zahrez Rharbi **82** 34 50N 2 55 E
Zaïr **82** 29 47N 5 51W
Zaïre ⤳ **88** 6 4 S 12 24 E
Zaïre, Rep. of ■ **88** 3 0 S 23 0 E
Zaječar **42** 43 53N 22 18 E
Zakamensk **59** 50 23N 103 17 E
Zakataly **57** 41 38N 46 35 E
Zakavkazye **57** 42 0N 44 0 E
Zākhū **64** 37 10N 42 50 E
Zákinthos **45** 37 47N 20 57 E
Zaklików **28** 50 46N 22 7 E
Zakopane **27** 49 18N 19 57 E
Zakroczym **28** 52 26N 20 38 E
Zala □ **27** 46 42N 16 50 E
Zala ⤳ **27** 46 43N 17 16 E
Zalaegerszeg **27** 46 53N 16 47 E
Zalakomár **27** 46 33N 17 10 E
Zalalövö **27** 46 51N 16 35 E
Zalamea de la Serena **31** 38 40N 5 38W
Zalamea la Real **31** 37 41N 6 38W
Zalău **46** 47 12N 23 3 E
Zalazna **55** 58 39N 52 31 E
Žalec **39** 46 16N 15 10 E
Zaleshchiki **56** 48 45N 25 45 E
Zalewo **28** 53 50N 19 41 E
Zalingei **81** 12 51N 23 29 E
Zalţan, Jabal **83** 28 46N 19 45 E
Zambeke **90** 2 8N 25 17 E
Zambeze ⤳ **91** 18 55 S 36 4 E
Zambezi **89** 13 30 S 23 15 E
Zambezi = Zambeze ⤳ **91** 18 55 S 36 4 E
Zambezia □ **91** 16 15 S 37 30 E
Zambia ■ **89** 15 0 S 28 0 E
Zamboanga **73** 6 59N 122 3 E
Zambrów **28** 52 59N 22 14 E
Zametchino **55** 53 30N 42 30 E
Zamora, Mexico **120** 20 0N 102 21W
Zamora, Spain **30** 41 30N 5 45W
Zamora □ **30** 41 30N 5 46W
Zamość **28** 50 43N 23 15 E
Zamość □ **28** 50 40N 23 10 E
Zamzam, W. **83** 31 0N 14 30 E
Zan **85** 9 26N 0 17W
Zanaga **88** 2 48 S 13 48 E
Záncara ⤳ **33** 39 18N 3 18W
Zandvoort **16** 52 22N 4 32 E
Zanesville **114** 39 56N 82 2W
Zangue ⤳ **91** 17 50 S 35 21 E
Zanjan **64** 36 40N 48 35 E
Zannone **40** 40 58N 13 2 E
Zante = Zákinthos **45** 37 47N 20 54 E
Zanthus **96** 31 2 S 123 34 E
Zanzibar **90** 6 12 S 39 12 E
Zanzūr **83** 32 55N 13 1 E
Zaouiet El-Kala = Bordj Omar Driss **83** 28 4N 6 40 E
Zaouiet Reggane **82** 26 32N 0 3 E
Zapadna Morava ⤳ **42** 43 38N 21 30 E
Zapadnaya Dvina **54** 56 15N 32 3 E
Zapadnaya Dvina ⤳ **54** 57 4N 24 3 E
Západné Beskydy **27** 49 30N 19 0 E
Zapadni Rodopi **43** 41 50N 24 0 E
Zapadočeský □ **26** 49 35N 13 0 E
Západoslovenský □ **27** 48 30N 17 30 E
Zapala **128** 39 0 S 70 5W
Zapaleri, Cerro **124** 22 49 S 67 11W
Zapata **117** 26 56N 99 17W
Zapatón ⤳ **31** 39 0N 6 49W
Zapodnyy Sayan **59** 52 30N 94 0 E
Zapolyarnyy **52** 69 26N 30 51 E
Zaporozhye **56** 47 50N 35 10 E
Zapponeta **41** 41 27N 15 57 E
Zara **64** 39 58N 37 43 E
Zaragoza, Coahuila, Mexico **120** 28 30N 101 0W
Zaragoza, Nuevo León, Mexico **120** 24 0N 99 46W
Zaragoza, Spain **32** 41 39N 0 53W
Zaragoza □ **32** 41 35N 1 0W
Zarand **65** 30 46N 56 34 E
Zărandului, Munţii **46** 46 14N 22 7 E
Zaranj **65** 30 55N 61 55 E
Zarasai **54** 55 40N 26 20 E
Zarate **124** 34 7 S 59 0W
Zaraysk **55** 54 48N 38 53 E
Zarembo I. **108** 56 20N 132 50W
Zaria **85** 11 0N 7 40 E
Zarisberge **92** 24 30 S 16 15 E
Zárkon **44** 39 38N 22 6 E
Żarów **28** 50 56N 16 29 E
Zarqā' ⤳ **62** 32 10N 35 37 E
Zaruma **126** 3 40 S 79 38W
Żary **28** 51 37N 15 10 E
Zarza de Alange **31** 38 49N 6 13W
Zarza de Granadilla **30** 40 14N 6 3W
Zarza, La **31** 37 42N 6 51W
Zarzaîtine **83** 28 15N 9 34 E
Zarzis **83** 33 31N 11 2 E
Zas **30** 43 4N 8 53W
Zashiversk **59** 67 25N 142 40 E
Zaskar Mountains **69** 33 15N 77 30 E
Zastron **92** 30 18 S 27 7 E
Žatec **26** 50 20N 13 32 E
Zator **27** 49 59N 19 28 E
Zavala **42** 42 50N 17 59 E
Zavarāh **65** 33 29N 52 28 E
Zavetnoye **57** 47 13N 43 50 E
Zavidovići **42** 44 27N 18 13 E
Zavitinsk **59** 50 10N 129 20 E
Zavodoski **5** 56 0 S 27 45W
Zavolzhsk **55** 57 30N 42 10 E
Zavolzhye **55** 56 37N 43 26 E
Zawadzkie **28** 50 37N 18 28 E
Zawichost **28** 50 48N 21 51 E
Zawidów **28** 51 1N 15 1 E
Zawiercie **28** 50 30N 19 24 E
Zāwiyat al Bayḑā **81** 32 30N 21 40 E
Zawyet Shammâs **86** 31 30N 26 37 E
Zâwyet Um el Rakham **86** 31 18N 27 1 E
Zâwyet Ungeîla **86** 31 23N 26 42 E
Zāyandeh ⤳ **65** 32 35N 52 0 E
Zayarsk **59** 56 12N 102 55 E
Zaysan **58** 47 28N 84 52 E
Zaysan, Oz. **58** 48 0N 83 0 E
Zaytā **62** 32 23N 35 2 E
Zāzamt, W. **83** 30 29N 14 30 E
Zazir, O. ⤳ **83** 22 0N 5 40 E
Zázrivá **27** 49 16N 19 7 E
Zbarazh **54** 49 43N 25 44 E
Zbąszyń **28** 52 14N 15 56 E
Zbąszynek **28** 52 16N 15 51 E
Zblewo **28** 53 56N 18 19 E
Zdolbunov **54** 50 30N 26 15 E
Ždrelo **42** 44 16N 21 28 E
Zduńska Wola **28** 51 37N 18 59 E
Zduny **28** 51 39N 17 21 E
Zeballos **108** 49 59N 126 50W
Zebediela **93** 24 20 S 19 7 E
Zeebrugge **16** 51 19N 3 12 E
Zeehan **97** 41 52 S 145 25 E
Zeeland □ **16** 51 30N 3 50 E
Ze'elim **62** 31 13N 34 32 E
Zeerust **92** 25 31 S 26 4 E
Zefat **62** 32 58N 35 29 E
Zegdou **82** 29 51N 4 45W
Zege **87** 11 43N 37 18 E
Zégoua **84** 10 32N 5 35W
Zehdenick **24** 52 59N 13 20 E
Zeila **63** 11 21N 43 30 E
Zeist **16** 52 5N 5 15 E
Zeitz **24** 51 3N 12 9 E
Żelechów **28** 51 49N 21 54 E
Zelengora **42** 43 22N 18 30 E
Zelenika **42** 42 27N 18 37 E
Zelenodolsk **55** 55 55N 48 30 E
Zelenogradsk **54** 54 53N 20 29 E
Zelenokumsk **57** 44 24N 43 53 E
Zelënyy **57** 48 6N 50 45 E
Zeleznik **42** 44 43N 20 23 E
Zell, Baden, Ger. **25** 47 42N 7 50 E
Zell, Rhld-Pfz., Ger. **25** 50 2N 7 11 E
Zell am See **26** 47 19N 12 47 E
Zella Mehlis **24** 50 40N 10 41 E
Zelów **28** 51 28N 19 14 E
Zelzate **16** 51 13N 3 47 E
Zembra, I. **83** 37 5N 10 56 E
Zémio **90** 5 2N 25 5 E
Zemlya Frantsa Iosifa **4** 81 0N 55 0 E
Zemmora **82** 35 44N 0 51 E
Zemoul, O. ⤳ **82** 29 15N 7 0W
Zemun **42** 44 51N 20 25 E
Zengbe **85** 5 46N 13 4 E
Zenica **42** 44 10N 17 57 E
Zenina **82** 34 30N 2 37 E
Žepče **42** 44 28N 18 2 E
Zeraf, Bahr ez ⤳ **87** 9 42N 30 52 E
Zerbst **24** 51 59N 12 8 E
Zerhamra **82** 29 58N 2 30W
Żerków **28** 52 4N 17 32 E
Zermatt **25** 46 2N 7 46 E
Zernez **25** 46 42N 10 7 E
Zernograd **57** 46 52N 40 19 E
Zerqani **44** 41 30N 20 20 E
Zestafoni **57** 42 6N 43 0 E
Zetel **24** 53 25N 7 57 E
Zeulenroda **24** 50 39N 12 0 E
Zeven **24** 53 17N 9 19 E
Zévio **38** 45 23N 11 10 E
Zeya **59** 53 48N 127 14 E
Zeya ⤳ **59** 53 13N 127 35 E
Zêzere ⤳ **31** 39 28N 8 20W
Zgierz **28** 51 50N 19 27 E
Zgorzelec **28** 51 10N 15 0 E
Zhabinka **54** 52 13N 24 2 E
Zhailma **58** 51 37N 61 33 E
Zhangguangcai Ling **76** 45 0N 129 0 E
Zhanghua **75** 24 6N 120 29 E
Zhangjiakou **76** 40 48N 114 55 E
Zhangping **77** 25 17N 117 23 E
Zhangpu **77** 24 8N 117 35 E
Zhangwu **76** 42 43N 123 52 E
Zhangye **75** 38 50N 100 23 E
Zhangzhou **75** 24 30N 117 35 E
Zhanhua **76** 37 40N 118 8 E
Zhanjiang **75** 21 15N 110 20 E
Zhanyi **75** 25 38N 103 48 E
Zhanyu **76** 44 30N 122 30 E
Zhao Xian **76** 37 43N 114 45 E
Zhao'an **77** 23 41N 117 10 E
Zhaoping **77** 24 11N 110 48 E
Zhaoqing **77** 23 0N 112 20 E
Zhaotong **75** 27 20N 103 44 E
Zhaoyuan **76** 37 20N 120 23 E
Zharkovskiy **54** 55 56N 32 19 E
Zhashkov **56** 49 15N 30 5 E
Zhdanov **56** 47 5N 37 31 E
Zhecheng **77** 34 7N 115 20 E
Zhejiang □ **75** 29 0N 120 0 E
Zheleznodorozhny **52** 62 35N 50 55 E
Zheleznogorsk **54** 52 22N 35 23 E
Zheleznogorsk-Ilimskiy **59** 56 34N 104 8 E
Zheltyye Vody **56** 48 21N 33 31 E
Zhen'an **77** 33 27N 109 9 E
Zhenfeng **77** 25 22N 105 40 E
Zheng'an **77** 28 32N 107 27 E
Zhengding **76** 38 8N 114 32 E
Zhenghe **77** 27 20N 118 50 E
Zhengyang **77** 32 37N 114 22 E
Zhengyangguan **77** 32 30N 116 29 E
Zhengzhou **77** 34 45N 113 34 E
Zhenjiang **75** 32 11N 119 26 E
Zhenlai **76** 45 50N 123 5 E
Zhenning **77** 26 4N 105 45 E
Zhenyuan, Gansu, China **76** 35 35N 107 30 E
Zhenyuan, Guizhou, China **75** 27 4N 108 21 E
Zherdevka **55** 51 56N 41 29 E
Zhigansk **59** 66 48N 123 27 E
Zhigulevsk **55** 53 28N 49 30 E
Zhijiang **75** 27 27N 109 42 E
Zhirnovsk **55** 50 57N 44 49 E
Zhitomir **54** 50 20N 28 40 E
Zhizdra **54** 53 45N 34 40 E
Zhlobin **54** 52 55N 30 0 E
Zhmerinka **56** 49 2N 28 2 E
Zhodino **54** 54 5N 28 17 E
Zhokhova, Ostrov **59** 76 4N 152 40 E
Zhong Xian **77** 30 21N 108 1 E
Zhongdian **75** 27 48N 99 42 E
Zhongshan **77** 22 26N 113 20 E
Zhongwei **76** 37 30N 105 12 E
Zhongxiang **77** 31 12N 112 34 E
Zhoushan Dao **77** 28 5N 122 10 E
Zhouzhi **77** 34 10N 108 12 E
Zhovtnevoye **56** 46 54N 32 3 E
Zhuanghe **76** 39 40N 123 0 E
Zhucheng **76** 36 0N 119 27 E
Zhugqu **77** 33 40N 104 30 E
Zhuji **77** 29 40N 120 10 E
Zhukovka **54** 53 35N 33 50 E
Zhumadian **75** 32 59N 114 2 E
Zhuo Xian **76** 39 28N 115 58 E
Zhupanovo **59** 53 40N 159 52 E
Zhushan **77** 32 15N 110 13 E
Zhuxi **77** 32 25N 109 40 E
Zhuzhou **75** 27 49N 113 12 E
Ziarat **68** 30 25N 67 49 E
Zibo **76** 36 47N 118 3 E
Zidarovo **43** 42 20N 27 24 E
Ziębice **28** 50 37N 17 2 E
Zielona Góra **28** 51 57N 15 31 E
Zielona Góra □ **28** 51 57N 15 30 E
Zierikzee **16** 51 40N 3 55 E
Ziesar **24** 52 16N 12 19 E
Zifta **86** 30 43N 31 14 E
Zigey **81** 14 43N 15 50 E
Zigong **75** 29 15N 104 48 E
Zigui **75** 31 0N 110 40 E
Ziguinchor **84** 12 35N 16 20W
Zikhron Ya'Aqov **62** 32 34N 34 56 E

Place	Map	Lat	Long
Zile	64	40 15N	35 52 E
Žilina	27	49 12N	18 42 E
Zillah	83	28 30N	17 33 E
Zillertaler Alpen	26	47 6N	11 45 E
Zima	59	54 0N	102 5 E
Zimane, Adrar in	82	22 10N	4 30 E
Zimapán	120	20 54N	99 20W
Zimba	91	17 20 S	26 11 E
Zimbabwe	91	20 16 S	30 54 E
Zimbabwe ■	91	20 0 S	30 0 E
Zimnicea	46	43 40N	25 22 E
Zimovniki	57	47 10N	42 25 E
Zinder	85	13 48N	9 0 E
Zinga	91	9 16 S	38 49 E
Zingst	24	54 24N	12 45 E
Ziniaré	85	12 35N	1 18W
Zinjibār	63	13 5N	45 23 E
Zinkgruvan	49	58 50N	15 6 E
Zinnowitz	24	54 5N	13 54 E
Zion Nat. Park	119	37 25N	112 50W
Zipaquirá	126	5 0N	74 0W
Zippori	62	32 45N	35 16 E
Zirc	27	47 17N	17 42 E
Žiri	39	46 5N	14 5 E
Žirje	39	43 39N	15 42 E
Zirko	65	25 0N	53 40 E
Zirl	26	47 17N	11 14 E
Zisterdorf	27	48 33N	16 45 E
Zitácuaro	120	19 28N	100 21W
Zitava →	27	48 14N	18 21 E
Žitište	42	45 30N	20 32 E
Žitsa	44	39 47N	20 40 E
Zittau	24	50 54N	14 47 E
Zitundo	93	26 48 S	32 47 E
Živinice	42	44 27N	18 36 E
Ziway, L.	87	8 0N	38 50 E
Zixi	77	27 45N	117 4 E
Ziyang	77	32 32N	108 31 E
Ziz, Oued →	82	31 40N	4 15W
Zizhong	77	29 48N	104 47 E
Zlarin	39	43 42N	15 49 E
Zlatar, Hrvatska, Yugo.	39	46 5N	16 3 E
Zlatar, Srbija, Yugo.	42	43 25N	19 47 E
Zlataritsa	43	43 2N	25 55 E
Zlatibor	42	43 45N	19 43 E
Zlatitsa	43	42 41N	24 7 E
Zlatna	46	46 8N	23 11 E
Zlatograd	43	41 22N	25 7 E
Zlatoust	52	55 10N	59 40 E
Zletovo	42	41 59N	22 17 E
Zlitan	83	32 32N	14 35 E
Złocieniec	28	53 30N	16 1 E
Złoczew	28	51 24N	18 35 E
Zlot	42	44 1N	22 0 E
Złotoryja	28	51 8N	15 55 E
Złotów	28	53 22N	17 2 E
Złoty Stok	28	50 27N	16 53 E
Zmeinogorsk	58	51 10N	82 13 E
Žmigród	28	51 28N	16 53 E
Zmiyev	56	49 39N	36 27 E
Znamenka	56	48 45N	32 30 E
Znamensk	54	54 37N	21 17 E
Žnin	28	52 51N	17 44 E
Znojmo	26	48 50N	16 2 E
Zoar	92	33 30 S	21 26 E
Zobia	90	3 0N	25 59 E
Zogno	38	45 49N	9 41 E
Zolochev	54	49 45N	24 51 E
Zolotonosha	56	49 39N	32 5 E
Zomba	91	15 22 S	35 19 E
Zongo	88	4 20N	18 35 E
Zonguldak	56	41 28N	31 50 E
Zorgo	85	12 15N	0 35W
Zorita	31	39 17N	5 39W
Zorleni	46	46 14N	27 44 E
Zornitsa	43	42 23N	26 58 E
Zorra Island	120	9 18N	79 52W
Zorritos	126	3 43 S	80 40W
Zory	27	50 3N	18 44 E
Zorzor	84	7 46N	9 28W
Zossen	24	52 13N	13 28 E
Zou Xiang	77	35 30N	116 58 E
Zouar	83	20 30N	16 32 E
Zouérate	80	22 44N	12 21W
Zousfana, O. →	82	31 28N	2 17W
Zoutkamp	16	53 20N	6 18 E
Zrenjanin	42	45 22N	20 23 E
Zuarungu	85	10 49N	0 46W
Zuba	85	9 11N	7 12 E
Zubair, Jazāir	87	15 0N	42 10 E
Zubia	31	37 8N	3 33W
Zubtsov	54	56 10N	34 34 E
Zuénoula	84	7 34N	6 3W
Zuera	32	41 51N	0 49W
Zuetina	83	30 58N	20 7 E
Zufar	63	17 40N	54 0 E
Zug	25	47 10N	8 31 E
Zugdidi	57	42 30N	41 55 E
Zugersee	25	47 7N	8 35 E
Zugspitze	25	47 25N	10 59 E
Zuid-Holland □	16	52 0N	4 35 E
Zuidhorn	16	53 15N	6 23 E
Zújar	33	37 34N	2 50W
Zújar →	31	39 1N	5 47W
Zújar, Pantano del	31	38 55N	5 35W
Zula	87	15 17N	39 40 E
Zulpich	24	50 41N	6 38 E
Zululand	93	28 0 S	32 0 E
Zumaya	32	43 19N	2 15W
Zumbo	91	15 35 S	30 26 E
Zummo	85	9 51N	12 59 E
Zungeru	85	9 51N	6 8 E
Zunhua	76	40 18N	117 58 E
Zuni	119	35 7N	108 57W
Zunyi	75	27 42N	106 53 E
Županja	42	45 4N	18 43 E
Zuqar	87	14 0N	42 40 E
Žur	42	42 13N	20 34 E
Zürich	25	47 22N	8 32 E
Zürich □	25	47 26N	8 40 E
Zürichsee	25	47 18N	8 40 E
Zuromin	28	53 4N	19 51 E
Zuru	85	11 20N	5 11 E
Žut	39	43 52N	15 17 E
Zutphen	16	52 9N	6 12 E
Zuwārah	83	32 58N	12 1 E
Zuyevka	55	58 25N	51 10 E
Žužemberk	39	45 52N	14 56 E
Zvenigorodka	56	49 4N	30 56 E
Zverinogolovskoye	58	54 23N	64 40 E
Zvezdets	43	42 6N	27 26 E
Zvolen	27	48 33N	19 10 E
Zvonce	42	42 57N	22 34 E
Zvornik	42	44 26N	19 7 E
Zwedru (Tchien)	84	5 59N	8 15W
Zweibrücken	25	49 15N	7 20 E
Zwenkau	24	51 13N	12 19 E
Zwettl	26	48 35N	15 9 E
Zwickau	24	50 43N	12 30 E
Zwiesel	25	49 1N	13 14 E
Zwischenahn	24	53 12N	8 1 E
Zwoleń	28	51 21N	21 36 E
Zwolle, Neth.	16	52 31N	6 6 E
Zwolle, U.S.A.	117	31 38N	93 38W
Żychlin	28	52 15N	19 37 E
Zymoetz →	108	54 33N	128 31W
Żyrardów	28	52 3N	20 28 E
Zyrya	57	40 20N	50 15 E
Zyryanka	59	65 45N	150 51 E
Zyryanovsk	58	49 43N	84 20 E
Żywiec	27	49 42N	19 10 E

Recent Place Name Changes

The following place name changes have recently occurred.
The new names are on the maps but the former names are in the index.

India

Former name	New name
Ambarnath	Amarnath
Arrah	Ara
Aruppukottai	Aruppukkottai
Barrackpur	Barakpur
Berhampore	Baharampur
Bokharo Steel City	Bokaro
Budge Budge	Baj Baj
Burdwam	Barddhaman
Chapra	Chhapra
Cooch Behar	Koch Bihar
Dohad	Dahod
Dhulia	Dhule
English Bazar	Ingraj Bazar
Farrukhabad-cum-Fatehgarh	Fategarh
Ferozepore	Firozpur
Gadag-Batgeri	Gadag
Gudiyatam	Gudiyattam
Hardwar	Haridwar
Hooghly-Chinsura	Chunchura
Howrah	Haora
Hubli-Dharwar	Dharwad
Kadayanallur	Kadaiyanallur
Manaar, Gulf of	Mannar, Gulf of
Maunath Bhanjan	Mau
Mehsana	Mahesana
Midnapore	Medinipur
Monghyr	Munger
Morvi	Morbi
Nabadwip	Navadwip
Nander	Nanded
Palayancottai	Palayankottai
Purnea	Purnia
Rajnandgaon	Raj Nandgaon
Santipur	Shantipur
Serampore	Shrirampur
Siliguri	Shiliguri
Sonepat	Sonipat
South Suburban	Behala

Iran

Former name	New name
Bandar-e Pahlavi	Bandar-e Anzalī
Bandar-e Shāh	Bandar-e Torkeman
Bandar-e Shahpur	Bandar-e Khomeynī
Dezh Shāhpūr	Marīvan
Gach Sārān	Gachsārān
Herowābād	Khalkhāl
Kermānshāh	Bakhtārān
Naft-e Shāh	Naftshahr
Rezā'īyeh	Orūmīyeh
Rezā'īyeh, Daryācheh-ye	Orūmīyeh, Daryācheh-ye
Shāhābād	Āshkhāneh
Shāhābād	Eslāmābād-e Gharb
Shāhī	Qā'emshahr
Shahrezā	Qomsheh
Shāhrud	Emāmrūd
Shahsavār	Tonekābon
Solţānīyeh	Sa'īdīyeh

Mozambique

Former name	New name
Augusto Cardosa	Metangula
Entre Rios	Malema
Malvérnia	Chicualacuala
Miranda	Macalogue
Olivença	Lupilichi
Vila Alferes Chamusca	Guijá
Vila Caldas Xavier	Muende
Vila Coutinho	Ulonguè
Vila Fontes	Caia
Vila de Junqueiro	Gurué
Vila Luísa	Marracuene
Vila Paiva de Andrada	Gorongoza

Zimbabwe

Former name	New name
Balla Balla	Mbalabala
Belingwe	Mberengwa
Chipinga	Chipinge
Dett	Dete
Enkeldoorn	Chivhu
Essexvale	Esigodini
Fort Victoria	Masvingo
Gwelo	Gweru
Hartley	Chegutu
Gatooma	Kadoma
Inyazura	Nyazura
Marandellas	Marondera
Mashaba	Mashava
Melsetter	Chimanimani
Mrewa	Murewa
Mtoko	Mutoko
Nuanetsi	Mwenezi
Que Que	Kwekwe
Salisbury	Harare
Selukwe	Shurugwi
Shabani	Zvishavane
Sinoia	Chinhoyi
Somabula	Somabhula
Tjolotjo	Tsholotsho
Umvuma	Mvuma
Umtali	Mutare
Wankie	Hwange